RECONCEIVING THE FAMILY

This book provides a critical examination of and reflection on the American Law Institute's *Principles of the Law of Family Dissolution: Analysis and Recommendations*, arguably the most sweeping proposal for family law reform attempted in the U.S. over the last quarter century. The volume is a collaborative work of individuals from diverse perspectives and disciplines who explore the fundamental questions about the nature of family, parenthood, and child support. The contributors are all recognized authorities on aspects of family law and provide commentary on the principles examined by the ALI – fault, custody, child support, property division, spousal support, and domestic partnerships, utilizing a wide range of analytical tools, including economic theory, constitutional law, social science data, and linguistic analysis. This volume also includes the perspectives of U.S. judges and legislators and leading family law scholars in the United Kingdom, Europe, and Australia.

Robin Fretwell Wilson is a Professor of Law at the University of Maryland School of Law. She is the co-editor of *The Handbook of Children, Culture & Violence* and has published articles on the risks of abuse to children in the *Cornell Law Review*, the *Emory Law Journal*, the *San Diego Law Review*, and the *Journal of Child and Family Studies*. Professor Wilson has testified on the use of social science in legal decision-making in Joint Hearings before the Federal Trade Commission and Department of Justice. A member of the Executive Committee of the Family and Juvenile Law Section of the Association of American Law Schools, Professor Wilson frequently lectures on violence to children, including presentations at Yale University's Edward Zigler Center for Child Development and Social Policy and the National Society for the Prevention of Cruelty to Children in London, England.

Reconceiving the Family

Critique on the American Law Institute's PRINCIPLES OF THE LAW OF FAMILY DISSOLUTION

Edited by

Robin Fretwell Wilson

University of Maryland School of Law

CAMBRIDGE
UNIVERSITY PRESS

CAMBRIDGE UNIVERSITY PRESS
Cambridge, New York, Melbourne, Madrid, Cape Town, Singapore, São Paulo

Cambridge University Press
32 Avenue of the Americas, New York, NY 10013-2473, USA

www.cambridge.org
Information on this title: www.cambridge.org/9780521861199

First published 2006

Printed in the United States of America

A catalog record for this publication is available from the British Library.

Library of Congress Cataloging in Publication Data

Reconceiving the family critique on the American Law Institute's Principles
of the law of family dissolution / edited by Robin Fretwell Wilson.
p. cm.
ISBN 0-521-86119-5 (hardcover)
1. Divorce – Law and legislation – United States. 2. Custody of children – United States.
3. Child support – Law and legislation – United States. 4. Equitable distribution
of marital property – United States. 5. Divorce settlements – United States.
I. Wilson, Robin Fretwell. II. Title.
KF535.R43 2006
346.7301′66 – dc22 2006010004

ISBN-13 978-0-521-86119-9 hardback
ISBN-10 0-521-86119-5 hardback

In Memory of Our Colleagues,

Lee Teitelbaum and David Westfall

Contents

Acknowledgments

I am grateful to Mary Ann Glendon for believing in this project, for chairing the October 2004 Workshop entitled "Critical Reflections on the American Law Institute's *Principles of the Law of Family Dissolution*" at Harvard Law School at which many of us refined our chapters, and for her quiet cheerleading throughout. I am also grateful to Carl Schneider for letting me take a page from his Workshop playbook. It is entirely appropriate that Mary Ann and Carl form the "book-ends" for this volume since it could not have happened without either of them.

I am indebted to the University of Maryland School of Law for providing a team of research assistants without whom this volume could not have been completed within my lifetime. Michael Clisham, Kevin Madagan, and Mikaela Rossman devoted an entire year to this project, while Tamiya Baskerville, Asher Chancery, Kristen King, Jennifer Martin, Rahul Narula, Mona Shah, Amy Siegel, and DelY'vonne Whitehead poured themselves into refining the final manuscript. Susan McCarty, Susan Herrick, and the late Ryan Easley of the University of Maryland Law Library provided citation verification and legal research. Yvonne McMorris provided tireless secretarial assistance and, more importantly, moral support throughout this project. Jack Duncan provided expert assistance during the editing cycle, which was made through support from the Institute for American Values. My former colleagues at the University of South Carolina also provided support and encouragement for this volume, both while I was with them at USC and well after I left. David Owen provided invaluable guidance on publishing an edited collection.

I am thankful for John Berger's advice in the formative stages of this project and for Ken Karpinski's careful, thoughtful copy-editing. I was especially sorry that Lee Teitelbaum could not join us at Harvard as originally planned, but am thankful to him for his warm support of this project and his mentoring.

I am indebted to the Family Law Council of the Institute for American Values for its generous support of the October 2004 Workshop, out of which came the corpus of this volume. I am especially grateful to David Blankenhorn for his commitment to bringing together interesting people who have something interesting to say, and letting them say it. Finally, I am indebted to and admiring of the American Law Institute and the reporters for the PRINCIPLES OF THE LAW OF FAMILY DISSOLUTION, Professors Ira Ellman, Grace

Blumberg, and Katherine Bartlett, for what is arguably the most significant family law reform attempted in generations.

This is for the Dream Team: Mark Ancell, Michael Clisham, Jack Duncan, Jennifer Hilker, Pamela Melton, and Ken Wilkinson. I could not have done it without you. And, of course, this is for Glen.

Foreword

Mary Ann Glendon

The late twentieth century was a time of unprecedented changes in family behavior, family law, and ideas about marriage and family life. Starting in the mid-1960s, in North America, Europe, and Australia, a quake erupted across the whole set of demographic indicators. It came on so rapidly that it caught even professional demographers by surprise: birth rates and marriage rates fell, while divorce rates, births of children outside marriage, and the incidence of nonmarital cohabitation rose steeply. The director of the French National Demographic Institute characterized the changes as widespread, profound, and sudden: widespread, because so many nations had been affected; profound, because the changes involved increases or decreases of more than 50 percent; and sudden, because they took place in less than twenty years.[1] Along with changes in family behavior came less quantifiable but no less momentous shifts in the meanings that men and women attribute to sex and procreation, marriage, gender, parenthood, kinship relations, and to life itself.

These developments were part and parcel of social processes that Francis Fukuyama has described collectively as "The Great Disruption": rising affluence, accelerating geographical mobility, increasing labor force participation of women (including mothers of young children), more control over procreation, and greater longevity.[2] By the 1990s, the demographic indicators had more or less stabilized, but they have remained near their new high or low levels, registering only modest rises or declines since then.[3] The legal and social landscape had been utterly transformed. Familiar landmarks had disappeared. We were living in a new world.

With hindsight, the question arises as to whether those years of turbulence provided a favorable climate for law revision. The fact is, however, that family law systems were completely overhauled, often very hastily, in the 1970s and 80s.[4] Family law became a testing ground for various ways of reimagining family relations, and an arena for struggles among competing ideas about individual liberty, human sexuality, marriage, and family life. Many unforeseen developments, notably a sharp increase in poor, fatherless families, now seem to have been influenced by legal changes that were often presented as merely "adapting the law to social reality." Relatively little attention was paid to the ways in which law also helps to shape social reality.

[1] Louis Roussel, *Démographie: deux décennies de mutations dans les pays industrialisés*, *in* I Family, State, and Individual Economic Security 27 (M.T. Meulders and J. Eekelaar eds., 1988).

[2] Francis Fukuyama, The Great Disruption (1999).

[3] Stephen Bahr, *Social Science Research on Family Dissolution: What it Shows and How it Might be of Interest to Family Law Reformers*, 4 J.L. & Fam. Stud. 5, 5–6 (2002).

[4] *See generally*, Mary Ann Glendon, The Transformation of Family Law (1989).

Of the legal developments that have transformed family law, several represent pronounced departures from past arrangements: the reconceptualization of marriage and the family under the influence of ideas about gender equality, individual rights, and neutrality toward diverse lifestyles; the trend toward lessened state regulation of marriage formation and dissolution as such (i.e., fewer restrictions on entry into marriage and fewer obstacles to terminating marriage); and, despite the rise of "children's rights," the creation of a more adult-centered system of family law.

When the entire complex of changes is viewed together, it is apparent that the story the law tells about family life has been substantially rewritten. The legal narrative now places much more emphasis on the rights of individual family members than on familial responsibilities. Marriage is treated less as a necessary social institution designed to provide the optimal environment for child rearing than as an intimate relationship between adults. This historic transition has taken place through piecemeal changes, with little deliberation concerning the likely social consequences of weakening the connections between marriage as a couple and marriage as a child-raising partnership.

In short, the affluent western nations have been engaged in a massive social experiment – one that has opened many new opportunities and freedoms to adults, but one that presents new risks where children and other dependents are concerned. By ratifying many changes in the sexual mores and marriage behavior of large numbers of adults, the law has played its role in transforming the very experience of childhood. An unprecedented proportion of children are now spending all or part of their childhoods in fatherless homes, often in poverty. In fact, female-headed families created by divorce, desertion, or single parenthood now constitute the bulk of the world's poverty population. As for intact child-raising families, their standard of living is generally lower than that of childless households, especially if the mother stays home to care for the children.

The political obstacles to more child-oriented policies, moreover, have increased. For, as the proportion of childless households grows, the culture has become ever more adult centered.[5] With declining birth rates, children are less visible in everyday life; adults are less likely to be living with children; and neighborhoods less likely to contain children. Support for measures that might address the needs of child-raising families becomes harder to rally. As the old saying goes, "Out of sight, out of mind."

It thus seems evident that among the most pressing issues for family law and policy in the future will be those arising from the impaired ability of families to socialize the next generation of citizens, and the diminished capacity of society's support institutions (families, government, mediating structures of civil society) to furnish care for the very young and other dependent persons. Even advanced welfare states still rely heavily on families for the care of the young, the frail elderly, the sick, and the severely disabled, but the capacity of families to perform these functions has been dramatically reduced everywhere. No society, for instance, has yet found a substitute for the care, services, and support formerly furnished by the unpaid labor of women. As the baby boom generation approaches retirement age, it is becoming apparent that the combination of declining birth rates, greater longevity, and shortage of caretakers has brought health care and pension systems to the brink of crisis.

[5] Peter Uhlenberg, *Changing Adulthood Changes Childhood*, (New York: Institute for American Values, Working Paper No. 57, 1998).

What makes all these problems especially thorny is that their resolution will require finding a just balance among competing goods. After all, many of the developments that have weakened legal and social family ties are unintended consequences of freedoms that modern men and women prize. No one, for example, wants to roll back the clock on women's rights. The challenges are thus formidable: How can society take account of children's needs (and the preferences of many, perhaps most, mothers) while still providing equal opportunities to women? How can society respond to the needs of persons in broken or dysfunctional families while strengthening, or at least not undermining, the stable families upon which every society depends for the socialization of its future work force and citizenry? How can policy makers develop adequate responses to families currently in distress while shifting probabilities so that fewer families will find themselves in distressed circumstances in the future? When do the advantages for individuals of unprecedented freedom begin to be outweighed or nullified by the social costs of the cumulative effects of individual choices on social and family life?

By the time the American Law Institute completed its PRINCIPLES OF THE LAW OF FAMILY DISSOLUTION in 2002, family law had already been substantially transformed in all western legal systems. The PRINCIPLES consolidated many of the transformative trends and recommended further, far-reaching changes. Thus, the present volume, with its comprehensive appraisal of that ambitious undertaking, could not have appeared at a more propitious moment. Now that we are in a period of relative demographic equilibrium, the time is ripe for analysis of how various innovations have worked out in practice, for evaluation of their consequences, and for charting future directions that will benefit individuals, families, the dependent population, and society as a whole. These are matters that need to be widely discussed and deliberated, not only among specialists, but among the people most directly affected. How fortunate we are, then, to have this rich collection of essays by so many distinguished judges, practitioners, and scholars. Their diverse viewpoints will surely raise the level of the national conversation about where family law has been, where it is now, and where it ought to be headed.

List of Contributors

Jane F. Adolphe is an Associate Professor of Law, Ave Maria School of Law. Her research largely concerns issues pertaining to the family and international law.

Katharine K. Baker is a Professor and Associate Dean at Chicago-Kent College of Law. She is the author of numerous articles on family law, feminism, and sexual violence.

Brian H. Bix is the Frederick W. Thomas Professor of Law and Philosophy, University of Minnesota. He works in Family Law, Jurisprudence, and Contract Law. He is one of the five authors of *Family Law: Cases, Text, Problems* (4th ed. 2004), and the author of *A Dictionary of Legal Theory* (2004), *Jurisprudence: Theory and Context* (4th ed. 2006), and *Law, Language, and Legal Determinacy* (1993).

Margaret F. Brinig is the William G. Hammond Professor of Law at the University of Iowa College of law. She has written a number of books, including *From Contract to Covenant: Beyond the Law and Economics of the Family* (2000), and many articles on family law.

June Carbone is the Associate Dean for Professional Development, and a Professor of Law at Santa Clara University. She served as Presidential Professor of Ethics and the Common Good at the University's Markkula Center for Applied Ethics from 2001 to 2003. She is the author of *From Partners to Parents: The Second Revolution in Family Law* (2000) and the third edition of *Family Law* (2005) with Leslie Harris and the late Lee Teitelbaum.

Justice Maura D. Corrigan was elected to the Michigan Supreme Court in 1998 and was the Chief Justice of that Court from 2001–2004. She currently serves on the Pew Commission on Children in Foster Care and on the U.S. Department of Health & Human Services' Advisory Task Force on Child Support. Previously, while a member of the Conference of Chief Justices, she co-chaired the Problem Solving Courts Committee.

John Eekelaar is a Fellow of Pembroke College, Oxford and was Reader in Family Law at Oxford University until 2005. He has written and researched on family law for many years. He is co-director of the Oxford Centre for Family Law and Policy, and a Fellow of the British Academy. He is now Academic Director of Pembroke College.

Martha M. Ertman is a professor at the University of Utah's S.J. Quinney College of Law. She is the author of a number of law review articles bridging commercial and family law, and edited the book *Rethinking Commodification: Readings in Law & Culture* (2005) with Joan Williams.

Scott FitzGibbon is a professor at Boston College Law School, a member of the American Law Institute, and a member of the International Society of Family Law. One of his major scholarly interests is jurisprudence and legal philosophy, with special attention to friendship and marriage in the Aristotelean tradition.

Marsha Garrison is Professor of Law at Brooklyn Law School. She is the coauthor of *Family Law: Cases, Comments and Questions* (5th ed. 2003) and has written many articles on a diverse range of family law issues.

Mary Ann Glendon is the Learned Hand Professor of Law at Harvard University. Her books include *A World Made New: Eleanor Roosevelt and the Universal Declaration of Human Rights* (2001), *A Nation Under Lawyers: How the Crisis in the Legal Profession is Transforming American Society* (1994), and *Rights Talk: The Impoverishment of Political Discourse* (1991).

John DeWitt Gregory is the Sidney and Walter Siben Distinguished Professor of Family Law at Hofstra University. He is the author or co-author of several books, including *Property Division in Divorce*

Proceedings: A Fifty State Guide (2003) (with Janet Leach Richards and Sheryl Wolf), and a number of articles.

Robert J. Levy is the William L. Prosser Professor of Law Emeritus at the University of Minnesota Law School. He is currently a Visiting Professor at Florida International Law School. Professor Levy is the author of several books about Family Law and several articles about the ALI PRINCIPLES. Professor Levy was a co-Reporter for the Uniform Marriage and Divorce Act.

David D. Meyer is a Professor and the Mildred Van Voorhis Jones Faculty Scholar at the University of Illinois College of Law. He has written widely at the intersection of constitutional law and family law.

Patrick Parkinson is a Professor and Head of the Law School at the University of Sydney, Australia. He is the Chair of the Family Law Council (the Australian Government's advisory body) and also chaired a review of the Child Support Scheme in 2004–05. He has written many books and articles on family law, child protection and the law of equity and trusts. He is a member of the Executive Council of the International Society of Family Law.

Marie T. Reilly is a Professor of Law at the University of South Carolina School of Law. She is a teacher and author of articles on bankruptcy and commercial law subjects.

Carl E. Schneider is the Chauncey Stillman Professor of Law and Professor of Internal Medicine at the University of Michigan. He is the co-author of a family-law casebook – *An Invitation to Family Law: Principles, Process and Perspectives* (2d ed. 2000) – and the author of *The Practice of Autonomy: Patients, Doctors, and Medical Decisions* (1998).

Elizabeth S. Scott is a University Professor and Class of 1962 Professor of Law at the University of Virginia. She was a founder and is co-director of the Center for Children, Families and the Law at the University of Virginia. She is a co-author with Ira Ellman and Paul Kurtz of a widely used casebook in Family Law, and has also co-authored (with Walter Wadlington, Charles Whitebread, and Samuel Davis) a casebook on children in the legal system.

Katharine B. Silbaugh is Professor of Law and Associate Dean for Academic Affairs at Boston University School of Law. She is author of numerous publications addressing family and employment law aspects of household labor and the work-family conflict.

Katherine S. Spaht is the Jules F. and Frances L. Landry Professor of Law at Louisiana State University. She is the author of a treatise on community property and three textbooks on family law and successions. She has authored numerous articles and chapters in books on the subject of marriage.

Barbara Stark. Professor of Law at Hofstra Law School, is the author of *International Family Law: An Introduction* (2005), editor of *Family Law and Gender Bias: Comparative Perspectives* (1992), and the author of over fifty articles and chapters on family law and human rights law.

Mark Strasser is the Trustees Professor of Law at Capital University Law School in Columbus, Ohio. He is the author of several books including *On Same-Sex Marriage, Civil Unions, and the Rule of Law: Constitutional Interpretation at the Crossroads* (2002) and *Legally Wed: Same-Sex Marriage and the Constitution* (1997).

Tone Sverdrup is Professor of Law, Faculty of Law, University of Oslo. She is the author of several books, including one on co-ownership in marriage and unmarried cohabitation, and the standard family law textbook in Norway (co-authored with Professor Peter Lødrup).

Jean Hoefer Toal is the Chief Justice of the Supreme Court of South Carolina and a former member of the South Carolina House of Representatives. She is the author of numerous law review articles and other scholarly works.

Lynn D. Wardle is a Professor of Law at the J. Reuben Clark Law School of Brigham Young University. He is a past president of the International Society of Family Law, and the author, co-author, or co-editor of many books and law review articles mostly addressing issues of family law, including *Marriage and Same-Sex Unions: A Debate* (Lynn D. Wardle et al. eds., 2003).

David Westfall held the John L. Gray and Carl F. Schipper, Jr. professorships at Harvard Law School, where he joined the faculty in 1955. His publications include *Estate Planning Law and Taxation* (4th ed. 2001); *Forcing Incidents of Marriage on Unmarried Cohabitants*: The American Law Institute's Principles of Family Dissolution, published in the *Notre Dame Law Review*; and *Family Law* (1994).

Robin Fretwell Wilson is a Professor of Law at the University of Maryland School of Law and a member of the Executive Committee of the Family and Juvenile Law Section of the Association of American Law Schools.

Introduction

Robin Fretwell Wilson

The family has undergone almost revolutionary reconfigurations over the past generation. In the space of a few decades, we have seen the universal recognition in the United States of no-fault divorce, the legal recognition of nonmarital fathers, the establishment of registration schemes and other claims between cohabitants, both heterosexual and homosexual, and the recognition as parents of adults who have neither a biological tie to a child nor an adoptive one.[1] Recently, the pace of these changes has become almost frenetic. Just this year, Canada legalized same-sex marriage through national legislation, as South Africa did by judicial opinion; New Zealand's Law Commission has recommended major changes to the legal rules that determine status as a parent so that certain egg or sperm donors could become a child's third parent; and Belgium formally recognized its first polygamous marriage.[2]

Family law is red hot. These subjects – divorce, cohabitation, same-sex relationships, and the nature of parenting and parenthood – are now the subject of intense public debate in newspaper articles, editorials, television talk shows, and legislation, at the federal, state, and local levels.

In this volume, you will find the first major critique of the intellectually formidable and influential PRINCIPLES OF THE LAW OF FAMILY DISSOLUTION: ANALYSIS AND RECOMMENDATIONS ("PRINCIPLES")[3] developed by the American Law Institute ("ALI") over an eleven-year period, ending in 2002. In the PRINCIPLES, the ALI carefully considers many of the significant and very controversial questions raised by these changing family forms. The ALI, the most prestigious law reform organization in the United States, is a collection of judges, lawyers, and academics established in 1923 "to promote the clarification and simplification of the law and its better adaptation to social needs."[4] The ALI has been

[1] Section of Family Law, American Bar Ass'n, *10 FAQs About Family Law,* http://www.abanet.org/family/faq.html (last visited Dec. 1, 2005); Leslie J. Harris, *Same-Sex Unions Around the World*, PROB. & PROP., Sept./Oct. 2005, at 31; Lehr v. Robertson, 463 U.S. 248 (1983); Leslie Joan Harris, *Reconsidering the Criteria for Legal Fatherhood*, 1996 UTAH L. REV. 461.

[2] Civil Marriage Act, 2005 S.C., ch.33 (Can.); Michael Wines, Same-Sex Unions To Become Legal In South Africa, N.Y. Times, Dec. 2, 2005, at A6; NEW ZEALAND LAW COMMISSION, REPORT No. 88, NEW ISSUES IN LEGAL PARENTHOOD, at xxv (2005), *available at* http://www.lawcom.govt.nz/UploadFiles/Publications/Publication_91_315_R88.pdf (Recommendation R10, describing "Legal parenthood for 'known' donor as a child's third parent"); Paul Belien, *First Trio "Married" in the Netherlands*, BRUSSELS J., Sept. 27, 2005, http://www.brusselsjournal.com/node/301.

[3] AMERICAN LAW INSTITUTE, PRINCIPLES OF THE LAW OF FAMILY DISSOLUTION: ANALYSIS AND RECOMMENDATIONS (2002) [hereinafter PRINCIPLES].

[4] American Law Institute, http://www.ali.org/ (last visited Dec. 1, 2005).

tremendously influential in the development of American law through its publications and Restatements of Law.[5] The PRINCIPLES promise to be no exception.[6] Indeed, because of their breadth, depth, and novelty, the PRINCIPLES are arguably the most sweeping proposal for family law change attempted in the United States over the last quarter century.

Published after four preliminary drafts, the PRINCIPLES represent a massive scholarly effort – 1,187 pages in total – which, if enacted, would leave few areas of family law untouched. They address fault, the division of property, alimony payments, child custody, child support, domestic partnerships, and private agreements between adults who cohabit or marry. Many of the proposals contained in the PRINCIPLES would change current law dramatically, as the contributors to this volume observe again and again. Many are extremely controversial. For example, the PRINCIPLES propose, as one of the drafters explains, to treat both heterosexual and homosexual couples who cohabit "as though they were married" when "their long-term stable cohabitations come to an end."[7] The PRINCIPLES also propose to award custodial responsibility according to past caretaking practices of the adults in the relationship – a proposal first made by Professor Elizabeth Scott, a contributor to this volume[8] – rather than according to the loosely-defined "best interests of the child" standard. The PRINCIPLES would also redefine spousal support and alter the division of marital property. They would greatly reduce judicial discretion in some areas of family law and greatly expand it in others. In short, the PRINCIPLES represent a major reworking of the law of marital dissolution and are, and will surely be long into the future, a major influence on the field.

Plainly, the subject matter of the PRINCIPLES is of enormous significance and, for this reason, the PRINCIPLES deserve what scholars call a "comprehensive examination;" that is, a lively, illuminating dialogue among some of the nation's foremost legal experts on the future direction of family law. Although a few law journals have published symposia examining aspects of the PRINCIPLES,[9] no one has examined them critically in a systematic, book-length effort. This volume fills that void. Here, some of the nation's leading intellectuals in family law provide an in-depth analysis of the principles and policy choices the ALI endorses and offer a fundamentally different vision for resolving the challenges facing state courts and legislators. For example, the PRINCIPLES seek in some areas to sharply limit judicial discretion with detailed rules, commentary, and illustrations. Professor John Eekelaar notes in his chapter that while "[c]ourts, and couples, do need principles to follow," those principles "need not be very elaborate. Arrangements for children should aim to sustain a

[5] Marygold S. Melli, *The American Law Institute Principles of Family Dissolution, the Approximation Rule and Shared-Parenting*, 25 N. ILL. U. L. REV. 347, 347–48 (2005) (observing that the ALI's "Restatements of the Law have been enormously influential in the development of American law"). It is difficult to overstate the degree of the ALI's influence. As of March 1, 2004, state and federal courts have cited the Restatements 161,486 times. AMERICAN LAW INSTITUTE, PUBLISHED CASE CITATIONS TO RESTATEMENTS OF THE LAW AS OF MARCH 1, 2004, *available at* http://www.ali.org/ali/AM04_07-RestatementCitations04.pdf (last visited Dec. 1, 2005).

[6] Robert Pear, *Legal Group Urges States to Update Their Family Law*, N.Y. TIMES, Nov. 30, 2002, at A1 ("The findings are likely to have a major impact, given the prestige of the [ALI].").

[7] Grace Ganz Blumburg, a drafter of the PRINCIPLES and professor at the University of California, Los Angeles. *Talk of the Nation, New Principles for Family Law* (National Public Radio broadcast, Jan.) ("These people live like they're married, even if they're not formally married. They share a life together as though they were married. Therefore, when their long-term stable cohabitations come to an end, we should treat them as though they were married.").

[8] Elizabeth S. Scott, *Pluralism, Parental Preference, and Child Custody*, 80 CAL. L. REV. 615 (1992).

[9] *See* Symposium, *ALI Principles of the Law of Family Dissolution*, 2001 BYU L. REV. 857; Symposium, *Gender Issues in Divorce: Commentaries on the American Law Institute's Principles of the Law of Family Dissolution*, 8 DUKE J. GENDER L. & POL'Y 1 (2001); *Symposium on the American Law Institute's Principles of the Law of Family Dissolution*, 4 J.L. & FAM. STUD. 1 (2002).

stable environment, reduce conflict and maintain, as far as possible, the child's beneficial relationships with parents or parent-figures, whose independent interests should be recognized as far as possible, but as being subordinate to those of the children." Although such principles "should provide sound guides for separating parties, their advisers, mediators and lawyers . . . , [s]ometimes decisions will need to be made which require the exercise of judgment on the application of the principles: the courts are there to make them."

The ALI's proposals did not emerge in a vacuum. They reflect similar developments in family law in the United Kingdom, Europe, Australia, and elsewhere. Several scholars in this volume adopt a deliberately comparative structure that highlights the very different policy decisions that have been made by jurisdictions outside the United States. The PRINCIPLES provide a rich substratum for exploring the merits of these competing visions about what makes a family, the nature of parenthood, and the basis for the obligation to support one's child and the duty, if any, to support a person with whom one has lived in an intimate relationship.

Because of the prestige of the ALI, judges will undoubtedly rely on the PRINCIPLES as they have relied on the ALI's Restatements. Legislators are also likely to turn, rightly or wrongly, to the PRINCIPLES for guidance because, in contrast to the Restatements, this work was designed to stimulate legislative reform. In the words of the ALI's Director, Lance Liebman, "much of the relevant law is statutory, and what seemed to be needed was guidance to legislators as well as to courts."[10] As the definitive scholarly appraisal of the ALI's proposals, this volume is intended to be on the shelf side-by-side with the PRINCIPLES to be consulted as a source of critical perspectives. Any judge or policymaker confronted with the adoption of a specific reform in the PRINCIPLES, and any organization seeking to defend or challenge the PRINCIPLES, will want to consult this volume as a first step.

In fact, the impact of the PRINCIPLES is already being felt. West Virginia statutorily adopted the proposed "past caretaking standard" as a substitute for the "best interests" standard that now prevails everywhere else.[11] In Florida, an intermediate appellate court attempted to adopt the "past caretaking standard" judicially, but was overruled.[12] Supreme Courts in Rhode Island and Massachusetts have looked favorably upon the PRINCIPLES' definition of "de facto parent" in justifying an award of custodial rights to long-time caregivers who lacked formal legal ties to a child.[13] Even those who disagree with the ALI's proposed reforms, as this volume argues they frequently should, will likely feel obliged to consider them and explain the basis of their disagreement.[14]

[10] Lance Liebman, *Director's Forward, in* PRINCIPLES, at xv.

[11] W. VA. CODE ANN. § 48-11-106 (LexisNexis 2004).

[12] A judicial advisor to the ALI's work on the PRINCIPLES purported to adopt the "approximate the time" standard for custody dispositions following divorce as a matter of common law. Young v. Hector, 740 So. 2d 1153 (Fla. Dist. Ct. App. 1999). At rehearing *en banc*, the District Court of Appeal of Florida withdrew the panel decision and rejected the ALI standard. *See* Young v. Hector, 740 So. 2d at 1158.

[13] *See, e.g.*, Rubano v. DiCenzo, 759 A.2d 959, 974–75 (R.I. 2000) (drawing support from PRINCIPLES for holding that "a person who has no biological connection to a child but has served as a psychological or de facto parent to that child may . . . establish his or her entitlement to parental rights vis-à-vis the child."); E.N.O. v. L.M.M., 711 N.E.2d 886, 891 (Mass. 1999) (relying in part on PRINCIPLES in holding that "the best interests calculus must include an examination of the child's relationship with both his legal and de facto parent[s]"), *cert. denied*, 528 U.S. 1005 (1999); Youmans v. Ramos, 711 N.E.2d 165, 167 n.3 (Mass. 1999) (adopting the ALI's definition of "de facto parent" in holding that child's former guardian was entitled to seek court-ordered visitation).

[14] For example, although the Maine Supreme Judicial Court recently refused to adopt the PRINCIPLES' conception of parenthood, it acknowledged that the PRINCIPLES will be extremely influential. C.E.W v. D.E.W., 845 A.2d 1146, 1152 & n.13 (Me. 2004) (declining to adopt the ALI's definition of parenthood).

The questions the ALI tackles are sufficiently weighty and complicated that they must be discussed broadly, from multiple perspectives. Perhaps the most remarkable aspect of this volume is the rich and deep diversity of views contained within it. Among our contributors are feminists and child advocates, social conservatives, liberals, and moderates. We have utilized a wide range of analytical tools including economic theory, constitutional law, social science data, and linguistic analysis.

We are privileged to have scholars in this collection who are extraordinarily well-respected in the field of family law to provide much-needed context for and commentary on the ALI's reform proposals. Many of our contributors have written in this area for decades and bring that depth of knowledge and expertise to bear in evaluating the PRINCIPLES, especially the ALI's more novel proposals. For instance, Professor David Westfall's chapter on property division upon divorce both demonstrates the depth of innovation that the ALI would have judges and legislatures embrace, and provides a critical evaluation of the ALI's approach.

The rising stars in family law are also well represented among our contributors. For example, Professor David Meyer's chapter on the new forms of parenthood proposed by the ALI provides fresh insight to this area of the law, as well as a helpful assessment of the proposal's constitutionality. This chapter should give lawmakers much-needed assurance when deciding whether or not to adopt the PRINCIPLES, provide judges confidence in rejecting the PRINCIPLES or applying laws based upon them, and give legal scholars and scholars of the family new food for thought.

Importantly, this volume includes reflections from "end-users" of the PRINCIPLES, the judges and legislators who will decide whether and to what extent to adopt the ALI's proposed reforms. Precisely because so much about the family is in flux, judges and legislators are obliged to reexamine rules that no longer neatly fit the constantly changing familial arrangements that people are forming and disbanding. How the old rules ought to apply, and whether they need to be reformulated, are unavoidable questions today. Because the PRINCIPLES are directed to both "rulemakers" and "decisionmakers,"[15] we thought it was essential to have them weigh in. Included in this volume are the immediate past Chief Justice of the Michigan Supreme Court, Maura Corrigan, who oversaw the wholesale revamping of Michigan's child support enforcement system, and the sitting Chief Justice of the South Carolina Supreme Court, Jean Toal, who served as a legislator for more than a decade. Both emphasize how removed the PRINCIPLES are from the everyday realities of legal decision-making and judicial administration. Chief Justice Toal argues, for instance, that the PRINCIPLES' domestic partnership scheme "is significantly weakened by some fundamental assumptions involving the formation of legal obligations. . . . , [and] would impose legal obligations in a highly unorthodox manner, significantly run afoul of concepts of freedom of contract, [and] restrict individual autonomy. . . . " She concludes that "[t]he law is ill-served by creating classes of unmarried cohabitants who, for reasons of 'fairness,' have to bear greater financial responsibility for a 'break-up' than others."

Many of our other contributors are not strangers to the difficulties posed by law reform and legal change. Three of our contributors acted as advisors to the drafters of the PRINCIPLES, and another six were members of the ALI's Consultative Group. Professor

[15] Ira Mark Ellman, *Chief Reporter's Forward, in* PRINCIPLES, at xvii (stating that some sections "are addressed to rulemakers rather than decisionmakers").

Robert Levy served as the Reporter for the Uniform Marriage and Divorce Act and Professor Lynn Wardle is the immediate past president of the International Society of Family Law.

Despite their stellar academic credentials, our contributors are not confined to the "ivory tower." Many of our authors provide in-depth academic reflections while remaining cognizant of real world pressures and influences. Professor Katharine Baker, for example, discusses the ALI's asymmetrical approach to parental rights and obligations, which would give a broad range of individuals the ability to assert parental rights to a child without recognizing a corresponding responsibility to financially support that child. Although she unmasks a considerable shortcoming of the PRINCIPLES, Professor Baker acknowledges that the ALI may have struck an appropriate balance between rights and obligations in light of the political realities in the United States today.

To better inform policy makers, this volume also offers comparative perspectives missing in many academic volumes on family law. Included here are the views of leading family law scholars in the United Kingdom, Europe, and Australia, jurisdictions that have experimented to varying degrees with the subjects of the PRINCIPLES' proposals. For example, every state in Australia has extended marital property rights to cohabitants who live together for at least two years or have a child in common.[16] France has adopted Civil Solidarity Pacts that permit couples to receive marriage-like benefits under the law.[17] And on July 3, 2005, Spain became the first European state to allow both same-sex marriage and adoption.[18] Each nation offers an experimental laboratory in which to test the ALI's assumptions and to evaluate the success and wisdom of efforts to reconceive the family. The reflections of Professors John Eekelaar, Patrick Parkinson, and Tone Sverdrup on the experiences of and very different policy decisions made by these jurisdictions should prove invaluable to policy makers in the United States and elsewhere.

Although each chapter in this volume grapples with a different aspect of the PRINCIPLES and elucidates the assumptions underlying the ALI's policy recommendations, a number of themes emerge independently from these critiques. Several contributors ask whether the ALI's attempts at wringing discretion out of the system will be successful. Professor Levy observes that "[f]or parents and for those anxious to increase doctrinal determinacy, the PRINCIPLES pose even more troubling problems. The exceptions to the rigid 'approximate the time spent' doctrine seem to give judges as much discretion as the 'best interests' test does." Echoing this, Professor Eekelaar believes the ALI's "quest for certainty [may have] been subverted by complexity of application."

But the problem of discretion goes deeper than this. To use an analogy from physics, like energy in a system, discretion cannot be removed entirely from these difficult decisions – we can only move it around between parents, judges, legislators, or others. A number of contributors suggest we should place it in the hands of the people who have the most information on the ground, closest to the circumstances: in some instances, the adults who

[16] *See* Lindy Wilmott et al., *De Facto Relationships Property Adjustment Law – A National Direction*, 17 AUSTL. J. FAM. L. 1 (2003) (describing differences in state rules).

[17] Law No. 99–944 of Nov. 15, 1999, Journal Officiel de la République Française [J.O.] [Official Gazette of France], Nov. 16, 1999, p. 16959; Daniel Borrillo, *The* "Pacte Civil de Solidarité" *in France: Midway Between Marriage and Cohabitation, in* LEGAL RECOGNITION OF SAME-SEX PARTNERSHIPS: A STUDY OF NATIONAL, EUROPEAN AND INTERNATIONAL LAW 475 (Robert Wintemute & Mads Andenæs eds., 2001).

[18] Law to Amend the Civil Code on the subject of the right to contract marriage (B.O.E. 2005, 157), *available at* http://www.boe.es/boe/dias/2005/07/02/pdfs/A23632–23634.pdf. *See also* Al Goodman, *First Gay Couple Marries in Spain*, CNN.COM, July 11, 2005, http://www.cnn.com/2005/WORLD/europe/07/11/ spain.gay/.

are involved themselves and in others, judges. Thus, Professor Katharine Baker faults the PRINCIPLES' fluid definition of parenthood for encroaching on parents: "By increasing the number of people who can assert relationship rights, the PRINCIPLES necessarily increase the likelihood that courts, not parents, will be deciding what is in a child's best interest." The ALI's domestic partnership proposals raise a similar concern for Professor Marsha Garrison: "[T]he ALI approach... eliminates choice by forcing those who are unprepared to make marital commitments to shoulder the very responsibilities that they have avoided; it discriminates by cramming relationships of many contours into a 'one-size-fits-all' marital mold,... [and it] deeply intrudes into relational privacy." She concludes that "[d]espite the liberal rhetoric that cloaks its illiberal character, the ALI proposal offers nothing more – or less – than a dramatic expansion of state paternalism and coercion."

Of course, to foreclose the use of judgment by parents and judges, we should have good reasons or data. Yet, numerous contributors ask "where's the evidence?" In her chapter on the ALI's domestic partnership scheme, Chief Justice Toal asks whether there is "any evidence that cohabitating couples, as a general rule, do not provide for a fair and equitable distribution of [their] losses when their relationship dissolves?" Without such evidence, she believes "it would seem a tremendous waste to, with one broad brushstroke, paint legal obligations on a group of people 'after the fact,' based simply on their 'status' while in a relationship." Similarly, in his chapter on child support, Professor Mark Strasser notes that "one would expect the justification [for the PRINCIPLES' irrebuttable presumption that residential parents will make correct child care decisions for the first six years of a child's life] to include studies indicating why six years of age is an important milestone developmentally or, perhaps, some other justification for giving the residential parent of a young child such great leeway." Professor June Carbone questions the PRINCIPLES' "source of authority for the imposition of particular terms on warring couples," a crucial concern, she argues, because the family acts as a buffer between individuals and the State.

Our contributors return repeatedly to the novelty of the ALI's recommendations. In Professor John Gregory's view, the PRINCIPLES' "radical application of [property] characterization rules and by extension the rules of property division to domestic partners, for the most part rejects prevailing law, which rarely applies equitable distribution rules to the property of unmarried cohabitants." Similarly, several authors discuss the PRINCIPLES' unprecedented proposal to recharacterize separate property as marital when a long-term marriage dissolves. The novelty of the PRINCIPLES did not escape the ALI's attention. Professor Barbara Stark's chapter examines the PRINCIPLES' attempt to define "piecemeal" the responsibilities that should survive a relationship's termination. Although the ALI premises these responsibilities on "an inchoate national or local consensus," the drafters "conced[e] that in fact such a consensus may not exist."

A surprising number of chapters revisit questions of fault that, as Professor Katharine Silbaugh notes, the ALI has largely "side-lined." Professor Silbaugh wonders whether there can be justice when fault is not considered "either as a ground for divorce or in financial settlements." As Professor Lynn Wardle aptly observes, "[i]f marital misconduct is not *the* prime motivating, behavior-shaping, legal-proceeding influencing factor in marital dissolution proceedings, it certainly is one of the most important, especially when the misconduct is serious." Professor Wardle urges that it "is both irrational and impractical... [f]or the law to simply ignore... a factual reality that is... so integral to why, when and how [individuals] initiate and pursue such proceedings, and that manifests itself in so many ways in the tactics, claims and defenses" they assert. Professor Brian Bix speculates that the ALI's "basic antagonism towards – or fear of – anything that seems to require a judicial finding of fault" explains its proposal to not enforce any agreement that would make fault a ground for divorce or the basis for penalizing the bad actor.

In closing, although the PRINCIPLES have begun to filter into American law, they are only beginning to receive the attention they will ultimately garner. In its monumental undertaking in the PRINCIPLES, the ALI asks all the big questions: among them, what entitles an adult to parental rights to a child; whether we should erase distinctions that have always been important in American family law, but are perhaps now outdated, between couples who marry and those who do not; and whether we can trust judges to make decisions affecting children and adults after a family fractures. Until this volume, there has been no resource to consult for a serious, comprehensive examination of the very controversial answers the ALI proffers to those questions. We hope that this volume will generate a robust discussion of the ALI's recommendations and the choices embedded within them.

PART ONE. FAULT

1 Beyond Fault and No-Fault in the Reform of Marital Dissolution Law

Lynn D. Wardle

For such a massive production, there are surprising gaps in the PRINCIPLES. Some of the most curious of these occur in Chapter 1. The ALI's vigorous repudiation of "fault" as a valid principle to be applied at dissolution and dissolution-related issues occupies the largest portion of Chapter 1. Yet there is no discussion or consideration of the numerous recently developed, ameliorative procedures and programs in marital dissolution cases. These two inconsistent decisions are in fact related to each other, reflecting a decades-old and perhaps worn-out generational perspective favoring the elimination of all obstacles, especially moral condemnation or social disapproval, to the exercise of individual autonomy in exiting marriage.

This chapter examines "fault" and "no-fault" in marital dissolution conceptually (asking whether "fault" is relevant to marital dissolution), jurisprudentially (asking how well the notions of "fault" and "no-fault" fit the premises of our legal system), and practically (asking whether rigid no-fault rules reflect the concerns of litigants in dissolution proceedings). Part I of this chapter reviews the discussion in the PRINCIPLES of marital misconduct, identifies several specific and general flaws, and argues that the "fault/no-fault" language utilized in the PRINCIPLES is dated, distorting, and inadequate conceptually as well as practically. It proposes that the language of accountability and responsibility be substituted for "fault" and "no-fault."

Part II of this chapter suggests that society, families, and individuals, including divorcing parties, have compelling interests in promoting alternatives to divorce, and that such policies can be implemented as a part of marital dissolution proceedings, without severely restricting access to divorce. A vibrant marriage revitalization movement is alive and well in the United States, led primarily by mental health professionals who are convinced that many effective alternatives to divorce are available for most, but not all, married individuals who are dissatisfied with their marriages. The failure of the PRINCIPLES to recognize and consider any possible legal tools to give couples in crisis the opportunity and encouragement to explore non-divorce options is an enormous and inexcusable hole in the scope and value of the PRINCIPLES.

Part III presents an alternative to the ALI's "fault or no-fault" paradigm. It proposes judicial recognition of clearly established community standards regarding minimally acceptable behavior of spouses in marriage, and suggests that violation of those standards should be considered in determining alimony and property awards. Such violations not only damage a unique relational interest of the other spouse, but they also injure the community. Legal compensation for such loss appropriately protects and deters further injury to both public and private interests.

I. The ALI's Faulty Critique of Fault

A. The Drafters' Critique of Fault in Chapter 1 of the PRINCIPLES

The drafters begin their explanation in Chapter 1, Topic 2, of why marital misconduct should not be considered in property allocation and alimony (which the drafters label "spousal compensation") awards by acknowledging that "American law is sharply divided on the question of whether 'marital misconduct' should be considered in allocating marital property or awarding alimony."[1] Historically, consideration of such "'fault' was almost universally allowed." But by 1970, when the Uniform Marriage and Divorce Act ("UMDA") rejected marital misconduct as a consideration in both contexts, a trend against considering fault in making such financial awards had begun, a position that now has been adopted by approximately half of the states.[2] The PRINCIPLES also adopt the no-marital-misconduct position primarily for three reasons, because of (1) "the goal of improving the consistency and predictability of dissolution law;" (2) "the core tenet that the dissolution law provides compensation for only the *financial* losses arising from the dissolution of marriage[;]"and (3) tort reforms limiting inter-spousal immunity now permit separate tort claims between former spouses for some marital misconduct and reduce the need to have those claims asserted in property and alimony contests.[3] The conclusion reached by the drafters is not surprising. The PRINCIPLES' primary drafter, Professor Ira Mark Ellman,[4] appears to have written more law review articles criticizing fault in dissolution proceedings than any other living legal commentator.[5]

The PRINCIPLES explain that only two kinds of marital misconduct are universally considered in property and alimony award claims in all states: (1) when one spouse engaged in the misconduct of "waste or dissipation of marital assets," and (2) when spousal misconduct directly affects the "need" of a spouse, as when domestic violence leaves a spouse with increased medical expenses.[6] The PRINCIPLES adopt both of these exceptions, which impact financial awards upon divorce.[7]

[1] PRINCIPLES § 1, Topic 2, at 42.

[2] PRINCIPLES § 1, Topic 2, at 43.

[3] PRINCIPLES § 1, Topic 2, at 43.

[4] *See* PRINCIPLES, at vii (Ira Mark Ellman is identified as Chief Reporter, with Katharine T. Bartlett and Grace Ganz Blumberg as Reporters. Professor Marygold S. Melli was an original Reporter from 1989–94, but was designated "Consultant" instead of "Reporter" in 1995.)

[5] *See generally* Ira Mark Ellman, *The Misguided Movement to Revive Fault Divorce, and Why Reformers Should Look Instead to the American Law Institute*, 11 INT'L J. L. POL'Y & FAM. 216 (1997); Ira Mark Ellman & Sharon Lohr, *Marriage as Contract, Opportunistic Violence, and Other Bad Arguments for Fault Divorce*, 1997 U. ILL. L. REV. 719, 772; Ira Mark Ellman, *Should The Theory of Alimony Include Nonfinancial Losses and Motivations?*, 1991 BYU L. REV. 259, 304 ("One piece of wisdom contained in the no-fault reforms was a skepticism about our ability to decide who was really at fault for marital failure. In the first case, for example, perhaps the husband's infidelity was bred by his wife's coldness. But then, perhaps her coldness resulted from his insensitivity. Can we tell which came first? Can we even tell whether he was really insensitive, or she was really cold? One might reasonably doubt whether there are accepted standards for judging such things."); Ira Mark Ellman, *The Place of Fault in a Modern Divorce Law*, 28 ARIZ. ST. L.J. 773 (1996) (arguing that fault should not be considered in alimony determinations); Ira Mark Ellman & Stephen D. Sugarman, *Spousal Emotional Abuse as Tort?*, 55 MD. L. REV. 1268 (1996). Another Reporter, Katharine T. Bartlett, has also voiced similar concerns. *See* Katharine T. Bartlett, *Saving the Family From the Reformers*, 31 U.C. DAVIS L. REV. 809, 815 & 825–26 (1998) (arguing that revival of no-fault divorce would harm women and children).

[6] PRINCIPLES § 1, Topic 2, at 43.

[7] PRINCIPLES § 1, Topic 2, at 43.

The drafters explain that the states' use of marital misconduct in awarding alimony and property upon dissolution falls into six categories:[8]

(1) Twenty states are described as *pure no-fault states* and "exclude consideration of marital misconduct entirely, subject to the two universal (financial cost) exceptions."
(2) Five states reportedly have *pure no-fault property,* [and] *almost pure no-fault alimony.*
(3) Three states are described as *almost pure no-fault* because the controlling law does not absolutely forbid consideration of marital misconduct, but it almost does, and few recent cases consider such fault.
(4) Seven states are described as *no-fault property,* [but] *fault in alimony,* giving courts broad discretion to consider marital misconduct in determining alimony awards.
(5) Fifteen states are described as *full-fault states,* in which courts have discretion to consider marital misconduct in both property and alimony contests.
(6) No state allows consideration of fault only in property division; twenty-eight states have embraced wholly or in large part the no-fault principle.[9]

In general, the drafters agree that "the states are divided evenly" on whether to allow consideration of marital misconduct in settling the adult financial consequences of divorce.[10] The community-property idea of joint ownership underlying marital property principles seems to influence property division and may underpin the rejection of marital misconduct, but alimony claims are based on equity rather than ownership, which may explain why consideration of misconduct continues to be common with alimony. In contrast, the PRINCIPLES suggest establishing "a presumption of entitlement to compensatory payments" and acceptance of that ownership-like notion should reduce support for considering misconduct in making alimony awards.[11]

The drafters examine two potential justifications for considering marital misconduct in dissolution and look to tort law as a source for guiding principles.[12] The first justification is the role of fault "as an agent of morality: rewarding virtue and punishing sin." However, the drafters assert that punishing misconduct is more appropriate for criminal law than dissolution law, and criticize that "many fault states [that] apply rules that cannot be explained as anything but punitive . . . [such as] the rule that inflexibly bars alimony awards to every adulterous spouse, without regard to any other facts of the case." The inflexibility of an absolute rule produces unjust results, while a vague rule fails to establish "clear behavioral standards" and gives too much discretion to the judge to determine what he or she personally considers "appropriate behavior in intimate relationships."

The drafters criticize the notion that "a fault-based award is justified because it allocates more of those costs to the spouse whose conduct caused them, by causing the dissolution," and because for marital misconduct "no losses are identified beyond the financial consequences present in nearly every dissolution." This seems to be "providing compensation, rather than imposing punishment, but "relies on slight of hand in application." "In the context of marital failure . . . the word 'cause' has no such [objective] meaning . . . . " It is not "a prior event (such as infection, or rust) without which the later event would not have occurred." Divorce for drunkenness or adultery is no different than divorce because a spouse grows fat or spends too much time at the office – in either case the offended spouse

[8] These categories are based on research that was done in 1996. PRINCIPLES § 1, Topic 2, at 44–48.

[9] PRINCIPLES § 1, Topic 2, at 46.

[10] PRINCIPLES § 1, Topic 2, at 47.

[11] PRINCIPLES § 1, Topic 2, at 48.

[12] PRINCIPLES § 1, Topic 2, at 49–51.

can either tolerate the "offensive conduct" or may show "unreasonable intolerance." "[T]he complexity of marital relations" prevents courts from "assessing the parties' relative moral failings[.]" It would require courts to trace the conduct and see what caused the offensive behavior. Inappropriate behavior by the other spouse may share some of the blame. So what is involved, in the drafters' view, is assessing comparative moral rectitude, not neutral causation. Violation of tort and criminal standards can be actionable separately, so there is no need to consider "cause" in marital dissolution and causation is just a cover for moral inquiry.

The second rationale for fault examined and rejected by the drafters is whether fault is "a source of compensation for harms caused by wrongful conduct."[13] However, financial loss traceable to marital misconduct is already compensated.[14] Thus, the only purpose of fault is to compensate for nonfinancial loss, but that would "employ standards that are simply too vague to serve any purpose clearly."[15] Marital misconduct would compensate only for either emotional loss or pain and suffering, both of which can be adequately compensated in tort, the drafters maintain.

The drafters dismiss further consideration of whether to allow assertion of tort claims in dissolution proceedings as a "procedural issue[] beyond the scope of these Principles."[16] It is not clear that allowing the joinder of tort claims with marital dissolution would lower "the procedural or transactional hurdles" to asserting such claims.[17] "Daily life is full of acts that meet the formal elements of battery [or other torts] . . . [and] which are not pursued to judgment" and this is a good thing, the drafters believe.[18] The drafters do not wish to "encourage more tort suits by allowing those otherwise disinclined to sue to add their possible claims to forms that the state requires them to file for other reasons."[19] The drafters consider the possibility of tort claims for marital misconduct and acknowledge that with the "general demise of inter-spousal tort immunity, battery claims between spouses face no special legal obstacles."[20] However, they admit that claims for intentional infliction of emotional distress ("IIED") are more complicated; they generally favor rejecting such claims if based only on emotional damage rather than physical battery because IIED claims boil "down to the one element of 'outrage.'" In cases of physical battery causing emotional harm as well, IIED claims are, for the drafters, merely redundant.

The drafters note, with approval, that IIED claims based on adultery have often been rejected, "as courts conclude that unfaithfulness in all its variations is inadequate to support recovery under the outrageousness standard."[21] "Regulation of commercial interactions can rely on established conventions of public behavior as well as the understanding that the actors enter the relationship with a financial purpose that both bounds and explains the range of acceptable conduct." Marriages, the drafters insist, are different.

The drafters review two cases that illustrate the degree of judicial intrusion into intimate relationship details necessary to establish IIED claims at divorce, and the subjectivity that is required in assessing such claims.[22] The drafters believe that if the "social norm against

[13] Principles § 1, Topic 2, at 52.
[14] Principles § 4.10.
[15] Principles § 1, Topic 2, at 52.
[16] Principles § 1, Topic 2, at 53.
[17] Principles § 1, Topic 2, at 53–57.
[18] Principles § 1, Topic 2, at 53.
[19] Principles § 1, Topic 2, at 54.
[20] Principles § 1, Topic 2, at 54 (footnote omitted).
[21] Principles § 1, Topic 2, at 56, 58.
[22] Principles § 1, Topic 2, at 58–61 (citing Hakkila v. Hakkila, 812 P.2d 1320 (N.M. Ct. App. 1991) and Massey v. Massey, 807 S.W. 2d 391 (Tex. App. 1991)).

spousal beating is sufficiently strong," recovery will be allowed for its violation under tort (battery) claims.[23] While they agree that emotional harms may also be inflicted, they ordinarily should not be the basis for any legal recovery since lawyers will "see more strategic advantage in making such claims," and family law should not "invite the kind of claims with which the tort law has had such difficulty."

The drafters also consider whether forfeiture might be an alternative to marital misconduct or tort claims as it "avoids the difficulty of placing a dollar value on misconduct."[24] Forfeiture might apply to a claimant who is tempted to murder his spouse, but only prohibits him from obtaining a share of the former spouse's interest – it does not require him to give up his own interest. The drafters oppose forfeiture because the results would not always do equal justice to the spouses or their families.

Thus, the drafters conclude that, apart from situations resulting in financial "waste" or causing special needs, marital misconduct should not be allowed in awarding property or alimony "because the potentially valid functions of a fault principle are better served by the tort and criminal law, and attempting to serve them through a fault rule risks serious distortions in the dissolution action."[25] "[P]unishment of bad conduct . . . is generally disavowed even by fault states" and "compensation for the nonfinancial losses imposed by the other spouse's battery or emotional abuse, is better left to tort law." Property allocation and alimony rules are designed for purposes for which consideration of marital misconduct is inappropriate. "In the dissolution of a short marriage, the dominant principle is to return the spouses to the premarital situations." In longer-duration marriages, a second purpose of dissolution law is to provide some remedy to the "financially more vulnerable spouse in recognition of their *joint responsibility* for the irreversible personal consequences that arise from investing many years in the relationship."[26]

"In a system of no-fault divorce . . . duration [of marriage] provides a valid benchmark for assessing the extent of this joint responsibility."[27] The drafters believe that it will be the "unusual case in which the fairness of the result will be improved by a judicial inquiry into the relative virtue of the parties' intimate conduct." The introduction of fault into dissolution will (1) provide a remedy less adequate than tort; (2) make the outcome of the dissolution litigation less predictable; and (3) give the parties an incentive to raise inappropriate misconduct claims.

B. Specific Problems with the Drafters' Critique of Fault

The discussion of marital misconduct in Chapter 1 of the PRINCIPLES makes several valid points. This includes the undesirability of giving parties an incentive to turn dissolution proceedings into "spitting matches" in which all the misbehaviors of the spouses are reviewed in excruciating detail to establish who did what embarrassing things and to obtain a declaration of comparative moral rectitude. The potential for abuse of discretion in comparative fault, the potential unfairness of subjective investigations into whether the parties violated their own subjective standards of appropriate spousal behavior, and the potential injustice of absolute rules are well described. For the most part, however, the drafters' treatment of fault largely mirrors the approach settled on twenty-five to thirty

[23] PRINCIPLES § 1, Topic 2, at 63.
[24] PRINCIPLES § 1, Topic 2, at 64–66.
[25] PRINCIPLES § 1, Topic 2, at 66.
[26] PRINCIPLES § 1, Topic 2, at 66 (emphasis added).
[27] PRINCIPLES § 1, Topic 2, at 66–67.

years ago,[28] and fails to address contemporary concerns about protecting community standards of minimum levels of spousal behavior.

There are a number of problems with the drafters' critique of fault in awarding property and alimony in dissolution proceedings. First, while there is a very strong and diverse literature considering fault in marital dissolution,[29] the PRINCIPLES fail to either adequately review or seriously engage the arguments that support the use of "fault" in various aspects of marital dissolution. Second, the reliability of factual data relied upon by the drafters is questionable in some cases. For example, the drafters' state-by-state characterization of

[28] *See* Uniform Marriage and Divorce Act, 9A U.L.A. Pts. I & II (2004–2005); Robert J. Levy, *A Reminiscence About the Uniform Marriage and Divorce Act and Some Reflections About Its Critics and Its Policies*, 1991 BYU L. REV. 43.

[29] *See, e.g.*, Peter Nash Swisher, *The ALI Principles: A Farewell to Fault – But What Remedy For the Egregious Marital Misconduct of an Abusive Spouse?*, 8 DUKE J. GENDER L. & POL'Y 213, 230 (2001) ("[L]egal consistency and predictability can be bought at too high a price, if there is no fault-based exception to the general rule for the serious or egregious marital misconduct of a spouse."); Michael A. Robbins, *Divorce Reform: We Need New Solutions, Not a Return to Fault*, 79 MICH. B.J. 190, 191 (2000) [hereinafter Robbins, *Divorce Reform*] ("If we really want to reduce the divorce rate, we need to find the causes of divorce and work on resolving them. This could be accomplished in three ways: [t]hrough education and counseling[;] [t]hrough reform of our divorce laws[;] [t]hrough reform of our court system[.]"); Jane Biondi, *Who Pays for Guilt?: Recent Fault-Based Divorce Reform Proposals, Cultural Stereotypes and Economic Consequences*, 40 B.C. L. REV. 611, 631 (1999) ("[T]he moral rhetoric of fault-based divorce reform serves to distract reformers from the economic inequality caused by gender-neutral divorce laws in a gender-biased world. Fault-based divorce laws and proposals do not necessarily allow for greater financial protection for women and children . . . Economic reforms must rest on guidelines designed to result in equal financial outcomes for both men and women after divorce to eradicate the post-divorce poverty that disproportionately affects women and children."); Laura Bradford, Note, *The Counterrevolution: A Critique of Recent Proposals to Reform No-Fault Divorce Laws*, 49 STAN. L. REV. 607, 635 (1997) (Bradford argues that "[t]he current divorce regime clearly requires reform" and that, although the "proposed fault-based schemes fall short," they are worth considering because many of them take into account mechanisms such as counseling, waiting periods, and education before both marriage and divorce); J. Herbie DiFonzo, *Alternatives To Marital Fault: Legislative and Judicial Experiments in Cultural Change*, 34 IDAHO L. REV. 1 (1997) (explaining that neither fault nor no-fault has proven healthy for society, and suggesting that perhaps the law should require mutual consent and/or waiting periods before divorce is finalized); Peter Nash Swisher, *Reassessing Fault Factors in No-Fault Divorce*, 31 FAM. L.Q. 269 (1997) (critique of absolute no-fault); Barbara Bennett Woodhouse, with Comments by Katharine T. Bartlett, *Sex, Lies and Dissipation: The Discourse of Fault in a No-Fault Era*, 82 GEO. L.J. 2525, 2526–27 (1994) [hereinafter Woodhouse, *Sex, Lies, and Dissipation*] (suspending the author's "'fear of fault'" and admitting that no-fault divorce "tends to reduce marriage to a calculus that considers economic harms, but not violations of physical integrity, intimacy, or trust" and suggests that no-fault divorce "seems in danger of forgetting both the rhetoric and the remedies for addressing good and bad marital conduct and abuses of trust in intimate relationships"); Lynn D. Wardle, *No-Fault Divorce and the Divorce Conundrum*, 1991 BYU L. REV. 79 [hereinafter Wardle, *Divorce Conundrum*] (presenting a critique of no-fault divorce for failing to achieve the goals of the divorce reform movement and recognizing the dilemma of making divorce accessible without making it so permissive as to undermine marriage); Margaret F. Brinig, *Status, Contract and Covenant*, 79 CORNELL L. REV. 1573, 1573 (1994) (family law should not be viewed as a "nexus of contracts" because doing so misses the critical roles families play in providing intimate human contact); Lynn D. Wardle, *Divorce Violence and the No-Fault Divorce Culture*, 1994 UTAH L. REV. 741, 774–75 [hereinafter Wardle, *Divorce Violence*] ("The nexus between violence and no-fault divorce litigation merits further examination. The theoretical and empirical connection between the no-fault divorce culture and the no-fault divorce legal system should be explored by social scientists as well as legal scholars."); Allen M. Parkman, *Reform of the Divorce Provisions of the Marriage Contract*, 8 BYU J. PUB. L. 91, 106 (1993) ("The introduction of no-fault divorce has resulted in a deterioration in the financial condition of many divorced women and their children and a reduction in the quality of family life . . . This situation could be improved by viewing marriage as a contract and recognizing that a contractual remedy can improve social welfare."); *see also* Catherine Mazzeo, Note, Rodriguez v. Rodriguez: *Fault as a Determinative Factor in Alimony Awards in Nevada and Other Community Property Jurisdictions*, 2 NEV. L.J. 177 (2002) (suggesting alternatives to either a pure fault-base or a pure no-fault-based method of determining alimony).

marital misconduct is treated with alimony and property division awards.[30] This material is very extensive but some of it is of questionable reliability. For example, the drafters classify Utah as a "pure no-fault property almost pure no-fault alimony state." However, as the Reporter's Notes indicate, a statute enacted in 1995, seven years before the PRINCIPLES were finally published, explicitly allows divorce courts to consider "the fault of the parties" in awarding alimony.[31] In 1998, four years before the PRINCIPLES were published, the Utah Court of Appeals explicitly affirmed that fault may be considered in awarding alimony.[32] In light of that statutory standard, as well as actual judicial application of it, the drafters' inaccurately characterized Utah as an "almost pure no-fault alimony" state.[33]

Similarly, the drafters emphasize the risk of barring alimony after adultery, but cite only four states that take that position. They cite eleven states in which adultery is an "appropriate consideration" that may reduce alimony but is not a complete bar, and two states somewhere in between these two positions.[34] Thus, the drafters base their fear of an absolute rule upon a straw man, selecting the most extreme form of the rule that was in effect in only four states at the time. The drafters finesse the point that the emotional loss and pain and suffering are not compensable under tort law in all states.

The drafters also suggest that marital misconduct consideration is waning in dissolution proceedings, while they admit that thirty states allow consideration of marital misconduct in both alimony and property disputes (fifteen states), or in alimony but not property contests (twenty-two always consider fault in alimony awards and eight rarely do).[35] The general description and conclusions drawn by the drafters sometimes contradict the data they provide. The drafters' evaluation of state law reflects some wishful thinking or strategic exaggeration, rather than accurate and unbiased presentation. Third, the consideration of punitive and tort dimensions of marital misconduct without any consideration of contract perspectives is a significant omission.[36] It is curious that the drafters do not analyze marital misconduct as a potential contract-based claim. Marriage is a contract, and breach of contract may be more apt than either tort or criminal law. Contract might also be a better analogy for marriage relations, insofar as it is viewed as containing some publicly-imposed contract elements which the parties cannot alter, much as minimum wage standards apply to employment agreements.

Finally, the drafters' emphasis on economic considerations is distorting. Endorsing tort claims in lieu of considering marital misconduct in dissolution, the drafters note that IIED claims have "most often been used to police relations between actors in a commercial context, enforcing a minimal requirement of decency and fair procedure as between landlords and tenants, creditors and debtors, and employers and employees."[37] Precisely! The fact

[30] PRINCIPLES § 1, Topic 2, at 68–82.

[31] PRINCIPLES § 1, Topic 2, at 74. This statute is now UTAH CODE ANN., § 30-3-5(8)(b) (2005) (internal quotation marks omitted).

[32] *See, e.g.*, Childs v. Childs, 967 P.2d 942, 946 (Utah Ct. App. 1998) ("Although not required, the court may consider fault in determining alimony."). Since then, another appellate decision has again confirmed the propriety of considering fault in Utah when allocating the economic effects of divorce. *Compare* Davis v. Davis, 76 P.3d 716, 718 n.1 (Utah Ct. App. 2003).

[33] PRINCIPLES § 1, Topic 2, at 74 (acknowledging that "[t]here are nonetheless threads of fault occasionally appearing in Utah law.").

[34] PRINCIPLES § 1, Topic 2, at 49 n.82, 53.

[35] PRINCIPLES § 1, Topic 2, at 43, 46.

[36] PRINCIPLES § 1, Topic 2, at 43, 51–54.

[37] PRINCIPLES § 1, Topic 2, at 57.

that tort remedies can enforce decency is not a justification for rejecting consideration of marital misconduct in divorce, but rather a reason why there is a need for something more than mere tort remedies.[38]

C. Defects in the ALI's Evaluation of Marital Misconduct in Dissolution Proceedings

The drafters' discussion of fault manifests seven general flaws. They are: (1) the disconnection of the PRINCIPLES from the lives and concerns of parties in dissolution actions, and other practical realities of dissolution proceedings; (2) the failure to recognize and protect the public interest in marriage; (3) the failure to recognize and protect the unique private interest that each spouse has in the marital relationship – apart from his or her interest in property and emotional and physical well-being; (4) inconsistency in discussing the proper role of moral considerations in marital dissolution proceedings; (5) misunderstanding of the ramifications of adopting no-fault divorce grounds; (6) misunderstanding of the role of discretion in marital dissolution; and (7) inconsistency regarding the problems of absolutism in divorce proceedings.

(1) Lack of Realism. The drafters' stance on fault is inconsistent with their general recommendation that predictability should be based upon the realities of "the concrete, individual patterns of specific families."[39] If marital misconduct is not *the* prime motivating, behavior-shaping, legal-proceeding influencing factor in marital dissolution proceedings, it certainly is one of the most important, especially when the misconduct is serious. Lawyers, judges, and other professionals who work with divorcing parties – indeed everyone who talks to people who recently have been involved in dissolution proceedings – understand that marital misconduct is a large part of what concerns them. Often it is a factor they wrestle with, frequently it is the motivation for the marriage's breakup, and sometimes it becomes the consuming obsession of their lives.[40] Like it or not, this is true; it is reality. For the law to simply ignore a factual reality that is so important in the lives of so many divorcing persons involved in the dissolution proceeding, that is so integral to why, when, and how they pursue such proceedings, and that manifests itself in so many ways in the tactics, claims, and defenses asserted, is both irrational and impractical. Pretending that serious marital misconduct does not matter flies in the face of reality. It matters mightily to the parties, and generally it matters more to the parties than most other considerations of which marital dissolution law does take account. It will not go away just because the ALI or existing law in some states ignores it. To disregard marital misconduct when it matters so

[38] Similarly, the drafters never explain why *procedural matters* are beyond the scope of the project. PRINCIPLES § 1, Topic 2, at 53. In fact, the PRINCIPLES recommend several significant procedurals rules and clerical provisions. *See, e.g.,* PRINCIPLES § 207 (requiring parenting plans); Principles § 3.05 (illustrating a marginal expenditure formula and worksheet); Principles § 6.03(2)-(3) (explaining the presumption concerning domestic partnership); Principles app. I, Model Provision Adopting Chapter 3; Principles app. II, Model Provision Adopting Chapter 5.

[39] PRINCIPLES § 1, Topic 1, at 3.

[40] *See generally* Paul Amato & Denise Wallin, *People's Reasons for Divorcing: Gender, Social Class, the Life Course, and Adjustment,* presented at the 63rd Annual Conference of the National Council on Family Relations (2001), *available at* http://biblioline.nisc.com (indicating that infidelity ranked as the number one cause of divorce); Mary A. Dolan & Charles D. Hoffman, *Determinants of Divorce Among Women: a Re-Examination of Critical Influences,* 28 J. DIVORCE & REMARRIAGE 97 (1998) (concluding that, regardless of socioeconomic status, women tend to list lack of emotional support and incompatibility as the primary causes of divorce); JUDITH S. WALLERSTEIN & SANDRA BLAKESLEE, SECOND CHANCES 15 (1989) ("Many adults still felt angry, humiliated and rejected, and most had not got their lives together again.").

much to the parties guarantees that divorce proceedings will be disconnected from reality. Disregarding fault may make the jobs of lawyers and judges simpler, but it makes dissolution law and legal proceedings surreal, less responsive to the key issues, and less connected to what is really happening in the parties' lives, and therefore it makes dissolution law less effective, less complete, and less just.

Moreover, a social consensus exists about many kinds of marital misconduct, as the drafters themselves acknowledge.[41] The drafters recognize this in their own recommendations to consider financial misconduct and domestic violence.[42] In those contexts, they recognize socially-established standards and respect the moral dimensions of that marital misconduct. But when it comes to sexual infidelity and other serious misbehavior, the drafters are unwilling to allow common consensus to be recognized or effectuated. This distinction between acceptable and unacceptable moral consensus considerations is both inconsistent and discriminates without justification.[43]

Moreover, abolition of fault in allocating alimony or property will not eliminate it from the dissolution proceeding. It merely forces it underground, to reassert itself as the underlying motivation for custody disputes, visitation contests, child support disagreements, and other aspects of marital breakup. It does the legal system no good to force such a powerful influence underground. It is much more problematic for courts and lawyers to deal indirectly with phantom factors than to deal directly and openly with factors that drive the parties and their litigation.[44]

The concern that if "fault" is considered in allocating economic consequences of divorce it will lead to the misuse of such claims is undoubtedly a valid concern. Divorcing parties and their lawyers already engage in a lot of "strategic" behavior. Because this is true, if some of the strategic behavior shifts to focusing on "fault," this will add little to the overall amount of strategic behavior that occurs in divorce cases. The consideration of marital misconduct can be regulated so that the incentive to engage in strategic behavior is limited, the court's ability to recognize and reject strategic behavior is maximized, the likelihood of profiting from such behavior is very small, and the prospect of negative litigation consequences resulting from such behavior offsets any temptation to engage in it. It is neither necessary nor wise to bar absolutely all consideration of noneconomic marital misconduct.

[41] A 1998 survey by the Washington Post revealed that 88% of Americans believe that adultery is immoral, while only 11% find it morally acceptable. Washington Post/Kaiser/Harvard Survey Project, American Values: *1998 National Survey of Americans on Values*, at 4, *available at* http://www.kff.org/kaiserpolls/upload/14655_1.pdf (last visited Jan. 29, 2005). A Princeton Survey Research Associates/Newsweek poll in September 1996 reported that only 2% of respondents thought that adultery was not wrong at all; 50% of those surveyed said it was wrong because it was immoral; 25% said it was wrong because it could cause pain or break up a marriage; and 17% said it was wrong because of the danger of AIDS or other diseases. The Roper Center for Public Opinion Research, University of Connecticut, Question ID USPSRNEW.092196.R15. Another comprehensive survey published in 1994 reported that across surveys 80% of all Americans strongly disapprove of adultery. Robert T. Michael et al., Sex in America: A Definitive Survey 84 (1994). *See also* Principles § 1, Topic 2, at 43.

[42] *See, e.g.*, Principles § 2.07(1)(c) (citing domestic violence as relevant in custody allocation); Principles § 1, Topic 2, at 43–44; Principles § 4.10; Principles § 5.02. *See generally* William J. Glucksman & Kristina C. Royce, *Determining Whether to Pursue Potential Interspousal Tort Actions*, 17(10) Matrim. Strategist 4 (1999) ("Most courts appear to be moving toward the more realistic understanding of what type of behavior is unacceptable in marriage, and have concluded that spousal abuse, although prevalent, is unacceptable.").

[43] *See infra*, Part II(C), and accompanying text.

[44] Wardle, *Divorce Conundrum*, *supra* note 29, at 105 ("[T]here are indications that no-fault grounds for divorce have only caused the lying to shift (as did the hostility) from the part of the proceeding dealing with the grounds for divorce to the collateral aspects, especially child custody and visitation disputes.").

(2) Failure to Recognize the Public Interest in Marriage. It has long been understood that there are both public interests and private interests in marriage. Nearly ninty years ago, Dean Roscoe Pound explained that those interests are separate, and that they should not be confused with each other.[45] Unfortunately, the drafters seem to conflate those separate interests. They simply do not recognize the validity or scope of the *public* interest in marriage. By comparing marital misconduct consideration to claims for IIED, the drafters worry that allowing marital misconduct to be considered in allocating the financial consequences of divorce would be very subjective, intrusive, and turn into a contest about comparative moral rectitude in marriage, attempting to determine who was the worse spouse.[46] These are certainly legitimate concerns. However, the drafters fail to recognize that the law can be structured to allow a less intrusive examination of individualized facts in a marital misconduct claim than now allowed for IIED claims. As the drafters point out, IIED claims reflect the variable and highly subjective "bounds of decency" set by the parties in particular relationships. But establishment of a marital misconduct claim could require proof that the spouse's behavior fell below public standards of minimum acceptable conduct for spousal treatment, rather than accepting spouses' subjective, personal standards.[47] The drafters apparently forgot that marriage is indeed a *public* status, and that it is a public institution with publicly determined standards of minimum acceptable treatment of one's spouse.

To the drafters, the content of marriage seems an entirely private subject, to be negotiated between the spouses, such that adultery or screaming abusively might be acceptable if the parties "negotiate" that and the victimized spouse receives in return some value for which he or she is willing to endure adultery, emotional outbursts or, arguably, any other kind of demeaning behavior. The drafters agree that there is a social consensus that physical battery between spouses is not acceptable,[48] and also that dissipation of assets is socially intolerable.[49] But they are unwilling to recognize any other generally accepted standards of minimum acceptable behavior for spouses. This is a huge factual and conceptual mistake.

The potential for abuse in consideration of marital misconduct, as the drafters' IIED cases illustrate,[50] only underscores the need to make the standard public, objective, and high – rather than private, subjective, and individualized. The failings and abuses in the IIED cases illustrate the need for a separate claim for marital misconduct and a different conceptual approach than tort.

(3) Misunderstanding Private Relational Interests. The drafters also fail to recognize that each spouse has a profound private interest in the *relationship* of marriage, and that spouses suffer losses other than financial and emotional losses when there has been a breach of minimum marital standards, such as infidelity.[51] Such breaches cause very real damage which goes beyond the damage that occurs when a husband and wife simply grow apart and decide to dissolve their marriage.[52] The loss is the loss of trust, and the wounds are

[45] Roscoe Pound, *Individual Interests in the Domestic Relations*, 14 MICH. L. REV. 177, 177 (1916) ("It is important to distinguish the individual interests in domestic relations from the social interest in the family and marriage as social institutions.").

[46] PRINCIPLES § 1, Topic 2, at 51, 58–61.

[47] PRINCIPLES § 1, Topic 2, at 60–61.

[48] PRINCIPLES § 1, Topic 2, 62–63; *see* PRINCIPLES § 2.03 cmt. h, at 126–27; *see also* PRINCIPLES § 5.02 Reporter's Notes to cmt. e, at 796–97.

[49] PRINCIPLES § 4.10.

[50] PRINCIPLES § 1, Topic 2, at 58–64.

[51] PRINCIPLES § 1, Topic 2, at 50.

[52] *See generally* Lynn D. Wardle, *Parental Infidelity and the "No-Harm" Rule in Custody Litigation,* 52 CATH. U. L. REV. 81 (2002).

different than those that result from the simple inability or lack of desire to make a marriage work.[53] The drafters view marital misconduct as merely a claim for private emotional harm or battery, or some other tort injury, and not as injury to the parties' unique relationship interest. Yet there is a separate individual interest in the marital relationship apart from the physical or financial interests.

The drafters' inadequate understanding of marriage reflected in Chapter 1 of the PRINCIPLES is based on the erroneous belief that there is no independent private interest in the marriage *qua* marriage. The drafters apparently do not believe that the spouse's interest in his or her marriage has any independent value that should be recognized in law. In that regard the drafters distinguish commercial relationships, believing that the law should protect commercial relationships but should not extend protection to marital relationships.[54] Yet, the social value and importance of marriage relations are just as great, if not much greater, than those of commercial relations. It is irrational for the law to deny compensation for real injuries done to the basic social unit of society.

(4) Inconsistency and Misunderstanding of Morality. The drafters try to distinguish causation from morality – favoring good, disfavoring evil. They fail to recognize that all causation assessment involves some moral dimension.[55] Any determination of what is "reasonable" requires an individual and/or community moral judgment. The drafters single out the search for causation in marital dissolution as inappropriately moralistic,[56] apparently forgetting that morality is an indispensable element of the search for "causation" in all legal inquiry.[57] Courts in all cases that find causation are, in fact, "rewarding virtue and punishing sin."[58] For example, the practice in short-lived marriages of returning the parties to the status quo ante, noted by the drafters,[59] has one significant qualification that the drafters fail to engage in their discussion of fault – this practice is subject to adjustment for any significant uncompensated disadvantage that the party has suffered as a result of

[53] *Id.* at 106.

[54] PRINCIPLES § 1, Topic 2, at 57–58.

[55] Roscoe Pound observed that "[l]aw cannot depart far from ethical custom nor lag far behind. For law does not enforce itself. Its machinery must be set in motion . . . and guided by individual human beings [rather than by] abstract . . . legal precept[s]." Roscoe Pound, Law and Morals 122 (Rothman Reprints, Inc. 1969) (1924), cited in J. Jack B. Weinstein, *Every Day Is A Good Day for a Judge to Lay Down His Professional Life for Justice*, 32 FORDHAM URB. L.J. 131, 143 (2004); *see also* J. Jack B. Weinstein, *Ethical Dilemmas in Mass Tort Litigation*, 88 NW. U. L. REV. 469, 568 (1994) ("Ethical and legal norms out of touch with real life lead not to morality but to hypocrisy, abuse, and waste.").

[56] PRINCIPLES § 1, Topic 2, at 51.

[57] John A. Robertson, *Causative vs. Beneficial Complicity in the Embryonic Stem Cell Debate*, 36 CONN. L. REV. 1099, 1104 (2004) ("Moral responsibility for a wrong requires both causation and complicity. One is not morally responsible for an event unless one has caused that event with the intention, knowledge, recklessness, or negligence necessary for moral culpability."); Keith N. Hylton, *Slavery and Tort Law*, 84 B.U. L. REV. 1209, 1249 (2004) ("Moral arguments should have a different flavor and should involve at least some norms that are not diminished by the mere passage of time or by every change of circumstances. Otherwise, corrective justice theory becomes a version of economics – practiced without the constraint of mathematical modeling."). *See also* Richard W. Wright, *The Principles of Justice*, 75 NOTRE DAME L. REV. 1859 (2000).

[58] PRINCIPLES § 1, Topic 2, at 51–52; *see also* Noel B. Reynolds, *The Enforcement of Morals and the Rule of Law*, 11 GA. L. REV. 1325, 1357 (1977) ("[S]ome enforcement of morals [in law] is inevitable, and possibly even desirable, in a society. Both sides of the traditional [debate] have admitted this."); *see generally* JOHN STUART MILL, ON LIBERTY (1859); JAMES FITZJAMES STEPHEN, LIBERTY, EQUALITY, FRATERNITY (1967); PATRICK DEVLIN, THE ENFORCEMENT OF MORALS (1965); H.L.A. HART, LAW, LIBERTY AND MORALITY (1963); H.L.A. Hart, *Positivism and the Separation of Law and Morals*, 71 HARV. L. REV. 593 (1958); Lon L. Fuller, *Positivism and Fidelity to Law – A Reply to Professor Hart*, 71 HARV. L. REV. 630 (1958); Ronald Dworkin, *Lord Devlin and the Enforcement of Morals*, 75 YALE L.J. 986 (1966); Rolf E. Sartorius, *The Enforcement of Morality*, 81 YALE L.J. 891 (1972); ROBERT P. GEORGE, MAKING MEN MORAL (1993).

[59] PRINCIPLES § 1, Topic 2, at 64; *see also* PRINCIPLES § 5.13.

the marriage or its breakup.[60] Thus, the spouse who dropped out of college to support a husband for three or four years before the marriage broke up is generally given rehabilitative alimony to allow her to recover for the educational loss resulting from her investment in a marriage that failed and which benefited the husband who was able to continue his education.[61] That is a significant moral consideration. Likewise, consideration of financial waste is a moral consideration.

Ignoring marital misconduct is inconsistent with the drafters' own position that breakup of the marriage should be considered in dividing income streams. Why should the fact of income disparity be considered at all in awarding one spouse part of the other's income, if not for moral considerations such as fairness, reliance, and protecting justified expectations? Marital misconduct may and usually does arise from and reflect exactly those same moral considerations. The drafters' rejection of moral misconduct generally, but acceptance of it when it will enhance the economic well being of one gender class of divorce litigants, seems to reflect an ideological or gender bias that neither the ALI nor the law should endorse. It is strange to award money damages for loss of economic benefits of a marriage, by allowing compensatory spousal alimony awards, but not award damages for the breach of minimum standards of interspousal behavior that hastened the marital breakdown and therefore caused the economic loss.

The drafters' description of marital breakup causation as "joint" accurately describes some divorces where the parties have just "drifted apart." However, it is simply erroneous to say all divorces are jointly caused, especially when one spouse violates clear community standards of minimum acceptable spousal behavior. In these situations, one party's unacceptable behavior is a much more serious cause of the breakup, and to suggest that the victim spouse jointly shares responsibility is erroneous. This is no different than telling the victim of domestic violence that her minor irritating words or behavior are "jointly responsible" for the explosion of domestic violence that put her into a hospital, or telling a rape victim that her flirting or immodest clothing make her "jointly responsible" for being raped. We distinguish daily between criminal domestic violence and inappropriate words, and between forcible sexual assault and foolish flirtatiousness. The gap between those categories of "misconduct" is so clear, and the social consensus is so great that we do not impute any "joint" responsibility to the victim of domestic violence or rape. Likewise, in other areas of interspousal misbehavior, such as adultery, abandonment, child abuse, or habitual alcohol or drug abuse, the social consensus that such behavior by married persons is unacceptable is so strong that it separates those behaviors from the ordinary minor indignities of imperfect marital living. To insist that causation for marital failure is always "joint" is simply wrong. Some divorce is overwhelmingly caused by the severely destructive behavior of one spouse. It is unjustifiable to exclude consideration of egregious marital misconduct and to base dissolution law on the false assumption that marital failure only results from joint, comparable fault.

The drafters are correct that the search for causation involves some element of moral judgment, but that is true of the search for causation in all contexts, such as asking whether a driver's action was "reasonable" under the circumstances. The PRINCIPLES would protect only economic expectations, but not other forms of behavioral or moral expectations of the parties.[62] However, when we allocate financial liability for an auto accident to

[60] PRINCIPLES § 5.13.

[61] PRINCIPLES § 5.13.

[62] This is in response to PRINCIPLES § 1, Topic 2, at 49–52.

the person who was driving drunk, we are making a moral statement. When we allocate contributory fault to the speeding driver, that is a moral determination that such behavior was inappropriate. The drafters fail to recognize the moral element of fault in other legal contexts, and seem oblivious to the moral dimension behind determinations of reasonableness, unreasonableness, liability, and immunity. The drafters' failure to recognize common morality in other legal contexts makes them think that recognizing moral dimensions of behavior in the marital breakup context is unique, when in fact it is not.

In the area of marriage it is especially important to recognize moral responsibility because one purpose of the law is to express minimum standards of acceptable conduct appropriate in marriage. While the law respects the parties' privacy to a great extent, it does not give them complete autonomy to do whatever they choose to do to each other. The law sets a number of moral standards for behavior with regard to the conduct of the spouses. The law does not allow the stronger spouse to abuse the weaker spouse, physically or emotionally. The law does not allow the richer spouse to leave the poorer spouse entirely destitute. We use the law to require the parties to support each other. The law does not allow either spouse to abandon mutual child support responsibilities. Both spouses are required to contribute to the extent they have the ability. At dissolution, the law enforces many of these standards by setting guidelines for determining child support, contact with the children of the marriage, awards of allocation of property, and so forth. The law allows the consideration of numerous moral factors in determining these allocations. Indeed, to consider economic fault, but not other kinds of fault, is a form of moral discrimination in favor of economic fairness over other fairness standards and discrimination in favor of financial responsibility over all other socially-established expectations regarding behavior in marriage.

The ALI position that only fault linked to the financial allocation of property or alimony on divorce is appropriate is far too simplistic. The "right" of one spouse to any financial allocation of property owned by the other or to an income stream belonging to the other depends upon a profound moral premise – that taking property or income belonging to one spouse and giving it to the other is appropriate under some conditions, such as to compensate for loss or to avoid inequity or recoup wasted assets. That is not a natural or "given" reality, but an a priori, morally-based public value premise. It depends upon and derives from community standards concerning morally acceptable marital outcomes. Thus, the award of alimony and property division in any case, and the adjustment of such awards because of waste or need-creating marital misconduct, derives from the very same moral source that underlies community norms about minimum acceptable (or unacceptable) marital misconduct such as adultery, domestic violence, or child abuse.

(5) Flawed Assumption That There Is No Place for "Fault" in "No-Fault" Divorce Systems. Another significant flaw in the drafters' analysis of marital misconduct is the foundational assumption that apart from cases of waste and special need, "fault" has no place in marital dissolution proceedings because "no-fault" grounds for divorce have been universally adopted.[63] Adoption of no-fault grounds for divorce was intended to protect privacy, to insure mutuality, to satisfy widespread concerns about forcing parties to air dirty laundry, and to restore integrity to the judicial dissolution process.[64] These considerations are

[63] PRINCIPLES § 1, Topic 2, at 66–67.

[64] Wardle, *Divorce Conundrum*, *supra* note 29, at 91–97.

inapposite in the discussion of marital misconduct claims in the context of alimony and property awards. These purposes do not preclude recognition of social standards of minimum acceptable marital behavior. No-fault grounds for divorce do not compel the repudiation of accountability for severe forms of marital misconduct in violation of clear community standards.

(6) Fear and Misunderstanding of Judicial Discretion. As the drafters note, "[p]redictable outcomes are insufficient ... unless they are also sound."[65] While rejection of marital misconduct may enhance consistency and predictability, it does so at the cost of fairness and justice. Yet, the drafters' insistence that rejection of marital misconduct consideration is necessary to curtail discretion contrasts sharply with their pervasive acceptance of judicial discretion in other parts of the PRINCIPLES.[66] As Professor Westfall observes elsewhere in this volume, the PRINCIPLES "make only a limited attempt to reign in the role of judicial discretion in determining [the] economic consequences" of divorce.[67]

Proper consideration of marital misconduct would allow discretion only in determining how much financial reallocation is appropriate for a spouse's violation of what are clearly community standards, such as the prohibition against adultery. It would not give judges discretion to determine subjectively what behavior is appropriate. Since the financial consequences ought to fit the circumstances and severity of transgression, it seems entirely appropriate to leave that to the discretion of judges to decide case by case. Finally, if the concern is that giving the judge generic power to determine "fault" or "moral misconduct" in the abstract is a problem, the obvious solution is to limit that discretion by identifying categories of morally unacceptable behavior by spouses toward each other.

(7) Inconsistency and Flaws About Absolutism. The argument that awards for marital misconduct will in some cases cause injustice is based in part on the belief that absolutes cause injustice. Thus, the drafters criticize states in which adultery precludes any award of alimony.[68] However, an absolute bar of consideration of noneconomic marital misconduct is also an absolute rule, and also causes injustice.

It is one thing to encourage people not to pursue all of the claims for battery or intentional infliction of emotional distress that they could pursue. It is altogether different and unjust to create a legal principle that would absolutely bar them from choosing whether to do so in the divorce proceeding, which is what the drafters propose.

[65] PRINCIPLES § 1, Topic 1, at 1.

[66] For example, in the realm of enforcement and adjustment of custodial responsibility, PRINCIPLES Section 2.15(1) states that "[A] court may modify a court-ordered parenting plan if it finds ... that a substantial change has occurred in the circumstances of the child or of one or both parents and that a modification is necessary to the child's welfare." According to Section 2.15(3), an "involuntary loss of income," parental "remarriage or cohabitation," and "a parent's choice of reasonable caretaking arrangements for the child" do not qualify as substantial changes requiring modification unless "harm to the child is shown." PRINCIPLES § 2.15(3). Section 2.15(2) allows courts to modify a parenting plan "[e]ven if a substantial change of circumstances has not occurred" provided the court finds "that the plan arrangements are not working as contemplated and in some specific way cause harm to the child." PRINCIPLES § 2.15(2). Section 2.16 permits the court to "modify a parenting plan without a showing of changed circumstances ... if the modification is in the child's best interests" and if the modification "reflects the de facto arrangement under which the child has been receiving care," "constitutes a minor modification, is necessary to accommodate the firm preferences of a child who has attained [a uniform age set by state law]," or "is necessary to change a parenting plan that was based on an agreement that the court would not have ordered ... had the court been aware of the circumstances at the time the plan was ordered, if modification is sought ... within six months of the issuance of the parenting plan." PRINCIPLES § 2.16.

[67] Westfall, this volume. *See also* David Westfall, *Unprincipled Family Dissolution: The American Law Institute's Recommendations for Spousal Support and Division of Property*, 27 HARV. J.L. PUB POL'Y 917, 922 (2001).

[68] PRINCIPLES § 1, Topic 2, at 49 n. 82.

As explained in Part III, the better approach is to recognize clearly established community standards about unacceptable marital misbehavior, and to consider evidence of that in marital dissolution cases.

II. The Principles' Neglect of Significant Developments in the Marriage Revitalization and Divorce Reform Movements

The other major flaw in Chapter 1 of the Principles is its failure to examine a host of ameliorative proposals that have been made (some of which have been adopted) in many states to make parties aware of alternatives to divorce and give them both the time and incentive to consider those options before getting onto the "fast-track assembly line" of unilateral no-fault divorce. Included are: (1) mandatory mediation,[69] (2) other forms of alternative dispute resolution,[70] (3) therapeutic jurisprudence,[71] (4) different procedures for parties with children than for parties without children,[72] (5) waiting periods,[73] (6) premarital counseling,[74] (7) covenant marriage approaches (now adopted in Louisiana, Arizona, and Arkansas),[75] (8) general marriage education

[69] *See, e.g.*, Maggie Vincent, Note, *Mandatory Mediation of Custody Disputes: Criticism, Legislation, and Support*, 20 Vt. L. Rev. 255, 263 (1995); Penelope E. Bryan, *Killing Us Softly: Divorce Mediation and the Politics of Power*, 40 Buff. L. Rev. 441, 523 (1992) (opposing mediation in divorce cases because it shifts focus "from rights to relatedness . . . [and thus it] endangers divorcing women and reinforces male dominance. Mediation proponents seductively appeal to women's socialized values by speaking softly of relatedness. Yet mediation exploits wives by denigrating their legal entitlements, stripping them of authority, encouraging unwarranted compromise, isolating them from needed support, and placing them across the table from their more powerful husbands and demanding that they fend for themselves."); *see also* Roselle L. Wissler, *The Effects of Mandatory Mediation: Empirical Research on the Experience of Small Claims and Common Pleas Courts*, 33 Willamette L. Rev. 565, 601 (1997); Margaret F. Brinig, *Does Mediation Systematically Disadvantage Women?*, 2 Wm. & Mary J. Women & L. 1, 33 (1995); Alison E. Gerencser, *Family Mediation: Screening For Domestic Abuse*, 23 Fla. St. U. L. Rev. 43, 68 (1995); Craig A. Mcewen et al., *Bring in the Lawyers: Challenging the Dominant Approaches to Ensuring Fairness in Divorce Mediation*, 79 Minn. L. Rev. 1317, 1322–23 (1995); Trina Grillo, *The Mediation Alternative: Process Dangers for Women*, 100 Yale L.J. 1545, 1610 (1991). These perspectives about mediation underscore the richness and diversity of the mediation literature that was simply ignored by the drafters.

[70] *See generally* Andre R. Imbrogno, *Arbitration as an Alternative to Divorce Litigation: Redefining the Judicial Role*, 31 Cap. U. L. Rev. 413 (2003); Jacqueline Kong & Jamie Olson, *Divorce in the Child's Best Interest: Alternative Dispute Resolution Methods for Resolving Custody Issues*, 4-SEP Haw. B.J. 36 (2000); Hanley M. Gurwin, *Divorce Arbitration in the 1990s*, 19-Spg. Fam. Advoc. 29 (1997). Faith-based conciliation services are also available. *See generally* Glenn G. Waddell & Judith M. Keegan, *Christian Conciliation: An Alternative to Ordinary ADR*, 29 Cumb. L. Rev. 583 (1999).

[71] *See generally* David B. Wexler & Bruce J. Winick, Essays in Therapeutic Jurisprudence (1991); C. J. Judith S. Kaye, Policy Essay, *Delivering Justice Today: A Problem–Solving Approach*, 22 Yale L. & Pol'y Rev. 125 (2004); *but see*, Morris B. Hoffman, *Therapeutic Jurisprudence, Neo Rehabilitationism, and Judicial Collectivism: The Least Dangerous Branch Becomes Most Dangerous*, 29 Fordham Urb. L.J. 2063, 2091–92 & n.120 (2002).

[72] *See generally* Betsy J. Walter, *Lesbian Mediation: Resolving Custody and Visitation Disputes when Couples End Their Relationships*, 41 Fam. Ct. Rev. 104, 109 (2003).

[73] *See, e.g.*, Elizabeth S. Scott, *Rational Decision-making About Marriage and Divorce*, 76 Va. L. Rev. 9, 76–78 (1990).

[74] The Florida Marriage Preservation and Preparation Act offers a reduction in the price of marriage licenses and waiver of the three-day waiting period to couples who undergo at least four hours of training in a "premarital preparation course," and requires couples who file for divorce to attend a "Parent Education and Family Stabilization Course" addressing the legal and emotional impact of divorce on adults and children, financial responsibility, laws on child abuse or neglect and conflict resolution skills. Fla. Stat. Ann. §§ 741.0305 (fee reduction); 741.04 (waiver of waiting period); 61.21 (parent education course).

[75] Katherine Shaw Spaht, *What's Become of Louisiana Covenant Marriage Through the Eyes of Social Scientists*, 47 Loy. L. Rev. 709 (2001) (providing an overview of covenant marriage in Louisiana).

programs,[76] and (9) special assistance for low-income or special-needs couples, such as those provided by the so-called "marriage initiatives" of the Clinton and Bush welfare reforms,[77] etc.

There is already a significant and growing marriage revitalization movement in the United States.[78] There is also, nationwide, a growing "trend toward offering families access to services to address their underlying problems, such as domestic violence, substance abuse, mental health issues [that] brings a host of service providers into the dispute,"[79] and to assist couples to address foundational issues, such as the parties' lack of communication skills, self-control skills, financial management skills, or patience, inadequate child rearing skills, and the inability to cope with the need to compromise. During the past decade, every American state has had at least one government program or policy change intended to strengthen marriage or two-parent families.[80] Three states have adopted and other states have considered adopting "covenant marriage" laws that allow couples to make a stronger commitment to marriage when they wed. Covenant marriage requires that couples: (1) obtain premarital counseling; (2) specifically choose covenant marriage; (3) seek marital counseling before filing for divorce; and (4) get divorced only for serious breaches of marital covenants like adultery or violence.[81] Other recent state marriage revitalization and divorce reform proposals include proposals to (1) replace no-fault grounds with marital misconduct-based divorce laws; (2) require premarital and/or predivorce counseling; (3) make fault a more substantial consideration in all economic aspects of divorce; (4) legalize private contract (precommitment) penalties and rewards to promote marriage-maintaining behavior; (5) give couples the option to choose a more committed form of marriage; or (6) impose additional divorce procedures or limitations when children are involved.[82]

Moreover, supporting and strengthening marriage is a highlight of President Bush's welfare reform "marriage initiatives." Pending legislation in the United States proposes at least $100 million in funding for healthy marriage education, including matching grants for high school marriage and relationship skills programs, marriage education skill development programs, premarital education for engaged couples, marriage enhancement programs, divorce reduction, and marriage mentoring.[83]

[76] Florida's Marriage Preservation and Preparation Act requires all high school students in the state to be given instruction in "marriage and relationship skills education." FLA. STAT. ANN. §§ 741.0305 (fee reduction); 741.04 (waiver of waiting period); 61.21 (parent education course).

[77] *See, e.g.*, Martha C. Nguyen, *Welfare Reauthorization: President Bush's Agenda*, 9 GEO. J. ON POVERTY L. & POL'Y 489 (2002); Personal Responsibility and Work Opportunity Reconciliation Act of 1996, Pub. L. No. 104–93, § 104 (codified at 42 U.S.C. § 601 (1996)).

[78] *See generally* Lynn D. Wardle, *Divorce Reform at the Turn of the Millennium: Certainties and Possibilities*, 33 FAM. L.Q. 783, 788–91 (1999) [hereinafter Wardle, *Divorce Reform*].

[79] Karen Oehme & Sharon Maxwell, *Florida's Supervised Visitation Programs: The Next Phase*, 78 FLA. B.J. 44 (2004).

[80] Theodora Ooms, Stacey Bouchet & Mary Parke, *Beyond Marriage Licenses: Efforts to Strengthen Marriage and Two-Parent Families. A State-by-State Snapshot*, Center for Law and Social Policy (2004), *available at* http://www.clasp.org/publications/beyond˙marr.pdf.

[81] *See* Spaht, *supra* note 75.

[82] Wardle, *Divorce Reform*, *supra* note 78.

[83] *See* Personal Responsibility, Work, and Family Promotion Act of 2003, H.R. 240, 109th Cong., 1st Sess. (2005); Personal Responsibility and Individual Development for Everyone Act, S. 667, 108th Cong., 1st Sess. (2005) ("PRIDE Act") (as of September 20, 2005, both bills were still in committee). *See also* Julia M. Fisher, Book Review, *Marriage Promotion Policies and the Working Poor: A Match Made in Heaven?* 25 B.C. THIRD WORLD L.J. 475, 477 (2005) ("The most current version of the welfare reform bill, presently stalled in the Senate, provides $100 million a year for "healthy marriage promotion activities," such as public advertising campaigns on the value of marriage, premarital education, and marriage skills programs."). *See also* National Public Radio,

There are literally hundreds of "grass-roots efforts aimed at strengthening marriage" in hundreds of "communities across the country."[84] Recent research suggests that these community-based education and renewal programs are achieving measurable gains in reducing divorce and strengthening marriage. For example, a recent independent evaluation of Marriage Savers, a church-based marriage mentoring initiative presently active in 186 U.S. cities, found that while divorce rates in matched counties without Marriage Savers declined by an average of 9.4 percent over the course of seven years, divorce rates in counties with Marriage Savers programs declined by an average of about 17.5 percent over the same period of time.[85]

These developments have not been happening in a forgotten corner. In 1996, four years before the adoption of the PRINCIPLES, the Clinton Administration adopted the first "marriage initiative" in welfare reform,[86] which has been continued and expanded under the Bush Administration. Furthermore, there has been extensive, lively, and widespread discussion in legal literature about the marriage revitalization movement in general,[87] and about various proposals and programs in particular,[88] which could not have escaped the drafters' attention. Yet there is no mention about these programs in the PRINCIPLES. Clearly, the drafters made a deliberate decision to ignore these developments.[89] In doing so, they performed a grave disservice to family law.

III. The Need to Recognize Community Standards of Minimum Acceptable Spousal Behavior Instead of "Fault" or "No-Fault"

The binary categories – fault and no-fault – are inadequate to capture the realities of marital dissolution or to provide an adequate foundation for justice in dissolution cases. These terms should be discarded in favor of more accurate and helpful operational concepts.

Morning Edition: Bush Seeks $1 Billion to Promote Marriage (Jan. 15, 2004), at http://www.npr.org/features/feature.php?wfld=1599045; U.S. Department of Health and Human Services, The Administration for Children and Families, The Healthy Marriage Initiative, at http://www.acf.dhhs.gov/healthymarriage/about/factsheets.html.

[84] What's Next for the Marriage Movement 6 (2004) (on file with author).

[85] Paul James Birch, Stan E. Weed & Joseph Olsen, *Assessing the Impact of Community Marriage Policies on County Divorce Rates*, 53 FAM. RELATIONS 495 (2004) (indicating that the dissolution rate in counties with community marriage programs is significantly lower than in matched counties without them, and that the rate of decline of divorce is significantly greater); The Institute for Research and Evaluation, Executive Summary March 2004, *available at* http://www.marriagesavers.org/Executive%20Summary.htm (last visited Oct. 4, 2004).

[86] Personal Responsibility and Work Opportunity Reconciliation Act of 1996, Pub. L. No. 104–93, § 104 (codified at 42 U.S.C. § 601 (1996)).

[87] *See generally* Katherine Shaw Spaht, *Revolution and Counter-Revolution: The Future of Marriage in the Law*, 49 LOY. L. REV. 1, 76–78 (2003); James Herbie Difonzo, *Customized Marriage*, 75 IND. L.J. 875, 962 (2000) (arguing that covenant marriage is the best option for revitalizing marriage because "[t]he attempt to restore culpability analysis to center stage in divorce proceedings will . . . succeed only in rendering divorces more antagonistic."); Robbins, *Divorce Reform, supra* note 29, at 191 (explaining that rather than returning to a dangerous fault-based system, states should combat the divorce problem through education, counseling, and non-fault based reform of the divorce system, together with a reform of the court system); Lynn D. Wardle, *Is Marriage Obsolete?*, 10 MICH. J. GENDER & L. 189, 235 (2003); Wardle, *Divorce Violence, supra* note 29, at 785; Penelope Eileen Bryan, *"Collaborative Divorce" Meaningful Reform or Another Quick Fix?*, 5 PSYCHOL. PUB. POL'Y & L. 1001, 1002 (1999); Pauline H. Tesler, *The Believing Game, The Doubting Game, and Collaborative Law A Reply to Penelope Bryan*, 5 PSYCHOL. PUB. POL'Y & L. 1018 (1999); MARTHA FINEMAN, THE ILLUSION OF EQUALITY: THE RHETORIC AND REALITY OF DIVORCE REFORM (1991).

[88] *See infra* Part III, and accompanying text.

[89] The drafters describe these profound developments as "largely procedural in nature, and . . . not within the scope of this project." PRINCIPLES § 1, Topic 2, at 67.

It is futile and unproductive to expend resources to re-solve the "fault-versus-no-fault" debate that consumed policy makers during the 1960s and 1970s. That debate is over; no-fault divorce has become the dominant, ubiquitous baseline standard for termination of marriage. There is a better way. Law reform proposals today like "covenant marriage," mediation, marriage education, and procedural reforms in cases involving children do not propose to abolish "no-fault" divorce, but to provide other options. Similarly, consideration of community consensus-based marital misconduct will not roll back access to divorce. Nor will it require an intrusive, subjective examination of the parties' comparative moral rectitude or of their many personal failings and misdeeds. While that may be required in tort if marital misconduct concerns public standards, in dissolution proceedings it can be objective, not subjective; specific, not general; and focused, not diffuse or expansive.

In dissolution cases, courts should attempt to vindicate, and reinforce', community standards of minimum acceptable spousal behavior. The purpose is not to sort out in excruciating detail the failings or moral defects of each party in order to reward the least morally culpable spouse. The goal is to determine, when either spouse asserts the claim,[90] whether any community standards about wholly unacceptable behavior in marriage have been violated. Considering such violations of strongly held, widely shared community standards would vindicate the social interest in marriage by reinforcing the community standards, would protect those values and social interests, and would potentially deter other spouses when they are tempted to engage in unacceptable marital behavior.

IV. Conclusion

In the PRINCIPLES, the drafters observe that "[o]ne expects a nation's family law to reflect its cultural values."[91] Yet, the PRINCIPLES clearly fail to do that because of the ALI's dogged refusal to consider marital misconduct, except in rare situations involving economic misconduct. While the discussion of fault in Chapter 1 is notable, it is incomplete. Chapter 1 reflects an ideological rejection of legal accountability for marital misbehavior in violation of clear community standards that simply refuses to engage in a full, vigorous discussion or analysis. Indeed, the PRINCIPLES reflect the cultural values of the small, ideological homogeneous group of drafters and ALI Advisors, rather than the values of the nation. This is clearly demonstrated by the drafters' refusal to consider a host of other proposals which may have the beneficial effect of strengthening some troubled marriages of unhappy couples, and which may reduce the animosity and injustice of divorce. Programs that have significant records of success should at least have been openly engaged and examined by the drafters. There is no doubting that the ALI intended the PRINCIPLES to be a comprehensive law reform proposal,[92] and clearly the drafters' work is encyclopedic in scope. However, the failure of the PRINCIPLES to consider or discuss basic, gateway requirements for filing

[90] Just because one spouse has committed domestic violence, adultery, or other socially unacceptable serious marital misconduct does not compel the other spouse to raise the issue in dissolution proceedings. For example, spouses may choose to privately negotiate, so as not to raise the issue, but the rule gives them a position from which to bargain fairly in the shadow of the law. Robert Mnookin & Lewis Kornhauser, *Bargaining in the Shadow of the Law*, 88 YALE L.J. 950 (1979).

[91] Ira Mark Ellman, *Chief Reporter's Foreword*, PRINCIPLES, at xvii.

[92] *See, e.g.*, PRINCIPLES OF THE LAW OF FAMILY DISSOLUTION: ANALYSIS & RECOMMENDATIONS, at 1–16 (Tentative Draft No. 3 pt. I, 1998).

for divorce, such as waiting periods, pre-filing requirements, early-diversion, mediation, and other forms of alternative dispute resolution, and ameliorative dissolution procedures constitutes a major gap in the PRINCIPLES. The failure to examine so many innovative and popular programs cannot be explained as inadvertent.

The drafters' "fear of fault," as Barbara Bennett Woodhouse calls it,[93] blinds them to many important and valuable developments in marriage-revitalization and divorce reform that could improve American dissolution law. This tunnel vision also blinds them to recognizing the need to, and strong public support for, recognizing minimum standards of spousal conduct in marriage.

The issue today is different than it was thirty-plus years ago. Then, the issue was whether a system of divorce that allowed individual failings and misconduct of the parties to dominate the divorce process should be perpetuated. That kind of spitting contest was not a particularly enlightened or pleasant way to effectuate the public interests in protecting the minimum standards of acceptable marital behavior, and it is not surprising that it was replaced by "no-fault" divorce reforms. But that is not the issue today, despite the drafters' fixation. Today, the issue is whether an absolute refusal to recognize severe violations of community norms regarding minimum acceptable and totally unacceptable behavior by spouses should be considered in marital dissolution proceedings. Unfortunately, the PRINCIPLES miss the key issues of substance and procedure by focusing on issues that were settled a generation ago. Consequently, the ALI's rejection of judicial consideration of marital misconduct in connection with property division and alimony is rigid, unfair, inadequate, out of touch with the needs of parties who file for dissolution, and oblivious to emerging dissolution law developments in many U.S. jurisdictions.

This chapter was prepared for the October 2004 Workshop entitled "Critical Reflections on the American Law Institute's *Principles of the Law of Family Dissolution*" held at Harvard Law School. Valuable research assistance was provided by Brinton Wilkins, Jonathan Wardle, Vanessa Stephens, Kevin Fiet, Eliza Ciccotti, and Ashley Valencic. Marcene Mason provided valuable production assistance.

[93] Woodhouse, *Sex, Lies, and Dissipation*, *supra* note 29, at 2526 (internal quotation marks omitted).

2 A City without Duty, Fault, or Shame

Scott FitzGibbon

Imagine all the people
Living for today...

Imagine there's no countries
It isn't hard to do
Nothing to kill or die for
And no religion too...

Imagine all the people
Sharing all the world...

You, you may say I am a dreamer
But I'm not the only one
I hope someday you'll join us
And the world will be as one.[1]

The PRINCIPLES avoid taking account of fault, as Professor Wardle details at length in this volume.[2] The PRINCIPLES in this respect extend a trend of the past several decades toward the development of the no-fault marriage, the no-fault family, and the no-fault legal system. There have also been tendencies toward the emergence of a no-fault public culture, a no-fault system of social morality,[3] and even perhaps toward a normative psychology which encourages the individual to maintain an attitude of continuous self-congratulation.

This chapter argues that the recognition of fault, in others and oneself, is actually a good thing because it is inextricably linked to the remedial side of certain basic personal and social goods. Recognition of fault has a special place with regard to marriage and the family.

How is the recognition of fault a good thing? This chapter approaches the question in three stages. First, it considers obligation, since fault relates to violation of duty, presenting

[1] John Lennon, "Imagine," *available at* http://lyrics.rockmagic.net/lyrics/lennon_john/imagine_1971.html#imagine (last visited Sep. 4, 2004).

[2] *See generally* Wardle, this volume.

[3] *See* CHRISTIE DAVIES, THE STRANGE DEATH OF MORAL BRITAIN 43 (2004) [hereinafter DAVIES, STRANGE DEATH]; P. S. ATIYAH, THE RISE AND FALL OF FREEDOM OF CONTRACT 649–59 (1979) (noting the "decline of principles" and of "[t]he sanctity of promises" in English life); Todd J. Zywicki, *Bankruptcy Law as Social Legislation*, 5 TEX. REV. L. & POL. 393, 399–400 (2001) (noting an explosive growth of bankruptcy filings by individuals and families, including many who could repay their debt without hardship). For a description of the repudiation of a "rigid" approach to the moral order among segments of the clergy, see MICHAEL S. ROSE, GOODBYE, GOOD MEN (2002). *See generally* John Eekelaar & Mavis MacLean, *Marriage and the Moral Bases of Personal Relationships*, 31(4) J. L. & SOC. 510 (2004).

an account of the goods involved in having an obligation, accepting it, and acting upon it. Second, it considers honor, broadly defined to encompass a social and political order's system of recognizing and appreciating the fulfillment of obligation. Third, this chapter considers shame and depicts the ways in which shame participates, in a remedial mode, in securing the goods of obligation and honor. The aim throughout this chapter is to develop a fairly "high" account of the goods involved, and one which is more than instrumentalist.

Several major tendencies in nineteenth- and twentieth- century thought have tended to detract from obligation, honor, and shame. One tendency, the relativist or ethical nihilist, has drawn into question the objectivity of ethics.[4] A second tendency, the romantic, has sometimes ascribed a harmful quality to obligation, in the Byronic view that man is best when he is wild and free. These tendencies also derogate from fault, for the obvious reason that if you have no obligations, you never fail to fulfill any. A third tendency enhances excuses, expanding the scope of doctrines relating to incapacity, or for example conscientious dissent, often out of a suspicion of anything "judgmental" and a general "remissive" disposition.[5] A fourth tendency narrows the writ of social and political authorities which might impose obligation and remedy fault, denying their legitimate application to private things and promoting the preeminence of individual choice. All of these trends make their appearance in writings about marriage and the family[6] and strains of them run through the PRINCIPLES' discussion of fault.[7] This chapter criticizes these trends, arguing that a well established legal and social order in general, and a well constructed morality of the family in particular, must include obligation, fault-finding, blame, retribution, and a thoroughly judgmental attitude.

I. Obligation

Fault arises from obligation. It is a condition of having had an obligation, having failed to fulfill it, and having had no excuse.[8] Thus, to understand fault, it is necessary to understand obligation. To understand the goods that may be connected to fault and its recognition,

[4] For materials on ethical relativism, *see* MOHAMMAD A. SHOMALI, ETHICAL RELATIVISM: AN ANALYSIS OF THE FOUNDATIONS OF MORALITY (2001); RELATIVISM: COGNITIVE AND MORAL (Jack W. Meiland & Michael Krausz eds., 1982).

[5] *See* Carl E. Schneider, *Marriage, Morals, and the Law: No-Fault Divorce and Moral Discourse*, 1994 UTAH L. REV. 503, 541–42 [hereinafter Schneider, *Marriage, Morals, and the Law*]:

> [T]he bountiful remissiveness of so much American thought. . . . grows importantly out of the psychologic view, which stresses the environmental causes of human behavior and the therapeutic possibilities of human life. This therapeutic remissiveness expresses itself in popular psychologic language. People are urged to give themselves "permission" to do things they feel constrained from doing, to avoid any feelings of guilt, to have high self-esteem (whatever their character or behavior might otherwise warrant), to accept themselves as they are for the valuable people they are. This remissiveness also expresses itself in the law. . . .

[6] Consider, for example, the "nonjudgmental" attitude recommended recently by a prominent sociologist:

> [Policymakers] could attempt to create policies to support and help people in whatever type of social structures they create, giving equal credence and respect to divorced and married people, cohabiting and married couples, to children born out of wedlock and children born to married couples, and to married and unmarried parents. * * * [S]ocial policies need to support people as they enter into, reside within, and move to whatever pair-bond structures fit their needs and goals. . . . Social policies must be based on respect for people's right to choose – to live . . . within any particular pair-bond structure.

William M. Pinsof, *The Death of "Till Death Us Do Part": The Transformation of Pair-Bonding in the 20th Century*, 41(2) FAM. PROCESS 135, 151 (2002).

[7] *See generally* Wardle, this volume.

[8] *See* Milliken v. Fenderson, 110 Me. 306, 86 A. 174, 175 (1913) ("[I]n the language of the law and in the interpretation of statutes, [fault] is held to signify a failure of duty, and deemed to be the equivalent of negligence.").

it is necessary to understand the goods involved in having obligations, recognizing them, and fulfilling them.

A. The Nature of Obligation

"To be under an obligation signifies being tied, required, or constrained to do (or from doing) something by virtue of a moral rule, a duty, or some other binding demand."[9] The derivation of "obligation" is "*obligatio*," a binding up.[10] To be under an obligation is to be tied. It is to be bound firmly rather than just pressed gently. To be under an obligation is to be subject to a norm which is not supererogatory – a "must" rather than a "perhaps you should."[11]

B. The Good of Having Obligations, Recognizing Them, and Fulfilling Them

To test what may be at stake here, imagine a world in which there is no obligation, or at least a world where no one ever recognizes obligation. A city like this makes an appearance in Plato's *Republic*:[12]

> [There is] license in it to do whatever one wants.... And where there's license, it's plain that each man would organize his life in it privately just as it pleases him.
>
> [T]he absence of any compulsion to rule in this city... even if you are competent to rule, or again to be ruled if you don't want to be, or to make war when the others are making war, or to keep peace when the others are keeping it, if you don't desire peace; and, if some law prevents you from ruling or being a judge, the absence of any compulsion keeping you from ruling or being a judge anyhow, if you long to do so – isn't such a way of passing the time divinely sweet for the moment?
>
> And... [i]sn't the gentleness toward some of the condemned exquisite? Or in such a regime haven't you yet seen men who have been sentenced to death or exile, nonetheless staying and carrying on right in the middle of things; and, as though no one cared or saw, stalking the land like a hero...?
>
> And [this city] spatters with mud those who are obedient, alleging that they are willing slaves of the rulers and nothings... while it praises and honors... the rulers who are like the ruled and the ruled who are like the rulers.... [A] father... habituates himself to be like his child and fear his sons, and a son habituates himself to be like his father and to have no shame before or fear of his parents... and metic is on an equal level with townsman and townsman with metic, and similarly with the foreigner.... [T]he

[9] The Oxford Companion to Philosophy 668 (Ted Honderich ed., 2nd ed., 2005). *See also* Germain Grisez, Christian Moral Principles 255 (vol. I of The Way of the Lord Jesus) (1983) ("Not all morally good acts are obligatory – for example, feeding the hungry is good yet not obligatory. The reason is that an act of this kind can have an alternative itself morally good."). Justinian's Institutes define "obligation," for legal purposes, "as a tie of law, by which we are so constrained that of necessity we must render something according to the laws of our state." D. J. Ibbetson, A Historical Introduction to the Law of Obligations 6 (1999).

[10] Charlton T. Lewis & Charles Short, A Latin Dictionary 1236 (1969).

[11] *See generally* David Heyd, Supererogation: Its Status in Ethical Theory (1982); Gregory Mellema, Beyond the Call of Duty: Supererogation, Obligation, and Offence (1991). *Cf.* The Oxford Dictionary of the Jewish Religion 211 (R. J. Zwi Werblowski & Geoffrey Wigoder eds., 1997) ("DUTY (Heb., *hovah*), an obligation or due.... *Hovah* is distinct from *mitsvah*, which can also signify a commendable, but not necessarily obligatory, action....").

[12] The Republic of Plato (Allan Bloom, translation, 2nd ed., 1968) [hereinafter Plato, Republic]. The excerpts quoted in this chapter appear in the same sequence as in the original, but with long elisions. Dots identify the elisions, even where the usual canons of style would call for asterisks. Here and throughout, passages are attributed to Plato when he himself attributes them to Socrates.

> teacher . . . is frightened of the pupils and fawns on them, so the students make light of their teachers. . . . [T]he old come down to the level of the young; imitating the young, they are overflowing with facility and charm, and that's so that they won't seem to be unpleasant or despotic. . . .
>
> Then, summing up all of these things together . . . do you notice how tender they make the citizens' soul, so that if someone proposes anything that smacks in any way of slavery, they are irritated and can't stand it? And they end up, as you well know, by paying no attention to the laws, written or unwritten, in order that they may avoid having any master at all.[13]

It is a city without *nomos*;[14] a city without the normal bonds between citizens; a city without duty. It is a city without what Plato calls, in a telling passage, the "necessary":

> [F]or the sake of a newly-found lady friend and unnecessary concubine [an inhabitant of this city] . . . will strike his old friend and necessary mother . . . [and] for the sake of a newly-found and unnecessary boy friend, in the bloom of youth, he will strike his elderly and necessary father. . . .[15]

"Necessary," ("*anankaion*,") is used here in a special sense. It does not refer to what an individual needs to keep himself alive, such as food and water, nor does it refer to what he must do to avoid trouble. That inhabitant no longer finds his mother and father necessary for purposes like those. Rather, the term refers to a bond or tie within a friendship or a family. The root of "*anankaion*" may be "*ankon*," – "arm" – and so perhaps the underlying concept is that "necessary" people are those who grip a man by the arm, obliging him to honor their wishes and to help them when they are in distress.[16]

This city will be referred to in this chapter as the "Formless City," following Professor Arlene Saxonhouse, to emphasize its "blurring of form" and "forgetting of form."[17] It is a Woodstock of a city.

There are worse places. Some people who might be crusty and paternalistic under a different regime are "overflowing with facility and charm" under these circumstances. Some souls that might be tough are "tender." Some inhabitants experience their lives to be "divinely sweet," or at any rate they feel this way "for the moment." The regime may be better than the oligarchy it supplanted, and it is certainly preferable to the tyranny to which it soon gives place.

On the other hand, Plato seems to imply that something is amiss, and the reader soon apprehends that things are not all that they should be in the Formless City. What does a city forfeit by jettisoning obligation? To approach this question, it helps to consider the Aristotlean distinction between things that are instrumentally good only and those that

[13] *Id.* at 557b–563d (Bloom translation at 235–42). The first sentence is presented as a question in the original: "And isn't there license in it to do whatever one wants?" But it is clear from the context that Socrates expects an affirmative answer. He receives one and builds on it.

[14] "*Nomos* " means "law," especially fundamental law.

[15] *Id.* at 574b–c (Bloom translation at 255) (Socrates poses the assertion as a question: "is it your opinion that . . . ?", but clearly expects to receive an affirmative answer and approves of it once he receives one).

[16] Or perhaps it refers to those whom you have grasped or embraced. *See* I CESLAS SPICQ, O. P., THEOLOGICAL LEXICON OF THE NEW TESTAMENT 97–100 (James D. Ernst, translation, 1994). *Cf.* DAVID WIGGINS, NEEDS, VALUES, TRUTH 26 (3d ed. "amended," 2002) (discussing Aristotle's treatment of the term in METAPHYSICS V: "Aristotle's contribution . . . resides in his having signaled . . . that *need* [necessity] is a modal concept of a special kind and imports the linked ideas of a situation and a non-negotiable . . . good, which *together* leave no alternative. . . . ").

[17] Arlene W. Saxonhouse, *Democracy, Equality, and* Eidê*: A Radical View from Book 8 of Plato's* Republic, 92(2) AM. POL. SCI. REV. 273, 280 (1998) [hereinafter Saxonhouse, *Democracy*].

are good non-instrumentally, between acts that we "choose for the sake of something else" and those that we choose for themselves.[18]

1. Instrumental Good

A city that forgets obligation impairs its ability to act in a decisive and coordinated manner. For the soldier to have no obligations undermines the good of national defense. For the parent to have no obligations undermines the good of well brought-up children. Obligation is good, in part, for instrumental reasons.

Instrumental accounts explain a lot. Associations that shoulder important goals, such as the military and fire department, often display highly articulated obligational structures, whereas organizations whose product is loosely defined, – university English departments, for example – often display looser ethical arrangements. A family that undertakes the task of raising upstanding members of the next generation is likely to develop firmer ideas of familial obligation than might parents who left it to the "village" to raise the children and regarded their marriage as mainly a refuge for the heart.[19]

2. Beyond Instrumentalism

It seems clear that instrumentalism cannot provide the entire explanation. Imagine a world in which there is no instrumental point to obligation. Suppose that all the good consequences at which action might aim – beauty, health, pleasure, and so forth – could be as well served without obligation as with it. Perhaps they have all been perfectly achieved already, or perhaps the world is populated entirely by persons who do just as well in the service of those goods without obligation as with it. Imagine that the city has no enemies and its food supply fattens in pastures and orchards without much effort by farmers. Suppose that children grow up perfect by nature, like flowers and butterflies. Suppose that when one citizen injures another in a vehicular accident, a wealthy treasury unhesitatingly pays for all the losses. Would the unfocused, feckless way of life of the Formless City then be optimal?

> [H]e . . . lives along day by day, gratifying the desire that occurs to him, at one time drinking and listening to the flute, at another downing water and reducing; now practicing gymnastic, and again idling and neglecting everything; and sometimes spending his time as though he were occupied with philosophy. Often he engages in politics and, jumping up, says and does whatever chances to come to him; and if he ever admires any soldiers, he turns in that direction; and if it's money-makers, in that one. And there is neither order nor necessity in his life, but calling this life sweet, free, and blessed he follows it throughout.[20]

Something is fundamentally amiss about the Formless City. It appears to have lost its hold on some basic good, and to float free. Its denizen seems to be "human being lite."

[18] *See* Aristotle, Nicomachean Ethics 1094a 18–22 (W. D. Ross, translation, revised by J. O. Urmson) in II The Complete Works of Aristotle 1729 (J. Barnes ed., 1984) ("If, then, there is some end of the things we do, which we desire for its own sake (everything else being desired for the sake of this), and if we do not choose everything for the sake of something else (for at that rate the process would go on to infinity, so that our desire would be empty and vain), clearly this must be the good and the chief good.") [hereinafter Aristotle, Nicomachean Ethics].

[19] *Cf.* E. J. Graff, What Is Marriage For? 251 (2004) ("Western marriage today is a home for the heart: entering, furnishing, and exiting that home is your business alone. Today's marriage – from whatever angle you look – is justified by the happiness of the pair.").

[20] Plato, Republic, *supra* note 12, at 561c–d (Bloom translation at 239–40).

3. Non-Instrumental Goods

Consider two troublesome characteristics of the denizen of the Formless City, unsteadiness and dreaminess.

There is no order in his life. "Jumping up," he "says and does whatever chances to come to him." This is why he seems to be "human being lite." To be fully human, a person must acquire a certain *gravitas.*

To possess and exercise any virtue in its wholeness, a person must enjoy a certain steadiness. To be fully virtuous, an action must, Aristotle states, "proceed from a firm and unchangeable character."[21] Only the self-governing, steady person, steadily reflecting and firmly choosing, "is at one mind with himself" when he acts and puts his entire self behind each action. Only the steady man acts "with an eye to [his] life in its entirety"[22] and so embeds his action in a "complete life."[23]

To recognize an obligation, especially when appetite protests, involves the subordination of the passions and the firm governance of the mind and will. Ignoring obligation strengthens the appetites and weakens the will. Obligation is a field for self-command.

In the *Summa Theologica,* Saint Thomas Aquinas makes this point when he discusses the good involved in taking a vow. What is the good of a vow, above and beyond the good of the things you vow to undertake? Why not just do the good things without the vow? Aquinas states that vowing adds a "necessity" which "strengthens the will."[24]

> "[A] vow fixes the will on the good immovably and to do anything of a will that is fixed on the good belongs to the perfection of virtue...."[25]

The Formless City displays a quality of unreality. It is "like a many-colored cloak decorated in all hues,"[26] "fair and heady."[27] More to the point, the denizen is himself "fair and many-colored"[28] and he is a dreamer, or rather he enjoys now while awake the life that was once the stuff of his dreams:

> [T]hose opinions he held long ago in childhood about fine and base things... are mastered by the opinions newly released from slavery, now acting as love's bodyguard.... These are the opinions that were formerly released as dreams in sleep when, still under laws and a father, there was a democratic regime in him. But once a tyranny was established by love, what he had rarely been in dreams, he became continuously while awake.[29]

[21] Aristotle, Nicomachean Ethics, *supra* note 18, at 1105b–1 (Ross translation at 1746).

[22] A. W. Price, *Aristotle's Ethical Holism,* 89(35) Mind, New Series 338, 342 (1980) ("it must take a lifetime to display [firm and unchangeable character] fully.").

[23] Aristotle, Nicomachean Ethics, *supra* note 18, at 1098a 18, 1100a 5 (Ross translation at 1735 & 1738) (stating that a "complete life" is a condition of *eudaimonia* (happiness)).

[24] St. Thomas Aquinas, Summa Theologica II–II, q. 88, a. 6, reply to objection 2 (Vol. II of the Fathers of the English Dominican Province translation, 1947, at 1571) (1265) ("According to the Philosopher, necessity of coercion, in so far as it is opposed to the will, causes sorrow. But the necessity resulting from a vow, in those who are well disposed, in so far as it strengthens the will, causes not sorrow but joy."). Thomas uses the term "vow" to mean a promise to God, but the point holds for promises generally.

[25] *Id.* a. 6c ("[J]ust as to sin with an obstinate mind aggravates the sin, and is called a sin against the Holy Ghost...." *See also* John Finnis, Aquinas: Moral, Political, and Legal Theory, 199 (1998) (asserting that, in a promise, an intention is affirmed in the sense of "asserted" and also in the sense of "made firm.")

[26] Plato, Republic, *supra* note 12, at 557c (Bloom translation at 235).

[27] *Id.* at 563e (Bloom translation at 242).

[28] *Id.* at 561e (Bloom translation at 240) ("[T]his man is all-various and full of the greatest number of dispositions, the fair and many-colored man, like the city.").

[29] *Id.* at 574d–e (Bloom translation at 255).

Their dreamy mentalities afford another reason for the denizens' "liteness." It would not be accurate to say that they have lost their minds altogether, but their cognition displays a disordered and episodic quality. Their thinking resembles feeling. If they attempted to account for their lives theoretically they might identify the good with "states of consciousness."[30] If they tried to compose their intellectual biographies, they might depict a series of swoops into one cluster of emotional experiences after another.[31]

Disregard of obligation may be the cause and recognition of obligation may be part of the cure. Obligation is a component of knowledge. To recognize an obligation is to practice the art of making firm distinctions. To conform to an obligation is to bring the matter into one's life and make it part of one's experiential self.[32]

The absence of obligation is part of what makes the city described in the *Republic* a place of "blurring of form" and "forgetting of form." The residents of the Formless City experience cloudiness of vision and thought for the same reason that they suffer from weakness of will. They see fewer distinctions because, having been brought up in an oligarchic regime where obligations were imposed for no good reason, they perceive no good reasons for drawing distinctions.[33] Furthermore, after they have lived the life of license for a while there are many important distinctions that they do not wish to recognize:

> [I]f someone says that there are some pleasures belonging to fine and good desires and some belonging to bad desires, and that the ones must be practiced and honored and the others checked and enslaved.... [the resident of this city] throws his head back and says that all are alike and must be honored equally.[34]

[30] *See generally* G. E. Moore, Principia Ethica §113 (rev. ed. 1903; Thomas Baldwin ed., 1993) ("By far the most valuable things, which we know or can imagine, are certain states of consciousness which may be roughly described as the pleasures of human intercourse and the enjoyment of beautiful objects. * * * [I]t is only for the sake of these things – in order that as much of them as possible may at some time exist – that any one can be justified in performing any public or private duty.... [T]hey are the *raison d'etre* of virtue.").

[31] As in the life of Bertrand Russell:

> Ever since my marriage, my emotional life had been calm and superficial.... Suddenly the ground seemed to give way beneath me.... Within five minutes I went through some such reflections as the following: the loneliness of the human soul is unendurable; nothing can penetrate it except the highest intensity of the sort of love that religious teachers have preached; whatever does not spring from this motive is harmful... it follows that war is wrong, that a public school education is abominable... and that in human relations one should penetrate to the core of loneliness and speak to that. * * * At the end of those five minutes, I had become a completely different person. For a time, a sort of mystic illumination possessed me. I felt that I knew the inmost thoughts of everybody that I met in the street.... Having been an imperialist, I became during those five minutes a pro-Boer and a pacifist.... A strange excitement possessed me, containing intense pain but also some element of triumph....
>
> I went out bicycling one afternoon, and suddenly, as I was riding along a country road, I realized that I no longer loved Alys [his wife for six or seven years]. I had had no idea until this moment that my love for her was even lessening.

I The Autobiography of Bertrand Russell 220–22 (1951).

[32] The Psalms use an experiential word – *yada* – when they praise the knowledge of the law. *See* John Paul II, The Theology of the Body: Human Love in the Divine Plan 99 (1997) ("'To know' (jadaq) in biblical language does not mean only a purely intellectual knowledge, but also concrete knowledge, such as the experience of suffering (cf Is 533), of sin (Wis 3:13), of war and peace (Jgs 3:1; Is 59:8). From this experience moral judgment also springs: 'knowledge of good and evil' (Gn 2:9–17).").

[33] Terence Irwin, Plato's Ethics 286 (1995) ("The democratic person assumes that any discrimination between desires involves arbitrary and unjustifiable force; for he sees that this is true of the oligarchic person's attitude, and sees no better basis for discrimination.").

[34] Plato, Republic, *supra* note 12, at 561c. The above is a medley of the Bloom translation at 239 and the translation in Arlene Saxonhouse's *Democracy, Equality, and* Eidê*: A Radical View from Book 8 of Plato's* Republic, *supra* note 17, at 280.

II. Honor

A. The Nature of Honor

Fault arises from a failure with regard to obligation, but the ascription of fault involves not only the wrongdoer but also those who assess his conduct. Fault and merit can be solitary, but the ascription of credit or discredit and the communication of its ascription is a social project. It relates to the system of honor. To understand the ascription of fault or credit it is necessary to consider the components of a system of honor.

Honor can be parsed into four components.[35] The first two are the most obvious: the honorable person fulfills his obligations;[36] and the community gives him credit for doing so,[37] according him respect, renown, praise, applause, and a generally high reputation.[38] To enjoy honor as a spouse is to be true to the family and faithful to the marriage and as a result to secure a position as a respected member of the community.

The third and fourth components involve hearts and minds. The third component pertains to those who acknowledge the honorable conduct of others, and stipulates that when the system of honor is functioning at its best, members of the society accord respect for the right reasons and because they themselves are virtuous people. In the exercise of wisdom and discernment they know of the excellences of others; and in the exercise of justice they bestow recognition and applause. The fourth component pertains to the person who receives respect, stipulating that when all is as it should be, he is well enough bonded to the community to respect its opinion and appreciate its recognition.

Honor is often signaled by the attitude of the head. The honoring person may bow. The honorable person "holds his head up" whereas the dishonored person holds it downwards. The denizen of the Formless City, caring neither about his own honor nor that of anyone else, "throws his head back."[39]

B. The Good of Honor

Imagine a world where people have obligations and fulfill them but where there is no system of honor. It is a world, perhaps, of conscientious but very private people. Each

[35] The following discussion owes much to PETER A. FRENCH, THE VIRTUES OF VENGEANCE 141–59 (2001) [hereinafter FRENCH, VIRTUES].

[36] The honorable person may also go far beyond the fulfillment of obligation. Often honors are conferred for heroism and other conduct beyond the call of duty. This aspect of honor has little connection with fault and shame.

[37] In an imperfect system, the community might instead honor "high birth . . . wealth . . . a great house, a grand procession of slaves and clients on the street, expensive clothes," a "proper accent" and "elegance." *See* J. E. LENDON, EMPIRE OF HONOUR: THE ART OF GOVERNMENT IN THE ROMAN WORLD 36–37 (1997) [hereinafter LENDON, EMPIRE OF HONOUR] (describing the "system of aristocratic honour" in ancient Rome).

[38] *Compare* DAVIES, STRANGE DEATH, *supra* note 3, at 43:

> [I]n the past to have a good name and a good character were both necessary and sufficient for self-esteem and for gaining the respect of others. . . . This kind of respect was available to everyone, but it had to be earned. Respect was not the cheap and impudent demand of today for automatic acceptance regardless of qualities of character or patterns of behavior.

See generally ARISTOTLE, NICOMACHEAN ETHICS, *supra* note 18, at 1095b 26–29 (Ross translation at 1731–32) ("[M]en seem to pursue honour in order that they may be assured of their merit; at least it is by men of practical wisdom that they seek to be honoured, and among those who know them, and on grounds of their excellence. . . . ").

[39] *See* Ertman, this volume, for a discussion of handshakes and embraces and what these communicate about the parties' relationship.

individual takes his duties to heart, but scrupulously refrains from "imposing his own morality" on his neighbors by thought, word, or deed. Furthermore, each cares little for what his neighbors think, looking for approbation or blame only in the mirror of his own conscience. What would be amiss? What does a community forfeit if it fails to develop an economy of honor?

1. Instrumental Good

Systems of honor provide carrots for those who fulfill their obligations and apply sticks to those who shirk. By doing so, they augment the instrumental goods of obligation. Elaborate systems of honor, complete with medals, ranks, and titles, are applied in the military and in other organizations that serve exigent purposes.

2. Beyond Instrumentalism

Imagine away once again the instrumental goods. Suppose that each citizen so thoroughly fulfills his obligations that enemies are repelled, conflagrations extinguished, and all other social requirements satisfied without the incentives of credit and blame. Imagine further that as a result, people abandon any effort to maintain an economy of honor. A hero is treated the same as a drudge; a wise leader or prophet is accorded no better recognition than a confused teenager. Should a villain wander in from another world and break a window, it is soon repaired for free, and should he light a match to burn a building, the fire is soon extinguished. Throughout, he continues to stalk the streets on the same footing as anyone else.

What is missing in such a world? What might be lost by abandoning the practices of honor? Plato's *Republic* again proves instructive, because the Formless City has neglected not only to fulfill obligation but also to sustain the social practices which recognize it. The city imposes no "compulsion" to rule; it acknowledges no "compulsion" to keep the peace; and it accords nothing but "gentleness" toward miscreants, allowing them to carry on "as though no one cared or saw." The odd, dreamy, "lite" quality of the inhabitants arises not only from the repudiation of obligation but also as a consequence of the deterioration of the system of honor.

3. Non-Instrumental Goods

A system of honor extends the non-instrumental goods of obligation, giving them special depth and a public dimension. It holds up a mirror in which the citizen can see himself reflected. It articulates judgments which he can consider when ruminating upon his own conduct. Through its eyes, he can see himself as others see him, understand himself as others do, and assess his achievements as others might. He can see and judge himself "from the outside," reflected in the eyes of others.[40] People care how they look and how

[40] *Cf.* Aristotle, Nicomachean Ethics, *supra* note 18, at 1095b 26–29 (Ross translation at 1731–32) (observing that those who pursue honor do so "in order that they may be assured of their merit" ("at least it is by men of practical wisdom that they seek to be honoured, and among those who know them, and on the ground of their excellence...."). But this reference to something evaluatative, "to be assured of their merit," seems to relate only to a very specific kind of knowledge, the sort that might be conferred by a grade on an exam. Well developed systems of honor give the honored person not only a sort of grade but also a substantive appraisal like a teacher's comments.

others judge their conduct if they are committed members of a community that maintains an economy of honor.[41]

Further, a system of honor adds to firmness of character, inviting people to fulfill their community's obligations, offering them participation in their community's strengths, and adding a social aspect to firmness of character. This is the condition that Pericles sought to instill when he advised the wartime Athenians:

> [Y]ou must yourselves realise the power of Athens, and feed your eyes upon her from day to day, till love of her fills your hearts; and then when all her greatness shall break upon you, you must reflect that it was by courage, sense of duty, and a keen feeling of honour in action that men were enabled to win all this, and that no personal failure in an enterprise could make them consent to deprive their country of their valour, but they laid it at her feet as the most glorious contribution that they could offer.[42]

Civil society is constituted by "*homonoia*" or unanimity in thought and intentionality.[43] Citizens agree on basic things – whether offices should be elective or whether to make an alliance. Citizens agree not just severally, as by chance strangers on a road might each intend to reach the same destination, but jointly and as a result of commonality of purpose and concurrence of thought. Citizens concur in a way which involves understanding and constancy:

> [T]hey are unanimous both in themselves and with one another, being, so to say, of one mind (for the wishes of such men are constant and not at the mercy of opposing currents like a strait of the sea)....[44]

The concordance of a community is sustained through reciprocity. Each member is invited to look into the eyes of others as into a mirror. It matters to each member that the others participate. It matters to each member whether others will understand, accept, and develop the firmness of character, which the community as a whole requires. The economy of honor is a component of this affiliational structure.

III. Shame

A. The Nature of Shame

Shame lies on the delictual side of obligation and on the opprobrious side of a system of honor. It is a reaction to the discernment of one's own delictual state, and involves the experience of dislocation between oneself and one's community. It follows upon the circumstances of having had an obligation, having failed inexcusably to fulfill it, having been detected and adversely assessed by the community, and having learned of one's exposure

[41] *Compare* John Rawls, A Theory of Justice 441–43 (1971) [hereinafter Rawls, Justice] ("[U]nless our endeavors are appreciated by our associates it is impossible for us to maintain the conviction that they are worthwhile.... * * * Thus what is necessary is that there should be for each person at least one community of shared interests to which he belongs and where he finds his endeavors confirmed by his associates. * * * This democracy in judging each other's aims is the foundation of self-respect in a well-ordered society.").

[42] Thucydides, The Peloponnesian War II 43 ((Crawley, translation, Modern Library ed., 1951, at 107).

[43] Aristotle, Nicomachean Ethics, *supra* note 18, at 1167b 2–4 (Ross translation at 1845) ("Unanimity [*homonoia*] seems, then, to be political friendship, as indeed it is commonly said to be; for it is concerned with things that are to our interest and have an influence on our life.").

[44] *Id.* at 1167b 6–8 (Ross translation at 1845).

and one's loss of good repute. Shame follows when the miscreant is sufficiently bound to the community to acknowledge and respect its judgment and to take it to heart.[45]

Of course, people often experience shame-like feelings for very different reasons. A mugger might experience shame as a result of having failed to steal a wallet – ashamed, in other words, of *not* having violated an obligation. Many people seem to become ashamed about things that are not disgraceful, such as being poor, unpopular, or unemployed. Therefore, the definition set forth above identifies a "high" or central case of shame, the sort of shame that can fit into the analysis which follows and which participates in the social good.[46] Defective economies of honor and shame are discussed briefly in Parts IV and V of this chapter.

B. The Good of Shame

Shame participates in the good of knowledge in one of its most painfully difficult forms, namely, knowledge of oneself as delictual, imperfect, and morally flawed. A society that develops an economy of honor and shame holds up a mirror to fallen mankind. It provides the external point of view that is necessary for the development of full self-knowledge. Gabrielle Taylor notes: "in feeling shame the actor thinks of himself as having become an object of detached observation, and at the core to feel shame is to feel distress at being seen at all."[47] Peter French observes: "It is that point of view – of seeing oneself as being seen or possibly being seen in a certain way, as exposed – that motivates the self-critical and self-directed judgment that produces shame reactions."[48] Shame leads to the reestablishment of modesty and the restoration of a character which is perceptive in self-appraisal and firm in matters of conduct.

Shame supports the legal order. As Plato says in *The Laws*, shame secures obedience: "[w]hen ignoble boldness appears, ... [the laws of a good lawgiver] will be able to send in as a combatant the noblest sort of fear accompanied by justice, the divine fear to which we give the name 'awe' and 'shame'."[49]

Shame, with its roots within the family, secures obedience in Plato's *Republic*, not in the Formless City but under another regime where:

> an older man will be charged with ruling and punishing all the younger ones.... And further, unless rulers command it, it's not likely that a younger man will ever attempt to

[45] *See* Aristotle, Rhetoric, at 1383b 13 *et. seq.*, in II The Complete Works of Aristotle 2152, 2204–05 (W. Rhys Roberts, translation, J. Barnes ed., 1984) ("Shame may be defined as pain or disturbance in regard to bad things... which seem likely to involve us in discredit; and shamelessness as contempt or indifference in regard to these same bad things. If this definition be granted, it follows that we feel shame at such bad things as we think are disgraceful to ourselves or those we care for. These evils are, in the first place, those due to badness.... [Examples include] having carnal intercourse with forbidden persons.... * * * Now since shame is the imagination of disgrace, in which we shrink from the disgrace itself and not from its consequences, and we only care what opinion is held of us because of the people who form that opinion, it follows that the people before whom we feel shame are those whose opinion of us matters to us. Such persons are: those who admire us, those whom we admire, those by whom we wish to be admired, those with whom we are competing, and those whose opinion of us we respect.").

[46] Arguments for an objectivist account of shamefulness and an objectivist/subjectivist account of self-respect are presented in Martha Craven Nussbaum, *Shame, Separateness, and Political Unity: Aristotle's Criticisms of Plato*, in Essays on Aristotle's Ethics 395, 398 et seq. (Amélie Oksenberg Rorty ed., 1980).

[47] Gabrielle Taylor, Pride, Shame and Guilt: Emotions of Self-Assessment 60 (1985).

[48] French, Virtues, *supra* note 35, at 152.

[49] The Laws of Plato 671d (Thomas L. Pangle, translation, 1980, at 53–54). *See generally* Eric A., Posner, Law and Social Norms (2000) ch. 6 ("Status, Stigma, and the Criminal Law").

> assault or strike an older one. And he won't, I suppose, dishonor one in any other way. For there are two sufficient guardians hindering him, fear and shame: shame preventing him from laying hands as on parents, fear that the others will come to the aid of the man who suffers it, some as sons, others as brothers, and others as fathers.[50]

A society that deploys awe and shame can often secure compliance with the laws in this way more effectively than through the threat of criminal sanctions. Shame is, as Plato says, a "guardian."

Shame is personal and involves the heart in a way that may not be the case with the penalties imposed by law. Pope John Paul II observed:

> [S]hame is a complex experience... in the sense that, almost keeping one human being away from the other (woman from man), it seeks at the same time to draw them closer personally, creating a suitable basis and level in order to do so.[51]

A system of honor facilitates restitution, reparation, reconciliation, and the other steps that may be necessary to set things straight. It includes the practices of acknowledging, confessing, apologizing, and repairing delicts. On the other side of the equation lie the practices of recognizing fault, accepting apologies, calibrating the appropriate sort of restitution, and letting bygones be bygones once restitution has been made. Shame leads to repentance, reconciliation, rehabilitation, and the recovery of honor. Shame leads on to redemption.

IV. Shamelessness and the Shameless City

The shameless person detaches himself from the system of honor. His disposition toward the ministrations of the authorities is mutinous. He does not care whether he leads an acceptable life or about how his community assesses his conduct. He has no intention of apologizing for his faults or making restitution for his wrongs, and he has no interest in reconciliation or redemption. Once again, the Formless City is instructive, since its denizen "has no shame before... his parents."[52] Shamelessness might be defined as indifference to the opinion of the community and a repudiation of its system of honor, at least insofar as that system generates adverse conclusions about oneself. Coriolanus exemplified shamelessness when he turned his back on the people of Rome.[53]

The trajectory of the Formless City extends to a point where shamelessness is not only individual but public, mutual, and collective. Persons who would normally exercise authority and reward merit with honor, and punish delictual conduct with disgrace and shame, no longer command respect and perhaps, eventually, no longer expect it. The rulers try to be like the ruled. "[T]he teacher... is frightened of the pupils and fawns on them.... [T]he old come down to the level of the young; imitating the young, they are overflowing with facility and charm.... "[54]

Public opinion – that commonality of will and reason which lies at the foundation of the political community[55] – decomposes to the extent that people no longer care whether

[50] Plato, Republic, *supra* note 12, at 465 a–b (Bloom translation at 144).

[51] John Paul II, Original Unity of Man and Woman: Catechesis on The Book of Genesis 93 (1981).

[52] Plato, Republic, *supra* note 12, at 562e (Bloom translation at 241).

[53] William Shakespeare, The Tragedy of Coriolanus act III, sc. 3.

[54] Plato, Republic, *supra* note 12, at 563 a–b (Bloom translation at 241).

[55] *Supra* Part II(B).

some avoid service when the city is at war or behave belligerently when the city is at peace or whether persons convicted of crimes take their places in the public square without distinction from the innocent. The political and social economy of honor deteriorates. Perhaps some cities follow this course because they lose confidence in the validity of moral conclusions generally, or because they conclude that it is an inappropriate exercise of political and social position to "inflict" judgments on other citizens, even in an informal way. Perhaps they set a very high value on self-esteem and concur on making their social order into one great mutual admiration society.[56]

The formation of conclusions as to merit and demerit is abandoned. The city accedes to what Christie Davies, in his recent book *The Strange Death of Moral Britain*, characterizes as "the cheap and impudent demand of today for automatic acceptance regardless of qualities of character or patterns of behavior."[57] The city no longer confers honor or dishonor, no longer discerns fault, and no longer inspires shame.[58]

A shameless denizen of a shameless city has no "critical audience," no external point of view from which to assess himself. The mirror reflects a wavering and dreamy image. Bereft of self-understanding, he has little hope of recovery. Inhabiting a city that lacks a well constructed system of honor, he finds at hand no facilities for rehabilitation.

V. The Shameful City

A city may develop a false economy of honor, according to which the meretricious accomplishments of temporary flute-players and pseudophilosophers earn everyone his five minutes of fame. Or progressing still further, a city might develop an economy of *dishonor*. In a shameful city, fulfillment of obligation incurs disrespect rather than admiration. The shameful city "spatters with mud those who are obedient, alleging that they are willing slaves of the rulers and nothings."[59] It assaults modesty. It rewards disregard of obligation and magnificence in the indulgence of vice with praise and admiration and perhaps even celebrity status.

VI. The Family

A. Obligation

To be a father or mother, or a son or daughter, or a husband or wife, is to be subject to special duties. Family, and especially marriage, is a field for the recognition and fulfillment

[56] *See* Rawls, Justice, *supra* note 41, at 442 ("[A]s citizens we are to reject the standard of perfection as a political principle, and for the purposes of justice avoid any assessment of the relative value of one another's way of life.... Thus what is necessary is that there should be for each person at least one community of shared interests to which he belongs and where he finds his endeavors confirmed by his associates. And for the most part this assurance is sufficient whenever in public life citizens respect one another's ends and adjudicate their political claims in ways that also support their self-esteem.").

[57] Davies, Strange Death, *supra* note 3, at 43 (2004).

[58] *Cf. id.* at 208 ("There has been a decline in moralism with its emphasis on autonomous individuals who were free to choose either virtuous innocence or deliberate guilt and to whose choices society responded with appropriate forms of reward, protection, and penalties. It was replaced by causalism ... namely the minimizing of harm regardless of moral status.").

[59] Plato, Republic, *supra* note 12, at 562d (Bloom translation at 241).

of obligation. Professor James Q. Wilson identifies this as a universal feature of human societies:

> In every community and for as far back in time as we can probe, the family exists and children are expected, without exception, to be raised in one. By a family I mean a lasting, *socially enforced obligation* between a man and a woman that authorizes sexual congress and the supervision of children.[60]
>
> [Society] embed[s] marriage in an elaborate set of rules.... Those rules are largely part of another universal feature of all human societies, the kinship system. * * * Every society... surround[s] the mother-father bond with a host of customary rules and legal provisions. * * * [E]very society imposes rules of courtship, provides for some kind of definition of marriage, restricts a man's access to other women, and in many instances requires that the marriage be arranged in advance by older family members.[61]

The non-instrumental goods of obligation are present in a special way within the family. As Professor Wilson concludes:

> [M]ore than a useful connection is produced by marriage, for the family, when it lasts, does for people what no other institution can quite manage. Every person wishes to form deep and lasting bonds with other people, bonds that will endure beyond the first blush of romance or the early urgings of sexual desire. The family is our most important way of creating intimacy and commitment.[62]

Nothing steadies the wild adolescent spirit so thoroughly as a sustained marriage.[63] You know nothing so well in life as the spouse whom you have loved faithfully for many years.

B. Honor

Family obligations are seldom entirely private; many are social obligations as well. As Professor Wilson states in the passage above, families involve "*socially enforced* obligation."

Societies perennially care about family obligations because they discern that the family is the "fundamental group unit of society," as the Universal Declaration of Human Rights calls it[64] and the family is "the foundation on which is erected the essential structure of

[60] James Q. Wilson, The Marriage Problem: How Our Culture Has Weakened Families 24 (2002) [hereinafter Wilson, The Marriage Problem].

[61] *Id.* at 30.

[62] *Id.* at 31–32.

[63] *See* Émile Durkheim, Suicide: A Study in Sociology 270–1 (John A. Spaulding & George Simpson translation, 1951):

> [B]y forcing a man to attach himself forever to the same woman [marriage] assigns a strictly definite object to the need for love, and closes the horizon. This determination is what forms the state of moral equilibrium from which the husband benefits. Being unable to seek other satisfactions than those permitted, without transgressing his duty, he restricts his desires to them.... Though his enjoyment is restricted, it is assured and this certainty forms his mental foundation.

Studies support this "moral equilibrium" thesis, establishing that married people are steadier employees – less likely to miss work, less likely to show up hung-over or exhausted, more productive, and less likely to quit – and are steadier in many other ways as well: less likely to overindulge in alcohol, drive too fast, take drugs, smoke, and get into fights. *See* Linda J. Waite & Maggie Gallagher, The Case for Marriage: Why Married People are Happier, Healthier, and Better Off Financially 47–64 and 97–109 (2000); Margaret F. Brinig, *Unmarried Partners and the Legacy of* Marvin v. Marvin, 76 Notre Dame L. Rev. 1311, 1316–17 (2001).

[64] Article 16(3), Universal Declaration of Human Rights, adopted December 10, 1948, G.A. Res. 217A (III), UN Doc. A/810 (1948).

social order" as Professor Wilson states.[65] A "core insight of the Western tradition" has been that:

> [M]arriage is good not only for the couple and their children, but also for the broader civic communities of which they are a part. The ancient Greeks and Roman Stoics called marriage variously the foundation of republic and the private font of public virtue. The church fathers called marital and familial love 'the seedbed of the city,' 'the force that welds society together.' Catholics called the family 'a domestic church,' 'a kind of school of deeper humanity.' Protestants called the household a 'little church,' a 'little state,' a 'little seminary,' a 'little commonwealth.' American jurists and theologians taught that marriage is both private and public, individual and social, temporal and transcendent in quality . . . a pillar if not the foundation of civil society.[66]

Similarly, it has been a core doctrine of the Confucian tradition that:

> It is only . . . when the person is cultivated that order is brought to the family; when order is brought to the family that the state is well governed; when the state is well governed that peace is brought to the world.[67]

Because societies care about family obligations they make them a part of their systems of honor:

> Marriage and parenthood are social institutions. A social institution is 'a pattern of expected action of individuals or groups enforced by social sanctions, both positive and negative.' * * * Social institutions are vital not just because they provide some forms for family life; they also embody specific norms that are thought to serve desirable social ends. In the American institution of the family, members are conventionally expected, among other things, to be affectionate, considerate, and fair, to be animated by mutual concern, to sacrifice for each other, and to sustain these commitments for life. These ideals compose a kind of social prescription for enduring, pacific, and considerate family relationships which people may generally benefit by following. They also form the basis for the social sanctions, positive and negative, which can sustain people in civilized family life when other incentives temporarily fail.
>
> Social institutions, then, offer patterns of behavior that channel people into family life, that support them in their efforts to fulfill the obligations they undertake, that help hold them to the commitments they make, and that constrain them from harming other family members.[68]

A society which, atypically, persuaded itself that the family was not a matter of civic relevance because its functions could be performed by schools or villages would likely leave it out of the system of honor, taking the view that marital disorders were not a matter for public concern, and that marital misconduct, even of a flagrant nature, was no obstacle to

[65] *See* Wilson, The Marriage Problem, *supra* note 60, at 66 ("The family is not only a universal practice, it is the fundamental social unit of any society, and on its foundation there is erected the essential structure of social order – who can be preferred to whom, who must care for whom, who can exchange what with whom.").

[66] John Witte, Jr., *The Tradition of Traditional Marriage,* in Marriage and Same Sex Unions: A Debate 47, 58 (Lynn D. Wardle, Mark Strasser, William C. Duncan, and David Orgon Coolidge eds., 2003). *See generally* John Witte, Jr., From Sacrament to Contract: Marriage, Religion and Law in the Western Tradition (1997).

[67] "The Great Learning," *quoted in* I Sources of Chinese Tradition From Earliest Times to 1600 at 331 (2d ed., Wm. Theodore de Bary & Irene Bloom, compilers, 1999).

[68] Schneider, *Marriage, Morals, and the Law, supra* note 5, at 571–72.

high office. A society which ceased to concur on a coherent understanding of the definition and purpose of family would experience the collapse of its economy of family honor.[69]

C. Shame

The ancient Romans provide a good example of the perennial connections between family obligation, family honor, and the experience of shame when family comes up short. Strongly emphasizing the role of the parent as a "transmitter of traditional morality"[70] and the function of the family as a transmitter of social rank and wealth,[71] the Romans set high standards of familial obligation[72] and accorded various legal privileges to those who married and begot children, including preference in appointment to office.[73] Acutely aware of the vicarious honor and dishonor that might be transmitted through family connections,[74] Cicero exhorted his brother to conduct himself in a creditable manner as governor of a province and to see to it that his household also behaved well, noting: "you are not seeking glory for yourself alone . . . you have to share that glory with me."[75]

In our own society, as Professor Wilson states, "[s]hame once inhibited women from having children without marrying and men from abandoning wives for trophy alternatives. Today it does much less of either."[76]

VII. Dissolution: The Family without Duty, Guilt, or Shame

The nonrecognition of obligation and the denial of fault have introduced the conditions of the Formless City into the moral order of the family. The dreamy, superficial fellow depicted by Plato makes an appearance as "husband lite" and perhaps "wife lite" in Judith Wallerstein's study *The Unexpected Legacy of Divorce*, in her description of the parents of "Billy":

> The marriage ended with a disquieting lack of feeling. Billy's mother had come to resent her husband's preoccupation with partying and business. After he started an affair and took no pains to conceal it, she asked him to leave. They shared one attorney and settlement negotiations were simple. Both felt it was a fair and compatible divorce. . . .
>
> Many people separate as coolly as this couple did. The marriage fails for any number of reasons but the partners are not particularly hurt or wounded by the divorce. Both

[69] *Compare* the impossibly elastic definitions of "family" presented in recent United Nations documents. *See* Maria Sophia Aguirre & Ann Wolfgram, *United Nations Policy and the Family: Redefining the Ties that Bind: A Study of History, Forces and Trends*, 16 B.Y.U. J. Pub. L. 113, 116 (2002).

[70] Suzanne Dixon, The Roman Mother 233 (1988) [hereinafter Dixon, Roman Mother] ("The central argument of this work has been that the Roman mother was not associated as closely with the young child or with undiscriminating tenderness as the mother of our own cultural tradition but was viewed primarily as the transmitter of traditional morality. . . . ").

[71] *See* Judith Evans Grubbs, Women and the Law in the Roman Empire: A Sourcebook on Marriage, Divorce and Widowhood 81 (2002) [hereinafter Grubbs, Women and the Law] ("The Romans considered marriage a partnership, whose primary purpose was to have legitimate descendants to whom property, status, and family qualities could be handed down through the generations.").

[72] The ancient Romans laid great emphasis on *pietas in parentes* to the extent that "Roman adults were expected to display great respect and even submissiveness to their parents." Dixon, Roman Mother, *supra* note 70, at 234.

[73] Grubbs, Women and the Law, *supra* note 71, at 84.

[74] Lendon, Empire of Honour, *supra* note 37, at 45 ("Although honour was a personal quality, its aura extended over household and connections by blood and marriage: a man's family was part and parcel of his social persona. Its members' conduct reflected on him, his on them. . . . ").

[75] Marcus Tullius Cicero, "Epistulae ad Quintum Fratrem" I i. 44 (W. Glynn Williams, translation, XXVIII Loeb Classics Series 435).

[76] Wilson, The Marriage Problem, *supra* note 60, at 217.

> believe their needs have changed or that they find each other boring and that they are moving on to livelier times.[77]

Even "Billy," in fourth grade at the time, seems at first to be "lite," based on what his parents say about him. "'Now I can get a dog,' his mother remembers him saying on receiving the news of his father's departure. His dad was allergic to dogs."[78] His father reports that actually "'Billy' is 'lucky.'[79] From now on, 'Billy' will have 'the bonus of two Christmases, two birthdays, and probably two daddies.'"[80]

VIII. Conclusion

The PRINCIPLES' rejection of considerations of fault and similar recent measures extend the tendency toward obliviousness to fault and the elimination of adverse judgment from the legal and social order that bears upon the hearth and home.[81] We may not yet have arrived at the point where abusers of spouses walk the streets unpunished, but if the PRINCIPLES' approach carries the day, we may have approached a social situation in which those who have deserted their indigent wives and neglected their deserted children and in other ways violated basic familial obligations are exempted from blame and opprobrium. Adultery prosecutions are unheard of; the tort of alienation of affections has been widely abolished.[82] Divorce is available merely by the consent of the parties, and indeed usually by the fiat of one party alone, however great his own wrongdoing and without regard to the harm that may be imposed on the other spouse. Public opinion may turn a blind eye. It is a regime of divorce by repudiation.

Some who guide public opinion are willing to recommend the dishonoring of obligations and the disregard of fault. In December 2003, the *Boston Globe* published an advice column in which a man inquired as to the advisability of leaving his wife in order to be with his mistress. His wife was a "good woman," he admitted, but did not fully share his interests. He and his wife also had a ten-year-old daughter. Based on these facts, the *Globe's* headline writer characterized the man's relationship with his wife as an "empty marriage" and the *Globe's* columnist advised him to make the break and leave his family.[83] (What about the

[77] JUDITH WALLERSTEIN, JULIA LEWIS, & SANDRA BLAKESLEE, THE UNEXPECTED LEGACY OF DIVORCE: A 25 YEAR LANDMARK STUDY 228–29 (2000).

[78] *Id.* at 228.

[79] *Id.* at 226.

[80] *Id.* at 228.

[81] *See* MARY ANN GLENDON, ABORTION AND DIVORCE IN WESTERN LAW: AMERICAN FAILURES, EUROPEAN CHALLENGES 107–08 (1987) (footnote omitted):

> In the United States the 'no-fault' idea blended readily with the psychological jargon that already has such a strong influence on how Americans think about their personal relationships. It began to carry the suggestion that no one is ever to blame when a marriage ends. . . . The no-fault terminology fit neatly into an increasingly popular mode of discourse in which values are treated as a matter of taste, feelings of guilt are regarded as unhealthy, and an individual's primary responsibility is assumed to be to himself. Above all, one is not supposed to be 'judgmental' about the behavior and opinions of others.

See also Schneider, *Marriage, Morals, and the Law, supra* note 5, at 569 ("[B]y declining to discuss divorce in moral terms, the law wrongly suggests that divorce is not a moral issue.").

[82] Michele Crissman, *Alienation of Affections: An Ancient Tort – But Still Alive in South Dakota*, 48 S.D. L. REV. 518 (2003).

[83] "Annie's Mailbox: Because of daughter, he stays in empty marriage," BOSTON GLOBE, Dec. 30, 2003, at E-2 col. 3 ("While divorce isn't the preferred option, children are quite resilient. . . . If counseling doesn't help, try a legal separation."). *See generally* MAGGIE GALLAGHER, THE ABOLITION OF MARRIAGE: HOW WE DESTROY LASTING LOVE (1996); BARBARA DAFOE WHITEHEAD, THE DIVORCE CULTURE: RETHINKING OUR COMMITMENTS TO MARRIAGE AND THE FAMILY (1998).

ten-year-old daughter? The columnist had only the following to say: “Children are quite resilient.”)

A no-fault legal and social order – a “city without fault,” – is also a legal and social order that is unable to recognize obligation. It impairs the firmness of character of its citizens and the security of knowledge and judgment that is the foundation of political and familial solidarity. A no-fault, no-obligation political and social order erodes the economy of honor. It no longer inspires shame in those who depart from good citizenship. It thus diminishes their capacity to see themselves in the eyes of a disapproving audience and to commence the painful process of self-rectification and rehabilitation. A city without fault is a city without redemption.

My thanks for assistance to James Gordley, Shannon Cecil Turner Professor of Jurisprudence, University of California at Berkeley; also, for assistance with matters pertaining to Plato's *Republic* in connection with a related article, to Professors Christopher Bruell, David Lowenthal, Francis McLaughlin, and Paul McNellis, S.J., of Boston College. Portions of this chapter extend and develop material in Scott FitzGibbon, *Marriage and the Good of Obligation*, 47 Am. J. Juris. 41 (2002) and *Marriage and the Ethics of Office*, 18 Notre Dame J.L. Ethics & Pub. Pol'y 89 (2004).

PART TWO. CUSTODY

3 Partners, Care Givers, and the Constitutional Substance of Parenthood

David D. Meyer

The PRINCIPLES suffer from no lack of ambition. In seeking to rethink family law from the ground up, the PRINCIPLES would discard age-old assumptions about family roles and identity and push society to give equal respect to a significantly broader range of family forms. The resulting innovations – equating committed cohabitation with marriage, same-sex and opposite-sex relationships, and non-marital property with marital property for some purposes of property distribution, among others – have inspired both alarm and admiration.[1]

True to form, the PRINCIPLES' approach to child custody disputes, set out in Chapter 2, proposes not merely to tinker with the criteria for selecting a child's custodian or the nature of custodial rights, but to rethink the very idea of parenthood. Care givers lacking any adoptive or biological ties to the child – dismissed by traditional family law as "legal strangers" – would gain the ability to preserve their child rearing role even over the objections of a child's legal parents. More provocatively, the PRINCIPLES would deem these care givers *parents* of the child. These new parents, moreover, would add to, rather than substitute for, any preexisting parents, so that a child might have at once three, four, or even more parents sharing in his or her upbringing.

The PRINCIPLES' provision for new routes to parenthood, in the form of "parenthood by estoppel" and "de facto parenthood," has drawn fire from a diverse group of critics. Predictably, some have objected that state action broadening the definition of parenthood would violate the constitutional rights of biological and adoptive parents.[2] By this view, the Constitution precludes the drafters' innovations because it fixes the concept of parenthood at its traditional boundaries. Others have located the constitutional defect not in the PRINCIPLES' assignment of parent identity to nontraditional persons, but rather

[1] For a small sampling of the PRINCIPLES' academic reception, *see* Symposium, *The ALI* Principles of the Law of Family Dissolution, 2001 BYU L. REV. 857; Symposium, *The American Law Institute's* Principles of the Law of Family Dissolution, 4 J.L. & FAM. STUD. 1 (2002); Symposium, *Gender Issues in Divorce: Commentaries on the American Law Institute's* Principles of the Law of Family Dissolution, 8 DUKE J. GENDER L. & POL'Y 1 (2001); Nancy D. Polikoff, *Making Marriage Matter Less: The ALI Domestic Partner Principles Are One Step in the Right Direction*, 2004 U. CHI. LEGAL F. 353; Julie Shapiro, *De Facto Parents and the Unfulfilled Promise of the New ALI Principles*, 35 WILLAMETTE L. REV. 769 (1999); David Westfall, *Unprincipled Family Dissolution: the American Law Institute's Recommendations for Spousal Support and Division of Property*, 27 HARV. J.L. & PUB. POL'Y 917 (2004); David Westfall, *Forcing Incidents of Marriage on Unmarried Cohabitants: The American Law Institute's Principles of Family Dissolution*, 76 NOTRE DAME L. REV. 1467 (2001).

[2] *See infra* notes 43–44 and accompanying text.

in its allowance for multiple persons to hold that identity concurrently.[3] By this view, the Constitution has relatively little bearing on the identity of the persons designated by the state as "parents," but strictly protects the traditional prerogatives that attend that status, including the prerogative to deny that role to other care givers.

This chapter charts a middle course between these understandings of the Constitution's protection of parenthood. The Constitution, this chapter argues, imposes meaningful limits on the state's ability to deny parenthood status to traditional parent figures and therefore significantly qualifies the state's freedom simply to reassign traditional parenting prerogatives to nontraditional care givers. At the same time, the Constitution imposes fewer limitations than is often assumed on the creation of new parenting roles. On these assumptions, the route taken by the PRINCIPLES – preserving the identity of traditional parents while simultaneously extending parenting status to additional, nontraditional care givers – is both constitutional and, quite possibly, the most that government can do to secure the welfare of children in some unconventional family settings.

This chapter proceeds in three parts. Part I describes the key features of the PRINCIPLES' approach to child custody and situates them in the context of recent trends in child-custody law. Part II examines leading criticisms of the PRINCIPLES' custody innovations, focusing particularly on constitutional objections. Finally, Part III explores the constitutional substance of parenthood in an effort to identify the relevant limits on the discretion allowed to states in defining parenting identity and roles.

I. The New Parenthood

Until recently, the legal idea of parenthood was generally stable. The boundaries of traditional parenthood could be defined with relative precision through rules respecting biology, marriage, and adoption. In recent years, however, the consensus that long supported enforcement of bright-line boundaries has weakened in the face of non-traditional child rearing arrangements that seem to defy basic assumptions underlying the old rules.[4] As a result, state courts and even some legislatures have begun to innovate by recognizing new routes to parenthood based on intention, partnership, and care giving. Among the proponents of this new parenthood, the PRINCIPLES are clearly in the vanguard.

A. The Place of Parenthood in Existing Custody Law

Child custody law has always made it essential to identify clearly a child's parents. The "tender years doctrine," favoring mother custody, and earlier law recognizing a custody

[3] *See* Emily Buss, *"Parental" Rights*, 88 VA. L. REV. 635 (2002); *cf.* Elizabeth Bartholet, *Guiding Principles for Picking Parents*, 27 HARV. WOMEN'S L.J. 323, 342–43 (2004) (urging caution about the idea of recognizing "a multiplicity of parents" on grounds that it may intrude improperly on values of "family privacy," though without expressly contending that to do so would be unconstitutional).

[4] *See* Katharine K. Baker, *Bargaining or Biology?: The History and Future of Paternity Law and Parental Status*, 14 CORNELL J. L. & PUB. POL'Y 1 (2004); June Carbone, *The Legal Definition of Parenthood: Uncertainty at the Core of Family Identity*, 65 LA. L. REV. 1295 (2005); June Carbone & Naomi Cahn, *Which Ties Bind?: Redefining the Parent–Child Relationship in an Age of Genetic Certainty*, 11 WM. & MARY BILL OF RIGHTS J. 1011 (2003); David D. Meyer, *Parenthood in a Time of Transition: Tensions Between Legal, Biological, and Social Conceptions of Parentage*, 54 AM. J. COMP. L.-(forthcoming 2006).

entitlement for fathers, assumed knowledge of the child's mother and father.[5] Although courts today use the more indeterminate "best interests of the child" standard to allocate custodial rights, status as a parent remains nearly as determinative as under the older, gender-specific presumptions.[6] Threshold determinations of parentage are vitally important because the law in every state strongly prefers, in some fashion, parents over nonparents in deciding child custody. In many states, for instance, a parent is entitled to custody in a contest with a nonparent unless the parent is affirmatively "unfit" to parent – effectively requiring the same showing that the state must make to terminate parental rights altogether.[7] In other states, a nonparent may be awarded custody in "extraordinary circumstances," typically construed to mean that custody with the parent would be harmful or seriously detrimental to the child.[8] Even in the rare cases in which courts nominally employ a "best interests" standard, status as a parent remains "a strong factor for consideration."[9]

This preference for parent custody has led courts to deny continuing custodial rights even to care givers who had assumed major parenting roles with the acquiescence of the legal parent.[10] For example, a New York court held that a man who had assumed the role of a girl's father since her birth nevertheless had no standing to seek custody or visitation after it was discovered that another man was actually the girl's biological father.[11] Even his acknowledgment of paternity years earlier, allegedly with the mother's full cooperation and consent, was legally ineffective against DNA evidence establishing the other man's reproductive role.[12] Similarly, courts in several states have reached the same result in cases

[5] *See* Jamil S. Zainaldin, *The Emergence of a Modern American Family: Child Custody, Adoption, and the Courts, 1796–1851*, 73 Nw. L. Rev. 1038 (1979).

[6] *See* Naomi R. Cahn, *Reframing Child Custody Decision-making*, 58 Ohio St. L.J. 1, 1 (1997) (noting that, while issues of "parentage and custody are interrelated," "pursuant to contemporary legal doctrines, the designation of parent inevitably dictates the rights of all parties involved"); Carbone & Cahn, *supra* note 4, at 1014.

[7] *See, e.g.*, Martin v. Neiman, 2004 WL 1909353 (Ky. App. Aug. 27, 2004) ("A non-parent seeking custody must show that the parent is unfit, and must meet the threshold requirements for an involuntary termination of parental rights."); David N. v. Jason N., 596 S.E.2d 266, 267–68 (N.C. App. 2004). Although the conduct constituting "unfitness" in each context appears to be substantially identical, the level of proof required may differ. To terminate parental rights, the state is constitutionally required to prove its grounds by clear and convincing evidence. *See* Santosky v. Kramer, 455 U.S. 745 (1982). However, to overcome the preference for parental custody, it is sufficient in some jurisdictions to prove a parent's unfitness by a preponderance of the evidence. *See, e.g.*, Shurupoff v. Vockroth, 814 A.2d 543, 554 (Md. 2003); Pecek v. Giffin, 2002 WL 549940 (Ohio App. Apr. 12, 2002).

[8] *See, e.g.*, Evans v. McTaggart, 88 P.3d 1078, 1983 (Alaska 2004); Hamers v. Guttormson, 610 N.W.2d 758, 759–60 (N.D. 2000).

[9] Rowles v. Rowles, 668 A.2d 126, 128 (Pa. 1995); *see also* Cahn, *supra* note 6, at 16 (discussing *Rowles*). The Pennsylvania Supreme Court recently explained that in custody disputes between a biological parent and a third party, "the burden of proof is not evenly balanced and . . . the evidentiary scale is tipped hard to the biological parent's side." T.B. v. L.R.M., 786 A.2d 913, 920 (Pa. 2001).

[10] *See, e.g.*, Ephraim H. v. Jon P., 2005 WL 2347727 (Neb. App. Sept. 27, 2005) (awarding custody, following death of 12-year-old boy's mother, to legal father who had not visited the boy prior to the mother's death rather than to stepfather who was concededly "the only father figure that [the boy] had ever known"); Multari v. Sorrell, 731 N.Y.S.2d 238 (App. Div. 2001) (mother's former cohabiting partner had no standing to seek visitation with 8-year-old boy he had helped raise since child was 18 months old). *See generally* James G. Dwyer, *A Taxonomy of Children's Existing Rights in State Decision-making About Their Relationships*, 11 Wm. & Mary Bill Rts. J. 845, 940–52 (2002) (discussing the myriad ways in which children's interests are often subordinated to the interests of parents in these and other custody disputes); Barbara Bennett Woodhouse, *Hatching the Egg: A Child-Centered Perspective on Parents' Rights*, 14 Cardozo L. Rev. 1747 (1993).

[11] Sean H. v. Leila H., 783 N.Y.S.2d 785 (Sup. Ct. 2004).

[12] *See id.* at 787–88; *see also* C.M. v. P.R., 649 N.E.2d 154 (Mass. 1995) (holding that a man who lived with a pregnant woman and who assumed in every way the role of father to child born during their relationship, but who was not the child's biological father, lacked standing to establish paternity or seek visitation).

involving the separation of same-sex partners who jointly raised a child born to one of the partners.[13] Despite evidence clearly demonstrating a joint undertaking to parent, these courts have concluded that the status and prerogatives of parenthood remain exclusively with the biological parent.

In recent years, some jurisdictions have begun to relax the traditional parental preference in recognition of the important roles played by many nonparent care givers.[14] A growing number of courts and legislatures now permit adults who assumed the functional role of a parent to preserve their relationship with a child despite the legal parent's preference for a clean break.[15] Describing them as "psychological parents" or "de facto parents," these courts have carved out a role for these care givers based on the rationale that the state's interest in protecting children from emotional harm is sufficiently strong to overcome parental rights.[16] Yet, although they may be permitted to preserve a "parent-like" relationship with the child in this way, these care givers continue to occupy the status of a nonparent.[17]

B. "De Facto Parenthood" and "Parenthood by Estoppel" Under the PRINCIPLES

The PRINCIPLES not only embrace the trend toward recognizing an ongoing custodial role for nonparent care givers, but they take it an important step farther. In addition to permitting such care givers to continue established child rearing roles, the PRINCIPLES would designate some of them "parents." Section 2.03 recognizes three classes of

[13] *See, e.g., In re* Thompson, 11 S.W.3d 913 (Tenn. Ct. App. 1999); Kazmierazak v. Query, 736 So.2d 106 (Fla. Dist. Ct. App. 1999); Lynda A.H. v. Diane T.O., 673 N.Y.S.2d 989 (App. Div. 1998); Titchenal v. Dexter, 693 A.2d 682 (Vt. 1997); *see also* Melanie B. Jacobs, *Micah Has One Mommy and One Legal Stranger: Adjudicating Maternity for Non-Biological Lesbian Coparents*, 50 BUFF. L. REV. 341 (2002); Nancy D. Polikoff, *This Child Does Have Two Mothers: Redefining Parenthood to Meet the Needs of Children in Lesbian-Mother and Other Non-Traditional Families*, 78 GEO. L.J. 459 (1990).

[14] *See Developments in the Law – Changing Realities of Parenthood: The Law's Response to the Evolving American Family and Emerging Reproductive Technologies*, 116 HARV. L. REV. 1996, 2052 (2003); Katharine T. Bartlett, *U.S. Custody Law and Trends in the Context of the ALI* Principles of the Law of Family Dissolution, 10 VA. J. SOC. POL'Y & L. 5, 41–44 (2002).

[15] *See, e.g.*, ARIZ. REV. STAT. § 25–415 (2004) (permitting non-parents who "stand in loco parentis to the child" to bring an action for custody or visitation); OR. REV. STAT. § 109.119 (2004) (permitting "any person... who has established emotional ties creating a child-parent relationship" to petition for custody or visitation); P.B. v. T.H., 851 A.2d 780 (N.J. Super. 2004) (holding that a neighbor helping to raise child with custodial aunt's encouragement was a "psychological parent" with standing to seek custody); Scott v. Scott, 147 S.W.3d 887, 896 (Mo. App. 2004) (holding that former partner of lesbian mother overcame parental presumption in custody dispute because the partner was "the person who has, for the life [the child] remembers, been his parent"); *In re* E.L.M.C., 2004 WL 1469410 (Colo. App. July 1, 2004) (holding a former partner of lesbian mother was a "psychological parent" with standing to seek custody and visitation); V.C. v. M.J.B., 748 A.2d 539 (N.J. 2001) (holding same).

[16] *See E.L.M.C.*, 2004 WL 146910 (Colo. App. July 1, 2004); *Scott*, 147 S.W.3d at 896–97; Holtzman v. Knott, 533 N.W.2d 419, 435 (Wis.), *cert. denied*, 516 U.S. 975 (U.S. 1995).

[17] *See* Clifford K. v. Paul S., 619 S.E.2d 138 (W. Va. 2005) (surviving lesbian partner of deceased biological mother had standing as a "psychological parent" to assume custodial responsibility of child she had helped raise, although she did not qualify as a "legal parent"); Riepe v. Riepe, 91 P.3d 312, 316–17 (Ariz. 2004) (emphasizing, in decision permitting a stepmother to seek visitation on grounds that she had formed a parent-like relationship with child, that "[a] person standing in loco parentis to a child is not a 'parent,' does not enjoy parental rights, and therefore does not become an 'additional parent'"); Solangel Moldanado, *When Father (or Mother) Doesn't Know Best: Quasi-Parents and Parental Deference After* Troxel v. Granville, 88 IOWA L. REV. 865, 893–97, 910–12 (2003) (arguing in favor of granting visitation rights to "quasi-parents" as third parties); Janet Leach Richards, *The Natural Parent Preference Versus Third Parties: Expanding the Definition of Parent*, 16 NOVA L. REV. 733, 760–66 (1992) (proposing legislation that would designate longtime care givers as "parents," but acknowledging that such an approach has almost no precedent in U.S. law).

"parents": "[A] *parent* is either a legal parent, a parent by estoppel, or a de facto parent."[18] A "legal parent" describes a person who would presently be classified as a parent under state law, such as an adoptive or biological parent.[19] A "parent by estoppel" is a person who, though not classified as a parent under traditional legal principles, assumed "full and permanent responsibilities as a parent" with the acquiescence of the child's legal parents.[20] For example, a man who lived with a child for at least two years under the mistaken belief that he was the child's biological father would be considered a "parent by estoppel," as would an individual who assumed for at least two years full parenting duties with the legal parent's agreement.[21] Finally, a "de facto parent" is an individual who, with the legal parents' acquiescence or spurred by their "complete failure or inability" to parent, lived with the child and performed caretaking functions equal to those of the child's legal parents for two years or longer.[22]

Under the PRINCIPLES, "parents by estoppel" would be accorded a parenting status fully equivalent to that held by traditional parents. Thus, in a custody dispute between an adoptive parent and a parent by estoppel, neither would enjoy any legal preference over the other. Instead, in the absence of a contrary agreement, the court should allocate to each a share of custodial responsibilities roughly equal to that exercised by the parties before the family's fracture.[23] "De facto parents," although considered true "parents," occupy a secondary status under the PRINCIPLES. In any dispute with a legal parent or a parent by estoppel, for instance, a de facto parent ordinarily cannot be assigned a majority of the caretaking functions.[24] Similarly, a de facto parent lacks the presumptive entitlement that legal parents and parents by estoppel enjoy to share in significant decisions involving the child's upbringing.[25] Otherwise, however, de facto parents are entitled to preserve established parenting roles alongside the child's other parents.

The ALI's approach creates the possibility that a child might have three or more parents all at the same time. No cap is imposed on the number of parents a child might have, although some limits are placed on the extent to which parenting responsibilities may be divvied up among these parents. For instance, the PRINCIPLES permit significant decision-making responsibility for a child to be assigned to no more than two parents jointly.[26] And the PRINCIPLES direct judges not to splinter custodial responsibilities among so many parents that the resulting arrangement would be "impractical."[27] Aside from those considerations, however, the PRINCIPLES seek generally to preserve and carry forward whatever fragmentation of child rearing roles prevailed before the family's fracture.

To date, while no jurisdiction has formally adopted the PRINCIPLES' expansive definitions of parenthood,[28] several states have begun to move tentatively in that direction. The

[18] PRINCIPLES § 2.03(1) (emphasis added).

[19] PRINCIPLES § 2.03(1)(a).

[20] *See* PRINCIPLES § 2.03(1)(b).

[21] PRINCIPLES §§ 2.03(1)(b)(ii), (iv).

[22] PRINCIPLES § 2.03(1)(c)(ii).

[23] PRINCIPLES § 2.08(1).

[24] PRINCIPLES § 2.18(1)(a). An exception is made for cases in which a child's other parents have failed to perform "a reasonable share of parenting functions" or in which granting a primary role to other parents would "cause harm to the child." *Id.* §§ 2.18(1)(a)(i)–(ii).

[25] *See* PRINCIPLES §§ 2.09(2), (4).

[26] PRINCIPLES § 2.09(1).

[27] PRINCIPLES § 2.18(1)(b) (stating that judges "should limit or deny an allocation [of custodial responsibility] otherwise to be made if, in light of the number of other individuals to be allocated responsibility, the allocation would be impractical in light of the objectives of this Chapter"); *see also id.* § 2.08(4) ("In determining how to schedule the custodial time allocated to each parent, the court should take account of economic, physical, and other practical circumstances. . . .").

[28] One state, West Virginia, has adopted the "approximation standard" as a substitute for the "best interests" standard that prevails elsewhere. *See* W. Va. CODE § 48-11-106 (2000). Section 2.08(1) of the PRINCIPLES embodies that

supreme courts of Maine, Massachusetts, and Rhode Island have looked approvingly to the PRINCIPLES' definition of "de facto parenthood" in justifying custodial awards to long time care givers who lacked formal legal ties to a child.[29] Of these, the Maine Supreme Court has inched perhaps the closest to accepting the PRINCIPLES' view of "de facto parents" as not merely suitable guardians or custodians but as true parents to a child.[30]

Of equal significance, courts in slightly more states have begun interpreting legal parenthood in nontraditional ways and, specifically, designating as parents adults who have no biological or adoptive ties to the child. This innovation occurs often in the context of new reproductive technologies, where courts have emphasized parenting intentions over genetic or biological contributions in deciding legal parentage.[31] In *Marriage of Buzzanca*,[32] for example, the California Court of Appeals held that a husband and wife were the legal parents of a child born to a surrogate because they intended to create the child as parents, even though they shared no biological relation with the child.[33] But the same trend is discernible outside the reproductive technologies context as well. For instance, men who have agreed with a pregnant woman to assume the role of father to her child have established paternity on that basis alone, despite the fact that all parties knew another man was the biological father.[34] Similarly, in a few states women agreeing to co-parent

standard, which was originally proposed in an article by Professor Elizabeth Scott. *See* Elizabeth S. Scott, *Pluralism, Parental Preference, and Child Custody,* 80 CAL. L. REV. 615 (1992). The Supreme Judicial Court of Massachusetts recently observed that Massachusetts' preexisting law shares the PRINCIPLES' emphasis on "approximation" as a primary goal of custody determinations. *See In re* Custody of Kali, 792 N.E.2d 635, 641 (Mass. 2003).

29 *See, e.g.,* C.E.W. v. D.E.W., 845 A.2d 1146, 1152 & n.13 (Me. 2004) (recognizing former lesbian partner of parent as a "de facto parent" entitled to seek an allocation of parenting responsibility); Rubano v. DiCenzo, 759 A.2d 959, 974–75 (R.I. 2000) (drawing support from the PRINCIPLES for holding that "a person who has no biological connection to a child but has served as a psychological or de facto parent to that child may... establish his or her entitlement to parental rights vis-à-vis the child."); E.N.O. v. L.M.M., 711 N.E.2d 886, 891 (Mass. 1999) (relying in part on the PRINCIPLES in holding that "the best interests calculus must include an examination of the child's relationship with both his legal and de facto parent[s]"), *cert. denied,* 528 U.S. 1005 (1999); Youmans v. Ramos, 711 N.E.2d 165, 167 & n.3 (Mass. 1999) (embracing the PRINCIPLES' definition of "de facto parent" in permitting child's former guardian to seek court-ordered visitation).

30 The Maine Supreme Court distinguished "de facto parents" from "third parties" – *i.e.,* nonparents who might otherwise be permitted to seek visitation with a child – in holding that a trial court may recognize as a "de facto parent" a stepfather who had helped to raise a daughter since she was a few months old, entitling him to an allocation of parenting responsibility. *See* Young v. Young, 845 A.2d 1144 (Me. 2004). For other recent Maine cases recognizing the custodial rights of "de facto parents," see Leonard v. Boardman, 854 A.2d 869 (Me. 2004); C.E.W. v. D.E.W., 845 A.2d 1146 (Me. 2004); Stitham v. Henderson, 768 A.2d 598 (Me. 2001). The Maine Supreme Court recently noted, however, that it has not yet formally "adopted" the PRINCIPLES' definition of parenthood. *See C.E.W.,* 845 A.2d at 1152 n.13.

31 *See* Johnson v. Calvert, 851 P.2d 776 (Cal. 1993), *cert. denied,* 510 U.S. 874 (1993); Richard F. Storrow, *Parenthood by Pure Intention: Assisted Reproduction and the Functional Approach to Parenthood,* 53 HASTINGS L.J. 597 (2002); John Lawrence Hill, *What Does It Mean to be a "Parent"? The Claims of Biology as the Basis for Parental Rights,* 66 NYU L. REV. 353 (1991); Marjorie Maguire Shultz, *Reproductive Technology and Intent-Based Parenthood: An Opportunity for Gender Neutrality,* 1990 WIS. L. REV. 297.

32 72 Cal. Rptr. 2d 280 (Ct. App. 1998).

33 *Id.* at 293 ("Even though neither Luanne nor John are biologically related to Jaycee, they are still her lawful parents given their initiating role as the intended parents in her conception and birth."); *see also In re* C.K.G., 2004 WL 1402560 (Tenn. App. June 22, 2004) (following *Johnson* and *Buzzanca* in finding that gestational mother was legal parent based on her intention to assume the responsibilities of parenthood, despite the lack of any genetic tie to the child); McDonald v. McDonald, 608 N.Y.S.2d 477 (App. Div. 1994) (holding same); Perry-Rogers v. Fasano, 715 N.Y.S.2d 19, 24 (App. Div. 2000) (concluding that couple whose embryo was mistakenly implanted in another woman should be regarded as child's parents based on their intent to become parents).

34 *See In re* Nicholas H., 46 P.3d 932 (Cal. 2002); Michael Higgins, *Man Ruled Father of Unrelated Boy,* CHI. TRIB., Sept. 17, 2004, at 1 (describing ruling of Illinois trial court).

children born to their same-sex partners have been deemed legal parents without any formal adoption proceeding.[35] This willingness to recognize legal parentage based solely upon the assumption of a parental role with the agreement of the child's biological parent shares a basic premise with the PRINCIPLES: that parenthood is essentially and predominantly "a functional status, rather than one derived from biology or legal entitlement."[36]

II. Criticisms of the PRINCIPLES' New Parenthood

While the ALI's work has drawn admiration from a number of academic observers for its care and crafting, and even some glimmers of acceptance in the courts, its allowance for multiple parenthood has met strong criticism from numerous quarters. While a few scholars suggest that the PRINCIPLES did not go far enough in acknowledging the parenting roles of nontraditional care givers,[37] more contend that the drafters were entirely too adventurous.[38] Critics raise a host of policy objections to the PRINCIPLES' expansive notions of parenthood, arguing that they represent an ideological assault on marriage and the traditional family,[39] encourage strategic behavior by adults that is detrimental to children,[40] and rest on thin empirical evidence about the benefits to children.[41] Even the

[35] *See* Elisa B. v. Superior Court, 117 P.3d 660 (Cal. 2005); A.B. v. S.B., 818 N.E.2d 126 (Ind. App. 2004), *vacated*, 837 N.E.2d 965 (Ind. 2005); *In re* Parentage of L.B., 122 P.3d 161 (Wash. 2005). In each of these cases, the couple contested parentage after breaking up. In *A.B.*, the Indiana appellate court held that "when two women involved in a domestic relationship agree to bear and raise a child together by artificial insemination of one of the partners with donor semen, both women are the legal parents of the resulting child." 818 N.E.2d at 131. The Indiana Supreme Court formally vacated that opinion but in remanding agreed that the trial court could "determine whether such a person has the rights and obligations of a parent." 837 N.E.2d at 967. The California Supreme Court in *Elisa B.* held that the same-sex partner of a biological mother could be established as a legal parent by virtue of having "receive[d] the child into [her] home and openly h[e]ld out the child as [her] natural child," based on a gender-neutral construction of the state's parentage act governing "presumed fathers." 117 P.3d at 667. In *L.B.*, the Washington Supreme Court sidestepped the state's parentage act altogether and held that the partner might nevertheless establish her "coparentage" as a "de facto parent" under the common law. 122 P.3d at 163, 176–77. The court noted that its conclusion was consistent with the PRINCIPLES' approach to parentage, although using "slightly different standards." *Id.* at 176 n.24.

In another parentage dispute involving a same-sex couple decided the same day as *Elisa B.*, the California Supreme Court recognized still another possible route to effective parentage rights. In *Kristine Renee H. v. Lisa Ann R.*, 117 P.3d 690 (Cal. 2005), the court held that a biological mother who initially consents to a stipulated judgment establishing joint parentage with her partner is estopped from later contesting the validity of the parentage judgment. Although the court did not decide whether the judgment itself was legally valid, the estoppel bar effectively shields the partner's "parent" status from its most likely avenue of attack. *See id.* at 695.

[36] Marsha Garrison, *Law Making for Baby Making: An Interpretive Approach to the Determination of Legal Parentage*, 113 HARV. L. REV. 835, 893 (2000); *see generally* JUNE CARBONE, FROM PARTNERS TO PARENTS: THE SECOND REVOLUTION IN FAMILY LAW (2000); NANCY DOWD, REDEFINING FATHERHOOD (2000).

[37] *See, e.g.*, Mary Ann Mason & Nicole Zayac, *Rethinking Stepparent Rights: Has the ALI Found a Better Definition?*, 36 FAM. L.Q. 227 (2002); Barbara Bennett Woodhouse, *Horton Looks at the ALI* Principles, 4 J. FAM. & L. STUD. 151 (2002).

[38] *See, e.g.*, F. Carolyn Graglia, *A Nonfeminist's Perspective of Mothers and Homemakers Under Chapter 2 of the ALI* Principles of the Law of Family Dissolution, 2001 BYU L. REV. 993; Gregory A. Loken, *The New "Extended Family" – "De Facto" Parenthood and Standing Under Chapter 2*, 2001 BYU L. REV. 1045; David M. Wagner, *Balancing "Parents Are" and "Parents Do" in the Supreme Court's Constitutionalized Family Law: Some Implications for the ALI Proposals on De Facto Parenthood*, 2001 BYU L. REV. 1175; Lynn D. Wardle, *Deconstructing Family: A Critique of the American Law Institute's "Domestic Partners" Proposal*, 2001 BYU L. REV. 1189, 1228–30.

[39] *See* Graglia, *supra* note 38, at 996–1002; Wardle, *supra* note 38, at 1228–29, 1232–33.

[40] *See* Loken, *supra* note 38, at 1058–61; Wardle, *supra* note 38, at 1229–30.

[41] *See* Loken, *supra* note 38, at 1062–63.

California Supreme Court, in decisions otherwise pushing the boundaries of traditional parenthood, has nevertheless balked at the notion of multiple parenthood.[42]

In addition, there are substantial questions about the constitutionality of the PRINCIPLES' enlargement of the concept of parenthood. Many court decisions suggest that the Constitution's regard for traditional parents – those who come by that status through the customary routes of biological reproduction, marital presumption, or adoption – precludes a state's extension of parental status to other adults.[43] These cases assume that the Constitution fixes the boundaries of parenthood protecting the parent-child relationship, leaving states with little room to innovate with new definitions. On this basis, a number of courts have held that equating "psychological" or "de facto parents" with legal parents impinges upon the constitutional rights of traditional parents and that the Constitution recognizes no countervailing claim of parental status on the part of nontraditional care givers.[44]

Other scholars have defended legal innovation in the assignment of parenting status, while raising a different set of concerns about the PRINCIPLES' approach.[45] Professor Emily Buss contends that the Constitution has little to say about the identity of the persons who may hold the status of "parent," but is strictly protective of the child rearing prerogatives enjoyed by whomever is given that title:

> [T]he Constitution should be read to afford strong protection to parents' exercise of child-rearing authority but considerably weaker protection to any individual's claim to parental identity. This means that a state has broad authority to identify nontraditional care givers as parents, and, if it does so, it must afford their child-rearing decisions the same strong protection afforded more traditional parental figures.[46]

[42] *See Elisa B.*, 117 P.3d at 665–66; Johnson v. Calvert, 851 P.2d 776, 781 & n.8 (Cal. 1993).

[43] *See, e.g.*, Sean H. v. Leila H., 783 N.Y.S.2d 785, 788 (Sup. Ct. 2004) (reasoning that the Supreme Court's decision in *Troxel v. Granville*, 530 U.S. 57 (2000), upholding the fundamental rights of parents to limit non-parent visitation, "strongly supports, from a constitutional perspective, [a] . . . narrow definition of 'parents' for the purpose of standing in custody and visitation cases"); *In re* Nelson, 825 A.2d 501, 503 (N.H. 2003) (rejecting the suggestion that "the status of parent should be extended to cover all persons who have established a parental relationship with a child through the *in loco parentis* or psychological parent doctrines" on the ground that doing so would violate the state constitutional rights of biological and adoptive parents); Kazmierazak v. Query, 736 So.2d 106 (Fla. App. 1999); *see also* John DeWitt Gregory, *Redefining the Family: Undermining the Family*, 2004 U. CHI. LEGAL F. 381, 392 (asserting that efforts to recognize "de facto parents, functional parents, parents by estoppel, and the like" as members of a child's family "threaten both the constitutional liberty interests of parents and children and the values that support them, including the presumption that fit parents in autonomous families are competent to rear, educate, and guide their children"); John DeWitt Gregory, *Family Privacy and the Custody and Visitation Rights of Adult Outsiders*, 36 FAM. L.Q. 163, 184–87 (2002) (criticizing court decisions granting custody or visitation rights to "de facto parents" as intruding upon the constitutional privacy rights of legal parents).

[44] *E.g., Nelson*, 825 A.2d at 503–04 (rejecting contention that "de facto" or "psychological parents" are entitled to their own constitutional rights as parents and concluding that granting equal custodial status to "de facto" or "psychological parents" would violate the fundamental rights of biological or adoptive parents under the state constitution); *In re* E.L.M.C., 100 P.3d 546, 561–562 (Colo. App. July 1, 2004); *In re* Thompson, 11 S.W.3d 913, 923 (Tenn. App. 1999); Liston v. Pyles, 1997 WL 467327, at * 8 (Ohio App. Aug. 12, 1997); *see also* Miller v. California, 355 F.3d 1172, 1175–77 (9th Cir. 2004) (holding that custodial grandparents who had served as "de facto parents" to their grandchildren had no substantive due process interest in maintaining a relationship with the children); Clifford S. v. Superior Court, 45 Cal. Rptr. 2d 333, 337 (App. Ct. 1995) (holding that a man who lived with and reared a daughter in mistaken belief that he was her biological father, and who thereafter continued to act as her "de facto parent," nevertheless lacked standing to seek reunification services or custody in a dependency proceeding involving the child; nor does Constitution require that "de facto parents" be accorded the same rights as legal parents).

[45] *See* Bartholet, *supra* note 3; Buss, *supra* note 3.

[46] Buss, *supra* note 3, at 636.

Similarly, Professor Elizabeth Bartholet suggests that while states enjoy "significant leeway to determine who is a parent," respect for values of family privacy should lead them to reject the idea of multiple parenthood.[47] By these views, the PRINCIPLES' custody provisions founder not because they assign parent status to nontraditional figures but because the parent status they confer simply carries too little substantive authority. By preserving a multiplicity of parenting roles, the PRINCIPLES end up carving the "parenting rights pie"[48] too thinly, giving each parent insufficient power to fulfill the child-welfare purposes underpinning the Constitution's grant of parental autonomy.[49] Consequently, the PRINCIPLES fail children and, under a child-centered conception of parental rights, the Constitution itself.[50]

III. Does the Constitution Define Parenthood?

This latter critique of the PRINCIPLES' custody provisions raises foundational questions about the nature and scope of parental rights under the Constitution. Does the Constitution focus its concern on the substantive prerogatives of parenthood while maintaining little interest in the identity of the persons assigned that role? If so, this narrows significantly the field of constitutional dispute over the ALI's approach to custody, and directs it away from the ground that many would find most controversial. It suggests that the constitutionality of the PRINCIPLES rests entirely on whether the Constitution permits the state to force parents to share their child rearing authority with others who build important relationships with a child; the PRINCIPLES' choice to designate that other care giver a parent rather than a guardian or "third-party" visitor, however, would present no independent constitutional issue of any significance. Indeed, on this account, given the Constitution's substantial indifference to how states assign parent status, the PRINCIPLES presumably could have gone farther still in favoring nontraditional care givers: rather than forcing biological or adoptive parents to share their parent status with unrelated care givers, the PRINCIPLES might simply have disposed with legal parents altogether, allowing the new parents to supplant the old.

This part considers in turn the dual premises of this understanding of parental rights. It concludes that the Constitution is probably somewhat less deferential than the account supposes concerning the assignment of parental identity while also somewhat more flexible than is often imagined concerning the substance of the prerogatives guaranteed to parents.

[47] *See* Bartholet, *supra* note 3, at 326–27, 342–43. Professor Katharine Baker has similarly criticized the PRINCIPLES' endorsement of multiple parenthood. *See* Baker, *supra* note 4, at 48–49.

[48] Bartholet, *supra* note 3, at 343.

[49] *See* Buss, *supra* note 3, at 640–41.

[50] Professor David Wagner advances a somewhat related criticism of the PRINCIPLES' extension of parenthood to nontraditional care givers, although he does not characterize it as a constitutional defect. Like Professors Bartholet and Buss, he concludes that the Constitution imposes no barrier to the assignment of parent status to care givers formerly regarded as "third parties" or "legal strangers." *See* Wagner, *supra* note 38, at 1185. Also like Professors Bartholet and Buss, Professor Wagner sees in the PRINCIPLES' willingness to spread parenting status and roles among a widening circle of care givers a danger of diluting the value of parenthood for those who hold that status, ultimately working to the detriment of children. *See id.* at 1184–86. Unlike Buss, however, Wagner frames his objection to this "parent inflation" solely as one of policy rather than of constitutionality. *See id.* at 1185. Professor Bartholet, while criticizing the assignment of multiple parenthood as inconsistent with the respect owed to family privacy, seems to stop short of saying explicitly that to do so would be unconstitutional. *See* Bartholet, *supra* note 3, at 342–43.

A. Constitutional Deference to State-Law Definitions of Parenthood

Consistent with the idea that the Constitution imposes few constraints on a state's initial choices concerning parent identity, several rulings of the U.S. Supreme Court suggest that parenting status for constitutional purposes rests on the definitions found in state law rather than on some meaning of parenthood embedded in the Constitution.

Prince v. Massachusetts,[51] one of the Supreme Court's earliest parental liberty cases, assumed that a nonparent guardian could assert constitutional parenting rights. *Prince* upheld a woman's conviction for permitting her nine-year-old niece to distribute religious magazines on a public street corner under Massachusetts' child labor law, but it did so on the ground that the state's interest in child welfare justified the intrusion on the aunt's constitutional "rights of parenthood."[52] Because state law granted the guardian the prerogatives of parenthood, the Supreme Court readily extended to her the constitutional prerogatives of parenthood. Likewise, there is no doubt that adoptive parents may similarly exercise parental rights under the Constitution. Even though adoptive parents may lack a biological tie to their children – a "natural bond" sometimes described as a basis for parental rights[53] – state law clearly defines them as parents and that is sufficient for the Constitution.[54]

Sixty years after *Prince*, the Supreme Court's recent opinion in the Pledge of Allegiance case, *Elk Grove Unified School District v. Newdow*,[55] seems to reflect the same principle. The Court in *Newdow* concluded that a father lacked standing to press constitutional objections to the recitation of the pledge at his daughter's public school because a state custody order gave ultimate decision-making authority over her upbringing to her mother.[56] Significantly, both Justice Stevens, writing for the Court, and Chief Justice Rehnquist, concurring in the judgment, assumed that Michael Newdow's standing to assert constitutional parental rights rested entirely on state law.

"Newdow's parental status," Stevens wrote, "is defined by California's domestic relations law."[57] The Court accepted that "state law vests in Newdow a cognizable right to influence his daughter's religious upbringing"[58] and that "the state cases create a zone of private authority within which each parent, whether custodial or non-custodial, remains free to impart to the child his or her religious perspective."[59] But the Court concluded that California law does not grant Newdow, as a noncustodial parent,[60] "a right to dictate

[51] 321 U.S. 158 (1944).

[52] *Id.* at 166.

[53] Judicial opinions routinely state that constitutionally protected rights in this context belong to the "biological" or "natural" parent. *See, e.g.*, W.T.M. v. S.P., 889 So.2d 572, 580 n.2 (Ala. Civ. App. 2003); *In re* Children of Schauer, 2003 WL 22481494, at * 4 (Minn. App. Nov. 4, 2003); *In re* Baby Girl L., 51 P.3d 544, 555 n.7 (Okla. 2002); *Greer v. Alexander*, 639 N.W.2d 39, 43–44 (Mich. App. 2001). The opinions also rationalize protection on the presumption that "natural bonds of affection lead parents to act in the best interests of their children." Parham v. J.R., 442 U.S. 584, 602 (1979).

[54] *See In re* Nelson, 825 A.2d 501, 502 (N.H. 2003) (noting that case law has "extended... protection [of parental rights under state constitution] to both natural and adoptive parents"); Owenby v. Young, 579 S.E.2d 264, 266 (N.C. 2003) (stating that the Constitution's protection of parents' rights "is irrelevant in a custody proceeding between two natural parents, whether biological or adoptive"). Without focusing specifically on constitutional law, courts have observed that "[o]nce the adoption is final, there is no distinction in law between the biological parent and the adoptive parent; they are parents to that child of equal rank and responsibility." Carter v. Carter, 546 S.E.2d 220, 221 (Va. App. 2001).

[55] 124 S. Ct. 2301 (2004).

[56] *See id.* at 2311–12.

[57] *Id.* at 2311.

[58] *Id.*

[59] *Id.*

[60] Newdow was nominally granted "joint legal custody," but the state custody order specified that the girl's mother, with whom she resided, would have final decision-making authority in the event of disagreements between the

to others what they may or may not say to his child respecting religion."[61] Because state law assigned that authority to the girl's mother as the custodial parent, Newdow could not object to state-sponsored religious indoctrination of his daughter on the ground that it violated his own constitutional rights as a parent. Although Chief Justice Rehnquist emphasized a different construction of California custody law that would have permitted Newdow to present his constitutional claim, he agreed with the majority that "[t]he correct characterization of respondent's [constitutional] interest [as a parent] rests on the interpretation of state law."[62]

In *Newdow*, the Supreme Court appeared not to contemplate that the Constitution itself might define the scope of Newdow's rights as a noncustodial parent. Even if the Constitution permitted states to define many aspects of a parent's noncustodial role, the Constitution might be thought to specify some floor of minimal participation in child rearing, to which Newdow would then be entitled. Instead, by suggesting that Newdow's constitutional interests in his daughter's upbringing depended entirely on the generosity of state custody law, the Supreme Court implied the existence of broad state authority to define the extent and scope of parenthood.

In this, *Newdow* might suggest a basic parallel between the ways in which parenthood and property are defined for constitutional purposes. Courts defer to state law when defining the "property" protected by the Due Process Clause. "Property interests," the Supreme Court has held, "are not created by the Constitution, 'they are created and their dimensions are defined by existing rules or understandings that stem from an independent source such as state law.' "[63] In the same way, the parenting "liberty" protected by the Due Process Clause might rest on a definition of parenthood independent of the Constitution and subject to the discretionary power of the state. Indeed, this is effectively how the Washington Supreme Court justified its decision to recognize as parents both members of a dissolved same-sex partnership: the court held that its own redefinition of parenthood through the common law effectively wiped away any constitutional privilege enjoyed by the biological mother.[64]

Of course, any suggestion of a correspondence between the rights of parents and the rights of property owners is certain to raise hackles.[65] And properly so, since the linkage implies the commodification of children, recalling darker periods in which widely

parents. *See id.* at 2310 n.6. As such, he was effectively a non-custodial parent despite his protestations to the contrary. *See id.* at 2315 n.1 (Rehnquist, C.J., concurring in the judgment) (noting Newdow's insistence "that he has never been a 'noncustodial' parent").

[61] *Id.* at 2311.

[62] *See id.* at 2315–16 (Rehnquist, C.J., concurring in the judgment).

[63] Cleveland Bd. of Educ. v. Loudermill, 470 U.S. 532, 538 (1985) (quoting Board of Regents v. Roth, 408 U.S. 564, 577 (1972)); *see* Town of Castle Rock v. Gonzales, 125 S. Ct. 2796, 2803 (2005); 3 Ronald D. Rotunda & John E. Nowak, Treatise on Constitutional Law: Substance and Procedure §17.5 (3d ed. 1999 & Supp. 2004).

[64] *In re* Parentage of L.B., 122 P.3d 161, 177–8 (Wash. 2005). The court explained:

> ... [O]ur holding ... regarding the common law status of *de facto* parents renders the crux of Britain's [the biological mother's] constitutional arguments moot. Britain's primary argument is that the State, through judicial action, cannot infringe or materially interfere with her rights as a biological parent in favor of Carvin's rights as a nonparent third party. However, today we hold that our common law recognizes the status of *de facto* parents and places them in parity with biological or adoptive parents in our state. Thus, if, on remand, Carvin can establish standing as a *de facto* parent, Britain and Carvin would *both* have a "fundamental liberty interest[]" in the "care, custody, and control" of L.B.

Id. at 178 (emphasis in original).

[65] *See* Baker, *supra* note 4, at 44–45 (advocating the use of property concepts in defining the rights of parents while acknowledging that "there is strong resistance to property rhetoric when it comes to characterizing family relationships – particularly relationships with children").

shared notions of child "ownership" rationalized considerable mistreatment.[66] Of course, all judges today disclaim any effort to liken children to property.[67] And, yet, the analogy may not be altogether malevolent. One enduring theory of property – which the Court suggested in *Board of Regents v. Roth* underlies the Constitution's protection of property rights[68] – offers a utilitarian foundation: by providing security to owners that they will capture the fruits of their investments, the institution of property encourages people to husband resources, increasing overall resource development to society's benefit.[69] This conception of property rights shares a core premise with some modern, child-centered theories of parental rights: that the promise of parental freedom from meddlesome state interference encourages parents to invest more generously in the nurture and development of their children, to the ultimate benefit of their children and all of society.[70]

Although the property analogy implicit in *Newdow*'s conception of parental rights might suggest reflexive deference to innovative redefinition of parenthood, such as is contemplated by the PRINCIPLES, it seems quite doubtful that states' discretion in this area is unbounded.

First, it is not certain that the Supreme Court really meant what it said in *Newdow*. Other factors may well explain *Newdow*'s readiness to defer to state-law definitions of parenting authority, particularly the Justices' eagerness to avoid deciding the merits of a messy and divisive religious-liberty controversy.[71] As Douglas Laycock neatly summed up the Court's dilemma, "*Newdow*... may have been politically impossible to affirm and legally impossible to reverse."[72] Prudential concerns about Newdow's standing provided a convenient exit.[73] In addition, the case presented an intractable conflict of constitutional rights within the family. Responding to Newdow's contention that all parents, regardless

66 *See* Barbara Bennett Woodhouse, "*Who Owns the Child?*": Meyer *and* Pierce *and the Child as Property*, 33 WM. & MARY L. REV. 995 (1992). As James Dwyer recently pointed out, such notions of child "ownership" are by no means entirely behind us. *See* Dwyer, *supra* note 10, at 985–86.

67 *See, e.g.*, Troxel v. Granville, 530 U.S. 57, 64 (2000) (plurality opinion of O'Connor, J.) (rejecting dissent's assertion that ruling striking down grandparent visitation order implied that " 'children are so much chattel'"); Collins v. Missouri Bar Plan, 157 S.W.3d 726, 738 (Mo. App. 2005) (Smart, J., concurring) (emphasizing state's strong policy against treating children like "chattels to be bartered or sold"); Baker v. Baker, 582 S.E.2d 102, 107 (Ga. 2003) (Benham, J., dissenting) ("I speak not of rights of ownership, for we can all agree that children are not chattel, but of the right to be recognized as a parent and to participate in the child's life.").

68 *See* Board of Regents v. Roth, 408 U.S. 564, 577 (1972) ("The Fourteenth Amendment's procedural protection of property is a safeguard of the security of interests that a person has acquired in specific benefits.... It is a purpose of the ancient institution of property to protect those claims upon which people rely in their daily lives.").

69 *See* Thomas W. Merrill, *Introduction: The Demsetz Thesis and the Evolution of Property Rights*, 31 J. LEG. STUD. 331, 331–32 (2002); Thomas W. Merrill & Henry E. Smith, *What Happened to Property in Law and Economics?*, 111 YALE L.J. 357, 360–62 (2001).

70 As Elizabeth Scott explained in advancing a "fiduciary model" of parental rights:

> Legal deference to parents' authority over child rearing plays a key role in the fiduciary model, because it serves as compensation for the job parents do.... Intrusive legal oversight of parents' behavior and rearing decisions would likely diminish role satisfaction considerably.... The fiduciary model of regulation clarifies that parental autonomy serves as an important function as a reward for satisfactory performance of the obligations of parenthood. Parental rights insure that the costly investment that parents make in rearing their children is afforded legal protection.

Elizabeth S. Scott, *Parental Autonomy and Children's Welfare*, 11 WM. & MARY BILL RTS. J. 1071, 1078–79 (2003); *see also* Elizabeth S. Scott & Robert E. Scott, *Parents as Fiduciaries*, 81 VA. L. REV. 2401 (1995); Margaret F. Brinig, Troxel *and the Limits of Community*, 32 RUTGERS L.J. 733, 765, 778–79 (2001).

71 *See The Supreme Court, 2003 Term Leading Cases – Federal Jurisdiction and Procedure*, 118 HARV. L. REV. 427 (2004).

72 Douglas Laycock, *Theology Scholarships, the Pledge of Allegiance, and Religious Liberty: Avoiding the Extremes But Missing the Liberty*, 118 HARV. L. REV. 155, 224 (2004).

73 *See Newdow*, 124 S. Ct. at 2316 (Rehnquist, C.J.) (describing the Court's standing concerns as "ad hoc improvisations" for avoiding the merits of Newdow's claim).

of their custodial status, have a constitutional right to be free from state interference in imparting values to their children, Justice Stevens stated that

> [t]he difficulty with that argument is that Newdow's rights, as in many cases touching upon family relations, cannot be viewed in isolation. This case concerns not merely Newdow's interest in inculcating his child with his views on religion, but also the rights of the child's mother.... And most important, it implicates the interests of a young child who finds herself at the center of a highly public debate....[74]

Interestingly, this is precisely the same concern that Justice Stevens raised four years earlier in *Troxel v. Granville*[75] when confronted with a parent's claim of a fundamental constitutional right to bar unwanted visits by a grandparent. In that case, he wrote separately to point out that a parent's constitutional liberty to control a child's family relationships may conflict with the constitutionally protected wishes of other family members, including those of children.[76] Stevens used this potential for intrafamily conflict to qualify the strength of constitutional protection afforded parental rights by balancing them against the rights of children and other family members.[77] In *Newdow*, Stevens returned to the same intrafamily conflict as a ground for avoiding decision altogether. At bottom, however, this avoidance reflects a judgment that parental rights must be assessed within the broader context of other constitutional rights-holders, not that family constitutional rights within the family are readily curtailed or reassigned by state law.

Second, the Supreme Court's cases addressing the constitutional rights of unwed fathers strongly suggest that the Constitution in fact provides its own parameters for parental status apart from a state's policy choices. In *Stanley v. Illinois*[78] and subsequent cases, the Supreme Court struck down state policy choices to withhold parental recognition from men the Constitution regarded as fathers.[79] In *Stanley*, for instance, the State of Illinois decided, as a matter of state policy, to deny parental status to unwed biological fathers. The Supreme Court, however, held that Peter Stanley, like "all Illinois parents," was "constitutionally entitled to a hearing on [his] fitness" before his children could be removed from his custody.[80] Implicit in this holding, of course, was a judgment that unwed biological fathers are constitutionally entitled to state recognition as parents.

Subsequent cases make clear that no single criterion determines parentage for constitutional purposes. While biological connection appeared significant in *Stanley*,[81] substantial emotional bonds figured prominently in *Lehr v. Robertson*.[82] From *Lehr*, it emerged that the

[74] 124 S. Ct. at 2310.

[75] 530 U.S. 57 (2000).

[76] *Id.* at 88–89 (Stevens, J., dissenting).

[77] *Id.* ("While this Court has not yet had occasion to elucidate the nature of the child's liberty interests in preserving established familial or family-like bonds, it seems to me extremely likely that, to the extent parents and families have fundamental liberty interests in preserving such intimate relationships, so, too, do children have these interests, and so, too, must their interests be balanced in the equation.") (citations omitted).

[78] 405 U.S. 645 (1972).

[79] Although the Court's opinions in some of these cases were framed in terms of procedural due process, the judgments unmistakably struck substantive rules of law that denied parental status on the basis of the Constitution's regard for the fundamental parenting rights of the men. *See* David D. Meyer, *Justice White and the Right of Privacy*, 52 Cath. U. L. Rev. 915, 931–32 (2003) (discussing the intertwinement of procedural and substantive due process in these cases).

[80] *See* 405 U.S. at 658.

[81] *See id.* at 651.

[82] 463 U.S. 248, 261–62 (1983) ("[T]he importance of the familial relationship, to the individuals involved and to the society, stems from the emotional attachments that derive from the intimacy of daily association, and from the role it plays in 'promot[ing] a way of life' through the instruction of children.").

constitutional claim to parent status depends on more than genetic contributions alone; it requires a willingness to make the emotional and other contributions required to raise a child. "The significance of the biological connection," the Court explained, "is that it offers the natural father an opportunity that no other male possesses to develop a relationship with his offspring. If he grasps that opportunity and accepts some measure of responsibility for the child's future, he may enjoy the blessings of the parent-child relationship and make uniquely valuable contributions to the child's development."[83]

Six years later, it appeared that even *Lehr*'s biology-plus-care giving formula would not always be enough to trigger constitutional recognition as a parent. For the plurality in *Michael H. v. Gerald D.*,[84] societal judgments about parenting and family identity were also important considerations. There, the Court held that California was not required to recognize as a parent a man who had demonstrated his willingness to care emotionally and financially for his biological daughter. Because the child was conceived in an extramarital affair and now lived in an intact marital family, the man's relationship with the child was not one society traditionally respected and considered worthy of constitutional protection.[85] As Justice Stevens later recounted, *Michael H.* "recognized that the parental liberty interest [i]s a function, not simply of 'isolated factors' such as biology and intimate connection, but of broader and apparently independent interest in the family."[86]

The concept of parenthood reflected in these cases is surely expansive enough to permit the conferral of parent status on nontraditional care givers.[87] But these cases also surely impose some ultimate limitations on the state's ability to deny parental status to those falling within the constitutional criteria.[88] Professor Buss rightly warns that "[a]ny simple formula – whether based on history, biology, or biology plus some relationship – that purports to establish to whom parental rights belong will fail, in some circumstances, to account for those who constitute a child's familial core."[89] And, she contends, "[a] constitutional protection reduced to any such formula will therefore disserve the important child-rearing interests the Constitution should be construed to protect."[90] It is undeniable that any constitutional entitlement to parental identity risks excluding some persons who have built care giving relationships of enormous importance to children, and will therefore sometimes scrape up hard against the interests of children. But it is doubtful that the Constitution's protection of parental rights is so exclusively child-focused. Instead, it seems likely that constitutional protection of parenthood, like other non-textual rights, is

[83] *Id.* at 261–62. A basic and lingering ambiguity in *Lehr* is whether it is enough for constitutional status as a parent that the biological father *sought* to involve himself constructively in the child's rearing or whether it is necessary for him actually to *succeed* in building emotional bonds. *See* David D. Meyer, *Family Ties: Solving the Constitutional Dilemma of the Faultless Father*, 41 Ariz. L. Rev. 753, 762–69 (1999). This distinction is crucial in determining the constitutional claims of so-called "thwarted fathers," men who are prevented from contributing to a child's upbringing because of their faultless ignorance of the child's existence or whereabouts. *See id.*

[84] 491 U.S. 110 (1989).

[85] *See id.* at 122–23 & n.3 (opinion of Scalia, J.).

[86] *Troxel*, 530 U.S. at 88 (Stevens, J., dissenting).

[87] *See* Buss, *supra* note 3, at 657 (reviewing the unwed father cases and concluding that they "suggest the state has considerable power to recognize nontraditional care givers as parents themselves"); Bartholet, *supra* note 3, at 326 (similarly concluding that "today's U.S. Supreme Court has signaled its willingness to provide the states with significant leeway to determine who is a parent and how prominently biology should figure in that determination").

[88] *See* Nancy E. Dowd, *Fathers and the Supreme Court: Founding Fathers and Nurturing Fathers*, 54 Emory L.J. 1271, 1306 (2005) (finding in the Supreme Court's unwed father cases a "definition of constitutional fatherhood," and concluding that "[t]he Court's cases reflect a definition of fatherhood that operates along several axes – marriage, biology, legitimization and nurture").

[89] Buss, *supra* note 3, at 662.

[90] *Id.*

bottomed on social value judgments that are more multidimensional. The presumption that parental prerogative will advance the welfare of children is a major premise of constitutional protection, but it is not the only one. A sense of justice for parents, a notion of desert rooted in the satisfaction of parental duty, is also a strong undercurrent in the Supreme Court's cases and in society's judgments about the privileged place of parents in relation to their children. This dual footing of parents' rights is a key reason why the Supreme Court's cases in turns seem to reflect both deference and skepticism toward state-law measures that redefine the role and identity of parents. The variation is not truly incoherence or indecision, but the product of an attempt to balance constitutional respect for the interests of children and adults in connection with a matter that affects them both profoundly.

If neither children's nor parents' interests can be categorically subordinated to the other for all purposes, then some means of accommodating them must be found. Perhaps the analogy to constitutional understandings of property is again apt. The Constitution readily permits state law to extend the boundaries of due process protection by recognizing new forms of property,[91] just as it permits an extension of parenting rights through state-law doctrines respecting adoption or de facto parenthood. But, just as there would be close scrutiny of any significant roll back of state-law definitions of what counts as "property" in order to avoid constitutional protections, any state-law curtailment of established understandings of parenthood would trigger a more searching examination.

Notwithstanding *Roth*'s essentially unqualified assertion that property is constitutionally defined by independent sources such as state law, the Supreme Court has come to recognize, at least implicitly, that there must be some limits on the states' power to rethink what counts as property. As Professor Thomas Merrill observes, *Roth*'s seemingly reflexive resort to state law to define the boundaries of a constitutional right poses a "positivist trap."[92]

> The trap arose because the Court's method effectively ceded the domain of constitutional property to governmental actors over which the Court, in its capacity as constitutional interpreter, had no control. In other words, *Roth* appeared to require the Court to go along with any and all contractions or expansions on the domain of property dictated by nonconstitutional law. This cession of control produced a "trap" because it could lead to either too little or too much property relative to other value commitments that were important to the Justices.[93]

In more recent cases, the Supreme Court seemingly has pulled back from the implications of unbridled deference to state-law definitions of property. For example, Professor Merrill finds in the Supreme Court's uneven attention in *Phillips v. Washington Legal Foundation*[94] to various legal sources an "intimat[ion] that perhaps long-established common-law rules are central to the identification of 'true' property interests, whereas rules enacted by regulatory agencies are not."[95] Similarly, in *Ruckelshaus v. Monsanto Co.*,[96] the Court held that corporate trade secrets qualified as property protected by the Takings Clause only by disregarding legal regulation that seriously undercut the claim of secrecy.

[91] *See, e.g.*, Goldberg v. Kelly, 397 U.S. 254 (1970) (recognizing property interests in welfare entitlements); *see also* Ruckelshaus v. Monsanto Co., 467 U.S. 986 (1984) (recognizing property interests in trade secrets).

[92] Thomas W. Merrill, *The Landscape of Constitutional Property*, 86 Va. L. Rev. 885, 922 (2000) (quoting Jerry Mashaw, *Administrative Due Process: The Quest for a Dignitary Theory*, 61 B.U. L. Rev. 885, 888 (1981)).

[93] *Id.* at 923.

[94] 524 U.S. 156 (1998).

[95] Merrill, *supra* note 92, at 898.

[96] 467 U.S. 986 (1984).

Merrill posits that the Court's refusal to apply *Roth*'s positivist test faithfully is driven by its conviction that to do so would deny protection to interests that, independent of the underlying legal sources, warranted protection as property.[97]

These and other cases suggest that, although states may extend the scope of property, they will not be permitted to contract property rights in ways that unsettle basic social expectations.[98] Similarly, social expectations about the nature of parenthood are likely to apply a constitutional brake on state-law efforts to withdraw and reassign parent status.[99] The unwed father cases provide markers of those expectations: the presence of genetic ties, emotional bonding, and traditional social consensus, for instance, are all relevant.[100] While the outer boundaries on the state's definitional power are not sharply drawn, it seems reasonably clear that denying parental status at least to adults meeting all three of these markers would cross the line.

California may soon provide a test case. In 2004, the California Supreme Court held that when multiple adults assert parental ties to a child, either on the basis of biology or past care giving, judges should weigh "considerations of policy and logic" in ascertaining the most "appropriate" parent.[101] This particular case involved a contest between two putative fathers. One, Heriberto, was the biological father of a two-year-old girl and had lived with the child and her mother for much of her life. The other, Paul, was married to the girl's mother; although he and the mother had been separated, the mother and her daughter nevertheless visited Paul periodically.[102] Both men qualified as "presumed

[97] Professor Merrill writes:

> Why was the [*Ruckelshaus*] Court reluctant to use the disclosure statute to defeat the manufacturer's claim that it had property? The best explanation would seem to be that a decision holding that the trade secrets were not property during the mandatory disclosure years was just too implausible–too jarring given general expectations about kinds of interests that are commonly regarded as being property in our society. The *Roth* approach, if applied by considering all relevant sources of nonconstitutional law, generated a result that the Court regarded as yielding too little property relative to what most observers would consider to be the intuitive result.

Merrill, *supra* note 92, at 939.

[98] In Merrill's assessment, the most coherent cases have adopted a "patterning approach," under which state law defines the substantive entitlements held by the private claimant, but *federal* law independently makes the ultimate determination whether those state-granted entitlements amount to "property" for purposes of federal constitutional protection. *See id.* at 926–28 (citing *Memphis Light, Gas & Water Division v. Craft*, 436 U.S. 1 (1978), and *Drye v. United States*, 535 U.S. 274 (1999)). The Supreme Court recently applied this approach in *Town of Castle Rock v. Gonzales*, 125 S. Ct. 2796, 2803–04 (2005), to conclude that a crime victim did not have a constitutional "property interest" in police enforcement of a protective order. For another recent case taking the same approach in the context of defining "property" for purposes of federal tax law, see *United States v. Craft*, 535 U.S. 274 (2002).

[99] *Cf.* Cass R. Sunstein, *The Right to Marry*, 26 Cardozo L. Rev. 2081, 2105 (2005) (suggesting that the Constitution would require heightened scrutiny of state measures to strip parental status from biological or adoptive parents, but not to measures merely withholding parental status from unconventional aspirants, because "for a biological or adoptive parent, state intervention imposes a loss that is distinctive in both degree and kind").

[100] Professor Katharine Baker argues that

> the most important factor in determining whether a genetic father will be entitled to constitutional protection of his parental rights is his relationship with the mother. In *Stanley* and *Caban v. Mohammed*, cases in which the Court protected the father's constitutional rights as a parent, one could readily find an implicit agreement between the mother and father to share parental rights.

Baker, *supra* note 4, at 34.

[101] *See In re* Jesusa V., 10 Cal. Rptr. 3d 205, 218–19 (Cal. 2004); *see also* Craig L. v. Sandy S., 22 Cal. Rptr. 3d 606, 612–14 (Ct. App. 2004). Other courts have similarly directed trial courts to weigh competing claims of biology and caregiving in selecting among presumed parents under the Uniform Parentage Act. *See* Dept. of Soc. Servs. v. Byer, 678 N.W.2d 586, 591–92 (S.D. 2004) (where paternity presumptions based on marriage and biology conflict, court should designate the father according to discretionary "best interests" determination); G.D.K. v. Dept. of Fam. Servs., 92 P.3d 834, 837–38 (Wyo. 2004); N.A.H. v. S.L.S., 9 P.3d 354, 366 (Colo. 2000); Doe v. Doe, 52 P.3d 255, 262 (Haw. 2002).

[102] *Jesusa V.*, 10 Cal. Rptr. 3d at 210–11.

fathers" under California's version of the Uniform Parentage Act, Heriberto on the basis of his genetic connection and Paul on the basis of his marriage to the mother. Additionally, each man could plausibly claim that he had "received the child into his home and openly held her out as his child."[103] Reasoning that it must choose between these men, the California Supreme Court ruled that "[t]he juvenile court thus was obliged to weigh all relevant factors – including biology – in determining which presumption was founded on weightier considerations of policy and logic."[104] It then upheld the juvenile court's conclusion that, at least on the particular facts of this case, " '[t]he man who provide[d] the stability, nurturance, family ties, permanence, is more important to a child than the man who has mere biological ties.'"[105] On that basis, Paul was made Jesusa's parent, relegating Heriberto to the sidelines after living nearly two years with her as father and daughter.

Although the California Supreme Court turned aside Heriberto's due process objections, the case nevertheless illustrates the constitutional limitations on state choices among aspiring parents. The court defended the constitutionality of its action, over strong dissent,[106] on two grounds: First, it asserted – somewhat implausibly under California law – that "the identification of another man as Jesusa's presumed father does not terminate Heriberto's parental relationship with the child."[107] Second, Heriberto had not done enough under *Lehr* to "'demonstrate[] a full commitment to his parental responsibilities' [so as] to merit constitutional protection."[108] Without passing on the merits of these assertions, the broader point is that each implies the existence of some independent constitutional limitation on state power to reassign parental status. That the court, in affirming the state's power to choose among competing father figures, felt it necessary to insist that the designation would not clearly foreclose an ongoing parental role for Heriberto implies a broader tolerance for adding new parents than for substituting them. Similarly, its assessment of whether Heriberto had done enough to "grasp the opportunity" to parent acknowledges that some men at least can indeed demand constitutional recognition as parents. If Heriberto had been a bit faster to seek a formal declaration of his paternity, or if Paul and Jesusa's mother had not married, then the court presumably might have been compelled to acknowledge Heriberto's status as a parent, notwithstanding the greater "stability, nurturance, family ties, [and] permanence" offered by Paul. This is not to say that the Constitution would necessarily bar the state from extending parent status to Paul, only that it might preclude extinguishing Heriberto's claim to parenthood without proving his unfitness or other grounds for termination.[109]

[103] *Id.* at 215, 219 (tracking statutory language of Fam. Code § 7611(d));

[104] *Id.* at 220.

[105] *Id.* at 220–21.

[106] *Id.* at 267–74 (Chin, J., dissenting) (contending that majority's assumption of the power to choose among prospective parents violated Heriberto's fundamental liberty interests as a fit biological parent who had lived with and cared for his child).

[107] *Id.* at 221 (emphasis in original). The assertion is dubious because in other cases, both before and after *Jesusa V.*, the California Supreme Court has made plain that a child may not have three parents under California law. *See* Elisa B. v. Superior Court, 117 P.3d 660, 666 (2005) ("[W]hat we considered and rejected in *Johnson* [*v. Calvert*, 851 P.3d 776 (Cal. 1993),] was the argument that a child could have three parents: a father and two mothers."). Consequently, acceptance of one man's claim to parentage implicitly precluded the other's. *See Jesusa V.*, 10 Cal. Rptr. 3d at 268–69 (Chin, J., dissenting).

[108] *Jesusa V.*, 10 Cal. Rptr. 3d at 222.

[109] In fact, as both the majority and dissent in *Jesusa V.* recognized, there were ample facts – including Heriberto's incarceration for brutally assaulting Jesusa's mother – that might support terminating Heriberto's parental rights, if any such rights existed. *See* 10 Cal. Rptr. 3d at 241 (Chin, J., dissenting).

B. New Parents and the Dilution of Parenting Authority

There will be many cases in which the Constitution is likely to require states to recognize the "parent" status of a biological parent in circumstances in which that parent opposes the ongoing involvement of a nontraditional care giver. In such cases, the only choices open to law will be to sacrifice the nonparent relationship – as state courts did, for example, in the cases of Baby Jessica[110] and Baby Richard[111] – or else to find some way to reconcile and accommodate the involvement of both.[112] The PRINCIPLES opt for the latter course and likely obtain the maximal involvement and status for nontraditional care givers permitted by the Constitution.

It is true that the addition of new parents who will share that status with a preexisting legal parent significantly intrudes on the child rearing liberty of traditional parents. But it is likely an intrusion the Constitution permits, at least in the limited circumstances under which the PRINCIPLES would recognize a "de facto parent" or "parent by estoppel."

As an initial matter, it is increasingly clear that something less than strict scrutiny applies in the context of substantive due process protection of parental rights. Although strict scrutiny is the usual test for state action that burdens a fundamental constitutional right, the Supreme Court's family privacy cases have repeatedly hedged in their description of the necessary scrutiny.[113] And the Supreme Court's most recent cases strongly confirm its commitment to a flexible, intermediate standard of review. *Troxel v. Granville*,[114] a case affirming the fundamental child rearing right of parents, eschews quite deliberately the usual strict-scrutiny search for "narrow tailoring" and "compelling interests" in favor of a more open-ended balancing of public and private interests.[115] The only general guidance the plurality offers to lower courts weighing nonparent visitation disputes is that they must give an unspecified "special weight" to a fit parent's reasons for wishing to limit contact with a nonparent.[116] The Court's decision more recently in *Lawrence v. Texas*[117] follows the same pattern, vindicating a fundamental privacy interest in intimate association without employing strict scrutiny.[118]

In place of strict scrutiny, the Supreme Court has used an intermediate form of review employing at least three factors to gauge the sufficiency of the state's justification for its intrusion on family privacy. The Supreme Court looks to (1) the degree of unity or fracture within the family unit affected by the state action; (2) the degree of the state's intrusion on

[110] *In re* B.G.C., 496 N.W.2d 239 (Iowa 1992).

[111] *In re* Petition of Kirchner, 649 N.E.2d 324 (Ill. 1995); *In re* Petition of Doe, 638 N.E.2d 181 (Ill. 1994).

[112] *See* Meyer, *supra* note 83, at 813–45 (proposing a form of non-consensual, open adoption as a means of accommodating parental roles for both adoptive and biological parents in this context).

[113] *See* Zablocki v. Redhail, 434 U.S. 374, 386–88 (1978); Moore v. City of East Cleveland, 434 U.S. 494, 499 (1977); David D. Meyer, *The Paradox of Family Privacy*, 53 VAND. L. REV. 527, 536–48 (2000) (reviewing cases and commentary).

[114] 530 U.S. 57 (2000).

[115] *See id.* at 80 (Thomas, J., concurring in the judgment) (noting that the plurality and other separate opinions "curiously" fail to apply strict scrutiny despite having found a burden on the parent's fundamental right to rear her children). For further discussion of the significance of this omission, and the "middle" standard applied in place of strict scrutiny, see Emily Buss, *Adrift in the Middle: Parental Rights After* Troxel v. Granville, 2000 SUP. CT. REV. 279; Stephen G. Gilles, *Parental (and Grandparental) Rights After* Troxel v. Granville, 9 SUP. CT. ECON. REV. 69 (2001); David D. Meyer, Lochner *Redeemed: Family Privacy After* Troxel *and* Carhart, 48 UCLA L. REV. 1125 (2001).

[116] 530 U.S. at 69 (plurality opinion).

[117] 539 U.S. 558 (2003).

[118] I defend this claim at greater length in David D. Meyer, *Domesticating* Lawrence, 2004 U. CHI. LEGAL F. 453. *See also* Laurence H. Tribe, *Lawrence v. Texas: The "Fundamental Right" That Dare Not Speak Its Name*, 117 HARV. L. REV. 1893 (2004).

private interests; and (3) historical and contemporary social consensus about the nature and value of family relationships.[119]

The PRINCIPLES' approach to custody appears well crafted to pass muster under these considerations.[120] The PRINCIPLES recognize new parents only when some family fracture led the disputants into court.[121] The presence of preexisting family discord lowers the justificatory burden for state intervention because presumably at least one party invited the state's role as mediator, lessening the intrusiveness of the state's action, and because family disputes frequently hasten a clash of competing privacy interests.[122] The latter concern, of course, is the same one cited in *Newdow* to justify its refusal to privilege the noncustodial father's child rearing wishes over the custodial mother's. This clash of interests also led Justice Stevens in *Troxel* to favor qualifying the strength of the Constitution's protection of parental prerogative in visitation disputes.[123]

Although the novelty of a government-sponsored scheme of multiple parenthood counsels some judicial skepticism,[124] an assessment of the degree of the PRINCIPLES' intrusion on privacy interests weighs strongly in its favor.[125] Indeed, the PRINCIPLES' preference for adding new parents without simply reassigning parent status and displacing the old,[126] as the California court effectively did in *Jesusa V.*, significantly bolsters its claim to constitutionality. Whereas a wholesale reassignment of exclusive parent status ordinarily extinguishes the former parent's family status, the addition of new parents only dilutes the prerogatives of preexisting parents. This is not to suggest that dilution is an insignificant incursion on parental prerogative – it surely is not – but it is a far lesser intrusion than that contemplated by a reassignment of exclusive parent status.

Finally, the benefits of the PRINCIPLES' parenthood provisions for children (and for adults who under traditional law are classified as "non-parent care givers" or "legal strangers") would be real and substantial. There are benefits that flow specifically from classifying a care giver as a "parent," rather than, as under current law, a "third-party" custodian or visitor. Empirical evidence seems to confirm what common sense would suggest: that children and their care givers form deeper and more mutually satisfying

[119] *See* Meyer, *supra* note 113, at 579–91 (discussing relevance and past judicial consideration of these factors). For lower court decisions applying similar approaches to calibrate the level of scrutiny in family privacy cases, see Guardianship of L.S., 87 P.3d 521, 527 (Nev. 2004); Kirkpatrick v. Eighth Jud. Dist. Ct., 64 P.3d 1056, 1061–62 (Nev. 2003); Patel v. Searles, 305 F.3d 130 (2d Cir. 2002), *cert. denied*, 538 U.S. 907 (2003); *cf.* Crowley v. McKinney, 400 F.3d 965 (7th Cir. 2005) (suggesting that strength of parental right varies depending upon nature of the asserted interest at stake and presence of conflicting interests within family).

[120] *See* David D. Meyer, *What Constitutional Law Can Learn from the ALI* Principles of Family Dissolution, 2001 BYU L. REV. 1075.

[121] *See* PRINCIPLES § 2.01 (stating that custody principles apply only when parents are separated or "when the circumstances underlying a child's residence with a de facto parent substantially change"). A comment accompanying this provision makes clear that it reflects a conscious desire by the drafters to avoid incursions on intact families. *See id.*, cmt. b.

[122] *See* Sandra Day O'Connor, *The Supreme Court and the Family*, 3 U. PA. J. CONST. L. 573, 575–76 (2001); Anne C. Dailey, *Constitutional Privacy and the Just Family*, 67 TUL. L. REV. 955, 982–89 (1993).

[123] *See supra* text accompanying notes 74–77.

[124] Although the multiple parenthood contemplated by the PRINCIPLES plainly constitutes a major departure from traditional assumptions about parenthood as an exclusive status belonging only to one father and one mother, *see* Katharine T. Bartlett, *Rethinking Parenthood as an Exclusive Status: The Need for Legal Alternatives When the Premise of the Nuclear Family Has Failed*, 70 VA. L. REV. 879 (1984), the allowance for second-parent adoptions, open adoption, and similar arrangements demonstrates that "some exceptions to [the traditional] rule have recently begun to develop." Perry-Rogers v. Fasano, 715 N.Y.S.2d 19, 25 n.1 (App. Div. 2000).

[125] *See* Meyer, *supra* note 120, at 1094–9.

[126] *See* PRINCIPLES §§ 2.03, 2.08 (providing for the allocation of custodial responsibility among multiple parents).

bonds when the law gives the fullest measure of security to the continuity of their relationship.[127] Where care givers lack the secure status of parenthood, and risk losing custody or contact under a legal regime that powerfully privileges parents' rights over "third-party" interests, they sometimes hold back, consciously or otherwise, from investing themselves fully in the intimate relation. The risks of emotional loss may simply seem too great.[128] Empirical research also amply demonstrates that inhibitions in the bonding between a child and parent can carry detrimental consequences for the child's attachment and overall development.[129]

Accordingly, although it cannot be doubted that spreading parental authority among a wider circle of parents would carry significant and genuine costs, including the potential for additional conflicts among a child's care givers and a diminution of the care giving satisfaction of the legal parents, these costs must be balanced against the benefits to children from the greater continuity and security of care giving relationships.

IV. Conclusion

As the Supreme Court has acknowledged, the "changing realities of the American family"[130] have made it clear that "[f]or many boys and girls a traditional family with two or even one permanent and caring parent is simply not the reality of their childhood."[131] Instead, many such children will be raised by caring adults whom they regard as their parents but who have not traditionally been treated as parents by the law. Attempts to vindicate children's interests by simply reassigning parent status from biological or adoptive parents to parent-like care givers are almost certain in some circumstances to collide with constitutional notions of parenthood that are tethered more closely to traditional social expectations. The custody provisions of the PRINCIPLES, by contrast, aim to give these children the most that likely can be given them in a society that remains deeply respectful of traditional parental roles and prerogatives. By conferring parental rights on those who play dominant child rearing roles while also preserving the ties that children have with fit but possibly more distant biological or adoptive parents, the PRINCIPLES do an admirable job of accommodating the respect the Constitution requires for traditional parents with the respect the Constitution allows for the needs of children growing up outside the boundaries of the conventional family.

The author gratefully acknowledges the support of the Ross and Helen Workman Law Research Grant in the preparation of this chapter.

[127] *See* Margaret F. Brinig & Steven L. Nock, *How Much Does Legal Status Matter? Adoptions by Kin Caregivers*, 36 FAM. L.Q. 449, 467–69 (2002) (documenting significant differences in well-being of children residing in foster and kinship care as opposed to those living with adoptive parents, and attributing the gap in part to "a lack of trust by participants [in the non-adoptive families] that the relationships will continue"); Meyer, *supra* note 83, at 798–803 (reviewing additional studies).

[128] *See, e.g.*, Lisa Belkin, *Now Accepting Applications for My Baby*, N.Y. Times, Apr. 5, 1998, § 6 (Magazine), at 58 (describing one couple's calculated "reserve" in caring for their prospective adoptive child).

[129] *See* Meyer, *The Modest Promise of Children's Relationship Rights*, 11 WM. & MARY BILL OF RIGHTS J. 1117, 1125–26 & n.44 (2003); Meyer, *supra* note 83, at 798–800.

[130] *Troxel*, 530 U.S. at 64 (plurality opinion).

[131] *Id.* at 98 (Kennedy, J., dissenting).

4 Custody Law and the ALI's PRINCIPLES: A Little History, a Little Policy, and Some Very Tentative Judgments

Robert J. Levy

The PRINCIPLES' analyses of custody law doctrines and family issues are much too well researched and documented, too rich and exhaustive, too elegantly drafted, to be described, much less analyzed, in a single chapter. This chapter seeks to put the PRINCIPLES' recommended standard for deciding divorce-custody disputes in an abbreviated historical context, one that focuses on the contention of many commentators (but fewer judges and lawyers) that the much-noted indeterminacy of traditional doctrinal standards should be minimized.[1] Part I provides that historical context; Parts II and III examine the architecture of two of the ALI's many proposals for improving the procedural norms of custody litigation, Parenting Plans and the appointment of a guardian ad litem or lawyers for the child. The chapter concludes that the product of the endeavor has substantially advanced public policy endeavors in both substantive and procedural areas of concern; the endeavor also creates new and difficult problems for custody doctrine formulation.

I. Substantive Standards for Awarding Custody: Policy Diversity and the ALI's "Approximate the Time" Proposal

Judges, divorce practitioners, forensically sophisticated mental health experts, as well as academic commentators agree about very little. But there does seem to be a consensus that the standards governing judicial determinations of post-divorce custody of children pose a most difficult and unresolved legal policy conundrum. Many commentators have suggested that the nature of custody litigation contributes significantly to the difficulties.[2]

[1] This chapter does not examine many of the traditional subsidiary rules that affect or frequently dispose of custody contests, such as the "maternal" or "tender years" presumption, the "blood is thicker than water" presumption, the "joint custody" preference, the "unfitness" disqualification, the "psychological parent" thesis, the rule against splitting siblings, and a host of other subsidiary doctrines. This chapter is a modified and expanded version of some chapters of NATIONAL INTERDISCIPLINARY COLLOQUIUM ON CUSTODY LAW, LEGAL AND MENTAL HEALTH PERSPECTIVES ON CUSTODY LAW (2005 Robert J. Levy, General Editor) (hereinafter cited as COLLOQUIUM, with page numbers).

[2] *See, e.g.*, Robert J. Levy, *Rights and Responsibilities for Extended Family Members?*, 27 FAM. L.Q. 189, 194 (1993) (including among custody adjudication's attributes "its intense emotionalism, how 'unfit' litigating parents often appear or are made to appear to judges, and the invitation the 'best interests' standard's indeterminate qualities offers to judges to award custody to those litigants whose attributes and values most resemble their own").

A path-breaking academic essay on custody law and practice pointed out:

> [U]nder the best interests principle the outcome in court will often be uncertain: each spouse may be able to make a plausible claim for custody, and it may be impossible to predict how a court would decide a disputed case.[3]

Mnookin and Kornhauser showed that uncertain rules, although apparently neutral in effect, have very different impacts on spouses' bargaining power, and therefore can differentially affect the negotiation of that enormous proportion (over 90 percent) of divorce cases that are "settled" by the spouses and their lawyers rather than litigated. It is now widely recognized that the nature of the guiding standard is central to custody negotiations; but that recognition has not helped legislatures, courts, or commentators to agree on an appropriate guiding standard. Rather, legislatures and courts have for generations struggled to establish a proper balance between doctrinal rule and judicial discretion.[4] Appellate courts and legislatures have regularly sought to make the standard less "indeterminate," to give greater guidance to trial judges mired in the emotional and legal difficulties of custody adjudication. Simultaneously and quite inconsistently, appellate courts and legislatures, in the interest of recognizing one or another "factor" deemed relevant to the "best interests" of particular children, have adopted rules that substantially increase "indeterminacy" and judicial discretion.[5]

In the nineteenth century, the father was deemed to have almost a property right in his children at the marriage's termination.[6] In the twentieth century, the "best interests" standard came to be associated with a presumption favoring the mothers of young children (often called the "tender years" presumption).[7] Some scholars supported the "tender years" standard, not because of the advantages it provided divorcing women, but because it helped to constrain the otherwise dangerous discretion the "best interests" standard gave judicial decisionmakers.[8] But in the 1970s, some scholars began to oppose the standard because it appeared to relegate women to a subservient, caretaker position in the family.[9] Eventually, a number of courts ruled the standard unconstitutional and almost every state legislature abolished it.[10]

Legal scholars of almost every intellectual persuasion and from almost every place on the political compass have tried to formulate doctrinal standards for custody litigation. Professor Mary Becker argued for a "maternal deference" standard under which judges would acquiesce to the mother's wishes as to custody in order to protect the greater commitment of mothers to the children of their marriages.[11] This proposal has gained no legislative

[3] Robert H. Mnookin & Lewis A. Kornhauser, *Bargaining in the Shadow of the Law: The Case of Divorce*, 88 Yale L.J. 950, 956 (1979).

[4] *See generally* Carl E. Schneider, *Discretion, Rules and Law: Child Custody and the UMDA's Best-Interest Standard*, 89 Mich. L. Rev. 2215 (1991).

[5] Colloquium, *supra* note 1, at 11–48.

[6] *See, e.g.*, Homer H. Clark, 2 Law of Domestic Relations in the United States 496 (2d ed. 1987).

[7] *See, e.g.*, Ramsay L. (Laing) Klaff, *The Tender Years Doctrine: A Defense*, 70 Cal. L. Rev. 335 (1982).

[8] *See* Phoebe C. Ellsworth & Robert J. Levy, *Legislative Reform of Child Custody Adjudication: An Effort to Rely On Social Science Data in Formulating Legal Policies*, 4 Law & Soc. Rev. 167 (1969).

[9] For discussion of the literature see, e.g., Robert J. Levy, *A Reminiscence About the* Uniform Marriage and Divorce Act – *and Some Reflections About Its Critics and Its Policies*, 1991 BYU L. Rev. 43, 49.

[10] *See, e.g.*, Ex Parte Devine, 398 So.2d 686 (Ala. 1981); Stephen J. Bahr, *Trends in Child Custody Awards: Has the Removal of Maternal Deference Made a Difference?*, 28 Fam. L.Q. 247 (1994).

[11] Mary E. Becker, *Maternal Feelings: Myth, Taboo and Child Custody*, 1 Rev. L. & Women's Stud. 133 (1992).

or policy group's support. Professor Andrew Schepard recommended that custody be determined by the spouses themselves with the aid of a mediator;[12] but Professor Trina Grillo warned that mediation poses grave risks to those many divorcing women who are subservient to their husbands in the marriage relationship.[13]

The "joint custody" movement, although separable from mediation, has often been associated with it. Joint custody enjoyed substantial legislative popularity for a time because its advocates claimed it kept noncustodial fathers involved in the post-divorce parenting of their children.[14] The theory is that if divorced fathers are not deprived of authority over their children they will continue to support them and stay emotionally attached to them, to the children's developmental advantage.[15] Although quite a few legislatures have passed joint custody statutes, most legal observers believe that only "joint legal custody" (sharing of legal decision-making authority) rather than "joint physical custody" (some kind of shared parenting) has or should become common.[16] Moreover, many lawyers and mental health experts believe that joint legal custody is often used more as a sop to fathers' egos than as an effective inducement to paternal participation in parenting. The doctrine has attracted substantial opposition.[17] Some scholars who identify with the "Children's Rights" movement argue that the stated preference of a child older than a specific age should determine the child's custody.[18] One observer, despairing that any rational standard can in fact be articulated, seriously argued that custody should be determined in most cases by flipping a coin, because the right result would be achieved just as often and much more efficiently.[19]

Mental health professionals have produced equally varied and inconsistent proposals for solving the enormous complexities of custody law. Some psychologists and psychiatrists, many lawyers believe, would be satisfied only by a standard that refers all custody disputes to a mental health expert. Thus, a psychiatrist recommended "the psychological best interests of the child" as the appropriate dispositional standard, believing that the standard's indeterminate qualities could be controlled with lavish advice from mental health experts.[20] A group of mental health professionals recommended that custody be awarded to "the psychological parent" – the adult whom the child identifies as

[12] Andrew I. Schepard, *Taking Children Seriously: Promoting Cooperative Custody After Divorce*, 64 TEX. L. REV. 726 (1985). *See also infra* p. 19 and the discussion of "Parenting Plans."

[13] Trina Grillo, *The Mediation Alternative: Process Dangers For Women*, 100 YALE L.J. 1545 (1991).

[14] *See generally* H. Jay Folberg and Marva Graham, *Joint Custody of Children Following Divorce*, 12 U.C. DAVIS L. REV. 523 (1979).

[15] *See* Beck v. Beck, 432 A.2d 63, 64 (N.J. 1981) ("Joint custody attempts to solve some of the problems of sole custody by providing the child with access to both parents and granting parents equal rights and responsibilities regarding their children.").

[16] *See* COLLOQUIUM, *supra* note 1, at 49–60.

[17] *See* Elizabeth S. Scott & Andre P. Derdeyn, *Rethinking Joint Custody*, 45 OHIO ST. L.J. 455 (1984); Lumbra v. Lumbra 394 A.2d 1139 (Vt. 1978) (instituting a presumption that joint custody is not in a child's best interests and should only be awarded in extraordinary circumstances).

[18] *See* Randy Francis Kandel, *Just Ask the Kid! Towards a Rule of Children's Choice in Custody Determinations*, 49 U. MIAMI L. REV. 299 (1994). *See also* Barbara Bennett Woodhouse, *Child Custody in the Age of Children's Rights: The Search for a Just and Workable Standard*, 33 FAM. L.Q. 815 (1999); Katherine Hunt Federle, *An Empowerment Perspective on the Rights of Children*, 68 TEMP. L. REV. 1585 (1995) (emphasizing providing lawyers for children who will help them to assert their interests independently and forcefully).

[19] *See* Jon Elster, *Solomonic Judgments: Against the Best Interests of the Child*, 54 U. CHI. L. REV. 1 (1987).

[20] Andrew S. Watson, *The Children of Armageddon: Problems of Custody Following Divorce*, 21 SYRACUSE L. REV. 55 (1969).

his or her parent.[21] This proposal and its implications were rigorously criticized in the literature.[22]

In recent years, influenced by mental health professionals, a number of legislatures have sought to obviate the "winner/loser" mentality that sometimes results when parents view custody disposition as a zero-sum game. In some states the terms "custody" and "custodian" as well as "visitation" have been abolished and replaced with a concept of actual and shared parenting.[23] The Washington statute has become the model for what is now often called the "Parenting Plan" formula:[24] a post-dissolution care and management plan for children of the marriage is conceived and executed primarily by the parents themselves with the aid of their choice of a mediator, a mental health specialist, or some other neutral, such as the judge. The plan is intended to make parents deal cooperatively with every aspect of the child's postdivorce life without requiring a choice between a "winning" and a "losing" parent.

The following paragraphs describe in greater detail two custody standard proposals that have attracted some judicial and legislative attention in recent years. The proposals both reflect legislative and judicial ambivalence as to the balance between rule and discretion. To some extent these proposals foreshadow the Institute's effort to achieve a more determinate standard as well as its concurrent effort to provide expansive and indeterminate "exceptions" to that standard.

A. The "Primary Caretaker" Doctrine

A number of scholars have urged a return to the "tender years" presumption to protect women from judges who sometimes use an indeterminate standard to discriminate against mothers.[25] Many judges and commentators have favored a "primary caretaker" presumption, acknowledging that in most families the mother's parenting role is dominant[26] – leading some lawyers and judges to describe it as the "degendered maternal presumption."

[21] *See* Joseph Goldstein, Anna Freud & Albert J. Solnit, Beyond the Best Interests of the Child (1973).

[22] *See, e.g.*, Nanette Dembitz, *Beyond Any Discipline's Competence*, 83 Yale L.J. 1304, 1310 (1974); Peter L. Strauss and Joanna B. Strauss, *Book Review*, 74 Colum. L. Rev. 996, 1004 (1974). In a more recent revision of the authors' work, the insistence that visitation by a noncustodial parent be at the sole discretion of the custodial parent was restated and given additional emphasis. *See* Joseph Goldstein, Albert J. Solnit, Sonja Goldstein & Anna Freud, The Best Interests of the Child: The Least Detrimental Alternative 23–24, nn.10–12 (1996).

[23] *See, e.g.*, Wash. Rev. Code § 26.09.184 (West Supp. 2004) (eliminating terms "custody" and "visitation" and using terminology of "permanent parenting plan," "residential" and "nonresidential" parent, and "decision-making authority"); Neb. Rev. Stat. § 43-2903 (1993) (referring to "parenting functions" rather than custody); Tex. Cam. Stat. Ann. § 153.001 (Vernon 2003) (referring to "primary" and "secondary" "conservator"). An earlier version of the Principles explains the drafters' choice to abandon the "power-laden terminology" of "custody" and "visitation" because it "symbolizes and helps to perpetuate the adversarial nature of the process of determining arrangements for children after family breakdown." Principles of the Law of Family Dissolution: Analysis and Recommendations 7–8 (Preliminary Draft No. 5, May 11, 1995). The Principles adopt the language "Allocation of Custodial Responsibility" and "Allocation of Significant Decision-making Responsibility." *See infra* note 45 and accompanying text.

[24] *See* Jane W. Ellis, *Plans, Protections, and Professional Intervention: Innovations in Divorce Custody Reform and the Role of Legal Professionals*, 24 U. Mich. J.L. Reform 65 (1990). The Principles also adopted a form of "parenting plan" regulation. *See infra* Part II.

[25] *See, e.g.*, Rena K. Uviller, *Father's Rights and Feminism: The Maternal Presumption Revisited*, 1 Harv. Women's L.J. 107 (1974); Martha Minow, *Consider the Consequences*, 84 Mich. L. Rev. 900, 908 (1986).

[26] *See* Garska v. McCoy, 278 S.E.2d 357 (W. Va. 1981); Mary Ann Glendon, *Fixed Rules and Discretion in Contemporary Family Law and Succession Law*, 60 Tul. L. Rev. 1165, 1179 (1986).

This formulation has not been praised by all commentators.[27] Nor have all state legislators been enthusiastic about the "primary caretaker" doctrine's effort to limit judicial discretion.[28]

Although the "primary caretaker" designation appears to lessen the indeterminacy of the "best interests" test, it produces problems that cause many critics to reject it. Determining which parent was in fact "primary" can cause as many proof problems as the "best interests" test. The test may cause unnecessary hostility and litigation early in the spouses' separation, just when "cooling down" should be encouraged. In addition, if the standard is measured at the time of the divorce, it may be unfair to a spouse who, in the interest of peace, gave up everyday contact with the child. Moreover, the standard may take too little account of changes in family roles, emotional attachments, and general behavior of parents when marriages break up. For example, the spouses may have decided that the breadwinner should spend an extraordinary amount of time away from home to achieve economic benefits for the family even at the expense of that parent's current time with the child. Although both spouses will frequently reassess their relative commitment to work and family after the breakup, the "primary caretaker" rule makes earlier commitments permanent and prevents either parent from making a new choice of priorities without the other's permission. In short, the effort to minimize discretion creates opportunities for unfair outcomes because divorce is often, if not always, the occasion for reconsideration by spouses of their parental roles.[29]

B. The "Friendly Parent" Doctrine

Although many proposals to "solve" the "indeterminacy" of custody laws have had a very short "half-life," one recent development may well persist: a criterion that awards custody to the parent more able and willing to foster the child's relationship with the other parent. This is sometimes described as the "friendly parent" doctrine.[30]

The criterion, obviously difficult to quantify in objective terms, at least partially captures an important element of divorced parents' necessary social intercourse. Indeed, observers often comment that many postdecretal modification contests might have been avoided if each parent's willingness to recognize and promote the child's relationship with the other parent could have been predicted and reliably measured. Yet the criterion also allows the decisionmaker easily to infuse his or her own personal values into its vague contours and encourages rather than discourages litigation. In short, legislators and judges who support the "friendly parent" doctrine promote "indeterminacy" in the service of one of the many facets of "best interests."

The sometimes unspoken foundation for the "friendly parent" doctrine posits that, ideally, a child should be raised, even after her parents' divorce, by two cooperative parents.

[27] *See, e.g.*, Gary Crippen, *Stumbling Beyond Best Interests of the Child: Reexamining Child Custody Standard-Setting in the Wake of Minnesota's Four Year Experiment With the Primary Caretaker Preference*, 75 Minn. L. Rev. 427 (1990) (giving author's perspective as a Minnesota intermediate appellate court judge).

[28] Following a series of decisions that adopted and then reaffirmed the primary caretaker presumption, the Minnesota legislature amended the statute to eliminate preferences: "The court may not use one factor to the exclusion of all others. *The primary caretaker factor may not be used as a presumption in determining the best interests of the child.*" Minn. Stat. Ann. § 518.17 (West 1990), *amended by* 1990 Minn. Laws, ch. 574, § 13.

[29] Professor Carl E. Schneider's extraordinarily thorough and thoughtful examination and criticism of a primary caretaker rule can be found at Schneider, *supra* note 4, at 2283–87.

[30] Colloquium, *supra* note 1, 21–6.

Judicial discussions hewing to this line often suggest that if a child cannot have two parents recognizing and promoting each other's roles in the child's life, then the child will be better off cared for by the parent who recognizes the other parent's importance or, at least, is not disposed to affect adversely the child's relationship with the other.[31] Yet the parent better able to foster the child's relationship with the other parent is not necessarily the parent better able to pilot the child across the huge sea of concerns that determine the child's health, happiness, and passage to successful adulthood. Indeed, because the "friendly parent" function is only one of innumerable aspects of good parenting (and, of course, only one of many criteria for determining the child's "best interests"), "friendly parent" concerns must be weighed, as they say, in the balance. The problem (often insoluble in similar contexts) is giving content to "friendly parentism" while minimizing the risk that its vague and indeterminate qualities will be misused to cover decisions based unduly on decisionmakers' personal values. Examination of evidence and proof problems becomes essential.

It is easy to interpret spousal skirmishes common in many divorces as evidence that the actor is an "unfriendly parent." Much parental behavior can be construed as indicative of parental alienation, even justified criticism of the other parent, as well as unjustified but unsuccessful undermining of a parent produced by the strained circumstances of a pending divorce. This is not to say that a custodial spouse who is upset because her former spouse never picks up the kids on time, arrives drunk, or brings the kids back late or exhausted or both, doesn't have something to complain about. But the risk of subsequent judicial misapprehension, disbelief or manipulation, in the context of an "unfriendly parent" claim, remains substantial.

Consider also the role that motive may play in the exploration of this criterion. A custodial parent who wants to kill the child's affection for the other parent has a greater chance of succeeding than does a parent trying to accomplish a healthy coparenting relationship. The postdecretal custodial spouse "relocation" cases indicate that, whatever dangers motives evidence pose, courts have been disposed to give such evidence great weight.[32] But judicial examination of an individual's emotional state – which an exploration of motive requires – is a difficult and chancy endeavor, easy to manipulate. It would be much fairer, if a "friendly parent" criterion is relevant, to eschew motive evidence and focus strictly on parental behavior and any impact that behavior has actually had on the other parent's relationship with the child.[33]

Yet whether the relevance inquiry is limited to violation of court orders, or broadened to include the slippery slope of parental motives, evidence of parental behavior must be assessed carefully in light of the family's dynamics. The relevance of parental behavior will inevitably differ in relation to the specific circumstances of the spouses and their children and a host of other matters. One parent's failure to send notices or reports from the child's

[31] *See, e.g.*, Seymour v. Seymour, 433 A. 2d 1005, 1008 (Conn. 1980).

[32] *See* Colloquium, *supra* note 1, at ch. 21, at 260–61.

[33] *See, e.g.*, Sigg v. Sigg, 905 P.2d 908, 914–15 (Utah App. 1995) (transferring custody from mother to father; the mother's constant efforts to foil father's exercise of visitation rights showed change of circumstances justifying change in custody).

A more severe form of "unfriendly parent" focus in recent years can be seen in some mental health professional testimony describing a "Parental Alienation Syndrome." *See* Richard Gardner, The Parental Alienation Syndrome: A Guide for Mental Health and Legal Professionals (Rev. 2d ed. 2000). For a powerful critique of the alienation hypothesis, see Carol Bruch, *Parental Alienation Syndrome and Parental Alienation: Getting it Wrong in Custody Cases*, 35 Fam. L.Q. 527 (2001).

school to the other may be unimportant if both parents have adequate opportunity to visit the school or the school customarily provides duplicate notices or reports. Similarly, one parent's insistence that child exchanges occur at a public place rather than at the spouses' residences could stem either from that parent's endeavor improperly to disparage the other parent's home, or, benignly, from an effort to divide transportation responsibilities more equally. The need to distinguish the real from only the manifest is no different in "friendly parent" contests than in other kinds of custody disputes. Testimony by one parent that the other parent is never denigrated is obviously self-serving; but it might nonetheless be true. On the other hand, anger and hostility are so common in custody litigation that drawing adverse "friendly parent" inferences from such testimony should be difficult at best: few divorce dockets are filled with parents who know how to cooperate in caring for their children. All participants in custody contests are painfully aware of the need to separate the wheat of real past behavior from the chaff of hostile and often over-blown allegations.

To an ever increasing extent, statutes and judicial decisions direct judges considering either initial or modification custody awards to consider which parent will promote the child's relationship with the other. The Uniform Marriage and Divorce Act ("UMDA") did not include a "friendly parent" custody provision.[34] The Missouri legislature adopted the UMDA but added a requirement that courts consider, among other factors in determining the best interests of the child, "which parent is more likely to allow the child frequent and meaningful contact with the other parent."[35] In states without a specific legislative directive, appellate courts have given impetus to the criterion.[36] Yet the criterion may be less influential in initial custody determinations than the legislatures and appellate courts intended: parents' relationship fostering skills are not likely to be substantially and fairly displayed or tested while the divorce action is pending or even immediately after the divorce while the spouses are struggling with continuing coparenting responsibilities. After the initial decree, the stability enhancing values recognized in modification doctrines make initial judicial custody decisions very difficult to change.[37] Nonetheless, "friendly parent" evidence can affect the vast number of modification contests in which the custodial parent's interference with or obstruction of the child's relationship with the noncustodial parent leads to a reexamination of the original custody determination.[38] Appellate cases reviewing trial court modification decisions often discuss the criterion – although not always in the guise of a "friendly parent" criterion.[39] Application of the doctrine has been unclear in part because appellate courts have not always distinguished between the "good cause" needed to reexamine a prior custody award from the "failure to foster" evidence that might justify a modification.

[34] *See* Uniform Marriage and Divorce Act § 402, 9A Pt. II U.L.A. 282 (1998) (custody provisions).

[35] Mo. Ann. Stat. § 452.375(2)(6) (Supp. 2000). *See also* Colo. Rev. Stat. Ann. § 14-10-124(f) (2003); Fla. Stat. Ann. § 61.13(3)(b)(j) (Supp. 2004); Cal. Fam. Code § 3040(a)(1). *See also* Nat'l Ctr. On Women and Family Law, Friendly Parent Provisions in Custody Determination, Women's Advoc. (Sept. 1992).

[36] *See, e.g.*, Myers v. DiDomenico, 657 A.2d 956, 960 (Pa. Super. 1995) (considering which parent would be most likely to foster an ongoing relationship with noncustodial parent as part of "best interests of the child").

[37] *See* Colloquium, *supra* note 1, at 233–40.

[38] *See, e.g.*, Fisher v. Fisher, No. 508944, 1996 WL 646758 (Conn. Super.) (stating that one parent's greater willingness to facilitate the other's relationship with the child is more significant than other factors for purposes of application of "best interests" standard in relocation cases).

[39] See the cases analyzed in Debra E. Wax, *Interference by Custodian of Child with Noncustodial Parent's Visitation Rights as Ground for Change of Custody*, 28 A.L.R. 4th 9 (1981).

Few would disagree with the empirically unverified hunch that a child of divorce will be better off reared cooperatively by two parents who support and respect each other and their individual roles. The corollary is also entitled to weight: children whose parents seek to undermine each other's parental roles cannot possibly be helped by such behavior and could be harmed emotionally by it. But moving from these propositions to the legal principle that the child's physical custody should ride on a comparative judgment of the cooperating and "other-parent-facilitating" skills of the parents is a very different and much more dubious proposition. Recalcitrant, "non-cooperator" parents might be encouraged, even compelled, to improve their behavior – but a "friendly parent" doctrine's physical custody modification threat is much too large a bludgeon to accomplish the purpose effectively. The "friendly parent" standard is no panacea for custody doctrine indeterminacy; indeed, "friendly parenting," as vague and capable of manipulation as "best interests," simply adds an additional arrow to trial judges' indeterminate criteria quiver.

C. The PRINCIPLES' "Approximate the Time" Standard

Professor Elizabeth Scott, a contributor to this volume, suggested that custody and visitation be awarded so as to approximate the time each parent spent with the child during the marriage.[40] Although the notion attracted few adherents initially, it has received substantially more attention since the drafters adopted the proposal.[41] This effort to give substantial and determinate substantive content to the "best interests" test gained traction when the West Virginia legislature surprised most commentators by adopting the approximation standard.[42] Because the drafters' proposal comes with the prestigious imprint of the American Law Institute, whose products in the past have attracted state Supreme Court approvals even without legislative enactment,[43] and because the proposal has already been enacted by one legislature, the scheme is likely to receive widespread legislative scrutiny.

The drafters claim that their analysis "is a refinement and rationalization of the elastic 'best interests of the child' standard set forth in the relevant statutes of every state, and may therefore be relied upon by courts in interpreting and applying their statutes."[44] The dispositive provisions construct an extremely complex and integrated policy designed to replace all previous law – changing doctrinal denominations like "custody" and "visitation" and "deconstructing" the several aspects of parenting responsibilities. The PRINCIPLES break down traditional post-divorce parental powers and responsibilities into two sources of authority, "Allocation of Custodial Responsibility," and "Allocation of Significant Decision-making Responsibility."[45] The former standard requires that "the proportion of time the child spends with each parent [approximate] the proportion of

[40] Elizabeth S. Scott, *Pluralism, Parental Preference, and Child Custody*, 80 CAL. L. REV. 615 (1992).

[41] *See* PRINCIPLES, ch. 2 (custody), §§ 2.08, .09, at 180–248.

[42] *See* W. VA. CODE §§ 48–11–101 (2001). At least one advisor for the PRINCIPLES, an opponent of the "primary caretaker" rule adopted previously by the West Virginia Supreme Court and a vigorous defender of "fathers' rights," testified that the approximation standard would give noncustodial fathers a larger role in their children's post-divorce lives than the "primary caretaker" rule. Personal communication to the author from Ronald Allen, Esquire.

[43] *See* Dupre v. Dupre, 857 A.2d 242 (R.I. 2004) (concerning parent relocation). In a Florida intermediate appellate court opinion, a judicial advisor for the PRINCIPLES purported to adopt as a matter of common law the PRINCIPLES' "approximate the time" standard for custody dispositions following divorce. Young v. Hector, 1998 WL 329401 (Fla. Dist. Ct. App., June 24, 1998). This effort proved unsuccessful when the court *en banc* withdrew the panel decision, rejected the PRINCIPLES' standard, and affirmed the trial court's award of custody to a practicing attorney mother rather than to the stay-at-home architect father.

[44] PRINCIPLES, Chief Reporter's Foreword, at xviii.

[45] PRINCIPLES §§ 2.08, 2.09.

time each parent spent performing caretaking functions for the child prior to the parents' separation."[46] Exceptions to the rule are designed to protect the child and one of the parents from the other parent's neglect or abuse, domestic violence, drug or alcohol abuse, or persistent interference with the child's access to that parent.[47] Additional indeterminate exceptions to the "approximate the time" rule include allocations designed: to "permit the child to have a relationship with each parent;" to accommodate the "firm and reasonable preferences" of a child who has reached a certain (but unspecified) age; to keep siblings together if necessary for their welfare; to protect the child's welfare from harm due to operation of the rule "because of a gross disparity in the quality of the emotional attachment between each parent and the child or in each parent's demonstrated ability or availability to meet the child's need" to avoid allocations that "would be extremely impractical or that would interfere substantially with the child's need for stability...;" and to accomplish the relocation objectives of the PRINCIPLES.[48]

Decision-making responsibility pertains to "significant life decisions on behalf of the child, including decisions regarding the child's education and health care."[49] The provision includes a presumption of a joint allocation to each parent, overcome by a history of domestic violence or child abuse, or "if it is shown that joint allocation of decision-making responsibility is not in the child's best interests."[50] The "approximate the time" provisions are tempered by separate sections supporting parental autonomy in custodial decision-making. The PRINCIPLES require that the parents file, separately or jointly, a "Parenting Plan" making the allocations the doctrine requires,[51] and that courts order provisions of a Parenting Plan agreed to by the spouses.[52] According to Dean Katherine Bartlett, one of the

[46] PRINCIPLES § 2.08. Section 2.03(5) defines "caretaking functions" as "tasks that involve interaction with the child or that direct, arrange, and supervise the interaction and care provided by others." A non-exclusive list of caretaking functions includes such matters as "satisfying the nutritional needs of the child," "directing the child's various developmental needs," "providing discipline," "supervising chores," "performing other tasks that attend to the child's needs for behavioral control and self-restraint," "arranging for the child's education," "providing moral and ethical guidance," and a host of other specified functions. *Id.* at § 2.03(5)(a)–(h). Section 2.03(3) makes clear that "custodial responsibility" "refers to physical custodianship and supervision of a child. It usually includes, but does not necessarily require, residential or overnight responsibility." Section 2.03(6) defines "parenting functions," a phrase which appears only in Section 2.09(2), to include "tasks that serve the needs of the child or the child's residential family," including "caretaking functions" and a diverse variety of other functions, ranging from "providing economic support," "yard work, and house cleaning," to "participating in decision-making regarding the child's welfare" and "arranging for financial planning."

[47] PRINCIPLES § 2.11. The last clause may be seeking to capture "friendly parent" policies. *See supra* note 30 and accompanying text.

[48] PRINCIPLES § 2.08.

[49] PRINCIPLES § 2.09. Note that education and health care are topics also included as caretaking functions. *See supra* note 46. The allocation can be to one parent or to both parents jointly and in accordance with the child's best interests in light of several factors, including the allocation of custodial responsibility, the level of each parent's participation in past decision-making, the parents' wishes, the level of ability and cooperation the parents have shown in past decision-making. *Id.*

[50] PRINCIPLES § 2.09(2). But Section 2.09(3) stipulates that "unless otherwise provided or agreed by the parents, a parent should have sole responsibility for day-to-day decisions for the child while the child is in that parent's custodial care and control, including emergency decisions affecting the health and safety of the child."

[51] PRINCIPLES § 2.05.

[52] PRINCIPLES § 2.06. Section 2.12 bars judges from "issuing orders" which "consider" such matters as the race or ethnicity of the child or parent, religious practices of parent or child "except to the minimum degree necessary to protect the child from severe and almost certain harm or to protect the child's ability to practice a religion that has been a significant part of the child's life," sexual orientation of a parent, extramarital sexual conduct of a parent "except upon a showing that it causes harm to the child," or the parents' relative earning capacity. It follows that such factors cannot be included in parenting plans. Of course, it almost goes without saying that these prohibitions can create problems for trial judges trying sincerely to serve the child's "best interests" under a variety of unique circumstances involving such "factors."

PRINCIPLES' drafters, these provisions differ from the "primary caretaker" presumption in both theory and practice:

> The primary caretaker presumption assumes as a fact that a primary caretaker existed,[53] and then assumes as a state norm that one parent should have primary custody at divorce. The PRINCIPLES' past-caretaking standard makes no such factual or normative assumption; in fact, it is indifferent to the nature of the past-caretaking arrangements. If parents equally shared caretaking responsibilities, that fact will be reflected in the custodial allocations; if there was a clear primary caretaker, that will also be reflected, as well as everything else in between. Under the PRINCIPLES' approach, past arrangements – whatever they were – are to guide post-divorce arrangements. To the extent courts adopt this approach, they are taking their cue not from some state-selected preference in favor of a certain custody ideal, but from the parents themselves. As the law moves in this direction, more weight is given to parental decision-making – in this case decision-making during the marriage – and less to the state itself.[54]

These provisions reflect the drafters' belief that the "best interests" test is a "policy goal and not an administrable legal standard."[55] Past caretaking has become an important factor for judges applying the best interests test;[56] and a number of state statutes specifically direct courts to make past caretaking an important factor in custody decision-making – although the extant statutes seldom prioritize among a great variety of factors.[57]

It is certainly true that what might be called a "pure" "approximate the time" standard is less indeterminate than "best interests," and the standard, if administered rigorously, would more effectively channel and limit judicial discretion than the traditional rule. But like the "primary caretaker" rule, the standard denies either spouse the opportunity without the other's permission, to expand contacts and his or her relationship with the child by changing roles when the marriage has factually terminated. Such role changes commonly occur long before the divorce action is filed and even longer before a judge must decide to whom custody should be awarded. Role changing spouses are gravely disadvantaged in divorce negotiations and the pre-divorce homemaker spouse is given as great a tactical advantage as the maternal presumption gave mothers.[58] Nor does this rigorous standard recognize that comparative time spent with the children may not reflect each parent's emotional relationship with them.

For parents and for those anxious to increase doctrinal determinacy, the PRINCIPLES pose even more troubling problems. The exceptions to the rigid "approximate the time spent" doctrine seem to give judges as much discretion as the "best interests" test does. How many trial judges, committed to "individualizing" justice and caring about the healthy development of the children, would ignore the discretion authorized by Section 2.09?

[53] In fact, the opinion in Garska v. McCoy, 278 S.E.2d 357, 363 (W. Va. 1981), the case that popularized the "primary caretaker presumption," incorporated a caveat that "in those custody disputes where the facts demonstrate that child care and custody were shared in an entirely equal way, then indeed no presumption arises and the court must proceed to inquire further into relative degrees of parental competence."

[54] Katherine T. Bartlett, *Custody Law and Trends in the Context of the ALI Principles of the Law of Family Dissolution,* 10 VA. JOURNAL OF SOCIAL POLICY & LAW 5, 18 (2002).

[55] *Id.* at 16.

[56] *Id.* at 17.

[57] *Id.* at 16–17. *See, e.g.,* WASH. REV. CODE ANN. § 26.09.187(3)(a)(1) (West Supp. 2004). See also the undifferentiated listing of factors in MICH. COMP. LAWS ANN. § 722.23 (West Supp. 2002).

[58] Section 2.08(2) of the PRINCIPLES specifically requires courts allocating custodial responsibility to ignore "the division of functions arising from temporary arrangements after the parents' separation, whether those arrangements are consensual or by court order."

Consider the provision which requires the judge to vary the custody award to "protect the child's welfare when the presumptive allocation . . . would harm the child because of a gross disparity in the quality of the emotional attachment between each parent and the child or in each parent's demonstrated ability or availability to meet the child's needs."[59] What good trial judge would not be able to reach any outcome consistent with the judge's view of the facts and beliefs as to the child's "best interests?"[60] How many judges could or would resist the siren call to avoid allocations that "would be extremely impractical or that would interfere substantially with the child's need for stability?"[61]

The drafters designed these exceptions as "escape hatches" to the rigorous commands of the "approximate the time" standard. And the exceptions were drafted carefully in an effort to limit their scope and use – with the inclusion of such limiting language as "harm the child because of a gross disparity," "extremely impractical," and "interfere substantially."[62] The important questions cannot be answered empirically now and probably never will be: To what extent will trial judges confronting an entirely new doctrinal custody regime, one which compels them to focus on "narrow" "escape hatches" to a determinate principle, change their habitual decision-making assumptions and styles? To what extent, under traditional doctrinal regimes, did judges decide custody disputes by masking their personal value preferences in the vague language of "best interests?" In how large a percentage of such decisions were the child's "best interests" in fact undermined? Even if these questions were subject to inquiry, varying hunches about the answers by scholars, lawyers, and judges would inevitably be based upon their own personal, familial, and legal backgrounds and political preferences. On the one hand, the law itself requires us to presume that judges will follow the legislature's command. On the other hand, academics and legislators have sought a more determinate standard for years for a reason. These efforts, outlined above, suggest the belief that "best interests" alone – or supplemented by the standard traditional presumptions – has been utilized by judges to introduce more individualized and personalized justice into custody determinations than may be morally appropriate or good for families.

[59] PRINCIPLES § 2.08(d).

[60] Professor Carl E. Schneider convincingly argues that any rigorous, legislatively crafted or judicially created custody rule will inevitably lead to the creation of subsidiary discretionary exceptions to the rule – of the kind included in the PRINCIPLES: "it may be a false proposition to say that we have a choice between rules and discretion. Rather, we may have a choice at the extremes between rules formally adopted and systematically applied and rules informally adopted and perhaps unsystematically applied. Outside those extremes, we have a choice between a mix of discretion and rules too complex to be denominated by one term or the other." Schneider, *supra* note 4, at 2290.

[61] PRINCIPLES § 2.08(1)(f). The provision specifies a number of circumstantial limitations: "in light of economic, physical or other circumstances, including the distance between the parents' residences, the cost and difficulty of transporting the child, each parent's and the child's daily schedules, and the ability of the parents to cooperate in the arrangement." Presumably, the drafters intended this clause to pertain to traditional visitation, a subject swallowed up in their broader concept of "custodial responsibility. *See* PRINCIPLES § 2.08 cmt. j, at 202. Yet precisely because traditional visitation is to be an aspect of "custodial responsibility" and affect the post-divorce lives of the spouses and their children, the exception will be "in play" in contested "custodial responsibility" cases.

[62] PRINCIPLES §§ 2.08(1)(d), (f). In addition, the drafters provide numerous illustrative cases to aid judges to limit the scope of the "escape hatches." These illustrations will assist judges only if they are available as part of the statute's legislative history and if the judges are willing to use them. *Cf. infra* note 63 and accompanying text. Since the drafters seemed committed to reducing the indeterminacy in custody decision-making, one wonders whether any of the "escape hatches," in Section 2.08 and in other provisions, reflected the difficulties of drafting determinate rules or were included because the drafters believed that the exceptions were necessary to purchase acceptance of the PRINCIPLES by the Council of the ALI, which governs the work of the drafters, as well as discussions of the ALI membership other than formal votes. Any bet on the subject would be speculative – and there is no legislative history.

It may well be true that a strict "approximate the time" standard is too rigid and difficult to allow fair administration. It may also be true that with its "escape hatches" the standard is as determinate as legislative compromise and precatory statutory language can achieve. In fact, it is much easier to criticize the indeterminacy of the PRINCIPLES' "escape hatches" than it is to draft a fair, administrable, and determinate standard to replace them. Nonetheless, it cannot be denied that the PRINCIPLES allow judges considerable discretion to accomplish the child's "best interests" as they perceive them.[63]

II. Parenting Plans under the PRINCIPLES

Regardless of the governing standard for determining custody, judges administering divorce calendars most often approve pro forma, without investigation or oversight, custody awards agreed to by the parents and their lawyers as a part of a broader negotiation and settlement of all the legal issues in the divorce.[64] It is true that in almost every state, trial judges are required by statute or decision to assure themselves that negotiated custody awards satisfy the "best interests" standard, and, very occasionally, judges will set aside or review "de novo" the parents' deal.[65] But rejected agreements are few and far between – and for good reason. To review a consensual parental custody decision, the trial judge would somehow have to become aware of the family's situation (through a social agency's evaluation, a mental health professional's report, or a disputed pretrial motion). In most cases settled by negotiation, the judge gets no notice of any reason to inquire about, much less overturn, the spouses' agreement.

The PRINCIPLES' "Parenting Plan" policy seems to acknowledge that "parents know best." Both procedurally and substantively, the policy builds on the principle of parental

[63] For the author's repeated judgment that trial judges regularly impose their own values in contested custody cases, see Robert J. Levy, *A Reminiscence About the* Uniform Marriage and Divorce Act – *and Some Reflections About Its Critics and Its Policies*, 1991 BYU L. Rev. 43, 73 n.103; Robert J. Levy, *Rights and Responsibilities for Extended Family Members?*, 27 FAM. L.Q. 191, 199 n.24 (1993). Describing the complex interaction of rule and discretion in custody doctrine and judicial practice, Professor Schneider concludes:

> I agree that the best-interest principle by itself does not dictate results in cases and that any grant of judicial discretion may be abused. And I agree that the best-interest principle sometimes gives courts too little guidance and that custody courts have sometimes abused their discretion . . .

Schneider, *supra* note 4, at 2297–98. Thus, the relationship between rule and discretion in any substantive area is forbiddingly complex.

> All this is true of custody adjudication. The critics are right in saying that the discretionary best-interest standard has its flaws and hazards. But they are too grudging in their recognition that the rules that might replace discretion likewise have their flaws and hazards and that discretion allows courts to do good as well as harm. The critics are right in saying that unfettered discretion is problematic. But they are wrong in believing that courts applying the best-interest principle exercise unfettered discretion.

Id.

[64] PRINCIPLES § 2.06. *See also* PRINCIPLES § 2.06. cmt a, at 156 ("The approach to parental agreements taken in these Principles assumes that courts have neither the time nor the resources to give meaningful review to all parental agreements. Even if greater time and resources were available, court review is unlikely to uncover concrete evidence that the agreement is not in the interests of the child, particularly in the face of a united front by the parents, or to lead to a better agreement than the agreement the parents have reached on their own. This section also assumes that a plan to which the parents agree is more likely to succeed than one that has been ordered by the court over the objection of one or both parents."). *See also* Marygold S. Melli, Howard S. Erlanger & Elizabeth Chambliss, *The Process of Negotiation: An Exploratory Investigation in the Context of No-Fault Divorce*, 40 RUTGERS L. REV. 1133, 1145 (1988) (showing that only one of 349 offered settlements was rejected by the court); Robert J. Levy, *Custody Investigations in Divorce Cases*, 1985 AMER. BAR FOUND. RES. J. 713 (estimating that somewhere close to or more than 90 percent of custody awards are consensual and not reviewed by judge).

[65] PRINCIPLES § 2.06 cmt. a, Reporter's Note, at 160–61.

autonomy and the goal of judicial efficiency: post-divorce parenting and parental relationships should be flexibly customized to fit each family's unique circumstances;[66] responsibility for the postdivorce futures of children should reside with their parents; parents who negotiate and plan cooperatively for their children's futures will overcome the hostility accompanying their divorce, be better parents, engage less frequently in postdecretal litigation, and despite their divorce enhance together their children's development to successful adulthood.[67] Although parental custodial autonomy should be limited by requiring parents to adopt a formal "plan" (subject to approval by the court) that recognizes and regularizes both parents' interest in and responsibility for their child, negotiated settlements will save judicial time and parental conflict by avoiding custody trials.[68]

A number of states had adopted some kind of formal Parenting Plan requirement before the policy was endorsed by the PRINCIPLES.[69] A few states mandate plans only when custody is contested; other states allow the judge unconstrained discretion to order a plan under any litigation circumstances and despite whatever custodial arrangement is contemplated by the parents. Some of the statutes are keyed to specific custody awards: litigants may be required to submit Parenting Plans when an award of joint physical custody is contemplated; some statutes allow judges to waive a plan if joint custody is contemplated.[70] The statutes vary both in the issues they require Parenting Plans to address and in the specificity of their requirements. Where Parenting Plans are mandatory, greater detail seems to be required.[71] The Illinois statute, which makes Parenting Plans mandatory for joint custody, requires the plan to specify "each parent's powers, rights and responsibilities for the personal care of the child and for major decisions such as education, health care and religious training," "a procedure by which proposed changes, disputes and alleged breaches may be mediated or otherwise resolved," and a provision for "periodic review of [the plan] by the parents."[72] In New Jersey, a "discretionary" state, the statute contains no specific instructions as to content and requires only that the parties file a "custody plan which the court shall consider in awarding custody."[73] Parenting Plan advocates have clearly been influenced by the mediation "movement." The PRINCIPLES apparently contemplate that professional mediators will play a role in helping the spouses to negotiate a plan successfully.[74] Thus, fashioning a plan, the PRINCIPLES claim, should provide greater flexibility in

[66] PRINCIPLES § 2.05 cmt. b, at 152 ("The parenting-plan concept presupposes a diverse range of child rearing arrangements and rejects any pre-established set of statutory choices about what arrangements are best for children.").

[67] *See* Dr. Robin Deutsch & Arlene S. Rotman, *Parenting Plans: How to Settle on Appropriate Access*, 26 FAM. ADVOC. 28 (2004) (stating that "children do best in school, in relationships, with self-esteem, and general adjustment when both parents are involved in their lives . . ."). The authors are a psychologist and a former family court judge. *See also* Michael E. Lamb, *Placing Children's Interests First: Developmentally Appropriate Parenting Plans*, 10 VA. J. SOC. POL'Y & L. 103 (2000) (stating that parenting plans should seek to "maximize positive and meaningful paternal involvement, rather than merely ensure minimal levels of visitation"). Dr. Lamb is the Head of the Section on Social and Emotional Health of the United States National Institute of Child Health and Human Development.

[68] The programs often eliminate terms deemed controversial, such as "custody" and "visitation," and replace them with terms thought not to raise "adversarial" concerns for parents. *See supra* note 23.

[69] The details about parenting plans in this and the following paragraph are summarized from Reporter's Notes, PRINCIPLES, Section 2.06, at 151–54.

[70] *See* COLO. REV. STAT. § 14–10–124(7) (2003); TEX FAM. CODE ANN. §§ 153.133, .134 (2004/05).

[71] PRINCIPLES § 2.05 cmt. b, at 152.

[72] 750 ILL. COMP. STAT. ANN. 5/602.1(b) (2003).

[73] N.J. REV. STAT. § 9:2–4(e) (2002).

[74] *See* PRINCIPLES § 2.07 and cmt. b, at 166–67 (providing additional criteria and conditions for negotiations in specific areas of concern). *See also* PRINCIPLES §§ 2.10–2.12. *See infra* notes 80, note 82 and accompanying text. *See also* WASH. REV. CODE § 26.09.184 (West Supp. 2004) (specifically requiring parents to negotiate their parenting plans with the help of a mental health professional, a mediator, or the judge).

postdivorce custodial and visitation arrangements, and enhance parental autonomy and cooperation in divorce negotiations and postdivorce relationships.[75]

Legislative and scholarly rhetoric concerning Parenting Plans emphasizes the promotion of parental autonomy and (the current buzz-word) "private ordering" – and the drafters clearly endorsed more than a semblance of parental autonomy.[76] Yet Parenting Plans under the PRINCIPLES are required to include specific understandings (such as "a process" for identifying and dealing with issues of domestic violence and suspected abuse of the children),[77] and must exclude others (such as a child support amount less than the amount legislatively authorized in exchange for a waiver of contest).[78] The judge may require that the Parenting Plan include methods for resolving important and difficult (and often postponable and wisely postponed) postdecretal issues, such as relocation of one of the parents, as well as provisions for modifying custody for specified future contingencies.[79]

[75] *See* PRINCIPLES § 2.07 cmt. b, at 166.

[76] PRINCIPLES, § 2.06 cmt. c, at 158 ("[T]his standard is different from traditional law which, as a formal matter at least, expects the court in every case to determine affirmatively if an agreement is in the child's best interests."). Although the PRINCIPLES do not rule out any particular agreement as per se harmful, *ibid.* Section 2.12 places "substantive" limitations on spouses' parenting plans and gives the court authority to deny enforcement to plans which are not knowing or voluntary, are "harmful to the child," or agreed to by parents when child abuse or domestic violence has occurred. *See infra* notes note 77–note 79 and accompanying text.

[77] Hearings as to the validity of a Parenting Plan are recommended if "credible information" is "presented to the court" that child abuse or domestic violence has occurred. PRINCIPLES § 2.06(2). In addition, the court may conduct an evidentiary hearing "on any basis it deems sufficient" to determine whether a parental agreement was either "not knowing," not "voluntary," or "would be harmful to the child." PRINCIPLES § 2.06(1). Mediators helping in the negotiation of Parenting Plans are specifically freed of any guarantee of confidentiality – which otherwise would attach to "information a parent has disclosed during mediation under a reasonable expectation of privacy" – with respect to information acquired about child abuse or domestic violence or about whether the agreement was knowing and voluntary or harmful to the child under Section 2.06. *See* PRINCIPLES § 2.07(5) and cmt. b, at 166. Moreover, Section 2.07(2) requires mediators to "screen for domestic violence and other conditions or circumstances that may impede a party's capacity to participate in the mediation process." If "credible evidence" of such conditions appears, the section recommends termination of the mediation unless steps are taken to ensure reasonable consent of the parties and to protect the safety of any victim. As to whether these rules comport with general notions of privilege and confidentiality, see generally *Note, Protecting Confidentiality in Mediation*, 98 HARV. L. REV. 441 (1984); *see also* McKinlay v. McKinlay, 648 So.2d 806 (Fla. App. 1995) (holding that wife seeking to set aside mediated divorce agreement on grounds of duress and intimidation waived statutory right to invoke statutory mediation confidentiality privilege). The *McKinlay* case does not necessarily authorize mediators to "screen" for domestic violence and for "other circumstances that may impede a party's capacity to participate in the mediation process" and report to the court, as PRINCIPLES § 2.07(2) authorizes. Clearly, the invitation to trial judges to initiate a hearing about a Parenting Plan "on any basis it deems sufficient" is expansive and expandable; the standards authorizing judicial rejection of a Parenting Plan are just as expansive. One wonders what is left of the PRINCIPLES' asserted commitment to parental autonomy and "deference" to parental agreements. *See supra* note note 64 and accompanying text.

The interlocking provisions concerning child abuse and domestic violence mentioned throughout this chapter suggest that the drafters thought that the judicial system and divorce lawyers have paid too little attention to such issues in the past. The drafters sacrificed their own commitment to "private ordering" and doctrinal determinacy to achieve more protection for abused women and children.

[78] Because they are "most problematic" (and despite the fact that consensual divorce "deals" frequently feature such provisions), the PRINCIPLES bar agreements for child support that provide for "substantially" less child support than would otherwise be awarded. PRINCIPLES § 2.06 cmt. c, at 158. If a parenting plan is rejected, the parents are permitted to negotiate a new agreement. PRINCIPLES § 2.06(3), at 155.

[79] See PRINCIPLES § 2.10 (requiring the court to include in the Parenting Plan "a process for resolving future disputes that will serve the child's best interests" unless "otherwise resolved by agreement of the parents"). The court is authorized to order a "nonjudicial process of dispute resolution" (evidently, by an arbitrator or mediator) without the parents' agreement; disputes resolved this way are subject to de novo review. In contrast, disputes resolved by a parentally chosen, nonjudicial system of review are binding on the parents unless the decision will result in "harm to the child" or is the product of "fraud, misconduct, corruption, or some other serious irregularity in the dispute-resolution process." PRINCIPLES §§ 2.10(2), (3). This clause provides another indeterminate "escape hatch."

The plan must be approved as to form and substance by the judge.[80] Judges have discretion to disallow agreements, after a hearing that judges can initiate despite parental agreement, if the agreement would be "harmful to the child" or is "not knowing or voluntary," both indeterminate standards.[81]

All in all, drawing on the "black letter" as well as the Comments, the PRINCIPLES arguably want it both ways – "private ordering" as well as discretionary and indeterminate judicial control. The ambivalence should not be surprising – every person's "sense" of the propriety of particular Parenting Plans reflects in some measure his or her approval or disapproval of the parental behavior and its predicted effect on the children.

In a sense, of course, the PRINCIPLES' limitations are not very different (but perhaps more determinate and concise) than many common law "public policy" limitations on contract negotiations.[82] Whether new and specific instructions to judges to review Parenting Plans will produce greater oversight of parents' "private ordering," more rejections of custody deals and less parental autonomy, is not yet known.[83] But prior judicial practice and the drafters' apparent effort to vindicate simultaneously both parental autonomy and discretionary judicial oversight of Parenting Plans suggests that lawmakers as well as judges are unsure about the proper balance between private ordering and judicial control of child custody dispositions.

Not enough is yet known about Parenting Plans to draw conclusions about any of the factual premises of their advocates. An early report on experience in Washington state, the first state to adopt the device, was enthusiastic, describing substantial increases in divorce decrees specifying joint parental decision-making, large increases in joint residence agreements, and modest declines in mother-only custody awards.[84] But a survey of lawyers showed close to an even split as to whether the statute had reduced hostility between parents.[85] A later study, by a group that included the psychiatrist influential in obtaining the plan's legislative acceptance, was less enthusiastic.[86]

[80] *See* PRINCIPLES § 2.05(3), (4), (5).

[81] PRINCIPLES § 2.06(1)(a), (b). The drafters point out that "the absence of voluntary and knowing consent is difficult to establish, as a practical matter, when the parties jointly submit a parental agreement to the court. Even if a hearing were held in each case, it would be the unusual case in which a court is able to determine, at the time for approval, that a jointly submitted plan was not freely consented to by the parents." PRINCIPLES § 2.06 cmt. d, at 158. Furthermore, "although the court is invited to look closely at whether consent to an agreement is voluntary and knowing, this inquiry does not permit the court free rein to ignore agreements it does not like. Thus, for example, unevenness of bargaining power, or an initial reluctance to sign the agreement, does not justify a determination that consent did not exist, or else an agreement might be in jeopardy simply because one parent had the negotiating advantage of having been the child's primary caretaker, or because one parent found the decision to accept the agreement a difficult one." *Id.* at cmt. b. This explanation does not do a great deal to make the exception determinate. *See also id.* at cmt. d (suggesting how courts can gather enough information about voluntariness and harm to initiate a hearing, including parental disclosures under Section 2.05(2)(f), court ordered investigations authorized by Section 2.13, and interviews of the child under Section 2.14). Similar problems are implicit in the exception for "harm to the child" – despite the drafters' assertion that the exception is "different from traditional law which, as a formal matter at least, expects courts in every case to determine affirmatively if an agreement is in the child's best interests" PRINCIPLES § 2.06 cmt. c. Judges determined to intervene would have little trouble interpreting this provision expansively. Imagine the primary custodial mother who establishes a post-separation home with another woman (despite the prohibition in PRINCIPLES Section 2.12(d) against consideration of a parent's "sexual orientation").

[82] *See generally* E. Allen Farnsworth, CONTRACTS 313–51 (4th ed. 2004).

[83] *See supra* note note 61 and accompanying text.

[84] *See generally* Jane W. Ellis, *supra* note 24.

[85] *Ibid.* PRINCIPLES § 2.05 cmt. a, Reporter's Notes, at 151 (describing study).

[86] Anna L. Davis et al., *Mitigating the Effects of Divorce on Children Through Family–Focused Court Reform* 29–30 (mimeo) (1997) (detailing then unpublished, small scale study by Dr. John E. Dunne, which "did not demonstrate any beneficial effects on the child's or the parents' adjustment to divorce, or in the post-divorce quality of the child's relationship with either parent," but which cautioned that "contemporaneous changes in the child-support

A cynic might claim that Parenting Plans will have the same future as many other divorce reforms: lawyers will mold the rules to their clients' dictates and demands for a rapid, relatively cheap, judicially unsupervised divorce, while custody bargaining will continue to be a prominent if unacknowledged aspect of divorce. Under the PRINCIPLES, judges in contested cases will receive whatever benefit comes from the lawyers' preparation and exchange of trial briefs describing the client's parenting strengths and custodial and visitation wish list – but now those briefs will be labeled the client's proposed Parenting Plan. In short, life will go on as before – with additional opportunities for mediators and other mental health professionals to feed at the divorce trough.

The world would be a finer and happier place if parents wanting to terminate their marriages could sit down together (perhaps with the help of their lawyers or a mental health professional) to plan and specify their own future circumstances, their children's, and the relationships between each of them for the indefinite future. For a jointly drafted Parenting Plan to work, parents must be able to work together to develop the plan, to place the child's interests before their own, and to change the plan as they and the child change and mature. Just as many parents arrange their divorces peacefully and successfully, so it is possible that some parents will be able to construct and successfully administer a Parenting Plan of the kind contemplated by advocates. But the simplistic and very general process recommendations offered by enthusiasts require interpersonal relationships that are agonizingly difficult to achieve in real life.

There is another side to this controversy. Negotiating a Parenting Plan might provide divorcing spouses an opportunity for healthy learning about the complexities of postdivorce life and an opportunity, despite anger, to strive for a negotiated compromise. Under the watchful eyes and concerned mentoring of sensitive and psychologically astute lawyers, something good might happen. Parenting plans are no panacea for the difficulties of divorce for parents, children, lawyers, or for the judges who must make custody decisions. But if lawyers are willing to grapple with their clients' shortcomings and the dynamics of their clients' marriages – and if judges are willing to use Parenting Plans for educational purposes and not to control spouses' deals and postdivorce lives – encouraging some form of Parenting Plan could be a useful adjunct to custody adjudication. This is a substantial group of assumptions. It is difficult to believe that hype alone will help to fulfill them.

III. Protecting the Separate Interests of Children in Divorce Litigation

Everyone agrees that the interests of the children can easily be forgotten or minimized in the heat of their parents' divorce. Spouses, consumed by animosity and their desire for financial retribution, ignore their children's desire to maintain a relationship with both parents; lawyers, anxious to make a killing for their clients but also to "settle" the divorce action short of trial, help parents treat their children as additional marital assets; judges, anxious to clear their dockets and avoid litigation, cavalierly approve parental custody

guidelines linking support obligations to nights spent with the child may have undermined the parenting plan's objective to reduce conflict between parents"). Dr. Dunne published the study using a larger sample after the drafters finished their work on the topic. *See* John E. Dunne, E. Wren Hudgins & Julia Babcock, *Can Changing the Divorce Law Affect Post–Divorce Adjustment?*, 33 J. DIVORCE & REMARRIAGE 35 (2000).

deals with little oversight. For both policy and efficiency reasons, parental agreements about their children's custody are rarely rejected on any ground.[87]

Nonetheless, judges and legislatures have created procedural devices to protect the interests of children in the process and the outcomes of divorce litigation. The Parenting Plan is one such device.[88] Another is the discretionary or required appointment of a custody evaluator to find facts about the children that might not come to light in an adversary trial.[89] A third is to allow or require judges to interview the children.[90] Another common method for satisfying the perceived need to protect children from the risks of divorce litigation is the discretionary or mandatory appointment by the judge of an independent "representative" for the child – a "guardian ad litem," perhaps, or a lawyer.[91]

The purposes served by these devices are theoretically disparate and distinguishable, ranging from neutral fact-finding to child protection to advocating for a child's wishes.[92] But both in legislative enactment and in practice from jurisdiction to jurisdiction, there has been conceptual and verbal confusion; the theories become intertwined and the roles of child representatives blend. In Wisconsin, for example, lawyers for children in custody disputes are specifically authorized by the enabling legislation to argue for what they perceive to be the client's best interests without regard to the client's desires.[93] Other jurisdictions place the lawyer in the role of advocating for the child's wishes unless these "would be seriously injurious," in which case the lawyer may resign.[94] The only serious effort to discover how lawyers for children actually behave suggests that judges should expect less than effective "adversarial lawyering" from lawyers appointed for children in divorce cases.[95]

Representation devices have been the subject of heated dispute both in legislatures and in the academic literature for some time.[96] The basic policy issue is how to balance properly parental prerogatives with the lawyer's or guardian's control as well as judicial control of custody decision-making. There is no doubt that most children could profit from, and many children need, intervention of some kind to insure that their interests are not

[87] *See* PRINCIPLES § 2.06 cmt a, Reporter's Notes, at 163 (2000). *See also supra* note 64.

[88] *See supra* notes 64–86 and accompanying text.

[89] Although PRINCIPLES Section 2.13 encompasses evaluators as well, this chapter will not discuss evaluators and evaluations. *See generally* Robert J. Levy, *supra* note 64. Some jurisdictions make use of "neutrals" – usually mental health professionals judicially appointed to investigate and report on the best interests of children. Such litigation helpers are akin to guardians ad litem. *See also infra* notes 91, 94.

[90] *See, e.g.*, Barbara A. Atwood, *The Child's Voice in Custody Litigation: An Empirical Survey and Suggestions for Reform*, 45 ARIZ. L. REV. 629 (2003).

[91] Linda D. Elrod, *Raising the Bar for Lawyers Who Represent Children: ABA Standards of Practice for Custody Cases*, 37 FAM. L.Q. 105 (2003).

[92] PRINCIPLES, *supra* note 1, § 2.13 cmt. a, at 317.

[93] *See* WIS. STAT. ANN. § 767.045(4) (2004) (holding that a guardian ad litem must be a lawyer who is "an advocate for the best interests of a minor child" and "shall consider, but shall not be bound by, the wishes of the minor child or the positions of others as to the best interests of the minor child").

[94] *See* Linda D. Elrod, *supra* note 91, at 120–21(discussing American Bar Association model standard); STATE OF NEW YORK, UNIFIED COURT SYSTEM, STATEWIDE ADMINISTRATIVE JUDGE FOR MATRIMONIAL MATTERS, LAW GUARDIAN DEFINITION AND STANDARDS (undated) (on file with author) (requiring a child's law guardian to report to the Court the child-client's "stated position," and directing the guardian to advocate for that position "if the law guardian, on his/her own or with the assistance of a mental health professional and after investigation and assessment of the situation, determines that the child is unimpaired").

[95] *See* Kim J. Landsman & Martha L. Minow, *Note, Lawyering for the Child: Principles of Representation in Custody and Visitation Disputes Arising from Divorce*, 87 YALE L.J. 1126 (1978) (noting in a partially anecdotal empirical investigation of eighteen private lawyers appointed to represent children in Connecticut divorce cases that some advocates did not even bother to meet with their clients).

[96] *See* Linda D. Elrod, *supra* note 95, at 105–12.

ignored in their parents' legal tussle. But it is also true that an independent representative for the children, if appointed by the judge when the parents have agreed or are likely to agree about the children's future, can severely impair the parents' ability to make family decisions. Moreover, a representative for the child might initiate and impose on the parents and perhaps the children the substantial emotional cost of extra conflict and litigiousness; and the resulting fees would add a significant cost to the already imposing expense of divorce for middle class families.[97] In addition, appointment of a representative for children detracts from the "family privacy" interest that underpins support for "private ordering" (by parents) of custody decision-making.[98] Perhaps most important, there is precious little evidence that a judicial custody award resulting from the efforts of a court-appointed guardian ad litem or lawyer for the children will serve the children's interests any better than a consensual parental agreement would.[99] Because American society is in fact committed to both of the perhaps inconsistent goals of "private ordering" and judicial protection of children's best interests, legislative forays and judicial decisions in this area often respond more to the individual facts of the cases than to doctrinal logic and consistency.

It is easy enough to chart the theoretical differences between the role of a guardian ad litem and the role of an attorney for the child. The advantage of a guardian is that she will focus on the best interests of both younger and older children, whatever they claim they want, and is less likely to overvalue the child's expressed wishes; the advantage of a lawyer is that she is less likely to substitute for the child's wishes a personal opinion of the child's best interests. Each representative's advantage is set off by a corresponding disadvantage: the guardian is more likely to substitute his personal opinion of best interests for the child's wishes; the lawyer is more likely to overvalue the child's expressed wishes, especially those which have been unduly (but cleverly) influenced by parental pressure.

The complex provisions of PRINCIPLES Section 2.13 give the judge discretion to order an investigation or appointment of a guardian but require clear specification of the scope of the endeavor.[100] In addition, discretion to appoint a lawyer for the child is authorized "if the child" is competent to direct the terms of the representation and the court has a reasonable basis for finding that the appointment would be helpful in resolving the issues in the case.[101]

[97] *But see* PRINCIPLES § 2.13(7) ("Appointments, investigations, evaluation services, or tests should not be ordered under this section unless at no cost to the persons involved, or at a cost that is reasonable in light of the financial resources of the parents. When one parent's ability to pay is significantly greater than the other's, the court should allocate the costs between them equitably.").

[98] Katherine Federle, *supra* note 18, at 1157–58 (arguing that appointments protect the personal rights of the child and "empower" the child to feel that she is respected in the decision). For a thoughtful and thorough investigation of the developmental literature and some doubts about the "empowering" children theory, see Emily Buss, *Confronting Developmental Barriers to the Empowerment of Child Clients*, 84 CORNELL L. REV. 895 (1999).

[99] *See supra* note 65. *See also* PRINCIPLES § 2.13 cmt. b, at 317–18 ("[T]he effort to obtain better information about, or representation for, the child can have a negative effect on the proceedings themselves.... In addition, it should not be assumed that an independent, court-ordered, investigation or evaluation will assure an outcome for the child that is 'best,' in some objective or neutral sense. Disagreements about the best interest of children among child advocates and among academic and clinical professionals are hard to explain apart from the value judgments and policy commitments that underlie them.").

[100] PRINCIPLES § 2.13(1) and (2).

[101] PRINCIPLES § 2.13(3). Subsection (9) recommends either an investigation or appointment of a guardian when 'substantial allegations' have been made or there is 'credible information' of domestic violence or child abuse or neglect." *See infra* note 115 and accompanying text. The court is authorized, subject to state law restrictions, to require persons with knowledge to provide information to an investigator, guardian, or lawyer for the child. *Id.* at § 2.13(5). There is an on-going debate about the extent of parents' and even children's medical (especially psychiatric) privilege in divorce custody cases. For a thoughtful review of the cases, see Kinsella v. Kinsella, 696 A.2d 556, 581 (N.J. 1997).

A good example of the tension between parental autonomy and judicial protection of children is afforded by the continuing debate over the circumstances under which the judge should have authority to appoint a lawyer for them. Most legislatures, most judges, and the PRINCIPLES prefer a discretionary appointment power.[102] By and large, advocates of universal appointment have been "children's rights" advocates, clinical law teachers, and individual members of organized bar groups and the bar groups themselves.[103] Given the financial resources of most divorcing families with children, it is not surprising that judges and most parents would be opposed to wholesale appointments of lawyers on behalf of the child empowered to conduct discovery and engage in every aspect of the divorce litigation on behalf of the child![104] Nor would it be surprising if divorce lawyers who see a need for additional business (and the bar association committees they monopolize) were to support compulsory or at least very common appointment of lawyers for children.

So when should the benefits of separate legal representation for children outweigh its actual and potential emotional and financial costs? There is good reason not to leave the choice solely to the judge's discretion – for all the reasons that indeterminate standards worry scholars of custody law and practice.[105] The trick, of course, is to find language which will at once give direction to judges and constrain their discretion without unduly "tying their hands" and precluding the accomplishment of justice in individual cases. The PRINCIPLES seek – and in my estimation achieve – a decent accommodation of the competing interests. Judges are allowed but not required to appoint counsel or a guardian and must limit the appointment of a lawyer to cases in which the child "is competent to direct the terms of the representation" *and* to those in which "the court has a reasonable basis for finding that the appointment would be helpful in resolving the issues of the case."[106] The provision demands, moreover, that in each case the "role, duties, and scope of authority" of the lawyer be specified in the order of appointment.[107] Although the comments are not terribly specific, the provision itself seems to make clear that the PRINCIPLES sought to cabin both the frequency of lawyer appointments generally and to preclude Wisconsin-like lawyer appointments.[108] The reference to the child's competence to direct the representation apprises judges as well as the lawyers they appoint that the child's and not the lawyer's judgment of "best interests" is to be pursued. The requirement that the representation's scope be specified is a way of compelling judges to circumscribe (or at least to pay attention to) the lawyers' activities as well as their fees. The "helpfulness" requirement seems to

[102] *See* Linda D. Elrod, *supra* note 91; PRINCIPLES § 2.13(3) cmt. a, Reporter's note, at 321–23 (describing the literature and arguments for and against mandatory appointment). *Cf.* Uniform Marriage and Divorce Act § 405, 9A Pt. II U.L.A. 386 (1998) (stating that the court has discretion to order custody evaluation but only in contested custody proceedings and in cases where a request is made by one of the parents).

[103] *See generally* American Academy of Matrimonial Lawyers, *Representing Children: Standards for Attorneys and Guardians ad litem in Custody and Visitation Proceedings*, 13 J. AM. ACAD. MATRIMONIAL L. 1 (1995); M. Guggenheim, *Reconsidering the Need for Counsel for Children in Custody, Visitation and Child Protection Proceedings*, 29 LOY. U. CHI. L.J. 299 (1998); Howard Davidson, *The Child's Right to be Heard and Represented in Judicial Proceedings*, 18 PEPP. L. REV. 255 (1991).

[104] *See* Linda D. Elrod, *supra* note 91, at 119–20 (noting that "[t]he lawyer should conduct discovery; develop a strategy of the case; stay apprised of other court proceedings affecting the child ... participate in and when appropriate, initiate negotiations and mediation; participate in depositions, pretrial conferences and hearings; [and] file or make petitions, motions or responses when necessary," and a long list of other responsibilities).

[105] *See* Part I *supra* (discussing problems of indeterminacy).

[106] *See supra* note 101 and accompanying text.

[107] PRINCIPLES § 2.13.

[108] *See supra* note 101 and accompanying text. PRINCIPLES § 2.13 cmt. (3), at 319. Although the court is required to specify the terms of the appointment of guardians ad litem as well, the guardian appointment provision contains no similar limiting terminology. Compare the Uniform Marriage and Divorce Act § 310, 9A, Pt. II U.L.A. 13 (1998) (authorizing the court to appoint a lawyer for a child in divorce cases without any limitation).

imply that where the spouses themselves will present all the information the judge needs to decide the issues, no appointment should be made. The provision also implies that appointments should not be made in cases where the parents have reached agreement as to their children's custody. Other sections make clear the drafters' commitment to parental negotiation and agreement.[109] Because the PRINCIPLES require mandatory appointments in specific situations,[110] in the absence of such situations it would be more difficult for the judge to claim a "reasonable basis" in consensual cases for a finding of "helpfulness."[111] As with any substantive standard, there is a risk that judges will ignore the constraints on appointment the PRINCIPLES have constructed.[112] But it is reasonable to believe that the risk is less here. Judges have important policy reasons for wanting cases to settle with minimal conflict. They are also committed (at least theoretically and often actually) to family autonomy, and parental agreements without interventions are efficient and save precious judicial time.

Either an investigation or the appointment of a guardian is recommended in cases in which "substantial allegations" of domestic violence or child abuse or neglect have been made, as well as in those in which "there is credible information" about such behavior.[113] The mandate is limited; no appointment need be made if "the court is satisfied that the information adequate to evaluate the allegations will be secured without such an order or appointment."[114] Notice that the statutory purpose for the mandatory investigation or appointment is specifically identified (and therefore limited); and the judge's appointment discretion is described relatively narrowly and therefore constrained. Better and even more specific limitations, and even narrower powers of discretionary appointment, certainly could and should have been proposed. For example, the "unless" clause in Section 2.13(4) – obviating appointment of an investigator or a guardian if the allegations can be adequately evaluated otherwise – could have been broader and less discretionary (further constraining those judges who appoint lawyers or guardians ad litem in wholesale fashion); "probable cause to believe" might have been substituted for "credible information" in the formula for unrequested intervention.[115] Those scholars and advocates who believe that too much domestic violence and child neglect is suppressed by lawyers and ignored by judges – and that decisions denying custody to battered women are often the consequence – will approve the PRINCIPLES' more inclusionary language.[116] Nonetheless, the important fact is that the PRINCIPLES make an effort to balance the need for intervention into the affairs of divorcing parents with respect for their autonomy.

The problem of representation for children is a difficult one that no code of regulations is likely to solve satisfactorily. Consider a contested custody case in which the judge has appointed a "neutral" forensic expert and a guardian or attorney for the child. Some judges claim that the ultimate decision plays to the scorecard: the parents' attorneys cancel each other out; if those seen as "neutral" or relatively neutral agree (that is, the guardian for the children and the mental health expert come out the same way), the case is over – appellate

[109] *See supra* notes 64–70 and accompanying text.

[110] *See infra* note 113 and accompanying text (discussing allegations of domestic violence).

[111] PRINCIPLES § 2.13(3).

[112] *See supra* note 63 and accompanying text.

[113] *See supra* note 101.

[114] PRINCIPLES § 2.13(4).

[115] *See supra* note 101.

[116] *See generally* Karen Winner, DIVORCED FROM JUSTICE: THE ABUSE OF WOMEN AND CHILDREN BY DIVORCE LAWYERS AND JUDGES (1996). *But see* Linda Kelly, *Disabusing the Definition of Domestic Abuse: How Women Batter Men and the Role of the Feminist State*, 30 FLA. ST. U. L. REV. 791 (2003).

courts always choose the judgment of "neutrals" rather than the trial judge's when he disagrees with them. To be sure, judges can be wrong as often as "neutrals" are – and the fact that two parties share a view opposed to the judge's should give the judge pause. Some judges believe that appellate courts are prone to give excessive weight to the guardian or attorney, and that person's views too often trump the views of a custody evaluator or even, occasionally, those of the trial judge. The appointment of an "adversarial lawyer" poses substantial risks. In difficult, hotly contested cases, many judges believe, children's expressed wishes are the product of undue parental pressure and the defeat of one parent's pressure by the other parent's advocacy. Because "adversarial lawyers" tend to overvalue their client's expressed wishes, and are not always either interested in or sophisticated enough to delve below the surface of those wishes, the contest can be contaminated by the "child's wishes" variable. Yet such threatened obstacles to proper assignments of custody and allocations of visitation indulge the assumption that in most cases judges know better than the lawyers judges appoint as representatives for children – not necessarily an intuitively correct proposition. Difficult problems, indeed.

A focus on parental autonomy at the expense of judicial control may well produce some cases where children's interests will be less well preserved than if some representative had been appointed. But the only way to prevent such losses is to appoint a representative in every case – and pay the cost of an unknown number of "false positives," that is, cases where the children and perhaps the family will be worse off as a result of the intervention than they would have been without it. Some cost-benefit analysis is required – but if the facts are not available or obtainable – and that is certainly true in this instance – it is necessary to rely on the relative social weight of the competing values.

IV. Conclusion

The three great public policy issues of custody law and practice are not difficult to identify. The first, of course, is how to construct the substantive standard. It is not clear that we have a social consensus on this subject. Are we willing to rely on judges' discretionary administration of an indeterminate standard? If not, what standard can we agree to and what value would that standard reinforce? Or is the endeavor a waste of time because parents, lawyers, and judges will – in a variety of ways and for a variety of inconsistent reasons in individual cases – undermine any feasible expression of any compromise?

A second, also contested, issue is whether the value to children of more shared parenting than most parents apparently adopt on their own is worth the cost of doctrinal and practice modification that accomplishing the change would require. A subsidiary issue is whether any proposed legal change would increase shared parenting or if, instead, doctrinal change would impose great transaction costs in lawyers' fees and judicial resources, and still be undermined by lawyers' and parents' resistance to change.

The third great public policy issue is the extent to which legislatures or judges should modify the traditional American commitment to "private ordering" – that is, to the acceptance of parental autonomy in determining post-dissolution custodial arrangements for children. It is true that judges have always had the authority to reject any custody and visitation arrangement agreed to by parents and their lawyers. But parentally arranged custody – as occurs with more than 90 percent of the custody awards from year to year[117] – takes

[117] *See supra* note 64 and accompanying text.

place with almost no judicial interference.[118] These practice policies have been adopted and maintained despite their obvious cost – that is, in some unknown proportion of the cases, one spouse will obtain an agreement from the other that was in some fashion coerced or might not have been the decision imposed by a judge if the case had been contested. The common policy response has been to prefer parental decision-making on grounds of efficiency – that judicial resources would be overwhelmed if all dissolution custody arrangements were to be subjected to real judicial oversight – and parental autonomy, which is prized as an independent value in a free society. The notion is that the benefit to children of legal representation and more active judicial supervision of parental decision-making would have to be provable and substantial to justify undermining the countervailing values.

Answers to these basic questions are not likely to be discovered easily. In any event, it is likely that custody law and procedure doctrines and practices will change, if at all, as legal doctrine in general does – in modest ways and with glacial slowness. Yet personal, parental, and marital values do seem to be changing, slowly, but in important ways. Only unscientific and unrepresentative examples are available: many airport men's rooms have added changing tables for infants to their decor during the last five years; expectations (and therefore values) about fathers' roles with young children are changing.[119] In recent years, moreover, a number of authors have complained that judges too frequently deny women custody of their children for inadequate or inappropriate reasons.[120] And there have been many new custody proposals – the "primary caretaker," the "maternal deference," the "approximate the time spent" standards – which seem to route the law implicitly in the direction of the maternal presumption of earlier days. There are a few signs that at least some judges' practices may be changing; but the extant empirical research seems to indicate that parents' practices (how parents actually allocate their children when they separate and divorce) have not changed all that much from earlier times.[121] These circumstances suggest that we may have entered a transitional period during which disputes about legal doctrines engage not only litigants, lawyers, and judges, but political and pressure groups, as well. One of the most interesting aspects of a potential shift in social mores is that the law may change in fact without any formal or overt change in the legal standard. The "best interests" test, with all its indeterminacy and lack of legal guidance, might provide cover for a basic sea-change in American social values and practices. Substantial legal doctrinal stability may be purchased at the cost of continued substantial discretion for judges during a period of slowly changing judicial values. The winners will be the judges who prize discretion, the lawyers who will be paid to litigate more contested cases, and those who favor doctrinal stability for its own sake; the losers will be those who value predictability and litigants' bank accounts.

[118] *See supra* notes 64 and 75 and accompanying text.

[119] *See*, e.g., Michelle Orecklin, *Stress and the Superdad*, TIME MAGAZINE, August 16, 2004; Ros Coward, *When Love Hurts*, THE GUARDIAN, September 19, 2003.

[120] *See, e.g.*, Karen Winner, *supra* note 116.

[121] *See* Eleanor Maccoby & Robert H. Mnookin, DIVIDING THE CHILD: SOCIAL AND LEGAL DILEMMAS OF CUSTODY(1992). *See also* PRINCIPLES § 2.12 Reporter's Notes, at 295 (reviewing the more recent literature and commenting that "much of the impetus for this literature [arguing for a return to some form of the maternal preference] comes from figures showing that while women obtain custody in a large proportion of custody cases, fathers have high success rates when they contest custody"). But, as the drafter's comments indicate, much of the data fail to support the need for formal change.

However the conflicting values are eventually accommodated, all sides of the policy and political debates will have the benefit of the PRINCIPLES' careful research and brilliant analysis, extraordinarily thoughtful, careful and objective articulation of doctrine, and brave and artful effort to deal with the problems.

This chapter is a considerably modified and expanded version of essays on these subjects I provided for a new interdisciplinary examination of custody law and practice prepared collaboratively by members of the National Interdisciplinary Colloquium on Custody Law, to be published in 2005. Although I am the General Editor of the Colloquium book, I am solely responsible for the views expressed in this chapter. *See generally* National INTERDISCIPLINARY COLLOQUIUM ON CUSTODY LAW, LEGAL AND MENTAL HEALTH PERSPECTIVES ON CHILD CUSTODY LAW: A DESKBOOK FOR JUDGES 9-35 (1998).

5 Undeserved Trust: Reflections on the ALI's Treatment of De Facto Parents

Robin Fretwell Wilson

In chapter 2 of the PRINCIPLES, the ALI proposes sweeping changes to the legal conception of parenthood. It would confer custody and visitation "rights"[1] on a stepparent or ex-live-in lover of a child's legal parent[2] who shared caretaking responsibility for a child for as little as two years ("Ex Live-In Partner").[3] Such an individual is recognized by the PRINCIPLES as a "de facto parent," a term the PRINCIPLES borrow from case law. The PRINCIPLES would significantly enlarge the rights these individuals receive under state law, however. With the same stroke, the ALI would dispossess legal parents of the prerogative to decide who continues to have contact with their child.[4]

In many ways, the ALI is engaged in an admirable undertaking: to provide children with enduring contact with the "only father [a] child ha[d] known."[5] But like much of our experience with "re-imagining" family relations, significant unintended consequences

[1] PRINCIPLES ch. 1, Topic 1.I (d), at 5–6.

[2] This chapter uses legal parent, as the PRINCIPLES do, to mean biological parents and adoptive parents. *See* PRINCIPLES § 2.03 cmt. a, at 110.

There are good reasons that legal parents have a constitutionally protected status. PRINCIPLES § 2.18, Reporter's Notes, cmt. b, at 389–90 (discussing natural parents). "[T]he autonomy of parents . . . is essential to their meaningful exercise of responsibility." PRINCIPLES ch. 1, Topic 1.I (d), at 5–6. Moreover, legal parents exhibit "maximum commitment to the parenting enterprise." PRINCIPLES ch. 1, Topic 1.I (d), at 5. This observation is grounded in a substantial body of social science. Part III.C *infra* discusses how the presence of one's mother is protective of children, while separation from one or both biological parents introduces risk. In the same vein, numerous studies find that adoptive parents invest in their children as heavily, or more heavily, than do biological parents. *See generally* Robin Fretwell Wilson, *Uncovering the Rationale for Requiring Infertility in Surrogacy Arrangements*, 29 AM. J. L. & MED. 337 (2003). Unlike other nongenetic caretakers, such as foster parents, stepparents, and mothers' cohabitants, there is little evidence that adoptive parents engage in more neglect or abuse of their children. *Id.*

[3] This chapter uses the term "Ex Live-In Partner" to describe the population of male "de facto parents" on whom the ALI would confer significantly expanded parental rights. The common denominator among this group of men is their previous status as coresidents of the child's mother, together with their performance of certain "caretaking functions." *See* PRINCIPLES § 2.03(c). As this chapter argues throughout, we cannot infer from the fact that these men have performed "caretaking functions" that they necessarily have undertaken to assume a level of care, permanency, and bonding in a child's life that warrants recognition and treatment as a parent. Performance of "caretaking" chores, this chapter argues, does little to discern how protective these men have been or will be. *See* Part IV *infra*. Moreover, the fact that they are unrelated is relevant to the risks posed to children with whom they may have continuing contact, *see* Part II.A. *infra*, as well as to the degree of benefit that continuing contact may hold for children, *see* Parts II.B. & III.E. *infra*.

[4] The drafters are candid about the ALI's proposal. They acknowledge that courts have used equitable doctrines, like estoppel, to extend "parental rights to an individual who otherwise would not qualify." PRINCIPLES § 2.03, Reporter's Notes, cmt. b, at 128. Like those equitable doctrines, the drafters seek to confer custody and visitation rights "over the opposition of the legal parent." PRINCIPLES § 2.03, Reporter's Notes, cmt. b, at 129.

[5] *See* PRINCIPLES § 2.03 cmt. b, at 129 (discussing equitable-parent cases).

may result.[6] The drafters, without substantiation, simply assume that continuing contact between a child and an Ex Live-In Partner – who will almost always be male[7] – will be an unadulterated good.

The story they tell reads like this: Giving parental rights to a "de facto parent" is necessary to conform to the lived experience of many children, who are "often cared for by adults other than parents[, such as] stepparents . . . and parental partners who function as coparents."[8] Continued contact with a de facto parent and his participation in the child's life, they explain, are "critically important to the child's welfare."[9] This is so because the de facto parent functioned as the child's primary parent or undertook equal caretaking duties.[10] Disregarding the connection between a child and this adult at break-up, they tell us, "ignores child-parent relationships that may be fundamental to the child's sense of stability."[11] Moreover, a de facto parent is entitled to legal recognition for serving in this capacity because it is fundamentally fair.[12] For these reasons, the drafters seek to imbue de facto parents with new "rights."[13]

[6] Mary Ann Glendon, *Family Law and Family Policies in a Time of Turbulence*, prepared for April 2004 Family Policies Congress of the Social Trends Institute. at 3 (on file with author). Loosening restrictions on access to divorce is one example of the creation of unintended consequences. At the same time that divorce has become easier to obtain, a growing body of literature documents its negative impact upon children, including dramatic economic decline, myriad behavioral problems, poorer performance in school, diminished earning capacity, and an increased probability of divorce as an adult. *See, e.g.*, Judith S. Wallerstein et al., The Unexpected Legacy of Divorce: A 25 Year Landmark Study (2000).

[7] The parties principally impacted by this reform are nonmarital children and children after divorce, the vast majority of whom live with their mothers. Of the children who live with either their mother or father only, 83 percent live with a mother. U.S. Census Bureau, America's Families and Living Arrangements: 2003, tbl.C2 (2004), http://www.census.gov/population/socdemo/hh-fam/cps2003/tabC2-all.pdf (reporting that approximately 16.8 million children living with mother only versus approximately 3.3 million living with father only). Among divorced and separated couples with children, mothers maintain over four times as many households as fathers. U.S. Census Bureau, America's Families and Living Arrangements: 2003, tbl.FG6 (2004), http://www.census.gov/population/socdemo/hh-fam/cps2003/tabFG6-all-1.pdf (showing that approximately 1.3 million maintained by father versus approximately 5.3 million maintained by mother). In single parent homes where the couple never married, the disparity is slightly greater. *Id.* (finding that 852,000 maintained by father versus approximately 4.4 million maintained by mother). Given these facts, the creation and enlargement of parental "rights" for de facto parents, over the objection of the legal parent, will disproportionately infringe on the parental prerogatives of women.

It will also tie the hands of minority women more often than white women. *See* Sarah H. Ramsey, *Constructing Parenthood for Stepparents: Parents by Estoppel and De Facto Parents Under the American Law Institute's* Principles of the Law of Family Dissolution, 8 Duke J. Gender L. & Pol'y 285, 287 (2001) (discussing how family formation patterns often differ by race).

[8] Principles ch. 1, Topic 1.I (d), at 5. The drafters are not alone in advancing the idea that what one does should count more than who one is. A number of commentators have argued that function should determine and define legal fatherhood more than mere biology. *See, e.g.*, Leslie Joan Harris, *Reconsidering the Criteria for Legal Fatherhood*, 1996 Utah L. Rev. 461, 480 (arguing that "functional paternity" should be the basis for legal rights and duties because functioning as a parent is congruent with current social mores, and encourages and supports individuals who take on responsibility for children); David L. Chambers, *Stepparents, Biologic Parents, and the Law's Perceptions of "Family" After Divorce, in* Divorce Reform at the Crossroads 102, 117 (Stephen D. Sugarman & Herma Hill Kay eds., 1990) ("[M]any individual stepparents do form strong emotional bonds with their stepchildren. They are seen by the child as 'parent.'"); Gilbert A. Holmes, *The Tie That Binds: The Constitutional Right of Children to Maintain Relationships with Parent-Like Individuals*, 53 Md. L. Rev. 358, 410 (1994) (arguing that the law should "grant[ ] parent-like individuals greater consideration than the current jurisprudence affords").

[9] Principles ch. 1, Topic 1.I (d), at 5.

[10] Principles § 2.03 cmt. c.

[11] Principles ch. 1, Topic 1.I (d), at 5–6.

[12] Principles ch. 1, Topic 1.I (d), at 5–6 ("Traditionally, parenthood is an exclusive, all-or-nothing status. A child can have only one mother and only one father; others have no rights, regardless of their functional roles.").

[13] The Principles would also extend parent-like rights to another category of adults who live with a child, parents by estoppel. The defining characteristic of this group is that they accept responsibility for the child. *See* Principles

My aim in this chapter is not to take issue with the presence of these posited goods.[14] No one doubts that some children will be made better off by preserving a connection with a de facto parent.[15] But this gain may not be as great as we might think it would be by extrapolating from biological parents. New, carefully constructed studies of parental investment suggest that the level of investments that fathers make in children varies with the fathers' biological relatedness to the child.[16] Moreover, whatever the magnitude of the gain for some children, it comes at a cost. A significant body of research suggests that giving men previously in relationships with a child's mother significant amounts of unsupervised parental access – as the ALI proposes to do – will result in more children being sexually exploited and physically abused.[17]

This chapter argues that before we grant Ex Live-In Partners new parental "rights," we must do more than simply posit good outcomes. Rather, policymakers, courts, and legislators should sum these probable effects, good and bad, to evaluate whether the approach is, on balance, a net good. Before any decisionmaker implements the ALI's proposed treatment of Ex Live-In Partners, they should be convinced that the ALI has met its burden of demonstrating that this creation and enlargement of parental rights would benefit children more than it would harm them. As Professor Eekelaar concludes so aptly with respect to the past caretaking standard, "But if it is to be *presumed* that an arrangement will be in a child's best interests, it must be clear that this will be so in an overwhelming majority of cases. In the absence of clear evidence that time matching will satisfy this, or even that this is what parents usually do by agreement, it fails as a presumption."[18]

In working out this calculus, this chapter discusses only one risk to children from conferring significantly expanded parent-like "rights" on Ex Live-In Partners: the possibility of sexual exploitation. This chapter focuses only on sexual abuse because it is sufficient to illustrate one probable harm some children will likely experience if we follow the ALI's recommendations. But sexual exploitation is by no means the only harm to which we would expose children by instituting a free-form, fluid conception of parenthood that encompasses every cohabitant with whom a woman shared equal caretaking responsibility for two years or more. Some of these children are likely also to experience punishing physical abuse and neglect.[19]

§ 2.03 cmt. b(ii), at 111–12. The legal recognition of parents by estoppel is justified in part by expectations of the parties. PRINCIPLES § 2.03 cmt. b(ii), at 112 ("When this reasonable good faith [that the individual is the parent] exists, the individual is seeking status based not solely on his functioning as a parent but on the combination of the parental functions performed and the expectations of the parties."). Legal recognition is also predicated on actions that are sufficiently clear and unambiguous to indicate parental status was contemplated by all. PRINCIPLES § 2.03 cmt. b(iii), at 114. Parents by estoppel will often have lived with the child since birth and believed themselves to be the child's biological parent. PRINCIPLES § 2.03 (1)(b)(ii),(iii); Seger v. Seger, 542 A.2d 424 (Pa. Super. Ct. 1988) (granting partial custody and visitation to stepfather who lived with child's mother for two years when she informed him she was pregnant with his child and who raised and supported the child after she revealed he was not the father, until the couple's break up). This is important from a risk assessment perspective and possibly also to the benefits we would predict to children of continuing contact. *See* Parts II & III *infra*. Consequently, the recommendations and critiques in this chapter are limited to the ALI's proposed treatment of de facto parents.

[14] The drafters assume that Ex Live-In Partners who performed caretaking tasks for a child have done so for benign reasons, not malign ones. As note 45 *infra* observes, the drafters confine their consideration of child abuse to abuse that "has occurred," neglecting the potential for future abuse.

[15] There is certainly no dearth of social science evidence suggesting some children will indeed benefit from continuing contact. *See infra* note 80.

[16] *See infra* Part II.

[17] *See infra* Part III.

[18] Eekelaar, this volume.

[19] Children living with unrelated males are more vulnerable to physical abuse and other forms of child abuse. For instance, British children living with their mother and a cohabitant are 33 times more likely to be physically abused

Because this argument hinges on the calculation of probable harms or goods resulting to children who have lived with a stepfather or the mother's unmarried live-in partner, it is necessarily limited. The research presented here sheds light only on the wisdom of giving to Ex Live-In Partners parent-like "rights" of access to children, without the moderating influence of a mother's presence. It cannot tell us anything at all about whether women in now-defunct relationships with a child's father should receive custody and visitation "rights," nor can it help us to evaluate whether to extend such rights to lesbian coparents. Both questions would involve a different set of calculations than presented here.[20]

This chapter evaluates whether the drafters' ballooning definition of parent has the potential for ill, as well as for good. Part I describes and critiques the ALI's proposed treatment of de facto parents. Part II reviews new studies that suggest that the upside to children of continuing contact with an Ex Live-In Partner may be more muted than the ALI assumes. Part III then provides a primer on factors affecting a child's risk of sexual abuse, and concludes that in this brave new world of newly anointed "parents," protective factors that might serve to shield a child from sexual victimization are not marshaled on behalf of the child. Part IV then examines the way in which sexual predators "groom" their victims and documents the significant overlap between "grooming" and the caretaking functions used to decide who qualifies as a de facto parent. Part V asks whether the test for de facto parents can be refined to select for "good risks," while culling out the bad and argues that an individualized decision based on the nature of the child's attachment to the Ex Live-In Partner would better promote the welfare of the children involved. Part VI concludes that the ALI – and more importantly, legislatures and courts that consider these proposals – should not base such sweeping changes in parental rights on unsupported assumptions

and 73 times more likely to be killed than children living in an intact family. *See* Robert Whelan, Broken Homes and Battered Children: A Study of the Relationship Between Child Abuse and Family Type, tbls.12 & 14 (1994) (reporting a risk of physical abuse for children living with two natural married parents of 0.23, compared to a risk of 7.65 for children living with their natural mother and a cohabitee and a risk of fatal abuse for children living with both natural, married parents of 0.31, compared to a risk of fatal abuse of 22.9 for children living with their natural mother and a cohabitee). A child in a stepparent household is 120 times more likely to be bludgeoned to death than a child living with his genetic father in an intact household. Owen D. Jones, *Evolutionary Analysis in Law: An Introduction and Application to Child Abuse*, 75 N.C. L. Rev. 1117, 1208 (1997). New research focusing on all forms of child maltreatment has found that "[c]hildren who had a father surrogate living in the home were twice as likely to be reported for maltreatment after his entry into the home than those with either a biological father (odds ratio = 2.6, 95% confidence interval = 1.4–4.7) or no father figure in the home (odds ratio = 2.0, 95% confidence interval = 1.1–3.5)". Aruna Radhakrishna et al., *Are Father Surrogates a Risk Factor for Child Maltreatment?*, 6 (4) Child Maltreatment 281 (November 2001).

Similarly, Ania Wilczynski reports in an English sample of child-killing that the "proportion of male parent-substitutes and male cohabitees [among child killers] were nine and fifty times" their respective rates in a national survey. Ania Wilczynski, Child Homicide 72–73 (1997). In an Australian sample, she found that nonbiological parents comprised 27 percent of the child-killers, although "only an estimated 7 percent of Australian children . . . lived in step or blended families." *Id.*

20 This is so because we know very little about child sexual abuse by women, other than it seems to occur very rarely. *See* Robin Fretwell Wilson, *The Cradle of Abuse: Evaluating the Danger Posed by a Sexually Predatory Parent to the Victim's Siblings*, 51 Emory L. J. 241, 245 n.13 (2002). Moreover, the principal risk to children of punishing physical abuse comes from father substitutes rather than from women. *See* Part III *infra*. It is worth noting, however, that an important impetus for permitting parental claims by de facto parents and parents by estoppel was to recognize same sex partners who cannot adopt one another's child or marry their partners. This desire to recognize same sex partners may have led to a number of unintended consequences and tensions explored here. To protect a mother's right to decide who has contact with her child without undermining the recognition many would like to extend to same-sex, non-biological parents may be tricky. Part V suggests that state legislators may want to address only the most compelling cases for significantly expanding rights for nonbiological caretakers – like the interests of same sex partners or of stepfathers who want to care for a child after the mother's death – and leave the less compelling cases untouched.

about the value of continuing contact with Ex Live-in Partners, but must instead take account of and respond to the empirical research that bears on the wisdom of such fundamental change.

I. The ALI Views Continuing Contact between Children and Ex Live-In Partners as an Unadulterated Good

This part demonstrates that the drafters view continuing contact between children and men who shared caretaking with a child's mother for two years or more – whether married or unmarried – as an unadulterated good. It first outlines the substantive and standing rights the ALI seeks to confer upon an Ex Live-In Partner, and then critiques this treatment of de facto parents.

A. ALI's Treatment of De Facto Parents

As noted earlier, the drafters want to ensure continuing contact between a child and former partner of the child's parent, without – they argue – "unnecessary and inappropriate intrusion into the relationships between legal parents and their children."[21] To accomplish this, their test for status as a de facto parent is, they urge, "strict:"[22]

(1) The individual must have lived with the child for a significant period of time (not less than two years), and acted in the role of a parent for reasons primarily other than financial compensation [described hereinafter as the "Residency Requirement"].
(2) The legal parent or parents must have agreed to the arrangement, or it must have arisen because of a complete failure or inability of any legal parent to perform caretaking functions [described hereinafter as the "Agreement Requirement"].
(3) In addition, the individual must have functioned as a parent either by (a) having performed the majority share of caretaking functions for the child, or (b) having performed a share of caretaking functions that is equal to or greater than the share assumed by the legal parent with whom the child primarily lives [described hereinafter as the "Caretaking Requirement"].[23]

Significantly, there is no requirement that treatment as a de facto parent be in the best interests of the child, as is required for certain parents by estoppel.[24]

The Residency Requirement functions to exclude "neighbors, nonresidential relatives, or hired babysitters,"[25] while the exclusion of relationships motivated by money is designed to cull out caretakers who are not "motivated by love and loyalty."[26] Although the drafters seek to recognize "long-term, substitute parent-child relationship[s]," coresidence for as little as two years may qualify an adult as a de facto parent.[27] The length of time that is considered "significant" will vary with the child's age, frequency of contact with the adult, and the intensity of their relationship.[28] For children under six, two years "is likely to qualify as significant" while longer periods "may be required" for school-aged children, and "even longer" if the child is an adolescent.[29]

[21] Principles § 2.03 cmt. c, at 119.
[22] Principles § 2.03 cmt. c, at 119.
[23] Principles § 2.03 cmt. c, at 119.
[24] *See* Principles § 2.03(1)(b)(iii).
[25] Principles § 2.03 cmt. c (i), at 119–20.
[26] Principles § 2.03 cmt. c (ii), at 120.
[27] Principles § 2.03 cmt. c (iii), at 122.
[28] Principles § 2.03 cmt. c (iv), at 122.
[29] Principles § 2.03 cmt. c (iv), at 122. The drafters seem unwilling to require additional years or to give clear signals that such additional amounts of time should be required. Instead they note that "[i]n some cases, a period longer

A de facto parent relationship, the drafters tell us, "cannot arise by accident, in secrecy, or as a result of improper behavior"[30] because it usually requires agreement. The Agreement Requirement limits de facto parent status generally "to those individuals whose relationship to the child has arisen with knowledge and agreement of the legal parent."[31] Lack of agreement may be evidenced by the failure of the partner to adopt the child, if adoption was an option,[32] as well as by the retention by the legal parent "of authority over matters of the child's care, such as discipline."[33]

Although the Agreement Requirement requires "an affirmative act or acts by the legal parent demonstrating a willingness and an expectation of shared parental responsibilities," agreement may be implied by the circumstances.[34] When two adults share roughly equal responsibility for a child, this equal caretaking by itself satisfies the agreement requirement. Consider illustration 22:

> For the past four years, seven-year-old Lindsay has lived with her mother, Annis, and her stepfather, Ralph. During that period, Ralph and Annis both worked outside the home, and divided responsibility for Lindsay's care roughly equally between them.
>
> Annis's sharing of responsibility for Lindsay's care with Ralph constitutes an implied agreement by her to the role assumed by Ralph.[35]

In short, any parent who acquiesces in her partner's decision to take on equal caretaking duties, would likely "have agreed" to the partner's claim of de facto parent status.

With respect to the Ex Live-In Partner's share of caretaking functions, he must have performed at least as much care as the legal parent herself provided.[36] Caretaking functions consist of the chores necessary for the "direct delivery of day-to-day care and supervision to the child."[37] They include "physical supervision, feeding, grooming, discipline, transportation, direction of the child's intellectual and emotional development, and arrangement of the child's peer activities, medical care, and education."[38] In the drafters' view, caretaking functions "are likely to have a special bearing on the strength and quality of the adult's relationship with the child" because they involve "tasks relating directly to a child's care and upbringing."[39]

The Caretaking Requirement is central not only to the de facto parent's qualification *qua* de facto parent, but also to the allocation of time with the child, which the drafters label "custodial responsibility."[40] Section 2.08 of the PRINCIPLES generally seeks after the break-up to "approximate" those caretaking arrangements that preceded it.[41] Thus, the

than two years *may be* required in order to establish that an individual has the kind of relationship that warrants recognition." PRINCIPLES § 2.03 cmt. c (iv), at 122 (emphasis added).

30 PRINCIPLES § 2.03 cmt. c (iii), at 121.

31 PRINCIPLES § 2.03 cmt. c (iii), at 121.

32 PRINCIPLES § 2.03 cmt. c, at 119 (noting that absence of adoption when available would not be dispositive, but would be "some evidence" of lack of intent to agree).

33 PRINCIPLES § 2.03 cmt. c (iii), at 121. No agreement is required where there has been a "total failure or inability by the legal parent to care for the child." *Id.*

34 PRINCIPLES § 2.03 cmt. c (iii), at 121.

35 PRINCIPLES § 2.03, illus. 22, at 122.

36 PRINCIPLES § 2.03 cmt. c (v), at 123. The one exception to this is where the legal parent is a noncustodial parent, in which case the parent's partner will not satisfy the criterion. *Id.*

37 PRINCIPLES § 2.03 cmt. g, at 125.

38 PRINCIPLES § 2.03 cmt. g, at 125.

39 PRINCIPLES § 2.03 cmt. g, at 125. The drafters themselves recognize this as "an assumption." *Id.*

40 *See* PRINCIPLES § 2.08(1), at 178.

41 *See* PRINCIPLES § 2.08(1) cmt. a, at 180. The drafters want to resist "express[ing] particular preferences about what is best for children," because rules favoring sole custody over joint, or vice versa, "do not reflect the preferences, experiences, or welfare of all families." *Id.* § 2.05 cmt. a, at 146 (explaining their selection of the approximation standard). No rule is neutral, however, even this default to past caretaking practices. The drafters have chosen not only to replicate past actions, but to give Ex Live-In Partners greater entitlement to partial custody.

"approximation" or "past caretaking" standard requires that "the proportion of time the child spends with each parent [approximate] the proportion of time each parent spent performing caretaking functions for the child prior to the parents' separation," unless an exception applies.[42] The justification for this arrangement is that "the division of past caretaking functions correlates well with other factors associated with the child's best interests, such as the quality of each parent's emotional attachment to the child and the parents' respective parenting abilities."[43] The rights of access that the PRINCIPLES would give to Ex Live-In Partners appear to include unsupervised visitation and overnight stays. Supervised visits are reserved for those instances when protecting the child or the child's parent is warranted, as when the courts finds "credible evidence of domestic violence."[44]

As Professor Levy notes in this volume, exceptions for departing from the past caretaking standard are available to protect the child or a parent from the other parent's neglect or abuse, domestic violence, or drug or alcohol abuse;[45] to accommodate an older child's preferences; to protect a child from the harm that would result from the rule's application "because of a gross disparity in the quality of the emotional attachment between each parent and the child or in each parent's demonstrated ability or availability to meet the child's need;" and to avoid allocations that "would be extremely impractical or that would interfere substantially with the child's need for stability...;" among other things.[46] Generally, however, if an Ex Live-In Partner puts in half the work involved in caring for a child, he gets as much as half the time,[47] subject to the practical constraints of splitting time with a child fifty-fifty, as explained more fully below.

[42] PRINCIPLES § 2.08. Section 2.03(5) defines "caretaking functions" as "tasks that involve interaction with the child or that direct, arrange, and supervise the interaction and care provided by others." A nonexclusive list of caretaking functions includes such matters as "satisfying the nutritional needs of the child," "directing the child's various developmental needs," "providing discipline," "supervising chores," "performing other tasks that attend to the child's needs for behavioral control and self-restraint," "arranging for the child's education," "providing moral and ethical guidance," and a host of other specified functions. *Id.* § 2.03(5)(a)–(h). Section 2.03(3) makes clear that "custodial responsibility" "refers to physical custodianship and supervision of a child. It usually includes, but does not necessarily require, residential or overnight responsibility." Section 2.03(6) defines "parenting functions," a phrase which appears only in Section 2.09(2) (*see infra* note 50), to include "tasks that serve the needs of the child or the child's residential family," such as "caretaking functions" and a diverse variety of other functions, from "providing economic support," "yard work, and house cleaning," to "participating in decision-making regarding the child's welfare" and "arranging for financial planning." PRINCIPLES § 2.03(6).

[43] *See* PRINCIPLES § 2.08(1) cmt. b, at 182.

[44] PRINCIPLES § 2.05, illus. 2., at 149.

[45] The drafters do care about child abuse, but the inquiry is essentially backward-looking, asking judges and others to identify only those cases "in which there is credible evidence that child abuse... has occurred." PRINCIPLES ch. 1, Topic 1.II(e), at 6–7. *See also* PRINCIPLES § 2.05(3), at 144 (outlining elements of parenting plan). Section 2.05(3) directs courts to screen cases for child abuse or domestic violence. A court-monitored screening process is necessary "[s]ince parents often are not forthcoming about the existence of child abuse and domestic abuse." PRINCIPLES § 2.05 cmt. c, at 147. During this screening process, the focus is on what already "has occurred." This phrase appears five times in Section 2.05(3) and comment c explaining it, while no mention is explicitly made about the potential for future abuse per se. If domestic violence is brought to a court's attention, the court must decide on whether abuse *has occurred* when considering a parenting plan. *See id.* § 2.11(1)(a), at 255.

[46] Levy, this volume.

[47] Parkinson, this volume (reviewing the drafters' illustrations of the past caretaking standard and exceptions to it, and concluding that while "it is accepted that if the parents have shared equally in the caretaking of the children, then an allocation of equal custodial time would ordinarily be warranted," most of the Illustrations focus on exceptions to the standard, rather than the standard's usual application, and therefore create some confusion about the strength of the past caretaking standard as a determinant of care arrangements after the adults break up). Professor Parkinson notes that at least one drafter shared the view that equal caretaking will generally result in roughly equal time. *Id.* (citing Katharine T. Bartlett, *U.S. Custody Law and Trends in the Context of the* ALI Principles of the Law of Family Dissolution, 10 VA. J. SOC. POL'Y & L. 5, 18 (2002) ("If parents equally shared caretaking responsibilities, that fact will be reflected in the custodial allocations.")).

Section 2.04 does two things: it allows an Ex Live-In Partner who lived with the child during the previous six months to bring an action,[48] and then it gives him substantive rights.[49] In terms of substantive rights, the Ex Live-In Partner will have a claim to an equal share of the custodial responsibility for a child, subject to three limits. First, a de facto parent may not receive a majority of the custodial responsibility for a child over the objection of the child's legal parent or parent by estoppel, unless that parent has not been performing a reasonable share of the child's parenting.[50] Second, although a de facto parent can receive some decision-making responsibility for a child, he is not presumptively entitled to this, as a legal parent or parent by estoppel would be.[51] Third, a de facto parent does not get presumptive access to a child's school or health records, as other parents do under the PRINCIPLES.[52] In addition to these specific limitations, there is the general exception to the past caretaking standard, noted above, that provides that a de facto parent should not receive an allocation of time with the child if making such an award would be impractical.[53]

To make this more concrete, consider illustration 1 to Section 2.18. There, Barbara marries Randall and for four years acts as the primary caretaker for his two children from a prior marriage.[54] Randall supports the family economically and provides backup care. At divorce, "assuming Barbara satisfies the definition of a de facto parent," she "may be allocated a coequal share of responsibility with Randall," or a "smaller share" if practicality so dictates.[55] However, because Randall has been performing a reasonable share of parenting functions, Barbara will not receive "the majority share of custodial responsibility for the children unless Randall agrees, or unless she shows that an

[48] Section 2.04 gives standing and notice rights to a de facto parent who "resided with the child within the six-month period prior to the filing of the action or who has consistently maintained or attempted to maintain the parental relationship since residing with the child." PRINCIPLES § 2.04 (1)(c), at 134. The six-month window is waived if the de facto parent "consistently maintained or attempted to maintain the parental relationship since no longer sharing the same residence." *Id.* § 2.04 cmt. d, at 136. This waiver "eliminate[s] the advantages of uncooperative or strategic behavior by the custodial parent." *Id.*

[49] PRINCIPLES § 2.04, Reporter's Notes, cmt. a, at 139–40.

[50] PRINCIPLES § 2.18. Parenting functions means "tasks that serve the needs of the child or the child's residential family," including not only caretaking functions but also "providing economic support; participating in decisionmaking regarding the child's welfare; maintaining or improving the family residence, including yard work, and house cleaning; doing and arranging for financial planning and organization, car repair and maintenance, food and clothing purchases, laundry and dry cleaning, and other tasks supporting the consumption and savings needs of the household; performing any other functions that are customarily performed by a parent or guardian and that are important to a child's welfare and development; arranging for health-care providers, medical follow-up, and home health care; providing moral and ethical guidance; and arranging alternative care by a family member, babysitter, or other child-care provider or facility, including investigation of alternatives, communication with providers, and supervision of care." PRINCIPLES § 2.03(6).

[51] PRINCIPLES § 2.09 cmt. c, at 240.

[52] PRINCIPLES § 2.09(4).

[53] Illustration 4 to Section 2.18 demonstrates the limitation that workability places upon the arrangements that a court may make. There, a child, Keith, has two parents who have received custodial rights after their divorce, Elena and Lee. Elena's second husband, Lincoln, also received every other weekend with Keith upon his divorce from Elena since he "assumed the majority of responsibility for Keith's upbringing while Elena returned to school to finish her medical training." Elena married Norman, who with Elena's consent provided as much care for Keith as Elena. The PRINCIPLES note that although Norman would ordinarily warrant an allocation of custodial responsibility if he meets the test for de facto parent, "[t]he court may determine that allocating custodial responsibility to four different adults now living in four different households is impractical and contrary to Keith's interests. If so, the court should limit or deny an allocation of responsibility to Lincoln, or Norman, or both of them." PRINCIPLES § 2.18, illus. 4.

[54] PRINCIPLES § 2.18, illus. 1.

[55] PRINCIPLES § 2.18, illus. 1 (concluding that Barbara "should be allocated whatever share of custodial responsibility for the children is determined to be appropriate under § 2.08, but as limited by § 2.18(1)," which prohibits the de facto parent from receiving a majority of the caretaking responsibility and limits allocations if they would be impractical).

allocation of the majority of custodial responsibility to Randall would be harmful to them."[56]

It is important to recognize the magnitude of the shift the ALI proposes. Without the ALI's proposed reforms, an Ex Live-In Partner would have standing only in a minority of jurisdictions.[57] Although a growing number of jurisdictions already give standing to nonparents, many of these limit standing only to grandparents or stepparents.[58] Very few permit unmarried cohabitants to initiate actions for custody or visitation.[59] Contrast the ALI's proposed reforms with the Uniform Marriage and Divorce Act, which allows an action by "a person other than a parent, ... but only if [the child] is not in the physical custody of one of his parents."[60] There, an emergency – the absence of legal parents – necessitates standing by others. Here, we have third parties, unrelated adults, given the opportunity to tread on the parental prerogatives of the legal parent. In the absence of the PRINCIPLES, an Ex Live-In Partner today would likely receive some limited visitation in certain jurisdictions with the child after the breakup, but nothing that approaches the allocations of time that the ALI proposes to give. As Professor Jane Murphy noted in a recent review of de facto parent cases, a "few states and a handful of courts have granted non-biological, non-marital caretakers such as stepfathers ... rights similar to those granted legal fathers," but "these cases generally limit the parental rights to visitation."[61]

Like all custody rules,[62] the rights the ALI seeks to create in some jurisdictions and enlarge in others only come into play when the legal parent does not willingly grant visitation to her ex-partner.[63] A mother can always decide voluntarily to provide visitation to those men she thinks will enrich her child's life.

Interestingly, the ALI would extract very little from Ex Live-In Partners in exchange for this significant enlargement of parental rights. As Professor Katharine Baker points out in this volume, the PRINCIPLES impose child support obligations on parents by estoppel but not on de facto parents.[64] This choice is perplexing since live-in partners benefit children by providing them with additional financial support during the intact adult relationship and presumably could do so to some degree afterwards.[65]

[56] PRINCIPLES § 2.18, illus.1.

[57] *See* PRINCIPLES § 2.04, Reporter's Notes, cmt. d, at 140 (noting the "traditional rule ... that a nonparent cannot file an action for custody or visitation without a showing that the parents are unfit or unavailable").

[58] PRINCIPLES § 2.04, Reporter's Notes, cmt. a, at 140.

[59] *See, e.g.*, Cooper v. Merkel, 470 N.W.2d 253, 255–56 (S.D. 1991) (denying visitation to mother's ex-boyfriend who as a father figure had assumed responsibility for raising her son for seven years); Engel v. Kenner, 926 S.W.2d 472 (Mo. Ct. App. 1996) (denying joint custody to boyfriend of mother who lived with mother and child for five months and helped support child for three years thereafter).

[60] UNIF. MARRIAGE & DIVORCE ACT § 401(d)(2), 9A U.L.A. 264 (1998).

[61] Jane Murphy, *Legal Images of Fatherhood: Welfare Reform, Child Support Enforcement, and Fatherless Children*, 81 NOTRE DAME L. REV. 325, 342–343 (2005).

[62] Of course, the problem extends beyond those instances in which the legal parent does not voluntarily grant visitation to her ex-partner. By conferring legal standing and "rights" on ex-partners to seek custody and visitation, the drafters make it all the more difficult for mothers to say no. *See* Robert H. Mnookin & Lewis Kornhauser, *Bargaining in the Shadow of the Law: The Case of Divorce*, 88 YALE L.J. 950 (1979).

[63] The drafters seek to confer custody and visitation rights "over the opposition of the legal parent." PRINCIPLES § 2.03, Reporter's Notes, cmt. b, at 129 (discussing equitable doctrines conferring such rights).

[64] Baker, this volume.

[65] *See* Sarah H. Ramsey, *Stepparents and the Law: A Nebulous Status and a Need for Reform, in* STEPPARENTING: ISSUES IN THEORY, RESEARCH AND PRACTICE 217, 228 (Kay Pasley & Marilyn Ihinger-Tallman eds., 1994).

The ALI's decision to give Ex Live-In Partners parental rights without requiring child support may also represent a missed child protection opportunity. The ALI could have limited standing as a de facto parent to those adults who voluntarily assume a child support obligation to a child, which would serve an important screening function. It

B. Critique of the ALI's Treatment of De Facto Parents

If state legislatures or courts institute these proposals, many mothers will find themselves unable to excise former lovers from their lives and the lives of their children. This should trouble us. As Professor Karen Czapanskiy observes: "For [the caregiver] to do the job to the best of her or his abilities, [they] need[] authority as well as responsibility.... The autonomy of the lead caregiver must be respected."[66] The Agreement Requirement is a weak reed of protection against such a dramatic and unexpected result. A partner's interest in and interaction with her children presumably is a desired goal of most women, and is likely to be warmly received. What mother would not allow her husband or live-in partner to read to her child, help put the child to bed and wake him or her up in the morning, and otherwise share caretaking responsibility? The fact that many of these actions may be undertaken with the legal parent's consent in an ongoing relationship seems to say very little about the legal parent's expectations after the relationship's demise.[67]

It was unnecessary to stretch the tent of parenthood this far. Many live-in partners who want to protect their interests in an existing adult-child bond after their relationship ends with the child's mother, can adopt the child.[68] Moreover, the drafters' provision of standing to nonparents when it serves the best interests of the child would have accommodated the most compelling claims for standing to seek custody and visitation with a child,[69] without encompassing every Tom, Dick, and Harry with whom a woman cohabits for two years and shares an equal caretaking load.

Despite acknowledging that legal parents exhibit the "maximum commitment to the parenting enterprise,"[70] the drafters make no inquiry, when providing standing and an allocation of custodial responsibility, into the reasons for the legal parent's objection.[71] Perhaps she ended the relationship because of his interaction with her child.[72] Other than stock observations about emotions running high at the time of breakup,[73] the drafters have no more reason to believe that when a mother withholds access she does so out of spite or selfishness than they do for believing that she is motivated

would promote continuing contact between children and those adults who have committed to a child in concrete, palpable ways – where continuing contact is likely to create the greatest gains for a child – while possibly helping to screen out "bad risks." *See* Parts II, III and IV *infra.*

[66] Karen Czapanskiy, *Interdependencies, Families, and Children*, 39 Santa Clara L. Rev. 957, 979–80, 1029 (1994).

[67] Contrast this with coparents who have set forth an understanding in writing about how a child will be parented, where it may well be the expectation of the parties to share parental responsibilities during the relationship *and* after. Principles § 2.03 cmt. c (iii), at 121.

[68] Principles § 2.03 cmt. c, at 119 (noting that adults can protect their interest in a relationship with a child by adopting the child "if available under applicable state law").

[69] Principles § 2.04(2) (giving the court discretion "in exceptional cases, ... to grant permission to intervene, under such terms as it establishes, to other individuals ... whose participation in the proceedings under this Chapter it determines is likely to serve the child's best interests").

[70] Principles ch. 1, Topic 1.I (d), at 5–6.

[71] The one exception to this is for past or ongoing abuse, but not mere queasiness that something is not right about a partner's interaction with a child.

[72] Diana E. H. Russell, The Secret Trauma: Incest in the Lives of Girls and Women 372 (1986) (reporting that one in four nonoffending mothers suspected the abuse shortly before the child's disclosure).

[73] Principles § 2.08 cmt. b, at 183 (observing, in a discussion of the rationale for the past caretaking standard, that the parties' "expectations and preferences are often complicated at divorce by feelings of loss, anxiety, guilt, and anger–feelings that tend not only to cloud a parent's judgment and ability to make decisions on behalf of the child, but also to exaggerate the amount of responsibility a parent wants to assume for a child, or the objections he or she has to the other parent's level of involvement in the child's life").

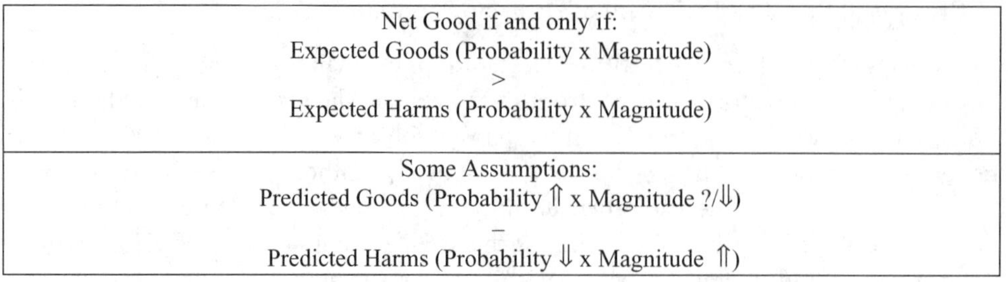

Figure 5.1. Assessing the ALI's Treatment of Ex Live-In Partners.

by concern for the best interests of her child.[74] Moreover, one can easily imagine that the rights the ALI seeks to confer on Ex Live-In Partners could be exploited not as an opportunity to stay in the children's lives, but as an opportunity to control a child or her mother.

Further, conferring new parental rights is not without cost. By granting standing to Ex Live-In Partners, we would encourage the adults involved to resolve problems in court, with all the costs and damaged relationships that result. We would also encourage litigation by conferring substantive rights on Ex Live-In Partners. It may be important to encourage continuing relationships with Ex Live-In Partners, but long, expensive custody fights – even where the mother wins – have financial and emotional costs that hurt her and the child. This is particularly worrisome as a risk because the definition of de facto parent requires such complex fact finding. Nonetheless, the drafters latch onto bright-line, easily verifiable time requirements in an effort to avoid expensive and, in their view, generally counterproductive inquiries into the qualitative nature of the relationship being preserved. Such inquiries are counterproductive both because they "draw[] the court into comparisons between parenting styles and values that are matters of parental autonomy not appropriate for judicial resolution,"[75] and because they require expert testimony which, in the "adversarial context, tends to focus on the weaknesses of each parent and thus undermines the spirit of cooperation and compromise necessary to successful post-divorce custodial arrangements."[76]

A time test also obscures the underlying "good" for which the time requirement serves as a proxy – the depth and quality of the adult-child relationship. Attachment may well safeguard a child who has contact with that adult after the breakup.[77] Yet it plays no part in the ALI's assessment of who counts as a de facto parent and has standing to seek such rights of access. Neither is attachment explicitly considered in awarding visitation and custody, unless there is a "gross disparity in the quality of the [child's] emotional attachment" with each parent.[78]

[74] As the PRINCIPLES observe, "[t]he law grants parents responsibility for their children based, in part, on the assumption that they are motivated by love and loyalty, and thus are likely to act in the child's best interests." PRINCIPLES § 2.03 cmt. c (ii), at 120.

[75] PRINCIPLES § 2.08 cmt. b, at 181–82 (making this observation about the "best interests" test and arguing that the approximation standard "yields more predictable and more easily adjudicated results, thereby advancing the best interests of children in most cases without infringing on parental autonomy").

[76] PRINCIPLES § 2.08 cmt. b, at 181–82.

[77] *See infra* Part V.

[78] *See* PRINCIPLES § 2.08(1)(d).

C. The ALI Fails to Take into Account the Repercussions of Including Ex Live-In Partners in Children's Lives

As noted above, the drafters construct a benign explanation for why an Ex Live-In Partner should have access to the child of their former partner. For the drafters, the impulse is at once selfless and selfish, grounded in a desire to continue an important parent-child relationship. Having largely assumed the possibility of an upside – one half of the calculus shown in Figure 5.1 – the drafters abruptly conclude that continuing contact between de facto parents and the children of their former lovers is an unqualified good for children.

Missing from this account is a critical, in-depth examination of the degree of gain children are likely to experience from continuing contact with an Ex Live-In Partner after the adults' relationship dissolves. Entirely absent from this account is the possible downside, the second half of the equation shown in Figure 5.1.[79] While we may expect that some children (perhaps even the overwhelming majority) will be made better off, to some degree,[80] we should also affirmatively expect that others will be made worse off, and profoundly so.[81] This is so because many sex offenders use adult relationships to gain sexual access to children,[82] and the PRINCIPLES could be employed to give them continuing access to child victims.

The next two parts argue that imbuing adults with parental rights merely because they resided with a child and shared equal caretaking chores may not yield the welfare benefits for children that we might hope for, especially in light of the fact that the rights of continuing contact do not carry a concomitant duty to financially support these children. Equally important, any gains for children will come at a price. The ALI proposal would stretch the "parenthood" tent so wide that it will necessarily encompass some men with less-than-admirable motives or impulses.

[79] Although they have not examined the particular set of risks being examined here, scholars generally agree that the "definition of parent should be expanded or curtailed only when doing so serves to further the child's interests." Janet Leach Richards, *Redefining Parenthood: Parental Rights Versus Child Rights*, 40 WAYNE L. REV. 1227, 1229 (1994).

[80] For an excellent recitation of the social science evidence that many children will benefit from continuing contact, see Katharine T. Bartlett, *Rethinking Parenthood as an Exclusive Status: The Need for Legal Alternatives When the Premise of the Nuclear Family Has Failed*, 70 VA. L. REV. 879, 902 (1984) (citing social science evidence that a "[n]ear consensus" exists that a child's healthy growth depends upon the continuing of his personal relationships). *See also* Holmes, *supra* note 8, at 389–90 (noting "the current consensus remains that children benefit from continued contact with non-custodial parents"); Kaas, *supra* note note 79, at 1119 (examining the "psychological harm to the child" that would result from a change in custody in favor of or contrary to a nongenetic caretaker).

Other scholars have analyzed the "findings of the recent research on the stepparent relationship," and concluded that "insofar as the needs of children are concerned, economic considerations suggest that remarriage is typically beneficial." Chambers, *supra* note 8, at 102, 108. The "surge of research on the stepparent relationship," *id.* at 102–03, is useful in determining whether a child benefits from stepparents who are in an intact relationship with the child's legal parent, but is less helpful in assessing the risks and benefits to a child of continuing contact after the adults break up.

[81] *See infra* note note 178 and accompanying text (noting that abuse inflicted by father substitutes is among the most depraved and injurious).

Of course, there are other costs to giving de facto parents parental rights. In her seminal article in the *Virginia Law Review*, Katharine Bartlett, one of the three drafters of the PRINCIPLES, concluded that the "key disadvantages of broadening access to parenthood" are the increase in "the number of adults making claim to a child and enhanc[ing] the indeterminacy that already exists in child custody law." Bartlett, *supra* note 80, at 945.

[82] *See infra* Part III.B.

II. Evaluating the Upside to Children from Continuing Contact with Ex Live-In Partners

"A limited but growing number of studies examine the social well-being of children living in cohabiting parent families."[83] Two recent, carefully constructed studies continue this work, using very different analytical tools. The first study, by Manning and Lamb, evaluates outcomes for children raised by biological and nonbiological fathers and compares these to outcomes for children raised only by their mothers.[84] The second study, by Hofferth and Anderson, examines differential investments in children by biological and nonbiological fathers.[85] As a pair, these studies provide a valuable lens for assessing the relative importance of biology as a factor affecting children's welfare and the incentive various fathers have to invest in children.

A. The Importance of Biological Ties for Child Well-Being

Manning and Lamb examined the well-being of adolescents in various families and asked (1) whether teenagers who live with their mother and her partner, whether married ("stepfathers") or unmarried ("mother's cohabitant"), do as well academically and behaviorally as teenagers living with two married, biological parents, and (2) whether these children fare better or worse than children living with single mothers.[86] The results of this analysis indicate that children living with a stepfather or mother's cohabitant are more likely than children living with two married, biological parents to be expelled from school, exhibit greater levels of delinquency, and encounter more school problems.[87] Additionally, these children are more likely to have a lower grade point average and generally greater odds of achieving lower grades; they also score lower on the Peabody Picture Vocabulary Test ("PPVT").[88] As the authors note, none of this is surprising. Children living in two married, biological parent families "generally fare better than teenagers living in any other family type."[89]

What was novel and perhaps even surprising were Manning and Lamb's findings when they shifted the frame of reference from two married, biological parent families to single

[83] Wendy D. Manning & Kathleen A. Lamb, *Adolescent Well-Being in Cohabiting, Married, and Single-Parent Families*, 65 J. MARRIAGE & FAM. 876, 878 (2003).

[84] Manning & Lamb, *supra* note 83, at 876.

[85] Sandra L. Hofferth & Kermyt G. Anderson, *Are All Dads Equal?: Biology Versus Marriage as a Basis for Paternal Investment*, 65 J. MARRIAGE & FAM. 213 (2003).

[86] Manning & Lamb, *supra* note 83, at 876. The authors evaluated data from the first wave of the National Longitudinal Adolescent Study of Adolescent Health (Add Health), which was based on interviews done in 1995 with students in grades 7 through 12 and their parents from a sample of 80 high schools and 52 middle schools in the United States. *Id.* at 880–81.

[87] *Id.* at 885–86 tbl. 3 (using married two parent families as a reference category, and finding that teens who lived with mother's cohabitant were more likely to be expelled from school (.80, $p < .001$), exhibit greater levels of delinquency (1.32, $p < .01$), and encounter more school problems (.76, $p < .001$); while children living with a stepfather were more likely to be expelled from school (.56, $p < .001$), exhibit greater levels of delinquency (.61, $p < .01$), and encounter more school problems (.69, $p < .001$)).

[88] *Id.* (using married two parent families as a reference category, and finding that teens who lived with mother's cohabitant were more likely to receive low grades (.64, $p < .001$) and have lower vocabulary scores (−2.36, $p < .01$); while children living with a stepfather were more likely to receive low grades (.52, $p < .001$), and have lower vocabulary scores although the difference was not statistically significant).

[89] *Id.* at 885; Robin Fretwell Wilson, *Evaluating Marriage: Does Marriage Matter to the Nurturing of Children?*, 42 SAN DIEGO L. REV. 847 (2005).

mother families. There they found that children living with stepfathers or mother's cohabitants "have similar odds of being suspended or expelled as their counterparts living in single-mother families."[90] Teens living with stepfathers had "lower levels of delinquency than teens living with single mothers," while teens living with mother's cohabitant experienced more delinquency, although the difference receded when other variables were taken into account.[91] Teens in all three households experience similar levels of trouble in school and possessed similar verbal skills and college expectations.[92]

Although they found "differences at the bivariate level... in terms of delinquency and low grades in school" between teens living with single mothers and those living with stepfathers, Manning and Lamb concluded that "teenagers living with unmarried mothers do not seem to benefit from the presence of their mother's cohabiting partner."[93] Consequently:

> [M]en's presence alone seems neither sufficient nor necessary to create positive outcomes for children. Indeed, our results show that stepfathers (married or cohabiting) provide limited benefit when contrasted with single-mother families. Our findings suggest that neither parental cohabitation nor marriage to a partner or spouse who is not related to the child (stepfamily formation) is associated with uniform advantage in terms of behavioral or academic indicators to teenagers living in single-mother families.[94]

Manning and Lamb note that their "results are consistent with research focusing on behavior problems."[95]

B. The Importance of Biological Ties for Paternal Investments

Studies of outcomes for children by family type suffer from an obvious limitation: a poorer outcome may be due to family form, but it may also be the result of other factors. For instance, differences in outcomes for children in two biological parent, married families versus those in cohabiting families may be attributable to a host of differences between these families, including income, relative youth of the parents, higher levels of stress and conflict,[96] role confusion, or a lack of clear expectations about parenting in cohabiting households.[97] Unlike outcome studies, a focus on investment avoids the multitude of reasons why groups of children may fare better or worse than others on average.[98]

[90] *Id.* at 886–87 & tbl.4 (using single mother households as a reference category, and finding that teens who lived with mother's cohabitant had similar odds of being expelled or suspended, whether in the bivariate model or the multivariate model)were more likely to be expelled from school (.80, $p < .001$), exhibit greater levels of delinquency (1.32, $p < .01$), and encounter more school problems (.76, $p < .001$); while children living with a stepfather were more likely to be expelled from school (.56, $p < .001$), exhibit greater levels of delinquency (.61, $p < .01$), and encounter more school problems (.69, $p < .001$)).

[91] *Id.* at 886–87 & tbl.4 (finding that teens who lived in single mother households experienced less delinquency (− .76, $p < .05$) than those who lived with mother's cohabitant, although the difference receded to a statistically insignificant –0.06 after a multivariate analysis).

[92] Manning & Lamb, *supra* note 83, *id.* at 886–87 & tbl.4 (noting that adolescents who live with stepfathers score higher on the vocabulary test than teens who live with mother's cohabitants but that this effect is marginally significant ($p = .06$) after a multivariate analysis).

[93] *Id.* at 890.

[94] *Id.* at 890.

[95] *Id.* at 890.

[96] Anne Case et al., *How Hungry is the Selfish Gene?*, 110 Econ. J. 781, 782 (2000) (making this observation about stepchildren versus children in nuclear families).

[97] *Id.* (making this observation about stepparent households).

[98] Robin Fretwell Wilson, A Review of *From Partners to Parents: The Second Revolution in Family Law* by June Carbone, 35 Fam. L.Q. 833 (2002).

Hofferth and Anderson examined levels of residential father involvement, comparing children living with biological fathers to children living with nonbiological fathers (stepfathers and mother's cohabitants).[99] They compared investments in children by married, biological fathers, stepfathers (married but nonbiological parents), and mother's cohabitant family (unmarried, nonbiological parents), all of whom resided with the child.[100] Hofferth and Anderson measured "parental involvement" in terms of time children spent actively engaged with their father;[101] weekly hours when the father was available to the child but not actively engaged with the child;[102] number of activities the father participated in with the child in the past month;[103] and "warmth" toward the child, as reported by fathers themselves.[104]

Hofferth and Anderson conclude that the investments fathers make in their children are significantly influenced by biological-relatedness.[105] They confirmed, as initially hypothesized, that children spent significantly more time actively engaged with a married, biological father than with a nonbiological father, whether a stepfather or mother's cohabitant. Specifically, married biological fathers spent 15.63 hours per week engaged with their child, compared to 9.15 hours for stepfathers and 10.10 for mother's cohabitants.[106] Hours available fell off for stepfathers when compared to married biological fathers, but increased for mother's cohabitants: 13.35 hours per week for married biological fathers, 10.94 hours for stepfathers and 17.24 for mother's cohabitants.[107] With regard to activities, children did significantly fewer activities with nonbiological fathers, whether stepfathers or mother's cohabitants. Married biological fathers engaged in 9.13 activities with their biological child over the course of a month, while stepfathers engaged in 8.22 activities and mother's cohabitants engaged in 7.43 activities.[108] Finally, with regard to warmth, biology correlated positively with fathers' own assessment of the warmth they felt toward the children with

[99] Hofferth & Anderson, *supra* note 85, at 223.

[100] *Id.* at 218–19. Hofferth and Anderson used data from the 1997 Child Development Supplement to the Panel Study of Income Dynamics, a 30-year longitudinal survey of a representative sample of United States men, women, children, and the families with whom they resided. The study sample represented 2,522 children who were reported by the primary caregiver to be living with an adult male, "either their biological father, a stepfather who is a nonbiological father married to the mother, or their mother's cohabiting partner." *id.* at 219.

[101] *Id.* This figure was obtained using a time diary of the child's activities, as reported by the child and/or the child's mother, including the question "[w]ho was doing the activity with [the] child?" The diary captured one weekday and one weekend day. Figures for the weekday (multiplied by five) were added to the figure for the weekend day (multiplied by two) to arrive at a weekly figure. *Id.* at 220.

[102] Hofferth & Anderson, *supra* note 85, at 219. This was also accomplished using the time diary, with the additional question, "[w]ho else was there but not directly involved in the activity?" *Id.*

[103] *Id.* at 220. The researchers analyzed thirteen activities: "going to the store; washing or folding clothes; doing dishes; cleaning house; preparing food; looking at books or reading stories; doing arts and crafts; talking about the family; working on homework; building or repairing something; playing computer or video games; playing a board game, card game, or puzzle; and playing sports or outdoor activities." These questions were only asked with respect to children three years and older, with the result that the sample sizes are lowest for this variable. *Id.*

[104] *Id.* The study measured warmth by the father's responses to six items: "how often in the past month the father hugged each child, expressed his love, spent time with child, joked or played with child, talked with child, and told child he appreciated what he or she did." *Id.*

[105] *Id.* at 213 ("Biology explains less of father involvement than anticipated once differences between fathers are controlled.").

[106] *Id.* at 223. Both findings were significant at a high level of confidence, with $p < .001$.

[107] *Id.* at 223 & tbl.3 (reporting significance levels for the stepfather finding of $p < .05$ and for the finding with respect to mother's cohabitants $p < .001$). Hofferth and Anderson surmised that these differences exist between biological and stepfathers because stepchildren may be receiving some or all of that time and attention from a nonresidential biological father, which "makes up for part of the shortfall with residential stepfathers." *Id.* at 223.

[108] *Id.* at 224 & tbl.3. Both findings were significant at a high level of confidence, with $p < .05$.

whom they lived. Self-reports of warmth for married biological fathers, 5.10, were significantly greater than for stepfathers and mother's cohabitants, 4.36 and 3.69, respectively.[109] Clearly, married biological fathers may be investing in their children more heavily than nonbiological fathers for reasons that have nothing to do with biology, but reflect instead wealth, educational levels, or other sociodemographic differences between these groups of men.[110] To evaluate whether these sociodemographic differences accounted for the differences in investment, Hofferth and Anderson controlled for race, father's age, child's gender and age, number of children, percentage of months lived with the father, father's work hours per week and earnings, and whether the father paid child support for children outside the house.[111]

The increased investment in biological children persisted after controlling for socioeconomic factors. Specifically, nonbiological fathers spent over five hours less a week on average with their children than married biological fathers.[112] Differences persisted for the second factor (hours available) only for stepfathers, who were available to the children 4.63 fewer hours than married biological fathers,[113] while stepfathers and mother's cohabitants performed significantly fewer activities with a child than married, biological fathers, 4.35 fewer and 5.79 fewer, respectively.[114]

When it came to warmth, significant differences emerged for mother's cohabitants but not for stepfathers. Mother's cohabitants rated themselves less warm toward their children than married biological fathers did; stepfathers also reported lower warmth scores, although the difference was not statistically significant.[115]

Hofferth and Anderson concluded that, "consistent with evolutionary theory," biology affects a father's level of engagement.[116] They concluded further that "fathers will not invest as much cognitively or emotionally in nonbiological as in biological offspring."[117] They cite several reasons for this difference:[118] (1) that, particularly with regard to stepfathers, expectations are that they will be less involved with children, (2) that, particularly with regard to boyfriends, "parental" behavior toward their partner's child is "so new that norms have not developed to guide nonmarital partners in parenting children,"[119] and (3) that men choosing to enter stepparent relationships may be positively or negatively selected depending on their motivation for becoming a de facto parent.[120] That is, Hofferth and Anderson suggest that nonbiological fathers make investments in children but they do so in part because it gains them favor with the child's mother, or "reproductive access."[121] Thus, the benefits gained by children living with nonbiological fathers may recede or disappear once the relationship between the child's mother and her partner ends. Therefore, Hofferth

[109] *Id.* at 223, tbl.3. Both findings were significant at a high level of confidence, with $p < .001$.

[110] *See generally* Wilson, *supra* note 89, at 854 (discussing differences in wealth, educational attainment, mobility, and other characteristics between married, two biological parent families and families in which a child lives with only one biological parent).

[111] Hofferth & Anderson, *supra* note 85, at 224, 225 tbl.5.

[112] *Id.* at 224, 225 tbl.5 (reporting that stepfathers spent 4.79 hours fewer per month engaged with their child than married biological fathers, $p < .01$, while mother's cohabitants spent 3.60 hours fewer, $p < .05$).

[113] *Id.* at tbl.5 ($p<.01$). Mother's cohabitants were available for slightly more hours every month than married biological fathers, 0.80, but the increase was not statistically significant.

[114] *Id.* at tbl.5 (reporting p values for both findings as $p < .001$).

[115] *Id.* (reporting that mother's cohabitants rated themselves as less warm, − 1.16, with a significance value of $p < .01$; while stepfathers also rated themselves as less warm, − 0.38, but this was not statistically significant).

[116] Hofferth & Anderson, *supra* note 85, at 224.

[117] *Id.* at 229.

[118] *Id.* at 229–30.

[119] *Id.*

[120] *Id.* at 230.

[121] *Id.* at 215.

and Anderson would predict that even if nonbiological fathers perform well in ongoing relationships, their performance may not be as strong when that relationship breaks up.[122]

In sum, these studies suggest that biology produces real differences in investment and outcomes for children. Because the studies used different data sets and comparison groups to isolate the impact of biology, the differences they uncover are surely more than statistical blips. Certainly, selection effects may explain the results in any correlational study.[123] Nonetheless, these studies further an emerging literature on nonbiological caretakers that suggests that, as a group, the gains children realize from living with nongenetic caretakers may not be as great as we would otherwise suppose, and may represent only modest welfare increases over living alone with their mothers.

Some may see this decreased investment by nongenetic caretakers as irrelevant since only adults who meet the equal caretaking criterion qualify under the ALI's standard. Nonetheless, the drafters have not shown that performing equal caretaking functions during an intact relationship necessarily predicts the types of investments after break-up that warrant parental rights.

The differential investment by biological and nonbiological parents is important for another reason as well. The ALI assumes a child will be made better off by any time spent with the Ex Live-In Partner. Like the bundle of sticks that represents one's rights in property, such as the ability to exclude a person from private property, taking a stick from the legal parent's parenting bundle diminishes it. Here, giving time to an Ex Live-In Partner necessarily reduces the time that the biological mother can spend with the child. We should do this as a matter of policy only if we believe that the value of time spent with the Ex Live-In Partner exceeds the value of time spent with the child's mother, or if we believe that the child would get more out of that time if spent with the Ex Live-In Partner, or if spending time with an Ex Live-In Partner is costless and does not detract from the legal parent's time. It is far from clear that any of these assumptions are warranted.

More fundamentally, these studies examine children's welfare and the paternal investments that occur during the adults' intact relationship when, as many commentators have urged, "[i]nvestment in their partner's child may be an important relationship strategy for cohabiting men who wish to have their own children."[124] The ALI proposes to extend parental rights to these nonbiological fathers in the aftermath of failed relationships, a proposal that may actually produce seriously detrimental consequences for some children, as the next part explains.

III. Evidence of Negative Repercussions to Some Children

This part examines the impact of various features of de facto parents, as they are envisioned by the drafters, on a child's risk of physical abuse and sexual violence. It explains that a significant risk of sexual abuse arises in part when unrelated men, not present in a child's life from birth or shortly thereafter, have unsupervised access to a child without the moderating presence of the child's mother.

[122] Although the PRINCIPLES lump stepparents and unmarried live-in partners together, whether a mother and her partner choose to marry matters greatly to the level of investment that he makes in her child. Manning and Lamb and Hofferth and Anderson found "marriage advantages" for marital children over nonmarital children. *See generally* Wilson, *supra* note 89.

[123] *See* Wilson, *supra* note 90.

[124] Hofferth & Anderson, *supra* note 85, at 215.

A. Risk of Sexual Victimization by Ex Live-In Partners

A child's exposure to unrelated men in her home plays a crucial role in determining her vulnerability to sexual victimization. Virtually every study of child sexual abuse reports that girls living with stepfathers are at high risk,[125] leading one researcher to conclude that the presence of a stepfather is "[t]he family feature whose risk has been most dramatically demonstrated."[126] While these studies differ in scope and the strength of their findings, they agree on one essential: the addition of an unrelated male "to a girl's family causes her vulnerability to skyrocket."[127]

In one long-term study, researchers in New Zealand found that children reporting childhood sexual abuse were more likely to live with a stepparent before the age of fifteen.[128] Of those children experiencing intercourse, nearly half (45.4 percent) were raised in a stepparent household.[129] Similarly, Diana Russell found in a community survey of 933

[125] Hilda Parker & Seymour Parker, *Father-Daughter Sexual Abuse: An Emerging Perspective*, 56 Am. J. Orthopsychiatry 531, 541 (1986).

It is not immediately apparent why researchers have found a heightened risk of sexual abuse to girls in non-traditional families, but not for boys. *See, e.g.*, David Finkelhor et al., *Sexual Abuse in a National Survey of Adult Men and Women: Prevalence, Characteristics, and Risk Factors*, 14 Child Abuse & Neglect 19, 24–25 tbl.7 (1990) ("It would seem that almost any long-term disruption of the natural parent situation is risky for girls *but not so for boys.*") (emphasis added); Jean Giles-Sims, *Current Knowledge About Child Abuse in Stepfamilies*, 26 Marriage & Fam. Rev. 215, 227 (1997) ("In summary, most studies of child abuse in stepfamilies indicate higher risks to children, particularly for sexual abuse of girls."). Because the heightened risk of abuse stems, in part, from abuse by Ex Live-In Partner, a disproportionate impact on girls should be expected. Ninety-nine percent of sexual abuse by a parent is perpetrated by fathers or father-substitutes, with the vast majority of these acts directed toward female children. Rebecca M. Bolen, Child Sexual Abuse: Its Scope and Our Failure 120 (2001).

This is not to say that boys are immune from sexual violations at the hands of their mother's partner. Andrea J. Sedlak & Diane D. Broadhurst, U.S. Dep't of Health & Human Services, Third National Incidence Study of Child Abuse and Neglect: Final Report 5 at 6–5, 6–6 tbl.6–2 (1996) (reporting in a 1993 congressionally-mandated study of 5,600 professionals in 842 agencies serving forty-two counties that one-fourth (25 percent) of sexually abused girls *and* boys were victimized by a parent substitute – defined to include in-home adoptive parents and stepparents, as well as parents' paramours). Moreover, as note 19 *supra* explains, the costs for boys of residing with unrelated males often takes the form of child homicide and punishing physical abuse and neglect.

[126] David Finkelhor, *Epidemiological Factors in the Clinical Identification of Child Sexual Abuse*, 17 Child Abuse & Neglect 67, 68 (1993).

[127] David Finkelhor, Sexually Victimized Children 122 (1979) [hereinafter Finkelhor, Sexually Victimized Children] (making the observation about stepfathers); *see also* Joseph H. Beitchman et al., *A Review of the Short-Term Effects of Child Sexual Abuse*, 15 Child Abuse & Neglect 537, 550 (1991) (observing in a review of forty-two separate publications that "[t]he majority of children who were sexually abused ... appeared to have come from single or reconstituted families"); Jocelyn Brown et al., *A Longitudinal Analysis of Risk Factors for Child Maltreatment: Findings of a 17-Year Prospective Study of Officially Recorded and Self-Reported Child Abuse and Neglect*, 22 Child Abuse & Neglect 1065, 1074 (1998) (finding in a longitudinal study of 644 families in upstate New York between 1975 and 1992 that disruption of relationships with biological parents and living in the presence of a stepfather increased girls' risk of sexual abuse); David M. Fergusson et al., *Childhood Sexual Abuse, Adolescent Sexual Behaviors and Sexual Revictimization*, 21 Child Abuse & Neglect 789, 797 (1997) (finding in a longitudinal study of 520 New Zealand born young women that child sexual abuse was associated with living with a stepparent before the age of fifteen); David Finkelhor & Larry Baron, *High-Risk Children*, *in* A Sourcebook on Children Sexual Abuse 60, 79 (David Finkelhor ed., 1986) ("The strongest and most consistent associations across the studies concerned the parents of abused children.... Girls who lived with stepfathers were also at increased risk for abuse."); John M. Leventhal, *Epidemiology of Sexual Abuse of Children: Old Problems, New Directions*, 22 Child Abuse & Neglect 481, 488 (1998) ("Studies have indicated that ... girls living with step-fathers are at an increased risk compared to girls living with biological fathers.... ").

[128] David M. Fergusson et al., *Childhood Sexual Abuse and Psychiatric Disorder in Young Adulthood: I. Prevalence of Sexual Abuse and Factors Associated with Sexual Abuse*, 35 J. Am. Acad. Child Adolescent Psychiatry 1355, 1359 tbl.2 (1996) (reporting results of a longitudinal study of 1,265 children born in Christchurch, New Zealand, who were studied from birth until the age of eighteen).

[129] *See id.* at 1358 tbl.1, 1359 tbl.2.

women in San Francisco that one in six stepdaughters growing up with a stepfather was sexually abused, making these girls over seven times more likely to be sexually victimized than girls living with both biological parents.[130] Indeed, of forty risk factors tested for association with child sexual abuse in an early study, the presence of a stepfather "remained the strongest correlate of victimization, even when all other variables were statistically controlled."[131]

Stepfathers and mother's cohabitants also represent a greater proportion of abusers than their incidence in the general population, suggesting that they are more likely to abuse girls in their care than are biological fathers. In their study of children molested by caretakers, Leslie Margolin and John Craft posited that stepfathers should account for 10.6 percent of all father abuse "[b]ased on the percent of children cared for by nonbiologically related fathers."[132] In fact, "they accounted for [41 percent] of all sexual abuse, or almost [four] times what would be expected based on the percent of children cared for by nonbiologically related fathers."[133] Multiple studies in North America have found similar results.[134] This overrepresentation appears to be an international phenomenon, consistent across

[130] RUSSELL, *supra* note 72, at 255 (1986) (reporting in a study of 930 women in the San Francisco area, that 2% of respondents reared by biological fathers were sexually abused, while "at least [17%] of the women in our sample who were reared by a stepfather were sexually abused by him before the age of fourteen"); *cf.* Parker & Parker, *supra* note 125, at 541 (finding risk of abuse associated with stepfather status to be almost twice as high as for natural fathers). Significantly, the risk of sexual assault by father-substitutes "who are around for short[er] lengths of time... may be considerably higher." RUSSELL, *supra*, at 268.

[131] DAVID FINKELHOR, CHILD SEXUAL ABUSE: NEW THEORY AND RESEARCH 25 (1984).

[132] Margolin & Craft, *supra* note 125, at 452.

[133] *Id.*

[134] *E.g.*, U.S. DEP'T OF HEALTH & HUMAN SERVICES, STUDY FINDINGS: NATIONAL STUDY OF THE INCIDENCE AND SEVERITY OF CHILD ABUSE AND NEGLECT 31 tbl.5–5 (1981) (finding in a stratified random sample of child protective services agencies in twenty-six counties within ten states that stepfathers were involved in 30 percent of the reported sexual abuse cases, while biological fathers were involved in 28 percent of the cases); Hendrika B. Cantwell, *Sexual Abuse of Children in Denver, 1979: Reviewed with Implications for Pediatric Intervention and Possible Prevention*, 5 CHILD ABUSE & NEGLECT 75, 77 tbl.1 (1981) (finding in a study of 226 substantiated cases of child sexual abuse in Denver, Colorado during 1979 that 27.5 percent of children were sexually victimized by a surrogate father, compared to 26.5 percent who were abused by their natural father); Gruber & Jones, *supra* note 127, at 21–22 (finding in a study of delinquent adolescent females that living with a stepfather or foster father "significantly discriminated the victim and nonvictim groups," with 85 percent of sexual abuse victims coming from single or stepparent families compared to 47 percent of psychiatric controls); Robert Pierce & Lois Hauck Pierce, *The Sexually Abused Child: A Comparison of Male and Female Victims*, 9 CHILD ABUSE & NEGLECT 191, 191–93, 194 tbl.2 (1985) (ascertaining from a review of 180 substantiated cases of sexual abuse reported to a child abuse hotline between 1976 and 1979 that 41% of the perpetrators against girls were the child's natural father, while 23 percent were the child's stepfather); Edward Sagarin, *Incest: Problems of Definition and Frequency*, 12 J. SEX RES. 126, 133–34 (1977) (concluding from a study of 75 cases of heterosexual incest involving 32 stepfathers and 34 biological fathers, that "it appears that the likelihood of a stepfather-stepdaughter relationship is far greater than [a] father-daughter [relationship]" because the "number of households in which there is a stepfather and stepdaughter is surely many times lesser than those in which there is a father and daughter"); *cf.* MARY DE YOUNG, THE SEXUAL VICTIMIZATION OF CHILDREN 3, 16 (1982) (finding in a study of eighty incest victims that 39 percent of the incest offenders were stepfathers, leading the author to conclude "that the introduction of a stepfather into a family does increase the possibility that the stepdaughter will become the victim of incest"); Mark D. Everson et al., *Maternal Support Following Disclosure of Incest*, 59 AM. J. ORTHOPSYCHIATRY 198, 198–99 (1989) (noting in a sample of eighty eight children recruited from eleven county social service agencies in North Carolina over a twenty-eight month period to study the effects of maternal support that 30 percent of the perpetrators were biological fathers, 41 percent were stepfathers, and 17 percent were mothers' boyfriends); Elizabeth A. Sirles & Pamela J. Franke, *Factors Influencing Mothers' Reactions to Intrafamily Sexual Abuse*, 13 CHILD ABUSE & NEGLECT 131, 133 & tbl.1 (1989) (finding in a maternal support study of 193 incest victims receiving counseling services in St. Louis, Missouri, that sixty-four children were molested by their father, with an equal number abused by a stepfather or a mother's live-in partner).

cultures.[135] A study of child abuse registers in the United Kingdom found that 46 percent of paternal offenders were nonbirth fathers, compared to 54 percent who were birth fathers.[136] Given the fact that during the study time frame only 4 percent of British children resided with nonbirth fathers, father-substitutes appear "substantially over-represented" among perpetrators.[137] As one researcher concluded, "a stepfather was five times more likely to sexually victimize his stepdaughter than was a genetic father."[138]

In more than one study, stepfathers actually outnumbered natural fathers as abusers, a telling result given the disproportionately greater number of biological fathers during the study time frames.[139] Christopher Bagley and Kathleen King estimate that "as many

[135] Michael Gordon & Susan J. Creighton, *Natal and Non-natal Fathers as Sexual Abusers in the United Kingdom: A Comparative Analysis*, 50 J. Marriage & Fam. 99, 100, 101, 104 (1988) (finding in a review of data collected by the National Society for the Prevention of Cruelty to Children that stepfathers and father substitutes "were disproportionately represented among perpetrators"); Russell P. Dobash et al., *Child Sexual Abusers: Recognition and Response*, *in* Child Abuse and Child Abusers: Protection and Prevention 113, 114–15, 124 fig.6.6, 126 (Lorraine Waterhouse ed., 1993) (finding in a study of fifty-three known perpetrators of child abuse in Scotland that 12.59 percent of child victims lived with their mother and her cohabitant, while 21.16 percent lived with their mother and a stepfather, leading the authors to conclude that "children living with step-fathers and [unrelated] male cohabitees appear to be much more at risk of sexual abuse than children living with both their natural parents"); Patricia J. Mrazek et al., *Sexual Abuse of Children in the United Kingdom*, 7 Child Abuse & Neglect 147, 150 (1983) (noting in a survey of 1,599 family doctors, police surgeons, pediatricians, and child psychiatrists in the United Kingdom that "[w]ithin the family, the natural father was most likely (48%) to be the perpetrator, with stepparents the next most common (28%)"); Heikki Sariola & Antti Uutela, *The Prevalence and Context of Incest Abuse in Finland*, 20 Child Abuse & Neglect 843, 846 (1996) (reporting that 3.7 percent of Finnish girls living with a stepfather reported being sexually abused by him, making stepfather-daughter abuse 15 times more common than father-daughter incest); S. N. Madu & K. Peltzer, *Risk Factors and Child Sexual Abuse Among Secondary School Students in the Northern Province (South Africa)*, 24 Child Abuse & Neglect 259, 260, 266 (2000) (reporting that having a stepparent in the family during childhood significantly predicted risk of child sexual abuse); S. Krugman et al., *Sexual Abuse and Corporal Punishment During Childhood: A Pilot Retrospective Survey of University Students in Costa Rica*, 90 Pediatrics 157, 157–58 (1992) (finding in a study of 497 Costa Rican university students that a stepfather caused 6.3 percent of the female abuse experiences, while natural fathers caused 3.2 percent); R. Chen, *Risk Factors for Sexual Abuse Among College Students in Taiwan*, 11 J. Interpersonal Violence 79, 88, 91 (1996) (discovering that those Taiwanese respondents "who did not live with both parents before college faced a higher risk [of childhood sexual abuse] than those who lived with both parents"); *see also* David Finkelhor, *The International Epidemiology of Child Sexual Abuse*, 18 Child Abuse & Neglect 409, 412 (1994) (reviewing international studies of child sexual abuse and debunking the notion that "the problem is more severe in North America").

[136] Gordon & Creighton, *supra* note 135, at 99, 100, 101, 104 (reviewing data collected by the National Society for the Prevention of Cruelty to Children).

[137] *Id. See also* David Thorpe, Evaluating Child Protection 1, 84, 115 (1994) (finding in a study of social service referrals in the UK and western Australia that parents were responsible for 27.7 percent of the sexual abuse cases; in contrast, stepparents and de facto parents accounted for 24.8 percent of cases); Mrazek et al., *supra* note 135, at 150 (noting in a survey of 1,599 family doctors, police surgeons, pediatricians, and child psychiatrists in the UK that "[w]ithin the family, the natural father was most likely (48%) to be the perpetrator, with stepparents the next most common (28%)"); Susan J. Creighton & Neil Russell, Voices From Childhood: A Survey of Childhood Experiences and Attitudes to Child Rearing Among Adults in the United Kingdom 45 tbl.14 (1995) (reporting that 8 percent of respondents in England, Scotland, and Wales were sexually abused by their fathers, while 7 percent were victimized by a stepfather); Dobash et al, *supra* note 135, at 120 (finding in an analysis of 501 sexual abuse case files taken from Scottish police and child protection agencies that 23 percent of identified abusers were the child's natural father while 23 percent were the victim's stepfather or father substitute).

[138] David Finkelhor, *Risk Factors in the Sexual Victimization of Children*, 4 Child Abuse & Neglect 265, 269 (1980) (reporting results of a study of college undergraduates).

[139] Vincent De Francis, Protecting the Child Victim of Sex Crimes Committed by Adults: Final Report 69 (1969) (finding in a study of 250 sexual abuse cases that the natural father committed the offense in 13 percent of the cases, whereas in 14 percent of cases the offense was committed by a stepfather or by the man with whom the child's mother was living); Gray, *supra* note 134, at 85 fig.4.10 (noting in a study of all cases of molestation filed in eight jurisdictions that 23.3 percent of accused perpetrators were stepfathers and boyfriends, while biological fathers accounted for 13.4 percent); Giles-Sims & Finkelhor, *supra* note 134, at 408 tbl.1 (reporting that 30 percent

as one in four stepfathers may sexually abuse the female children to whom they have access."[140]

Rebecca Bolen's research on multiple risk factors solidifies the connection between sexual victimization and living with unrelated men.[141] She used statistical tools to distinguish the effect of living without both natural parents from other aspects of household composition.[142] When all other variables were held constant, she found "children living with males in the household after separation [of their parents] were more than seven times more likely to be abused" than "children living with only females after separation."[143] In hard numbers, "over half of these children were sexually abused."[144]

Bolen's findings suggest that the heightened risk to girls does not result from the breakup of a traditional nuclear family itself,[145] but "[i]nstead, living with a male in the household after separation . . . appeared to be the more important predictor."[146] As Bolen observes, "for children living with a male in the household, rates of abuse appeared to be better explained by (a) living with a stepfather or (b) being separated from one's natural mother."[147]

B. The Attractiveness of Single Mothers to Sex Offenders Who Target Children

That sex offenders might use adult relationships in order to gain access to child victims is firmly established. One sex offender's "guide" to molesting children begins with finding

of abusers in the study were stepfathers, outnumbering natural father abusers, who constituted 28 percent of the abusers).

140 Christopher Bagley & Kathleen King, Child Sexual Abuse: The Search for Healing 75–6 (1990). The risk of abuse to girls from an Ex Live-In Partner is even greater than these comparisons suggest because these girls "are also more likely than other girls to be victimized by other men." Finkelhor, *supra* note 131, at 25. For example, stepdaughters are five times more likely to be abused by a friend of their parents than are girls in traditional nuclear families. *Id.* Thus, stepfathers "are associated with sexual victimization not just because they themselves take advantage of a girl, but because they increase the likelihood of a nonfamily member also doing so." Finkelhor, Sexually Victimized Children, *supra* note 127, at 130. *See also* Bagley & King, *supra*, at 91 (citing study finding that girls separated from one parent "were also at risk for sexual victimization by more than one adult"). Because the risk of sexual abuse is cumulative, one researcher found that "[v]irtually *half* the girls with stepfathers were victimized by someone." Finkelhor, *supra* note 131, at 25.

141 *See* Rebecca M. Bolen, *Predicting Risk to Be Sexually Abused: A Comparison of Logistic Regression to Event History Analysis*, 3 Child Maltreatment 157 (1998).

142 *Id.* (performing multivariate analyses of data from Diana Russell's survey of 933 adult women in the San Francisco area).

143 *Id.*

144 *Id.* at 163 (reporting that 53 percent were sexually abused).

145 Some may see the risks to children in fractured and blended families as a deficit of their family form (i.e., whether they have two parents). These statistics would not support such an inference – an intact family does not immunize a child from sexual exploitation. *E.g.*, Finkelhor, *supra* note 126, at 68 ("[T]he presence of both natural parents is certainly not an indicator of *low risk* in any absolute sense."); P. E. Mullen et al., *The Long-Term Impact of the Physical, Emotional, and Sexual Abuse of Children: A Community Study*, 20 Child Abuse & Neglect 7, 18 (1996) (conceding that "[i]ntact families do not guarantee stability"). *See generally* Wilson, *supra* note 20.

146 Bolen, *supra* note 141, at 167.

147 *Id.* at 166. While "the addition of a stepfather to a girl's family causes her vulnerability to skyrocket," Finkelhor, Sexually Victimized Children, *supra* note 127, at 122, it is overly simplistic to assume that the mother's remarriage or cohabitation is a necessary predicate to victimization. A girl's long-term separation from her father – a risk factor "strongly associated" with childhood victimization – is sometimes, *but not always*, followed by the introduction of unrelated males into the household. Bagley & King, *supra* note 140, at 91 (reporting results from several research studies).

"some way to get a child living with you."[148] Anna Salter's interviews of sex offenders include a particularly chilling account by a sex offender who deliberately dated women in order to rape their children.[149] These men are not alone in taking this approach. Asked about their modus operandi in selecting victims, seventy-two incarcerated child molesters indicated they deliberately targeted "passive, quiet, troubled, lonely children from broken homes," since these characteristics indicate a child's vulnerability to the offender's advances.[150]

As one child molester explains, by selecting a child "who doesn't have a happy home life," it is "easier to groom them and to gain their confidence."[151] This should come as no surprise. At least for those children who have experienced divorce, the emotional void created by the loss of a parent sometimes opens the child up to the abuser's predations,[152] making them less able to say "no" to unwanted sexual advances.[153] Offenders then simply exploit "a child's normal need to feel loved, valued and cared for."[154] Family fragmentation offers offenders a second advantage as well: it often isolates the child from social supports that existed before the divorce.[155]

This heightened vulnerability may also stem, in part, from a lack of supervision, as single and separated parents navigate the taxing process of parenting alone and rebuilding their lives.[156] Many custodial and single mothers must work outside the home to support their family, diminishing the opportunity to supervise their children.[157] As Judith Wallerstein

[148] *See* Jon R. Conte et al., *What Sexual Offenders Tell Us About Prevention Strategies*, 13 CHILD ABUSE & NEGLECT 293, 298 (1989) (asking sex offenders to describe their methods).

[149] Videotape: *Truth, Lies, and Sex Offenders* (Anna C. Salter 1996) (on file with author).

[150] Lee Eric Budin & Charles Felzen Johnson, *Sex Abuse Prevention Programs: Offenders' Attitudes About Their Efficacy*, 13 CHILD ABUSE & NEGLECT 77, 79, 84 (1989). Similarly, one study of twenty adult sexual offenders in a Seattle, Washington, treatment program found that offenders selected victims based on the child's vulnerability, with vulnerability "defined both in terms of children's status (for example living in a divorced home or being young) and in terms of emotional or psychological state (for example a needy child, a depressed or unhappy child)." Conte et al., *supra* note 148, at 293. For a particularly chilling account by a sex offender who deliberately dated women in order to rape their children, see Videotape: *Truth, Lies, and Sex Offenders* (Anna C. Salter, 1996) (on file with author).

[151] Conte et al., *supra* note 148, at 298. Children in single and reconstituted families are a subset of a broader group of children who are more vulnerable to sexual abuse as a result of family circumstances. For instance, children who live in households marked by domestic violence, drug and alcohol abuse, mental health issues, and other problems all face elevated risks of sexual abuse. *See* BOLEN, *supra* note 125, at 136 tbl.81 (cataloging studies finding parental alcohol and drug abuse as a risk factor for child sexual abuse); Margaret F. Brinig, *Choosing the Lesser Evil: Comments on Besharov's "Child Abuse Realities,"* 8 VA. J. SOC. POL'Y & L. 205 (2000) (discussing empirical evidence showing a relationship between parental substance abuse or domestic violence and the abuse of children).

[152] Lucy Berliner & Jon R. Conte, *The Process of Victimization: The Victims' Perspective*, 14 CHILD ABUSE & NEGLECT 29, 35–36, 38 (1990) (finding in interviews of twenty-three child victims of sexual abuse that "[i]n many cases the sexual abuse relationship filled a significant deficit in the child's life.... The children were troubled and/or their parents were not resources for them.").

[153] *See, e.g.*, Conte et al., *supra* note 148, at 299 (describing ways in which sexual predators "manipulate ... [a child's] vulnerability as a means of gaining sexual access").

[154] Berliner & Conte, *supra* note 152, at 35–36, 38 (interviewing twenty-three child victims of sexual abuse).

[155] *See, e.g,* Sue Boney-McCoy & David Finkelhor, *Is Youth Victimization Related to Trauma Symptoms and Depression After Controlling for Prior Symptoms and Family Relationships?: A Longitudinal, Prospective Study*, 64 J. CONSULTING & CLINICAL PSYCHOL. 1406, 1415 (1996) (finding in a national telephone survey of children that a child's prior symptoms of depression increased a child's risk of later sexual victimization, "perhaps because anxious children are less able to protect themselves and may present easier targets for victimization"); Budin & Johnson, *supra* note 150, at 77, 79 (reporting that child molesters deliberately selected victims who had "no male figures in their lives").

[156] FINKELHOR, SEXUALLY VICTIMIZED CHILDREN, *supra* note 127, at 124 (speculating that the custodial parent's new relationship may take "time and energy and actually mean less supervision of the child than previously").

[157] *See, e.g.*, Saul Hoffman & Greg Duncan, *What Are the Economic Consequences of Divorce?*, 25 DEMOGRAPHY 641, 644 (1988) (showing a decline in economic status of about one-third for women and children after divorce); Ross Finnie, *Women, Men, and the Economic Consequences of Divorce: Evidence from Canadian Longitudinal Data*, 30

has explained, "[i]t's not that parents love their children less or worry less about them [after divorce, but rather that] they are fully engaged in rebuilding their own lives – economically, socially and sexually."[158]

C. Risk of Sexual Abuse when a Child's Mother is Absent

The ALI's efforts to secure continuing contact between children and Ex Live-In Partners after the breakup of the adult relationship is problematic for other reasons, as well. These men will typically have access to the children outside the presence of their mothers.[159] The mere absence of a girl's mother heightens her risk for sexual exploitation.[160] For instance, researchers have compared girls who lived without their mother before the age of sixteen to those who remained with their mother throughout childhood. The sexual vulnerability of the estranged girls was nearly 200 percent greater than that of other girls, leading one researcher to conclude that "missing a mother is the most damaging kind of disruption."[161]

This pattern of a girl's heightened vulnerability in mother-absent households is repeated in multiple studies.[162] In their investigation of father-daughter incest, Judith Herman and Lisa Hirschman found that risk of incest was particularly acute in families in which mothers were absent from the home due to hospitalization or other reasons.[163] Another study found that "[f]or women abused by someone outside of the family, the significant predictors [included] . . . mother's death[] and having an alcoholic mother."[164] The authors speculate that a mother's absence, in the form of her death or mental illness, "may place the child at risk of neglect that involves a lack of supervision."[165] In one of the few longitudinal studies

CANADIAN REV. SOC. & ANTHROPOLOGY 205, 206 (1993) (reporting that the income-to-needs ratio for women drops just over 40 percent in the first year of divorce, followed by a moderate rise in subsequent years); Richard R. Peterson, *A Re-Evaluation of the Economic Consequences of Divorce*, 61 AM. SOC. REV. 528, 528 (1996) (noting one study of women in Los Angeles that estimated that women's standard of living declined 73 percent after divorce).

158 WALLERSTEIN ET AL., *supra* note 6, at xxix.

159 *See* FINKELHOR, SEXUALLY VICTIMIZED CHILDREN, *supra* note 127, at 124 (noting that for many mothers divorce necessitates working outside the home to support their families, diminishing the time and attention previously showered on their children); WALLERSTEIN ET AL., *supra* note 6, at xxix (that the presence of a new man in a mother's life takes up time and energy previously shown to the children).

160 Most studies analyzing the "mother-absent" factor have examined situations in which the mother was absent for prolonged and sustained periods for time, due to health, mental illness, or death. The risk remains particularly acute in reconstituted families because the child's mother will be absent for certain periods of time and will rely on a nongenetic caretaker for supervision of the children, therefore magnifying the established baseline risk of having such an individual in the child's life by giving him access to that child outside her presence.

161 FINKELHOR, SEXUALLY VICTIMIZED CHILDREN, *supra* note 127, at 121.

162 *See, e.g.*, RUSSELL, *supra* note 72, at 363 (enumerating studies that have "shown that many mothers of incest victims are sick, absent, or in powerless or abusive situations themselves"); Alexander, *supra* note 127, at 185 (citing research documenting that maternal unavailability is among the "most significant predictors for increased risk for all kinds of sexual abuse"); Michael Gordon, *The Family Environment of Sexual Abuse: A Comparison of Natal and Stepfather Abuse*, 13 CHILD ABUSE & NEGLECT 121, 128 (1989) (noting that "a girl whose mother is absent or passive is more vulnerable to abuse than a girl whose mother is present and active"); Mullen et al., *supra* note 145, at 18 (concluding that "having a close and confiding relationship with the mother seemed to confer a degree of protection").

163 *See* Herman & Hirschman, *supra* note 125, at 968. Herman and Hirschman found that "[m]others in the incestuous families were more often described as ill or disabled and were more often absent for some period of time." *Id.* Specifically, "[f]ifty percent of the women in the incest group but only [15 percent] of the comparison group reported that their mothers had been seriously ill." *Id.* With regard to maternal absence, 38 percent of the women in the incest group reported separation from their mothers for some period of time during childhood, while none of the comparison group had been estranged from their mothers. *Id.*

164 Jillian Fleming et al., *A Study of Potential Risk Factors for Sexual Abuse in Childhood*, 21 CHILD ABUSE & NEGLECT 49, 50, 55 (1997) (enumerating factors possibly associated with childhood sexual abuse, including "living apart from their mother at some time during their childhood").

165 *Id.* at 56.

of a general population, David Fergusson and his colleagues followed 1,265 children from birth until the age of sixteen.[166] They found that 66.5 percent of the victims of sexual abuse came from families that "experience[d] at least one change of parents before age 15," compared to 33.5 percent of children who did not experience abuse.[167] The only national survey in the United States to examine risk factors for child sexual assault at the time found higher rates of abuse among women who reported living for some period of time without one of their biological parents.[168] At least a dozen other studies confirm that sexual victimization occurs more often in disrupted families.[169] Those studies estimating

[166] Fergusson, *supra* note 128, at 1356 (following a cohort of children born in Christchurch, New Zealand in 1977 and asking them at age eighteen to provide retrospective reports of molestation experiences during childhood). *See, e.g.*, Bagley & King, *supra* note 140, at 90 ("It is not typical for sexual abuse to occur independently of other aspects of family dysfunction. It occurs with greater frequency in homes disrupted by parental absence or separation ..."); Alexander, *supra* note 127, at 185 ("[C]ertain family characteristics are the most significant predictors for increased risk for all kinds of child sexual abuse, [including] absence of a biological parent."); Christopher Bagley & Richard Ramsey, *Sexual Abuse in Childhood: Psychosocial Outcomes and Implications for Social Work Practice, in* Social Work Practice in Sexual Problems 42 (James Gripton & Mary Valentich eds., 1986) (stating that molestation "occurs with greater frequency in homes which are disrupted by the child's separation from one or both parents," but cautioning that "sexual abuse is not[,] in statistical terms, a direct function of family variables"); Brown et al., *supra* note 127, at 1075 (finding in a study of 644 families in upstate New York surveyed on four occasions between 1975 and 1992 that disruption in a child's relationship with her biological parent increases her risk of sexual abuse); Ann W. Burgess et al., *Abused to Abuser: Antecedents of Socially Deviant Behaviors*, 144 Am. J. Psychiatry 1431, 1433 (1987) (finding in follow-up studies of two groups of adolescents who participated in sex rings as children, that 70 percent of adolescents who participated in the sex rings for more than one year were from single-parent families, compared to 47 percent of the adolescents who were involved for less than a year); Fergusson et al., *supra* note 127, at 797 (finding in a longitudinal study of 520 New Zealand-born children that "[y]oung women who reported [child sexual abuse] were more likely [than nonabused children] to have experienced at least one change of parents before the age of [fifteen]"); David Finkelhor, *Current Information on the Scope and Nature of Child Sexual Abuse*, Future of Child., Summer/Fall 1994, at 31, 48 ("In many studies ... children who lived for extended periods of time apart from one parent have been found to bear elevated risks for sexual abuse."); Finkelhor, *supra* note 126, at 68 (concluding that "[i]n general, children who are living without one or both of their natural parents are at greater risk for abuse"); Giles-Sims, *supra* note 125, at 218 (noting that the "sexual abuse literature is more consistent ... in finding that children not living with both natural parents run higher risks of child sexual abuse both from family members and others, but the exact magnitude of reported risk varies across studies"); Parker & Parker, *supra* note 125, at 532 ("Reconstituted families, stepparent and broken families, with mother's male companions in the home, seem to be vulnerable."); Anne E. Stern et al., *Self Esteem, Depression, Behaviour and Family Functioning in Sexually Abused Children*, 36 J. Child. Psychol. & Psychiatry & Allied Disciplines 1077, 1080 & 1081 tbl.1 (1995) (finding in a comparison of eighty-four sexually abused children and their families to nonabused controls that the abused group had more marital breakdown and change of parents than the nonabused group).

[167] *Id.* at 1359 tbl.2. Fergusson reports, moreover, that 60 percent of children who experienced intercourse as part of the abuse experience had been exposed to parental divorce or separation. *Id.* However, in a regression analysis, investigators found that five factors – gender, marital conflict, parental attachment, parental overprotection, and parental alcoholism – were predictive of reported abuse. *Id.* at 1360 & 1360 tbl.3.

[168] Finkelhor et al., *supra* note 125, at 24 (finding in a national survey of 2626 adult men and women that separation from a natural parent for a major portion of one's childhood is a risk factor for sexual victimization).

[169] *E.g.*, De Francis, *supra* note 139, at 50 (finding in a study of 250 sexual abuse cases that in 60 percent of the families, the children's natural father or natural mother was not in the home – "an extraordinary high incidence of broken homes"); Russell, *supra* note 72, at 103, 104 tbl.8–1 (revealing that "women who were reared by both of their biological or adoptive parents were the least likely to be incestuously abused"); S. Kirson Weinberg, Incest Behavior 49 (1955) (finding in a study of 203 incest cases in the State of Illinois that 40.3 percent of the fathers were widowed or separated from their wives at the start of incestuous relationships with their daughters); Raymond M. Bergner et al., *Finkelhor's Risk Factor Checklist: A Cross-Validation Study*, 18 Child Abuse & Neglect 331, 334 (1994). (finding that "separation from mother during some period" discriminated between abused and nonabused subjects in a study of 411 female college students); Bolen, *supra* note 141, at 157, 164 (finding in a multivariate analysis of Diana Russell's survey data on 933 adult women in the San Francisco area that "[r]espondents living with both natural parents prior to the age of fourteen had the lowest rates of abuse"); Finkelhor & Baron, *supra* note 127, at 60, 73, 79 (noting the "impressive number of studies with positive findings on the question of parental absence" and concluding that "[t]he strongest and most consistent associations across the studies concerned the parents of abused children," and that "[g]irls who are victimized are ... more likely to have lived without their

the incidence of sexual abuse find that as many as half the girls in fractured families report sexual abuse as a child.[170]

Although we have scant research on the risks to girls in father-custody households,[171] what is available underscores the significance of a mother's absence, both temporary and long term. One national survey in the United States found significantly elevated risk of molestation for girls following divorce, "particularly when living alone with [their] father."[172] In that study, 50 percent of female children residing solely with their father reported sexual abuse by someone, although not necessarily their father.[173] Similarly, a 1995 poll of parents about child maltreatment found an annual rate of child sexual abuse for boys and girls in single-father households equal to forty-six victims per one thousand children.[174] In comparison, parents in two-parent households reported a rate of eleven victims per one thousand children.[175]

It is unclear how much weight should be given to the studies of mothers' absence since under the ALI's proposal, a child's legal parent would be presumptively entitled to half the custodial responsibility for a child. In one sense, the mother remains present

natural fathers"); Kenneth J. Gruber & Robert J. Jones, *Identifying Determinants of Risk of Sexual Victimization of Youth: A Multivariate Approach,* 7 CHILD ABUSE & NEGLECT 17, 21 tbl. 2 1983) (discovering in a sample of delinquent adolescent females in Western North Carolina that victims of child sexual assault were less likely to be living with both natural parents – 15 percent of the abused children lived with both natural parents while 52 percent of nonabused children did so); Marcellina Mian et al., *Review of 125 Children 6 Years of Age and Under Who Were Sexually Abused,* 10 CHILD ABUSE & NEGLECT 223, 227 (1986) (finding that 67 percent of the victims of intrafamilial abuse came from families in which parents had separated or divorced, compared to 27 percent of the children abused by perpetrators outside of the family); Mullen et al., *supra* note 145, at 8–9, 18 (reporting, in a study of 2,250 randomly selected adult women in New Zealand, that sexual, physical, and emotional abuse "occurred more often in those from disturbed and disrupted home backgrounds"); Nancy D. Vogeltanz et al., *Prevalence and Risk Factors for Childhood Sexual Abuse in Women: National Survey Findings,* 23 CHILD ABUSE & NEGLECT 579, 586 (1999) (finding, after using statistical analysis to unravel the effects of multiple risk factors, that not living with both biological parents by the age of sixteen ranked among those factors "significantly associated with increased risk of [child sexual abuse]"); Patricia Y. Miller, Blaming the Victim of Child Molestation: An Empirical Analysis (1976) (unpublished Ph.D. dissertation, Northwestern University) (on file with author) (discovering that biological father's absence "directly influence[d] molestation" and constituted the "variable [with] the largest direct effects on . . . victimization"); *cf.* Kristin Anderson Moore et al., *Nonvoluntary Sexual Activity Among Adolescents,* 21 FAM. PLAN. PERSP. 110, 113 tbl.3 (1989) (ascertaining in a study of white female adolescents that having parents who are "separated, divorced or never-married" doubles the likelihood of sexual abuse, although the association was not significant when other factors were controlled).

170 *E.g.,* FINKELHOR, SEXUALLY VICTIMIZED CHILDREN, *supra* note 127, at 125 (discovering that 58 percent of the girls who at some time before the age of sixteen had lived without their mothers had been sexually victimized, three times the rate for the whole sample, making these girls "highly vulnerable to sexual victimization"); Bagley & Ramsey, *supra* note 166, at 37 & 38–39 tbl.1 (reporting that 53 percent of women separated from a parent during childhood reported sexual abuse).

171 The absence until recently in child sexual abuse studies of "raised by father only" and "raised by father and stepmother" categories reflects the historical preference for maternal custody. *See, e.g.,* HOMER H. CLARK, JR., THE LAW OF DOMESTIC RELATIONS IN THE UNITED STATES § 19–4, at 803 (2d ed. 1988).

172 Finkelhor et al., *supra* note 125, at 24–25, tbl.7. *See also* Giacomo Canepa & Tullio Bandini, *Incest and Family Dynamics: A Clinical Study,* 3 INT'L J. L. & PSYCHIATRY 453, 459 (1980) (discussing the recurrence of several factors in nine case histories of father–daughter incest, with a stepmother's presence occurring in two of the nine case histories).

173 *See* Finkelhor et al., *supra* note 125, at 25 tbl.7.

174 *See* GALLUP ORG., DISCIPLINING CHILDREN IN AMERICA: A GALLUP POLL REPORT 16 (1995) (reporting results of poll of 1,000 parents); *see also* Desmond K. Runyan, *Prevalence, Risk, Sensitivity, and Specificity: A Commentary on the Epidemiology of Child Sexual Abuse and the Development of a Research Agenda,* 22 CHILD ABUSE & NEGLECT 493, 495 (1998) (observing that "[a]n obvious area of research is to sort out the additional risk [for male and female children of] being victimized in single parent households and why the rate is higher in male-headed households").

175 GALLUP ORG., *supra* note 174, at 16.

because the child returns home after visits with the de facto parent. In another sense, however, the mother is absent for those periods when the child is in the custody of the de facto parent, away from the mother's watchful, discerning eyes. There are good reasons, moreover, to avoid contexts that permit illicit desires to gain ground and manifest themselves. Many abused children never disclose the abuse; many outwardly display no telltale symptoms.[176] In fact, the abuse most likely to remain shrouded in secrecy often occurs at the hands of a father figure,[177] while violations by father figures are among the most depraved.[178]

D. Risks to Children Who Have Not Resided with an Adult from Infancy

Children also face a disproportionate risk from adults who have not resided with them from infancy, whether those adults have a biological connection to the child or not. Child abuse researchers have always been perplexed by runaway rates of incest in Navy families, an obvious conundrum for those who believe that a biological tether insulates a child from sexual exploitation. In a comparison of paternal caretaking among 118 incestuous fathers and 116 closely matched nonincestuous fathers, Williams and Finkelhor found that incestuous fathers were significantly less likely to have been in the home or involved in child-care activities during the child's first three years of life.[179] They concluded that involvement in non-bodily caretaking activities, like reading stories, during the first three to six years of a child's life serves to inhibit incest to the greatest degree.[180] While early care giving inhibits incest, it does not do so by inhibiting sexual arousal.[181] Rather, the inhibitory effect stems from the enhancement of parental impulses, developed when the child is very young, that allow the adult to view the child as his own.[182] Thus, the Residency Requirement may be protective if residency were required during a child's infancy but is not a be-all-and-end-all itself.

While high involvement in care giving during a child's early years is protective against incest, "being the sole care-giver for a daughter for at least 30 consecutive days was [also]

[176] Mian et al. found that the rate of purposeful (as opposed to unintentional) disclosure by the child decreased significantly when the perpetrator was intrafamilial. Mian et al., *supra* note 169, at 226 tbl.5. In fact, a greater proportion of children victimized by family never tell (17.7%) than occurs with children who are the victims of extrafamilial abuse (10.9%). *See* Donald G. Fischer & Wendy L. McDonald, *Characteristics of Intrafamilial and Extrafamilial Child Sexual Abuse*, 22 Child Abuse & Neglect 915, 926 (1998).

Physical manifestations one might expect are also frequently absent. A third of sexually abused children have no apparent symptoms. K. A. Kendall-Tackett et al., *Impact of Sexual Abuse on Children: A Review and Synthesis of Recent Empirical Studies*, 113 Psychol. Bull. 164, 167 (1993). Roughly half fail to display the classic, most characteristic symptom of child sexual abuse: "sexualized" behavior. *Id.*

[177] "The more severe cases [are] the ones most likely to remain secret." Russell, *supra* note 72, at 373. Russell reports that in 72 percent of the cases in which mothers were unaware of the abuse, more severe abuse had occurred. *Id.* at 372.

[178] Abuse by father-figures occurs with greater frequency, over a longer time frame, and is more likely to include penetration, physical contact, force, and threats of force than abuse by others, surpassing the "norm" for child sexual abuse. *See* Robin Fretwell Wilson, *Children at Risk: The Sexual Exploitation of Female Children After Divorce*, 86 Cornell L. Rev. 251, 274–77 (2001).

[179] Linda Williams & David Finkelhor, *Parental Caregiving and Incest: Test of a Biosocial Model*, 65 Am. J. Orthopsychiatry 101, 102, 107 (1995) (comparing parental involvement for two groups of incestuous fathers, one recruited from the U.S. Navy and one recruited from civilian sources, with a closely matched group of control fathers).

[180] *Id.* at 109.

[181] *Id.* at 111.

[182] *Id.* (noting that early involvement in non-bodily caretaking reinforces positive parenting skills and attitudes in fathers, creating nurturing parental responses).

found to increase the risk of later [father-daughter] incestuous abuse."[183] This is so because many incestuous fathers engage in high levels of caretaking as part of their efforts to "groom" the child. Intensive caretaking creates the conditions – time alone, unusual dependence, and the child's acceptance of intimate physical touch – that allow and encourage the child's tolerance of later sexual contact.[184]

In many ways, the presence of caretaking among the most bonded parents, and the least – those who seek to exploit a child sexually – is a lot like the classic antitrust problem in which two gas stations operate directly across from each other, charging the same price for gasoline. The fact of an identical price is consistent with either collusion or perfect competition.[185] The problem is that price alone cannot tell us which of the two, collusion or competition, is operating. Likewise, the fact of caretaking does little to discern the adult's motivation and commitment to parenting. And unfortunately, the fate of a vulnerable child hangs in the balance.

Unlike many parents by estoppel, de facto parents do not believe that they were the child's biological father for a significant period of time after the child's birth. In the classic parent by estoppel case, the deceit serves the useful purpose of allowing the "parent" to bond with the child as if the child was his own biological child. Blossoming during this time are those mechanisms that dissuade most men from harming their "own."[186]

E. Continuing Contact Is Not an Unqualified Good to Children

Clearly, the risk factors for child sexual abuse are complex and interlinked. Despite this complexity, what we do know is that coresidence with an unrelated male and separation from one or both biological parents matter greatly to a child's risk of sexual abuse. We also know that the inability to bond with a child at birth, or shortly thereafter, elevates a child's later risk of incest with the biological father or father-substitute. Finally, a mother's protective presence mitigates this risk.

Under the PRINCIPLES, not a single one of these mechanisms, which are known to protect a child from abuse, is necessarily present with de facto parents. An Ex Live-In Partner gains time with the child without the moderating presence of the child's mother; without the protection afforded by a biological or adoptive tie; without necessarily having bonded with the child at a young age; and without any guarantee that the adult is properly attached to the child and the child is attached to him. In short, the test for de facto parenthood brings none of these protective measures to bear on behalf of the children being laid claim to.

While the incest mechanism is complex and difficult to tease out, we do understand the long-term social, psychological, and economic effects of sexual abuse and exploitation to children. By advocating for rights that do not presently exist, the drafters are gambling with the lives of those children. The stakes are high. Sexual abuse at the hands of a parent

[183] *Id.* at 103, 108.

[184] *Id.* at 110; *see also* John R. Christiansen & Reed H. Blake, *The Grooming Process in Father-Daughter Incest, in* THE INCEST PERPETRATOR: A FAMILY MEMBER NO ONE WANTS TO TREAT 88, 91–92 (Anne L. Horton et al. eds., 1990) (noting that pedophiles within the home use "boundary violations" – bathing, dressing, and bathroom behavior – in "grooming" their daughters to participate in sexual activities, as acts of incest within the home overwhelmingly use coercion and not outright force).

[185] *See* Donald F. Turner, *The Definition of Agreement Under the Sherman Act: Conscious Parallelism and Refusals to Deal,* 75 HARV. L. REV. 655, 659 (1962).

[186] Presumably, the benefits of this bonding carry forward even after the deceit is exposed.

figure has devastating, corrosive effects on the child well into adulthood.[187] The harsh consequences to child victims counsel against expanding parental rights without additional safeguards.[188]

IV. The ALI's Test for De Facto Parents Does Not Separate the Good Risks from the Bad

Importantly, the test developed by the drafters to decide who counts as a de facto parent is poorly designed to exclude those individuals who pose the most significant risks. The very same conduct that would delight most women about their partner's interest in and interaction with her children, is also used to garner her trust and that of her child. Of the drafters' sixteen illustrative caretaking functions, eight overlap with and mirror those behaviors pedophiles engage in when "grooming" child victims, as Table 5.1 demonstrates. Child molesters read to children, child molesters bathe children, child molesters dress children, child molesters discipline children, child molesters shower children with attention and gifts.

Clearly, we are looking for the wrong things here, at least if we are concerned about mitigating the possibility of this risk for children. Instead of looking for time-in-residence as a proxy for the bonded, dependent relationship, the PRINCIPLES should look for that relationship itself. Admittedly, this inquiry would be less administrable, and involve greater cost, but it would more meaningfully respond to the risks this new entitlement poses for its intended beneficiaries.

Wisconsin allows a court to award visitation, but not custody, to individuals who formed "a relationship similar to a parent-child relationship[s] with [a] child."[189] In this formulation, what matters is whether the *raison d'etre* for awarding visitation is present: a bonded, dependent relationship that is parental in nature. Likewise, Oregon grants rights to "a person who establishes emotional ties creating child-parent relationship or ongoing personal relationship" with a child.[190]

V. Can the ALI's Test Be Refined to Minimize Harms while Preserving the Goods?

In any revised test for de facto parent, attachment should figure more prominently. If the child is improperly attached to the adult, then the benefits of continuing contact to the child will be small, and the risks will be high. Rather than using disproportionate attachment only as grounds for departure from the past caretaking standard, as the ALI does, attachment could be used to decide who has standing to seek time with the child after the adults'

[187] *See* Joseph H. Beitchman et al., *A Review of the Long-Term Effects of Child Sexual Abuse*, 16 CHILD ABUSE & NEGLECT 101 (1992) (describing the impact of child sexual abuse on its victims).

[188] Legal parents should retain the prerogative to decide who has unsupervised access to their children even when no indication of risk is present at break up. Even if the mother's ex-partner never previously touched the child, he may do so when the child is outside the mother's discerning view.

Handing out parental rights to an Ex Live-In Partner ties the mother's hands in important ways. Consider the mother who ends a relationship because she suspects her partner might abuse her child in the future and who, acting on this concern, subsequently denies him access. Prior to the onset of actual abuse, she probably could not substantiate her concerns and even if she could, the concern may not rise to the level of abuse, as defined in state law. PRINCIPLES § 2.03(7). But he could prove her denial of visitation, which could then be used against her under Section 2.11(1)(d), and ultimately give him even greater access to her child as a result.

[189] WIS. STAT. ANN. § 767.245 (West 2001).

[190] OR. REV. STAT. § 109.119 (2003).

Table 5.1. *ALI caretaking functions and grooming of child victims: a comparison*

ALI Caretaking Functions	Grooming Behaviors
Grooming[1]	Bathing[3,4]
Washing[1]	Bathing[3,4]
Dressing[1]	Dressing[3,4]
Toilet Training[1]	Bathroom Behavior[3]
Playing with child[1]	Attention[2,3,6] Affection[2,6]
Bedtime and Wakeup[1]	Being around child at bedtime[6]
Satisfying Nutrition Needs[1]	
Protecting child's safety[1]	
Providing transportation[1]	
Directing development[1]	
Discipline[1]	Discipline[6]
Arranging for education[1]	
Helping to develop relations[1]	
Arranging for health care[1]	
Providing moral guidance[1]	Assure child of rightness;[3] telling child that acts would not hurt them[3]
Arranging alternate care for child[1]	
	Bribes[2,3,5,6]
	Trust[2,3,6]
	Alienating child from peers and family[3,6]
	Secrecy[3,4,6]
	Sexually Explicit and Vulgar Conversation[3,6]

Sources:
[1] PRINCIPLES § 2.03 cmt. g., at 125.
[2] DAVID FINKELHOR, CHILD SEXUAL ABUSE: NEW THEORY AND RESEARCH (1984).
[3] John R. Christiansen & Reed H. Blake, *The Grooming Process in Father-Daughter Incest, in* THE INCEST PERPETRATOR: A FAMILY MEMBER NO ONE WANTS TO TREAT (Anne L. Horton et al. eds., 1990).
[4] Patricia Bell, *Factors Contributing to a Mother's Ability to Recognise Incestuous Abuse of Her Child*, 25 WOMEN'S STUD. INT'L F. 347 (2002).
[5] Jon R. Conte, *The Nature of Sexual Offenses Against Children, in* CLINICAL APPROACHES TO SEX OFFENDERS AND THEIR VICTIMS (Clive R. Hollin & Kevin Howells eds., 1991).
[6] Jon R. Conte et al., *What Sexual Offenders Tell Us About Prevention Strategies*, 13 CHILD ABUSE & NEGLECT 293 (1989).

breakup. If used in this way, an Ex Live-In Partner would not have standing at all unless he was the psychological parent. This is the approach taken in *V.C. v. M.J.B*, in which the court concluded that the psychological parent of the child had standing to proceed in a custody case.[191] The psychological parent-child bond arguably is a more effective sorting mechanism than time in residence as an equal caretaker. Including a "psychological parent" requirement would remove many men who pose risks, while perhaps allowing continuing contact only with those men with whom a child would benefit, on balance. However states choose to define de facto parents, it should "surely be limited to those adults who have fully and completely undertaken a permanent, unequivocal, committed, and responsible parental role in the child's life."[192] These are the relationships that should be preserved and continued.

Alternatively, the PRINCIPLES could give courts the discretion to allow nonparents to go forward when they deem it is in the best interests of the child, as occurs with

[191] 748 A.2d 539 (N.J. 2000).
[192] C.E.W. v. D.E.W., 845 A.2d 1146, 1152 (Me. 2004).

intervention.[193] At least this would be an individual-specific inquiry, rather than the conferral of possible rights wholesale on Ex Live-In Partners. Or, like the drafters' treatment of intervention by third parties in Section 2.04(2), de facto parents could be given the ability to intervene in pending actions, but not the right to initiate actions unilaterally.

The ALI's proposal raises not just a question of who counts. It also raises questions about what they should receive. The ALI's proposal ratchets up the "rights" of de facto parents, via the past caretaking standard, entitling them to as much as an equal share of custody since they performed equal caretaking. While a real 50/50 split is impracticable, the use of the past caretaking standard would permit courts to award Ex Live-In Partners much more unsupervised time than de facto parents presently receive in most states.

Obviously, one problem with any approach is underinclusiveness: removing too many good men from the tent of "de facto parenthood." Yet even these good men would have some recourse – they could file a complaint for custody under the traditional third-party custody standard, which generally requires exceptional circumstances or unfitness of the legal parent.[194] Or they could secure a voluntary agreement after the breakup with the legal parent.[195] With the latter, of course, the question becomes how many good men will be unable to secure an agreement with the child's mother. If the relationship between the child and the mother's ex-partner is good for the child, we can expect lots of mothers will want to preserve that relationship.

It is certainly true that many of the de facto parent cases are very sympathetic and raise claims that require a response, both out of fairness to the adult and out of concern for the child – for instance, those cases in which the de facto parent survives the child's legal parent and is willing to continue caring for a child after the death but is challenged in this by a biological father who has been largely absent or by a more distant relative. In this instance, a continuing relationship with the de facto parent may shield the child from even greater dislocation following the parent's death and may be a source of comfort and continuity. Moreover, the de facto parent and mother may have had a biological child in common, so that removing the mother's child from the de facto parent's care jeopardizes that child's relationship with his or her siblings. Indeed, the de facto parent may well represent the best adult available to care for this child. Preserving this relationship is very different, however, from providing continuing contact with a mother's ex-partner outside her supervision and over her veto, while carving into the time that she spends with the child. States are always free to address the claims of adults in only the most compelling cases, without diluting the value of these reforms by reaching cases in which it is far less clear how children will fare.

VI. Conclusion

By sleight of hand, designating more and more adults as "parents" to whom custodial responsibility may be given, the ALI glosses over significant differences in the protective capacities of legal parents and other caretakers – as well as their desires to exploit children.

[193] *See* PRINCIPLES § 2.04, Reporter's Notes, cmt. g, at 142 (noting that courts in some states "have considerable discretion to allow nonparents to intervene in custody disputes"); *Id.* § 2.04 cmt. a, at 135 (allowing individuals to intervene whose participation, the court finds, "is likely to serve the child's best interests").

[194] *See generally* Murphy, *supra* note 61.

[195] PRINCIPLES § 2.05 cmt. f, at 150 (noting that separating adults are "free to settle any issues they wish on their own").

The drafters see continuing contact between de facto parents and the children of their former partners as a good in itself, or a net good.

Only when we consider the evidence of possible harms to children do we realize how irresponsible it is – without sound evidence or additional safeguards – to cling to the ideal of "neutrality toward diverse lifestyles"[196] and to confer parent-like rights upon the adults involved. Some of these adults may well be good risks, as legal parents are.[197] Others may not.

Obviously, concerns about sexual and physical abuse should not overwhelm other values. Nonetheless, the sorts of concerns raised here should be included in any cost-benefit analysis of promoting continuing contact between children and Ex Live-In Partners. Legislators should evaluate, for example, what portion of the adults who seek to continue their relationship with children do so for malign reasons, and what portion for benign ones. They should also ask how much better off some children would be, and weigh this against how much worse off others would become. Unfortunately, the ALI has not done this important work in the PRINCIPLES for legislators and policymakers.

We have not had gleaming results thus far from our grand social experiment in redesigning the family. Now, arguably, we do not bear collective responsibility for those consequences we could never have anticipated.[198] But we can and will be judged for putting into motion changes that we should reasonably expect will make some children worse off, and profoundly so. We should institute such reform only if we think the ALI has met its burden of proof – namely, that the gains far exceed the costs.[199] The ALI has not convincingly demonstrated that extending parental rights to every Ex Live-In Partner who shares caretaking duties for a child for as little as two years would benefit children more than it harms them.

An earlier version of this chapter was presented at the October 2004 Workshop, "Critical Reflections on the American Law Institute's *Principles of the Law of Family Dissolution*," held at the Harvard Law School and to 12th World Conference of the International Society of Family Law. I am indebted to the Workshop and ISFL participants, to an anonymous outside reviewer, and to Jane Murphy, John Lopatka, and Pamela Melton for comments on an earlier draft, as well as to Michael Clisham for his diligent and cheerful research assistance.

[196] Glendon, *supra* note 6, at 3.

[197] The drafters repeatedly pay homage to the ability of legal parents to safeguard children. For instance, they explain their use of parenting plans as "locat[ing] responsibility for the welfare of the child in the first instance in parents rather than in courts." PRINCIPLES § 2.05 cmt. a, at 145.

[198] For example, we presumably could not have discovered, ex ante, the link between the breakup of the parental relationship and instability in a child's own relationships as an adult. *See, e.g.*, WALLERSTEIN ET AL., *supra* note 6 (showing that children of divorced parents have marriages that dissolve at higher rates than children whose parents did not divorce).

[199] As the Maine Supreme Court said in *Merchant v. Bussell*, 27 A.2d 816, 818 (Me. 1942). "The natural right of a parent to the care and control of a child should be limited only for the most urgent reasons."

PART THREE. CHILD SUPPORT

6 Asymmetric Parenthood

Katharine K. Baker

What is it that makes someone financially responsible for a child? Surprisingly, this is a remarkably difficult question for the law or common consensus to answer. There are certainly some situations in which it is relatively easy to decide that someone should be responsible for a child. These usually occur in the context of what is, in the United States a normative ideal: A man and woman, married to each other, who had reproductive sex with each other in order to produce and raise a child, and who proceed to do so.[1] This chapter refers to this norm as the binary biological ideal. Society's allegiance to this ideal is so strong that it acts as the model for child support obligations, despite the fact that well over half of the children in this country do not spend their childhood in such families.[2] Given that reality, it is not obvious that the law should continue to use this model in all situations. The more varied and diverse the reality of parenthood becomes, the more policymakers need to understand why it is that certain people have obligations to children while others do not.

The drafters of the PRINCIPLES seem remarkably uninterested in explaining why someone should be financially responsible for a child. This lack of analysis contrasts, quite sharply, with the drafters' interest in exploring why someone might have custodial rights to a child.[3] The different treatment of nontraditional parents' rights and obligations presents an obvious asymmetry in the drafters' picture of parenthood.

Part I of this chapter explores the different treatment of rights and obligations. It contrasts how chapter 2 of the PRINCIPLES bestows custody and visitation rights with how chapter 3 imposes child support obligations. Put simply, the PRINCIPLES significantly expand the class of people entitled to parental rights; while barely altering the traditional rules regarding who should be responsible for children. Part II analyzes the implications of those differences. First, it shows how the binary biological ideal rejected in the PRINCIPLES' custody provisions is deeply embedded in its child support provisions, both in determining who is obligated and in determining how much an obligated parent owes. That is, the child support provisions not only limit parenthood to two people, they treat as irrelevant all

[1] This seemingly detailed and dry description of the binary biological ideal is necessary. As this chapter shows, how a child's conception happened matters greatly, especially with respect to whether the parties were married, whether they intended to produce a child, and whether they willingly accepted parental responsibility.

[2] SARA MCLANAHAN & GARY SANDEFUR, GROWING UP WITH A SINGLE PARENT: WHAT HELPS, WHAT HURTS 2 (1994) ("Well over half of all children born in 1992 will spend all or some of their childhood apart from one of their parents."). There have not been significant enough changes in either the divorce rate or the rate of children born to unmarried parents to suggest that the numbers today are any different than they were in 1992. U.S. Dept. of the Census, Population and Family Characteristics: March 2002 (2003).

[3] *Compare* PRINCIPLES, ch. 2 (discussing custody) *with* PRINCIPLES, ch. 3 (discussing child support).

functional aspects of parenthood.[4] Functional relationship does not give rise to obligation; and the obligation the PRINCIPLES impose is based on what is often an entirely hypothetical idea, that the two legal parents actually lived together and shared resources. Second, the PRINCIPLES' expansion of the custody and visitation rights of nontraditional parents, which expands the state's role in child rearing, is not accompanied by greater state responsibility for children. By increasing the number of people who can assert relationship rights, the PRINCIPLES necessarily increase the likelihood that courts, not parents, will be deciding what is in a child's best interest. Although parents' rights are diminished and the state's power increased, the PRINCIPLES make no provision for diminishing parental obligation or increasing state responsibility. Third, by protecting established emotional relationships without protecting established financial relationships, the PRINCIPLES prioritize children's emotional needs over their financial needs. The drafters opt to protect emotional reliance more than financial reliance without any justification or explanation as to why. Finally, the one justification offered by the drafters for finding nontraditional parents liable for support, an intent to accept responsibility as a parent, is strikingly inconsistent with the drafters' concurrent reliance on state parentage acts, which reject intent as a basis for parenthood.[5] Intent as a basis for obligation is also inconsistent with the treatment of obligation elsewhere in the PRINCIPLES.[6] These inconsistencies cause a good deal of confusion about when and why intent to parent should matter in determining parental obligation. In sum, Part II shows how the PRINCIPLES' treatment of rights rejects the supremacy of biology, while embracing increased state participation in children's emotional well-being. In contrast, the PRINCIPLES' treatment of obligation endorses the binary parent model and the supremacy of biology while eschewing state responsibility for children's financial well-being.

Finally, Part III concludes by exploring some tentative justifications for this asymmetry. Given the political realities of child support and the uncertainty about certain empirical questions, it may be that the drafters have struck an appropriate balance. We may be better off living with an asymmetric understanding of parenthood than living with either a restrictive understanding, which limits both rights and obligations or a more capacious model that expands both rights and obligations.

I. The Categories

This part will explore the key differences between chapter 2 of the PRINCIPLES, which details who has the right to petition a court for custody or visitation with a child, and chapter 3 of the PRINCIPLES, which explains who shoulders the obligation to support a child.

A. Relationship Categories for Purposes of Custody and Visitation

Chapter 2 of the PRINCIPLES outlines who has standing to assert relationship rights with a child, that is, who may ask the state to protect his or her relationship with a child.[7] Chapter 2

[4] PRINCIPLES § 3.02(1)(defining parent for purposes of the child support provisions).

[5] *See e.g.* Unif. Parentage Act § 204; 750 III. Comp. State 45/5 (2003); Cal. Fam. code § 7611(c) (2004) (none of them mention intent).

[6] *See infra*, notes 127–128.

[7] PRINCIPLES § 2.04 delineates who may "bring an action under this Chapter" and/or "be notified of any participate as a party in an action filled by another." PRINCIPLES § 2.04(1).

bestows relationship rights on four categories of people: legal parents, parents by estoppel, de facto parents, biological parents who are not legal parents, and any individual who has custodial rights under an existing parenting plan.[8] The fourth category, a biological parent who is not the legal parent, is the most straightforward. A birth mother or sperm donor who does not intend to be the legal parent but wants to retain, through contract, certain relationship rights, can do so.[9] The first category, legal parents, may seem clear cut, though as the next part makes clear, this category is far more fluid and contextual than one might initially presume. The other categories codified in Section 2.03 need more explanation.

A parent by estoppel is someone who (a) lived with the child for at least two years or since the child's birth and (b) either reasonably believed he was the biological father of the child and accepted responsibility as father of the child, found out he was not the biological father of the child after believing he was but continued to accept responsibilities as the child's father, or accepted responsibilities as the child's parent pursuant to an agreement with the child's other parent or parents.[10] The parent by estoppel category was created in order to prevent legal parents from blocking a functional parent's potential custodial rights on the basis of biology or legality. For the most part, the PRINCIPLES treat parents by estoppel and legal parents comparably,[11] though parents by estoppel may not hold the full panoply of constitutional rights that legal parents do.[12] Nonetheless, both legal parents and parents by estoppel have a presumptive right to that amount of custodial time allocated to legal parents under state law.[13] Both also have the right to object if a de facto parent seeks a majority of the custodial time.[14]

A de facto parent is someone who, for not less than two years, lived with the child and, for reasons other than financial compensation and pursuant to an agreement with the legal parent to form a parent-child relationship, performed at least as much of the caretaking for the child as the legal parent performed.[15] This category allows people who have developed a substantial emotional relationship with a child to assert custodial rights. De facto parents have a form of lesser parental status. They may petition for custodial time, but this right is temporally limited – they generally must assert it within six months of having lived with

[8] Technically, there is a fifth category for individuals who have custodial rights under an existing parenting plan, but because anyone in this fifth category must have originally fallen into one of the other four categories, a separate discussion of the fifth category is not necessary.

[9] Some ambiguity nonetheless surrounds what constitutes biological parent. Is an egg donor who did not carry the child to term, or a gestational surrogate who did not provide an egg, a biological parent? The ALI preserves rights for biological parents who, through prior agreements with the child's legal parent(s), have retained some parental rights or responsibilities, PRINCIPLES §§ 2.04(1)(d), 2.18(2)(b), but they do not define biological parent. *See* PRINCIPLES § 2.03 cmt. a, Reporter's Note at 128; § 2.04 cmts. a, e, at 135, 137–138 for definitions.

[10] PRINCIPLES § 2.03(1)(b). If the child is under age two, the agreement with the child's parent must have been formed prior to the child's birth. PRINCIPLES § 2.03(1)(b)(iii).

[11] PRINCIPLES § 2.03 cmt b, at 110 ("A parent by estoppel is afforded all of the privileges of a legal parent under this Chapter.").

[12] For instance, it is not clear whether a parent by estoppel should be considered a parent for constitutional purposes, and thereby protected from certain forms of state interference. *See* Emily Buss, *Parental Rights*, 88 VA. L. REV. 635, 642 (2002) ("[T]he ALI gives no indication that the custody proceeding can transform parents by estoppel into the sort of parents entitled to special constitutional protection under the Due Process Clause. . . . ").

[13] PRINCIPLES § 2.08(1)(a) (providing that "a legal parent or a parent by estoppel who has performed a reasonable share of parenting functions [is entitled to] . . . not less than a presumptive amount of custodial time set by a uniform rule of statewide application"). *See also* PRINCIPLES, § 2.03 cmt. f, at 99.

[14] PRINCIPLES § 2.18(1)(a).

[15] PRINCIPLES § 2.03(1)(c).

the child.[16] Unlike parents-by-estoppel, de facto parents cannot assert a right based on the provision of food or shelter or services; they must have provided caretaking.[17] The PRINCIPLES specifically state that a de facto parent's entitlement is less than that of a legal parent or parent by estoppel.[18]

B. Obligation Categories for Purposes of Child Support

Chapter 3 of the PRINCIPLES outlines who should be held responsible for child support and how much they should pay. The PRINCIPLES recognize only three categories of potential obligors: legal parents, parents by estoppel, and people required by state law to support a child despite termination of their parental rights.[19] To make matters particularly confusing for the uninitiated, the PRINCIPLES do not define parents by estoppel in Section 3.03 the same way the PRINCIPLES define parents by estoppel in Section 2.03. Whereas Section 2.03 is designed to prevent a legal parent from barring a nonlegal parent from asserting custodial rights, Section 3.03 is designed to estop a nonlegal parent from denying a support obligation.[20] Anyone who is estopped from denying a child support obligation under Section 3.03 is entitled to custodial rights as a parent by estoppel under Section 2.03, but the obverse does not hold.[21] In other words, the obligor is always entitled to rights, but the rights holder is not always obligated to pay.

The PRINCIPLES make very clear that nonlegal parents should only rarely be obligated to pay child support. The first part of Section 3.03 states that a parenthood by estoppel for support purposes should be found only "in exceptional" circumstances, and only in cases in which the potential obligor's "affirmative conduct" renders estoppel appropriate.[22] The drafters were clear that obligation should grow from deliberate action, not circumstance.[23]

The second part of Section 3.03 limits even further the circumstances in which a parent by estoppel can be found for support purposes. Section 3.03(2) discourages the imposition of

[16] PRINCIPLES § 2.04(1)(c) (imposing a 6 month requirement unless the de facto parent consistently maintained or attempted to maintain his or her parental relationship since residing with the child). *See also* PRINCIPLES § 2.04 cmt. d, at 136.

[17] Parenting functions include caretaking functions, but they may also encompass providing economic support, noncaretaking labor for the household, and decision-making. PRINCIPLES § 2.03(6).

[18] PRINCIPLES § 2.18(1)(a) (providing that a court "should not allocate the majority of custodial responsibility to a de facto parent over the objection of a legal parent or a parent by estoppel who is fit and willing").

[19] PRINCIPLES § 3.02(1). This last category is probably limited to those rare instances in which a state terminates someone's parental rights (probably for reasons of abuse or neglect) but nonetheless demands a support obligation from that person. PRINCIPLES § 3.02 cmt. b, at 412. In any other instance it would be inconsistent with other provisions of the PRINCIPLES to make someone pay support for a child without allowing that person to assert custodial rights. *See* PRINCIPLES, § 3.03 cmts. d, e, and discussion *infra* note 21.

[20] *Compare* PRINCIPLES § 2.03 cmt. b, at 110 *with* PRINCIPLES § 3.03 cmt. a, at 415–16.

[21] *See* PRINCIPLES § 3.03 cmt d, at 420 ("In some cases estoppel may be mutual, but in other cases it may not be. Whether the parties are estopped to deny parenthood for the purpose of custodial responsibility is determined by Chapter 2 . . . However, estoppel is always mutual if a child-support obligation is actually imposed under [Chapter 3].").

[22] PRINCIPLES § 3.03(1).

[23] PRINCIPLES § 3.03 cmt. a, at 415. Moreover, by specifically stating that a parent by estoppel for purposes of custody is not necessarily a parent by estoppel for child support purposes, the drafters must have meant "accepting full and permanent responsibilities as a parent, pursuant to an agreement with the child's parent(s)," PRINCIPLES § 2.03(1)(B)(iv), which entitles one to custody rights should not mean the same thing as "affirmative conduct" constituting "an explicit or implicit agreement or undertaking . . . to assume a parental support obligation" PRINCIPLES § 3.03(1)(a) which obliges one to pay child support.

an obligation if the potential obligor did not "[supplant] the child's opportunity to develop a relationship with an absent parent and to look to that parent for support."[24] Nor should an obligation be found if there are two other parents "who owe the child a duty of support and are able and available to provide support."[25]

The concern about supplanting the child's opportunity to develop a relationship with his or her legal father expressed in Section 3.03(2) parallels, or perhaps gives content to, the affirmative conduct requirement in Section 3.03(1). It does so, however, without clearly defining what constitutes action sufficient to warrant an obligation. Although Illustration 2 to Section 3.03 explains that an obligation can be imposed if a stepfather counsels his wife not to pursue child support against the legal father and urges her to pursue termination of the legal father's support obligation,[26] the far more likely scenario involves less dramatic action. Suppose the stepfather simply assumes the duty to support so that the legal mother does not bother to pursue child support. The stepfather may even say he is happy to help, which can be true but still fall far short of encouraging the legal parent not to pursue child support. The stepparent may also develop a bond with the child, though not because he deliberately tried to exclude the legal father. It is common for the legal father to simply drift away.[27] The nonlegal parent's "affirmative conduct" in this very common situation often consists of little more than filling the vacuum left by a legal parent's absence. Once established, however, that stepparent relationship can be a powerful and important presence in both the child's and the custodial legal parent's life.[28] It is a relationship that entitles the stepparent to relationship rights as a de facto parent, but apparently does not entitle the child or his mother to a right of support.

The restrictive conditions under which the PRINCIPLES are willing to impose obligations on nonlegal parents demonstrate a desire to rely on extant legal determinations of parental identity in order to determine child support obligations. Although this might seem like an appropriate, clear rule – only legal parents should be obligated to pay, an examination of how the law of parental identity operates shows that the category of "legal parent" is much messier than one might expect. The Uniform Parentage Act, and virtually all state parentage acts, presumes certain people to be legal parents. For women, the rule works without incident most of the time: whoever gives birth to the child is the mother.[29] Fatherhood is, and always has been, more complicated. Most parentage acts incorporate the common law presumption that a man married to the mother at the time of birth or conception is the child's father.[30] The man listed on the birth certificate is also often presumed to be

[24] PRINCIPLES § 3.03(2)(b). [25] PRINCIPLES § 3.03(2)(c).

[26] *See* PRINCIPLES, § 3.03 illus. 2, at 416.

[27] FRANK FURSTENBURG & KATHLEEN MULLAN HARRIS, WHEN FATHERS MATTER / WHY FATHERS MATTER: THE IMPACT OF PATERNAL INVOLVEMENT ON THE OFFSPRING OF ADOLESCENT MOTHERS IN THE POLITICS OF PREGNANCY: ADOLESCENT SEX AND PUBLIC POLICY 217 (D. Rhode ed. 1993).

[28] Children living with stepfathers are more likely to identify their stepfather as part of their family than they are to identify their biological father as a family member. Frank Furstenburg and Christine Nord, *Parenting Apart: Patterns of Childbearing After Marital Disruption*, 47 J. MARRIAGE & FAM. 893, 899 (1985).

[29] Surrogacy arrangements can make motherhood determinations equally complicated. A gestational surrogate may well not be the genetic mother of a child. An intending mother who gets impregnated using an ovum from another woman is not a genetic mother either. Almost all of these new arrangements are accompanied by private contracts that spell out the parental rights of the relevant parties. For the most part, courts accept the legitimacy of these contracts and let private ordering determine both rights and obligations. *See* Katharine K. Baker, *Bargaining or Biology: The History and Future of Paternity Law and Parental Status*, 14 CORNELL J. L. & PUB. POL'Y 1, 26–30 (2004).

[30] Unif. Parentage Act §§ 204(a)(1) and (2) (2002); 750 ILL. COMP. STAT. 45/5(a)(1) (2003).

the legal father,[31] as is a man who resides with a newborn child and "openly holds out the child as his natural child."[32] It is not uncommon for these presumptions to clash with each other or with biological evidence.[33] In cases where nonbiological presumptions clash, courts sometimes rely on biological evidence,[34] but other times they simply make a best interest of the child determination in order to determine paternity.[35] Comparably, in cases in which there has already been a paternity judgment without genetic testing, courts can refuse to order such testing even if a legal father has new reason to believe that he is not the genetic father.[36] Thus, neither the rules themselves nor judicial interpretation of those rules suggest that the "legal parent" is easily defined.

The confusion enveloping legal parentage determinations has important implications for the PRINCIPLES. Although legal parents have custodial rights under the PRINCIPLES, one's status as legal parent can change quickly. Section 2.04(1)(e) states that once a person has been allocated "custodial responsibility or decision-making authority" under chapter 2, he or she has continued standing to assert custodial rights.[37] Contrast this with what occurs when someone initiates a proceeding as a legal parent and finds out before an adjudication is final that he is not a legal parent.[38] The child support obligation under chapter 3 attaches automatically at the legal determination of paternity, but that legal determination can easily change after custodial rights have been established. Consequently, someone who received custodial rights as legal father would retain those rights after a new legal father had been found but would shed his obligation to pay.

C. Summary

The PRINCIPLES create different categories of individuals who may have custody and visitation rights to children under chapter 2 or financial obligation to children under chapter 3. The PRINCIPLES give custody and visitation rights to legal parents, biological parents who contracted for them, de facto parents, and parents by estoppel. Chapter 3 limits financial responsibility almost exclusively to legal parents, with minor allowances for some parents by estoppel and abusive parents.[39] A person who has a right to estop a legal

[31] *See, e.g.*, 750 ILL. COMP. STAT 45/5(a)(2) (2003); ALA. CODE §§ 26–17–1 to 26–17–21 (1975); CAL. FAM. CODE §§ 7611(c)(I) (2004).

[32] *See, e.g.*, CAL. FAM. CODE § 7611(d)(2004); COLO.REV.STAT. § 19–4–105(1)(d) (2003).

[33] NAH v. SLS, 9 P.3d 354, 357 (Colo. 2000) (considering the legal fatherhood status of a husband who was identified on the birth certificate as the father and accepted the child as his own, although genetics testing showed another man was the biological father); Davis v. La Brec, 549 S.E.2d 76 (Ga. 2001) (Man in a long term relationship with the mother was named as the father on the birth certificate and obtained full legal custody of the child, but a DNA test years later proved another man was the biological father); County v. R. K., 757 A.2d 319 (N.J. Super. Ct. Ch. Div. 2000) (requiring continued child support from a man who signed a voluntary admission of paternity and was believed to be the father for ten years although a later paternity test revealed he was not).

[34] In re Marriage of Rebecca & David R., 62 Cal.Rptr.2d 730 (Cal. Ct. App. 1997).

[35] *See* NAH v. SLS, and Davis v. La Brec, *supra* note 33.

[36] In re Paternity of Cheryl, 746 N.E.2d 488 (Mass. 2001).

[37] PRINCIPLES § 2.04(1)(e).

[38] *See* In re Roberts, 649 N.E.2d 1344 (Ill. 1995) (concluding that a husband had standing to pursue custody and visitation even though in the midst of a divorce and custody battle over a child whom the husband and legal father presumed to be his own, the court determined that the husband was not the legal father of the child; the court reasoned that the husband had standing in the custody battle because at the initiation of the suit, he was the legal father).

[39] PRINCIPLES § 3.03. It also provides for the very limited category of parents who are ordered to pay child support despite the severing of their legal status as parents. *See supra* note 23.

parent from contesting his parental status receives custodial rights under the PRINCIPLES equal to a legal parent,[40] but that same person is not necessarily himself estopped from denying a support obligation in chapter 3.[41] By comparison, a person who was a legal parent at the time custodial rights were originally determined will always have standing to assert parental rights, but if that same person loses his status as legal parent, he may well be relieved of his support obligation.[42]

The best way to summarize the distinctions between chapter 2 and chapter 3 of the PRINCIPLES may be to understand how each chapter deals with the concept of legal parentage. The comments to child support provisions state that the determination of legal paternity is "a matter outside the scope of these PRINCIPLES."[43] Presumably, in passing over that question, the drafters meant to avoid the messy determinations involving competing presumptions of fatherhood just discussed, but there is at least a partial tautology involved in doing so. The reason courts determine legal parentage is to determine who has rights and responsibilities with regard to a child. The purpose of custody and child support provisions of the PRINCIPLES is to determine who has rights and responsibilities with regard to children. In determining rights and responsibilities, the law determines parenthood. Thus, in a very practical sense, the purpose of the PRINCIPLES is to determine legal parentage. How could the very purpose of the PRINCIPLES be beyond their scope? The answer to this question lies in the way in which the PRINCIPLES sever rights and responsibilities. Traditionally, whoever had rights had responsibilities and the only people who had rights and responsibilities were parents.[44] The PRINCIPLES now suggest a very different structure. People can have rights without having responsibilities, and a determination of legal parentage really only matters for the imposition of responsibility. The custody provisions lay out who should be entitled to rights without much care for who the legal parents are. In doing so, these provisions do a great deal of work in determining who is able to enjoy the benefits of parenthood and why.[45] Parentage determinations are thus not outside the scope of the custody provisions. The child support provisions, on the other hand, restrict responsibility to legal parents and those rare individuals who have, in exceptional circumstances, willingly agreed to assume full parental responsibilities.[46] By leaving it to others, that is, those deciding legal parentage, to decide who should shoulder the responsibilities of parenthood,[47] the child support provisions ignore the very questions that the custody provisions resolve.

[40] PRINCIPLES § 2.03 cmt. b, at 110.

[41] PRINCIPLES § 3.03 cmt. d, at 420.

[42] PRINCIPLES § 3.03 probably allows a court to impose an obligation on such a man, but it does not compel it. If the "subsequent" father can support the child, § 3.03(2)(c), and if the "first" father did not actively "supplant[] the child's opportunity to develop a relationship" with the "subsequent parent," § 3.03(2)(b), then the "first" father should escape obligation.

[43] PRINCIPLES § 3.03 cmt. d, at 418.

[44] *See* Katharine Bartlett, *Rethinking Parenthood as an Exclusive State: The Need for Legal Alternatives When the Premise of the Nuclear Family Has Failed*, 70 Va. L. Rev. 870, 883 (1984) ("Parents' rights and duties are ordinarily both exclusive and indivisible. They are exclusive in that only a child's legal parents will have rights and duties ordinarily considered parental; non-parents cannot acquire them. They are indivisible in that each parent, with respect to his or her own child, will have every right and duty generally available to parents.").

[45] PRINCIPLES § 2.03(1). Notably, those nontraditional categories of people who are now entitled to parental rights all have the word "parent" in them:, "parents-by-estoppel," "de facto parents," and "biological parents who have a prior agreement with legal parents." *Id.*

[46] PRINCIPLES §§ 3.02, 3.03.

[47] The "others" would presumably be the drafters of state parentage acts, the legislators who enact the acts, and the judges who interpret them.

II. The Implications

Analysis of the different treatment of rights and obligations detailed above reveals curious inconsistencies and policy choices implicit in the PRINCIPLES' framework. The binary biological ideal is, for the most part, discarded for purposes of custody and visitation rights, but remains important and normative for purposes of obligation. Functional relationships are critical for determining custody and visitation rights, but largely irrelevant to support obligations. The custody and visitation rules increase state participation in child rearing decisions and emphasize children's emotional reliance, while the obligation rules eschew state support for children and discount the need to protect children's financial reliance. Moreover, the obligation rules, by making intent to parent relevant for some determinations of parental obligations, seem to reject their own embrace of extant parentage statutes, while ignoring the extent to which obligation grows regardless of intent in other provisions of the PRINCIPLES. This part explores all these tensions.

A. Two-Parent Model

By adopting an expansive view of parental rights, the PRINCIPLES reject the binary parent model. More than two people can have custody or visitation rights to children. This is evident not only in the extension of such rights to de facto parents, but in the incorporation of biological parents who are not legal parents but have an agreement with a legal parent to reserve some parental rights.[48] The PRINCIPLES even contemplate the idea that two parents could agree to have a third party assume full parental duties and thereby become a parent-by-estoppel.[49]

The child support chapter is far less receptive to the idea of multilateral responsibility. As discussed, nonlegal parents can only be held responsible in exceptional circumstances and are particularly unlikely to be held accountable if there are "two [other] parents who owe the child a duty of support."[50] More practically, the Child-Support Formula adopted in Section 3.05 embodies not only a two-parent norm, but also a two-parents-who-have-shared-a-household norm. "The marginal expenditure measure requires that a child support obligor continue to contribute to the marginal support of the child as he would if he were sharing a home with the child and the other parent."[51] The amount a person owes his or her child is determined by the standard of living the child would enjoy if the obligor were living with the residential parent and the residential parent was not living with somebody else. This formula may well reflect the best way to ensure fair and efficient transfer of resources to

[48] PRINCIPLES § 3.03(1)(a).

[49] PRINCIPLES §§ 2.03(b)(iii) and (iv) suggests that a biological mother and father (who would be the legal parents of the child) could enter into a coparenting agreement with a third person who agrees to raise the child with full parental rights and responsibilities. If such an agreement was in place, the third party would acquire parent-by-estoppel status if he or she had lived with the child since birth or for at least two years. The notes to chapter 2 suggest that it is unlikely that a parent-by-estoppel relationship will be formed if there are two legal parents, but it is not impossible. PRINCIPLES § 2.03 cmt. a(iii), at 115.

[50] PRINCIPLES § 3.03(2)(c).

[51] PRINCIPLES § 3.05 cmt. d, at 444. *See also* PRINCIPLES § 3.05 cmt. f, at 427 (stating that a nonresidential parent "[has] an interest in contributing no more to the support of a child than if he were living with the child in a two-parent household, that is, in not being required to pay any more than he would were the family intact."). *See also* PRINCIPLES § 3.05 cmt. e, at 445 ("Base percentages... may be selected... from estimates of marginal expenditure on children... in two-parent families.").

children born to the binary biological ideal, but it uses as a baseline a non-majoritarian norm. Children are just as likely *not* to live in a family composed of two biologically-related parents and biological siblings as they are to live within that model.[52] Thirty percent of the children in this country are born to nonmarried mothers.[53] To base the entire child support structure on the binary biological ideal when it is so transparently not reality for millions of children seems odd.

Allocating responsibility based on this model without considering the behavior and circumstances that led to the obligation also seems odd. A man who never wanted and never intended to have a child, but sired one in a one night stand, owes the same amount of child support as a comparably-earning man who intended to sire and willingly reared his child. The quality and content of the adult-child relationship that are critical to the assessment of custody and visitation rights under the PRINCIPLES are irrelevant to the assessment of obligation. In addition, what the man in the one night stand owes is a function of an entirely hypothetical situation. Section 3.05 asks a court to determine what he would contribute if he were living and sharing resources with the mother and child, despite the fact that he has never lived with the mother or the child.

The drafters assert that this scheme will alleviate the "economic plight of children in single-parent households,"[54] for whom the drafters expressed great concern: "[w]idespread economic inadequacy in one-parent families is not only a grievous harm to children; it is also an unwise under investment in a vital social resource."[55] For sure, though, part of the grievous harm could be alleviated by simply casting the obligor net wider. The drafters would not even have to cast it in arbitrary directions. They could simply net in the very same people who are entitled to custody and visitation rights under the PRINCIPLES.

Such an approach would not only deepen the pool of resources available to children, it would better reflect parental reality as it is experienced by both adults and children. In many communities, serial fatherhood is the norm. "The responsibilities of fathers are carried from one household to the next as [men] migrate from one marriage to the next. Some men who become stepparents or surrogate parents in a new household often transfer their loyalties to their new family."[56] "For men, marriage and coresidence usually define responsibilities to children. Regardless of their biological ties to children, men share time and resources with the children of their wives or female partner."[57] Of children who live in mother-only households, 20 percent live with an adult male.[58] Of children that live in father-only households, 40 percent live with an adult female.[59] Of children in single-parent households generally, another 20 percent live with an adult of the same sex as their residential parent.[60] Literally millions of children do not live the biological binary parent ideal but they are living with at least two adults, many of whom will be entitled to parental

[52] Stacy Furukawa, U.S. Dep't of Commerce, Current Population Reports, Series P70, No. 38, The Diverse Living Arrangements of Children: Summer 1991, at 1 (1994). This study, based on 1991 data, found that only one out of two children lived with their biological parents and their biological siblings. *See also* NANCY DOWD, IN DEFENSE OF SINGLE PARENT FAMILIES (New York University Press, 1997) at 27 (using 1994 data to reach the same conclusion).

[53] National Center for Health Statistics (2003), http://www.nchs/04facts/birthrates.htm (last visited March 6, 2006).

[54] PRINCIPLES § 3.04 cmt. h, at 429.

[55] PRINCIPLES § 3.04 cmt. b, at 424.

[56] Furstenburg and Harris, *supra* note 27, at 217.

[57] Judith Seltzer, *Consequences of Marital Dissolution For Children*, 20 AM. REV. SOCIOL. 235, 237 (1994).

[58] DOWD, *supra* note 52, at 28.

[59] *Id.*

[60] *Id.*

rights.[61] The child support provisions ignore these functional relationships and instead link obligation to determinations of legal parenthood made elsewhere and to a model of parental relationships that applies to less than half of the children in this country.

B. The Expansion of State Power

In granting relationship rights to nonlegal parents, the PRINCIPLES also endorse an expanded view of state power. The state has the right to protect a child's emotional well-being by ensuring the continuation of certain relationships even if the custodial parent(s) want to end or diminish the strength of those relationships.[62] With this expansion of state power comes a diminishment of negative parental rights – that is, the right to be free of state interference in the parent-child relationship.

Others have written about the PRINCIPLES' weak allegiance to parental rights.[63] By giving nonparents rights to petition for custody and decision-making authority, the PRINCIPLES weaken "the primary role of the parents in the upbringing of their children."[64] Traditionally, parents were protected from state interference into upbringing decisions.[65] Only if the state could prove by clear and convincing evidence that a parent was abusing or neglecting her children, could the state usurp a parent's role.[66] In the famous string of substantive due process cases announcing parental rights, the justification that emerged for protecting parental rights rested on the belief that parents, not the state, should socialize children.[67] States would not be particularly good at socializing a diverse population,[68] and parents have a protected interest in socializing their children as they want to.[69] Moreover, parents

[61] The most recent data suggest that forty-four percent of children who live with a single parent also have another adult present in the household. U.S. CENSUS BUREAU, CURRENT POPULATION REPORTS, CHILDREN'S LIVING ARRANGEMENTS AND CHARACTERISTICS: MARCH 2002 5 (2003).

[62] Theoretically, the state can do this pursuant to its *parens patraie* power, which allows the state to act on behalf of children because children are not fully able to protect themselves. *See* Prince v. Massachusetts, 321 U.S. 158, 162 (1944).

[63] *See* Buss, *supra* note 12.

[64] Wisconsin v. Yoder, 406 U.S. 205, 232 (1972).

[65] Parents had the right to make decisions about discipline, religion, education (within limits), and association. *See* Bartlett, *supra* note 44. Mandatory school attendance laws abridge a parent's right to not educate his or her child, but parents are given wide latitude to provide whatever education they want. And, if the parent's reasoning seems sound enough, they can be exempted from mandatory school attendance laws. *See also* Wisconsin v. Yoder, *supra* note 64.

[66] Santosky v. Kramer 455 U.S. 745 (1982).

[67] The string includes Meyer v. Nebraska, 262 U.S. 390 (1923), Pierce v. Society of Sisters, 268 U.S. 510 (1925), Prince v. Massachusetts, *supra* note 62; Wisconsin v. Yoder, *supra* note 64. The Supreme Court's recent decision, Troxel v. Granville, 530 U.S. 57 (2000), suggests a much more limited enthusiasm for parental rights.

[68] "[A]ffirmative sponsorship of particular ethical, religious or political beliefs is something we expect the state *not* to attempt in a society constitutionally committed to the ideal of individual liberty and freedom of choice." Bellotti v. Baird, 443 U.S. 622, 638 (1979). In Meyer v. Nebraska, *supra* note 67, the Supreme Court noted if the state were to assume the job of socializing children, the result would be a kind of homogeneity that is "wholly different from [the individualism] upon which our institutions rest." *Id.* at 402. In Moore v. East Cleveland, 431 U.S. 494, 503–04 (1977), the Court observed "[i]t is through the family that we inculcate and pass down many of our most cherished values, moral and cultural." *See also* Bartlett, *supra* note 44, at 890 (describing the view that protecting parental rights serves instrumental goals).

[69] Justice Stewart has argued:

> If a State were to attempt to force the breakup of a natural family, over the objections of parents and their children, without some showing of unfitness and for the sole reason that to do so was thought to be in the children's best interest, I should have little doubt that the State would have intruded impermissibly on the private realm of family life which the state cannot enter.

are likely to know their children best and therefore be best able to act in their children's best interest.[70] By allowing nonparents to compete with others to socialize children, the PRINCIPLES diminish the control and the ability of parents to "bring up [a] child in the way he should go."[71]

Arguably, however, the negative parental rights that the substantive due process clause protects have never extended to nonmarried parents.[72] That is because a nonmarried parent has the positive parental right to invoke the state's judgment when challenging a decision of another parent.[73] When nonmarried parents disagree, the state must make the very decisions that negative parental rights prevent the state from making for married parents.[74]

The rights that a parent by estoppel or de facto parent asserts under the custody and visitation provision will likely be asserted against a nonmarried parent, that is, someone whose negative parental rights are already severely restricted by the positive parental rights of another parent. Thus, by giving rights to parents by estoppel and de facto parents, the PRINCIPLES may not be infringing that significantly on a parent's negative parental rights because those rights are already compromised by her single status.[75]

Because the custody and visitation entitlements will emerge in situations in which the negative parental rights of the parent(s) can already be challenged, they may not pose a particularly large threat to the parenting practices of legal parents. There is at least one group of parents whose rights are likely to be significantly restricted though, the single custodial parent who has an absentee-but-still-legal coparent. Ironically, this is the same, often poor, custodial parent that the comments to child support provisions say we must help.[76] The absentee-but-still legal parent does not usually challenge the parenting decisions of

Smith v. Org. of Foster Families for Equality and Reform, 431 U.S. 816, 862–63 (1977) (internal citations omitted). *See also* Stephen Gilles, *On Educating and Rearing Children: A Parentalist Manifesto*, 63 U. CHI. L. REV. 937 (1996) (arguing that the parental rights doctrine protects critical expressive rights for parents because raising children is a form of self-expression).

[70] Parham v. J. R., 442 U.S. 584, 602 (1979) (stating parents are entitled to a presumption that they are acting in the best interest of their children.).

[71] *See* Prince v. Massachusetts, 321 U.S. at 164.

[72] All of the parents who won in the original parents rights cases, *see supra* notes 64–71, were married and asserting their parental rights jointly. The recent case that gave only a lukewarm endorsement to the notion of negative parental rights, *Troxel v. Granville*, involved a parent who had never married the father of her children and who separated from him before he died.

[73] *See* Katharine K. Baker, *Property Rules Meet Feminist Needs: Respecting Autonomy by Valuing Connection*, 59 OHIO ST. L. J. 1523, 1545–46 (1998).

[74] *See, e.g.*, Mentry v. Mentry, 190 Cal.Rptr. 843, 850 (Cal. Ct. App. 1983) (evaluating decisions about religious practices); Felton v. Felton, 418 N.E.2d 606, 611 (Mass. 1981); Jarett v. Jarett, 400 N.E.2d 421, 427 (Ill. 1980) (custodial mother loses custody because of her belief that she need not marry her sexual partner); Peterson v. Peterson, 434 N.W.2d 732, 737 (S.D. 1989) (explaining that it is up to court to determine "realistic needs of the children."). Moreover, the Supreme Court has just held that an unmarried noncustodial father does not have standing to challenge unconstitutional state practices that affect his daughter, *see* Elk Grove Village v. Newdow 542 U.S. 1 (2004), although the constitution clearly affords standing to married parents if they proceed together. *See* Yoder, *supra* note 64; Meyer, *supra* note 67.

[75] It is unlikely that either parents by estoppel or de facto parents will infringe on the parental prerogatives of married parents. To be a parent by estoppel, one has to have lived with the child for two years or since birth, and "accepted full and permanent responsibility as a parent" as part of a coparenting agreement with the child's parents, *see* PRINCIPLES § 3.03(1)(b)(3). As noted above, it is possible, but not likely, that two married parents would agree to have a third person accept full and permanent responsibility. To be a de facto parent, one has to have lived with the child for two years and assumed as great a share of the caretaking functions as the legal parent. PRINCIPLES § 2.03(c). Again, it is possible that a married couple would welcome someone like this into their home, but not particularly likely. Thus, de facto parents are not likely to be competing with married parents either.

[76] *Supra* note 51.

the custodial single parent because his or her absence precludes it. This absence gives the custodial single parent freedom, but it also often compels that single parent to look for caretaking help from a de facto parent.[77] The person who (for free) provides that caretaking help can become a de facto parent and thereby diminish the rights of the single parent.[78]

To be sure, there is a certain justice to diminishing the single parent's rights in these situations. If a parent has asked a nonparent to share caretaking burdens, she may have to be prepared to share caretaking rights. Moreover, the PRINCIPLES' de facto rules sometimes do little more than curtail the rights of the absentee-but still-legal parent.[79]

There are other situations in which the assertion of such rights is considerably more controversial. *Painter v. Bannister*,[80] the famed U.S. case, is an example. In *Painter*, maternal grandparents who had taken care of their grandson after their daughter's death were able to retain custody of the child even after the father asked to have his son back. The case generated considerable commentary,[81] many people thinking it perfectly appropriate for the father to ask for help from his in-laws and not at all fair to deprive him of custody years later. It is clear that the PRINCIPLES would treat the grandparents in *Painter* as de facto parents, with standing to assert a custody claim.[82]

Consider also what would happen if the facts of one of the PRINCIPLES' examples changed slightly. Suppose, as Illustration 3 to the child support provisions does, that a mother has been institutionalized with a mental illness.[83] The father has custodial rights but because of his work schedule, the child resides with his maternal grandmother during the week (or gets dropped off at grandmother's before breakfast and picked up after the child has gone to sleep). The PRINCIPLES state that the grandmother in this situation would qualify as a de facto parent, while also stressing that as a caretaker, not a parent, the grandmother "ordinarily, [would have] no duty of support."[84] If the father begins to disagree with how Grandmother is raising the child or if he remarries and would like to have the child stay in his home during the day because his new wife is happy to assume the role of caretaker, the grandmother will be able to challenge his parenting decisions legally.[85]

[77] De facto parents are also likely to emerge in situations in which one divorced parent remarries a person who assumes primary caretaking responsibility for a child from the first marriage. In this instance, the relative infringement caused by the stepparent is small because the custodial parent's parenting decisions are already subject to challenge by the other legal parent as a result of the divorce decree.

[78] PRINCIPLES §§ 2.03(c), and § 2.03 cmt. b, at 110.

[79] The illustration to section 2.18 provides a good example. Three-year-old Perry lived with his mother, Lois, and grandmother, Glenna, since birth. Lois performed more than half of the caretaking. The legal father, Hank, had seen Perry only six times and had never provided child support. When Lois went to jail, Glenna had standing as a de facto parent and could be awarded a majority of the custodial responsibility. *See* PRINCIPLES § 2.18 illus. 2, at 386. If she did not have standing, Hank would have had sole rights and responsibility for Perry. Making room for Glenna to assert rights in this case seems unquestionably sound.

[80] Painter v. Bannister, 140 N.W.2d 152 (Iowa 1966).

[81] For a discussion of *Painter's* influence, see Gilbert A. Holmes, *The Tie That Binds: The Constitutional Rights of Children to Maintain Relationships with Parent-Like Individuals*, 53 MD. L. REV 358, 384 (1994).

[82] Under the PRINCIPLES there would be a presumption against awarding them a majority of the custodial time, but they might well end up with custody. Painter lived in California; the Bannisters lived in Iowa. Section 2.18 permits a court to award a majority of the custodial responsibility to a de facto parent over the objection of a legal parent if the "available alternatives would cause harm to the child." PRINCIPLES § 2.18(2)(c).

[83] *See* PRINCIPLES § 3.02 illus. 3, at 414.

[84] PRINCIPLES § 3.02 cmt. g, at 414.

[85] The grandmother will have standing in any custodial hearing and if the parties disagree, the PRINCIPLES offer competing guidance: grandmother should not get a majority of the custodial time because she is "only" a de facto parent, PRINCIPLES § 2.18(a), but if the parties disagree, the court should look to past practices, PRINCIPLES § 2.08. Past practices suggest that grandmother should get a majority of the custodial time. Thus, it is unclear what the grandmother would get, but could easily receive substantial custodial time over the wishes of the primary parent.

Regardless of one's view of the merits of granting custody or visitation to de facto parents in these situations, one fact is plain. Giving de facto parents rights increases the state's involvement in the child rearing process. The more people who can claim relationship rights, the more people there are who can petition a court to alter or solidify a custodial arrangement, and the more courts end up deciding what is in a child's best interest.

Giving the state authority in these situations and recognizing that the state routinely exercises its authority in cases involving unmarried parents, evinces the drafters' comfort with the state's participation in child rearing decisions. This expansive view of custody and visitation rights, coupled with changing norms with regard to marriage and parenting, means that the state would have ultimate decision-making authority for at least half of the children in this country.[86] The custody provisions soundly endorse this increased state participation, while the support provisions specifically eschew any increased state financial responsibility for children.[87] The PRINCIPLES diffuse parents' rights without diffusing their obligation.[88]

C. Emotional Over Material Needs

The drafters explicitly acknowledge that their goal in expanding custody and visitation rights in chapter 2 is to protect children's emotional well-being.[89] Embracing an expansive approach to children's emotional health while at the same time maintaining a restricted, traditional approach to children's financial well-being suggests one of two things: Either the drafters thought children's emotional health was more important than their financial health or they thought diminishment of traditional parental rights was not as significant a state interference as imposing financial obligation on nontraditional parents.

Consider Illustration 4 in chapter 3 of the PRINCIPLES, precisely the kind of scenario in which someone is likely to have custody or visitation rights as de facto parent under chapter 2, but not have financial responsibility for a child under chapter 3. Fred, a widowed father of two, cohabited with Allen for five years before separating.[90] During their cohabitation Fred and Allen shared their earnings and the children benefited from the increased household income. Assume also that Fred and Allen shared caretaking responsibilities, with Allen doing as much as Fred.[91] Allen would have custodial rights as a de facto parent[92] but, absent "affirmative conduct [indicating] . . . an agreement to assume a parental support obligation" and even then only in "exceptional" circumstances, Allen would not be responsible for any child support.[93]

[86] *See supra* note note 2.

[87] *See supra* note note 20.

[88] The state could diffuse parents' obligation either by assuming some of the support duty itself, as virtually every other industrialized country does, or by imposing support obligations on the people who are dissipating traditional rights. *See* Social Security Administration, Research Report #65, SSA Publication No. 13–11805, Social Security Programs Throughout the World – 1997 xxvi xx–xxxv, xxvi.

[89] PRINCIPLES § 2.02 cmt. e, at 98 ("The continuity of existing parent-child attachments after the break-up of a family unit is a factor critical to the child's well-being. Such attachments are thought to affect the child's sense of identity and later ability to trust and form healthy relationships.").

[90] PRINCIPLES § 3.03 illus. 4, at 417.

[91] There could be any of a number of reasons for this, including the rather benign one that Allen's schedule afforded him more flexibility and therefore it was easier for him to attend to the children's schedules.

[92] PRINCIPLES § 2.03(c).

[93] *See* PRINCIPLES § 3.03(1). The Comments state that Allen is not responsible for child support even though Fred is a widower. There is no other parent available to provide support, Illust. 4.

Perhaps this makes sense because a child's emotional well-being is simply more important than his material well-being. Generations of happy, productive people who were raised without many resources by loving parents or other adults might compel such a conclusion. It is odd, though, that the PRINCIPLES do not cite any data supporting this conclusion, nor do they even mention that they are treating emotional relationships as more important than financial ones. Perhaps then the PRINCIPLES rest on another premise: that, regardless of what actually is more important to the child, the child perceives the emotional relationship as more important. In other words, the child relies on the emotional relationship in an important psychological sense. Various scholars have advanced this argument in advocating for expansive notions of parenthood.[94] The problem with this as a rationale for the PRINCIPLES is that the custody and visitation provisions specifically reject reliance as a rationale. The "focus [is] on function, rather than on detrimental reliance."[95] To the extent that the custody provisions invoke a concept other than function, they suggest that the "expectation of the parties" as to the relationship's continuance can be relevant.[96] Why not, then, ground a continuing support obligation on function and expectation also? If the concern is consistency, certainly Fred's children will experience more consistency if they can count on some financial assistance from Allen, rather than suffer a significant decline in their standard of living.[97] Empirical work underscores that it is the relative decline in income, rather than the absolute income level, that is most likely to hurt children.[98] The recent trend among courts that impose support obligations on nontraditional parents has been to look to the extent of reliance by the child, the custodial parent, or both.[99] The PRINCIPLES reject this trend. By refusing to let obligation grow out of function, reliance, or expectation, the PRINCIPLES preference emotional connections over financial ones without giving a reason why.

Perhaps, then the drafters simply thought it less intrusive for the state to interfere with traditional parental rights than it was for the state to impose nontraditional obligations. The liberty taken from traditional parents by diminishing their rights might be seen as

[94] *See* Bartlett, *supra* note 44 at 903–906; Naomi Cahn, *Reframing Child Custody Decision-Making*, 58 OHIO ST. L J. 1, 49–50 (1997).

[95] PRINCIPLES § 2.03 cmt. b, at 110 ("While these circumstances typically contain a component of reliance by the individual claiming parent status, the goal of the Chapter is to protect parent-child relationship presumed to have developed under these various circumstances rather than reliance itself. Accordingly, the requirements of Section 2.03(1)(b) focus on function, rather than on detrimental reliance.").

[96] PRINCIPLES § 2.03 cmt. (b)(ii), at 112.

[97] Judith Seltzer, *Consequences of Marital Dissolution for Children*, 10 Am Rev. Sociol. 235, 250 (1994) ("Stepfathers are an important source of children's income... Children who live with stepfathers generally benefit from these men's investments in improved housing and neighborhood location and from step father contributions to daily needs.").

[98] *See* MCLANAHAN & SANDEFUR, *supra* note 2, at 94 ("These finding provide strong evidence that it is not just low income per se but the *loss* of economic resources associated with family disruption that is a major source of lower achievement of children of divorce."). *See also* J. S. WALLERSTEIN & J. B. KELLY, SURVIVING THE BREAK-UP: HOW CHILDREN AND PARENTS COPE WITH DIVORCE (1980) and J. S. WALLERSTEIN & S. BLAKESLEE, SECOND CHANCES: MEN, WOMEN AND CHILDREN A DECADE AFTER DIVORCE (1990) (noting that children feel and resent the sense of loss associated with the decreased standard of living after separation).

[99] *In re* Paternity of Cheryl, *supra* note 36, ("Cheryl knew and relied on [the man who had been supporting her] as her father"); Monmouth County v. R.K., 757 A2d 319, 331 (NJ Super. Ct. Ch. Div 2000) ("[child] has been financially reliant upon [man who had been supporting her]"); Wright v. Newman, 467 S.E.2d 533, 535 (Georgia 1996) (finding both mother and child "relied upon [man's] promise to their detriment"); Markov v. Markov, 758 A.2d 75, 83 (Md. 2000)("[I]t is incumbent upon Appellee... to prove sufficiently that her reliance upon Appellant's prior conduct and verbal representations has resulted in a... loss.").

less important than the property taken from nontraditional parents if the state imposed a child support obligation on them. Construing the relationship of rights and obligation in this way, particularly in light of the fact that divorce and nonmarital births have already dissipated the strength of parental rights, may make some sense. But this construction actually reverses both traditional liberal thinking and more contemporary communitarian thinking. John Locke observed, "[t]he power... that parents have over their children, [arises] from that duty which is incumbent on them, to take care of their offspring during the imperfect state of childhood."[100] In other words, the duty comes first. One has rights to bring up the child "in the way he should go"[101] because one has an obligation to the child. Hegel reached the same conclusion, writing that what gave parents the right to their children's services was the parents' obligation to provide for them.[102] This tether between rights and responsibilities is also a common feature of communitarian thinking. Amitai Etzioni contends that the rights that society bestows on its members "requires community members to live up to their social responsibilities."[103]

For sure, Locke and Hegel viewed rights to children in very different terms than we do today. Children no longer provide parents with the kind of services that they once did.[104] Nonetheless, as every person who fights for custodial privileges will attest, children are still critically valuable resources, not just to society but also to the individuals who wish to maintain relationships. Being able to take a child to the park may be the modern day equivalent of being able to use a child's labor on the farm, but in both cases the adult gains value from the child. The PRINCIPLES ignore the foundational thinking about the relationship between rights and responsibilities.

The only explicit reason the PRINCIPLES give for inverting the traditional relationship between rights and obligations emerges from a close reading of the Reporter's Notes, which cite *Miller v. Miller*, a New Jersey case.[105] There, the court explained that imposing a support obligation on stepparents would discourage too many people from becoming stepparents.[106] In other words, if Allen is worried that he might someday be responsible for child support, he will never move in with Fred and start supporting his children. The children then will lose both the temporary support that Allen can provide and the chance for long term support that Allen would provide if he and Fred stayed together.

There are several problems with this rationale. First, it is not at all clear that potential stepparents' demand curves are as elastic as the reasoning suggests. When someone moves in with or marries another adult with children, potential future liability is often a distant and not particularly relevant concern. Common experience and available data suggest people are wildly optimistic about relationships in their early stages.[107] The drafters' own call for scrutiny of prenuptial agreements in the PRINCIPLES is based on people's tendency to overvalue present benefits, over-discount future benefits, and treat low probability events

[100] JOHN LOCKE, 2 TWO TREATISES OF GOVERNMENT § 58 308 (Laslett, ed.)(1988).

[101] Prince v. Massachusetts, 321 U.S. 158, 164 (1944).

[102] GEORG WILHELM FREDRICH HEGEL, ELEMENTS OF THE PHILOSOPHY OF RIGHT' 174 (A. Wood, ed. 1991).

[103] Amitai Etzioni, *The Responsive Community: A Communitarian Perspective*, 199 AM SOCIO. REV. 1, 9 (1996).

[104] Naomi Cahn, *Perfect Substitutes or the Real Thing*, 52 DUKE L. J. 1077, 1988 (2003) (finding children were economically valuable until the middle of the 19th century).

[105] PRINCIPLES § 3.03 cmt. b, reporter's note at 420 (citing Miller v. Miller, 478 A.2d 351 (N.J. 1984)).

[106] Miller, *supra* note.

[107] Lynn A. Baker & Robert E. Emery, *When Every Relationship is Above Average: Perceptions and Expectations of Divorce at the Time of Marriage*, 17 LAW & HUM. BEHAV. 439, 443 (1993).

as having zero probability.[108] If potential stepparents behave like everyone else, they will heavily discount the chances of breaking up and so are unlikely to be dissuaded by any potential child support obligation that might result.

Second, the *Miller* logic assumes that the potential obligors care more about foregoing obligation than embracing rights. The chance to live with and provide for children allows potential obligors to enjoy all of the relationship benefits that lead adults to fight for custodial privileges in chapter 2. Some courts that have imposed child support obligations on nonlegal parents have done so precisely because the nonlegal parent enjoyed the benefits of parenthood.[109] The PRINCIPLES reject this rights/obligation trade-off for fear that too few people will enter into relationships with children if they are worried about future liability. One wonders, however, why the drafters are so eager to award someone custody or visitation rights if that same person would not have developed the relationship had she known that there might be a financial cost. How strong can a person's emotional commitment to a relationship be if she would let its financial implications dictate her decision to start it or stay in it?

In sum, the preference for protecting children's emotional interests over their financial interests is inconsistent with liberal and communitarian thinking about the relationship between parental rights and obligations, and seems somewhat blind to the recognition that the very same concerns for consistency and expectation that underlie the expansion of custody and visitation rights could support the expansion of financial obligation. It also assumes, without support, that potential future obligation will significantly detract from one's willingness to parent a child.

D. Obligation From Volition

The PRINCIPLES reject the idea that obligation can flow from functional relationship, but endorse the idea that obligation can flow from an express intent to provide support. To impose a support obligation under the PRINCIPLES, a court must find "affirmative conduct," and a clear agreement to assume the support obligation either before or after the child's birth.[110] Marriage or cohabitation at the time of the child's birth, coupled with affirmative conduct, can also trigger responsibility.[111] Agreeing to marry or cohabit with a pregnant woman serves as a proxy for agreeing to support the child. For the most part, the intent to agree to support a child must be obvious to all concerned.[112]

Initially, this may seem like a sensible structure for parental obligation. The law should bind as parents only those people who agree to be parents. If one does not intend to be a parent to a child, one should not be saddled with the obligations of a parent. Further

[108] PRINCIPLES § 7.05 cmt. b, at 986.

[109] *See* Wade v. Wade, 536 So.2d 1158 (Fla. Dist. Ct. App. 1988) (finding "the benefits of his representations as the child's father, including the child's love and affection, his status as father . . . and the community's recognition of him as the father" justify imposing a support obligation.); Gonzalez v. Andreas, 369 A.2d 416, 418 (Pa. Super. Ct. 1976).

[110] Section 3.03(1) requires "an explicit or implicit agreement or undertaking by the person to assume a parental support obligation to the child." Section 3.03(1)(c) requires that the child be "conceived pursuant to an agreement between the person and the child's parent that they would share responsibility for raising the child."

[111] PRINCIPLES § 3.03(1)(b).

[112] The PRINCIPLES intimate that one need not make one's intent explicit. An "*implicit* agreement or undertaking to assume a parental support obligation" can make a person responsible in exceptional circumstances, but that implicit agreement still has to involve "affirmative conduct." PRINCIPLES § 3.03(1)(a). As discussed earlier, just what constitutes "affirmative conduct" is an open question. *See supra* text accompanying notes 22–23. "Exceptional" circumstances probably include those in which a second parent is not available.

scrutiny reveals the limitations of this notion. The PRINCIPLES' reliance on notions of *legal* paternity in the support provisions strongly suggest that intent should not be determinative of parenthood and intent can be trumped if there is another parent in the picture.[113] Moreover, other sections of the PRINCIPLES suggest that obligation can and should grow from function as well as intent.

First, fatherhood based on intent for support purposes is inconsistent with the PRINCIPLES' reliance on extant notions of legal and biological parenthood.[114] Traditional paternity rules have never required a finding of intent to parent or intent to provide support before saddling someone with child support payments. For unmarried men, biological connection, not intent, was traditionally and still is the single most important factor in determining paternity. Boys who are statutorily raped[115] and men whose partners lie to them about their use of birth control[116] are held responsible for child support despite the fact that they had no intent to parent. The justification for these rules is usually that the right to child support is the child's right and therefore the mother's malfeasance should not defeat the child's right to support.[117] In one recent case, a Florida man entered into a "Preconception Agreement" with his partner before having intercourse. In the Agreement, she promised not to identify him as the father or sue him for paternity.[118] He was nonetheless held responsible for child support after a paternity adjudication because, the court held, "the rights of support and meaningful relationship belong to the child, not the parent; therefore neither parent can bargain away those rights." It is hard to imagine a more complete rejection of intent as a basis of parenthood.

To be fair, the PRINCIPLES' reliance on intent to determine obligation is consistent with one growing segment of parentage cases, those involving assisted reproduction. For children born as a result of any process other than heterosexual intercourse, preconception intent is emerging as the predominant paradigm for determining parentage.[119] If friends get together and informally agree that one will donate sperm so that the other can get pregnant, the preconception intent of the parties, as manifested in explicit or implicit agreements, governs who will be held financially responsible.[120] If parties sign a surrogacy contract or participate in another arrangement that relies on the variety of reproductive technologies now available, most courts enforce those contracts in the name of respecting the parties' intent.[121] Thus, the reproductive process is critical to determining whether intent to parent

[113] PRINCIPLES § 3.03 cmt. d, reporter's note at 421.

[114] According to most state parentage acts, legal and biological paternity goes hand in hand. The biological father is the legal father. Courts often reject this tautology, however, in an effort to award the "better" father with parental rights. *See supra* notes 33–38 and accompanying text.

[115] Kansas ex. rel. Hermesmann v. Sayer, 847 P.2d 1273 (Kan. 1993); San Luis Obispo v. Nathaniel J., n. 57 Cal. Rptr. 2d 843 (Cal. Ct. App. 1996); Mercer County Dep't of Social Servs. on behalf of Imogene T. v. Alf M., 589 N.Y.S.2d 288 (N.Y. Misc., 1992).

[116] Wallis v. Smith, 22 P.3d 682 (N.M. 2001) (holding father cannot sue in tort to recover compensatory damages stemming from girlfriend's misrepresentation about birth control); Moorman v. Walker, 773 P.2d 887, 889 (Wash. 1989); Pamela P. v. Frank S., 449 N.E.2d 7134, 715 (N.Y. 1983).

[117] *See supra* notes 114–115.

[118] Budnick v. Silverman, 805 So.2d 1112, 1113 (Fla. Dist. Ct. App. 2002).

[119] *See* Baker, *supra* note 29, at 26–28.

[120] *See* R.C. v. J.R. 129 P.2d 27 (Colo. 1989) (reviewing the legal commentary on the subject and most of the decided cases, and holding that the determinative question for support purposes is whether the sperm donor and the mother "at the time of insemination agree that [the sperm donor] will be the natural father.").

[121] *See* Johnson v. Calvert, 851 P.2d 776 (Cal. 1993); McDonald v. McDonald, 608 N.Y.S.2d 477 (N.Y. App. Div. 1994). *See also* John Lawrence Hill, *What does it Mean to be a Parent? The Claims of Biology as the Basis for Parental Rights*, 66 N.Y.U. L. REV. 353 (1991); Lori Andrews, *Legal and Ethical Aspects of New Reproductive Technologies*, 29 CLIN. OBSTET. & GYN. 190 (1986). *But see* Marsha Garrison, *Law Making for Baby Making: An Interpretive Approach to*

matters. For babies born the old-fashioned way, as in *Budnick*, intent to parent is irrelevant. For babies born the modern way, as with surrogacy or artificial insemination, intent to parent is determinative. By relying so heavily on extant legal definitions of paternity, the PRINCIPLES embrace this inconsistency. Parentage statutes continue to use blood and presumptions and "Best Interest of the Child" determinations,[122] none of which necessarily measure intent, while reproductive technology contracts and the exceptional circumstances contemplated by the PRINCIPLES rely on intent to determine parental obligation.

Also, relying on intent seems inconsistent with the PRINCIPLES' position that a nontraditional parent should not be liable for child support if there is another source of income for the child. The PRINCIPLES caution against finding a support obligation if "the child otherwise has two parents who owe the child a duty of support and are able and available to provide support."[123] It is not clear, from either a child-centered perspective or an obligor-centered perspective, why this alternative source of revenue should be relevant to the responsibility of the volitional actor.

From a child-centered perspective, the potential parent by estoppel may be providing critical amounts of support before the adults break up. As discussed earlier, a stepparent or cohabitant can provide a child with a standard of living to which the child becomes accustomed and the loss of which could cause the child significant harm.[124] Another legal parent who is "able and available to provide support" may be able to provide only a fraction of what the potential parent-by-estoppel can provide.[125] This difference in the ability to provide appears to make little difference to the drafters.

From an obligor-centered perspective, the support duty seems arbitrary, despite its volitional character. One's ultimate responsibility depends not on what others relied on or on what one promised or actually did. It depends on the availability of another payor whom one likely does not know and may never have met. Consider the not-so-uncommon situation of a man who finds out that he is not the biological father of his wife's or girlfriend's child.[126] He can accept that child as his own, provide for the child financially, develop or continue a relationship with the child, and still be relieved of obligation if the biological father surfaces.[127] If the biological father does not surface, he can be held responsible. His obligation is based largely on the chance finding of the biological parent.

Finally, chapter 3's insistence on volition is inconsistent with the treatment of obligation elsewhere in the PRINCIPLES. The domestic partnership provisions allow obligation between cohabitants to grow from either "losses that arise from the changes in life opportunities and expectations caused by the adjustments individuals ordinarily make over the course of a relationship"[128] or from "disparities in the financial impact of a short

the Determination of Legal Parentage, 113 HARV. L. REV. 835 (2000) (arguing that parental determinations in cases of reproductive technologies should be governed by existing family law rules, many of which do not honor intent).

[122] *See supra* notes 30–36.

[123] PRINCIPLES § 3.03(2).

[124] *See supra* note 98.

[125] The amount an obligor owes is based on what the obligor earns. If the legal parent does not have much, there is not much to get from him. *See* § 3.05(3).

[126] *See, e.g.*, Markov v. Markov, *supra* note 99 (considering the support obligation of a husband who did not know he was not the biological father of twins born 10 months into the marriage; In re Cheryl, *supra* note 36 (considering the support duties of an ex-boyfriend who was told and believed that he was the biological father of the child).

[127] *See* Markov v. Markov, *supra* note 99 (finding that the husband's responsibility for child support depends on whether the biological father can be found); Monmouth County v. R. K., *supra* note 99, citing Miller v. Miller, *supra* note 105.

[128] PRINCIPLES § 6.02(1)(b)(ii).

relationship on the partners' post separation [sic] lives."[129] Thus, a former cohabitant can incur an ongoing duty of support despite having never manifested an intent to assume that obligation. This is so because the PRINCIPLES recognize that adults adjust their lives and expectations in the course of sharing a household with someone. This chapter endorses the view that the law should mitigate some of the harshness that can follow when a household breaks up, regardless of whether the parties agreed to provide for each other after they separated. Ironically, this means that it is actually easier under the PRINCIPLES to become obligated to an adult who theoretically has some ability to provide for him or herself, than it is to become obligated to a child who has no such ability.

III. Conclusion

In embracing the case-by-case functional approach to custody and visitation rights, the PRINCIPLES quote a Maryland court with approval: "Formula or computer solutions in child custody matters are impossible because of the unique character of each case and the subjective nature of the evaluation and decisions that must be made."[130] The drafters offer no reason for why particular obligations are rooted less in unique or subjective factors than are custody decisions, but as the foregoing makes clear, the PRINCIPLES clearly reject the case-by-case functional approach to child support obligations. Severing the approach to rights and responsibilities in this way, even if done without explanation, may nonetheless make sound, risk-averse policy sense. If the state is unwilling to accept responsibility; if men will not form relationships with women or children if those relationships could lead to obligation; if policy makers have so little faith in judges' ability to make case-by-case support determinations, then the PRINCIPLES' approach may be the best option.

The most straightforward way to alleviate the harm done by too few financial resources for children would be for the United States, like almost all industrialized countries, to develop a more comprehensive system of state support for children. This kind of system would correspond to the PRINCIPLES' expansion of state control over child rearing decisions in its custody and visitation provisions. Politically, though, as the drafters acknowledge, the United States is a long, long way from accepting significantly more communal responsibility for children.[131] Tinkering with the traditional approach to child support obligations without enlisting the state as a guarantor in the end may be simply too risky.

Moreover, once a child support system ceases holding traditional parents automatically accountable and starts relying instead on notions of function, expectation, reliance, or intent, it runs the risk that no one other than a primary parent will actually incur the legal obligation to support a child. Perhaps, as the *Miller* court warned with respect to stepparents, nonbiological fathers will not marry or move in with women who already have children. Perhaps men will cease providing for children in the way they do now. Perhaps grandparents, like the Bannisters, and grandmothers everywhere will cease forming bonds with children out of fear that such bonds will lead to financial obligations. If these fears are realistic, then the PRINCIPLES' asymmetric approach to rights and obligation may protect children in the best way we can. That is, we protect children's emotional expectations

[129] PRINCIPLES § 6.02(1)(b)(iii).

[130] PRINCIPLES § 2.02 cmt. c, reporter's note at 104.

[131] *See* PRINCIPLES § 3.04 cmt. g, at 429 ("What distinguishes the United States from other wealthy western countries is its disinclination to act as a primary guarantor of children's economic adequacy.").

and not their financial ones because the protection of their financial expectations would undermine the very existence of potential emotional relationships.

A support system based more on notions of function, expectation, or reliance, would also require a return to less mechanistic measures of obligation. The binary parent formula offered in the PRINCIPLES may be based on an idealized and unrealistic binary biological model of parenthood but, like all child-support formulas adopted in the last thirty years, it takes away the discretion and bias that led to wildly inconsistent and often unacceptably small child support awards.[132] Premising a support system on function, reliance, or expectation would require tailoring different support awards to reflect the extent of function, reliance, and expectation. This type of case-by-case analysis would preclude the use of formulas. It might be that we have so little faith in the judiciary's ability to formulate and enforce case-specific orders that we are better off living with formulas based on counterfactual norms than with theories of support based on parenthood as lived.

The rigidity of the ALI's proposed model does diminish the likelihood that the parties, negotiating on their own, will trade custody for support. A bright line rule with regard to support, like the one offered in the PRINCIPLES, reduces the opportunities for strategic bargaining. Although the comments barely acknowledge this concern it may have played a role in their strict allegiance to a formula.[133] There are several ways to expand or incorporate certain formulas (thus reducing strategic behavior) while recognizing the heterogeneous nature of contemporary parenthood, however. First, the formula could still be used in situations involving the binary biological ideal or in all divorce proceedings. Second, alternative models that allocated responsibility based on a percentage of custody or visitation time would provide enough clarity to reduce strategic bargaining while incorporating different theories of obligation. Third, states could adopt a presumption in favor of a primary formula, but allow that presumption to be overcome in the type of cases that lead to multiple parenthood under the PRINCIPLES' custody and visitation provisions. In short, it is perfectly possible to minimize strategic behavior with regard to bargaining over custody, without forgoing multiple nontraditional sources of parental obligation.

Finally, the PRINCIPLES' ambivalent treatment of intent to provide support for a child may be necessary in light of the uncertainty surrounding men's behavior in the absence of biological obligation. Embracing intent as the standard by which society should determine parenthood – the way courts now do in the reproductive technology area and the way the PRINCIPLES reluctantly do by allowing affirmative conduct plus agreement to lead to obligation – may erode traditional paternity law. Traditional paternity law roots obligation in genetic connection. If the law uses intent, not blood, as the lynchpin of parenthood, then some men could escape parental obligation. Men who are unwilling to forego reproductive sex but have no intent to parent can currently be held responsible for child support. If we dispensed with biology, these men could have reproductive sex without having to worry about supporting any child who results. Of course, currently, most of these men probably

[132] *See* Nancy Thoennes et. al., *The Impact of Child-Support Guidelines on Award Adequacy, Award Availability and Case Processing Efficiency*, 25 FAM. L.Q. 325, 326 (1991) (citing studies).

[133] Illustration 3 in Section 3.13 does mention the problem with bargaining, but suggests that the strong presumptions with regard to custody and visitation in chapter 2 diminish the likelihood of oppressive bargaining. As long as the presumption in chapter 2 is solid enough, there is less need to worry about parties bargaining away child support in return for custody.

end up living with and fathering either their own biological issue or someone else's.[134] A child support system rooted in function, reliance, or expectation would still find these men responsible, but it might be seen as too risky.

* * *

Changes in both social norms and technology have altered, fundamentally, how people become and function as parents. It defies reality to assume that children will be cared or provided for within the confines of a binary biological norm. The binary biological model may still express our ideal but it does not reflect our world. The custody and visitation provisions of the PRINCIPLES embrace this reality. In contrast, the PRINCIPLES' child support provisions hold on tight to the traditional ideal, unwilling to answer the question of what should make someone responsible for a child, and perhaps fearful of how little support a child would actually receive if our child support system embraced the truth about contemporary parenting.

I'd like to thank the contributors to this volume for helpful comments and suggestions.

[134] *See* Furstenburg and Nord, *supra* note 27, at 903; DOWD, *supra* note 52.

7 Paying to Stay Home: On Competing Notions of Fairness and the Imputation of Income

Mark Strasser

The PRINCIPLES' child support provisions[1] try to respect and give weight to the interests of the parents while minimizing damage to the child or children at issue. The result is an impressive, balanced treatment in an area fraught with difficulty. This chapter focuses on one specific issue which helps illustrate some of the competing interests and rationales which are involved when decisions about child support must be made – namely, the conditions under which the ALI and various jurisdictions in the United States believe income should be imputed to a stay-at-home parent.

A number of important, competing considerations are at issue when deciding income attribution questions. As a general matter, jurisdictions believe that children should not be put at a disadvantage merely because their parents are no longer living together.[2] They also believe that where practicable all parents should maintain close relationships with and contribute to the support of their children.[3] In many instances, these goals conflict and compromises must be reached. It is not surprising, then, that different jurisdictions reach different conclusions about how to weigh these sometimes competing considerations and thus have adopted different policies with respect to when income should be attributed to a stay-at-home parent.[4]

One confusing aspect of the ALI proposal is that the reasons offered in support do not fit tightly with the drafters' recommendations.[5] While sensible and legitimate, the considerations articulated by the drafters support both the policy proposed and a number of other policies. One cannot help but suspect that the real reasons underpinning the ALI's particular recommendations were not articulated. While it would be too much to ask for all of the reasons and their respective weights to be clearly and explicitly articulated, the recommendations may have been more persuasive had the drafters spelled out the justifications more fully.

The difficulty created by failing to spell out all of this more clearly is that a large number of different policies take the considerations identified by the drafters into account to a greater or lesser degree. Without an explicit weighting or a more detailed discussion of

[1] PRINCIPLES ch. 3.

[2] *See* In re Marriage of Rottscheit, 664 N.W.2d 525, 530 (Wis. 2003) (explaining that the purpose of child support is to ensure to the degree possible that a child's standard of living will not be adversely affected because the parents are no longer living together).

[3] *See* Kay v. Ludwig, 686 N.W.2d 619 (Neb. Ct. App. 2004) (discussing legislative finding that it is in the best interests of the child to have ongoing involvement in the life of the child by both parents).

[4] *See infra* Part II (B) and accompanying text.

[5] *See infra* Part II and accompanying text.

how to balance some of these considerations, the jurisdictions deciding whether or how to modify existing policy are not aided in deciding which policy to adopt.

Part I of this chapter discusses the conditions under which income will be imputed to a stay-at-home parent, focusing on the respects in which residential and nonresidential parents are treated dissimilarly. Part II discusses the ALI's rationales for its policy proposals, suggesting that the rationales do not justify choosing the recommended policies rather than any of a host of alternatives, which factor in the same considerations, although giving them somewhat different weights. The chapter concludes that, while the ALI has pointed to many of the relevant considerations, it has provided too little guidance with respect to how these competing considerations should be balanced against each other, leaving that very difficult task for others.

I. Imputation of Income to Stay-at-Home Parents

The PRINCIPLES' child support provisions discuss the conditions under which it is appropriate to impute income to a parent, offering a number of recommendations about what to do when a parent is underemployed or unemployed. The intuitions behind the recommendations are eminently sensible, for example, that individuals who seek retraining to better provide for their children should not be prevented from doing so,[6] or that individuals who refuse to work in order to avoid paying child support should not be rewarded by being excused from paying that support.[7] Notwithstanding the reasonableness of these intuitions, one might nonetheless disagree with some of the particulars of the policies suggested. Courts and legislatures sometimes take approaches to these issues which differ from that of the ALI, at least in part, because of different emphases on different policy goals.

A. When May Income Be Imputed?

The PRINCIPLES' child support provisions suggest that as a general matter it is appropriate to attribute income to a parent if "the court finds that a parent is voluntarily unemployed or underemployed."[8] As an initial matter, it may be helpful to consider what would count as being unemployed or underemployed. An individual who is not earning money will be considered unemployed whether that individual is taking care of children or ill parents,[9] or spending time in other ways the individual finds valuable.[10] An individual who earns less money than that person might reasonably be expected to earn might be viewed as

[6] *Cf.* Stufflebean v. Stufflebean, 941 S.W.2d 844, 847 (Mo. Ct. App. 1997) ("To prohibit a custodial parent who is attending school from having her child care expenses considered for child support purposes would, in effect, discourage a custodial parent from attending college to better equip herself to obtain employment and, thus, eventually contribute to the support of the children.").

[7] *Cf. id.* at 846 ("A spouse may not escape responsibility to her or her minor children by deliberately limiting his or her work to reduce income.") (citing Jensen v. Jensen, 877 S.W.2d 131, 136 (Mo. Ct. App. 1994)).

[8] PRINCIPLES § 3.14(5), at 521.

[9] *See In re* Z.B.P., 109 S.W.3d 772, 783 (Tex. Ct. App. 2003) ("The evidence showed that part of the reason for her unemployment was that she took care of her elderly and sick parents who lived next door.").

[10] *See* Pharo v. Trice, 711 S.W.2d 282, 284 (Tex. Ct. App. 1986) (Pharo "currently spends her time researching genealogy, working with the library, working with the Dallas Medical County Medical Auxiliary, playing tennis, being involved with the Park Cities Tennis Association, and helping a friend put together a cookbook.").

underemployed – for example, spending too few hours at work[11] or, perhaps, working at a different, less well-paying job even if working full time.[12]

If a parent is unemployed or underemployed, "the court may impute income to the parent on the basis of the parent's demonstrated earning capacity," or if "there is no reliable basis for earnings, gainful earnings may be imputed at the prevailing minimum wage."[13] However, certain exceptions applicable to both residential and nonresidential parents are offered when, for example, the parents seek retraining to make themselves more marketable.[14] In addition, there are separate exceptions applicable only to residential parents.[15]

B. Special Exceptions for Residential Parents

Section 3.15 of the PRINCIPLES discusses the limitations on attribution to residential parents, stating:

> The child support rules should provide that the court may impute income to the residential parent . . . [w]hen the residential parent is not caring for a child of the parties under the age of six and is earning less than the parent could reasonably earn considering the parent's residential responsibility for the children of the parties.[16]

Thus, the PRINCIPLES suggest that residential parents should not have income imputed when either of two conditions applies:

(a) The residential parent cares for a child of the parties under the age of six, or
(b) The residential parent earns all that might reasonably be expected, given the parent's residential duties.

Condition (a) is self-explanatory. Indeed, the provision proposes an absolute ban on the imputation of income to residential parents if the child to be benefited by the order has not yet reached school age.[17] The drafters do not wish "to second guess the hard choices

[11] *Cf.* Saussy v. Saussy, 638 So.2d 711 (La. Ct. App. 1994) (discussing an individual who took a job requiring fewer hours at least in part because he could then visit his children on alternate weekends).

[12] *See, e.g.*, PRINCIPLES § 3.14 cmt. e, illus. 5, at 526 (discussing an individual who wishes to resign his partnership in a firm to become a supervising attorney at a legal aid office where he would earn roughly 38 percent of what he would have earned as a partner).

[13] PRINCIPLES § 3.14(5).

[14] *See* PRINCIPLES § 3.14(5).

Gainful earnings should not be imputed to an unemployed or underemployed parent to the extent that such unemployment or underemployment is attributable to:

(a) a parent's pursuit of education, training, or retraining in order to improve employment skills so long as the pursuit is not unreasonable in light of the circumstances and the parent's responsibility for dependents
(b) a parent's change of occupation so long as the child support award based upon the parent's employment in the new occupation does not unreasonably reduce the child's standard of living taking into account the child's total economic circumstances.

[15] *See* PRINCIPLES § 3.14(5)(c).

> [A] parent's residential responsibility for a child of the parties. A parent's unemployment or underemployment should be deemed attributable to a parent's residential responsibility for a child of the parties when a parent would not be subject to income imputation under § 3.15(1)(a). The court may also find, in other circumstances, that a parent's unemployment or underemployment is attributable to a parent's residential responsibility for a child of the parties.

[16] PRINCIPLES § 3.15(a).

[17] *See* PRINCIPLES § 3.15 cmt. b, at 535. ("The PRINCIPLES do not impute earnings to the residential parent when a child who is the subject of the child support order has not yet reached primary-school age.").

facing parents with residential responsibilities for preschool children,"[18] understanding "the difficulties of securing adequate day care and meeting employer expectations while serving as the residential parent of a young child."[19] Certainly, it cannot be doubted that parents have difficult choices to make, with numerous competing considerations to weigh and balance, when deciding who should be caring for their children.

The ALI recognizes that the difficulties involved in securing adequate day care and meeting employer expectations do not end once the child reaches school age.[20] Nonetheless, the PRINCIPLES argue that the difficulties "lessen substantially at that point"[21] and, consequently, would permit imputation of income when the child is six years of age or older. It is a mistake, however, to believe that the drafters are comfortable with imputation when the child reaches six. The ALI is plainly reluctant to prescribe which choices a parent should make, describing the practice of imputation as "problematic in concept and effect,"[22] because it allegedly "expresses a judgment about how [parents] should allocate their time between gainful employment and child rearing, a matter normally left to the decision-making of parents."[23] The PRINCIPLES further caution that, "to the extent that income is merely imputed, but not realized, the effect is to penalize the child economically for the parent's decision to give the child more rather than less direct parental care."[24] The drafters conclude their commentary by suggesting that the decision about whether to attribute income should be made "with due respect for the residential parent's reasonable parenting choices."[25]

C. On Making Good Choices

While due respect should, of course, be given to a parent's reasonable parenting choices, it is not at all clear that the justifications offered by the PRINCIPLES can do all of the work intended. For example, decisions about child care are difficult in the best of circumstances, and as a general matter parents can be presumed to care more than the state about the welfare of their children.[26] Indeed, one argument that might underlie the ALI's position is that parents are more likely to have the best interests of the child at heart than is the state, and thus should be presumed to be doing what is best for the child.

While it is reasonable to presume that parents have the best interests of the child at heart, employing this presumption does not resolve whether income should be imputed in a particular case, since parents may themselves disagree about what would be best. In many cases, if the nonresidential parent supported the residential parent's decision to stay home with the child, the nonresidential parent presumably would not request that income be imputed to the residential parent. Yet, if parents disagree about what is best for the child, the presumption that parents have the best interests of the child at heart will not resolve whether income should be imputed. To resolve this issue, one might have to assume, for example, that a residential parent had the best interests of the child at heart but that the nonresidential parent did not.

[18] PRINCIPLES § 3.15 cmt. b, at 535.

[19] PRINCIPLES § 3.15 cmt. b, at 535.

[20] PRINCIPLES § 3.15 cmt. b, at 535 (noting that the difficulties "do not entirely disappear when a child enters school").

[21] PRINCIPLES § 3.15 cmt. b, at 535.

[22] PRINCIPLES § 3.15 cmt. b, at 535.

[23] PRINCIPLES § 3.15 cmt. b, at 535.

[24] PRINCIPLES § 3.15 cmt. b, at 535.

[25] PRINCIPLES § 3.15 cmt. b, at 535.

[26] *Cf. In re* Marriage of Horner, 2004 WL 1403306, *5 (Wash. 2004) (discussing the "traditional presumption that a fit parent will act in the best interests of her child").

It is possible that the nonresidential parent would agree that the child is better off with child care provided by the residential parent, but nonetheless may not want to pay for that care (i.e., wants income to be imputed to the residential parent), just as it is possible that the nonresidential parent does not care what would best promote the interests of the child and instead simply wishes to minimize the support payments. Yet, the state should not presume that the nonresidential parent does not have the child's interests at heart, just as the state should not presume that a parent who wishes to stay home to care for children is merely trying to avoid working outside of the home. Each parent may be seen by the other as undervaluing the importance of the child's interests, but the state should certainly not be making assumptions about whether, as a general matter, residential parents are more willing than nonresidential parents to put their child's interests first. If the state is unwilling to make these assumptions, however, then the ALI's proposal on income imputation may be even harder to justify than might first appear.

A few points should be made clear. The claim here is neither that nonresidential parents always have the best interests of their children at heart, nor that nonresidential parents are more likely than residential parents to have the best interests of their children at heart. The claim is merely that the state should not presume, much less irrefutably presume, that residential parents will make the correct decisions regarding child care for the first six years of the child's life.

A number of factors may go into a decision regarding what child care arrangement would be best. Indeed, imputation of income might affect the relevant calculus – all things considered, it might be best for the child for the residential parent to stay home if income would not be imputed, but not best for the child if income would be imputed. Thus, one way to understand the ALI's proposal is as a suggestion that certain financial considerations be taken off the table when the parent of a child under six is making child care decisions. Yet, if this accurately reflects the ALI's position, one would expect the justification to include studies indicating why six years of age is an important milestone developmentally or, perhaps, some other justification for giving the residential parent of a young child great leeway.[27] Instead, the justifications offered – for example, that this is the kind of decision which should be left up to the parent rather than made by the state[28] – apply to residential parents generally. The justifications do not offer persuasive support for an absolute ban on imputation for residential parents with very young children.

D. The Role of Adequate Child Care Alternatives

As a general matter, the relevant question in income imputation cases is not really whether the residential parent is making the "correct" decision – the question instead is whether the parent is rejecting an "adequate" alternative. This is a more difficult test for the residential parent to meet, since the decision to stay at home with the child may be correct decision, but the parent may nonetheless be subject to income imputation because a different, suboptimal but adequate child care alternative is available.

[27] States vary in the cut-off age they use for imputation to the residential parent. Compare Ky. Rev. Stat. Ann. § 403.212(2)(d) (2003) (instituting an age 3 cut-off) with W.Va. Code Ann. § 48-1-205(c)(1) (2004) (instituting preschool cut-off).

[28] *See supra* note 18 and accompanying text.

Let us assume that it would be best for a particular child if his residential parent were to stay home with him. Even if the parent did not want to choose the adequate but suboptimal choice of daycare outside the home, the parent might nonetheless have a difficult decision to make, since staying at home with the child would not be cost-free. Not only might the parent have to forego the income that would have been received by working outside of the home, but income might be imputed as well. Thus, while the imputation of income is not as great an intrusion as, for example, the parent being told that the child must be put in some kind of daycare, the effect of an imputation should not be minimized. For some families, the fact that income is being imputed will be enough to change the family's financial picture and will therefore require the residential parent to make a different, suboptimal daycare decision.

Yet, the issue at hand is not whether this decision may be a difficult one for some parents. Instead, the issue is why residential parents with children under six years of age are treated differently from parents with older children. For parents with children at least six years of age, the PRINCIPLES suggest that income be imputed if the parent "is earning less than the parent could reasonably earn considering the parent's residential responsibility for the children of the parties."[29] Residential responsibility for an eight-year-old might require that a parent not work if the child has special needs,[30] but many parents can fulfill their residential responsibilities even if working outside of the home by finding acceptable, even if suboptimal, child care. More justification needs to be offered to establish why, for income imputation purposes, complete deference should be given to the residential parent of the five-year old but not to the parent of the six-year-old. While difficulties for the residential parent may lessen once the child reaches school age, it is not at all clear that this change in degree justifies going from an absolute ban on imputation to considering residential responsibilities as merely one factor which might justify a refusal to impute income.

Presumably, one of the intuitions underlying the recommendation that parents with school-age children be subject to imputation is that once a child reaches school age, a parent does not have to worry about child care during school hours. Yet, it is true that some employer flexibility would still be required when, for example, a child is ill, and a parent still needs to worry about after-school activities for the child. Thus, the factors cited to support absolute deference to the residential parent's decision when the child is under six years of age would also support absolute deference when the child is six or older.

Residential parents of children under six are not similarly situated in all relevant respects to residential parents of older children. Yet, the issue here is not whether the best decision for a parent with a younger child would mirror the best decision for a parent with an older child, but only who should be allowed to decide, free from the effects of income imputation. Even if a residential parent with an older child factors into the calculation the fact that the child is now attending school during part of the day, that parent arguably should also be free to make the best decision without feeling the pressure of a possible income imputation.

[29] PRINCIPLES § 3.15(a).

[30] *Cf. In re* Marriage of Pote, 847 P.2d 246 (Colo. Ct. App. 1993) (holding that a mother was not voluntarily under-employed, given the needs of her Downs Syndrome Child) (superceded by statute on a different matter). *See also* Petcu v. Petcu, 1997 WL 695615, *5 (Wash. Ct. App. 1997) (imputed income diminished because of behaviorally difficult child born of the marriage).

Differentiating between residential parents based on a child's age is presumably based on the assumption that older children will attend school outside of the home. A growing number of parents have decided to home school,[31] a development with potentially significant implications for the PRINCIPLES' support proposal, especially if, as seems likely, the ALI would be loath to label home schooling as an unreasonable choice.[32]

While the difficulties in finding adequate daycare and in meeting employer demands are appropriately considered, the PRINCIPLES fail to make the case that these considerations justify a ban on imputation of income when a child under six years of age is a subject of a support order. A position which seems at least as plausible is that these factors might be given differing weights depending upon the circumstances, sometimes being dispositive, sometimes considered but not dispositive, and sometimes not even relevant.

Suppose that a residential parent with a child under six were to hire someone to stay with the child, but nonetheless did not work for pay outside the home, choosing instead to spend time performing tasks that involved neither caring for the child nor earning wages.[33] The PRINCIPLES suggest that income should not be imputed in such a case without even considering whether good daycare was available or whether employment could be secured which was compatible with residential responsibilities.

Perhaps the parent in this example decided that the added flexibility afforded by not having a paying job was worth forgoing the additional income. While such a judgment might be correct, it does not seem to be the kind which should be immune from challenge. Ironically, the PRINCIPLES do not even consider the possibility that residential parents might decide neither to work for pay outside the home nor to provide daycare for their children.

Presumably, most parents would not make the choice described above, even though it is and should be a choice that a residential parent might make. That said, however, Section 3.14 of the PRINCIPLES does not have the flexibility to permit a court to impute income in such a case, which means that the nonresidential parent must subsidize this kind of choice. At the very least, this seems to be the kind of decision that should be open to review, at least in the sense that income might be imputed.

E. The ALI's Position of Neutrality

The ALI does not want to "express[] a judgment about how [parents] should allocate their time between gainful employment and child rearing, a matter normally left to the decision making of parents."[34] While the ALI makes no express judgment, the PRINCIPLES' incentive structure is not neutral, since residential parents are offered incentives to stay

[31] *See* Carolos A. Ball, *Lesbian and Gay Families: Gender Nonconformity and the Implications of Difference*, 31 CAP. U. L. REV. 691, 722–23 (2003) (noting that there "is a growing number of parents in this country who, because of religious beliefs or because of the perceived poor quality of public schools in some areas (or both), are choosing to educate their children at home").

[32] In Bennett v. Commonwealth, 472 S.E.2d 668 (Va. Ct. App. 1996), the court refused to impute income to a mother who was home schooling her two children, although the court justified this by pointing to the special needs of a third child. *See id.* at 672. In Donna G. R. v. James B. R., 877 So.2d 1164 (La. Ct. App. 2004), a Louisiana appellate court held that home schooling was not in the best interests of the children at issue and that support issues would have to be reevaluated because the stay-at-home mother would now be free to work.

[33] *Cf.* Pharo v. Trice, 711 S.W.2d 282, 284 (Tex. Ct. App. 1986) ("Although she . . . [has] an infant daughter, Pharo is able to devote her time to these [non-paying] activities because she employs a full-time baby sitter.").

[34] PRINCIPLES § 3.15 cmt. b, at 535.

home with their children.[35] Perhaps this merely reflects other legal practices which arguably favor stay-at-home parents.[36] In any event, whether or not favoring stay-at-home parents is good public policy, the PRINCIPLES have not adopted a neutral position on this matter.

Mothers remain significantly more likely to be awarded custody after a divorce, which introduces an additional complicating factor.[37] Some might see the PRINCIPLES as advocating that mothers should stay home with their children. Bracketing the merits of these differing views, the ALI position will likely not be seen as neutral,[38] and implicit claims about wishing to remain neutral will not do much to bolster the articulated position.

Consider a different but related matter, namely, the degree of deference that should be given to residential parents' decisions about who will provide daycare for their children. Are such decisions reviewable, at least in the sense that nonresidential parents can challenge the need to pay those costs? This question might arise, for example, if part of a child support order includes a specified amount for child care. One infers that the ALI would recommend complete deference if the child were under six years of age and the costs were not already built into the award.[39]

In *In re Marriage of Scott*,[40] the mother was awarded custody of the children following the divorce.[41] She was working part time and needed day-care for her youngest child.[42] Her ex-husband sought to be excused from paying day-care costs because his mother would provide such services without charge.[43] The mother thought that they would be better off with a different day-care provider, alleging that the paternal grandmother abused alcohol.[44] Finding that the charges against the grandmother were not credible, in part because the grandmother was providing child care for the youngest child at the time of the hearing,[45] the court excused the husband from having to pay day-care costs.

The *Scott* decision does not stand for the proposition that nonresidential parents will only be forced to pay child care costs equivalent to the least expensive services available. The *Scott* court noted that if there was evidence that the grandmother was not suitable, the court would reconsider day-care costs.[46] However, the *Scott* decision does stand for

[35] There is an incentive in that income will not be imputed and also in that child care costs may already have been built into the support. *See* PRINCIPLES § 3.05 cmt. j, at 461.

[36] *Cf.* Adrien Katherine Wing & Laura Weselmann, *Transcending Traditional Notions of Mothering: The Need for Critical Race Feminist Praxis*, 3 J. GENDER RACE & JUST. 257, 258 (1999) ("The law rewards the self-sacrificing, nurturing, married, white, solvent, stay-at-home, monogamous, heterosexual, female mother.").

[37] *See* Martha A Ertman, *Reconstructing Marriage: An Intersexional Approach*, 75 DENV. U. L. REV. 1215, 1220 n.25 (1998) ("Mothers are much more likely to be awarded custody of children of the marriage upon divorce."); Leslie Joan Harris, *The ALI Child Support Principles: Incremental Changes to Improve the Lot of Children and Residential Parents*, 8 DUKE J. GENDER L. & POL'Y 245, 246 (2001) ("most of the time children live with their mothers").

[38] It is not clear that courts are free of notions about the proper roles of the sexes. For example, in Brody v. Brody, 432 S.E.2d 20 (Va. Ct. App. 1993), the court noted that if "the roles had been reversed, and the father chose to leave his job and stay at home to care for the children of another marriage, we would not, without more, uphold an elimination of his obligation to support his other children." *See id.* at 22. One infers that the court would be less willing to countenance a father's staying home with children, although the court did not discuss this at length because it was not before the court.

[39] This is assuming that such costs have not already been built into the support award. *See* PRINCIPLES § 3.05 cmt. j, at 461 ("[T]he ALI formula already includes the nonresidential parent's fair contribution to child-care expenditure necessary to enable the residential parent to pursue gainful employment or vocational training.").

[40] 952 P.2d 1318 (Kan. 1998).

[41] *Id.* at 1319.

[42] *Id.* at 1320.

[43] *Id.*

[44] *Id.* at 1321.

[45] *Id.* at 1320.

[46] *Id.* at 1322 ("If Renee's concerns about the grandmother turn out to be valid, she may request a modification of child support and introduce evidence that work-related outside child care is necessary and should be included in the child support calculations.").

the proposition that courts may second-guess a residential parent's child care decisions, at least insofar as the costs will be shouldered by the nonresidential parent.[47]

II. Justifying These Policy Choices

Understanding that the recommendations treat residential and nonresidential parents differently, the PRINCIPLES offer justifications for that policy choice. Regrettably, these justifications do not adequately support the choices made, which means that those states needing to decide whether or how to change their policies will have too little guidance with respect to what they should do.

A. Treating Residential and Nonresidential Parents Differently

The drafters write that the

> [I]mplications of earnings imputation differ significantly according to whether imputation is to the nonresidential or residential parent, that is, the support obligor or the support obligee. Imputation to the obligor and the obligee differ with respect to (i) the goals sought to be achieved and the harms averted by imputation; (ii) the impact of imputation on a child support award; and (iii) the consequences of error, that is, the consequences of imputing earnings to a parent who will not or cannot earn the amounts imputed by the court.[48]

It is certainly true that residential and nonresidential parents are not similarly situated in all respects, and that imputation of income to each may well have different implications for the children benefited by support orders. When income is imputed to residential parents, the amount of court-ordered child support will decrease, and either the residential parent will have to work more outside the home or the household will have to find another way to absorb or make up for the decrease in child support. When income is imputed to the nonresidential parent, the amount of court-ordered child support will increase, so that the nonresidential parent will have to work more hours, change jobs, or find some other way to pay the increased support or risk legal sanction for failing to do so.[49]

Yet, that said, it is not so clear that "imputation to the obligor and the obligee differ with respect to . . . the goals sought to be achieved and the harms averted by imputation."[50] Presumably, the goal of imputation as a general matter is to make each parent shoulder a fair share of the burden of supporting their child, and the harm to be averted is the imposition of an unfair burden on one of the parents. It may well be that as a result of imputation, a parent, whether residential or nonresidential, may have to change how time is being spent, for example, working outside the home, getting a different job, or working more hours at the same job, but this does not establish that the goals or even the effects differ.

[47] *Id.* at 1322 ("Renee does not have to take the children to the paternal grandmother for child care if she does not feel that this is in the children's best interests. Renee may secure any type of care she desires. The trial court simply decided that the cost of outside child care was unnecessary and David should not have to share in the expense.").

[48] PRINCIPLES § 3.14 cmt. e, at 524.

[49] PRINCIPLES § 3.14 cmt. e, at 524 ("Failure to pay child support may have serious legal consequences for the obligor.").

[50] PRINCIPLES § 3.14 cmt. e, at 524.

Comment e to Section 3.14 suggests that "[i]mputation to the nonresidential parent is designed to increase child support payments to the child's residential household."[51] It is probably more accurate to suggest that imputation of income to the nonresidential parent is designed to make that parent shoulder a fair support obligation, which will have the effect in many cases of increased payments to the residential household.

Consider how the ALI's rationale would analogously be applied in a case involving income imputation to a residential parent. Presumably, some jurisdictions would deny that the *goal* of such an income imputation would be to decrease support payments to the residential household, and would instead suggest that the goal is to make parents shoulder a fair support obligation, while admitting that one effect of income imputation to residential parents is that support payments would decrease in amount.

Even jurisdictions unwilling to discuss the goals of imputation in terms of justice or fair burdens would likely reject the PRINCIPLES' characterization, and would opt instead for a description applicable to both residential and nonresidential parents. For example, they might suggest that the goal of imputation as a general matter is to increase the income of the residential household, either through additional support payments that result when income is imputed to a nonresidential parent or through the increased salary that a residential parent has been induced to earn, even after the costs of daycare have been taken into account, when income is imputed to a residential parent. While it is of course true that the benefits will not be realized if the imputation does not induce a residential parent to seek employment outside the home,[52] that is hardly the goal of the imputation.

As a separate matter, it is at the very least surprising that the PRINCIPLES would define error as "the consequences of imputing earnings to a parent who will not or cannot earn the amounts imputed by the trier of fact."[53] Such a definition obscures an important difference between "will not" and "cannot." Because imputed income is the income that a parent might reasonably be expected to make, it would certainly be an error to impute an amount which cannot be made. Imputing an amount which *will* not be made, however, might simply involve a decision by a residential or nonresidential parent that it is better to continue the employment status quo, all things considered, notwithstanding the change in the support order. For example, for a parent who has remarried and whose spouse is earning a good income outside of the home, the fact that the parent chooses not to earn more may not mean that the imputation is an error, but simply that the family has decided to absorb the costs imposed by the changed support order. Such a family might be contrasted with, for example, a single residential parent with three children whose disposable income as a family might be severely affected by an income imputation.

The drafters should have been more careful when describing what would constitute error, precisely because the character of families potentially subject to income imputation may differ so dramatically. That a parent will not earn the income imputed to him or her says nothing about whether the imputation was erroneous. Rather, error should be determined in light of some independent criterion, for instance, that the trier of fact wrongly assessed how much a parent could reasonably make, or whether that a parent could work outside of the home given existing residential responsibilities.

[51] PRINCIPLES § 3.14 cmt. e(i), at 524.

[52] *See* Stanton v. Abbey, 874 S.W.2d 493, 499 (Mo. Ct. App. 1994) ("[T]he income generated by attribution is often fictional and, therefore, no benefit to the children.").

[53] PRINCIPLES § 3.14 cmt. e, at 524.

This chapter does not argue that differences between residential and nonresidential parents are minimal, or that they must be deemphasized. Nor is the claim that it is easy to put a value on the different opportunities or responsibilities afforded to each parent. Indeed, the PRINCIPLES implicitly understate both the difficulty of putting a value on the experiences of residential or nonresidential parents, as well as the difficulty in comparing their experiences. For example, the comments suggest that a "residential parent's disproportionate responsibility for a child might . . . be assumed to be roughly counterbalanced by the disproportionate relational benefits concomitant with residential child care."[54] While that assessment is probably accurate for some parents, it may well not capture the experience of a residential parent who is struggling to make ends meet, if only because that parent may be so exhausted and overworked that it is too difficult to reap the relational benefits.[55]

By the same token, the comments capture the experience of some parents but not others, by suggesting that a "nonresidential parent's possible loss [with respect to the relationship with the child] might be considered roughly counterbalanced by the residential parent's disproportionate responsibility and provision of child care."[56] This would depend upon the relative degrees to which (a) a residential parent finds it burdensome to provide a disproportionate amount of childcare,[57] and (b) a nonresidential parent finds it burdensome to have a diminished or nonexistent relationship with his or her child.[58]

Presumably, the PRINCIPLES "decline to measure and weigh the many incalculable and incommensurate non-financial costs and benefits incident to family dissolution"[59] because of the inherently subjective nature of these benefits and burdens and the inherent difficulties in measuring them. If that is so, however, the PRINCIPLES should suggest that these matters not be reviewed because of the great if not insurmountable difficulties involved in placing a reasonable value on them, rather than implying that they cancel each other out.

It might be argued that it does not matter why these assessments are being taken off the table – the important point is that they are being withdrawn from the court's consideration. Yet, one of the underlying issues suggested by the PRINCIPLES involves who should be given the benefit of the doubt in close cases. On this question, the PRINCIPLES implicitly favor the residential parent.[60] By implying that the benefits and burdens of residential care cancel each other out, and that the burdens and missed opportunity costs borne by

[54] *See* PRINCIPLES § 3.04 cmt. g, at 428.

[55] *Cf.* Karen Syma Czapanskiy, *Parents, Children and Work First Welfare Reform: Where Is the C in TANF*, 61 MD. L. REV. 308, 353 (2002) (discussing some of the difficulties for the parent-child relationship where the parent cannot earn much money).

[56] PRINCIPLES § 3.04 cmt. g, at 428.

[57] *Cf.* Reva Siegel, *Reasoning from the Body: A Historical Perspective on Abortion Regulation and Questions of Equal Protection*, 44 STAN. L. REV. 261, 377 (1992) (suggesting that there are very heavy costs for the primary caretaker).

[58] *See* Mary Ann Mason & Nocole Sayac, *Rethinking Stepparent Rights: Has the ALI Found a Better Definition*, 36 FAM L.Q. 227, 251 (2002) (discussion the great range in the visitation rates by nonresidential parents). Even if some of this could be explained by the residential parent's interfering with visitation; *see* Daniel Pollack & Susan Mason, *Mandatory Visitation: In the Best Interests of the Child*, 42 FAM CT. REV. 74, 76 (2004) (discussing the claim by many nonresidential parents that this is the reason that they have seen their children less often than they otherwise would have), it seems reasonable to believe that this is at least partially caused by some nonresidential parents placing a far greater value on continued visitation with their children than do other nonresidential parents).

[59] PRINCIPLES § 3.04 cmt. g, at 428.

[60] *Cf.* PRINCIPLES § 3.15 cmt. b, at 536 ("While both forms of imputation [i.e., to the residential and the nonresidential parent] should be approached with caution, imputation of earnings to the residential parent should be approached with even more circumspection.").

residential parents are canceled out by those experienced by nonresidential parents, the PRINCIPLES undermine one of the justifications for giving residential parents the benefit of the doubt, namely, that a residential parent bears a greater share of the responsibility for a child.

Certainly, the PRINCIPLES offer other justifications for favoring residential parents on a variety of issues.[61] Yet, many of these justifications are themselves suspect, leaving the ALI's recommendations without adequate support. As the next part illustrates, the drafters' analysis of the role of shirking, while initially appealing, is ultimately unpersuasive and may actually undercut the ALI's proposal.

B. Shirking Obligations

One of the ALI's justifications for treating residential and nonresidential parents differently is that nonresidential parents might seek to shirk their obligations, but residential parents would not. "Imputation to support obligors expresses concern that the obligor may be concealing income or shirking gainful labor in order to avoid payment of child support. The residential parent lacks those motivations because that parent in any event shares all resources with the residential children."[62] This claim, while initially appealing, is ultimately unhelpful because it implicitly misrepresents both the conditions under which income might be imputed and the ways in which one might shirk one's obligations.

As an initial point, many jurisdictions are unwilling to limit income imputations to cases in which a parent is avoiding gainful labor in order to avoid having to pay support.[63] One would also expect the drafters to reject such a limitation. Consider the nonresidential parent who does not work outside of the home because that parent is caring for children from a second marriage. In this case, the parent is not shirking but instead is fulfilling child care responsibilities, even if the children receiving the care have no connection to the parent's previous spouse.

Two issues must be distinguished: (1) Is a nonresidential parent who wishes to stay home with children from a subsequent marriage "shirking" an obligation to support the children of a prior marriage?, and (2) Should a nonresidential parent who wishes to stay home with children from a subsequent marriage nonetheless be subject to income imputation?

Courts and jurisdictions are much more divided about the second issue than they are about the first. Numerous courts describe the parent who wishes to stay home with children as laudable, and would be loath to describe this as shirking responsibilities.[64] A separate issue is whether such a parent should have income imputed. In *Rohloff v. Rohloff*,[65] a Michigan appellate court noted that the "plaintiff left the job market in good faith and for the arguably laudable goal of strengthening her newly entered marriage,"[66] but nonetheless suggested that she was not "entirely free to make financial decisions which are allegedly in

[61] *See, e.g.*, Part II(B) (discussing the ALI's analysis of shirking); Part II(C) (discussing the ALI's analysis of fairness and responsibility).

[62] PRINCIPLES § 3.14 cmt. e(ii), at 524.

[63] *See infra* notes note 64–102 and accompanying text.

[64] *See* Rohloff v. Rohloff, 411 N.W.2d 484 (Mich. Ct. App. 1987); McAlexander v. McAlexander, 1993 WL 420206 (Ohio Ct. App) *6 ("The decision of a parent to stay home in order to care for and raise a newly born child, and not return to the workforce, cannot be criticized."); *In re* Marriage of Pollard, 991 P.2d 1201, 1204 (Wash. Ct. App. 2000).

[65] 411 N.W.2d 484 (Mich. Ct. App. 1987).

[66] *Id.* at 488.

the best interest of her new family, but which abrogate her responsibilities to her existing family."[67] The court noted that it "would be inequitable to allow the children of her first marriage to suffer merely so that her second marriage can purportedly prosper."[68] Thus, the nonshirking parent can have income imputed, notwithstanding a lack of moral blameworthiness, because of the opportunity costs that the parent's non-supported children would otherwise be forced to bear.

Pennsylvania recognizes a nurturing parent doctrine, and does not distinguish between children who are the subjects of the support order and children born in a subsequent relationship.[69] Other jurisdictions are more ambivalent about whether to distinguish between such children. For example, in *McAlexander v. McAlexander*,[70] an Ohio appellate court had to decide whether to impute income to a woman who wished to stay home with her newborn from a subsequent marriage. The court was neither willing to hold that "in all such cases in the future that choice by the parent would be, by itself, a per se reason to terminate all child support obligation without imputation of any income to that parent whatsoever,"[71] nor to hold that "the simple determination by a parent to stay home and care for a newborn child would never be a reason to completely terminate a child support obligation on the part of such a parent."[72] The court explained that the "decision of a parent to stay home in order to care for and raise a newly born child ... cannot be criticized, [since the] benefit to the newborn child in such cases is unquestionable [and] ... all society benefits from that parental decision, not just the child and the parent."[73] Nonetheless, the court worried that "the parent and the newborn child [might be] ... living in the lap of luxury, due to inheritance, the income of the new spouse, a big win in the lottery, etc., and the other children [might be] ... destitute."[74] Whether to impute income in such cases, the court concluded, would have to be decided on a case-by-case basis.

In a different case, an Ohio appellate court considered whether a mother's decision to stay home with children from a subsequent marriage excused her from child support. In *Addington v. Addington*,[75] the court explained that "any impairment of [the former Mrs. Addington's] earning ability represented by her decision to bear additional children constitutes a voluntary impairment to her earning ability, which does not entitle her to shift to [Mr.] Addington an increased share of the support necessary for the children of her marriage to [him]."[76] Thus, within Ohio, different courts have taken very different approaches, with some refusing to impute income when a parent wishes to stay at home with children from a subsequent marriage and others suggesting that imputation is required in such cases.

New Jersey courts have also exhibited some ambivalence with respect to how these cases should be treated. In *Thomas v. Thomas*,[77] the court was unwilling to impute income to a woman who wished to stay home with children born in a subsequent marriage. The court

[67] *Id.*

[68] *Id.*

[69] *See* Bender v. Bender, 444 A.2d 124, 126 (Pa. Super. 1982); Atkinson v. Atkinson, 616 A.2d 22, 23 (Pa. Super. 1992); Hesidenz v. Carbin, 512 A.2d 707, 710 n.4 (Pa. Super. 1986) ("[W]e have held that the fact that the child to be nurtured is not the subject of the support order does not necessarily remove the case from the application of the 'nurturing parent' doctrine.").

[70] 1993 WL 420206 (Ohio. Ct. App.).

[71] *Id.* at *5.

[72] *Id.*

[73] *Id.* at *6.

[74] *Id.* (citing Boltz v. Boltz, 31 Ohio. Ct. App.3d 214 (1986)).

[75] 1995 WL 599886 (Ohio Ct. App.).

[76] *Id.* at *1.

[77] 589 A.2d 1372 (N.J. Ch. Div.).

explained that "the defendant is not engaged in the job market because she is fulfilling a unique and important role in providing a nurturing environment for her extremely young children," and noted that "plaintiff's decision to remain at home with her two-month old and three-year old sons is entitled to great deference."[78] The court implied that reasonable parents might disagree about whether to stay home with a child, but that courts should not second-guess parents' decisions in such cases. "While the costs and benefits of such a decision to stay at home may be fairly debated, no court should overrule a parent's decision in that regard or punish the decision by the imposition of a monetary award."[79] The *Thomas* court distinguished between parents who choose not to work outside of the home, to raise children, and parents who choose not to work outside of the home for different reasons, noting, "[w]hile the latter does not excuse an obligation to support children monetarily, the former does. To rule otherwise would, in effect, determine that monetary contributions to children living with another is more important than providing care to children in the obligor's custody."[80]

In *Bencivenga v. Bencivenga*,[81] a New Jersey appellate court explicitly rejected the *Thomas* approach.[82] The court noted that a decision to stay at home with children from a subsequent marriage might be "made possible by the ample income or resources of her new husband," and that "the benefits of her decision to devote a share of the current family resources to her second family's care [should not be allowed in such a case to] work so much to the disadvantage of her first children."[83] The court was therefore willing to impute income in appropriate circumstances.[84]

Jurisdictions vary about whether to attribute income to a parent who wishes to stay home with children born of a subsequent marriage, at least in part, because they do not agree about whether a showing of bad faith is necessary before income can be imputed. In *In re Marriage of LaBass*,[85] a mother with custody of her school age children argued that "for policy reasons, [a] wom[a]n who ha[s] primary custody of the children should never be subject to . . . income imputation"[86] where "the refusal to realize her earning potential is motivated by her perception of 'the best interests of the children.' "[87] She worked only part time because she wanted to spend more time with her children,[88] notwithstanding the availability of day care.[89] The California appeals court rejected the notion that good motivation immunizes an individual from imputation.[90] Similarly, in *Guskjolen v. Guskjolen*,[91] the nonresidential parent, who subsequently remarried and had two children with her new husband, testified that she felt "a moral obligation to not work fulltime outside her home

[78] *Id.* at 1373.

[79] *Id.*

[80] *Id.*

[81] 603 A.2d 531 (N.J. Ct. App. 1992).

[82] *See id.* at 532.

[83] *See id.* at 533.

[84] *See id.* at 532–33.

> [I]t may be that a mother's decision to stay home with her new children is made possible by the ample income or resources of her new husband. It seems odd that the benefits of her decision to devote a share of the current family resources to her second family's care could work so much to the disadvantage of her first children. We do not hint that we think this is the case here. We merely point out that such facts should, where present and pertinent, be considered, and might be sufficient to affect the outcome of a custodial parent's effort to secure an order for support.

id.

[85] 66 Cal.Rptr.2d 393 (Cal. Ct. App. 1997).

[86] *Id.* at 398.

[87] *Id.*

[88] *Id.* at 397.

[89] *Id.* at 398.

[90] *See id.* at 397 (stating that a "parent's motivation for not pursuing income opportunities is irrelevant.").

[91] 499 N.W.2d 125 (N.D. 1993).

so that she [could] personally be with and care for her current family."[92] The North Dakota Supreme Court cast no doubt on the sincerity of her belief, merely noting instead that she also had an obligation to support her child from her previous marriage.[93]

In *In re Marriage of Padilla*,[94] a California appeals court explained why bad faith would not be required to impute income.

> Once persons become parents, their desires for self-realization, self-fulfillment, personal job satisfaction, and other commendable goals must be considered in context of their responsibilities to provide for their children's reasonable needs. If they decide they wish to lead a simpler life, change professions or start a business, they may do so, but only when they satisfy their primary responsibility: providing for the adequate and reasonable needs of their children.[95]

The PRINCIPLES rightly suggest that "the residential parent's choices about labor force participation often involves trade-offs between providing the children with care and pursuing gainful employment. Limitation of gainful employment may benefit the children and pursuit of gainful employment may work to their detriment."[96] Yet, it does not follow from these observations that "imputation of earnings to the residential parent cannot generally be justified by reference to the interests of children."[97] The ALI seems to ignore that children might be benefited by their residential parent's working rather than staying at home, for example, because of the improved standard of living that might result from the residential parent's working. Because, all things considered, some children would receive a net benefit and others would not as a result of a residential parent's decision to refrain from working outside of the home, the ALI needs to offer much more to justify this recommendation.

Courts have recognized that residential parents sometimes shirk their responsibilities when avoiding gainful employment.[98] For example, in *LaBass*, the California appeals court described a residential parent's decision to work part time as "a lifestyle choice in derogation of her duty to support her children.[99] The court recognized that "the only qualification to the discretionary imputation of income is that it be consistent with the children's best interest"[100] and affirmed the imputation,[101] presumably because the court believed that the children would be benefited by the improved standard of living which would result if the mother was induced to enter the workforce.[102]

Clearly, residential parents can and do make sacrifices for their children. Nonetheless, courts should not assume, as a matter of law, that residential parents cannot shirk their obligations to support their children. If residential parents can shirk their obligations, or if states are willing to impute even when a parent has a legitimate or laudable reason for being unemployed or underemployed, such as staying at home with a child born during

[92] *Id.* at 128.

[93] *Id.*

[94] 45 Cal.Rptr.2d 555 (Col. Ct. App. 1995).

[95] *Id.* at 560.

[96] PRINCIPLES § 3.14 cmt. e(ii), at 524–25.

[97] PRINCIPLES § 3.14 cmt. e(ii), at 525.

[98] *See* Stanton v. Abbey, 874 S.W.2d 493, 499 (Mo. Ct. App. 1994) ("[S]taying at home to care for children may constitute volitional unemployment.").

[99] *LaBass*, 66 Cal.Rptr.2d at 399.

[100] *Id.* at 398.

[101] *Id.* at 399.

[102] *See* Stanton v. Abbey, 874 S.W.2d 493, 499 (Mo. Ct. App. 1994) (stating that a factor favoring attribution is that it might be "minimizing the economic impact of family breakup on children by discouraging parental unemployment or underemployment").

a subsequent relationship, then it will be more difficult to distinguish between residential and nonresidential parents for income imputation purposes.

C. On Responsibility

A much different kind of rationale might be offered to justify the choice to distinguish between stay-at-home residential and stay-at-home nonresidential parents, namely, that children born of a marriage are the responsibility of both parents, whereas children born of a subsequent marriage are not the responsibility of the ex-spouse. On the surface, appealing to the parents' respective obligations seems like a ready way to justify imputation to nonresidential, but not to residential, parents.

Suppose that a nonresidential parent remarries and stays at home at the request of the new spouse. Courts have often been unwilling to accept this as a sufficient reason to justify a modification in the child support owed by the stay-at-home nonresidential parent.[103] In such cases, courts are not suggesting that the nonresidential parent intends to harm the children from a former marriage, but merely that the motivation, however laudable, does not justify lowering the standard of living of the children from the previous marriage. For example, in *Roberts v. Roberts*,[104] a Wisconsin court upheld an income imputation when a mother quit her job to stay home with a child born of a subsequent marriage.[105] The court did not suggest that the mother's decision was made in bad faith,[106] but merely that the mother was voluntarily staying at home[107] and thus would not be relieved of her obligation to support her children from her previous marriage.[108]

While appealing to the respective obligations of stay-at-home residential and nonresidential parents might seem promising, at first, to justify treating these parents differently for imputation purposes, it is a less attractive rationale upon closer examination. Just as one can justify imputing income to a stay-at-home nonresidential parent, one can also justify imputing income to a stay-at-home residential parent, since "both parents must shoulder the task of providing support for their children."[109] If the reason that income should not be imputed to a stay-at-home residential parent is that the obligation to provide support is suspended when a residential parent wishes to stay at home with a very young child, then the same might be said of the nonresidential parent who wishes to stay home with a newborn. Indeed, if a parental support obligation is owed to society as a whole,[110] then there should be no cause for complaint should society decide to suspend that obligation

[103] *See* Boltz v. Boltz, 509 N.E.2d 1274, 1276 (Ohio Ct. App. 1986) (concluding that new spouse's wanting wife not to work did not suffice to justify relief from obligation to support her children).

[104] 496 N.W.2d 210 (Wis. Ct. App. 1992).

[105] *See id.* at 212–13.

[106] *Id.* at 213 ("It was not a decision made in bad faith.").

[107] *Id.* at 212–13 ("Roach's obligation to support the Roberts children continued despite her voluntary choice to remain at home with a child of a subsequent marriage.").

[108] *See In re* Marriage of Jonas, 788 P.2d 12, 13 (Wash. Ct. App. 1990) ("The record discloses nothing to suggest that either parent was voluntarily unemployed for the purpose of avoiding child support obligations. No matter how legitimate their reasons, however, each is accountable for earnings forgone in making the choice to be unemployed."). *See also id.* ("Jonas, who is unemployed while attending school, contends primarily that the court erred in determining and then considering his income potential while refusing even to determine Carrie's. Carrie is capable of employment, but she has chosen to stay at home to care for her children.").

[109] *In re* Z.B.P. 109 S.W.3d 772, 782 (Tex. Ct. App. 2003).

[110] *See* Boltz v. Boltz, 509 N.E.2d 1274, 1275 (Ohio Ct. App. 1986) ("The obligation to support one's own children is one owed to the public generally.").

when one has children below a certain age, regardless of whether the ex-spouse played a role in producing the child.

Consider the residential parent who wishes to stay home with an older child. The PRINCIPLES suggest that "imputation seeks to express a principle of fairness: Child-support obligors should not be required to assume more than their fair share of the economic burdens of child support."[111] To the extent that a nonresidential parent's "child support obligation is a function of the residential parent's unwarranted failure to pursue gainful employment, earnings should be imputed to the residential parent."[112] The drafters worried about the "residential parent who unwarrantedly declines to engage in gainful employment when the earnings from such employment would serve to reduce the nonresidential parent's support obligation."[113]

Of course, the question then is when a parent's choice to stay at home would be unwarranted. If, for example, that would only be when the children would be better off in terms of their care if the parent works, then there would presumably be relatively few instances in which imputation is warranted. Yet, the children might be better off, all things considered, if the residential parent were to work, because any differences in care would be outweighed by the improved standard of living. It is simply unclear whether this reasoning is what the drafters had in mind when discussing an unwarranted failure to pursue gainful employment and, if so, why the same analysis would not apply for younger children as well. In both kinds of cases, the residential parent presumably feels that the trade-off in working is not worthwhile.

The following case illustrates some of the difficulties here. Suppose that the children would be equally well off when (a) the children were put in day care so that the residential parent could work, or (b) the children were taken care of by the residential parent and the nonresidential parent paid more in support. Would it be fair for the nonresidential parent to be forced to pay more?

One difficulty illustrated by this scenario is the apparent incommensurability of (a) caring for one's child and (b) receiving additional income so that one's standard of living is improved. Yet, judgments will have to be made about this if we are ever to say that a parent who would be the optimal care giver nonetheless should work. The difficulties only increase when attempting to figure out the nonresidential parent's obligations of support, given that the nonresidential parent might also wish to stay home, for example, with children born of a subsequent marriage. Thus, a nonresidential parent might have very different reactions to whether it is fair to be forced to pay more so that the residential parent could stay home, depending upon whether the nonresidential parent acquired additional obligations resulting from a subsequent relationship. The drafters pay short shrift to such considerations, noting that "these Principles implicitly give priority to the first family,"[114] believing such a policy to be justifiable because the parent comes "to a second family already economically diminished by obligations to a prior family" and "[p]rior obligations should not, as a general matter, be retroactively reduced in light of obligations subsequently taken."[115] Yet, the PRINCIPLES do not give sufficient weight to the

[111] PRINCIPLES § 3.14 cmt. e(ii), at 525.

[112] PRINCIPLES § 3.14 cmt. e(ii), at 525.

[113] PRINCIPLES § 3.14 cmt. e(iii), at 525.

[114] PRINCIPLES § 3.14 cmt. i, at 528.

[115] PRINCIPLES § 3.14 cmt. i, at 528. While this policy might seem reminiscent of the discredited policy of primogeniture, they are distinguishable in that here, the differentially treated children do not have the same set of parents, while in the case of primogeniture, the differentially treated children did have the same parents. *See* HENRY CAMPBELL BLACK ET AL, BLACK'S LAW DICTIONARY 1191 (6th ed. 1990) (defining primogeniture as "[t]he state of being born

burden that children in the subsequent family might then be forced to bear. Moreover, by offering this justification for treating the families differently, the drafters implicitly reject the notion that shirking or avoidance are the sole justification for imputation. On the contrary, the PRINCIPLES suggest that an obligation exists to support the first family, and that the amount that the nonresidential parent should pay is not appropriately reduced even if that parent has a legitimate, nonshirking reason to seek this reduction, such as support for or care of a subsequent family. Acceptance of this claim, however, undercuts the ALI's justification for treating residential and nonresidential stay-at-home parents differently.

Perhaps the drafters were worried that individuals who remarry may be too willing to spend time or dollars on the current family to the detriment of the former family. Yet, this is the kind of case-specific consideration which could be better handled by giving courts discretion to impute income, rather than by adopting a blanket rule that requires imputation regardless of whether the parent is privileging the second family.

In *Tetreault v. Coon*,[116] the Vermont Supreme Court explained that there is a split of authority on whether courts should impute income when a parent wishes to stay at home with children born from a subsequent relationship.[117] The court outlined the competing policy considerations.[118] "On the one hand, imputing income to a stay-at-home parent creates an economic disincentive to remarriage and child conception, punishes children for the action of their custodial parent, does not support the nurturing of young children, and requires consideration of income that is often fictional."[119] The refusal to impute income has its drawbacks, too. "On the other hand, the policy [of imputing income] discourages parental unemployment or underemployment, recognizes the volitional aspect of conceiving subsequent children, and does not require the obligor to pay more because of the presence of a second family the obligor is not required to support."[120]

The Vermont Supreme Court made clear that there are a number of factors to consider when deciding whether to impute income and implied that whether the child was the subject of the support order would be given relatively little weight.[121] The court gave this factor relatively little weight because subsequent children are considered in requests for modification of child support orders.[122]

One difficulty with the PRINCIPLES is that it is unclear what states should do if they reject the ALI's position on the primacy of the first family. If, for example, a state is willing to reduce an obligor's support payments because of support orders to children in other families[123] or because of obligations the parent has to support children in his or her current family,[124] then it is simply unclear what other recommendations in the PRINCIPLES should also be rejected.

among several children of the same parents; seniority by birth in the same family. The superior or exclusive right possessed by the eldest son, and particularly, his right to succeed to the estate of his ancestor, in right of his seniority by birth, to the exclusion of younger sons.").

[116] 708 A.2d 571 (Vt. 1998).

[117] *Id.* at 576.

[118] *Id.*

[119] *Id.*

[120] *Id.*

[121] *See id.* ("The factors apply . . . whether the stay-at-home parent is rearing children of the parties to the support order, or additional children of a parent other than the child support obligor.").

[122] *See id.* at 575–76 ("The Legislature's intent is that the economic effects of additional dependents should be considered in establishing child-support awards.").

[123] *See* GA. CODE ANN. § 19-6-15(c)(6) (2004).

[124] *See* REV. REV. CODE WASH. ANN. 26.19.075(1)(c)(v)(e) (West Supp. 2005).

Regardless of whether we are considering the claims of residential or nonresidential parents, it is of course true that parental claims about unemployment or underemployment being for the sake of the children need not be credited. For example, in *McHale v. McHale*,[125] the court imputed income to a father who left a lucrative job in Florida to take a much less well-paying job in Louisiana, allegedly to be nearer his children.[126] The trial court discounted McHale's stated motivation, in part because he had "failed to fully exercise his visitation rights"[127] and because he had not been consistent in providing them court-ordered support.[128] This voluntary reduction in salary was not excused and income was imputed.[129] However, the court was not imputing income regardless of why McHale was no longer making as much money as he once was. The court noted, for example, that a reduction in earnings resulting from a bad economy would be involuntary and might justify a decrease in court-ordered child support.[130]

In cases in which unemployment or underemployment is for the sake of the children, however, it is not at all clear that the age or parentage of the children should play the decisive role envisioned by the PRINCIPLES. Many of the PRINCIPLES' articulated goals can be realized by using a more flexible approach, which allows courts to give differing weights to the various factors depending upon the circumstances.

III. Conclusion

The PRINCIPLES offer one possible way to handle a vexing problem – namely, whether and when to impute dollars to a parent who wishes to stay home with children rather than to work outside of the home. There is no clearly correct way to handle this situation, especially because the available resources in such a situation must now support two households rather than one. Furthermore, either or both of the parents may have started new relationships, and may have had children in such relationships.

The PRINCIPLES suggest that residential parents with children six years of age or older should, as a general matter, be subject to income imputation if unemployed or underemployed. Yet, the reasons the drafters offer to justify no imputation for stay-at-home residential parents with children under six years of age also support not imputing income even if the children are older. The reasons offered to justify imputation in cases involving older children also justify imputation in cases involving younger children. By the same token, many of the reasons offered to impute income to a nonresidential parent who stays home with a young child also support imputation to a residential parent who stays home with a young child.

While all of the considerations cited in the PRINCIPLES are appropriately factored into its analysis, it is not at all clear that the implicit weighing of these considerations is correct. Further, some considerations militate in favor of one policy, while other considerations militate in favor of a conflicting one. Thus, the ALI does not offer persuasive reasons to adopt

[125] 612 So.2d 969 (La. Ct. App. 1993).

[126] *Id.* at 974.

[127] *Id.* at 973.

[128] *Id.* ("Mr. McHale has a long record of accruing arrearages in his child support obligations requiring his former spouse to bring him back into court on numerous occasions to have the arrearages made executory."). *Cf.* Moore v. Tseronis, 664 A.2d 427 (Md. Ct. Spec. App. 1994) (stating that an individual who moved to a less affluent area would not have the income imputed to him that he likely would have earned had he remained in a more affluent area).

[129] *McHale*, 612 So.2d at 974.

[130] *See id.*

its proposal over the multitude of other proposals which also take these considerations into account. Jurisdictions deciding whether or how to modify their own policies will not be helped much by the PRINCIPLES.

Perhaps the difficulty in establishing a plausible, coherent policy is simply inherent in these kinds of cases because, in many of them, individuals who have done nothing wrong – such as children born of the various relationships – would have to forgo opportunities that might otherwise have been open to them. One cannot help but think that the ALI might have offered reasons for its recommendations in the PRINCIPLES that were more closely tied to its recommendations, thereby helping jurisdictions to understand why these recommendations are best, or at least giving jurisdictions more guidance if they reject some of the recommendations but embrace others. With regard to imputation, the PRINCIPLES, although helpful because they highlight many of the considerations that should enter into this kind of policy analysis, are disappointing because they leave too much of the difficult work yet to be done.

PART FOUR. PROPERTY DIVISION

8 The ALI Property Division Principles: A Model of Radical Paternalism

John DeWitt Gregory

This chapter addresses the ALI's proposals regarding property division upon dissolution.[1] Consideration of this single well-worn subject might at first glance appear to be a fairly routine exercise. After all, there are currently a great many books, written for the edification of practicing lawyers,[2] that treat various aspects of the subject of property division at divorce, together with a number of treatises, outlines, and handbooks for students that deal with the subject,[3] and a slew of law review articles dissecting myriad issues relating to property distribution that defy classification or accurate numbering.[4] Anyone who takes comfort from the fact that this glut of material exists to address the subject of property division is in for a rude and dismaying awakening when first confronting the PRINCIPLES recommended by the ALI.

The PRINCIPLES are set out in a volume that consists of more than a thousand pages of text. Concededly, a reader's focus on any number of provisions in any single chapter, including many of those in the property division chapter, will aid the reader's comprehension of the subject matter that the provision purports to address. At the same time, however, there are critical and often complex relationships between the property division chapter and several other chapters of the PRINCIPLES. The reader who devotes his or her attention only to the property division principles will surely fail to see a number of snakes hiding in the tall grasses of other provisions. For example, one cannot deal in an intelligible way with the ALI's approach to property division in chapter 4 without considerable familiarity with chapter 5, which covers what practitioners know as alimony or maintenance but which the drafters label as "compensatory spousal payments."[5] Also, the property division provisions are relevant, if not critical, to an understanding of chapter 6, which deals with,

[1] PRINCIPLES ch. 4.

[2] *See, e.g.*, JOHN DEWITT GREGORY, JANET LEACH RICHARDS & SHERYL WOLF, PROPERTY DIVISION IN DIVORCE PROCEEDINGS: A FIFTY STATE GUIDE (2004); BRETT R. TURNER, EQUITABLE DISTRIBUTION OF PROPERTY (1994 & SUPP.); THOMAS J. OLDHAM, DIVORCE, SEPARATION AND THE DISTRIBUTION OF PROPERTY (1987); JOHN DEWITT GREGORY, THE LAW OF EQUITABLE DISTRIBUTION (1989).

[3] *See, e.g.*, HARRY D. KRAUSE & DAVID D. MEYER, FAMILY LAW §§ 22.1–22.7 (2003); JOHN DEWITT GREGORY, PETER SWISHER & SHERYL L. WOLF, UNDERSTANDING FAMILY LAW §§ 10.01–10.12 (2d ed. 2001).

[4] *See, e.g.*, Robert J. Levy, *An Introduction to Divorce Property Issues*, 23 FAM. L.Q. 147 (1989); Thomas J. Oldham, *Tracing, Commingling and Transmutation*, 23 FAM. L.Q. 219 (1989); Joan M. Krauskopf, *A Theory for "Just Division of Marital Property in Missouri,"* 41 MO. L. REV. 165 (1976); Alan L. Feld, *The Implications of Minority Interest and Stock Restrictions in Valuing Closely-Held Shares*, 122 U. PA. L. REV. 934 (1974).

[5] PRINCIPLES ch. 5. *See* James Herbie Di Fonzo, *Toward A Unified Field Theory of the Family: The American Law Institute's Principles of the Law of Family Dissolution*, 2001 BYU L. REV. 923 (observing that "the financial aftershocks of marital dissolution, traditionally termed alimony (or maintenance) and property division, have virtually melded into one integrated financial scheme governing all domestic fractures").

among other matters, property division between unmarried cohabitants.[6] Again, matrimonial and family law practitioners everywhere certainly know that property division is, as a practical matter, inextricably linked with prenuptial and antenuptial agreements between the spouses. Yet, the PRINCIPLES carve this subject out from property division and relegate it to chapter 7 on "Agreements." Also, and certainly not less importantly, the ALI's scheme for the division of property requires familiarity with the black letter law addressing, whether marital misconduct, or fault, ought to be considered as a factor in allocating property upon dissolution, a discussion contained in chapter 1 of the PRINCIPLES.[7] The drafters, in response to this question, reach a radically different conclusion from the one that underlies the statutory and case law that a significant number of American courts and legislatures, after many years of careful reflection, have established. Accordingly, although this chapter is concerned with property division, it will at some points cross reference other provisions of the PRINCIPLES.

Let me note in passing why this chapter uses the single word "dissolution" to refer to the proceeding that in most states, if not in all, is called either "divorce" or "dissolution of marriage." This usage is compelled by the approach of the PRINCIPLES themselves, which, as their title suggests, purport to deal with dissolution of the family, broadly defined.[8] Indeed, one critic of the PRINCIPLES rightly asserts that "[w]hile some of the PRINCIPLES are very familiar to law professors who teach family law, many of the proposals go far beyond existing law and recommend significant policy changes, including official recognition of homosexual and extramarital concubine-like domestic partnership agreements, on an economic par with marriage."[9] The wholesale importation of the property division proposals, which are the subject of this chapter, into the provisions that deal with domestic partners is among the most far-reaching and arguably most controversial proposals to be found in the PRINCIPLES.[10]

Before dealing with some of the many questions raised by the PRINCIPLES' property division provisions, a few comments are in order with respect to the context in which those provisions and others were adopted. Some commentators have expressed concern and, indeed, strong reservations about the ALI's processes or procedures. Professor David Westfall, for example, in a critique of the treatment of unmarried cohabitants in one of the earlier drafts of the PRINCIPLES, published before the final version was adopted by the ALI, observed:

> If there were any persuasive reason to believe that the PRINCIPLES actually reflected the views of a substantial majority of the almost three thousand distinguished judges, lawyers, and law teachers who are members of the American Law Institute, I would hesitate to write a critical essay. In fact, however, there is no way to know whether the PRINCIPLES reflect the views of more than a minor fraction of the membership.[11]

[6] PRINCIPLES ch. 6, at 907.

[7] PRINCIPLES ch. 1, at 42.

[8] *See* John DeWitt Gregory, *Redefining the Family: Undermining the Family*, 2004 U. CHI. LEGAL F. 381.

[9] Lynn D. Wardle, *Deconstructing Family: A Critique of the American Law Institute's "Domestic Partners" Proposal*, 2001 BYU L. REV. 1189, 1192. (observing further that "[m]ost of the chapters of the Family Dissolution Principles contain provisions that deconstruct, level, or redefine 'family' relationships," citing several chapters of the PRINCIPLES that "contain provisions that either significantly redefine currently protected family relationships or radically alter existing family law doctrines").

[10] PRINCIPLES, ch. 6, at 907.

[11] David Westfall, *Forcing Incidents of Marriage on Unmarried Cohabitants: The American Law Institute's Principles of Family Dissolution*, 76 NOTRE DAME L. REV. 1467 (2001).

Describing the quorum requirement for the ALI's membership meetings, Professor Westfall notes in this volume that "fundamental matters of policy may be decided by a handful of votes, and may reflect the views of only a tiny fraction of the membership."[12] Consequently, "although the PRINCIPLES represents the official position of the ALI, it may not reflect the views of even a substantial minority of the membership."[13] After a detailed review and analysis of the provisions relating to unmarried cohabitants, or as the drafters style them, "domestic partners," Professor Westfall concludes that "[t]he PRINCIPLES reflect policies favored by a small group of legal academics, rather than the mainstream of developing American law governing cohabitants."[14]

Another critique of the process by which the ALI adopted the PRINCIPLES laments similarly that:

> [t]he prestige of the [ALI], and the fact that many well-placed lawyers, distinguished law professors, and influential judges belong to the ALI guarantees that [the PRINCIPLES] will have some impact. Even before the PRINCIPLES were adopted by the ALI, the draft provisions had been cited and discussed in dozens of law review articles. Yet, despite the great potential impact of the PRINCIPLES and despite (or perhaps, because of) the gerrymandering of the scope of this project, the PRINCIPLES show little imprint of serious conceptual criticism. The ALI's process of crafting and approval left the few critics in the ALI feeling that their views were simply not heard and disregarded.[15]

Indeed, if an anecdotal comment is appropriate, anyone who attended the ALI's membership meetings during which the PRINCIPLES were debated could not help but notice the rush of ALI members from the meeting room to the hallways and coffee lounge when debates about corporate matters concluded and were then followed on the meeting agenda by discussion of the PRINCIPLES.

The PRINCIPLES were developed over a period of more than ten years, during which time the ALI published a number of drafts, and were adopted by the ALI in 2002. From the project's inception until the final adoption and promulgation of the PRINCIPLES, they were discussed, criticized, and analyzed in several law review articles. Curiously, the provisions relating to custody[16] and domestic partners[17] have thus far engendered considerably more attention in law review literature and significantly more controversy than other chapters, including the PRINCIPLES' property division proposals. This may not be surprising. As the Director's Foreword to the PRINCIPLES points out, "nearly everything in the PRINCIPLES can be found in the current law of some states, as well as in that of other countries with a common law tradition."[18] Similarly, the Chief Reporter's Foreword notes that "[s]ome provisions function as traditional Restatement rules. They are addressed to courts

[12] Westfall, this volume. [13] Westfall, *supra* note 11, at 1469.

[14] *Id.* For criticisms of other recent work of the ALI, see *id.* at 1469, n.12.

[15] Lynn D. Wardle, *Introduction to the Symposium*, 4 J.L. & FAM. STUD. 1 (2002).

[16] *See, e.g.*, Linda Jellum, *Parents Know Best: Revising our Approach to Parental Custody Agreements*, 65 OHIO ST. L.J. 615 (2004); Robert F. Kelly and Shawn Ward, *Social Science Research and the American Law Institute's Approximation Rule*, 40 FAM. CT. REV. 50 (2002); Margaret S. Osborne, *Legalizing Families: Solutions to Adjudicate Parentage for Lesbian Co-Parents*, 49 VILL. L. REV. 363 (2004).

[17] *See, e.g.*, Margaret F. Brinig and Steven L. Nock, *What Does Covenant Mean for Relationships*, 18 NOTRE DAME J.L. ETHICS & PUB. POL'Y 137 (2004); Katherine M. Franke, *The Domesticated Liberty of Lawrence v. Texas*, 104 COLUM L. REV. 1399 (2004); Mark Strasser, *Some Observations about DOMA, Marriages, Civil Unions and Domestic Partnerships*, 30 CAP. U. L. REV. 363 (2002).

[18] PRINCIPLES, Director's Foreword, at xv.

in their function as decisionmakers in individual cases, and identify 'the considerations that courts, under a proper view of the judicial function, deem it right to weigh.'"[19] These comments are particularly applicable to a number, but by no means all, of the provisions relating to property division on dissolution.

I. Placing the Property Division Proposals in Context

The PRINCIPLES treat the definition and characterization of property in a conventional manner, classifying property acquired during marriage as marital property, and gifts and inheritances, together with property acquired in exchange for separate property, as separate property.[20] This dual property scheme for classification of property at divorce is consistent with the approach taken in a majority of states.[21] The PRINCIPLES also recommend a conventional cut-off date for the acquisition of marital property, which is property acquired "after the commencement of marriage and before the filing and service of a petition for dissolution (if that petition ultimately results in a decree dissolving the marriage)," absent facts "establishing that use of another date is necessary to avoid a substantial injustice."[22] Prevailing law on this point may be summarized as follows:

> A problem unique to dual property jurisdictions is the point in time at which property is to be classified as marital, and hence subject to distribution, or separate, and therefore assignable to the party in whose name title is held. That is, for the purposes of classifying property acquired "during the marriage" as marital property, when does the marriage end? In various jurisdictions, the point in time at which classification occurs is found in (1) an explicit exception to the definition of marital property, (2) the definition of separate property, or (3) the definition of marital property. These three variations in wording achieve the same effect, excluding from distribution property acquired after the legal separation of the parties. In states in which the statutes are silent, property is generally subject to distribution at the time of legal separation; some courts, however, have selected alternative dates to determine when the marital partnership ends.[23]

After reading these Restatement-like provisions, it is startling to find a provision of the PRINCIPLES governing characterization of property that sets out the following requirement: "Property acquired during a relationship between the spouses that immediately preceded their marriage, and which was a domestic-partner relationship as defined by [Section] 6.03 is treated as if it were acquired during the marriage."[24] This provision is entirely at odds with the holdings of judicial decisions in the vast majority of jurisdictions that have addressed the question, which have refused to classify property acquired by parties before marriage or in contemplation of marriage as marital property.[25]

Simply stated, this radical application of characterization rules and by extension the rules of property division to domestic partners, for the most part rejects prevailing law, which rarely applies equitable distribution rules to the property of unmarried cohabitants.

[19] PRINCIPLES, Chief Reporter's Foreword, at xvii.

[20] PRINCIPLES § 4.03, at 649–50.

[21] *See* JOHN DEWITT GREGORY, JANET LEACH RICHARDS & SHERYL WOLF, PROPERTY DIVISION IN DIVORCE PROCEEDINGS: A FIFTY STATE GUIDE § 2.02 (2004) ("A slim majority of statutes employ a dual property approach. In these dual property states, marital property or community property, as the case may be, is divisible. Separate property, on the other hand, is retained by the spouse who has title.").

[22] PRINCIPLES § 4.03, at 650.

[23] *See* GREGORY, THE LAW OF EQUITABLE DISTRIBUTION § 2.06 (1989).

[24] PRINCIPLES § 4.03(6), at 650.

[25] *See* GREGORY, *supra* note 23, at § 2.03[2].

Decisions by courts in a small minority of states sometimes divide property acquired shortly before marriage for use as the marital residence, theorizing that the property was acquired in contemplation of marriage. In *In re Marriage of Altman*,[26] for example, the Colorado Court of Appeals stated:

> Where . . . a family residence is selected and acquired within a few days of the parties' marriage, in contemplation of that marriage, and the equity accumulated therein results from contributions by both parties, we hold that the court does not err in treating the residence and all equity obtained therein as marital property. In order to obtain the status of separate property . . . , it must appear that the property was acquired prior to marriage with the intent that it become the separate property of Husband.[27]

But cases in an overwhelming majority of states hold that a literal reading of the definition of marital property in property division statutes does not permit distribution of property acquired by unmarried cohabitants.[28]

There are other provisions in the PRINCIPLES, not all of which can be addressed in this chapter, that would, unlike a Restatement, radically change or entirely reject rules, factors, and presumptions that state courts have developed through careful reflection during the many years since equitable distribution of property became law in almost all jurisdictions. In a number of instances, the drafters made a choice between conflicting rules of property division adopted by American legislatures or courts, sometimes favoring a rule not accepted in the majority of jurisdictions, or rejecting one developed by states, again after many years of legislative or judicial reflection.

In light of such inconsistencies between the PRINCIPLES and the well-established law in a good many jurisdictions, it is appropriate to ask several questions. It would be useful to know, for example, if the PRINCIPLES relating to property division in divorce proceedings have had any significant impact on state statutory law or court decisions relating to distribution of property, during either the ten or so years when the ALI was publishing numerous drafts or the years following the adoption and promulgation of the PRINCIPLES in their final form. Another relevant question is whether one may reasonably expect that the PRINCIPLES, insofar as they do not restate current law but call for significant and arguably radical changes, will have an observable impact on a body of law that state courts and legislatures have developed during at least the last three decades. Also, one may usefully ask whether the theoretical foundations of the PRINCIPLES accord sufficient respect to the practical considerations that animate state property division law. To put it more sharply, one must wonder whether the approaches to property division under the PRINCIPLES will have a strong or lasting impact on American matrimonial law; or will they eventually come to be regarded as merely an academic exercise or, indeed, another one of those "thought experiments" of which some legal academics have recently become so fond.

One example of the drafters picking and choosing among various property division or equitable distribution doctrines that are well established in virtually all American jurisdictions is its treatment of marital misconduct or fault. In most states, equitable distribution statutes list dissipation of assets, sometimes called waste or financial misconduct, as one of the factors that a court must consider when making a fair and equitable distribution of marital property.[29] There is not complete agreement, however, with respect to the

[26] 530 P.2d 1012 (Colo. Ct. App. 1984).

[27] *Id.* at 1013.

[28] *See* GREGORY, *supra* note 23, at § 2.03[2].

[29] *See* GREGORY ET AL., *supra* note 3, § 10.12 [D][1]–[4].

conduct that will constitute dissipation, so that the facts in each case may well determine whether a party's conduct constitutes waste or dissipation. The Supreme Court of Illinois has examined the elements of dissipation carefully and in the greatest detail. Several other states have relied on that court's approach, which is exemplified by the Illinois Supreme Court's opinion in *In re Marriage of O'Neill*,[30] where the court stated: "[T]he term 'dissipation'... refers to the use of marital property for the sole benefit of one of the spouses for a purpose unrelated to the marriage at a time that the marriage is undergoing an irreconcilable breakdown."[31]

While one frequently encounters the Illinois approach in cases decided by other courts, some courts have not adopted the requirement that dissipation will be a property division factor only if it occurs when the marriage is breaking down. Also, some decisions suggest that there must be an intent to dissipate marital assets. An excellent example is *Robinette v. Robinette*,[32] in which the Court of Appeals of Kentucky stated:

> We believe the concept of dissipation, that is, spending funds for a non-marital purpose, is an appropriate one for the court to consider when the property is expended (1) during a period when there is a separation or dissolution impending, and (2) where there is a clear showing of intent to deprive one's spouse of his or her proportionate share of marital property.[33]

State courts also are not in agreement with respect to remedies for dissipation.[34] With some frequency courts will try to compensate the innocent party. In *In re Partyka*[35] for example, the Appellate Court of Illinois stated the approach that one most frequently encounters in state court opinions that deal with the issue. The court stated: "Where a party has dissipated marital assets, the court may charge the amount dissipated against his or her share of the marital property so as to compensate the other party."[36] But other state courts have declined to include dissipated assets in the marital estate since such assets no longer exist. Some courts, rather, consider dissipation of assets as a factor to be considered in distribution, as did the Montana Supreme Court in affirming a division of 70 percent of the marital property to the wife and 30 percent to the husband because of the husband's dissipation of marital assets.[37]

The PRINCIPLES explicitly treat dissipation of distributable assets under the rubric of "Financial Misconduct as Grounds for Unequal Division of Marital Property."[38] In the black letter, the PRINCIPLES specifically identify several kinds of misconduct that by and large have been treated by the courts as dissipation under prevailing law, and in most cases provide the remedy of augmentation or enlargement of the innocent party's share of the marital property. Also, the PRINCIPLES generally provide a limited period of time during which rules relating to dissipation are applicable,[39] which would appear to be an improvement on the arguably over broad requirement that cognizable dissipation occur during the breakdown of the marriage, the application of which has given courts considerable difficulty.

[30] 563 N.E.2d 494 (Ill. 1990).
[31] *Id.* at 498–99.
[32] 736 S.W.2d 351 (Ky. Ct. App. 1987).
[33] *Id.* at 354.
[34] *See* GREGORY ET AL., *supra* note 3, § 10.12(D)(4).
[35] 511 N.E.2d 676 (Ill. App. Ct. 1987).
[36] *Id.* at 680.
[37] *See In re* Marriage of Merry, 689 P.2d 1250 (Mont. 1984).
[38] PRINCIPLES § 4.10, at 750.
[39] PRINCIPLES § 4.10, at 750 ("fixing a period of time specified in a rule of statewide application").

There is a sharp departure from generally prevailing law, however, in cases of dissipation where there is insufficient marital property to achieve the remedy favored by the PRINCIPLES. There, the PRINCIPLES allow invasion of a spouse's separate property.[40] In the states that have adopted the dual property approach to classification of property, also accepted by the PRINCIPLES as preferable to an all property or "hotchpot" system,[41] equitable distribution statutes that permit invasion of separate property are rare, and permit invasion under very limited circumstances, as in cases of undue hardship or in order to balance the equities between the parties.[42] To the extent that such statutes apply, they are not significantly different from those in all property or "hotchpot" states. For the most part, then, the treatment of dissipation of marital property, or financial misconduct as the PRINCIPLES label it, is in harmony with state laws and decisions because dissipation of assets, a kind of economic fault, is uniformly taken into consideration when dividing marital property.

The PRINCIPLES are not so harmonious with generally prevailing state law, however, when one compares them with the law in a significant number of states relating to misconduct that is not financial, commonly referred to as marital fault. A number of state legislatures have barred any consideration of marital fault in property distribution at divorce, adopting the Model Marriage and Divorce Act, formerly known as the Uniform Marriage and Divorce Act, requirement that spousal property be divided "without regard to marital misconduct"[43] by adopting the same language in their property division statutes.[44] This is also the all-or-nothing approach that the PRINCIPLES recommend.[45] At the opposite end of the spectrum one finds statutes that contain a mandate that the court consider "the conduct of the parties during the marriage" or "the respective merits of the parties."[46] A few states adopt a third approach, variously worded, which considers only misconduct that causes or leads to divorce or to the breakdown of the marriage, and there are others that are silent with respect to fault, leaving it within the discretion of the courts to determine whether fault is a relevant property division factor. Finally, some statutes list among the factors that the court must consider when distributing marital property a so-called catchall factor, exemplified by the New York statutory requirement that the court consider "any other factor which the court shall expressly find to be just and proper."[47] Construing this provision in *O'Brien v. O'Brien*,[48] New York's highest court stated:

> Except in egregious cases which shock the conscience of the court, ... [marital fault] is not a "just and proper" factor for consideration in the equitable distribution of marital property.... That is so because marital fault is inconsistent with the underlying assumption that a marriage is in part an economic partnership and upon its dissolution the parties are entitled to a fair share of the marital estate, because fault will usually be difficult to

[40] PRINCIPLES § 4.10(6), at 751.

[41] Curiously, the PRINCIPLES adopt the term "hotchpot" rather than the familiar "all property" states to identify jurisdictions in which all property held at the time of dissolution, sometimes with exceptions, is subject to distribution, in contrast with "dual property" states that permit distribution of property acquired during the marriage. *See* GREGORY ET AL., *supra* note 3, § 10.03.

[42] See GREGORY, THE LAW OF EQUITABLE DISTRIBUTION § 2.05 for illustrative statutes and cases that permit invasion of separate property in dual property states. GREGORY ET AL., *supra* note 2.

[43] UNIFORM MARRIAGE AND DIVORCE ACT § 307, 9 U.L.A. 238 (1987).

[44] *See, e.g.*, COLO. REV. STAT. § 14-10-113 (2004).

[45] *See* Wardle, this volume.

[46] *See, e.g.*, MO. REV. STAT. § 452.330(1) (2004); WYO. STAT. ANN. § 20-2-114 (2004).

[47] *See* N.Y. DOM. REL. LAW § 236B(5)(d)(13) (McKinney 2004).

[48] 489 N.E.2d 712 (N.Y. 1985).

> assign and because introduction of the issue may involve the courts in time-consuming procedural maneuvers relating to collateral issues.[49]

Unlike the common-sensical treatment of fault in *O'Brien*, the PRINCIPLES adopt a position that rejects consideration of marital fault in every circumstance, no matter how egregious the conduct of one of the spouses.[50] Leaving the black letter silent with respect to the issue, the PRINCIPLES provide a lengthy essay in the introductory chapter that asks "whether marital misconduct should be considered in property allocation and awards of compensatory payments" and concludes that it should not.[51] One commentator, Professor Peter Nash Swisher, has characterized as "questionable" the three premises upon which the PRINCIPLES reject "the application of any fault-based non-financial factors in determining the allocation of marital property," which he identifies as follows: 1) utilizing fault factors "as an agent of morality" in effect "rewards virtue and punishes sin;" 2) judicial discretion would be "inherently limitless if no finding of economic harm to the claimant is required to justify [such an] award or its amount;" and 3) compensation for serious harm caused by the wrongful conduct of a spouse is "better left" to a separate criminal law or tort law remedy rather than a concomitant fault-based divorce remedy.[52]

This chapter will not rehearse Professor Swisher's persuasive analysis, and criticism of, and challenge to, these three assumptions, except to say that I concur entirely in his conclusion that states that have provided a remedy for egregious marital misconduct should continue to do so, and that relegating compensation for serious harm by an abusive spouse to remedies under tort law or criminal law is not only insufficient but what is more, it is unfair. Even a cursory reading of New York decisions that apply the principle that egregious harm should be a relevant factor in the division of marital property at divorce shows clearly that "state courts generally have applied such fault based remedies in a serious and responsible manner."[53] This point is readily illustrated with two New York cases.

In one unpublished New York case, the facts reveal that the husband, during the divorce proceedings, returned to his Middle East country of origin, taking the parties' minor children of the marriage with him.[54] The law provided no remedy to compel the return to New York of the husband or the children, so that the effect was to deny the mother and children any contact with each other for the rest of their lives. The court took the husband's egregious fault as a factor that justified a property division that awarded all of the marital property to the wife and nothing to the derelict husband.

In another New York case, *Havell v. Islam*,[55] the trial court addressed the question whether the offensive conduct of the husband should be taken into account in making an equitable distribution of marital property accumulated during the twenty-one years of the parties' marriage, which had produced six children whose ages ranged from nine to twenty years. The court posed the following question:

> In considering the equitable distribution of marital property, may the court properly admit evidence at trial of a pattern of domestic violence in a marriage of long duration,

[49] *Id.* at 719.

[50] PRINCIPLES, Chapter 1, Topic 2, at 42–85.

[51] PRINCIPLES, Chapter 1, Topic 2, pts I–VI, at 42–67.

[52] Peter Nash Swisher, *Commentary: The ALI Principles: A Farewell to Fault-But What Remedy for the Egregious Marital Misconduct of an Abusive Spouse*, 8 DUKE J. GENDER L. & POL'Y 213, 216, 219–220 (2001) (citations omitted).

[53] *Id.* at 216.

[54] Safah v. Safah, 1892 NYLJ p. 28, col. 5 [Sup. Ct. Suffolk Co.].

[55] 718 N.Y.S.2d 807 (Sup. Ct. 2000).

> pursuant to [the New York statute](which directs the court to consider "any other factor which the court shall find to be just and proper") and the standard set forth in ... *O'Brien.*"[56]

The testimony at trial revealed, among other things, that one evening the wife told the husband that she wanted a divorce, and "[t]hereafter the husband repeatedly struck the wife about the face and head with a barbell."[57] Besides this atrocious assault, the court lists twenty-one other instances of the husband's outrageous conduct, including striking and beating several of the children on a number of occasions; telling the children "the wife was a whore because she had previously been married;"[58] walking about the house morning and night "in drawstring pajamas with the drawstring opened to an extent that his sexual organs were exposed with the children and their friends in the home;"[59] grabbing the wife and twisting the wife's arm "in 'an excruciating painful way' causing her housekeeper to intervene;" spanking their six year old child for crying, and calling their child, who had learning difficulties "stupid and an idiot;" and beating the child's head and face.[60] After examining judicial decisions in other states and reviewing relevant law review literature, the court concluded:

> Upon consideration of the foregoing case law, statutes, and literature, it is the opinion of this court that a pattern of domestic violence, properly proven by competent testimony and evidence, is a "just and proper" factor to be considered by the court in connection with the equitable distribution of property pursuant to [the New York Domestic Relations Law].[61]

Accordingly, the court awarded 90 percent of the marital property to the wife and 10 percent to the husband.

I find it difficult to fathom on what basis anyone would consider it fair and equitable to prohibit a court from reaching the results in the two cases just discussed or would insist on leaving the wronged and abused women in these cases to remedies that tort law and criminal law supposedly would provide. As Professor Swisher concludes, after cataloging reasons why remedies in tort are an insufficient response to egregious marital misconduct:

> [A]nother major problem with the Principles' advocacy of an independent tort action for serious or egregious marital misconduct is that separate marital tort claims would foster a costly, onerous, unnecessary, and largely unsuccessful multiplicity of lawsuits–especially for injured spouses of modest means. Moreover, serious procedural questions of whether a tort claim should be joined in a divorce action, and under what applicable procedural guidelines, continue to trouble a number of courts and commentators.[62]

Leaving recompense for egregious marital fault to the criminal justice system is at least as questionable, if not more so. Significantly, the husband in *Havell v. Islam*[63] who, it will be recalled, broke his wife's jaw with a barbell, was indicted for attempted murder and first degree assault. After pleading guilty to only the second charge, he received a prison sentence of eight and one-third years, which he was serving in a state prison at the time of the divorce proceeding.[64] One might speculate about whether or not the wife was comforted

[56] *Id.* at 808.
[57] *Id.*
[58] *Id.* at 809.
[59] *Id.*
[60] *Id.*
[61] *Id.* at 811.
[62] Swisher, *supra* note 52, at 229.
[63] 718 N.Y.S.2d 807 (Sup. Ct. 2000).
[64] *Id.* at 808.

by this result, but she surely was not compensated. Crimes are, in principle, an offense against society, rather than against a particular victim, and whatever function criminal punishment may serve is often vitiated and compromised by factors such as prosecutorial discretion and plea bargaining.

Prosecutorial discretion, an essential component of the criminal justice system, has been defined as "[a] prosecutor's power to choose from the options available in a criminal case, such as filing charges, prosecuting, plea bargaining, and recommending a sentence to the court."[65] It would appear to be a truism that "[p]rosecutors... have the most to say about whether to file charges against a suspect and which charges to select... [I]n the end, the prosecutor can overrule police charging decisions without interference."[66] As one commentary points out:

> The prosecutor's broad charging discretion has a long history in the common law, both in England and in the United States. Judges today explain their reluctance to become involved in charging decisions on three grounds: (1) under the separation of powers doctrine, the executive branch has the responsibility to enforce the criminal law; (2) judges are poorly situated to make judgments about the allocation of limited prosecutorial resources; and (3) overbroad provisions in criminal codes require selection of from among the possible charges that could be filed.[67]

In *United States v. Armstrong*, the Supreme Court of the United States, rejecting a claim of selective prosecution, invoked separation of powers principles that support the broad discretion of prosecutors in the enforcement of criminal laws.[68] Similarly, in *Newton v. Rumery*, the Court emphasized that matters such as evaluation of the merits of a case and allocation of resources are within the province of the prosecutor and not the judiciary.[69] Again, in *Wayte v. United States*, the Supreme Court emphasized that "[s]uch factors as the strength of the case, the prosecution's general deterrence value, the Government's enforcement priorities, and the case's relationship to the Government's overall enforcement plans are not readily susceptible to the kind of analysis the courts are competent to undertake."[70] State court decisions also reflect the wide berth afforded to prosecutors with respect to discretion in charging,[71] as well as in declination to charge and in diversion decisions.[72] Furthermore, even the concern that "criminalization of innocuous behavior" may occur because of broad provisions in the criminal law "is muted in the American justice system by prosecutorial discretion. Prosecutors need not prosecute every case that presents a potential violation of the criminal law."[73]

Simply stated, it is highly questionable that the criminal justice system is an appropriate place in which to place such social problems as domestic violence. It is also worth noting

[65] Bryan A. Gardner, A Handbook of Criminal Law Terms (2000).

[66] *See* Nora V. Demleitner, Douglas A. Berman, Marc L. Miller & Ronald F. Wright, Sentencing Law and Policy 802 (2004).

[67] *Id.*

[68] 517 U.S. 456, 464 (1996).

[69] 480 U.S. 386, 396 (1987).

[70] 470 U.S. 598, 607 (1985). *See also* Marshall v. Jerrico, 446 U.S. 238, 148 (1980) (noting in connection with a complaint against the Secretary of Labor: "Our legal system has traditionally accorded wide discretion to criminal prosecutors in the enforcement process... and similar considerations have been found applicable to administrative prosecutors as well").

[71] *See, e.g.*, State v. Peters, 525 N.W.2d 854 (Iowa 1994).

[72] *See, e.g.*, Wilson v. Renfroe, 91 So.2d 857 (Fla. 1956); Cleveland v. State, 417 So.2d 653 (Fla. 1982).

[73] Vikramaditya S. Khanna, *Corporate Crime Legislation: A Political Economy Analysis*, 82 Wash. U. L.Q. 95, 128 (2004).

that domestic violence may be more difficult to prove in a criminal case than it would be in a divorce proceeding. Such cases frequently involve years of repeated violent incidents. In a criminal proceeding, prosecutors are required to plead and to prove beyond a reasonable doubt specific instances of violence at specific times. A pattern of violence during a marriage might not be susceptible of such proof. Thus, absent a prompt report to the police or at least to a medical provider, such cases are almost impossible to prove.[74]

II. Gauging The Impact of the Property Division Proposals

In view of the considerable amount of time and effort that was devoted to the ALI property division proposals, it is fair to ask what impact they have thus far had on legislatures and courts, and how seriously they have been taken by members of the organized matrimonial bar, who deal with property division issues on a day-to-day basis. As of this writing, the response to such an inquiry is more than a little disappointing. A survey of bar association journals around the country has unearthed a single article, appearing in an American Bar Association ("ABA") publication, that so much as mentions the ALI property division proposals.[75] The author's only observation about the subject of property division (in an article based in large part on an interview with Professor Ira Mark Ellman, the chief drafter for the PRINCIPLES), is that the ALI "suggests that decisions about maintenance and division of property be made without regard to marital misconduct such as adultery.... [T]hose are just a few of the sweeping changes presented in the ALI's wide-ranging, 1,200-page report recommending overhaul of divorce law."[76] Just two other articles, also found in ABA journals, deal with the treatment of domestic partners [77] and alimony under chapter 5 of the PRINCIPLES.[78] The impact of the ALI property division proposals on the decisions of state courts also has been insignificant as of this writing. Several decisions cite various drafts of the PRINCIPLES when they are conveniently consistent with or supportive of prevailing rules in a particular state. In *Blanchard v. Blanchard*,[79] for example, a case involving retirement benefits, the Supreme Court of Louisiana cited a draft provision of the PRINCIPLES that was consistent with the law of several other community property states.[80] Similarly, the Supreme Court of Vermont, in *Damone v. Damone*,[81] pointed out that the defendant's approach to classification of personal injury awards was endorsed by the ALI.[82]

[74] This insight is attributed to Professor Alafair Burke based on her experience as a prosecutor.

[75] *See* Mark Hansen, *A Family Law Fight: ALI Report Stirs Hot Debate Over Rights of Unmarried Couples*, 89 A.B.A.J. 20 (June 2003).

[76] *Id.* The article also notes sharp criticisms directed against other provisions of the PRINCIPLES. Hansen reports, for example, that "Brigham Young University law professor Lynn D. Wardle, a member of the ALI and one of the project's chief critics, says the entire project reflects a strong ideological bias against marriage." He also notes that "another leading critic, David Blankenhorn, founder and president of the Institute for American Values, a pro-family think tank, say the ALI proposals, if enacted, would undermine the institution of marriage." Also, "Ronald K. Henry, a child advocacy lawyer in Washington, D.C.... opposes the report's child support and child custody provisions, both of which he says contain a built-in bias against fathers." *Id.*

[77] John J. Sampson, *Preface to the Amendments to the Uniform Parentage Act*, 37 FAM. L.Q. 1 (2003).

[78] *See* Brenda L. Storey, *Surveying the Alimony Landscape: Origin, Evolution and Extinction*, 25 FAM. ADVOC. 10 (2003).

[79] 731 So.2d 175 (La. 1999).

[80] *Id.* at 181.

[81] 782 A.2d 1208 (Vt. 2001).

[82] *Id.* at 506, n.1 ("While not necessary to this decision, we acknowledge the trend in the country to adhere to defendant's suggested approach. [ALI] endorses this approach as well and recognizes the personal nature of a loss which gives rise to a claim for pain and suffering. *See* PRINCIPLES OF THE LAW OF FAMILY DISSOLUTION: ANALYSIS AND RECOMMENDATIONS § 4.08(2)(a) (ALI, Proposed Final Draft, Part I, February 14 (1997)). Accordingly, the ALI would treat this type of property as the separate property of the injured spouse. *See also* Doucette v. Washburn, 766 A.2d 378 (Me. 2001) (citing the same section of the PRINCIPLES).

A justice of the Supreme Court of Kentucky, in a concurring opinion, cited the ALI property division proposals in support of his view, consistent with the rule in other jurisdictions, that there is a presumption that debts that occur during the marriage are marital property.[83] Again, in *Holman v. Holman*,[84] the Kentucky Supreme Court, ruling on the characterization of disability payments, adopted the approach of the majority of other jurisdictions while noting that it was also the approach recommended by the ALI.[85] The Supreme Court of North Dakota, in *Weber v. Weber*[86] reiterated the generally prevailing principle that trial courts should recognize agreements between the parties when distributing property. The court noted, however, in the course of striking down the agreement before it as unconscionable, that trial courts "should not... blindly accept property settlement agreements," citing case law and the PRINCIPLES.[87]

As of this writing, the most recent case from the highest court of a state that cites the property division principles was rendered by the Massachusetts court after the PRINCIPLES were adopted and promulgated in their final form. The Supreme Judicial Court of Massachusetts, in *Kittridge v. Kittridge*,[88] finding no definition of "dissipation" in its own case law, reviewed the way in which courts in other jurisdictions defined the concept, together with a supporting citation from the PRINCIPLES.[89]

III. Conclusion

This brief review of cases that the highest state appellate courts have decided as various drafts of the PRINCIPLES became available and following their publication in final form, reveals that state courts have yet to fall under the sway of the ALI property division recommendations. As this chapter has shown, a few judges have cited the PRINCIPLES, but without much elaboration, when they are consistent with principles already established in state law. A skeptical reader might suspect that such otiose references to the work of the prestigious American Law Institute serves to add intellectual cachet to otherwise routine judicial opinions. In any event, apart from these occasional sops, it appears that state courts have largely ignored the drafters' property division proposals. Also, as this chapter

[83] *See* Neidlinger v. Neidlinger, 52 S.W.3d 513, 524 (Ky. 2001).

[84] 84 S.W.3d 903 (Ky. 2002).

[85] *Id.* at 906–07 ("In addition to the approaches noted by the Tennessee Supreme Court is an approach recommended by the American Law Institute which, similar to the 'analytical approach' or 'purpose analysis' classifies such benefits according to the nature of the property they replace rather than by the source of the funds used to acquire the benefit: 'Disability pay and workers' compensation benefits are marital property to the extent they replace income or benefits the recipient would have earned during the marriage but for the qualifying disability or injury.' Such benefits are therefore classified 'as marital property to the extent they replace earnings during the marriage and as separate property to the extent they replace earnings before or after the marriage, without regard to how or when the benefit was acquired.'") (citations omitted). *See also* Terwiliger v. Terwiliger, 64 S.W.3d 816, n.18 (Ky. 2002) (citing PRINCIPLES § 4.03, cmt. c, (Proposed Final Draft, Part I, February 14, 1997) ("When tracing yields only ambiguous results, the property is typically treated as marital.").

[86] 589 N.W. 2d 358 (N.D. 1999).

[87] *Id.* at 360 (citing PRINCIPLES OF THE LAW OF FAMILY DISSOLUTION: ANALYSIS AND RECOMMENDATIONS § 4.01, Tentative Draft No. 2, A.L.I. (1996) for the proposition that "[a]greements between spouses have traditionally been subject to various procedural and substantive rules beyond those which apply to contracts generally").

[88] 803 N.E.2d 306 (Mass. 2004).

[89] *Id.* at 36–37 (citing the PRINCIPLES § 4.10 (2) and comment C, which recommend that property division be adjusted to account for marital property lost or destroyed through spouse's "intentional misconduct" occurring during a fixed period of time prior to commencement of proceedings, noting that "only transactions during a period immediately preceding commencement of a dissolution action should ordinarily be considered").

discussed earlier, if one judges by bar association publications, the ALI property division proposals remain largely irrelevant not only to state courts, but also to national and state bar associations as well as family and matrimonial law practitioners.

The Director's Foreword notes that the PRINCIPLES were "undertaken in the 1990s, when the law on these subjects was still in flux" and that this project was written as reform movements swirled.[90] With respect to property division at least, the PRINCIPLES for better or for worse do not appear to have had more than a whit of influence on these swirling reform movements. Viewed as theoretical academic scholarship, the ALI property division proposals are gracefully presented, and one might say elegant. As legal standards to which legislators, judges, and practicing lawyers might repair, however, these provisions are seriously, and one might say abysmally, flawed. The property division proposals seem to be a pretty good example of the old adage that "the mountain has labored and produced a mouse."[91]

I am grateful to Alexis Collentine and Lisa Spar for assistance in preparing this chapter.

[90] PRINCIPLES, Director's Foreword, at xv.

[91] *See* Jean de la Fontaine Fables, V "La Montagne qui accoucche" ("A mountain in labour shouted so loud that everyone . . . ran up expecting . . . a city bigger than Paris; she brought forth a mouse.").

9 Unprincipled Family Dissolution: The ALI's Recommendations for Division of Property

David Westfall

The PRINCIPLES reflect eleven years of work by a massive team of drafters, advisors, and consultative groups.[1] A former director of the ALI described the project as "among the most important that the [ALI] has ever undertaken."[2] The task took on Herculean dimensions. Unfortunately, the final result is profoundly disappointing, particularly in contrast to the ALI's outstanding work in the Restatements, which have often exerted a strong positive influence on major areas of law.[3]

The PRINCIPLES, published with the prestigious imprimatur of the ALI, may impede much needed reforms and even lead the legislators, judges, and rule makers to whom they are addressed to adopt unsound policies. In seeking to ward off these potentially harmful effects, this chapter first analyzes exactly what the ALI's imprimatur on the PRINCIPLES really means and then demonstrates why their uncritical acceptance as guideposts would be unwise. The PRINCIPLES contain serious deficiencies that should be corrected.

At the outset, it is crucial to examine the procedures under which the PRINCIPLES were passed. Although ALI's bylaws require authorization by the membership and approval by the ALI for publication of any work intended to represent the ALI's position,[4] the bylaws also provide that "[a] quorum for any session of a meeting of the members is established by registration during the meeting of 400 members. . . . "[5] Thus, a quorum is conclusively deemed to be present for all sessions of a meeting as soon as a little over 10 percent of the approximately 3,800 members[6] have registered, even though the number present and voting at a given session may be minimal. "A majority of the members voting on any question during any meeting or session is effective as action of the membership,"[7] and there is no proxy voting. As a result, fundamental matters of policy may be decided by a

[1] My own minuscule role, both in the "Members Consultative Group" for the PRINCIPLES and as a member of the ALI, had no effect on the final result. After one meeting, it became clear that both the Group and the drafters were marching to a very different beat and that my efforts to alter their views would be futile. I tried again at the May 2000 Annual Meeting, introducing three motions to amend Chapters 6 and 7, but they were all defeated by voice votes. *See* 77 A.L.I. PROC. 67–88 (2000).

[2] PRINCIPLES OF THE LAW OF FAMILY DISSOLUTION: ANALYSIS AND RECOMMENDATIONS, at xi (Tentative Draft No. 3 pt. I, 1998) (Director's Foreword by Geoffrey Hazard).

[3] As of April 1, 2002, the number of published case citations to the Restatements was just under 155,000. Over forty percent of these citations were to the particularly influential RESTATEMENT OF TORTS. *See* 2002 A.L.I. ANN. REP. 11.

[4] *See* 2002 A.L.I. ANN. REP. app. 1, at 56.

[5] *Id.* at § 3.02.

[6] First Vice President Harper referred to the former quorum requirement of one fifth of the voting members as approximately 760. *See* 78 A.L.I. PROC. 14 (2001).

[7] *See* 2002 A.L.I. ANN. REP. app. 1, at 54.

handful of votes,[8] and may reflect the views of only a tiny fraction of the membership. Yet, the PRINCIPLES are published as the position of the ALI, with no indication of the number of members who actually voted on any given portion or the narrow margin by which they were adopted. Even a careful reader of the Proceedings of the ALI's Annual Meeting may learn no more than that a given motion was adopted (or defeated) by a voice vote, with no way of knowing how many voices were heard.

If the PRINCIPLES are to guide legislative action or judicial decision, it should be either because of their inherent merit or the reputations of the drafters themselves,[9] rather than the eminence of the many distinguished lawyers, judges, and academics listed as members but largely absent from the meetings at which the PRINCIPLES were approved. To emphasize their source, I will often refer here to "the drafters," rather than to "the PRINCIPLES."

I. Why Serious Reform of Family Law Is Needed

This chapter deals with only one aspect of divorce, as well as of "domestic partnerships" between unmarried cohabitants, the termination of which the drafters would generally treat like divorce:[10] the division of property. It is an area in which family law cries out for serious reform. The economic consequences of divorce in a given state are often highly unpredictable because of statutes and court decisions that accord trial judges a large measure of discretion in allocating property between the spouses,[11] as well as lengthy lists of factors that judges often are either directed or authorized to consider.[12]

Because of the unpredictability this judicial discretion creates, spouses and their lawyers may have little guidance in negotiations for settlement of their claims, and the more risk averse party may suffer a substantial disadvantage as a result.[13] In addition, the negotiating process is likely to be more time-consuming and expensive because of the large number of factors to be considered and the parties' uncertainty as to how they will be viewed by the

[8] For example, at the 1995 Annual Meeting, a member moved to recommit a highly controversial proposed provision – not presently the law in any state – that would change the character of a spouse's individual property to marital property based merely on the passage of time since the property was acquired, thereby causing the recharacterized property to be equally divided between them on dissolution of their marriage. By a vote of only 101 to 95, the motion to recommit was defeated. *See* 72 A.L.I. PROC. 128–42 (1995). This challenged section is, therefore, included in the PRINCIPLES and bears the ALI's imprimatur, even though a change of only four votes – just over one tenth of one percent of the membership – would have caused the section to be recommitted. *See* PRINCIPLES § 4.12.

[9] The primary drafter of the PRINCIPLES, Professor Ira Ellman, was identified by the Director of the ALI as responsible for drafting chapters dealing with division of property and "compensatory spousal payments," commonly known as alimony or maintenance. Geoffrey C. Hazard, Jr., *Foreword* to PRINCIPLES OF THE LAW OF FAMILY DISSOLUTION: ANALYSIS AND RECOMMENDATIONS, at xiii, xiv (Proposed Final Draft pt. I, 1997). Dean Katharine T. Bartlett drafted the chapter dealing with "residential responsibility" or child custody, and Professor Grace Ganz Blumberg drafted the chapter dealing with child support. Geoffrey C. Hazard, Jr., *Foreword* to PRINCIPLES OF THE LAW OF FAMILY DISSOLUTION: ANALYSIS AND RECOMMENDATIONS, at ix, xi (Tentative Draft No. 3 pt. I, 1998).

[10] *See* PRINCIPLES § 1, Topic 1, Overview of Chapter 7, pt. II, at 39. *See also* PRINCIPLES § 6.03 (setting forth criteria to determine whether couples are "domestic partners"). For a discussion of these criteria, see David Westfall, *Forcing Incidents of Marriage on Unmarried Cohabitants: The American Law Institute's Principles of Family Dissolution*, 76 NOTRE DAME L. REV. 1467, 1478–80 (2001).

[11] *See infra* Part I(C).

[12] *See infra* Part I(C).

[13] *See* Robert H. Mnookin & Lewis Kornhauser, *Bargaining in the Shadow of the Law: The Case of Divorce*, 88 YALE L.J. 950, 979 (1979) (discussing risk aversion in the context of custody disputes).

particular judge who hears the case. Additionally, if the spouses do not settle, a trial may be even more costly if the parties seek to introduce relevant evidence for all of the factors that the judge may consider.

A further result of this unpredictability is that both the parties and the general public often may perceive the results to be unfair, with couples who appear to be similarly situated experiencing vastly different economic consequences from divorce. The inevitable result is diminished respect for the legal system and reduced confidence that justice will be done in family law cases, which constitute one third of the civil actions filed in state courts.[14]

Even if the rules were clear in each state, however, wide variations in state law would produce major disparities in results for married couples divorced in different states. And the consequences of ending the kind of cohabitation that the PRINCIPLES treat as a "domestic partnership" are even more unpredictable, because of the absence of relevant statutes,[15] as well as the paucity of judicial decisions, dealing with claims of former cohabitants after the end of their relationship.[16]

The quest for a uniform law of marriage and divorce goes back at least as far as the formation of the National Conference of Commissioners on Uniform State Laws in 1892,[17] but did not lead to the promulgation of the Uniform Marriage and Divorce Act ("UMDA") until 1970.[18] Although the UMDA was adopted by only eight states,[19] it embodied fundamental changes that are now reflected in the laws of many other states. It "totally eliminated the traditional concept that divorce is a remedy granted to an innocent spouse, based on the marital fault of the other spouse which has not been connived at, colluded in, or condoned by the innocent spouse."[20] This principle is now generally accepted with the widespread adoption of provisions for no-fault divorce, although many states merely added a no-fault alternative to existing fault-based grounds.[21] New York is a prominent exception that stands by the old rule.[22]

[14] *See* COURT STATISTICS PROJECT, NATIONAL CENTER FOR STATE COURTS, EXAMINING THE WORK OF STATE COURTS, 2001, at 16, 36 (Brian J. Ostrom et al. eds., 2001) (indicating that domestic relations cases comprise 5.2 million of the nearly 15 million cases filed).

[15] Notable exceptions are those statutes that deny enforcement of agreements between cohabitants that are not in writing. *See, e.g.*, MINN. STAT. §§ 513.075–513.076 (2002) (stripping the state's courts of jurisdiction over claims rooted in cohabitation, absent a written agreement); TEX. FAM. CODE ANN. § 1.108 (Vernon 1998).

[16] The best known decision recognizing cohabitants' capacity to contract with each other and offering them a variety of remedies for claims relating to the incidents of their relationship is, of course, *Marvin v. Marvin*, 557 P.2d 106 (Cal. 1976). For decisions in other states, see Westfall, *supra* note 10, at 1472–73, 1475 nn. 51–54 (2001).

[17] *See* UNIF. MARRIAGE AND DIVORCE ACT prefatory note (amended 1973), 9A U.L.A. 160 (1998).

[18] *See id.*

[19] *See id.* at 159 tbl. The adopting states are Arizona, Colorado, Illinois, Kentucky, Minnesota, Missouri, Montana, and Washington. There have been no more adoptions since 1977, when Illinois was added to the list. *See* 750 ILL. COMP. STAT. §§ 5/101–5/102 (2002).

[20] UNIF. MARRIAGE AND DIVORCE ACT prefatory note (amended 1973), 9 U.L.A. 161 (1998).

[21] *See* Herma Hill Kay, *Equality and Difference: A Perspective on No-Fault Divorce and its Aftermath*, 56 U. CIN. L. REV. 1, 5–6 & n.20 (1987).

[22] *See* N.Y. DOM. REL. LAW ANN. § 170(1)–(4) (McKinney 1999) (requiring proof of a specified kind of fault, or that the parties have lived separate and apart for a year or more, pursuant either to a decree or a separation agreement, and that the plaintiff has substantially performed the terms of the decree or agreement). The latter provision for a so called "conversion divorce" in effect authorizes divorce by mutual consent. *See id.* § 170(5)–(6).

A. Basic Flaws in the ALI's Response

The ALI's attempt at family law reform falls short in three major respects:

(1) it fails to promote interstate uniformity, such that under the proposed system the economic consequences of divorce would continue to vary greatly depending upon which state grants the divorce;
(2) it would curtail the autonomy of prospective spouses, domestic partners, and divorcing couples to structure the economic consequences of their relationship or its termination to meet their individually perceived needs; and
(3) it would make only a limited attempt to limit the role of judicial discretion in determining those economic consequences.

Unlike the UMDA, the drafters' objective is not uniformity (except within a state).[23] Rather, it is "to promote . . . the law's 'clarification,' its' 'better adaptation to social needs,' and its' securing of 'the better administration of justice.' "[24] The ALI does recommend rules that would make some issues clearer, but often leaves to the rule-making authority the determination of both the requisite threshold for a rule's application and the rate at which its effect increases.[25] In addition, the PRINCIPLES sometimes offer no guidance at all as to the choice between contrasting rules.[26] While complete unanimity among the states on the economic consequences of divorce is not a realistic goal, the drafters should have done more to guide policy makers and to encourage conformity, rather than inviting individual variations.

The law of family dissolution could serve another important goal: confirming that spouses, prospective spouses, and domestic partners may, if reasonable requirements to protect the parties' interests are satisfied, structure the terms of their divorce to meet their individually-perceived needs. Instead, the PRINCIPLES would curtail the increased autonomy granted to prospective spouses and divorcing couples by the Uniform Premarital Agreement Act[27] and the UMDA.[28] This unhappy consequence follows from provisions in the PRINCIPLES permitting more intrusive judicial review of the parties' agreements at

[23] *See* PRINCIPLES § 1, Topic 1, Overview of Chapters 4 and 5, pt. II, cmt. c, at 29 (discussing "[t]he value of statewide rules establishing presumptive results").

[24] Ira Mark Ellman, *Chief Reporter's Foreword* to PRINCIPLES, at xvii (quoting from the ALI's charter).

[25] *See, e.g.*, PRINCIPLES § 5.04(2) (suggesting that the rule-making authority specify both the duration of marriages and the degree of spousal income disparity necessary to qualify a spouse for a presumption of entitlement to compensation for loss of the marital living standard).

[26] *See, e.g.*, PRINCIPLES § 5.04 cmt. f, at 814 (permitting the definition of spousal income for purposes of determining compensatory spousal payments to "be based on pretax or after-tax income," as it is for child support calculations under Section 3.14(7)).

[27] *See* UNIF. PREMARITAL AGREEMENT ACT § 3(a)(3)–(4), 9C U.L.A. 43 (2001). Section 3(a)(3) authorizes parties to contract, *inter alia*, with respect to the disposition of property upon marital dissolution and, under Section 3(a)(4), with respect to "the modification or elimination of spousal support[.]" However, if such provisions dealing with support cause one party "to be eligible for support under a program of public assistance at the time of separation or marital dissolution, a court . . . may require the other party to provide support to the extent necessary to avoid that eligibility." *id.* § 6(b).

[28] *See* UNIF. MARRIAGE AND DIVORCE ACT § 306(a)–(b) (amended 1973), 9A U.L.A. 248–49 (1998). Section 306(a) authorizes the parties to provide in a written separation agreement, *inter alia*, for the disposition of property and for maintenance, and Section 306(b) makes such provisions binding on the court unless it finds "that the separation agreement is unconscionable."

the time enforcement is sought.[29] A far better alternative would be to protect the more vulnerable party by requiring independent advice when the agreement was made in order for it to be enforceable against that party, without creating continuing uncertainty about its validity.[30]

In contrast, when enforcement of a premarital or marital agreement is sought after the death of a spouse, Section 9.4 of the recently published RESTATEMENT (THIRD) OF PROPERTY: WILLS AND OTHER DONATIVE TRANSFERS[31] makes no provision for judicial review either of its fairness or of the various other factors that may be taken into account in states that provide for equitable distribution of property upon divorce. As one of the drafters of the Restatement pointed out, "the idea of extending the equitable distribution system into the area of elective-share law was rejected because of the discretionary and unpredictable nature of the results under that system."[32]

The appropriate role of judicial discretion, and the persistent failure of the PRINCIPLES to recommend needed limitations on its exercise in the context of any of the four major aspects of their recommendations discussed below,[33] is sufficiently pervasive to merit consideration here as a separate topic. But before doing so, it is important to note that in addition to these lost opportunities to move the law forward, the PRINCIPLES are plagued with three recurring deficiencies:

(1) the PRINCIPLES are internally inconsistent, at times to the point of incoherence;[34]
(2) the PRINCIPLES rely on the comforting but inaccurate assumption that no-fault divorce is freely available to spouses everywhere;[35] and
(3) the treatment of business and economic matters and income tax considerations is surprisingly uninformed and incomplete.[36]

[29] *See* PRINCIPLES § 7.05. In contrast, comment k to Section 9.4 of the RESTATEMENT (THIRD) OF PROPERTY: WILLS AND OTHER DONATIVE TRANSFERS (2003) treats a premarital or marital agreement as "unenforceable if it was unconscionable when it was executed." Professor Melvin Eisenberg endorses a second-look approach to prenuptial agreements because of the parties' "limits of cognition." Melvin Aron Eisenberg, *The Limits of Cognition and the Limits of Contract*, 47 STAN. L. REV. 211, 254 (1995). Professor Eisenberg, however, fails to acknowledge that increased uncertainty about the enforceability of such agreements may prevent marriages from taking place despite the belief of both prospective spouses that marriage on the proposed terms is preferable to not marrying.

[30] *See* Michael Trebilcock & Steven Elliott, *The Scope and Limits of Legal Paternalism: Altruism and Coercion in Family Financial Arrangements, in* THE THEORY OF CONTRACT LAW 45, 64–67 (Peter Benson ed. 2001).

[31] *See* RESTATEMENT (THIRD) OF PROP.: DONATIVE TRANSFERS § 9.4 (2003).

[32] Lawrence W. Waggoner, *Marital Property Rights in Transition*, 59 MO. L. REV. 21, 51 (1994).

[33] *See infra* Part II.

[34] *Compare* PRINCIPLES § 5.02 cmt. a, at 789 (endorsing "*compensation for loss* rather than *relief of need*" as a basis for interspousal payments after divorce), *with* PRINCIPLES § 5.09 cmt. a, at 876 (referencing "the policy purpose of an alimony award, which is relief of need"); *compare* PRINCIPLES § 4.12 cmt. a, reporter's notes at 782–83 (noting that an award of separate property to the nonowner spouse will reduce any spousal support award, which is based on disparity of income), *with* PRINCIPLES § 5.04 cmt. f, at 815 ("Spousal income from marital property allocated at dissolution between the spouses should not be considered."). Thus, spousal income from separate property is considered in making a spousal support award, but spousal income from marital property is not.

[35] *See, e.g.*, PRINCIPLES § 4.10 cmt. b, at 753 (noting that "[t]he legal remedy available to a spouse who finds a marriage unacceptably burdensome or inequitable is exit. Modern divorce law allows either spouse to end the marriage"). *But see supra* note 22 (noting the unavailability of no-fault divorce in New York). Comments to Section 5.02 take a more realistic view of the possibility that "nonlegal ties" may "keep persons in unhappy relationships." PRINCIPLES § 5.02 cmt. c, at 791. Religious beliefs may also have that effect.

[36] The absence of any recognition of the special factors involved in determining whether, and to what extent, stock options granted to corporate executives and other employees are to be treated as marital property is the most prominent example. *See infra* Part II(B)(2). Similarly, the treatment of goodwill as divisible marital property does not adequately reflect the relevance of postdivorce services of a spouse in estimating the value attributable to goodwill

It is important to bear in mind that, in recommendations for division of property and "compensatory spousal payments" (commonly known as alimony or maintenance), the PRINCIPLES embody dramatic departures from the mainstream of American family law.[37] These departures are at least as striking in their treatment of nonmarital partners' rights against each other, as well as agreements by cohabitants and prospective spouses to modify those rights.[38] After exploring the appropriate role of judicial discretion in determining the economic consequences of divorce, this chapter analyzes the drafters' recommendations for the characterization and division of property on divorce.

B. The ALI's Failure to Reign in Judicial Discretion

The PRINCIPLES extol the virtues of statewide rules establishing presumptive results as ensuring consistency and predictability,[39] but would impair their effectiveness by unjustified and unnecessary authorization of judicial departures from presumptive results to avoid "a substantial injustice."[40] The PRINCIPLES assert: "Clearly, the presumptions established under the required statewide rules must be rebuttable, to allow the trial court or other decisionmaker to respond to the unusual case presenting factual variations no governing statute could anticipate."[41] The prevalence of broad judicial discretion in determining the economic consequences of divorce is all too familiar. It is said, for example, that in the vast majority of states today, the normal approach is "to give broad discretion . . . to trial courts to assign to either spouse property acquired during the marriage, irrespective of title, taking into account the circumstances of the particular case and recognizing the value of the contributions of a nonworking spouse or homemaker to the acquisition of that property."[42] Although greater use is being made of guidelines and rules of thumb in determining alimony, the former often are limited to one or more counties in a state.[43]

Arguments for firm rules or discretionary standards in the context of divorce have been explored extensively by Professor Marsha Garrison from both an analytical and an empirical perspective.[44] She notes that "discretionary standards will typically, through the development of informal rules of thumb and formal precedents, become more rule-like. . . . In contrast to the channeling tendency of discretion, rules tend to produce exceptions."[45]

of a business or professional practice. *See infra* Part II(B)(1). Furthermore, the discussion of the relationship between property division and compensatory payments ignores the difference in their treatment for income tax purposes. *See infra* Part I(D).

[37] *See* Silbaugh, this volume (discussing recharacterization of separate property as marital property). *But see* J. Thomas Oldham, *ALI Principles of Family Dissolution: Some Comments*, 1997 U. ILL. L. REV. 801, 802 (asserting that the property proposals generally restate prevailing law).

[38] *See generally* Westfall, *supra* note 10.

[39] *See* PRINCIPLES § 1.01 cmt. a, at 86–87.

[40] PRINCIPLES § 1.01 cmt. b, at 87.

[41] PRINCIPLES § 1.01 cmt. b, at 87 (internal quotation marks omitted).

[42] John DeWitt Gregory, THE LAW OF EQUITABLE DISTRIBUTION § 1.03 (1989).

[43] *See* Virginia R. Dugan & Jon A. Feder, *Alimony Guidelines: Do They Work?*, 25 FAM. ADVOC. 20, 20–22 (Spring 2003).

[44] *See* Marsha Garrison, *How do Judges Decide Divorce Cases? An Empirical Analysis of Discretionary Decision-Making*, 74 N.C. L. REV. 401 (1996).

[45] *Id.* at 514. Professor Garrison also states that the costs of discretionary and rule-based decision-making are quite different. Discretionary rules impose greater information costs on private parties, while rule-based decision-making burdens the rule-making authority with costs in searching for the right rule and imposes costs on all of the affected parties if the search is unsuccessful. *Id.* at 516–18.

Professor Mary Ann Glendon has pointed out that "[f]amily law . . . is characterized by more discretion than any other field of private law."[46]

In contrast, intestacy statutes, including provisions for an elective share for the surviving spouse, are a clear illustration of reliance on fixed shares. Another is the generally mandated equal division of community property on divorce or on death in California, Louisiana, and New Mexico.[47] Indeed, the 1990 revision of Article II of the Uniform Probate Code ("UPC"), already adopted in nine states,[48] retains the traditional rule that neither intestate shares nor the elective share of the surviving spouse are subject to discretionary modification by the probate court.[49] Similarly, UPC Section 2–202[50] implements a partnership or marital-sharing theory of marriage by increasing the elective-share percentage of the augmented estate so that it gradually reaches the maximum level of 50 percent after a marriage has lasted fifteen years.[51]

The UPC could have followed the ALI's approach in dealing with compensatory payments in Chapter 5 and treated intestate and elective shares as merely rebuttable presumptions.[52] The UPC could have authorized the court to modify these shares to take into account such factors as (1) the size of the decedent's transfers to others, (2) the wealth and anticipated needs of the surviving spouse, (3) the needs of children and other dependents of the decedent, (4) the opportunity of each claimant to acquire assets and income in the future, and (5) the conduct toward the decedent of all potential claimants, by analogy to many state statutes dealing with alimony and distribution of property on divorce.[53] Courts could also be given discretion to deal with more unusual cases, such as the groom who drops dead minutes before the minister pronounces the couple man and wife.[54]

But the cost of doing so would be high, and the Joint Editorial Board for the UPC rejected extending equitable distribution into the law of elective shares "because of the discretionary and unpredictable nature of the results under that system."[55] Today, the public accepts the use of fixed rules in determining the elective share of the surviving spouse, as well as shares in cases of intestacy.[56] Furthermore, the UPC responds to unusual situations by express

[46] Mary Ann Glendon, *Fixed Rules and Discretion in Contemporary Family Law and Succession Law*, 60 Tul. L. Rev. 1165, 1167 (1986).

[47] The drafters refer to the three community property states that generally divide community property equally on divorce, but understandably treat division at death as being beyond the Principles' scope. Principles § 4.02 cmt. a, at 647.

[48] *See* Unif. Probate Code (amended 1997), 8 U.L.A. 76 (1998).

[49] The provision in UPC § 2–404 for a "reasonable allowance" for support of the "surviving spouse and minor children whom the decedent was obligated to support and children who were in fact being supported by the decedent" during the estate's administration does allow for some judicial discretion, but it is likely to be of minor importance in an estate of more than modest size. Wisconsin, a non-UPC state, authorizes the court to provide for the support and education of dependent minor children and for support of the surviving spouse in some cases. *See* Wis. Stat. Ann. § 861.35 (2002). Oregon likewise has limited statutory provisions for the support of the decedent's spouse and dependent children. *See* Or. Rev. Stat. § 114.01-114.055 (2001).

[50] *See* Unif. Probate Code §2–202 (amended 1990), 8 U.L.A. Pt. I 102–03 (1998).

[51] "Augmented estate," as defined in UPC § 2–203 includes not only the decedent's probate estate, but also the decedent's nonprobate transfers to others, *see id.* § 2–205, and to the surviving spouse, *see id.* § 2–206, as well as the decedent's own property and similar transfers.

[52] Principles §§ 5.04, 5.05.

[53] *See, e.g.*, Mass. Gen. Laws ch. 208, § 34 (1998) (listing 14 mandatory factors that must be taken into account in assigning property and, in addition, two discretionary factors that courts may take into account).

[54] *See* In re Neiderhiser's Estate, 2 Pa. D. & C.3d 302 (1977) (holding the bride to be the deceased groom's widow, entitling her to letters of administration on his estate).

[55] *See* Waggoner, *supra* note 32, at 51.

[56] A plausible explanation for the emphasis on rules in probate law is that, having been derived from property law, its focus is on rights, their protection, and their clarification to provide greater certainty, *see* Garrison, *supra* note 44,

provision, such as in the denial of benefits to the felonious and intentional slayer of the decedent.[57] If distribution of intestate estates were controlled by rebuttable presumptions, rather than fixed rules, the application of judicial discretion to vary the rules would surely lead to much popular discontent.

In contrast to a grant of broad judicial discretion, there is good reason to believe that the public prefers the prevailing regime of specified shares in cases of intestacy and the generally firm rules of state probate codes. Succession law is "the traditional stronghold of fixed rules[.]"[58] This system, which in almost all of the non-community property states provides a defined share for the surviving spouse who elects against the decedent's will, has withstood calls for reform by several different constituencies. Some favor forced shares for children; others favor free testation, with no minimum for the surviving spouse; and a third group would allow a judge, in his or her discretion, to increase the share of an applicant who "has not received reasonable provision" out of the estate.[59]

In opposing the creation of such discretionary power, Professor Glendon concludes that the current body of law "functions well on a day-to-day basis – facilitating private planning, producing little unnecessary litigation and operating in accordance with the needs and desires of most of the persons it affects."[60] She contends that judicial discretion in probate "ignores the intent of the testator, promotes intra-family litigation, depletes estates, and brings disarray into a relatively smooth-functioning area of the law."[61] Indeed, "ease of administration and predictability of result are prized features of the probate system," according to the Commissioners on Uniform State Laws.[62]

C. The ALI's Rationales for "Property Division"

At the outset, the PRINCIPLES summarize the evolution of existing law governing alimony (renamed "compensatory spousal payments")[63] and division of property, and then purport to derive three "[l]essons from [t]his [h]istory":[64]

(1) The importance of establishing a coherent justification for alimony;
(2) Recognizing the relationship between property allocation and alimony; and
(3) The value of statewide rules establishing presumptive results.[65]

However, their recommendations actually reflect only the last of the three. The ALI treats the relationship between property allocation and alimony as "appropriately decided by rules that rely more on practical considerations and less on basic principle."[66]

The discussion that follows this surprising statement makes no reference to the important differences in income tax treatment of property transfers incident to divorce and alimony payments. The former is neither includible in income by the recipient nor

at 418, whereas divorce law in modern times originated as an equitable remedy and hence relied on discretion. *Id.* at 419.

[57] *See* UNIF. PROBATE CODE § 2–803 (amended 1997), 8 U.L.A. 459 (1998).

[58] *See* Glendon, *supra* note 46, at 1185.

[59] *Id.* at 1185–86.

[60] *Id.* at 1186.

[61] *Id.* at 1191.

[62] UNIF. PROBATE CODE art. II, pt. 2, cmt. (amended 1990), 8 U.L.A. 96 (1998) (explaining the decision to use a mechanically determined elective share rather than one that would require the exercise of judicial discretion to determine whether property held by the spouses was marital property or separate property).

[63] PRINCIPLES § 1, Topic 1, Overview of Chapters 4 and 5, pt. II, at 27–28.

[64] *See* PRINCIPLES § 1, Topic 1, Overview of Chapters 4 and 5, pt. II, at 27.

[65] PRINCIPLES § 1, Topic 1, Overview of Chapters 4 and 5, pt. II, at 27–30.

[66] PRINCIPLES § 1, Topic 1, Overview of Chapters 4 and 5, pt. II, cmt. b, at 28.

deductible by the transferor, but the latter generally has both characteristics.[67] Moreover, to find no principled difference between the two major spousal claims on divorce is to ignore their sharply contrasting nontax characteristics. Property division is a disposition of spousal assets, often limited to those acquired during marriage,[68] and ordinarily is final. In contrast, alimony, which is premised on an otherwise unequal sharing of losses from dissolution of the marriage, is both today and under the ALI's recommendations subject to automatic suspension,[69] termination,[70] or judicial modification.[71]

The ALI would generally eliminate fault as a factor in awarding alimony and determining property division, with exceptions for specified forms of financial misconduct, including unilateral gifts of marital property.[72] In this regard, the ALI follows the UMDA, which provides that both the disposition of property[73] and alimony[74] should be determined "without regard to marital misconduct."[75] However, the drafters' survey of state law found that only twenty states are "pure" no-fault both in dividing property and in determining alimony.[76] Fifteen states authorize courts to take marital misconduct into account for both purposes,[77] and the remainder do so in varying degrees.[78] The drafters conclude that all states, including those classified as "pure" no-fault, allow misconduct to be taken into account "to the extent it enlarges either spouse's need."[79] The ALI's rejection of marital behavior as a relevant factor includes all forms of misbehavior (with the exception just noted), including those which today in over half the states may cause one spouse's claims to be reduced or denied, or enhance the claim of the other.[80]

The PRINCIPLES rigorously apply the premise that disfavored conduct of spouses should not affect the financial results of divorce, even if this conduct is the murder and attempted murder of one spouse by the other![81] This is in contrast to statutory and case law in well over half the states denying specified benefits to a person responsible for the felonious and intentional killing of another.[82] The rationale for this conclusion that murder should not affect property division or alimony claims is a distaste of forfeitures, and the

[67] *See* I.R.C. §§ 71, 215 (2003). *See generally* DAVID WESTFALL & GEORGE P. MAIR, ESTATE PLANNING LAW AND TAXATION § 12.08 (4th ed. 2001).

[68] In a minority of states, the divorce court also has authority to assign property individually owned at the time of marriage. *See, e.g.*, MASS. GEN. LAWS ch. 208, § 34 (1998).

[69] *See* PRINCIPLES § 5.09(3) (generally providing for suspension of periodic payments when "the obligee maintained a 'common household'... with another person" for a specified minimum continuous period).

[70] *See* PRINCIPLES § 5.07 (generally providing for automatic termination of compensatory payments on the death of either party or the remarriage of the obligee).

[71] *See* PRINCIPLES § 5.08.

[72] *See* PRINCIPLES § 4.10; *see also infra* Part II(C).

[73] UNIF. MARRIAGE & DIVORCE ACT § 307 (amended 1973), 9A U.L.A. 288–89 (1998) (Alternatives A and B). Alternative B was added in 1973 because commissioners from community property states represented that their states "would not wish to substitute, for their own systems, the great hotchpot of assets created by Alternative A...." *See id.* cmt. at 289. Under Alternative A, all assets of either spouse are distributable, rather than being limited to community property or assets acquired during marriage.

[74] UNIF. MARRIAGE & DIVORCE ACT § 308 (amended 1973), 9A U.L.A. 446 (1998).

[75] UNIF. MARRIAGE & DIVORCE ACT §§ 307[a], 308[b] (amended 1973), 9A U.L.A. 446 (1998).

[76] *See* PRINCIPLES § 1, Topic 2, pt. II, cmt. a, at 45.

[77] *See* PRINCIPLES § 1, Topic 2, pt. II, cmt. e, at 46.

[78] *See* PRINCIPLES § 1, Topic 2, pt. II, cmts. b–d, at 45–46.

[79] PRINCIPLES § 1, Topic 2, pt. II, at 43.

[80] *See* PRINCIPLES § 4.09 cmt. e, at 737.

[81] *See* PRINCIPLES § 1, Topic 2, pt. V, at 64–66. *See also Actions Taken with Respect to Drafts Submitted at 1996 Annual Meeting*, 19 A.L.I. REP., Fall 1996, at 1, 4. A motion to give the court the power to deny compensatory spousal payments and a share of marital property to a spouse who committed a violent felony against the other spouse or a child of the other spouse was rejected... [as was the addition of a provision making] violent felony a ground for unequal division of marital property, and increased compensatory payments for the victim of a violent crime. *Id.*

[82] *See* RESTATEMENT (THIRD) OF PROP.: DONATIVE TRANSFERS § 8.4 Reporter's Notes (2003).

incongruity the drafters perceive in allowing a murderer to keep his separate property while denying a murdering spouse her claim to a share of the marital property they own together.[83]

A provision analogous to UPC Section 2–803, denying benefits to someone who feloniously and intentionally kills the decedent, would seem highly appropriate.[84] If financial misconduct, including certain gifts to third parties, affects the division of property on divorce,[85] surely an attempted slaying does not merit more favorable treatment.

Section 5.12 of the PRINCIPLES allows reimbursement for financial contributions to the other spouse's education or training under specified circumstances.[86] This is consistent with the ALI's refusal to treat educational degrees and professional licenses as marital property for purposes of division on dissolution.[87] This provision belongs in Chapter 4, Division of Property Upon Dissolution, as the reimbursement is an offset to the asset that the educated or trained spouse will possess after the divorce.

Surprisingly, Section 5.12 refers to education or training that was "completed" within a specified period prior to divorce.[88] This may mean that a Ph.D. candidate can receive support from his or her spouse for an almost interminable period without becoming subject to a claim for reimbursement if they divorce, and the fourth year medical student may similarly avoid liability if the divorce is granted before he or she receives the degree. It would seem to be more appropriate to take into account periods of education or training aggregating a year or more, even though no degree was received, if a spouse satisfies the requirement in Section 5.12(1)(8) that earning capacity was substantially enhanced as a result.[89]

II. Characterization and Division of Property on Dissolution

Having asserted that "recognizing the relationship between property allocation and [alimony]"[90] is one of the three lessons derived from history, the drafters nevertheless analyze property claims separately. The starting point, in Section 4.03, is the definition of marital and separate property.[91] This definition follows the uniformly held principle in community property states and in a majority of common law states that property either acquired before marriage or as gifts (or inheritances) from third parties during marriage is the separate property of the acquiring spouse and hence not subject to division upon divorce.[92] Under Section 4.04, income and appreciation in the value of separate property is also separate unless it is recharacterized either because of its enhancement by spousal labor or under Section 4.12, which provides for gradual recharacterization of such property in marriages that last a minimum of five years.[93]

The general rule contained in Section 4.09(1), mandating an equal division of marital property[94] and marital debts, is eminently reasonable, as are the provisions permitting an

[83] PRINCIPLES § 1, Topic 2, pt. V, at 65.

[84] *See* UNIF. PROBATE CODE § 2–803 (amended 1990), 8 U.L.A. 211–13 (1998).

[85] PRINCIPLES § 4.10.

[86] PRINCIPLES § 5.12.

[87] *See* PRINCIPLES § 4.07(2).

[88] PRINCIPLES § 5.12.

[89] PRINCIPLES § 5.12(1)(8).

[90] PRINCIPLES § 4.07(2).

[91] PRINCIPLES § 4.03.

[92] *See* ANN OLDFATHER ET AL., VALUATION & DISTRIBUTION OF MARITAL PROPERTY §§ 20.03[1][a], 18.05[1]. (2003).

[93] *See* PRINCIPLES § 4.04; *see also* PRINCIPLES § 4.12.

[94] PRINCIPLES § 4.09(1). A troubling qualification of the general rule requiring equal division is the authorization in Section 4.09(2)(c) for the court to award an enhanced share of marital property as compensation for a loss

unequal division of debts where they exceed the marital assets under specified circumstances,[95] and requiring that educational loans be treated as the separate obligation of the spouse whose education they financed.[96]

Section 4.10 appropriately makes specified kinds of financial misconduct that occur within some period prior to divorce, grounds for an unequal division of marital property,[97] but is seriously flawed in its failure to provide sound guidance to govern that period. The PRINCIPLES suggest that "only transactions during a period immediately preceding the commencement of a dissolution action should ordinarily be considered," and that "the time period can be drawn from a statute of limitations applicable to a comparable transaction, such as misfeasance by a trustee."[98] This is inaccurate, as the more flexible doctrine of laches, which provides no fixed time period, often applies to such claims.[99]

The ALI correctly states the principle that should determine whether property is marital, and hence divisible on divorce:

> [M]arriage alone should not affect the ownership interest that each spouse has over property possessed prior to the marriage or received after the marriage by gift or inheritance.... [But] marriage alone *is* sufficient to support a spousal claim of shared ownership at divorce to property earned by... (labor performed during marriage by a spouse).[100]

However, there are serious flaws in the ways the PRINCIPLES would determine:

(1) the extent to which the value of a spouse's separate property has been enhanced by either spouse's labor and hence is marital;
(2) the extent to which property at divorce was either derived from earnings before marriage or represents future earnings and hence is separate;
(3) the extent to which separate property should be recharacterized as marital property because of the passage of time since it was acquired; and
(4) claims for contributions to the other spouse's education or training.

In dealing with these issues, courts, spouses, and counsel need rules that are reasonably clear and at the same time evenhanded in their treatment of the spouses' competing claims. The ALI's recommendations are neither.

A. Enhancement of Separate Property by Spousal Labor

Section 4.05(1) provides that "[a] portion of any increase in the value of separate property is marital property whenever either spouse has devoted substantial time during marriage to the property's management or preservation."[101] Obviously, the controlling factors are the definition of "substantial time," and, if that threshold is crossed, how the resulting "portion" that constitutes marital property is determined.

recognized in the spousal support chapter, Chapter 5. This is inappropriate with respect to losses recognized because of a disparity of expected post-divorce incomes under Sections 5.04, 5.05, and 5.11, as awards under these sections are subject to modification under Section 5.08 in light of subsequent changes in the parties' financial capacity, but an award of marital property is not.

95 PRINCIPLES §§ 4.09(2)(b–c).

96 PRINCIPLES § 4.09(2)(d).

97 PRINCIPLES § 4.10.

98 PRINCIPLES § 4.10 cmt. c, at 755.

99 *See* 3 AUSTIN WAKEMAN SCOTT & WILLIAM FRANKLIN FRATCHER, THE LAW OF TRUSTS § 219 (4th ed. 1987).

100 PRINCIPLES § 4.03 cmt. a, at 650.

101 PRINCIPLES § 4.05(1).

1. The Definition of "Substantial Time"

Usually, cases dealing with enhancement of separate property, whether from community property or common law states,[102] involve a spouse's full-time service managing either a business which was his or her separate property[103] or the spouse's investment portfolio.[104] In those cases, the question is merely whether, and in what form, the interest of the community or marital estate should be recognized, either by an award of an interest in the business or by recognition of a dollar claim for the value of the owner's services. However, the ALI would take this sound principle to extremes by applying it in cases where the amount of spousal labor on separate property was quite small but is nevertheless deemed to be substantial, reasoning that:

> [T]he marital community has a dominant claim on the labor of the spousal owner of separate property. If time spent tending separate property intrudes on that commitment, then the marital labor is substantial. . . . It is a different case when that tending time merely takes the place of the few hours each week that the spousal owner might otherwise spend on nonremunerative activities.[105]

Illustration 4 indicates that three hours per week by the owner spouse is not substantial, and hence does not result in a portion of the increase in value being treated as marital property.[106] However, the threshold is lowered if the nonowner spouse performs the work, so that a smaller amount of expended time would result in the creation of marital property.[107] Illustration 7 treats a portion of the increase in value of a mutual fund as marital property where one spouse "read[s] several books on investing"[108] and solicits the advice of knowledgeable friends before purchasing mutual funds with the other spouse's money.[109]

This treatment of minor amounts of spousal time represents a vast and unwarranted expansion of the case law dealing with marital labor that enhances separate property. It is an open-ended invitation to interrogatories and discovery to determine exactly how many hours a week were spent by either spouse tending to investments over the course of a marriage. Ultimately, the exercise of judicial discretion would be required to determine both the extent that the market value of the property increased during the marriage and the amount by which that increase exceeded the growth in value of "assets of relative safety requiring little management."[110]

The PRINCIPLES envision a comparison of the market value of the separate property at the beginning of the marriage, or when acquired if later, with its value when sold or at the end of the marriage, as if such values are readily capable of proof.[111] Valuation is often highly controversial, particularly in the case of small businesses, such as closely held corporations. To prove many years later the value of any kind of property (other than

[102] Many of the cases are collected in the Reporter's Notes. *See* PRINCIPLES § 4.06 cmts. a–c, reporter's notes at 690–93.

[103] *See, e.g.*, Jensen v. Jensen, 665 S.W.2d 107, 110 (Tex. 1984) (remanding for a determination of the reimbursement due the community for the services of the husband toward enhancement of the stock of a holding company in whose operation he was the key man).

[104] *See, e.g.*, Beam v. Bank of Am., 490 P.2d 257, 267 (Cal. 1971) (finding that, although the husband spent the majority of his time managing his investment portfolio, family expenses absorbed any resulting community property).

[105] PRINCIPLES § 4.05 cmt. d, at 672.

[106] PRINCIPLES § 4.05 illus. 4, at 673.

[107] PRINCIPLES § 4.05 illus. 4, at 673.

[108] PRINCIPLES § 4.05 illus. 3, at 673.

[109] PRINCIPLES § 4.05 illus. 7, at 675.

[110] PRINCIPLES § 4.05 cmt. b, at 670 (internal quotation marks omitted).

[111] *See* PRINCIPLES § 4.05 cmt. h, at 678–79.

listed securities) that a spouse owned at the time of marriage may be challenging, but often is inevitable in property allocation on divorce. However, a more realistic definition of "substantial time" would reduce the frequency of such inquiries and more adequately reflect the fact that, as the drafters point out, "all capital requires some minimal amount of management."[112]

2. The Determination of the Marital Property Portion

Analytically, the increase in the value of separate property may have three components: (1) the return on the separate property itself, (2) the labor of either or both spouses, and (3) the synergetic gains from the combination of the other two factors.[113] The ALI is far from evenhanded in its allocation of these elements of gain. As noted above, marital property includes all gain in excess of "the amount by which capital of the same value would have increased over the same time period if invested in assets of relative safety requiring little management."[114] This standard "does… [not] specify a particular benchmark investment…. No fundamental principle compels the choice between intermediate-term Treasury bonds and an indexed mutual fund."[115] This surprising *ipse dixit* is followed by an even more startling assertion: "The returns on capital invested in comparable businesses, or in aggressive growth funds, would not be appropriate because these are not assets 'of relative safety requiring little management.' "[116]

Both statements are wholly at odds with the realities of financial markets and the choices market participants make among alternative investments. In the real world, the return on capital is higher for risky investments that are profitable, not solely because they sometimes require more management than assets "of relative safety,"[117] but also because investors demand a premium for assuming a greater risk of loss. If the value of a spouse's separate property declines, the loss is suffered by him or her alone and is not shared with the marital estate.[118] Indeed, the drafters do not foreclose the possibility that gains and losses from separate property on which a spouse labored are to be treated item by item, with the marital estate sharing gains but not suffering losses.[119] Because losses are not shared, the risk premium, in the form of the additional return an investor demands because of the greater risk of loss, should inure solely to the owner of the property.[120]

The price of Treasury securities does not include a risk premium, although the price is affected by market participants' expectations about future interest rates as well as by the supply and demand for such securities and other factors. The price of indexed mutual funds presumably includes a risk premium, so such funds would clearly be a more valid benchmark in determining the portion of appreciation comprising separate property.

With respect to the marital interest derived from spousal labor, the drafters explicitly reject any comparison, in the case of separate property held in corporate form, with

[112] Principles § 4.05 cmt. d, at 672.
[113] *See* Principles § 4.05 cmt. b, at 669–71.
[114] Principles § 4.05(3).
[115] Principles § 4.05 cmt. b, at 670.
[116] Principles § 4.05 cmt. b, at 670.
[117] Principles § 4.05 cmt. b, at 670 (internal quotation marks omitted).
[118] Principles § 4.05 cmt. c, at 671–72.
[119] Principles § 4.05 cmt. d, at 672.
[120] Cases in other contexts have recognized this principle. *See, e.g.*, First Nat'l Bank of Chi. v. Standard Bank & Trust, 172 F.3d 472, 480 (7th Cir. 1999) (holding that the lower court abused its discretion to award prejudgment interest at treasury bill rate because it does not reflect the true cost of capital); Fishman v. Estate of Wirtz, 807 F.2d 520, 580–81 (7th Cir. 1986) (Easterbrook, J., dissenting in part) (arguing that when calculating damages in an antitrust case, "[i]t is a fantastic assumption" that the "cost of… capital was the rate available on T-Bills, a riskless investment").

"compensation of other executives in comparable posts."[121] The result is to attribute to the labor component the entire synergetic portion of gain resulting from the combination of separate capital and marital labor. A more evenhanded treatment would be to divide that portion between the separate and marital interests.

In any event, the drafters rationalize allocating the higher return on higher-risk investments to the marital interest on the ground that "[s]uccess in higher-risk investments may be derived . . . from insights or information gained through the application of the investor's labor or talent[.]"[122] The drafters assert that treating the excess return as marital "is consistent with the commonly accepted principle that when separate and marital property are irreversibly commingled, the entire amount is treated as marital. . . ."[123] This *ipse dixit* – or assertion without proof – is at odds with the drafters' recognition in Section 4.06(1)(b) that property acquired for marital and separate property consists of proportionate shares of each.[124]

B. Property Derived from Earnings Before Marriage or After Divorce

Spousal earning capacity, skills, postdissolution labor, occupational licenses, and educational degrees should not be subject to division on divorce, and Section 4.07 so provides.[125] Two important kinds of property, which may be derived from earnings before marriage or reflect anticipated earnings after divorce are goodwill[126] and employee stock options.[127]

1. Goodwill

The ALI's treatment of goodwill in Section 4.07(3) is troublesome because it is often difficult to differentiate and measure an increase in value during marriage of a marketable business or the spouse's professional goodwill. Because compensatory spousal payments under the PRINCIPLES already take into account any substantial disparity in postdissolution spousal incomes,[128] treatment of professional goodwill as marital property is likely to give the other spouse an interest in postdivorce earnings of the professional.[129] Although some courts nevertheless treat "nonmarketable goodwill"[130] as property to be valued and considered, to do so undermines the principled exclusion from property division of earning capacity and skills.[131]

A theoretical argument can be made for an exception, as comment d suggests,[132] for the non-marketability of a professional practice that stems from regulatory restrictions. Individual law practices are common examples because ethical rules in most states bar their sale. Comment d suggests that "[i]f market data is available by which to fix a value for the

[121] *See* PRINCIPLES § 4.05 illus. 12, at 677.

[122] PRINCIPLES § 4.05 cmt. b, at 670.

[123] PRINCIPLES § 4.05 cmt. b, at 670.

[124] PRINCIPLES § 4.06(1)(b).

[125] PRINCIPLES § 4.07.

[126] *See* PRINCIPLES § 4.07 cmt. d, at 699–704.

[127] *See* PRINCIPLES § 4.07 cmt. b, at 698.

[128] PRINCIPLES § 5.04.

[129] *But cf., e.g.*, Nail v. Nail, 486 S.W.2d 761, 764 (Tex. 1972) (arguing that the goodwill of the husband's medical practice was not property because its value depends upon his survival and future work).

[130] PRINCIPLES § 4.07 cmt. d, at 700 (internal quotation marks omitted).

[131] Courts refusing to recognize professional goodwill as marital property frequently express concern that its value will be counted twice, once as property and again as future earning capacity for purposes of maintenance and child support awards. *See* Helga White, *Professional Goodwill: Is It a Settled Question or Is There "Value" in Discussing It?*, 15 J. AM. ACAD. MATRIM. LAW. 495, 503 (1998).

[132] PRINCIPLES § 4.07 cmt. d, at 699–704.

practice that is distinct from the value of the seller's personal skills and future labor, then this value is marital property. . . ."[133] No guidance is provided, however, as to the nature of the required data. In its absence, recognition of the exception creates the risk that it will become merely another bargaining chip in negotiations between the parties, and another ambiguity for lawyers to exploit. There may be no persuasive way to quantify a claim based on professional goodwill that may not legally be transferred, and hence for which there cannot be market data.[134]

2. Employee Stock Options

Employee stock options may take an almost infinite variety of forms, and employers' motivations in granting them may be quite complex. The PRINCIPLES do not discuss the treatment of this kind of property, which presumably is encompassed by the general discussion in the PRINCIPLES of intangible assets. The PRINCIPLES generally exclude property claims to certain intangible assets "because their value is inextricably intertwined with spousal skills or earning capacity, or post-marital spousal labor."[135] Analytically, however, an option may be granted both as compensation for current or past services and as an inducement for future services, which may include a period after the divorce. For example, a corporate executive may be granted an option to buy the company's stock at any time within the next five years at a price of $10 a share. Even if the stock is selling for less than $10 a share at the time of divorce, the option obviously has value as a call on the stock for the remainder of its term. Whether all of that value should be treated as earnings during marriage is debatable, as the option may have been granted in part to motivate the employee both to continue working for the employer for five years and to work harder to increase the stock's value.

Since a case-by-case analysis of employer motivation would not be feasible, an even-handed approach might treat as marital that proportion of the option's value that the time held during marriage bears to the option's total duration. But a full treatment of the varied forms of options in property division on divorce is beyond the scope of this chapter.[136] The fact that the ALI ignores this vital subject altogether leaves an important gap in the PRINCIPLES.

Treatment of stock options upon divorce should be addressed in order to provide guidance to courts which may be asked by the parties to (a) retain jurisdiction until the options

[133] PRINCIPLES § 4.07 cmt. d, at 704.

[134] The time-honored way in which a lawyer "sells" his practice without violating ethical rules is to admit to partnership or to employ as an associate a younger lawyer who is in effect the "buyer," with the understanding that the buyer will do a disproportionately large share of the work in relation to the buyer's compensation for a period of time while the "seller" introduces the buyer to the clients. Over time, the "seller's" share of both work and compensation will gradually decrease. In order to establish a value for the "seller's" goodwill, it would seem to be necessary to establish the value at the time of divorce of the amount by which the "seller's" compensation while this arrangement continues exceeds what the seller is able personally to bill clients for during this period. But how to determine this amount with even plausible accuracy is elusive.

[135] PRINCIPLES § 4.07 cmt. b, at 698.

[136] For a comprehensive discussion of the valuation of options, see generally RICHARD A. BREALEY & STEWART C. MYERS, PRINCIPLES OF CORPORATE FINANCE (7th ed. 2003). For specific applications in the context of divorce, see David S. Rosettenstein, *The ALI Proposals and the Distribution of Stock Options and Restricted Stock on Divorce: The Risks of Theory Meet the Theory of Risk*, 8 WM. & MARY J. WOMEN & L. 243 (2002); David S. Rosettenstein, *Exploring the Use of the Time Rule in the Distribution of Stock Options on Divorce*, 35 FAM. L.Q. 263 (2001).

are exercised or expire, (b) assume a more definite value for the options, or (c) impose a constructive trust on the options in lieu of distributing them in kind.[137] These solutions are said to avoid the unfairness of a particularly low or high valuation of the options at the time of dissolution, which does not correspond to the value the options eventually assume. If the value at the time of dissolution is high, the holder may be forced to exercise the options early or sell other property in order to pay the other spouse his or her share of the marital property. When the valuation at dissolution is low, the other spouse may lose out on subsequent appreciation merely because of a temporary downturn in the market or for other seemingly arbitrary reasons.

This argument, however, would apply to all risky assets, as well as to other assets that may not appear to be risk-laden but, with the omniscience of hindsight, may prove to have been. It also fails to take into account the desirability of separating the spouses' financial interests. Use of an appropriate formula to value the option at the time of divorce should provide evenhanded treatment for the spouses, just as use of the market price for a stock does so, even though the price may thereafter change dramatically.

C. Financial Misconduct as Grounds for Unequal Division of Marital Property

The ALI departs from the general principle that marital conduct should be irrelevant in determining financial consequences of divorce if three forms of financial misconduct occur during the waning days of the marriage: (1) certain gifts made without the other party's consent, (2) property lost, expended, or destroyed through intentional misconduct, and (3) property lost or destroyed through negligence after the service of the dissolution petition.[138] The PRINCIPLES suggest that conduct of the first and second type should be relevant if it occurs six months prior to the service of the dissolution petition, while conduct of the third type is relevant if it occurs within a year prior. This limits the retrospective assessment of the fairness of the marriage's financial arrangements.[139]

The reason given for the general rule excluding retrospective accounting, to which these are very limited exceptions, is that "[t]he legal remedy available to a spouse who finds a marriage unacceptably burdensome or inequitable is exit. Modern divorce law allows either spouse to end the marriage."[140] New York, with its refusal to adopt no-fault divorce, remains a prominent exception to this generalization,[141] as are other states which may require separation for as much as two years in order to secure a no-fault divorce.[142] In states with a lengthy waiting period, the fact that spouses do not have an unqualified unilateral right to a reasonably prompt divorce may justify an accounting period as long as the minimum waiting period for a no-fault divorce.

137 *See* Charles P. Kindregan, Jr. & Patricia A. Kindregan, *Unexercised Stock Options and Marital Dissolution*, 34 SUFFOLK U. L. REV. 227, 234 (2001).

138 PRINCIPLES §§ 4.10(1), 4.10(2), and 4.10(3).

139 PRINCIPLES § 4.10 illus. 8–9, at 757–58. *Compare* PRINCIPLES § 4.10 cmt. c, at 755 (suggesting that a "time period can be drawn from a statute of limitations applicable to a comparable transaction, such as misfeasance by a trustee."). However, the more flexible doctrine of laches often applies to such claims. *See supra* note 99 and accompanying text.

140 PRINCIPLES § 4.10 cmt. b, at 753.

141 *See supra* note 22.

142 *See, e.g.*, TENN. CODE ANN. § 36–4–101 (2003) (requiring married couple to live in separate residences, without any cohabitation, for two years before permitting no-fault divorce).

D. Recharacterization of Separate Property as Marital Property under Section 4.12

As noted above, a motion to recommit an earlier version of Section 4.12 was narrowly defeated.[143] The rationale proffered to support the recharacterization of separate property is based on the subjective expectations of the spouses: "After many years of marriage, spouses typically do not think of their separate-property assets as separate.... Both spouses are likely to believe ... that such assets will be available to provide for their joint retirement, for a medical crisis of either spouse, or for other personal emergencies."[144] Although the comments to this section refer to "many years,"[145] Section 4.12 is not so limited. It provides for partial recharacterization in marriages that last no more than five years.[146]

The drafters' notes to Section 4.12 acknowledge that the ALI's supporting premise remains untested.[147] The drafters point out in the minority of states in which all property of the spouses, not merely marital property, is divisible on divorce,[148] the courts are more likely to divide inherited or premarital property upon dissolution of a lengthy marriage.[149] At present, no state explicitly provides for such recharacterization.

With respect to separate property owned at the time of marriage, the drafters' argument for its gradual recharacterization as marital property would have some force if the admittedly untested premise about the spouses' expectations is accurate and if this were truly a default rule. But the parties' freedom to contract out of it is seriously constrained by the drafters' strict procedural and substantive regulation of premarital agreements, as well as the extensive judicial review of them.[150]

Additional problems arise from the drafters' treatment of gifts and bequests during marriage, which are subject to recharacterization at an accelerated rate "that takes into account both the marital duration and the holding period of the property in question."[151] The PRINCIPLES suggest that for such property, the rate should be (a) 4 percent for each year after five years from the date the property is acquired, plus (b) half the number of years that passed between the fifth year of marriage and the year it was acquired.[152] Thus, if Spouse A acquires $100,000 by gift at the end of the twentieth year of marriage and files for dissolution at the end of thirty years of marriage, the rate would be (a) 20 percent (4 percent × 10 years between acquisition of the gift and filing for dissolution, minus five years) plus (b) 30 percent (4 percent × 20 years of marriage prior to the gift, again minus five years, with the resulting percentage divided by 2). This yields a total of 50 percent. Consequently, $50,000 of the gift would be treated as marital property.

The drafters provide no persuasive justification for recharacterization of gifts and bequests received by a spouse during marriage. As with property owned at the time of marriage, it is expressly stated as a default rule. Section 4.12(5) provides: "The provision of a will or deed of gift specifying that a bequest or gift is not subject to claims under this section should be given effect."[153] A donor or testator who wished to make a gift to both spouses could readily say so, by transferring the property to "John and Mary," rather

[143] *See supra* note 8.

[144] PRINCIPLES § 4.12 cmt. a, at 771.

[145] PRINCIPLES § 4.12 cmt. a, at 771.

[146] *See generally* PRINCIPLES § 4.12 cmt. b, at 772–74.

[147] PRINCIPLES § 4.12 cmt. a, reporter's notes at 781.

[148] *See supra* notes 82–84 and accompanying text.

[149] PRINCIPLES § 4.12 cmt. a, reporter's notes at 781.

[150] *See* PRINCIPLES §§ 7.04 and 7.05. *See generally* Westfall, *supra* note 10, at 1480–90; Carbone, this volume; *see also* Brian H. Bix, *Premarital Agreements in the ALI Principles of Family Dissolution*, 8 DUKE J. GENDER L. & POL'Y 231, 244 (2001) ("[T]he Principles will block and deter some of the more egregious forms of procedural unfairness....").

[151] PRINCIPLES § 4.12(2)(a).

[152] PRINCIPLES § 4.12 illus. 1, at 774.

[153] PRINCIPLES § 4.12(5).

than simply "Mary." One might expect that the latter form would keep Section 4.12 from applying to the gift. However, the drafters make clear that such plain words should not be given their ordinary effect, as Section 4.12(5) requires an explicit reference barring claims under the section.[154] The result is to create a trap for the unwary donor or testator whose lawyer does not make such a reference because of oversight, because the Section has not been enacted in her state when she draws the will or deed of gift, or because she does not anticipate that Mary will be divorced in another state that has enacted the section. It creates a similar trap for donors who make gifts of cash or other property to a married child without a lawyer's help.

Lawyers would have to advise their clients that whenever such a gift is made, an accompanying letter should specify that it is not subject to Section 4.12 if that is the client's intention. Under Section 4.12(4), the recipient can also give notice that the gift will remain separate property, although he or she may be reluctant to do so because of the possible adverse effect on the relationship between the spouses.[155]

Of course, intestate shares would be subject to Section 4.12 unless the recipient spouse gave the requisite notice within the specified time period that his or her share was not to be subject to recharacterization. Distributions from a trust would be similarly recharacterized unless the trust provided otherwise or the recipient gave notice. Trusts already in existence when Section 4.12 was enacted would be unlikely to refer to the section. Compensation during marriage for services performed before marriage and personal injury awards, both of which are separate property under Section 4.08,[156] would also be subject to recharacterization in the absence of such notice by the recipient.[157]

In addition to the computational complexities involved in applying Section 4.12 to a series of gifts and distributions from trusts, another cogent objection is the pall it could cast over relationships within a family. Unless the spouses or domestic partners make a premarital agreement that effectively negates its application, the requirement of notice by the recipient or specific exclusion of the section by the donor may serve as a continuing reminder of the possibility that either a spouse or a donor has doubts about the durability of the marriage or domestic partnership, or the completeness of her commitment to the relationship. Being required to express those doubts may hasten the relationship's demise.

III. Conclusion

The PRINCIPLES are a failed effort at family law reform and may not even enjoy the support of most of the members of the ALI. In dealing with compensatory spousal payments, they fall short of providing for divorcing spouses the predictability of economic consequences that the public has shown it prefers in probate, by making results overly dependent on detailed judicial fact finding and the extensive exercise of judicial discretion. Moreover, the PRINCIPLES are plagued with internal inconsistencies and are seriously uninformed in their treatment of business and economic matters and tax considerations. Finally, the PRINCIPLES would curtail the ability of spouses, prospective spouses, and nonmarital cohabitants to structure the terms of their relationship to meet their individually perceived needs.

[154] PRINCIPLES § 4.12(5).

[155] *See* PRINCIPLES § 4.12(4).

[156] PRINCIPLES § 4.08.

[157] PRINCIPLES § 4.12.

Although the PRINCIPLES are too seriously flawed to serve as guideposts for the reform of family law, they are useful in highlighting many of the issues that potential reforms should address. For this purpose, the notes and commentary to the PRINCIPLES can serve as important research tools. Perhaps someday a revised edition of PRINCIPLES may be more successful in serving the purposes that the present version fails to achieve.

Elizabeth Bartholet, Charles Donahue, Mary Ann Glendon, Robert Levy, and Lawrence Waggoner provided many helpful suggestions. I am also grateful for excellent research assistance by Jeremy Younkin, of the Harvard Law School Class of 2002, Jared G. Jensen, Sorelle A. Merkur, and Nathan B. Oman, of the Harvard Law School Class of 2003, and Matthew J. Caccamo, K. Alejandro Camara, Jeanine Kerridge, and Robert A. Schroeder, of the Harvard Law School Class of 2004.

10 You and Me against the World: Marriage and Divorce from Creditors' Perspective

Marie T. Reilly

Legal regulation of families has two aspects. The first defines the rights and obligations of family participants *inter se*. It addresses who may marry or otherwise form a legally recognized family and resolves issues that arise when that family breaks up. The second aspect addresses the effect of legal family status on the participants' relationships with outsiders such as credit card issuers, tort claimants, taxing authorities, and medical care providers. The PRINCIPLES focus exclusively on the *inter se* relationships of family members with each other, particularly with respect to responsibility for and financial support of dependent family members.[1] The PRINCIPLES do not address individual family members' relationships with their creditors, either during marriage or following divorce.

This omission is understandable. As an academic subject, family law addresses family relationships. The interaction of family members with outsiders is addressed in other areas of law, for example contract, tort, and tax law. Although it makes sense that the PRINCIPLES do not consider the external effect of family relationships, it is a mistake to infer that changes in family law will have no ramifications outside the family on credit relationships. The predominant focus of this volume is on how the PRINCIPLES would affect family members' relationships with each other. This chapter takes a different approach and considers how legal regulation of marriage appears from the outside looking in. By looking at families the way creditors do, we can begin to understand how changes to the legal regulation of family members' relationships *inter se* will affect the relationships between family members and their nonfamily creditors.

Part I explains how an individual's marital relationship affects his or her relationship with creditors. It explains how an individual debtor can shield wealth within marriage from his creditors by acting alone or with the cooperation of his spouse. A variety of legal devices facilitate wealth-shielding behavior while other legal devices protect creditors from the effect of this behavior. Whenever creditors challenge marital wealth-shielding behavior, courts balance the social value of the marriage against the rights of the spouse's creditors. To the extent that the balance tips in favor of the debtor's spouse, creditors subsidize marital collaboration. Part II explains how the law governing spouses' rights against each other during marriage and upon divorce facilitates marital wealth shielding. Part III makes some observations about the PRINCIPLES' potential effect on the balance between the rights of creditors and the adults in marital or cohabiting relationships. The law governing creditors' rights against married people has all the complications of creditors' rights law

[1] *See* PRINCIPLES chs. 3 (Child Support), 4 (Division of Property Upon Dissolution), 5 (Compensatory Spousal Payments), 6 (Domestic Partners), and 7 (Agreements).

plus the exponential complication of an array of special rules that apply only to married people's credit relationships. Given this legal environment, sweeping predictions about the effect of change in marital and divorce law on creditors are appropriately suspect. We can conclude, however, that creditors' law and marital law are intimately related. Neither can be fully understood without consideration of the other.

I. Individual Liability and Marital Wealth

Spouses join together in marriage, but continue to interact with creditors as individuals. In their capacity as individuals, spouses owe credit card issuers, home mortgage lenders, medical care providers, taxing authorities, and tort claimants. A person who signs a promissory note incurs personal liability under contract law. Similarly, an adult who drives his car over his neighbor's mailbox incurs personal liability in tort. In neither case does the person's marital status affect his personal liability to a creditor.

Although spouses remain legal individuals in their relationships with creditors, their collaborative relationship with each other affects those credit relationships. The fact that two persons are married might prompt them to share the cost and benefits of a debt to a third party, and become jointly liable as codebtors. Or they could agree that one of them will be principally liable to the creditor, with the other serving as a surety.[2] The two cases, codebtors or principal/surety, differ only in the agreement the spouses make with each other. The terms of their relationship do not control their common creditor's rights against either of them.[3] Their creditor can sue either of the spouses for the full amount of the debt regardless of the spouses' agreement between themselves as to whose debt it is primarily, and without regard to any subsequent change in the spouses' relationship.

A collaborative relationship between two persons can affect their credit relationships in another way. One person can become liable for another person's obligation to a third party by operation of law because of a legally sufficient connection between the person and the debtor. If a person commits a tort as an agent of another person within the scope of an agency relationship, the principal is liable vicariously to the injured person under the doctrine of respondeat superior. If the debtor's liability is consensual, a second person who did not expressly assent to liability can nonetheless become liable upon a finding that the debtor incurred the liability both for himself and as agent for the second person.[4]

[2] *See generally* Restatement (Third) of Suretyship § 1 (1995) (stating the criteria for one person to be a surety for another). Using Restatement vocabulary, a person becomes a surety for another person by contract (the "secondary obligation") under which the surety (the "secondary obligor") agrees to be liable to a creditor (the "obligee") with respect to an obligation (the "underlying obligation") of another person (the "principal obligor") to that same creditor. The principal and secondary obligor agree between themselves that the principal obligor ought to perform the underlying obligation. Although both the principal and secondary obligors are liable, the creditor is entitled to only one performance.

[3] *Id.* § 3(1) cmt. on subs. 1. Their creditor cares about the existence of a suretyship relationship between the debtor/spouses only in the unusual case where a defense based on a spouse's status as a surety applies. *See also id.* §§ 37–49; U.C.C. § 3–605 (amended 2002).

[4] *See generally,* Alan Q. Sykes, *The Boundaries of Vicarious Liability: An Economic Analysis of the Scope of Employment Rule and Related Legal Doctrines*, 101 Harv. L. Rev. 563, 563 (1988) (defining "vicarious liability" as the "imposition of liability upon one party for a wrong committed by another party"); Eric Rasmussen, *Agency Law and Contract Formation*, 6 Am. L. & Econ. Rev. 369, 371 (2004) (distinguishing the problem of spreading contract liability from an agent to a principal from that of spreading tort liability under the doctrine of vicarious liability); Restatement (Second) of Agency § 257 (1958) (providing that one person may be liable through the agency of another even though she did not participate in the wrongdoing).

Creditors can only enforce an obligation against a person who is liable for it and against that person's property. A judgment in favor of a creditor merely establishes the personal liability of the defendant. It does not alone permit the creditor to help himself to the debtor's property to satisfy his claim. To do this, a creditor must have a security interest or judgment lien on particular items of the debtor's property. A creditor obtains a property interest in the debtor's property by the debtor's consent to a security interest or mortgage, or by following foreclosure procedure to create judgment lien. A creditor with an interest in the debtor's property is a "secured creditor," while an "unsecured creditor" has the personal liability of the debtor, but no interest in or recourse to any of the debtor's property. The secured creditor's reward for obtaining an interest in the debtor's property is a priority right in it over the debtor's unsecured creditors.[5]

To a creditor, the wealthier the debtor, the lower the risk that the debt will go unpaid. Conversely, in a competitive market, the lower the risk of loss to the creditor, the lower the cost of borrowing to the debtor. Significantly, neither party can estimate risk precisely. The debtor's wealth can change over the term of the credit, while the terms of a credit relationship are relatively static. Creditors who can bargain with the debtor can set the interest rate sufficiently high to compensate themselves for the possibility of changes in the debtor's wealth. Some creditors bargain for the additional liability of a second person. Or they obtain a lien in some or all of the debtors' property to control the debtors' wealth directly. These adjustments do not completely eliminate creditors' risk, however. All negotiated debt relationships involve some terms that do not perfectly take into account changes in the debtor's wealth. Moreover, in many credit relationships the creditor has no opportunity to negotiate for compensation for bearing risk, or for control over changes in risk. Tort creditors, tax authorities, emergency medical care providers, and others who become creditors reluctantly and without a bargain must take their debtors as they find them.[6]

Given these characteristics of credit relationships, the debtor's strategy is plain: obtain credit at a low cost that reflects high wealth (and correspondingly low risk to creditors). If the debtor defaults, he wants to expose a different, lower amount of wealth to his creditors. In economic terms, the debtor seeks to externalize the risk of loss to creditors without compensating them to bear it. The debtor's goal is to hold wealth so that he effectively controls it while it is legally shielded from his creditors' claims if he defaults.

One familiar wealth-shielding technique is for the debtor to hold property in certain forms legally designated as "exempt."[7] The purpose of exemption laws is to protect from creditors the types of property lawmakers deem necessary for a "fresh start."[8] Although

[5] In a bankruptcy proceeding, holders of secured claims are paid in full from the value of their collateral before unsecured creditors receive anything. *See generally*, Charles Jordan Tabb, The Law of Bankruptcy 538 (1997).

[6] *See generally*, Lynn M. LoPucki, *The Unsecured Creditor's Bargain*, 80 Va. L. Rev. 1887, 1896–98 (1994) (noting that both individual and business debtors have nonadjusting creditors).

[7] A significant form of exempt property is "homestead" referring to real or personal property used as a principal residence. *See, e.g.*, 11 U.S.C. § 522(d)(1) (2005); *Homestead Exemptions, at* http://www.assetprotectionbook.com/homestead_exemptions.htm (last visited March 5, 2006) (state by state links to homestead statutes). *See also* 11 U.S.C. §§ 522(d)(10)(A) (social security, veterans, and disability benefits), 522(d)(10)(E) (life insurance and annuities) (2005); *Life Insurance and Annuity Exemptions*, http:/www.assetprotectionbook.com/life_insurance_exemptions.htm (last visited March 5, 2006).

[8] *See, e.g.*, Elizabeth Warren & Jay Westbrook, The Law of Debtors and Creditors 104 (4th ed. 2001) (noting that exemption laws reflect sympathy for debtors and a social desire to protect the "social fabric of the community," expressing concern that a creditor not leave a debtor unable to rehabilitate himself financially, and recognizing that some personal property has great use value to the debtor but little liquidation value to the creditor).

jurisdictions vary widely in what is exempted, these laws reflect legislative concern not only for the debtor's fresh start, but also for the financial rehabilitation of the debtor's family.[9] Exemption laws do not generally protect a debtor's property from the claims of consensual secured creditors. Thus, mortgagees and car lenders that have obtained a security interest in the debtor's property with his consent can safely ignore his right to assert an exemption as to that property.[10]

Some jurisdictions recognize a special right to exempt property available only to married people. In these jurisdictions, married couples have the option of holding property jointly as tenants by the entirety.[11] A creditor of only one spouse cannot seize the individual spouse's interest in that property.[12] Nor can the debtor transfer his interest in property held as a tenancy by the entirety to a third party without his spouse's consent.[13]

Community property jurisdictions afford married persons a similar wealth-shielding opportunity.[14] These jurisdictions characterize a married couple's assets as either separate (his or hers) or belonging to the "community."[15] The legal metaphor that the "community" holds property during the marriage becomes problematic for creditors of the individual spouses while they remain married because no jurisdiction recognizes the "community" as a separate legal entity that can incur indebtedness. Although community property jurisdictions vary in their approach, generally a creditor of an individual spouse can satisfy its claim only from that individual's separate property.[16] And a creditor who has the personal liability of both spouses can satisfy its claim from each spouse's separate property as well as from the spouses' community property. Community property jurisdictions diverge widely on whether a creditor of one spouse can satisfy its claim from the debtor's share of community property, but most restrict a creditor's access in some way.[17]

To illustrate how tenancy by the entirety title and community property laws create a place for married people to shield assets from their creditors, suppose a bank loans money to Mr. Green individually. At the time he defaults, he owns an undivided one half interest in Redacre with his wife, Ms. Blue, as tenants in common. The bank can foreclose on Redacre and sell it to liquidate Mr. Green's interest in it. Ms. Blue is entitled to half of the proceeds. Now change the character of the couple's respective ownership interest in Redacre from tenants in common to tenants by the entirety. Now the bank cannot sell and

[9] For example, the Texas statute permits a debtor to exempt certain types of personal property "provided for a family" up to a total of $60,000 in value, whereas a debtor who is not a member of a family can exempt only $30,000 in value. TEX. PROP CODE ANN. § 42.001 (Vernon 1999 & Supp. 2000).

[10] An exception to the invulnerability of secured creditors to exemptions arises in the debtor's bankruptcy case with respect to certain exempt personal property. *See* 11 U.S.C. § 522(f) (2005).

[11] Thirty states afford married people the option to hold property as tenants by the entirety. Richard R. Powell et al., 7 POWELL ON REAL PROPERTY § 52.01 at 52–4 to 52–12 (Michael Allen Wolf ed., 1999). Thirteen states have abolished it. The status of the remaining seven states' status is uncertain. *See generally*, Peter M. Carrozo, *Tenancy in Antiquity: A Transformation of Concurrent Ownership for Modern Relations*, 85 MARQ. L. REV. 423, 445–446 (2001).

[12] The creditor's interest in the debtor's interest in a tenancy by the entirety interest is subject to his spouse's right of survivorship, greatly diminishing the market value of the debtor/spouse's interest. 41 AM. JUR. 2d *Husband and Wife* § 75 (1995).

[13] *Id.* at § 41.

[14] The community property system of marital law appears in the law of nine states and the Commonwealth of Puerto Rico. W.S. McClanahan, COMMUNITY PROPERTY LAWS IN THE UNITED STATES §§ 1.8, 14.4 (1982 and Supp. 1992).

[15] McClanahan, *supra* note 14 at §§ 4.10–4.15.

[16] *See id.* at § 10.6.

[17] *Id.* at § 10.7.

partition Redacre without Ms. Blue's consent, effectively shielding Mr. Green's interest in Redacre.[18]

The outcome would be roughly the same if the couple held Redacre as community property, although creditors' rights vary among jurisdictions. Some states prevent a creditor from reaching community property to recover on an individual spouse's contract obligation entered into after he marries,[19] but would permit this for tort liability.[20]

Any two people can collaborate to hide wealth from creditors, even without the special advantages afforded spouses in tenancy by the entirety and community property jurisdictions. One of the collaborators arranges for the other to hold his property outside the reach of his creditors, but within his control by virtue of his relationship with the collaborator. For example, suppose Mr. Green holds sole legal title to a beach house. To protect his interest in it from the claims of potential tort creditors of a risky business venture, he transfers sole title to the beach house to his collaborator, Ms. Blue. She agrees that Mr. Green may continue to enjoy the beach house as though he were a co-owner. Their shared strategy is to allocate debt to one collaborator who bears risk but is legally insolvent, and property to the other, who legally incurs no debt.[21] Mr. Green and Ms. Blue share both property and debt, adopting a private distribution of wealth to their advantage and at the expense of creditors. As discussed above, creditors who can bargain with the debtor can limit the effectiveness of this kind of wealth-shielding conduct. This kind of wealth-shielding strategy is, however, potentially effective against reluctant creditors who cannot protect themselves from it by bargain.

From creditors' perspective, the debtor's participation in a collaborative relationship can be both a positive and a negative factor in assessing the riskiness of the credit. To engage in wealth-shielding behavior, Mr. Green and Ms. Blue must act together to achieve a common goal. The broader the scope of their collaboration, the more interrelated are their fates. If Mr. Green and Ms. Blue's collaboration encompasses both personal and financial goals, we recognize them as engaged in "marital like" collaboration. Their mutual investment in this kind of broad and intimate collaboration creates a powerful incentive on each of them to monitor the performance of the other in order to protect their collective investment. Creditors are sensitive to this positive effect of collaboration. A creditor exploits it expressly by obtaining the liability of the collaborator along with the debtor either as a joint primary obligor or as a guarantor.[22]

[18] *See* John V. Orth, *Tenancy By the Entirety: The Strange Career of the Common-Law Marital Estate*, 1997 BYU L. Rev. 35, 43–47. In at least eight jurisdictions, the couple's tenancy by the entirety changes at their divorce into a joint tenancy with right of survivorship in both spouses, thus permitting partition. *Id.* at 44.

[19] *See, e.g.*, Zork Hardware Co. v. Gottlieb, 821 P.2d 272 (Ariz. Ct. App. 1991) (spouse who signs promissory note alone cannot subject the community to liability or give payee access to community assets on foreclosure); Humphrey v. Taylor, 673 S.W.2d 954 (Tex. App. 1984) (holding that wife was not liable for husband's debt on a note where wife did not assent to loan or receive benefit from it).

[20] *See, e.g.*, Selby v. Savard, 655 P.2d 342, 349 (Ariz. 1982) (holding community not liable for one spouse's intentional torts unless the other spouse consented or the community benefited); Carlton v. Estate of Estes, 664 S.W.2d 322 (Tex. 1983) (holding community property subject to tort liability of either spouse during the marriage).

[21] True, the transfer to Ms. Blue exposes Mr. Green's former legal interest in the beach house to her creditors. So part of their strategy will require that only Mr. Green will be liable to creditors of the risk generating business, and not also Ms. Blue. For instance, Ms. Blue should not exercise control over the risk generating business or take other actions that might justify her vicarious liability and expose her separately held assets.

[22] *See generally* Avery Weiner Katz, *An Economic Analysis of the Guaranty Contract*, 66 U. Chi. L. Rev. 47, 51–52 (1999) (noting first that creditors should prefer to acquire a guarantor when the guarantor can monitor the debtor's performance more cheaply than the creditor can; second, that a person will prefer to serve as guarantor rather than

The negative effect of collaboration is wealth-shielding conduct. But even reluctant creditors are not defenseless against it. Reluctant creditors must rely on *post hoc* legal tools to deter and undo wealth-shielding collaboration. One way creditors challenge wealth-shielding conduct is to point to the collaborative relationship itself as grounds to impose liability on the debtor's collaborator. For example, Mr. Green's creditor may argue that Ms. Blue is vicariously liable for Mr. Green's tort because she is a partner in his business and he is her agent. If successful with this liability spreading argument, the creditor would obtain Ms. Blue as a debtor and could foreclose on the beach house to satisfy what now is their joint tort obligation.

Another creditor response is to point to the connection between the collaboration and a property transfer as grounds to invalidate the transfer. Consider again Mr. Green's transfer of the beach house to Ms. Blue. If after the transfer Mr. Green's creditor finds that Mr. Green has no property to satisfy his debt, it can avoid the transfer of the beach house to Ms. Blue on proof that Mr. Green made it with the actual intent to "hinder, delay, or defraud" his creditors.[23] Alternatively, a creditor can avoid the transfer as a constructive fraud, regardless of Mr. Green's intent, on proof that it took place while Mr. Green was insolvent or that it rendered him insolvent, and that Ms. Blue paid "less than a reasonably equivalent value" for the beach house.[24] If Mr. Green's creditor is successful, Ms. Blue must relinquish the beach house or its value to satisfy the creditor's claim.

Although married people enjoy a wealth shielding advantage over nonmarried people because of their exclusive access to tenancy by the entirety and community property regimes, this advantage is tempered by a legal doctrine that creditors can use only against married collaborators. Under the doctrine of necessaries, a creditor can impose an obligation on an insolvent debtor's spouse to the extent the liability is for "necessaries" the creditor provided on credit.[25] One possible legal justification for the doctrine is that in the purchase of "necessaries," one spouse acts as agent for the other to further the interest of the family.[26] But, the doctrine of necessaries is broader than simple agency. Even if one spouse publicly disavows any agency by the other, courts bypass an inquiry into actual agency to find a spouse, the husband, liable under a "compulsory agency" theory, or as a quasicontractual obligation deriving from his marital obligation to support his wife and family.[27]

As a result of modern equal protection scrutiny, the expanded role of women in the wage labor force, and reform of divorce law, some jurisdictions have expanded the doctrine of

primary lender when her transaction costs (including cost of liquidity) exceeds a third party lender's; and third, that the primary lender attaches a higher value to a direct right of action against the principal debtor than the guarantor does).

23 *See, e.g.*, 11 U.S.C. § 548(a)(1) (2005); Uniform Fraudulent Transfer Act (UFTA) § 4(a)(1), 7A pt. II U.L.A. 266 (1984).

24 *E.g.*, 11 U.S.C. § 548 (a)(2) (2005); UFTA § 4(a)(2) (1984).

25 *See generally*, 5 Samuel Williston, A Treatise on the Law of Contracts § 11:9 (4th ed. 1993).

26 *See, e.g.*, Phillips, Nizer, Benjamin, Krim and Ballon v. Rosensteil, 490 F.2d 509, 517 (2d Cir. 1973) (discussing doctrine of necessaries at common law); *See generally*, Robert C. Brown, *The Duty of the Husband to Support the Wife*, 18 Va. L. Rev. 823–24 (1932). The scope of the term "necessaries" varies among jurisdictions. *E.g.*, DuBois, Sheehan, Hamilton and DuBois v. DeLarm, 578 A.2d 1250 (N.J. Super. Ct. App. Div. 1990) (rendering legal fees "necessary" where family may be negatively affected by incarceration).

27 *See, e.g.*, Gessler v. Gessler, 124 A.2d 502, 505 (Pa. Super. Ct. 1956) ("A husband is under a legal duty to support his wife and children, and where he neglects this duty, one who supplies necessaries for their support may recover their cost in an action under the common law, which raises an implied promise, on the part of the husband, to pay.").

necessaries to impose liability on either the husband or the wife for necessaries acquired on credit by the other. In these jurisdictions, the liability incurring spouse is conclusively the agent for both as to liability for designated "necessaries" or "family expenses" – without regard to who actually incurred the obligation, on whose credit the creditor relied, or any agreement between spouses as to which of them would be liable for family support obligations.[28] To creditors' delight, this expansion of the doctrine of necessaries makes all nonexempt property available to satisfy either spouse's creditor's claim for "family" liability. Other jurisdictions have modified the common law doctrine, which recognized only the husband's liability for necessaries furnished to the wife, by imposing liability on the nondebtor spouse regardless of gender but only as a surety for necessaries furnished to the other.[29] A few jurisdictions have found the doctrine of necessaries a violation of the fourteenth amendment equal protection clause, and have eliminated it as to both spouses.[30]

As for liability other than for necessaries or statutorily designated family expenses, creditors rely on the collaborative nature of marriage coupled with the law of agency to spread liability from one spouse to the other. The parties' marital status is not dispositive, but the nature of the marital collaboration is relevant.[31] For example in *Cockerham v. Cockerham*,[32] the court found the husband liable on his wife's debt incurred to finance her dress business because the husband invested in the business and the couple filed a joint tax return claiming deductions for its losses.[33] Some courts find spousal agency for contractual obligation when the nondebtor spouse simply enjoyed the benefits of the business for which the loan was incurred.[34] Some courts find vicarious tort liability only if the spouse had an ability to control the tortfeasor spouse by virtue of a master-servant type agency relationship between them.[35] Instances in which courts find implied agency between spouses are exceptions but not the rule. Unlike the collaboration among

[28] *See, e.g.*, Colo. Rev. Stat. § 14–6–110 (1987); 40 Ill. Comp. Stat. § 1015 (2004); Iowa Code Ann. § 597.14 (West 2001); Wash. Rev. Code § 26–16–205 (1986); Montana Code Ann. § 40–2–210 (2004) (holding both spouses liable for "necessary articles"). For judicial adoption, *see, e.g.*, Cooke v. Adams, 183 So.2d 925 (Miss. 1986); Marcus L. Moxley, Survey, *North Carolina Baptist Hospitals, Inc. v. Harris: North Carolina Adopts a Gender-Neutral Approach to the Doctrine of Necessaries*, 66 N.C. L. Rev. 1241, 1246 (1988).

[29] *See, e.g.*, Memorial Hosp. Inc. v. Hahaj, 430 N.E.2d 412 (Ind. Ct. App. 1982) (holding wife primarily liable and husband secondarily liable for medical care provided to wife); Jersey Shore Med. Ctr. v. Estate of Baum, 417 A.2d 1003, 1010 (N.J. 1980) ("[A] creditor should have recourse to the property of both spouses only where the financial resources of the spouse who incurred the necessary expense are insufficient . . . granting some protection to a spouse who has not expressly consent to that debt.").

[30] *See, e.g.*, North Ottowa Community Hosp. v. Keift, 578 N.W.2d 267 (Mich. 1998); Emanuel v. McGriff, 596 So.2d 578 (Ala. 1992).

[31] *See, e.g.*, Lake Mary Ltd. Partnership v. Johnston, 551 S.E.2d 546, 555–56 (N.C. Ct. App. 2001) ("No presumption arises from the mere fact of the marital relationship that the husband is acting as agent for the wife.").

[32] 527 S.W.2d 162 (Tex. 1975).

[33] *Id.* at 172. *See also*, Zukowski v. Dunton, 650 F.2d 30, 34 (4th Cir. 1981) (considering husband agent for wife where she was a codirector in the family business). *Compare* Nelson v. Citizens Bank and Trust Co. of Baytown, Texas, 881 S.W. 2d 128, 131 (Tex. Ct. App. 1994) (recognizing no agency where nondebtor spouse was not involved in debtor spouse's separately incorporated business).

[34] *E.g.*, DuBose Steel, Inc. v. Faircloth, 298 S.E.2d 60, 61 (N.C. Ct. App. 1982) (nondebtor spouse liable for husband's business indebtedness because she deposited business funds in her personal checking account). *But see*, Zickgraf Hardwood Co. v. Seay, 298 S.E.-2d 208, 210–211 (N.C. Ct. App. 1982) (holding wife who worked as a bookkeeper in family business not liable for husband's debt, because the benefit she received was "the maintenance and support which she was entitled to receive from her husband under the law").

[35] *See, e.g.*, Gist v. Vulcan Oil Co., 640 So.2d 940 (Ala. 1994) (wife's agency for purpose of vicarious liability of her husband depends on whether wife acted "under the control" of the husband); Smith v. Myrik, 442 S.E.2d 236 (Ga. Ct. App. 1992) (husband not agent for wife where his wrongful acts were not in furtherance of his wife's business).

unmarried business partners, spouses are not presumptively agents for each other, thus collaboration through marriage provides an important, if not impervious, shield against creditors' claims.[36]

II. How Creditors View Marriage and Divorce

Because of their personal relationship, Mr. Green and Ms. Blue (whether married or not) can shield wealth by transferring the beach house to Ms. Blue subject to their private understanding that Mr. Green can use and enjoy it. Their strategy succeeds only if the transfer cuts off Mr. Green's creditors' right to obtain an interest in the beach house if Mr. Green defaults. This question turns on the nature of Mr. Green's interest in the beach house after the transfer, which in turn depends on who is asking.

To illustrate, suppose things go badly between Ms. Blue and Mr. Green and she excludes Mr. Green from the beach house. He may be able to enforce their agreement against her by asserting breach of an implied contract or an equitable property interest in the house. Now, suppose that things go swimmingly between Ms. Blue and Mr. Green, but that Mr. Green's tort creditor attempts to seize and liquidate Mr. Green's interest in the beach house notwithstanding the fact that Ms. Blue holds legal title to it. Whether Mr. Green's creditors can take advantage of the arguments Mr. Green could raise against Ms. Blue is a very different story.

In the first case, it is Mr. Green who is asking the court to evaluate the nature of his interest in the beach house given his relationship with Ms. Blue. The court focuses on the "equities" in the relationship between Ms. Blue and Mr. Green and the alleged breach of their trust. In this context, the court may recognize an enforceable interest for Mr. Green and modify Ms. Blue's legal rights accordingly. In the second case, Mr. Green's creditor is asking the court to evaluate Mr. Green's interest in the beach house in light of his relationship with Ms. Blue. Although the court's focus remains on the relationship between Mr. Green and Ms. Blue, the fight is now between the creditor and Ms. Blue. Ms. Blue will urge the court to characterize the transfer of the beach house to her as an unconditional gift from Mr. Green and a commendable expression of his commitment to and affection for her. In contrast, Mr. Green's creditor will cast their relationship in an unfavorable light and argue that the transfer was the fruit of a fraudulent scheme between colluders set on hiding wealth from his creditors.[37] If Mr. Green was not obviously making the transfer to blunt a creditor's collection effort, and if he was not insolvent or rendered insolvent at the time of the transfer, the creditor's action to avoid it will likely fail, even though the effect is to enrich Mr. Green at his creditors' expense. If Mr. Green's creditor asserts that Ms. Blue is vicariously responsible for Mr. Green's liability, the court will balance the value of their collaborative relationship and their collective interest in the beach house against the rights of Mr. Green's creditor. Given the diversity of views about spousal agency among the states, it is difficult to predict how a court would decide these two cases. But it is not difficult to imagine that a court would not reach the same result in both.

Marital collaboration is set apart legally from other kinds of collaborative forms due to the legal construct of the spouses' relationship. While they are married, spouses cannot enforce their expectations against each other by legal action. For example, one spouse

[36] *See, e.g.*, 1 Alan R. Bromberg & Larry E. Ribstein, Bromberg & Ribstein on Partnership § 4.01(b)(1)(2005).

[37] *See* discussion regarding the avoidance of fraudulent transfers in text accompanying notes 23–24.

cannot sue the other for breach of a promise to purchase a new car.[38] Their legal rights against each other spring into existence only upon divorce. The non-enforceability of spousal expectations except at divorce serves a judicial screening function. For small disputes not worth divorcing over, married people must sort out their relationship on their own. The "love it or leave it" feature of marriage is an analog to the "exclusivity of remedy rule" in partnership law, which denies a partner a legal remedy against the partnership or other partners except as part of an accounting on dissolution of the partnership.[39]

The exclusivity of remedy for spouses and partners is not absolute. Courts occasionally recognize that partners and spouses can contract with each other outside the scope of their relationship if they make their intention to do so clear.[40] In both settings, the court must determine whether the claimant incurred a particular loss as a partner or a spouse (to which the exclusivity rule would apply), or as an individual interacting with the other party outside their partnership or marriage. The determination that a particular event or relationship between partners is outside the scope of the partnership is easier than the analogous determination as between spouses. The scope of a partnership is confined to a business venture, whereas a marriage is thought to encompass all aspects of the couple's lives.

Another effect of the rule that makes divorce the nearly exclusive remedy for disappointed marital expectations is to create incentive for one spouse to exploit the other who has more to lose if the marriage ends in divorce.[41] Where one spouse values the continuation of the marital relationship (notwithstanding disappointed expectations) by an amount greater than the distribution she expects at divorce, she will stay in the marriage and overlook her spouse's failures. The spouse with less to lose by divorce can behave badly during the marriage at the other spouse's expense by exploiting the other spouse's reluctance to divorce.[42]

If we change our focus to the spouses' relationship with their creditors, a less obvious feature of marriage, and divorce as a nearly exclusive remedy, appears. Creditors of either spouse cannot disrupt the ongoing relationship in order to seize and liquidate wealth that is locked in the relationship in the form of marital expectations. Suppose that Mr. Green

[38] *See generally*, Saul Levmore, *Love It or Leave It: Property Rules, Liability Rules and Exclusivity of Remedies in Partnership and Marriage*, 58 Law & Contemp. Probs. 221, 225–26 (1995); McGuire v. McGuire, 59 N.W.2d 336 (Neb. 1953). Marriage and partnership differ in this respect from the corporate form. A shareholder can sue a corporate agent while continuing to own stock in the corporation.

[39] *See* 2 Alan R. Bromberg & Larry E. Ribstein, Bromberg and Ribstein on Partnership § 6.08(b) (2005).

[40] For example, one partner can sue another partner if they have agreed the transaction giving rise to the claim is outside the scope of the partnership. *Id.* at § 6.08(c) n. 52 (citing cases involving claims by a partner against another partner that arose from personal and not partnership relationship). *See also* Revised Uniform Partnership Act (RUPA), 6 U.L.A. §§ 405(b) (1994) (partners can enforce "rights and interests arising independently of the partnership relationship" without an accounting upon dissolution). In rare cases, one spouse can enforce a contract right against another. *E.g.*, Department of Human Resources v. Williams, 202 S.E.2d 504 (Ga. 1973) (wife's surrender of legal right to seek outside employment and care for her totally disabled husband was consideration for his promise of a salary). In most jurisdictions, spouses can bring some tort actions against each other. *See* Dan B. Dobbs, The Law of Torts § 279 at 751–53 (2000).

[41] *Cf.* Levmore, *supra* note 38 at 222 (stating that divorce as the exclusive remedy for spouses "can leave wrongs uncorrected and in this way permit an unhealthy degree of exploitation of a minority partnership interest").

[42] *See, e.g.*, Margaret F. Brinig, *"Money Can't Buy Me Love:" A Contrast Between Damages in Family Law and Contract*, 27 J. Corp. L. 567, 581 (2002) (discussing how divorce courts find it difficult to measure damages for aggrieved spouse who financed her spouse's education); Margaret F. Brinig & Steven M. Crafton, *Marriage and Opportunism*, 23 J. Legal Stud. 869, 879–81 (1994) (explaining how the marriage "contract" has become illusory through the availability of no-fault divorce and equitable property distribution regimes).

faithfully supports his wife, Ms. Blue, as they agreed he would, consistent with a duty imposed on him by the state to support her as an incident of their legal marriage. Further suppose that Ms. Blue incurs a huge liability to a casino. Even though she reasonably treats support from her husband as her wealth, her creditor, the casino, cannot seize and liquidate Mr. Green's commitment to her to satisfy its claims. While they are married, she enjoys his loving generosity. But, Ms. Blue's creditors have no right to butt into the ongoing relationship between Ms. Blue and Mr. Green. Although Ms. Blue will be entitled to an equitable distribution of marital property if they divorce, until they actually do and the court orders a transfer of property from Mr. Green to her, her reasonable expectation of an equitable distribution of their wealth upon their divorce is of no value to her creditors. The non-enforceability of spousal expectations prevents those expectations from becoming market commodities. But by characterizing spousal expectations this way, the law opens a wealth hiding place for married people vis-à-vis their creditors.

The wealth-shielding potential of marriage's "love it or leave it" nature is amplified by bankruptcy law. A married debtor may file for bankruptcy individually and obtain discharge of his debts. The estate in bankruptcy that is available to satisfy claims against him consists of his legal and equitable interests in property, but not expectations of income or property from his spouse.[43] This enables a married debtor to obtain a discharge of his individual debt while shielding from his individual creditors the wealth intrinsic in his relationship with his spouse. Most obligations one spouse owes to a former spouse pursuant to a divorce proceeding are not dischargeable, and usually receive priority payment in a bankruptcy case.[44] The effect is a wealth transfer from the debtor's unsecured creditors to the nondebtor spouse.[45]

If Mr. Green and Ms. Blue divorce, the divorce court commodifies Ms. Blue's expectations of financial support from Mr. Green. Their divorce will affect their creditors in different ways, depending on the nature of the creditor's rights at the time of the divorce. Creditors who hold liens and interests in property survive divorce relatively unscathed by the distribution on dissolution of the marriage.[46] To illustrate, suppose Mr. Green and Ms. Blue are both debtors on a loan, secured by a lien on a car titled in the name of Mr. Green. Suppose the divorce court orders that Ms. Blue take title to the car, and that Mr. Green take over the payments for it. After the divorce, the creditor can enforce the loan against Ms. Blue and repossess the car from her if Mr. Green defaults. She will lose the car to the creditor, whose security interest in the car has priority over her interest in it by way of the divorce distribution. To the extent of her loss, Ms. Blue becomes an unsecured creditor of Mr. Green under the hold harmless obligation imposed on him by the divorce court.

While secured creditors like the car lender in this hypothetical example ride through divorce relatively indifferent to it, a transfer of property ordered by the divorce court does

[43] *See* 11 U.S.C. § 541(a) (2005). *See generally* Mechele Dickerson, *To Love, Honor, and (Oh!) Pay: Should Spouses Be Forced to Pay Each Other's Debts?*, 78 B.U. L. Rev. 961 (1998).

[44] *See* 11 U.S.C. §§ 523 (a)(5) (discussing nondischargeability of domestic support obligations), 523 (a)(15) (discussing nondischargeability of obligations to a spouse or former spouse other than those provided for in (a)(5)); 507 (a)(1) (covering priority distribution for unsecured domestic support obligation claims)(2005).

[45] Dickerson, *supra* note 43 at 1011 (arguing that bankruptcy policy should recognize the debtor spouse's expectation of support as his property and require nondebtor spouses to contribute income to repay the debtor spouse's creditors; and noting without discussion that neither creditors nor society receive a "tangible, objective benefit" from the current subsidy for married people in bankruptcy).

[46] *See* Brett R. Turner, Equitable Distribution of Property § 9.05 (2d ed., 1994).

affect the spouses' unsecured creditors. Suppose Mr. Green was liable to a tort creditor at the time of his divorce from Ms. Blue. Suppose also that Mr. Green owned shares in Acme Company in his own name prior to the divorce, but that the divorce court ordered him to transfer the shares to Ms. Blue. The tort creditor had no interest in the shares before the divorce and has none afterwards. But, to the extent that court ordered transfer of the shares leaves Mr. Green with less property for the tort creditor to seize in satisfaction of his claim, the tort creditor is negatively affected.

The challenges that unsecured creditors can raise against debtor's wealth-shielding conduct outside of divorce are ineffective in divorce cases. The court's function in a divorce proceeding is to allocate property and debt between the divorcing spouses without regard to the effect of the distribution on their creditors. Non family creditors are not parties to the divorce proceeding and have no opportunity to be heard.

After the divorce proceedings conclude, an unsecured creditor could challenge the transfer of the shares from Mr. Green to Ms. Blue as a fraudulent transfer. Although not a mainstream occurrence, an unsecured creditor's challenge to an "equitable" distribution as an avoidable fraudulent transfer is not implausible.[47] The divorce court evaluates the "fairness" of the transfer solely from the perspective of the spouses without expressly considering the "fairness" of that transfer to either spouse's reluctant creditors. On the other hand, the fact that the divorce court ordered the transfer as part of an adversarial proceeding between the spouses tends to negate the inference that the divorce transfer was a sham undertaken to hide assets from Mr. Green's creditors.

The final blow that divorce makes to unsecured creditors is the debtor's postdivorce bankruptcy discharge. After the divorce court strips Mr. Green of property to afford Ms. Blue an equitable distribution, Mr. Green can shield his future income permanently from the claims of many of his prebankruptcy creditors by obtaining a bankruptcy discharge.[48]

III. Some Observations on the Effect of Changes in Divorce Law on Creditors' View of Marriage

Thinking about marriage as a tool for wealth shielding may strike some as perverse or foolishly off the point. Most couples marry and divorce because of their perceptions regarding their relationship with each other, and not to achieve a strategic advantage vis-à-vis their unsecured creditors. Although couples probably do not seriously take the wealth-shielding potential of their marital collaboration into account, the legal environment of marriage and divorce unquestionably facilitates marital wealth shielding at the expense of creditors. Even though spouses do not deliberately plan for it, their creditors subsidize their investment in marriage whenever the law treats a creditor's rights in an individual's wealth as legally subordinate to his spouses' interest in it.

The law governing the effect of collaboration on creditors is complex and varies widely among jurisdictions. Some legal doctrines, such as spousal title, favor marital collaborators over their creditors. Other doctrines, such as the doctrine of necessaries, and application of agency and vicarious liability principles to the marital relationship, limit the subsidy for spouses. The interface between policy that favors marital collaboration and policy that

[47] *See* In re Fordu, 201 F.3d 693 (6th Cir. 1999); In re Lankry, 263 B.R. 638 (Bankr. M.D. Fla. 2001).

[48] 11 U.S.C. §§ 523 (nondischargeable claims), 524 (effect of discharge) (2005).

protects creditors from unfair marital wealth shielding is too complex to be susceptible to generalization. The variation within creditors' rights law about the effect of marriage reflects a social perception that marriage is appropriately idiosyncratic, and that intimate relationships between persons ought not be susceptible to generalization. For these reasons, it is difficult to draw broad conclusions about how courts should strike the balance between the rights of spouses or domestic partners and their creditors.

One justification for a policy that facilitates collaborative wealth shielding is concern for the injury that might befall the debtor's spouse or partner if a creditor could force a liquidation of property, such as the family home.[49] This concern derives from the stereotypical view of marriage as placing one participant in a position of financial dependency relative to the other. To the extent the stereotype holds true, spousal title regimes may be justifiable on efficiency grounds. Some of the fruits of investment in household management and child rearing are public goods. To the extent financial dependency is a cost of these projects, the cost arguably should be borne publicly. Creditors can generally spread the cost of dependency more efficiently over a large group of participants in the market for credit.

The problem with this justification is that a legal regime that favors a debtor's spouse over his creditors goes too far whenever the stereotype of dependency does not hold. The fact that two persons are married no longer supports an inference that one is financially dependent on the other, and in need of protection at the expense of the other's creditors. Moreover, even when one person in the relationship is financially dependent on the other, that dependency is not always socially desirable. Recognizing this, the PRINCIPLES offer a framework of rules for compensating a financially dependent spouse in some but not all situations.[50] This scheme creates an incentive for spouses to become financially dependent only when it is socially desirable that they do so.

Nor is it obvious that only *marriage* creates socially desirable financial dependency. The PRINCIPLES recognize that one cohabitant may also be financially dependent on the other and that society should facilitate this dependency. To this end, the PRINCIPLES would expand the reach of laws governing property distribution and compensatory payments at dissolution to couples in a "domestic partnership."[51]

A legal regime that affords a blanket subsidy to spouses or cohabitants without regard to whether the nondebtor is in fact financially dependent on the debtor spouse or cohabitant, or whether the dependence is socially desirable, imposes the risk of loss on a spouse's or cohabitant's reluctant creditors without an obvious efficiency gain. When the balance is to be struck between a financially independent person and a hapless tort creditor of her conveniently insolvent spouse or cohabitant, which party should win out becomes obscure.

The arguments for treating domestic partners as though they were married upon dissolution may be compelling. However, because domestic partners' creditors would be

[49] *See*, McClanahan, *supra* note 14 at 489–90. After the debtor spouse's one half interest in the community is applied to reduce the creditor's claim, the nondebtor spouse would arguably have a right of reimbursement against the debtor spouse, raising "substantial difficulties" in the event of their subsequent divorce. *Id.* at 490.

[50] *See, e.g.*, PRINCIPLES § 5.02(3) (authorizing court to consider "[t]he loss of earning capacity arising from a spouse's disproportionate share of caretaking responsibilities for children or other persons to whom the spouses have a moral obligation").

[51] *See, e.g.*, PRINCIPLES § 6.02(b)(i) (applying to domestic partners the provisions governing spousal compensatory payments in Section 5.02(3)).

affected by the ALI's domestic partnership proposal, it is not satisfactory to evaluate the merits of the ALI's proposal based solely on whether it would benefit domestic partners as a group. The availability of a relatively predictable, equitable allocation of wealth between domestic partners when they break up would lower the cost and increase the benefits of wealth shielding strategies for domestic partners, but at their creditors' expense.[52] The net effect on creditors of expanding remedies upon dissolution to domestic partners will ultimately depend on how the law governing creditors' rights develops. States who choose to adopt the PRINCIPLES' domestic partnership provisions should determine whether to extend to domestic partners the same option to hold property as members of a community or as tenants by the entirety that local law extends to married persons. They should also consider whether to harmonize the rules that govern domestic partners' rights to enforce expectations against each other by legal actions prior to dissolution of the domestic partnership with the rules that govern spouses' rights, Moreover, states should consider the impact of federal bankruptcy laws on the rights the PRINCIPLES would create between domestic partners. Although a debtor currently may not discharge in bankruptcy most obligations to a spouse, bankruptcy law does not currently recognize obligations between unmarried domestic partners as nondischargeable because they are not obligations to a "spouse."[53]

IV. Conclusion

The PRINCIPLES never consider the effect of marital and dissolution law on creditors, an understandable omission. Even without the ALI's proposed reforms, this area of the law is complicated. States vary widely regarding creditors' access to debtors' property as well as in their treatment of creditors' tools to address marital wealth-shielding behavior, such as the doctrine of necessaries, spousal agency, and vicarious liability. The PRINCIPLES ignore these complications and instead view the law of dissolution only through the perspective of the spouses and their dependents.[54] Despite the ALI's decision to limit the scope of the PRINCIPLES' to *inter se* claims between the parties to a relationship and their dependents, the rights the ALI would create or enforce necessarily impact creditors and credit relationships. This impact is perhaps most dramatic with respect to the new rights the ALI would create between domestic partners. The interests of the adults and their dependents are not the only interests affected by their relationship and subsequent break up. To view marriage and domestic partnerships accurately, we must pause to see these relationships through creditors' eyes.

52 Unmarried partners generally do not enjoy access to judicially supervised divorce. Instead, they must rely on uncertain outcomes from contract and restitutionary claims, and the vagaries of nonjudicial enforcement mechanisms. PRINCIPLES chief reporter's forward, at xix. *See generally* 69 A.L.R. 5th 219 (2005).

53 11 U.S.C. § 523(a)(5) (providing for nondischargeability of a "domestic support obligation"); 11 U.S.C. § 101(14A) (defining "domestic support obligation" as an obligation "owed to or recoverable by – (i) a spouse, former spouse, or child of the debtor. . . .) (2005); Defense of Marriage Act, 1 U.S.C. § 7 (2000) ("marriage," as it appears in federal statutes, refers to "only a legal union between one man and one woman as husband and wife").

54 PRINCIPLES § 4.09, cmt b.

PART FIVE. SPOUSAL SUPPORT

11 Back to the Future: The Perils and Promise of a Backward-Looking Jurisprudence

June Carbone

Family law once regulated sex and family by providing bright-line definitions of status (marriage principally among them) that served to inculcate and reinforce the prevailing norms of the day. In contrast, the PRINCIPLES would replace the nineteenth century insistence on the marital monogamous family as "the foundation of civilization" with a rush not to judge. The PRINCIPLES strive to treat all families and intimate relationships on equal terms and insist on few, if any, preconditions for the recognition of family relationships. Rather than police rigid status boundaries – and the draconian consequences that follow from them – they suspend judgment, moral and practical, long enough to create a private space for the creation of relationships free from the historical weight of family regulation. When families break down, however, the PRINCIPLES do not hesitate to intervene, to secure protection of the vulnerable and to provide a foundation for family members to continue on the basis of what has come before.

To do so, the PRINCIPLES necessarily rest on existential uncertainty with respect to the legal obligations they would enforce. After all, what is the status of a premarital agreement, valid when entered, whose enforceability can only be determined at the time of implementation? Or of an intimate relationship whose partners have exchanged no formal promises and forged no understandings, but who may be substantially obligated to each other when the relationship ends? Or of an adult-child relationship, in which the adult has no biological or legal ties to the child until enough time has passed that the assumption of the responsibilities of parenthood gives rise to legal recognition? The PRINCIPLES are most distinctive as a system of family regulation in their insistence that with each of these and other decisions, the legal consequences cannot be fixed until the point at which the relationship dissolves.

As a result, the PRINCIPLES envision a family law jurisprudence that is backward-looking in at least three respects. First, the PRINCIPLES resolve disputes at dissolution on the basis of circumstances that exist as a consequence of the parties' relationship, rather than the parties' understandings or position at the outset. The fairness – and thus the enforceability – of a premarital agreement may, for example, depend on whether the parties have managed to maintain two careers or whether one spouse suffers from an unexpected illness.[1] Similarly, a custody decree may most decisively reflect the division of parental responsibility in the period preceding dissolution.[2] Second, the PRINCIPLES adopt an explicitly *ex post* rather than an *ex ante* perspective. The most striking example may be their insistence on imposing similar financial obligations on couples breaking up after long term relationships,

[1] PRINCIPLES § 7.05.

[2] PRINCIPLES § 2.05(2)(c).

irrespective of marriage and the empirical data that underscores the different understandings marital and nonmarital couples have about the nature of their relationships.[3] Finally, the PRINCIPLES are backward-looking in that they are more intent on providing for the multiplicity of existing relationships – cementing the decades-long movement away from traditional notions of family morality – than on laying the foundation for a new regime.[4]

This approach has much to commend it. Rather than undertaking a comprehensive approach to family governance, the PRINCIPLES set out to bring order to the "current disarray in family law" by selecting from among existing decisions those "emerging legal concepts" that recognize family diversity.[5] The refusal to judge – or to appear to insist on a new moral order – is ideal for a law of transition. Family law varies considerably from state to state, and as the developments with respect to same-sex relationships attest, no consensus has emerged on a new approach.[6] Indeed, some issues (*e.g.*, civil unions) are characterized by increasing polarization while others (*e.g.*, premarital agreements) have been the subject of zig-zag developments even within individual jurisdictions.[7] In the face of dogged adherence to older principles in some quarters and determined resistance in others, the PRINCIPLES attempt to sidestep irreconcilable positions by emphasizing process, practicality, and fairness. It is hard to object to the recognition of unconventional parenthood, for example, if the alternative rejects the only father a six-year-old has ever known. Facts on the ground, especially when no basis exists to judge them in advance, can be very persuasive. Moreover, in selecting among emerging legal concepts, the PRINCIPLES gives voice to doctrines like *de facto* parenthood less likely to be reflected in model legislation.

Legislation and uniform acts such as the Uniform Premarital Agreement Act,[8] and the Uniform Parentage Act,[9] must, by their nature, appeal to the broadest common denominator of state legislatures. Case-by-case decisions, such as those recognizing parenthood by estoppel or the financial obligations of unmarried cohabitants, enjoy greater flexibility.[10] The ALI has long sought to give voice to such emerging legal developments within the common law tradition. Although the PRINCIPLES depart more than many restatements from existing case law, and although they combine case-based principles with proposals for legislation, they perform their greatest service in articulating concepts unlikely to be popular in state legislatures. After all, legislation best addresses that which the ALI has eschewed, *viz.*, the forward looking creation of legal regimes designed to shape behavior rather than simply resolve existing disputes.

While the PRINCIPLES may thus do yeomen service for a family law of transition, to succeed on a more permanent basis, they must ultimately give way to a more

[3] *See* Parts II.C and D, *infra*. *See also* Brinig, Garrison, this volume.

[4] PRINCIPLES, Director's Foreword at xv.

[5] PRINCIPLES OF THE LAW OF FAMILY DISSOLUTION: ANALYSIS AND RECOMMENDATIONS, Foreword at xiii (Proposed Final Draft 1997). The purpose and content of the PRINCIPLES understandably evolved over time. Provisions from the early drafts that did not stay in the final version are included here principally for the insight they provide into the drafters' motivation.

[6] Indeed, Naomi Cahn and I argue that we may be moving toward two internally coherent, but irreconcilable systems, one that continues to encourage early marriage and the regulation of sexuality, and a second that places greater emphasis on later marriage and financial independence while deregulating adult sexual relations altogether. For a preliminary version of this argument, see June Carbone and Naomi Cahn, *The Biological Basis of Commitment: Does One Size Fit All?*, WOMEN'S RTS. L. REP. 223, 244–9 (2004).

[7] *See, e.g.*, LESLIE J. HARRIS, LEE E. TEITELBAUM AND JUNE CARBONE, FAMILY LAW 738–40 (3rd ed. 2005) (discussing recent California developments).

[8] UNIF. PREMARITAL AGREEMENT ACT (2000).

[9] UNIF. PARENTAGE ACT (2002).

[10] *See, e.g.*, Holtzman v. Knott, 533 N. W.2d 419, 421 (Wis. 1995), *cert. denied*, 516 U.S. 975 (1995).

forward looking jurisprudence. Two considerations compel this conclusion. First, the backward looking nature of the PRINCIPLES papers over tension about the source of authority for imposing particular terms on warring couples. Like many of the legal rules imposed on private parties, these terms tend to be justified in one of two ways: either they reflect the couples' agreement, express or implied, or they represent society's collective judgment about the best way to conduct family life.[11] Although both rationales require due process and notice as an element of fairness, the notice that can be said to come from one's behavior may be quite different from the implied notice of societal conventions. The failure to address the differences between the two rationales may ultimately undermine the legitimacy of both. Second, both justifications, contract and societal conventions, are more effectively implemented when they are made explicit. Efficiency considerations suggest, for example, that if the parties are uncertain about the enforceability of their agreement before marriage, they will be less likely to enter into agreements, less likely to rely on the agreements they do enter, less likely to feel obliged to honor their terms, and more likely to engage either in strategic behavior that exploits later opportunities or hedging behavior that anticipates possible breach. For example, a wealthy heiress who believes her premarital agreement with a younger beau may not be enforced may be more likely to transfer assets to her children.

The more compelling concern, however, has been the role of family law in creating understandings about family behavior. State mandated statuses have served as a channeling function, directing intimate relationships along lines that serve societal ends.[12] If the ALI is engaged in an effort to impose a new set of societally-mandated obligations, as it arguably is, then making explicit at the relationship's start the responsibilities it carries is ultimately necessary to encourage widespread acceptance. Consider, for example, an executive husband and a homemaker wife filing for divorce after the wife informs the husband that her casual affair has persuaded her that she no longer loves him. If couples were informally surveyed, they might agree that in such a case the wife who decides to call it quits without cause should be held responsible for the consequences of the dissolution. The PRINCIPLES concerning spousal support, which require couples to share the "losses" that arise at dissolution, would reflect a societal insistence that a wealthier spouse provide for a destitute partner, rather than an implied contract to deal with the circumstances of the split.[13] Making that obligation explicit, and articulating the reasons why intimate relationships necessarily involve a sharing of wealth as well as pleasure, will prompt greater acceptance of both the sharing norm itself and the PRINCIPLES as an enduring legal framework.

This chapter first documents the disarray in family law that made a backward looking jurisprudential approach attractive to the drafters. Second, it explores in depth those PRINCIPLES dealing with the property division, spousal support, cohabitating couples,

[11] *See, e.g.*, Carl E. Schneider, *Moral Discourse and the Transformation of American Family Law*, 83 MICH. L. REV. 1803, 1807–08 (1985) (discussing the regulatory role of family law in guiding behavior in accordance with societal norms). *Cf.* Elizabeth S. Scott, *Marriage, Cohabitation and Collective Responsibility for Dependency*, 2004 U. CHI LEGAL F. 225, 259 (arguing that presumed agreement to default principles can serve as a basis for contract-based imposition of responsibility).

[12] *See* Schneider, *supra* note 11 (distinguishing two primary themes in the post-fault evolution of the American law: "a diminution of the law's discourse in moral terms about the relations between family members, and the transfer of many moral decisions from the law to the people the law once regulated").

[13] *See* PRINCIPLES §§ 5.02–5.04 (explaining that the objective of Chapter 5 is the allocation of the losses that arise from the end of the relationship, including the continued access to the other spouse's income).

and premarital agreements to illustrate the pervasively backward looking nature of the ALI approach.[14] Third, it critiques the legitimacy of a system that rejects both contract and regulatory rationales, and fails to systematically provide for the precommitment practices that make both individual agreements and societally sanctioned mandates more likely to be implemented. Finally, this chapter concludes that the ALI recommendations implicitly rest on forward looking principles, and explores the possibilities for restating the obligations in aspirational terms.

I. The Current Disarray in Family Law and the ALI's Backward-Looking Approach

The drafters began the project emphasizing the "current disarray in family law,"[15] which purportedly justified an articulation of emerging principles rather than a restatement, and made it difficult for the Reporters to embrace either a regulatory or a contractual approach to family law. At the project's outset, the cycle of family law change and renewal had brought both into disrepute.

Older principles of family law – that is, the dominant family law jurisprudence of the latter half of the nineteenth and the first half of the twentieth centuries – embraced a regulatory model. The United States Supreme Court declared the monogamous family to be the foundation of civilization in 1888.[16] Accordingly, the state had a significant interest in policing the boundary between licit and illicit sexuality, regulating marriage as the foundation of family life, and addressing the dependence that came with child rearing and a sexual division of family responsibilities. The state oversaw marriage, restricted divorce, drew clear distinctions between legitimate and illegitimate children, and distributed resources in conformance with the era's family norms.[17]

The transformations during the latter half of the twentieth century undermined the earlier model. First, paternalistic notions about the dependence of women (and the need to protect them from one-sided arrangements) became obsolete as women assumed greater roles in the workforce.[18] Couples acquired greater freedom to manage their own affairs on terms of their choosing. Second, less financial vulnerability lay the foundation for no-fault divorce, and abandonment of the principle that couples could not dissolve their unions by agreement alone.[19] Adoption of pure no-fault systems, in which fault considerations became irrelevant not only to granting divorce but also to the financial considerations

[14] The same critique could be applied to the principles of custodial decision making, but because those decisions necessarily involve third parties, namely the children, I will limit this discussion to the financial portion of the PRINCIPLES. The issue of precommitment strategies, however, applies with similar force to undertaking parenthood.

[15] PRINCIPLES OF THE LAW OF FAMILY DISSOLUTION: ANALYSIS AND RECOMMENDATIONS, Foreword at xiii (Proposed Final Draft 1997).

[16] Maynard v. Hill, 125 U.S. 190, 211 (1888) (Marriage "is an institution, in the maintenance of which in its purity the public is deeply interested, for it is the foundation of the family and of society, without which there would be neither civilization nor progress.").

[17] *See, e.g.*, Brian H. Bix, *Premarital Agreements in the Principles of Family Dissolution*, 8 DUKE J. GENDER L. & POL'Y 231, 231 (2001). Those who emphasize the public status of marriage argue that "the state, and the state alone, should set the terms for the marriage," including rules for entry, rules during the marriage, and the terms on which the marriage can be dissolved.

[18] For a more general discussion of the interaction between financial independence and divorce rates, see JUNE CARBONE, FROM PARTNERS TO PARENTS: THE SECOND REVOLUTION IN FAMILY LAW 99 (2000).

[19] Alicia Brokars Kelly, *The Marital Partnership Pretense and Career Assets: The Ascendancy of Self Over the Marital Community*, 81 B.U. L. Rev. 59, 67 (2001).

thereafter, for all intents and purposes eliminated the legal obligation to stay married, and much of the stigma associated with divorce.[20]

The sexual revolution completed the transformation. Whereas society once recognized marriage as the only legitimate locus for sexuality, contemporary public opinion supports the sexual autonomy of the unmarried.[21] The United States Supreme Court has long since declared unconstitutional any legal distinctions between marital and nonmarital children. While nonmarital childbearing remains controversial, nonmarital births have become commonplace and single parent families widespread.[22] As a result, the disabilities once attached to "bastardy" are now seen as "pointless and savage."[23] The United States Supreme Court's decision in *Lawrence v. Texas*,[24] which extended a zone of privacy to same-sex relationships, effectively completed the deregulation of sexuality between consenting adults.

These elements made a paternalistic system of family law untenable, and at least initially pointed toward greater acceptance of intimate agreements. The Pennsylvania Supreme Court in *Simeone v. Simeone* emphasized that women's greater equality eliminated the primary objection to premarital bargaining.[25] Critics argued, however, that the new order involved neither true equality,[26] nor a contractual regime that might incorporate voluntarily assumed, but nonetheless long term, commitment. Instead, it involved a new ideology of the "Love Family," based on choice, voluntary affiliation, and transitional associations with another adult rather than the permanent commitment traditionally associated with marriage.[27] While the *Simeone* court tied greater gender equality to greater willingness to enforce premarital agreements,[28] other courts limited the amount and duration of spousal support even in the absence of agreements.[29] These courts viewed the imposition of continuing obligations after divorce as a relic of fault-based paternalism, and the idea of contract became associated with the dismantling rather than the enforcement of domestic obligations.

[20] For a summary of these developments, see Barbara Dafoe Whitehead, The Divorce Culture (1997), and Carbone, *supra* note 18, at viii.

[21] *See, e.g.*, Bruce Fretts, "THE EW POLL: Better Parent? Murphy Beats Dan!," *BPI Entertainment News Wire*, June 2, 1992 (finding in a telephone survey of 600 Americans taken for Entertainment Weekly on May 22–25 by the Gallup Organization, with a sampling error of plus or minus 4%, that 65% of the American public did not believe that Murphy Brown set a bad example by having a nonmarital child).

[22] Carbone, *supra* note 20, at xiii.

[23] Leslie J. Harris & Lee E. Teitelbaum, Family Law 1014 (2nd ed. 2000).

[24] 539 U.S. 558 (2003).

[25] 581 A.2d 162, 165 (Pa. 1990) ("Society has advanced, however, to the point where women are no longer regarded as the 'weaker' party in marriage, or in society generally. Indeed, the stereotype that women serve as homemakers while men work as breadwinners is no longer viable. Quite often today both spouses are income earners. Nor is there viability in the presumption that women are uninformed, uneducated, and readily subjected to unfair advantage in marital agreements. Indeed, women nowadays quite often have substantial education, financial awareness, income, and assets.").

[26] Of course, women's equal legal status is not the same thing as practical equality in access to equal wages, working conditions, or opportunities. *See id.* (Papadakos, J., concurring).

[27] *See* Whitehead, *supra* note 20. *See also* Naomi R. Cahn, *The Moral Complexities of Family Law*, 50 Stan. L. Rev. 225, 232 (1997); Elizabeth S. Scott & Robert E. Scott, *Marriage As Relational* Contract, 84 Va. L. Rev. 1225, 1239 (1998) (summarizing the view of many communitarians that an understanding of the marriage relationship in contractual terms is inevitably linked to limited commitment motivated by selfish interest, to a unilateral right of termination, and to policies promoting a clean break without regret when marriage ends).

[28] Whitehead, *supra* note 20.

[29] *See* Joan Krauskopf, *Theories of Property Division/Spousal Support: Searching for Solutions to the Mystery*, 23 Fam. L.Q. 253 (1989).

By the time the ALI undertook its work on the PRINCIPLES, the new regime of contract, choice, and autonomy had come under withering attack. *The Divorce Culture* argued that the emphasis on adult satisfaction contributed to family instability and lack of long term commitment to children.[30] Martha Fineman led a generation of feminists who critiqued society's failure to provide for the dependence that inevitably accompanies child rearing, if not gender per se.[31] Any number of commentators explored the intermingling of lives and finances that occurs with almost all intimate relationships of any substantial duration.[32] They argued that just as contract principles in the commercial context acknowledged the possibility of unfair bargaining power, family law should also do so.[33]

At the time the ALI began its reexamination of family dissolution, uniform and model legislation provided the primary vehicles to systematize family law across the fifty states.[34] Many of the Uniform Acts, particularly the Uniform Premarital Agreement Act,[35] and the Uniform Marriage and Divorce Act[36] were identified with the era of autonomy and contract. Three minority lines of cases, however, began to recognize financial vulnerability rooted in family arrangements rather than gender. First, some states departed from standard contract principles to judge the validity of premarital agreements at the time of enforcement rather than at the time of contracting.[37] Second, a number of states recognized estoppel principles as a basis for acknowledging nonbiologically-based parenting.[38] Finally, the line of cases that began with *Marvin v. Marvin*[39] provided some relief for unmarried partners who never entered into express agreements.[40] Taken together, however, these cases did not provide a coherent alternative view of family obligation. Rather, they provided a limited dissent from the failure of existing family doctrine to meet the needs of a broader range of family arrangements. The time was ripe for a farther-reaching examination of family dissolution, which the ALI undertook over an eleven-year period.

The ALI defined its mission in three ways. First, as noted above, it elected to issue principles rather than a restatement to give "greater weight to emerging legal concepts."[41] "Restating" the law of family dissolution to portray a coherent sense of the law across the fifty states would in any event have been impossible; defining the project in terms of the articulation of principles gave the drafters permission to choose which line of cases to emphasize.[42]

[30] *See generally* Whitehead, *supra* note 20.

[31] *See, e.g.*, MARTHA FINEMAN, THE NEUTERED MOTHER, THE SEXUAL FAMILY AND OTHER TWENTIETH CENTURY TRAGEDIES (1996).

[32] *See, in particular*, June Carbone and Margaret F. Brinig, *Rethinking Marriage: Feminist Ideology, Economic Change, And Divorce Reform*, 65 TUL. L. REV. 953 (1991).

[33] Brian Bix, *Bargaining in the Shadow of Love: The Enforcement of Premarital Agreements and How We Think of Marriage*, 40 WM. & MARY L. REV. 145, 182, 188 (1998).

[34] Congress also passed national legislation designed to increase the efficacy of child support enforcement, but the issues associated with those efforts go well beyond the scope of this chapter. For an excellent review, see Ann Laquer Estin, *Federalism and Child Support*, 5 VA. J. SOC. POL'Y & L. 541 (1998).

[35] UNIF. PREMARITAL AGREEMENT ACT (2000).

[36] UNIF. MARRIAGE & DIVORCE ACT, 9A U.L.A. 282 (1998).

[37] *See* Judith T. Younger, *A Minnesota Comparative Family Law Symposium: Antenuptial Agreements*, 28 WM. MITCHELL L. REV. 697 (2001).

[38] *See, e.g.*, *Holtzman*, 533 N.W.2d at 421.

[39] 18 Cal.3d 660 (1976).

[40] For a summary of these developments, see Harris, Teitelbaum and Carbone, *supra* note 7, 246–66.

[41] PRINCIPLES OF THE LAW OF FAMILY DISSOLUTION: ANALYSIS AND RECOMMENDATIONS, Foreword at xiii (Proposed Final Draft 1997) at xiii, xv.

[42] PRINCIPLES, Director's Foreword (emphasizing that "[s]ometimes ALI work systematizes legal change that has already occurred. This project was written as reform movements swirled").

Second, the ALI limited its mission to principles of *dissolution*. Geoffrey Hazard, former director of the ALI, noted in his Foreword to the Proposed Final Draft of the PRINCIPLES, that:

> The project deals not with the grounds for divorce, but rather with the issues of property division, post-dissolution support, and child custody. These are usually referred to as the "incidents" of dissolution. Today all states in some way allow divorce without regard to proof of fault, so that the grounds for divorce are rarely an issue. The "incidents" of the family law dissolution process now constitute the overwhelming mass of family law litigation.[43]

The ALI approached family law dissolution as a process that stands on its own.

Third, the PRINCIPLES sought to achieve an equitable sharing of the financial losses from the dissolution of the family relationship.[44] Note that the losses are described as the losses from dissolution, not from the relationship – a curious conclusion for PRINCIPLES that urge the abolition of fault and, thus, the end of a legally enforced obligation to remain married. While the ALI appropriately recognized that abolishing fault makes management of dissolution that much more important practically, it also meant that the ALI produced principles of family law dissolution without crafting principles of family law creation or governance.

The emphasis on dissolution, together with the disarray among the states, yielded an *ex post* perspective that permeates the PRINCIPLES' treatment of everything from premarital agreements to definitions of parenthood. If family dissolution is considered independently of creation, then the relevant inquiry concerns the facts at the end of the relationship. Marriage, which the PRINCIPLES has bracketed as outside the scope of the project, cannot be treated as a fixed status with understood terms; parenthood is neither defined by nor limited to marriage, biology, or adoption. Moreover, states continue to vary with respect to whether to treat unmarried cohabitants as candidates for domestic partnership benefits or arrest for fornication. The question for state legislators, family court judges, legal scholars, and others interested in the family is whether the PRINCIPLES, in providing for dissolution, reflect tenable assumptions about, or lay a foundation for, family creation, as well. This requires consideration of how the individual parts of the PRINCIPLES fit together, which the next Part examines.

II. Sharing PRINCIPLES and the Allocation of Resources

The cornerstone of the PRINCIPLES is a recognition that partner's lives become increasingly commingled over the course of a relationship. Such recognition, however, could be rooted in any number of jurisprudential approaches: express assumption of responsibilities associated with marriage, an implied contract arising from the parties' actual arrangements, default terms changeable by express agreement, or societally mandated terms justified by gender disparities, the obligations of caretaking, or the desire to protect the public fisc. This Part argues that fairness principles justified by societal concerns dominate the

[43] PRINCIPLES, Director's Foreword.

[44] PRINCIPLES, Director's Foreword. Section 4.02 emphasizes the objective of equitably sharing the financial losses from dissolution of marriage while Section 6.02 emphasizes the division of the financial losses occurring from dissolution of a relationship equitably and predictably. PRINCIPLES §§ 4.02, 6.02.

PRINCIPLES, although the drafters do not necessarily embrace a single view of society's interest in regulating family life.

A. The Property Division

The property provisions of the PRINCIPLES overwhelmingly reflect a concept of marital property that is an amalgam of the community property and marital property regimes already in place in most states. Both regimes divide the property acquired over the course of marriage into (1) that property acquired during marriage as a result of the spouses' labor which is labeled either "marital property" or "community property," and (2) separate property, typically that property held by the parties before marriage or acquired during marriage by gift or inheritance.[45] Section 4.12, however, innovatively recharacterizes separate property as marital property at the dissolution of a long term marriage.[46] In practice, this provision, if adopted, would increase the assets available at dissolution without the open-ended discretion courts in many states already enjoy with respect to marital property.[47]

The rationale underlying Section 4.12 provides insight into the drafters' overall approach. The drafters comment that:

> After many years of marriage, spouses typically do not think of their separate-property assets as separate, even if they would be so classified under the technical property rules. Both spouses are likely to believe, for example, that such assets will be available to provide for their joint retirement, for a medical crisis of either spouse, or for other personal emergencies. The longer the marriage the more likely it is that the spouses will have made decisions about their employment or the use of their marital assets that are premised in part on such expectations about the separate property of both spouses.[48]

This explanation stands in contrast to the two primary justifications for alternative models of dividing property at divorce, the partnership model of marriage and an approach based on need.

Many commentators believe the partnership model of marriage "pervades and dominates the law of marriage and divorce."[49] In fact, the Uniform Marriage and Divorce

[45] Section 4.03 of the PRINCIPLES, which follows the majority rule among the states, adopts the following definitions:
(1) Property acquired during marriage is marital property, except as otherwise expressly provided in this Chapter.
(2) Inheritances, including bequests and devises, and gifts from third parties, are the separate property of the acquiring spouse even if acquired during marriage. PRINCIPLES § 4.03.

[46] PRINCIPLES § 4.12.

[47] For a comparison in Nebraska, see Craig W. Dallon, *Reconsidering Property Division in Divorce Under Nebraska Law in Light of the* ALI's PRINCIPLES *of the Law of Family Dissolution: Analysis And Recommendations*, 37 CREIGHTON L. REV. 1, 58 (2003). *See also* Craig W. Dallon, *The Likely Impact of the ALI Principles of the Law of Family Dissolution on Property Division*, 2001 BYU L. Rev. 891, 894–95 (noting that equitable distribution may permit the distribution of all property in some states, or just marital property in other states, but that distributions limited to marital property need not be 50/50, giving the courts considerable discretion).

[48] PRINCIPLES § 4.12, cmt. a, at 771.

[49] Kelly, *supra* note 19. *See also* Cynthia Starnes, *Divorce and the Displaced Homemaker: A Discourse on the Playing with Dolls, Partnership Buyouts and Dissociation Under No-Fault*, 60 U. CHI. L. REV. 67, 136–37 (1993); Marjorie E. Kornhauser, *Theory Versus Reality: The Partnership Model of Marriage in Family and Income Tax Law*, 69 TEMP. L. REV. 1413, 1413 (1996) ("Current legal theory in both family and tax law accepts the belief that a marriage is like a partnership."); Milton C. Regan, Jr., *Market Discourse and Moral Neutrality in Divorce Law*, 1994 UTAH L. REV. 605, 637 ("The economic partnership model of marriage has become perhaps the governing vision in legal determinations. . . . "); Jana B. Singer, Divorce Reform and Gender Justice, 67 N.C.

Act explicitly embraced the partnership theory as the basis for the property division at divorce.[50] The partnership model presumes that the parties enter into marriage committing themselves, explicitly or implicitly, to a relationship built on mutual care and concern:

> A myriad of thoughts and feelings fill [the couple's] minds. Despite the sobering statistics that one in two marriages end in divorce, they believe they will beat the odds: hope and optimism for their future together predominate. Whatever life's challenges and joys, they envision their lives united: a partnership forged of love and commitment that will provide solace and nourishment in the years to come.[51]

This image illustrates partnership as an *ex ante*, not an *ex post*, undertaking. Professor Alicia Kelly explains that: "The theory provides that spouses are partners who each make a set of meaningful, although perhaps different, contributions to the marital enterprise."[52] Accordingly, "each spouse is entitled to share in the marital estate because each participated in its acquisition. Under this view, the economic resource is apportioned, not based on need or status, but because it has been earned."[53]

Within this theory, partnership is a specialized form of contract.[54] Partners enter into a voluntary association accepting the explicit or implied terms that come with the relationship. These terms are understood from the beginning and are expected to engender reliance. The terms themselves may be default rules, applicable unless changed, that proceed from the parties' presumed bargain or they may reflect public policies designed "to compensate, and thus implicitly to promote, the kind of sharing, and at times altruistic behavior in spouses that is deemed essential for the preservation of marriage."[55] In either event, the partnership model anticipates a conscious choice to enter a relationship with established understandings.

L. Rev. 1103, 1114 (1989) ("One promising theory . . . is an investment partnership model of marriage and divorce."); Bea Ann Smith, *The Partnership Theory of Marriage: A Borrowed Solution Fails*, 68 Tex. L. Rev. 689, 696 (1990) ("Nearly every state currently embraces the community-property concept of marriage as a partnership" (citations omitted)). For a list of cases nationwide that explicitly treated marriage as a partnership or shared enterprise, see Lee R. Russ, Annotation, *Divorce: Equitable Distribution Doctrine*, 41 A.L.R. 481, 489 (1985 & Supp. 2000).

[50] Unif. Marriage & Divorce Act Prefatory Note (amended 1973), 9A U.L.A. 161 (1998).

[51] Kelly, *supra* note 19, at 60.

[52] *Id.* at 69.

[53] *Id.* at 69–70. Similarly, Professor Sally Sharp observes:

> The partnership ideal does stand for the proposition that property acquired by the single enterprise of the marital unit, to which both spouses often are presumed to contribute equally, should be equally shared when the unit is dissolved by divorce. Partnership principles seek to compensate, and thus implicitly to promote, the kind of sharing, and at times altruistic behavior in spouses that is deemed essential for the preservation of marriage. In particular, the concept creates a means for recognition of the contribution of the dependent spouse, who may have sacrificed his or her own career potential for the sake of the other or for the marriage itself. At one level then, the partnership ideal enunciates a public policy of promoting sharing behavior. . . . It also seeks to ensure that each estate is compensated fairly for its investment in the marriage.

Sally Burnett Sharp, *The Partnership Ideal: The Development of Equitable Distribution in North Carolina*, 65 N.C. L. Rev. 195, 199 (1987).

[54] Indeed, the proponents of the partnership model emphasize its similarity to commercial bargains, even though commercial bargains, unlike marriage, do not have to be dissolvable at will. *See* Kornhauser, *supra* note 51, at 1416–17 (noting that partnership model of marriage is an Idealized version of the equivalent two-person commercial partnership model); *Kelly, supra* note 19 at 75 ("No-fault divorce itself also reflects partnership theory. Similar to a commercial partnership, which is a voluntary association, under no-fault divorce, spousal partners can terminate their relationship at will.").

[55] Sharp, *supra* note 53, at 197.

Need is the alternative ground for a division of marital assets.[56] The Uniform Marriage and Divorce Act, in encouraging a "clean break" between the couple, suggested that the property division might be used to address not only the respective contributions of the couple, but their postdivorce needs.[57] The statute accordingly authorized courts to exercise discretion to divide the property into unequal shares in order to eliminate the need for support.[58] The justification for an unequal division then mirrored that for spousal support.[59]

The PRINCIPLES, in contrast, do not depend on the parties' understanding of or commitment to sharing as part of their relationship, although they could be said to reflect an assumption of sharing behavior within marriage and they may have the practical effect of addressing need.[60] For the PRINCIPLES, it suffices that the longer the marriage lasts, the more likely the parties are to treat separate assets as jointly owned.[61] A commitment to do so at the beginning of the relationship is unnecessary.[62] This approach solves a number of practical problems. The PRINCIPLES expand the available assets as the marriage progresses without introducing substantially more judicial discretion. But the approach fails to address the question: on what basis beyond convenience is the transformation of separate into marital property made and does this basis require a particular view of marriage?[63]

[56] Historically, the title theory prevalent in the common law states awarded property to the title holder. Where this resulted in the award of most of the marital assets to a single party, typically the husband, the other party's "need" might serve to justify support. *See* Kelly, *supra* at 51. Carbone and Brinig have argued, however, that support within this system reflected specific performance of the marital duty of support rather than a true division of assets. *See* Carbone and Brinig, *supra* note 32.

[57] UNIF. MARRIAGE AND DIVORCE ACT § 30, 9A U.L.A. 282 (1998). *See, in particular*, Suzanne Reynolds, *The Relationship Of Property Division And Alimony: The Division Of Property To Address Need*, 56 FORDHAM L. REV. 827, 838 (1988).

[58] UNIF. MARRIAGE AND DIVORCE ACT § 307, 9A U.L.A. 282 (1998).

[59] *Id.* at 839.

[60] Commentators vary in their description of the parties' expectations about the treatment of separate property. Susan Gary maintains that "In contrast with marital partnership theory, research indicates that a couple in an ongoing first marriage are likely to view their marriage as a sharing not just of property earned during the marriage but of all their property." Susan N. Gary, *Marital Partnership Theory and the Elective Share: Federal Tax Law Provides a Solution*, 49 U. MIAMI L. REV. 576, 572–73 (1995) (citing a 1978 survey describing treatment of property at death). Professor Robert Levy, on the other hand, argues that: "It may not be universal, but it is certainly not uncommon for couples to view income that either of them produced during the marriage as 'of the marriage' and different from funds or assets brought by one of the spouses to the marriage or acquired by one of the spouses during the marriage by gift or inheritance." Robert Levy, *An Introduction to Divorce-Property Issues*, 23 FAM. L.Q. 147, 152 (1989).

[61] The drafters note further that "Another premise of this section, that after 30 or 35 years of marriage most people will expect that property their spouses brought into the marriage will be available to them jointly upon retirement or in an emergency, remains untested. However, the courts of hotchpot states may share this assumption, for they appear more likely to allocate inherited or premarital property to the other spouse at the dissolution of a lengthy marriage than at the dissolution of a short one." PRINCIPLES § 4.12, Reporter's Notes, cmt. a, at 781.

[62] Indeed, the drafters observe that "it may be pointless to ask about the parties' expectations at the time of their marriage as to the disposition of their property should they divorce, for they probably have no expectation at all because they do not expect to divorce. The data suggest that economic decisions made during marriage are largely premised on the assumption that the marriage will continue, which is a premise of this section." PRINCIPLES § 4.12, Reporter's Notes, cmt. a, at 781.

[63] Although the principles use the language of expectation ("the longer the marriage the more likely it is that the spouses will have made decisions about their employment or the use of their marital assets that are premised in part on such expectations about the separate property of both spouses"). UNIF. MARRIAGE & DIVORCE ACT PREFATORY NOTE (amended 1973), 9A U.L.A. 161 (1998). The drafters make it clear that the parties' most common "expectation" is the often unrealistic one that they will not divorce, rather than a legally enforceable expectation that the marriage will continue. *See* notes 62 and 63, *supra*. The drafters similarly refer to the idea of "reliance," but that reliance is most commonly reliance on the continuation of a relationship legally terminable at will. *Id.*

The PRINCIPLES take the question seriously enough to attempt a comprehensive answer only when they approach the topic of compensatory payments.

B. Compensatory Payments

The PRINCIPLES acknowledge that the issues are identical; that the "same rationale that suggests that a long term spouse should usually share in the other spouse's greater post-dissolution earnings also suggests that long term spouses should usually share in one another's greater assets."[64] The PRINCIPLES then go to great lengths to set forth a rationale for their approach to compensatory payments.

The PRINCIPLES establish the primary objective for compensatory payments as the allocation of the "financial losses that arise at the dissolution of a marriage."[65] In a marriage of significant duration, the PRINCIPLES recognize that a central loss, and potentially the most controversial, is "the loss in living standard experienced at dissolution by the spouse who has less wealth or earning capacity."[66]

The PRINCIPLES explain that the objective of compensatory payments is to insure that the financial losses that typically follow the division of one household into two are equitably distributed.[67] In defining losses, the comments note that "a principle that compensates a spouse for loss of the marital living standard could instead be said to protect the gain in living standard that spouse obtained from the marriage. The choice of language is of course less important than the underlying rule it describes."[68] That rule, in turn, is tied once again to the length of the relationship. The PRINCIPLES describe the basic rule as one that "the claimant has been married to a person of greater wealth or earning capacity and therefore experiences a loss of the marital living standard at dissolution, and the marriage 'was of sufficient duration that equity requires that some portion of the loss be treated as the spouses' joint responsibility.'"[69]

The PRINCIPLES again reject a number of the conventional rationales for why one spouse has an obligation to the other for the loss of the living standard that existing during the marriage. First, the PRINCIPLES acknowledge that protection of the standard of living during the marriage could correspond to the expectation interest in contract damages, but this ordinarily requires identification of the breaching party and is thus inconsistent with the PRINCIPLES' no-fault approach.[70] Second, the PRINCIPLES note that while the lesser earning spouse often contributes to the higher earning spouse's income potential, such contributions are difficult to prove.[71] Finally, while the PRINCIPLES report that the historic justification for alimony has been relief of need, they intentionally term their

64 PRINCIPLES § 4.12, cmt. a.

65 PRINCIPLES § 5.02(1).

66 PRINCIPLES §§ 5.03(2), 5.04. The PRINCIPLES also provide for compensation for the losses associated with primary caretaking, contributions to the other spouse's education or training, and other matters. *See* PRINCIPLES §§ 5.05, 5.12 and 5.13. This Chapter focuses, however, only on Section 5.04 as the best illustration of the rationales underlying the PRINCIPLES. For a more in-depth examination of the compensatory payments, *See* June Carbone, *The Futility of Coherence: The ALI's* Principles of the Law of Family Dissolution, *Compensatory Spousal Payments*, 4 J. L. FAM. STUD. 43 (2002).

67 PRINCIPLES § 5.02 cmt a, at 788.

68 PRINCIPLES § 5.02 cmt a, at 788.

69 PRINCIPLES § 5.04 cmt a, at 806.

70 PRINCIPLES § 5.04 cmt b, at 806–07.

71 PRINCIPLES § 5.04 cmt b, at 806–07. The PRINCIPLES state further that "It must be emphasized that the difficulty of showing that the homemaker has "contributed" to the other spouse's earning capacity or comfort does not cast doubt on the observation that, in assuming that role, the homemaker incurs a significant economic loss. It merely reveals that a different rationale is needed to explain why the law may require the other spouse to provide compensation for that loss." PRINCIPLES § 5.04 cmt b, at 808.

provisions "compensatory payments" in order to transform "the claimant's petition from a plea for help to a claim of entitlement."[72]

With rejection of the two most conventional justifications for spousal support, need and partnership, the PRINCIPLES turn to the same factors used to validate the transformation of separate property into marital property over time. The drafters observe that:

> [T]he cases reflect an enduring intuition that the homemaker in a long-term marriage has some claim on the other spouse's post-divorce income. That intuition does not depend on any assumption that the parties made explicit promises to one another, but on the belief that the relationship itself gives rise to obligations.... Some [duties] may be waivable by contract and some not, but few are dependent upon contract to establish their existence. They emerge from entry into the relationship itself, whether or not the parties expressly adopt them. The relationship of husband and wife is of this kind, but more so. Its effects may accrete slowly, but with great impact as the spouses' lives become entwined over time.[73]

These comments emphasize the privileging of the *ex post* perspective. Spouses in a long term marriage have an obligation to share the "losses from dissolution," which are defined as the loss of the standard of living the marriage made possible. These sharing obligations do not arise from an exchange of promises, from the "marriage ceremony alone" or from any particular "conception of marriage."[74] Instead, the obligations arise from the fact that "over time... the parties' lives become entwined."[75]

The PRINCIPLES might have justified their result by a partnership ideal that included a duty to share earning capacity as well as income. Both contributions to the marriage that enhanced one party's income and sacrifices that reduced the other party's earning potential might be recognized as obligations of the marriage. Income sharing proposals that equalize income for a period proportionate to the length of the marriage effectively, then, become a property division that balances jointly acquired gains and losses without requiring proof in individual cases.[76]

[72] PRINCIPLES § 5.02 cmt a, at 790.

[73] PRINCIPLES § 5.04 cmt c, at 808–09. The comment continues:

> The remedy is proportional to the marital duration because the obligations recognized under this section do not arise from the marriage ceremony alone, but develop over time as the parties' lives become entwined. That is, this Chapter does not rely upon a conception of marriage as a contract whose terms require the equitable remedies it provides, but rather sees the obligations of spouses to one another as arising from their sharing of their lives over time. *See* PRINCIPLES § 5.02, cmt. f. As a marriage lengthens, the parties assume roles and functions with respect to one another. In sharing a life together, they mold one another. Spouses married for 35 years are different people than they were before marriage, and also different than they would have become had they not married. Their choices about their education and their work are likely to have been affected, as are their expectations, their tastes, and perhaps their beliefs. To leave the financially dependent spouse in a long marriage without a remedy would facilitate the exploitation of the trusting spouse and discourage domestic investment by the nervous one. PRINCIPLES § 5.04 cmt c, at 809.

[74] PRINCIPLES § 5.04 cmt c, at 808–09.

[75] PRINCIPLES § 5.04 cmt c, at 808–09.

[76] This approach treats the spouses' earning capacity as an item of marital property. For additional explorations of this approach, see Joan M. Krauskopf, *Comments on Income Sharing: Redefining the Family in Terms of Community*, 31 HOUS. L. REV. 417 (1994); Joan Williams, *Is Coverture Dead? Beyond a New Theory of Alimony*, 82 GEO L. J. (1994); Susan Moller Okin, *Economic Equality After Divorce: "Equal Rights" or Special Benefits*, 38 DISSENT 383 (1991); Cynthia Starnes, *Divorce and the Displaced Homemaker: A Discourse on Playing with Dolls, Partnership Buyouts and Disassociation Under No-Fault*, 60 U. CHI. L. REV. 67 (1993); Jane Rutherford, *Duty in Divorce: Shared Income as a Path to Equality*, 58 FORDHAM L. REV. 539 (1990).

While the PRINCIPLES acknowledge the close relationship between their approach and income sharing, they reject the property rubric on which the latter is based.[77] Instead, they repeatedly come back to the perspective of dissolution and the idea of merger over time. It is the facts on the ground rather than the agreement to create those facts – the fairness of providing for the circumstances that exist at dissolution – that underlies the duty to provide compensatory payments. The PRINCIPLES can thus embrace an expansive theory of postdivorce obligation without elaborating on a concept of marriage.

C. Domestic Partnerships

If a particular conception of marriage is not necessary to the ALI's remedies, and they are not based on the implied consent of the parties, then the same PRINCIPLES should arguably apply to nonmarital relationships with similar characteristics. The ALI, which systematically addresses nonmarital as well as marital relationships, agrees.

In what is perhaps the PRINCIPLES' greatest departure from existing law, the drafters declare that "[t]he primary objective of Chapter 6 [governing domestic partnership] is fair distribution of the economic gains and losses incident to termination of the relationship of domestic partners."[78] The PRINCIPLES define domestic partners as "two persons of the same or opposite sex, not married to one another, who for a significant period of time share a primary residence and a life together as a couple."[79] Those who meet the definition of domestic partners are then subject to the same property and compensatory payment terms as married couples, and are permitted to modify their arrangements in accordance with the same principles that govern premarital and marital agreements.[80] The effect of such parity is to largely eliminate the distinctions between marital and nonmarital couples, at least in their obligations toward each other.[81] Indeed, marriage might effectively become irrelevant to the imposition of financial obligations. A couple who lived together for ten years, married, and divorced a year later would be treated as domestic partners from the point that they first shared a residence.[82] The 'entitlement' to marital property and support would extend all the way back to the beginning of cohabitation, and the marriage in year ten might have no affect on their obligations to each other at all.

This extension of the marital property and compensatory payments scheme to unmarried partners is absolutely consistent with the ALI's approach more generally. The domestic partnership chapter, the drafters observe, "is premised on the familiar principle that legal

[77] The PRINCIPLES observe that:

> Some authors have urged remedies under the property rubric, by treating the earning capacity of divorcing spouses as an item of marital property. *E.g.*, Joan C. Williams, *Married Women and Property*, 1 VA. J. SOC. POL'Y & L. 383 (1994). While the property approach is rejected by these PRINCIPLES, *see* § 4.07, that rejection is grounded upon the availability of a remedy under this Chapter that is substantively equivalent and that can fit more coherently within the general framework of dissolution remedies.

PRINCIPLES § 5.04, Reporter's Notes, cmt c, at 826.

[78] PRINCIPLES § 6.02(1).

[79] PRINCIPLES § 6.03(1).

[80] PRINCIPLES §§ 6.04–6.06.

[81] The PRINCIPLES note the major difference between married and unmarried relationships under the PRINCIPLES is the effect on third parties, which must recognize marriage, but not necessarily domestic partnerships, in providing benefits, liability, and other matters. *See* PRINCIPLES § 6.02 cmt b, at 915–16.

[82] PRINCIPLES § 6.04(2).

rights and obligations may arise from the conduct of parties with respect to one another, even though they have created no formal document or agreement setting forth such an undertaking."[83] The purpose of the chapter then becomes the equitable allocation of the gains and losses that arise from termination of a relationship in which the parties have intermingled their affairs.[84]

In the drafters' view, relationships often unfold over time without conscious direction. Some couples "begin a casual relationship that develops slowly into a durable union, by which time a formal marriage ceremony may seem awkward or even unnecessary," while others belong to ethnic and social groups with a substantially lower incidence of marriage.[85] Those who deliberately choose not to marry are easily dismissed as the unsympathetic cases of individuals who either have been "unhappy in prior marriages and therefore wish to avoid the form of marriage even as they enjoy its substance with a domestic partner," or who are in a stronger position socially or economically than their partner, "which allows the stronger partner to resist the weaker partner's preference for marriage."[86]

Missing from this list of unmarried cohabitants are those who choose not to marry because they are unwilling to make a long term commitment to the other party. Under the PRINCIPLES, if they stay in the same household long enough, they will have assumed such commitments whether they ever realized it or not.[87] This is not surprising. An approach that looks backward from dissolution to determine how to allocate gains and losses arising from the relationship's failure has no principled basis on which to distinguish between married and unmarried cohabitants.

D. Premarital Agreements

Particularly in their discussion of domestic partnerships, the drafters emphasize that the parties are free to contract around the results.[88] But they quickly add that such bargains are subject to the same provisions that govern other domestic agreements.[89] The provisions governing family agreements adopt the same backward looking approach, privileging the *ex post* perspective and undercutting the certainty of such bargains. The ALI's backward looking perspective on the forward looking topic – contract – illustrates its deep commitment to a new, noncontractual conception of family.

In approaching the validity of premarital contracts, the drafters start with the uncertainty of existing law. They explain that under fault-based divorce premarital agreements were

[83] PRINCIPLES § 6.02 cmt a, at 915.

[84] PRINCIPLES § 6.03 cmt b, at 918–19.

[85] PRINCIPLES § 6.02 cmt a, at 914.

[86] PRINCIPLES § 6.02 cmt a, at 914.

[87] Indeed, although this section achieves a measure of fairness more directly than the tortured decisions based on other rationales that have started to move in this direction, the major criticism has been the element of surprise. Couples who intentionally choose not to marry may not realize that they have been bound to comparable terms. *See, in particular*, Margaret F. Brinig, *Domestic Partnership: Missing the Target?* 4 J. L. FAM. STUD. 19 (2002) (arguing that empirical studies show that "cohabiting couples are less specialized than married couples, are less inter-dependent, and have far more embedded equality goals," and that imposing default rules unlikely to reflect the preferences of the parties is bad policy).

[88] PRINCIPLES § 6.02 cmt a, at 914–16, states:

> The Chapter does not impose all the consequences of recognition as domestic partners on every couple that falls within its definition because domestic partners may, by agreement, avoid the rules that this Chapter would otherwise apply. However, the freedom to contract with respect to a domestic relationship is not unlimited. It is subject, under traditional law as well as under Chapter 7, to some limitations not generally applicable to other contracts.

[89] PRINCIPLES § 6.02 cmt a, at 914–16.

unenforceable.[90] They then acknowledge that existing law provides greater ambit for such agreements, but without a consensus on the appropriate rules to apply, observing that:

> [T]here is today widespread agreement, in principle, that such agreements may be enforceable. This change followed in the wake of the widespread adoption of no-fault divorce. *See* § 7.01, cmt a. However, there is considerable variation in the willingness of courts to enforce particular agreements that may appear harsh or oppressive at dissolution. Some courts routinely enforce them as they would a business contract, while others deny enforcement, generally by distending ordinary contract principles or developing special exceptions applicable only to premarital agreements.[91]

In other words, existing law recognizes contract as the starting point for premarital agreements and then finds a way to enforce them selectively on the basis of noncontractual regulation.

The drafters do not wish to jettison all use of contract, particularly since they are eager to encourage parting couples to take charge of their own affairs. The drafters acknowledge that premarital bargaining encourages the parties to think realistically about their relationship, to plan for contingencies, and to secure greater certainty about the future.[92] In addition, the drafters note that enforceable contracts allow parties to meet the needs of their particular relationships when those relationships do not easily or appropriately fit the terms of more conventional arrangements.[93] Accordingly, the drafters embrace rather than resolve the ambiguity between the two approaches they identify in existing law. The drafters characterize their proposals as "a position between the English rule that premarital contracts are not binding, and a rule that would enforce them on the same basis as ordinary business contracts."[94] In adopting a middle position, they propose to balance the advantages of contracting autonomy with the special circumstances that apply to family agreements.

The drafters nonetheless take pains to distinguish family relationships from commercial bargains.[95] They assume that parties entering into commercial contracts are engaged in arms length transactions, with their eyes wide open to the conflicting interests of the other parties and possible contingencies that may confound their plans.[96]They have no such illusions about intimate partners. Fiancées are in a relationship of trust. The PRINCIPLES observe that "[p]ersons planning to marry usually assume that they share with their intended spouse a mutual and deep concern for one another's welfare. Business people negotiating a commercial agreement do not usually have such expectations of one another."[97] They do not believe that their relationships will end or that their needs will change years into the future. And the subject matter of their agreement – the family – affects not just the contracting parties, but their children, and thus the larger society. Accordingly, the drafters conclude that contract principles alone cannot adequately deal with the interests at stake.[98]

[90] *See generally* PRINCIPLES § 7.01, cmt a. Curiously, though, the drafters attribute unenforceability to the doctrine that invalidated premarital agreements that contemplated divorce, and not to the farther reaching concerns for the provision of women and children. *Compare* Simeone v. Simeone, *supra* note 27.

[91] PRINCIPLES § 7.02 cmt. a, at 954.

[92] PRINCIPLES § 7.02 cmt. a, at 954.

[93] PRINCIPLES § 7.02 cmt. a, at 954.

[94] PRINCIPLES § 7.02 cmt. a, at 955.

[95] PRINCIPLES § 7.02 cmts. a and b, at 955–58.

[96] PRINCIPLES § 7.02 cmts. a and b, at 955–58.

[97] PRINCIPLES § 7.02 cmt c, at 956.

[98] PRINCIPLES § 7.02 cmt c, at 956. For the suggestion that contract principles, in fact, offer more flexible consideration of such circumstances, see Brian H. Bix, *Premarital Agreement*, *supra* note 17, at 236.

The drafters deal with these competing concerns by using procedural safeguards to address the initial validity of the agreements, but reserving final judgment about substantive concerns until the time of enforcement. Both the procedural requirements and the substantive review raise the bar for the enforceability of premarital agreements, presumably to advance public policy rationales.

Traditional contract concerns might justify the procedural requirements. Commercial contracts, after all, must also be voluntary and free. The PRINCIPLES make explicit the procedural protections some courts have recognized, providing that "a party seeking to enforce an agreement must show that the other party's consent to it was informed and not obtained under duress."[99] A rebuttable presumption arises that the agreement was not signed under duress when the party seeking to enforce the agreement shows that:

(a) it was executed at least 30 days before the parties' marriage;
(b) both parties were advised to obtain independent legal counsel, and had reasonable opportunity to do so, before the agreement's execution; and,
(c) in the case of agreements concluded without the assistance of independent legal counsel for each party, the agreement states, in language easily understandable by an adult of ordinary intelligence with no legal training,
  (i) the nature of any rights or claims otherwise arising at dissolution that are altered by the contract, and the nature of that alteration, and
  (ii) that the interests of the spouses with respect to the agreement may be adverse.[100]

These requirements address the most common circumstances alleged to constitute coercion in the premarital bargaining, specifically, the presentation of the proposed agreement on the eve of the wedding, to a party unrepresented by counsel, who may not be aware either of the other party's assets or the legal provisions applicable in the absence of an agreement.

The drafters acknowledge, however, that the proposed protections exceed those mandated by contract principles. They maintain that:

> This heightened scrutiny is appropriate. Most parties contemplating marriage focus their attention on the life they anticipate sharing with their intended spouse, not on the financial aspects of a marital dissolution they do not expect to occur. Moreover, premarital agreements typically alter claims the parties would otherwise have on one another under applicable law, while parties to a commercial agreement typically have no obligations to one another other than those established by their agreement. It is appropriate for the law to apply a more demanding standard of contractual consent to an agreement altering established legal rights than it applies to an agreement that does not displace otherwise applicable public policies.[101]

And therein lies the rub. The drafters believe the PRINCIPLES would establish legal rights and address public concerns designed to protect the more vulnerable parties at

[99] PRINCIPLES § 7.04(2). [100] PRINCIPLES § 7.04(3).

[101] PRINCIPLES § 7.04 cmt b, at 962. The PRINCIPLES conclude that:

> In sum, nearly all premarital agreements involve special difficulties arising from unrealistic optimism about marital success, the human tendency to treat low probabilities as zero probabilities, the excessive discounting of future benefits, and the inclination to overweigh the importance of the immediate and certain consequences of agreement – the marriage – as against its contingent and future consequences.

PRINCIPLES § 7.05 cmt b, at 987.

dissolution. Having systematically crafted such protections, the drafters are reluctant to permit the more powerful and sophisticated party in an intimate relationship to dismantle them. Accordingly, the PRINCIPLES prescribe not only heightened procedural protections at the time of contracting, but a determination at the time of enforcement of whether the agreement would work a "substantial injustice."[102]

The restriction of contract is critical to the success of the ALI approach. Having expanded the obligations of marriage, it is essential not to make nonmarital cohabitation too attractive. And having expanded the obligation of cohabitants, it becomes important to limit their ability to contract around them.

The ALI could, however, have accomplished their goals through an *ex ante* approach. It could specify, for example, that waivers of compensatory payments, or the failure to provide for an incapacitated spouse are *prima facie* unconscionable. Instead, the PRINCIPLES adopt a wait-and-see approach. Such agreements are invalid only if by the time of dissolution the circumstances that would make them unfair have come to pass. This approach is consistent with the idea that it is the passage of time rather than the parties' implied consent that gives legitimacy to the results.

III. Back to the Future: When Does a Backward-Looking Jurisprudence Need to Become Forward-Looking?

The ALI serves a family law in transition precisely because it avoids the hardest questions at its core. It effectively distances itself from the most pervasive criticisms of traditional marriage, namely, that marriage encourages gender–based dependency through the creation of a privileged status that celebrates a sexual division of labor, and stigmatizes and penalizes the most vulnerable alternative family forms, unmarried households.[103] It also rejects the excesses of the other extreme, that is, a contract approach that treats family issues as private matters governed only by the agreements of its members, which leaves the most vulnerable and unprotected from exploitation by the relatively more powerful. It simultaneously does both by maintaining a detached neutrality toward the creation of family: all family forms are equal; none are to be encouraged or discouraged, but the members are responsible for the consequences of the arrangements undertaken, with the consequences determined from the perspective of dissolution. This backward looking approach, while it sidesteps many of the politically-charged controversies in family law, avoids two of family law's enduring issues: what is the source of authority for the imposition of the PRINCIPLES on family members and what future behavior will (and should) the ALI encourage.

The source of authority for the regulation of family matters is a matter of concern because the family stands at the crux of the divide between public and private.[104] On the one hand, the state has long been seen as having an essential stake in the family as the foundation of society and as a regulator of sexuality morality.[105] On the other hand,

[102] PRINCIPLES § 7.05. The ALI specifies such circumstances emphasizing the passage of time, the birth of children, and events the parties did not foresee.

[103] *See, in particular*, Scott, *supra* note 11, at 234 (Critics claim that marriage can not escape its history as a patriarchal institution that oppressed women who married and harshly discriminated against those who did not).

[104] *See generally*, June Carbone, *Morality, Public Policy And The Family: The Role Of Marriage And The Public/Private Divide*, 36 SANTA CLARA L. REV. 265 (1996).

[105] *See, e.g.*, Maynard v. Hill, 125 U.S. 190, 211 (1888); Loving v. Virginia, 388 U.S. 1, 12 (1967) (marriage is a basic right, "fundamental to our very existence and survival").

over the last two centuries the courts have also recognized a zone of privacy extending to family matters,[106] and finally to sexuality itself.[107] The state has historically mediated the tension between regulation and privacy by strictly regulating the incidents of marriage, after which it recognized the autonomy of family members within that sphere while pervasively regulating identical conduct outside of marriage.[108]

In rejecting the privileged status of marriage, the ALI has rejected the creation of a state-regulated status as the source of authority for its principles of dissolution. Many commentators have emphasized that this makes the imposition of state-mandated obligations at the dissolution of a domestic partnership "illiberal."[109] The same argument, however, can be made of the ALI approach toward marriage itself. The historic regulation of marriage is not "illiberal" in the sense of imposing a set of terms on unconsenting adults because marriage has been treated as a brightline status in which the parties can be held to an understanding of the prescribed terms. Domestic partners who sign no agreements, file no forms,[110] and participate in no ceremonies are different because they may find themselves bound to obligations that did not arise until the decision to end the relationship, and which are not tied to any clear point in the relationship.

The same thing, however, can be said of the ALI treatment of marriage. The property and compensatory payment provisions that the ALI applies to married couples at the dissolution of their union stem from behavior over the course of the marriage.[111] The ALI does not ground its provisions on an exchange of promises, a promise to remain married, or breach of the union's understood terms. Instead, the source of obligation for married and unmarried couples is identical, that is the "sharing of their lives over time" whether the parties elect such provisions or not.[112] For the married as well as the unmarried,

[106] The 19th century coupled strict regulation of marriage with a strict policy of nonintervention within. *See generally* Frances E. Olsen, *The Family and the Market: A Study of Ideology and Legal Reform*, 96 Harv. L. Rev. 1497, 1498–1500 (1983), Martha Albertson Fineman, *Symposium: Privacy and the Family: PANEL III: What Place for Family Privacy?*, 67 Geo. Wash. L. Rev. 1207 (1999) (family privacy is a legacy of the separate spheres distinguishing the public sector of market and state from the private sector of home and family, and limiting state intervention in the latter).

[107] *Compare* State v. Jones, 205 A.2d 507, 509 (Conn. Cir. Ct. 1964) (observing that "the standards of society are such that sexual relations or lascivious actions by persons who do not have the benefit of marriage to one another are regarded as obscene, unchaste and immoral") *with* Lawrence v. Texas, 539 U.S. 558 (1993) (holding that the liberty clause of the Constitution protects private sexual behavior, including homosexual sodomy, between consenting adults).

[108] Naomi Cahn notes that "Privacy within family law has two primary, and interrelated, meanings. First, privacy can mean privatization, the use of internal rather than external norms, and thus, the legal ability to control the rights and responsibilities that attach to any familial relationship. Second, privacy can denote a protected sphere, the right to engage in any activities that one chooses within that sphere." Naomi Cahn, *Symposium: Privacy and the Law: Models of Family Privacy*, 67 Geo. Wash. L. Rev. 1225, 1225 (1999). So, too, privacy in the context of the Principles can mean treating the family as an arena for private decision-making, with contract (i.e., provisions agreed upon by the parties) the only basis for state intervention, or it can mean autonomy to enter into whatever statuses the parties choose with intervention justified only at the breakup of the status.

[109] Scott, *supra* note 11, at 250. *See also* Marsha Garrison, Is Consent Necessary? An Evaluation of the Emerging Law of Cohabitant Obligation, 52 UCLA L. Rev. 815 (2005); Brinig, *supra* note 87.

[110] Statutory civil unions and domestic partnerships are quite different in that, like marriage, they require registration, and thus offer a bright line determination of status. *See* Harris, Teitelbaum and Carbone, *supra* note 8, at 267–77.

[111] Principles §§ 4.09–4.12 and § 5.03.

[112] *See* Principles § 5.04 cmt c, at 809. Also see the domestic partnership chapter, Chapter 6, which "is premised on the familiar principle that legal rights and obligations may arise from the conduct of parties with respect to one another, even though they have created no formal document or agreement setting forth such an undertaking." Principles § 6.02 cmt. a, at 915.

the results may bring surprise. Consider the following variation on a classic divorce case:

> Sam and Sally marry at twenty-nine. She is an airline pilot; he is a travel agent who earns two-thirds of her salary. They have no children and both remain employed in the same jobs throughout the marriage. After sixteen years of marriage, Sam tells Sally that he has had an affair and he is leaving her. Sally is devastated. She consults a lawyer and learns that, under the Principles, Sam is entitled to half of the assets accumulated over the marriage, which largely are the savings from Sally's earnings, a portion of the inheritance Sally received from her parents, who died shortly after the marriage began, and compensatory payments of several thousand a month (she now earns three times as much as Sam) for the next nine years.[113]

If Sam and Sally had cohabitated without marriage, Sally might be shocked to discover that the PRINCIPLES would impose almost the same financial obligations on her.[114] With marriage, Sally should be less surprised to discover that they must share their combined savings. She would presumably be more distressed to learn that Sam could leave her with impunity,[115] and be entitled to a substantial share of her inheritance and future earnings despite the fact that their lives were relatively unentwined – no children, no career sacrifices, no contributions to the other's earning potential.[116] If marriage comes with an exchange of promises, fixed commitments, or default provisions, the result might be more palatable, but the grounds for the ALI's conclusion, which roots Sally's obligations in assumptions about her relationship that might not be true, are unsatisfying and murky. Why should Sally accept an obligation to Sam that does not correspond to the promises they made to each other at the beginning of the relationship, their understandings of marriage as an institution, or the particular circumstances of their relationship?

At the end of the day, the ALI should identify more directly the source of the obligations the PRINCIPLES impose, and consider the implications for the beginning as well as the end of relationships. In more precisely defining the sources of obligation, the ALI must ultimately revisit the two sources it is so eager to reject: contract and noncontract, that is, either the voluntary assumption of responsibilities by parties free to contract around them or the imposition of state-mandated terms justified by the state interest in the relationships themselves. To rehabilitate these sources of obligation, it is necessary to distill their functional differences and, even more crucial, to build consent – and ultimately commitment – back into the undertaking.

The drafters' marginalization of contract turns on an extraordinarily narrow definition of what contract entails. The drafters are certainly correct that married couples expect their relationship to last, whatever the divorce statistics show.[117] They are also right that the "cognitive" limitations of bargaining make it unlikely that the parties will realistically

[113] While the PRINCIPLES leave to the states the precise calculations, one illustration to Section 5.06 used a statewide presumption of nine years of payments after a 15 year marriage. *See* PRINCIPLES § 5.06 cmt. b, at 851.

[114] The principle difference would be the treatment of her inheritance. *See* PRINCIPLES § 6.04.

[115] I have argued at length elsewhere that this scenario arises from the determination to make fault irrelevant to the proceeding, and that the elimination of fault is on balance justifiable in part because the marriages in which one party earns substantially more than the other after a long term marriage are the ones where the lower earning party is least likely to be the one to call it quits. *See* Carbone, *supra* note 66.

[116] The ALI deals separately with career sacrifices. *See* PRINCIPLES §§ 5.05, 6.06(1).

[117] *See* Lynn Baker & Robert Emery, *When Every Relationship is Above Average: Perceptions and Expectations of Divorce at the Time of Marriage*, 17 LAW & HUM. BEHAV. 439, 439 (1993).

anticipate or plan for future events.[118] They accurately cite the long line of cases since *Marvin v. Marvin* that use the uncertainty of intimate understandings as a reason to find no obligations whatsoever.[119] Nonetheless, the drafters ignore the contract-based provisions for addressing these difficulties in the context of other relational contracts.[120]

Only one essential element separates contractual from non-contractual sources of obligation: that is, the voluntary assumption of that responsibility by the parties, whether express or implied. This consent does not require that for each transaction the parties directly negotiate express terms. It does not even require that the parties anticipate future events. Instead, the law may supply, as it does for contracts generally, default terms that operate in the absence of the parties' agreement to the contrary.[121] Of course, there is no reason why the default terms could not come from the PRINCIPLES as drafted. If the PRINCIPLES were refashioned to use this "contractual" approach, only a few adjustments would be necessary. The most basic change would be one of perspective. If the PRINCIPLES' provisions were described as default terms, parties would then be encouraged to embrace them as central to the undertaking. Such a modification would be consonant with an *ex ante* partnership approach to relationships that treats marriage (and domestic partnerships, as discussed below) as a contract in which the sharing principle is central to the relationship.[122] If marriage were understood to mean a comingling of the partners' lives and finances and acceptance of responsibility for the result, then a coequal division of the property accumulated during the marriage, a gradual transformation of separate into marital property, and some acceptance of responsibility for the disparities in earning power at the end of the relationships can be easily justified.[123] The parting couple would be obligated to each other for postdivorce disparities because they undertook that responsibility as part of their relationship, not just because the disparities arose over the course of time together.

A more difficult issue would be the enforceability of express contracts that depart from these terms. If the cornerstone of marital obligation were voluntary agreement, then the parties should ordinarily be free to vary the terms. While even the most commercial of ordinary contracts, however, are limited by principles of unconscionability, contract

[118] PRINCIPLES § 7.05, cmt. b (Cognitive flaws and contractual integrity).

[119] PRINCIPLES § 6.03, cmt. b; *See also* Ira Ellman, *Unmarried Partners and the Legacy of Marvin v. Marvin: "Contract Thinking" was Marvin's Fatal Flaw*, 76 NOTRE DAME L. REV. 1365 (2001).

[120] Scott, *supra* note 11 at 259–60, n.110; *See also* Scott and Scott, *supra* note 27.

[121] Scott and Scott, *supra* note 27, at 1251, observe, for example, that:

> Most people contemplating marriage don't bargain explicitly over the terms that will govern the performance of their marital obligations, or consciously select among different enforcement options to ensure that each will behave in the future in ways that advance their shared goals. It is tempting to conclude, therefore, that the idea of a "marital bargain" is entirely hypothetical. But the fact that people seldom bargain explicitly over marriage is, in large part, a function of the relative harmony between their preferences and the societal norms and legal default rules that form the common understandings about marital behavior and of the relative immaturity of tailor-made alternatives to the standard marital regime. People who marry approach the relationship with a baseline of expectations that are a function of existing societal norms and of the existing legal regime. To incorporate all these expectations into their own relationship, they need only to exchange marital vows in a legally endorsed ceremony.

[122] *See* discussion, *supra* at notes 53 to 57, and accompanying text.

[123] The hardest aspect element to justify is not the PRINCIPLES' particular terms, but the decision to impose the terms without consideration of fault. The terms, however, can be justified as addressing the role of fault in the cases where it is most likely to occur, without the difficulties presented by individual adjudications. *See* Carbone, *supra* note 66, at 74–75 (arguing, for example, that compensatory payments were likely to be most important in long-term marriages in which higher earning men left lower earning women, and these types of cases were also the ones most likely to involve traditional fault grounds (adultery, cruelty, or the unexcused decision to leave) by the higher earning partner).

unconscionability is ordinarily determined at the time of the agreement.[124] The difficulty with the ALI approach, which accepts the presumptive legitimacy of private bargains, is that it determines their enforceability only with the passage of time. Accordingly, the ALI message is a mixed one: you are free to write whatever agreement you want, but the validity of your bargain depends on what happens later. The bargain is necessarily tentative; the parties are not encouraged to rely on its terms.

The ALI could, however, keep the same principles and state them in *ex ante* terms. California, for example, recently decided a case in which the wife, who had been married for eight years at the time of the divorce, suffered a horrific automobile accident during the marriage that left her permanently incapacitated.[125] The court held that while not all waivers of spousal support are unenforceable, this one was unconscionable at the time of enforcement.[126] The court emphasized that public policy does not permit the discarding of disabled spouses without support.[127] While this type of ruling is often given as an example of the type of case where an agreement is held unconscionable only at the time of enforcement, it could also be stated as a prospective rule: that waivers of spousal support that fail to provide for the other spouse's incapacity are prima facie unconscionable at the time of contracting.[128] If, in fact, the ALI has a robust conception of the public policy responsibilities of intimate couples, why not articulate such obligations as part of the initial determinations of enforceability so that the parties can take such concerns into account in their bargaining?[129] The drafters dealt with the limitations of voluntary consent by specifically providing for the circumstances such as the surprise agreement presented on the eve of the wedding that most commonly occur in the case law; they could craft comparable provisions that define substantive unconscionability from the outset of the relationship.[130]

The hardest issue, however, is the selection of default terms parties are unlikely to choose on their own. Marrying couples may largely be willing to accept relationship terms that make each responsible for the other.[131] Unmarried cohabitants are far more likely to be unmarried because they do not wish to assume the responsibilities of marriage.[132] Moreover, for those who wish to vary the institution's terms, the marriage ceremony itself is

[124] It has been noted, for example, that contract law routinely polices the bargaining process for duress and unconscionability, and often prescribes mandatory terms. *See* Scott and Scott, *supra* note 27, at 1258.

[125] Rosendale v. Rosendale, 119 Cal. App. 14th 1202, 15 Cal. Rptr. 3d 137 (2004).

[126] *Id.* at 1213–14.

[127] *Id.*

[128] Indeed, the relatively procontract UMDA had a provision rendering a waiver of spousal support that left a spouse dependent on public assistance unenforceable as a matter of public policy. PRINCIPLES § 7.01, cmt. d.

[129] Howard Fink and June Carbone, *Between Private Ordering and Public Fiat: A New Paradigm for Family Law Decision-making*, 5 J. L. FAM. STUD. 1, 28–29 (2003) (arguing that "good lawyers" include some provision for shared property and spousal support as a way to enhance the validity of the agreements they draft).

[130] *See* PRINCIPLES § 7.04(3). Contractual unconscionability is determined at the time of contracting, not at the time of enforcement, in accordance with a relatively open-ended standard. Nonetheless, the drafters have dealt with what would be termed procedural unconscionability in the contract context by providing explicit guidance on the most common circumstances, and there is no reason why they could not take the same approach to the substantive issues. *See* Fink and Carbone, *supra* note 129, at 28–29, giving examples of such terms, and explaining how they can be applied in an *ex ante* proceeding.

[131] *See* Steven L. Nock, *A Comparison of Marriages and Cohabiting Relationships*, J. FAM. ISSUES 16 (January 1995); Baker and Emery, *supra* note 117.

[132] Nock, *supra* note 131, at 53; Marin Clarkberg et al., *Attitudes, Values, and the Entrance into Cohabitational versus Marital Unions*, 74 SOC. FORCES 609, 621–24 (1995) (reporting that cohabitation is preferred to marriage by those segments of the population who desire more flexibility in their relationships and reject the constraints of marriage).

likely to inspire a flurry of contract drafting. Unmarried cohabitants, in contrast, experience no single moment likely to prompt a trip to the lawyer (or even the form shop). Thus, while the PRINCIPLES, as applied to married couples, can overwhelmingly be justified as default terms the parties likely would select for themselves, subject to relatively minor public policy limitations, anchoring the imposition of duties on unmarried cohabitants on contract is much less plausible.[133] This raises the question: can the ALI terms be directly justified on public policy grounds, and, if so, are domestic partners on notice of the terms?

The ALI's treatment of unmarried partners appears to be motivated by two concerns. First, the ALI wishes to distance the PRINCIPLES from the historic stigma associated with nonmarital intimate relationships.[134] Instead, it wishes to acknowledge such relationships and treat them on something closer to equal terms. Second, the ALI is concerned with the potential exploitation of the more vulnerable partner, and seeks to mandate terms to prevent that result.[135]

The historic approach to the disadvantages associated with a gendered division of labor and the dependency associated with child rearing was to treat marriage as the solution.[136] If the parties were to undertake the rigors of family life, then they needed to do so within marriage both to insure protection of the vulnerable and to ensure a claim on societal resources, public and private, for assistance. This, of course, is the very system that the PRINCIPLES seek to dismantle.

Instead, the ALI wishes to turn on its head the relationship between legal obligation and the assumption of family responsibilities. It treats all family forms on equal terms. The parties are welcome to qualify their commitments, switch partners as often as they like, and receive recognition for their parental undertakings, but if they stay together long enough, they cannot deny responsibility for each other. Let us, however, return to the case of Sam and Sally. If instead of marrying, they live together in an uncommitted relationship for sixteen years and, like many cohabitating couples, do not have children or influence each other's careers, can they really be said to have assumed such responsibilities? When? Why?

To gain acceptance for its approach, the PRINCIPLES must ultimately spark a transformation of family law that is forward looking in at least three respects. First, rather than taking parties as they find them, the PRINCIPLES must contribute to the remaking of the norms intimate couples bring to the table. Second, to do so, the PRINCIPLES must influence the understandings that attend the creation and not just the dissolution of relationships. Finally, the PRINCIPLES must move beyond rejection of decaying doctrines of the past to lay the foundation for the rebuilding of the family law norms of the future.[137]

IV. Creating Commitment

Professor Robert Frank in a symposium on precommitment theory, explored the relationship between norms, moral emotions, and commitment. He observed that the rational

[133] As Nock observes, "We lack consensus over what it means to be a cohabiting partner." Nock, *supra* note 131, at 56.

[134] For fuller development of this issue, *See* Scott, *supra* note 11, at nn. 17–30, and accompanying text.

[135] *See* Part C, *supra*, particularly note 89 and accompanying text.

[136] For a feminist critique of this system, see Fineman, *supra* note 31.

[137] The idea that legal rules may influence social norms is hardly new. *See* Lawrence Lessig, *Social Meaning and Social Norms*, 144 U. PA. L. REV. 2181 (1996); Cass R. Sunstein, *On the Expressive Function of Law*, 144 U. PA. L. REV. 2021 (1996); Richard H. McAdams, *The Origin, Development, and Regulation of Norms*, 96 MICH. L. REV. 338, 380–81 (1997). I predict that, to the extent the PRINCIPLES depart from existing norms, they will either wither on the vine or prompt reconsideration of the norms.

actor model, which predicts that individuals will act in their own self-interest, cannot explain why large numbers of people vote, leave tips in restaurants far from home, or donate to charity.[138] His answer, which he terms adaptive rationality, is that many (but not all) people have a taste for cooperation, and that "if moral sentiments can be reliably discerned by others, then the complex interaction of genes and culture that yields human preferences can sustain preferences that lead people to subordinate narrow self-interest to the pursuit of other goals."[139] In other words, if we effectively internalize norms associated with cooperative behavior, and reliably signal to others our willingness to live by such norms, we encourage the type of cooperation that makes at least one party more vulnerable, but produces better results for everyone.[140]

Does this apply to intimate relationships? Of course. Professor Elizabeth Scott describes the production of commitment as central to her conception of marriage, which she describes as:

> [A] status available to individuals who want to formally undertake a long-term commitment to another person of the same or opposite sex, to live together in an intimate and exclusive family union – a union dissolvable only through formal legal action. The exchange of marriage vows represents each party's implicit agreement to be bound by a regime of informal social norms underscoring their commitment to the relationship and by a set of legal rights and obligations affirming that the union is one of economic sharing and mutual care. These obligations include the duty to care for one another and for any children who become part of the family, to share property and income acquired during the union, and to provide support to dependent family members should the union dissolve. Couples who undertake this formal commitment to one another become eligible to receive any array of government benefits and privileges, recognizing that their relationship of mutual care and support benefits society as well as themselves.[141]

Marriage in Professor Scott's terms succeeds when it assists couples to internalize norms associated with economic sharing and mutual care. It does so in part through a public affirmation of the spouses' bonds with each other, and their obligation to respect their vows for the benefit not only of each other, but of friends, family, community, and state. In this sense, marriage is a human institution adapted for the production of cooperative behavior.

For Professor Scott, marriage entails an assumption of responsibility for the vulnerabilities produced by the relationship and its dissolution, a view that is similar to the ALI's. The principal difference between these views is that, for Professor Scott, the obligation arises from the commitment the parties make to each other at the beginning of their relationship, not something produced by the unforeseeable unfolding of events. The distinction is important if the objective is not just to impose minimal obligations on those who fall within the ALI's definition, but to instill norms that encourage acceptance of the responsibility as part of what it means to enter into an intimate relationship. Scott emphasizes, as noted above, that nonmarital relationships differ significantly from marital ones.[142] They are less likely to endure, more likely to be characterized by infidelity and domestic violence,

[138] Robert H. Frank, *Commitment Problems in the Theory of Rational Choice*, 81 Tex. L. Rev. 1789 (2003).
[139] *Id.* at 1793.
[140] Frank emphasized that his observations of human rationality are designed to solve a variety of commitment problems. *Id.*
[141] Scott, *supra* note 11, at nn. 36–37, and accompanying text.
[142] *Id.* at nn. 62–66, and accompanying text.

and less likely to produce individuals who are happy with their relationship.[143] In addition, cohabitating couples are less likely to share assets or intermingle finances. This suggests both that cohabiting couples enter their relationships with different understandings from spouses and that the understandings they have are less likely to fit with the PRINCIPLES.

Does this mean the PRINCIPLES should be rejected? Not necessarily. The PRINCIPLES do reflect a family law in disarray. The test of their success will be if they help bring order to the chaos. In asking whether the PRINCIPLES will assist or undercut future efforts at commitment, it is important to inquire more deeply into the following issues suggested briefly by the drafters.

1. What Will Be the Impact on Marriage of the Principles That Deal with Cohabitation?

The drafters observe that: "It is not an objective of [the domestic partnership] Chapter to encourage parties to enter a non-marital relationship as an alternative to marriage. On the contrary, to the extent that some individuals avoid marriage in order to avoid responsibilities to a partner, this Chapter reduces the incentive to avoid marriage because it diminishes the effectiveness of that strategy."[144] To the extent the drafters are correct, they may reinvigorate the case for marriage. But that effect requires acceptance of their basic principle: that all of those entering into an enduring intimate relationship must assume responsibility for each other. If an older generation passed judgment on those engaging in sexual intercourse without marriage (reserving, of course, the greatest stigma for women), the ALI is passing judgment on those who engage in cohabitation without assuming a level of responsibility comparable to marriage. Ultimately, the ALI's message may be renewed insistence on committed relationships as the *sine qua non* of responsible intimate partnerships.

2. Has the ALI Effectively Sidestepped the Problem of Fault?

The greatest difficulty with the example of Sam and Sally is the problem of fault. If they are married, they have promised to remain together for life, and Sam has breached that obligation to Sally's distress. Why should she be responsible for the loss Sam experiences from leaving a relationship he ended? If Sam and Sally have not married, the problem is greater since Sam has no reasonable reliance on the continued existence of a relationship and no basis on which to claim a contribution to Sally's higher income. I have concluded elsewhere that at least for married couples, the drafters are right that bringing fault back into the equation is not worth the vindictiveness it is likely to engender.[145] The interaction of several sections of the PRINCIPLES, however, raises at least three opportunities to mitigate the potential unfairness without explicit recognition of fault:

First, Section 4.12(6), which allows the recharacterization of separate into marital property, is subject to a limitation that allows consideration of "substantial injustice." The example given involves an inheritance of great sentimental value, such as a watch, that cannot be easily divided. It is conceivable that substantial injustice is influenced by the circumstances of the breakup, albeit *sub silentio*.

Second, a court, upset by Sam's desertion of Sally, may conclude that they were never domestic partners. The more flexible standards for domestic partners, which emphasize

[143] *Id.*

[144] PRINCIPLES § 6.02, cmt. b, at 916.

[145] Carbone, *supra* note 66, at 72–73.

sharing "a primary residence and life together as a couple," might be interpreted in a backward looking way to reflect the court's conclusion about the fairness of the proposed financial division.[146]

Third, the provisions that hinge on the length of the relationship coexist with provisions that depend on the presence of children, lost career opportunities, and the like.[147] If courts place more emphasis on the provisions that follow from a relationship's particular arrangements and less on the mere passage of time, the determination of responsibility for the end of the relationship will matter less.[148] If Sam forewent his own earnings potential to care for the children or to facilitate Sally's career, he should be entitled to compensation irrespective of the reasons for the relationship's dissolution. In the end, however, enforcement of sharing principles without consideration of fault is likely to be tenable only if the enforcement primarily occurs in circumstances that correspond to our perceptions of fairness.[149]

3. Can the ALI Provisions Be Restated as the Terms of Marital Partnership?

The ALI effectively embraces an ethic of sharing that grounds its financial dissolution provisions in the type of partnership rationale that justifies joint ownership – and mutual commitment. While the drafters eschew property rhetoric almost as much as they do contract doctrine, the PRINCIPLES lay a foundation for a revitalized conception of partnership – applied at a minimum to married couples, unmarried couples barred from marriage by legal disabilities such as a same-sex relationship, those undertaking nonmarital child rearing, and domestic partners without children who choose not to marry. For all but the latter, the law could establish bright-line moments when partnership obligations begin.[150] The challenge for the long term success of the PRINCIPLES is whether the insistence on including this latter group will ultimately undermine or advance recognition of new terms for the beginning as well as the end of family relationships.

V. Conclusion

The PRINCIPLES ultimately rest on a deeply held normative vision that parties in a long term intimate relationship should be responsible for each other. It is obligation without formality, and obligation without fault, but it is clearly obligation, nonetheless. The PRINCIPLES, whether or not they are enacted into law, should prompt renewed attention to the ideals of mutual responsibility and commitment. With systematic articulation of the ideal, the PRINCIPLES should also encourage renewed consideration of the mechanisms that prompt broad acceptance of their principles, individual internalization of the values on which the principles rest, and fidelity to the principles in practice.

I would like to thank Jaqueline Hand for her comments on earlier drafts for this chapter, and Alexander Weddle for his research support.

[146] PRINCIPLES § 6.03.

[147] *See, e.g.*, PRINCIPLES § 5.05.

[148] *See* Carbone, *supra* note 66, at 69 (lost earning capacity can be awarded on no-fault basis).

[149] *Id.* at 75. Long term marriages are most likely to end because of the decision or infidelity of the higher earning party.

[150] Indeed, childbirth is likely to be as emotionally intense an experience as marriage. Given the formal registration of legal parents, it provides an opportunity to identify couples embarking on a joint enterprise. Same-sex couples are easily subsumed under comparable regimes for married couples, with registration or joint parenting creating a basis for the recognition of their relationships.

12 Money as Emotion in the Distribution of Wealth at Divorce

Katharine B. Silbaugh

The ALI's PRINCIPLES take an incoherent body of law governing the treatment of nonfinancial contributions to wealth accumulated during marriage, a body of law with many unresolved tensions, and treat it as might be expected. To the ALI's credit, the PRINCIPLES' treatment of nonfinancial matters, although it too is incoherent, is more thoughtful than the underlying law it seeks to organize and describe. Nonetheless, this chapter examines one deeply flawed choice animating the PRINCIPLES, the attempt to separate financial and nonfinancial matters.[1]

The PRINCIPLES attempt to separate emotional and personal aspects of a marriage from financial ones in numerous places.[2] The drafters' approach is to acknowledge and settle financial issues between the parties, but to leave nonfinancial disputes without legal remedy. The drafters aim to avoid dealing with the more emotional issues surrounding marital dissolution by removing nonfinancial matters from consideration.[3] This approach is problematic for several reasons. First, most marriages include countless negotiations and bargains weighing financial matters against nonfinancial matters. Remedies that fail to capture those bargains are likely to be unfair. Second, this approach fails to appreciate how emotional the financial issues can become within marriages and at the time of marital dissolution. Finances are not distinct from emotions in relationships, but are an avenue through which spouses express emotions. Finally, even if it were well advised, the drafters' attempt to sever nonfinancial matters from divorce proceedings is futile. Despite the drafters' strong commitment to ignoring nonfinancial matters, the PRINCIPLES lapse sporadically back into accounting for them in various financial formulas.[4] Although we may wish that legal remedies at divorce could unfold without the thorniest nonfinancial matters coming into the litigation, those matters are essential to the broken bargain and impossible to remove from consideration. The drafters do a disservice to divorce litigation by attempting to bury issues that will inevitably resurface in different forms. In a few places, the drafters seem to acknowledge that financial and nonfinancial aspects of marriage cannot be separated. We must decide whether to view this as an inconsistency, or instead, as an inevitability.

[1] Although the drafters' resolution of the financial/nonfinancial divide is not satisfactory, the drafters deserve genuine respect for the skill, wisdom, and intelligence with which they have approached this problem.

[2] *See, e.g.*, Principles §§ 5.02 cmt. b, at 790 (discussing spousal support) and 7.08 (governing premarital agreements).

[3] Principles § 5.02 cmt. b, at 790.

[4] *See, e.g.*, PRINCIPLES § 5.07 (compensating for a spouse's loss in earning capacity as a result of caring for a dependent child or relative).

This chapter does not argue that the drafters failed to consider the complexities of the problem. Instead, it argues that they have dealt with one of the thorniest issues in family law by choosing simply to take it off the table. This choice does not necessarily lack courage. But I believe it represents wishful thinking. This chapter argues that it is impossible to separate money from emotion, as the PRINCIPLES strive to do. While this chapter does not offer a better solution, the choice the drafters make bears understanding and analysis.

This chapter maps out the PRINCIPLES' treatment of nonfinancial matters in property division, alimony awards, and premarital agreements in Section I. It examines first the consequences and next the rationale for the ALI's exclusion of nonfinancial matters in Section II. In Section III, the chapter examines one provision of the PRINCIPLES which governs financial misconduct. It uses this example to illustrate the impossibility of excluding nonfinancial matters from consideration, as nonfinancial matters become masked as financial ones.

I. How the PRINCIPLES Manage Nonfinancial Matters

It is first necessary to illustrate the drafters' approach to the separation of financial and nonfinancial matters. While the PRINCIPLES draw the line between nonfinancial and financial matters in many provisions, a few examples will suffice here.

A. Compensatory Spousal Payments

The clearest and most significant example of line-drawing between financial and nonfinancial matters comes in Section 5.02, which explains Compensatory Spousal Payments.[5] The very purpose of compensatory payments or alimony is to "allocate financial losses that arise at the dissolution of a marriage."[6] Imagine the sentence without the term "financial."[7] Some people would assume it was limited to financial losses, while others would imagine an open-ended inquiry into the conditions of the marriage. However, the drafters' choice to include the term "financial" makes it clear that they know that these losses are only one slice of the losses associated with the end of a marriage. The term is inserted to clarify the limited scope of the remedy, that is, the cognizable losses for which a court can account.

The PRINCIPLES devote comment b in Section 5.02 to explaining the exclusion of nonfinancial losses. That comment acknowledges the reality of nonfinancial gains and losses as it chooses to ignore them: "[d]ivorce also imposes emotional losses and emotional gains, but these PRINCIPLES do not recognize these as an element of awards."[8] The decision to recognize only financial losses rests on the notion that financial issues and emotional issues are separate: "[t]he pains and joys that individuals find from divorce are not commensurable with its financial costs..."[9]

The notes to comment b refer readers to an influential law review article written by the PRINCIPLES' chief reporter, Professor Ira Ellman, on the same subject.[10] Here, as elsewhere in the PRINCIPLES, there is every sign that the drafters know that financial issues

[5] PRINCIPLES § 5.02.

[6] PRINCIPLES § 5.02(1).

[7] *Id.*

[8] PRINCIPLES § 5.02 cmt. b, at 790.

[9] *Id.*

[10] *Id.* (citing Ira Mark Ellman, *Should the Theory of Alimony Include Nonfinancial Losses and Motivations?*, 1991 B. Y. U. L. REV. 259).

and emotional issues are entirely intertwined in reality, but incommensurable for legal purposes.

B. Marital Agreements

While compensatory spousal payments are the best example of the drafters' commitment to this separation, there are others. Consider the treatment of marital agreements in Chapter 7 of the PRINCIPLES.[11] In keeping with state law, the PRINCIPLES allow for the enforcement of agreements governing finances, while rejecting enforcement of agreements that govern what are in essence the nonfinancial elements.[12] Section 7.08 bars enforcement of agreements that would provide for a financial penalty if divorce follows marital misconduct – agreements that would institute for the couple the fault-regarding distribution systems still alive in some states.[13] The PRINCIPLES also reject enforcement of agreements that hinge financial payments on particular conduct within marriage, such as fidelity, or some other nonfinancial benefit.[14]

C. Fault-Blind Divorce and Division of Assets

The sidelining of nonfinancial matters is also expressed in the drafters' decision not to account for contributions to a marriage in dividing assets,[15] and not to consider fault either as a ground for divorce or in financial settlements.[16]

II. Evaluating the Separation of the Financial from the Nonfinancial

Once the drafters concede that separating the nonfinancial elements is not the same thing as denying that they exist, several questions arise. First, is it a large or a small matter to address and remedy only financial issues? Is the separation justified and if so, how? Can there be justice with the two separated? Should we assess the justice question abstractly, or gauge it more practically by the litigants' satisfaction? Does the satisfaction of other actors in the system, primarily divorce attorneys and judges, take precedence over the litigants' satisfaction? This Part considers each of these questions.

A. Is the Exclusion of Nonfinancial Matters a Large or Small Matter?

The relationship between financial and nonfinancial matters is not simply an attribute of marriage. It is perhaps the defining attribute of marriage.[17] Marriage is the constant exchange of financial and nonfinancial things, monetary and nonmonetary ones. Some of

[11] PRINCIPLES § 7.

[12] PRINCIPLES § 7.08(2) (making unenforceable agreements to limit or enlarge grounds for divorce or agreements requiring a court to evaluate marital misconduct in awarding alimony or dividing marital property.)

[13] PRINCIPLES § 7.08 cmt. b, at 1005.

[14] *Id.*

[15] PRINCIPLES § 4.09 cmt. b, at 734. This is an area where most states have at least formally considered nonfinancial contributions.

[16] PRINCIPLES § 4.09 cmt. e, at 734.

[17] For further discussion, see Katharine B. Silbaugh, *Turning Labor into Love: Housework and the Law*, 91 NW. U. L. REV. 1 (1996) [hereinafter Silbaugh, *Turning Labor Into Love*]; Katharine B. Silbaugh, *Marriage Contracts and the Family Economy*, 93 NW. U. L. REV. 65 (1998) [hereinafter Silbaugh, *Marriage Contracts*]; Katharine B. Silbaugh, *Commodification and Women's Household Labor*, 9 YALE J. L. & FEMINISM 81 (1997); Katharine B. Silbaugh, *Gender*

those nonmonetary ones are well understood to be "economic," such as household labor that provides material benefits. Some nonmonetary exchanges are not as often characterized as financial, including the exchange of counseling, support, love, sex, companionship, loyalty, compliments, or entertainment. These exchanges can result from overt bargaining as well as simple reciprocity. The exchanges are a defining attribute of family relationships.

Often, money in marriage is exchanged for a nonmonetary benefit, as when a wage is brought home and shared in exchange for homemaking. Family law has come to recognize and account for this exchange, as evidenced by the homemaker provisions in equitable distribution statutes.[18] But that exchange is not the only instance where there is a relationship between money and marital conduct. They are more deeply inseparable than that near-labor contract would suggest. Even the giving of money is the giving of nonmonetary benefits: people given money within marriage may experience it as care for them and for the relationship. People who give money may do so as an expression of love, making the giving of money in effect the giving of love. The withholding of money can imply the inverse. Money is fully imbued with the emotions of the marriage. When a marriage later falls apart, it is no wonder that feelings of betrayal and loss include financial betrayal and resentment. The financial unwinding of a marriage is not distinct from the emotional accounting rejected by the PRINCIPLES. It is one very significant element of it. The best that can be said, then, is that the drafters selectively reject nonfinancial matters, since financial ones are so laden with nonfinancial attributes as to be easily classified as emotional and nonfinancial in nature.

From the drafters' comments, it appears that they appreciate the countless ways in which marriage can be thus characterized as an exchange. Has comment b to Section 5.02 correctly characterized these other gains and losses when it calls them the "emotional losses and gains?"[19] I have argued that financial losses are emotional losses. Money, both during and after marriage, is emotional and intimate. People work to provide money to their families, and consider that act an expression of commitment and love. Couples fight about money more than they fight about anything else in marriage.[20] Divorcing couples themselves judge the financial outcome of a divorce in light of marital conduct, no matter how many times their lawyers tell them fault does not matter.

Policy makers might have particular concerns about paying attention to financial but not nonfinancial matters. The nonfinancial versus financial aspects of marriage are significantly gendered.[21]

There is another concern. The parties may continue to exchange some nonfinancial benefits after dissolution, although this exchange will not appear as such under the Principles. While the PRINCIPLES acknowledge homemakers and primary caretakers who give up earning capacity to care for dependents, their analysis is limited to loss of earning capacity, not the ongoing flow of benefits from unpaid labor. Consider ongoing child care by a custodial parent after a divorce. Child support pays for expenditures that will need to be made on a child's behalf, but not for the actual labor of raising the child. If such labor impairs a

and Nonfinancial Matters in the ALI Principles of the Law of Family Dissolution, 8 DUKE J. GENDER L. & POL'Y 203 (2001).

[18] *See, e.g.*, UMDA § 307.

[19] Principles § 5.02 cmt. b, at 790.

[20] *See* PHILIP BLUMSTEIN & PEPPER SCHWARTZ, AMERICAN COUPLES: MONEY, WORK, AND SEX 53, 77–93, (1983); *see generally* Silbaugh, *Marriage Contracts, supra*, at 109–11 & nn. 165–66.

[21] *See generally* Silbaugh, *Turning Labor into Love, supra* note 17; Silbaugh, *Marriage Contracts, supra* note 17.

parent's earning capacity, that may be addressed through compensatory payments.[22] But there is a continued flow of labor to the benefit of the noncustodial parent, who still has continued responsibility for the child's welfare. It is possible to pretend to offset that labor against the noncustodial parent's sense of loss from not living with his or her child, which the PRINCIPLES allude to.[23] But the grounds for assuming an equal exchange of financial and nonfinancial benefits during the marriage, if there ever were any, no longer exists postdivorce. The only assurance given by the PRINCIPLES that the exchange of financial and nonfinancial benefits is equal during marriage is that if it were not, one spouse would exit.[24] Because exit has already happened after divorce, the ongoing postdivorce flow of nonfinancial benefits needs a better account than the PRINCIPLES give.

B. Is the Exclusion of Nonfinancial Matters Justified?

The drafters justify the exclusion of nonfinancial matters from compensatory spousal payments in comment b to Section 5.02 as follows:

> The reasons for this exclusion are pragmatic as well as principled. The pains and joys that individuals find from divorce are not commensurable with its financial costs, so that there is no method for determining the extent to which compensation for a financial loss should be reduced or enlarged to reflect nonfinancial gains or losses. Any effort to consider the emotional consequences of divorce would also require evaluation of the parties' marital conduct. A spouse may experience relief or even joy from having terminated an oppressive marriage, but we presumably would not wish to reduce that spouse's financial claims by assigning monetary value to these emotional gains. So also if joy came from the freedom to pursue an intimate relationship with a third person that had begun during the marriage, unless we distinguish the cases on grounds of fault.... To include consideration of emotional losses and gains would require a more general examination of marital misconduct, which this section rejects.[25]

To summarize this rationale: first, nonfinancial losses are not commensurable with financial losses; that is to say, there is no common metric between them. That is what is meant by "there is no method for determining the extent to which compensation for a financial loss should be reduced or enlarged to reflect nonfinancial gains or losses."[26] Second, counting nonfinancial gains and losses would be inconsistent with a core tenet of the PRINCIPLES, the elimination of the fault determination.[27] That is what is meant by "To include consideration of emotional losses and gains would require a more general examination of marital misconduct, which this section rejects."[28]

These two justifications appear in other provisions where the PRINCIPLES limit nonfinancial losses. For example, in arguing against the enforcement of marriage agreements pertaining to nonfinancial matters, the PRINCIPLES say that courts would find themselves "policing the details of intimate relationships," a task that the drafters believe is inconsistent with the elimination of fault-based divorce.[29]

This subpart considers these two rationales, incommensurability and the no-fault philosophy, in reverse order. It then concludes with one of the drafters' mitigating assumptions:

[22] PRINCIPLES § 502(3)(a).

[23] PRINCIPLES § 5.02 comment b, at 791.

[24] PRINCIPLES § 5.02, comment c, at 791.

[25] PRINCIPLES § 5.02 cmt. b, at 790.

[26] *Id.*

[27] PRINCIPLES § 1, Topic 2, pt. I, at 42–43.

[28] PRINCIPLES § 5.02 cmt. b, at 790.

[29] PRINCIPLES § 7.08 cmt. a, at 1004.

that the give and take of financial and nonfinancial matters within marriage evens out in the end, because otherwise couples would divorce.[30]

1. The Fault Inquiry

While this chapter does not advocate the reintroduction of fault per se, the PRINCIPLES' use of the no-fault concept to justify the exclusion of nonfinancial matters is nonetheless troubling. A glaring circularity marks the rationale offered by the PRINCIPLES. The drafters give two reasons for excluding fault:

> [T]he position taken by the PRINCIPLES on this question follows from both the goal of improving the consistency and predictability of dissolution law, and the core tenet that the dissolution law provides compensation for only the *financial* losses arising from the dissolution of marriage.[31]

The PRINCIPLES have failed completely on one of the two explanations offered for ignoring nonfinancial matters: that consideration would too closely resemble an evaluation of fault. At the same time, the drafters reject consideration of fault because it resembles compensating for nonfinancial matters. These justifications are completely circular: considering fault looks too much like considering nonfinancial matters, while considering nonfinancial matters looks too much like considering fault. If the similarity to fault fails as an independent reason to sideline nonfinancial matters, only consistency and predictability are offered to justify eliminating fault, and incommensurability to justify ignoring nonfinancial losses and gains.

Consider, then, the impact of the position on fault taken by the PRINCIPLES. The distaste for fault extends well beyond eliminating fault grounds for divorce. It includes rejecting any inquiry that reminds us of a fault inquiry. Thus the PRINCIPLES disallow marital agreements governing marital conduct because the inquiry could be similar to a fault inquiry.[32] The equation of the two bases glosses over significant differences between adjudicating fault where the parties have asked a court to, as is the case with a marital agreement governing fault, and adjudicating fault where one or both parties resist it. To the drafters the elimination of fault grounds for divorce is adequate to justify the elimination of any adjudication that could resemble fault-based determinations.

A driving motivation for marginalizing nonfinancial matters is an unwillingness to investigate the details of intimate relationships. The fault debate will continue to be had elsewhere. But to understand the way in which avoiding fault inquiries motivates and bleeds into all sorts of other decisions within the PRINCIPLES, it is crucial to unmask the precise objection here: is it squeamishness about investigating these details? Is it concerns about privacy and, if so, whose privacy: lawyers, judges (disrespect for the court system), or litigants, children, and other family members? Is the objection about indeterminacy? Or does the objection stem from a belief that conduct that appears "wrong" outwardly might not be so wrong, such as adultery that happens after the marriage is ruined in fact, if not formally. Surely, the reason for avoiding inquiries into nonfinancial matters should influence the reach of this policy. For example, if a couple's privacy is the driving concern, then explicit marital agreements inviting a court to adjudicate fault should be permissible.

[30] PRINCIPLES § 4.09, comment b.

[31] PRINCIPLES § 1, Topic 2, Part I, at 43.

[32] PRINCIPLES § 7.08 cmt. b, at 1005.

The PRINCIPLES have not clearly articulated which concern motivates the aversion to examining marital conduct. I would presume the aversion is motivated by indeterminacy, or a real lack of social consensus about marital conduct. Certainly, that lack of social consensus complicates the task the drafters set out to accomplish. But if that is the reason it is not possible to consider marital conduct, then the PRINCIPLES suffer from a significant limitation, since issues about appropriate marital conduct are decided by default when ignored. It is true that allowing each individual judge to resolve disputes according to the judge's version of marital expectations is a nightmare. However, it is not obvious that the ALI is a less arbitrary decisionmaker when it comes to matters of social values.

Thus, in an attempt to eliminate one problematic inquiry, the PRINCIPLES arguably have eliminated the good with the bad. Although few favor the reinstitution of fault-based divorce, if the only way to eliminate fault is to ignore the nonfinancial aspects of marriage, the price is just too high.

The PRINCIPLES have thus overreacted to the fault issue, with consequences. It is not clear that the law must stamp out all remaining vestiges of an investigation of marital conduct in order to eliminate fault divorce grounds. The PRINCIPLES take a crimped view of fault: just as the PRINCIPLES refer to nonfinancial losses as "emotional" losses,[33] missing other nonfinancial aspects of marriage, the PRINCIPLES refer to questions of fault as questions of "morality," "virtue," and "sin," missing other attributes of fault.[34]

Attempting to eliminate everything that resembles fault makes it difficult to manage some of the more important distributive issues at divorce. This chapter argues below that even the PRINCIPLES are not prepared to go as far as their stated ideal. The best example occurs in Section 4.10, dealing with property distribution, which establishes an exception to the equal division rule in the case of financial misconduct.[35] First, however, this chapter considers the other justification for avoiding the evaluation of nonfinancial matters: incommensurability.

2. The Incommensurability Problem

The use of incommensurability to justify ignoring nonfinancial matters is equally unsatisfying.[36] On its face, the argument is almost nonsensical, as the law routinely provides remedies for losses that are in some way incommensurable with financial metrics: pain and suffering, emotional distress, reputational loss, and loss of consortium are just a few examples. All but the most mechanical economists acknowledge that measuring those types of losses in dollar terms is an artificial process. But the law accommodates this fiction because it is better than the alternative, which is not recognizing the losses at all. To shore up the argument made in the PRINCIPLES, the drafters must supplement the incommensurability idea. Incommensurability between finances and other relationship issues must be different than the incommensurability between finances and physical pain or emotional distress in tort, for example.

One possible way to distinguish incommensurabilities occasioned by divorce is by labeling them "not worth it," in the sense that the size of the loss is smaller than the pain of the litigation. The drafters may simply be arguing in this case that using a financial metric for nonfinancial matters does not beat the alternative. The PRINCIPLES hint at this when they suggest that nonfinancial matters during marriage can be presumed to have

[33] PRINCIPLES § 5.02 cmt. b, at 790.

[34] PRINCIPLES § 1, Topic 2, pt. III(a).

[35] PRINCIPLES § 4.10.

[36] PRINCIPLES §§ 5.02, cmt. B, at 790; 4.09, cmt. C, at 736.

been offered in an equal exchange, since an unequal bargain would have led to divorce before.[37] This argument seems weak in part because, as the PRINCIPLES acknowledge, there are many barriers to divorce: religious commitments, sunk costs, and children, for example, that make it probable that people will stay in a bad bargain. More particularly, courts only examine the questions the PRINCIPLES raise after a marital split has actually ensued, making it almost certain that the bargain was in fact a bad one in that particular marriage. If the spouses have any regard for marriage or any psychological attachment to the marriage's success, the bargain likely has been bad for a significant amount of time.

The PRINCIPLES elsewhere suggest that the return is not worth the effort of finding a metric. In its justification for rejecting premarital agreements that insert fault-based divorce by consent, the PRINCIPLES suggest that fault inquiries may not be a good use of judicial time.[38] Also, in the explanation for adopting a presumption of equal property division, the PRINCIPLES emphasize how burdensome and intrusive such an inquiry would be.[39] Thus, the drafters may not be resting their argument on the presumed equality of exchange, meaning the outcome's presumed justice, so much as on an aversion to examining nonfinancial matters in the legal process. Evaluating nonfinancial matters in marriages is an ugly process for litigants, judges, and lawyers, and perhaps this explains the aversion, regardless of the justice of the matter.[40]

Thus aversion and intrusion may be one thing the PRINCIPLES seem to mean by incommensurability, rather than that it is not possible to find a financial metric. But there is another possibility. The drafters may be advancing a distinct point, that it is impossible to agree on what was a loss and what was a gain in marriage. This position holds that evaluating marriages is a hopelessly relativistic, values-based process. The difference between calculating losses in divorce and pain and suffering in tort law is that there are deep differences of perspective on how valuable various nonfinancial elements of a marriage are. In tort, it is the artificiality of money as a proxy for the loss that is the concern. No one doubts, however, the existence or severity of pain. But with divorce, the contested terrain concerns the very pluralism of family life in the United States, the pluralism of meanings about family. Maybe the challenge of finding a common metric is greater here because it implicates all the contests at the heart of the "family values" debates. Maybe the drafters despair, as so many do, of coming to any conclusion on those matters. Hence, the PRINCIPLES try to show wisdom by concluding that settling nonfinancial matters is impractical.

However, an equally plausible understanding of the same dilemma is that the PRINCIPLES advocate putting our heads in the sand. Deciding not to confront these cultural contests does not eliminate them. A formula that takes the worst contests out of the legal system may make the legal process less contentious. Yet, one of the main benefits of a civil legal system is providing a proper forum for resolving the knottiest conflicts in society. It seems possible that the PRINCIPLES will provide predictability by avoiding the nonfinancial issues, but a coin toss also provides predictability. The real question is whether it fairly resolves the dispute between litigants. By taking the enormous and deep conflicts over nonfinancial

[37] PRINCIPLES § 502 comment c; Section 4.10, Comment b.

[38] PRINCIPLES §§ 7.08 comment b, at 1005 "Such a state law may reflect institutional judgments about the allocation of judicial time").

[39] PRINCIPLES § 4.09, cmt. b, at 763 ("Even though the presumption [of an equal division] will sometimes be incorrect, case-by-case measurement offers no promise of greater accuracy. Moreover, the measurement attempt itself would require a retrospective examination of the parties' marital life that would often be burdensome and intrusive, as well as futile in its purpose.").

[40] *Id.*

matters within marriage, perhaps the most significant matters in a divorce, out of the legal system, the PRINCIPLES do not eliminate those conflicts. Instead the PRINCIPLES leave us asking where else those inevitable conflicts will express themselves.

There are circumstances when even the rationalist PRINCIPLES admit that nonfinancial matters require redress, as in the cases where one spouse has been a primary caretaker of children in a marriage.[41] In these instances, the PRINCIPLES seem to walk a tightrope. The drafters acknowledge marital conduct but insist that there is a special financial-ness to this particular problem. There does have to be compensation, and the dispute does relate to nonfinancial roles and behaviors during marriage, if the term "nonfinancial" can be used at all. The PRINCIPLES solve the problem by arguing that the compensatory payments in that case are justified by loss of financial earning power.[42] But illogically, the payments are tied to both spouses' incomes.[43] If the payments were to be justified on the basis offered by the PRINCIPLES – loss of the care giver's earning capacity – the payments should be tied to the difference between the care giver spouse's earning capacity before care giving and her earning capacity after care giving. Instead, the PRINCIPLES pay attention to the breadwinner's earnings as well. In other words, although the PRINCIPLES assert that they are just managing a financial loss to the earning capacity of the care giver, it looks like they are responding to a nonfinancial matter – the role commitments made within that type of marriage. The property illustration that follows makes this point even more clearly: the drafters can argue that they are only managing financial losses that arise from divorce, but they cannot help but do more than that if the PRINCIPLES are to retain any claim to fairness.

3. The Assumption That Nonfinancial Matters Do Not Outlive the Marriage

Finally, the PRINCIPLES utilize a device that the drafters believe will make this tension acceptable: an assumption that the financial and nonfinancial aspects of marriage resulted in an equal balance of benefits and burdens during the marriage.[44] If that were not the case, couples would get divorced. That theoretical equality serves as a justification for not examining exchanges during the marriage. At the same time, the PRINCIPLES forthrightly acknowledge the inadequacy of that theory to describe actual marriages, as explained in comment c to Section 5.02:

> Divorcing individuals are likely to believe that the allocation of resources and responsibilities during their marriage was unfair. It would seem certain that some are correct. But the divorce law cannot provide general relief for unfair conduct in marriage.... The no-fault divorce law of most states gives spouses the legal power to terminate the marriage unilaterally. In principle, this power makes it impossible for either spouse to impose an inequitable arrangement on the other, at least in the long term. In practice, this may not be true. Parties may be bound together by nonlegal ties that keep persons in unhappy relationships. There is little the law can do to alter that.[45]

This position is obviously very cold consolation: there are injustices of a nonfinancial nature, they are to be acknowledged, but the law cannot address them. As a practical

[41] PRINCIPLES § 5.03(2)(b).

[42] PRINCIPLES § 5.02(3).

[43] PRINCIPLES § 5.05.

[44] PRINCIPLES §§ 4.10 cmt. b, at 753 ("The legal remedy available to a spouse who finds a marriage unacceptably burdensome or inequitable is exit."); 4.09, cmt. c, at 736 ("In considering the reasonableness of the presumption of equality, some comfort may perhaps be taken in the observation that under a legal regime of no-fault divorce in which either spouse can unilaterally terminate the marriage, individuals who believe their relationship is seriously one-sided can terminate it.").

[45] PRINCIPLES § 5.02 cmt. c, at 791.

matter, the PRINCIPLES ultimately do not manage to not address nonfinancial matters very effectively, as this chapter demonstrates, despite the fact that the drafters are highly motivated to ignore them.[46]

In short, the PRINCIPLES formally address only postdissolution losses, while responding to the occasional postdissolution consequence of roles during the marriage, as with the compensatory spousal payments for primary care givers. Nonfinancial matters are a real and crucial aspect of the exchange during marriage, but are also assumed to be equally distributed when money is factored in, and unmeasurable, and therefore unremediable postdivorce.

Consider Section 4.10, comment b:

> The equitable importance of differences in the spouses' financial contributions or consumption could not be evaluated in isolation from the marriage as a whole, because the financial and non-financial threads of marriage cannot ordinarily be unraveled. A retrospective assessment of the marriage for the purpose of determining a fair allocation of property would require examining the emotional and personal benefits and burdens that the marriage provided each spouse, as well as the financial burdens and benefits. Individuals may derive great benefit, overall, from a marriage that is a net financial loss. But such an inquiry into the entire marriage is not *and should not* be part of the process by which marital property is allocated. The law employs a general rule of equal division because an individualized assessment of each marital relationship is not normally possible.... The legal remedy available to a spouse who finds a marriage unacceptably burdensome or inequitable is exit.[47]

As an aside, it is worth noting something counterculture about this remedy. Policymakers generally bemoan the apparent commitment problems of adults today, expressed through the ease with which people leave marriage to meet their personal needs. The drafters, on the other hand, use the easy availability of divorce to justify legal unwillingness to delve into the complexity of marriage. It is as if the PRINCIPLES endorse divorce for those who are unhappy, a position that may be correct, but is certainly controversial.

More to the point, it is unclear whether all nonfinancial goods are consumed during the marriage. Are there no lingering effects or lingering exchanges? Children live on and are provided countless benefits, financial and nonfinancial, that inure to the benefit of both parents. Marital decisions about where to reside can linger postdivorce, emotional opportunities with third parties passed up during marriage can have postdivorce effect, and betrayal lives on, as anyone who has known someone after a bitter divorce knows. That is to say that the exclusion of nonfinancial matters is artificial even postdivorce. Given that the nonfinancial and financial were entwined and continue to be entwined, a sense of a just financial settlement that ignores nonfinancials is hard to achieve. This leads to the question of whether the ALI's solution is just, to which this chapter now turns.

C. Is the Exclusion of Nonfinancial Contributions Just?

Suppose two children are each given ten dollars in quarters. They are told that they can pool their money and spend it, making any kind of deal with each other they would like, or they can each spend their ten dollars separately. But they are also told that at the end

46 *See* Part III *infra*.

47 PRINCIPLES § 4.10 cmt. b, at 752–53 (emphasis added).

of the day, all that is left in either pile will be divided equally between them. The children have been given a set of rules that are clear, rules that have predictability as a virtue. But this rule does not embody any particularly deep values, and it creates odd incentives for each child to spend instead of save. While this may not be a great analogy for marriage, parts of it may shed light on our family law system, particularly with respect to rewarding consumption over savings. What the illustration asks is whether, when crafting a rule that is easy to administer but avoids the intractable questions around values and values conflict, it is possible to call such a rule just or successful by any important measure.

The PRINCIPLES raise other particular concerns about justice and injustice. The PRINCIPLES replicate a convention in the law of making some things inappropriate material for legal exchange – love, care of one's children, emotional support, and sex, for example. To the extent, however, that such things actually are exchanged in some form, failing to enforce the deal simply weakens the bargaining hand of the individual who offers the item for exchange.[48] A real advantage-taker who brings nothing financial to the table, but nothing nonfinancial either, may benefit from the PRINCIPLES' willingness to give him or her half the money anyway on the assumption that he or she must have brought something more to the deal than feeding the other spouse's masochism. At the same time, someone who brings plenty of nonfinancial contributions to the table would barely know she had offered anything to the deal under this scheme, and may find little refuge in the PRINCIPLES' justification that she was always free to get a divorce.[49]

III. Is This the Only Choice? The Problem of Financial Misconduct

Are the PRINCIPLES just accommodating reality or practicality? As this chapter has already argued, nonfinancial matters are routinely dealt with in law. In addition, simply taking the really hard questions out of the equation does not make them go away. Finally, it is important to consider whether excluding the nonfinancial in fact accommodates reality. If so, why do states cling to the use of fault or other evaluations of various kinds of conduct within marriage, both beneficial, like savings, and harmful, like desertion?

These are difficult questions. The most generous view of the PRINCIPLES' choice is to ask: could anything have been done differently? Perhaps exclusion is a lousy choice, but better than all the other ones. There is plenty of support for this idea. Recall that the drafters justify the separation of these elements in large part with arguments from practicality. Those arguments include the impracticality of finding good measurements for nonfinancial losses, the incommensurability claim. They also include the impracticality of expecting predictable or accurate independent evaluation of marital conduct or the no-fault argument. There is much that is persuasive about this perspective.

But the belief that the choice to exclude nonfinancial contributions is practical or inevitable is itself questionable. So, too, is the related claim that accounting for the full range of marital conduct, gains, and losses is idealized and impractical. The law repeatedly returns to accounting for some kinds of marital conduct of a nonfinancial nature, and the PRINCIPLES are no exception. Even with a strong commitment to avoiding this evaluation, the PRINCIPLES have been unable to stick to its mission. If the PRINCIPLES, apparently strongly committed at the abstract level to the elimination of these factors, are unable

[48] For further discussion see generally Silbaugh, *Marriage Contracts*, *supra* note 17.

[49] PRINCIPLES § 4.10 cmt. b, at 753.

to execute that principle, perhaps it cannot be done. Money is not as transparent as the drafters thought. Instead, it is laden with the same emotional content as anything else that happens within a marriage.

As a primary example, consider some rules with regard to the distribution of property, though there are other examples.[50] In particular, consider Section 4.10, Financial Misconduct as Grounds for Unequal Division of Marital Property. What this section does is create an exception to the rule that divides property fifty–fifty without regard for marital conduct. That exception allows for offsets when one spouse engages in what is called "financial" misconduct.[51] Specifically, if one spouse makes a gift of marital property to a third party, such as a paramour or a parent or sibling, or spends or loses money through "intentional" misconduct and does so within a time period before the dissolution marked by a rule of statewide application (a year, two years, for example), that gift is counted back into the assets available for fifty–fifty divide.[52] The same rule applies to financial losses, even from negligence, that occur after service of a dissolution petition.[53]

This section may appear to be different because the misconduct is financial. But that is not so clear. First, the PRINCIPLES elsewhere ignore explicitly financial conduct that occurred during marriage.[54] The drafters must take this position if they are to exclude the consideration of nonfinancial matters: once the law asks who spent too much, or saved or earned or consumed too much during the marriage itself, it immediately finds itself considering the many items of exchange – services, well-being, support, and so forth – that are at the center of the storm for those seeking to avoid nonfinancial matters. Comment b to Section 4.10 admits as much:

> The general rule that the allocation of property at divorce is not based upon a retrospective accounting of the parties' relative expenditures arises from the same basic analysis that explains why unequal earnings do not rebut the rule that marital property is divided equally at divorce. The equal-division principle is not grounded upon a factual assumption that the parties made equal financial contributions to the marriage, or equal financial demands upon it. It is therefore not rebutted by a contrary factual showing.... [T]he financial facts could not alone govern the assessment of whether an equal division is fair. The equitable importance of differences in the spouses' financial contributions or consumption could not be evaluated in isolation from the marriage as a whole, because the financial and non-financial threads of marriage cannot ordinarily be unraveled. A retrospective assessment of the marriage for the purpose of determining a fair allocation of property would require examining the emotional and personal benefits and burdens that the marriage provided each spouse, as well as the financial burdens and benefits. Individuals may derive great benefit, overall, from a marriage that is a net financial loss. But such an inquiry into the entire marriage is not and should not be part of the process by which marital property is allocated.... The legal remedy available to a spouse who finds a marriage unacceptably burdensome or inequitable is exit.[55]

[50] Perhaps the most obvious of a rule that considers marital conduct is the PRINCIPLES' compensation for losses in earning capacity only for those who cared for dependents of various kinds – an inquiry into positive marital conduct, albeit one with some objective criteria. PRINCIPLES § 5.03(2)(b+c). Another example is the termination of these payments upon remarriage of the recipient, which is a behavioral rather than a financial judgment. PRINCIPLES § 5.07.

[51] PRINCIPLES § 4.10.

[52] PRINCIPLES §§ 4.10(1) and 4.10(2).

[53] PRINCIPLES § 4.10(3).

[54] *See, e.g.*, PRINCIPLES § 4.10, cmt. c.

[55] PRINCIPLES § 4.10 cmt. b, at 752–53 (internal citation omitted).

The drafters argue for ignoring the financial conduct during marriage, then, because they realize that financial and nonfinancial conduct are inseparable. But the types of financial misconduct anticipated in the exception crafted in Section 4.10 absolutely typify the ways in which financial and nonfinancial matters are completely and inextricably intertwined. There is no principled way to contain the insight of Section 4.10. The comments to Section 4.10 admit this strikingly with the illustrations chosen.[56]

The most obvious example is Illustration 11.[57] In this illustration, a husband is found guilty of forcible rape and sentenced to prison. His wife does not have to share in the expense of his legal defense in the divorce that follows because the expenditure resulted from intentional misconduct on his part. It turns out that this is true even if that conduct took place before the window of time when financial misconduct matters; even if, for example, she stands by him while he claims his innocence, and seeks the divorce later when he admits to her his guilt.[58] Paragraph 5 of Section 4.10 says that these provisions can go back before the fixed period set forth in the rule of statewide application, "if facts set forth in written findings of the trial court establish that their application to the earlier incidents is necessary to avoid a substantial injustice."[59]

Other classic examples, offered up in the illustrations, are of gambling expenditures and of money spent on adulterous relationships.[60] These expenditures, too, can be backdated under Paragraph 5 to before the rule of statewide application, to avoid a substantial injustice.

Whether a spouse is a convicted rapist, or just a profligate spender on particularly insulting causes like affairs or gambling, there is room in the PRINCIPLES to account for his or her conduct. The drafters maintain that the exception is cabined by the financial nature of this misconduct – these are cases where, in their view, the conduct is just about the money. But how is it possible to know that the spending was wrong – that it was "financial misconduct"? Comment e suggests that prevailing case law will apply to conventional financial misconduct, such as concealing assets, as well as to "a wider group of fact patterns that also include gambling losses and funds spent on an adulterous relationship ...."[61] In other words, an existing body of law outlines conventional nonfinancial misconduct or fault.

The explanatory comment notes that these rules reflect prevailing law in most states.[62] The PRINCIPLES are arguably just bowing to reality here: this is prevailing law in most states because courts are simply unable to ignore this kind of misconduct, and the PRINCIPLES will not seem like a credible alternative to current law if they fail to accommodate this reality.

Why is this the prevailing law in most jurisdictions? It is inevitable that some forms of conduct and misconduct will play a role in financial settlements at divorce. This is because everyone knows – the drafters, the judges, lawyers, people getting divorced, people who are married – that financial misconduct is wrapped up in facts about the relationship: the adultery, the consumption, the gambling, or as Illustration 11 posited, even the rape.[63] This is not to say that fault evaluations are good, just that they are inevitable. It is impossible to think or talk about dissolution without considering these issues in every case. The law

[56] *See* PRINCIPLES § 4.10 illus. 1–4, at 753–4.

[57] PRINCIPLES § 4.10 illus. 11, at 759.

[58] PRINCIPLES § 4.10 cmt. e, at 759.

[59] PRINCIPLES § 4.10(5).

[60] PRINCIPLES § 4.10, illus. 8–9, at 757–58.

[61] PRINCIPLES § 4.10 cmt. e, at 757.

[62] *Id.*

[63] PRINCIPLES § 4.10 illus. 11, at 759.

can choose to ignore them, but if it does so, participants in the process are likely to feel as though the system is not just or realistic.

What are the implications of this analysis of Section 4.10? The narrowest point that can be made here is that Section 4.10 is an exception to the no-fault principle, causing the PRINCIPLES to fall short of their commitment to no-fault in this single provision.[64] But this provision illustrates more than this; indeed, it nicely captures many of the impossibilities and practicalities of family law.

First, nonfinancial conduct and financial conduct are intertwined. Before a divorce, as a couple is drifting apart, the wife might begin to invest in a hobby that is an assertion of independence from the marriage. Perhaps that hobby would be cycling, which increasingly occupies her free time. She buys a $6,000 bicycle one year before the marriage ends. It is expensive, but for a cycling enthusiast it may not be outrageous. This expenditure is probably not misconduct under the provision, even though the cycling may be wrapped up in her emotional exit from the marriage. However, if she spends that money buying jewelry for her paramour, then that purchase is considered misconduct under the provision. So what is the outrage – spending valuable cash outside the marital unit, or spending it in adultery? It seems obvious that it is the latter: adultery is bad enough, but spending money on it puts salt in the wound. This is the kind of insult to injury that an ordinary judge will recognize and feel the need to remedy.

Money is not distant and cold, but instead is integrally wrapped up in the personal aspects of marriage. This is illustrated most clearly when there is spending on adultery, and the drafters provide a remedy for that situation. But despite the drafters' decision to provide no remedy when one spouse is a saver and one a spender, the saver feels personally betrayed by the spender, often emotionally betrayed. I have analyzed before the odd legal doctrines governing marriage contracts that consider financial matters distant enough from marriage to be an appropriate subject of contract without damaging the core of marriage, while other nonfinancial conduct is so central to marriage that it cannot be reduced to contract. I responded that money is not naturally unemotional, but the legal rules that distance it from emotions themselves commodify money.[65] The drafters repeat that characterization by making financial matters seem tame enough for courts, by comparison to nonfinancial ones. The drafters pretend money is colder or less fraught with emotion or more rational than it is; that would seem to be the only way to justify treating nonfinancial matters differently. But when it comes to compensating a spouse when his or her ex spent money on a lover, it is a thin reed of respectability to claim that the reason that the spouse needs to be compensated is that his or her bank account has been reduced.

If the drafters have in fact been unable to hold nonfinancial matters at bay, it is important to ask whether that was inevitable. Think of the implications: the drafters, the ALI, and maybe the whole Family Law bar, have been prepared to concede that after all these years of experience with fault, there is no good way to take marital conduct into account. The drafters profess, in comment c to Section 5.02: "the divorce law cannot provide general relief for unfair conduct in marriage."[66] Yet on the other hand, there may be no way to avoid taking account of marital conduct. That may be the real tension, or incoherence, of family law – the impossibility, but the necessity, of looking into the marriage.

[64] PRINCIPLES § 4.10.

[65] Silbaugh, *Marriage Contracts*, *supra* note 17, at 124.

[66] PRINCIPLES § 5.02 cmt. c, at 791.

IV. Conclusion

Of course, the drafters are aware of the ways in which the financial and nonfinancial are entwined. The PRINCIPLES finesse the problem: it is precisely because they cannot be disentangled that we cannot try to.

Then what is the PRINCIPLES' real relationship to the financial versus the nonfinancial aspects of marriage? The PRINCIPLES express conflicting attitudes. At times, the PRINCIPLES appear to resolve the tension by proclaiming that the law can only or should only deal with financial issues. But at other times, the PRINCIPLES explain the treatment of financial issues in terms of other, nonfinancial considerations, as in the case of compensatory payments for care giver spouses or offsets for financial misconduct. Maybe this is the best we can do: it is pragmatic. It may also be predictable. However, it is not coherent, despite the fact that coherence was a prominent goal of the drafters. Legislators in particular should consider whether the value of predictability is high enough to overcome results that will not be satisfying to litigants in real cases.

I would like to thank the participants in the October 2004 Workshop at the Harvard Law School for helpful comments, as well as Masataka Scanlan for his research assistance.

13 Postmodern Marriage as Seen through the Lens of the ALI's "Compensatory Payments"

Katherine Shaw Spaht

The "no-fault" divorce revolution, begun in the late 1960s, stalled in many states in the United States with the stubborn persistence of fault as a factor in alimony awards and the division of marital property after divorce.[1] In the Introduction to the PRINCIPLES, the drafters assert that "American law is sharply divided on the question of whether 'marital misconduct' should be considered in allocating marital property or awarding alimony."[2] During the 1970s, many states not only retained fault for purposes of the financial incidents of divorce but also combined a new no-fault ground for divorce with existing fault grounds. Thus, divorce law of many states, as well as the law governing ancillary matters, remains "mixed," with both fault and no-fault grounds for divorce, and fault taken into consideration as a factor in alimony or property awards or both.

As a means of completing the stalled no-fault revolution,[3] achieving unity among state laws that was not accomplished by the Uniform Marriage and Dissolution Act ("UMDA"),[4] and providing a coherent theory justifying awards to a spouse after divorce,[5] the PRINCIPLES propose a set of provisions that would compensate a spouse for certain losses attributable to the marriage and its termination.[6] Loss would substitute for the almost universal criterion today of need, and fault would be eliminated almost entirely[7] from

[1] PRINCIPLES § 1, Topic 2, pt. II, cmts. a–e, at 45–7; *see* Wardle, this volume (demonstrating that a majority of States consider fault at dissolution in some form).

[2] PRINCIPLES § 1, Topic 2, pt. I, at 42–43. *See also* PRINCIPLES § 1, Topic 2, pt. II, cmt. e, at 47 ("The dominant position of no-fault rules in property allocation, as compared to the even division in alimony, appears to reflect a difference in the underlying rationale for each of them, at least in many states."). In an earlier article, Professor Ira Ellman, the primary drafter of the PRINCIPLES, stated that "[o]nly a small minority of states today allow fault generally to enter into the determination of whether and how much alimony should be due . . . ," although he did acknowledge that a greater number of states do consider one particular form of fault, adultery. Ira Mark Ellman, *Should the Theory of Alimony Include Nonfinancial Losses and Motivations?*, 1991 BYU L. REV. 259, 262.

[3] PRINCIPLES § 1, Topic 2, pt. I, at 43.

[4] PRINCIPLES § 1, Topic 2, pt. I, at 43 ("The Uniform Marriage and Divorce Act (UMDA), initially approved in 1970, provides unambiguously that both allocation of marital property and determinations of spousal maintenance be made 'without regard to marital misconduct.' Published surveys typically report that approximately half the states now share the Uniform Act's position. These Principles do as well."). At least half of the states in the United States have not chosen to adopt the UMDA position promulgated at least thirty years ago. *See also* Lynn Wardle, *No-Fault Divorce and the Divorce Conundrum*, 1991 BYU L. REV. 79; James Herbie DiFonzo, *Toward a Unified Field Theory of the Family: The American Law Institute's Principles of the Law of Family Dissolution*, 2001 BYU L. REV. 923.

[5] PRINCIPLES § 1, Topic 1, Overview of Chapters 4 and 5, pts. I & II, cmts. b, c, at 24–28 ("The approach of these PRINCIPLES is to refocus the alimony inquiry from *need* to *loss*, a shift that some cases have already begun to adopt."). *But see* June Carbone, *The Futility of Coherence: The ALI's Principles of the Law*, 4 J. L. & FAM. STUD. 43 (2002).

[6] PRINCIPLES § § 5.01–5.14.

[7] *See* Wardle, this volume.

consideration in the PRINCIPLES.[8] The substitution of loss for need rhetorically recasts the view of the judge from an assessment of the future affected by the past, to a selective and constricted consideration of the past as it affects the future.[9] In evaluating the past, the judge may not consider whose act caused the injury that is being suffered, even if it is the claimant's act. The ALI believes that the "punishment" of marital misconduct more properly belongs to the law of torts and crimes, if anywhere,[10] even though this treatment would reach only a very narrow range of marital misconduct,[11] is inefficient, and, in the case of criminal law, depends upon the discretionary decision by a local district attorney.[12]

> *Despite ongoing societal reconsideration of the ease of divorce*, the ALI PRINCIPLES exclude consideration of fault or any other dissolution-delaying mechanism. Considered together these features fuse to form the backbone of a unified field theory of the family, one whose unspoken aim is finally to consolidate the no-fault divorce revolution.[13]

Many scholars have carefully analyzed and evaluated the compensatory spousal payments provisions, as detailed in Part IIb. The primary drafter of the PRINCIPLES, Professor Ira Ellman, has written extensively about the role of fault in property and spousal support determinations, defending its elimination and forging a new theoretical underpinning for awards to a former spouse after divorce.[14]

"Working backward,"[15] the particular rules governing the financial incidents of divorce create a theory and a vision of marriage that many scholars lament,[16] or resignedly accept,[17] or embrace with only qualified enthusiasm.[18] This theory of marriage and its potential

[8] PRINCIPLES § 1, Topic 1, pt. II, cmt. a, at 27–28. *See* PRINCIPLES § 5.02(2) ("Losses are allocated under this Chapter without regard to marital misconduct, but nothing in this Chapter is intended to foreclose a spouse from bringing a claim recognized under other law for injuries arising from conduct that occurred during the marriage."); PRINCIPLES § 5.02, cmt. e, at 792.

[9] *See* Carbone, this volume (characterizing the ALI proposal this way).

[10] *See* PRINCIPLES § 5.02, cmt. c, at 792. Ellman, *supra* note 2, at 305–06 ("One can recover in tort for all kinds of things that no one knows how to measure: emotional distress, pain and suffering, and the loss of dignity involved in an 'offensive' touching. Perhaps therein lies the real arena for adjusting imbalances in the nonfinancial gains and losses of marriage, or providing recovery for outrageous or improper spousal conduct. *I am not sure I favor that solution myself; the problems do not go away by labeling them tort – they just seem more tolerable.*") (emphasis added). *See also* J. Thomas Oldham, *ALI Principles of Family Dissolution: Some Comments*, 1997 U. ILL. L. REV. 801.

[11] Criminal law and, in most states, tort law does not punish adultery, abandonment, mental cruelty, some acts of physical cruelty, intentional nonsupport, public defamation, and habitual intemperance. *See* Oldham, *supra* note 10, 801 (discussing a growing recognition in some states that an action is needed to punish "outrageous marital misconduct").

[12] *See* DeWitt Gregory, this volume.

[13] DiFonzo, *supra* note 4, at 925 (emphasis added). *See also* JAMES HERBIE DIFONZO, BENEATH THE FAULT LINE: THE POPULAR AND LEGAL CULTURE OF DIVORCE IN TWENTIETH CENTURY AMERICA (1997).

[14] *See* Wardle, this volume.

[15] *See* Carl E. Schneider, *Rethinking Alimony: Marital Decisions and Moral Discourse*, 1991 BYU L. REV. 197. *See also* Carbone, *supra* note 5.

[16] *See* Wardle, *supra* note 4, and to a lesser extent, Schneider, *supra* note 15. *See also* Lynn D. Wardle, *Divorce Violence and the No-Fault Divorce Culture*, 1994 UTAH L. REV. 741.

[17] DiFonzo, *supra* note 4 ("Naked divorce in America has gone too far."). *Compare* DiFonzo, *supra* note 4, at 958 ("Given the historical failure of marital fault as a screen for rational divorce, the ALI position appears justified on policy grounds as well.").

[18] *See* Herma Hill Kay, *From the Second Sex to the Joint Venture: An Overview of Women's Rights and Family Law in the United States During the Twentieth Century*, 88 CAL. L. REV. 2017, 2020, 2090 (2002) (recognizing that although she envisions the institution of marriage as a "joint venture, formed for a specific transaction, and renewable at the pleasure of the venturer[s]," this concept of marriage "is not yet an appropriate model for all couples"). *See also* Carbone, *supra* note 5.

effects on marital behavior and quality deserve more explicit scrutiny. Some defenders of the PRINCIPLES prefer to critique only the PRINCIPLES' ability to influence marital behavior.[19] Other defenders would prefer to focus exclusively on the type of losses that should be compensated[20] or claim that the PRINCIPLES should be evaluated by a single yardstick, that being whether the alimony provisions eliminate disincentives for marital sharing.[21] Most importantly, defenders want critics of the PRINCIPLES to concede that the moral relations of the parties cannot be gauged[22] and that fairness must be judged without "reference to qualities of the marital relationship"[23] because they are impossible to measure. Despite its refusal to consider the moral relations of the spouses themselves, the PRINCIPLES elsewhere recognize the moral responsibilities of a spouse to a third person as relevant to recovery of alimony or "compensatory payments."[24] Having experience in a legal tradition that unambiguously relies on moral relations between persons even in contract law,[25] I refuse to concede that the moral relations of the parties cannot be "gauged" and that fairness to the marital partners excludes the "qualities of the marital relationship." This legal theory of marriage implied in the PRINCIPLES is objectionable.

If there is one lesson to be learned from the four decades since the no-fault divorce revolution began, it is the importance of caution with respect to social experimentation on the family. This caution is supported by a growing body of social science literature.[26] During the decades before the no-fault revolution, some of the legal barriers protecting marriage, both external and internal, were slowly and incrementally dismantled.[27] This

[19] Ira Mark Ellman, *Brigette M. Bodenheimer Memorial Lecture on the Family: Inventing Family Law*, 32 U.C. DAVIS L. REV. 855, 885 (1999) ("There was a time when I was younger and even less sensible than I am now, when I thought family law might be important for the impact it had on how people conducted their marriages. Devise the right rules of family law and perhaps people will treat one another better, have happier marriages, or be better parents. I have long since moved away from such views.").

[20] *See* Ellman, *supra* note 2, at 259. *See also* Schneider, *supra* note 15, at 256 ("The abolition of alimony is certainly not unthinkable.").

[21] Ellman, *supra* note 2, at 302–03 (conceding in a response to a critique by Professor Carl E. Schneider, *supra* note 15, that "[t]he *Theory of Alimony* is not perfect, even when tested against its own rationale of eliminating disincentives to marital sharing behavior. Some disincentives will remain and, in many other cases, nonfinancial motivations will swamp the financial considerations with which *The Theory* deals"). Some scholars hope that the PRINCIPLES also discourage bad marital behavior, i.e., opportunism based on pure self-interest. *See, e.g.*, Allen M. Parkman, *The ALI Principles and Marital Quality*, 8 DUKE J. GENDER L. & POL'Y 157 (2001).

[22] Ellman, *supra* note 2, at 305 ("Yet, if we concede that we are not in fact capable of gauging these things, then we must ask a second question: what is the fairest way to proceed when we cannot fully gauge parties' 'moral relations'?").

[23] *Id.* ("Although Professor Schneider is correct that *The Theory* is grounded primarily on an incentive rather than a fairness rationale, *The Theory* may also be a reasonable approximation of a fair system *once we accept that fairness must be judged without reference to qualities of the marital relationship that we cannot measure.*") (emphasis added).

[24] PRINCIPLES § 5.02(3)(a) ("Equitable principles of loss recognition and allocation should take into account all of the following: ... The loss of earning capacity arising from a spouse's disproportionate share of caretaking responsibilities for children or *other persons to whom the spouses have a moral obligation....*) (emphasis added).

[25] Louisiana is a civil law jurisdiction with European codifications as models, especially France. Louisiana law borrows from that tradition. Contract law incorporates natural obligations, defined historically as binding in conscience and natural justice and now defined as a particular moral duty. LA. CIV. CODE ANN. art. 1760 (2005). If a person promises in fulfillment of a natural obligation, the contract is onerous, which means that no form is required. LA. CIV. CODE ANN. art. 1761 (2005). The contract (offer and acceptance) is by law deemed not gratuitous; the promise was made because the person making it was morally obligated. For other examples, *see* notes 72–80, *infra*, and accompanying text.

[26] *See, e.g.*, PAUL AMATO & ALAN BOOTH, A GENERATION AT RISK: GROWING UP IN A TIME OF FAMILY UPHEAVAL (1997).

[27] Katherine Shaw Spaht, *The Last One Hundred Years: The Incredible Retreat of Law from the Regulation of Marriage*, 63 LA. L. REV. 243 (2003). *See also* Francis Cardinal George, *Law and Culture*, 1 AVE MARIA L. REV. 1 (2003).

incremental dismantling of barriers culminated in the drastic event of the enactment of no-fault divorce in California. Marriage was finally left naked and legally unprotected. Before the adoption of any further family law reform, particularly one that solidifies the no-fault revolution,[28] there are certain questions that first need answers: "what assumptions about human nature underlie family law generally and the trend toward diminished moral discourse particularly. . . . [H]ow [does] man respond to the absence of social controls, how [does] he react[] to a more spontaneous and active emotional life, what [is] the nature of his need for privacy . . . to what extent [may] his behavior [be] deliberately reformed, [and] to what extent [does] he need aspirations beyond himself and attachments to his community[?]"[29]

This Chapter seeks to answer these questions as they relate to the treatment of alimony in the PRINCIPLES. Part I analyzes the alimony provisions of the PRINCIPLES by examining their purposes and the kinds of loss that are compensable and noncompensable. Part II examines the vision of marriage conveyed by the PRINCIPLES' alimony provisions: is it a joint venture for a limited purpose as some scholars assert and is it likely that both parties who enter a marriage understand its inherent nature? Part III poses the query whether marriage can be conceived differently from that reflected in the PRINCIPLES for the purpose of offering greater legal stability to the institution and greater legal protection, which facilitates more effective choices by the spouses. Ultimately, the answer is yes.

I. Analysis of the PRINCIPLES' Alimony Provisions

A. Purposes

As with the entire project, the objective of the provisions governing alimony, which the PRINCIPLES label compensatory spousal payments, "is to allocate financial losses that arise at the dissolution of a marriage according to equitable PRINCIPLES [subsequently defined] that are consistent and predictable in application."[30] In a comment, the drafters explain that "[e]arly in the no-fault reform era, [the Uniform Marriage and Divorce Act] described alimony as an award meant to provide support for the spouse in 'need' who is 'unable to support himself through appropriate employment.' With time it has become apparent that this conception of alimony's purpose has two principal difficulties."[31] Those difficulties are the lack of a rationale supporting the imposition of the obligation of support on former spouses, "rather than on their parents, their children, their friends, or society in general," and "the law's historic inability to provide any consistent principle for determining when, and to what extent, a former spouse is 'in need.'"[32]

[28] In a "counter-revolution," many scholars in social science and in law now consider the no-fault revolution a failure that has increased rather than decreased the suffering of children and their parents. See, for example, JUDITH WALLERSTEIN, THE LEGACY OF DIVORCE: A 25-YEAR LANDMARK STUDY (2000); BARBARA DAFOE WHITEHEAD, THE DIVORCE CULTURE (1999); MAGGIE GALLAGHER, THE ABOLITION OF MARRIAGE: HOW WE DESTROY LASTING LOVE (1996); Margaret E. Brinig & F. H. Buckley, *No-Fault Laws and At-Fault People*, 18 INT'L REV. L. & ECON. 325 (1998); Peter Nash Swisher, *Reassessing Fault Factors in No-Fault Divorce*, 31 FAM. L.Q. 2679 (1997).

[29] Carl E. Schneider, *Moral Discourse and the Transformation of American Family Law*, 83 MICH. L. REV. 1803, 1878 (1985).

[30] PRINCIPLES § 5.02(1).

[31] PRINCIPLES § 5.02, cmt. a, at 789 (explaining that the UMDA initially intended for alimony to provide support for an unemployed spouse in need) (internal citation omitted).

[32] PRINCIPLES § 5.02, cmt. a, at 789.

Because of these two principal failings, the reconceptualization of alimony "recharacterize[s] the remedy it provides as compensation for loss rather than relief of need. . . . The intuition that the former spouse has an obligation to meet that need arises from the perception that the need results from the unfair allocation of the financial losses arising from the marital failure."[33] In explaining how that intuition becomes an obligation extending beyond marriage, Professor Ellman comments that "there is also a widespread *intuition* that marriage alone does not create an obligation of one spouse to provide the other with post-marital financial support, the way that parentage alone creates the child support obligation. . . . [T]he sense that one spouse has an obligation to meet the other's post-dissolution needs arises from the recognition that the need results *at least in part from an unfair distribution of the financial losses arising from the marital failure.* Alimony thus becomes a remedy for unfair loss allocation. . . ."[34]

Under the PRINCIPLES, marital misconduct is explicitly excluded from consideration at dissolution,[35] yet nothing precludes a spouse from seeking redress for injuries "arising" from such conduct "under other law."[36] For the ALI, fault, "an agent of morality,"[37] serves to punish sin and reward virtue, which is problematic. For example, one problem fault creates is discrepancies among judges' conceptions of what conduct constitutes fault by a spouse, resulting in the sort of unpredictable outcomes that result from a purely discretionary award.[38] The drafters explain that "the effect is to empower each judge to employ matrimonial law to punish conduct that society is unwilling to reach explicitly in the criminal law."[39] Punishable conduct need not, of course, be criminal; the entire body of tort law operates to provide remedies that criminal law often does not. State repeal of the criminal punishment of adultery does not mean there should be no civil remedy for breach of the obligation to be sexually faithful to a spouse. As offensive as adultery is,[40] contemporary society considers adultery to be an offense principally against the other spouse rather than society at large. Family law, which imposes the obligation of fidelity implicitly or explicitly upon spouses during marriage,[41] has traditionally provided a remedy for the breach, not tort law.

[33] PRINCIPLES § 5.02, cmt. a, at 789.

[34] Ellman, *supra* note 19, at 878, 879 (emphasis added). *See also* PRINCIPLES § 5.02 cmt. f, at 793 ("Marriages can give rise to duties that continue even though the marriage itself has been terminated on the petition of one or both spouses.").

[35] PRINCIPLES § 5.02(2) ("Losses are allocated under this Chapter without regard to marital misconduct. . . .").

[36] PRINCIPLES § 5.02(2).

[37] PRINCIPLES § 1, Topic 2, pt. III, cmt. a, at 49–50.

[38] PRINCIPLES § 1, Topic 2, pt. III, cmt. a, at 50. ("The vagueness of the [discretionary] approach [in which judges determine what is marital misconduct] does [insure some indefensible results] because the moral standards by which blameworthy conduct will be identified and punished will vary from judge to judge, as each judge necessarily relies on his or her own vision of appropriate behavior in intimate relationships."). Of course, there is a distinction between what constitutes fault, a legal issue, and whether a discretionary award applying statutory factors amounts to an abuse of discretion.

[39] PRINCIPLES § 1, Topic 2, pt. III, cmt. a, at 50.

[40] Some scholars encourage restoration of the action for alienation of affections. *See, e.g.*, William C. Corbett, *A Somewhat Modest Proposal to Prevent Adultery and Save Families: Two Old Torts Looking for a New Career*, 33 ARIZ. ST. L.J. 985 (2001) *and* Nehal A. Patel, *The State's Perpetual Protection of Adultery: Examining Koestler v. Pollard and Wisconsin's Faded Adultery Torts*, 2003 WIS. L. REV. 1013.

[41] LA. CIV. CODE art. 98 (2005) ("Married persons owe each other fidelity, support, and assistance."); Elizabeth S. Scott, *Social Norms and the Legal Regulation of Marriage*, 86 VA. L. REV. 1901, 1919 (2000) (describing sexual fidelity as a "relational norm" developed by the couple over time but is also broadly applicable and enforced by the community as well as the couple). Fidelity is the hallmark of marriage and distinguishes marriage from mere cohabitation, both in law and in fact. *See* Garrison, this volume. However, the PRINCIPLES blur the line between them by recognizing that domestic partners may also have the right to alimony. PRINCIPLES § 6.01 *et seq.*

Another reason the drafters offer support for eliminating fault is "the concern that evaluation of marital misconduct requires too nuanced an understanding of the marital relationship."[42] In oft-repeated illustrations[43] intended to demonstrate such nuances, the drafters pair adultery by one spouse with a different type of conduct by the other. According to the drafters, the use of fault in alimony awards is premised on an attempt to determine whose fault "caused" the breakdown, which cannot be established objectively.[44] By contrast "the cause of chicken pox, or of a plumbing failure" can be determined objectively.[45] Considering fault in the context of marital failure "masks a moral inquiry with a word pretending a more objective assessment."[46]

> Some individuals tolerate their spouse's drunkenness or adultery and remain in their marriage. Others may seek divorce if their spouse grows fat, or spends long hours at the office. Is the divorce "caused" by one spouse's offensive conduct, or by the other's unreasonable intolerance? In deciding that question the court is assessing the parties' relative moral failings, not the relationship between independent and dependent variables. And the complexity of marital relations of course confounds the inquiry. *The fading of affective ties makes spouses less tolerant of one another.*[47]

"One piece of wisdom contained in the no-fault reforms was a skepticism about our ability to decide who was really at fault for marital failure."[48]

Identifying fault in an adultery hypothetical probably represents the easiest refutation of the difficulty of determining who was at fault. Adultery is an example where the social norm, fidelity, continues to be "quite robust."[49] That adultery threatens the stability of marriage is reflected in a 2003 study, in which adultery was the most frequently cited cause for divorce among divorcees.[50] Judges generally have no difficulty identifying adultery. Historically, the inquiry was not whether the other spouse's "getting fat" or "coldness"[51] was the "cause" of the adultery or whether the adultery caused the "coldness" or weight gain. Adultery was the only cognizable fault, regardless of what psychological or emotional motivation spurred the adulterer. Society confidently punished adultery because the essential feature of monogamous marriage is sexual fidelity, an obligation imposed

[42] PRINCIPLES § 1, Topic 2, pt. III, cmt. a, at 49–50.

[43] PRINCIPLES § 5.02 Reporter's Notes, cmt. e, at 796–97.

[44] PRINCIPLES § 5.02 Reporter's Notes, cmt. e, at 796–97 ("The problem of devising rules of marital conduct and then applying them can be seen by examining adultery, which is still treated as 'fault' by many states that otherwise determine alimony by no-fault rules, undoubtedly because even in the modern world one still finds general agreement that marriage entails a commitment to sexual fidelity. Yet justice is hardly served by treating one spouse's adultery as relevant to the alimony inquiry without also examining the other spouse's conduct, the tacit understandings between them, and the conduct of both before and after the adulterous episode. Deciding which, if either, to condemn is difficult and relating that moral judgment to the claim for support or the allocation of marital property is necessarily arbitrary.").

[45] PRINCIPLES § 1, Topic 2, pt. III, cmt. a, at 50.

[46] PRINCIPLES § 1, Topic 2, pt. III, cmt. a, at 51.

[47] PRINCIPLES § 1, Topic 2, pt. III, cmt. a, at 49–50 (emphasis added).

[48] Ellman, *supra* note 2, at 304.

[49] Elizabeth S. Scott, *Marriage, Cohabitation and Collective Responsibility for Dependency*, 2004 U. CHI. L. FORUM 225. *See also* Elizabeth S. Scott, *Social Norms and The Legal Regulation of Marriage*, 86 VA. L. REV. 1901, 1919 (2000).

[50] Paul Amato & Denise Previti, *People's Reasons for Divorcing: Gender, Social Class, the Life Course, and Adjustment*, J. FAM. ISSUES 602 (July 2003).

[51] Ellman, *supra* note 2, at 304 ("[P]erhaps the husband's infidelity was bred by his wife's coldness. But then, perhaps her coldness resulted from his insensitivity. Can we tell which came first? Can we even tell whether he was really insensitive, or she was really cold? One might reasonably doubt whether there are accepted standards for judging such things.").

on the spouses by law or social norms even in this postmodern world.[52] Adultery was considered sufficiently serious to permit a spouse the choice of a legal separation and later divorce, despite society's overarching interest in the stability of marriages. Considering the relevance of the psychological cause of the adultery is a twentieth century phenomenon, a phenomenon increasingly influential, especially over the last four decades.

"The rise of psychologic man"[53] had profound effects on family law, and those effects continue to influence the view of many Americans. This view explains the PRINCIPLES' reference to nuance in marital relationships. To suggest that there is nuance in whether a wife's coldness or getting fat precipitated or caused the husband's adultery and thus was the true cause of the breakdown of the marriage, merely scratches the surface.

> The problem is even more complicated than the text suggests. Perhaps ... the mistake was in ever thinking they loved one another; who is responsible for that? Suppose the husband tried to make the marriage last even after it seemed that mutual affection had been lost, but was not able to make his emotions follow this determination. Is he then liable for his coldness or insensitivity? More examples can be given; the point is simply that *human relations are too complex to be susceptible to such inquiries.*[54]

To describe human relations as "too complex to be susceptible to such inquiries" is to adopt the view that personal affairs should be viewed from a psychological perspective, not a moral one.[55] Combined with changing sexual mores, the psychological perspective, Professor Schneider observed, "has sharpened our appreciation of the enforcement problem, and it shapes and is shaped by the tradition of liberal individualism."[56] The psychologic view and the ideas it promotes, moral skepticism and relativism,[57] have replaced "moral thought with therapeutic thought."[58] Those who adopt the psychologic view endorse an individual's need for "privacy," defined as the right to conduct one's affairs autonomously, free of unnecessary constraint so as to pursue self discovery, which is the goal of human existence.[59] Such a view rejects the idea that human conduct should be discussed in moral terms:

> "No-fault" divorce ... captures neatly the psychologic attitude toward the latter belief: There ought to be no sense of guilt when a marriage doesn't work, because there was simply a technical dysfunction; there ought to be no sense of prolonged responsibility, because that would itself be dysfunctional; and there ought to be no regulation of those technical problems except, possibly, a technical one, i.e., counselling[sic].[60]

[52] PRINCIPLES § 5.02, Reporter's Notes, cmt. e, at 796. *See also* Scott, *supra* note 49, at 241–42 ("[M]any marital norms (loyalty, *fidelity*, trust) create behavioral expectations for both husband and wife that underscore their mutual commitment to the relationship.... Marital status also signals the community that the spouses are not available for other intimate relationships, and thus discourages outsiders interested in intimacy from approaching married persons. *In general, the fidelity norm is quite robust*; the spouse contemplating adultery will anticipate costs associated with guilt and community disapproval.") (emphasis added).

[53] Schneider, *supra* note 29, at 1845–63.

[54] Ellman, *supra* note 2, at 305, n. 84 (emphasis added).

[55] Schneider, *supra* note 29, at 1845.

[56] *Id.* at 1835–45 (identifying the tradition of noninterference in the family and liberal individualism as cultural forces transforming family law).

[57] *Id.* at 1867 ("The Court's attitude in *Roe* fits well with the moral skepticism and relativism that are part of psychologic man's world views."). *See also* Carl E. Schneider, *Marriage, Morals and the Law: No-Fault Divorce and Moral Discourse*, 1994 UTAH L. REV. 503 (exploring moral relativism and its manifestation among students at Michigan Law School).

[58] *Id.* at 1847.

[59] *Id.* at 1861, 1851.

[60] *Id.* at 1853.

Not surprisingly, the psychological view of relationships leads to nonbinding commitments:[61]

> [T]he view that a relationship should be maintained only if it 'works,' that 'options' should be kept numerous and open to 'facilitate personal growth,' and that living in a family is a matter of psychological adjustment, a technical matter of finding happiness, not a matter of moral relations. This view prefers temporary marriages, temporary nonmarital arrangements. . . .[62]

Classical liberalism and its "economic man" share the same goal, that is, "the greatest good for the greatest number is to be had by allowing the market, in goods or in 'interpersonal relations,' to work as free of government regulation as possible."[63] As Professor Ellman expresses it,

> [F]or a marriage to endure, both spouses must see the marriage as yielding a benefit to them. . . . However we define 'benefit' – to include financial factors or not – both spouses derive a benefit from the intact marriage, or it will not remain intact.[64]

The goal of egalitarianism within the married family encourages the focus of the law to be on the individual, rather than the family unit, just as the psychological perspective does.[65] As a practical matter if the family is viewed as a unit someone must speak for it and "historically, when the family has spoken, the voice has been the husband's."[66] Despite the modern view of the family unit as composed of the two spouses who are seen as equals, the eradication, which was appropriate, of the partriarchal concept of the family "has perhaps led to a form of egalitarianism whose effects can be atomistic."[67] Egalitarianism in its most radical form envisions each spouse as obligated "to maintain their independence, to be their own person."[68] Yet, as Professor Thomas Oldham observes, there is obvious concern by the drafters for "the plight of homemakers at the dissolution of a long marriage."[69] One argument advanced is that "as women age it is more difficult for them to find new partners than it is for men," and "many married women earn less than their husbands," thus, "the cost of divorce is higher for older women than for men."[70] If this is true, then clearly egalitarianism in married life has not yet been achieved.[71]

Before no-fault divorce, a coherent theory of alimony existed in civil law jurisdictions.[72] Posing the question, "[u]pon what idea is founded persistence of the obligation of support between two persons who have nothing in common?" Marcel Planiol, the great French treatise writer, answered, "Whatever act of man causes damage to another obliges him by whose fault it happened to repair it."[73] For civil law jurisdictions, alimony after divorce

[61] *Id.* at 1848.

[62] *Id.* at 1855.

[63] *Id.* at 1863.

[64] Ellman, *supra* note 2, at 281. *But see* Lee E. Teitelbaum, *The Family as a System: A Preliminary Sketch*, 1996 UTAH L. REV. 537 (arguing that Professor Ellman assumes rational decision-making during marriage, which in fact does not occur in any explicit way).

[65] Schneider, *supra* note 29, at 1859 ("Finally, psychologic man's view of families as made up of individuals is encouraged by and encourages egalitarianism.").

[66] *Id.* at 1859. *See also* Elizabeth S. Scott, *Social Norms and the Legal Regulation of Marriage*, 86 VA. L. REV. 1901 (2000).

[67] *Id.* at 1860.

[68] Schneider, *supra* note 57, at 514.

[69] Oldham, *supra* note 10, at 808. *See also* Teitelbaum, *supra* note 64.

[70] Oldham, *supra* note 10, at 808.

[71] *See* discussion in text at notes 127–32, *infra.*

[72] Apparently, coherence did not exist in common law jurisdictions. Schneider, *supra* note 29; Ellman, *supra* note 2.

[73] Planiol, TRAITE ELEMENTAIRE DE DROIT CIVIL, Vol. 1-Part 1, No. 1259 at 696 (LA. ST. L. INST. transl. 1959).

when the parties were no longer spouses was founded in the law of tort – the "duty is to make pecuniary amends for the consequences of an illicit act."[74]

Because fault is excluded from consideration, the theory underlying compensatory spousal payments in the PRINCIPLES obviously cannot rest on tort. Neither can it rest on contract. Even though the spouses made promises to each other in their wedding vows,[75] under the PRINCIPLES the court will not specifically enforce these[76] unless the "breaching party" caused certain financial losses. If marriage were a contract with implied terms based upon social norms,[77] such as the norm that marriage is for life,[78] the spouse who terminated the marriage by no-fault divorce would violate the terms of the contract. That spouse would be required to restore to the other spouse "that part of the bargain that can be reduced to economic terms."[79] It would be inconceivable in a contractual action for the "breaching party" to be able to recover damages. Furthermore, to be the "breaching party" would require an assessment of who violated the terms of the contract, whose fault constituted the breach.[80] But, how can one be a "breaching party" if the implied terms of the contract do not obligate either of the parties to "stay married?" If the law in the form of unilateral no-fault divorce permits a spouse at any time for any reason to terminate the marriage, there can be no implied obligation to stay with a spouse.[81]

Not even a quasicontractual remedy such as unjust enrichment can supply a basis for this obligation since that remedy, too, requires an inquiry as to why the claim exists and why the enrichment is not just.[82] Even more importantly, it requires proof that one party

[74] *Id.* at 696–97 (citing FR. CIV. CODE art. 1382, which corresponds to LA. CIV. CODE art. 2315) ("As long as the marriage lasted it gave each of the spouses an acquired position upon which each could count. The community of life permitted the spouse without means to share the welfare of the other. Suddenly through no fault of the spouse in question, he or she finds himself or herself devoid of resources and plunged into poverty. It is manifestly in such a case as this that the guilty party should be made to bear the consequences of his wrongful act.... This obligation subsisting after divorce partakes, in the highest degree, of the nature of an indemnity. It is intended to restore to the spouse without means something of the resources of which he or she is thenceforth deprived through the other's fault.... This indemnity nevertheless merely counter balances the privation of the right to support which was vested in the spouse. It becomes transformed into alimony....").

[75] Scott, *supra*, note 49 at 240 ("Each party's choice to marry signals to the partner and to the community that he/she is what Eric Posner [in *Family Law and Social Norms*, The Fall and Rise of Freedom of Contract (ed F. H. Buckley 1999)] calls a 'good type' – a responsible party ready to undertake a *long term* commitment to an *exclusive* intimate affiliation.")(emphasis added).

[76] Maggie Gallagher, END NO-FAULT DIVORCE? YES, FIRST THINGS: A MONTHLY JOURNAL OF RELIGION AND PUBLIC LIFE 24 (1997).

[77] Scott, *supra* note 49.

[78] *Id.*; *see also* Schneider, *supra* note 57, at 509 ("[T]he understanding he and his wife had almost surely entertained when they married that they were making a lifetime commitment to each other, that they were forsaking all others until death them did part.").

[79] Schneider, *supra* note 29, at 1859. Louisiana uniquely allows for the recovery of nonpecuniary damages for the breach of certain types of contract. LA. CIV. CODE art. 1998 (2005). *See* notes 102–12, *infra.*

[80] *See, e.g.,* LA. CIV. CODE art. 1994 (2005) ("An obligor is liable for damages caused by his failure to perform a conventional obligation [contract].").

[81] Carbone, *supra* note 5, at 76 ("Neither the PRINCIPLES nor existing law provide enough of an award to allow [the primary caretaker of children] to realize the expectation that she could continue to devote the major part of her energies to care of the children. I believe that this result follows from the decision *not to recognize the obligation to stay married as a substantive,* rather than a procedural or administrative issue. The failure to recognize fault ratifies the conclusion that both parties are free to leave the relationship at will.")(emphasis added).

[82] *See, e.g.,* LA. CIV. CODE art. 2298 (2005) ("A person who has been enriched without cause at the expense of another person is bound to compensate that person. The term 'without cause' is used in this context to exclude cases in which the enrichment results from a valid juridical act or the law. The remedy declared here is subsidiary and shall not be available if the law provides another remedy for the impoverishment or declares a contrary rule. The amount of compensation due is measured by the extent to which one has been enriched or the other has been impoverished, whichever is less.").

was enriched and the other impoverished, with a causal connection between the two. Yet, each of the instances of compensable loss under the PRINCIPLES rests upon the intuition, or theory, that to deny recovery would cause an unfair allocation of losses attributable to the marriage and its termination. Why are the losses in Chapter 5 of the PRINCIPLES unfair and other losses are not? Is it possible to resort to established notions of equity to support each instance of loss for which compensation is due?

B. Kinds of Compensable Loss

The PRINCIPLES' explicit goal of substituting specific instances of compensatory loss for the concept of alimony, which is largely discretionary, has instant appeal for a lawyer from a jurisdiction in which private law is codified. Yet, at the same time a legal system of codified private law usually formulates legislation in relatively broad statements of general principles, adopting fixed rules to implement those principles where a great degree of social consensus exists and general assumptions about human behavior are warranted.[83]

In Chapter 5, the PRINCIPLES recognize five categories of compensable loss: (1) for marriages of significant duration, there is a compensable loss when one spouse with less wealth or earning capacity suffers the loss of a higher living standard after divorce; (2) for a caretaker spouse who bore a disproportionate share of the care of children and suffered a loss of earning capacity during marriage that continues after divorce; (3) for a caretaker spouse who cared for "a sick, elderly, or disabled third party, in *fulfillment* of a *moral obligation* of the other spouse or of both spouses jointly" and suffered a loss of earning capacity during marriage that continues after divorce; (4) for a spouse who invests in the other spouse's earning capacity and suffers a loss when the marriage is dissolved before that spouse "realizes a fair return from his or her investment in the other spouse's earning capacity;" and (5) for a spouse in a short marriage who suffers an unfair and disproportionate loss because of her inability to recover her "pre-marital living standard after divorce."[84]

Critics offer a number of observations about these provisions. First, the narrow, exclusive range of losses compensated are simultaneously over- and underinclusive in view of the drafters' theory for such payments.[85] Second, the desire to remove disincentives for opportunistic behavior during marriage is not fully accomplished because the provisions only recognize loss from economically rational marital sharing behavior.[86] Third, the incentives and disincentives contained in the PRINCIPLES require that people know the law and its details, something that very few do.[87] Fourth, the theory is narrow and its

[83] In Louisiana, one such system within the United States, the law governing the incidental effects of divorce contains some clear fixed rules, such as the equal ownership and division of community property (LA. CIV. CODE arts. 2336, 2369.1 (2005)); some extremely specific, formulaic rules, such as those in child support (LA. CIV. CODE arts. 141–42; 215–237 (2005), including the particularized child support guidelines in LA. R.S. 9:315, *et seq* (2005); some less specific rules implementing a general principle that nonetheless channels the judge's discretion, such as with child custody (LA. CIV. CODE arts. 131–33 (2005) (read together, these articles establish a hierarchy directing the judge in determining what constitutes the best interest of the child); and finally, some rules that give wider discretion to the judge, such as those for determining spousal support and a claim for contributions to a spouse's education or training (LA. CIV. CODE arts. 111–17 (2005)).

[84] PRINCIPLES § 5.03; PRINCIPLES § 5.03, cmt. c, at 801 (emphasis added).

[85] Carl E. Schneider, *Rethinking Alimony: Marital Decisions and Moral Discourse*, 1991 BYU L. REV. 197 (citations omitted). *See generally* David Westfall, *Unprincipled Family Dissolution: The American Law Institute's Recommendations for Spousal Support and Division of Property*, 27 HARV. J.L. PUB. 917 (2004).

[86] Schneider, *supra* note 85; *see also* Teitelbaum, *supra* note 64.

[87] Schneider, *supra* note 85, at 205; DiFonzo, *supra* note 4, at 956.

application and calculation are very complex and speculative, both in applying the criteria for an award[88] and in calculating the sum due for the loss.[89] Fifth, the assumptions about marriage and the spouses as "self-interested bargainers" in purely economic terms are not accurate nor are they supported by empirical data.[90] Sixth, the provisions ignore marital exchange to decide if the investment was a genuine loss and thus can result in injustice.[91]

Other critiques offer more specific suggestions, such as (1) adopting a pure restitution theory;[92] (2) abolishing recovery for loss based upon duration of the marriage and the loss of a higher standard of living at divorce;[93] (3) abolishing compensation for inability to recover a premarital standard of living in a short, childless marriage;[94] (4) removing the period of time for caretaking of children that is required to qualify for a compensatory payment under § 5.06;[95] (5) eliminating a compensatory payment when the caretaking of children involved the claimant's child from another marriage;[96] and (6) permitting a claim for spousal support in every divorce "for a very short period ... in those states where a divorce can be obtained before a spouse has had an opportunity to adjust to the new situation."[97] In an attempt to assist the ALI in persuading others to adopt the PRINCIPLES, Professor June Carbone suggests that the ALI first "acknowledge the substantive grounds for rejecting fault," which should be the changed nature of marriage rather than the fact that fault is too difficult to determine; second, rest the theory for compensatory payments on "restitution for lost career opportunities and other marital contributions;" third, conduct a more thorough exploration of the "different nature of marital assets;" and last, "explicitly acknowledge the continuing role of public as well as private rationales for the financial resolutions made at divorce."[98]

Despite these critiques, almost every author applauds the result of the PRINCIPLES as an improvement over the current state of the law governing alimony, especially when considered in conjunction with the law of equitable distribution.[99] There seems to be general consensus that narrow rules that fix the criteria and the calculation of the sum due with greater certainty, thus predictability, are especially desirable. Virtually every critique, whether reluctantly or enthusiastically, approved of the specific elimination of fault as an element in the financial consequences of divorce.[100] Yet, no one should be surprised

[88] The PRINCIPLES require, for example, a determination of "earning capacity," "disproportionate share," "caretaking," "moral obligation to a third party," and "significant duration."

[89] Schneider, *supra* note 85, at 209, 225.

[90] *Id.*, at 212-15, 242; Ann Estin, *Love and Obligation: Family Law and the Romance of Economics*, 36 WM. & MARY L. REV. 989 (1995); Ann Estin, *Marriage and Belonging*, 100 MICH. L. REV. 1690 (2002); DiFonzo, *supra* note 4, at 951.

[91] Schneider, *supra* note 85, at 220–21.

[92] Both Professors Carbone and DiFonzo suggest restitution as the appropriate theory. *See* Carbone, *supra* note 5, at 77; DiFonzo, *supra* note 4, at 945–51.

[93] Oldham, *supra* note 10, at 807–10; PRINCIPLES § 5.04.

[94] Oldham, *id.*, at 829.

[95] *Id.* at 812.

[96] *Id.* at 830.

[97] *Id.*

[98] Carbone, *supra* note 5, at 77–78 ("Fault rested historically on the nature of marriage as a lifelong commitment made by the couple not only to each other, but to God and community."); Parkman, *supra* note 21.

[99] Two authors postulate that the provisions of the PRINCIPLES are too intertwined and interrelated that they must be adopted *in toto* or not at all. DiFonzo, *supra* note 4, at 959; Oldham, *supra* note 10.

[100] Schneider, *supra* note 85, at 257; Oldham, *supra* note 10, at 829 (generally approving of the elimination of fault for purpose of compensatory awards at divorce, but recognizing that "[i]t may also be wise to bar a claimant from receiving post-divorce sharing if guilty of outrageous behavior"); Carbone, *supra* note 5 (critiquing the PRINCIPLES' lack of coherence but arguing that introducing greater coherence might inflict more damaging costs by requiring a recognition and consideration of fault). Only Professor Schneider lamented the loss of alimony and its historical foundation, the moral responsibility of each spouse for the other that deepens and strengthens over time as their lives become increasingly intertwined.

if under the rubric of "substantial injustice" or "equity" a judge chooses to consider the moral relations of the parties and to deny any recovery to the claimant, who otherwise satisfies the criteria for a compensatory payment.[101]

C. Non-Compensable Losses: Expectation and Non-Pecuniary Damages

Only a narrow range of pecuniary loss at divorce is compensable under the PRINCIPLES.[102] Neither expectation loss recoverable for breach of contract[103] nor nonpecuniary loss – that is, damage of a moral nature which does not exert a tangible impact[104] – is compensable under the PRINCIPLES. To include expectation loss, as is common in cases of breach of contract, would require one to identify the implied terms of the marriage contract and then determine who breached the contract, necessarily assigning blame to the spouse whose fault caused the damage.[105] Because either spouse is free to leave at any time, there is no implied term for how long the marriage will last.[106] As a consequence, a primary caretaker in a short marriage under the PRINCIPLES will be unable to recover for "the expectation that she could continue to devote the major part of her energies to care of the children."[107] The advice to the custodial parent following divorce is "You're on your own, baby. Look to your own career or a new relationship for your future, not to the promise to remain married."[108]

No one doubts that emotional, psychological, and social losses are engendered by divorce and that the suffering brought on by such losses often outlasts the other injuries inflicted by divorce. After all, the opportunity to inflict harm and the unique vulnerability of persons in intimate relationships makes such injury likely and potentially severe. Yet, recognition of such claims "would require examining the reasons for divorce – who is at fault, who 'breached'"[109] the contract and that is impossible. Stressing the impossible once again, Professor Ellman observes,

> [s]uch emotional losses are properly excluded.... Even if one believes they should be compensable, since the rationale for allowing recovery would necessarily be quite different.... Emotional pain one spouse inflicts upon the other would surely require a finding

[101] PRINCIPLES § 5.02(3) ("Equitable principles of loss recognition and allocation *should* take into account all of the following....") (emphasis added). Note that *should* is aspirational, and the sentence fails to use "only."

[102] Ellman, *supra* note 2, at 283.

[103] The Louisiana Civil Code measures damages as the "loss sustained by the obligee and *the profit of which he has been deprived*." LA. CIV. CODE art. 1995 (2005) (emphasis added). Furthermore, a distinction is drawn between the obligor who breached the contract in good faith and one who breached the contract in bad faith with the former liable only for the damages "that were *foreseeable* at the time the contract was made." LA. CIV. CODE art. 1996 (2005).

[104] LA. CIV. CODE art. 1998 (2005) ("Damages for nonpecuniary loss may be recovered when the contract, *because of its nature*, is intended to *gratify a nonpecuniary interest* and, because of the *circumstances surrounding the formation or the nonperformance of the contract*, the obligor knew, or should have known, that his failure to perform would cause that kind of loss. Regardless of the nature of the contract, these damages may be recovered also when the obligor intended, through his failure, to aggrieve the feelings of the obligee.") (emphasis added); *id.* cmt. b (defining nonpecuniary loss).

[105] Carbone, *supra* note 5, at 76–77 ("The second expectation interest that suffers from these formulations is that of the higher earning spouse whose mate leaves him after a long marriage, with a right not only to half of their accumulated assets, but a substantial share of his post-divorce earnings.... The PRINCIPLES make some effort to limit the potential injustices from failure to recognize which party precipitated the divorce [by providing for some deviations from the formula in cases of injustice].").

[106] Carbone, *supra* note 5, at 73.

[107] *Id.* at 76.

[108] *Id.*

[109] Schneider, *supra* note 85, at 225 (internal citations omitted).

> that the claimant's emotional loss flowed from some conduct of the defendant's that one is prepared to label as blameworthy.[110]

Professor Ellman doubts that a rational system could be devised to include nonrational and nonfinancial losses without a determination of fault so he would leave nonfinancial losses at the courthouse door.[111] Ironically, Professor Schneider argues that it is impossible to construct a system of "alimony" in "morally neutral terms" that will preclude a judge from considering the parties' moral relations.[112] The law of contract, tort, and quasi contract surely cannot.

Why is it, then, that only in marriage, a relationship that includes economic, emotional, psychological, and child rearing goals for one's entire life, the PRINCIPLES would preclude an examination of the moral relations of the parties? Has the nature of marriage changed, as Professor Carbone suggests, and what vision of marriage does the PRINCIPLES' treatment of alimony endorse?

II. Vision of Marriage Conveyed by the PRINCIPLES: Joint Venture for a Limited Purpose?

> [T]he law cannot easily escape the need to adopt and apply a moral theory of marriage.... The gravitational pull of no-fault divorce, however, has exacerbated the trend away from *moral discourse and left the law of alimony*... unsupported by any satisfactory moral understanding of marriage.[113]

Divorce laws shape our understanding of marriage, "the nature, expectations and success" of marriage; to what extent and in combination with what other cultural and social forces is unclear and controversial, however.[114] Social science research can assist in evaluating the current state of marriage and divorce and assessing whether solidifying the no-fault divorce revolution is a desirable goal. There now exists a significant body of research studying the life course of those impacted by divorce. "Low-discord" marriages that end in divorce, that is, marriages that would be "good enough" from a child's perspective, are increasing proportionately and it is those divorces among "good enough" marriages which are the most harmful for children.[115] As Elizabeth Scott observes:

> [I]t is possible that no-fault divorce reforms may have contributed to the inclination of parents in "good enough" marriages to divorce by inadvertently destroying restrictions on divorce that served as useful precommitment mechanisms.[116]

[110] Ellman, *supra* note 2, at 283. *See* discussion in text at notes 102–12 *supra*.

[111] *Id.* at 270.

[112] Schneider, *supra* note 85.

[113] Schneider, *supra* note 57, at 556. (emphasis added).

[114] Wardle, *supra* note 4, at 120. For an example of scholarship suggesting other social forces, *see* Nancy E. Dowd, *Law, Culture, and Family: The Transformative Power of Culture and the Limits of Law*, 78 CHI.-KENT L. REV. 785 (2003).

[115] Paul R. Amato, *Good Enough Marriages: Parental Discord, Divorce, and Children's Long-Term Well-Being*, 9 VA. J. SOC. POL'Y & L. 71 (2001). *See also* PAUL R. AMATO & ALAN BOOTH, A GENERATION AT RISK (1997); Margaret F. Brinig and Douglas W. Allen, *"These Boots Are Made For Walking": Why Most Divorce Filers are Women*, 2 AM. L. & ECON. REV. 126 (2000) (reporting that self-interest drives filing behavior, which is motivated especially by the feeling of being exploited within the marriage, and finding that many filers used no-fault divorce, "supporting the theory that bare restrictions on exit from marriage would be particularly costly to women"). Of course, anecdotal evidence suggests that the decision whether to use the no-fault ground is ordinarily one made by the attorney, not the client. *See also* ELIZABETH MARQUARDT, BETWEEN TWO WORLDS (2005) (discussing the myth of the "good divorce" for the children).

[116] *See also* Elizabeth Scott, *Rational Decision-making about Marriage and Divorce*, 76 VA. L. REV. 9 (1990).

By imposing substantial costs on the decision to divorce (the requirement of proving fault), divorce law discouraged unhappy spouses from leaving a marriage because of transitory dissatisfaction or routine stresses – boredom, mid-life crises, and the like.[117] If social norms supporting commitment in marriage have weakened, in part because the law erects no internal or external barriers to protect marriage, and more "good enough" marriages end in divorce, which harms children, the view of marriage implied in any proposed new law must be carefully and deliberately considered.

What view of marriage do the provisions of the PRINCIPLES, particularly the chapter on compensatory spousal payments, portray? For the ALI, "[f]amily breakdown is accepted as a given [because either no one is at fault or both individuals share blame], and an appropriate basis for dissolution, and the legal framework surrounding the Project's implementation is oriented towards fair treatment that is nonpunitive, nonsexist, nonpaternalistic...."[118] It is a simple fact that Americans have accepted "serial marriage."[119] This being true,

> a more realistic analogy for marriage in the twenty-first century is the joint venture, given the unilateral nature of no-fault divorce. A joint venture is defined in the commercial setting as '[a] legal entity in the nature of a partnership engaged in the joint undertaking of a particular transaction for mutual profit.' A joint venture differs from a partnership in that it 'does not entail a continuing relationship among the parties.' *At first glance, the joint venture may seem to be the exact antithesis of a stable relationship and therefore poorly suited as a conceptualization of an enterprise that typically involves the rearing of children.*[120]

Completing the analogy, Professor Herma Hill Kay observes that (1) in a joint venture the model is one of "spouses who are self-sufficient at the outset of the undertaking;" (2) a joint venture "requires a community of interest in the performance of the subject matter," such as having children and rearing them; (3) a joint venture presupposes "'a right to direct and govern' the undertaking;" and (4) "[*t*]*he most attractive aspect*... the possibility of renewal" at each stage of completion of the project of family life.[121] Renewal involves a decision by the couple "whether the venture should be continued to the next stage,"[122] always with the "recognition that either spouse is free to terminate the undertaking."[123]

How many couples who marry envision their marriages as a joint venture defined by these four distinct features? How many married couples live out marriage as a joint venture with the possibility of renewal? When is there a "stage of completion" and how does one "renew?" Professor Kay admits that "a concept of marriage as a joint venture is not yet an

[117] Elizabeth S. Scott, *Divorce, Children's Welfare, and the Culture Wars*, 9 VA. J. SOC. POL'Y & L. 95, 103 (2001). *See also* Peter Nash Swisher, *Reassessing Fault Factors in No-Fault Divorce*, 31 FAM. L. Q. 269 (1997); Spaht, *supra* note 27 (discussing the dismantling of barriers).

[118] Herma Hill Kay, *From the Second Sex to the Joint Venture: An Overview of Women's Rights and Family Law in the United States During the Twentieth Century*, 88 CAL. L. REV. 2017, 2073 (2000). Earlier, Professor Kay observed that "[d]ivorce by unilateral fiat is closer to desertion than to mutual separation." *Beyond No-Fault: New Directions in Divorce Reform*," HERMA HILL KAY, DIVORCE REFORM AT THE CROSSROADS 8 (1990).

[119] Oldham, *supra* note 10, at 827. *See also* BARBARA DAFOE WHITEHEAD, THE DIVORCE CULTURE 188 (1999).

[120] Kay, *supra* note 118, at 2089 (emphasis added).

[121] *Id.* at 2089 (emphasis added). *See also* Carbone, *supra* note 5, at 76 (arguing that the conception of marriage as a joint venture "would provide a stronger framework for the ALI approach than the conclusion that the otherwise relevant consideration of fault is simply too difficult to define").

[122] *Id.* at 2089.

[123] *Id.*

appropriate model for all couples."[124] However, she believes that "[t]he trend towards independence and self-sufficiency for women... has made clear... that traditional marriage is not well-adapted to dual-career couples."[125] Yet, even though a joint venture analogy may be more suitable to dual career couples, Professor Kay concedes that the "vision of equality between men and women in the home as well as the market-place... has not yet been realized."[126]

Equality in the home may never be realized. Professor Ellman observes that an economist interested in maximizing production would not predict egalitarian marriage, that is, "a marriage in which the spouses share domestic tasks equally, and have equal market labor commitments...."[127] This is so because specialization by the spouses creates a gain that is lost in egalitarian marriage.[128] Working wives continue to shoulder an unequal share of housework, a phenomenon that "must in some sense result from the interaction of common preferences of men and women, whether or not one regards the preferences as unfairly or improperly constrained."[129] Such common preferences would include a wife's preference for more of the domestic role and a preference for a husband with higher earnings who is not domestically inclined to permit her to perform that role.[130]

> [I]t may be that if one looks at what people actually do, rather than at what they say, one finds a pattern that is more consistent *with the continuing durability of traditional gender roles.* Perhaps, then, the tension is between what people think they ought to want, and what they actually want: we *ought* to want gender equality, which perhaps means we *ought* to want to abolish gender roles in marriage. But one may believe that eliminating gender roles in marriage is an important societal aspiration but have preferences in the conduct of one's own marriage that are not entirely in accord.[131]

Professor Ellman concludes that "[h]umans are enormously adaptable, but our preferences may be less malleable than our tactics."[132]

If egalitarian marriage is unlikely to materialize because of the preferences of men and women, can we afford to adopt joint venture as a theory of marriage when it neither reflects the reality nor the aspirations of married life? Who might suffer most from the adoption of such a theory that promotes temporary commitments requiring constant renewals?

[124] *Id.*

[125] *Id.* at 2090 ("Laws governing married names, domicile, and marital property all assume a primary breadwinner/dependent homemaker model of marriage."). *See also* Ira Mark Ellman, *Divorce Rates, Marriage Rates, and the Problematic Persistence of Traditional Marital Roles*, 34 FAM. L.Q. 1, 18 (2000) ("Feminists can be comfortable with the idea that the traditional patriarchal marriage relied for its survival on a socialization process that constrained women's choices within boundaries set by a marital role of financial dependency.").

[126] Kay, *supra* note 118, at 2090.

[127] Ellman, *supra* note 125, at 19.

[128] *See* Brinig & Allen *supra* note 115, at 150 (predicting that the bargaining during marriage after the birth of children is likely to disfavor wives and permit husbands to exploit their labor as nurturers, leading wives trapped in these "unhappy" marriages to want to flee).

[129] Ellman, *supra* note 125, at 19.

[130] *Id.* at 20 & n. 48. *See also* Paul R. Amato, David R. Johnson, Alan Booth, & Stacy J. Rogers, *Continuity and Change in Marital Quality Between 1980 and 2000*, 65 J. MARR. & FAM. 1 (Feb. 2003) (revealing that "[i]ncreases in husbands' share of housework appeared to depress marital quality among husbands but to improve marital quality among wives"); STEVEN RHOADS, TAKING SEX DIFFERENCES SERIOUSLY 248 (2004).

[131] Ellman, *supra* note 125, at 36–37.

[132] *Id.* at 39.

III. Marriage Differently Conceived: More Legal Stability and Protection to Facilitate Effective Choices by Wives and Mothers

> [W]e cannot adopt a theory of alimony until we construct a theory of marriage. The task before us, then, is to ask what we want of marriage as a social institution.[133]

If we adopted a view that emphasized "the separateness of the spouses rather than their unity,"[134] such a view would represent the ultimate triumph of individual autonomy in its radical form.[135] It would represent the primacy of the therapeutic culture[136] where self-actualization and perfectability trump marital stability.[137]

There are small but encouraging signs that Gen Xers are rebelling against their Baby-Boomer parents' casual treatment of marriage. A recent study conducted by Professor Paul Amato and colleagues documents the perceived cohesiveness by couples of their marriages in terms of rewards, barriers, and alternatives. The most frequently mentioned psychological barrier to divorce was "staying married for the sake of the children," a finding that suggests the beginning of a process of reversal of Americans' views about the primacy of personal autonomy and self-fulfillment. Even more encouraging is the reversal of a long-term trend among Americans: another barrier mentioned by couples was, "the commitment to the norm of lifelong marriage."[138] The reason the mention of the barrier of commitment to the norm of lifelong marriage is so encouraging is because, "the undermining of commitment" operates "as a primary mechanism underlying the intergenerational transmission of marital instability."[139] Even a small hint of a possible interruption in the intergenerational transmission of divorce is reason for encouragement.

[133] Schneider, *supra* note 85, at 257.

[134] *Id.*

[135] Schneider, *supra* note 29.

[136] Schneider, *supra* note 29.

[137] Wardle, *supra* note 4. For a contrary view of marriage, *see* Jane Adolphe, this volume.

[138] Paul Amato & Denise Previti, *Why Stay Married? Rewards, Barriers, and Marital Stability*, 65 J. MARR. & FAM. 561, 570 (Aug. 2003) ("[S]taying married for the sake of the children was the most commonly mentioned barrier, being cited by 31% of all respondents. Other barriers included a lack of financial resources, religious beliefs, commitment to the norm of lifelong marriage, and the maintenance of traditional breadwinner-homemaker roles."). *See also* Paul R. Amato, *Good Enough Marriages: Parental Discord, Divorce, and Children's Long-Term Well-Being*, 9 VA. J. SOC. POL'Y & L. 71 (2001); Elizabeth S. Scott, *Divorce, Children's Welfare, and the Culture Wars*, 9 VA. J. SOC. POL'Y & L. 95 (2001). Another study compared marital quality and divorce proneness among couples in 1980 and couples in 2000. Although the authors found little change in the intervening twenty years, couples in 2000 reported that marital interaction declined significantly. *See* Paul R. Amato, David R. Johnson, Alan Booth, and Stacy J. Rogers, *Continuity and Change in Marital Quality Between 1980 and 2000*, 65 J. MARR. & FAM. 1, 19 and 21 (Feb. 2003). ("[T]he lives of husbands and wives are becoming more separate, with couples being less likely to share activities such as eating meals, shopping, working on projects around the house, visiting friends, and going out for leisure activities."). The authors' explanation for this small change was that offsetting trends in the intervening twenty-year period improved marital quality. These trends include increases in economic resources, decision-making equality, nontraditional attitudes toward gender, and support for the norm of lifelong marriage. The authors concluded that "[i]ncreased support for the norm of lifelong marriage may have had positive implications for multiple dimensions of marital quality."

[139] Paul R. Amato & Danelle D. DeBoer, *The Transmission of Marital Stability Across Generations: Relationship Skills or Commitment to Marriage?*, 63 J. MARR. & FAM. 1038-57, 1049–50 (Nov. 2001). In Paul R. Amato and Stacy J. Rogers, *Do Attitudes Toward Divorce Affect Marital Quality?*, J. FAM. ISSUES 69, 70 (Jan. 1999), the authors observe: "Although most Americans continue to value marriage, the belief that an unrewarding marriage should be jettisoned may lead some people to invest less time and energy in their marriages and make fewer attempts to resolve marital disagreements. In other words, a weak commitment to the general norm of life-long marriage may ultimately undermine people's commitments to particular relationships."

There has to be a competing vision of marriage to that offered by the PRINCIPLES, one that does not undermine the norm of lifelong marriage and marital commitment.[140] Envisioning marriage as a joint venture for a limited purpose terminable at will by either "venturer" without significant penalty is a risky proposition, especially for women interested in child rearing.[141] Louisiana, Arizona, and Arkansas[142] are experimenting with an alternate vision of marriage – covenant marriage. It is a small, cautious experiment that permits the parties to choose a covenant marriage at their option. A covenant marriage contains essentially three unique features: mandatory premarital counseling after which the two parties sign a Declaration of Intent with an accompanying affidavit that they received counseling and attach the counselor's attestation; a legal obligation contained in the Declaration of Intent that the parties will take all reasonable steps to preserve their marriage if marital difficulties arise; and more restrictive divorce grounds requiring serious fault or that the parties live separate and apart for two years, rather than, for example, the shorter period of 180 days for no-fault divorce in Louisiana.[143]

To date the percentage of married couples selecting the optional covenant marriage remains very small, in part attributable to implementation problems.[144] Data accumulated from a five-year study of covenant couples in Louisiana, the first state to enact covenant marriage, support the more general observation about women's desire for long-term relationships:[145] "women are the 'leaders' in selecting covenant marriage, particularly women with a vested interest in childbearing who apparently feel the need for the protection of stronger divorce laws."[146] Covenant couples have a forceful conviction about the importance of the choice they are making that "standard" married couples do not.[147] Covenant couples, who are more educated than the standard married couples studied, believe "that

140 Allen M. Parkman, *supra* note 21, at 157 ("Most adult Americans believe that having a successful marriage and family life is very important, yet many of them fail in their attempts. A subtle, but important reason for their failures is the laws governing the dissolution of marriage. The combination of unilateral, no-fault grounds for divorce, with financial arrangements at divorce – that usually disregard the effect of marriage on the spouses' income earning capacity... have encouraged spouses to be more concerned about their own self-interest and less concerned about their family's welfare.").

141 Allen M. Parkman, *Bringing Consistency to the Financial Arrangements at Divorce,* 87 KENT L.J. 59, 76 n.116 (1998–99). ("Because no-fault divorce permits unilateral divorce often accompanied by limited financial compensation for women who have limited their careers to benefit their families, married women have been forced to take steps to protect themselves from the potential adverse effects of divorce. Since they are acting in their best interest rather than that of their families, this lack of protection for their investments often induces them to make inefficient decisions for their families because the benefits do not exceed the costs.").

142 LA. REV. STAT. §§ 9:272–75.1; 293–98; 307–09; ARIZ. REV. STAT. §§ 25–901–04 (1998); ARK. CODE ANN. §§ 9–11–801–08 (2001).

143 *See* Katherine Shaw Spaht, *Louisiana's Covenant Marriage Law: Social Analysis and Legal Implications,* 59 LA. L. REV. 63 (1998).

144 Laura Sanchez, Steven L. Nock, James D. Wright, Jessica W. Pardee, & Marcel Ionescu, *The Implementation of Covenant Marriage in Louisiana,* 9 VA. J. SOC. POL'Y & L. 192 (2001); Katherine Shaw Spaht, *What's Become of Louisiana's Covenant Marriage As Seen Through the Eyes of Social Scientists,* 47 LOY. L. REV. 1 (2003); Margaret F. Brinig & Steven L. Nock, *What Does Covenant Mean for Relationship?* 18 NOTRE DAME J.L. ETHICS & PUB. POL'Y. 137 (2004). Obviously, couples choosing covenant marriage are self-selecting, so that self-selection effects must be considered in any empirical review.

145 *See* RHOADS, note 130 *supra,* at 248.

146 Katherine Shaw Spaht, *Revolution and Counter-Revolution: The Future of Marriage in the Law,* 49 LOY. L. REV. 1, 52 (2003) (citing Laura Sanchez, Steven L. Nock, James D. Wright, Julia C. Wilson, *Social Demographic Factors Associated with Couple's Choice Between Covenant and Standard Marriage in Louisiana* (draft report presented May, 2002 and on file with author).

147 *Id.*

they are making a powerful social statement about marriage as an institution."[148] Couples in a covenant marriage "are far more likely to choose communication strategies that do not revolve around attacking or belittling their partner. [They] are less likely to respond to conflict with sarcasm or hostility, two communication strategies that ... are particularly strongly associated with poor marriage outcomes."[149]

In follow-up surveys after two years of marriage, covenant couples "'described their overall marital quality as better than did their Standard counterparts.' Covenant couples were more committed to their marriage two years after the ceremony than at the time of their marriage; whereas, their standard counterparts had changed little in their level of commitment."[150]

> With the growing centrality of marriage for covenant couples, they experienced "higher levels of commitment ... higher levels of agreement between partners ... fewer worries about having children ... and greater sharing of housework." It is not too early ... to conclude that covenant marriages are better marriages.... Steven Nock, the director of the study, expresses the view that internally the [covenant] marriages are vastly better, and covenant couples agree about who does what, the fairness of things, etc. much more than standard couples."[151]

As participants in this "new" form of marriage, covenant couples recognize that a covenant marriage "preserves the traditional, conventional, and religious aspects of the traditional institution, but also resolves the various inequities often associated with gender in marriages."[152] A key difference that "discriminates between the two types of unions ... [is] sanctification of the marriage," which simply reflects the couple's view that "the marriage warrants consideration apart from the individualistic concerns of either partner. In regard to some matters, covenant couples appear to defer to the interests of their marriage even when the individual concerns of the partners may appear to conflict. And this orientation to married life ... helps resolve the customary problems faced by newly married couples in regard to fairness and equity."[153] Covenant couples view marriage institutionally, which "elevates the normative (expected) model of marriage to prominence in the relationship."[154] What accounts for this institutional view? "[T]he centrality accorded religion by the couple"[155] and "beliefs about the life of marriage independently of the individual...."[156] Thus, covenant couples understand two autonomous individuals do not make a strong marriage; a strong marriage requires a set of guiding principles around which the two persons organize their lives and orient their behavior.

The Louisiana legislature has since enacted new provisions to enhance the covenant marriage legislation by addressing more explicitly the content of the covenant marriage

[148] *Id.*

[149] *Id.* at 52–53 (internal quotations omitted)

[150] *Id.* at 53; Brinig & Nock, *supra* note 144, at 175 ("What is interesting is that these couples feel *more* strongly about the concept three years into marriage, and that the difference in how they feel is significantly greater than the difference in how the standard marriage couples feel about the same statement."); *see also* Margaret F. Brinig & Steven L. Nock, *"I Only Want Trust": Norms, Trust, and Autonomy*, 32 J. Socio-Econ. 471–87 (2003).

[151] Spaht, *supra* note 146, at 53.

[152] Steven L. Nock, Laura Sanchez, James D. Wright, *Intimate Equity: The Early Years of Covenant and Standard Marriages* 7 (presented at annual meeting of the Population Assoc. of America, May 2003, on file with the author). *See also* Steven L. Nock, Laura Sanchez, Julia C. Wilson, James D. Wright, *Covenant Marriage Turns Five Years Old*, 10 Mich. J. Gender & L. 169 (2003).

[153] Nock, *supra* note 152, at 6. (emphasis added). *See also* Brinig & Nock, *supra* note 144.

[154] Nock, *supra* note 152.

[155] *Id.* at 7.

[156] *Id.*

relationship. The new legislation contains more specificity about the rights and responsibilities of covenant spouses, which supplements the law regulating all married couples. Under current law each spouse, in a covenant or standard marriage, owes to the other fidelity, support, and assistance,[157] legal terms of art which impose obligations upon the spouses toward each other. Fidelity has both negative aspects, not to have sex with another, and positive aspects, the obligation to submit to the reasonable sexual desires of the other spouse absent illness or grave cause, consisting almost always of fault by the other spouse.[158] Support means furnishing the other spouse with the necessities of life, which include "not only ... food, clothing and shelter, but also ... such conveniences as telephones, home appliances, and an automobile."[159] Assistance requires at the very least that personal care be given to an ill or infirm spouse and, more broadly, "defined," assist each other in the tasks of daily living required to promote cooperative living. As to children of the marriage, "[s]pouses mutually assume the moral and material direction of the family, exercise parental authority, and assume the moral and material obligations resulting therefrom."[160]

In addition to these obligations that all married spouses in Louisiana owe to each other, in a covenant marriage the law of separation and divorce speak to appropriate marital conduct. Each spouse is to "conduct himself so as not to bring dishonor and shame to the family formed by the marriage, which could occur by adulterous affairs, outrageous or felonious behavior, and constant intemperance."[161] Furthermore, in a covenant marriage neither spouse should leave the other [abandonment] and by so doing deny to the other spouse support and assistance. Nor should either spouse physically or sexually abuse the other spouse or a child of the parties.[162]

The new legislation also contains general principles about the content of marriage, "some with legal consequences intended to constrain or punish and others intended to be simply hortatory or examples of the expressive function of law."[163] The new legislation restores a vision of marriage that is more complete, and by doing so, asserts a public interest in marriage, expressed in its collective voice, the law. Consider the vision of marriage rhetorically communicated by some of these provisions, which obligate the covenant spouses to give "each other love and respect, ... commit to a community of living," and "attend to the satisfaction of the other's needs," as well as "live together, unless there is good cause otherwise," by determining "the family residence [through] mutual consent, according to their requirements and those of the family."[164] It is an egalitarian vision of marriage. "The management of the household shall be the right and the duty of both spouses" and the spouses "make decisions relating to family life" by "mutual consent after collaboration," guided by "the best interest of the family."[165] Furthermore, it is also focused on the child: "The spouses are bound to maintain, to teach, and to educate their children born of the marriage in accordance with their capacities, natural inclinations, and aspirations, and

[157] La. Civ. Code Ann. art. 98 (2005).

[158] *Id.* cmt. (b).

[159] *Id.* cmt. (c).

[160] La. Civ. Code Ann. art. 99 & cmt. 1987 (2005) ("This article is new. It states a general principle of equality between the spouses in the moral and material direction of the family.").

[161] Katherine Shaw Spaht, *supra* note 27, at 294.

[162] La. Rev. Stat. §§ 9:307A (3)(4) (2005).

[163] Katherine Shaw Spaht, *How Law Can Reinvigorate a Robust Vision of Marriage and Rival its Post-Modern Competitor*, 2 Geo. J.L. & Pub. Pol'y 449, 460 (2004); *see also* Katherine Shaw Spaht, *A Proposal: Legal Re-Regulation of the Content of Marriage*, 18 Notre Dame J.L. Ethics, & Pub. Pol'y 243 (2004).

[164] La. Rev. Stat. §§ 9:294-5 (2005).

[165] La. Rev. Stat. §§ 9:296-7 (2005).

shall prepare them for their future."[166] A competing vision of marriage emerges that bears little resemblance to a joint venture for a limited purpose.

IV. Conclusion

> Preserving a language through which the law can recognize the moral elements of family life may well be a desirable goal in a number of areas.[167]

Is marriage an area where the law should recognize the moral elements of family life? The ALI rejects a moral view of the marital relationship, setting aside as too messy the moral relations of the spouses. In so doing, the ALI accepts the basic principle that neither the spouses nor their conduct should be constrained by law and thus by society. Human nature often precludes altruistic decision-making that weighs the interests of others more heavily than one's own self–interest. Without constraint, human beings respond spontaneously and impulsively and identify freedom from constraint as a right to "privacy."

People, in all endeavors including marriage, need aspirations beyond self. The ALI's decision to wash its hands of morality fails to inspire and fails to seriously consider the saliency of attachments to the community. Couples deserve a transcendent view of "marriage," not a hollowed out one, and they deserve the active support of their community.

[166] La. Rev. Stat. § 9:298 (2005).

[167] Schneider, *supra* note 57 at 584, 583 ("We therefore need to recall that language matters, and that it is difficult to talk one way and act another. Thus it is legitimate to wonder how long people may be expected to act well without the spur and sustenance moral language provides.").

14 Domestic Partnership and Default Rules

Margaret F. Brinig

The domestic partnership chapter of the PRINCIPLES "both over-and undershoots its target."[1] That is, by assuming cohabitation and marriage were similar, but only legislating for the limited purpose of dissolution, the PRINCIPLES create a default rule that few would want. As may be obvious from their title, the PRINCIPLES do not attempt to directly influence ongoing family relationships. Thus, "In view of the scope of these Principles, Chapter 6 is limited to the following question: What are the economic rights and responsibilities of the parties to each other at the termination of their nonmarital cohabitation? Chapter 6 does not create any rights against the government or third parties."[2] Unprotected parties who would marry if they were able to (and for whom the chapter was presumably intended) would not get enough relief because there would be no protection upon death of one of them, nor is there a requirement of mutual support during the relationship. This stands in contrast to the Canadian rule, as Canadian law still enforces the duty to support during the "common law" relationship.[3] Moreover, parties who did not want to get married but wanted to cohabit would find themselves with a set of responsibilities on dissolution that they did not want to assume; if they had wanted these responsibilities, they would have married. Contrast this with Norway, where about 25 percent of couples are unmarried, but "[u]nlike married couples, cohabiting couples have no legal responsibility to provide for each other."[4]

Couples may not even see the importance of the step they take in "just living together."[5] One or both members of a cohabiting couple may even cohabit, rather than marry, in order to side-step difficult disagreements about the meaning and future of their relationship.

Some individuals who live together undoubtedly see cohabitation as an alternative to marriage, perhaps because they cannot marry, sometimes because they do not see the need for marrying, and sometimes because they see an overwhelming dark side to the institution of marriage itself. In some couples, one or both partners may see cohabitation as a prelude to marriage. One or both may wish to cohabit simply because it is a convenient way to live until the wedding or because, like the transition from dating to going steady to wearing his class ring to engagement, living together seems to be another stage in a

[1] Margaret F. Brinig, *Domestic Partnership: Missing the Target?*, 4 J. L. & FAM. STUD. 19, 20 (2002).

[2] PRINCIPLES § 1, Overview of Chapter 6, at 32.

[3] Modernization of Benefits and Obligations Act, S.C. 2000, c. 12.

[4] Truid Noak, *Cohabitation in Norway: An Accepted and Gradually More Regulated Way of Living*, 15 INT'L J. L. POL'Y. & FAM. 102, 110 (2001).

[5] JUST LIVING TOGETHER: IMPLICATIONS OF COHABITATION ON FAMILIES, CHILDREN AND SOCIAL POLICY (Alan Booth & Ann C. Crouter, eds.) (2002).

deepening relationship. Finally, a person may cohabit to test the relationship: Can I live with this partner without squabbling about cleanliness or sharing household chores?[6] Will we still find each other sexually attractive lounging in threadbare gym clothes? Can we really spend all our leisure time together without being bored of one another?

The problem, as noted above, is that the PRINCIPLES propose a default that no one wants. This, in and of itself, is a significant shortcoming. In commercial law, default rules are typically set to reflect what the parties would have chosen had they thought about it in advance, or what most people would want.[7] Alternatively, default rules, whether coming from legislatures or courts, may be designed to fill contractual gaps in socially efficient ways.[8] Marriage is theoretically an efficient arrangement. The economic model of marriage concludes that what should be maximized is "household production," or some combination of consumer goods and the leisure time to enjoy them.[9] I have argued elsewhere that the PRINCIPLES' domestic partnership proposal neither matches what most people would want nor fills contractual gaps in socially efficient ways.

This chapter tests another possibility. What if the ALI domestic partnership rules instead operate as a set of "penalty default rules," designed to insure that the parties would contract around them, or at least that they would reveal privately held information? This theoretical possibility was suggested in the commercial context by Professors Ian Ayres and Robert Gertner.[10] The idea with a penalty default rule is that when, for example, the Uniform Commercial Code ("UCC") sets a default quantity at "zero," it forces the parties to specify some other quantity.[11] Similarly, setting the availability of consequential damages at "zero" forces the party for whom they matter to contract for their recovery, probably at a higher contract price.[12] Certainly the ALI meetings themselves and the Reporter's Comments do not reflect any thinking along these lines.[13] The Comments state that Section 6.03 "does not require . . . that the parties had an implied or express agreement, or even that the facts meet the standard requirements of a quantum meruit claim. It instead relies, as do the marriage laws, on a status classification. . . . "[14] The Comments also suggest that this approach "places the burden of showing a contract on the party wishing to avoid such fairness-based remedies, rather than imposing it on the party seeking to claim

[6] PAMELA J. SMOCK & SANJIV GUPTA, *Cohabitation in Contemporary North America, in* Booth & Crouter, *supra* note 5, at 53, 68–69 (reporting that, surprisingly, cohabiting men do the same amount of housework as married men – on average 19 and 18 hours per week, respectively – while cohabiting women do 31 hours of housework per week compared to 37 for married women).

[7] Charles Goetz & Robert Scott, *The Mitigation Principle: Toward a General Theory of Contractual Obligation*, 69 VA. L. REV. 967, 971 (1983).

[8] Promotion of efficient outcomes, as opposed to what the parties most often want, is the other justification commonly given for default rules. *See, e.g.*, Alan Schwartz, *The Default Rule Paradigm and the Limits of Contract Law*, 3 S. CAL. INTERDISC. L.J. 389 (1993) (discussing various kinds of efficiency-producing norms); Charles J. Goetz & Robert E. Scott, *The Limits Of Expanded Choice: An Analysis Of The Interactions Between Express And Implied Contract Terms*, 73 CAL. L. REV. 261 (1985).

[9] ROBERT A. MOFITT, *Female Wages, Male Wages, and the Economic Model of Marriage: The Basic Evidence, in* THE TIES THAT BIND: PERSPECTIVES ON MARRIAGE AND COHABITATION 302, 303–06 (Linda J. Waite ed., 2000).

[10] Ian Ayres & Robert Gertner, *Filling Gaps In Incomplete Contracts: An Economic Theory Of Default Rules*, 99 Yale L.J. 87, 89 (1989).

[11] *Id.* at 95–96.

[12] *Id.* at 101–03. *See also*, William Bishop, *The Contract-Tort Boundary and the Economics of Insurance*, 12 J. LEGAL STUD. 241, 254 (1983); Lucien Bebchuk & Steven Shavell, *Information and the Scope of Liability for Breach of Contract: The Rule of Hadley v. Baxendale*, 7 J. L. ECON. & ORGAN. 284 (1991) .

[13] *See, e.g.*, Wardle, this volume; Gregory, this volume; Westfall, this volume.

[14] PRINCIPLES § 6.03(b) cmt. b, at 919.

them."[15] The Comments thus suggest that the drafters wanted to recognize that at least some cohabiting couples were in a "status" not substantially different from marriage and, consequently, that one of the classical rationales for default rules – filling contractual gaps in a socially efficient way – applied. This chapter shows, however, that neither the classical nor even the "penalty default" explanation for the ALI domestic partnership proposal is likely to work as a practical matter.

I. Does Family Law Operate like the Law of Commercial Contract?

It is important to consider whether family law operates like the law of commercial contract. The law and economics view of commercial contracts is that they operate in a place where there is a real market, and where information flows freely and rapidly. Contracting parties in commerce are thought to be relatively sophisticated, to have clear ideas about their options and to be able to rationally decide what to put in the contract and what to leave until later or to chance.[16] They can follow several schemes to minimize loss from this contract: they can hold a portfolio of such contracts or they can insure against risk.[17] They can breach if they wish to cut their losses.[18] They can choose to isolate their investments from the rest of their wealth (by choosing a corporate form, or by investing only as limited partners) in a way that married couples, certainly, cannot do easily. Married couples can do so by contracting beforehand or by keeping title strictly in the name of the spouse wishing to retain the asset. Cohabiting couples, in contrast, can do this quite easily – they typically will not be responsible for each others' debts nor their support or medical care.

In commercial contracts, it is not necessary to worry about the effects on third parties, since "third parties may be able to protect themselves without immutable rules."[19] Of course this safeguard does not work in the family context if there are children, who are legally unable to make contracts. Professors Ayres and Gertner note that "immutable rules are justifiable if society wants to protect parties outside the contract,"[20] and conclude that "immutability is justified only if unregulated contracting would be socially deleterious because parties internal or external to the contract cannot adequately protect themselves."[21]

The PRINCIPLES' domestic partnership scheme is not likely to work as a penalty default rule for several reasons. First, unlike commercial contract makers, the domestic partners have no ability to get insurance. In fact, to offer insurance might give at least some incentive to break up, which would certainly be against public policy. Hedging in this context through

[15] PRINCIPLES § 6.03(b) cmt. b, at 919.

[16] Charles J. Goetz & Robert E. Scott, *Principles of Relational Contract*, 67 VA. L. REV. 1089, 1089–90 (1981) ("Parties in a bargaining situation are presumed able, at minimal cost, to allocate explicitly the risks that future contingencies may cause one or the other to regret having entered into an executory agreement."). Note that "The corporation's choice of governance mechanisms does not create substantial third party effects – that is, does not injure persons who are not voluntary participants in the venture." Frank H. Easterbrook & Daniel R. Fischel, *The Corporate Contract*, 89 COLUM. L. REV. 1416, 1429–30 (1989). That's because "investors, employees, and others can participate or go elsewhere." *Id.* at 1430.

[17] Allan Schwartz & Robert E. Scott, *Contract Theory and the Limits of Contract Law*, 113 YALE L.J. 541, 559 (2003)("This is because buyers in general are better insurers against lost valuations of specialized investments than are sellers; buyers usually are better informed than sellers about the consequences of sellers' breach. Excusing the seller requires the buyer either to insure on the market or to reveal its valuation to the seller.").

[18] This is called the doctrine of "efficient breach." *See, e.g.*, RICHARD A. POSNER, ECONOMIC ANALYSIS OF LAW 118–20 (4th ed. 1992); Ian Macneil, *Efficient Breach of Contract: Circles in the Sky*, 68 VA. L. REV. 947 (1982).

[19] AYRES & GERTNER, *supra* note 11, at 88.

[20] *Id.*

[21] *Id.*

multiple similar relationships is at best nonproductive, unlike some of the family forms envisioned by Professor Martha Ertman,[22] monogamy is the point.[23] Further, the alternative of "bargaining around" set rules hurts the relationship: there can be no "efficient breach" of a serious relationship, especially when children are involved.[24] Finally, very few people seriously contemplate the "worst case" of breakup at the beginning of cohabitation, just as couples during engagement are convinced that their particular marriage will not end in divorce, although they are aware that half of all marriages will.[25] Further, having to bargain about finances or other details takes some of the bloom off the love relationship.[26]

Perhaps more fundamentally, the law and economics default scholarship assumes some sort of contracting is going on. The ALI domestic partnership proposal triggers effects at times when people are not otherwise contracting – the obligations ripen and entitlements vest after some period of time when the cohabitants are in the midst of their relationship. In contrast, other default provisions of the PRINCIPLES, such as the custody approximation principle,[27] will only take conscious effect when the parents are bargaining at the time of divorce. Does explicit contracting take place in cohabitation?[28] Explicit contracting (other than for the engagement itself) is quite unusual before marriage, and should be even less so in these arrangements, which are entered into with much less planning or social import. Finally, obligations under the PRINCIPLES ripen only at some specified time after the couple's relationship begins. Default rules usually work best when parties are actively making contracts anyway.[29] While couples at the time they marry arguably are not thinking in contract-mode,[30] it is even less likely that couples who move in together will be doing so some years down the line when the state-defined "cohabitation period"[31] of Section 6.03(3) or the "cohabitation parenting period"[32] ends and their relationship ripens from mere cohabitation into "domestic partnership."[33]

[22] Martha M. Ertman, *The ALI Principles' Approach to Domestic Partnership*, 8 DUKE J. GENDER L. & POL'Y 107, 115–16 (2001).

[23] *See* PRINCIPLES § 6.03 (1) ("For the purpose of defining relationships to which this Chapter applies, domestic partners are two persons of the same or opposite sex, not married to one another, who for a significant period of time share a primary residence and a life together as a couple."). Life together as a couple includes "the extent to which the parties' relationship was treated by the parties as qualitatively distinct from the relationship either party had with any other person." PRINCIPLES § 6.03 (7)(g). *See also*, Garrison, this volume.

[24] Margaret F. Brinig, *"Money Can't Buy Me Love": A Contrast Between Damages in Family Law and Contract*, 27 J. CORP. L. 567, 589 (2002).

[25] Lynn A. Baker & Robert E. Emery, *When Every Relationship Is Above Average: Perceptions and Expectations of Divorce at the Time of Marriage*, 17 LAW & HUM. BEHAV. 439, 443 (1993).

[26] Marjorie Maguire Shultz, *Contractual Ordering of Marriage: A New Model for State Policy*, 70 CAL. L. REV. 204, 209 (1982).

[27] PRINCIPLES § 2.08.

[28] Sometimes, of course, explicit contracting may take place. *See e.g., Kozlowski v. Kozlowski*, 403 A.2d 902 (N.J. 1979).

[29] If the default rules surround commercial contracts, and they reflect what most people would rationally choose otherwise, they are not problematic. *See, e.g.*, U.C.C. § 1–102 (3) (2005) ("The effect of provisions of this Act may be varied by agreement, except as otherwise provided in this Act. . . . ")

[30] Couples understand neither the legal regimes of marriage and divorce nor the likelihood that their own marriage will falter. *See* Baker & Emery, *supra* note 26.

[31] PRINCIPLES § 6.03(3).

[32] PRINCIPLES § 6.03(2).

[33] Similar problems of proof plague persons attempting to establish common law marriage, since the requisite agreement to be married "in words of the present tense" must have existed. *Staudenmayer v. Staudenmayer*, 714 A.2d 1016, 1020 (Pa. 1998). Many times couples will move in together gradually and will not form an intent either to set up a domestic partnership or to be married at common law until a later time. Such problems of intent are considered in *Shrader v. Shrader*, 484 P.2d 1007 (Kan. 1971); *Conklin v. Millen Oil Corp*, 557 N.W.2d 102 (Iowa App. 1996) and *Goldin v. Goldin*, 426 A.2d 410 (Md. Ct. Spec. App. 1981).

Professor Lon Fuller once wrote that legal formalities could serve a channeling function which would allow parties to channel their contractual agreements toward legal or nonlegal enforcement.[34] The lack of regulation suggests a channeling of cohabitants toward marriage involving, of course, legal formalities, or toward nonlegal enforcement.[35]

II. How Should Legislatures View the ALI Domestic Partnership Proposal?

Legislatures thinking of adopting the ALI domestic partnership proposal should consider a group of questions, as follows:

(1) Does society want heterosexual cohabitants to behave like married couples? To the extent that cohabitants do not behave in this "traditional" fashion, they are less likely to produce the kind of wealth – in terms of financial wealth, health, and even sexual satisfaction – that researchers have observed among married couples.[36]
(2) Are they likely to contract around the default?[37]
(3) If they do, would contracting hurt the relationship?[38]
(4) Is the protection that the PRINCIPLES would provide at dissolution a sufficient remedy?
(5) And does the state really want to encourage cohabitation despite the drafter's claim that they are not?[39]

Legislators should be greatly assisted with these questions by the substantial research about cohabiting couples that has been conducted since the mid 1980s, which has revealed a number of empirical facts. First, there are growing proportions of cohabiting couples, particularly among African Americans.[40] Second, the relationships themselves last a shorter time than marriage, even if there are children.[41] Third, cohabitation followed by marriage (particularly when the couple cohabits without being engaged) leads to less stable marriages when compared to marriages that were not preceded by living together.[42] Fourth, cohabiting couples experience a larger incidence of domestic violence than do married ones.[43]

[34] Lon Fuller, *Consideration and Form*, 41 COLUM. L. REV. 799, 801–03 (1941).

[35] Of course, express promises can be legally enforced in the line of cases following *Marvin v. Marvin*, 557 P.2d 106 (Cal. 1976). In addition, unmarried couples can enforce agreements that pertain to the couple's business rather than to their domestic partnership. See, e.g., *Bass v. Bass*, 814 S.W.2d 38 (Tenn. 1991), where a couple cohabiting following their divorce established a business partnership.

[36] Linda J. Waite, *The Importance of Marriage is Being Overlooked*, USA TODAY MAG., Jan. 1999, at 46, ; Linda J. Waite, *The Negative Effects of Cohabitation*, 10 THE RESPONSIVE COMMUNITY 31 (Winter 1999–2000).

[37] A survey completed in 1995–96 suggests that less than half of same-sex couples, who have no option but to contract, had written agreements affecting their relationship (47% of 393 responding couples). *See* Attitudes Toward Legal Marriage, *at* http://www.buddybuddy.com/survey-p.html (last visited March 6, 2006).

[38] *See*, Margaret F. Brinig, *The Influence of Marvin v. Marvin on Housework During Marriage*, 76 NOTRE DAME L. REV. 1311,1333–34, 1337–38 (2001)(detailing a number of these problems for the marriage relationship and arguing that to the extent one views the relationship as based on exchange, as opposed to love and obligation, the relationship becomes more transitory).

[39] PRINCIPLES § 6.02 cmt b.

[40] Andrea G. Hunter, *(Re)Envisioning Cohabitation: A Commentary on Race, History, and Culture, in* Booth & Crouter, *supra* note 5, at 41, 42.

[41] Kathleen Kiernan, *Cohabitation in Western Europe: Trends, Issues, and Implications, in* Booth & Crouter, *supra* note 5, at 171; Smock & Gupta, *supra* note 6, at 59 ("Given the wide variation in data, samples, measures of marital instability, and independent variables, the degree of consensus about this central finding is impressive.").

[42] Larry L. Bumpass & Hsien-Hen Lu, *Trends in Cohabitation and Implications for Children's Family Contexts in the United States*, 54 POP. STUD. 29 (2000).

[43] Susan Brown & Alan Booth, *Cohabitation Versus Marriage: A Comparison of Relationship Quality*, 58 J. MARRIAGE & FAM. 668 (1996).

The United States Department of Justice reports "those who never married became violent crime victims at more than four times the rate of married persons."[44] Fifth, compared to married couples who have been together for the same length of time, those in informal (cohabiting) unions are less committed to their partnership. They see fewer costs should the relationship end, and report poorer quality relationships with one another and with the cohabitants' parents.[45] Scholars debate whether to view such findings as healthy adaptations to the constantly changing institution of marriage or as a sign of social decline and growing impermanence in the intimate lives of children and adults.[46] Still, "[c]ohabitation is an incomplete institution. No matter how widespread the practice, nonmarital unions are not yet governed by strong consensual norms or formal laws."[47] As such, it is not a social institution; marriage is. In sharp contrast to cohabitation, marriage is surrounded by legal, social, and cultural beliefs about the broad contours of the relationship. This is the defining difference between legal marriage and informal cohabitation.[48] Thus, not only do scholars have difficulty pinning down the meaning of cohabitation, but so do cohabitants themselves.

III. Cohabitation Differs from Marriage

The cohabiting relationship itself is qualitatively different from marriage. This set of effects is hard to sort out. Do couples cohabit because they are precisely the sort who are less likely to be dependent upon one another, or are they less likely to depend on each other because they cohabit? For some couples, this may be exactly what they wanted: an alternative to marriage. Couples who cohabit, though they may boast of the strength of their love as the Marvins did,[49] express less interdependence than typical married couples. The strong health effects seen by married couples – especially by men, but also by women, too – are not as pronounced.[50] Sex is reportedly not as good for cohabitants, on average.[51] Fathers are less likely to stay involved with their children, or to support them.[52]

Many of these undesirable features may represent something more than just "selection effects" – meaning that they stem at least in part from cohabitation itself rather than from the characteristics of the cohabitants themselves. Nonetheless, proving this thesis

[44] United States Department of Justice, Bureau of Justice Statistics, 2002, *at* http://www.acvcc.state.al.us/asads/victimcharacter.htm (last visited march 6, 2006).

[45] Steven L. Nock, A Comparison of Marriages and Cohabiting Relationships, 16 J. Fam. Issues 54, 74 (1995).

[46] *Compare* Martha A. Fineman, *Why Marriage?*, 9 Va. J. Soc. Pol'y & L. 239 (2001) *and* Judith Stacey, *Good Riddance to "The Family": A Response to David Popenoe (in An Exchange on American Family Decline)*, 55 J. Marriage & Fam. 545–47 (1993) *with* Steven L. Nock, *'Why Not Marriage'*, 9 Va. J. Soc. Pol. & L. 273 (2001) *and* David Popenoe, *American Family Decline, 1960–1990: A Review and Appraisal*, 55 J. Marriage & Fam. 527 (1993).

[47] Nock, *supra* note 45.

[48] Nock, *supra* note 45.

[49] *Marvin v. Marvin*, 557 P.2d 106 (Cal. 1976) (Opinion of the Trial Court on Remand, Superior Court of Los Angeles County (1979), reprinted in Carl Schneider & Margaret F. Brinig, An Invitation to Family Law at 501, 504 (2d ed., 2000):

> On cross-examination, plaintiff testified that they were "always very proud of the fact that nothing held us. We weren't – we weren't legally married." After the breakup she declared to an interviewer: We used to laugh and feel a great warmth about the fact that either of us could walk out at any time.

[50] Brown & Booth, *supra* note 43.

[51] Linda J. Waite & Kara Joyner, *Emotional and Physical Satisfaction with Sex in Married, Cohabiting, and Dating Sexual Unions: Do Men and Women Differ?*, *in* Sex, Love, and Health in America 239 (E. O. Laumann & R. T. Michael, eds.) (2001).

[52] Wendy D. Manning, *The Implications of Cohabitation for Children's Well-Being*, *in* Booth & Crouter, *supra* note 5, at 121, 143.

definitively is difficult. To begin with, studies in the United States simply have not collected the right data. Empirically, causation is difficult to tease out.[53] For example, did a particular couple cohabit and then break up because they were less dependent on each other, or did the smaller degree of interdependence cause the instability, or are both true? Alternatively, did the cohabitation produce some other effects that led to unhappiness, which led to a split only because the couple was not dependent on one another?

Because the meaning of cohabitation is difficult to establish and the consequences of cohabitation difficult to prove, the social policy implications have been the subject of considerable debate.

While U.S. data show couples who live together prior to marriage are actually more likely to divorce than couples who marry without first cohabiting, the European experience is different. Professor Kathleen Kiernan points out that in some Western European countries, marriages preceded by cohabitation evidenced "little difference in the risk of dissolution of converted unions compared with direct marriages."[54] She goes on to discuss the stages through which Sweden passed in recognizing cohabitation. During the first stage, cohabitation emerges:

> as a deviant or avant-garde phenomenon practiced by a small group of the single population, while the great majority of the population marries directly. In the second stage, cohabitation functions as either a prelude to or a probationary period where the strength of the relationship may be tested prior to committing to marriage and is predominantly a childless phase. In the third stage, cohabitation becomes socially acceptable as an alternative to marriage and becoming a parent is no longer restricted to marriage. Finally, in the fourth stage, cohabitation and marriage become indistinguishable with children being born and reared within both, and the partnership transition could be said to be complete. Sweden and Denmark are countries that have made the transition to this fourth stage. At any time, cohabitation may have different meanings for the men and women involved.[55]

It is possible, of course, that for Western European nations, enough time has passed to move through these various stages. In the United States, where cohabiting couples were first counted in the 1970s,[56] we may simply be at an earlier phase. It is equally possible that the social support given to cohabiting couples elsewhere, particularly those with children, make these relationships attractive and possible when they would not be in the United States.[57] The Netherlands, at the beginning of 1998, instituted formal registration of partnerships for both heterosexual and homosexual couples and made legally registered cohabitation functionally equivalent to marriage (except that cohabiting couples do not have the right to adopt).[58] Denmark instituted legal registration of same-sex partnerships in the early 1990s.

[53] *See, e.g.*, Smock & Gupta, *supra* note 6, at 59–60 (reviewing other studies).

[54] Kiernan, *supra* note 41, at 5, 16 (reporting that Switzerland, Austria, and East Germany had lower rates of dissolution, or the difference was not statistically significant).

[55] *Id.* at 5 (citing Dorien Manting, *The Changing Meaning of Cohabitation and Marriage*, 12 Eur. Soc. Rev. 53 (1996)).

[56] Lynn M. Casper et al., *How Does POSSLQ Measure Up? Historical Estimates of Cohabitation* (U.S. Census Bureau, Population Division Working Paper No. 36 1999) http://www.census.gov/population/www/documentation/twps0036/twps0036.html.

[57] Chong-Bum An, Robert Haveman & Barbara Wolfe, *Teen Out-of-Wedlock Births and Welfare Receipt: The Role of Childhood Events and Economic Circumstances*, 75 Rev. Econs. & Stats. 195 (1993); Robert Moffitt, *Incentive Effects of the U.S. Welfare System: A Review*, 30 J. Econ. Lit. 1 (1992).

[58] W. M. Schrama, *Registered partnerships in the Netherlands*, 13 Int'l J. L. Pol'y & Fam. 315 (1999).

Alternatively, the reason that cohabitation is closer to marriage in Europe than in the United States may be that in Europe marriage, per se, has been gradually and effectively deinstitutionalized.[59] To the extent that marriage is no longer a legal status carrying differential privileges or obligations, and to the extent that such legal changes were in response to popular opinion, we may say that the cultural script that defined marriage as a distinct relationship has been rewritten to equate marriage and cohabitation. If marriage in Europe is treated in law and culture as the functional equivalent of cohabitation, it may no longer produce distinctive results. To the extent that this has happened as it may well have in many Western European countries, cohabitation would be treated in law and custom as marriage. Alternatively, marriage would come to be viewed as one more alternative form of cohabitation.

Policymakers are unlikely to want to provide default rules for cohabitation that would encourage cohabitation as an alternative to marriage since empirical studies show it is far less stable than marriage.[60] Further, the partners invest less in each other or in the relationship than they do if married. In other words, cohabitation does not promote "economic efficiency" in the same way marriage does. For example, when men marry, they do much better financially than if single or cohabiting,[61] presumably either because their wives "nag" them into more responsible behavior[62] or because the wives contribute "backup" support that makes the men's labor force participation more focused.[63] Cohabitants are more likely than married couples to share household tasks relatively more equally, though still with less sharing and more gendered behavior than one would expect, and to generally value gender equality.[64]

Cohabiting partners have less commitment to each other than do married spouses, and are more likely to think in terms of short-term rather than long-term consequences. In fact, cohabitation is usually an exchange relationship, which produces less satisfaction[65] than one taking an "internal stance"[66] which is central to a meaningful interpersonal relationship. In marriage, a relationship centered upon short-run gains signals instability.[67]

Even the landmark cohabitation decision, *Marvin v. Marvin*, noted that "the structure of society itself largely depends upon the institution of marriage, and nothing we have said in this opinion should be taken to derogate from that institution."[68] As a community, we in effect do not give the cohabitation this kind of trust, so why treat cohabitation as though we do? Professors Brinig and Nock in their recent work have found that where young people grow up in areas where there is a higher percentage of divorced people, the males delay first marriages and their first "union," which is not likely to be delayed, is

[59] Kiernan, *supra* note 41 at 26–27.

[60] Larry L. Bumpass, James A. Sweet & Andrew Cherlin, *The Role of Cohabitation in Declining Rates of Marriage*, 53 J. Marriage & Fam. 913 (1991); Bumpass & Sweet, *infra* note 87, at 620–21.

[61] Victor Fuchs, Women's Quest for Economic Equality 58–60 (1988); Nock, *supra* note 45, at 66, 143.

[62] Linda J. Waite & Maggie Gallagher, The Case for Marriage: Why married People are Happier, Healthier, and Better Off Financially (2000); Linda J. Waite, *Does Marriage Matter?* 32 Demography 483, 496 (1995).

[63] Joan C. Williams, UnBending Gender: Why Family and Work Conflict and What to Do About It (2000).

[64] Nock, *supra* note 45, at 16.

[65] Gary L. Hansen, *Moral Reasoning and the Marital Exchange Relationship*, 131 J. Soc. Psych. 71 (1991).

[66] Milton C. Regan, Alone Together: Law and the Meaning of Marriage 24 (1999).

[67] *See* Steven L. Nock & Margaret F. Brinig, *Weak Men and Disorderly Women: Divorce and the Division of Labor, in* The Law and Economics of Marriage and Divorce: 171 (Dnes and Rowthorn, eds. 2002).

[68] *Marvin v. Marvin*, 557 P.2d 106, 122 (Cal. 1976).

cohabitation.[69] Thus, one of the effects of a relatively high divorce rate seems to be a higher rate of cohabitation. As noted earlier, among Americans, marriages entered into after cohabitation are less, not more, stable, than the marriages of couples who do not cohabit first.[70] Generally speaking, the presence of a child increases union stability,[71] though boys apparently stabilize relationships more than do girls .[72]

In sum, by using a default rule that is not what people would most likely agree to in advance, as the ALI proposes to do, we force those who do not want this type of relationship into contract-mode. This stifles the relationship, forcing over-planning and destroying "covenantal" thinking as the parties focus on what they can get out of the venture and how long it will last.[73] As any follower of family law cases knows, couples in committed relationships are unlikely to resort to contract. For instance, as of 1995 10 percent or less of same-sex couples, who have very high incentives to contract, had written agreements.[74] Data for married couples is nearly impossible to obtain, since it will not be filed anywhere unless the marriage dissolves.[75] An article written in 1988 suggests that there are "more" such agreements than before.[76]

IV. Current Law Governing Cohabitation

There is no requirement that during the relationship, cohabiting partners support one another or provide medical care.[77] California law attempted to fill this gap with its domestic

[69] Margaret F. Brinig & Steven L. Nock, *"I Only Want Trust": Norms, Trust, and Autonomy*, 32 J. Socio-Econ. 471, 483 & Tbl. 4 (2003).

[70] William G. Axinn & Arland Thornton, *The Relationship Between Cohabitation and Divorce: Selectivity or Causal Influence?*, 29 Demography 357 (1992).

[71] Bumpass, Sweet & Cherlin, *supra* note 60.

[72] Aphra R. Katzev, Rebecca L. Warner and Alan C. Aycock, *Girls or Boys? Relationship of Child Gender to Marital Instability*, 56 J. Marriage & Fam. 89 (1994).

[73] *See* Spaht, this volume (discussing covenant marriages).

[74] *The Advocate Survey* (1994–95). This survey is no longer available on line. However, as of 1990, 9% of women and 10% of men in same-sex partnerships had written agreements. *See* http://www.buddybuddy.com/survey.html (last visited March 6, 2006).

[75] By definition, we cannot know how often American couples write antenuptial contracts. Even if we were to survey individuals, the numbers writing antenuptial contracts would probably be too small to permit meaningful analysis. Further, those who rely on such contracts are so unrepresentative (and perhaps more inclined to divorce) that such a query would be tremendously expensive. It is impossible to rely on divorce records because those with antenuptial agreements may be more likely to divorce anyway. Therefore, any research on this issue would face daunting problems in establishing a causal connection.

[76] Sheryl Nance, *'Til Some Breach Doth Them Part*, National Law Journal, at 1 (November 7, 1988). For example, Ill. Sta. Ch. 750 § 15/1 provides in § 1 that:

> Every person who shall, without any lawful excuse, neglect or refuse to provide for the support or maintenance of his or her spouse, said spouse being in need of such support or maintenance, or any person who shall, without lawful excuse, desert or neglect or refuse to provide for the support or maintenance of his or her child or children under the age of 18 years, in need of such support or maintenance, shall be deemed guilty of a Class A misdemeanor and shall be liable under the provisions of the Illinois Public Aid Code.

[77] The Illinois Statute has been rewritten, and now appears as 750 Ill. C.S. 16/1 (2005). It provides:

> § 15. Failure to support.
> a. A person commits the offense of failure to support when he or she:
>   1. willfully, without any lawful excuse, refuses to provide for the support or maintenance of his or her spouse, with the knowledge that the spouse is in need of such support or maintenance, or, without lawful excuse, deserts or willfully refuses to provide for the support or maintenance of his or her child or children in need of support or maintenance and the person has the ability to provide the support....
> b. Sentence. A person convicted of a first offense under subdivision (a)(1) or (a)(2) is guilty of a Class A misdemeanor. A person convicted of an offense under subdivision (a)(3) or (a)(4) or a second or subsequent offense under subdivision (a)(1) or (a)(2) is guilty of a Class 4 felony.

partnership provisions, which apply to same-sex couples and to persons over 62, and allow registration of domestic partnerships in which partners must agree to assume joint responsibility for each other's "basic living expenses."[78] These provisions authorize state and local employers to offer health care coverage and other benefits to domestic partners of employees and require health-care facilities to permit visits by a patient's domestic partner. Nonetheless, in addition to the general rule that cohabitants are not responsible for each other's medical care, they do not enjoy the privileges of confidential communications[79] or tort immunities. They cannot hold property as a community or by the entireties. If one of them dies, the other does not have the benefit of intestacy laws, as would a putative spouse who mistakenly believes he or she is legally married and would be, but for some defect in the ceremony.[80] Supporting children does not become a common enterprise because of the adults' relationship. In contrast, if a couple marries, the stepparent may well have support obligations for the children of the spouse at least during the pendency of the relationship.[81] Former cohabitant fathers seem to provide support less often than noncustodial fathers following divorce.[82]

The current rule, which is the default in the absence of the PRINCIPLES, is that no one recovers upon dissolution of a cohabiting relationship – you take what you already have clear title to. This is particularly unfortunate in the case of same-sex couples, who must enter into hundreds of little contracts to avoid this result. For them, marriage, civil union, or a formal state domestic partnership law, like California's or Hawaii's, works better. Note that these alternatives require a voluntary commitment, as does marriage.

The Comments for Chapter 6 suggest that the ALI wanted to protect same-sex couples and some adults who would otherwise fall between the cracks, such as putative spouses, victims of fraud and deceit, and those who are not legally married but should be estopped from claiming otherwise.[83] Others have discussed the PRINCIPLES as they apply to same-sex partners, so this chapter will concentrate on heterosexual couples.

[78] Cal. Fam. Code § 297 (2000).

[79] Milton C. Regan, *Spousal Privilege and the Meanings of Marriage*, 81 VA. L. REV. 2045 (1995).

[80] Schneider & Brinig, *supra* note 49, at 488.

[81] *See, e.g.*, WASH. REV. CODE § 26.16.205 (2005) ("The expenses of the family and the education of the children, including stepchildren, are chargeable upon the property of both husband and wife, or either of them, and they may be sued jointly or separately. When a petition for dissolution of marriage or a petition for legal separation is filed, the court may, upon motion of the stepparent, terminate the obligation to support the stepchildren."); N.D. CENT. CODE § 14–09–09 (a) (2005) ("A stepparent is not bound to maintain the spouse's dependent children, as defined in Section 50–09–01, unless the child is received into the stepparent's family. If the stepparent receives them into the family, the stepparent is liable, to the extent of the stepparent's ability, to support them during the marriage and so long thereafter as they remain in the stepparent's family."). *But see Wood v. Woods*, 184 Cal. Rptr. 471 (Cal. Ct. App. 1982) (finding no requirement that stepparent repay county for aid to families with dependent children). *Compare Johnson v. Johnson*, 617 N.W.2d 97 (N.D. 2000) (holding parent liable under doctrine of equitable adoption) *with Bagwell v. Bagwell*, 698 S.2d 746 (La. Ct. App. 1997) (finding no obligation by stepparent after divorce). But under current law, no such obligation exists for the child of a cohabitant. Under the PRINCIPLES, whether a child support duty lasts beyond dissolution of a marital or cohabitating relationship depends upon whether the stepparent has become a de facto parent or parent by estoppel. *See* Baker, this volume.

[82] Manning, *supra* note 52, at 143.

[83] *See* PRINCIPLES § 6.01 (1) (providing in part that "Domestic partners are two persons of the same or opposite sex, not married to one another. . . . "); PRINCIPLES § 6.01 cmt d. at 911–12 (discussing the difference between the traditional putative spouse doctrine and the PRINCIPLES); PRINCIPLES § 6.01 Reporter's Notes, cmt. d., at 912.

Table 14.1. *PCT22. Unmarried-Partner Households and Sex of Partners*

	United States
Total	105,480,101
Unmarried-partner households	5,475,768
Male householder and male partner	301,026
Male householder and female partner	2,615,119
Female householder and female partner	293,365
Female householder and male partner	2,266,258
All other households	100,004,333

[1] Data Set: Census 2000 Summary File 2 (SF 2) 100-Percent Data[84]

For heterosexual couples, who will be the vast majority of those affected by the ALI proposal,[85] being treated by each other as though they were married, as the PRINCIPLES would do, probably is not what they want. Most heterosexual cohabiting couples fall into one of two groups. "There is no single answer to whether cohabitation is a late stage of courtship or an early stage of marriage. It is the former for couples who are uncertain about their relationship but are considering marriage, the latter for those who would marry immediately were it not for some practical constraint, and neither for couples who do not want to marry each other."[86] Cohabitants thus may be on their way to marriage. In these cases, the abolition of heart-balm actions by legislatures and courts suggests a public policy to treat them differently from married persons since they are nowhere given the support relief afforded to married persons upon dissolution.[87]

Another set of heterosexual couples affirmatively wish to reject marriage, as the PRINCIPLES recognize.[88] Professor Nicholas Bala of the Queen's University Faculty of Law argues:

> The motivations for living together outside of marriage are complex, but these relationships frequently arise because one party (often the man) is unwilling to make the commitment of marriage and does not want to under-take the legal obligations of marriage. If the period of cohabitation is short, it may be quite fair to have no obligations arise from the relationship. However, if the relationship is longer term, the expectations of the parties may change over time, even if they do not marry. One partner, most commonly the woman, may "invest" more in the relationship and any children.[89]

[84] Available at http://factfinder.census.gov/servlet/DTTable?_bm = y&-geo_id = 01000US&-reg = DEC_2000_SF2_U_PCT022:001&-ds_name = DEC_2000_SF2_U&-_lang = en&-_mt_name = DEC_2000_SF2_U_PCTO22&-format = &-CONTEXT = dt (last visited October 1, 2005).

[85] *See* Table 14.1 *infra.* Estimates of the numbers of same-sex couples vary, but the low and high estimates seem to be between two and ten percent of the general population. The CURRENT POPULATION SURVEY of March, 1998, Table 8, at 71, *at* http://www.census.gov/population/www/socdemo/ms-la.html.

[86] *See, e.g.*, Larry L. Bumpass & James A. Sweet, *National Estimates of Cohabitation*, 26 DEMOGRAPHY 615 (1989).

[87] The two heartbalm actions that typically involved engaged couples were breach of marriage promise and seduction. For a recent case discussion, see *Miller v. Ratner*, 688 A.2d 976 (Md. Ct. App. 1997); *Compare* Katherine T. Silbaugh, *Turning Labor into Love: Housework and the Law*, 91 NW. U. L. REV. 1 (1995) (documenting that contracts for household services are not enforced when couples are married). *See also* Contracts in which sexual services predominate are not enforced because akin to prostitution. *See, e.g.*, *Hewitt v. Hewitt*, 394 N.E.2d 1204, 1208 (Ill. 1979).

[88] PRINCIPLES § 6.02 cmt. b, at 916 ("On the contrary, to the extent that some individuals avoid marriage in order to avoid responsibilities to a partner....").

[89] MARGARET F. BRINIG, FROM CONTRACT TO COVENANT: BEYOND THE LAW AND ECONOMICS OF THE FAMILY (2000), *reviewed by* Nicholas Bala, 2 ISUMA 2 (2001) available at http://www.isuma.net/v02n02/bala/bala_e.shtml.

The PRINCIPLES "diminishes the effectiveness of that strategy" of avoiding responsibility.[90] The application of the benefits and obligations of domestic partnership law to ongoing relationships is a major difference between domestic partners under the PRINCIPLES, who have no support obligation while the relationship continues, and couples who are "common law partners" in Canada[91] or who live in civil union in Vermont and Connecticut, who are bound by precisely the same obligations as are married persons. To the extent that the goal of Chapters 3 and 4 of the PRINCIPLES governing Compensatory Payments and Property Division is to encourage specialization of labor between spouses and investment in the family,[92] applying the same rules to dissolving domestic partnerships flies in the face of reality: cohabiting couples are less specialized than married couples, are less interdependent, and have far more embedded equality goals.[93] They thus fail to satisfy one criterion usual for setting default rules, efficiency.

If the ALI really wanted to help same-sex couples, it would seem much better to do so straightforwardly, and more completely, than to provide them limited benefits upon dissolution while also extending these rights to heterosexual cohabitants. One problem, for some, with advancing the limited relief provided by the PRINCIPLES is that it may in fact eventually lead to same-sex marriage as a matter of equal protection.

The ALI might have been unintentionally pushing toward same-sex marriage by creating equal rights on dissolution for unmarried couples. Similar legislative activities have set up claims for same-sex couples in both the United States and Canada. While some may feel this is entirely justified for couples who currently cannot marry, like same-sex couples, dragging along the much larger group of heterosexual cohabitants,[94] for whom the equality argument is nowhere near as strong, is the wrong way to accomplish that goal.

For example, in *Baker v. State*,[95] same-sex couples brought a successful declaratory judgment action under the Common Benefits clause of the Vermont constitution.[96] These couples claimed, among other things, "that Vermont law affirmatively guarantees the right to adopt and raise children regardless of the sex of the parents, and challenge[d] the logic of a legislative scheme that recognizes the rights of same-sex partners as parents, yet denies them–and their children–the same security as spouses."[97] The *Baker* court found that the asserted state goal of promoting the procreation of children could not in that case support the denial of the numerous benefits of marriage since the couples were not dissimilar to many heterosexual couples who could not or would not have children.[98] More germane to the present discussion, however, was the court's conclusion that the exclusion of same-sex couples from marital rights was inconsistent with the earlier granting of rights as parents:

> The argument, however, contains a more fundamental flaw, and that is the Legislature's endorsement of a policy diametrically at odds with the State's claim. In 1996, the Vermont General Assembly enacted, and the Governor signed, a law removing all prior

[90] PRINCIPLES § 6.02 cmt. b, at 916.

[91] The CANADIAN CRIMINAL CODE § 215(1)(b) punishes those who do not furnish necessaries to the common law partner.

[92] The proper goals for alimony are discussed in a large number of articles. Perhaps the best known is by the Reporter for the ALI PRINCIPLES. Ira Ellman, *The Theory of Alimony*, 77 CAL. L. REV. 1 (1989).

[93] For a thorough empirical discussion of these points, *see* Steven L. Nock, *Commitment and Dependency in Marriage*, 57 J. MARRIAGE & FAM. 503 (1995).

[94] *See* Table 14.1 *infra*.

[95] *Baker v. State*, 744 A.2d 864 (Vt. 1999).

[96] VT. CONST. ch. I, art. 7.

[97] *Baker v. State*, 744 A.2d 864, 870 (1999) (citations omitted).

[98] *Id.* at 883–84.

> legal barriers to the adoption of children by same-sex couples. At the same time, the Legislature provided additional legal protections in the form of court-ordered child support and parent-child contact in the event that same-sex parents dissolved their 'domestic relationship.' In light of these express policy choices, the State's arguments that Vermont public policy favors opposite-sex over same-sex parents or disfavors the use of artificial reproductive technologies are patently without substance.[99]

The *Baker* court similarly defused the argument that same-sex relationships were legally disfavored in Vermont. The court noted: "[W]hatever claim may be made in light of the undeniable fact that federal and state statutes – including those in Vermont – have historically disfavored same-sex relationships, more recent legislation plainly undermines the contention."[100]

The kind of reasoning followed in *Baker* was not lost to the Connecticut court in *Rosengarten v. Downes*[101] when it denied interstate recognition of a Vermont civil union. The court carefully distinguished the Vermont environment from the Connecticut one, noting:

> It becomes clear from a careful reading of the floor debate on this legislation in both houses, that a number of legislators were opposed to adoption of this legislation [allowing adoption by same-sex partners] if it were to be used later in any way as a wedge by appellate or trial courts to require recognition of civil unions in Connecticut in the manner they ascribed to the Vermont Supreme Court in *Baker v. State.* Members of the General Assembly in their floor debate in each house did not make explicit mention of *Baker.* It is clear, however, that several legislators were concerned, as a result of the Vermont experience, that in overriding the ruling in the *In re Baby Z.* case by permitting adoption of a child who already had a natural or adoptive parent by another person of the same sex who was not lawfully married to that parent, they did not allow an appellate court to use that legislative enactment as a wedge to bring down the laws of Connecticut concerning who may marry.
>
> The *Baker* court had done just that by citing the Vermont legislature's enactment of a same sex couple adoption law as one of the reasons why there was no proper governmental purpose under the common benefits clause of the Vermont constitution to restrict marriage to unions between a man and a woman. After discussing what it termed the "reality" that some persons in same-sex relationships were conceiving children by artificial means, the Vermont court so used the enactment by the Vermont legislature of that change in the law when it stated: "The Vermont Legislature has not only recognized this reality, but has acted affirmatively to remove legal barriers so that same-sex couples may legally adopt and rear the children conceived through such efforts."[102]

Notably, Connecticut adopted civil union by statute in 2005.[103]

V. The Success of the Unequal Treatment Argument in Canada

Using precisely this pattern of attack, same-sex couples achieved what is perhaps their greatest success in the line of cases that has triggered Canadian legislation opening marriage to all two-person couples. The initial onslaught appeared in the case of *M. v. H.*[104]

[99] *Id.* at 884–85. (citations omitted).
[100] *Id.* at 885–86.
[101] *Rosengarten v. Downes,* 802 A.2d 170 (Conn. App. Ct. 2002).
[102] *Id.* at 181.
[103] 2005 Conn. Pub. Act 05–10.
[104] *M. v. H.,* [1999] 2 S.C.R. 3.

Previously, the Ontario legislature had opened support to unmarried couples.[105] In this case M, who had lived with her partner (and business associate) for more than 25 years sought support when the relationship dissolved. She successfully argued that Article 15(1) of the Canadian Charter of Rights and Freedoms, the antidiscrimination section, guaranteed her the rights of a "spouse." The Court held that benefits granted to heterosexual cohabitants under the definition of "spouse" under Section 29 of the Family Law Act – which grants benefits to separating cohabitants who have lived together at least three years or who have a common child and have lived together in a relationship of some permanence – must be extended to same-sex couples as a matter of equality. After *M. v. H.*, legislation passed in 2000, the Modernization of Benefits and Obligations Act, required that the definition of "common law partner" for purpose of numerous federal benefits and obligations include those in a conjugal relationship for one year or more. Section 215(1)(b) of the Canadian Criminal Code punishes those who do not furnish necessaries to the common law partner. Again, the application of the benefits and obligations of domestic partnership law to ongoing relationships is a major difference from Chapter 6 of the PRINCIPLES, which do not impose a support obligation while the relationship continues. This is also a difference between the PRINCIPLES and Vermont's Civil Union statutes, enacted in response to *Baker*.[106]

But, looking straightforwardly at the unequal treatment of the unmarried produced conflict with antidiscrimination rules. As *M. v. H.* noted, Ontario had set up such a classification.[107] The Modernization of Benefits and Obligations Act[108] was enacted in response to *M. v. H.*[109] This legislation, which contained 340 sections, amended virtually every area of nationwide public law to grant rights to unmarried as well as married couples. The Act extends federal benefits and obligations to all unmarried couples that have cohabited in a conjugal relationship for at least one year, regardless of sexual orientation. The Act did not purport to be a federal statutory definition of marriage and did not change the common law definition of marriage.[110]

In *Halpern v. Toronto*,[111] the Ontario Court of Appeals took the next logical step, holding that the common law definition of marriage violated Section 15(1) of the Canadian Charter. The *Halpern* court held:

> As recognized in *M. v. H.*, same-sex couples are capable of forming "long, lasting, loving and intimate relationships." Denying same-sex couples the right to marry perpetuates the contrary view, namely, that same-sex couples are not capable of forming loving and lasting relationships, and thus same-sex relationships are not worthy of the same respect and recognition as opposite sex relationships.

[105] S.C. 2000, c. 12. This legislation responded to *Egan v. Canada*, [1995] 2 S.C.R. 513 (granting survivor rights to partner of deceased same-sex recipient under the Old Age Security Act). Arguably *Egan* is the first directly relevant case in this line.

[106] Bala, *supra* note 88.

[107] The point was made in argument that same-sex couples were much less likely to need spousal support than their married (heterosexual) counterparts: Same-sex couples are much less likely to adopt traditional sex roles than are opposite-sex couples: M. Cardell, S. Finn, & J. Marecek, *Sex-Role Identity, Sex-Role Behavior, and Satisfaction in Heterosexual, Lesbian, and Gay Male Couples*, 5 PSYCHOL. WOMEN Q., 488, 492–93 (Spring 1981). Indeed, "research shows that most lesbians and gay men actively reject traditional husband-wife or masculine-feminine roles as a model for enduring relationships" L. A. PEPLAU, *Lesbian and Gay Relationships*, *in* HOMOSEXUALITY: RESEARCH IMPLICATIONS FOR PUBLIC POLICY 183 (J. C. Gonsiorek and J. D. Weinrich, eds. 1991).

[108] S.C. 2000, c. 12.

[109] *Halpern v. City of Toronto*, [2003], 65 O.R.3d 161.

[110] *Halpern* at 172.

[111] *Halpern v. Canada*, [2003] 65 O.R.3d 161.

> Accordingly, in our view, the common law requirement that marriage be between persons of the opposite sex does not accord with the needs, capacities and circumstances of same-sex couples.
>
> ... Historically, same-sex equality litigation has focused on achieving equality in some of the most basic elements of civic life, such as bereavement leave, health care benefits, pensions benefits [sic], spousal support, name changes and adoption. The question at the heart of this appeal is whether excluding same-sex couples from another of the most basic elements of civic life – marriage – infringes human dignity and violates the Canadian Constitution.[112]

Similarly, in *Egale v. Canada,*[113] the limitation of marriage definitions to heterosexual couples was successfully challenged under the Canadian Charter. The Canadian Parliament enacted C-38 in July 2005, allowing any two persons to marry, regardless of whether they are same-sex or heterosexual.

VI. Conclusion

In conclusion, the PRINCIPLES' domestic partnership chapter seems to fail as both a normal type of contractual default rule and as a "penalty default" causing parties to take remedial steps or reveal information. What it does perhaps do best is set the road in place for same-sex marriage, as similar legislative enactments did in Canada. But this comes at the price of pulling substantially larger numbers of heterosexual couples into a relationship that most find substantially inferior to marriage.

Many thanks the other members of the Harvard Workshop, particularly Marsha Garrison and Elizabeth Scott, and to Steven L. Nock. Portions of this chapter draw on Margaret F. Brinig, *Domestic Partnership: Missing the Target?*, 4 J.L. & FAM. STUD. 19 (2002).

[112] [2003], 65 O.R.3d 161, 168 and 187.

[113] *Egale v. Canada,* [2003] 225 D.L.R. (4th) 472. *See also* Dunbar and Edge, 2004 YTSC 54 (Yukon, 7/30/04), available at www.egale.ca/yukon.pdf; *Hendricks v. Québec* (Procurer Général), [2002] J.Q. 3816 (QL) (mandating marriage since the state has no legitimate "equal protection" interest in denying it). The opinion in Dunbar and Edge issued July 30, 2004, states: "I do not consider it open to the Attorney General of Canada to ask this Court to defer to the Reference and to Parliament. The Attorney General of Canada is not divisible by province. The office of the Attorney General of Canada is responsible for federal law. The capacity to marry is a federal issue. To paraphrase paragraph 28 of Hendricks, it is legally unacceptable in a federal constitution area involving the Attorney General of Canada for a provision to be inapplicable in one province and in force in all others ... [t]o fail to act now in the face of an acknowledged constitutional violation will result in an unequal application of the law ... [i]n my view, with respect to the Attorney General of Canada, the approach it has taken is so fundamentally inconsistent with the approach it took in the other provinces and, indeed, with the approach that is acknowledged to be correct in the Supreme Court of Canada, that solicitor client costs should be awarded against the Attorney General of Canada." *Id.* at 13.

15 Private Ordering under the ALI PRINCIPLES: As Natural as Status

Martha M. Ertman

The PRINCIPLES begin by observing that "[o]ne expects a nation's family law to reflect its cultural values."[1] But left unspecified are the particular cultural values that the PRINCIPLES incorporate. Freedom of contract, also known as private ordering, is one important cultural value that is expressed. This chapter identifies a number of provisions that incorporate private ordering, namely the ALI's domestic partnership, parenthood by estoppel, and de facto parenthood proposals, and articulates reasons that deference to private ordering makes sense. The strengths of private ordering are both functional and linguistic. Functionally, family law doctrine already defers to private ordering in many instances, and indeed increasingly tends toward privatization.[2] Moreover, private ordering can facilitate equality in families and accounts for the fact that people form families in different ways.

The linguistic point requires a bit more explanation. Abstract ideas, such as family – understood as the kind of social affiliation that the law recognizes as legitimate – can only be discussed in metaphorical terms because it is difficult, if not impossible, to explain complex concepts like intimate affiliation and legal recognition without resorting to other concepts.[3] While metaphors imperfectly capture the notion of family and other abstractions, they are the best tools we have, making analysis of their mechanics particularly important.[4] Metaphors work by identifying a target problem and then identifying a source analog to understand it. For example, scientists wondering how sound works (the target) compared it to waves of water (the source), concluding that the metaphor of sound waves works because both sound and water waves exhibit periodicity and amplitude. Obviously, the

[1] PRINCIPLES, Ira Mark Ellman, *Chief Reporter's Foreword*, at *xvii.*

[2] For a concise description of status-based family law that gave way to individualism and contractarianism, see MARY ANN GLENDON, THE TRANSFORMATION OF FAMILY LAW: STATE, LAW, AND FAMILY IN THE UNITED STATES AND WESTERN EUROPE 291 (1989). Discussions of deference to private ordering in family law include Robert H. Mnookin & Lewis Kornhauser, *Bargaining in the Shadow of the Law: The Case of Divorce*, 88 YALE L. J. 950 (1979); Jana Singer, *The Privatization of Family Law*, 1992 WIS. L. REV. 1443; Brian Bix, *Bargaining in the Shadow of Love: The Enforcement of Premarital Agreements and How We Think About Marriage*, 40 WM. & MARY L. REV. 145 (1998–1999); Margaret F. Brinig, *Unhappy Contracts: The Case of Divorce Settlements*, 1 REV. L. & ECON. 241 (2005).

[3] George Lakoff, *The Contemporary Theory of Metaphor, in* METAPHOR AND THOUGHT 205 (Andrew Ortony ed., 2d ed. 1993) (observing that "as soon as one gets away from concrete physical experience and starts talking about abstractions . . . metaphorical understanding is the norm").

[4] Thomas W. Joo, *Contract, Property, and the Role of Metaphor in Corporations Law*, 35 U. C. DAVIS L. REV. 779, 799 (2002) (observing that "[i]n reality, nothing is the same as anything else. Mapping can be done only between abstractions, not between messy realities. Because analogy and metaphor use abstracted portraits to stand in for more complex real phenomena, they always make use of a kind of metonymy . . . the name of a thing or concept is used to refer to something less than the whole and that essentialized part is taken to stand for the whole.").

sound wave metaphor is not an equation; waves of sound are neither blue-green, wet, nor cool. But that particular metaphor works because there are deep structural commonalities between sound and waves of water.[5]

Because this volume and the PRINCIPLES concern families, the relevant metaphoric investigation identifies the target as "what constitutes a family," in particular whether cohabitants and intimates of legal parents who assume parental responsibilities count as family. This chapter contends that contract is an appropriate source for metaphors relating to family, and further that legal regulation already adopts this metaphor through rules that embrace private ordering.

Contractarianism in its various forms employs at least two distinct understandings of contract, which Thomas Joo has labeled "K" and "R." "K," following the law school classroom abbreviation, refers to a legally enforceable agreement, while "R," the understanding of contract that prevails among economists, refers to "a voluntary 'relationship[] characterized by reciprocal expectations and behavior.'"[6] The contractarianism discussed in this chapter includes both "K" and "R", but focuses more on the latter.

Some metaphors are never really accepted, such as the economic model of families as firms.[7] But the metaphor of marriage and contract is already deeply rooted in legal and social discourse, its adoption having begun more than 150 years ago as part of the general pattern of status giving way to contract.[8] Just as sound waves and water waves share structural similarities, both family and contract bring to mind voluntariness, reciprocity, and bodies, in particular bodily proximity. This third structural commonality between families and contract, bodily proximity, may seem counterintuitive. But further consideration confirms the similarity. An image commonly associated with contract – a handshake – best illustrates the structural commonality.[9] A handshake is the meeting of two bodies to represent or enact the meeting of the minds of two people entering an agreement.[10] In other words, handshakes and families both involve parties voluntarily binding themselves to a reciprocal relationship.[11] The richness and power of the handshake image is further explained by cognitive linguistic theory suggesting that people often think in metaphors that relate to the body, investing the handshake image with imaginative force.[12] Once we

[5] For an elaboration of the sound wave metaphor, see *id.* at 785.

[6] Joo, *supra* note 4, at 789 (quoting Melvin Eisenberg, *The Conception that the Corporation is a Nexus of Contracts and the Dual Nature of the Firm*, 24 J. CORP. L. 819, 822–23 (1999)).

[7] MARGARET BRINIG, FROM CONTRACT TO COVENANT 138 (2000).

[8] HENRY SUMNER MAINE, ANCIENT LAW 168–70 (1996). For a critique of the focus on individuals in family law, see Glendon, *supra* note 2, at 297–302. The metaphor of marriage as a partnership contract informs various statutes, including the Uniform Probate Code and the Uniform Marriage and Divorce Act. Martha M. Ertman, *The Business of Intimacy*, *in* FEMINISM CONFRONTS HOMO ECONOMICUS: GENDER, LAW, & SOCIETY 467, 476 (Martha Albertson Fineman & Terence Dougherty eds., 2005). Of course, contractual notions of relationships regarding children differ from discussions of contract in marriage. For a discussion of how contractarianism affects parent-child relationships, see notes 11 and 21–24, *infra*, and associated text.

[9] Contract might bring to mind other images, such as a signature on a dotted line. *See* Specht v. Netscape Communication, 150 F. Supp. 2d 585 (2001).

[10] For a discussion of mutual assent in contract law, see JOSEPH M. PERILLO, CALAMARI AND PERILLO ON CONTRACTS 26–27 (5th ed. 2003).

[11] Of course children do not voluntarily bind themselves to their parents. This pattern coheres with contractualism, in that children lack the capacity to enter legally binding agreements. AMERICAN LAW INSTITUTE, RESTATEMENT (SECOND) OF CONTRACTS § 14 (1981).

[12] GEORGE LAKOFF, WOMEN, FIRE AND DANGEROUS THINGS: WHAT CATEGORIES REVEAL ABOUT THE MIND (1987) (hereinafter LAKOFF, WOMEN, FIRE AND DANGEROUS THINGS); GEORGE LAKOFF & MARK JOHNSON, METAPHORS WE LIVE BY (1980). Other linguists might counter Lakoff's claims regarding the mapping metaphors onto bodily

consider these structural similarities between family and contract, it becomes apparent that contractual metaphors are as natural a model as any other, such as status, for regulating family.

This chapter first describes the ways that domestic partnership, parenthood by estoppel, and de facto parenthood rely on principles of private ordering, and then briefly applies George Lakoff's cognitive linguistic research on metaphors to demonstrate how private ordering provides a coherent conceptual basis for these provisions. The chapter concludes by observing how the PRINCIPLES' private ordering provisions are consistent with current doctrine as expressed in a trio of California cases that recognize a range of ways that same-sex couples can, through various kinds of agreement, become families in which both parents have full parental rights and responsibilities.[13] This exercise suggests that the PRINCIPLES' provisions on private ordering resonate with existing legal doctrine by accounting for the way real-world families are structured.

I. The Elasticity of Contract

What is private ordering? Certainly, private ordering includes formal contracts such as the premarital and postmarital agreements governed by Chapter 7 of the PRINCIPLES – agreements that could be described in shorthand as "K." But private ordering also includes less formal arrangements, arrangements that focus on voluntariness and reciprocity and might be evidenced by, in place of formalities, conduct and implicit understanding. These agreements can be distinguished from those defined by legal enforceability by using the shorthand "R," as already noted. In short, contract provides a conceptual frame that reflects the PRINCIPLES' general tendency to defer to arrangements partners and parents have reached on their own.[14]

Thus contract informs the PRINCIPLES' doctrine and the theory behind it. Contract serves this function in other areas. Just as contract is a well-established metaphor for understanding corporations,[15] it provides a powerful heuristic in philosophical discussions of the social contract. No one seriously contends that our ancestors entered an actual contract that binds us to pay taxes and obey laws. Instead, John Rawls and other social contractarians analyze a *hypothetical* agreement, asking what we would have agreed to had such a negotiation occurred.[16] The continued vitality of social contract theorizing reflects the elasticity of contract-based analysis, in particular the way that contractual concepts embrace both actual and metaphoric agreements.[17]

experience with arguments that language, and signs generally, are arbitrary. *See, e.g.*, FERDINAND DE SAUSSURE, COURSE IN GENERAL LINGUISTICS 74 (Charles Bally & Albert Harris, translation 1990) (1916).

[13] Elisa B. v. Emily B., 117 P.3d 660 (Cal. 2005); Kristine H. v. Lisa R., 117 P.3d 690 (Cal. 2005); and K. M. v. E. G., 117 P.3d 673 (Cal. 2005).

[14] For example, the PRINCIPLES' Introduction begins by defining a "primary challenge" in family law as facilitating "thoughtful planning by cooperative parents," PRINCIPLES at 1, and explains that it does this in part by giving preference to private ordering by parents over judicial supervision. PRINCIPLES at 4, 8.

[15] For a description and critique of the nexus of contracts approach to corporations, see Joo, *supra* note 4.

[16] JOHN RAWLS, A THEORY OF JUSTICE 11–12 (1971).

[17] *See, e.g.*, Jeremy Waldron, *John Locke: Social Contract Versus Political Anthropology*, *in* THE SOCIAL CONTRACT FROM HOBBES TO RAWLS 51 (David Boucher & Paul Kelly eds., 1994); Ann Cudd, *Contractarianism*, The Stanford Encyclopedia of Philosophy, (Edward N. Zalta ed. Spring 2003) (*available at* http://plato.stanford.edu/archives/spring2003/entries/contractarianism); Fred D'Agostino, *Contemporary Approaches to the Social Contract*, The Stanford Encyclopedia of Philosophy (Edward N. Zalta ed. Spring 2003) (*available at* http://plato.stanford.edu/archives/sum2003/entries/contractarianism-contemporary). It is worth noting that philosophical

This chapter similarly exploits the many meanings of contract. Most concretely, it addresses explicit agreements between parties, which courts may enforce. But it also includes parties acting as if they have entered an agreement, and perhaps also entering informal agreements, which the law might recognize. Most abstractly, at the level of metaphor, a handshake operates as a symbolic embodiment of contract and family norms such as consent, affiliation, and the freedom to order one's own affairs. I use the terms contract, private ordering, and agreement variously to invoke these meanings, all of which might be summed up as contractarianism.

Contractarianism already appears in family law generally and the PRINCIPLES in particular.[18] For example, Section 2.03 of the PRINCIPLES provides that by making a coparenting agreement with the legal parent and "accepting full and permanent responsibilities as a parent," a person can become a parent by estoppel.[19] The private ordering of Section 2.03 does not require a written contract, but instead turns on a prior coparenting agreement which may not satisfy the requirements of contract doctrine (such as offer, acceptance, consideration, and a writing),[20] since domestic arrangements tend to lack the formality of commercial life.

To be sure, private ordering is not the only cultural value expressed in the PRINCIPLES. Status-based values, such as protecting children because of their vulnerability, are expressed, for example, in the provisions providing that agreements limiting child support will not receive the same deference as other agreements.[21] Moreover, being designated as a parent by estoppel, based on a coparenting agreement, requires that the agreement be in the child's best interests.[22] However, even to the extent that status remains a strong operating principle, it is blended with contractual arrangements.[23] For example, the PRINCIPLES set the amount of child support by guidelines,[24] but allow a child to have two mothers, two fathers, or even three parents by virtue of private ordering.[25] Along the same lines, the PRINCIPLES' domestic partnerships provisions create rights and liabilities between the intimates themselves, which need not be recognized by third parties such as the State or

approaches to contractarianism have been distinguished from contractualism, with the latter holding "that rationality requires that we respect persons, which in turn requires that moral principles be such that they can be justified to each person. Thus, individuals are not taken to be motivated by self-interest but rather by a commitment to publicly justify the standards of morality to which each will be held." Cudd, *supra*. Contractualism may be especially pertinent to family contexts, in which love and obligation accompany self-interested behavior.

18 *See* notes 2 and 14, *supra*, and associated text.

19 PRINCIPLES § 2.03.

20 RESTATEMENT (SECOND) OF CONTRACTS §§ 17, 24, 50, 71, 110 (1981).

21 PRINCIPLES § 7.06 ("The right of a child to support may not be affected adversely by an agreement."). The PRINCIPLES show similar solicitude for victims of domestic violence. PRINCIPLES Introduction 10–11; PRINCIPLES §§ 2.06(2) & 2.07(3).

22 PRINCIPLES § 2.03(b).

23 While this chapter focuses on contractarianism, one also might say that the PRINCIPLES' provisions on domestic partnership, parenthood by estoppel and de facto parenthood adopt status models that are grounded in contract principles, or that the provisions elevate agreement to the level of status through state recognition.

24 PRINCIPLES ch. 3.

25 For example, a lesbian can have a baby with a gay male friend, and also have a female partner with whom she raises the child, pursuant to a coparenting agreement. In these circumstances the PRINCIPLES provides that the child can have two legal parents (a biological mother and father) and either a de facto parent or parent by estoppel. *See* PRINCIPLES §§ 2.03(b)(iii) and (iv) (providing that coparenting agreements must be with child's legal parent "or, if there are two legal parents, both parents" for parenthood by estoppel to arise). *See also* PRINCIPLES § 2.03 cmt. b(iii), at 114–15 (suggesting that either two women or two men can be parents of the same child under the parenthood by estoppel provisions, skirting the ban on same-sex couples adopting in some jurisdictions and noting that the number of parents is not dispositive, and further that the real issue is the strength of bonds with the child, and the extent of parental involvement).

employers.[26] In doing so, the PRINCIPLES retains a special status for marriage, and relegates domestic partners to a contract-like relationship that centers on the partners themselves rather than third parties. This braiding of contract and status is consistent with the nearly universal recognition that families, and thus family law, include elements of both status and contract.[27]

II. Private Ordering under the PRINCIPLES: Domestic Partnership, Parenthood by Estoppel, and De Facto Parenthood

Domestic partnership, parenthood by estoppel, and de facto parenthood are instances of private ordering in the PRINCIPLES.[28] This part elaborates the private ordering elements of each, focusing on how private ordering recognizes the differences in the way that people order their lives. Recognizing different kinds of agreements is consistent with contract law. The Uniform Commercial Code "UCC," a staple of contract law, is predicated on the idea that there are different kinds of agreements and that the sale of goods, debtor-creditor relations, and contracts relating to negotiable instruments are governed by different rules.[29] This approach recognizes that life, commercial and social, is too complex to fit into one tiny little box.[30]

At first glance, it seems that domestic partnership is a status rather than a contract because it does not require parties to make an implied or express agreement.[31] However, further analysis reveals that domestic partnership rests in large part on contract. The PRINCIPLES acknowledge as much, explaining that the definition "identifies the circumstances that would typically lead . . . a court to find a contract, and defines those circumstances as giving rise to a domestic partnership."[32]

Section 6.03 of the PRINCIPLES begins by providing that two people, same-sex or opposite sex, are domestic partners if they are not married to one another and "for a significant period of time share a primary residence and a life together as a couple."[33] One way to share a life together as a couple is to live with a common child for a statutorily determined time, which the comments suggest could be two years, and the other way is to cohabit for a statutorily determined time, which the comments suggest could be three years.[34] However, merely living together for the requisite period is insufficient; the presumption of domestic partnership can be rebutted by evidence that the parties did *not* share a life together,

[26] PRINCIPLES § 6.01 cmt. a, 908 (noting that the PRINCIPLES' proposals "are confined to the inter se claims of domestic partners").

[27] *See, e.g.*, DeMatteo v. DeMatteo, 762 N. E.2d 797, 809 (Mass. 2002); Ertman, *supra* note 8, at 469; Katharine B. Silbaugh, *Marriage Contracts and the Family Economy*, 93 NW. U. L. REV. 65, 110–111 (1998).

[28] Not everyone agrees. *See* Marsha Garrison, *Is Consent Necessary? An Evaluation of the Emerging Law of Cohabitant Obligation*, 52 U. C. L. A. L. REV. 815 (2005); Carbone, this volume (contending that domestic partnership imposes a status on unwilling cohabitants rather than deferring to people's private ordering).

[29] UNIFORM. COMMERCIAL CODE (2005) [hereinafter UCC].

[30] For a discussion of how law could recognize a range of intimate affiliations as it recognizes a range of business entitles, see Ertman, *supra* note 8.

[31] PRINCIPLES § 6.03 cmt. b, at 919.

[32] PRINCIPLES § 6.03 cmt. b, at 918–19.

[33] PRINCIPLES § 6.03(1). One can see the burden-shifting framework of the domestic partnership provisions as recognizing that certain cohabitants have the status of domestic partners if they share a life together as a couple. If, however, they do not share a life together as a couple, the person resisting this label can assert facts set out in Section 6.03(3) and (7) to counteract the presumption of domestic partnership that arises once the parties live together for the requisite time.

[34] PRINCIPLES § 6.03(3) and cmt. d, at 921.

based on thirteen factors.[35] These factors indicate that a domestic partnership comes into being when parties either form agreements related to sharing a life together as a couple, or act as if they have. Four of these factors seem quite contractual: making statements or promises to each other regarding the relationship; naming one another as beneficiary of an insurance policy or will; participating in a commitment ceremony or registering as domestic partners; and entering a void or voidable marriage.[36] The other nine factors rest on implied agreements to share a life together as a couple, including intermingling finances; becoming economically dependent or interdependent; specializing in roles; changing life circumstances due to the relationship; treating the relationship as qualitatively different from other relationships; being emotionally or physically intimate; being known in the community as a couple; having a child, adopting, or jointly assuming parental functions toward a child; and maintaining a common household.[37]

It makes sense to infer an agreement to share gains and losses from sharing a life together as a couple. When business partners intermingle finances as they jointly operate a business for profit, the law recognizes the joint entity thus created.[38] Just as would-be business partners can contract out of that status, cohabitants can contract out of domestic partnership under the PRINCIPLES.[39] Some cohabitants maintain financial and other kinds of independence, thus contracting out of domestic partnership informally, through conduct. But when cohabitants do share a life together as well as a mailbox, it makes more sense for the law to treat them as partners than as strangers.

[35] PRINCIPLES §§ 6.03(3) and (7). These factors are:

(a) the oral or written statements or promises made to one another, or representations jointly made to third parties, regarding their relationship;
(b) the extent to which the parties intermingle their finances;
(c) the extent to which their relationship fostered the parties' economic interdependence, or the economic dependence of one party upon the other;
(d) the extent to which the parties engaged in conduct and assumed specialized or collaborative roles in furtherance of their life together;
(e) the extent to which the relationship wrought change in the life of either or both parties;
(f) the extent to which the parties acknowledged responsibilities to each other, as by naming the other the beneficiary of life insurance or of a testamentary instrument, or as eligible to receive benefits under an employee-benefit plan;
(g) the extent to which the parties' relationship was treated by the parties as qualitatively distinct from the relationship either party had with any other person;
(h) the emotional or physical intimacy of the parties' relationship;
(i) the parties' community reputation as a couple;
(j) the parties' participation in a commitment ceremony or registration as a domestic partnership;
(k) the parties participation in a void or voidable marriage that, under applicable law, does not give rise to the economic incidents of marriage;
(l) the parties' procreation of, adoption of, or joint assumption of parental functions toward a child; [and]
(m) the parties' maintenance of a common household[.]

PRINCIPLES § 6.03(7).

[36] PRINCIPLES §§ 6.03(7)(a), (f), (j), (k).

[37] PRINCIPLES §§ 6.03(7)(b–e), (g–i), (l–m). "Persons *maintain a common household* when they share a primary residence only with each other and family members; or when, if they share a household with other unrelated persons, they act jointly, rather than as individuals, with respect to management of the household." PRINCIPLES § 6.03(4) (emphasis added).

[38] UNIFORM PARTNERSHIP ACT § 202(a) (1997), 6 U. L. A. 53 (Supp. 2000).

[39] PRINCIPLES §6.01(2). Further demonstrating the contractual nature of the domestic partnership scheme, parties can contract into domestic partner status pursuant to Section 6.01(3), even if their circumstances do not satisfy the other elements of Section 6.03. *See also* PRINCIPLES § 7.01(2) (noting that the provisions governing agreements apply also to domestic partners).

Parenthood by estoppel represents another instance of private ordering because it turns on a prior coparenting agreement. Sections 2.03(b)(iii) and (iv) provide that a parent by estoppel is someone who lived with a child, either from birth or for at least two years, and assumed "full and permanent responsibilities as a parent" as part of a "prior agreement with the child's legal parent (or, if there are two legal parents, both parents)."[40] This is clearly private ordering. It may be a contract in the "R" sense that focuses on voluntariness and reciprocity rather than the "K" sense that focuses on legal enforceability, because it is subject to the child's best interest. However, to the extent that the law *does* recognize the prior coparenting agreement, it *is* enforceable, at least more so than under prior law, which treated coparents who were not legal parents as strangers to the children.[41] The comments to Section 2.03(b) clarify the importance of a coparenting agreement, providing that where a lesbian couple "decided to raise a child together" and "agreed that... [they] would be equally involved and responsible for" the child, the nonbiological mother is a parent by estoppel.[42] In contrast, a nonbiological mother is not a parent by estoppel where she "agreed to help out, but she assumed no financial responsibilities."[43]

A third instance of private ordering is de facto parenthood. A de facto parent under Section 2.03(c) is someone who lives with a child "for a significant period of time not less than two years," doing as much or more caretaking of the child than the legal parent "with the agreement of a legal parent to form a parent-child relationship."[44] Illustration 22 demonstrates that the agreement necessary to become a de facto parent is considerably less formal than the coparenting agreement necessary for parenthood by estoppel since it rests merely on the division of caretaking responsibility:

> For the past four years, seven-year-old Lindsay has lived with her mother Annis and her stepfather, Ralph. During that period, Ralph and Annis both worked outside the home, and divided responsibility for Lindsay's care roughly equally between them. Annis's sharing of responsibility for Lindsay's care with Ralph constitutes an implied agreement by her to the role assumed by Ralph.[45]

However, if Annis, as the legal parent, retains authority over all important matters such as discipline, bedtime, television, after-school activities, and friends, Ralph does not become a de facto parent.[46] The distinction rests on the nature of the relationship agreed to,

[40] PRINCIPLES § 2.03(b) (defining a "parent by estoppel" as "an individual who, though not a legal parent... (iii) lived with the child since the child's birth, holding out and accepting full and permanent responsibilities as a parent, as part of a prior coparenting agreement with the child's legal parent (or, if there are two legal parents, both parents) to raise a child together each with full parental rights and responsibilities, when the court finds that recognition of the individual as a parent is in the child's best interests; or (iv) lived with the child for at least two years, holding out and accepting full and permanent responsibilities as a parent, pursuant to an agreement with the child's parent (or, if there are two legal parents, both parents), when the courts finds that recognition of the individual as a parent is in the child's best interests"). Section 2.03(b)(i) also provides that a person obligated to pay child support is a parent by estoppel.

[41] Melanie B. Jacobs, *Micah Has One Mommy and One Legal Stranger: Adjudicating Maternity for Nonbiological Lesbian Coparents*, 50 BUFF. L. REV. 341 (2002).

[42] PRINCIPLES § 2.03 cmt. b(iii), illus.9, at 115.

[43] PRINCIPLES § 2.03 cmt. b(iii), illus.11, at 116.

[44] PRINCIPLES § 2.03(c) ("A *de facto parent* is an individual other than a legal parent or a parent by estoppel who, for a significant period of time not less than two years, (i) lived with the child and (ii) for reasons primarily other than financial compensation, and with the agreement of a legal parent to form a parent-child relationship, or as a result of a complete failure or inability of any legal parent to perform caretaking functions, (A) regularly performed a majority of the caretaking functions for the child, or (B) regularly performed a share of caretaking functions at least as great as that of the parent with whom the child primarily lived.") (emphasis added).

[45] PRINCIPLES § 2.03 cmt. c, illus.22, at 122.

[46] PRINCIPLES § 2.03 cmt. c, illus.23, at 122.

glorified babysitter or de facto parent.[47] This distinction allows parties to privately tailor their arrangements to suit their needs. It is, in short, private ordering.

III. Private Ordering as a Conceptual Basis for Family Law

Private ordering provides a key conceptual basis for both family and family law because it can account for life's complexities. Other chapters in this volume raise the importance of a clear conceptual basis for legal doctrine.[48] This is an important issue, since the success of other projects synthesizing and updating a legal area, such as the UCC, has turned on the project having one or more central themes. The key concept around the UCC, more evident in some Articles than in others and perhaps more evident in the original Articles than in more recent revisions, is a legal realist idea that agreements are formed both formally and informally and that legal doctrine provides gap-fillers to make up for the fact that people often do not even consider some terms of their agreement.[49] This idea translates into a common sense rule for sales of goods that if buyers and sellers act as if they have an agreement – if they deliver goods, for example, or pay for them – then legal doctrine treats them as having entered into a contract, even if the boilerplate terms of a preprinted form say otherwise.[50] In other words, if it looks like a duck, walks like a duck, and talks like a duck, the law treats it as a duck, even if it is wearing a collar saying "this is not a duck."

Admittedly, not all contracts are alike: there is a big difference between buying a car and getting married. Accordingly, different bodies of law govern the two transactions. Still, a contractual principle, a legal realist view that the law should recognize people's conduct as well as their words, could, and arguably does, inform family law.[51] The major competitor to this view is status, a theme that historically dictated that one's condition of birth, such as sex, determined rights and responsibilities, such as child custody and alimony.[52] If there is a coherent theme to the PRINCIPLES, contractual or status-based, this project might be as successful as the UCC. If not, the PRINCIPLES may share the fate of other uniform law efforts, languishing unadopted by courts or legislators.[53] The next part argues that private ordering provides a conceptual basis for provisions governing domestic partnership and parental rights, leaving for another day the question of whether it provides a conceptual basis for the PRINCIPLES as a whole.

IV. Equality, Plurality, and Nature

The benefits of private ordering are twofold. First, private ordering can account for equality and plurality within relationships, and among different kinds of relationships. Second,

[47] Of course these are extremes, and the messy realities of actual lives tend to fall somewhere between babysitter and full parent. *See* cases discussed at notes 102–17, *infra*, and associated text.

[48] *See, e.g.*, Garrison, this volume; Carbone, this volume; Scott, this volume.

[49] UCC § 1–303 cmt. 1 (2003) (rejecting a conveyancer's reading of a commercial agreement, and providing instead that "the meaning of the agreement of the parties is to be determined by the language used by them and by their action, read and interpreted in the light of commercial practices and other surrounding circumstances."). *See also* Randy E. Barnett, ... *And Contractual Consent*, 3 S. CAL. INTERDISC. L. J. 421, 429 (1993); Michael Korybu, *Searching for Commercial Reasonableness Under the Revised Article 9*, 87 IOWA L. REV. 1383, 1454 (2002).

[50] UCC § 2–207 (2000).

[51] *See* note 2, *supra.*

[52] Danaya C. Wright, *The Crisis of Child Custody: A History of the Birth of Family Law in England*, 11 COLUM. J. GENDER & L. 175, 195 (2002).

[53] *See, e.g.*, UNIFORM. LAND SECURITY INTERESTS ACT, 7A U.L.A. 403 (1999).

based on both common sense and cognitive linguistic theory, private ordering is as natural as other ways of thinking about families. This part addresses each point in turn.

Aristotle defined equality as treating likes alike and treating nonalikes differently.[54] Private ordering facilitates this kind of equality among different types of relationships.[55] Equality, of course, does not require that every married couple be treated the same for all purposes, since people have different kinds of families. Bill and Hillary Clinton, for example, seem quite independent of each other, while George and Laura Bush seem more interdependent. But both couples are married, which means that there is a need for legal rules that account for the different ways that spouses order their lives. For example, legal doctrine could recognize the significance of Laura Bush's more modest income-producing potential after divorce and grant her part of George Bush's postdivorce income.

Private ordering also furthers equality among different types of relationships by requiring that the State recognize a range of intimate relationships, rather than have regulation that functions like an on/off switch, recognizing only one relationship, that of spouses, and treating the participants in all other kinds of relationships as strangers to one another.[56] Spouses and domestic partners are more "like" one another than "unlike" in that they share a life together by cohabiting, perhaps raising children and/or intermingling finances, and thus merit similar, if not identical, treatment.[57] This distinction between similar and identical treatment is key and routine for law. All property owners are taxed, for example, but the amount differs depending on factors such as the property's value and the owner's status as an individual or a business. If a relationship is really "unlike" committed long term relationships – a casual dating relationship, for example – legal doctrine can treat it differently without violating principles of equality.

Private ordering thus accounts for plurality among different kinds of relationships, providing a conceptual basis for recognizing the different ways they function. Unlike marriage, domestic partnership under the PRINCIPLES does not require the parties to comply with the formality of filing a document with the State. Functionally, this difference in formality signifies a difference in kind, namely that domestic partnership is simply less formal, just as business partnerships are less formal than corporations.[58] This difference

[54] 3 ARISTOTLE, NICOMACHEAN ETHICS 1131a-1131b (2d ed.,Terence Irwin translation, 1999).

[55] At the metaphorical level, private ordering can serve equality within relationships by treating the members of a couple, male or female, as similarly capable of engaging in wage labor, raising children, and other things. Status, in contrast, suggests men and women are "unlike" and therefore should be governed by different rules that, for example, give fathers custody of children because of their greater capacity to engage in moral reasoning. NORMA BASCH, IN THE EYES OF THE LAW: WOMEN, MARRIAGE AND PROPERTY IN NINETEENTH-CENTURY NEW YORK (1982). In addition, couples whose relationships are not legally recognized, such as same-sex couples, can create rights and obligations through contract to share wealth and thus create a more equitable balance of power in the relationship than provided under background legal rules. *See, e.g.*, Posik v. Layton, 695 So.2d 759 (Fla. App. 1997). However, private ordering can also facilitate inequality in couples, as when a socially and economically powerful partner won't marry unless the other, less powerful partner, executes a prenuptial agreement waiving entitlements to support or property upon divorce. Mary Becker, *Problems with the Privatization of Heterosexuality*, 73 DENV. U. L. REV. 1169 (1996).

[56] On the incongruity of treating intimates as if they were strangers, see Milton C. Regan, *Spouses and Strangers: Divorce Obligations and Property Rhetoric*, 82 GEO. L. J. 2303 (1994).

[57] *But see* Garrison, *supra* note 28. Professor Garrison overlooks the difference between identical and similar in suggesting that recognizing any rights of cohabitants treats cohabitation exactly the same as marriage. There are various kinds of long-term committed intimate relationships, some married and some not. The law could and should recognize both similarities and differences among various kinds of committed long-term relationships. Contractual reasoning accommodates this kind of plurality. Ariela Dubler, *In the Shadow of Marriage*, 112 YALE L. J. 1641, 1710 (2003).

[58] A business partnership comes into being when two or more people jointly operate a business for profit. A corporation, in contrast, cannot come into existence until the people forming it file Articles of Incorporation with the

between an arrangement that arises by default, as opposed to formal opting-in, justifies treating domestic partners differently from spouses. Logically, Chapter 6 of the PRINCIPLES makes domestic partners responsible to one another but does not mandate recognition by third parties, such as the State or employers.[59] But there is a problem with this analysis, because in every U.S. state except Massachusetts, only opposite-sex couples can marry.[60] If marriage was open to all couples, it would make sense to allow people to select more or less formal arrangements. Setting aside for the moment the unfairness of banning same-sex marriage, a position that can be partly justified by the fact that legislation and litigation are pending in several jurisdictions to recognize same-sex marriage, it does make sense to govern different kinds of relationships with different rules. We are complex social beings who organize our lives in different ways. The sheer number of ways to order coffee at Starbucks indicates that there are a lot of ways to approach even minor aspects of life. How odd it would be if intimate affiliation came in one size when we can order a double shot skinny latte with no foam.

Indeed, major parts of statutes such as the Uniform Marriage and Divorce Act and the Uniform Probate Code go some distance toward adopting contractual metaphors for family by embracing the partnership model of marriage.[61] Yet many people resist this way of thinking about intimate affiliation.[62] This resistance may erode once people realize that private ordering is no less natural than other models. The natural link between private ordering and family becomes clear when one considers the work of cognitive linguist George Lakoff, who suggests that people often think in terms of body-based metaphors.[63] Using the association of handshakes with contracts, the next part illustrates that private ordering is far more intimately associated with family than most people imagine.

V. Body-Based Metaphors, Families, and Private Ordering

Professor Lakoff's theory of embodied cognition contends that common bodily experiences inform thought and language by providing metaphors to describe that experience. For example, anger creates physiological effects, including increased body heat and increased blood pressure and muscular pressure.[64] Consequently, people think and talk about anger in ways that reflect this embodied experience. Idioms relating to anger (i.e., "he lost his cool," "he was foaming at the mouth," "you make my blood boil," and "he's just letting off steam") refer back to the physiological experience of anger.[65] Under Professor Lakoff's analysis, one would also expect metaphors for intimate affiliation to refer to the body.[66]

State. In this way, cohabitation is more like a partnership, and marriage is more like a corporation. *See generally* Ertman, *supra* note 8.

[59] PRINCIPLES § 6.02 and cmt. b, at 915–16.

[60] *See generally* Goodridge v. Department of Public Health, 798 N.E.2d 941 (Mass. 2003).

[61] For further discussion of the partnership analogy to intimate affiliation, see Ertman, *supra* note 8, at 476.

[62] *See, e.g.*, Ann Laquer Estin, *Can Families Be Efficient?*, *in* FEMINISM CONFRONTS HOMO ECONOMICUS 423 (2005).

[63] LAKOFF, WOMEN, FIRE AND DANGEROUS THINGS, *supra* note 12.

[64] *Id.* at 381.

[65] *Id.* at 380–81. In America, anger also is associated with wild animals ("he has a *ferocious* temper") and insanity ("I'm *mad*"). According to Lakoff, all of these metaphors refer to bodily experiences associated with anger, such as increased body heat, increased internal pressure – blood pressure and muscular pressure – agitation, and interference with accurate perception. *Id.* at 381–94.

[66] I use the term metaphor loosely, while linguists distinguish among metaphor, analogy, and metonym. *See* LAKOFF, WOMEN, FIRE AND DANGEROUS THINGS, *supra* note 12, at 19. A metaphor is a figure of speech in which a term is transferred from the object it ordinarily designates to another object by implicit comparison, such as "foot of the mountain." *Id.* at 825. Analogy is defined as a logical inference that if two things are alike in some respects they

And they do. We talk about a one-time sexual encounter as a one night stand, for example, invoking the image of standing up and, presumably, being ready to go. When a person falls in love, she might be head over heels, that is until she falls out of love. Body-based metaphors, Professor Lakoff contends, are not limited to social relations; even if I miss a step in my analysis of private ordering, that very turn of phrase supports his premise that much of our cognition rests in metaphors whose meaning lies in the body.

Clearly, we think of family in terms associated with bodies and bodily proximity. For census and tax purposes, for example, there are heads of households, and it is sometimes said that the kitchen is the heart of a home. Wedding vows include promises "to have and to hold," invoking images of arms and bodily proximity.[67]

In law, this bodily proximity is sometimes expressed with reference to nature. Family law refers to "natural mother[s]" and "natural children," meaning people bound together by biology,[68] and estates and trusts law uses the phrase "natural beneficiaries" of one's bounty to describe close relations, such as a spouse or child.[69] Proximity, however, is not always deemed natural; statutes have dubbed skin-to-skin proximity between people of the same sex a "crime against nature."[70] The category "natural" is further complicated by the fact that nature is generally set up in opposition to culture, and family is commonly understood as being both natural and cultural. Less ambiguously, bodies, especially unclothed bodies, are conceived as being on the natural side of the equation. One possible manifestation of this linking of bodies, nature, and families is the importance of bodily intimacy in families. In families, we care for the sick, we nurse babies, we have sex, we roughhouse with siblings and children.

Logically, then, legal doctrines have generally used metaphors relating to the body to give a coherent conceptual basis to those doctrines.[71] In order to take hold, a metaphor should feel like a familiar and convincing way to think about families and intimacy. One long standing and old fashioned metaphor is coverture, which provided a conceptual basis for family law until the late nineteenth century. According to the OXFORD ENGLISH DICTIONARY, coverture refers to a cover, specifically a bed cover.[72] It is not surprising that marriage would be associated with beds, which invoke rich images of home, warmth, safety, rest, and comfort, as well as sex.[73]

are alike in other respects. AMERICAN HERITAGE DICTIONARY 47 (New College ed. 1979). A metonym, in contrast, exists when a part of a whole stands for the whole, as when a nurse says "the C section in Room 107 needs meds." LAKOFF, WOMEN, FIRE AND DANGEROUS THINGS, *supra* note 12, at 77.

[67] The etymology of this vow, however, stems from terms of conveyance in property law, echoing the sale-like qualities in a wedding ceremony; "to have and to hold" originally referenced the decidedly unromantic notion of possessing and controlling. Maya Grosz, *To Have and to Hold: Property and State Regulation of Sexuality and Marriage*, 24 N.Y.U. REV. L. & SOC. CHANGE 235 (1998).

[68] *See, e.g.*, Johnson v. Calvert, 5 Cal.4th. 84 (1993).

[69] *See, e.g.*, Nygaard v. Peter Pan Seafoods, Inc., 701 F.2d 77, 80 (9th Cir. 1983).

[70] Bowers v. Hardwick, 478 U.S. 186 (1986), *rev'd by* Lawrence v. Texas, 539 U.S. 558 (2003). A rich body of literature challenges the conventional wisdom that crimes against nature were extramarital, since a genealogy of sodomy and other crimes against nature indicate that the common law proscribed sexual acts such as anal penetration regardless of whether the people performing them were married to one another.

[71] Attempts to use the firm as a metaphor for the family have been largely unsuccessful, perhaps because of the lack of association with bodies. *See* BRINIG, *supra* note 7.

[72] I OXFORD ENGLISH DICTIONARY 535 (New Shorter ed. 1993). It also refers to a garment, or other covers (a lid, canopy, or disguise). *Id.*

[73] This last association is particularly important as it brings to mind the image of a man covering a woman in what is commonly known as the missionary position. If a central concern of marriage is sexual exclusivity, as Professor Spaht argues in this volume, then under coverture it is the exclusive covering by men of women, both literally and figuratively. Katherine Spaht, this volume.

Under coverture, married women had no independent legal identity so that the man, literally and figuratively, covered the woman. This lack of independence has been on the decline since the nineteenth century, when Sir Henry Maine famously declared that the move in progressive societies was one from status to contract.[74] Family law, like other areas, has followed this trajectory, increasingly recognizing the independent personhood of women and children. This tremendous transformation both spawned and required a new metaphor. Contract emerged as that metaphor to replace the status-based system of coverture, and to reflect the alteration of household arrangements due to the abolition of slavery and the increased equality of women.[75] Part of this transition involved the passage of Married Women's Property Acts, which authorized married women to make and enforce contracts. Thus, contract has been increasingly central to our thinking about family, especially about spouses, for over a century.[76] As a result, married women now have an independent legal identity. Indeed, the demise of coverture and the rise of contractual understandings of intimate affiliation were necessary for married women to enjoy that identity. The images associated with the metaphors for coverture and contract, a bed cover and a handshake, reveal the sharp contrast between the old and new regimes. Coverture, the bed cover, is based on vertical, hierarchical, status-based understanding of marriage, while contract, as illustrated by the image of the handshake, is based on a horizontal, equal, consensual view of marriage. While either could be called natural, since that term is used to describe a wide range of things,[77] most people persist in thinking of coverture metaphors of family as more "natural" than contract.[78]

The main obstacle to seeing that contract is a natural way to describe family, as natural as status, is that contract implies distance as much as bodily closeness.[79] Contracts are, to use another body-based metaphor, arm's length transactions. Professor Lakoff suggests that the phrase "to keep someone at arm's length" means "to keep someone from becoming intimate, so as to avoid social or psychological harm."[80] However, he also notes that an idiom can have nearly opposite meanings: the phrase "a rolling stone gathers no moss"

[74] See note 8, *supra.*

[75] AMY DRU STANLEY, FROM BONDAGE TO CONTRACT (1998); LINDA K. KERBER, NO CONSTITUTIONAL RIGHT TO BE LADIES: WOMEN AND THE OBLIGATIONS OF CITIZENSHIP (1998). These transformations, however, were not complete, as courts and legislatures often constrained the new rights. *See* Reva Siegel, *Why Equal Protection No Longer Protects: The Evolving Forms of Status-Enforcing State Action,* 49 STAN. L. REV. 1111 (1997).

[76] Contract, despite its increased importance, does not exhaust the metaphors we associate with marriage and family; the focus on marriage as sacrament – one body taking another body, albeit a divine one, metaphorically into itself – continues to be foundational for opponents of same-sex marriage. George W. Dent, Jr., *The Defense of Traditional Marriage,* 15 J.L. & POL. 581, 617 (1999). Another example of noncontractual analysis in family law is the PRINCIPLES' proposals about alimony or "compensatory payments," which is grounded in the idea of compensation for losses rather than contractual analysis. PRINCIPLES § 5.04 cmt. b, at 807–08.

[77] *See* JOHN STUART MILL, *Nature, in* THREE ESSAYS ON RELIGION 64–65 (1969).

[78] One example of the prevalence of status-based understandings of marriage, and resistance to private ordering, is the fact that most states and the federal government have passed Defense of Marriage Acts, which define marriage as a relationship between one man and one woman, and further refuse to recognize same-sex marriages entered in other jurisdictions. *See, e.g.,* 28 U.S.C. § 1738C (2000). These measures defend the special status of opposite-sex marriage, and thus of heterosexuals, as well as men and women, since the only reason to mandate that every marriage include one man and one woman in marriage is to mandate that the husband play the role of *the* man and the wife play the role of *the* woman. Andrew Jon-Peter Kelly, Note, *Act of Infidelity: Why the Defense of Marriage Act is Unfaithful to the Constitution,* 7 Cornell J. L. & Pub. Pol'y. 203 (1997). A contractual understanding of marriage, in contrast, recognizes the importance of choice and autonomy, and allows spouses to order their intimate lives in different ways, for example with less rigid division of labor along gendered lines.

[79] Indeed, coverture arguably is less closely associated with the body than contract given that the bed cover is neither a human body nor a part of one, while a handshake is a connection between two bodies.

[80] LAKOFF, WOMEN, FIRE AND DANGEROUS THINGS, *supra* note 12, at 448.

suggests both that moss is good, representing stability or roots in a community, and that moss is bad, representing encumbrance or lack of freedom.[81] The legal phrase "arm's length transaction" similarly seems to connote both distance and closeness. As discussed above, not all contracts are the same. Some, like employment contracts, are more about an ongoing connection than about separation. Others, like discrete, one-time transactions – buying a Coke, for example – are more about distance. Even so, the phrase "arm's length" connotes closeness, since being a mere arm's length away – within spitting distance – is quite close. This invocation of connection by the phrase "arm's length *transaction*" is a function of the last word in the phrase, since parties would not be in a transaction in the first place unless they wanted or needed to bind themselves together. While others have articulated the ways that contractual metaphors signal separation, and thus inadequately capture love and obligation inherent in family life,[82] there are ways in which contract can involve at least as much connection as separation. A handshake, the image associated with contract, demonstrates this closeness, since it represents a literal connection of two bodies.

Mythic handshakes illustrate the importance of hands touching. The high drama of Michelangelo's famous depiction of the Creation on the ceiling of the Sistine Chapel, for example, centers on the image of the two hands coming together, one divine and one human, signaling both closeness and separation at the moment of Creation. Part of the excitement generated in that image turns on the fact that the hands are not quite touching, so Creation has either just occurred, or is about to occur, and we do not know which. This

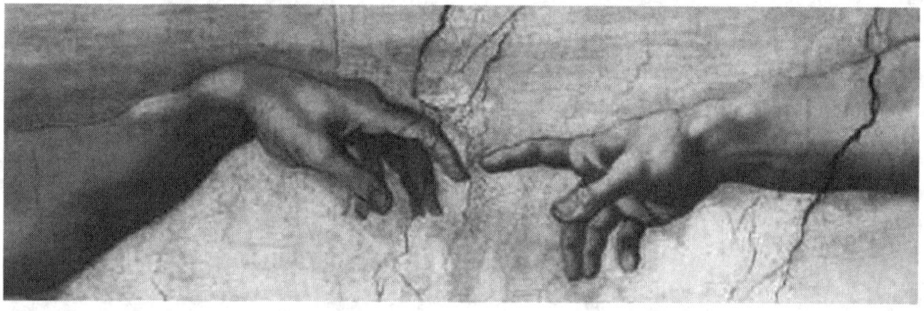

image of a highly stylized handshake, implying a covenant between God and humanity, perhaps, is extraordinarily moving because it is simultaneously immanent and transcendent, human and aspirational, just like intimate affiliation.

But that is Creation. What are the associations of a handshake with marriage? A young man traditionally asks for a woman's hand in marriage. If accepted – note the contractual term – he takes her hand, and she gives her hand. Not surprisingly, putting the ring on the fourth finger, known as the ring finger, is a key part of both engagement and the wedding ceremony. The importance of hands in marriage is further illustrated by the fact that a newly engaged woman sometimes shakes hands with her left hand to show off her ring and new status. Even phrases that seem unrelated to hands can be traced back to handshake images. For example, the phrase "tying the knot" derives from a Celtic ritual called hand fasting in which people getting betrothed or married bind their hands together as a central part of the ceremony.[83] Moreover, in most faiths and in civil ceremonies, contractual terms

[81] *Id.* at 451.

[82] Ann Laquer Estin, *Love and Obligation: Family Law and the Romance of Economics*, 36 Wm. & Mary L. Rev. 989 (1995).

[83] Clan Ross Association of Canada, Inc., *Hand Fasting*, in *Contemporary Items, Notes and FAQs*, *available at* http://www.greatclanross.org/htext8~Q4.html (last visited August 3, 2005).

define a marriage ceremony: each person makes vows and consents to take the other as a spouse. At a minimum, marriage is a relational contract.[84]

The history of handshakes further demonstrates the rich association of marriage with contract. Historically, convention dictated that only equals would shake hands. Men would shake other men's hands, but a master and servant would not shake hands, nor would a man and woman, nor a black man and a white man.[85] Instead, at least among men and women of a particular class, men might kiss a hand in greeting, signaling social hierarchy and status.[86] Indeed, one way to trace the evolution of civil rights is through the expansion of who gets to shake hands, which in turn tells us who had the capacity to form contracts and other kind of agreements. In the last fifty years, roughly the period of the second wave of the women's movement and the black civil rights movement, there probably has been more handshaking across sex and race than ever before. Not coincidentally, during this period, the U.S. Supreme Court also overturned state bans on interracial couples marrying and Massachusetts lifted the ban on same-sex marriage.[87]

Moreover, unlike a man kissing a woman's hand, a handshake signals physical contact but not necessarily sexual contact. Consistent with the expanding range of intimate affiliations, there is a trend away from coverture's sexual imagery of covering and toward recognizing non-sexual unions. Yet this idea is not entirely new. The biblical story of Ruth and Naomi is often read at weddings, despite the fact that Ruth and Naomi, as a couple, were neither hetero nor sexual, but instead mother-in-law and daughter-in- law: "Whither thou goest I will go; and where thou lodgest, I will lodge; thy people shall be my people, and thy God my God: Where thou diest I will die and there will I be buried."[88] Although not a sexual affiliation, these vows state the aspirational goals of marriage. Professor Martha Fineman persuasively articulates this vision, suggesting that our understandings of family be retooled to center not around sexual unions but around dependency, mainly between mothers and children.[89] Legal doctrine increasingly recognizes this pattern. Hawaii and Vermont, for example, both recognize that people can be "reciprocal beneficiaries." This status covers people who are barred from marrying and conveys some rights usually accorded to spouses, such as hospital visitation.[90] While the two states define reciprocal beneficiary differently, both states include non-sexual affiliates, such as a widowed mother and her adult son.[91] Similarly, some de facto parents under the PRINCIPLES are non-sexual affiliates of the

[84] Elizabeth S. Scott & Robert E. Scott, *Marriage as Relational Contract*, 84 VA. L. REV. 1225 (1998).

[85] C. DALLETT HEMPHILL, BOWING TO NECESSITIES: A HISTORY OF MANNERS IN AMERICA, 1620–1860 185 (1999); BERTRAM WILBUR DOYLE, THE ETIQUETTE OF RACE RELATIONS ON THE SOUTH: A STUDY IN SOCIAL CONTROL 13 (1971); STETSON KENNEDY, JIM CROW GUIDE TO THE U.S.A. 212 (1959) ("Under no circumstances does interracial etiquette permit you to shake hands with a person of the other race anywhere in segregated territory.").

[86] HEMPHILL, *supra* note 85, at 27, 191, 200, 203.

[87] *See, e.g.*, Loving v. Virginia, 388 U.S. 1 (1967); *see also* Goodridge v. Dept. of Pub. Health, 798 N.E.2d 941 (Mass. 2003). Other states, such as Vermont, Connecticut, and California, recognize many of the rights of marriage through relationships called civil unions and domestic partnerships. VT. STAT. ANN. tit. 15, §§ 1201–1207 (2002); 2005 CONN. PUB. ACT No. 05–10, An Act Concerning Civil Unions (effective Oct. 1, 2005); CAL. FAM. CODE §297.5 (West. Supp. 2004).

[88] HOLY BIBLE, BOOK OF RUTH 16–17. The popularity of this material for weddings is evident by its listing at http://www.ezweddingplanner.com.

[89] MARTHA ALBERTSON FINEMAN, THE NEUTERED MOTHER, THE SEXUAL FAMILY, AND OTHER TWENTIETH CENTURY TRAGEDIES (1995).

[90] HAW. REV. STAT. §§ 572C-1–7 (1997); VT. STAT. ANN. tit. 15, §§1301–06 (2002).

[91] In Hawaii, reciprocal beneficiaries are any two people barred from marrying, such as relatives and same-sex romantic partners. HAW. REV. STAT. §§ 572C-1–7 (1997). In Vermont, reciprocal beneficiaries must be barred from marrying and also from entering civil unions (thus precluding same-sex romantic partners from being reciprocal beneficiaries). VT. STAT. ANN. tit. 15, §§ 1301–06 (2002).

legal parents – for example, grandparents caring for their grandchildren in a parent-like relationship.[92]

Like the plurality of relationships, handshakes take different forms. Cognitive science suggests that most categories include both basic examples and radial examples. For something to be a basic example, there must be other, less central, instances of the same thing. For example "chair" is the basic level example of the category "furniture" because it is the best example of that category – the thing that comes to most people's mind when asked to give an example of furniture. In contrast, "rocker" is a radial example, a variant of the central category.[93] So while "dog" is the basic level example of "animal," "retriever" is a radial example.[94] While general categories (furniture, animals) are not characterized by specific images or associated motor actions, people do have an abstract mental image of the basic level example of the category. Thus, people have an abstract image in their mind of a chair that does not fit any particular chair, as well as a general motor action for sitting in chairs.[95] Radial level examples (rocker, retriever) are too specific to be basic examples of something. Setting aside for the moment the normative problem of seeing one form of relationship as better than others,[96] Professor Lakoff's rubric of basic level and radial categories provides a way to understand why contractual ordering of families makes sense. Most interesting, this scheme of basic and radial categories helps explain both why private ordering is a natural metaphor for the family, and why some people resist thinking about family in this way.

The quintessential handshake is the kind of image that might show up in a PowerPoint presentation at a business meeting: two white hands, meeting horizontally, both apparently

[92] Principles § 2.03(c).

[93] Lakoff, Women, Fire and Dangerous Things, *supra* note 12, at 91. Variants are generated one by one, by convention, rather than through general rules. *Id.*

[94] *Id.* at 46, 51. Lakoff further explains that basic-level categories "are 'human-sized.' They depend not on objects themselves, independent of people, but on the way people interact with objects: the way they perceive them, image them, organize information about them, and behave toward them with their bodies." *Id.* at 51.

[95] *Id.* at 51–52.

[96] Of course, labeling something a basic example always raises the spectre giving primacy to it, colluding with systems of invidious discrimination, just as dated definitions of marriage as between persons of the same race spawned the old ban on interracial marriage.

male and equal as indicated by the cuff of a button-down shirt and suit jacket. It is the quintessential handshake because it is the first thing that many people think of when hearing the term "handshake." It could be described in Professor Lakoff's terms as a basic category. But being a basic category, the best example of something, does not mean that this quintessential handshake is the only item in the category.

According to cognitive science research, most people agree on what constitutes the basic category for many things. For example, people who are shown 320 paint chips tend to agree that the best example of red is a particular shade that cognitive scientists call "focal red."[97] Researchers believe that neurons fire in a particular way in response to focal colors, so that this designation of focal red as the best example of red is determined partly by biology.[98] Thus, although burgundy is a shade of red, focal red represents the best example of the color.

A rash of statutes and constitutional amendments banning same-sex marriage at both the state and federal level reflect an intense anxiety on the part of many heterosexuals about the definition of marriage. One can see this anxiety as an investment in the basic category of marriage, and in particular a fear that a radial category, whether same sex marriage or domestic partnership, will destroy that basic category. In the terms of cognitive linguistics, these "defenders" of marriage seek to create a world in which there is only a basic category by abolishing radial categories, the equivalent of outlawing burgundy to protect the special status of focal red, or banning high fives to protect the special status of handshakes. This position cannot withstand scrutiny, at least if one accepts the legal realist premise that law should reflect the way people actually live.

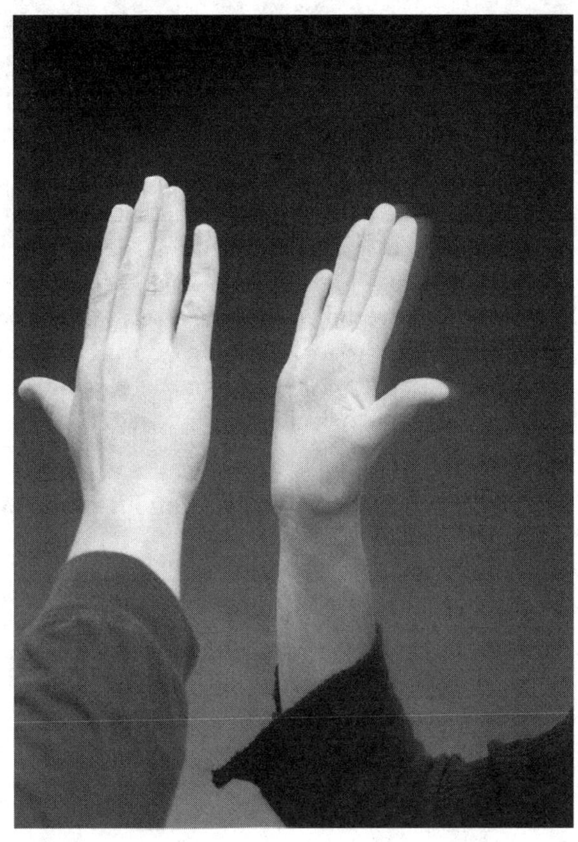

Just as there is more than one shade of red, there is more than one kind of intimate relationship. Handshakes mirror this plurality. There is the high five, there is the neighborhood handshake for urban hipsters, there is the feminine handshake in which one offers only fingers for clasping instead of a whole hand. Children pinky swear.[99]

As with relationships, this very plurality is inextricably linked to the basic category.

[97] Lakoff, Women, Fire and Dangerous Things, *supra* note 12, at 26.

[98] *Id.* at 26–29. The best examples are also determined by culture, as evidenced by the fact that focal colors are not uniform across languages. *Id.*

[99] Interestingly, pinky swearing is typically done by people who lack contractual capacity, perhaps indicating that pinky swearing is a kind of minicontract.

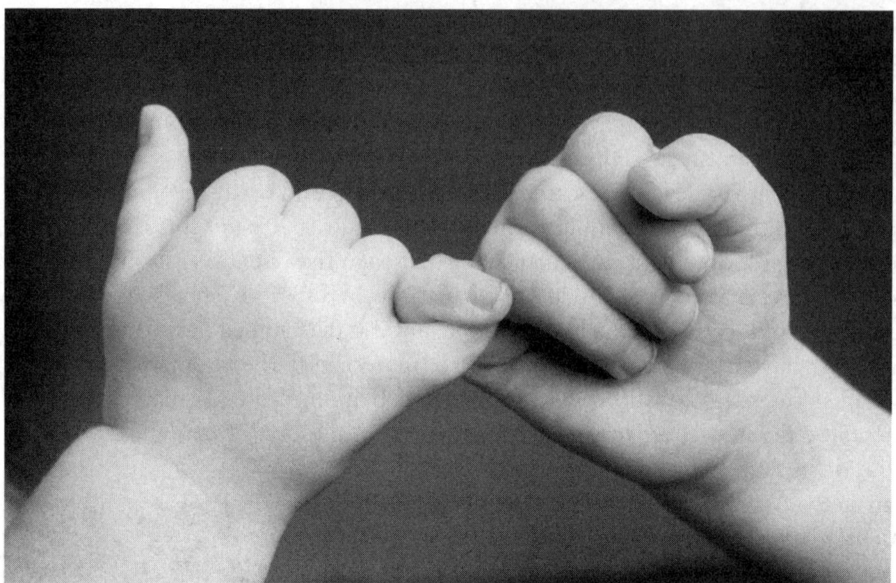

Basic and radial categories in families further illustrate this point. The basic level example of "mother" is a woman who gives birth and raises a child. Radial extensions of this category include "adoptive mother," "birth mother," "foster mother," and "surrogate mother."[100] A legal doctrine that recognizes only marriage – ignoring, penalizing, or banning all other relationships – is as woefully inadequate as one that refuses to recognize the unique situations of adoptive, birth, foster, and surrogate mothers. Indeed, legal doctrine regulates these forms of motherhood because ignoring them would create uncertainty and encourage opportunism.[101] In short, law has to recognize both basic level and radial categories to provide orderly and principled dispute resolution.

VI. Applying the Private Ordering Elements of the PRINCIPLES

Three recent cases decided by the California Supreme Court illustrate the ways that private ordering, as evidenced in the PRINCIPLES, reflects current trends in domestic relations law.[102] While the court did not cite to the PRINCIPLES in reaching its conclusions, it did recognize that romantic couples can agree to be parents in a range of ways. Because these decisions turn on parties' agreements and intent rather on than marriage or, with one possible exception, biological ties to children, they incorporate private ordering, as much

[100] LAKOFF, WOMEN, FIRE AND DANGEROUS THINGS, *supra* note 12, at 91. Basic level categories include assumptions. For example, the basic level example of "bachelor" includes assumptions about marriageability and the desire to marry. Thus, John Kennedy, Jr. was often described as a bachelor prior to his marriage, while Liberace and the Pope were not. *Id.* at 70. Legal doctrine can and does regulate both basic and radical categories of motherhood. Carol Sarger, *Separating from Children*, 96 COL. L. REV. 375, 491–94 (1996).

[101] Even if the state refrains from dictating rights and obligations of, say, surrogate mothers, that silence is a regulation in that it ratifies the state of affairs absent government involvement. Frances Olsen, *The Family and the Market*, 96 HARV. L. REV. 1497 (1983). While refusing to enforce cohabitation agreements, along the same lines, might be laissez faire regulation, it also rewards parties with title to property for keeping title in their own name, and punishes those who invest in property without getting title formally changed.

[102] Elisa B. v. Emily B., 117 P.3d 660 (Cal. 2005); Kristine H. v. Lisa R., 117 P.3d 690 (Cal. 2005); and K. M. v. E. G., 117 P.3d 673 (Cal. 2005).

as status. A brief review of the cases reveals the natural progression of this line of reasoning, and further that these cases facilitate both equality and plurality, as well as the children's best interests.

In *Elisa B. v. Emily B.*, the court imposed child support obligations on a woman whose former lesbian partner had borne twins while the two were together.[103] The two women had been inseminated with sperm from the same donor, Emily bearing the twins and Elisa also giving birth to a child. Emily stayed home with all three children, while Elisa (whose income at the time of trial was $95,000 a year) worked to support the family.[104] One of the twins had Down's syndrome; after the breakup Emily went on public assistance. The court's analysis turned on agreement and conduct reflecting an agreement that both women would be parents to the twins:

> A woman who *agreed* to raise children with her lesbian partner, supported her partner's artificial insemination using an anonymous donor, and received the resulting twin children into her home and held them out as her own, is the children's parent under the Uniform Parentage Act and has an obligation to support them.[105]

This focus on agreement, as opposed to marriage or biology, allows contract to supplement and redefine parental status. Status reasoning is hardly absent; the court recognized Elisa as the parent of her former partner's biological children because she acted like a parent. In this way, Elisa's conduct – which might be described as sharing a life together as coparents – gave rise to a set of legal rights and obligations in a similar way that sharing a life together gives rise to a domestic partner relationship under the PRINCIPLES:

> All three children were given the same hyphenated surname. As they had planned, Emily stayed home and cared for the three children, while Elisa worked to support the family. Elisa claimed all three children as dependents for tax purposes, and on an application for health insurance, and she described herself in a job interview as the mother of triplets.[106]

In short, the California Supreme Court did what it might have done in an analogous contract dispute. Just as contract law binds parties to a contract when their conduct indicates that they believe they have a contract (such as a buyer paying for goods, or a seller delivering goods), even if their standard forms say that they do not,[107] the court held that a woman who agrees to have children with her partner and then engages in parenting functions is treated as a parent under California law. This is not to say that every person who lives with a mother becomes a parent of the child living with them – the California Supreme Court carefully limited the application of its holding to those who wish to become parents by this route.[108] In short, like the PRINCIPLES' provisions on parenthood by estoppel and de facto parenthood discussed above, merely cohabiting is

[103] Elisa B. v. Emily B., 117 P.3d at 662–64.

[104] *Id.* at 664.

[105] *Id.* at 662 (emphasis added).

[106] *Id.* at 672 (Kennard, J., concurring).

[107] UNIF. COMM. CODE. 2–207 (2003).

[108] Elisa B. v. Emily B., 117 P.3d at 670 ("We were careful in *Nicholas H* therefore, not to suggest that every man who begins living with a woman when she is pregnant and continues to do so after the child is born necessarily becomes a presumed father of the child, even against his wishes. The Legislature surely did not intend to punish a man like the one in *Nicholas H.* who voluntarily provides support for a child who was conceived before he met the mother, by transforming that act of kindness into a legal obligation.") (internal citation omitted).

insufficient to establish parenthood; there must be some kind of agreement with the other parent before the mother's romantic partner will become a parent.

Had the court refused to recognize that agreement can give rise to a parental relationship, it would have countenanced inequality between partners (giving Emily the power to cut off Elisa's access to the twins, and Elisa the power to cut off financial support), and also harmed the children by depriving them of financial and emotional support from the woman they knew as a parent since birth. Only the principle of plurality, which recognizes that families come to be in various ways, can counteract such opportunism.

Similarly, *Kristine H. v. Lisa R.* involves the California Supreme Court recognizing a lesbian couple's agreement to coparent a child by holding that Kristine, the biological mother, was estopped from denying her former partner's parental status.[109] When Kristine was seven months pregnant, the two women jointly filed a "Complaint to Declare Existence of Parental Rights" in Superior Court to declare that Lisa was "the joint intended legal parent" of the child.[110] When the couple separated three years later, Kristine attempted to set aside the stipulated judgment. While the court did not use the language of contract or even intent, the parties could not have entered the stipulation absent an agreement to coparent. Thus its estoppel-based conclusion, based in equity, provides that Kristine was estopped from denying Lisa's parenthood because she agreed to coparent with Lisa and acted in ways that were consistent with that agreement.[111]

In contrast to the first two cases, the third case, *K. M. v. E. G.*, employs status-based reasoning to the extent that it recognizes a genetic mother's parenthood in the face of resistance by the woman, her former partner, who gestated their twins.[112] However, contractual reasoning is central to the opinion, since the crucial question is whether a preprinted form on which the genetic mother waived parental rights (and also promised not to have any contact with the gestational mother) trumps the genetic mother having intended to coparent the twins, which she in fact did for the first five years of their lives. In short, the case resolves a conflict between a writing waiving parental rights and years of conduct in which both women acted like parents. Inevitably, contractual reasoning would be central to its conclusion.

K. M. and E. G. undertook to conceive a child through E. G. gestating K. M.'s eggs, intending to raise the children in their common household.[113] The parties disagreed, however, as to whether they intended that they would both be legal parents in that household. E. G. contended that they orally agreed that she would be the sole legal parent, a claim that K. M. denied.[114] The strongest evidence supporting E. G.'s claim that K. M. waived her parental relationship to the twins was K. M. having signed the form at the beginning of the IVF procedure waiving her parental rights, which also included the statement "I agree not to attempt to discover the identity of the recipient[.]"[115] During the five years they

[109] Kristine H. v. Lisa R., 117 P.3d 690 (Cal. 2005).

[110] *Id.* at 692.

[111] *Id.* at 696. ("Kristine then stipulated to entry of a judgment naming Lisa as the child's other parent, obtained a birth certificate naming Lisa as the child's other parent, and co-parented the child with Lisa for nearly two years.").

[112] K. M. v. E. G., 117 P.3d 673 (Cal. 2005).

[113] *Id.* at 678.

[114] *Id.* ("K. M. contends that she did not intend to donate her ova, but rather provided her ova so that E. G. could give birth to a child to be raised jointly by K. M. and E. G. E. G. hotly contests this, asserting that K. M. donated her ova to E. G., agreeing that E. G. would be the sole parent. It is undisputed, however, that the couple lived together and that they both intended to bring the child into their joint home.").

[115] *Id.* at 676. The women's doctors knew that the women were partners. But E. G. swore K. M. to secrecy about the twins' parentage; E. G. claimed she did it because she was the only legal parent, and K. M. claimed she did it because E. G. worried that she would not be recognized as the "real" mother if people knew that K. M. was the

raised the twins together their social circle – friends, their nanny – viewed both women as mothers, although K. M.'s genetic tie to them remained a secret pursuant to E. G.'s request.

The women split up at least in part because K. M. wanted to be recognized as the girls' genetic mother. The trial and appellate courts refused to recognize K. M. as a legal parent, relying heavily on the form waiver she signed in the hospital.[116] The California Supreme Court redefined the question from whether they intended to be legal parents to whether they intended to raise the children together in their common home:

> even accepting as true E. G.'s version of the facts (which the superior court did), the present case... does not present a "true 'egg donation'" "situation.... K. M. did not intend to simply donate her ova to E. G., but rather provided her ova to her lesbian partner with whom she was living so that E. G. could give birth to a child that would be raised in their joint home.[117]

Intent, a central component of private ordering, was key to this reasoning. The court determined intent in a way that could be dubbed legal realist since it focused on the partners' intent to raise the children together in a common home, rather than a more legal formalist intent to become legal parents as determined by the hospital's waiver form. In analysis not so different from that used in a contractual battle of the forms, the court gave greater weight to conduct between domestic partners raising children together than to a waiver of parental rights in the hospital's preprinted form.[118] In short, it paid attention to how the parties actually shared a life together.

These three cases illustrate that the California Supreme Court is heading in much the same direction as the PRINCIPLES, at least to the extent that it recognizes that families come into existence in a range of ways and that coparents' agreements play a crucial role in distinguishing between family – those who have continuing rights and responsibilities after a romantic relationship sours – and others. Thus contractual reasoning allows legal doctrine to recognize a range of relationships, and in doing so promotes equality within relationships as well as between types of relationships. In addition, it serves the central purpose of family law in protecting children by recognizing functional parenthood and

twins' genetic mother. To support her claim that they orally agreed that she would be the sole parent, E. G. relied heavily on the consent form. K. M. disagreed, saying she saw the consent form for the first time a few minutes prior to beginning the egg retrieval procedure and viewed the form as "something for the clinic – it wasn't anything between my partner and me. We were having a family." Peggy Orenstein, *The Other Mother*, NEW YORK TIMES MAGAZINE July 25, 2004, at 27. The facts support both women's claims. On the one hand, both women went to every prenatal appointment. K. M. cut the umbilical cord. E. G. proposed to marry K. M. shortly after the birth, and the two exchanged rings under the Christmas tree in a private ceremony. There is evidence that the twins called both women "Mama" and also called K. M.'s parents "Granny" and "Papa." Moreover, E. G. listed K. M. as a "co-parent" on school forms and both women took the children to pediatric appointments. K. M. took off Fridays to spend with the girls. Both women paid for lessons, haircuts, birthday parties, and child care. On the other hand, E. G. added the children as beneficiaries to her life insurance policy and to her retirement plan, while K. M. did not, though K. M. may not have done this because her health problems may have prevented additional life insurance. K. M. was not listed on the birth certificate, but said that the hospital would not list two mothers. Similarly, K. M. was not listed on the baptismal certificate, nor was she mentioned at the ceremony. Moreover, the twins have Irish names after E. G.'s grandmothers, as well as her last name. But the girls have the two mothers' names as their middle names.

[116] K. M. v. E. G., 13 Cal. Rptr. 3d 136, 146 (Cal. App. 1st. Dist. 2004) (emphasis in original).

[117] K. M. v. E. G., 117 P.3d at 679 (citation omitted).

[118] UCC § 2–207.

thus protecting children who would otherwise lose not only the emotional relationship of someone central to their formative years, but also financial support.[119]

VII. Conclusion

The Principles do not radically depart from the ways that people form families, nor even from legal doctrine. Rather, they build on a trend to move away from a unitary status and more toward private ordering of intimate affiliation. Doing so is consistent with the way people think about family, grounded as it is in images of handshakes, which in turn account for equality, consent, physical closeness, and plurality. Thus private ordering is as natural as any other conceptual basis for regulating intimate affiliation. Professor Wardle observes in this volume that "if we ignore fault, we are inconsistent with what is happening in people's lives."[120] Similarly, ignoring the range of the way people are living in relationships is inconsistent with what is happening in people's lives. If the State mandates that there is only one kind of legitimate intimate affiliation, and treats everyone else in other relationships as strangers, it fails to govern all citizens on an equal basis, failing its essential purpose.

I owe thanks to Beth Clement, Leslie Francis, Laura Kessler, and Kathryn Stockton for comments on an earlier draft and Tiffany Pezzulo for invaluable research assistance.

[119] One potential downside of contractual reasoning is that it also allows a range of rights and responsibilities to children. *See* Katherine Baker, this volume (criticizing the Principles' allocation of child support to parents by estoppel but not de facto parents).

[120] *See* Wardle, this volume.

16 Marriage Matters: What's Wrong with the ALI's Domestic Partnership Proposal

Marsha Garrison

Twenty-five years ago, the *Marvin* decision and its progeny[1] stood the law of nonmarital cohabitation on its head. The law's prior inhibitory approach, which disallowed even explicit agreements between cohabitants, gave way to a contractual model that permits the parties both to enforce their understandings and to rely on an extensive battery of quasicontractual remedies.[2] The ALI's new "domestic partnership" proposal would again stand the law of nonmarital cohabitation on its head: based on a domestic partnership finding, it would impose on the cohabiting couple who have chosen to avoid marriage obligations virtually identical to those the couple would have incurred had they elected to marry.[3] The net effect of the ALI proposal would be to partially assimilate cohabitation to marriage.[4]

The ALI proposal is not novel. Although its approach is rare in the United States,[5] several other nations have adopted rules that impose on cohabitants some or all of the

[1] Marvin v. Marvin, 557 P.2d 106 (Cal. 1976); J. Thomas Oldham, Divorce, Separation and the Distribution of Property § 1.02 (2002) (listing decisions following *Marvin*); Joel E. Smith, Annot., *Property Rights Arising from Relationship of Couple Cohabiting Without Marriage*, 69 A.L.R. 5th 219 (2005) (surveying states).

[2] Under *Marvin*, a cohabitant may recover when she can show an express contract "or some other tacit understanding." *Marvin*, at 665. Some states have accepted the *Marvin* court's contractual approach but permit recovery based only on an express contract. *See, e.g.*, Morone v. Morone, 50 N.Y.2d 481 (1980); Tapley v. Tapley, 122 N.H. 727 (1982). A few states permit recovery based only on an express, written agreement. *See* Minn. Stat. Ann. § 513.075 (West 2005); Tex. Fam. Code Ann. § 1.108 (2004); Posik v. Layton, 695 So. 2d 759, 762 (Fla. Dist. Ct. App. 1997); Kohler v. Flynn, 493 N.W.2d 647, 649 (N.D. 1992). A number of courts have also endorsed the use of constructive trust and *quantum meruit* claims. *See infra* notes 87–88 and accompanying text.

[3] Principles § 6.01 et seq.

[4] The ALI's scheme extends to cohabitants classed as domestic partners all the rules applicable to married couples except those governing recharacterization of separate property. The ALI scheme governs only private rights and obligations attached to marital status; domestic partners thus would remain unmarried and could not claim statutory benefits, such as the right to file a wrongful death action or obtain Social Security Survivor's benefits. *See* Principles § 6.01 et seq.

[5] The Washington courts have utilized such an approach. *See* In re Marriage of Lindsey, 678 P.2d 328 (Wash. 1984); Connell v. Francisco, 898 P.2d 831 (Wash. 1995). An Oregon appellate court has also held that judges have "equitable powers" to reach a "fair result" at the end of a period of cohabitation. *See* Wilbur v. De Lapp, 850 P.2d 1151, 1153 (Or. Ct. App. 1993).

legal obligations assumed by marriage partners,[6] and other nations are considering such innovations.[7]

The ALI proposal is undesirable. In this chapter, I argue that the ALI has failed to make a convincing argument in favor of the conscriptive approach it advocates. My conclusion is grounded in a large body of evidence establishing that cohabitation is simply not, as the ALI argues, the functional or expressive equivalent of marriage.[8] Because marriage and cohabitation have different social meanings and rest on different personal understandings, the ALI proposal would undermine the consistency, fairness, and integrity of family law. Adoption of the ALI proposal would also necessitate individualized, post-relationship litigation to determine a couple's obligations to each other, an approach that would virtually ensure expense, fraud, loss of privacy, and uncertainty. Adoption of the proposal would diminish personal autonomy. And, by falsely signaling the equivalence of marriage and cohabitation, it would devalue one of our most fundamental social institutions and risk serious harm to the interests of both adults and children. For all these reasons, the ALI domestic partnership proposal should be rejected.

I. The Case for the Domestic Partnership Proposal: Evaluating the Evidence

A. The ALI Argument: Equivalence and Practicality

The ALI begins its argument in favor of the domestic partnership proposal by noting that "society's interests in the orderly administration of justice and the stability of families are best served when the formalities of marriage are observed...."[9] This is not a controversial proposition; formal marriage has long been favored because it clearly, efficiently, and publicly establishes the parties' mutual intention to assume marital status and corollary obligations. By contrast, the common law marriage doctrine – which permits the establishment of a marriage based on a private agreement to be married and a public "holding out" of a marital relationship – has fallen from favor because fact-based determination

[6] All of the Canadian provinces except Quebec now impose a support obligation on cohabitants who have lived together for periods ranging from one to three years. *See* Nicholas Bala, *Controversy Over Couples in Canada: The Evolution of Marriage and Other Adult Interdependent Relationships*, 29 Queen's L. J. 41, 45–49 (2003) (describing provincial support rules). All of the Australian states have adopted legislation that extends marital property rights to cohabitants who have a common child or have lived together for at least two years. *See* Dorothy Kovacs, De Facto Property Proceedings in Australia 10–11 (1998); Lindy Willmott et al., *De Facto Relationships Property Adjustment Law – A National Direction*, 17 Aust. J. Fam. L. 1, 2–5 (2003) (describing differences in state rules). New Zealand has extended all of the rights and obligations of marriage to couples who have been "de facto partners" for three years. *See* Property (Relationships) Amendment Act 2001, http://www.legislation.govt.nz/browse_vw.asp?content-set=palstatutes; Bill Atkin, *The Challenge of Unmarried Cohabitation – The New Zealand Response*, 37 Fam. L.Q. 303 (2003); Virginia Grainer, *What's Yours Is Mine: Reform of the Property Division Regime for Unmarried Couples in New Zealand*, 11 Pac. Rim L. & Pol'y. J. 285 (2002).

[7] *See* Sarah Lyall, *In Europe, Lovers Now Propose: Marry Me, A Little*, N.Y. Times, Feb. 15. 2004, at A3 (describing Norwegian legislation that would extend inheritance rights to cohabitants who have lived together for five years or have a common child and permit a surviving partner to retain a shared residence regardless of a contrary disposition in the decedent partner's will, and Italian legislation that would permit a surviving cohabitant to remain in a shared residence for a period equal to the length of the relationship).

[8] See Part I.A *infra*.

[9] Principles § 6.02 cmt. a, at 914.

of marital commitment "leads to fraud and uncertainty in the most important of human relationships."[10]

If family stability and the orderly administration of justice are best served by formal marriage, if common law marriage has fallen from favor because it cannot avoid fraud and uncertainty, why would we want to adopt rules that require courts to conduct individualized, fact-based inquiries into the nature of a cohabiting couple's relationship whenever they have lived together – or one partner asserts that they have – for a state-defined period? The ALI rests its case for this unlikely reform on one proposition: "the absence of formal marriage," the PRINCIPLES urge, "may have little or no bearing on the character of the parties' domestic relationship and on the equitable considerations that underlie claims between lawful spouses at the dissolution of a marriage."[11] The ALI approach thus "reflects a judgment that it is usually just to apply to both groups the property and support rules applicable to divorcing spouses, that individualized inquiries are usually impractical or unduly burdensome, and that it therefore makes more sense to require parties to contract out of these property and support rules than to contract into them."[12]

Ultimately, then, the ALI domestic partnership proposal is based on claims of equivalence and practicality. The ALI asserts that the relationships of cohabitants on whom it would impose marital obligations are sufficiently marriage-like that "it is usually just" to treat them as marital relationships. The ALI also contends that individualized inquiries are sufficiently "impractical" or "burdensome" that "it ... makes more sense to require parties to contract out [of marital obligations] ... than to contract in."

B. The Claim of Equivalence: The Research Evidence

The ALI's assertion that "it is usually just" to impose marital obligations on unmarried cohabitants rests on its claim of equivalence. If "the absence of formal marriage" *does not* typically denote a significant difference in the "character of the parties' domestic relationship and ... the equitable considerations that underlie claims," then it would be fair to treat these relationships the same way.[13] Of course, the converse is also true: if the absence of formal marriage *does* typically denote a significant difference in the parties' relationship and the equitable considerations that underlie their claims, then it would be unfair to treat these relationships the same way.

Surprisingly, the ALI offers no evidence whatsoever to support its claim of equivalence. That does not mean that evidence is unavailable. The increased incidence of cohabitation has produced a large and rapidly growing body of empirical research. But that research definitively demonstrates that the relationships of married and cohabiting couples are *not* equivalent. Instead, the behaviors, understandings, and attitudes of cohabitants typically differ dramatically from those of married couples.

The first significant fact established by recent research is that cohabitation is usually a short-lived state. Although the likelihood that cohabitation will lead to marriage is

[10] *See* HOMER H. CLARK, JR. THE LAW OF DOMESTIC RELATIONS IN THE UNITED STATES 59 (2d ed. 1988); Cynthia Grant Bowman, *A Feminist Proposal to Bring Back Common Law Marriage*, 75 OR. L. REV. 709, 732–51 (1996).

[11] PRINCIPLES § 6.02 cmt. a, at 914–15.

[12] PRINCIPLES § 6.03 cmt. b, at 919.

[13] PRINCIPLES § 6.02 cmt. a, at 914–15.

declining,[14] approximately 60 percent of all U.S. cohabitants and 70 percent of those in a first, premarital cohabitation marry within five years.[15] More tellingly, only about 10 percent of all U.S. cohabitants who do not marry are still together five years later.[16] By contrast, 80 percent of first marriages survive five or more years and two-thirds survive for at least ten years.[17] Cohabitation thus represents, for most couples, a brief transitional stage on the way to either marriage or separation.[18]

Cohabitants tend to be younger[19] and less prosperous than married couples.[20] More importantly, they do not typically follow the relational norms associated with marriage. Cohabitants are much less likely than married couples to have children together,[21] to pool their resources,[22] to feel secure and unconflicted in their

[14] *See* Larry L. Bumpass, *The Changing Significance of Marriage in the United States, in* THE CHANGING FAMILY IN COMPARATIVE PERSPECTIVE: ASIA AND THE UNITED STATES 63, 71 (K. O. Mason et al. eds., 1998).

[15] *See* M. D. BRAMLETT & W. D. MOSHER, COHABITATION, MARRIAGE, DIVORCE, AND REMARRIAGE IN THE UNITED STATES 22 & tbl.9 (2002).

[16] *See* Pamela J. Smock, *Cohabitation in the United States: An Appraisal of Research Themes, Findings, and Implications,* 26 ANN. REV. SOCIOL. 1, 3 (2000); Larry L. Bumpass & Hsien-Hen Lu, *Trends in Cohabitation and Implications for Children's Family Contexts in the United States,* 54 POP. STUD. 29, 33 (2000). *See also* BRAMLETT & MOSHER, *supra* note 15, at 22 & tbl.15. Trends outside the U.S. appear to be consistent. *See, e.g.,* Kathleen Kiernan, *Cohabitation in Western Europe,* 96 POP. TRENDS 25, 29 tbl.6 (1999) (showing median duration of first-union cohabitations in ten western European countries was 26 months or less, while Sweden had a 48-month median duration); Zheng Wu & T. R. Balakrishnan, *Dissolution of Premarital Cohabitation in Canada,* 32 DEMOGRAPHY 521, 526 tbl.1 (1995) (finding in Canada, that 28% of female respondents' and 25% of male respondents' cohabiting relationships that did not lead to marriage survived five years).

[17] *See* BRAMLETT & MOSHER, *supra* note 15, at 17–18, tbl.21.

[18] *See* Patrick Heuveline & Jeffrey M. Timberlake, *The Role of Cohabitation in Family Formation: The United States in Comparative Perspective,* 66 J. MARRIAGE & FAM. 1214,1223 tbl.2 (2004) (reporting median duration of cohabitation in the United States as 1.17 years). Nor is the average duration of cohabitation increasing. *See* Bumpass & Lu, *supra* note 16, at 33; Andrew J. Cherlin, *Toward a New Home Socioeconomics of Union Formation, in* THE TIES THAT BIND: PERSPECTIVES ON MARRIAGE AND COHABITATION 126, 135 (Linda J. Waite ed. 2000) [hereinafter THE TIES THAT BIND].

[19] *See* BRAMLETT & MOSHER, *supra* note 15, at 11 tbl.C (finding that of women aged 20–24, 11% were cohabiting and 27% were married; among women 35–44, less than 5% were cohabiting and 68% were married). The proportion of youthful cohabitants has declined in recent years, however. *See* LYNNE M. CASPER & SUZANNE M. BIANCHI, CONTINUITY AND CHANGE IN THE AMERICAN FAMILY 44–45 (2002) (showing in 1978 that 35% of cohabiting women and 38.5% of cohabiting men were age 35 or higher; in 1998, 44% of cohabiting women and 48% of cohabiting men were 35 or older).

[20] At least among men, cohabitants have less education and lower socioeconomic prospects than their married counterparts. *See* CASPER & BIANCHI, *supra* note 19, at 52–53 tbl.2.3; Steven L. Nock, *A Comparison of Marriages and Cohabiting Relationships,* 16 J. FAM. ISSUES 53, 66 tbl.1 (1995). *See also* Bumpass & Lu, *supra* note 16, at 32; Smock, *supra* note 16 at 4. Income potential is also an important predictor of whether a man will marry. *See, e.g.,* Valerie K. Oppenheimer, *Cohabiting and Marriage During Young Men's Career-Development Process,* 40 DEMOGRAPHY 127 (2003); Yu Xie et al., *Economic Potential and Entry into Marriage and Cohabitation,* 40 DEMOGRAPHY 351, 361 tbl.3 (2003). But there is some evidence that the association between male income and marriage is declining. *See* Sharon Sassler & Frances Goldsheider, *Revisiting Jane Austen's Theory of Marriage Timing: Changes in Union Formation Among American Men in the Late 20th Century,* 25 J. FAM. ISSUES 139 (2004).

[21] *See* Judith A. Seltzer, *Families Formed Outside of Marriage,* 62 J. MARRIAGE & FAM. 1247 (2000) (summarizing evidence). The percentage of U.S. cohabitants who bear children together has increased substantially, however. *See* Bumpass & Lu, *supra* note 16, at 34 tbl.4 (cohabiting couples had 29% of nonmarital births in the early 1980s and 39 percent a decade later). Despite this increase, only 2.9 percent of U.S. children lived with a cohabiting parent in 2002. *See* LAURA WHERRY & KENNETH FINEGOLD, MARRIAGE PROMOTION AND THE LIVING ARRANGEMENTS OF BLACK, HISPANIC, AND WHITE CHILDREN 5, tbl.1 (Urban Inst. No. B-61, 2004), *at* http://www.urban.org/UploadedPDF/311064_B-61.pdf.

[22] *See* BLUMSTEIN & SCHWARTZ, AMERICAN COUPLES: MONEY-WORK-SEX 94–100, figs.8–9 (1985) (showing among survey group that 37 percent of male and 44% of female cohabitants opposed income pooling, as compared to 12 percent of wives and 8% of husbands); Martin Clarksberg et al., *Attitudes, Values, and Entrance into*

relationships,[23] to value commitment, or to express commitment to their partners.[24] They are more likely than married couples to be in a physically abusive relationship,[25] and less likely to demonstrate sexual fidelity.[26]

Cohabitational versus Marital Unions, 74 Social Forces 609 (1995); Helen Glezer & Eva Mills, *Controlling the Purse Strings*, 29 Fam. Matters 35 tbl. 2 (1991) (reporting that 27 percent of Australian cohabitants and 71% of married couples combined their incomes); Kristen R. Heimdal & Sharon K. Houseknecht, *Cohabiting and Married Couples' Income Organization: Approaches in Sweden and the United States*, 65 J. Marriage & Fam. 525, 533 tbl. 2 (2003) (finding in the U.S. that 17 percent of married and 46 percent of cohabiting couples report keeping their money separate); R. S. Oropesa et al., *Income Allocation in Marital and Cohabiting Unions: The Case of Mainland Puerto Ricans*, 65 J. Marriage & Fam. 910 (2003) (married Puerto Rican men pooled income more often than cohabiting men); Anne E. Winkler, *Economic Decision-Making by Cohabitors: Findings Regarding Income Pooling*, 29 App. Econ. 1079 (1997) (observing that most cohabitants, particularly those without children and in short-term relationships, do not pool their incomes). *See also* K. J. Bauman, *Shifting Family Definitions: The Effect of Cohabitation and Other Nonfamily Household Relationships on Measures of Poverty*, 36 Demography 315 (1999) (reporting that income of a cohabitant was significantly less to alleviate material hardship than income of a spouse).

[23] *See* Larry L. Bumpass et al., *The Role of Cohabitation in Declining Rates of Marriage*, 53 J. Marriage & Fam. 913, 922–23 (1991) (finding that compared with married respondents and adjusted for duration and age differences, cohabitants were almost twice as likely to report that they have thought their relationship was in trouble over the past year; in three of four cohabiting relationships, at least one partner reports having thought the relationship was in trouble); Susan L. Brown & Alan Booth, *Cohabitation Versus Marriage: A Comparison of Relationship Quality*, 58 J. Marriage & Fam. 668, 674 tbl.1 (1996) (reporting that cohabitants report significantly more fights and less fairness in their relationships than married couples).

[24] See Blumstein & Schwartz, *supra* note 22, at 184 fig.26 (54% of male cohabitants and 67% of female cohabitants said that "private time away from one's partner" was "very important," as compared to 32% of husbands and 46% of wives); William G. Axinn & Arland Thorton, *The Relationship Between Cohabitation and Divorce: Selectivity or Causal Influence?*, 29 Demography 357, 358–59 (1992) (illustrating that surveyed cohabitants tended to express a low opinion about the value of commitment); Clarksberg et al., *supra* note 22, at 621–24 (noting that cohabitation is preferred to marriage by those who desire more flexible relationships and reject marital constraints); Nock, *supra* note 20 at 65–67 tbl.1, 73 (1995) (demonstrating that cohabiting men and women reported lower levels of commitment and lower levels of commitment appeared to "foster poorer assessments of the relationship"); S. M. Stanley et al., *Interpersonal Commitment and Premarital or Nonmarital Cohabitation*, 25 J. Fam. Issues 496 (2004) (reporting in a national random sample that premarital and nonmarital cohabitation were associated with lower levels of interpersonal commitment to partner); Elizabeth Thomson & Ugo Colella, *Cohabitation and Marital Stability: Quality or Commitment*, 54 J. Marriage & Fam. 259 (1992) (noting that cohabitants were more likely than married couples to value individual freedom). Cohabitants with the lowest level of commitment are also the most likely to split up. *See* Casper & Bianchi, *supra* note 19, at 59 tbl.2.5.

[25] *See, e.g.*, Linda J. Waite & Maggie Gallagher, The Case for Marriage 155 (2000) (finding based on analysis of National Survey of Families and Households data, that "married people are much less likely than cohabiting couples to say that arguments between them and their partners had become physical in the past year (4% of married people compared to 13% of the cohabiting). When it comes to hitting, shoving, and throwing things, cohabiting couples are more than three times more likely than the married to say things get that far out of hand"); Sonia Miner Salari & Bret M. Baldwin, *Verbal, Physical, and Injurious Aggression Among Intimate Couples Over Time*, 23 J. Fam. Issues 523, 535–36 tbl.1 (2002) (showing that 24% of cohabiting and 7.3% of married couples reported one of two most serious forms of physical aggression); Jan E. Stets, *Cohabiting and Marital Aggression: The Role of Social Isolation*, 53 J. Marriage & Fam. 53 (1991) (showing that nearly 14% of cohabitants and 5% of married individuals admitted to hitting, shoving or throwing things at their partner in the past year; difference remained even after controlling for factors such as education, age, occupation, and income); Todd K. Shackelford, *Cohabitation, Marriage and Murder*, 27 Aggressive Behavior 284 (2001) (arguing that Canadian and U.S. studies show that women in cohabiting relationships are about nine times more likely than married women to be killed by a partner). *See also* D. A. Brownridge, *Understanding Women's Heightened Risk of Violence in Common-Law Unions – Revisiting the Selection and Relationship Hypotheses*, 10 Violence Against Women 616 (2004).

[26] *See* Blumstein & Schwartz, *supra* note 22, at 274–75 (both male and female cohabitants were less likely to be sexually faithful than married men and women at all relationship-duration levels; greatest gap was between long-duration married and cohabiting couples); Renata Forste and Koray Tanfer, *Sexual Exclusivity Among Dating, Cohabiting, and Married Women*, 58 J. Marriage & Fam. 33 (1996) (finding in National Survey of Women that 4% of married women and 20% of cohabiting women reported sexual infidelity); Judith Treas & Deidre Giesen, *Sexual Fidelity Among Married and Cohabiting Americans*, 62 J. Marriage & Fam. 48 (2000) (presenting evidence that even after controlling for permissive values about extramarital cohabitation, twice as many cohabitants as married

These behavioral differences reflect starkly divergent relational attitudes. The contrasting relational perspectives of cohabitants and married couples emerge in many ways, but attitudes toward money are particularly revealing. Blumstein and Schwartz, who conducted a pioneering survey of American couples, found that "married couples unconsciously assume a commingling of money and . . . cohabitors assume separate finances."[27] To explicate this attitudinal difference, Blumstein and Schwartz offer representative conversations in which couples "discuss[ed] how they would – together – spend six hundred dollars that they were to pretend [the researchers] would give them."[28] The married couple immediately focused on a shared goal:

> Caroline: I think we should spend it on ourselves.
> Chris: Okay, what do we need?
> Caroline: We have things we need. Let's spend it on something we both want, not just something one or the other wanted . . . I've been thinking of something like airline tickets to Hawaii. You've been wanting to go to Maui. I think it would be nice for us.
> Chris: Okay, that's perfect. Sold.

The cohabiting couple immediately focused on individual wants:

> Mark: I'm ready.
> Susan: Split it fifty-fifty, right?
> Mark: Exactly.
> Susan: We're finished.
> Mark: Same as always.
> Susan: Fifty-fifty.
> Mark: I'll spend at least two hundred dollars on photographic equipment . . . and probably pay off something to Visa. . . .
> Susan: And I'll spend mine my way. Very simple.[29]

Blumstein and Schwartz conclude that cohabitants, "striving to be independent, . . . avoid the interdependence that pooling brings," while "[t]he marriage contract . . . allows [married couples] to trust each other enough to work as a financial team."[30] Put somewhat differently, the "what's mine is yours" expectation that arises from marriage simply does not arise from the fact of cohabitation.

Marital expectations do not typically arise from cohabitation because, at least in the United States, cohabitants overwhelmingly see cohabitation as a substitute for being single, not for being married. More than 90 percent of cohabiting U.S. respondents report that they plan to marry at some point,[31] and about three-fourths say that they will marry their current

individuals had engaged in recent infidelity); Linda J. Waite & Kara Joyner, *Emotional and Physical Satisfaction in Married, Cohabiting, and Dating Sexual Unions: Do Men and Women Differ?*, *in* SEX, LOVE, AND HEALTH IN AMERICA: PRIVATE CHOICES AND PUBLIC POLICIES 239 (E. Laumann and R. Michael eds. 1999) (showing in national sex survey that 4% of married men, 1% of married women, 16% of cohabiting men, and 8% of cohabiting women reported sexual infidelity during the past year).

[27] BLUMSTEIN & SCHWARTZ, *supra* note 22, at 98.

[28] *Id.* at 98.

[29] *Id.*

[30] *Id.* at 110.

[31] *See* John D. Cunningham & John K. Antill, *Cohabitation and Marriage: Retrospective and Predictive Comparisons*, 11 J. SOC. & PERSONAL RELATIONSHIPS 77, (1994). *See also* Cherlin, *supra* note 18, at 135 ("The typically short durations in the United States, along with expressed preferences for marriage, suggest that marriage is still the goal for most young adults and cohabitation is still seen as an intermediate status.")

partner.[32] But these cohabitants do not report that their relationships are already marital. In a cohabitant survey conducted during the late 1980s, only 10 percent of respondents reported that cohabitation was a "substitute for marriage," while 61 percent said that it was a precursor to or "trial" period to assess marital compatibility, and 29 percent described it as a form of coresidential dating.[33] Since the 1980s, the attitudes of cohabitants seem to have shifted even further from a marital perspective. In a recent, small survey of New York City cohabitants, the primary reasons that respondents offered for their decisions to cohabit were finances, convenience, and housing needs – all practical considerations of the sort one would consider in deciding whether to obtain a roommate or take in a boarder. Only two of twenty-five interviewees mentioned discussing marriage prior to moving in with their partners.[34] Those respondents who had talked about marriage with their partners typically had cohabited for about two years before doing so, but the researchers also found "substantial variation in the tempo of relationship development. . . . "[35] In a larger 2002 survey, Professors Wendy Manning and Pamela Smock found that none of the cohabitants they interviewed were deciding between marriage and cohabitation at the time they began living together. Decision-making instead focused on "whether to cohabit or to remain single, with marriage not seriously entering the picture."[36] Moreover, the line between cohabitation and living alone was often "quite blurry, with the movement into cohabitation often described as a gradual or unfolding process that occurs over a week, or even months."[37] Many interviewees had difficulty defining when they started living together, and those who had broken up often had difficulty pinning down when the relationship ended. The processes that lead to cohabitation thus "appear[] to differ in important ways from processes determining entry into marriage."[38]

Because of its relative rarity, long-term cohabitation has produced much less evidence. But the research suggests that even the couples in this small, atypical group rarely see their relationships as marital.

First, although one economist who employed a labor-supply model to infer cohabitant behavior did find evidence of some income pooling in long-term cohabitation,[39] surveys of cohabitants themselves do not show that lengthier periods of cohabitation are associated with more sharing or higher expectations of sharing. In Blumstein and Schwartz's survey, couples who had cohabited for a period between two and ten years were no more likely

[32] *See* Wendy Manning & Pamela J. Smock, *First Comes Cohabitation, Then Comes Marriage*, 23 J. Fam. Issues 1065, 1973 tbl.1 (2002); Brown & Booth, *supra* note 23, at 673. *See also* Bumpass et al., *supra* note 23, at 922 tbl.10 (reporting that 81% of never-married cohabitants and 61% of previously married cohabitants said that they had "definite plans" or "think they will marry" their current partner).

[33] *See* Casper & Bianchi, *supra* note 19, at 59 tbl.2.5.

[34] *See* Sharon Sassler, *The Process of Entering Into Cohabiting Unions*, 66 J. Marriage & Fam. 491, 498–501 (2004).

[35] *Id.* at 502.

[36] *See* Wendy Manning & Pamela J. Smock, *Measuring and Modeling Cohabitation: New Perspectives from Qualitative Data*, 67 J. Marriage S. Fam. 989, 998 (2005).

[37] *Id.* at 995.

[38] *Id.* at 1000. *See also* Eleanor Macklin, *Heterosexual Cohabitation Among Unmarried College Students*, Fam. Coordinator 463, 466 (1972), *quoted in* Manning & Smock, *supra* note 36, at 29 (explaining that the decision to cohabit typically derived from "gradual, often unconscious, escalation of emotional and physical involvement" that "was seldom the result of a considered decision, at least initially").

[39] *See* Winkler, *supra* note 22 (drawing inferences from a "generalized model of labour supply" applied to data from the 1993 Current Population Survey and 1987 National Survey of Families and Households and reporting that "[t]hese data sets provide evidence that cohabitors, taken as a group, do not pool all income. However, there is also evidence that cohabitors are not homogeneous in their behavior; income pooling is not rejected for cohabitors in longer-term relationships and for those who have a biological child together." *Id.* at 1079.

to pool their funds than those whose relationships had endured less than two years.[40] A cross-national survey also revealed that Swedish cohabitants, whose relationships are typically longer than the American norm, were not more likely to pool resources than their American counterparts.[41]

Second, a longer cohabitation period is not positively associated with either the quality or stability of the relationship. One researcher who utilized a large national survey found that long-term marriage typically produced the perception of relationship stability while cohabitation which did not lead to marriage tended instead to produce a high level of perceived instability.[42] Another research team found that the duration of a cohabiting relationship was significantly – and negatively – correlated with several variables related to relationship quality.[43] The research data thus offer nothing to support the hypothesis that the passage of time breeds either marital commitment or understandings.

The evidence also fails to show that childbearing during cohabitation produces or results from such understandings. Childbearing during cohabitation is far more likely to be unplanned than it is during marriage.[44] Although a Canadian researcher found that childbearing significantly enhanced the stability of cohabitants' relationships,[45] U.S. researchers have generally failed to find such an effect.[46] One U.S. researcher did find that the conception of a child during cohabitation was associated with greater stability in the parents' relationship – but only if the couple married before the child was born; children conceived and born during cohabitation had no impact whatsoever on the stability of their parents' relationships.[47]

Unmarried parents also tell us that they believe marriage and cohabitation to be fundamentally different. The U.S. Fragile Family Study, which sponsored in-depth interviews of a nationally representative group of unmarried parents, found that cohabiting parents overwhelmingly believe both that "marriage is better for children" and that they are

[40] *See* Blumstein & Schwartz, *supra* note 22, at 95 fig.8.

[41] *See* Heimdal & Houseknecht, *supra* note 22.

[42] *See* Susan L. Brown, *Relationship Quality Dynamics of Cohabiting Unions*, 24 J. Fam. Issues 583, 598 (2003). Professor Brown also found that plans to marry were associated with lower levels of relationship instability in short relationships, but not in long ones. "This finding implies that cohabitors with marriage plans expect that their unions will be transformed quickly into marriages. When these expectations are not met, cohabitors perceive greater instability. In contrast, couples who do not desire marriage gain confidence over time that their relationships will remain intact." *Id.* at 595–96. Likewise, Professors Brown and Booth also found that plans to marry are an important factor in differentiating among cohabiting relationships. Although cohabitants, in general, reported lower-quality relationships than married couples, those cohabitants with plans to marry reported relationships of similar quality. *See* Brown & Booth, *supra* note 23, at 675.

[43] Brown & Booth, *supra* note 23, at 674. *See also* Bumpass et al., *supra* note 23, at 922 tbl.10 (showing that a higher proportion of cohabitants whose relationships had lasted at least three years said that, during the past year, they had "thought that [their]... relationship might be in trouble" than cohabitants whose relationships had lasted less than one year).

[44] *See* The Best Intentions: Unintended Pregnancy and the Well-Being of Children and Families 31–32 tbl.2.2 (Sarah S. Brown & Leon Eisenberg eds., 1995) (finding that 88% of never-married, 68.5 percent of previously-married, and 40 percent of married women's pregnancies are unplanned; never-married women (75 percent) and previously-married women (53 percent) were far more likely than married women (26%) to terminate an unintended pregnancy through abortion); Wendy D. Manning, *Childbearing in Cohabiting Unions: Racial and Ethnic Differences*, 33 Fam. Planning Perspectives 217, tbl.5 (2001) (reporting that 18 percent of married, 44% of cohabiting, and 61 percent of single, noncohabiting women said that their first birth was unintended).

[45] *See* Zheng Wu, *The Stability of Cohabitation Relationships: The Role of Children*, 57 J. Marriage & Fam. 231 (1995).

[46] *See* Wendy D. Manning, *Children and the Stability of Cohabiting Couples*, 66 J. Marriage & Fam. 674 (2004) (summarizing research).

[47] *See id.*

likely to eventually marry their current partners.[48] But outside of marriage, "most of these cohabiting pairs espouse a strong *individualistic ethic*... in which personal happiness and fulfillment hold the highest value."[49] The researchers offer two quotes from cohabitants that "illustrate this ethos particularly well, and describe how sharply cohabitation differs from marriage":

> The first tells us, "Most people feel like with their boyfriend or girlfriend, when they get into an argument they can just leave. Most of them feel like, OK, when you're married you can't just walk away and leave like that." The second says, "With me and Victor, we have a commitment. But he can still decide this is not working for [him]. But if you go as far as getting *married*, there you need to know you're really *with* the person."[50]

These respondents did not think that marriage was only a piece of paper. Far from it, they saw marriage as a fundamental shift in commitment and relational values.

Taken as a whole, the evidence thus demonstrates that the personal commitments and sharing expectations that arise from marriage – and which underlie the law of divorce entitlements[51] – do not arise from the decision to cohabit. To the contrary, the evidence strongly suggests that cohabitation typically reflects an implicit decision not to share or make a commitment. As a male cohabitant interviewed by Manning and Smock put it,

> "I wasn't ready, I mean to get... that close to somebody and I mean I lived with her but we still had our freedom we still let each other do what we wanted to do so I had my space and she had her space."[52]

Cohabiting relationships in which individuals are committed to preserving their freedom and their space are simply not equivalent to marital relationships in which individuals are committed to maintaining an enduring partnership. Events such as childbearing and the passage of time may well alter a couple's relationship. But we have no evidence that such events are typically transformative or that they denote marital intention.

Although most of the research reports come from the United States, the evidence from abroad is generally consistent with the American pattern. In Canada, the Pacific, and Western Europe, cohabitation again tends to be a comparatively short-lived state.[53] It is

[48] *See* Christina Gibson et al., High Hopes But Even Higher Expectations: The Retreat from Marriage among Low-Income Couples tbl. 3 (Ctr. Research Child Welfare Working Paper 03–06-ff, 2003) (reporting that, in Fragile Families survey, 79 percent of unmarried mothers and 84 percent of unmarried fathers living together at childbirth say that there is at least a good or certain chance that they will marry); Kathryn Edin et al., *A Peek Inside the Black Box: What Marriage Means for Poor Unmarried Parents*, 66 J. Marriage & Fam. 1007, 1010 (2004) 1010 (reporting data from Fragile Families Study showing that two-thirds of new unmarried mothers and three quarters of new unmarried fathers agreed with the statement "marriage is better for children"). *See also* Gregory Acs & Heather Koball, TANF and the Status of Teen Mothers under Age 17 fig.7 (Urban Inst. Series A, No. A-62, 2003) (http://www.urban.org/ UploadedPDF/310796_A-62.pdf) (reporting that a majority of surveyed unmarried parents said that their chances of marriage were good or almost certain).

[49] Edin et al., *supra* note 48 at 1011 (emphasis in original).

[50] *Id.*

[51] The modern law of divorce entitlements rests on the notion that marriage is a partnership of equals. *See* Marsha Garrison, *Good Intentions Gone Awry: The Impact of New York's Equitable Distribution Law on Divorce Outcomes*, 57 Brooklyn L. Rev. 621, 630 n. 29 (1991) (citing sources describing partnership model as basis of modern divorce law).

[52] Manning & Smock, *supra* note 36.

[53] *See, e.g.*, John Ermisch & Marco Francesconi, *Cohabitation in Great Britain: Not for Long, but Here to Stay* 6 (ISER, University of Essex, 1998), http://www.iser.essex.ac.uk/pubs/workpaps/pdf/98-1rev.pdf (median length of U.K. cohabiting relationships is under two years and only 4 percent of cohabiting relationships last more than 10 years);

much less likely than marriage to produce children or to induce resource pooling;[54] it does not demonstrate rejection of formal marriage, as many cohabitants report that they are likely to ultimately marry their partners.[55]

I do not mean to suggest that cohabitation never resembles marriage. As the ALI notes, "some ethnic and social groups have a substantially lower incidence of marriage and a substantially higher incidence of informal domestic relationships than do others."[56] In New Zealand and Australia, for example, formal marriage is "culturally alien" to the native Aborigine and Maori populations, who typically enter into informal marital unions.[57] Scholars have also reported that informal marriage is extremely common in Latin America,[58] and demographers have identified a few industrialized nations in which a significant number of couples appear to choose long-term cohabitation as a marriage substitute.[59]

The ALI is also right when it asserts that some cohabiting relationships "develop[] slowly into a durable union, by which time a formal marriage ceremony may seem awkward or even unnecessary." Professor Ira Ellman, primary drafter of the Principles, offers the case of Terri and Eliot Friedman[60] as an example of a relationship that develops over time into a marital union, and it is an excellent example.[61] Not only did the Friedmans' relationship endure for twenty-five years and produce two children, but Terri and Eliot also "vowed to be husband and wife and to strive to be partners in all respects 'without any sanction by the State'"[62]; they took title to property as husband and wife, filed joint income tax returns, and "Mrs." Friedman assumed a marital name.[63]

Heuveline & Timberlake, *supra* note 18 at 1223 tbl.2 (median duration of cohabitation by age 45 across 17 industrialized nations was 2.39 years).

[54] *See* Grainer, *supra* note 6, at 313 (1996 New Zealand census data show that 49% of women in de facto relationships did not have children, compared to 12% of married women); Clara H. Mulder, *The Effects of Singlehood and Cohabitation on the Transition to Parenthood in the Netherlands*, 24 J. Fam. Issues 291 (2003) (finding that cohabitation was associated with a significantly smaller long-term likelihood of becoming a parent and positing higher dissolution rate of cohabitations as a reason); Heimdal & Houseknecht, *supra* note 22 at 534 (Swedish cohabitants were not significantly more likely to pool income than U.S. cohabitants, despite longer duration of relationships); Helen Glezer & Eva Mills, *Controlling the Purse Strings*, 29 Fam. Matters 35 tbl.2 (1991) (27% of Australian cohabitants and 71% of married couples combined their incomes).

[55] *See* Lixia Qu, *Expectations of Marriage Among Cohabiting Couples*, Fam. Matters 35, 36 (Aust. Inst. of Fam. Stud. 2003) (in survey of more than 1,300 Australian cohabitants, 57% of men and 52% of men said that they were likely or very likely to marry their current partner, while roughly one-fourth felt marriage to be unlikely or very unlikely); Lyall, *supra* note 7 (describing attitudes of European cohabitants who chose to register their partnerships instead of marrying). *But see* Lynn Jamieson et al., *Cohabitation and Commitment: Partnership Plans of Young Men and Women*, 50 Sociol. Rev. 357, 362 tbl.2 (2002) (72% of never-married 20 to 29-year-old Scottish cohabitants said that they had (set up a home because (I wanted to commit myself to our relationship).

[56] Principles § 6.02 cmt. a, at 914 (emphasis added).

[57] *See* Ken Dempsey & David de Vaus, *Who Cohabits in 2001? The Significance of Age, Gender, Religion and Ethnicity*, 40 Aus. J. Sociology 157 (2004).

[58] *See* Teresa Castro Martin, *Consensual Unions in Latin America: Persistence of a Dual Nuptuality System*, 33 J. Comp. Fam. Stud. 35 (2002) (arguing that nonmarital cohabitations in Latin America are "best described as surrogate marriages").

[59] For example, in France, half of children living with cohabiting parents do so for at least 9.43 years and only 23.8% of cohabiting relationships involving children terminate in marriage. Demographers Patrick Heuveline & Jeffrey Timberlake conclude that a substantial minority of French parents thus seem to choose long-term cohabitation as an alternative to marriage. Heuveline & Timberlake, *supra* note 18 at 1225 & tbl.3.

[60] Friedman v. Friedman, 24 Cal. Rptr. 2d 892 (Cal. Ct. App. 1993).

[61] *See* Ira M. Ellman, *"Contract Thinking" Was* Marvin*'s Fatal Flaw*, 76 Notre Dame L. Rev. 1365, 1371 (2001). For comparable fact patterns, *see, e.g.*, Morone v. Morone, 413 N.E.2d 1154 (N.Y. 1980); Hewitt v. Hewitt, 394 N.E.2d 1204 (Ill. 1979).

[62] *Friedman*, at 894, 902.

[63] *See Friedman*, at 894–95, 901–02.

The Friedmans and other cohabitants who make informal marriage vows undeniably have marriage-like relationships. Indeed, in a state recognizing common law marriage, a court would likely find that these couples *were* married. Conduct can evidence consent, and courts thus tend to rely on "the duration and character of the relationship" as a means of inferring whether there was a marital agreement and "making good the bona fide expectations of the parties."[64]

However, the existence of some cases of marriage-like cohabitation does not justify the imposition of marital obligation on cohabitants whose relationships are not marriage-like. And the evidence simply does not show that marriage and cohabitation typically, or even frequently, involve equivalent behaviors, expectations, and commitments. The ALI's claim that "it is usually just to apply to both groups the property and support rules applicable to divorcing spouses"[65] thus lacks any basis in the evidence.

C. The Claim of Practicality: Problems Associated with Individualized Determination

The claim that the domestic partnership proposal is practical has no sounder basis than the claim that cohabitation and marriage are functional equivalents.

Perhaps because the research does not support the uniform imposition of marital obligations on cohabitants, the ALI proposal relies largely on presumptions. Except in the case of a couple who "have maintained a common household . . . with their common child . . . for a continuous period that equals or exceeds a duration . . . set in a rule of statewide application," the PRINCIPLES presume that a couple not related by blood or adoption are "domestic partners" when "they have maintained a common household" for a state-specified period.[66] Either party may rebut the presumption with "evidence that the parties did not share life together as a couple, as defined by Paragraph (7),"[67] and paragraph (7) lists thirteen different factors – all of which would require individualized inquiry by the fact-finder – that might singly or in combination provide the basis for such a rebuttal.[68]

[64] CLARK, *supra* note 10, at 50–51.

[65] PRINCIPLES § 6.03 cmt. b, at 919.

[66] *See* PRINCIPLES at § 6.03.

[67] PRINCIPLES § 6.03(3).

[68] Paragraph 7 lists the following factors:

(a) the oral or written statements or promises made to one another, or representations jointly made to third parties, regarding their relationship;
(b) the extent to which the parties intermingled their finances;
(c) the extent to which their relationship fostered the parties' economic interdependence, or the economic dependence of one party upon the other;
(d) the extent to which the parties engaged in conduct and assumed specialized or collaborative roles in furtherance of their life together;
(e) the extent to which the relationship wrought change in the life of either or both parties;
(f) the extent to which the parties acknowledged responsibilities to each other, as by naming the other the beneficiary of life insurance or of a testamentary instrument, or as eligible to receive benefits under an employee-benefit plan;
(g) the extent to which the parties' relationship was treated by the parties as qualitatively distinct from the relationship either party had with any other person;
(h) the emotional or physical intimacy of the parties' relationship;
(i) the parties' community reputation as a couple;
(j) the parties' participation in a commitment ceremony or registration as a domestic partnership;

Thus, far from avoiding individualized inquiry, the ALI approach almost ensures its necessity.

This is an odd choice because, as we have seen, common law marriage has fallen from favor in large part because of the evidentiary problems that individualized fact-finding entails. At one time, nearly two-thirds of the states recognized common law marriage; by 2002, only eleven U.S. jurisdictions did so,[69] and two of the eleven had adopted strict limitations on its establishment.[70] Common law marriage demands factual inquiry on only two issues, whether there was a present agreement to be married and whether the couple publicly held themselves out as married. If these two facts are so hard to determine that the potential for fraud and uncertainty outweighs the benefit of the doctrine, then one must assume that the ALI's "anything relevant to life as a couple" approach would produce even more fraud and uncertainty, with even less off-setting benefit: the factor list invites the decisionmaker to investigate virtually every aspect of the couple's relationship; while all of the thirteen listed factors are relevant, none is determinative; most of the listed factors require an incremental assessment, but none identifies a threshold level of significance.

The uncertainty inherent in such an open-ended inquiry is enhanced by the fact that cohabitants often disagree about the nature of their relationship. In 20 to 40 percent of cohabiting relationships, partners express different views on whether they plan to marry each other.[71] Many cohabiting couples also disagree on the amount of time they spend together and on whether their relationship is a happy one.[72]

Adding to these evidentiary problems, the PRINCIPLES fail to provide models of relationships that should produce obligation and those that should not. Significantly – and despite the claim that cohabitation is a functional equivalent of marriage – the proposed rule does not mandate any showing of marital intention or conduct. We thus cannot assume that a relationship must be "marriage-like" in order for a court to find that it has produced marital obligations; indeed, we must assume the opposite. But the ALI never specifies how close to marriage – in commitment, sharing, expectations – a relationship should be in order to qualify as a domestic partnership that gives rise to marital obligations.

In sum, while the PRINCIPLES' highly contextual, fact-based approach avoids the peril of rigid, counterfactual classification, it necessitates time-consuming and expensive litigation to determine a couple's status. This approach virtually ensures uncertain and inconsistent

(k) the parties' participation in a void or voidable marriage that, under applicable law, does not give rise to the economic incidents of marriage;
(l) the parties' procreation of, adoption of, or joint assumption of parental functions toward a child;
(m) the parties' maintenance of a common household, as defined by Paragraph (4).
PRINCIPLES § 6.03(7).

[69] *See* HARRY E. KRAUSE ET AL., FAMILY LAW: CASES, COMMENTS, AND QUESTIONS 87 (5th ed., 2003).

[70] *See* TEX. FAM. CODE ANN. § 2.402 (2005) (requiring affirmation of the marriage in a state "declaration form"); UTAH CODE ANN. § 30-1-4.5(2) (2004) (requiring establishment of common law marriage within one year of its dissolution).

[71] *See* Susan L. Brown, *Union Transitions Among Cohabiters: The Significance of Relationship Assessment and Expectations*, 62 J. *Marriage* & *Fam.* 833, 838 (2000); Bumpass et al., *supra* note 23, at 923; Sharon Sassler & James McNally, *Cohabiting Couple's Economic Circumstances and Union Transitions: A Re-Examination Using Multiple Imputation Techniques*, 32 SOC. SCI. RES. 553 (2004) (reporting that 42% of surveyed couples disagreed about the future of their relationship).

[72] *See* Brown, *supra* note 71 (finding that about a third of surveyed couples disagreed about whether the couple spent a lot of time together and 40% gave contrasting answers about whether they felt a high degree of happiness with the relationship).

outcomes. It fails even to tell us what sort of relationship it intends to capture, let alone provide structured guidance on how to separate the right sort from the wrong sort.

Although the ALI scheme does give cohabitants the right to opt out of the obligations that go along with a finding of domestic partnership, there are many reasons to doubt that this will solve the problems. First, few cohabiting couples currently enter into relationship contracts even though they are legally empowered to do so.[73] Second, because cohabitation often develops over time, there is no obvious event that signals the need to contract out. Third, many couples will not perceive the need to contract out; some will be unrealistically optimistic about the relationship, some will be uncomfortable discussing dissolution, and some will simply not understand the law.[74] Those who do perceive the desirability of opting out may be inhibited by the time and cost of entering into an agreement. And even if all cohabitants who should opt out did so, the associated discomfort, expense, and inconvenience weigh heavily against the ALI approach.

Of course, the problems inherent in the ALI approach would be reduced with rules that demand a lengthy relationship; given that 90 percent of cohabiting relationships end or result in marriage within five years,[75] a statute that required, say, a six-year cohabitation period as a precondition to establishing a domestic partnership would automatically eliminate the vast majority of those who might be affected. Professor Elizabeth Scott has recommended alteration of the ALI proposal along these lines.[76] Under her model, a relationship of five or more years would establish a presumption of intent to undertake marital obligations.[77] Professor Scott's proposal offers two advantages over the ALI approach: it would have much less impact on individuals and courts; it would require the fact-finder to focus squarely on marital commitment instead of undertaking a fishing expedition into all aspects of a couple's relationship.

Despite these clear improvements, Professor Scott's proposal does not avoid the problems of uncertainty and inconsistency inherent in the ALI model; it merely confines these difficulties to a smaller group of cases. Individuals who do not know how long their relationships will endure must still contract out of obligations in order to avoid the possibility of expensive, time-consuming litigation. The potential for fraud, expense, uncertainty, and inconsistency is still high. A long-duration ALI model cannot avoid the problem of determining when cohabitation commenced and ended. Nor, most importantly, can it ensure that those conscripted into marital obligation intended to assume those obligations.

[73] The primary drafter of the PRINCIPLES, Professor Ira Ellman, notes that "[r]eal data on the frequency of contracting are scarce, but the basic claim is not in serious dispute. Certainly written agreements between cohabitants are rare among the reported cases . . . [and an experienced attorney] whose practice focuses on unmarried couples. . . . told [the author]. . . . that in his experience the proportion of such couples who enter written agreements is 'miniscule'." *See* Ellman, *supra* note 61, at 1367 n.17. *See also* Kirsti Strom Bull, *Nonmarital Cohabitation in Norway* 30 SCANDINAVIAN STUD. L. 31 (1986) (reporting that 5% of surveyed Danish and Norwegian cohabitants had entered into contracts). Ironically, contracts seem to be more frequently employed by couples with committed relationships. *See* Jennifer K. Robbennolt & Monica Kirkpatrick Johnson, *Legal Planning for Unmarried Committed Partners: Empirical Lessons for a Preventative and Therapeutic Approach*, 42 ARIZ. L. REV. 417 (1999) (finding in a survey of 169 "committed" cohabiting couples, that 29% had written agreements).

[74] *See* Bala, *supra* note 6, at 54–55 ("People are generally not psychologically prepared to make contracts about their personal relationships, and the evolving roles and expectations of the partners in non-marital relationships in any event tend to make contracts problematic when dealing with familial rights and obligations.").

[75] *See* sources cited in note 15, *supra*.

[76] *See* Scott, *infra*. *See also* Elizabeth S. Scott, *Marriage, Cohabitation and Collective Responsibility for Dependency*, 2004 U. CHI. LEGAL F. 225 (2004).

[77] *See* Scott, this volume. *See also* Scott, *supra*.

Professor Scott asserts that, "[f]or most parties in relationships of long duration, the presumption that the union is marriage-like probably represents accurately the parties' explicit or implicit understanding about property sharing and support, and thus the [suggested] framework simply functions as a standard majoritarian default."[78] But as we have seen, there is simply no evidence to support the supposition that couples who have cohabited for five years have marital understandings about property, sharing, or support: the research evidence does not show that longer periods of cohabitation are correlated with more resource pooling;[79] the evidence does show that longer periods of cohabitation are negatively correlated with variables related to relationship stability and quality.[80] This evidence does not definitively disprove the proposition that long-term relationships are more like marriage than short-term relationships. But if long-term cohabitation is not positively associated with more sharing or higher expectations of stability, we should be extremely skeptical of the proposition that it is associated with marital understanding, which connotes both sharing and stability.[81] Certainly, a presumption in favor of marital intention based on cohabitation for five or more years lacks any basis in the research data.

Such a presumption would also reintroduce – with a vengeance – all of the evidentiary problems that gave common law marriage a bad name. There is no reason to suppose that a presumption in favor of marital intent would produce any less litigation, fraud, uncertainty, or inconsistency than has the common law marriage presumption against marital intent. Indeed, because Professor Scott's proposal does not include a publicity requirement, courts would often have little more than subjective, self-interested accounts of "who said what to whom" as a basis for their intent findings. It is hard to see how this represents an improvement over the traditional common law marriage doctrine.

Whether or not the domestic partnership proposal is modified as Professor Scott has suggested, the ALI's claim of practicality thus appears to have no sounder evidentiary basis than its claim of equivalence. Instead of reducing the need for individualized inquiry, the ALI approach vastly expands it. The multifactor inquiry required by the PRINCIPLES would force a considerable loss of individual privacy.[82] It would ensure uncertainty, expense, fraud, and inconsistency.

II. Public Policy Disadvantages Inherent in the ALI Approach

Not only does the evidence fail to support the ALI's claims of equivalence and practicality, but its uncertain, status-based approach entails serious public policy disadvantages.

[78] *Id. See also* Scott, this volume.

[79] *See* BLUMSTEIN & SCHWARTZ, *supra* note 22, at 95 fig.8.

[80] *See* Brown & Booth, *supra* note 23, at 674. *See also* Bumpass et al., *supra* note 23, at 922 tbl.10 (reporting that a higher proportion of cohabitants whose relationships had lasted at least three years said that, during the past year, they had "thought that [their] . . . relationship might be in trouble" than cohabitants whose relationships had lasted less than one year).

[81] Blumstein & Schwartz, *supra* note 22 (discussing sharing in marriage); BRAMLETT & MOSHER , *supra* note 15 (discussing stability in marriage).

[82] *Cf.* Patricia A. Cain, *Imagine There's No Marriage*, 16 QUINNIPIAC L. REV. 27, 53 (1996) (noting that a "bright line test such as marriage . . . protect[s] privacy. If courts are asked to make determinations on a case by case basis, they will have to review evidence that supports the couple's claim that they are committed to a shared life . . . [,] produc[ing] obvious privacy costs to the couple").

A. Adoption of the Domestic Partnership Proposal Would Erode the Integrity of Our Law

Marriage, throughout the ages, has been contractual.[83] Of course, the content of the marital contract and the criteria for marriage eligibility and exit have varied widely. Marriage has variously been defined as a patriarchal relationship with all governance rights concentrated in the husband and as a partnership of equals. It has encompassed polygamy as well as monogamy and suttee as well as no-fault divorce. But at all times marriage has been predicated on an agreement to enter the married state. Unless marriage partners say, "I do," they are not married; a "de facto" marriage is nothing more than an oxymoron.

The consensual nature of marriage is evident in the common law marriage doctrine, which requires evidence of a present agreement to marry.[84] It is also evident in the rules for exiting a marital relationship. The grounds for annulment – incapacity, based on mental state or age; fraud, based on a material misrepresentation or physical incapacity; duress, either physical or mental – are all contract defenses. Fault-based divorce grounds represent contract breaches rather than defenses, but the consensual conception of marriage is still central. And, while modern no-fault divorce has expanded the content of the marriage agreement to include spousal compatibility in addition to the traditional elements, it has not altered the view of marriage as a legally binding contract which can neither be imposed without consent nor exited without risk of legal sanctions. Indeed, the contractual view of marriage has gained new force; today marriage partners may individually negotiate with respect to their property rights and, to a lesser but still significant extent, their support obligations.[85]

The contractual view of marriage is not unique to the common law tradition. Under the civil law, marriage was and is contractual.[86] Under Catholic, Jewish, and Islamic law, marriage was and is contractual.[87] Under Roman law, marriage was contractual.[88] Even

[83] *See, e.g.*, 1 WILLIAM BLACKSTONE, COMMENTARIES ON THE LAWS OF ENGLAND ch. 15 ("[O]ur law considers marriage in no other light than as a civil contract"); JOHN LOCKE, TWO TREATISES OF CIVIL GOVERNMENT § 78 (Peter Laslett ed. 1988) ("[C]onjugal society is made by a voluntary compact between man and woman"). One commentator has urged that, "[i]n premodern English law, the use of the term contract was often synonymous with marriage, and it was from the law of spousals that many of the doctrines of modern contract law were first taken[, i]n particular, rules relating to capacity, to duress, to consideration, to offer and acceptance in praesentia and in absentia, to present and future intent, and to the plea of non est factum...."); Peter Goodrich, *Habermas on Law and Democracy: Critical Exchanges: Part II: Communication and Miscommunication: Habermas and the Postal Rule*, 17 CARDOZO L. REV. 1457, 1470 (1996).

[84] *See* CLARK, *supra* note 10; Bowman, *supra* note 10.

[85] *See* KRAUSE ET AL., *supra* note 69, at 178–79 ("Today all states agree that a premarital agreement is enforceable if it meets certain requirements.").

[86] SAMUEL PUFENDORF, OF THE LAW OF NATURE AND NATIONS bk. 6, ch. 1, §§ 12, 14 (1672) ("[C]onsenting and not bedding makes a marriage."). *See also* Hans W. Baade, *Marriage Contracts in French and Spanish Louisiana: A Study in "Notarial" Jurisprudence*, 53 TUL. L. REV.3 (1978); Rodolfo Batiza, *The Actual Sources of the Marriage Contract Provisions of the Louisiana Civil Code of 1808: The Textual Evidence*, 54 TUL. L. REV. 77 (1979).

[87] *See* REUVEN P. BULKA, JEWISH MARRIAGE: A HALAKHIC ETHIC 23–24 (1986); DAWOUD SUDQI EL ALAMI & DOREEN HINCHCLIFFE, ISLAMIC MARRIAGE AND DIVORCE LAWS OF THE ARAB WORLD 5–6 (1996); JOHN WITTE, JR., FROM SACRAMENT TO CONTRACT: MARRIAGE, RELIGION AND LAW IN THE WESTERN TRADITION 25–26 (1997).

[88] *See* Susan Treggiari, *Divorce Roman Style*, *in* MARRIAGE, DIVORCE, AND CHILDREN IN ANCIENT ROME (Beryl Rawson ed. 1991). *See also* Goodrich, *supra* note 83 at ("[In medieval England]... marriage was subject to the jurisdiction of ecclesiastical courts and judges trained in civil law, and it is that Roman inheritance which the common lawyers subsequently admitted into English law.").

the Babylonian Code of Hammurabi provided that, "[i]f a man take a wife and does not arrange with her the proper contracts, that woman is not his legal wife."[89]

The pattern of relational obligation that arises from marital commitment is not out of step with traditional principles of legal responsibility: virtually all other legally enforceable fiduciary obligations – that of guardian to ward, conservator to incompetent, trustee to beneficiary – arise, not by default, but from the voluntary assumption of a particular role in relation to a particular individual.[90] And, as with marriage, the role expectations attached to these various statuses inhibit other relational opportunities and induce detrimental reliance: neither the beneficiary with a trustee, nor the ward with a guardian, can easily replace the individuals who have assumed fiduciary obligations toward them; the assumption of these statuses precludes their assumption by others and induces reliance on role performance.

Given the law's consistent reliance on commitment as a source of private legal obligation, adoption of the ALI proposal would force our family law to "endorse principles to justify part of what it has done that it must reject to justify the rest."[91] This kind of "checkerboard" law making violates the ethical norm that like cases receive like treatment. It denies "what is often called 'equality before the law.'"[92]

B. The ALI Proposal Conflicts with the Ideal of Individual Autonomy

The ALI domestic partnership proposal also runs counter to one of the most important values in modern liberal societies, the ideal of individual autonomy. The autonomy ideal presupposes that individuals should be free to make life choices based on their own goals and values unless the state has some substantial basis for interference. It views the state's rightful role as preventing harm to others, not imposing majoritarian values on those who have chosen a different life course.[93]

In keeping with this view, the U.S. Supreme Court has ruled that decision-making about marriage, procreation, parenthood, and family relationships is included within the liberty protected under the Fourteenth Amendment. It has held that "these matters, involving the most intimate and personal choices a person may make in a lifetime . . . are central to the liberty protected by the Fourteenth Amendment" and concluded that "beliefs about these matters could not define the attributes of personhood were they formed under compulsion of the State."[94]

Given the high likelihood that cohabiting couples would often neglect to contract out of obligations imposed by the PRINCIPLES' domestic partnership scheme, many would lose the freedom to choose when, how, and whether to marry; instead, the state – after the

[89] Babylonian Code of Hammurabi, *quoted in* KRAUSE ET AL., *supra* note 69, at 33.

[90] The obvious exception is parenthood, where obligation is widely understood to derive from dependency-causation. *See* Marsha Garrison, *Is Consent Necessary? An Examination of the Emerging Law of Cohabitant Obligation*, 52 UCLA L. REV. 1, 12–14 (2005).

[91] RONALD DWORKIN, LAW'S EMPIRE 183–84 (1986).

[92] *Id.* at 185. *See also* See JOSEPH RAZ, THE AUTHORITY OF LAW: ESSAYS ON LAW AND MORALITY 180, 201–06 (1979); CASS R. SUNSTEIN, LEGAL REASONING AND POLITICAL CONFLICT 96–100 (1996).

[93] *See* JOHN STUART MILL, ON LIBERTY 13, 82–83 (Bobbs-Merrill ed. 1956).

[94] Planned Parenthood v. Casey, 505 U.S. 833, 851 (1992). *See also* Kenneth Karst, *The Freedom of Intimate Association*, 89 YALE L. J. 637, 637 (1980) ("It is the choice to form and maintain an intimate association that permits full realization of the associational values we cherish most").

fact – would decide for them.[95] This approach represents a form of state paternalism that our legal system generally rejects and which ordinarily demands a showing of harm to others.

There is no evidence that such a massive curtailment of liberty is warranted. In addition to the contract option made available under *Marvin* and its progeny, most courts permit cohabitants to rely on equitable doctrines – constructive trust,[96] purchase money resulting trust,[97] *quantum meruit*[98] – to avert unjust enrichment in cases where a cohabitant has made significant uncompensated contributions or has been induced to rely on continuation of the relationship to his or her detriment. In general, courts have held that compensation for unpaid services is appropriate "in those situations where it would be reasonable to expect compensation"[99] and when compensation during the relationship was inadequate.[100] With the ability to privately create contractual obligations and rely on a panoply of equitable remedies, few cohabitants need additional legal protection to avoid exploitation and satisfy legitimate expectations.

Of course, contractual and quasicontractual remedies do not establish marital status and the public benefits that accompany that status. They are thus inadequate for same-sex couples who want to marry and for heterosexual couples, like the Friedmans, who make private, nonceremonial marriage vows. But the logical reforms are a means for same-sex couples to register marital vows and a revivified, more objective common law marriage doctrine.[101] Both of these reforms would ensure that the law honors commitments; both reforms would enhance individual autonomy; both would provide couples with marital status as well as its public and private benefits. By contrast, the ALI domestic partnership

[95] Principles § 6.03.

[96] Constructive trust "is the name given a flexible remedy imposed in a wide variety of situations to prevent unjust enrichment. When property has been acquired in such circumstances that the holder of the legal title may not in good conscience retain the beneficial interest, equity converts him into a trustee. A constructive trustee is under a duty to convey the property to another on the ground that retention of the property would be wrongful. The usual requirements for imposition of a constructive trust are: 1) a confidential or fiduciary relationship; 2) a promise, express or implied, by the transferee; 3) a transfer of property in reliance on the promise; and 4) unjust enrichment of the transferee. But the constructive trust remedy is not limited to these circumstances... [and] may be imposed in situations where... the court is moved simply by the desire to prevent unjust enrichment." Jesse Dukeminier & Stanley M. Johanson, Wills, Trusts, and Estates 585 (6th ed., 2000). *See also* 5 Austin W. Scott, Trusts §§ 461–552 (William F. Fratcher ed., 4th ed. 1987). A number of courts have endorsed the use of constructive trust principles in cases involving unmarried cohabitants. *See, e.g.*, Bright v. Kuehl, 650 N. E.2d 311 (Ind. Ct. App. 1995); Watts v. Watts, 405 N.W.2d 303 (Wis. 1987).

[97] A purchase money resulting trust arises when one person pays the purchase price for property and causes title to the property to be taken in the name of another person. *See* Restatement (Third) of Trusts §§ 7–9 (2003).

[98] "[C]ourts use *quantum meruit* to compensate a person for services rendered in the absence of a contract.... [The doctrine] lacks readily ascertainable rules for the determination of the proper amount of compensation. The technique used to determine recovery varies according to the circumstances of each case." Jeffrey L. Oakes, Comment, *Article 2298, the Codification of the Principle Forbidding Unjust Enrichment, and the Elimination of the* Quantum Meruit *as a Basis for Recovery in Louisiana*, 56 La. L. Rev. 873, 874–75 (1996). *See generally* Judy Becker Sloan, Quantum Meruit: *Residual Equity in Law*, 42 De Paul L. Rev. 399 (1992) (surveying history and usage of *quantum meruit* doctrine). A number of courts have endorsed the use of *quantum meruit* principles in cases involving unmarried cohabitants. *See, e.g.*, Maglica v. Maglica, 78 Cal. Rptr. 2d 101 (Cal. Ct. App. 1998); Mason v. Rostad, 476 A.2d 662 (D. C. Cir. 1984).

[99] Krause et al., *supra* note 69, at 229. For examples of cases applying this principle, see, for example, Tapley v. Tapley, 449 A.2d 1218 (N.H. 1982) (limiting recovery to business services); Whorton v. Dillingham, 248 Cal. Rptr. 405 (Cal. Ct. App. 1988) (finding that services as a bodyguard, secretary, and real estate counselor are compensable).

[100] *See, e.g.*, Tarry v. Stewart, 649 N. E.2d 1 (Ohio Ct. App. 1994) (refusing cohabitant's reimbursement claim for improvements made to house due to benefit received from living in house during relationship).

[101] For more detailed proposals for each reform, *see* Garrison, *supra* note 90, at 75–83.

proposal adds nothing to the contractual and quasicontractual remedies that are already available: the obligations that accompany a finding of domestic partnership remain uncertain until tested in the courts and, even if the parties are ultimately declared domestic partners, they are not married and thus cannot claim the public benefits associated with marriage.

In sum, the ALI proposal diminishes personal liberty and privacy; individuals are forced into a marital mold whether or not that family form comports with their own goals and personal choices. This massive curtailment of freedom is unjustified by any public or private interest.

C. The ALI Proposal Conveys False Information about Marriage and Cohabitation

The ALI proposal also sends the wrong message about marriage and cohabitation. The extension of marital obligations and rights to those who have not made marital commitments signals – inaccurately – that marriage and cohabitation are the same. Such a signal discourages marital commitment and investment. It also devalues marriage, a status of enormous symbolic importance to most citizens and one associated with greater health, wealth, happiness, and stability, for both adults and children, than is cohabitation.

The symbolic importance of marriage is easily demonstrated by recent attempts to legalize same-sex marriage. The strong feelings of both those who oppose and those who favor same-sex marriage make it abundantly clear that marriage matters. Marriage remains the preferred – some would argue the only – method of signaling full relational commitment to a partner and the world.[102] Marriage vows both establish a new, publicly recognized family and unify the marriage partners' families of origin.[103]

Americans believe that marriage matters. They fill reams of newsprint with announcements of their marital intentions. They receive gifts to mark the occasion. They invite friends and relatives to witness their marital commitments and spend tens of billions of dollars every year on the wedding festivities that celebrate those vows.[104] They report that marriage connotes a more certain and "special" status than does cohabitation.[105] They tell us, in sum, that marriage remains an extraordinarily meaningful life event. Academics may question whether marriage still matters, but individual Americans do not.

[102] *See* William N. Eskridge, Jr., The Case for Same-Sex Marriage 71 (1996) ("Getting married signals a significantly higher level of commitment, in part because the law imposes much greater obligations on the couple and makes it much more of a bother and expense to break up.... Moreover, the duties and obligations of marriage directly contribute to interpersonal commitment.")

[103] In a 2004 national survey, 28% of respondents said that marriage was "mostly a legal matter," 46% that it was "mostly a religious matter," and 22% that it was "both equally." Four percent reported no opinion. *See* Roper Ctr. for Pub Opinion Research, Question Id. USPSRNEW.022104 R26 (Princeton Research Assoc., Feb. 19, 2004).

[104] In the United States, $72 billion is spent each year on weddings and $8 billion on honeymoons. *See* http://honeymoons.about.com/cs/eurogen1/a/weddingstats.htm (last visited march 8, 2006). There is evidence that marriage ceremonies reinforce marital role transitions by reducing uncertainty about new roles and by providing approval for norm-guided behavior. *See* M. Kalmijn, *Marriage Rituals as Reinforcers of Role Transitions: An Analysis of Weddings in The Netherlands*, 66 J. Marriage & Fam. 582 (2004).

[105] Weddings profiled in the *New York Times* contain a gold mine of information on attitudes toward marriage and cohabitation. One couple – who had been together for seventeen years – told a *Times* reporter that they had decided to marry, in part, because of their ambiguous social status. As the Husband put it, "I felt the ambiguity was not worth the price of having to explain to other people what was going on.... Iconoclastic rebellion didn't seem important any more." Eric V. Copage, *Weddings/Celebrations/Vows: Madeline Schwartzman and Jeffrey Miles*, N.Y. Times, Feb. 2, 2003, at § 9 p. 9. Another stressed the "special" status that marriage connotes: "we had to check the 'other' box in referring to our relationship [on a medical form].... We realized 'other' wasn't special enough." *Weddings/Celebrations/Vows: Judy Shapiro and Joe Garber*, N.Y. Times, Aug. 15, 2004, at § 9, p. 11.

Young American adults continue to describe a good marriage as one of their most important life goals[106] and believe that marriage confers a wide range of private and public benefits.[107] The evidence justifies their enthusiasm. Those who are married live longer and are less likely to become disabled than the unmarried; they get more sleep, eat more regular meals, visit the doctor more regularly, and abuse addictive substances less frequently.[108] Even after controlling for age, married men earn more than either single men or cohabitants,[109] and they are less likely to lose their earnings through compulsive gambling.[110] Married couples also have a higher savings rate and thus accrue greater wealth than the unmarried.[111] Married individuals rate their happiness and mental health more highly than the unmarried.[112] They experience less domestic violence and greater physical security.[113] Although a high divorce rate, rising rates of cohabitation, and later marriage have all weakened both the stability and status linked with marriage,

[106] *See* Barbara Dafoe Whitehead & David Popenoe, *Changes in Teen Attitudes Toward Marriage, Cohabitation and Children 1975–1995* (Nat. Marriage Project Next Generation Project), *at* http://marriage.rutgers.edu/Publications/pubteena.htm (showing that respondent teenagers overwhelmingly reported that they would marry and approximately three-fourth reported that a good marriage is "extremely important").

[107] *See* Kelly Raley, *Recent Trends and Differentials in Marriage and Cohabitation, in* THE TIES THAT BIND, *supra* note 18, at 34 (reporting that most young adults age 20–29 tend to believe that they would be happier, "more economically secure, have more emotional security, a better sex life, and a higher standard of living if they were married").

[108] *See* WAITE & GALLAGHER, *supra* note 25, at 47–64 (summarizing research). However, the evidence is conflicting on whether the married rate their health more highly than the unmarried. *See* Linda J. Waite, *Trends in Men's and Women's Well-Being in Marriage, in* THE TIES THAT BIND, *supra* note 18, at 368, 375–9; Zheng Wu et al., *"In Sickness and in Health": Does Cohabitation Count?*, 24 J. FAM. ISSUES 811 (2003). Selection effects may also account for some of the reported differences between married and cohabiting couples. *See id.*

[109] "[T]he general consensus in the literature is that controlling for other observable characteristics, married men are simply more productive than unmarried men." Jeffrey S. Gray & Michel J. Vanderhart, *On the Determination of Wages: Does Marriage Matter?*, in THE TIES THAT BIND, *supra* note 18, at 356. Married men also tend to work longer hours and to choose higher-paying jobs and professions. *See* WAITE & GALLAGHER, *supra* note 25, at 99–105; Oppenheimer, *supra* note 20. The male "marriage premium" has declined, however, for reasons that are poorly understood. *See* Philip N. Cohen, *Cohabitation and the Declining Marriage Premium for Men*, 29 WORK & OCCUPATIONS 346 (2002).

[110] *See* J. W. Welte et al., *Gambling Participation and Pathology in the United States – A Sociodemographic Analysis Using Classification Trees*, 29 ADDICTIVE BEHAVIORS 983 (2004) (finding in a national U.S. telephone survey that the most frequent gamblers were divorced, widowed, or cohabiting men, and that nonpoor, married, or widowed whites were least likely to be problem gamblers).

[111] *See* Joseph Lupton & James P. Smith, *Marriage, Assets, and Savings, in* MARRIAGE AND THE ECONOMY: THEORY AND EVIDENCE FROM ADVANCED INDUSTRIAL SOCIETIES 129 (Shoshana Grossbard-Schechtman ed. 2003).

[112] *See* Waite, *Trends, supra* note 108, at 368, 374–75 tbl.19.2 (showing that the reported happiness levels of married individuals exceeded those of never married, previously married, and cohabiting individuals (which tended to be comparable), and "the happiness advantage of the married [is] ... roughly similar ... for men and women ... [and] has not changed over the past 35 years"); Susan L. Brown, *Moving from Cohabitation to Marriage: Effects on Relationship Quality*, 33 J. SOC. SCI. RES. 1 (2004) (reporting in national sample that cohabitants who married reported higher levels of relationship happiness as well as lower levels of relationship instability, disagreements, and violent conflict than those who remained cohabiting, net of time-1 relationship quality and sociodemographic controls). *See also* Susan L. Brown et al., *The Significance of Nonmarital Cohabitation: Marital Status and Mental Health Benefits among Middle-Aged and Older Adults*, J. GERONTOLOGY: SOC. SCI. (2004) (finding that male, but not female, cohabitants reported significantly higher depression scores than married men and women after controlling for sociodemographic variables); Russell P. D. Burton, *Global Integrative Meaning as a Mediating Factor in the Relationship Between Social Roles and Psychological Distress*, 39 J. HEALTH & SOC. BEHAVIOR 201 (1998); Kathleen A. Lamb et al., *Union Formation and Depression: Selection and Relationship Effects*, 65 J. MARRIAGE & FAM. 953 (2003); Nock, *supra* note 20, at 68–69 tbl.1.4.

[113] *See* sources cited in note 22, *supra*; Waite, *Trends, supra* note 108, at 381 tbl.19.6 (cohabitants with no plans to marry are "substantially and significantly" more likely to report couple violence than either married or engaged couples).

marriage is still associated, across nations and cultures, with higher levels of subjective well-being.[114]

Some of the benefits of marriage undoubtedly result from "selection" effects rather than marriage itself; to the extent that those who marry are healthier, wealthier, and happier to begin with, they should maintain these advantages after marriage. The jury is still out on the extent to which the marriage "premium" derives from preexisting characteristics or the married state. Undoubtedly, preexisting characteristics are important and explain away some significant part of the marital advantage. However, researchers who have controlled for obvious confounding factors like age and education continue to report marital advantages,[115] and longitudinal studies have also found significant health, income, and behavioral effects associated with marriage.[116] Researchers thus almost universally agree that some, as yet undetermined, fraction of the marital "premium" stems from marriage itself.[117]

Marriage is also associated with important advantages to children. As a group, children born to married parents experience much greater stability than children born to unmarried parents; indeed, cross-national research shows that children born to cohabiting parents are two to four times more likely to see their parents separate than are children of parents married at the time of birth.[118] Because of the greater stability provided by marriage, marital

[114] *See* Ed Diener et al., *Similarity of the Relations Between Marital Status and Subjective Well-Being Across Cultures*, 31 J. Cross-Cultural Psychol. 419 (2000) (finding in a 42-nation survey that the positive relationship between marital status and subjective well-being did not differ by gender and was "very similar" across the world); Steven Stack & J. Ross Eshleman, *Marital Status and Happiness; A 17-Nation Study*, 60 J. Marriage & Fam. 527 (1998) (observing that "married persons have a significantly higher level of happiness than persons who are not married. This effect was independent of financial and heath-oriented protections offered by marriage and was also independent of other control variables including ones for sociodemographic conditions and national character." Although cohabitants had a higher level of happiness than single persons, their happiness level was still "less than one quarter of [that] of married persons"). *See also* Arne Mastekaasa, *The Subjective Well-Being of the Previously Married: The Importance of Unmarried Cohabitation and Time Since Widowhood or Divorce*, 73 Soc. Forces 665, 682 (1994).

[115] *See* Nadine F. Marks, *Flying Solo at Mid-Life: Gender, Marital Status, and Psychological Well-Being 10–11*, CDE Working Paper 95–03 (http://www.ssc.wisc.edu/cde/cdewp/95-03.pdf) (reviewing research data on impact of selection effects in explaining higher happiness levels of married individuals).

[116] Longitudinal studies show that the transition to marriage is significantly associated with greater psychological well-being and healthier behaviors, while the transition out of marriage is associated with less well-being and less healthy behaviors. *See* Nadine F. Marks & James D. Lambert, *Marital Status Continuity and Change Among Young and Midlife Adults: Longitudinal Effects on Psychological Well-Being*, 19 J. Fam. Issues 652 (1998); Allan V. Horowitz et al., *Becoming Married and Mental Health: A Longitudinal Study of a Cohort of Young Adults*, 58 J. Marriage & Fam. 652 (1998); H. K. Kim & P. C. McHenry, *The Relationship Between Marriage and Psychological Well-Being – A Longitudinal Analysis*, 23 J. Fam. Issues 885 (2002) (presenting data that "confirmed the strong effects of marital status on psychological well-being, supporting the protection perspective," and indicated that "the transition to cohabiting did not have the same beneficial effects as marriage for psychological well-being," but which produced "weak and inconsistent" evidence of selection effects). And at least for men, marriage brings a sharp reduction in social evenings at bars or taverns and an enormous increase in involvement with relatives and church-related activities. Men's first marriages are also associated with measurable positive changes in annual income, weeks worked, and occupational prestige. *See* Steven L. Nock, Marriage in Men's Lives 82, 94–95, 112–18 (1995).

[117] *See, e.g.*, Pamela J. Smock et al., *The Effect of Marriage and Divorce on Women's Economic Well-Being*, 64 Am. Sociol. Rev. 794, 809 (1999) ("[T]he economic benefits of marriage are large, even above and beyond the characteristics of those who marry. . . . "); Donna K. Ginther & Madeline Zavodny, *Is the Male Marriage Premium Due to Selection? The Effect of Shotgun Weddings on the Return to Marriage*, 14 J. Pop. Econ. 313 (2001) (finding that, "at most 10% of the estimated marriage premium [in men's wages] is due to selection") and sources cited in note, supra.

[118] *See* Cynthia Osborne et al., Instability in Fragile Families: The Role of Race-Ethnicity, Economics, and Relationship Quality 9, tbl.2 (CRCW Working Paper 2004-17FF, 2004) (in nationally representative U.S. sample, 40% of children born to cohabiting parents and 20% of children born to married parents experienced their parents' separation within three years of birth); Bumpass & Lu, *supra* note 16, at 38 tbl.6 (reporting that children born to married parents spend 84% of their childhood in two-parent families; children born to cohabiting parents "may spend about a quarter

children are exposed to fewer financial,[119] physical,[120] and educational[121] risks. Unsurprisingly, lower risk is associated with higher levels of childhood well-being.[122] There is also evidence that the advantages conferred by marital childbearing and rearing transcend the specific benefits associated with residential and economic stability. Married fathers appear to spend more time with their children than unmarried fathers; if parental separation occurs, they see their children more often and pay child support more regularly.[123]

of their childhood years with a single parent, a quarter with a cohabiting parent, and less than half with married parents"); Patrick Heuveline et al., *Shifting Childrearing to Single Mothers: Results from 17 Western Countries*, 29 Pop. & Dev. Rev. 47 (2003) (explaining that in most countries, children born to cohabiting parents are two to four times more likely to see their parents separate than are children of parents married at the time of birth); Kiernan, *supra* note 16 (reporting that within 5 years of the birth of a child, 8% of married couples in the United Kingdom have split up, compared to 52% of cohabitants and 25% of those who marry after the birth).

[119] *See* Casper & Bianchi, *supra* note 19, at 111–12 fig.4.3 (reporting that in 1998 poverty rate of married-parent households was 6.9% and that of single-mother households was 38.7%); Urban Inst., Wedding Bells Ring in Stability and Economic Gains for Mothers and Children, http://www.urban.org/Template.cfm?Section=ByTopic&NavMenuID=62&template=/TaggedContent/View Publication.cfm&PublicationID=7858 (reporting that three related studies found that "[m]arriage, even a shotgun wedding, significantly improves the living standards of mothers and their children.... Families with two married parents encounter more stable home environments, fewer years in poverty, and diminished material hardship.") Noncustodial divorced and never-married parents are also less likely to pass wealth on to their adult children. *See* Frank F. Furstenberg, Jr. et al., *The Effect of Divorce on Intergenerational Transfers: New Evidence*, 32 Demography 319 (1995) (showing that divorce during childhood years was associated with sharp decrease in transfers by fathers); Nadine F. Marks, *Midlife Marital Status Differences in Social Support Relationships with Adult Children and Psychological Well-Being*, 16 J. Fam. Issues 5 (1995) (finding that remarried and single parents professed less belief in parental financial obligation and were less likely to provide support to adult children than first-marriage parents).

[120] Rates of physical and sexual abuse are much higher when children live with an adult stepparent or cohabitant. *See* Robin Fretwell Wilson, *The Sexual Exploitation of Female Children After Divorce*, 86 Cornell L. Rev. 251 (2001); Martin Daly & Margo Wilson, *Child Abuse and Other Risks of Not Living with Both Parents*, 6 Ethology & Sociobiology 197 (1985); Leslie Margolin, *Child Abuse by Mothers' Boyfriends: Why the Overrepresentation?*, 16 Child Abuse & Neglect 541 (1992).

[121] *See* Sara McLanahan & Gary Sandefur, Growing Up with a Single Parent: What Hurts, What Helps 39–63 (1994) (reviewing evidence); Wendy Sigle-Rushton & Sara McLanahan, *Father Absence and Child Well–Being: A Critical Review*, *in* The Future of the Family 116, 120–22 (Daniel P. Moynihan et al. eds. 2004) (same).

[122] *See* Paul R. Amato & Jacob Cheadle, *The Long Reach of Divorce: Divorce and Child Well-Being Across Three Generations*, 67 J. Marriage & Fam. 191, 193 (2005) (summarizing studies); Sigle-Rushton & McLanahan, *supra* note 121 at 122–25 (same). *See also* Casper & Bianchi, *supra* note 19, at 46 (finding children whose parents never married see their fathers less frequently after parental separation); Susan L. Brown, *Family Structure and Child Well-Being: The Significance of Parental Cohabitation*, 66 J. Marriage & Fam. 351 (2004) (reporting children living in two cohabiting biological-parent families experienced worse outcomes, on average, than those residing with two married biological parents; among children age 6–11, economic and parental resources attenuated these differences. Among adolescents ages 12–17, parental cohabitation was negatively associated with well-being, regardless of the levels of these resources. Child well-being did not significantly vary among cohabiting versus married stepfamilies, cohabiting two-biological-parent families versus cohabiting stepfamilies, or either type of cohabiting family versus single-mother families).

[123] *See* Casper & Bianchi, *supra* note 19, at 46 (reporting that children whose parents never married see their fathers less frequently after parental separation); Marcy Carlson et al., Unmarried But Not Absent: Fathers' Involvement With Children After a Nonmarital Birth (CRCW Working Paper 2005–07) (finding that parents' relationship status at the time of the child's birth is a key predictor of subsequent involvement: fathers in cohabiting unions were much more likely to be involved in their child's life three years later than other unmarried fathers. Parents' relationship quality was also linked to greater father involvement for some outcomes, and domestic violence, a history of incarceration, and having children by other partners were significantly associated with lower involvement); Lingxin Hao, *Family Structure, Private Transfers, and the Economic Well-Being of Families with Children*, 75 Social Forces 269 (1996) (finding that married fathers were more likely to pay child support). *See also* Susan L. Brown, *Family Structure and Child Well-Being: The Significance of Parental Cohabitation*, 66 J. Marriage & Fam. 351 (2004) (reporting that children living in two cohabiting biological-parent families experienced worse outcomes, on average, than those residing with two married biological parents; among children age 6–11, economic and parental resources attenuated these differences. Among adolescents ages 12–17, parental cohabitation was

The advantages of marriage may even extend to later generations. A number of studies have found that both men and women who experience a single-parent household as children are more likely than others to divorce or separate as adults.[124] Researchers who examined links between divorce in the grandparent generation and outcomes for grandchildren have also reported that grandparental divorce is significantly associated with less education, more marital discord, more divorce, and greater tension in early parent-child relationships.[125]

The marital advantage also appears to be universal. Even in the Scandinavian nations, which have the longest experience with cohabitation as a mainstream family form and a high level of support for single-parent families, demographers continue to find that marital childbearing is associated with greater childhood stability[126] and smaller risks to adult welfare.[127]

Of course, marriage is not always associated with advantage, for either children or adults. Violent marriages are clearly dangerous, and even verbal marital conflict appears to be harmful to both adults and children.[128]

negatively associated with well-being, regardless of the levels of these resources. Child well-being did not significantly vary among cohabiting versus married stepfamilies, cohabiting two-biological-parent.).

[124] *See* Paul R. Amato & Alan Booth, A Generation at Risk: Growing Up in an Era of Family Upheaval 106–117 (1997) (summarizing studies); Amato & Cheadle, *supra* note 122 at 192–93 (same); Jay D. Teachman, *The Childhood Living Arrangements of Children and the Characteristics of Their Marriages*, 25 J. Fam. Issues 86 (2004) (finding that "any time spent in an alternative [i.e., nonmarital] family increases the likelihood that a woman [will herself] form[] a union with characteristics that decrease the likelihood of a successful union"). Parental divorce or separation is also significantly correlated with likelihood of premarital cohabitation. *See* Kiernan, *supra* note 16, at 55 tbl.3.8 (showing significant increase in likelihood of cohabitation before marriage among those whose parents divorced or separated across fourteen European nations).

[125] *See* Amato & Cheadle, *supra* note 122.

[126] *See* An-Magritt Jensen & Sten-Erik Clausen, *Children and Family Dissolution in Norway: The Impact of Consensual Unions*, 10 Childhood 65 (2003) (stating that children of cohabiting parents run a much higher risk of dissolution compared to children in marital unions and "this risk is not diminishing as cohabitation becomes more widespread").

[127] *See* Gunilla Ringback Weitoft et al., *Mortality, Severe Morbidity, and Injury in Children Living with Single Parents in Sweden: A Population-Based Study*, 361 Lancet 289 (2003) (showing that based on analysis of national register data in almost a million cases, Swedish children in single-parent households showed significantly increased risks of psychiatric disease, suicide or suicide attempt, injury, and addiction. Even after controlling for socioeconomic status factors such as parental addiction or mental disorder, children in single-parent families still exhibited "significant increases in risk" for all adverse outcomes); Jan O. Jonsson & Michael Gahler, *Family Dissolution, Family Reconstitution, and Children's Educational Careers: Recent Evidence for Sweden*, 34 Demography 277, 287 (1997) (finding that even after controlling for all independent variables, children of divorced and separated parents and children living in reconstituted families have low school-continuation propensities compared to children living with both biological parents); Helen Hansagi et al., *Parental Divorce: Psychosocial Well-Being, Mental Health and Mortality During Youth and Young Adulthood: A Longitudinal Study of Swedish Conscripts*, 10 Eur. J. Pub. Health 335 (2000) (reporting that in a group of Swedish conscripts, several indicators of low levels of well-being and mental illness, including alcoholism, were significantly correlated with parental divorce even after adjustment for antecedents and other factors). *See also* Taru H. Makikyro et al., *Hospital-Treated Psychiatric Disorders in Adults with a Single-Parent and Two-Parent Family Background: A 28-Year Follow-Up of the 1966 Northern Finland Cohort*, 37 Fam. Process 335 (1998).

[128] *See* Amato & Booth, *supra* note 124 at 219–20 (reporting that "parents' marital unhappiness and discord have a broad negative impact on virtually every dimension of offspring well-being" and that parental divorce actually "benefits children in certain ways if it removes them from a discordant parental household"; Debra Umberson et al., *You Make Me Sick: Marital Quality and Health Over the Life Course*, PRC Working Paper No. 03-04-05, 2005), http://www.prc.utexas.edu/working_papers/wp_pdf/03-04-05.pdf (reviewing evidence); J. K. Kiecolt-Glaser & T. L. Newton, *Marriage and Health: His and Hers*, 127 Psychol. Bull. 472 (2001) (finding that unhappy marriages have negative physical-health consequences); Kristina Orth-Gomer et al., *Marital Stress Worsens Prognosis in Women With*

We also lack an understanding of the process by which the benefits associated with marriage are produced, and some demographers have argued that they may result simply from stronger and more committed partnerships being selected into marriage.[129] It is possible that this supposition is correct; certainly, it is extremely hard to prove or disprove. But given the plentiful and consistent research showing the married state to be associated with significant benefits to adult partners, their children, and the public, lawmakers should be extremely wary of adopting standards based on the supposition that marriage is irrelevant. There is too much evidence suggesting that marriage does matter, and that it has the capacity to confer important advantages on marriage partners and their families.

III. The Domestic Partnership Proposal Is Not a Liberal Reform

Even with the various advantages I have described, marriage is undeniably less important than it once was. Socially acceptable sex and childbearing are no longer confined to marital relationships.[130] Marriage is no longer women's primary source of adult economic security. Young adults are marrying later.[131] Increasing numbers will not marry at all.[132] Even those who do marry often live in nonmarital households for substantial periods of time.[133] Modern marriage thus represents only one possible choice among a range of familial and nonfamilial alternatives.

Modern marriage is also more variable than traditional marriage. Some husbands and wives continue to play traditional marital roles; many others reject those roles outright. Some want and raise many children, while others reject child bearing and rearing altogether. Some share each and every aspect of their lives together, and others live in widely separated cities, leading largely separate lives. Some enter into premarital agreements

Coronary Heart Disease, 284 JAMA 3008 (2000) (reporting that, among married and cohabiting women, marital stress was associated with a 2.9-fold increased risk of recurrent coronary events after adjustment for confounding variables, but work stress did not significantly predict recurrent coronary events).

[129] *See* Kathleen Kiernan, *Unmarried Cohabitation and Parenthood: Here to Stay? European Perspectives, in* THE FUTURE OF THE FAMILY, *supra* note 121, at 66, 91.

[130] In 2002, 33.8% of U.S. births were nonmarital, as compared to 3.8% in 1940. *See* U.S. NAT. CTR. HEALTH STATISTICS, NONMARITAL CHILDBEARING IN THE UNITED STATES 1940–99, 48 Nat. Vital Statistics Rrts. No. 16, available at http://www.census.gov/statab/hist/HS-14.pdf. The increase in nonmarital births reflects a large increase in premarital sex. The National Survey of Family Growth found that, in 1970, 40% of unmarried 18-year-old women said that they had engaged in sexual intercourse. By 1988, the proportion had risen to 70%. This trend has reversed in recent years, and in 1995 the proportion of 18-year-old women who reported having had sex fell to 63%. *See* Douglas Besharov & Karen Gardiner, *Trends in Teen Sexual Behavior*, 19 CHILD & YOUTH SERV. REV. 328 (1997), available at http://www.aei.org/publications/pubID.17756/pub_detail.asp.

[131] Between 1950 and 2002, the median age at first marriage increased for U.S. men by 4.1 years (from 22.8 to 26.9) and for women by 5 years (from 20.3 to 25.3). Median age at first marriage for U.S. men today is close to the median in 1890 (26.1 for men and 22 for women). *See* http://www.infoplease.com/ipa/A0005061.html (citing U.S. census data).

[132] Between 1950 and 1996, the U.S. marriage rate per 1,000 population declined from 11.1 to 8.8. *See* U.S. BUREAU OF THE CENSUS, STATISTICAL ABSTRACT OF THE UNITED STATES 2001 59 tbl.68. More strikingly, between 1970 and 2002, the proportion of U.S. adults aged 40–44 who reported that they had never been married increased among men from 4.9% to 16.7% (an increase of more than 300%) and among women from 6.3% to 11.5%. *See* http://www.infoplease.com/ipa/A0763219.html (citing U.S. census data).

[133] Between 1970 and 2004, the proportion of U.S. households that included a married couple declined from 70.6% to 54%. *See* Steve Rawlings, *Households and Families, available at* http://www.census.gov/population/www/pop-profile/hhfam.html (reporting U.S. census data).

limiting their marital entitlements, and others enter into covenant marriages that restrict options for exiting their relationships.[134] While there have always been atypical marriages, the number, and even our conception of typicality, has almost certainly expanded significantly.

Some commentators rely on the greater variability and lesser social importance of marriage as a basis for the claim that marriage should lose its privileged legal status. They argue that "[l]aw should adapt to these changes by protecting all relationships that serve family functions by abandoning its elevation of the status of formal marriage."[135] These commentators claim that current law discriminates against the unmarried. They contend that regulatory models like the ALI domestic partnership approach serve to ensure nondiscrimination, state neutrality, and relational choice.[136]

The rhetoric of choice and nondiscrimination that often appears in encomiums on behalf of the ALI domestic partnership proposal and like standards suggests that this regulatory model serves a liberal agenda. But let there be no mistake here. The ALI approach does not foster choice and nondiscrimination: it eliminates choice by forcing those who are unprepared to make marital commitments to shoulder the very responsibilities that they have avoided; it discriminates by cramming relationships of many contours into a "one-size-fits-all" marital mold. The ALI proposal deeply intrudes into relational privacy. It dramatically expands state control over private life.[137] Despite the liberal rhetoric that cloaks its illiberal character, the ALI proposal offers nothing more – or less – than a dramatic expansion of state paternalism and coercion.

The ALI domestic partnership proposal would impose marital obligations on those who have not undertaken them. Yet there is nothing to support the supposition that individual men and women do not know what they are doing when they decide to marry and when they decide not to. Nor is there any obvious public policy justification for state paternalism with respect to marital decision-making. The fact that marriage is more variable than it once was cannot justify such massive state intrusion into personal relational choices. The fact that marriage is less important socially and economically cannot justify such intrusion either. If anything, these changes in the institution of marriage suggest less state intervention in marital decision-making, not more. While the evidence does show that cohabitation is associated with fewer advantages than marriage both for adults and children,[138] this evidence is surely not so compelling as to justify a legal regime that forces those who have elected not to marry into shotgun, post hoc marital relationships. Nor is it likely that such a regime could replicate the benefits of marriage for those whom it affects, anyway. The evidence suggests that much of the marital premium flows from relational stability and the expectation of continued stability, but cohabitants who might be conscripted into marital obligation will not know their status until the relationship has ended and its character investigated through litigation. Conscription simply

[134] *See* Wardle, this volume.

[135] *See* Scott, this volume. *See also* Martha Fineman, The Autonomy Myth: A Theory of Dependency (2004).

[136] *See* Garrison, *supra* note 90, at 850 (quoting and citing commentators).

[137] *Cf.* Anita Bernstein, *For and Against Marriage: A Revision*, 102 Mich L. Rev. 129, 212 (2003) (arguing that elimination of marriage would ultimately produce more "control [of] citizens' private lives . . . [by] the state or capital. . . . No blithe, freeing, choice-affirming alternative to this extraordinary institution is available."); Cain, *supra* note 82.

[138] *See* text at notes 115, 124, *supra*.

cannot substitute for the commitments and role reinforcement that flow from formal marriage.

Modern marriage, for all its greater variability and lesser social significance, consistently differs from cohabitation in one large and important respect: Marriage partners have publicly assumed binding obligations to each other that restrict other marital opportunities, inhibit participation in other sexual and economic relationships, structure public and private expectations about their relationship, and burden exit from it. Cohabitants have not. This fundamental difference distinguishes marital relationships, for all their variability, from nonmarital relationships. This difference explains why marriage continues to foster "shared expectations for appropriate behavior within the partnership" while cohabitation remains an "incomplete institution" offering "no widely recognized social blueprint . . . for the appropriate behavior of cohabitors, or for the behavior of the friends, families, and other individuals and institutions with whom they interact."[139] This difference provides a sound basis for state enforcement of both marital commitments and decisions not to make such commitments. State enforcement of marital obligation thus rests not on an "elevation" of marriage over other types of intimate relationships, but instead on the voluntary assumption of obligation that marriage partners have undertaken.

In sum, it is not obvious why some commentators associate liberal principles with the ALI domestic partnership proposal. There is nothing liberal here.

IV. Conclusion

If and when the fact of cohabitation routinely implies marital commitment, cohabitation should give rise to marital obligation. But the ALI's assertion that marriage and cohabitation are equivalent relational states is unsupported by the evidence: Married and cohabiting couples tend to behave and view their relationships quite differently. Cohabitants are much less likely than married couples to share or pool resources. Cohabitation usually functions as a substitute for being single, not for being married.

The ALI's claim that it is practical to require cohabitants to contract out of marital obligations is also unfounded. Individualized inquiry into a couple's understandings and behavior is likely to produce highly uncertain and inconsistent results that can only be determined after time-consuming and expensive litigation. Status-based rules that infer marital obligation from easily ascertained facts such as a common child or the maintenance of a common residence for a defined period avoid much of the uncertainty and expense inherent in individualized inquiry, but create serious risks of misclassification.

The domestic partnership proposal would introduce discordant values into the law of relational obligation. It would diminish personal autonomy and falsely signal that marriage and cohabitation are equivalent relational states. Because marriage is advantageous both for adults and children, legal standards should foster marital commitments. By diminishing their importance, the ALI approach risks harm to individual interests and the public good.

The ALI's proposed reforms are not needed either to protect genuine marital commitments or avert unjust enrichment. Policymakers thus should affirm what is already

[139] Casper & Bianchi, *supra* note 19, at 40. *See also* Nock, *supra* note 20, at 74 ("Cohabitation is an incomplete institution. No matter how widespread the practice, nonmarital unions are not yet governed by strong consensual norms. . . . ")

obvious to most of the public: Marriage matters. Family law should reflect and reinforce that fundamental fact.

Research for this chapter was supported by Brooklyn Law School's Faculty Research Fund. The chapter draws heavily on my article *Is Consent Necessary? An Evaluation of the Emerging Law of Cohabitant Obligations*, 52 UCLA L. Rev. 1 (2005), which provides a more detailed analysis of cohabitant-obligation laws like that proposed by the ALI and offers an alternative reform proposal.

17 Domestic Partnerships, Implied Contracts, and Law Reform

Elizabeth S. Scott

The domestic partnership chapter of the PRINCIPLES is the shortest chapter, but, as the contributions to this volume suggest, among the most interesting to many people. The legal regulation of informal intimate unions generally and particularly the PRINCIPLES' approach of creating a status that carries the legal rights and obligations of marriage between cohabiting parties have generated considerable debate. In some quarters, the domestic partnership provisions are admired as an effective mechanism to protect dependent partners in marriage-like unions who otherwise may be unable to establish claims to property and support when their relationships end.[1] Others praise the PRINCIPLES for acknowledging the diversity of contemporary families and legitimizing a nonmarital family form for both same-sex and opposite-sex couples.[2] Some critics of the PRINCIPLES oppose domestic partnership status for exactly this reason, arguing that the legal recognition of informal intimate unions – including same-sex unions – undermines traditional marriage, and that this is bad.[3] Others object on practical grounds that the PRINCIPLES will generate a flood of litigation because of the complexity of the proposed legal standard and the need to establish domestic partnership status before a claim is considered.[4]

This chapter also expresses skepticism about the domestic partnership provisions, but for reasons that differ from those of most critics. The goal of providing partners in long-term unions with more effective means of enforcing financial obligations between themselves is laudable, as is the PRINCIPLES' inclusion of same-sex as well as opposite-sex unions. Domestic partnership status can provide greater financial security to dependent partners in informal unions than they have under current law, avoiding the harsh inequity that can result when one partner seeks to exploit the other by enjoying the benefits of an intimate union without incurring financial obligations. Although the enforcement of agreements between cohabitants has been possible since the California Supreme Court decided

[1] The drafters, Grace Blumberg and Ira Ellman, have long argued that domestic partnership status provides more effective protection to dependent partners than does contract law. *See* notes 47 & 48, *infra.*

[2] Nancy Polikoff, *Making Marriage Matter Less: The ALI Domestic Partnership Principles Are One Step in the Right Direction*, 2004 U. CHI. LEGAL F. 353.

[3] Lynn Wardle, *Deconstructing Family: A Critique of the American Law Institute's "Domestic Partners" Proposal*, 2001 BYU L. REV. 1189; Lynne Kohm, *How Will Proliferation and Recognition of Domestic Partnerships Affect Marriage?*, 4 J. L. & FAM. STUD. 105 (2002).

[4] Marsha Garrison, *Is Consent Necessary? An Evaluation of the Emerging Law of Cohabitant Obligation*, 52 UCLA L. REV. 639 (2005). Like Professor Garrison, this chapter argues that relationships between adults must be grounded in consent.

Marvin v. Marvin in 1976[5] courts have struggled with only limited success with these issues.[6] This chapter raises two concerns about the PRINCIPLES and domestic partnership status. The first is not a criticism, *per se*, but a general concern about this family form. Some observers applaud the declining popularity of marriage as a family form[7] and the blurring of the legal line between marriage and cohabitation. Yet, informal unions, including the PRINCIPLES' domestic partnerships, provide uncertain protection to financially dependent family members because the right to a share of property and support is legally established only after the relationship ends.[8] In contrast, marriage is a status based on registration under which rights and obligations attach at the outset with the exchange of vows. In part for this reason, marriage offers better protection to financially dependent family members than cohabitation. Thus, although enforcement of financial obligations between long-term cohabitants is useful in affording some protection to dependent family members, lawmakers might legitimately favor marriage over cohabitation and be concerned about diluting the distinctions between formal and informal unions.[9] Second, the approach of the domestic partnership provisions in which a marriage-like status attaches automatically at the end of a cohabitation period,[10] without consent or knowledge, and even against the wishes of the individuals involved, is coercive and paternalistic. In theory, partners who do not want to be subject to the property distribution or support rules that apply to marriage can opt out through express agreement.[11]However, the PRINCIPLES' provisions on agreements treat the contracts of cohabiting couples in the same way as premarital agreements, giving courts considerable discretion to set them aside based on a judgment that enforcement would "work a substantial injustice."[12] When taken together with the domestic partnership provisions, the effect is to restrict the freedom of unmarried couples to live together in unions of limited commitment and obligation, a stance that is discordant with contemporary social values.

The paternalistic stance of the domestic partnership provisions is normatively unappealing. It is also unnecessary as a means to provide financial protection to dependent partners in cohabitation unions. This chapter argues that contract theory supports a default rule framework that presumes that property acquired during long-term informal unions is shared and that support is available to dependent parties when these relationships

[5] In *Marvin v. Marvin*, the California Supreme Court held that express and implied contracts between cohabiting parties are enforceable. 557 P.2d 106 (Cal. 1976).

[6] *See infra* Part I.

[7] Patricia A. Cain, *Imagine There's No Marriage*, 16 QUINNIPIAC L. REV. 27 (1996); Nancy D. Polikoff, *supra* note 2; MARTHA ALBERTSON FINEMAN, THE NEUTERED MOTHER, THE SEXUAL FAMILY AND OTHER TWENTIETH CENTURY TRAGEDIES (1995). Marriages have actually increased in numbers in recent years but at a far slower rate than cohabitation. Between 1980 and 2002, the total number of cohabiting heterosexual couples in the United States more than tripled, from 1,589,000 to 4,898,000. U.S. Census Bureau, Table UC–1, *Unmarried Couple Households, by presence of Children: 1960–Present*, June 12, 2003, *at* http://www.census.gov/ population/socdemo/hh-fam/tabUC–1.pdf. During that time the number of marriages increased from 49,112,000 to 56,747,000. U.S. Census Bureau, *Table HH-1, Households by Type: 1960-Present*, June 12, 2003, *at* http://www.census.gov/population/socdemo/ hh-fam/tabHH-1.pdf. The 2000 Census also reported almost 600,000 same-sex couples. U.S. Census Bureau, *Married Couple and Unmarried Partner Households: 2000* 1 (Feb 2003), *at* http://www.census.gov/prod/2003pubs/censr-5.pdf.

[8] PRINCIPLES § 6.02(1).

[9] The drafters do not hold up domestic partnerships as superior to marriage. In fact, they suggest that the obligations that domestic partners would incur removes any incentive to avoid marriage, a valid point. *See* PRINCIPLES § 6.02 cmt. b, at 916.

[10] PRINCIPLES § 6.03.

[11] PRINCIPLES § 6.01(2).

[12] PRINCIPLES § 7.05.

dissolve.[13] Couples who do not wish to be bound by the default rules can opt out by agreement. Default rules that likely reflect the implicit understandings of most couples in marriage-like unions will mitigate the inequity that results today when courts decide that parties' understandings were too ambiguous for contractual enforcement. This autonomy-based framework is based on consent and, in this regard, is superior to the coercive approach of the PRINCIPLES. Moreover, because this approach builds on conventional contract doctrine, it is likely to be more palatable to legal authorities than the innovation proposed by the ALI.

Part I of this chapter describes the legal and social background that led to the adoption of the PRINCIPLES' domestic partnership provisions. Since *Marvin*, courts have been only modestly successful in responding to a growing number of compelling claims by cohabitants. The drafters of the PRINCIPLES perceived a need for legal reform to provide these parties with financial security.[14] Part II describes the key elements of the domestic partnership provisions and explains how they operate in conjunction with the provisions governing agreements to impose what may be an unwanted legal status on many couples. Part III proposes a contract default rule framework and argues that this approach will protect dependent partners in much the same way as the domestic partnership provisions, while respecting the freedom of individuals to order their intimate lives. Part IV examines the domestic partnership provisions as ex post family construction and explains why this approach provides less protection to dependent partners than a registration model, such as marriage.[15]

I. Courts and Cohabitation: *Marvin* and Beyond

The California Supreme Court decided *Marvin v. Marvin*[16] in 1976 against a backdrop of social and demographic change in American society. In less than a generation, a society in which marriage was the only socially sanctioned venue for an intimate relationship had evolved into one in which couples' living arrangements increasingly were viewed as a matter of personal choice. *Marvin* pointed to these changes in social norms, noting that many Americans had abandoned the moral compunctions about nonmarital unions that supported the traditional judicial hostility to contractual claims by these parties; this left no public policy justification for refusing to enforce cohabitants' agreements. The *Marvin* court concluded that express and implied contracts regarding property-sharing and support should be enforceable under ordinary contract principles.[17]

Since *Marvin*, couples in increasing numbers have chosen to live together in informal unions. Census figures report about 5 million cohabiting couples in 2002, three times as many as in 1980.[18] Most of these relationships are of relatively brief duration; one half last a year or less before the couple either terminate the union or marries.[19] However, about

[13] For a discussion of default rules regulating divorce, *see* Elizabeth Scott & Robert Scott, *Marriage as Relational Contract*, 84 VA. L. REV. 1225 (1998). The default rule framework regulating long-term cohabitation unions proposed here is similar in many regards.

[14] PRINCIPLES, Director's Foreword, at xv.

[15] As Part II A *infra* explains, domestic partnership status provides greater protection when the couple has a child together.

[16] *Marvin supra* note 5, at 122.

[17] *Id.*

[18] *See* statistics in note 7 *supra.*

[19] Larry L. Bumpass & Hsien-Hen Lu, *Trends in Cohabitation and Implications for Children's Family Contexts in the United States*, 54 POPULATION STUDIES 29 (2000).

10 percent of cohabiting couples live together for five years or more.[20] Litigation in the quarter century since *Marvin* mostly involves parties in these long-term unions;[21] as the number of cohabiting couples has increased, so have the claims.

Although the claims and stories vary, the reported cases follow a pattern. Often, the couple lived together for many years in a relationship very much like marriage; their friends and neighbors may have assumed that they *were* married.[22] Many of these cohabiting couples had children together and adopted traditional marital roles. The woman typically fulfilled household responsibilities, caring for the children and perhaps helping in a family business, while the man typically was the primary income earner. When the relationship ended, he held title to most of the property acquired during their time together and had a much higher earning capacity. The typical claim is brought in contract by the woman for a share of the property acquired during the union, compensation for services (either domestic or to a business owned by the other party), or for financial support.

Courts generally have been sympathetic to these claims, at least in principle, sometimes noting that claimants in these marriage-like unions would be entitled to a share of property and support if the couple in fact had married. Following *Marvin*, most courts have held that express agreements between cohabitants are enforceable.[23] Only three states, citing the traditional public policy grounds, have refused to enforce these contracts altogether in opinions that today seem outdated and moralistic.[24] Most states will enforce oral as well as written agreements, although a few states, by statute, require that agreements between cohabitants must be in writing.[25]

The response to financial claims by cohabitating parties based on conduct rather than express promise have been mixed.[26] Under general contract doctrine, contracts implied in fact are legally enforceable if the conduct is promissory – that is, if it is sufficiently clear to demonstrate an understanding between the parties that an obligation exists. A number of courts have followed *Marvin* in holding that implied contracts should be recognized in this

[20] *Id.*

[21] A casual survey of reported cases suggests that most claimants lived together for more than 10 years – often 15, 20, or more years. *See, e.g.*, Hay v. Hay, 678 P.2d 672 (Nev. 1984); Morone v. Morone, 413 N.E.2d. 1154 (N.Y. 1980); Friedman v. Friedman, 24 Cal. Rptr. 892 (Cal. Ct. App. 1994); Cook v. Cook, 691 P.2d 664 (Ariz. 1984); Recigno v. Recigno, No. A-2023–01t5 (N.J. Super. Ct. App. Div. Jan. 7, 2003). The seven year relationship in *Marvin* is far shorter than most, perhaps the substantial financial stakes resulting from Lee Marvin's successful acting career Ied Michelle to sue.

[22] *Id.*

[23] Ira Ellman et. Al., Family Law: Cases, Texts, Problems, 890–91, 4th ed. (2004).

[24] Illinois, Georgia, and Louisiana courts have declined to enforce cohabitation contracts since *Marvin*, although none of the cases is very recent. *See* Hewitt v. Hewitt, 394 N.E.2d 1204 (Ill. 1979); Schwegman v. Schwegman, 441 So. 2d 316 (La. App. 1983); Rehak v. Mathis, 238 S.E.2d 81 (Ga. 1977).

[25] *See* Kozlowski v. Kozlowski, 403 A.2d 902 (N.J. 1979) (finding an express oral contract for support in the man's statement during the relationship that he would support the woman for the rest of her life if she would return to live with him). Other courts have recognized express oral contracts to share property. *See* Cook v. Cook, 691 P.2d 664 (Ariz. 1984); Knauer v. Knauer, 470 A.2d 553 (Pa. Super. Ct. 1984). Statutes requiring that agreements be in writing include Minn. Stat. § 513.075 (2003).

[26] Although some courts have insisted that only express contracts between cohabitants will be enforced, many have been more open to implied contracts. *Compare* Morone v. Morone, 413 N.E.2d. 1154, 1159 (N.Y. 1980); Merrill v. Davis, 673 P.2d 1285 (N.M. 1983); Tapley v. Tapley, 449 A.2d 1218 (N.H. 1982) (enforcing only express contracts) *with* Goode v. Goode, 396 S.E.2d 430 (W. Va. 1990); Boland v. Catalano, 521 A.2d 142 (Conn. 1987); Watts v. Watts, 405 N.W.2d 303 (Wis. 1987); Hay v. Hay, 678 P.2d 672 (Nev. 1984); Marvin v. Marvin, 557 P.2d 106, 122 (Cal. 1976) (finding express and implied-in-fact contracts enforced). *See also* Kozlowski v. Kozlowski, 403 A.2d 902, 907–08 (N.J. 1979).

context.[27] In evaluating implied contract claims to share property, courts have pointed to the parties' extensive financial intermingling and claimants' substantial contributions to income and property acquisition as conduct that supports enforcement, but some courts also emphasize the nature of the cohabiting relationship and evidence of marriage-like sharing generally.[28] Duration is also important; courts only find implied contracts in unions of long duration.[29]

Even in these cases, however, many claims fail. Although a few courts have implicitly suggested that living together in a long-term marriage-like union is evidence of the parties' intentions to undertake marriage-like sharing of property,[30] others have emphasized that cohabitation, *per se*, is not conduct that implies financial sharing.[31] Moreover, even courts that emphasize the duration and the marriage-like nature of the relationship often also require substantial intermingling of assets and mutual contribution by claimants to the acquisition of property.[32] Thus, even where the parties' conduct mirrored that of a long-time married couple, and evidence suggests that they had some understanding about the sharing of property acquired while they were together, courts often conclude that the parties' understandings were too indefinite for contractual enforcement.[33]

Former cohabitants seeking compensation for domestic services or postdissolution support on the basis of implied contract have been less successful than those making property claims, as courts have declined to infer promissory conduct from the parties' adoption of marital roles.[34] Indeed some courts have adopted an implicit default rule presuming that services provided by one cohabiting party to the other are gratuitous.[35] Thus, the traditional marital role division in which one partner performs household services and the other provides support while investing in his own human capital carries no promissory meaning regarding future support – although this is precisely the situation in which spousal support is ordered. Indeed, it is unclear what conduct would be deemed sufficient to sustain such an implied contract claim for support.[36]

[27] Wallender v. Wallender, 870 P.2d 232, 234 (Or. Ct. App. 1994); *Glasgo* v. Glasgo, 410 N.E.2d at 1325 (Ind. Ct. App. 1980). *See also supra* note 26.

[28] An Oregon appellate court suggested that the determination of whether the parties implicitly agreed to share assets equally should be based *inter alia* on "how the parties held themselves out to the community, the nature of the cohabitation, [and] joint acts of a financial nature, if any . . . and the respective financial and non-financial contributions of each party." *Wallender*, 870 P.2d at 234. *See also Glasgo*, 410 N.E.2d at 1325 (finding intent in situation and relation of parties). Courts also point to a course of conduct between the parties as evidence of an oral agreement. *See Cook*, 691 P.2d at 667. Professor Ann Estin points out that the line between express oral agreements and agreements implied from conduct is murky, but can be quite important in jurisdictions that recognize the former but not the latter. *See* Ann Laquer Estin, *Ordinary Cohabitation*, 76 Notre Dame L. Rev. 1381 (2001). *See also* Morone v. Morone, 413 N.E.2d. 1154 (N.Y. 1980).

[29] *See* Ann Estin, *supra* note 28. A Nevada court, reviewing a claim by a woman whose twenty-three-year union dissolved, concluded that an agreement by the couple to hold property as if they were married could be found by looking at the "purpose, duration and stability of the relationship and the expectations of the parties." Hay v. Hay, 678 P.2d 672, 674 (Nev. 1984). The court went on to say that where it is "proven that there was an agreement to acquire and hold property as if the couple was married, the community property laws of the state will apply by analogy." *Id.*

[30] *Hay*, 678 P.2d 672.

[31] *See* Ann Estin, *supra* note 28, at 1393.

[32] Wallender v. Wallender, 870 P.2d 232, 234 (Or. Ct. App. 1994);

[33] *See, e.g.*, Morone v. Morone, 413 N.E.2d. 1154 (N.Y. 1980).

[34] Friedman v. Friedman, 24 Cal. Rptr. 2d 892, 899 (Cal. Ct. App. 1993).

[35] This of course defeats claims for compensation for those services and excludes evidence of the provision of household services in implied contract claims for support.

[36] In *Friedman*, 24 Cal.Rptr. at 899, a California appeals court noted that, although implied contract claims are recognized in California, no support order based on implied contract has been upheld on appeal.

Friedman v. Friedman, a post-*Marvin* California case, demonstrates the difficulties that claimants face in when they seek post-dissolution support in the absence of an express written contract – even in a jurisdiction that is relatively open to implied contract claims.[37] The Friedmans lived together for 21 years beginning in 1967 and had two children. Believing that marriage was unnecessary for a lifelong commitment, they vowed to be "husband and wife . . . partners in all respects without any sanction from the state."[38] In 1979, Elliott went to law school and pursued a successful career as a lawyer. Terri's plans to complete college fell through due to their child's illness; during the union, she cared for the children and home. A plan to get married in 1982 was postponed and the marriage never took place. Nonetheless, the couple held themselves out as husband and wife to the IRS, and in acquiring insurance and real estate. When they separated, Elliott continued to make voluntary monthly support payments to Terri for four years in the total amount of $190,000. The California appeals court rejected Terri's claim for support, declining to infer promissory conduct from the couple's adoption of marital roles or from Elliott's support payments. The court emphasized that the couple chose to live "without any sanction of the state," in support of its conclusion that they did not intend to be bound by state laws pertaining to support. Finally, in the court's view, ordering support in cases like *Friedman* would have the effect of resurrecting common law marriage, which had been abolished by the legislature.[39]

Some courts go a step further, limiting enforcement to express agreements. For example, in *Morone v. Morone*, the New York Court of Appeals rejected an implied contract claim for compensation for domestic and business services arising out of a twenty-five-year relationship in which the couple lived together as husband and wife and had two children.[40] The court noted the presumption that domestic services are offered gratuitously.[41] Beyond this, however, the Court found implied contracts to be simply too amorphous to enforce.

> For courts to attempt through hindsight to sort out the intentions of parties and affix jural significance to conduct carried out within an essentially private and non-contractual relationship runs too great a risk of error. Absent an express agreement . . . [t]here is . . . substantially greater risk of emotion-laden afterthought, not to mention fraud, in attempting to ascertain by implication what services, if any, were rendered gratuitously, and what compensation, if any, the parties intended to be paid.[42]

Courts sometimes have adopted other theories in efforts to achieve fair outcomes in cases involving financial claims by cohabitants. Some courts have relied on equitable principles such as constructive trust or common law (or implied) partnership in ordering property distribution to both cohabitants, where one party holds title to property that was acquired or improved through the contribution of both parties.[43] Even where one party tried to protect assets from future claims by the other, courts occasionally will recognize contribution as a basis of recovery on equitable grounds.[44] Finally, restitution and *quantum*

[37] *Id.*

[38] *Id.* at 894.

[39] This is clearly a weak argument, since common law marriage is recognized as marriage for all purposes, including state benefits. Terri Friedman, in contrast, made a narrow *inter se* claim for support.

[40] Morone v. Morone, 413 N.E.2d 1154 (N.Y. 1980).

[41] *Id.* at 1157.

[42] *Id.*

[43] Pickens v. Pickens, 490 So.2d 872 (Miss. 1986); Shuraleff v. Donnelly, 817 P.2d 764 (Or. Ct. App. 1991).

[44] *Shuraleff*, 817 P.2d at 764.

meruit are sometimes available to cohabiting partners who make financial investments in business ventures or real estate, or who provide services in a partner's business.[45]

Despite efforts by courts to achieve fairness in financial disputes between cohabitants, claimants have not had an impressive record of success in the post-*Marvin* period. Although express written contracts are routinely enforced today, it seems likely that few cohabiting couples execute written agreements clarifying their intentions regarding property sharing and support on the dissolution of their relationship. Oral agreements are also generally enforceable, but present proof problems of the "he-said, she-said" variety. Finally, although many courts recognize implied contracts in principle, and claimants sometimes prevail on this theory, enforcement of contracts based on conduct in general has been an uncertain business.

In part, the enforcement problem derives from the reality that cohabiting couples have varying expectations about financial interdependency. Some couples may assume that property and income acquired while the couple lives together are not shared – this may be the reason they did not marry. Some may engage in income pooling, but expect that property is separate, while others may assume that income and property are shared, but that the support obligation ends when the relationship dissolves. Still other unmarried couples may view their mutual obligations as indistinguishable from marriage. Finally, the parties may not even have the *same* expectations about financial sharing, particularly upon dissolution. One may believe that the union is marriage-like, while the other prefers cohabitation over marriage as a means of enjoying the benefits of marriage while limiting financial obligations. Given this variety of possibilities, it is not surprising that courts have difficulty determining accurately the parties' expectations about financial sharing and support on the basis of their conduct.

In part for these reasons, enforcement of implied contracts by cohabitants has been uncertain and costly. Even where the parties hold themselves out as a married couple for many years, courts may conclude that their understandings were not sufficiently definite for contractual enforcement.[46] Moreover, the process of adjudicating these claims is costly and cumbersome, as parties present evidence of behavior over many years that was, or was not, implicit with promise. The unpredictability of outcomes discourages settlements. The upshot is that although post-*Marvin* courts generally have been sympathetic to these claims, the results have been unsatisfactory from the perspective of protecting financially vulnerable parties.

II. The Status Alternative: The ALI's Domestic Partnership Principles

In response to the legal developments described in Part I, some observers concluded that contract doctrine was inadequate as a framework for enforcing financial obligations between parties in informal unions. Among the most outspoken critics were Professors Ira Ellman and Grace Blumberg. Professor Ellman, a long-time skeptic about the use of contract as a mechanism for regulating financial obligations in intimate relationships

[45] Kaiser v. Fleming, 735 N.E.2d 144 (Ill. App. Ct. 2000); Salzmann v. Bachrach, 996 P.2d 1263 (Colo. 2000).

[46] E. Allan Farnsworth, Contracts § 3.27, at 207–09 (Aspen 3d ed. 1999) (discussing indefiniteness of contract terms as basis for non-enforcement). *See also* Friedman v. Friedman, 24 Cal. Rptr. 2d 892, 899 (Cal. Ct. App. 1993) (finding insufficient evidence of agreement to provide support).

generally, has challenged the feasibility of using a contract framework in this setting.[47] He argues that unmarried couples do not think in contractual terms, and seldom have understandings about financial obligations upon dissolution that are sufficiently clear to permit legal enforcement as contract terms. Similarly, in a 1980 article, Professor Blumberg criticized *Marvin* and implied contract, and argued instead that cohabitation should be treated as a status that carries financial obligations.[48] As Chief Reporter of the PRINCIPLES and Reporter of the Domestic Partnership chapter, respectively, Professors Ellman and Blumberg are the intellectual architects of the ALI's domestic partnership status.[49] Not surprisingly, the PRINCIPLES embody their rejection of a contract framework and substitute a nonconsensual status as the mechanism for enforcing financial obligations between intimate partners.

A. Creating Domestic Partnerships under the PRINCIPLES

At the outset, it should be noted that a domestic partnership under the PRINCIPLES differs considerably from the standard version of this status, which is available through registration and typically carries relatively limited government benefits.[50] The PRINCIPLES, in contrast, offer a standard by which courts can evaluate financial disputes between intimate partners when informal unions dissolve: If the court determines ex post that the relationship was a domestic partnership, it is subject to the rules for property division and compensatory support payments that apply to marriage.[51] In this regard, the PRINCIPLES' partnership status is like common law marriage, but the PRINCIPLES' status affects only obligations between the parties; it does not affect government benefits or otherwise create a privileged legal status.[52]

Under the PRINCIPLES, same- or opposite-sex couples who live together for a prescribed cohabitation period are presumed to be domestic partners.[53] The Comments suggest that a three year cohabitation period is a "reasonable choice" for couples without children but do not urge states to adopt any particular period.[54] If the status is contested, the presumption that the couple were domestic partners can be rebutted by a demonstration that they did

[47] Ira Mark Ellman, *"Contract Thinking" Was Marvin's Fatal Flaw*, 76 NOTRE DAME L. REV. 1365 (2000–01). Professor Ellman has also rejected contract as a theory to justify spousal support obligations. *See* Ira Mark Ellman, *The Theory of Alimony*, 77 CAL. L. REV. 1 (1989).

[48] Grace Blumberg, *Cohabitation Without Marriage: A Different Perspective*, 28 UCLA L. REV. 1125 (1981). Professor Blumberg points to what she views as the artificiality of finding intent in this context, and also to the unfairness of contract given the unequal bargaining power of the parties. *See also* Grace Blumberg, *The Regularization of Non-Marital Cohabitation*, 76 NOTRE DAME L. REV. 1265 (2001).

[49] Professor Ellman was the Chief Reporter of the PRINCIPLES and Professor Blumberg was the Reporter for Chapter 6 on Domestic Partners.

[50] Many domestic partnership laws take the form of municipal ordinances designed to provide limited government benefits (health and life insurance for partners of government employees) for same-sex couples. In 2003, California enacted a comprehensive domestic partnership statute which extends to same-sex couples who register as domestic partners the legal "rights, protections, benefits and responsibilities" that are granted to spouses. California Registered Domestic Partners Rights and Responsibilities Act of 2003, Cal. Fam. Code §297 et seq. (West 2005). Several European countries have adopted comprehensive "registered partnership" laws, which extend marital rights to same-sex couples. *See* IRA ELLMAN, ET. AL, *supra* note 23 at 913.

[51] PRINCIPLES § 6.05–6.06.

[52] PRINCIPLES § 6.01, cmt. a.

[53] PRINCIPLES § 6.03.

[54] For parties with children, a two year cohabitation period is suggested. *See* PRINCIPLES § 6.03 cmt. d, at 921.

not "share a life together as a couple," a determination that can involve a broad ranging inquiry into the nature of the relationship.[55] Factors that can be considered include whether the couple intermingled finances, maintained a "qualitatively distinct relationship," shared emotional or physical intimacy, assumed specialized roles, or acknowledged a commitment to one another.[56]

Where domestic partners have a common child, the status is established when the cohabitation period passes, and cannot be challenged thereafter on other grounds.[57] The Comments suggest that the cohabitation period should be of shorter duration in these cases.[58] Thus, for the couple with a common child, the PRINCIPLES create a bright line rule – in contrast to the standard that applies to couples without children.

Domestic partnership status is imposed automatically at the end of the cohabitation period, without the parties' consent or, it seems likely, even their knowledge in many cases.[59] Couples who do not want to be subject to the property distribution and support obligations of marriage can opt out through express agreement – at least in theory.[60] However, Chapter 7 treats agreements between cohabitants the same as premarital agreements, giving judges broad discretion regarding enforcement.[61] This authority is triggered if enforcement would "work a substantial injustice" and either a certain number of years has passed since the agreement was executed or a significant change of circumstances has occurred that was not anticipated at the time of execution.[62] A "substantial injustice" can be found under the standards if a large disparity exists between the financial distribution under the agreement and the outcome otherwise prescribed by law.[63]

B. Evaluating the ALI Approach

Domestic partnership status under the PRINCIPLES promises to provide greater financial protection to dependent parties in informal unions than is available under contemporary contract doctrine.[64] Today, in the absence of a written agreement, a heavy burden falls on the claimant to establish the parties' understanding. In contrast, the PRINCIPLES create a useful presumption that financial obligations attach after a set period of cohabitation.[65] This approach will mitigate real hardship and unfairness by enforcing expectations in

[55] PRINCIPLES § 6.03(3).

[56] PRINCIPLES § 6.03(7). Other factors include: oral and written statements regarding the relationship; the extent to which the relationship fostered economic interdependence or the economic dependence of one party on the other; naming in a life insurance policy, will, or in an employee benefits plan; and the extent to which the relationship "wrought change in the life of either or both parties." *Id.*

[57] PRINCIPLES § 6.03(2).

[58] PRINCIPLES § 6.03 cmt. c, at 921.

[59] PRINCIPLES § 6.03.

[60] PRINCIPLES § 6.01(2). However, Chapter 7 of the PRINCIPLES regulates agreements between parties that opt out of the obligations established under the PRINCIPLES. PRINCIPLES § 7.02.

[61] PRINCIPLES §§ 7.04, 7.05. The Commentary in Chapter 7 of the PRINCIPLES emphasizes that contracts dealing with the consequences of family dissolution cannot be enforced under standard contract doctrine that applies to commercial contracts because married individuals are subject to cognitive limitations in their capacity to anticipate dissolution, and also because of the differences between intimate and commercial relationships. *See* PRINCIPLES § 7.02 cmt. a and b, at 954–55.

[62] PRINCIPLES § 7.05(2).

[63] *Id.* at (2)(c).

[64] PRINCIPLES § 6.05–6.06.

[65] PRINCIPLES §§ 6.02, 6.03.

long-term marriage-like unions and by discouraging exploitation by parties with greater financial sophistication and resources.

For couples with common children, the PRINCIPLES create an efficient bright line rule, which offers certainty to dependent partners (after a set period) about their entitlement to a share of property and support under the rules that apply to married couples.[66] The PRINCIPLES offer benefits to children of cohabiting couples that are available to children of married parents, implicitly recognizing that after divorce, spousal support, and marital property function to supplement child support as a means of providing financial security to children.[67] Under the domestic partnership provisions, the tangible evidence of the child's existence suffices to establish the claim once the cohabitation period passes. Thus, litigation is discouraged and settlement promoted. Moreover, the PRINCIPLES' treatment of agreements virtually invites courts to set aside agreements executed before children are born.[68] One downside exists: The status may have the unintended destabilizing effect of encouraging some parents to leave the home before the cohabitation period runs to avoid the legal obligations imposed on domestic partners. On the whole, however, the PRINCIPLES offer a relatively efficient mechanism to create financial entitlements for vulnerable partners and their children.

For couples without children, the mechanism is much more cumbersome and applying the standard to determine whether a union qualifies as a domestic partnership is costly, intrusive, and fraught with uncertainty. In jurisdictions that adopt a three-year cohabitation period, as suggested in the Comments,[69] the new status may generate a flood of litigation by hopeful claimants. With a cohabitation period of such modest duration, it seems likely that many marginal claims will arise when informal unions dissolve, given the indeterminacy of the standard and the payoff for successful claimants. Moreover, under the complex and indeterminate standard for testing the presumption of domestic partnership status, expensive and intrusive inquiries often will be necessary to discern whether the relationship qualifies as a domestic partnership. (Precisely what evidence will be offered of the parties' emotional and physical intimacy?) The upshot is that although the PRINCIPLES offer greater financial protection than currently constructed contract law, domestic partnership status provides only modest financial security to dependent partners through a costly process that is likely to burden the justice system as well as the claimants.

More problematic is the nonconsensual nature of the status and the coercive constraints on opting out. In contemporary American society, the freedom of individuals to order their intimate lives without undue government interference is well accepted – and protected by law.[70] Adult relationships are assumed to be grounded in consent. In this context, the imposition of an unchosen and often unwanted status on couples who have opted not to marry challenges contemporary social values. Especially if the suggested three-year cohabitation period is adopted, the obligations of marriage will be imposed on many couples whose relationships involve a more casual commitment.[71] To be sure, the imposition

[66] PRINCIPLES §6.04(2).

[67] PRINCIPLES §§6.04, 6.05, 6.06.

[68] PRINCIPLES § 7.05(2)(b).

[69] PRINCIPLES § 6.03, cmt. c, at 921.

[70] In *Lawrence v. Texas*, 123 S. Ct. 2472 (2003), the U.S. Supreme Court found that a criminal statute that prohibited sodomy between consenting adults violated privacy rights protected by the Due Process Clause of the Fourteenth Amendment.

[71] Part III *infra* argues that a presumption of marriage-like commitment may arise in unions of longer duration. *See* t.a.n. notes 53–54.

of obligations may be warranted when the interests of children are affected; assigning domestic partnership status to cohabiting parents can be justified on this ground. Where only the interests of autonomous adults are implicated, however, the ALI's stance is harder to justify.

Given the beneficial purposes of domestic partnership provisions, however, the automatic imposition of partnership status might seem like a small price, were it not for the obstacles that confront couples who seek to contract out. The PRINCIPLES give courts far broader power to review agreements between cohabitants than does current law.[72] Thus, parties who want relationships of more limited commitment and obligation than marriage can have no assurance that their understandings will be enforced.[73] They must recognize that in the future a court can set aside their agreement for unfairness if it decides that circumstances have changed or even if a number of years have passed.[74] Under this approach, much of the benefit of contracting is lost and some parties may be unwilling to enter informal unions on these terms. The PRINCIPLES do not recognize that some couples may choose cohabitation over marriage *because* they desire a union of limited commitment. Interestingly, this possibility is not included in a laundry list of reasons that cohabiting couples fail to marry offered in the Comments.[75] At least implicitly, the PRINCIPLES take the normative position that cohabiting couples should not be free to choose long-term relationships of limited commitment, and that the future claimant is better off without the relationship should her partner decide against cohabitation in the face of the uncertainty of contract enforcement under the PRINCIPLES.[76] And yet, it seems likely that some individuals would knowingly choose to risk financial insecurity in the future for a relationship that they value and the support it provides while intact.[77]

The core deficiency of the PRINCIPLES' approach to agreements, in my view, is that contracts between cohabitants are treated like premarital agreements. There may be good reasons to constrain the freedom of individuals who marry from opting out of their obligations to one another, by giving courts some discretionary authority over enforcement of premarital agreements. Marriage is a status with a clear social meaning and with extensive social and legal privileges that rewards spouses for undertaking a commitment to support and care for one another, a commitment that relieves society of some of the burden of dependency.[78] Legal regulations that restrict the freedom of married couples in this context

[72] Under traditional law, courts routinely refused to enforce premarital agreements on grounds of substantive unfairness. Today, however, many states have adopted the Uniform Premarital Agreement Act, under which premarital agreements can be set aside for flaws in execution, but not for unfairness at the time of enforcement. As described earlier, clear agreements between cohabitants are now routinely enforced by courts, and it is unlikely that courts would set agreements on grounds of substantive unfairness.

[73] PRINCIPLES § 7.05.

[74] PRINCIPLES § 7.05.

[75] PRINCIPLES § 6.02 cmt. a, at 914. The Comment mentions the following as reasons that couples do not marry: objections to the institution of marriage due to a bad experience in a prior marriage, awkwardness at changing status after living together a long time, religious and ethnic group norms, inequality of bargaining power that allows one party to resist marriage, and state law prohibitions of same sex marriage.

[76] Imagine the situation in which Lee Marvin is advised by his attorney that he cannot count on enforcement of a cohabitation agreement with Michelle and decides not to continue cohabitation on that basis. The PRINCIPLES seem to take the position that Michelle would not rationally choose the relationship of limited commitment that is the only one Lee is offering, and that she cannot be allowed to do so.

[77] For Michelle Marvin, for example, the prospect of living a glamorous life with a famous movie star for some time might be worth the cost of adjusting to life without Lee and his money in the future.

[78] This argument is developed in Elizabeth Scott, *Marriage, Cohabitation and Collective Responsibility for Dependency*, 2004 U. CHI. LEGAL F. 225.

can be justified on this ground.[79] Paternalistic restrictions on contracts between cohabitants cannot be similarly justified. Those couples who execute opt-out contracts are announcing thereby that their relationship is not the same as marriage. Effectively, the PRINCIPLES preclude this choice, narrowing the spectrum of legally sanctioned relationship options. In a context in which social and legal norms favor neutrality toward individual choices in the realm of intimate association, such paternalism is not justified.

III. Enforcement of Obligations in a Contract Default Rule Framework

The coercive approach of the domestic partnership provisions is not only incompatible with contemporary values; it is also unnecessary as a means to provide financial protection to dependent partners. In this Part, I argue that the drafters too quickly abandoned contract for status. A framework of contract default rules grounded in consent can largely accomplish the same objectives as domestic partnership status without heavy-handed paternalism. Contract law can provide efficient default rules that clarify the implied understandings about property and support obligations between parties in long-term intimate unions, facilitating legal enforcement and simplifying the judicial evaluation of these claims.

The simple premise of the default framework proposed here is that where a couple provides clear evidence through their conduct that the relationship is marriage-like, an agreement to assume marital obligations can be inferred – and legally enforced. A couple who live together for many years, sharing a life and financial resources, and holding themselves out as husband and wife can be presumed to intend to share the property acquired during the relationship.[80] Further, it is a sound presumption that a couple who assume traditional marital roles of wage earner and homemaker over a long period of time intend to provide the financially dependent partner with "insurance" in the form of support, should the relationship dissolve, regardless of which party ends the union.[81] The legal obligations of spousal support and property sharing represent the default terms of the marriage contract implicitly undertaken by spouses; these obligations should also be incurred by parties in long-term marriage-like informal unions.

The challenge is to design clear criteria that separate marriage-like unions from those in which the parties are not married because they do not want marital commitment or obligations. The framework should be as simple as possible, in order to clarify obligations and promote certainty for both courts and parties. The PRINCIPLES' approach to couples with children satisfies this criterion.[82] For couples without children, a cohabitation period of substantial duration is the best available proxy for commitment, and the only practical means to avoid an intrusive and error-prone inquiry in the effort to distinguish marriage-like relationships from more typical informal unions that involve less financial

[79] This regulation comes in the form of the greater authority of courts to set aside premarital agreements than they have in the context of commercial contracts. *See* Scott, *id.*

[80] Some courts have implicitly adopted this approach. In *Recigno, supra* note 22, at *5, the court, in recognizing a joint venture and dividing the assets between a couple who lived together for twenty-six years, emphasized the extent to which the parties had conducted themselves as husband and wife in every aspect of their lives. The court stated that "the nature of the relationship was truly a joint venture of a personal and business nature ... it was the mutual intent of the parties to be partners." *Id.*

[81] *See* Scott & Scott, *supra* note 13, at 1247 (arguing that parties in a hypothetical bargain before marriage would agree to provide postdissolution support as insurance against the risks of assuming a marital role that results in financial vulnerability regardless of fault or either party's role in ending the union).

[82] *See* PRINCIPLES § 6.03(5).

interdependency. A cohabitation period of at least five years, for example, supports a presumption that the relationship was marriage-like and also discourages opportunistic and marginal claims. A five-year period will significantly limit the category of claimants, because most informal unions do not last this long.[83] Thus, a default rule based on this duration promises to be a relatively accurate sorting mechanism for separating marriage-like relationships from casual unions. Although some deserving parties will not receive the benefit of this durational default rule, dependent partners in long-term unions present the most compelling claims, and these parties will be protected.

The proposed default rule framework represents a significant improvement over current contract doctrine. Today, as Part I explained, many claims fail, although it seems likely either that the parties had some agreement or that one partner misled or exploited the other. Default rules clarify that the conduct of couples in long-term unions will be deemed promissory unless the parties opt out of the rule. The framework functions effectively whether or not the parties have similar understandings of the terms of their commitment to one another. In most unions of long duration, the presumption that the relationship is marriage-like probably represents accurately the parties' explicit or implicit understanding about property sharing and support, and thus the framework simply functions as a standard majoritarian default. Where the default rule does not reflect both parties' expectations, it has a useful information-forcing function, putting the burden on the party who opposes enforcement of the default rule to identify himself explicitly as a "non-committer."[84] This will protect dependent individuals from exploitation by partners who are motivated to withhold information about their intentions for strategic purposes.

The risk of exploitation is substantial today. In contrast to marriage, cohabitation in itself provides no clear signal of commitment, and it may be difficult for individuals to discern whether their partner's intentions are the same as their own. Under current doctrine, a primary wage earner who does not wish to undertake legal obligations to his homemaker partner can withhold this information, allowing her to assume that they will share property acquired during the time they are together and that he will provide support should the relationship end.[85] Meanwhile, he is free to structure financial arrangements in ways that undermine her future claims.[86] In this way, he can reap substantial benefits from the relationship, and incur no obligations when it ends.

The proposed framework presents the primary wage earner with two options: He can (perhaps grudgingly) accept the legal obligations that follow from the application of the default rule as the cost of being in a long-term intimate union, or, if this is unacceptable, he can disclose to his partner his intentions not to engage in financial sharing[87] and seek

[83] Only about 10% of cohabitants who do not marry are still together five years later. Larry L. Bumpass & Hsien-Hen Lu, *supra* note 19. Clearly, parties can enter a cohabitation union with marriage-like commitment from the outset, but duration is the only practical means by which third parties can identify marriage-like unions ex post.

[84] Majoritarian default rules, in general, have this information-forcing property as applied to parties who want to opt out. For a discussion of default rules generally and their information-forcing properties, see Ian Ayres & Robert Gertner, *Filling Gaps in Incomplete Contracts: An Economic Theory of Default Rules*, 99 Yale L. J. 87 (1989–90). *See also* Robert Scott, *A Relational Theory of Default Rules for Commercial Contracts*, 19 J. L. Stud. 597, 606–13 (1990).

[85] The male pronoun is used because typically (although clearly not always) men in cohabitation unions are primary wage earners and property owners.

[86] He may do this by maintaining separate bank accounts and by acquiring real and personal property titled only in his name.

[87] Ayres and Gertner argue that penalty default rules can function to influence parties who strategically withhold information to disclose (so that they will not be bound by the default rule), leading to more efficient contracts.

to persuade her to opt out.[88] In the latter situation, the partner can make an informed choice about whether to end the union or to assume a role that leaves her financially vulnerable.[89] In any event, the default rule allows the parties to act upon more complete information about the financial terms of their relationship, reducing misunderstanding and exploitation.[90]

In comparison to current contract doctrine, the default rule approach simplifies the judicial determination of financial obligations between cohabitants; it avoids an open-ended inquiry into the parties' expectations in every case. Although fact finding will sometimes be complex, the framework provides a means to enforce the sometimes opaque financial understandings between cohabiting partners.[91] The default framework offers far greater financial security than does current law to the vulnerable partners who otherwise may be exploited or misled – or who may simply have a different understanding of the relationship than the primary wage-earning partner. To enhance this protection, courts can require a written agreement as clear evidence of the parties' intentions to opt out of their financial obligations to one another.[92]

The contract-based default framework has some advantages over the PRINCIPLES' approach, although outcomes under each would often be quite similar. First, the five-year time period proposed here will function more effectively than the shorter period suggested by the PRINCIPLES to separate casual from committed unions and to reduce litigation.[93] A more important advantage of the proposed contract default framework is that it builds incrementally on conventional legal doctrine regulating contract claims by parties in informal unions that has developed over the past generation. Indeed, a few

Ayres and Gertner, 99 YALE L. J. at 87. In the context of intimate unions, nondisclosure by the noncommitter is likely more efficient at least from a social welfare perspective, in that it will result in a contract based on the default rule.

[88] A rule that requires a written agreement to opt out of the default rule affords better protection of vulnerable parties, and simplifies and narrows the scope of relevant evidence. *See infra* note 92 and accompanying text.

[89] The dependant party has another alternative; she can adapt her role in the relationship so that she is more financially self-sufficient. Herma Hill Kay, *Equality and Difference: A Perspective on No-Fault Divorce and Its Aftermath*, 56 U. CIN. L. REV. 1 (1987) (arguing that adaptation of marital roles toward egalitarian sharing of parenting and other domestic duties will reduce women's dependency and encourage financial self-sufficiency).

[90] Although not all parties will be aware of the default rules, the partner who owns property and is the primary wage earner is likely to be more legally and financially sophisticated than the dependent partner. Thus, a default rule that puts the burden on the former to initiate an agreement to opt out is superior to current law, under which that party benefits if the default rule is applied.

[91] Professor Carol Rose's famous distinction between "crystal" and "muddy" rules in property law is apt in this context. Carol M. Rose, *Crystals and Mud in Property Law*, 40 STAN. L. REV. 577 (1988). Rose observes that human behavior cannot be compelled by "perfect specification of unchanging rights and obligations." *Id.* at 607. Although clear rules defining property rights generally are to be preferred, Professor Rose argues, they can sometimes function to allow the powerful to take advantage of the weak and gullible. When that happens, courts resort to "muddy" rules to achieve equitable solutions. In the realm of intimate unions, lawmakers legitimately might prefer that all couples choose marriage, a "crystal" category, but provide the protection of "muddy" default rules for unmarried parties who otherwise may be taken advantage of by their partners.

[92] An analogy is the implied warranty of merchantability (U.C.C. § 2–314 (1998), which is a default term in every contract for the sale of goods by a merchant seller. This warranty can be waived, but only by written agreement. This approach affords better protection to consumers, whose claims otherwise may face challenges that the warranty was verbally waived by the seller. In the cohabitation context, unless a written agreement is required to opt out of duties in informal unions, higher-earning partners can simply argue that they had made clear to the partner during the union that they had no intention to share property or provide support upon termination of the union. *See* Friedman, *supra* note 34.

[93] The PRINCIPLES do not urge the shorter cohabitation period and jurisdictions are free to adopt a five year (or more) period. *See supra* note 69 and accompanying text.

courts considering implied contract claims by cohabitants have come close to adopting the proposed default rule, finding promissory conduct in the marriage-like character of the relationship.[94] In contrast, the PRINCIPLES' domestic partnership status represents a bold innovation that legislatures and courts are likely to view with some wariness. This may explain the tepid response to these proposals to date.[95] Despite considerable academic interest, legal authorities have paid little attention to the domestic partnership provisions of the PRINCIPLES – in contrast to the response to other provisions.[96]

Finally, and most fundamentally, a contractual framework is compatible with liberal values, and thus has a normative appeal that the PRINCIPLES' status-based approach lacks. The proposed default rules rest on realistic empirical assumptions about the intentions of many couples in long-term informal unions, while at the same time offering protection to naïve parties whose expectations may not be shared by their partners. The framework recognizes, however, that sometimes one party will reject financial sharing as a condition of continuing the relationship, and his or her partner will agree – willingly or grudgingly – and choose to remain in the union. Parties are free to contract out of default rules and courts will enforce their agreements. The PRINCIPLES' approach implicitly assumes that financially vulnerable partners would (or should) always choose no relationship over a relationship without financial security;[97] in fact, some may prefer a shared life without financial entitlements. Adults with full information should be free to make these choices. To be sure, sometimes the outcome under the default framework may result in inequity; dependent partners may be persuaded to waive financial entitlements that they otherwise would receive. However, the alternative of paternalistically imposing financial obligations on unchoosing (and even unwilling) parties after a certain period of cohabitation is even less satisfactory. Although an imposed status may sometimes beneficially deter exploitation of dependent partners, it does so at a considerable cost to individual freedom.

Not so long ago, both law and morality narrowly circumscribed the freedom of individuals to make choices about intimate affiliation. Today, some people are nostalgic about a society in which marriage was the only acceptable intimate union. Most modern persons, however, endorse the core liberal principle that government should not interfere with the freedom of individuals to pursue their goals for personal happiness, absent some evidence that their choices will cause harm to others. Some couples may want to live together without commitment or obligation in long-term relationships. As long as each partner voluntarily chooses this arrangement and is free to leave the relationship, paternalistic government restrictions that inhibit freedom in this private realm are hard to justify.

[94] *See, e.g.*, Hay v. Hay, 678 P.2d 672 (Nev. 1984);. *See also Friedman, supra* note 34, dissenting opinion.

[95] Although at least one state, Washington, has adopted status-based approach to cohabitation unions, *see* Marriage of Lindsey, 678 P.2d 328 (Wash. 1984); Connell v. Francisco, 898 P.2d 831 (Wash. 1995), the overwhelming majority have sought to resolve financial disputes between cohabiting parties within a contractual framework. Moreover, no state combines recognition of a cohabitation status, with judicial discretion to set aside agreements between cohabiting parties.

[96] It is premature, of course, to judge the impact of the PRINCIPLES, which were only adopted in 2002, although drafts were available and cited by courts for a number of years before their official adoption by the ALI. A search turned up only one case citing the domestic partnership provisions, and that addressed a peripheral point. In contrast, some chapters have had an important impact on law reform. The custody chapter (Chapter 2), for example, is frequently cited by courts, particularly the sections on relocation and de facto parenthood. *See* David D. Meyer, *Partners, Caregivers, and the Constitutional Substance of Parenthood*, this volume.

[97] Although parties can opt out of the obligations of domestic partnership status through contract, courts have considerable latitude to set aside their contracts, as discussed *supra*, at t.a.n. 72 to 76. *See* PRINCIPLES §§ 6.01(2), 7.05.

IV. Informal Unions and Marriage: Should the Line Be Dissolved?

The PRINCIPLES' drafters make no claim that domestic partnership status would be a substitute for marriage or that its purpose is to encourage couples to live together in nonmarital unions. The Comments emphasize that domestic partnership status would affect only *inter se* claims between cohabitants; it is not a revival of common law marriage.[98] Neither are the PRINCIPLES offered as a superior alternative to civil unions or marriage for same-sex couples.[99] Indeed, given that the drafters' assignment from the ALI was to develop principles for the law of family *dissolution*,[100] the focus on ex post remedies was jurisdictional and inevitable.

Nonetheless, both supporters and opponents view the PRINCIPLES as part of a trend toward neutral legal recognition of many family forms and a diminishment in the status of marriage. Critics such as Professors Martha Fineman and Nancy Polikoff oppose marriage as an outmoded family form that is the source of women's oppression.[101] Professor Polikoff applauds the PRINCIPLES in part for "making marriage matter less."[102] Professor Lynn Wardle, on the other hand, opposes the PRINCIPLES for undermining the institution of traditional marriage.[103]

The tangible impact of the domestic partnership provisions on marriage is unclear. On the one hand, assigning marital obligations to nonmarital relationships blurs the distinction between formal and informal unions and dilute the uniqueness of marriage as a family form. It also recognizes and implicitly endorses the recent demographic trend under which many couples choose to cohabit rather than marry. On the other hand, because domestic partners are not common law spouses, the PRINCIPLES confer a more limited status than marriage.[104] Moreover, as the Comments suggest, the status removes a deterrent to marriage for those parties who currently might choose to live in informal unions to avoid marital obligations.[105]

Ultimately, legal facilitation of claims by cohabiting parties may undermine the distinct status of marriage somewhat, by extending legal recognition and some marital rights to informal unions. This cost is justified, however, as a means of protecting vulnerable individuals in these unions. Nonetheless, critics of marriage who applaud the domestic partnership provisions *because* they undermine marriage fail to appreciate the way in which formal unions function more effectively to protect dependent family members than do informal relationships. In marriage, two individuals undertake a formal commitment to one another to fulfill mutual obligations of care, support, and sharing; their expectations are incorporated in the legal rights and duties that regulate marriage and its dissolution,

[98] Spouses in common law marriages, in theory, are entitled to all the legal privileges and benefits of marriage. For example, they may qualify for government death benefits and for health and life insurance. *See* ELLMAN, ET. AL, *supra* note 23 at 83–85.

[99] PRINCIPLES § 6.03 cmt. g, Reporter's Note, at 936 ("When a registered partnership entails the rights and obligations established by this Chapter for domestic partners, this Chapter is of course unnecessary for registered partners.").

[100] PRINCIPLES, Director's Forward.

[101] Martha Albertson Fineman, *Cracking the Foundational Myths: Independence, Autonomy, and Self-Sufficiency*, 8 AM. U. J. GENDER SOC. POL'Y & L. 13 (2000).

[102] Nancy Polikoff, *Making Marriage Matter Less: The ALI Domestic Partnership Principles Are One Step in the Right Direction*, 2004 U. CHI. LEGAL F. 347 (2004).

[103] Lynn Wardle, *supra* note 3.

[104] The Comments emphasize that domestic partnerships are not common law marriages. PRINCIPLES § 6.02 cmt. a, at 914.

[105] PRINCIPLES § 6.02 cmt. b, at 916.

including the marital duties to share property and provide financial support to dependent spouses and children.[106] For this reason, marriage offers greater security to financially dependent spouses than their counterparts in informal unions enjoy.

To be sure, marital duties are seldom legally enforced in intact families.[107] For the most part, however, legal enforcement is unnecessary because a combination of affective bonds and the powerful social norms regulating marriage usually is sufficient to encourage the fulfillment of marital obligations. In contrast, couples living in cohabitation unions have varying expectations about financial sharing and no strong norms encourage mutual support.[108]

The formal legal status becomes more important as a source of financial protection to dependent family members when marriages end in divorce. The default rules that regulate support and property distribution on divorce can best be understood as the dissolution terms of the marriage contract.[109] The exchange of marriage vows represents an agreement by the spouses to be bound by the legal obligations embodied in these rules and offers to each the assurance that the other spouse is also bound.[110] The financial rules regulating divorce prescribe with relative certainty the entitlement of dependent spouses to property and (together with minor children) financial support when marriage ends. To be sure, the quality of financial protection extended to vulnerable spouses and children on divorce depends on the extent and certainty of obligations under divorce doctrine, and contemporary law is far from optimal in this regard. Criticism of current law, however, should not obscure the fact that the legal framework regulating divorce can (and, to an extent, does) serve as an effective mechanism to define financial obligations on the basis of marital roles when marriage ends.

Informal unions, as I have argued elsewhere, function far less effectively to afford financial protection to vulnerable family members, in part because these unions lack a legal framework that defines and enforces financial obligations.[110a] The domestic partnership provisions and my proposed default rule framework both mitigate this problem to some extent, promising greater financial protection to dependent parties in informal unions than is available under current law. Both would mitigate hardship and unfairness by enforcing expectations in long-term, marriage-like unions and by discouraging exploitation by parties with greater financial sophistication and resources. However, these beneficial ends are

[106] Robert Scott and I have argued that the legal default rules regulating marriage and divorce constitute many of the terms of the marriage contract, and that optimal rules can be designed (and existing rules evaluated) within a hypothetical bargain framework. Scott & Scott, *supra* note 13, at 1251.

[107] *See, e.g.*, Kilgrow v. Kilgrow, 107 So.2d 885 (Ala. 1958).

[108] Researchers have described cohabitation as "underinstitutionalized," meaning that, in contrast to marriage, no template of behavioral expectations guides couples in informal unions. *See* Stephen Nock, *A Comparison of Marriages and Cohabiting Relationships*, 16 J. Fam. Issues 53, 56–7 (1995).

[109] Scott & Scott, *supra* note 13, at 1263. Marriage also has more subtle protective effects that protect family members after dissolution. Divorced noncustodial parents comply with child support payment orders at a much higher rate than their unmarried counterparts, and are more likely to maintain relationships with their children. *See* Elaine Sorenson and Ariel Halpern, *Child Support Enforcement Is Working Better Than We Think*, Urban Institute Report No. A–31 (Mar 1999), *at* http://www.urban.org/url.cfm?ID = 309445.

[110] Some critics of marriage challenge the text statement by pointing out that individuals exchanging marriage vows have little knowledge about the financial obligations imposed by law on married couples. Polikoff, *supra* note 2. While it is surely true that individuals entering marriage typically do not know the specifics of their legal obligations, most surely view marriage as a legal and financial commitment to the spouse and understand generally that they are undertaking financial obligations to that person.

[110a] See Scott, note 78.

accomplished through means that are more costly, intrusive, and uncertain than are the legal enforcement tools available to spouses.

Any ex post determination of status will function less effectively than marriage to afford protection to dependent partners in intimate unions.[111] This is because the nature of the parties' commitment to one another and the contours of their legal obligations are ascertained only when the relationship ends. Domestic partnership status is triggered after the cohabitation period passes, but it is formally established only after the couple separates. If the status is contested, the court must undertake an inquiry into the nature of the relationship under a multifactored standard to decide whether the union qualified as a domestic partnership, entitling the claimant to property distribution and support.[112] Similarly, although my proposed contract default rules may be more determinate than the ALI's approach, here also, claims are brought only upon dissolution of the union. As is always true with ex post inquiries, the parties are likely to offer conflicting accounts of their relationship and courts must try to sort out the truth.

Of course, this is not to say that courts should reject property and support claims by dependent partners in long-term cohabitation unions. Enforcing the expectations of these parties and preventing exploitation are important goals that support legal enforcement, despite the messiness of the process. This is so, even if enforcement may blur the line between marriage and cohabitation, a cost that, in my view, is outweighed by the benefit to vulnerable unmarried claimants. However, it is important to be clear that ex post determinations of family obligations in informal unions offer only limited protection to dependent family members – whether under the domestic partnership provisions or through a regime of contract default rules. The partner who chooses to undertake a specialized family role that leaves her financially vulnerable can hope that she will receive support and a share of property should the relationship end, but that will happen only if a court concludes that the criteria for a domestic partnership or contractual obligation have been met.

As compared to cohabitation or domestic partnership status, marriage has significant advantages as a family form that can offer financial protection to vulnerable family members because the status carries financial rights and duties that attach ex ante through the concrete act of registration. Substantial individual and social benefits follow if couples formalize their commitment through marriage rather than living together informally. At that point, the terms of their commitment and the scope of their mutual financial obligations are clear and need not be determined through ex post inquiry.[113]

The way that marriage benefits dependent spouses has not been recognized in recent scholarship – for understandable reasons. Historically, legal marriage has functioned to reinforce gender hierarchy, oppressing women who married and relegating those who did not to low social status and often desperate financial circumstances. Most social observers would agree that marriage today is a far more egalitarian institution than it once was. Nonetheless, because of its unfortunate' history, many feminists are wary of marriage and

[111] Under a default rule framework, the "status" is the threshold determination of whether the couple belongs to the category of relationships to whom the default rules apply.

[112] Principles § 6.03(7). The factors that are considered in this inquiry are discussed in note 56 *supra* and accompanying text. Under my contract default rule framework, issues may arise about the duration of the cohabitation or other factors.

[113] The details of the spouses' financial obligations may be subject to adjudication at divorce, but the existence of obligations and their basic scope are based on the law of spousal support and property distribution, and thus implicitly part of the marriage contract.

some are quite ready to abolish it altogether.[114] This is unfortunate, in my view. To be sure, contemporary legal regulation of marriage is less than optimal, and calls for reform are justified. However, egalitarian marriage, available to both same-sex and opposite-sex couples, holds considerable promise as a contemporary family form.[115] Those who favor policies that promote the welfare of vulnerable family members should reconsider their rejection of marriage – or at least of formal legal commitment – as a means of attaining this goal.

V. Conclusion

The domestic partnership provisions represent an admirable law reform effort that aims to benefit individuals who need legal protection. An almost unnoticed social cost of the demographic changes of the past generation has fallen on individuals who assume marital homemaker roles in informal intimate unions. To date, the law has responded inadequately to their financial claims when their relationships end. Domestic partnership status represents a new family form that would provide greater financial security to these individuals and deter exploitation by their partners.

Unfortunately, the means by which the drafters seek to accomplish these admirable goals are unnecessarily heavy handed and paternalistic. This chapter has argued that much of the protection to vulnerable partners afforded by domestic partnership status can be provided through contract default rules. This framework offers substantial advantages over the coercive approach taken in the PRINCIPLES, because it is grounded in the consent of the parties and because it builds seamlessly on conventional contract doctrine. In a society that highly values personal autonomy and respects the freedom of individuals to order their intimate lives, consent is superior to coercion as a principle guiding the legal regulation of relationships between adults.

This chapter draws in part on an earlier paper, *Marriage, Cohabitation and Collective Responsibility for Dependency*, 2004 U. CHI. LEGAL F. 225.

[114] MARTHA ALBERTSON FINEMAN, *supra* note 7. For a discussion of feminist critiques of marriage, see Scott, *Marriage, Cohabitation and Collective Responsibility for Dependency*, *supra* note 78.

[115] The legitimacy of marriage as a privileged legal status depends on its availability to same-sex as well as opposite sex couples. *See* Scott, *supra* note 78.

18 The PRINCIPLES and Canada's "Beyond Conjugality" Report: The Move toward Abolition of State Marriage Laws

Jane Adolphe

This Chapter evaluates two law reform initiatives in North America: the PRINCIPLES and the 2001 Canadian Law Commission's report entitled "Beyond Conjugality: Recognizing and Supporting Close Personal Relationships" ("Beyond Conjugality").[1] The PRINCIPLES move "away from the idea that there can be public standards guiding marriage and parenthood. Instead it says that the central purpose of family law should be to protect and promote family diversity."[2] In particular, the PRINCIPLES introduce rules pertaining to pre-marital agreements and domestic partnerships that undermine the very essence of marriage and present it as one of many equally valid family forms.

In this regard, the PRINCIPLES follow in the footsteps of Beyond Conjugality, which proposes a revolutionary reconstitution of family law that would make State marriage laws superfluous. Beyond Conjugality promotes a registration scheme for all close adult relationships, which would include, for example, a person with disabilities and her care giver. Beyond Conjugality describes "the possibility of removing the state from the marriage business" as "worthwhile."[3] It models the registration scheme on marriage providing elements of both contract and status and then opens up registration to numerous types of relationships which are promoted as equally worthy of protection and assistance from the State.

The chapter is divided into three parts. Part I briefly sets the groundwork for a comparative analysis of the PRINCIPLES and Beyond Conjugality. Drawing from the work of canon lawyers about natural marriage, it demonstrates that the essence of marriage takes into consideration the universal nature of the human person and the proper role of the State.[4] Part II reviews the impact of the PRINCIPLES on the institution of marriage, giving

[1] LAW COMMISSION OF CANADA, BEYOND CONJUGALITY: RECOGNIZING AND SUPPORTING CLOSE PERSONAL ADULT RELATIONSHIPS (Dec. 21, 2001), *available at* http://www.lcc.gc.ca/research_project/cpra-en.asp (last viewed August 10, 2005) [hereinafter BEYOND CONJUGALITY]. For more information about the Commission generally, see the Commission's main website, *available at* http://www.lcc.gc.ca/about/default-en.asp.

[2] DAN CERE, THE FUTURE OF FAMILY LAW: LAW AND THE MARRIAGE CRISIS IN NORTH AMERICA 5 (Institute for American Values, 2005). *See also* Lynn D. Wardle, *Deconstructing Family: A Critique of the American Law Institute's "Domestic Partners" Proposal*, 2001 BYU L. REV. 1189, 1194 [hereinafter WARDLE, DECONSTRUCTING FAMILY] ("[T]he ideological bias against marriage and marriage-based family relations is reflected in many chapters of the *Family Dissolution Principles.*").

[3] BEYOND CONJUGALITY, *supra* note 1, at 124.

[4] The work is drawn from canon lawyers within the Catholic tradition. Natural marriage and sacramental marriage are distinct but interrelated realities. Natural marriage is the foundation of sacramental marriage. Natural marriage has been raised to the level of a sacrament for baptized persons. The Code of Canon Law in can. 1055 (1) provides: "The marriage covenant, by which a man and a woman establish between themselves a partnership of their whole life, and which of its own very nature is ordered to the well-being of the spouses and to the procreation and

special attention to the PRINCIPLES' proposals on agreements and domestic partnerships. Part III then turns to an analysis of Beyond Conjugality. This chapter concludes that ALI proposals concerning premarital agreements and domestic partnerships do not enforce essential characteristics of natural marriage, but rather, undermine them in a way that puts the PRINCIPLES on the same path as Beyond Conjugality, which favors the eventual abolition of State marriage laws.

I. The Essence of Marriage

No complete evaluation of law reform and its effect on marriage can occur without consideration of the human person, the nature of marriage itself, and the role of the State.[5] Any positive law ought to be founded on "the common nature of man and the course of action it indicates."[6] This ought to be the primary measure of all positive laws and rights.[7] Indeed, this has been the starting point for many discussions about human rights on an international level.[8] As Professor Pannikar states, "At the basis of the discourse on Human Rights there is the assumption of a *universal human nature* common to all peoples...."[9]

The universal essence of man, that which transcends the limits of culture and history, rests in the fact that all human beings are born male and female, endowed with reason and free will, and are inherently social.[10] Not every choice, however, is congruent with human dignity or worthiness of the human person (e.g., theft, murder). Authentic freedom is

upbringing of children, has, between the baptized been raised to a sacrament." (CODEX IURIS CANONICI auctoritate Ioannis Paulii PP. II promulgatus (1983). English translation from E. CAPARROS ET AL., CODE OF CANON LAW ANNOTATED (2d. 2004)). For an explanation of the meaning of sacrament see THE CATECHISM OF THE CATHOLIC CHURCH, ¶ 774 (2d ed. 1997).) For those concerned about a Church-state issue, see note 5 *infra*.

[5] This part rests on a number of authorities that include those associated with the Catholic intellectual tradition. However, the arguments made here do not depend upon religious convictions. Obviously some religious doctrines are in harmony with religiously based considerations about the human person, culture, and society. As the United States Supreme Court has observed in its Establishment Clause jurisprudence: "[T]he 'Establishment' Clause does not ban federal or state regulation of conduct whose reason or effect merely happens to coincide or harmonize with the tenets of some or all religions. In many instances, the Congress or state legislatures conclude that the general welfare of society, wholly apart from any religious considerations, demands such regulation. Thus, for temporal purposes, murder is illegal. And the fact that this agrees with the dictates of the Judeo-Christian religions while it may disagree with others does not invalidate the regulation." *McGowan v. Maryland*, 366 U.S. 420, 442 (1961).

[6] RAYMOND F. BEGIN, NATURAL LAW AND POSITIVE LAW 42 (1959).

[7] *Id.* at 50.

[8] The 1948 Universal Declaration of Human Rights recognizes and proclaims universal rights flow from the inherent dignity of the human person. Universal Declaration of Human Rights, G.A. Res. 217 A (III), U.N. GAOR, 3rd Sess., U.N. Doc. A/810 (1948) [hereinafter UDHR]. *See* Mary Ann Glendon, *Knowing the Universal Declaration of Human Rights*, 73 NOTRE DAME L. REV. 1153, 1153 (1998) ("The United Nations' [sic] Universal Declaration of Human Rights of 1948 is the single most important reference point for cross-cultural discussion of human freedom and dignity in the world today."); PONTIFICAL COUNCIL FOR THE FAMILY, THE FAMILY AND HUMAN RIGHTS (Nov. 15, 2000), *available at* http://www.vatican.va/roman_curia/pontifical_councils/family/documents/rc_pc_family_doc_20001115_family-human-rights_en.html (last viewed Sept. 24, 2005). For a more detailed study of the Declaration and its drafting process, see MARY ANN GLENDON, A WORLD MADE NEW: ELEANOR ROOSEVELT AND THE UNIVERSAL DECLARATION OF HUMAN RIGHTS (2001).

[9] Raimundo Pannikar, *Is the Notion of Human Rights a Western Concept*, *in* HENRY J. STEINER & PHILIP ALSTON, INTERNATIONAL HUMAN RIGHTS IN CONTEXT: LAW, POLITICS, MORALS: TEXT AND MATERIALS 384 (2000).

[10] *See* SAINT THOMAS AQUINAS, SUMMA THEOLOGICA, Part I, Q. 76, art. 3 & Q. 79 (intellect); Q. 83 (free will) (Maryland: Christian Brothers, 1981), [hereinafter AQUINAS, SUMMA THEOLOGICA]. *See also* UDHR Article 1 (providing that "All human beings are born free and equal in dignity and rights. They are endowed with reason and conscience and should act towards one another in a spirit of brotherhood."); Lynn D. Wardle, *The Bonds of Matrimony and the Bonds of Constitutional Democracy*, 32 HOFSTRA L. REV. 349 (2003) (arguing that marriage is a fundamental civic good which constitutes virtuous citizens).

exercised only when it is directed toward those goods that are fitting to the human person who comes from others and depends upon others.[11] One of these essential goods is natural marriage. Distinct from other animals, the human person discovers herself or himself to be more than the mere visible, a physical body and part of an exclusively biological world, yet seeks dialogue with the invisible world through ethics, morals, spirituality, faith, and religion. Additionally, the human being finds "the most radical communal dialogue between persons in so far as they are human," namely, the personal relationship between a man and a woman.[12]

Sexuality is a constitutive part of the human person, which means that it is not a purely physical reality but reveals the personal being in all of its aspects.[13] "The sexual dimension touches upon the more ample and more profound aspects of the person (temperament, sensibility, mentality, psychic structure, etc.)," so that when a person exercises all his or her faculties, it is achieved via a peculiar sexual modality.[14] Both personal beings – male and female – are equal in dignity but complementary in their diverse sexual dimensions. They form a marital union or community of life and overcome the human person's primary solitude in the visible world.[15] Having said that, the manner in which human persons live out their own masculinity and femininity may change within various cultural contexts, such as the type of dress or work.[16] Recognizing the importance of sexuality does not equate the value of women with their natural capacity to procreate or relegate them to the household, nor does it imply that women should be unjustly discriminated against in social, cultural, economic, and political sectors of society.[17] Consequently, one must distinguish between

[11] John J. Coughlin, *Natural Law, Marriage, and the Thought of Karol Wojtyla*, 28 FORDHAM URB. L.J. 1771, 1782 (2001). With regard to the notion of "good," supporters of David Hume argue that reason cannot tell us what we ought to desire, only how we can satisfy our desires. ROBERT P. GEORGE, IN DEFENSE OF NATURAL LAW 17–30 (1999) [hereinafter GEORGE, IN DEFENSE OF NATURAL LAW]. Followers of Aristotle and St. Thomas Aquinas believe, in contrast, that right reason can tell us what we ought to desire and how we can satisfy our desires.

[12] PEDRO JUAN VILADRICH, THE AGONY OF LEGAL MARRIAGE 87 (1990) [hereinafter VILADRICH, AGONY].

[13] JOAN CARRERAS, LE NOZZE: FESTA, SESSUALITÀ & DIRITTO 111 (2001).

[14] VILADRICH, AGONY, *supra* note 12, at 91 (explaining that intelligence and free will, essential properties of the human person, are in themselves neither masculine nor feminine, but are exercised in a manner that give a tonality to a particular way of feeling, reasoning, and willing).

[15] *Id.* at 88; *See also* GEORGE, IN DEFENSE OF NATURAL LAW, *supra* note 11, at 139–53, 140–41, and 161–83. Professor George argues that the true dignity of the human person requires that he or she be treated as a whole – as a physical, intellectual, emotional, and spiritual being. In some activities, individual males and females are complete in and of themselves, such as when they eat, speak, or think. But reproduction requires a man and woman to communicate through a bodily union. Such sexually reproductive-type acts reaffirm the couple's communion, whether or not they are capable of conceiving children. Only reproductive-type acts can be "truly unitive, and thus marital[0]," since reproduction is the only act that is performed by the married pair as an organic whole.

[16] This statement is not meant to promote "gender ideology" which reduces the human person to a completely subjective reality and in so doing actually demeans the richness of humanity. The ideology of gender views one's biological sex as natural but all other sex-related differences, such as masculinity, femininity, manhood, womanhood, motherhood, fatherhood, and heterosexuality as culturally constructed "gender roles." Hence, they are artificial and arbitrary. *See, e.g.*, DALE O'LEARY, THE GENDER AGENDA: DEFINING EQUALITY 120 (Vital Issues Press 1997).

[17] VILADRICH, AGONY,*supra* note 12, at 57–58. The Holy See, the governing body of Vatican City and the Catholic Church, has consistently reaffirmed the proposition that differences in the sexes should be understood and celebrated instead of labeled or treated as inferior or superior. *See, e.g.*, Congregation for the Doctrine of the Faith, *Letter to the Bishops of the Catholic Church on the Collaboration of Men and Women in the Church and in the World* (July 31, 2004), *available at* http://www.vatican.va/roman_curia/congregations/cfaith/documents/rc_con_cfaith_doc_20040731_collaboration_en.html (stating the following: "'*Man is a person, man and woman equally so*.... Their equal dignity as persons is realized as physical, psychological and ontological complementarity, giving rise to a harmonious relationship of 'uni-duality.... Sexuality characterizes man and woman not only on the physical level, but also on the psychological and spiritual, making its mark on each of their expressions'.

that which forms part of marriage and that which amounts to disturbing appendages to marriage, like sexual inequality or domestic violence.

Marriage is formed at the moment of consent, traditionally, publicly manifested[18] because of the unique human and social significance that transcends the couple.[19] It is not founded upon having sexual intercourse, or living together, or upon mere instinct and sentiment. Instead, it is founded on something more profoundly related to what it means to be human, a free act of intelligence and will. Spouses consent to the reciprocal and mutual exchange of each other as persons in their respective masculinity and femininity.[20] This exchange creates a "bond in justice"[21] whereby spouses owe a duty to love, a love that is conjugal[22] precisely because it is the result of a commitment by a man as man and a woman as woman. Since there is an actual exchange of persons or self-gift of the persons in his or her totality as a man and woman, respectively, the marriage created is permanent, monogamous, and open to life.[23] In other words, permanence, exclusivity, and procreative orientation are fundamental to marriage.[24] They are goods that make marriage attractive

It cannot be reduced to a pure and insignificant biological fact, but rather 'is a fundamental component of personality, one of its modes of being, of manifestation, of communicating with others, of feeling, of expressing and of living human love'."); Pope John Paul II, *Letter to Women*, (June 29, 1995), *available at* http://www.vatican.va/holy_father/john_paul_ii/letters/documents/hf_jp-ii_let_29061995_women_en.html; Pope John Paul II, Apostolic Letter *Mulieris dignitatem* (August 15, 1988), *available at* http://www.vatican.va/holy_father/john_paulnii/apost_letters/documents/hf_jp-ii_apl_15081988_mulieris-dignitatem_en.html; Pope John Paul II, *Letter to Families for the International Year of the Family, available at* http://www.priestsforlife.org/magisterium/papal/94-02-02lettertofamilies.htm (Feb. 2, 1994); John Paul II Post-Synodal Apostolic Exhortation, *Familiaris Consortio, available at* http://wf-f.org/FamCons.html (Nov. 22, 1981).

[18] This has been borne out in history. In the Judeo-Christian legal tradition, this formal and public manifestation traditionally took place through the celebration of a wedding ceremony within the community, without involvement of the Church or State; certain formalities (a priest and two witnesses) were later established by canon law in response to clandestine weddings. With the separation of Church and State, these laws evolved into State laws with respect to solemnization. *See Decree on the Reformation of Marriage*, Chapter I, *in* The Council of Trent – The Twenty-Fourth Session, The Canons and Decrees of the Sacred and Ecumenical Council of Trent 192–232 (J. Waterworth ed. & translation, 1848); Garrison, this volume (discussing the role of wedding vows).

[19] Viladrich, Agony, *supra* note 12, at 152–54.

[20] *Id.* at 160. *See also* Cormac Burke, *The Object of Matrimonial Consent: A Personalist Analysis*, 9 Forum 39, 49–50 (1998) [hereinafter Burke, Object of Matrimonial Consent] ("A true gift implies a transfer, from the giver to the receiver, of ownership of what is given. But it is obvious that each spouse does not transfer ownership of his or her person to the other. Such a transfer would in fact be impossible... Similarly, the spouse receiving the conjugal gift does not become owner of the 'self' of the other, entitled to dispose of it as he or she wishes. No spouse owns the other: not the 'self' of the other, not even the body of the other... The donation of one's person necessarily affects only the person's activity but not the person himself. And not even all of the person's activity can be the object of the gift.").

[21] Viladrich, Agony, *supra* note 12, at 160.

[22] *Id.* at 82 and 94. Viladrich explains that marital love is the culmination of three degrees of love: instinctive, sensitive, and rational. Each degree of love is sexual in so far as it refers to the other person as a man or woman. First, there is a basic sexual instinct, which founds the initial attraction felt between a man and a woman. The sexual instinct tends to render masculinity attracted to femininity and vice versa. Then, the goods known by the senses about a particular femininity and masculinity found and sustain a set of sentiments, for instance about the beauty of one's eyes, or the gracefulness of one's walk. Finally, the intelligence and will of the person grasps the exclusive goods of the loved one's personal dimension as unique and unrepeatable, where the instinctive and sensitive are integrated into the personal encounter with the other. Because instinct and sentiment have nothing to do with intelligence and will, it is this last level of love that unifies or brings the other levels to full conjugal love, through the person's rational understanding and free will to make a decision or commitment to love the other, or in other words, to donate himself or herself and all that he or she is to love the other. *See id.* at 128–33.

[23] *Id.* at 165–67. Marriage also implies a relationship that is exclusive: the same gift cannot be made to more than one person at the same time. *Id.* at 107.

[24] *Id.*

to human understanding.[25] Permanency and exclusivity correspond to the deepest aspirations of the human heart – "I will love you forever."[26] It is indissoluble because the object of man's and woman's consent is the donation of their masculine and feminine being, namely the gift of self, which thereby implies a permanent donation and not a loan.[27] It is exclusive because the same gift cannot be made to more than one person at the same time.[28] It is open to life because marriage inherently implies a sexual relationship (engaging in reproductive like acts). Man and woman *bind* themselves together with the "I do" but actually *give* themselves when they unite to produce a "new you and me... My gift does not simply become yours, nor yours mine. They unite to become a new being that is not just yours or mine, but *ours*, our child."[29] Engaging in reproductive type acts is good for spouses because it is unitive and it renders the sexual gift an authentic self-gift when such acts are open to life and are characterized by permanency and exclusivity, and therefore truly conjugal.[30] In sum, marriage does not exist, then, if any of these fundamental goods are excluded by either of the parties. This would be contrary to the spousal gift of self.

Marriage has a special status because it is tied to the social nature of the human person, which can be understood as an opening toward others that unfolds through sexual relations. This occurs on essentially three levels.[31] First, human persons are free to publicly commit to establish a personal and loving community between a man and woman that becomes the conjugal community. Second, the union between a man and woman leads to a community between parents and their children that becomes the parent-child community. Third, the family, as a subject of rights and duties, cooperates and collaborates with the state and becomes the fundamental unit of society.[32] Marriage, then, is the natural foundation upon which the family rests and, like the family, is therefore entitled to protection and support from society.[33] Marriage is a state in life that has a profound public relevance because it naturally creates the publicly acknowledged fundamental unit of society, the family, with its roles of husband and wife, mother and father, brother and sister, and so forth.[34]

The State's concern for marriage is founded on its importance for the development of the human person and society, as well as the strong link between law and culture.[35] The State's central role is the protection and promotion of the common good of society, which by

[25] BURKE, OBJECT OF MATRIMONIAL CONSENT, *supra* note 20, at 70.

[26] *Id.* at 67.

[27] *Id.* at 67.

[28] *Id.* at 69.

[29] *Id.* at 61.

[30] *Id.* at 107.

[31] VILADRICH, AGONY, *supra* note 12, at 63–64.

[32] Professor Viladrich uses the expression "family community." This chapter substitutes the term "parent-child community" in order to minimize confusion. The family is created at the moment of the valid exchange of consent, rather than with the birth of children. The fact that spouses are unable to bear children does not mean that they are not a family.

[33] Domestic laws in Western legal cultures evidence the State's role in promoting the common good through the protection and assistance of marriage. In some countries, such laws have included penal sanctions against sodomy, fornication, and adultery; norms regarding the establishment and rupture of the juridical bonds of marriage, procreation, and child custody; and norms determining the reciprocal rights and duties of the spouses, their relatives, and descendents. PIUS EHEOBU O. OKPAQLOKA, LEGAL PROTECTION OF MARRIAGE AND THE FAMILY INSTITUTIONS: A COMPARATIVE STUDY OF MAJOR NORMATIVE SYSTEMS WITH SPECIAL FOCUS ON NIGERIA-AFRICA 50 (2002). *See also* The Convention on Consent to Marriage, Minimum Age for Marriage and Registration of Marriages, G.A. Res. 1763 A (XVII U.N. GAOR, (1962) (illustrating attempts to codify legal norms concerning natural marriage on an international level as well as domestically).

[34] VILADRICH, AGONY, *supra* note 12, at 64.

[35] *See e.g.* Francis Cardinal George, *Law and Culture*, 1 AVE MARIA L. REV. 1 (2003) [hereinafter GEORGE, LAW AND CULTURE] (discussing how law is integrally bound up with culture and morals with particular reference to American society).

definition is centered on the human person.[36] The common good requires social conditions that allow human persons to freely develop and flourish. Consequently, the State is in the business of making distinctions that may require the prohibition of certain behaviors such as sexual intimacy with a minor; the toleration of behaviors such as cohabitation; and the promotion of some behaviors such as natural marriage. Further, the state must distinguish between the substance or essence of marriage, born at the public moment of consent between one man and one woman, and its legal positivist appearances, such as the marriage license.[37] These legal formalities presuppose the essential content of marriage, which, as described above, is a deeply profound reality. The State does not create marriage, which is founded on a human act of consent. Therefore, the State cannot change or redefine the essential goods or elements of marriage. The state must instead protect and support marriage because it is a *sui generis* contract.[38] In other words, it is much more than a mere contract. The contract contemplates the foundational moment of marriage, but fails to express the essence of marriage. A contract may be changed even in its essential terms upon consent of the parties, and may also be terminated. But this positivist legal notion does not capture the essence of the juridical bond that constitutes a permanently sealed debt in justice between a man and woman. In brief, it is *sui generis* because it cannot be fully compared to positive legal notions of contract without obscuring the essence of marriage.

II. The Principles

The Principles equate marriage to domestic partnerships and allow both spouses and domestic partners to accommodate their particular needs by contractually altering or confirming legal rights and duties, subject to public policy constraints and the parties' capacity to contract. The Principles' proposals regarding agreement and domestic partnerships do not reinforce the essential properties of marriage, but rather undermine them.

A. Premarital Agreements

Certainly there is a danger presented with the use of premarital contracts in so far as they reinforce the anticipation of marital breakdown, and therefore contribute to a divorce mentality. A good argument, however, can be mounted that a prenuptial agreement does not invalidate consent in natural marriage, per se. Since an individual consents to marriage

[36] Aquinas, Summa Theologica, *supra* note 10, at Part II, Q. 90, art 2. *See also* Jacques Maritain, The Person and the Common Good 39 (John J. Fitzgerald translation 1947) (explaining that "[t]here is a correlation between the notion of the *person* as a social unit and the notion of the *common good* as the end of the social whole. They imply one another"). Professor Maritain posits that the human person finds himself in serving the group, and the group attains its goal only by serving the person. *Id.* at 37–41. Part of the group's service of man is the realization that every human being has aspects which go beyond the group like spirituality, as well as, an ultimate calling that the group does not encompass. *Id.* at 52, 72–76. According to Maritain, that which constitutes the common good and promotes the perfection of man's life and liberty includes public services (i.e. roads, schools), structures (i.e., governmental bodies, military power), good customs, just laws, wise institutions, cultural treasures and heritage. *Id.* at 42. Perhaps most importantly, the common good also includes the promotion of basic human virtues, and civic rights and responsibilities. *Id.* The term "common good," therefore, does not refer to the sum total of individual interests, but rather, to an assessment of particular virtues and their integration with other values in balanced association with the human person in conformity with his or her rational, free, and social nature.

[37] Viladrich, Agony, *supra* note 12, at 143.

[38] *Id.* at 189–90 (summarizing this view).

as a whole and not to its individual elements, in order to render consent invalid an individual must specifically intend to avoid the marriage itself or one of its essential goods. For example, there is arguably a difference between a person who intends to divorce and one who does not intend to divorce but promises not to take certain assets upon divorce. In the latter case, it is possible to conceive of a situation where a person consents to a premarital agreement in order to appease the other party or his or her relatives, and were a divorce to be pursued by the other party, never intends to remarry recognizing that he or she is permanently bound. Furthermore, prenuptial agreements may be used to reinforce the essential goods of marriage: permanence, exclusivity, and procreative orientation.

The procedural and substantive requirements in Chapter 7 attempt to provide a workable set of rules for judges and lawyers based on the presumption that premarital agreements cannot be treated like standard business contracts.[39] This is congruent with the fact that marriage is a *sui generis* contract[40] as described above. Section 7.04 sets out procedural rules to protect against overreaching.[41] This section creates a "rebuttable presumption"[42] of informed consent and the absence of duress if certain preconditions are met.[43] Section 7.05 determines substantive fairness at the time of execution of a premarital agreement,[44] unless this would "work a substantial injustice."[45] Section 7.05's overall purpose is "to permit a substantial-justice inquiry in a subset of cases in which there is special reason to

[39] PRINCIPLES §§ 7.04–7.05. *See also* Sally Burnett Sharp, *Fairness Standards and Separation Agreements: A World of Caution on Contractual Freedom*, 132 U. PA. L. REV. 1399, 1430 (1984) (arguing that the relationship between a husband and wife is more akin to a partnership and should be treated as such, and questioning "the adequacy of contract law as a vehicle for the elimination of unfair bargaining tactics between spouses.")

[40] Classically, the understanding is that a contract is "a promise or set of promises for the breach of which the law gives a remedy, or the performance of which the law in some way recognizes as a duty." RESTATEMENT (SECOND) OF CONTRACTS § 1 (1981). Basically, contracts involve 1) a commitment that *something* shall or shall not be done; 2) an exchange of *something* of value between the parties (consideration); and 3) legal sanctions. JOHN EDWARD MURRAY JR., CONTRACTS: CASES AND MATERIALS 4–5 (2000). For further discussion of contract theory as it relates to family relations, see Alain Roy, *Mariage et contrat: fiction ou complémentarité?*, *in* LES FICTIONS DU DROIT 43 (Ysolde Gendreau ed., 2001) (discussing new contract theories and their improvements on classical contract theory by promoting contracts as flexible, person friendly, and evolving).

[41] See Bix, this volume; *See also* Brian H. Bix, *Premarital Agreements in the ALI Principles of Family Dissolution*, 8 DUKE J. GENDER L. POL'Y 231, 237 (2001) [hereinafter BIX, PREMARITAL AGREEMENTS].

[42] PRINCIPLES § 7.04 cmt. b, at 962–63. The PRINCIPLES put the burden of proof on the party who is seeking the benefit of the agreement. PRINCIPLES § 7.05(3).

[43] PRINCIPLES § 7.04. These conditions require that (1) the agreement be executed at least thirty days in advance of the marriage; (2) both parties be advised of the need for independent counsel and have had a reasonable opportunity to do so; and (3) where one of the parties lacks independent counsel, clear language is used regarding the rights waived and the adverse interests between the parties.

[44] *See* Judith Younger, *Antenuptial Agreements*, 28 WM. MITCHELL L. REV. 697, 718 (2001); Robert Roy, *Modern Status of Views as to Validity of Premarital Agreements Contemplating Divorce and Separation*, 53 A.L.R. 4TH 22 (2003); BIX, PREMARITAL AGREEMENTS, *supra* note 41.

[45] PRINCIPLES § 7.05(2)(a)–(c). The PRINCIPLES drop the term "unconscionable." The inquiry into substantial injustice arises in two stages. First, triggering events must exist. PRINCIPLES § 7.05(2)(a)–(c) (indicating that a certain number of years must have passed (as set by the State), a child must have been born or adopted since execution, or unanticipated change in circumstances must have had a substantial impact on the parties or child). Second, the court must determine whether enforcement would work a substantial injustice by considering a number of specified factors. PRINCIPLES § 7.05(3)(a)–(d) ("(a) the magnitude of the disparity between the outcome under the agreement and the outcome under otherwise prevailing legal principles; (b) for those marriages of limited duration in which it is practical to ascertain, the difference between the circumstances of the objecting party if the agreement is enforced, and that party's likely circumstances had the marriage never taken place; (c) whether the purpose of the agreement was to benefit or protect the interests of third parties (such as children from a prior relationship) whether that purpose is still relevant, and whether the agreement's terms were reasonably designed to serve it; (d) the impact of the agreement's enforcement upon the children of the parties").

test the parties' capacity to assess their self-interest, without casting doubt generally on the enforceability of premarital agreements."[46] According to the Comments, "[t]his approach achieves a nuanced accommodation between the benefits of contractual autonomy, and concerns for the special context in which bargaining over the terms of family relationship tends to occur."[47] Professor Brian Bix observes: "The American Law Institute's Principles of the Law of Family Dissolution offers an approach to premarital agreements which tries to respect both the status and private-ordering aspects of marriage."[48]

But on a closer analysis a question is raised as to whether the PRINCIPLES, in fact, respect both private ordering and the status of marriage. The marriage contract under the PRINCIPLES is acknowledged as *sui generis* although the reason given is because it is founded on "*family relationships.*"[49] As noted above, marriage is *sui generis* because the positivist legal notion that a contract can be changed by the parties, even its essential terms, does not capture the essence of the juridical bond that constitutes a permanently sealed debt in justice. Further, this bond of justice is created through the nature and will of the spouses. Using the term "family relationships" can mean, in contemporary terminology, a broad range of intimate living arrangements,[50] not just marriage between a woman and man.

The public status of marriage is reduced to protecting the economic interests of individuals (e.g., spouses and their children). Comment *a* to Section 7.02 explains that the State's only task is "to maintain, or even strengthen, its role as guardian of the economic interests of divorcing spouses and their children."[51] In this way, marriage as a status, in the natural sense, has virtually disappeared from public discourse. Public status of marriage is not tied to the social nature of the human person as unfolding through sexual relations – husband-wife, parent-child, or family-society – where biology and bond are in the same person(s).

Further, the PRINCIPLES are indifferent and at times hostile to the possibility of citizens working with the State to reaffirm marriage as an indissoluble and faithful union. Comment *a* to Section 7.08 states: "In principle, a state could adopt laws that allowed parties to choose... the rules that would govern its potential dissolution. This section neither

[46] PRINCIPLES § 1, Overview of Chapter 7 (Agreements), pt. I (Premarital and Marital Agreements), at 39. Of course, this is in line with the Uniform laws, which reflect an acceptance of premarital agreements contemplating dissolution of marriage, such as the Uniform Marriage and Divorce Act, the Uniform Marital Property Act, and the Uniform Premarital Agreement Act. *See* Roy, *Modern Status of Views*, *supra* note 44, at 2a.

[47] PRINCIPLES § 7.02 cmt. a, at 955.

[48] BIX, PREMARITAL AGREEMENTS, *supra* note 41, at 231.

[49] PRINCIPLES § 7.02 cmt. a, at 955 (emphasis added). ("This Chapter incorporates standard contract principles.... However, a comprehensive treatment of the principles of family dissolution must also take account of the unique and specialized character of contracts affecting rights and responsibilities flowing from family relationships and their dissolution.... This Chapter takes a position between the English rule that premarital contracts are not binding, and a rule that would enforce them on the same basis as ordinary business contracts.").

[50] *See, e.g.*, BIX, PREMARITAL AGREEMENTS, *supra* note 41, at 231 (stating that "[m]arriage is a public status grounded on an intimate relationship"). For further discussion about redefinition of the family by the courts in Canada, see Mary Jane Mossman, *Conversations About Families in Canadian Courts and Legislatures: Are There "Lessons" for the United States?*, 32 HOFSTRA L. REV. 171 (2003) [hereinafter MOSSMAN, CONVERSATIONS ABOUT FAMILIES]; for a review of the redefinition of the family on the international level, see Maria Sophia Aguirre & Ann Wolfgram, *United Nations Policy and the Family: Redefining the Ties that Bind: A Study of History, Forces and Trends*, 16 BYU J. PUB. L. 113, 116–17 (2002).

[51] PRINCIPLES § 7.02 cmt. a, at 955; *see also* James Herbie DiFonzo, *Unbundling Marriage*, 32 HOFSTRA L. REV. 31, 32 (2003) (who would likely view this focus on economic rights in marriage as an unbundling of the traditional view of marriage whereby legal marriage is reconfigured by the "discrete groupings, or 'bundles,' of rights and responsibilities. These new configurations of marriage's elements are highlighted in the development of civil unions and domestic partnerships, which replicate the privileges and pains of marriage in a marriage-like status").

endorses nor opposes this possibility."[52] The Comment notes that, historically, States have offered little choice.[53] In a more hostile stance, Section 7.08(3) would prohibit a court from penalizing a party for petitioning for divorce.[54] No mention is made of covenant marriage in the commentary to this section, notwithstanding the fact that citizens in three states (Louisiana, Arizona, and Arkansas) may now bind themselves to one another in this way.[55] Covenant marriage, a special contract authorized by law, has the force of law similar to ordinary contracts for prospective spouses who promise to take reasonable steps to preserve natural marriage. This contract begins at the moment of marital difficulties, and lasts until the rendering of a divorce judgment, save for exceptional circumstances such as sexual abuse of a spouse or a child. Covenant marriage differs from other State marriage laws in that it requires premarital counseling, reasonable efforts to preserve the marriage, and restricted grounds for divorce or a lengthy separation period prior to divorce.[56]

Furthermore, since the law is unclear as to whether there is a constitutional right to divorce,[57] a question arises as to why parties cannot reaffirm the indissolubility of natural marriage pursuant to state law. Reluctance to permit such terms could possibly be overcome. For example, state law could require the parties to include a clause giving access to civil annulment procedures for lack of consent or other grounds and providing for separate maintenance in certain cases, such as abuse or adultery. In this instance, couples would continue to acknowledge their marriage commitment but would alter their residential arrangements.[58] Even though only a minority of citizens would likely take advantage of such legislation, the State has an important role to play in protecting and assisting marriage. Moreover, such a law is didactic. Law participates in forming culture because of its tight interrelationship with culture.[59]

[52] PRINCIPLES § 7.08 cmt. a, at 1004.

[53] PRINCIPLES § 7.08 cmt. a, at 1004–05 ("In at least one state, no final decree of divorce can be granted if the party seeking the divorce refuses to cooperate in steps 'solely within his or her power' necessary to allow the other party to remarry in compliance with the religious requirements of the denomination of the clergyman who solemnized the marriage.").

[54] PRINCIPLES § 7.08(3).

[55] *See* Katherine Shaw Spaht, *The Last One Hundred Years: The Incredible Retreat of Law from the Regulation of Marriage*, 63 LA. L. REV. 243, 302 (2003) (describing Covenant Marriage as a state-authorized prenuptial option "which permits spouses to contract for a stronger form of marriage, imposing the legal obligation to submit to counseling prior to divorce and a more restricted 'right' to divorce."); *see also* Katherine Shaw Spaht, *Revolution and Counter-Revolution: The Future of Marriage in the Law*, 49 LOY. L. REV. 1, 49 (2003). *See* LA. REV. STAT. ANN. §§ 9:272–309 (West 2000); ARIZ. REV. STAT. ANN. § 25–901–04 (West 2000 & Supp. 2004); ARK. CODE ANN. §§ 9-11-801-11 (Michie 2002 & Supp. 2003) (providing examples of legislation in three states that have enacted covenant marriage laws including Louisiana (1997), Arizona (1998), and Arkansas (2001)). For a more extensive list of articles pertaining to covenant marriage, see DiFonzo, *Toward a Unified Field Theory of the Family*, 2001 BYU L. REV. 923.

[56] For a discussion of the fault versus no-fault divorce debate, see Craig W. Dallon, *The Likely Impact of the ALI Principles of the Law of Family Dissolution on Property Division*, 2001 BYU L. REV. 891, 917. *Cf.* Peter Nash Swisher, *Reassessing Fault Factors in No-Fault Divorce*, 31 FAM. L.Q. 269 (1997); Barbara Bennett Woodhouse & Katharine T. Bartlett, *Sex, Lies, and Dissipation: The Discourse of Fault in a No-Fault Era*, 82 GEO. L. J. 2525 (1994); Katherine Shaw Spaht, *Louisiana's Covenant Marriage: Social Analysis and Legal Implications*, 59 LA. L. REV. 63 (1998). *See also* DiFonzo, *Toward a Unified Field Theory of the Family*, *supra* note 55, at 954 n.145.

[57] *Boddie v. Connecticut*, 401 U.S. 371 (1971).

[58] Unlike divorce, the separation agreement does not cut off the marriage relationship. *See, e.g.*, MICH. COMP. LAWS § 552.7 (1971).

[59] *See* GEORGE, LAW AND CULTURE, *supra* note 38 (discussing the law and culture interrelationship); *See also* Katherine Shaw Spaht, *Covenant Marriage Seven Years Later: Its As Yet Unfulfilled Promise*, (forthcoming) (making the same point that marriage needs to be reinforced by the law).

On the question of whether parties may include terms requiring a judgment of marital misconduct, Section 7.08(2) permits the State to set its own public policy, as long as it does not impact property allocation and spousal compensation.[60] However, marital fidelity should be taken into account because it is fundamental to marriage, although it is rejected as a factor by the drafters. Taking marital infidelity into consideration is an important way to educate adulterers and the greater public about the deleterious effects of such conduct. Indeed, as Professor Lynn Wardle points out in this volume, there is no persuasive argument why marital infidelity should not be considered alongside the moral values the drafters prefer to take into account, such as dissipation of marital assets or domestic violence.[61] Additionally, if Professor Scott FitzGibbon is correct in arguing in this volume that fault is tied to the concept of obligation and that marriage is an institution with inherent obligations, then nonrecognition of fault (e.g., marital infidelity) will lead to nonrecognition of obligation. This, in turn, will undermine the institution of marriage.[62]

B. Domestic Partnerships

The ALI domestic partnership proposal contains six sections. Section 6.01 identifies the scope of the chapter, namely, to govern claims of any two unmarried persons in terms of any financial issues existing at termination of the relationship. It is subject to express opt-out contracts under Chapter 7 of the PRINCIPLES and may not be applied to compromise the marital claims of the lawful spouse of the domestic partner. Section 6.02 articulates the ALI's twin objectives in addressing domestic partnership: fair economic distribution and societal protection from unfair social welfare burdens.

Section 6.03 defines three ways in which parties may be deemed domestic partners. Generally speaking "domestic partners are two persons of the same or opposite sex, not married to one another, who for a significant period of time share a primary residence and a life together as a couple."[63] Individuals are irrebutably considered domestic partners when "they have maintained a common household[64] . . . with their common child[65] . . . for a continuous period that equals or exceeds" a state-specified cohabitation period.[66] A rebuttable presumption applies if individuals are "not related by blood or adoption . . . [and] have maintained a common household" for a minimum cohabitation period that is also set by the State.[67] Individuals would also be domestic partners with proof "that for a significant period of time the parties shared a primary residence and a life together as a couple" in light of thirteen categorical considerations, such as oral statements, commingled finances,

[60] PRINCIPLES § 1, Topic 2 (Whether Marital Misconduct Should Be Considered in Property Allocations and Awards of Compensatory Payments), pt. I (Introduction), at 42–43.

[61] Wardle, this volume. Dissipation of marital assets and domestic violence is discussed in the PRINCIPLES § 1, Topic 2 (Whether Marital Misconduct Should Be Considered in Property Allocations and Awards of Compensatory Payments), pt. II (Introduction), at 43.

[62] FitzGibbon, this volume.

[63] PRINCIPLES § 6.03(1).

[64] PRINCIPLES § 6.03(2). Additionally, Section 6.03(4) defines a "common household" as "shar[ing] a primary residence . . . [in which] they act jointly . . . with respect to management of the household."). PRINCIPLES § 6.03(4).

[65] PRINCIPLES § 6.03(2). Additionally, Section 6.03(5) defines a "common child" as one where each adult "is either the child's legal parent or parent by estoppel. . . . " PRINCIPLES § 6.03(5).

[66] PRINCIPLES § 6.03(2).

[67] PRINCIPLES § 6.03(3).

and so forth.[68] Section 6.04(1) defines domestic partnership property as that which would have been marital property during the relevant period. Section 6.05 allocates domestic partnership property in virtually the same way as marital property.[69] Section 6.06(1) ensures that a domestic partner is entitled to compensatory payments on the same basis as a spouse.

Clearly, the PRINCIPLES reconstitute family law.[70] Unlike Canadian courts,[71] American courts which have promoted equal treatment for married and nonmarried couples have not been as influential on state legislatures.[72] Instead, as the PRINCIPLES acknowledge, "for the last 25 years American law has applied the rubric of contract, rather than family

[68] PRINCIPLES at §§ 6.03(6)–(7).

[69] Westfall, this volume.

[70] It is noteworthy that only a small number of states have adopted laws recognizing and requiring benefits for domestic partnerships. *See* Connecticut Civil Union Act, 2005 Conn. Acts. 05-10 (effective Oct.1, 2005), *available at* http://www.cga.ct.gov/2005/act/Pa/2005PA-00010-R00SB-00963-PA.htm (last viewed Sept. 30, 2005); New Jersey Domestic Partnerships Act, N.J. STAT. ANN. 26:8A–1 (2004); CAL. FAM. CODE §§ 297–98 (West Supp. 2002); CAL. GOV'T CODE §§ 22867–77 (West 2004); CAL. HEALTH & SAFETY CODE § 1261 (West 2001); Vermont Civil Union Act, VT. STAT. ANN. tit. 15, § 1201(2)–1207 (2003); *id.* tit. 18, § 5160–69 (2000); Hawaii Reciprocal Beneficiaries Act, HAW. REV. STAT. § 572C (1997), *available at* http://www.capitol.hawaii.gov/hrscurrent/Vol12_Ch0501-0588/HRS0572C/ (last viewed Sept. 30, 2005). For a good overview and critique of the laws in Hawaii, California, and Vermont, see William Duncan, *Domestic Partnership Laws in the United States: A Review and Critique*, BYU L. REV. at 961–92 (2001).

[71] On July 20, 2004, the Civil Marriage Act, which formally recognizes same-sex marriage in Canada, received royal assent, completing the final step in a movement to equalize benefits between married and non-married opposite and same-sex couples. *Bill C-38 – The Civil Marriage Act – Receives Royal Assent*, Press Release by the Canadian Parliament (July 20, 2005), *available at* http://canada.justice.gc.ca/en/news/nr/2005/doc_31578.html (last viewed August 12, 2005). *See also* the main body of the Civil Marriage Act (sections 1 through 4), S.C. c. 33 (2005)(Can.) (*available at* http://www.parl.gc.ca/38/1/parlbus/chambus/house/bills/government/C-38/C-38_4/C-38-4E.html) (last visited Sept. 26, 2005). The Act is in response to Reference re: Same-Sex Marriage, 2004 SCC 79, which is in turn a response to the trilogy of cases considering same-sex marriage in the provinces of Quebec, British Columbia, and Ontario: *Hendricks v. Quebec*, [2002] R.J.Q. 2506; *EGALE Can. Inc. v. Can. (A.G.)*, [2003] 13 B.C.L.R. 2d 1; *Halpern v. Canada*, [2003] 65 O.R. 3d. 161 (Ont. C.A.). These cases found that marriage as defined in law prohibited same-sex marriage and therefore was in breach of art. 15 (1) and not saved by s. 1 of the Charter of Rights and Freedoms. For an overview of the same-sex marriage debate in Canada, see Jane Adolphe, *The Case Against Same-Sex Marriage in Canada: Law and Policy Considerations*, 18 BYU J. PUB. L. REV. 479 (2004).

[72] In contrast to the Canadian situation, thirteen states have amended their respective constitutions to restrict marriage to opposite-sex couples without the prompting of any judicial decisions in their respective jurisdictions but quite likely in response to judicial decisions in other jurisdictions. *See* ARK. CONST. amend. 83, § 1; GA. CONST. art. I, § IV, I(a); KY. CONST. § 233a; LA. CONST. art. XII, § 15; MICH. CONST. art. I, § 25; MISS. CONST. art. 14, § 263A; MO. CONST. art. I, § 33; MONT. CONST. art. XIII § 7; N.D. CONST. art. XIXI, § 28; OH. CONST. art. XV, § 11; OKL. CONST. art. II, § 35(A); OR. CONST. art. XV, § 5A; UTAH CONST. art. I, § 29. In other cases, where courts have invalidated such practices, the state legislature has quickly responded by initiating state constitutional amendments to protect traditional or natural marriage. The Alaskan people responded by amending its Constitution. ALASKA CONST. art I, § 25. The Hawaiian constitution was also amended. HAW. CONST. art. I, § 23. It is noteworthy that, following the ratification of the constitutional amendment, the Hawaii Supreme Court reversed the lower court without opinion. *Baehr v. Miike*, 994 P.2d 566 (1999) (Table). A small number of state courts have found that efforts to define marriage as between one man and one woman or to restrict marriage to such relationships are impermissible under either state or federal law. The most recent of these decisions have not yet spurred significant legislative or judicial reaction. *See, e.g.*, Hernandez v. Robles, No. 103434/2004 (N.Y. Sup. Ct. 2005), *available at* http://www.lambdalegal.org/binary-data/LAMBDA_PDF/pdf/378.pdf (last viewed Sept. 30, 2005); Marriage Cases, Judicial Council Coordination Proceeding No. 4365, Tentative Decision (Cal. Sup. Ct. 2005), *available at* http://www.lambdalegal.org/binary-data/LAMBDA_PDF/pdf/452.pdf (last viewed Sept. 30, 2005); Citizens for Equal Protection v. Bruning, 368 F. Supp.2d 980 (D. Neb. 2005); Castle v. State of Washington, No. 04-2-00614-4, Memorandum Opinion on Constitutionality of RCW 26.02.010 & RCW 26.02.020 (Wash. Sup. Ct. 2004), *available at* http://www.co.thurston.wa.us/Superior/Recent%20Opinions/Recent_Opinions.htm (last viewed Sept. 30, 2005).

law, to the rights and obligations of nonmarital cohabitants."[73] Equitable principles such as implied contract, unjust enrichment, *quantum meruit*, putative spouse doctrine, and constructive trust "have long proven useful to remedy the problem of economic injustice" resulting from the breakup of nonmarital sexually intimate relationships.[74] The use of contractual and equitable remedies plays an important pedagogical role, by educating the public about how such relationships depart from marriage and do not enjoy the legal preference shown to marriage.

Instead of fine tuning such principles and doctrines to ensure that they are sufficient to provide recovery,[75] the PRINCIPLES create in Chapter 6 a new relationship status that reduces marriage to one of many family forms, while significantly expanding the forms the family can take. Professor Lynn Wardle succinctly describes the change in the following manner:

> The fact that one or both of the parties is (or are) married to another (or others), or that the parties could not otherwise be legally married to each other (for example, consanguinity laws, or incest laws [that] would prohibit their marriage or sexual union) is no bar to finding that he, she or they are also domestic partners.[76]

In brief, the ALI domestic partnership proposal conveys the message that marriage is equivalent to domestic partnerships by providing the nearly same remedies upon dissolution.[77] Such a position is buttressed by the introductory chapter of the PRINCIPLES, which states that "the American family (whether marital or nonmarital) serves vital economic functions."[78] The PRINCIPLES reiterate this point, emphasizing that "family law should be concerned about relationships that may be indistinguishable from marriage except for the legal formality of marriage"[79] and describing domestic partnerships as "marriage-like cohabitation."[80] The message is "nonmarital cohabitation of almost any two persons (same-sex partners, incestuous partners, adulterous partners, and all other nonmarital cohabitants) is just as valuable to society, just as important to protect and encourage in law, as marriage."[81] As Professor Wardle aptly concludes, this position is "neither supported nor supportable."[82] In particular, it goes against what one can know through right

[73] PRINCIPLES § 1, Topic 1 (Summary Overview of Chapters 2, 3, 4, 5, 6–7), Overview of Chapter 6 (Domestic Partners), at 34.

[74] WARDLE, DECONSTRUCTING FAMILY, *supra* note 2, at 1211. For a brief overview of these remedies, see Scott, this volume.

[75] WARDLE, DECONSTRUCTING FAMILY, *supra* note 2, at 1212.

[76] *Id.* at 1196. *Cf.* PRINCIPLES § 6.03(7)(k) and cmt. d; PRINCIPLES § 6.01(5) and cmts.c–d. For other articles raising similar concerns with respect to domestic partnerships in the PRINCIPLES, see William C. Duncan, *Domestic Partnership Laws in the United States: A Review and Critique*, 2001 BYU L. REV. 961; Carolyn Graglia, *A Nonfeminist's Perspective of Mothers and Homemakers Under Chapter 2 of the ALI Principles of the Law of Family Dissolution*, 2001 BYU L. REV. 993.

[77] Scott, this volume.

[78] PRINCIPLES § 1, Topic 1 (Summary Overview of Chapters 2, 3, 4, 5, 6–7), Overview of Chapter 6 (Domestic Partners), at 31–32.

[79] PRINCIPLES § 1, Topic 1 (Summary Overview of Chapters 2, 3, 4, 5, 6–7), Overview of Chapter 6 (Domestic Partners), at 33 (footnote omitted).

[80] PRINCIPLES § 1, Topic 1 (Summary Overview of Chapters 2, 3, 4, 5, 6–7), Overview of Chapter 6 (Domestic Partners), at 34.

[81] WARDLE, *Deconstructing Family*, *supra* note 2, at 1210.

[82] *Id.* Wardle's article contains an in-depth study attacking the faulty assumptions underlying the position that domestic partnerships are equivalent to marriage.

reason, as laid out in Part I of this chapter, and empirical data[83] about the interrelationship between human flourishing and natural marriage.

III. Beyond Conjugality

The president of the Canadian Law Reform Commission believes that Beyond Conjugality raises two important issues: 1) the extent to which governments should influence the formation of close personal relationships and 2) whether there is a principled approach as to why other relationships should be protected and supported by the State.[84] With regard to the first, the Commission believes that government must "put in place the conditions in which people can freely choose their close personal relationships."[85] The value of autonomy and equality are compromised if the state promotes one relationship status (e.g., marriage) by granting more benefits or legal support than others or, conversely, if the state imposes more burdens.[86] To flesh out this reasoning and how it is similar or different compared to the PRINCIPLES, this section will briefly give an overview of the report before discussing the four legal models for living.

A. The Report

Chapter One of Beyond Conjugality highlights the diversity of personal adult relationships. The fundamental argument is that in a pluralistic society, the State should ensure whenever possible that all close personal relationships share in State resources, including conjugal relationships, nonconjugal relationships between relatives and nonconjugal relationships between nonrelatives, such as, persons with disabilities and their care givers.[87] In Canada, the scheme is not restricted to those who live together because "There is no similar restriction on marriage: married couples do not have to live together for the marriage to

[83] *See e.g.*, Norval D. Glenn et al., *Why Marriage Matters: Twenty-One Conclusions from the Social Sciences*, 5 AMER. EXPERIMENTAL Q. 34, 36 (2002), *available at* http://www.amexp.org/aeqpdf/AEQv5/aeqv5n1/AEQv5n1various.pdf (last viewed Sept. 24, 2005) (assessing the effect of marriage on families, economics, physical health of both parents and children, mental health, crime, and domestic violence, when compared with single-parent, divorced, or cohabitating arrangements, and concluding that "[m]arriage is an important social good, associated with an impressively broad array of positive outcomes for children and adults alike" but that "[c]ohabitation is not the functional equivalent of marriage"). *See also* DAVID POPENOE & BARBARA DAFOE WHITEHEAD, SHOULD WE LIVE TOGETHER? WHAT YOUNG ADULTS NEED TO KNOW ABOUT COHABITATION BEFORE MARRIAGE: A COMPREHENSIVE REVIEW OF RECENT RESEARCH (1999).

[84] Nathalie Des Rosiers, *Message of the President of the Law Reform Commission on the topic: Beyond Conjugality* (Mar. 12, 2002), available at http://www.lcc.gc.ca/president/conjugality-en.asp (last viewed Sept. 24, 2005) (arguing that the key question is whether the State should be in the bedrooms of the nation) [hereinafter DES ROSIERS, MESSAGE]; Nathalie Des Rosiers, *Speech of the President of the Law Commission of Canada on the topic of Beyond Conjugality* (Jan. 29, 2002) *available at* http://www.lcc.gc.ca/president/speeches-en.asp?id = 23 (last viewed August 12, 2005).

[85] BEYOND CONJUGALITY, *supra* note 1, at Ch. II, 18.

[86] *Id. See also* DES ROSIERS, MESSAGE, *supra* note 84 (arguing that eligibility for benefits has depended upon "one's marital status because it was presumed that married persons shared resources" and that as a result the granting of benefits was tied with the calculation of both spouses' income. However, governments presently extend "spousal benefits" to common law and same-sex couples because they "share the same characteristics of interdependence as married spouses." This has been necessary in order to eliminate discrimination on the basis of marital status and sexual orientation. It is now time to reflect upon the necessity for presumptions based on the existence of conjugal relationships).

[87] BEYOND CONJUGALITY, *supra* note 1, at Ch. I, 1–11.

be valid. There is, then, no compelling reason to impose such a restriction on registered relationships."[88]

The term "conjugal" is never defined in the report, but has been defined by the Supreme Court of Canada. In *M. v. H.*, the majority concluded that conjugality no longer means a couple holding themselves out as husband and wife, but rather is made up of a series of characteristics such as "shared shelter, sexual and personal behaviour, services, social activities, economic support and children as the societal perception of the couple."[89] This functional notion of conjugality made it possible for the Court to equate cohabitating same-sex couples with cohabitating opposite-sex couples. In that case, the Court found these two sets of relationships "functioned" the same, and then held that they should be entitled to the same legal benefits.

Like *M. v. H.*, Beyond Conjugality states that attention should be paid to close personal relationships: "emotional and economically important relationships outside of marriage and conjugality . . . for the quality of care and support they provide."[90] Beyond Conjugality argues that Canadian laws have been underinclusive. "A more principled and comprehensive approach is needed to consider not just the situation of spouses and common-law partners, but also the needs of persons in non-conjugal relationships, including caregiver relationships."[91]

The second chapter of Beyond Conjugality addresses the report's underlying philosophy, which is grounded in the twin values of equality and autonomy. Equality is not explicitly defined, but breaks down into two components, "relational equality" or the same treatment between relationships, and "equality within relationships" or the same treatment between people in a relationship.[92] Autonomy is defined as "[t]he freedom to choose whether and with whom to form close personal relationships[. . . .]"[93] Passing references are made to the values of privacy, personal security, freedom of conscience and religion, coherence, and efficiency.[94]

Chapter Three of the report divides the discussion about methodology for reconsidering the relevance of personal adult relationships into two parts. The chapter first provides a four step methodology "for rethinking the way in which relationships have been regulated."[95] The methodology is then applied to ten federal statutes.[96] The methodology is as follows:

[88] *Id.* at Ch. IV, 117.

[89] *M. v. H.*, [1999] 2 S.C.R. 3, ¶ 59. The main issue in *M. v. H.* was whether the term "spouse" in s. 29 of Ontario's *Family Law Act* discriminated against same-sex partners by denying them the possibility of seeking relief under the *Family Law Act* in violation of s. 15(1) of the Canadian Charter of Rights and Freedoms, and whether it could be saved by s. 1. The Court found that the *Family Law Act* failed to accord cohabiting same-sex couples the same benefits as cohabiting opposite-sex couples on the basis of sexual orientation, an analogous ground of enumeration under the equality provision. The decision led to significant changes in federal legislation. The *Modernization of Benefits and Obligations Act*, R.S.C., ch. 12 (2000) (Can) amended 68 federal statutes to extend federal benefits and obligations to all unmarried couples who have cohabited in a conjugal relationship for at least one year, regardless of their sexual orientation. The Court in *M. v. H.* stated that the appeal had "nothing to do with marriage *per se*." *Id.* at ¶ 52. And Federal officials made assurances that the new Federal Act would preserve opposite sex marriage. Adolphe, *supra* note 71 at 495–96. But the decision eventually paved the way for the trilogy of same-sex marriage cases which culminated in the *Civil Marriage Act*. *See* discussion *supra* note 71.

[90] Beyond Conjugality, *supra* note 1, at Introduction, xxiii.

[91] Beyond Conjugality, *supra* note 1, at Ch. II, 7.

[92] *Id.* at Ch. II, 13–17.

[93] *Id.* at Ch. II, 17.

[94] *Id.* at Ch. II, 19–25.

[95] *Id.* at Introduction, xxv.

[96] *Id.* at Ch. III, 37–111 (The Marine Liability Act (family compensation); The Canada Labour Code (employment leave); The Immigration Act (family sponsorship); The Canada Evidence Act (spousal evidence); The Employment Insurance Act (fraud prevention); The Bankruptcy and Insolvency Act (protecting creditors' interests); The Bank

> First Question: Does the law pursue a legitimate policy objective? If not, the law ought to be repealed or fundamentally reconsidered.
>
> Second Question: If the law's objectives are sound, do relationships matter? Are the relationships that are included important or relevant to the law's objectives? If not, revise the law to consider the individual and to remove the unnecessary relational reference.
>
> Third Question: If relationships do matter, could the law allow individuals to choose which of their own close personal relationships they want to be subject to the law? If so, revise the law to permit self-definition of relevant relationships.
>
> Fourth Question: If relationships do matter, and public policy requires the law delineate the relevant relationships to which it applies, can the law be revised to more accurately capture the relevant range of relationships? If so, revise the law to include the appropriate mix of functional definitions and formal kinds of relationship status.[97]

To understand how the methodology is applied to particular statutes, consider two examples from Beyond Conjugality. The evidentiary rule renders a spouse incompetent to testify if his or her spouse is the accused in a criminal prosecution. Beyond Conjugality argues that this rule fails to promote a legitimate objective since the objective of marital harmony is "repugnant to ideals of equal respect and dignity." [98] Beyond Conjugality also argues that the law "demeans the individual who may be forced to remain silent regardless of a desire to give evidence"[99] and ultimately finds that "[t]estimonial competence is a mark of personhood."[100]

Consider another example concerning the martial communications privilege. Beyond Conjugality concludes that there is a valid legislative objective in preserving confidences between spouses, but that the rule as articulated is underinclusive. The objective should be to promote candor and trust in all "emotionally supportive personal relationships."[101] This objective would better be achieved if it were attached not to the witness but to all communications made with an expectation of confidentiality, and would therefore "survive the end of a relationship, and control over the divulgence of a communication should rest with the speaker not the listener."[102]

Chapter Four discusses the four legal frameworks for personal relationships: private law, ascription, registration, and marriage. The role of the State is not to pursue the common good but rather to provide (1) "legal mechanisms for people to be able to achieve . . . private understandings" and (2) to "respect the values . . . [of] equality, autonomy and choice."[103] This chapter promotes registration of domestic partnerships as providing the essential characteristics of marriage: "voluntariness, stability, certainty and publicity."[104] Marriage is described as a mere "legal mechanism" of the State,[105] a mere legal tool, implying that it was produced by the State, can be used by the State, and can even be discarded or replaced by the State.

By way of critique, the capacious view of the human person produced in Part I of this Chapter is replaced in Beyond Conjugality by the perspective of the autonomous chooser who expects that the State's sole role is to facilitate human choice. With this approach,

Act and The Income Tax Act (economic transactions between related persons); The Old Age Security Act (benefits) and The Canada Pension Plan (survivor's, veteran's, and employee's pensions)).

[97] *Id.* at Ch. III, 30.

[98] *Id.* at Ch. III, 49.

[99] *Id.*

[100] *Id.*

[101] *Id.* at Ch. III, 52.

[102] *Id.* at Ch. III, 53.

[103] *Id.* at Ch. IV, 113.

[104] *Id.*

[105] *Id.*

the social nature of the human person is obscured. As discussed in Part I of this chapter, the human person is social, born male and female with a natural capacity for marriage to establish the fundamental unit of society. Further, the notions of conjugality in both *M. v. H.* and Beyond Conjugality differ greatly from that presented in Part I: love is conjugal when the man and woman with their respective rational understanding and free will make a commitment for the purpose of reciprocal self-donation, creating a bond in justice whereby each owes the other duties of permanence, faithfulness, and procreative orientation.

Further, in Beyond Conjugality, marriage is just one type of relationship among many equally valuable close personal relationships. This approach fundamentally contradicts marriage, since no other relationship naturally brings together the essential elements which mark an authentic notion of conjugality. This is not to say that the State ought to legislate every moral good, for example by creating some sort of screening mechanism to ensure that couples do not lack the intent to stay married, to participate in reproductive acts open to children, or to be faithful.[106] The State is a prudent legislator when it presumes that couples have such intent. Further, the State, as part of its care for the common good, ought to assist in educating the public about the fundamental elements of marriage, and marriage's integral tie to human flourishing. To this end, the State ought to remain open to reform possibilities, for example, divorce or welfare reform initiatives that are linked to the promotion of healthy marriages. Lastly, the State should not be apologetic about giving preferential treatment to marriage as something worthy of special protection and assistance because of marriage's importance for the common good.

Moreover, Beyond Conjugality develops a methodology to review legislation that could assist the State in evaluating other relationships if reframed. The State should ask whether they contribute to the common good, and whether they will harm marriage by reducing the State's resources, leaving less money for initiatives promoting marriage, or by obscuring the signal that marriage is the optimal environment for human flourishing. One could envision a methodology that asks the following questions:

> First Question: Taking into consideration the fact that marriage is the bedrock of the family, the fundamental unit of society, and is therefore entitled to special protection and assistance, does the law pursue a legitimate policy objective? If not, the law ought to be repealed or fundamentally reconsidered.
>
> Second Question: If the law's objectives are sound, do non-marital relationships matter: do they have public relevance and do they serve the common good? If the law does not include other relationships should other relationships be included which have public relevance and contribute to the common good, taking into consideration the importance of marriage, the resources needed to protect and assist it, and the message that needs to be transmitted through the legislation about the marriage?
>
> Third Question: If inclusion of non-marital relationships has public relevance, and fosters the common good, how should the law be revised in a way that does not limit the resources available for promotion of marriage or otherwise obscure the message about the importance of marriage for society?

[106] Aquinas, Summa Theologica, *supra* note 10, at Part II, Q. 96, art. 2 ("Now human law is framed for a number of human beings, the majority of whom are not perfect in virtue. Wherefore human laws do not forbid all vices, from which the virtuous abstain, but only the more grievous vices, from which it is possible for the majority to abstain; and chiefly those that are to the hurt of others, without the prohibition of which human society could not be maintained: thus human law prohibits murder, theft and such like.").

Each methodology has its own moral bias. Beyond Conjugality favors diversity of relationships. Such preference is evident in the underlying philosophy and methodology in action, while my proposed methodology clearly favors natural marriage. The existence of any bias illustrates the fallacy of State neutrality.[107] Beyond Conjugality promotes diversity as the right moral choice over the long established legal tradition favoring marriage, a tradition founded in common sense and supported by empirical data about what we know is good for human flourishing.[108]

B. The State's Legal Models for Living

1. Marriage

Ironically, the Commission rejects marriage as the sole "model"[109] while using it as a "model" to evaluate other possible schemes, such as private law, ascription, and registered domestic partnerships.[110] Beyond Conjugality argues that marriage's main characteristics are "voluntariness, stability, certainty, and publicity."[111] While these terms are not defined or explained in any great detail, it is possible to glean the following from the report: voluntariness means freely choosing the relationship and the rights and duties that flow from it; stability stands for commitment recognized in law; certainty refers to legal rights and duties known by the parties themselves and third parties; and publicity is official State status that is made possible through registration.[112] These four elements may be further consolidated into two: (1) contract, and (2) status, that is publicity or official status which leads to stability and certainty.

Although, Beyond Conjugality notes that marriage is both a contract and a status, there is no acknowledgement that marriage is a *sui generis* contract – something much more profound than a contract founded as it is in the human person. Neither does it acknowledge that marriage status is founded in the unfolding of sexual relationships, rendering it the fundamental unit of society and therefore worthy of public recognition, protection, and assistance. Further, Beyond Conjugality warns that introduction of the registration scheme should not be seen as a policy alternative to allowing same-sex couples to marry.[113] To this end, it recommends the creation of a new entity called "civil marriage."[114] Clearly, a reading of this section suggests there is no concept of natural marriage as something connected to the sexual complementarity between one man and one woman and the essential goods of procreative orientation, permanency, and fidelity. In sum, Beyond Conjugality's vision of marriage is much more deconstructed than that in the PRINCIPLES, which view marriage as a *sui generis* contract and status, although the significance of the terms do not

[107] Moral neutrality on the part of a government has been refuted by both conservative and liberal scholars. *See* GERARD V. BRADLEY, *Same-Sex Marriage: Our Final Answer in Same-Sex Attraction 124* 14 ND J. L. Ethics & Public Pol'y 729, 734 (2003) (claiming that "law ought to be morally neutral about marriage, or anything else for that matter, is itself a moral claim"); Robert George, *Same-Sex Marriage and Moral Neutrality in* MARRIAGE AND THE COMMON GOOD 81 (Kenneth D. Whitewood ed. 2001) (making a similar claim); *See also* LIBERALISM AT THE CROSSROADS (Christopher Wolfe ed., 2d ed. 2003) (providing an overview of the thought of various scholars (*e.g.*, Joseph Raz and William Galston) who defend perfectionist liberalism that sees the goal of political action as the pursuit of what is truly good and in so doing reject the anti-perfectionist neutrality position).

[108] *Supra* note. 81.

[109] BEYOND CONJUGALITY, *supra* note 1, at Ch. IV, 114.

[110] *Id.* at Ch. IV, 115–18.

[111] *Id.* at Ch. IV, 113.

[112] *Id.* at Ch. IV, 113–14.

[113] *Id.* at Ch. IV, 130.

[114] *Id.* at Ch. IV, 128–29.

correlate exactly to natural marriage laid out in Part I. Neither do the PRINCIPLES promote same-sex marriage as a needed law reform (see discussion *infra*).

2. Private Contracts

Beyond Conjugality criticizes the option of allowing people to enter into private contracts, such as care giving agreements or cohabitation arrangements, primarily because these contracts lack an official status which offers guarantees of certainty and efficiency.

> Throughout our consultations, it became clear that simply allowing people the option to enter into private contracts... was insufficient because it did not always have the official or public aspect that was needed, nor did it offer sufficient guarantee of certainty. In addition, the lack of official record of such private arrangements prevents the efficient administration of laws...[115]

This bias against using private contracts to regulate affairs is similar to that contained in the PRINCIPLES, which bar at least those clauses that reaffirm the essential elements of marriage: permanence, fidelity, and procreative orientation.

3. Ascription

Beyond Conjugality also rejects ascription as the best model to regulate personal relationships. Ascription "refers to treating unmarried cohabitants as if they were married, without their having taken any positive action to be legally recognized."[116] In other words, the model is presumptive, not voluntary. A set of duties and rights are imposed on people in conjugal relationships, so that they are unable "to define for themselves the terms of their relationships[.]"[117] Beyond Conjugality argues that ascription unfairly "treats all conjugal relationships alike, irrespective of the level of emotional or economic interdependency that they may present."[118] Curiously, ascription is said to offend the value of autonomy, because people "are not always aware" that they have autonomy to "opt out of certain statutory provisions governing their relationships," for example, by private agreement.[119]

The Canadian ascription system differs in its development from that set up under the PRINCIPLES. The Canadian system was established by a series of constitutional challenges in the courts that changed the face of family law.[120] As a result, cohabiting couples, both same-sex and opposite sex, enjoy the same benefits that are available to married couples.[121] In contrast, the PRINCIPLES, a law reform initiative, would introduce an ascription system even though American constitutional law gives legal preference to the family founded on marriage.[122] Because the benefits of this new status are limited to property

[115] *Id.* at Ch. IV, 114. Other ancillary concerns relate to equality (contracts require lawyers and not everyone has equal access due to differences in wealth), efficiency (too few people will bother negotiating the terms), and costliness (parties need to avail themselves of the courts for remedies) *Id.* at Ch. IV, 114–15.

[116] BEYOND CONJUGALITY, *supra* note 1, at Ch. IV, 116.

[117] *Id.*

[118] *Id.*

[119] *Id.*

[120] For a brief review of the case law, see MOSSMAN, CONVERSATIONS ABOUT FAMILIES, *supra* note 50, at 32–36 ("Equality is a prominent theme in Canadian family law – equality for different kinds of families... Reflecting the goals of both human rights legislation and s. 15 of the Canadian Charter... family law principles have increasingly extended benefits to opposite-sex and same-sex cohabitees that were once reserved only for married couples.").

[121] *Id. See also* The Modernization of Benefits and Obligations Act, R.S.C., ch. 12 (2000) (Can).

[122] *See* David D. Meyer, *What Constitutional Law Can Learn From the ALI* Principles of Family Dissolution, 2001 BYU L. REV. 1075, 1075–85 (acknowledging this constitutional bias in favor of the natural family, but criticizing it through his analysis of the PRINCIPLES). For a contrary opinion that the constitutional bias in favor of the natural family is justified, see WARDLE, DECONSTRUCTING FAMILY, *supra* note 2.

and alimony rights between parties residing together and only upon dissolution and do not extend to the distribution of State benefits, the PRINCIPLES have not gone as far as the Canadian ascription model in erasing distinctions between married and cohabitating couples.

4. Registered Domestic Partnership

Beyond Conjugality promotes the Registered Domestic Partnership ("RDP") as the preferred model because it provides two elements. It is a contract because it "affirm[s] the capacity of people to establish for themselves the terms of their relationships" and a status because it is a legal model with public recognition.[123] "Such schemes allow individuals to express their commitment publicly and voluntarily choose to be included within a range of legal rights and responsibilities."[124] This differs from the PRINCIPLES, which use a combination of the rebuttable presumption, irrebuttable presumption, and proof after the fact. In this way, RDPs are promoted as a status with the missing element of contract or voluntariness.

Like the PRINCIPLES, Beyond Conjugality includes many express references to marriage in fleshing out the topic of RDPs. Beyond Conjugality argues that when people register their relationships, they opt into a full range of rights and responsibilities, "often similar to marriage."[125] The registration regime in some countries began as "a parallel to marriage, in which the state is promoting a similar set of objectives in the recognition and support of personal relationships."[126] In regard to who can register, the scheme is not restricted "to conjugal couples or to same-sex couples or, indeed, only to couples,"[127] but rather is "available to conjugal and non-conjugal couples alike,"[128] such as two adult siblings. In Canada, the scheme should not be restricted to those who live together. "There is no similar restriction on marriage: married couples do not have to live together for the marriage to be valid. There is, then, no compelling reason to impose such a restriction on registered relationships."[129] The legal consequences of any registration regime set up in Canada could involve a number of issues such as "property and support obligations both during and after the relationship.... [and] determinations for care arrangements, consent to treatment or other aspects of the relationship."[130] Unilateral termination of RDP is reluctantly permitted only because marriage laws allow for no-fault divorce.[131] Beyond Conjugality ultimately recommends that:

> Parliament and provincial/territorial legislatures should pass laws enabling adults to register their relationship.... The registration should not be restricted only to conjugal relationships. It should provide for a set of commitments, which could include caring arrangements, consent to treatment dispositions, support and sharing in property from which the parties may opt out.[132]

123 BEYOND CONJUGALITY, *supra* note 1, at Ch. IV, 116.

124 *Id.* at Ch. IV, 117. BEYOND CONJUGALITY leaves it to the State to define some of the rights and obligations upon registration. The report reviews three possibilities: (1) predetermination of rights and duties with the choice of adopting those similar to spouse or common law partners; (2) making a more flexible model that may respond better to care giving situations; and (3) allowing private contract which can include: "support obligations... care arrangements, consent to treatment or other aspects of the relationship."

125 *Id.*

126 *Id.*

127 *Id.* at Ch. IV, 119.

128 *Id.* at Ch. IV, 120.

129 *Id.*

130 *Id.* at Ch. IV, 121.

131 *Id.*

132 *Id.* at Ch. IV, 122.

In terms of how RDPs will fare in relation to existing paradigms, Beyond Conjugality anticipates them existing alongside the use of private contracts to regulate a couple's affairs. RDPs will also coincide with the use of the nonconsensual ascription model because it expects that "the number of people who choose to register their relationships may not be significant."[133]

Beyond Conjugality also considers the ongoing viability of marriage after RDPs are instituted. The report asks whether in time "[c]reating a registration scheme . . . could eliminate the need for marriage" and "whether our marriage laws continue to meet the needs of our evolving society."[134] Beyond Conjugality clearly favors abolishing State marriage laws, but appreciates that Canadians are not ready for this reform. While "removing the state from the marriage business is worthwhile, we do not believe that this is a viable reform option at this time" because removal would undermine the choice of conjugal couples who continue to consider marriage as fundamental to their commitment.[135]

Having concluded that, for now, State marriage laws will continue to exist, Beyond Conjugality introduces the means by which marriage can be further deconstructed. It duly notes how State marriage laws have obscured the essential elements of natural marriage, especially permanency and procreative orientation. "Marriages are no longer legally indissoluble: the availability of no-fault divorce makes the continuation of a marital union a matter of mutual consent."[136] Beyond Conjugality also states: "[n]ow federal legislative policy and constitutional norms dictate equal treatment of married spouses and unmarried conjugal cohabitants."[137] Marriage, as a legal arrangement, is "not the only place where parenting is performed."[138] Further, Beyond Conjugality warns that introduction of the registration scheme should not be seen as a policy alternative to allowing same-sex couples to marry.[139] To this end, it recommends the creation of a new entity called "civil marriage" defined as a mere "means of facilitating in an orderly fashion the voluntary assumption of mutual rights and obligations by adults [including same-sex couples] committed to each other's well-being."[140] Beyond Conjugality also recommends a clear break between civil marriage and religious marriage, so that the latter will no longer have any civil effects as regards solemnization.[141]

How is this relevant to the PRINCIPLES? Beyond Conjugality discloses a well-defined strategy for reconstruction of family law. A similar path may be followed in U.S. jurisdictions, where promotion of other relationships as equal to marriage will ultimately lead to a discussion about the necessity of State marriage laws. The PRINCIPLES would also create a domestic partnership system that virtually equates domestic partnerships (nonmarital relationships) to marriage. This can only lead to a further deconstruction of marriage in the public square.

[133] *Id.*

[134] *Id.* at Ch. IV, 123.

[135] *Id.* at 124.

[136] *Id.* at Ch. IV, 127.

[137] *Id.* This has been greatly facilitated through changes in legislation allowing for same-sex adoption and access to artificial reproduction technology. *See, e.g.*, the discussion by Martha A. McCarthy, *Family Law for Same-Sex Couples: Chart(er)ing the Course*, 15 CAN. J. FAM. L. 101 (1998); *see also* Assisted Human Reproduction Act, Statutes of Canada, 2004, c.2, art 2 (e) ("persons who seek to undergo assisted reproduction procedures must not be discriminated against, including on the basis of their sexual orientation or marital status") *available at* http://laws.justice.gc.ca/en/A-13.4/2389.html (last visited October 7, 2005).

[138] *Id.*

[139] *Id.* at Ch. IV, 130.

[140] *Id.* at Ch. IV, 129. *See also* the discussion about same-sex marriage. *Id.* at 129–31.

[141] BEYOND CONJUGALITY, *supra* note 1, at Ch. IV, 128–29. For a discussion about the relationship between natural marriage and "religious marriage," see note 4 *supra*.

IV. Conclusion

With any comparative analysis of the law reform initiatives, it is important to examine the concept of law promoted by the law reform agencies under discussion. Professor Roderick Macdonald of McGill University argues that both supporters and skeptics of institutionalized expert law reform bodies share at least one basic misconception about the nature of law, namely, that the "highest type of law" is that made by legislatures.[142] Professor Macdonald laments that this assumption "rest[s] on an impoverished view of law and normativity."[143] And he is correct. Such a perspective denies a more capacious view of the human person, reducing the complexity and the profundity of the human being to an autonomous chooser. A number of deleterious effects flow from a strictly legal positivist view, which Professor Viladrich refers to as the "agony of matrimonial legality."[144] The legal positivist paradigm is founded on a flawed anthropology and does not inextricably link human flourishing to marriage. Additionally, marriage is embedded in a divorce system that is supported and promoted by a culturally accepted divorce mentality as well as a sexually liberal one. This feeds into a legal system, which favors the emptying out of the words "I do," which can be revoked at any moment. This supports the false idea that marriage "is an act of social conformity" to obtain permission to have sexual relations or to bear children with "social honorability."[145] It also presents the distorted picture that the State is free to completely ignore the essential reality of marriage and to instead call any type of union a marriage.[146] The end result is that marriage is stripped of its content and left to be nothing more than a legal document, leading one to question the necessity of State marriage laws.

Special thanks to those who took the time to read and comment on the chapter: Professors Lynn Wardle, Patrick Quirk, Father John Coughlin, and Ed Lyons.

[142] Roderick A. Macdonald, *Recommissioning Law Reform*, 35 ALBERTA L. REV. 831, 851 (1997).

[143] *Id.* at 851.

[144] VILADRICH, AGONY, *supra* note 12, at 147.

[145] *Id.*

[146] *Id.* at 141–47. Professor Viladrich explains that marriage does not come into being simply because the couple carried out a wedding ceremony in accordance with State laws. For example, two persons of the same sex may possess a marriage certificate but such a "marriage" as a natural law reality does not exist nor could it ever exist. If marriage was constituted by the mere legal formality, then there would be little difference between a man and woman who live in a *de facto* union and a man and a woman who marry in accordance with positive law requirements. The difference would be superficial. It would be a matter of social conformity based solely on the legal ceremony. As a result, this would render marriage nothing more than the legislature's view on how sexual relations should be conducted.

19 The ALI Principles and Agreements: Seeking a Balance between Status and Contract

Brian H. Bix

This chapter analyzes Chapter 7 of the Principles, which deals with agreements. It contrasts the ALI's treatment of premarital, marital, and separation agreements[1] with both current doctrine and arguments for respecting greater private ordering regarding marriage. While largely agreeing with the ALI's approach, this chapter urges an approach somewhat more respectful of party choice and more sensitive to the variety of marriage-related agreements.

The current treatment of premarital, marital, and separation agreements reflects a view that, in a world where entrance into marriage and exit from it is largely within the control of the partners, it seems consistent to allow the partners some choice regarding the nature of the marriage they decide to enter, or not to exit. Part I of this chapter deals with premarital agreements; Part II with marital agreements; and Part III with separation agreements. Each part begins with an overview of current law, followed by a summary of the Principles' position, and an evaluation of that position.

I. Premarital Agreements

A. Overview and Current Doctrine

Premarital agreements, also called "antenuptial" and "prenuptial" agreements, are entered into when marriage is imminent, to settle, create, or modify certain rights between the parties during their marriage, upon the death of one of the partners, or upon divorce. The following discussion focuses on premarital agreements meant to modify the rights of the spouses upon divorce.

Until the 1970s, premarital agreements were generally treated as unenforceable as contrary to public policy because they modified state-imposed terms of marriage or were said to encourage divorce. In the course of the 1980s and 1990s, every jurisdiction in the United States changed its laws to allow enforcement of premarital agreements in some

[1] Chapter 7's rules are to be applied to certain domestic partners in a way analogous to married partners. *See* Principles §§ 6.01, 6.05, 6.06 (delineating marriage-like rights for domestic partners); § 7.01(2) (applying rules regarding agreements to domestic partners). This chapter focuses only on the application of Chapter 7 to married couples. For a critique of Chapter 7's application to domestic partners, see David Westfall, *Forcing Incidents of Marriage on Unmarried Cohabitants: The American Law Institute's* Principles of Family Dissolution, 76 Notre Dame L. Rev. 1467, 1480–90 (2001).

circumstances.[2] This result was "hastened" by the 1983 promulgation by the National Conference of Commissioners of Uniform State Laws of the Uniform Premarital Agreement Act ("UPAA"), the provisions of which were more favorable for the enforcement of premarital agreement than the prior law in many states.[3] Twenty-six jurisdictions have adopted the UPAA, although some have added terms meant to be protective of vulnerable parties, making the enforceability of premarital agreements less likely and perhaps also less predictable.[4]

While I am aware of no systematic data regarding premarital agreements – how many are entered into each year, who uses them, the motivations behind them, what percentage are contested, what percentage of contested agreements are upheld, and so forth – there is certainly a standard view of such agreements, reflected in media and academic discussions. The standard story is that most premarital agreements are initiated by wealthy partners who are unwilling to share their wealth should their marriages fail.[5] It is sometimes noted that a minority of such agreements are entered into for the seemingly more laudable purpose of protecting the interests of children born of a prior marriage.[6] Both story lines are reflected in the PRINCIPLES' treatment of premarital agreements.

The current law on premarital agreements is not easy to summarize, because rules vary from state to state. Even when courts (whether in the same or different states) apply the same law, they often do so in ways which differ significantly in levels of deference or distrust. Of course, much of the reaction in particular cases is likely a response to the facts and parties before the court that day. Perhaps the broad equitable standards in current U.S. law are meant to encourage just such individualized responses to the cases before the court. That noted, in the vast majority of jurisdictions, there will be some sort of "fairness" or "reasonableness" inquiry. In all but a few states[7] this entails a more

[2] The history of the enforceability of divorce-focused premarital agreements is summarized in Brian Bix, *Bargaining in the Shadow of Love: The Enforcement of Premarital Agreements and How We Think About Marriage*, 40 WILLIAM & MARY L. REV. 145, 148–58 (1998).

The PRINCIPLES argue that the greater acceptance of premarital agreements is connected with the abandonment of a purely fault-based divorce system, asserting that the opposition to premarital agreements had been based on equating such agreements with the divorces by agreement, or "collusion," that were not allowed by pure fault-based systems. PRINCIPLES, *Introduction*, at 36. While there certainly might be a connection between the acceptance of premarital agreements and the move to no-fault – *e.g.*, through a belief motivating both positions that the state should not be so intrusively involved in marriage – the equation of premarital agreements with collusive divorce seems unjustified, and there is little evidence of any perceived equation in the early cases rejecting the enforceability of premarital agreements.

[3] UNIFORM PREMARITAL AGREEMENT ACT, 9C U.L.A. 35 (2001 & Supp. 2005); *see id.* at 36–37 (Prefatory Note discussing the objective of the UPAA, as encouraging greater "certainty and sufficient flexibility" through the greater enforcement of premarital agreements).

[4] *See id.* at 35 (listing adopting jurisdictions). For examples of significantly altered versions of the UPAA, see, *e.g.*, CAL. FAM. CODE §§ 1612, 1615 (West 2004) (limiting right to waive alimony, and making access to independent legal counsel central to determining voluntariness of agreement); CONN. GEN. STAT. ANN. § 46b-36g(2) (West 2004) (unconscionability to be tested not just at time of execution but also at time of enforcement).

[5] *See, e.g.*, Jan Hoffman, *To Have and to Hold*, N.Y. TIMES, Magazine, at 104, Nov. 19, 1995 (carrying the subtitles "How They Keep It" and "For the wealthy about to wed, the prenuptial agreement is the vow that gets honored first. Ten lawyerly ways to say you care.").

[6] *See, e.g.*, Shelia Poole, *'I do' – with Fineprint*, DES MOINES REGISTER, Business, at 3, Dec. 14, 1997 (listing protecting assets for children of prior marriage as one reason for having a premarital agreement).

[7] The Pennsylvania case, Simeone v. Simeone, 581 A.2d 162 (Pa. 1990), may be an exception. In *Simeone*, the Pennsylvania Supreme Court concluded that premarital agreements should generally not be treated differently from conventional commercial agreements, though even that decision requires a level of financial disclosure one

paternalistic and substantive test for enforceability than would be the case for a commercial agreement.[8]

Most jurisdictions require premarital agreements to be in writing, as does the UPAA.[9] Most jurisdictions also require a full or substantially full disclosure of assets by the party seeking enforcement of an agreement.[10]

With respect to the fairness of an agreement's terms, under the UPAA, the "fairness inquiry" is a question of voluntariness[11] or of unconscionability relative to the time the agreement was signed.[12] This standard may include a requirement that signing parties have a reasonable opportunity to consult independent counsel.[13] Some states look at the unfairness or unconscionability of the agreement relative to the time of enforcement, either in addition to an examination of initial fairness or instead of it.[14] Premarital agreements are also subject to challenge under the doctrines that apply to all contracts, including misrepresentation, undue influence, and mutual mistake.[15]

"Fairness," however expressed, is a vague standard at the best of times. With premarital agreements, the key inquiry is "relative to what?" An agreement could be seen, on one hand, to give comfortable provision to a former spouse, but could simultaneously be seen as quite stingy relative to what that former spouse enjoyed during the marriage or would have received under the default statutory guidelines. Courts disagree about the relevance of these comparisons.[16]

Of course, what a fair provision is at the time of divorce itself raises difficult questions that may be unrelated to the specific issues of premarital agreements. What of a spouse who suffers severe and costly health problems during the course of the marriage, problems not directly related to the marriage or the other spouse? Should the healthy spouse be

would not have with a conventional commercial agreement. *See id.* at 167. Also, a few states that have adopted the UPAA read its requirements of "voluntariness" and "not unconscionable" in a narrow, proenforcement way, leading to a standard of oversight (or lack of oversight) similar to that for commercial agreements. *See*, for example, Marriage of Bonds, 24 Cal.4th 1, 5 P.3d 815, 99 Cal. Rptr.2d 252 (Cal. 2000), whose proenforcement reading of the UPAA resulted in a legislative amendment to state law (discussed, *supra*, in note 4).

[8] *See, e.g.*, DeMatteo v. DeMatteo, 762 N.E.2d 797, 805 (Mass. 2002) (summarizing Massachusetts law, which requires that premarital agreements be "fair and reasonable" at the time of enforcement).

[9] The same sorts of exceptions to the Statute of Frauds in other contexts are sometimes allowed for premarital agreements. *See, e.g.*, Dewberry v. George, 62 P.3d 525, 528–30 (Wash. Ct. App. 2003) (allowing the enforcement of an oral premarital agreement under the general partial performance exception to the Statute of Frauds).

[10] The state may require something short of complete and detailed disclosure, as long as the disclosure gives a general picture of the other party's financial situation. *See, e.g.*, In re Estate of Lopata, 641 P.2d 952, 955 (Colo. 1982). Also, some states allow the disclosure requirement to be overcome by an express waiver by the other party or by a showing that the other party had actual knowledge of the assets. *See, e.g.*, Sanford v. Sanford, 694 N.W.2d 283, 294 (S.D. 2005) (adequate knowledge of property may come either from disclosure or from independent knowledge).

[11] UPAA § 6(a)(1), 9C U.L.A. at 48; *cf. In re* Estate of John Albert Hollett, 834 A.2d 348 (N.H. 2003) (rejecting on "voluntariness" grounds agreement presented to partner on eve of marriage).

[12] UPAA § 6(a)(2), 9C U.L.A. at 49; *see* In re Marriage of Maifield, 2004 WL 61108 (Iowa App.) (finding reasonableness to be determined at the time the agreement is entered into, not when enforcement is sought). The UPAA seems to go even further than conventional contract law in requiring the party challenging enforcement to prove not only unconscionability, but also that the challenging party did not have or was not provided adequate knowledge of the other party's resources. UPAA § 6(a)(2), 9C U.L.A. at 49.

[13] *See, e.g.*, *In re* Marriage of Maifield, 2004 WL 61108 (Iowa App.).

[14] *See, e.g.*, Hardee v. Hardee, 585 S.E.2d 501, 504 (S.C. 2003); McKee-Johnson v. Johnson, 444 N.W.2d 259, 264–67 (Minn. 1989); Rider v. Rider, 669 N.E.2d 160, 164 (Ind. 1996); Gross v. Gross, 464 N.E.2d 500 (Ohio 1984).

[15] For a recent case applying a conventional contract law understanding of unconscionability to a premarital agreement, see *In re* Marriage of Drag, 762 N.E.2d 1111, 1115 (Ill. App. 1002).

[16] *See, e.g.*, DeMatteo v. DeMatteo, 762 N.E.2d 797, 809–13 (Mass. 2002) (rejecting comparisons of premarital agreement with what party would have received under statutory standards).

obligated to pay for the other's medical treatment, even after divorce? Does it matter how long the parties were married?[17] The answer to such questions will do much to determine whether one thinks the waiver of spousal support is unconscionable as applied to a spouse who has suffered severe medical problems.[18]

There are limits to the coverage of premarital agreements. Most prominently, they are not enforceable when they purport to cover child custody, child support, or visitation; and they cannot add or subtract from the grounds available for divorce, a point discussed in Part I.C.(1) below.

B. ALI Proposal

The PRINCIPLES seek to balance respect for party choice with a recognition of the "bounded rationality" that may be at work in many premarital agreements and the fact that changes may occur in the spouses' lives that make enforceability unfair. The "bounded rationality" reflects empirical work that shows that at the beginning of a relationship (whether that relationship is one of employment or romance), most people have trouble thinking realistically about the likelihood that the relationship will turn out badly – and that this barrier to self-protection may be particularly true given the altruism and commitment that, for many, mark the early stages of a marriage.[19] Also, unlike most other agreements, premarital agreements potentially cover a long time-period; and unlike other long-term agreements, premarital agreements occur in a context where risks are hard either to ascertain with precision or to hedge against.[20]

As part of the balance between protecting choice and protecting the vulnerable, the PRINCIPLES establish a number of procedural guidelines. Meeting the guidelines will significantly increase the likelihood that a premarital agreement will be enforced, but by no means will ensure such enforcement.[21]

The criteria for determining the enforceability of premarital agreements[22] are: agreements must be in writing[23] and they must have been entered into with informed consent and not while under duress.[24] Informed consent and an absence of duress are rebuttably presumed if certain procedural requirements were met: the agreement was entered into at least thirty days before the marriage, the parties were advised to obtain independent legal counsel and had reasonable opportunity to do so, there was plain language explaining the nature of the rights altered by the agreement (for agreements where one party did not have independent legal counsel),[25] and a party waiving rights

[17] *Cf. In re* Marriage of Wilson, 247 Cal. Rptr. 522 (Cal. Ct. App. 1988) (refusing to impose permanent alimony after short marriage where wife suffered permanent disability during the marriage).

[18] *See In re* Marriage of Rosendale, 15 Cal. Rptr. 3d 137 (Cal Ct. App. 2004) (holding such a provision unconscionable at the time of enforcement).

[19] *See* PRINCIPLES § 7.05 cmt. b, at 986–87.

[20] *See id.*

[21] This balance is summarized in PRINCIPLES § 7.02.

[22] All of these requirements are in addition to the requirements contract law doctrines impose on agreements generally. *See* PRINCIPLES § 7.01(4).

[23] PRINCIPLES § 7.04(1).

[24] PRINCIPLES § 7.04(2).

[25] PRINCIPLES § 7.01(3). In such circumstances, the PRINCIPLES also indicate that the agreement should state in plain language "that the interests of the spouses with respect to the agreement may be adverse." PRINCIPLES § 7.04(3)(c). In the context of a discussion of the application of Chapter 7 to domestic partners, Professor Westfall warns that this standard could potentially create traps for the unwary. Westfall, *supra* note 1, at 1483–84.

to alimony or property had at least approximate knowledge of the other party's assets and income.[26]

Even if an agreement is held to have been entered into voluntarily and with informed consent, the PRINCIPLES hold that it should not be enforced to the extent that the agreement, or one of its terms, would "work a substantial injustice."[27] A court's discretion in this judgment is somewhat cabined. First, a judge can only consider the question if one of three things has occurred since the signing of the agreement: a certain number of years have passed,[28] a child was born to or adopted by the couple, or there has been some unexpected change of circumstances "that has a substantial impact on the parties or their children."[29] These factors do not prove the substantial injustice, they simply open the question for a judge's consideration.

A comment in the PRINCIPLES indicates that the section on "substantial injustice" was meant to codify and add structure to what many courts were already doing when they conducted "fairness reviews" of premarital agreements.[30] As noted above, a number of jurisdictions test for fairness at the time of enforcement – or, more precisely, as to whether "the facts and circumstances [have] changed since the agreement was executed, so as to make its enforcement unfair and unreasonable."[31]

The PRINCIPLES instruct courts considering the "substantial injustice" question to consider the following factors: (1) the difference between the outcome under the agreement and the outcome under the generally applicable rules and principles; (2) in short marriages, the difference between the circumstances of the parties if the agreement is enforced and the parties' likely circumstances had they never married; (3) whether the purpose and effect of the agreement was to protect the interests of third parties,[32] and how well the agreement now serves those purposes; and (4) the impact of enforcing the agreement on the couple's children.[33]

The first factor seems straightforward, but it is not always obvious when (or even why) a disparity between the outcome under an agreement and the outcome under statutory standards should merit nonenforcement. Even jurisdictions known to be suspicious of premarital agreements and protective of weaker parties have upheld quite disparate outcomes where the disparity was clearly foreseeable at the time the agreement was entered.[34] This position seems reasonable, and perhaps inevitable, once one accepts that premarital agreements can at least sometimes be enforceable, for the whole purpose of these agreements is to

[26] PRINCIPLES §§ 7.04(3), (5). Westfall argues that this standard, in practice, could be deceptively difficult to meet. See Westfall, *supra* note 1, at 1484–85.

[27] PRINCIPLES § 7.05. An agreement to waive the rule requiring the gradual recharacterization of separate property as marital property is expressly exempted – it may not be challenged on "substantial injustice" grounds. PRINCIPLES § 7.05(5).

[28] It is to be "more than a fixed number of years . . . that number being set in a rule of statewide application," PRINCIPLES § 7.05(2)(a), and the Comments suggest that 10 years might be appropriate. *See* PRINCIPLES § 7.05 cmt. b, at 987.

[29] PRINCIPLES § 7.05(2)(c).

[30] PRINCIPLES § 7.05 cmt. a, at 984.

[31] Hardee v. Hardee, 585 S.E.2d 501, 503 (S.C. 2003).

[32] PRINCIPLES § 7.05(3). Children from a prior relationship would constitute third parties for this purpose. PRINCIPLES § 7.05(3)(c).

[33] PRINCIPLES § 7.05(3)(d). The party challenging enforcement of the agreement carries the burden of proof under this section. PRINCIPLES § 7.05(3).

[34] *See, e.g.*, Richard v. Richard, 2004 Minn. App. LEXIS 1475, at 24 review denied, 2005 Minn. LEXIS 150 (Minn. Mar. 15, 2005) (affirming distribution based on agreement, which left husband with $858,366 and wife $60,450; wife argued that under Minnesota law the outcome would likely have been much different, but the court upheld the distribution "in light of the parties' individual financial circumstances and the language of the agreement").

ensure outcomes significantly different than that reached under statutory guidelines. A similar observation might be mode regarding the second factor.

The third and fourth factors are of particular interest. The third factor, third-party interests, relates to a point raised earlier: that premarital agreements are sometimes entered with the purpose of protecting children from a prior marriage,[35] a purpose which might strike courts (and others) more favorably than agreements entered into merely to reduce alimony obligations or to allow one party to retain more of the property acquired during the marriage than state law would otherwise permit. In any event, the equitable claims of such third parties would have to be considered in any claims of injustice by a spouse now challenging enforcement of an agreement he or she had signed.

The fourth factor, the impact on children, reflects an unfortunate reality regarding modern marriage and divorce. In principle, the financial provisions between current and former spouses should be separable from the financial support of the children – because child support is set by guidelines (which attempt to set adequate levels of funding for the children) or by the parties in separation agreements reached in the shadow of those guidelines. The reality, however, is that (a) child support is frequently not paid in full; and (b) even when paid in full, the support payments may often fall short of what is needed. Thus, there is a real chance that children born to a couple who has signed a premarital agreement can be harmed when a custodial spouse receives less property or alimony.

C. Special Cases

1. Covenant Marriage Agreements

In three states, couples have the option of entering a "covenant marriage."[36] This is meant to be a more binding form of marriage, requiring counseling prior to marriage and any divorce, and restricting the grounds on which divorce can be granted. Such restrictions usually lengthen significantly the time of separation required before a no-fault divorce can be granted.

Covenant marriages can be seen as a kind of state-sponsored alternative agreement or alternative form for marriages. The statutory covenant marriage option raises the issue of whether couples about to marry should be able to enter enforceable agreements of this kind, limiting their rights to divorce as a way of creating a stronger commitment to the marriage, even in the absence of express statutory authorization. The PRINCIPLES provide that such agreements should not be enforceable.[37] This conclusion is generally consistent with the sparse caselaw on the subject, but there has been some scholarly commentary urging a different result.[38]

[35] *Cf. In re* Estate of John Albert Hollett, 834 A.2d 348, 350 (N.H. 2003) (noting evidence that premarital agreement for second marriage was suggested or "insisted upon" by husband's first wife).

[36] ARIZ. REV. STAT. ANN. §§ 25-901 to 25-906 (West 2000 & Supp. 2004); ARK. CODE ANN. §§ 9-11-801 to 9–11–811 (Lexis 2002 & Supp. 2003); LA. REV. STAT. ANN. §§ 9:272–76 (West 2000 & Supp. 2005). For a general discussion, see Katherine Shaw Spaht, *Louisiana's Covenant Marriage: Social Analysis and Legal Implications*, 59 LA. L. REV. 63 (1998). While generally an option for couples about to marry, these laws also allow couples already married to "convert" their marriage to a covenant marriage. *See, e.g.*, ARIZ. STAT. ANN. § 25-902 (West Supp. 2004).

[37] PRINCIPLES § 7.08(1) ("A term in an agreement is not enforceable if it limits or enlarges the grounds for divorce otherwise available under state law.").

[38] *See, e.g.*, Eric Rasmusen & Jeffrey Evans Stake, *Lifting the Veil of Ignorance: Personalizing the Marriage Contract*, 73 IND. L.J. 453 (1998).

The PRINCIPLES do state in a comment: "In principle, a state could adopt laws that allowed parties to choose, at the time of their marriage, the rules that would govern its potential dissolution. This section neither endorses nor opposes this possibility."[39] However, this neutrality seems inconsistent with the text of Section 7.08(1), which, if adopted, would make just such agreements unenforceable.[40] The comment justifies the Section's position by noting that states have historically refused to recognize such agreements.[41] However, this seems a timid response for the drafters, who certainly elsewhere do not limit themselves simply to restating current state law.

There is much to be said in favor of premarital agreements through which parties commit themselves to a more binding form of marriage, despite the dangers and difficulties. It might have been useful had the PRINCIPLES at least encouraged states to consider the enforceability of such agreements on a case-by-case basis, rather than continuing a per se rule of unenforceability.

2. Traditional Religious Agreements

One difficult, but rarely discussed issue for the legal enforcement of premarital agreements involves agreements the terms of which are set by religious doctrine.[42] The prominent examples are the Jewish *ketubah* and the Islamic *mahr*. The *ketubah* is signed as part of the Jewish marriage ceremony, but it is commonly treated in courts as a premarital agreement.[43] Many modern *ketubahs* have terms requiring a husband, upon obtaining a civil divorce, to agree to cooperate in obtaining a religious divorce (a *get*), without which the former wife would not be allowed to marry under religious law.[44] The *mahr* similarly is part of the Islamic marriage, and involves a promise to pay money to the wife, an obligation that may not become due until the termination of the marriage.[45] A few courts have interpreted

[39] PRINCIPLES § 7.08 cmt. a, at 1004.

[40] The PRINCIPLES recognize that there is at least one well-known case of a court enforcing an agreement limiting the grounds for divorce. PRINCIPLES § 7.08 Reporter's Notes, cmt. a, at 1007, citing Masser v. Masser, 652 A.2d 219 (N.J. Super. Ct. App. Div. 1994). *Masser* enforced an agreement by which one party agreed only to seek a no-fault ground of divorce in return for the other party's vacating the marital home. This had the effect of delaying divorce for a significant period, as New Jersey's law at the time required an 18 month separation for no-fault divorce. *Id.* However, as the PRINCIPLES point out, the court was careful to note that such an agreement would not preclude a fault-based divorce based on conduct occurring after the agreement was entered. *See id*; Masser, 652 A.2d at 223.

[41] *See* PRINCIPLES § 7.08, Reporter's Notes, cmt. a, at 1006–07.

[42] Among the few articles on the topic are the following: Jodi M. Solovy, *Civil Enforcement of Jewish Marriage and Divorce: Constitutional Accommodation of a Religious Mandate*, 45 DEPAUL L. REV. 493 (1996); Jessica Davidson Miller, *The History of the Agunah in America: A Clash of Religious Law and Social Progress*, 19 WOMEN'S RTS L. REP. 1 (1997); Ghada G. Qaisi, *Religious Marriage Contracts: Judicial Enforcement of Mahr Agreements in American Courts*, 15 J. L. & RELIGION 67 (2001); Lindsey E. Blenkhorn, *Islamic Marriage Contracts in American Courts: Interpreting Mahr Agreements as Prenuptials and Their Effect on Muslim Women*, 76 S. CAL. L. REV. 189 (2002).

[43] PRINCIPLES § 7.08 Reporter's Notes, cmt. a, at 1008.

[44] *See* Avitzur v. Avitzur, 446 N.E.2d 136 (N.Y. 1983) (enforcing *ketubah* term requiring parties to appear before religious tribunal and accept its decision regarding a religious divorce). New York also has a statute requiring similar cooperation. NEW YORK DOM. REL. § 253 (McKinney 1999 & Supp. 2004).

[45] Apparently there is some dispute as to whether or under what circumstances a wife might lose her right to the payment if she initiates a divorce. *Compare* Dajani v. Dajani, 204 Cal. App. 3d 1387, 1389, 151 Cal. Rptr. 871, 872 (Cal Ct. App. 1988) (summarizing expert witness testimony that wife forfeits right to *mahr* payment if she initiates the divorce) *with* Zubair Fattani, *Islamic Mahr, available at* www.islamicacademy.org/html/Articles/English/Islamic_Mehr.htm (last visited Aug. 11, 2005) (summarizing other interpretations of Islamic law under which the wife only forfeits the payment if she has "no reason" for separating from her husband).

the *mahr* as supplanting any other financial claims the wife has against the husband on divorce.[46]

Religious premarital agreements raise two distinct problems. First, their enforcement may raise constitutional issues because of possible entanglement of the civil courts with religion; and second, because these agreements are thought to be required by one's religion and the terms are therefore set by tradition or authority, the parties' consent to the individual terms is arguably less than complete. Also, many of these agreements may have been entered into when the couple was living in another country, raising further considerations of comity in determining whether the law of the U.S. state in which the agreement is being litigated should govern the validity of such an agreement.[47]

The PRINCIPLES say little about religious premarital agreements.[48] Presumably the "standard form" of such agreements would receive the same treatment (neither better nor worse) as more individualized conventional premarital agreements.[49]

It appears a mistake to treat religious premarital agreements the same as secular, individually negotiated agreements. Religious agreements are form contracts, the terms of which are set by religious tradition or current religious teachings. At the same time, while this is the case, and while constitutional doctrine indicates that religious beliefs do not trump state regulation of domestic practices,[50] it would still seem wiser to presume the enforceability of such agreements. Thus, for example, a *mahr* might be presumptively enforceable if the payments required are within a reasonable range relative to the means of the parties; enforceability should be questioned, however, if the *mahr* payment is small and construed as preempting other court assignments of property or orders of alimony.

D. General Analysis and Discussion

As mentioned earlier, the PRINCIPLES' discussion of premarital agreements represents an effort to balance competing interests: the values of autonomy and predictability on the side of enforcing such agreements, and concerns about bounded rationality and protecting the vulnerable on the side of nonenforcement.

While the problem of bounded rationality is a real one with premarital agreements – it is hard to think clearly about the financial terms of the end of a romantic relationship when one is at an early period of the relationship – it is possible to overstate the problem here. Parties entering premarital agreements are not like some arbitrary group of newlyweds who understate their likelihood of getting divorced.[51] These are people who have been

[46] *See* Chaudry v. Chaudry, 388 A.2d 1000 (N.J. Super. Ct. App. Div. 1978).

[47] *See* Fattani, *Islamic Mahr, supra* note 45.

[48] Some *ketubahs* may require both parties to cooperate in obtaining a religious divorce, if a civil divorce has been set. The PRINCIPLES state that Chapter 7 does not render such provisions unenforceable if they are "otherwise enforceable under applicable legal principles." PRINCIPLES § 7.08 cmt. a, at 1004–05. *See also* PRINCIPLES § 7.08 reporter's notes, cmt. a, at 1008.

[49] As discussed above, *supra* note 48, the PRINCIPLES expressly approve the enforcement of *ketubah* provisions requiring cooperation in obtaining a religious divorce, if in those states where such provisions are otherwise enforceable.

[50] *See, e.g.*, Reynolds v. United States, 98 U.S. 145 (1878) (upholding application of law prohibiting polygamy to individuals whose religious faith required polygamy).

[51] See Lynn A. Baker & Robert E. Emery, *When Every Relationship Is Above Average: Perceptions and Expectations of Divorce at the Time of Marriage*, 17 LAW & HUM. BEHAV. 439, 443 (1993) (showing that students of family law course had low estimate of their own chance of divorcing, despite knowing the high rate of divorce nationwide).

given divorce-related financial agreements, frequently with the instruction that the marriage will not go ahead unless certain divorce-focused financial rights are waived. Thus, the best analogy is probably *not* employment agreements that include posttermination restrictive covenants. With premarital agreements, the waiver of rights is not tangential to the agreement or hidden at the end, as it may be with an employment agreement that includes a posttermination restrictive covenant. With an employment agreement, the focus of both parties is understandably on the wages and other present terms of the job, not the possibility of eventual termination and its consequences. With a premarital agreement, the possibility of termination and its consequences are the sole purpose of the agreement. Thus, a better analogy might be living wills and similar advance medical directives: while healthy people might not be able to think cogently about choices in extreme states of illness, at least the individual's thinking is clearly directed to the issue. Thus, the extent to which cognitive defects are likely to infect the parties' evaluation of premarital agreements is not as great as some claim.[52]

In considering the proper approach to enforcement of premarital agreements, the potential costs and benefits of enforcement must also be considered.[53] On the benefit side are many of the advantages associated with the enforcement of agreements generally. First, individuals have increased autonomy when they can enter binding agreements. Second, social welfare increases when parties, who usually have the greatest understanding of what is in their best interests, are able to make binding arrangements and exchanges among themselves.

On the cost side are three concerns. First, people are not always able to protect their own interests, and, as discussed, premarital agreements may be one area where such "bounded rationality" or "cognitive defects" may be most prevalent.[54] Second, there are frequently third parties, mostly children, who could be harmed by the enforcement of certain premarital agreements. Third, there are arguably social benefits to the way the state has structured marriage – such as the benefits that might come from the guarantee of an equal, or near-equal, division of marital resources upon divorce – benefits that might be lost if parties are allowed to alter the state-supplied terms.

Of course, a mixture of costs and benefits arises for those marriages that will be entered into or not because of the likelihood (viewed from the time the agreement would be entered into) that premarital agreements will be enforced. This chapter returns to this point after clarifying the idea of enforceability.

Relative to the time of signing, one could judge the eventual enforceability of premarital agreements along a spectrum: from certainly unenforceable (as they were in most jurisdictions until the last decades of the twentieth century), to uncertain regarding their enforceability, to certainly enforceable. In nearly every U.S. jurisdiction, and under the PRINCIPLES, agreements are uncertain in their enforceability, though the level of uncertainty may vary significantly, from highly likely to be enforced, to hard to predict, to highly unlikely to be enforced.[55] The "substantial injustice" provisions of the PRINCIPLES

[52] Professor Westfall makes a similar point. *See* Westfall, *supra* note 1, at 1487. It is probably for example true that people underestimate how children will change their lives. However, given the ready evidence from friends, relatives, coworkers, and strangers, this knowledge should be easily available. It is not clear that the law should protect parties who avoid such knowledge in a way that might border on self-delusion.

[53] *See* Westfall, *supra* note 1, at 1488 (raising an analogous point).

[54] Melvin Aron Eisenberg, *The Limits of Cognition and the Limits of Contract*, 47 STAN. L. REV. 211 (1995).

[55] PRINCIPLES § 7.05.

would seem to create significant uncertainty regarding enforceability, though of course, this perception might be altered by the way the provisions are interpreted by judges in a jurisdiction adopting them.[56] Finally, in a small number of jurisdictions – principally, jurisdictions that have adopted the UPAA as written, and Pennsylvania[57] – the enforcement of premarital agreements is as nearly certain as the enforcement of most conventional commercial agreements.

There are people who will not get married unless a premarital agreement is signed and they are confident that the agreement will be enforced.[58] There are others who will only get married if there is no agreement, or if they are confident that any agreement signed will not be enforced. There is currently no data regarding how many people are in which group, so any discussion of the effects of enforceability on marriage is necessarily speculative. Any level of enforceability is likely to affect who gets married and under what conditions: certain or near-certain enforceability will cause some to get married who otherwise would not, but may deter other marriages that might otherwise have occurred. The same result may be expected with certain or near-certain nonenforcement. Interestingly, where enforceability is highly uncertain, this may allow parties who want an enforceable agreement and those who do not, to sign such an agreement based on their individual best guesses about what a court would eventually do, with one party assuming enforcement and the other nonenforcement.

Whether having more marriages or fewer is in fact a benefit requires further discussion. While religious leaders and political leaders have both promoted marriage, it is not obvious that marriage is always a good thing, either for the individuals involved or for society generally.[59] At the least, it is far from clear that every marriage is an unmitigated good, whatever its underlying terms and facts might be. There is certainly an argument to be made that if a premarital agreement is sufficiently one-sided, marriage on such terms is worse than no marriage at all (to the parties involved and to society generally).

The PRINCIPLES' set of procedural requirements at the formation stage are welcome – both for clarifying vague standards in some jurisdictions, and for encouraging more overview of procedures in those jurisdictions that had not done so before. The vague after-the-fact "injustice" test is, however, less helpful. Under that test, judges have discretion to reconsider the enforceability of a very broad range of agreements, and their eventual decision whether to enforce will be hard to predict, even at the time of litigation. The factors listed for the judge's consideration in determining whether an agreement should be enforced will do little actually to channel the exercise of discretion, although they may give structure to the court's opinion. In fairness, however, this complaint could be made about many multifactor standards in family law judicial decision-making.

There are inevitably costs and benefits to any approach to the regulation of premarital agreements, whether choosing, as the PRINCIPLES do, to favor the protecting of the vulnerable, or choosing, as the UPAA does, to favor the values of autonomy and predictability.

[56] For a discussion about the way that the PRINCIPLES leave their terms open to quite different applications, and thus, effectively, creates significant judicial discretion, see Robert J. Levy, *Ellman's "Why Making Family Law is Hard": Additional Reflections*, 35 ARIZ. ST. L.J. 723, 724–40 (2003).

[57] Pennsylvania has a significant proenforcement decision by its supreme court. *See* Simeone v. Simeone, 581 A.2d 162 (Pa. 1990), discussed *supra* note 7.

[58] *Cf.* DeMatteo v. DeMatteo, 762 N.E.2d 797, 801 (Mass. 2002) ("[T]he husband was 'very clear that such an agreement was necessary.'").

[59] For an overview of this debate, see Anita Bernstein, *For and Against Marriage*, 102 MICH. L. REV. 129 (2003).

Reasonable minds can differ on this matter. It may be better to protect parties through a combination of formation standards like those in the PRINCIPLES, and standard contract doctrines, while protecting the interests of children primarily through the rules of child support which can more easily be updated and more effectively enforced. Other unforeseen misfortunes are arguably better seen as the responsibility of society generally rather than of the former spouse alone.

II. Marital Agreements

A. Overview and Current Doctrine

The category of "marital agreements" covers any agreement between the spouses entered after marriage, but not in contemplation of separation or imminent divorce. This usually means an agreement which purports to affect significantly the property rights of the spouses during the marriage or after, or alimony claims after divorce. A commercial agreement between spouses raises distinctive legal issues not considered in this chapter.[60]

Some states apply the same principles to marital agreements that they apply to premarital agreements.[61] Other states impose different requirements on marital agreements than they do on premarital agreements.[62] The basis for this difference may be as simple as the fact that the UPAA applies to premarital agreements but, by its own terms, does not apply to marital agreements[63]; or there may be a more contextual analysis, concluding that premarital agreements are more likely to be "arms-length" negotiations,[64] while marital agreements are more likely to be coercive.[65]

Sometimes the legal treatment of these agreements turns on their factual context and the intentions with which they were entered. In particular, some jurisdictions treat "reconciliation agreements" as a special form of agreement, deserving some respect and deference.[66] In such agreements, the parties agree to reconcile or to resume cohabitation, conditioned on some modification of their marital or post-dissolution property arrangements. These agreements may be enforceable in jurisdictions where other marital agreements are not,

[60] Among the questions here is whether the spouses intended their agreement to be legally binding or whether (because they are married) they prefer that the agreement not result in legally enforceable obligations. *See, e.g.*, Balfour v. Balfour, [1919] 2 K.B. 571 (C.A. 1919) (denying enforcement to an agreement between spouses); *see generally* E. ALLAN FARNSWORTH, CONTRACTS § 3.7, at 119 (4th ed., 2004) (discussing the modern approach to such agreements).

[61] *See, e.g.*, N.Y. DOM REL. LAW § 236, Part B(3) (McKinney 1999 & Supp. 2004); N.C. GEN. STAT. § 52–10(a) (2003); WIS. STAT. ANN. § 766.58 (West 2001 & Supp. 2004); Bratton v. Bratton, 136 S.W.3d 595, 599–601 (Tenn. 2004); Flansburg v. Flansburg, 581 N.E.2d 430, 433 (Ind. Ct. App. 1991).

[62] *See* MINN. STAT. § 519.11, subd. 1a (2002 & Supp. 2003); LA. CIV. CODE ANN. Civil Code art. 2329 (West 1985 & Supp. 2004); *In re* Marriage of Grossman, 82 P.3d 1039, 1043 (Or. Ct. App. 2003) (holding that marital agreements are subject to a "more vigilant" fairness overview than are premarital agreements); Pacelli v. Pacelli, 725 A.2d 56, 61–62 (N.J. Super. Ct. App. Div. 1999) (finding a need for greater scrutiny for fairness in a marital agreement).

[63] *See, e.g.*, Davis v. Miller, 7 P.3d 1223, 1229–30 (Kan. 2000) (holding that the Kansas version of the UPAA does not apply to marital agreements, but that the parties can, through express choice of law provisions, have their marital agreements judged under UPAA standards).

[64] *See In re* Marriage of Grossman, 82 P.3d 1039, 1043 (Or. Ct. App. 2003).

[65] *See* Pacelli v. Pacelli, 725 A.2d 56, 59 (N.J. Super. App. Div. 1999).

[66] *See, e.g., In re* Estate of Duggan, 639 So. 2d 1071 (Fla. Dist. Ct. App. 1994) (finding valid as reconciliation agreement a marital agreement involving waiver of estate interests). Special treatment of reconciliation agreements, allowing their enforcement, has roots that are relatively ancient. *See, e.g.*, Annot., *Validity and Enforceability of Agreement Designed to Prevent Divorce, or Avoid or End Separation*, 11 A.L.R. 277 (1921).

because of the state's interest in couples remaining married.[67] Thus, if it turns out that one party's manifested intention to reconcile was false, the resulting agreement will not receive favorable treatment, and may be voidable on grounds of fraud.[68]

As a matter of general contract law, enforceable agreements must be supported by adequate legal consideration.[69] This is not a problem with most commercial agreements (where the payment by one party, and the goods or services of the other party, would constitute the necessary consideration), nor is it a problem with separation agreements where both parties are waiving potential claims. Neither is it a problem with premarital agreements, where the decision to marry is the consideration. However, it can potentially be a serious issue with marital agreements, at least those in which the decision to reconcile is not the consideration.[70]

With such cases, consideration should arguably not be seen as a technical requirement designed to trip up the unwary. Rather, it is an indirect way of determining whether there is a true bargain, or just a coerced transfer of goods or rights. Consideration once played a similar role in commercial law, trying to help determine whether modifications of agreements were reasonable accommodations or coerced "hold-ups" by parties who suddenly found themselves, midperformance, with bargaining leverage.[71] Today, this function in commercial law is done by direct inquiries into "good faith" and "coercion."[72] Contract law has moved beyond formalistic inquiries into consideration in modification cases, in large part because modifications of commercial agreements are considered a normal part of daily business, with the understanding that such "one-sided changes" are frequently grounded in good reasons and good faith.[73] Accommodations in commercial arrangements are needed for unexpected changes in supply, costs of resources, and difficulty in completion. However, in the marital context, it is harder to think of good-faith reasons for mid-"performance" adjustments of terms, at least outside the context of reconciliation agreements. Thus, requiring consideration might serve a useful purpose for marital agreements (though not all jurisdictions require it[74]). Additionally, neither the formality of consideration, nor the focus on a general structure of reconciliation, can always distinguish the wronged or disenchanted spouse who is reluctantly persuaded to reconcile, from the bad faith spouse who uses a false claim of estrangement and threat of divorce to coerce a favorable property settlement from his or her partner.[75]

This analysis may seem inconsistent with earlier arguments. On one hand, this chapter has urged courts to reject on grounds of duress marital agreements where one spouse effectively states that he or she will continue the marriage only on more favorable economic terms. On the other hand, nothing similar was urged for apparently comparable situations

[67] *See, e.g.*, Flansburg v. Flansburg, 581 N.E.2d 430, 437 (Ind. Ct. App. 1991).

[68] *Cf.* Fogg v. Fogg, 567 N.E.2d 921, 923 (Mass. 1991) (refusing to enforce particular reconciliation agreement where wife lied about her motivation to reconcile, but not deciding the general enforceability of reconciliation agreements).

[69] *See, e.g.*, FARNSWORTH, *supra* note 60, § 2.2, at 47.

[70] *See, e.g.*, Bratton v. Bratton, 136 S.W.3d 595, 600 (Tenn. 2004) (refusing to enforce marital agreement in part because of absence of consideration).

[71] See, for example, the discussions in the classic "hold-up" consideration case of Alaska Packers' Ass'n v. Domenico, 114 F. 99 (N.D. Cal. 1902).

[72] *See, e.g.*, FARNSWORTH, *supra* note 60, §§ 4.21-4.22, at 267–74.

[73] *See, e.g.*, U.C.C. § 2–209(1) (1977) (requiring no consideration for a binding modification for sales of goods).

[74] *See, e.g.*, FLA. STAT. ANN. ch. 732.702(3) (West 1995 & Supp. 2004) (expressly rejecting a consideration requirement for either marital or premarital agreements).

[75] *See* Pacelli v. Pacelli, 725 A.2d 56, 58 (N.J. Super. App. Div. 1999) (concluding husband used a threat of divorce to coerce a favorable marital agreement).

with premarital agreements, where a potential spouse states that he or she will only enter marriage on certain financial terms reflected in a premarital agreement. However, the different legal treatment would be justifiable: a "take it or leave it" offer to marry on certain terms is usually less coercive than a "take it or leave it" offer to stay married, especially where the divorce would be perceived as harming the children or leaving the spouse who accepts it in a precarious social or financial condition.[76]

B. ALI Proposal

The PRINCIPLES offers relatively little on the topic of marital agreements. Section 7.01(b) defines a "marital agreement" as "an agreement between spouses who plan to continue their marriage that alters or confirms the legal rights and obligations that would otherwise arise under these Principles or other law governing marital dissolution." The text goes on to affirm that the same principles that apply to premarital agreements would apply to marital agreements.[77]

To make the treatment of marital agreements roughly comparable to that of premarital agreements (where execution thirty days prior to marriage is an integral part of creating a rebuttable presumption of voluntariness[78]), the PRINCIPLES allows either party to rescind the marital agreement within thirty days of signing.[79]

C. Special Cases

One category of reported case that seems to be appearing with greater frequency, and one that is specifically discussed, albeit briefly, in the PRINCIPLES, are agreements where the parties agree to attach specific financial sanctions to certain behavior.[80] For example, in *Mehren v. Dargan*, a couple separated due in large part to the husband's problems with cocaine addiction.[81] The parties reunited, and entered an agreement under which the husband agreed not to use illegal drugs, and further agreed that if he violated this promise, he would lose his community property right to certain property.[82] The husband violated the agreement, but the California Court of Appeal held the agreement to be unenforceable because contrary to public policy: it conflicted with the principles behind the state's no fault divorce laws.[83]The court also noted that such a contract would also fail for lack of consideration, as there is an existing legal obligation to refrain from using illegal drugs.[84]

[76] *See id.* at 59. The one situation in which a premarital agreement might be as coercive as a reconciliation agreement is where the premarital agreement is presented on the eve of the marriage, when expensive wedding arrangements have been irrevocably made and guests have already arrived. A number of courts have, correctly, invalidated premarital agreements presented this late under the rubric of duress or voluntariness. *See, e.g., In re* Marriage of Maifield, 2004 WL 61108 (Iowa App.). The PRINCIPLES make such a late presentation a reason for doubting the voluntariness of an agreement. *See* PRINCIPLES § 7.04(3)(c) & cmts. c, at 963 & d, at 966–67.

[77] PRINCIPLES § 7.01(3). *See also* PRINCIPLES § 7.01 Reporter's Notes, cmt. e, at 953.

[78] PRINCIPLES § 7.04(3)(a).

[79] PRINCIPLES § 7.04(4)(b) (stating that "if the other party previously parted with anything of value pursuant to the agreement, the rescinding party must restore it promptly upon rescission, or the rescission is not effective").

[80] PRINCIPLES § 7.08(2).

[81] Mehren v. Dargan, 13 Cal. Rptr. 3d 522, 522–23 (Cal. Ct. App. 2004).

[82] *Id.* at 523.

[83] *Id.* at 524–25.

[84] *Id.* at 525–26.

The PRINCIPLES reach a similar outcome. An agreement cannot "require or forbid a court to evaluate marital conduct in allocating marital property or awarding compensatory payments, except as the term incorporates principles of state law that so provide. . . ."[85]

Two substantial arguments support this approach. First, as the California court in *Mehren* argued, to allow parties to agree to such sanctions permits them effectively to circumvent the public policy that fault not play a significant role in the division of marital assets. Second, enforcing such agreements potentially opens up the court to being the overseer of an endless number of petty matters.[86]

On the other hand, one might argue that marital agreements should not be treated so differently from similar agreements outside of marriage. It is standard contract law that one party may make an enforceable promise to pay a second person if that second person does not smoke for five years, or walks across the Brooklyn Bridge, or the like.[87] Assuming one can avoid the consideration problem in *Mehren* – that is, the activity being proscribed cannot be one already legally prohibited or, conversely, the activity required cannot be one already legally required[88] – why should married partners not be able to promise one another rewards or sanctions for behavior?

Consider again the *Mehren* case, but assume that the agreement deals with a legal activity like drinking alcohol rather than an illegal activity like using cocaine. In that case, the possibility of entering an enforceable agreement with significant sanctions for violation facilitated the parties' reconciliation. Without the husband's ability to enter an enforceable agreement, whereby his promise carried the weight of real financial risk, the wife might have been unwilling to give him another chance. If we are interested in parties staying married, then refusing to enforce agreements of this sort may do more harm than good.

Here one needs to be careful in discussing how agreements of this sort would be treated outside of marriage. As stated, a contract involving one person's promise to pay a friend if that friend refrains from drinking alcohol for a set period of time is clearly enforceable. However, a simple promise by one person not to drink combined with a second promise to pay a large sum of money if he or she breaks the first promise, would face a number of hurdles to enforcement. First, the recipient of the promise does not seem to provide any consideration – though this difficulty would be overcome in the reconciliation context, where returning to the marital household would be consideration.[89] Second, promises to pay a large sum for breach are usually viewed as "penalty" clauses.[90]

Though a number of prominent commentators have argued for the enforceability of penalty clauses, under U.S. contract law such clauses are universally treated as unenforceable.[91] At the same time, where a preset sanction is in fact a reasonable estimate of the

[85] PRINCIPLES § 7.08(2).

[86] Imagine an agreement which provides that "loss or right to a marital asset will occur if . . . the wife's mother visits more than once a week or the husband does not do at least four hours of housework each week."

[87] *See* Hamer v. Sidway, 27 N.E. 256 (N.Y. 1891); FARNSWORTH, *supra* note 60, § 2.4, at 51–52 (discussing *Sidway*).

[88] Promises of that sort would not be legal consideration because there would be no detriment to the promisor. *See, e.g.*, JOHN EDWARD MURRAY, JR., MURRAY ON CONTRACTS § 56, at 243 (4th ed., 2001) (discussing "Absence of Detriment").

[89] The agreement to return to the marital home may comprise an express counterpromise or, if not, may nonetheless serve as reliance sufficient to make the promise enforceable. *See* RESTATEMENT (SECOND) OF CONTRACTS § 90 (1981).

[90] *See, e.g.*, Aaron S. Edlin & Alan Schwartz, *Optimal Penalties in Contracts*, 78 CHI. KENT L. REV. 33 (2003).

[91] *See* FARNSWORTH, *supra* note 60, § 12.18, at 811–13.

damages that the innocent party might suffer in case of breach, such a provision will be enforced as "liquidated damages."[92] In the context of a reconciliation agreement, one can imagine a partner saying that he or she will take a risk, and give the relationship one more chance, understanding that the spouse's future failure would cause harm in the form of disappointment, heartache, or wasted time; as a consequence, a certain fee, while obviously not a full equivalent, would be a reasonable estimate of that loss.

It seems clear that the PRINCIPLES veered away from enforcement of these sorts of marital agreements for the same reason that they rejected enforcement of private covenant marriages: the PRINCIPLES have a basic antagonism toward – or fear of – anything that seems to require a judicial finding of fault.[93]

D. Analysis

The PRINCIPLES apply the premarital agreement rules to marital agreements. As noted, current law sometimes distinguishes between circumstances in which marital agreements are entered, and appropriately so. If one's concern relates to cognitive defects, then one should certainly distinguish between an agreement entered in the early and optimistic days of a marriage and an agreement entered as part of a "reconciliation," at a point when one or both partners has seriously considered divorce.

At the same time, marital agreements can raise special factors arguing either for or against their enforcement, depending on the context in which they are entered. If enforceability of a marital agreement can make such an agreement instrumental to reconciling parties who might otherwise divorce, this would usually seem like a good thing. On the other hand, marital agreements create special opportunities for subtle coercion, paired with a sort of vulnerable sacrifice, which may warrant paternalistic intervention.[94]

In any event, there seem to be strong reasons for having rules that distinguish between the legal treatment of marital agreements and the legal treatment of premarital agreements (and separation agreements). There may also be good reasons for distinguishing among marital agreements, according to the context in which they are entered.

Unsurprisingly, one's attitude toward marital agreements will likely reflect one's general attitude to contracting between partners. The increasingly favorable legal treatment of premarital agreements seems to reflect a belief that parties should be able to structure the legal and financial contours of their marriage to reflect their interests and values coming in. This same view would seem to justify enforcing agreements that reflect changing interests and values held by those same couples.

Consider the California case, *Borelli v. Brusseau.*[95] In the case, a wife claimed that her late husband orally agreed to leave her certain properties in exchange for her agreement to care for him personally during his illness. The alleged agreement involved giving the wife certain property and money that the wife might have had claims to under state law had she not earlier signed a premarital agreement waiving some of her rights.[96] The court

[92] *See id.*, § 12.18, at 811–20 (summarizing the rule).

[93] This antipathy is clearest in the discussion of the role that marital misconduct should play in determining the financial terms after divorce. *See* PRINCIPLES, Topic 1, Overview of Chapter 7, pt. III, at 42–67.

[94] For a good discussion of these dynamics, and their repercussions for legal regulation, see Michael J. Trebilcock & Steven Elliott, *The Scope and Limits of Legal Paternalism: Altruism and Coercion in Family Financial Arrangements*, *in* THE THEORY OF CONTRACT LAW: NEW ESSAYS 45–85 (Peter Benson ed., Cambridge, 2001).

[95] 12 Cal. App. 4th 647, 16 Cal. Rptr. 2d 16 (1993).

[96] *Id.* at 650, 16 Cal. Rptr. 2d at 17 (describing the premarital agreement). Because California is a community property state, the wife would have an equal partnership interest during the marriage in wealth acquired during the marriage

refused to enforce the marital agreement of property for services because the agreement lacked consideration and was contrary to public policy – both conclusions were based on the argument that under California law spouses owe one another an obligation of care, and the wife here was merely promising to do what she already had an obligation to do.[97] Without claiming that this was precisely the case in the marriage in *Borelli*, it is easy to imagine a situation where bargaining leverage shifts from one party to the other during the relationship. For instance, a woman may want to get married, and her partner is indifferent on the subject, and on that basis a premarital agreement is entered into in which she waives some rights in order to persuade him to marry. Years into the marriage, the bargaining leverage may shift, either because he wants special personal care or because he wants the marriage to continue more than she does. On that basis, he transfers certain rights to her in exchange for her staying or for her personal care. The question in both sorts of cases is what we think about one partner using the partner's current bargaining advantage to get something that partner wants while offering something significant in return.

At least in the case where one party is offering to "return" rights waived in the premarital agreement, there is likely a strong intuition for enforcement – either as a matter of fairness, or because of a feeling of "poetic justice." Our inclinations might differ where one party uses bargaining leverage for the first time during the marriage, precisely when the other spouse is particularly vulnerable.

There will always be a difficult fact-sensitive judgment necessary to decide whether the marital agreement is being entered for good reasons, and as a good-faith accommodation, or whether the agreement is in fact a bad-faith coercion. But family law would be wise to look to conventional contract law, where the structure of analysis is already well worked out in the analogous context of modifications of existing contractual terms.

III. Separation Agreements

A. Overview and Current Doctrine

Separation agreements are agreements entered into when legal separation or divorce is imminent, with the purpose of settling the terms of the dissolution. In the vast majority of divorces, an estimated 75 percent to over 90 percent,[98] the terms of divorce are settled by the parties in "the shadow of the law" – that is, aware of the terms a court would likely impose if the divorce was tried.[99] This is, of course, not unusual; outside of family law disputes, many more cases end by settlement rather than litigated verdict. Settlement is favored in divorce cases, not only because it saves party and judicial resources, but because

by either party (except property acquired by gift, bequest, or inheritance), absent a premarital agreement. CAL. FAM. CODE §§ 751, 752, 760, 770 (West 1994 & Supp. 2004). Also, she would have inherited at least half of that "community property" upon her husband's death. *See* CAL. PROB. CODE § 6401 (West 1991 & Supp. 2004).

[97] The dissenting opinion argued that by promising to care for her husband personally, the wife promised more than her statutory obligation. *Borelli*, 12 Cal. App. 4th at 659–60, 16 Cal. Rptr. 2d at 26–27 (Poche, J., dissenting). There is reason to believe that the true ground for the court's decision was its fear that the alleged oral agreement never existed. *See id.* at 654, 16 Cal. Rptr. 2d at 20 ("There is as much potential for fraud today as ever, and allegations like appellant's could be made every time any personal care is rendered."). The dissent also discusses the issue of fraud. *See id.* at 659, 16 Cal. Rptr. 2d at 23 (Poche, J., dissenting).

[98] *See, e.g.*, LAURA W. MORGAN & BRETT R. TURNER, ATTACKING AND DEFENDING MARITAL AGREEMENTS 6 & n. 10 (2001); PRINCIPLES § 7.09, Reporter's Notes, cmt. b, at 1019.

[99] *See* Robert H. Mnookin & Lewis Kornhauser, *Bargaining in the Shadow of the Law: The Case of Divorce*, 88 YALE L.J. 950 (1979).

the parties might be more willing to live with an arrangement they themselves helped to work out, and because settlement prevents unpleasant court battles that might harm any children involved.

In most jurisdictions, the separation agreement must be presented to a court for its approval.[100] While separation agreements tend to deal with all aspects of the divorce, courts are usually instructed to be deferential to the aspects of separation agreements dealing with financial matters between the parties, but not deferential to terms involving children (custody, visitation, and child support).[101] Courts are frequently authorized by statute or case law to reject or ignore separation agreements if their terms are unfair,[102] but most observers indicate that this rarely happens.[103]

For the terms relating directly to children, courts are to check that the best interests of the children are adequately protected by the agreement. However, according to many accounts, courts tend to rubber-stamp all but the most one-sided terms in such agreements, especially if neither partner objects when the agreement is submitted to the court.[104]

Challenges to separation agreements after signing but before court approval are usually tested under standard contract law doctrines, considering defenses like duress, misrepresentation, undue influence, and mutual mistake. Attacks on the substantive fairness of the agreements are heard either under the standard contract law doctrine of "unconscionability,"[105] the standard suggested by the Uniform Marriage and Divorce Act,[106] or under a general standard of "fairness."[107] Such substantive reviews frequently compare the financial terms of the separation agreement with what the parties would have received under statutory guidelines.[108]

Courts are also open to defenses based on irregularities in negotiation, as least those that can be wedged into general contract law defenses. A difficulty here is that, in contrast to conventional commercial agreements, separation agreements, by their nature, are entered into under extremes of emotion and pressure. Aware of this, courts tend to be reluctant to void agreements that in another context might raise tenable claims of duress or undue influence.[109] In sufficiently extreme circumstances, however, including when negotiations have occurred in a context of domestic abuse, courts will find the agreements to be void or voidable.[110]

[100] The parties may also ask for the terms of the separation agreement to be merged into the final divorce decree. When an agreement is merged into the divorce decree, the agreement's terms become enforceable by contempt orders but also become subject to later modification (though a number of jurisdictions allow the parties to agree by express language to limit or forbid such modifications). *See, e.g.*, Moseley v. Mosier, 306 S.E.2d 629 (S.C. 1983). Where an agreement is not merged into the decree, it is still enforceable by a conventional breach of contract action. *See, e.g.*, Morgan & Turner, *supra* note 98, at 341–45.

[101] *See, e.g.*, Morgan & Turner, *supra* note 98, at 35–53; Uniform Marriage and Divorce Act (UMDA), § 306(b), 9A (Part I) U.L.A. 159, 249 (1998 & Supp. 2005).

[102] *See, e.g.*, *In re* Marriage of Grossman, 82 P.3d 1039, 1042–43 (Or. Ct. App. 2003).

[103] *See, e.g.*, Morgan & Turner, *supra* note 98, at 132–38.

[104] *See, e.g.*, Mnookin & Kornhauser, *supra* note 99, at 954–55.

[105] *See, e.g.*, Weber v. Weber, 589 N.W.2d 358, 361 (N.D. 1999) (rejecting a separation agreement on unconscionability grounds).

[106] UMDA § 306(b), 9A (Part I) U.L.A. at 249 (1998 & Supp. 2005).

[107] *See, e.g.*, Gaw v. Sappett, 816 N.E.2d 1027, 1037 (Mass. App. Ct. 2004) (judicial duty "to ensure the fairness and reasonableness" of financial terms of separation agreement).

[108] *See, e.g.*, Weber v. Weber, 589 N.W.2d 358, 361–62 (N.D. 1999).

[109] *See, e.g.*, Flynn v. Flynn, 597 N.E.2d 709, 714 (Ill. App. Ct. 1992) ("The anxiety inherent in ... [reaching a separation agreement] does not, by itself, constitute coercion.").

[110] *See, e.g.*, Putnam v. Putnam, 689 A.2d 446, 449–50 (Vt. 1996). The threat by an Orthodox Jewish man not to give his former wife a religious divorce (thus leaving her unable to remarry) has been held to constitute duress, making a one-sided separation agreement voidable. Perl v. Perl, 512 N.Y.S.2d 372 (N.Y. App. Div. 1987).

The courts' more favorable treatment of separation agreements relative to premarital agreements (both historically and presently) is due in part to their different contexts. Because separation agreements are entered into knowing that legal separation or divorce is imminent, it is less likely that the parties will be too clouded by romantic feelings or optimism to protect their own interests.[111]

B. ALI Proposal

The PRINCIPLES generally track current doctrine regarding the enforceability of separation agreements. In one way, the PRINCIPLES are even more proenforcement than the doctrinal rules of many jurisdictions, in that judicial approval is not required of the terms of separation agreements dealing with property division or alimony unless one party objects to those terms.[112]The PRINCIPLES recognize that this is more a difference of form than substance,[113] since oversight in the approval process, even when required, tends to be perfunctory where neither party objects.

The general requirements for enforceability under the PRINCIPLES are that any such agreement be in writing and entered only after "each party [has] had full and fair opportunity to be informed of the existence and value of the parties' marital and separate assets, each party's current earnings and prospects for future earnings, and the significance of the terms of the agreement."[114] These last procedural requirements may be a bit stronger than the rules in some jurisdictions, but any difference is unlikely to be significant in practice.

A "parenting plan" regarding the terms of child custody and visitation is to be accepted unless the agreement is "not knowing or voluntary" or "would be harmful to the child."[115] An agreement on child support is to be accepted by the court unless it "provides for substantially less child support than would otherwise be awarded."[116] These standards reflect the general doctrine and practice in most jurisdictions.

The PRINCIPLES seem to deviate most sharply from current law in Section 7.09(2), where the text authorizes courts to set aside terms of a separation agreement where those terms "substantially limit or augment property rights or compensatory payments [alimony] otherwise due under law, and enforcement of those terms would substantially impair the economic well-being of a party who has or will have (a) primary or dual residential responsibility [or custody] for a child or (b) substantially fewer economic resources than the other party."[117] Section 7.09(2) then immediately adds: "Nevertheless, the court may enforce such terms if it finds, under the particular circumstances of the case, that enforcement of the terms would not work an injustice."[118]

The combined effect of those two provisions is to give courts broad discretion in a large number of separation agreements regarding whether or not to enforce the agreement's

[111] *See, e.g.*, PRINCIPLES, Overview of Chapter 7, at 40.
[112] *Id.* at 41.
[113] *See id.*
[114] PRINCIPLES § 7.09(1). "The party opposing enforcement of the agreement has the burden of proving that this requirement was not satisfied." PRINCIPLES § 7.09 cmt. e, at 1013.
[115] PRINCIPLES §§ 7.09(5); 2.06(1).
[116] PRINCIPLES §§ 7.09(5). Even in such a circumstance, a court might still accept the agreement if it determines that when "read with the agreement as a whole, [the child support terms] are consistent with the interests of the child." *See also* PRINCIPLES § 3.13(1).
[117] PRINCIPLES § 7.09(2).
[118] *Id.*

terms or to enforce them in part.[119] The Reporter's Notes indicate that the PRINCIPLES are primarily attempting only to codify and constrain results that courts were already reaching indirectly through other doctrines.[120]

C. General Analysis and Discussion

Some commentators have urged less judicial deference to separation agreements than to other forms of contracts. They argue for a greater judicial willingness to modify or ignore separation agreements, where either the terms seem unfair relative to the time they were signed or because of a change of circumstances.[121]

One commentator, Professor Gillian Hadfield, correctly points out that the reliance interest of the other spouse[122] in a separation agreement is significantly less than that of other parties seeking the enforcement of agreements.[123] It is hard to see how the other party would have significantly changed his or her position in reliance on the agreement or its likely enforcement, in the relatively short time between when an agreement is signed and when it is presented to the court. The only likely alternatives at the point of signing the agreement were negotiating an agreement on different terms, or going to court. Moreover, an agreement on different terms, and terms imposed by the court, are exactly what will likely result if a separation agreement is not enforced.[124] Contrast premarital agreements, in which a party might rely on the agreement by marrying when he or she would otherwise have stayed single, as well as marital agreements, in which the parties are frequently deciding whether to reconcile or not.

Similarly, there is reason to believe that a judicial willingness to modify or reject separation agreements judged to be unfair would not necessarily deter such agreements. As the law currently stands, little to no deference is given to the terms in separation agreements covering child custody, child support, or visitation, yet divorcing couples frequently reach agreement on such terms.[125]

This argument seems to support an unexpected conclusion. While as a matter of doctrine and practice, separation agreements are much more likely to be enforced as written, compared to marital agreements and premarital agreements, policy arguments grounded in reliance might support a contrary approach.

The argument of "no reliance" works best when speaking of challenges brought to separation agreements prior to the entry of divorce. It applies less well to the type of case Professor Hadfield considered in her article: challenges brought to separation agreements long after the entry of divorce, when subsequent events show a waiver of alimony to have

[119] PRINCIPLES § 7.09(4)(authorizing courts to review separation agreements on their own motion even if the agreement has not been challenged by one of the parties). PRINCIPLES § 7.09(6) directs that courts should "ordinarily" allow the parties to renegotiate the agreement if one or more terms have been found to be unenforceable.

[120] PRINCIPLES § 7.09 Reporter's Notes, cmt. h, at 1019–1020. The Notes add that the PRINCIPLES "might be understood to add slightly" to caselaw here, in that Section 7.09(2) applies in principle to the overly generous separation agreement as well as the unfairly stingy agreement. *Id.*

[121] *See, e.g.*, Gillian K. Hadfield, *An Expressive Theory of Contract: From Feminist Dilemmas to Reconceptualization of Rational Choice in Contract Law*, 146 U. PA. L. REV. 1235, 1242–44, 1270–76 (1998).

[122] Professor Hadfield consistently refers to husbands enforcing agreements against wives, and it is a central part of her argument that women's interests can be both advanced and undermined by the enforcement of contracts in various situations. *See id.* This chapter leaves the gendered aspects of the debate for another day.

[123] *Id.* at 1272.

[124] *Id.*

[125] *See* Carol Rogerson, *They are Agreements Nonetheless*, 20 CAN. J. FAM. L. 197, 201 (2003).

been unwise.[126] With the passage of time since the entry of divorce, it is easy to imagine ways in which a party could, and likely would, reasonably and substantially rely on an agreement, and subsequent court order, stating that the financial obligation to an ex-spouse was "this much, and no more."

The discussion of whether to enforce or modify both premarital agreements and separation agreements is often couched in terms of autonomy interests versus the ongoing obligations of marriage that survive its breakup.[127] In a larger context, the question turns on whether the support of individuals is to be delegated or "privatized" to the family, or is to be maintained by the community.[128]

In any event, by most accounts, the current treatment of separation agreements "ain't broke," and so the PRINCIPLES wisely chose not to "fix it."

IV. Conclusion

Premarital agreements, marital agreements, and separation agreements raise significantly different questions regarding enforcement.

In its treatment of these agreements, the PRINCIPLES tries to maintain a balance between respecting the parties' autonomy on one hand, and, on the other hand, being cognizant of bounded rationality problems with these sorts of agreements, and of the unfairness that would result if we encourage or enforce one-sided arrangements or one-sided outcomes.

At the same time, the PRINCIPLES are sometimes insufficiently sensitive to important differences in context: for example, how marital agreements are usually formed for significantly different reasons, and within a quite different power dynamic, from premarital agreements; how traditional religious premarital agreements should be analyzed separately from other premarital agreements; and how true reconciliation agreements might warrant different treatment from other marital agreements.

Of course, there is a sense in which these criticisms are unfair: limitations of space and time may not have allowed this level or elaboration or precision of detail – the PRINCIPLES were not, after all, a treatise on marital agreements, but rather an ambitious rethinking of the "Principles of the Law of Family Dissolution," for which the discussion of marital agreements was but one small section. Nonetheless, this chapter is offered as a pointer to where further work and discussion might be fruitful.

An earlier version of this chapter was presented at the October 2004 Workshop, "Critical Reflections on the American Law Institute's *Principles of the Law of Family Dissolution*," held at the Harvard Law School. I am grateful to Mary Anne Case, June Carbone, Robert J. Levy, Katherine Shaw Spaht, David Westfall, Robin Wilson, and the participants at the Workshop, for their comments and suggestions.

[126] *See* Hadfield, *supra* note 121, at 1242–44 (describing fact situations). By contrast, the PRINCIPLES do not consider challenges to separation agreements long after the divorce has been finalized.

[127] *See, e.g.*, PRINCIPLES, *Introduction*, at 37; Rogerson, *supra* note 125, at 198–200.

[128] *Cf.* MARTHA ALBERTSON FINEMAN, THE AUTONOMY MYTH: A THEORY OF DEPENDENCY 208–09 (2004) (discussing "the optimal or appropriate distribution of responsibility for dependency across societal institutions").

20 The PRINCIPLES on Agreements: "Fairness" and International Human Rights Law

Barbara Stark

> [W]hile most courts still decline to enforce premarital agreements on the same basis as commercial contracts, no consensus emerged on the appropriate rules to apply, much less on the rationale that might be offered to explain them. These questions are the principle topic of this chapter.[1]

Family law is again in turmoil, and the PRINCIPLES are an ambitious and sometimes inspired effort to increase clarity and fairness. This turmoil can be attributed to two major factors. First, to paraphrase Professor June Carbone, family law is ground zero in the gender wars.[2] Second, family law is reeling from the upheavals of globalization. These factors provide the backdrop against which the dilemmas addressed in Chapter 7 pertaining to agreements play out.

As the introductory quotation from the PRINCIPLES suggests, Chapter 7 focuses on a particularly intriguing tension between commercial contracts and premarital agreements. This tension is grounded in the broader tension between American views on freedom of contract and autonomy in general, on the one hand, and on freedom of contract and autonomy in the specific context of the family, on the other. While the emphasis on freedom of contract may be peculiarly American, tension between legal regimes and private contractual regimes governing the family is quite common from an international perspective. As it is in the United States, the tension between competing regimes in other countries reflects deep cultural tensions. Rather than being grounded in the sacrosanct principles of autonomy and contractual freedom, however, private contractual regimes in other countries are generally grounded in religious or customary practices.[3] Prominent examples include the Islamic and Jewish marriage contracts.[4]

While these tensions have been addressed by a broad range of domestic courts relying on domestic law, here and abroad,[5] this chapter focuses on the mediation of these competing

[1] PRINCIPLES § 7.01 cmt. a, at 947.

[2] *See* June Carbone, *Has the Gender Divide Become Unbridgeable: The Implications for Social Equality*, 5 J. GENDER RACE & JUST. 31, 52 (2001) ("Custody is ground zero in the gender wars.").

[3] Courtney W. Howland, *The Challenge of Religious Fundamentalism to the Liberty and Equality Rights of Women: An Analysis Under the United Nations Charter*, 35 COLUM. J. TRANSNAT'L L. 271, 283–85 (1997) (explaining how religious fundamentalist laws require the obedience of women, contrary to the U.N. Charter norms of equality); Symposium, *Roman Catholic, Islamic, and Jewish Treatment of Familial Issues, including Education, Abortion, In Vitro Fertilization, Prenuptial Agreements, Contraception, and Marital Fraud*, 16 LOY. L.A. INT'L & COMP. L. REV. 9, 60–74 (1993) (setting out religious perspectives on prenuptial agreements).

[4] DAWOUD SUDQI EL ALAMI, THE MARRIAGE CONTRACT IN ISLAMIC LAW (1992).

[5] Ann Laquer Estin, *Toward a Multicultural Family Law*, 38 FAM. L.Q. 59 (2004).

interests under international law. International law addresses these conflicts through private international law, such as the Convention on the Recognition of Foreign Judgments,[6] and through public international law, specifically international human rights law.[7] This chapter argues that the PRINCIPLES' treatment of agreements should incorporate, and be subject to, the relevant human rights law.

While there are certainly good reasons for incorporating human rights law in all areas of family law, there are especially strong reasons for adopting it here. First, any consensus regarding "appropriate rules" must be grounded in a coherent rationale. Because of the stature of the norms to which they are an exception, including constitutionally-protected religious freedoms, the underlying rationale to justify different treatment between marital and nonmarital contracts should be grounded in law of commensurate stature. Second, because of the growing diversity of the American population, and the proliferation of different cultural norms, that law should not be grounded in the amorphous and irrelevant conceptions of equity, but in well-established and widely accepted international human rights law. To the extent that the PRINCIPLES already incorporate that law, albeit tacitly, they represent an important step forward. To the extent that the PRINCIPLES function in a legal context in which that law is ignored, however, vital interests – recognized in the rest of the world as "rights" – remain at risk.

Part I of this chapter first explains the need for a more robust rationale for deciding which agreements to enforce. Second, it explains why such a rationale is appropriately grounded in international human rights law. Finally, it explains how the goals of the PRINCIPLES with respect to agreements would be furthered by the explicit incorporation of international human rights law. Part II compares and contrasts the treatment under the PRINCIPLES of private contractual regimes, including religious or customary regimes, with the treatment of such regimes under the Convention on the Elimination of All Forms of Discrimination Against Women ("Women's Convention").[8] Part III compares the treatment of these regimes under the PRINCIPLES with their treatment under the International Covenant on Economic, Social, and Cultural Rights ("Economic Covenant").[9] This chapter concludes that although international human rights law is hardly a panacea,[10] its incorporation into the law of agreements would promote the development of U.S. law and extend the influence of that law abroad, at least in this particular context.

I. Why the PRINCIPLES Need Human Rights Laws

A. The Need for a More Robust Rationale

As Professor Ira Ellman, the primary drafter of the PRINCIPLES, explains, the drafters "bit the bullet" to adopt certain rules in order to create clearer, better boundaries for

[6] Concluded 1 Feb. 1971, entered into force 20 Aug. 1979 *available at* http://www.hcch.net/index_en.php?act=conventions.text&cid=78 (last visited October 29, 2005).

[7] *See* Part IV, *infra*.

[8] Convention on the Elimination of All Forms of Discrimination Against Women, G.A. Res. 180, 34 U.N. GAOR, 2d. Sess., Supp. No. 21, at 889, U.N. Doc. A/34/46 (1981) (hereinafter *Women's Convention*).

[9] International Covenant on Economic, Social and Cultural Rights, *opened for signature* Dec. 16, 1966, 993 U.N.T.S. 3 (hereinafter *Economic Covenant*).

[10] *See generally* MARY ANN GLENDON, RIGHTS TALK (1991) (describing over-reliance on, and degradation of, "rights talk"). In a recent work, Professor Glendon has affirmed the continuing importance of human rights. *See* MARY ANN GLENDON, A WORLD MADE NEW: ELEANOR ROOSEVELT AND THE UNIVERSAL DECLARATION OF HUMAN RIGHTS (2001) (describing the compassion and determination of the early human rights movement).

family lawyers and family law courts: "Fairness concerns set boundaries around our choice[s]. . . . The problem is that those boundaries are very wide."[11] As Professor Ellman concedes, however, these boundaries are very rough and somewhat arbitrary. Another choice is at least as fair.

There are two important justifications for circumscribing the ability of parties to enter into family law agreements, according to the PRINCIPLES. First, there are limits on the "cognitive capacity"[12] of those likely to enter into family contracts; namely, they are typically in love and unreasonably optimistic about the likelihood of their marriage enduring. Second, public policies, especially those that protect children and spouses left vulnerable after long marriages, are apt to be abrogated.[13]

These rationales for limiting agreements are necessary, but not sufficient. First, as noted above, the fairness parameters within which they function are so broad, and so loose, that they provide little real guidance for decision makers. Equally important, the minimal guidance they do provide assumes that the status quo is "fair;" it assumes that men and women entering into marriage or domestic partnerships are on a level playing field. This normalizes and perpetuates existing inequalities.

Neither of these flaws is likely to be corrected by the minimal limits on agreements imposed by the PRINCIPLES. Assuming procedural fairness, agreements may be put aside only if they are "unconscionable" as understood in the law of contracts. This explicitly includes "substantive unconscionability, or a gross one-sidedness in terms."[14] Further, under Section 7.05, the parties may be relieved of their obligations under the agreement, when enforcement "would work a substantial injustice."[15] Such a finding, however, is only possible under three specific circumstances: where 1) "more than a fixed number of years have passed," 2) the couple has had a child, or 3) there has been an unanticipated change of circumstances.[16] As Professor Ellman summarizes, "[H]opefully law can provide remedies that correct gross injustices. . . . "[17]The law is more likely to do so, however, where it provides frameworks for identifying such "gross injustices." Such frameworks, conspicuously lacking in the PRINCIPLES, may be found in international human rights law.

Moreover, as determined under the PRINCIPLES, "fairness" often depends on implied bad faith. In both the "Carol and Doug"[18] and the "Bugfree Software" illustrations,[19]for example, one spouse pressures the other into entering into an agreement granting significant benefits to the pressuring spouse, who is planning to leave the unsuspecting partner. What if Carol has no old boyfriend waiting in the wings, but has simply grown tired of being a doctor's wife? What if the waiver by the nonprogrammer spouse in the software illustration was insisted upon by the programmer's business partner, whose own marriage was in trouble and who was concerned about family court interference in the business? In both instances, the result is the same – the unsuspecting partner gives us statutory benefits – but there is no bad faith. "Fairness," as the PRINCIPLES acknowledge, may be in the eye of the beholder.

A more robust rationale is needed, especially to counter constitutionally-protected freedom of religion and norms, such as freedom of contract, to which courts have historically deferred. In the United States, religious freedom is expressly protected under the

[11] Ira Ellman, *Why Making Family Law is Hard*, 35 ARIZ. ST. L.J. 699, 701–02, 707 (2003).

[12] PRINCIPLES § 7.05 cmt. b, at 985–8.

[13] PRINCIPLES § 7.05 cmt. c, at 990–91.

[14] PRINCIPLES § 7.01 cmt. e, at 948.

[15] PRINCIPLES § 7.05(1)(b).

[16] PRINCIPLES § 7.05(2)(a).

[17] Ellman, *supra* note 11, at 707.

[18] PRINCIPLES § 7.01, illus. 3, at 950–51.

[19] PRINCIPLES § 7.01, illus. 2, at 949.

Establishment Clause of First Amendment, which assures the separation of church and State.[20] The question whether religious marriage contracts can be enforced by secular courts without violating this principle, however, has been a contentious one. Some courts have held that a State would be impermissibly promoting religion to enforce such contracts.[21] Others have found ways to circumvent such changes.[22]

In many other countries, however, such circumvention is unnecessary because there are no bars to enforcement of religious agreements. Indeed, in some States,[23] such as Israel and Kenya, responsibility for at least some areas of family law has been explicitly delegated to religious authorities.[24] Religious agreements, accordingly, are recognized and enforceable. The question thus becomes whether a particular marriage contract, clearly implicating the right to practice one's religion, is in conflict with other, equally clear, human rights norms, such as the norm against nondiscrimination.

The right to religious freedom is not as well developed in international law as some other human rights. In fact, although the U.N. General Assembly adopted a Declaration on the Elimination of All Forms of Intolerance and of Discrimination Based on Religious Belief without a vote on November 25, 1981,[25] no legally-binding convention has yet come into force on the subject. Nevertheless, the prohibition against discrimination on the basis of religion is well-established.[26] By identifying competing human rights norms of comparable stature, international human rights law directly confronts the dilemma of competing rights. This has produced rigorous and useful frames of analysis, such as that proposed by Donna Sullivan to resolve competing claims between gender equality and religious freedom.[27]

Sullivan begins by observing that the peremptory norms of human rights law, including norms against genocide, slavery, and torture, clearly trump claims of religious freedom. Thus, she argues, the Hindu practice of burning a widow on her husband's funeral pyre cannot be sanctioned. Where there are no peremptory norms at stake, she urges a balancing test, focusing on the relative importance of the competing rights in the particular context. Specifically, she asks how important the particular right is in terms of the "overarching goal of gender equality."[28] Second, she asks how important the particular religious practice

[20] U.S. CONST. amend. I.

[21] *See* Aflalo v. Aflalo, 685 A.2d 523 (N.J. Super. Ct. Ch. Div. 1996) (refusing to enforce agreement because order requiring husband to give wife a *get*, which is a religious divorce, would violate his first amendment rights). *See also, e.g.*, Kaddoura v. Hammound 168 D.L.R. 4th 503 (1998) (refusing to enforce terms of Muslim marriage certificate). *See generally* Rostain, *Permissible Accommodations of Religion: Reconsidering the New York Get Statute*, 96 Yale L.J. 1147 (1987).

[22] *See, e.g.*, Goldman v. Goldman, 554 N.E.2d 1016 (Ill. App. Ct. 1990) (requiring husband to provide *get*).

[23] In this chapter, "state" refers to a constituent unit of a federal entity, such as New York, while "State" refers to a nation state, such as China.

[24] BARBARA STARK, INTERNATIONAL FAMILY LAW: AN INTRODUCTION 126 (2004) (describing five separate family law systems in Kenya, three of which are religious); Frances Raday, *Israel – The Incorporation of Religious Patriarchy in a Modern State*, in GENDER BIAS AND FAMILY LAW COMPARATIVE PERSPECTIVES 209 (Barbara Stark ed., 1992) (describing the role of religion in Israeli Family Law).

[25] G.A. Res. 36/55, 36 U.N. GAOR, Supp. No. 51 (1981), U.N. Doc. A/36/684 (1981).

[26] Such discrimination is explicitly prohibited in Article 2 of the Universal Declaration of Human Rights, G.A. Res. 217A, U.N. GAOR, 3d Sess., Supp. No. 3, at 572, 575, U.N. Doc. A. 810 (1948) (hereinafter "Universal Declaration"); Article 2.2 of the Economic Covenant, *supra* note 9; Article 2.1 of the International Covenant on Civil and Political Rights, *entered into force* March 23, 1976, art. 2.1, 999 U.N.T.S. 171.

[27] Donna J. Sullivan, *Gender Equality and Religious Freedom: Toward a Framework for Conflict Resolution*, 24 N.Y.U. J. INT'L. L. & POL. 795 (1992).

[28] *Id.*

at issue is to the right of religious freedom.[29] Additional factors include the cumulative impact of each upon the other and, once it has been determined that a restriction on the religious practice is appropriate, an assessment of the proportionality of the restriction.

The explicit adoption of human rights norms could similarly clarify the debate about private agreements in the PRINCIPLES. Freedom of contract is not specifically addressed in the U.S. Constitution. However, as constitutional law expert Professor Norman Dorsen and his coauthors explain in their book *Comparative Constitutionalism*, the privileged place of freedom of contract in American jurisprudence has largely remained unchallenged: "[I]n the liberal economies of the nineteenth century, contractual freedom was uncontested."[30] This extreme deference to the principle of freedom of contract was not seriously challenged until the Great Depression.[31] The desperate plight of millions of Americans simply made it untenable to maintain freedom of contract as a paramount norm.

The same concern that justified abrogation of freedom of contract there, the need to protect the vulnerable, is applicable here. Concern for the vulnerable is particularly important where, as here, the vulnerable are least likely to protect themselves. As noted above, they are unlikely to do so for several reasons, including the social expectations of the parties and the typical assumption (especially, perhaps, among those who have not previously been divorced) that the marriage will endure. These reasons have historically led courts to treat contracts in family law differently.[32] The PRINCIPLES treat family contracts more like commercial contracts, to the detriment of the most vulnerable. Incorporation of human rights norms would restore historical protections, but only for those whose human rights were actually violated by privileging autonomy in this context.

B. Why Look to International Human Rights Law

The PRINCIPLES should look to international human rights law because it offers a normative framework for an increasingly multicultural America in an increasingly globalized world. Globalization is transforming family law. As the United Nations notes, families are the primary unit of social organization,[33] and families are changing, trying to adapt to new demands and taking advantage of new mobility. Women seek new lives in arranged marriages or as "mail order brides." They also seek asylum as refugees, fleeing domestic violence. Workers follow jobs, leaving their families behind and sometimes starting new families in their new countries. Child abduction has become a growing threat as parents of different nationalities divorce, and both want their children to be raised in their own national traditions.

Even as ties to such traditions become increasingly attenuated, their appeal may become stronger for some. Local religious leaders may insist on even stricter adherence to local customs, especially those related to marriage, divorce, and the care and custody of children, as their authority is challenged by competing customs and international norms. In many

[29] *Id.*

[30] NORMAN DORSEN ET AL, COMPARATIVE CONSTITUTIONALISM 1191 (2003). As I have explained elsewhere, it was not necessary to include the right to property in the Bill of Rights because it was not only implicit, but privileged. *See* Barbara Stark, *Deconstructing the Framers' Right to Property: Liberty's Daughters and Economic Rights*, 28 HOFSTRA L. REV. 963 (2000). Freedom of contract, specifically the right to enter into binding agreements regarding one's property, was similarly privileged.

[31] DORSEN ET AL, *supra* note 36.

[32] *See generally* Brian Bix, this volume.

[33] *See infra* notes 37, 46 (discussing the Universal Declaration of Human Rights and the Economic Covenant).

States, such as Saudi Arabia, family law is basically left to religious authorities. This reflects both its relatively low importance to national governments, compared to matters of trade and finance, for example, and its paradoxically high importance to those who seek to shape the national identity. As Article 9 of the Basic Law of Saudi Arabia states, "The family is the kernel of Saudi society, and its members shall be brought up on the basis of Islamic faith."[34] There are powerful trends and countertrends everywhere, and competing norms of family law are at the heart of each. The impact of this on family law practice has been noted by family law practitioners.[35] Family law is no longer limited by national boundaries. Indeed, starting with the first paragraph of the Chief Reporter's Foreword,[36] references to foreign law pervade the PRINCIPLES. The explicit incorporation of international human rights law would be a natural next step.

Human rights law represents a rough consensus among divergent national systems. More than 180 States have ratified the Civil Covenant, the Economic Covenant, the Women's Convention and the Convention on the Rights of the Child.[37] By incorporating human rights law, domestic law accedes to an international bottom line. Domestic law incorporating human rights norms accordingly is likely to be compatible with a broad range of foreign law that also incorporates these norms. As a corollary, it is increasingly likely to resonate with an increasingly mobile population.

Human rights law is grounded in the Universal Declaration of Human Rights ("Universal Declaration") drafted in 1948.[38] Under the Universal Declaration, parties recognized that "[t]he family is the natural and fundamental group unit of society and is entitled to protection by society and the State."[39] The Universal Declaration was merely aspirational, however; the parties did not intend it to be legally binding.[40] Rather, it was expected that a binding convention would be drafted in due course.[41] Because of the East/West split, and the emerging consensus that different kinds of rights could be better implemented by different mechanisms, two international treaties followed instead of one legally binding convention. The rights and obligations set out in the Universal Declaration were defined with greater specificity in the legally-binding Economic Covenant and International Covenant on Civil and Political Rights ("Civil Covenant").[42] Together with the Universal Declaration, these definitions comprise the International Bill of Rights.

There is some overlap between the two covenants. For example, Article 23 of the Civil Covenant expressly reiterates the State's obligation to protect the family as "the natural

[34] BARBARA STARK, INTERNATIONAL FAMILY LAW: AN INTRODUCTION 2 (2004).

[35] The ABA Section on Family Law has recently devoted an entire issue to the subject. *See The Impact of Diverse Cultures on Family Law*, 27 FAM. ADVOCATE (Fall 2004) (introducing range of topics confronting family lawyers).

[36] PRINCIPLES, Foreword at xvii ("One expects a nation's family law to reflect its cultural values. In America, those cultural values include a strong tradition of family privacy, with both common-law and constitutional roots. French laws bars parents from giving their child a name that does not appear on a government-approved list. Mexican family courts are empowered to settle disputes between spouses about their respective employment.").

[37] LOUIS HENKIN ET AL., BASIC DOCUMENT SUPPLEMENT TO INTERNATIONAL LAW CASES AND MATERIALS 151, 146, 174, 188 (3rd ed. 1993). In 1948, when the Universal Declaration was adopted, only 56 countries were parties. Forty-eight countries voted in favor of the Universal Declaration, none opposed and eight abstained. *Id.* at 143. The Child's Convention has been ratified by 192 countries, *available at* http://www.unhchr.ch/html/menu3/b/k2crc.htm (last visited October 29, 2005).

[38] *See* Universal Declaration, *supra* note 26.

[39] *Id.* at art. 16.3.

[40] Many argue that certain provisions in the Universal Declaration have since become binding as a matter of customary international law. HENKIN ET AL., *supra* note 37, at 322.

[41] Barbara Stark, *United States Ratification of the Other Half of the International Bill of Rights*, in HUMAN RIGHTS IN THE UNITED STATES: LOOKING INWARD AND OUTWARD 75 (David Forsythe ed., 2000).

[42] Civil Covenant, *supra* note 26.

and fundamental group unit of society"[43] as set out in the Universal Declaration.[44] Article 10 of the Economic Covenant similarly provides that "[t]he widest possible protection and assistance should be accorded to the family, which is the natural and fundamental group unit of society, particularly for its establishment and while it is responsible for the care and education of dependent children."[45] This arguably requires the State to enact laws protecting vulnerable parties, especially women and children, upon dissolution of marriage.

For the most part, however, the Civil Covenant addresses negative obligations of the State; it imposes limits on State interference with individuals. The Economic Covenant, in contrast, basically addresses affirmative obligations of the State, including the provision of welfare and social security benefits. The Economic Covenant requires the State to affirmatively assure its people an adequate standard of living, healthcare, education, and employment. In Article 10 of the Economic Covenant, for example, the State recognizes that mothers are entitled to "special protection" before and after childbirth, including paid leave. Thus, a State party would be required to incorporate into domestic law either welfare provisions assuring compensation or a requirement that private employers do so.

There are two obvious obstacles to the incorporation of international human rights law in the PRINCIPLES. First, the United States is not a party to the Economic Covenant or the Women's Convention, although it has signed both.[46] Second, human rights law historically focuses on the individual's rights vis-á-vis the State, that is, the State's treatment of its people, rather than individuals' obligations to each other. Indeed, the State's interference with those obligations has historically been rejected on the ground that the State is violating family privacy.[47]

The U.S. failure to ratify the human rights conventions does not preclude their incorporation here. International human rights norms have been used in a broad range of contexts to provide normative guidance – from adoption by municipalities, such as San Francisco, and states, such as Massachusetts, to signal support for human rights,[48] to the adoption by multinational corporations of Model Codes of Conduct, both to signal support for human rights and, it has been suggested, to preempt binding regulation. Even if particular human rights instruments are not ratified or acceded to by a particular country, in short they may be relied upon as nonbinding "soft law." The Sullivan Principles in South Africa are a well-known example of the use of soft law to promote human rights.[49]

C. Human Rights Law Would Further the Goals of the PRINCIPLES

The explicit incorporation of international human rights would create clearer, better boundaries for family lawyers and courts. This is supported by two distinct but converging trends: first, the increasing receptivity of U.S. courts to human rights in general,

[43] *See* Universal Declaration, *supra* note 26, at art. 16.3.

[44] Article 16.3 of the Universal Declaration provides, "The family is the natural and fundamental group unit of society and is entitled to protection by the society and the State."

[45] Economic Covenant, *supra* note 9, at 7.

[46] President Jimmy Carter signed the Economic Covenant and the Women's Convention. Neither of these has been ratified by the Senate, however. HENKIN ET AL, *supra* note 37, at 784.

[47] *See, e.g.*, Kilgrow v. Kilgrow, 107 So.2d 885 (Ala. 1958).

[48] *See* Crosby v. National Foreign Trade Council, 530 U.S. 363 (2000) (holding Massachusetts law barring trade with Burma because of human rights violations invalid under the Supremacy Clause).

[49] *See generally* SANCTIONS AGAINST APARTHEID (Mark Orkin ed. 1989). The Sullivan Principles challenged apartheid in South Africa.

and second, the increasing application of human rights norms to family law issues, by human rights bodies as well as domestic courts throughout the world.

The new openness of United States' courts to human rights is shown in two recent Supreme Court decisions. In *Grutter v. Bollinger*,[50] the United States Supreme Court upheld the affirmative action program at the University of Michigan Law School. Justice Ginsburg, joined by Justice Breyer, began her concurring opinion by setting out "the international understanding of [the office of] affirmative action"[51] in the International Covenant on the Elimination of All Forms of Racial Discrimination,[52] to which the United States is a party, and the Women's Convention, to which the United States is a signatory. In *Lawrence v. Texas*,[53] which struck a Texas sodomy statute, the Court again cited an international human rights instrument. The majority explicitly referred to the European Convention for the Protection of Human Rights and Fundamental Freedoms, for the proposition that homosexual activity should not be criminalized.[54] At least some members of the Court are showing what Justice Blackmun, citing the Declaration of Independence, referred to as a "decent respect to the opinions of mankind."[55] *Lawrence* also shows the Court's recognition that human rights norms are pertinent to intimate relationships, which have historically been the province of family law.

The *Lawrence* decision is consistent with, and may be understood as a part of, the increasingly frequent application of human rights norms to family law issues throughout the world. Examples range from the requirement that Ireland permit the dissemination of information about abortion pursuant to the European Convention on Human Rights to the procedural safeguards to protect surrendering parents in international adoptions under the Convention on Intercountry Adoption.[56] In some cases, international human rights support domestic law, such as the UNICEF Report on Child Marriage,[57] which strongly affirms India's Child Marriage Restraint Act of 1929.[58] In other cases, human rights norms serve as a counterweight to local law. In Kenya, for example, customary law regarding marital property leaves Kenyan women destitute and without recourse at divorce, in violation of the Women's Convention.[59]

Indeed, it can be argued that the incorporation of these norms is particularly important in the instant context precisely because of the U.S. failure to ratify the three human rights conventions, which has created an unfortunate and anomalous lacuna in American family law. As human rights and family law scholars have pointed out,[60] international human rights law has already had a major impact on family law. The incursion of the State into the traditionally private sphere of the family, for example, has been justified on the grounds

[50] 539 U.S. 306, 342 (2003).

[51] *Id.* at 342.

[52] International Covenant on the Elimination of All Forms of Racial Discrimination, *entered into force* Jan. 4, 1969, 660 U.N.T.S. 195.

[53] 539 U.S. 558 (2003).

[54] *See id.* (citing European Convention for the Protection of Human Rights and Fundamental Freedoms, *entered into force* Sept. 3, 1953, 213 U.N.T.S. 22).

[55] Harry A. Blackmun, *The Supreme Court and the Law of Nations: Owing a Decent Respect to the Opinions of Mankind*, 88 Am. Soc'y Int'l L. Proc. 383 (1994). Others, notably Justice Scalia, remain more parochial. In a recent case, Justice Scalia dismissed evidence of the rejection of the death penalty throughout the western world, explaining that the court should only be concerned with American values.

[56] Stark, *supra* note 24, at 51–60, 163.

[57] UNICEF, *Early Marriage Child Spouses*, March 2001 (available at http://www.unicef-icdc.org/publications/pdf/digest7e.pdf) (last visited October 29, 2005).

[58] Stark, *supra* note 24, at 16.

[59] *Id.* at 59–60 (discussing work of Human Rights Watch).

[60] Berta Hernandez-Truyol, *Asking the Family Question*, 38 Fam. L.Q. 481 (2004); Estin, *supra* note 5.

of the significant human rights at stake. Professor Ellman's examples of such incursions – domestic violence, abortion, and same-sex relationships[61] – have all been recognized and championed as human rights issues.

In addition, the goals of the PRINCIPLES with respect to agreements would be furthered by the incorporation of international human rights law in at least three important ways. First, human rights law provides normative support for the recognition of gay and lesbian relationships explicitly recognized in the PRINCIPLES.[62] Second, recognition of human rights law would promote increased American participation in private international law regimes that incorporate human rights norms, such as the pending Convention on Maintenance.[63] Third, recognition of human rights law by American courts would encourage greater respect for the decisions of American courts by foreign courts.

II. The PRINCIPLES and the Women's Convention

A. Why the Women's Convention?

The tension between American views on freedom of contract and autonomy in general, on the one hand, and American views on freedom of contract and autonomy in the specific context of the family, on the other, is grounded in the historical view of the family as a protected zone. In this view, ordinary rules can and should be suspended for the benefit of vulnerable family members, particularly women and children. This historical truism has been challenged, however, by a broad range of theoretical arguments as well as practical developments. Some claim marital regimes do not in fact protect the vulnerable members of the family; rather, they perpetuate traditional patterns of domination and subordination.[64] Others suggest that protection is no longer necessary.[65] Finally, the case has been made that the fundamental structure of family law itself is not only gendered, but bad for women.[66]

Whether contractual regimes are better or worse than marital regimes is similarly debated. As many commentators have observed, the religious authority for contractual family regimes is often profoundly gendered, especially where such authority is shaped by patriarchal cultural norms.[67] It has similarly been argued that despite their ostensible neutrality, freedom of contract and autonomy are also gendered.[68] While the precise ways in which family law is gendered, and the extent to which anyone benefits, are contested, it is clear that family law affects men and women differently.

[61] Ellman, *supra* note 11, at 701–02.

[62] Same-sex relationships are encompassed by the PRINCIPLES' domestic partnership proposals and by the provisions governing agreements to the extent that the parties deviate from the legal default by agreement.

[63] STARK, *supra* note 24, at 118–21.

[64] CATHARINE A. MACKINNON, FEMINISM UNMODIFIED 32–45 (1987)

[65] *See, e.g.* Orr v. Orr, 440 U.S. 268 (1979) (rejecting "old notion" that the man was responsible for providing a home as gender discrimination). *But see*, Donald G. McNeil Jr., *Real Men Don't Clean Bathrooms*, N.Y. TIMES, Sept. 19, 2004 § 4, 1 (summarizing recent report of Bureau of Labor Statistics, documenting persistence of gendered division of labor).

[66] MARTHA FINEMAN, THE NEUTERED MOTHER AND OTHER TRAGEDIES OF THE TWENTIETH CENTURY (1995); Frances E. Olsen, *The Family and the Market: A Study of Ideology and Legal Reform*, 96 HARV. L. REV. 1497 (1983).

[67] *See, e.g.*, IS MULTICULTURALISM BAD FOR WOMEN? (Joshua Cohen et al. eds. 1999); Raday, *supra* note 24; MERLE WEINER & MARIANNE BLAIR, FAMILY IN THE WORLD COMMUNITY (2003); FAMILY LAW AND GENDER BIAS: COMPARATIVE PERSPECTIVES (Barbara Stark ed. 1992).

[68] Linda McClain, *"Atomistic Man" Revisited: Liberalism, Connection, and Feminist Jurisprudence*, 65 S. CAL. L. REV. 1171 (1992); Clare Dalton, *An Essay in the Deconstruction of Contract Doctrine*, 94 YALE L.J. 997 (1985).

The underlying premise here is that, as Aristotle explained, it is just as unfair to treat people who are not similarly situated the same, as it is to treat those who are similarly situated differently.[69] Another premise here is that "gender-related behaviors are a process of individual and social construction."[70] Incorporation of the Women's Convention is simply a mechanism by which to recognize the ongoing gender discrimination in the marketplace and civil society and the ways in which such discrimination operates to delegate private sphere responsibilities to women,[71] especially when they are mothers.[72] The male partner, who has enjoyed some of the benefits of this discrimination, should in fairness assume some of the costs.

Two examples of this ongoing gender discrimination are: 1) domestic violence and 2) the persistence of a gendered wage gap. No data are available regarding domestic violence or the persistence of a gendered wage gap among the concededly small, self-selected portion of the population affected by the PRINCIPLES' provisions governing agreements. No empirical studies have focused on the incidence or severity of either among those who enter into premarital or marital agreements. But the prevalence of both domestic violence and a gendered wage gap in the general population makes it reasonable to expect to encounter both in this context as well. This is especially likely when considering particular segments of the population likely to enter into such agreements, such as mail-order brides or young women entering into marriages arranged by their families, in which the wife is especially likely to be younger, poorer, and less well-educated than her husband.[73]

1. Domestic Violence

As Professor David Westfall argues in this volume, there are many good reasons for taking domestic violence into account at divorce.[74] Under the ALI's framework in Chapter 7,

[69] JOAN WILLIAMS, UNBENDING GENDER: WHY FAMILY AND WORK CONFLICT AND WHAT TO DO ABOUT IT 205 (2000). *See generally*, Christine A. Littleton, *Reconstructing Sexual Equality*, 75 CAL. L. REV. 1279, 1296 (1987) ("[Acceptance] asserts that eliminating the unequal consequences of sex differences is more important than . . . trying to eliminate them altogether.").

[70] Kay Deaux & Brenda Major, *A Social-Psychological Model of Gender*, in THEORETICAL PERSPECTIVES ON SEXUAL DIFFERENCE 91(Deborah L. Rhode ed. 1979).

[71] Amy Wax, *Bargaining in the Shadow of the Market: Is There a Future for Egalitarian Marriage?* 84 VA. L. REV. 509, 513 (1998) ("Although both partners benefit from marriage, men on average have more power in the relationship. That is, men are in a position to 'get their way' more often and to achieve a higher degree of satisfaction of their preferences."). Thus, even when the law is gender neutral, like the Family and Medical Leave Act of 1993, 29 U.S.C. § 2601 et seq. (Supp. 1997), it is nevertheless likely to perpetuate gendered norms.

[72] As Professor Williams points out, current wage gap data "seriously underestimate the extent of women's marginalization in the workforce, because they compare the wage rates of *full-time* women with those of *full-time* men in an economy where more than half of mothers do not work full-time." Williams, *supra* note 69, at 274; *see also* Samuel Issacharoff & Elyse Rosenblum, *Women and the Workplace: Accommodating the Demands of Pregnancy*, 94 COLUM. L. REV. 2154 (1994).

[73] Official records are not kept identifying those who come to the United States as mail order brides or pursuant to arranged marriages. Recent census data indicate large and growing numbers of spouses of U.S. citizens, and legal permanent residents, which would include members of both groups. *See Table 26. Nonimmigrants admitted by class of admission: selected fiscal years 1985–2002*, Fiscal Year 2002 Yearbook of Immigrant Statistics, *available at* http://uscis.gov/graphics/shared/aboutus/statistics/TEMP02yrbk/temp2002tables.pdf; *Table 26. Nonimmigrants admitted by selected port of entry and region and country of citizenship*, Fiscal Year 2003 Yearbook of Immigrant Statistics, *available at* http://uscis.gov/graphics/shared/aboutus/statistics/TEMP03yrbk/2003TEMP tables.pdf (last visited March 5, 2006). Some of these data include children of citizens and permanent residents. Experts estimate relatively small, but not insignificant, numbers of mail order brides, approximately 4,000 per year; Robert J. Scholes, *The Mail Order Bride Industry and its Impact on U.S. Immigration available at* http://uscis.gov/graphics/aboutus/repsstudies/Mobappa.htm (last visited October 29, 2005).

[74] Westfall, this volume (discussing property division).

however, it would have to be shown that because of domestic violence in the relationship, it would be "unconscionable" to uphold the agreement. As Professor Brian Bix observes, the framework is elastic, and a judge could certainly find unconscionability under such circumstances.[75] But this leaves the burden on the abused partner, almost always the woman, to articulate the objection and prove her claim. It is well known, moreover, that domestic violence takes place along a continuum, ranging from criminal assault, to murder, to verbal abuse. Sometimes the batterer, usually the husband, maintains control through subtle threats, establishing a pervasive, if unspecified, atmosphere of menace. Under the "unconscionability" framework of the PRINCIPLES, it would be difficult to show why a wife should not be held to an agreement merely because she was afraid of her husband.

2. Persistent Wage Gap

As shown in U.S. Census data, the ratio of women's to men's median earnings has significantly increased in the last forty-two years.[76] In 1960, full-time women workers earned only $.60 for every dollar earned by full-time men workers. In 2002, such women were earning $.77 for every dollar earned by such men.

This is not as good for women as it might appear, however. First, because fewer women than men are engaged in full-time paid work – in part, of course, because of their ongoing unpaid work in the home – women's income as a percentage of men's remains roughly constant.[77] This is consistent with the disproportionate number of women living in poverty. As the Center on Hunger and Poverty at Brandeis University recently reported, female-headed households showed the highest levels of food insecurity and hunger in 2002, with 32 percent of such households experiencing food insecurity and 11 percent of such households experiencing hunger.[78]

Poverty grew in the United States in 2004, affecting approximately 12 percent of the population, mostly women and their children.[79] Because of the ongoing gendered disparity of wealth and income in this country, as well as women's ongoing child care and elder care responsibilities, women remain disproportionately dependent on social safety nets. Moreover, since such safety nets are "hung low and full of holes in the United States,"[80] women remain economically dependent on men. To the extent that the Women's Convention focuses on the factors responsible for women's ongoing economic subordination, it shifts the frame created by the PRINCIPLES. It situates the disputed agreement within the larger context of ongoing discrimination.

The Women's Convention would not necessarily protect women from such discrimination in this context, because it could only do so by shifting the entire burden to the husband. Where the husband was neither responsible for such discrimination nor directly benefited from it, this would not be fair. Thus, for example, a male doctor divorcing a female nurse would not be considered responsible for the gendered wage disparity between doctors and

[75] Bix, this volume (discussing premarital and marital agreements).

[76] David Leonhardt, "Poverty Grew in 2004, While Income Failed to Rise for 5th Straight Year," NY TIMES Aug 31, 2005 (citing recently released Census Bureau figures). Women's median income was $31,200; men's median income was $40,800.

[77] *Id.*

[78] Center on Hunger and Poverty *available at* http://www.centeronhunger.org/hunger/facts.html (last visited October 29, 2005).

[79] Leonhardt, *supra* note 76.

[80] *U.S.Courts as Magnet, in* CHARLES BALDWIN ET AL., INTERNATIONAL DISPUTE RESOLUTION (2003).

nurses. At the same time, however, this is not a gender-neutral scenario, and the incorporation of the Women's Convention would help decision makers avoid the mistake of treating it like one. Where an agreement involved a mail order bride or an arranged marriage, the Women's Convention would be even more important, focusing the court on the global inequalities that are the backdrop to such agreements.

B. How the Women's Convention Would Further the PRINCIPLES

The Women's Convention provides a useful and constructive framework for recognizing and reallocating the costs of ongoing gender discrimination. It begins by defining the phrase "discrimination against women" to mean "*any* distinction, exclusion or restriction made on the basis of sex which has the *effect or purpose* of impairing or nullifying the recognition, enjoyment or exercise by women . . . of human rights and fundamental freedoms in *the political, economic, social, cultural, civil or any other field*."[81] Article 2 of the Women's Convention further requires the State "[t]o take all appropriate measures, including legislation, to modify or abolish existing laws, regulations, customs and practices which constitute discrimination against women."[82] This effectively holds the State responsible for all discrimination on the basis of gender, whether through State policy or private prejudice.[83] Thus, the Women's Convention imposes an affirmative obligation on the State to take whatever steps are necessary to counteract discrimination against women, especially with respect to women's rights within marriage.[84]

III. The Economic Covenant and the PRINCIPLES

A. Why the Economic Covenant?

As noted in the Comment to Section 7.02, premarital agreements regarding property and maintenance are not binding on English courts and some Canadian courts.[85] Rather, the court's "power to do economic justice at divorce" trumps.[86] It is this basic notion of "economic justice," absent not only from the PRINCIPLES but from American law in general, that it is so crucial here. Procedural requirements, set out in Section 7.04, roughly replicate procedural due process requirements under domestic law.[87] These are similar to rights set out in the Civil Covenant. Section 7.04(3)(a) of the PRINCIPLES which requires that the agreement be executed at least thirty days before the parties' marriage, roughly corresponds

[81] *See* Women's Convention, *supra* note 8, at 16 (emphasis added).

[82] *Id.*

[83] *See* Rebecca J. Cook, *State Accountability Under the Convention on the Elimination of All Forms of Discrimination Against Women*, in HUMAN RIGHTS OF WOMEN: NATIONAL AND INTERNATIONAL PERSPECTIVES 228, 236–38 (Rebecca J. Cook ed., 1994). *Cf.* Susan Moller Okin, *Is Multiculturalism Bad for Women?*, *in* IS MULTICULTURALISM BAD FOR WOMEN?, *supra* note 67 at 7, 22 (noting that "[t]he subordination of women is often informal and private. . . . At least as important to the development of self-respect and self-esteem is *our place within our culture*. And at least as pertinent to our capacity to question our social roles is *whether our culture instills in us and forces on us particular social roles*").

[84] *Id.* Art 16.1(e), 1249 U.N.T.S. at 41. More States have taken reservations to Article 16 than to any other article in the Convention. Rebecca J. Cook, *Reservations to the Convention on the Elimination of All Forms of Discrimination Against Women*, 30 VA. J. INT'L L. 643, 702 (1990).

[85] PRINCIPLES § 7.02.

[86] PRINCIPLES § 7.02 cmt. a, at 955.

[87] PRINCIPLES § 7.04. *See, e.g.*, JOHN NOWAK AND RONAL ROTUNDA, CONSTITUTIONAL LAW 593, et seq. (7th ed. 2004).

to the "notice" requirement in the Civil Covenant.[88] Similarly, Section 7.04(3)(b), requiring that both parties be advised to obtain independent counsel, roughly corresponds to a right to counsel.[89] In striking contrast, the PRINCIPLES have very little to say about substantive requirements. Indeed, unless there is either proof of "unconscionability" or an explicit finding of "substantial injustice," grounded in one of three carefully limited circumstances noted above, the agreement must be enforced. This is neither workable nor adequate. Nor would it be the result if the Civil Covenant were applied in this context.

B. How the Economic Covenant Would Further the PRINCIPLES

The substantive requirements set out in Section 7.05, discussing *When Enforcement Would Work a Substantial Injustice*, fall far short of both the rights set out in the Economic Covenant and reflected in the English and Canadian conceptions of "economic justice."[90] As noted above, the Economic Covenant assures basic economic and social rights, including the right to health and the right to an adequate standard of living.[91] Unlike the Civil Covenant, it has no counterpart in U.S. jurisprudence.[92] Article 10 of the Economic Covenant addresses "family rights."[93] By affirming that States "recognize that... [t]he widest possible protection and assistance should be accorded to the family, which is the natural and fundamental group unit of society,"[94] Article 10 establishes the scope of the State's duty. Considered in conjunction with Articles 2 and 3, which require States to "ensure the equal rights of men and women to the enjoyment of all economic, social and cultural rights,"[95] Article 10 can be understood as a powerful safeguard for economic rights during marriage and at its dissolution.

In addition to the minimal restrictions set out in the PRINCIPLES, it could be argued that if the agreement exacerbates or creates economic inequalities between the parties, it should be barred – at least in those situations where the less well-off spouse would be unable to enjoy an "adequate standard of living" if the agreement were enforced. This is consistent with provisions in the PRINCIPLES governing alimony which treat "any significant disproportionality in income-earning capacity that evolved during the marriage as

[88] PRINCIPLES § 7.04(3)(a). *See, e.g.*, NOWAK AND ROTUNDA, *supra* note 98, at §13.8.

[89] PRINCIPLES § 7.04(3)(b). NOWAK AND ROTUNDA, *supra* note 98, at § 11.6.

[90] PRINCIPLES § 7.02.

[91] *Id.* Art 11–12, 993 U.N.T.S. at 7–8. *See also* Asbjorn Eide & Allan Rosas, *Economic, Social, and Cultural Rights: A Universal Challenge, in* ECONOMIC, SOCIAL AND CULTURAL RIGHTS 15, 17 (Asbjorn Eide, et al., eds., 1995) (viewing economic, social and cultural rights as raising "question[s] of income distribution" and "protection of vulnerable groups such as the poor"); Danilo Turk, *The United Nations and the Realization of Economic, Social and Cultural Rights, in* The Implementation of Economic and Social Rights: National International and Comparative Aspects 95, 106–07 (Franz Matscher (ed.), 1991) (employing term "economic" as part of set of "economic, social and cultural rights" that guarantee minimum welfare system).

[92] *Cf.* Charles L. Black, Jr., *Further Reflection on the Constitutional Justice of Livelihood*, 86 COLUM. L. REV. 1103, 1104–05 (1986) (arguing that economic rights can be grounded in Constitution). For a thoughtful analysis of the Supreme Court's resistance to economic rights, see Jonathan R. Macey, *Some Causes and Consequences of the Bifurcated Treatment of Economic Rights and "Other" Rights Under the United States Constitution, in* ECONOMIC RIGHTS 141, 151–70 (Ellen Frankel Paul, et al. eds., 1992).

[93] Economic Covenant, *supra* note 9, at 7.

[94] *Id.*

[95] *Id.* at 5. Article 2 provides that "[t]he States Parties to the present Covenant undertake to guarantee that the rights enunciated in the present Covenant will be exercised without discrimination of kind as to race, colour, sex... or other status." *Id.* However, Article 2 appears to apply only to rights "recognized" in the Covenant. *See* MATTHEW C. CRAVEN, THE INTERNATIONAL COVENANT ON ECONOMIC, SOCIAL AND CULTURAL RIGHTS: A PERSPECTIVE ON ITS DEVELOPMENT 26 (1995).

a marriage–caused loss and require[ing] payments to reduce it in accordance with the length of the marriage."[96] It is also consistent with well-established norms, at least in some American jurisdictions, that refuse to enforce agreements where doing so will leave one of the spouses destitute.[97] Current law in the United States is mixed on this issue, reflecting the lack of consensus and the often incorrect assumption that women now have "equal opportunity" in the workforce.[98]

It could also be argued, however, that the Economic Covenant does not require such a result. Rather, the Economic Covenant imposes obligations on the *State*. Indeed, there are no readily available examples in which the Economic Covenant has been relied upon to prevent enforcement of a separation agreement.[99] This is not surprising. Most countries which have ratified the Economic Covenant, and which take it seriously, also have domestic legislation implementing it in specific contexts. This legislation may have been enacted pursuant to the State's ratification, reflecting the same cultural norms about a society's responsibility to its most vulnerable members that would lead a State to ratify the Economic Covenant. In some cases, there are additional national or regional human rights instruments, consistent with and supportive of the Economic Covenant, but more closely tailored to national or regional needs and circumstances. In Canada, for example, economic rights are more likely to be protected under the Canadian Charter of Rights and Freedoms.[100] Similarly, In the United Kingdom, economic rights are more likely to be protected under the European Social Charter.[101] Such protection may well take the form of family law requiring "economic justice" to be taken into account at divorce, regardless of the parties' earlier intentions, as it is in England and Canada.[102]

IV. How the Incorporation of International Law Would Actually Work

There are two basic ways in which countries deal with international treaties.[103] In monist legal systems, such as that of The Netherlands, once human rights instruments are ratified, they are incorporated into domestic law. As part of domestic law, the substantive provisions of the instruments may be relied upon as substantive domestic law. In dualist legal systems, such as that of the United States, human rights instruments (as well as other international treaties) do not become part of domestic law until – and unless – domestic implementing legislation is enacted. This is further complicated in the United States by the doctrine of self-executing treaties. That is, certain treaties (such as friendship, commerce, and navigation treaties) are considered self-executing and no domestic legislation is required.[104] Since none of the human rights treaties are self-executing, however, this does not change the

[96] Katherine T. Bartlett, *Saving the Family from the Reformers*, 31 U.C. DAVIS L. REV. 809, 847 (1998).

[97] *See, e.g.*, Button v. Button, 388 N.W.2d 546 (Wis. 1986) (refusing to enforce agreement on the ground that, under the circumstances, it would be unfair to enforce it at divorce).

[98] Women still earn only $.77 for every dollar men earn. *See* text accompanying n. 60–61.

[99] *But see* STARK, *supra* note 24, at 136–43 (discussing CEDAW Comments on the Marital Property Regime in Kenya).

[100] *Available at* http://laws.justice.gc.ca/en/charter (last visited October 29, 2005).

[101] European Social Charter, *entered into force* Feb. 26, 1965, 529 U.N.T.S. 89.

[102] *See* text accompanying note 57, *supra*.

[103] For a rigorous analysis of the ways in which several States have incorporated international treaty norms related to gender, see Ruth Rubio-Marin & Martha Morgan, *Constitutional Domestication of International Gender Norms*, in GENDER AND HUMAN RIGHTS 113 (Karen Knop ed. 2004).

[104] Asakura v. City of Seattle, 265 U.S. 332 (1924).

basic analysis here. Even in countries where domestic legislation is not legally required, moreover, as a practical matter it may be necessary. As Arthur Chaskalson, Chief Justice of the South African Supreme Court, recently explained, courts are ill-equipped to enforce broad statements of economic rights.[105]

Under this proposal, the specified human rights instruments would function like the international human rights instruments function in monist systems. In such systems, each State has the option of enacting implementing legislation. Human rights are not an issue in every enforcement action as agreements under the PRINCIPLES. Consideration of human rights would only be triggered if either party made a good faith claim that enforcement in a particular case would in fact violate human rights under the cited instrument. Mail-order brides or women in arranged marriages may be able to avoid agreements that may not be "unconscionable" under traditional conceptions of equity. The notion of autonomous bargainers, implicit in such conceptions, may well be completely alien to such women. The burden would be on the party claiming a violation to establish it to the court's satisfaction.

In support of their arguments, aggrieved parties could rely on jurisprudence of the monitoring bodies, the Committee on the Elimination of Discrimination Against Women and the Committee on Economic, Social and Cultural Rights, and, where available, decisions of other national courts and tribunals. Professor Elizabeth Scott asks whether an agreement that perpetuated existing inequalities would be stricken under this standard.[106] Where such inequalities were so extreme, or the parties so poor, that enforcement would leave one without healthcare[107] or an adequate standard of living,[108] it could be challenged. But this is hardly the situation in most of the reported cases, as Professor John DeWitt Gregory has observed.[109] Application of international law does not eliminate freedom of contract, of course. It simply limits it in a few egregious cases.

V. Conclusion

The incorporation of human rights law makes sense in this context because it provides normative parameters conspicuously lacking in American jurisprudence. These are norms that support the security and well-being of those who need it most. As Professor Ellman observes, such law is unnecessary when there is affection between the parties who recognize a complex range of rights and responsibilities flowing between them.[110] Some of these, according to the PRINCIPLES, should survive the termination of the relationship. Which ones? Why? The PRINCIPLES answer these questions piecemeal, seeking to articulate an inchoate national or local consensus while conceding that in fact such a consensus may not exist.

International human rights law, in contrast, articulates the rough global consensus regarding that which is owed to the most vulnerable. This is the international version of

[105] Arthur Chaskalson, *Remarks at Columbia Law School* (Nov. 3, 2004).

[106] Comments of Professor Mary Ann Glendon, *Workshop on the PRINCIPLES*, Cambridge, Massachusetts (Oct. 16, 2004).

[107] Economic Covenant, *supra* note 9, at 8.

[108] *Id.* at 7.

[109] Comments of Professor John DeWitt Gregory, *Workshop on the PRINCIPLES*, Cambridge, Massachusetts (Oct. 16, 2004) (referring to the PRINCIPLES as "the *PRINCIPLES* for the rich and famous," which resonated strongly for many of those at the Workshop).

[110] Ellman, *supra* note 11, at 700.

what Professor Mary Ann Glendon has referred to as the "sub-strata, the common norms that hold everything up."[111] Our reluctance to ratify the human rights instruments reflects, in part, our continuing resistance to the idea that the vulnerable have a claim against society in general. This is grounded, in part, in our sometimes exaggerated deference to freedom of contract and autonomy. But as the PRINCIPLES affirm elsewhere, we have long recognized that the vulnerable have claims against their families.

I am deeply grateful to Mary Ann Glendon and Robin Fretwell Wilson for organizing the Harvard Workshop and for inviting me to participate, and to the other participants for their thoughtful presentations. The questions raised by Brian Bix, John DeWitt Gregory, Marsha Garrison, and Elizabeth Scott were particularly helpful. Warm thanks to Betty Black Leonardo for her skillful preparation of the manuscript.

[111] Comments of Professor Mary Ann Glendon, *Workshop on PRINCIPLES*, Cambridge, Massachusetts (Oct. 16, 2004).

21 A Formula for Fool's Gold: The Illustrative Child Support Formula in Chapter 3 of the ALI's PRINCIPLES

Maura D. Corrigan

This chapter offers a vision of negotiation and compromise in domestic relations litigation, and especially in child support matters, that is drawn from my own experience as the Chief Justice of the Michigan Supreme Court from 2001–2004. In that capacity, I shared with our governor the administrative oversight responsibility for Michigan's child support enforcement system.[1]

I became Michigan's Chief Justice in January 2001. My own initial introduction to child support law was sudden and a bit frightening. The first day on my new job brought word from the state budget director that the Judiciary should expect significant budget cuts because the federal government had penalized Michigan $39 million for failing to comply with a federal mandate to create a statewide computerized child support enforcement system. Michigan, a state whose population barely tops 10 million, currently has more than 800,000 open cases involving children who are entitled to receive support from noncustodial parents pursuant to orders issued in divorce and paternity cases.[2] The penalties for not complying with the federal mandate would have increased exponentially in subsequent fiscal years. Although we had many excuses and explanations,[3] we had exhausted the federal government's patience and so faced crippling economic penalties if we did not create a functioning statewide system almost from scratch in just two years, by September 30, 2003.

We did it, and the federal certification authorities later dubbed our effort the "Michigan Miracle" because no other state had been able to create a certification-worthy system in so little time. The federal government then waived most of the previously imposed penalties and refunded $34 million. I learned most of what I know about child support law during

[1] In Michigan, child support enforcement is administered jointly by the Judiciary and the Executive. In contrast to many other states, our longstanding practice had been to handle child support enforcement at the county level. That work was done cooperatively by the Judiciary through county "Friend of the Court" offices and the Executive through county "Family Independence Agency" offices. Each county had its own unique enforcement system and computer software.

[2] U.S. DEP'T HEALTH & HUMAN SERVICES, ADMINISTRATION FOR CHILDREN & FAMILIES, OFFICE OF CHILD SUPPORT ENFORCEMENT, DIVISION OF PLANNING, RESEARCH & EVALUATION, CHILD SUPPORT ENFORCEMENT, FY 2004, PRELIMINARY REPORT (2005), at Table 4, *at* http://www.acf.hhs.gov/programs/cse/pubs/2005/reports/ preliminary_report/table_4.html.

[3] As you can imagine, it is no easy task to design and build a functional statewide computer system that can handle all the details of child support enforcement work. Michigan's record for collecting child support had been excellent, at least when compared to other states. Because our county-based system worked well, no one was eager to switch to a federally mandated statewide system that was certain to be less productive (for many years) than the system we already had.

those thirty harrowing months. But it was a crash course, and my knowledge remains incomplete.

As Chief Justice, I also have an interest in using alternative dispute resolution ("ADR") processes to resolve or avoid litigation. If our courts can do a better job on a smaller budget, I want to explore how that can be done.[4] Domestic relations litigation, especially ongoing postjudgment litigation, accounts for a high percentage of the caseload in Michigan's general jurisdiction courts. In 2003, our circuit courts received 335,501 new-case filings.[5] Almost two-thirds of those were family-law filings, including 23,802 new divorce-with-children complaints,[6] 10,718 paternity complaints, 11,803 in-state support complaints, 2,833 interstate support enforcement complaints, and 7,001 "other domestic" filings.[7] These numbers show the disproportionate burden that domestic relations cases impose on our justice system. Resolving these disputes without a judge's long-term involvement is a win-win deal for everyone. It was through these two lenses – my personal interest in child support matters and my administrative interest in reducing the burden that domestic relations litigation places on the judicial system – that I viewed the ALI's reform proposals, especially as they relate to child support.

I see two principal problems with our present system. First, it aids and abets conflict between parents. Our adversarial litigation system facilitates, and often requires, courtroom warfare. In domestic relations cases, this warfare wastes money, burns emotional bridges, and does great harm to children. Second, and erring in the opposite direction, when a child's parents do not have an ongoing relationship and the authorities find it difficult to locate the noncustodial parent, we are too quick to resort to default proceedings.[8] Although the resulting default judgments may satisfy the bureaucratic need to establish paternity and obtain a support order, default judgments do not immediately produce any actual money. They do saddle the judgment debtors, who are often children themselves, with what are sometimes unrealistic, unpayable support obligations that do little to bind these fathers to their children.

To offer real help to families after dissolution, we need to do more than just fine tune the rules for awarding child support. Real progress will require changing the essential "culture" of domestic relations litigation. This chapter proposes a better way to resolve child support disputes – and all the other issues that arise when a family dissolves and litigation ensues. The reforms proposed here would substitute a conciliatory, child-focused process for our current adversarial, parent-focused process. Under this proposal, a court would issue the judgment of divorce or paternity, but the specific provisions of the judgment, including its child-support provisions, would reflect an agreement between the parties, not a decision

[4] I have long believed that mediation-like procedures should be used to resolve many disputes that now consume our courts' resources. That belief led me to working with the International Centre for Healing and the Law ("ICHL"), which "dedicates itself to healing and peace in our society, and provides opportunities for legal professionals to explore and reflect upon the deeper meaning of their vocation and their lives." *See* http://www.healingandthelaw.org. For the same reasons, I also cochair the Joint Problem-Solving Courts Committee of the Conference of Chief Justices and the Conference of State Court Administrators, the work of which is discussed in greater detail at the end of this chapter.

[5] Michigan Supreme Court, 2003 Annual Report, Circuit Court Statistical Supplement (2004), at 4, *at* http://courts.michigan.gov/scao/resources/publications/statistics/2003/circuitcaseloadreport2003.pdf.

[6] Childless married couples filed 22,628 divorce complaints. *Id.* at 3.

[7] *Id.* at 3. In addition to divorce, paternity, and child support cases, the family-court total also includes juvenile proceedings and personal protection order cases. *See generally id.*

[8] *See* 42 U.S.C. § 666(a)(5)(H) (1999). *See also* Sorensen, *infra* note 56, at 16–17.

imposed on the parties by a judge. Such a process has been explored and implemented in varying degrees on questions of custody in the United States, but not with respect to child support, although it is being explored even as to child support in Australia.[9]

This chapter begins in Part I with some brief observations about the PRINCIPLES' child support proposals. Parts II and III then discuss the root causes of the real problem underlying child support enforcement, the fragmentation of the family, focusing both on the economic impact on children and the emotional impact. I argue that any efforts at reforming the law of family dissolution should modify the law in ways that will contain and abate the crisis caused by family dissolution. I suggest that the PRINCIPLES, rather than containing the crisis, may accelerate it. Part IV discusses the very difficult problem of default judgments, which the PRINCIPLES would do little to address. Part V then argues that problem-solving courts should be established to assist families at the time of dissolution, as well as parents that never formed families. These courts would help the parents establish realistic child support obligations by mutual agreement, in much the same way that mediation is used now to structure custody and visitation arrangements. These problem-solving courts would be guided by a rule like the one summarized in Part V that presently is under consideration for adoption by the courts in St. Joseph County, Indiana. Finally, Part VI concludes that, although a standardized child-support formula like that proposed in Chapter 3 of the PRINCIPLES is a necessary feature of any domestic-relations legal system, specialized problem-solving courts and innovative mediation techniques hold far greater promise for helping the children and parents who must pass through that system.

I. The ALI's Child Support PRINCIPLES

As a threshold matter, the drafters are certainly correct in their basic premise that most current child support formulas allocate too little money to the household in which the children reside.[10] If finances were the sole concern, then this commentary could begin and end by saying that when the noncustodial parent has significant income, the PRINCIPLES'

[9] *See* Patrick Parkinson, Family Relationship Centres: A New Approach To Resolving Conflicts About Parenting, presented to the (12th) World Conference of the International Society of Family Law, Salt Lake City, Utah, July 19–22, 2005; Family Law (Shared Parental Responsibility) Bill 2005 (authorizing establishment of Family Relationship Centres in sections of the Bill relating to Family Dispute Resolution), *available at* www.aph.gov.au/house/committee/laca/familylaw/index.htm; Explanatory Statement issued by the Attorney-General, 2005 (discussing the role of Family Relationship Centres), *available at* www.aph.gov.au/house/committee/laca/familylaw/index.htm.

[10] *See, e.g.*, PRINCIPLES § 3.04 cmt. h, at 429–30 (regarding the problems of child poverty in single parent families). *See also* Grace Glanz Blumberg, *Balancing the Interests: The American Law Institute's Treatment of Child Support*, 33 ABA FAM. L. Q. 39 (1999); Karen Syma Czapanskiy, *ALI Child Support Principles: A Lesson in Public Policy and Truth-Telling*, 8 DUKE J. GENDER L. & POL'Y 259 (2001); Marsha Garrison, *The Economic Consequences of Divorce: Would Adoption of the ALI Principles Improve Current Outcomes?*, 8 DUKE J. GENDER L. & POL'Y 119 (2001); Theresa Glennon, *Expendable Children: Defining Belonging In a Broken World*, 8 DUKE J. GENDER L. & POL'Y 269 (2001); Leslie Joan Harris, *The Proposed ALI Child Support Principles*, 35 WILLAMETTE L. REV. 717 (1999); Leslie Joan Harris, *The ALI Child Support Principles: Incremental Changes to Improve the Lot of Children and Residential Parents*, 8 DUKE J. GENDER L. & POL'Y 245 (2001); J. Thomas Oldham, *Limitations Imposed by Family Law on a Separated Parent's Ability to Make Significant Life Decisions: A Comparison of Relocation and Income Imputation*, 8 DUKE J. GENDER L. & POL'Y 333 (2001).

The article by Professor Blumberg is particularly important because she served as one of the three drafters for the PRINCIPLES and is the principal author of Chapter 3. This article was published while the ALI was still reworking the PRINCIPLES. It includes some valuable work-in-progress insights into how Chapter 3 evolved that are not found in the PRINCIPLES' official Comments and Reporters Notes.

formula will deliver more of that money to the children.[11] Increasing resources for children is a good result, and the drafters are to be commended for their proposal.

Less commendably, the PRINCIPLES' child support formula assigns a high priority to the noncustodial parent's *right*, which the drafters call an "interest," to live better than his or her children.[12] A parent who will pay only what a judge orders is not likely to voluntarily surrender a societally-approved higher living standard. For this reason, and because the children are my primary concern, I question the ALI's basic premise on this issue – though I do acknowledge that there is a point of diminishing return beyond which further increasing the support obligation can eliminate a selfish parent's incentive to work.

As commentators have noted, even the PRINCIPLES' comparatively modest child support increases will be a hard sell politically.[13] Thus, it seems unlikely that any state will adopt support guidelines that require noncustodial parents to pay even more support than the drafters recommend. For those reasons, we probably will have to acknowledge a higher-income nonresidential parent's "right" to the higher standard of living. But there is a difference between having a right and doing right. A surprising number of noncustodial parents voluntarily pay more than their state's formula requires.[14] They do that because it helps their children, a consideration that would prevail more often in a system that encouraged parents to negotiate rather than litigate, as the reforms proposed at the end of this chapter would do.

In other parts of the PRINCIPLES' Chapter 3, I would resolve some minor issues differently than the ALI, but those quibbles are too insignificant to raise here. Besides, the PRINCIPLES do not purport to enact or restate law. They merely offer recommendations that each state may fine tune to reflect local policy preferences.[15]

Although I have no major quarrel with Chapter 3's general direction, I was greatly disappointed by the PRINCIPLES generally because they do not acknowledge the root cause of our child support problems, let alone propose corrective actions. The ALI could have offered a significant contribution to family law had the PRINCIPLES focused on the national crisis that creates the need for child support payments: the too-frequent dissolution of American families and the sad truth that so many children never live in a two-parent family.[16] Instead, Chapter 3 tinkers with child-support formulas and nibbles around the edges of that national crisis. Even worse, other chapters of the PRINCIPLES recommend

[11] *See* Karen Syma Czapanskiy, *ALI Child Support Principles: A Lesson in Public Policy and Truth-Telling*, 8 DUKE J. GENDER L. & POL'Y 259 (2001).

[12] *See* PRINCIPLES § 3.04 cmt. d, at 425 ("[T]he higher-income parent... has an *interest* in benefiting disproportionately, as compared to other family members, from the fruits of his or her own labor. These Principles accord considerable deference to this interest.... It is generally not subject to compromise in the balancing process.") (emphasis added).

[13] Harris, *supra* note 4, at 755–57.

[14] Judges and child support enforcement workers often tell me this. The PRINCIPLES make the same observation. *See* PRINCIPLES § 3.04 cmt. F, at 426. The PRINCIPLES would allow courts to approve parental agreements that depart from the child-support formula unless the agreed amount is "substantially less" than the formula calls for and "is not consistent with the interests of the child." PRINCIPLES § 3.13 cmt. a, at 517.

[15] PRINCIPLES, Chief Reporter's Foreword, at xviii.

[16] In this volume, Professor Lynn Wardle also faults the drafters for ignoring gate-keeping procedures that could ameliorate the incidence of divorce. He also criticizes the PRINCIPLES for failing to recognize the public's interest in enforcing "generally accepted standards of minimum acceptable behavior for spouses." Wardle, this volume. Professor Wardle believes – and I agree – that society should enforce those minimum standards by, for example, authorizing courts to consider the parties' adherence to them when the courts allocate the financial consequences of divorce.

changing the law in ways that would endorse and encourage the root causes of the crisis.

The crisis of which I speak is the decline of the two-parent family. Professor James Q. Wilson has labeled this crisis "the Marriage Problem:"[17]

> The [marriage] problem lies at the heart of the emergence of two nations [within the United States].... [T]here have been times in our history when unemployment was high and public schools barely existed. Yet in those days we were not two culturally opposed nations.... Today, we are vastly richer, but the money has not purchased public safety, racial comity, or educational achievement.
>
> The reason, I think, is clear: It is not money but the family that is the foundation of public life. As [that foundation] has become weaker, every structure built upon it has become weaker....
>
> The evidence concerning the powerful effect of this familial foundation is now so strong that even some sociologists believe it.[18]

We should be thinking about how to either enforce or modify current law in ways that will contain and abate this crisis. Implementing many of the ALI's recommendations would actually exacerbate the problem.[19] In short, modifying our current approach to child support formulas is worth doing, but we have much more important business to attend to, as this chapter explains.

II. The Sad Economic Truth of Family Fragmentation

If a child's parents do not live together, that child's standard of living will be lower than if the parents shared one household.[20] No surprise there. Economists question only the degree of economic harm to the child.

Divorce actually does the greatest economic harm to middle class families. If separating parents are wealthy, the economic harm to their children will likely be slight and need not concern us. But most families feel a financial pinch from paying just one set of household bills. If a splintered family must now maintain two separate households, then the resulting inefficiencies and duplicative costs make the financial pinch painful for even those parents who earn a middle-class income. Divorce can reduce struggling middle class families to poverty. For them, and for families at lower rungs on the income ladder, the dual-household pinch causes severe economic pain.

Many studies have demonstrated that children who grow up in single-parent or unmarried parent households are much more likely to live in poverty or near-poverty.[21] Most of the illustrations in the PRINCIPLES that accompany the ALI's proposed formula assert that it is superior to others because it will allow the child's residential household to live at (100 + X)

[17] JAMES Q. WILSON, THE MARRIAGE PROBLEM: HOW OUR CULTURE HAS WEAKENED FAMILIES (2002).

[18] *Id.* at 7.

[19] Wardle, this volume; Carbone, this volume (considering the impact on marriage of the domestic partnership provisions); Scott, this volume (observing that legal facilitation of claims by cohabiting parties may undermine marriage somewhat by extending legal recognition and some marital rights to informal unions).

[20] PRINCIPLES § 3.04 cmt. c, at 424 (noting the financial losses that typically follow the division of one household into two).

[21] David Popenoe, *The State of Our Unions 2004: The Social Health of Marriage in America* (The National Marriage Project, Rutgers University, 2005), at 17. (citation omitted).

percent of the federal poverty level instead of a lower (100 + Y) percent level produced by the "first-generation formulas" still used in most states.[22] At those near-poverty levels, any additional money for the child helps, as does shifting more of the unavoidable economic hardship to the noncustodial parent. But how significant can that improvement be if we must measure it relative to the federal poverty level? For me, reading the PRINCIPLES' hypothetical illustrations one after another made me despair for the children who lose so much if their parents cannot live together under the same roof.

How did we arrive at this sad state of affairs? In THE MARRIAGE PROBLEM, Professor Wilson says that American society has, over several decades, drifted toward a majority view that marriage is merely one of several acceptable options for a man and a woman who want a long-term sexual relationship.[23] Getting married now is merely an "option," as is staying married.

When a couple is childless, their marriage and divorce choices directly affect only themselves. But our major concern involves the children of divorced or never-married parents. They are the economic victims of their parents' decisions to divorce or not to marry in the first place. For these children, the human and economic costs are staggering. According to data from the National Center for Health Statistics, out-of-wedlock births in the United States numbered 1,365,966 during 2002,[24] nearly 34 percent of all the children born that year.[25] The majority of children who grow up outside married families will experience at least one childhood year of "dire" poverty.[26] U. S. Census Bureau data for *all* single-parent households show that, in 2002, families with a female head of household and no husband present accounted for one-half of all American families living in poverty.[27]

The poverty rate for custodial-parent families is four times greater than the rate for intact married families with children.[28] More than 31 percent of custodial parents have never been married.[29] More than 27 percent of all children live apart from one of their parents.[30] An estimated 13.4 million parents have custody of 21.5 million children whose other parent lives elsewhere.[31]

When parents live separately, the custodial parent's own income and the noncustodial parent's child support payments are supposed to, together, substitute for the financial support that an intact family would provide. But this is a poor substitute. The nonwealthy simply cannot maintain an intact family's living standard when parents live separately. So, child support payments seldom provide an adequate economic substitute even when the noncustodial parent pays as ordered. Now consider the numbers for unpaid child support. A recent accounting by the Office of Child Support Enforcement in the U.S. Department of Health and Human Services (HHS) showed that $96 billion of post-1975 court-ordered child support remained unpaid as of June 30, 2003.[32] By now, the total surely exceeds $100 billion.

[22] *See, e.g.*, PRINCIPLES § 3.05 illus., at 442.

[23] WILSON, *supra* note 17, at 3–5, 41.

[24] CENTERS FOR DISEASE CONTROL, NATIONAL CENTER FOR HEALTH STATISTICS, NATIONAL VITAL STATISTICS REPORT, BIRTHS: FINAL DATA FOR 2002 (2003), at 8, *at* http://www.cdc.gov/nchs/data/nvsr/nvsr52/nvsr52_10.pdf.

[25] *Id.* at 4.

[26] Popenoe, *supra* note 21, at 17. (citation omitted).

[27] U.S. CENSUS BUREAU, POVERTY IN THE UNITED STATES: 2002 (2003), at 13, *at* http://www.inequality.org/census˙poverty˙report.

[28] *Id.* at 3.

[29] U.S. CENSUS BUREAU, CUSTODIAL MOTHERS AND FATHERS AND THEIR CHILD SUPPORT: 2001, (2003), at 3, *at* http://www.census.gov/prod/2003pubs/p60-225.pdf.

[30] *Id.* at 1.

[31] *Id.*

[32] ADMINISTRATION FOR CHILDREN & FAMILIES, OFFICE OF CHILD SUPPORT ENFORCEMENT, U.S. DEP'T OF HEALTH & HUMAN SERVICES, CHILD SUPPORT ENFORCEMENT FY 2003, PRELIMINARY DATA REPORT,

Of the $96 billion that was unpaid as of 2003, almost half was "owed to the government" as reimbursement for government payments to custodial parents.[33] The good news is that government payments had partially substituted for the support that noncustodial parents failed to pay. That safety-net assistance at least averts starvation and homelessness. The bad news is that it cannot lift the children to an economic level from which they can realistically contemplate and aspire to a better life. Further, any fraction of the arrearage that the government retains as reimbursement for past government payments represents money paid by the noncustodial parent that will not go to the custodial household. Consequently, the delinquent noncustodial parent has less family-oriented incentive to pay the arrearage.

III. The Sad Emotional Truth of Family Fragmentation

Although many successful and emotionally healthy adults have grown up in one-parent households – usually thanks to heroic efforts of the residential parent – those children and parents have succeeded against the odds. They are the proverbial exceptions that prove the rule. That "rule" says that the best recipe for raising children requires two married parents who live together until one of them dies.[34] If we despair when contemplating the economic prospects of a child whose parents live separately, then we should feel even worse about the emotional handicaps imposed on children who never have experienced life in a two-parent household or who have watched their parents separate and have intuitively blamed themselves for being the wedge that split apart their parents.[35]

That last point, that children often subconsciously blame themselves for their parents' interpersonal strife, provided much of the impetus for the proposed court rules discussed in Part V of this chapter. Acrimony within a household is frightening for children; therefore, the legal processes that we use to formalize divorces, paternity determinations, and child support obligations should be designed to minimize the children's trauma. Adults may be able to "move on" from a broken marriage or relationship, but their minor children must stay behind and live among the remnants. They, and also the parents, need something better than our legal system now provides.

Attorneys and judges observe and know intuitively that lengthy and bitter domestic relations litigation harms the children who become trapped between their warring parents. Empirical research confirms that parents' separation-related conflicts increase their children's risk of experiencing an array of psychological harms, including self-blame, serious depression, chronic anxiety and distrust, inability to achieve essential developmental tasks, academic failure, dangerous relationships, and drug and alcohol experimentation.[36]

Preface: The Story Behind the Numbers: Who Owes the Child Support Debt? (2004), *at* http://www.acf.hhs.gov/programs/cse/pubs/2004/reports/ preliminary_data/#preface.

[33] *Id.*

[34] Robin Fretwell Wilson, *Evaluating Marriage: Does Marriage Matter to the Nurturing of Children?*, 42 San Diego L. Rev. 847 (2005); William H. Doherty et al., Why Marriage Matters: Twenty-One Conclusions from the Social Sciences (Institute for American Values, 2002), *at* http://www.marriagemovement.org/wmm/wmm_print.htm.

[35] Teyber, *infra* note 36.

[36] *See, e.g.*, Doherty et al., *supra* note 34; Constance Ahrons, We're Still Family: What Grown Children Have to Say about Their Parents' Divorce (2004); Paul R. Amato & Alan Booth, A Generation at Risk: Growing Up in an Era of Family Upheaval (1997); Debbie Barr, Children of Divorce: Helping Kids When Their Parents Are Apart (1992); Susan Blyth Boyan & Ann Marie Termini, Cooperative Parenting and Divorce: Shielding Your Child from Conflict: A Parent Guide to Effective Co-Parenting (1999); E. Mark Cummings & Patrick Davies, Children and Marital Conflict: The Impact of Family Dispute

Children suffer great emotional harm when their parents fight, separate, and then litigate the terms of their separation. But the broader legal community seems more concerned with parsing the parents' individual interests. When challenged to prove an assumed truth, attorneys often say that the assumption is "too obvious to require citation." But sometimes the truth is not obvious to all, or at least not as obvious as the proponent believes.[37] That is why it is essential to restate and establish the premise that parental conflict harms children emotionally, as these scholars do:

> Divorce presents many children with an unprecedented problem.... Not only are the children facing the greatest crisis of their young lives, but they are doing so without the emotional support of their parents.[38]
>
> [Divorce is] the knife that slashes not only [the child's] family but his world into pieces.[39]
>
> High conflict between parents not only causes children immense suffering, it causes serious problems in their development. They soon have the sense that they cannot trust any adults." *** Children caught in the flames of a high-conflict divorce have been referred to as 'children of Armageddon' – victims of the final war on earth. They are true casualties. Parents trapped in mutual anger often become heedless of anything else.[40]

The effects on children of family fragmentation are the same when never-married parents end their relationship. Younger children's known universe of "Mommy, Daddy, and me" doesn't take account of a marriage license. Although our legal system cannot fully shield children from the emotional pain caused by their parents' separation, the system should offer more protection than it currently does.

> When fighting continues after the divorce, children become disillusioned and disgusted. When parents divorce, children hope the fighting will go away so that they can have some peace in their lives. Many times I have heard children say that they wouldn't mind the divorce so much if their parents would finally learn to get along better. After the divorce, all children really want is for their parents to act grown up, leave them in peace, and let them love the other parent. Instead, when conflicts worsen, children are left with many wounds.[41]
>
> The thing that stresses children most, sometimes for many years, is lingering conflict between their parents.[42]

AND RESOLUTION (1994); KAREN FAGERSTROM ET AL., DIVORCE: A PROBLEM TO BE SOLVED, NOT A BATTLE TO BE FOUGHT (1997); CARLA B. GARRITY & MITCHELL A. BARIS, CAUGHT IN THE MIDDLE: PROTECTING THE CHILDREN OF HIGH-CONFLICT DIVORCE (1994); MARY ELLEN HANNIBAL, GOOD PARENTING THROUGH YOUR DIVORCE (2002); ARCHIBALD D. HART, CHILDREN AND DIVORCE: WHAT TO EXPECT – HOW TO HELP (1989); PHILIP M. STAHL, PARENTING AFTER DIVORCE: A GUIDE TO RESOLVING CONFLICTS AND MEETING YOUR CHILDREN'S NEEDS (2000); EDWARD TEYBER, HELPING CHILDREN COPE WITH DIVORCE (2001); SHIRLEY THOMAS, PARENTS ARE FOREVER: A STEP-BY-STEP GUIDE TO BECOMING SUCCESSFUL COPARENTS AFTER DIVORCE (2004); JUDITH S. WALLERSTEIN & SANDRA BLAKESLEE, WHAT ABOUT THE KIDS? (2003); RICHARD A. WARSHAK, DIVORCE POISON (2001).

[37] Whenever someone says that some assertion is "too obvious to need [supporting] citation," it brings to mind the story of the law professor who always told his first-year students about a memorable experience he had as a young associate at a prestigious New York law firm. The firm had just been retained to handle a major First Amendment case. The senior partner convening the firm's initial strategy session was widely recognized as a constitutional scholar. Nevertheless, the partner began the meeting by suggesting, "I think that we should start by reading the First Amendment to see exactly what it says." Similarly, we do well here to remind ourselves of the emotional distress felt by the children of divorced or separated parents.

[38] BARR, *supra note* 36, at 21.

[39] BOYAN & TERMINI, *supra* note 36, at 2.

[40] WALLERSTEIN & BLAKESLEE, *supra* note 36, at 204, 213–214.

[41] STAHL, *supra* note 36, at 19–20.

[42] AHRONS, *supra* note 36, at 80.

When it comes to "*lingering* conflict," there is nothing quite like a child support dispute, which can provide up to eighteen years' worth of new excuses for parents to renew old fights.

> Our data show that the long-term consequences of inter-parental discord for children are pervasive and consistently detrimental ... [and] have a broad negative impact on virtually every dimension of offspring well-being. ...[43]

It is tragically ironic that, after parents have created vulnerable children who depend on them totally, one or both parents so often conclude that a personal quest for happiness justifies ending the parents' relationship with each other, frequently terminating one parent's relationship with the children. The parental separation may indeed be justified, and in some cases even essential to personal safety.[44] But why does the law so unquestioningly facilitate the adults' quest for contentment while according comparatively little weight to the consequences felt by their children? I believe that the law should do more to encourage or require the parents to accept economic and emotional responsibility for the children that they have created.

The courts can help to reduce conflict by encouraging the parents to resolve child support (and other) issues by rational negotiation.[45] That is how the parents should "fight" if they want to protect their children.

Unlike the custody provisions of the PRINCIPLES, which embrace mediation,[46] mentions of mediation are virtually absent from the child support discussion in Chapter 3. This is not surprising given the history of child support, where guidelines have been instituted to constrain the judicial discretion that led to arbitrary and often insufficient child support awards.[47] Yet,

> The most important reason for working out a contentious relationship is that high conflict has far-reaching negative effects on children. Those who witness intense bitterness between their parents and are caught repeatedly in loyalty binds are at high risk for later emotional disturbance. Parental conflict interrupts many of the critical tasks of psychological development.
>
> ... As adults, these children typically experience problems with intimate relationships, conflict resolution, and self-identity. ... [C]hildren of high-conflict divorce are frequently unable to maintain their own marriages successfully. Not having learned the skills of communicating, cooperating, and resolving disputes, they lack problem-solving strategies and tools for handling conflict in an intimate relationship. ... These children often face hard struggles in defining their own identity. As they struggle over time to fit into the two polarities represented by their feuding parents, the result is often one of confusion. These children experience a great deal of identity diffusion, liking and accepting some parts of themselves and devaluing other parts.[48]

[43] AMATO & BOOTH, *supra* note 36, at 219.

[44] *See* Naomi Cahn, *Child Witnessing of Domestic Violence, in* HANDBOOK OF CHILDREN, CULTURE & VIOLENCE (Nancy Dowd, Dorothy G. Singer & Robin Fretwell Wilson, eds., 2006); Robin Fretwell Wilson, *Removing Violent Parents from the Home: A Test Case for the Public Health Approach*, 12 VA J. SOC. POL'Y & L. 635 (2005).

[45] Mnookin, Robert H. & L. Kornhauser, *Bargaining in the Shadow of the Law*, 88 YALE L.J. 950 (1979).

[46] The PRINCIPLES embrace ADR as a tool for resolving disputes between the parents after divorce, *see, e.g.*, PRINCIPLES § 2.10 (requiring dispute resolution mechanisms in parenting plans), and permit parents to resolve many issues by mutual agreement, *see, e.g.*, PRINCIPLES § 3.13 (providing that a parental agreement regarding child support should be adopted by the court unless it results in substantially less child support than would result by applying the PRINCIPLES).

[47] *See* Levy, this volume.

[48] GARRITY & BARIS *supra* note 36, at 26, 27.

If feuding parents do not comprehend how their actions affect their children in the here and now, then they surely will not pause to consider that they also are lengthening the future odds against their children having successful marriages of their own and raising the grandchildren within intact families.[49] But society should perform that calculation for its own sake. The ever-increasing numbers of divorces and never-married parents bode ill for our society, which needs a critical mass of productive adult citizens. Just as children who depend on government financial assistance are more likely to remain poor as adults,[50] so are the children of failed marriages or relationships more likely to fail in their adult relationships. Couples caught up in emotional warfare are unlikely to consider those long-term societal consequences; therefore, society must act to save itself. The ADR-based court rule proposal endorsed in Section V would contribute to that effort.

Parents who now bring their disputes to the courts will not be able to change tactics without firm guidance from the legal system. These parents are as human and almost as emotionally vulnerable as their children. Just as children need guidance from their parents, separating parents need guidance that our legal system does not currently provide.

> We can understand and empathize with the spouse who feels wronged and wants revenge, or the spouse who is overwhelmed with anxiety at the thought of losing the children, or the spouse who prefers to forget that the marriage ever was. But using the children to get revenge, to cope with anxiety, to erase the past, is unacceptable. Parents must hold themselves to a higher standard. They must have the courage to face what they are doing to their children. They must honor their mission to safeguard their children's welfare, even when the darkest feelings beckon them.... Divorce poison must be left in the bottle.[51]

Those parents inclined to choose litigation over compromise are too consumed by their own emotions to appreciate how much their courtroom battles harm their children. And the children are powerless. So, if the "divorce poison" is to be kept in the bottle, our legal system must assume that responsibility.

IV. The Default Problem

Thus far, I have criticized our present system because it aids and abets conflict between parents. But there is a second major systemic flaw, one that errs in the opposite direction. When a child's parents do not have an ongoing relationship and the authorities find it difficult to locate the noncustodial parent, we are too quick to resort to default proceedings.[52] Although the resulting default judgments may satisfy the bureaucratic need to establish paternity and obtain a support order, default judgments do not immediately produce any actual money. Worse, obtaining a support order by default actually lengthens the odds against the noncustodial parent ever paying support or establishing a parent-child relationship.[53]

Especially in the last ten years, our child-support enforcement efforts have become much more effective thanks to the many federal-state-interstate partnerships. An outright

[49] *See* Paul R. Amato & Jacob Cheadle, *The Long Reach of Divorce: Divorce and Child Well-Being Across Three Generations*, 67 J. MARR. & FAM. 191 (2005).

[50] DOHERTY ET AL., *supra* note 34, at 3–5.

[51] WARSHAK, *supra* note 36, at 22–23.

[52] *See* 42 U.S.C. § 666(a)(5)(H) (1999). *See also* SORENSEN, *infra* note 56, at 16–17.

[53] *Id.*

refusal to pay will land the nonpayer in jail. Flight across state lines no longer is a surefire avoidance tactic. We can seize tax refunds. We can require even small businesses to withhold wages. But this federally directed, one-size-fits-all enforcement system has some negatives. The states are under intense and constant federal financial pressure to make paternity determinations and establish support obligations by whatever means that requires.

Consider, for example, a 17-year-old unemployed male who fathers a child and then disappears from the mother's life. If we can find him just once, personal service of a paternity complaint will enable the mother or a prosecutor to obtain a support order. Or, if we cannot find him initially, a government agency that pays welfare benefits to the mother will start the meter running on a support bill that will be presented to the father for payment if the mother or the government can locate him sometime in the future.[54] Either way, without the father actually participating in the case from the beginning, the court or government agency often will calculate the support obligation with little regard for the father's real ability to pay.[55]

In some cases, a judgment by default may be the best that we can do. To say that our resources are "limited" is generous. We do try to find and serve fathers initially. But when that proves difficult, I think that we turn to default proceedings too early and too often just because they satisfy the federal government's requirements and are easy and cheap in the short run. That approach is "penny wise but pound foolish." Instead of defaulting the father and setting a too-high support obligation that virtually assures that the young family will fail, we should instead invest more effort and money in trying to find the father early on, compel him to participate in the paternity proceedings, and encourage him to establish a relationship with his child.

As we now conduct business, the default judgment creates a support obligation that grows to an impossible size before we confront the father in a meaningful way. Barring a lottery win or a pro sports contract, the long-absent father almost certainly will not have the ability to pay the accrued arrearage. Meanwhile, we also have given him a strong incentive to hide within a large city or to flee to another state. Those avoidance tactics also remove him from his child's life until it is too late for normal father-child bonding. While the scenarios I have just painted involve young, unmarried parents, default proceedings can cause most of the same problems when a married parent files for divorce and then obtains a default judgment that includes a support order.

Instead of worrying about paperwork quotas, we should take steps that will encourage all parents to "buy in" to the process and their children's futures. We can do that by involving the fathers in the process from the outset, and then by facilitating parental cooperation instead of confrontation. The PRINCIPLES' improved child support formula can help, but only at the margins.

How badly do the flaws in our current judicial processes hurt child support collections? Some facts emerge from a recent "collectibility study" that analyzed California's child support enforcement problems.[56] That state's arrearage stood at $14.4 billion as of March 2000.[57] The study's authors projected that only 25 percent of that arrearage would ever

[54] 42 U.S.C. § 654(4) (1999) and 42 U.S.C. § 656 (1997). [55] SORENSEN, *infra* note 56, at 17.

[56] ELAINE SORENSEN ET AL., THE URBAN INSTITUTE, EXAMINING CHILD SUPPORT ARREARS IN CALIFORNIA: THE COLLECTIBILITY STUDY (2003).

[57] *Id.* at 1.

be collected, and even that low estimate assumed that no additional surcharges – that is, interest – would be added to the arrearage total.[58] The reasons for this anemic estimate included the fact that: (1) much of the debt is owed by low-income or no-income noncustodial parents; (2) many of the support orders were entered by default, which means that the court often had no knowledge of the noncustodial parents' whereabouts, let alone their ability to pay support; and (3) about 20 percent of the arrearage is owed by noncustodial parents who do not live in California.[59]

Interstate collection is very difficult if the noncustodial parent seeks to avoid paying.[60] We only compound the difficulties with adversarial litigation, unrealistically large default judgments, and punitive interest assessments – all of which encourage noncustodial parents to "disappear" across state lines and thus to disappear from their children's lives.

V. We Need a Better Way

That is no way to run a court system. Courtroom battles are harmful for all the reasons summarized earlier. At the other extreme, serving notices by publication and taking judgments by default can expedite case processing, but they do little to help children and custodial parents. To address both of those flaws (excessive conflict and too many defaults) we need more than a judicial paper mill that creates uncollectible debts. We need processes that will establish realistic support obligations and also instill in noncustodial parents a sense of their obligation to make regular support payments.

To any objective observer, the need for broad systemic change should be obvious. If change is to come, it must be sponsored by the system's permanent residents, our judges and attorneys. They have an informed perspective acquired over many years and from many cases. They can see the current system's flaws. But they also are accustomed to doing things the traditional way. Most do not seriously consider that there may be a better way.

Some judges suggest that the best way to instill that sense of obligation is to involve the noncustodial parent early on in a conciliatory process that determines the support amount. As one jurist phrased it in 2004, "Where there is harmony, people are more likely to pay support."[61] A formal study has shown that mediation-like procedures enhance litigants' perceptions of the process and help create that harmony.[62]

Sadly, the legal system has often defaulted on its responsibilities to contain the poison of divorce and family disintegration and to tether unmarried parents to their children,

[58] The Collectibility Study reported that California previously charged above-market interest rates on its arrearage. Since many of those who owe the arrearage would struggle to pay even the original assessment, adding interest at a punitively high rate serves only to enlarge the arrearage and further discourage payment. On the other hand, interest at a realistic rate would account for the fact that money received five years from now is worth less than the same amount received today. But monetary interest cannot compensate for the fact that child support collected when a child is 25 will not pay for things that the child needed at age 10.

[59] *Id.* at 5.

[60] I predict that the federal government will soon attach another condition to federal child-support funds, mandating that all states use the same child support formula. That would reduce the incentives for parents to choose their domicile based on a particular state's guideline generosity and willingness to enforce another state's higher or lower award.

[61] Domestic relations Referee Betty Lowenthal, who hears cases in Oakland County, Michigan's second largest county.

[62] Nancy Thoennes, Center for Policy Research, Mediating Disputes Involving Parenting Time and Responsibilities in Colorado's 10th Judicial District: Assessing the Benefits to the Courts (2002).

both financially and emotionally. There are, of course, some plausible excuses. Our judges and lawyers are schooled in Anglo-American jurisprudence and thus operate from the assumption that the adversarial process, though imperfect, is the best way to seek truth and do justice. That assumption may be correct for criminal prosecutions and other civil disputes, but it is the wrong way to handle domestic relations litigation.

There was a time when attorneys acted mostly as counselors and facilitators who guided their less well-educated clients through necessary interactions with governments and businesses. Today, many attorneys too often obstruct rather than facilitate, something they have been taught to do. Since domestic relations cases are largely governed by the same rules as other civil litigation, most attorneys see their job as fighting within those rules to obtain as much as possible for their client. That thinking is understandable, but flawed.

> A divorce is a funeral for a marriage, and the lawyers are but pallbearers. No one would think of congratulating a pallbearer at an actual funeral about "winning" by carrying his side of the casket better than the pallbearers on the opposite side. So why would anyone try to "win" at divorce?[63]

We need a better way to resolve those disputes without a judge's long-term involvement. This would be a win-win deal for everyone. It frees the courts' time and resources for other business. More important, it benefits children in three ways. First, they are spared the pain of being caught between warring parents. Second, our experience has been that more child support gets paid when the parents negotiate the support obligation. Third, involving both parents in the process – instead of setting the support obligation by default – promotes closer ties between the children and the noncustodial parent.

When people have hurt each other emotionally, their desire to fight may be natural. We tell them that they must not resort to physical violence and most listen.[64] But we also tell them that the proper way to fight is to hire lawyers and "tell it to a judge." That may be sound advice for commercial disputants, but it disserves parents who are hurting. They may claim to want only a fair and final decision by a judge, but a part of them may just want to fight – or we may actually encourage them to fight by dumping them into the adversarial arena that we provide. These parents are hurting, and society tells them that fighting in court is the right thing to do. We then officiate their fight until their money runs out, but we do not provide a satisfactory emotional resolution.

A mutually satisfactory end to the emotional distress is what these litigants need, but too few understand that. Nearly all believe in their hearts that they can achieve emotional peace only by winning a total courtroom victory, a rare event in the real world. Sadly, even a total courtroom victory may not end the emotional warfare.

Even if domestic relations litigants could understand how counterproductive our current court procedures are, they lack the power either to change those rules or to disobey them. Litigants are only temporary visitors to the courts. While visiting, they focus on their personal disputes. When their cases end, they have no continuing interest in improving a system from which they are eager to escape.

[63] Robert D. Lee, Indiana family law attorney, *at* http://www.uptoparents.org/files/OurAgreedCommitmentstoJessica.pdf.

[64] *See* Cahn, *supra* note 44; Robin Fretwell Wilson, *supra* note 44. *See also generally*, Clare Dalton & Elizabeth Schneider, Battered Women and the Law (2001).

Domestic relations cases require targeted problem-solving courts and special rules designed to handle domestic relations cases much differently than we do now. A "problem-solving court" is a specialized court (or special procedures for an existing court) designed to address an intractable human problem. "Drug courts" are perhaps the most common and successful example of problem-solving courts. The Conference of Chief Justices ("CCJ") and the Conference of State Court Administrators ("COSCA") have a Joint Problem-Solving Courts Committee, which I cochair. Our committee recommended that CCJ/COSCA apply the problem-solving court concept beyond drug cases to other problematic areas. The CCJ and COSCA unanimously endorsed that recommendation by joint resolutions adopted in 2000 and again in 2004.[65]

For family law cases, this would be a substantial improvement over the status quo. Most states have a few special rules for domestic relations cases;[66] many have special courts or special divisions within their traditional courts.[67] However, apart from a courtesy nod to mediation or other ADR techniques, even those specialized rules and courts use the traditional adversarial methods. That is not good enough. For the children's sake, we must change the very culture of domestic relations litigation.

How might that be done? The lodestar for all concerned should be a desire to protect the children from further emotional trauma. That one overarching principle

[65] The 2004 joint resolution provides in relevant part:

WHEREAS, the Joint Problem-Solving Courts Committee found that:

- There is evidence of broad support for the principles and methods commonly used in problem-solving courts, including ongoing judicial leadership, integration of treatment services with judicial case processing, close monitoring of and immediate response to behavior, multidisciplinary involvement, and collaboration with community-based and government organizations;
- These principles and methods have demonstrated great success in addressing certain complex social problems . . . that are not effectively addressed by the traditional legal process; and
- The application of these principles advance the trust and confidence of the public; and

WHEREAS, CCJ and COSCA adopted [the 2000 resolution] that agreed to:

1. Call these new courts and calendars 'Problem-Solving Courts,' recognizing that courts have always been involved in attempting to resolve disputes and problems in society, but understanding that the collaborative nature of these new efforts deserves recognition.
2. Take steps nationally and locally, to expand and better integrate the principles and methods of well-functioning drug courts into ongoing court operations.
3. Advance the careful study and evaluation of the principles and methods employed in problem-solving courts and their application to other significant issues facing state courts.
4. Encourage, where appropriate, the broad integration [of problem-solving court techniques into other litigation categories].
5. Support national and local education [about those techniques].
6. Advocate for the resources necessary to advance and apply [those techniques] in the general court systems of the various states.
7. Establish a national agenda consistent with this resolution that includes [seeking funding from HHS, seeking design and implementation assistance from the National Center for State Courts, and sponsoring national and regional conferences to educate judges and other government officials].

NOW, THEREFORE, BE IT RESOLVED [in 2004] that CCJ and COSCA reaffirm their commitment to these [2000 resolution] action items; and

BE IT FURTHER RESOLVED that CCJ and COSCA agree to develop a national agenda that includes [eleven specific "action items" developed from the more general suggestions in No. 7 above].

Adopted as proposed by the CCJ/COSCA Problem-Solving Courts Committee at the 56th Annual [Joint] Meeting [of CCJ and COSCA] on July 29, 2004, available *at* http://ccj.ncsc.dni.us/CourtAdminResolutions/ProblemSolvingCourtPrinciplesAndMethods.pdf.

[66] *See, e.g.*, Michigan Court Rules (MCR) Subchapter 3.200; MCR 3.201 *et seq.* (1993 *et seq.*).

[67] *See, e.g.*, MICH. COMP. LAWS §§ 600.1021 (2002), 712A.1 (2001), 712A.2 (2001), and 712A.2a (1998).

requires that we take these cases out of the adversarial process and create a process that encourages – indeed requires – that the adults (including the attorneys and judges) act as true adults by discussing, negotiating, and compromising.[68]

Starting from that core principle, a problem-solving court for domestic relations could take many different forms. I offer as one good model a rule (hereinafter Proposed Court Rule) presently under consideration in Indiana.[69] That rule requires that the parties to a domestic relations case prepare for mediation and court appearances by visiting one of three free interactive websites where they must read and then either accept or reject certain "commitments" to their children.[70] It provides that "[n]either parents nor attorneys may use pleadings, contested hearings, custody evaluations, trials, or other judicial proceedings to resolve a dispute unless the parents and their attorneys have made good faith efforts in both private discussion and mediation."[71] The negotiation requirement is waived only for motions for protective orders or to collect child support or maintenance arrearages, and "other instances found by the court, to be clearly inappropriate for mediation due to safety concerns or other exceptional circumstances."[72] Significantly, "[p]redictions that mediation will not be successful are not grounds for dispensing with this mediation requirement."[73] The rule "expects all parents and attorneys "to consistently observe (a) *personal responsibility*, i.e., to act on one's own opportunities to improve circumstances rather than find and report the alleged fault of others; [and] (b) *cooperation*, i.e., to define and pursue the best interests of all family members," "among other things.[74] The rule's extensive INTRODUCTORY COMMENTARY functions as both a sales pitch for the rule and an orientation to the rule's innovative requirements. That INTRODUCTORY COMMENTARY is a terrific starting place for readers interested in this approach.

I am mindful that mediation may take longer than entering a default judgment. Also, interim orders for support may be necessary to assure that the children are provided for while the long-term support amount is being mediated. Interim orders, too, can be entered by stipulation when that is possible, or by a judge's order when it is not. These concepts will not work in every case, but they will work in most cases if we can succeed in changing our fundamental assumptions about the "culture" of family law cases.

VI. Conclusion

A more sensitive approach to handling domestic relations cases will not let us dispense with child support formulas, even if federal law would allow that. To the contrary, new problem-solving court procedures will need an accompanying child support formula, like

[68] There of course will be some parents so intransigent that the court will have to intervene. But our current system effectively encourages intransigence when it ought to do the opposite by every possible means.

[69] See the Proposed Court Rule (and a memo on resources for implementing the rule), *available at* www.UpToParents.org via that site's "Professionals Corner" link. That proposed court rule language is now being considered for adoption by the courts in St. Joseph County, Indiana. Charlie Asher, a South Bend attorney and the principal author of the proposed rule, has graciously allowed me to share his work in this chapter. He and his wife cofounded FREEDOM 22 FOUNDATION, a charity dedicated to several social projects, including initiatives in family dispute resolution and minority education. The American Bar Association's Dispute Resolution Section recognized Charlie's work with its 2003 "Lawyer as Problem Solver Award."

[70] These websites are www.UpToParents.org for married parents with no hope of reconciling, www.WhileWeHeal.org for married parents who might reconcile, and www.ProudToParent.org for unmarried parents. *See* Proposed Court Rule § D(1).

[71] *See* Proposed Court Rule § C(4).

[72] *See* Proposed Court Rule § C(4).

[73] *See Id.*

[74] *See* Proposed Court Rule § C(2).

that proposed by the ALI in Chapter 3, for the same reason that "good cop" and "bad cop" interrogators need each other. The formula's message will be that nothing can be gained by litigating over child support because, if the parents cannot agree, then the court will order what the formula requires. For that limited role as the "bad cop," the PRINCIPLES' model formula is superior to existing formulas because it delivers more money to the children. But our children deserve better, and our court system must do better. Meaningful systemic reforms are in order.

I especially thank and commend the excellent research assistance of Glen Gronseth and the staff of the Friend of the Court Bureau.

22 A Response to the PRINCIPLES' Domestic Partnership Scheme

Jean Hoefer Toal

South Carolina, a state that celebrated its Tri-Centennial thirty-six years ago in 1970, has always been a place where traditions are revered. South Carolina is one of the few remaining states that continue to recognize common law marriage, at one time a widely recognized doctrine in the United States. Our legal doctrine of common law marriage, hoary in some circles, remains vibrant and relied upon today by citizens of South Carolina.[1]

While the recognition of common law marriage brings with it certain inherent difficulties which have contributed to the decline of the doctrine elsewhere, common law marriage continues to serve an important function by recognizing relationships that are marital in character, but lack the necessary predicate of a formal marriage license. This legal recognition acknowledges that important property distribution rights and support obligations attach when a relationship of this character dissolves. Without doubt, the extensive scholarship that resulted in the publication of the PRINCIPLES focused on serving much of this same protective function. As a Chief Justice who well remembers her prior life as a state legislator, however, I am forced to cast a skeptical eye on the PRINCIPLES' proposed reforms.

This chapter focuses on the PRINCIPLES' approach to property division and support obligations, especially as these concepts are applied to unmarried cohabitating couples.[2] It explains why I think that imposing legal obligations such as these is better done through the doctrine of common law marriage. While there are inherent problems associated with recognizing common law marriages, I am not in favor of the ALI's approach to property division and support obligations suggested in the PRINCIPLES. As a starting point, it is necessary to review with the existing law on common law marriage.

I. Common Law Marriage in South Carolina

In South Carolina, common law marriage is simply a mutual agreement to live together and assume the relation of husband and wife.[3] Stated differently, a common law marriage

[1] Callen v. Callen, 620 S.E.2d 59 (S.C. 2005).

[2] It is essential to note that this analysis of the PRINCIPLES is limited in scope. In the context of domestic relations, in South Carolina, property division rights and support obligations arise only from the marriage relationship. As it applies to these rights and obligations, a marriage, in South Carolina, is simply a state-sanctioned contract between a man and a woman whereby they become reorganized under law as husband and wife. The marriage contract can be created only in one of two ways: by the issuance of a marriage license, *see* S.C. CODE ANN. § 20-1-210 (1976); or through common law marriage. This analysis is thus confined to an analysis of how the PRINCIPLES' proposals compare with this scheme. It is my view that using a scheme like the PRINCIPLES as a vehicle to recognize property distribution rights and support obligations in a relationship that is incapable, under existing law, of constituting a marriage would be improper.

[3] Barker v. Baker, 499 S.E.2d 503, 506 (S.C. Ct. App. 1998) (*citing* Rodgers v. Herron, 85 S.E.2d 104, 113 (S.C. 1954)).

is created by the present and mutual intent to enter into a marriage contract.[4] It is essential that the intention to be married be both a present intention and a mutual intention; this is so because in South Carolina, mere cohabitation without such intentions does not constitute marriage.[5] Such an agreement creates a valid marriage, and no other ceremony is necessary.[6] Intuitively then, were a common law marriage to dissolve, the property division and spousal support obligations arising from the dissolution would be exactly the same as those arising from the breakup of the traditional, more formal marriage.

Though the law of common law marriage in South Carolina is easily summarized in a few short sentences, determination of the existence of a common law marriage is not always a simple task. South Carolina's law of common law marriage is based on the contractual theory of the marriage relationship. In the most basic sense, we describe a contract as an agreement between two or more people to do or not do something for valuable consideration. It is equally well recognized that what makes the common law marriage area difficult is that, unlike the typical contractual relationship, there is not likely to be a written or public declaration expressing the parties' intentions to enter into a marriage agreement. Thus, the existence of a common law marriage frequently is proved by circumstantial evidence.[7] Proof by circumstantial evidence requires that we address certain problematic topics such as "burden of proof" and "standard of review."[8] While these situations typically require courts to rely on evidence establishing that the parties lived together for an extended period of time and publicly held themselves out to be husband and wife, "even cohabitation and repute will not avail where the proof is clear that the parties were never married."[9] Thus, the linchpin is, and remains, the parties' intentions.

II. The Principles' Approach

In the Principles, the ALI suggests that unmarried cohabitants should share legal obligations based on "status" and not contract.[10] The drafters' suggestion is premised "on the familiar principle that legal rights and obligations may arise from the conduct of parties with respect to one another, even though they have no formal document or agreement setting forth such an undertaking."[11] More specifically, this approach allegedly "follows more recent trends that treat persons as having entered into a relationship with legal significance when they live together and share a life together for a sufficient period of time."[12]

The Principles' imposition of legal obligations turns on the classification of a cohabitating couple as "domestic partners."[13] Once a couple shares a primary residence and "a

[4] *Id.* at 506.

[5] Johnson v. Johnson, 112 S.E.2d 647, 651 (S.C. 1960).

[6] *Barker*, 499 S.E.2d at 506–07 (*citing* 52 Am. Jur. 2d *Marriage* § 42 (1970)).

[7] *Barker*, 499 S.E.2d at 368; Rodgers v. Herron, 85 S.E.2d 104, 113 (S.C. 1954).

[8] A common law marriage must be proved by the "preponderance of the evidence." Ex parte Blizzard, 193 S.E.2d 633, 634 (Ga. Ct. App. 1937). The existence of a common law marriage is a question of law, and appellate review is therefore limited to a determination of whether there is any evidence to support the trial judge's findings. Tarnowski v. Lieberman, 560 S.E.2d 438, 440 (S.C. Ct. App. 2002).

[9] *Barker*, 499 S.E.2d at 368; *Johnson*, 112 S.E.2d at 652.

[10] Marsha Garrison, *Is Consent Necessary? An Evaluation of the Emerging Law of Cohabitant Obligation*, 52 UCLA L. Rev. 815, 815 (2005); Principles ch. 6.

[11] Principles, § 6.02 cmt. a.

[12] Ira Mark Ellman, *ALI Family Law Report* (Sept. 11, 2000), *at* http://papers.ssrn.com/sol3/papers.cfm?abstract_id=241418.

[13] Principles § 6.03 (1).

life together as a couple" for a significant period of time, the PRINCIPLES would classify the couple as a "domestic partnership." Under the PRINCIPLES, domestic partners are entitled to alimony (labeled compensatory payments) and property division remedies that overlap almost entirely with those rights and obligations as they occur in the traditional marriage relationship.[14] Based upon a belief that the "contract" method of determining rights and obligations between parties is inherently impractical and unduly burdensome, the ALI concludes that it makes more sense to require parties to contract out of these property and support rules than for the parties to contract into them.[15]

The PRINCIPLES' classification scheme involves a series of factual scenarios and circumstances which, when present, presumptively give rise to a domestic partnership, with its incident legal obligations. Specifically, the PRINCIPLES recommend that if parties have maintained a "common household" with a "common child" for a certain period of time, suggested to be two years, there should be a presumption that the parties are domestic partners.[16] If the parties do not have a common child, the PRINCIPLES would raise the same presumption if the parties have maintained a common household for a slightly longer period of time, suggested in this case to be three years.[17] The parties may rebut only the presumption raised when there is no common child. This rebuttal requires evidence that the parties did not "share life as a couple."[18] Finally, two parties who do not meet the requirements to raise either of these presumptions may still qualify, under the PRINCIPLES, as domestic partners if the parties have, for a "significant period of time," shared a primary residence and life as a couple.[19]

Similar, perhaps, to the doctrine of common law marriages, the PRINCIPLES' analytical method seems straightforward at first. But the view becomes less focused the deeper we look. A "common household," we are told, is when two individuals "share a primary residence only with each other and family members; or when, if they share a household with other unrelated persons, they act jointly, rather than as individuals, with respect to management of the household."[20] Persons have a "common child" when each is either the child's legal parent or parent by estoppel, as defined elsewhere in the PRINCIPLES.[21] Whether persons share "life together as a couple" is determined by reference to all of the circumstances, including: promises to one another, intermingling of finances, the extent to which the relationship fostered economic interdependence, the extent to which parties assumed collaborative roles in furtherance of their lives together, changes in the lives of the parties, acknowledging responsibilities to each other, intimacy of the parties' relationship, recognition in the community as a couple, participation in a commitment ceremony, participation in a void or voidable marriage ceremony, procreation or adoption of a child, and maintenance of a common household.[22] Finally, a "significant period of time" is determined in light of all of the "life as a couple" indicators and, particularly, the extent to which these circumstances wrought changes in the life of one or both parties.[23] A couple may enter into a contract that waives or modifies claims that would otherwise arise under the PRINCIPLES, or a couple may contract to provide additional remedies other than those

[14] *Id.*; Ira Mark Ellman, *ALI Family Law Report*, *supra* n.10.

[15] PRINCIPLES § 6.03 cmt. b.

[16] PRINCIPLES § 6.03 (2) cmt. d.

[17] PRINCIPLES § 6.03 (3) cmt. d.

[18] PRINCIPLES § 6.03 (3).

[19] PRINCIPLES § 6.03 (6).

[20] PRINCIPLES § 6.03 (4).

[21] PRINCIPLES § 6.03 (5).

[22] PRINCIPLES § 6.03 (7) (a)–(m).

[23] PRINCIPLES § 6.03 (6).

provided in the PRINCIPLES, but such a contract would be subject to the PRINCIPLES' chapter on enforcement of agreements.[24]

III. Response to the PRINCIPLES-Approach

As a general proposition, legislation should be written so that laws will be applied with a degree of certainty and predictability. Like cases must receive like treatment; rules must uniformly reflect policy goals; and policy goals must express current perceptions of relational obligation.[25] Though statutes that leave doubt as to their applicability in given situations may be painted with a "judicial gloss" to provide clarity,[26] the scheme envisioned by the PRINCIPLES is significantly weakened by some fundamental assumptions involving the formation of legal obligations. The PRINCIPLES' scheme would impose legal obligations in a highly unorthodox manner, significantly run afoul of concepts of freedom of contract, restrict individual autonomy, and essentially expand the doctrine of common law marriage.

A careful examination of the scheme outlined in the PRINCIPLES leads to some simple conclusions. We traditionally think of legal obligations as arising out of either duty or contract. Obligations arise out of duty in a number of situations; for example: a voluntary undertaking, a special relationship, an employment situation, and when individual conduct poses foreseeable risks to foreseeable victims.[27] Conversely, obligations arise out of contracts only when the obligation is a part of the basic assumption of the contract. The first simple conclusion after examining the PRINCIPLES' approach to property and support remedies is that the imposition of legal obligations in these scenarios does not fit into either analytical rubric.

The PRINCIPLES, in effect, retroactively look at the circumstances of a couples' relationship and determine that the relationship shared should give rise to legal obligations upon its dissolution. The imposition of obligations in this situation cannot be the result of some duty, via either a special relationship or a voluntary undertaking, because in the case of simple cohabitation, there is no well-established authority relationship, no substantial risk of serious harm, and no overt voluntary act. Certainly parties who live together in these types of situations made a decision to live together, and there must be some degree of closeness between them, but neither the decision to share a residence with someone nor the participation in a romantic relationship with a roommate are situations in which we can say traditional legal theory would impose property division and support obligations upon the relationship's dissolution. Similarly, any obligations imposed in these cases cannot legitimately arise out of contract because there is a complete lack of mutual assent (or meeting of the minds) as to any of these obligations. Indeed, under the PRINCIPLES, it seems quite possible for parties to incur substantial obligations much to their mutual chagrin.

The drafters of the PRINCIPLES explain that the primary purpose of this scheme is the fair distribution of the economic gains and losses incident to termination of the relationship of

[24] PRINCIPLES § 6.01 (2).

[25] Marsha Garrison, *Is Consent Necessary? An Evaluation of the Emerging Law of Cohabitant Obligation*, 52 UCLA L. Rev. 815, 820 (2005) (*citing* Benjamin N. Cardozo, THE NATURE OF THE JUDICIAL PROCESS 33 (1949)).

[26] U.S. v. Lanier, 520 U.S. 259, 266, 117 S.Ct. 1219, 1225 (1997) (stating that clarity at the requisite level may be supplied by judicial gloss).

[27] *See* F. P. Hubbard and R. L. Felix, THE SOUTH CAROLINA LAW OF TORTS (2nd ed. 1997).

domestic partners.[28] The more interesting question analytically is why cannot we trust the parties themselves to fairly distribute these gains and losses? To carry the question further; is there any evidence that cohabitating couples, as a general rule, do not provide for a fair and equitable distribution of these losses when their relationship dissolves? Without such evidence, it would seem a tremendous waste to, with one broad brush stroke, paint legal obligations on a group of people "after the fact," based simply on their "status" while in a relationship.

Though, as noted above, the contract analogy for marriage is not perfect, the analogy solves most of these analytical problems because of the presence of a critical feature: mutual assent. Where the PRINCIPLES' approach becomes particularly undesirable is not in its adoption of standards for classifying types of relationships and obligations per se, nor is it in the intensive consideration of circumstantial evidence which the court is bound to have to undertake. The critical element weighing against the PRINCIPLES' scheme is its neglect to focus on the intentions of the parties.

The empirical evidence suggests that most couples choose to cohabitate because they do not want to be married.[29] Though we cannot know the precise reasons why couples choose cohabitation over marriage, it must be fair to assume that part of the reason is that these couples do not want to be bound by the rights and obligations that are intrinsic in the marriage relationship. Furthermore, the evidence suggests that cohabitation is typically not a phase of a relationship that begins (or ends) at a definite moment in time.[30] A couple may gradually start spending more and more time together, spend more time sleeping at one party's place of residence, and eventually transition into full cohabitation. At best, it would take a wild theory of contract to impose legal obligations on each party as a result of such a gradual and piecemeal course of conduct that can hardly be said to constitute a true binding form of consent.

The PRINCIPLES' approach to altering the obligations it proposes is also greatly perplexing. Given that cohabitation is a stage that does not generally begin at a precise, definite time, and given that a relationship may evolve significantly over the course of time, it seems counterintuitive to suggest that if parties want to alter or modify these obligations, the parties are expected to expressly contract out of them.[31] Indeed, in one survey of cohabitants, the primary reasons people gave for cohabitation were finances, convenience, and housing needs.[32] Interestingly, in the same survey, only two of the twenty-five interviewees responded that they discussed marriage with their partners prior to cohabitating.[33] Imposing a scheme that requires people to expressly alter specific rights and obligations with particularity seems completely at odds with, and impractical in light of, the gradual process by which most of these relationships appear to evolve.

While there certainly may be situations in which one party to a cohabitating relationship sacrifices career opportunities, financial resources, other property, or undergoes some noneconomic hardship in maintaining this type of relationship, the PRINCIPLES suggest that courts should engage in an extensive scheme of presumptions, inquiries, and guesswork to discover what is "fair." In my view, this is exactly the sort of inquiry that a court recognizing common law marriage undertakes. However, as an advantage, a court seeking to discover the presence of a common law marriage instead asks a critical question that

[28] PRINCIPLES § 6.01 (1).
[29] *See* Garrison, this volume.
[30] *Id.*
[31] *See* PRINCIPLES § 6.01 (2).
[32] Garrison, this volume.
[33] *Id.*

carries with it a point of legal significance: did the parties intend to be married? The law is ill-served by creating classes of unmarried cohabitants who, for reasons of "fairness," have to bear greater financial responsibility for a "breakup" than others. By making the linchpin of the inquiry a focal point with traditional legal significance, the process remains defensible from an analytical perspective. You say to the parties "you were married, so you are bound by these rules;" not "it seems fair for you to pay." "Liberty finds no refuge in a jurisprudence of doubt."[34]

Again, the strength of the doctrine of common law marriage is the emphasis on mutuality and intent. Admittedly, couples who are common law married will rarely make an overt declaration of present intention to be married. The court then has to perform the often tedious task of weighing the circumstantial evidence in an effort to determine if the couple intended to be married.[35] As stated previously, the PRINCIPLES' adoption of the same investigative methods certainly offers no advantage to this process from the standpoint of judicial economy or conservation of time and resources. Additionally, since the PRINCIPLES presumptively impose these obligations on a group of people, the PRINCIPLES' approach may in fact exacerbate the "circumstantial evidence" gathering function that historically has been the major criticism of common law marriage. Indeed, all couples meeting the presumptions of domestic partnership will be subject to this extensive evidence gathering process. If reforms are in order, I am not sure that presumptively applying legal obligations to a category of people is the proper solution.

While the PRINCIPLES are an indication that a difficult area of family law is receiving some much needed attention, the approach to property division and support obligations the PRINCIPLES recommend seem an extremely confusing bandage to apply as courts and legislatures continue to search for a cure for this ailment. It is one thing to say that a relationship imposes moral obligations on its participants, but it is quite another thing to say that parties in a relationship should share legal obligations between each other. Though I admire the resources and scholarship brought to bear in producing the PRINCIPLES, I do not think that the picture of interrelational obligations needs such drastic touch-up as a shift in focus from evidence of the parties' manifested intentions to judicial discovery and analysis of the subtle nuances of relationships to determine what is fair in light of parties' "status."

IV. Conclusion

When people marry, they say "I do." Though there is a lot involved in those two words, there is, at the most basic level, an overt assumption of the rights and obligations flowing therefrom. Through the formal marriage ceremony, couples make a verbal manifestation of the intent to be married so that the entire community is on notice of the beginning of this legally significant relationship. The PRINCIPLES' approach to the rights and obligations that can arise over the course of a romantic relationship correctly recognizes that there are situations in which the rights and obligations associated with the marriage relationship should be imposed in relationships that would traditionally be nonmarital in character. In South Carolina, courts impose these rights and obligations on parties if, though the parties never participated in a formal marriage ceremony, there is a mutual agreement to

[34] Planned Parenthood of Southeastern Pa. v. Casey, 505 U.S. 833, 844, 112 S.Ct. 2791, 2803 (1992).

[35] *Barker*, 499 S.E.2d at 368; *Rodgers*, 85 S.E.2d at 113.

live together and assume the relation of husband and wife.[36] Though courts deciding this question typically have to engage in the cumbersome process of considering circumstantial evidence of the parties' intentions, I think that common law marriage offers a more attractive approach than the scheme suggested in the PRINCIPLES. In my opinion, when society engages in the tedious task of weighing circumstantial evidence to determine what the states of the parties' minds were, we are better served by a system focused on the evidence of intention, and not simple considerations of fairness.[37]

[36] *Barker*, 499 S.E.2d at 506 (*citing* Rodgers v. Herron, 85 S.E.2d 104, 113 (S.C. 1954)).

[37] A bill providing that common law marriage will no longer be recognized in South Carolina after January 1, 2006 has passed the South Carolina House of Representatives and is currently pending in the South Carolina State Senate. H.R. 3588, 2005 Leg., 116th Sess. (S.C. 2005).

23 Empowerment and Responsibility: The Balance Sheet Approach in the PRINCIPLES and English Law

John Eekelaar

During the last quarter of the twentieth century, the long "welfarist" era stretching from the Enlightenment seemed to be being displaced by a dual-track strategy proclaiming the promotion of individual empowerment and responsibility.[1] The drive for empowerment is seen in the increasing significance of the discourse of rights, which has undermined, or at least destabilized, the institutions through which welfarism operated. This destabilization in turn set up a new problem of the legitimacy upon which the rights-claims and related responsibilities were grounded, for if institutions, such as marriage or parenthood, lose their authority as sources for rights and obligations, it is necessary to find an alternative basis for their binding force. This chapter assesses how far the PRINCIPLES and some recent developments in English family law[2] fit in with this picture, and, if they do, how they seek to resolve the problem of legitimacy, that is, the source of authority for such rights and obligations. This chapter concludes that they do broadly fit the picture. The approach to the legitimacy problem is hard to characterize. This chapter suggests that the PRINCIPLES seem to approach the question of legitimacy through a method which, for want of a better term, this chapter calls the "balance sheet" approach. This chapter also offers a view about this method.

I. Compensatory Spousal Payments and Division of Property

This part examines the ALI approach to alimony and property division and contrasts it with the approach taken in England and Wales.

A. The Rejection of Needs and the Balance Sheet Approach

A major conceptual innovation claimed by the PRINCIPLES is recasting the basis of alimony from the relief of need to payment of compensation. Under the PRINCIPLES, loss of marital living standard after dissolution is compensable when a marriage exceeds a duration threshold, as defined by state law, and when the less well-off spouse has foregone financial opportunities in order to care for children.[3] It will immediately be obvious that, although

[1] "*The End of an Era*?" *in* SANFORD N. KATZ, JOHN EEKELAAR, AND MAVIS MACLEAN, CROSS CURRENTS: FAMILY LAW AND POLICY IN THE US AND ENGLAND (Oxford University Press, 2000), ch. 29; (2003) 28 J. J. FAM. HIST. 108.

[2] "English" is used here as shorthand for English and Welsh. This chapter does not cover Scotland or Northern Ireland.

[3] PRINCIPLES § 5.04–5.

located in the institution of marriage, the justifications for imposing this obligation are found primarily elsewhere, in the length of cohabitation or of child care, either of which can be satisfied outside marriage. And so it turns out that the PRINCIPLES also apply this obligation to unmarried domestic partners.[4] Furthermore, since both the amount of compensation to be paid and its duration are directly related to the length of cohabitation and child care, the PRINCIPLES do not attempt to estimate the actual loss suffered by the obligee flowing from having entered this particular, now failed, relationship. There are a number of measures for measuring actual loss, such as comparing one party's standard of living with that of an unmarried professional woman or man of the same age, or some other standard,[5] but these measures are simply too speculative because we do not know what would have happened if the relationship had not happened. Rather, the PRINCIPLES' rationale seems to be a complex one, which commingles a sense of mutual obligation that arises over time with a view that a disparate financial outcome fails to reward the obligee adequately for the amount of time and effort invested in the relationship, and the compensation is for this shortfall. As the PRINCIPLES state: "To leave the financially dependent spouse in a long marriage without a remedy would facilitate the exploitation of the trusting spouse and discourage domestic investment by the nervous one."[6]

Yet compensation is not premised solely on the sense of obligation because that could extend to a feeling that the better off former spouse should meet future needs of the other, for example, where the former spouse experiences hardship caused by an accident or unexpected illness. But the PRINCIPLES reject that.[7] Nor is it solely a compensation for investment of personal capital, because the obligee is under a duty to mitigate the loss by realizing the obligee's earning potential. It is perhaps best conceptualized as a balance sheet of sorts, detailing on one side what each party is taking out of the marriage (including earnings and earning capacity), and on the other the investment each partner put into the relationship in terms of personal capital. If the difference between what the parties take out is greater than the difference between what they put in, then the worse off party should receive compensation for the shortfall. To do this requires an accounting methodology of some complexity.

The allocation of spousal property demonstrates the same technique. Marital or "domestic-partnership" property is acquired by spousal or partner labor during the relationship and is presumptively divisible equally on dissolution.[8] The rationale for this does not seem to lie in the commitments of marriage, for (with one exception) the rule applies also to domestic partnerships,[9] but in a mixture of reasons: a compromise between satisfying needs and recognizing contributions, and plain convenience.[10] The fact that each partner can expect to acquire equivalent capital gains as their property holding increases over time shows that the PRINCIPLES treat the contributions of each to their common life as earning them an equal share in those acquisitions. Separate property remains separately owned, but is recharacterized as marital over the course of time according to a formula.[11]

[4] PRINCIPLES § 6.06.

[5] For an example of this approach, *see* Kahleen Funder, "*Australia: A Proposal for Reform*" *in* Lenore Weitzman and Mavis Maclean (eds.), ECONOMIC CONSEQUENCES OF DIVORCE: THE INTERNATIONAL PERSPECTIVE (Oxford, Oxford University Press, 1992), pp. 143–63.

[6] PRINCIPLES § 5.04.

[7] PRINCIPLES § 5.02 cmt. (a).

[8] PRINCIPLES §§ 4.09 (dividing marital property), 6.05 (dividing property of domestic partners).

[9] PRINCIPLES § 6.05.

[10] PRINCIPLES § 4.09.

[11] PRINCIPLES § 4.12. *See also* Westfall, this volume, for an explanation and critique of the formula for recharacterization.

Here the rationale is that over time the spouses come to see separate property as available for the benefit of both jointly in the future "for their joint retirement, for a medical crisis of either spouse, or for other personal emergencies."[12] Although many married couples might regard such separate property in the same way immediately after marrying, this rationale could of course also form the basis for an obligation to make payments to meet such needs after separation. However, as noted earlier, that notion is rejected in favor of a compensatory model. So an alternative rationale may be the same as that which underlies the calculation of compensatory payments: a return on the investment of personal effort. That the rationale is reward for such investment seems supported by the PRINCIPLES' treatment of enhancements in the value of separate property. If a spouse devotes substantial time to increasing the value of that spouse's separate property, the increased value becomes marital property,[13] because, it seems, that time might have been spent furthering the interests of both rather than, as in fact happened, of that spouse. But the owner of the separate property can devote minor amounts of time tending to (his) separate property without its value becoming marital, while the same amount of time spent on that property by the nonowning spouse would render the increase marital.[14] The balance sheet is becoming very detailed, now allowing a kind of virement – in accounting, this involves an administrative transfer of budgetary funds – between the efforts a spouse might have put into the relationship but, in fact, put into his separate interests and the extent to which those interests can now be treated as available to both. But if one partner puts effort into enhancing his educational qualifications, thus raising that spouse's earning capacity, that effort and its financial consequences are kept off the balance sheet with regard to property allocation, but could reenter the balance sheet when considering possible compensatory payments, which match the gap between respective postseparation incomes of the partners with the duration of the relationship.

B. England and Wales: A "Balanced" Rather Than "Balance Sheet" Approach or Just Disarray?

As regards property allocation, English law epitomizes the "equitable distribution" systems rejected by the PRINCIPLES. The governing statute[15] sets out the considerations that courts must take into account when exercising their jurisdiction to make property and financial orders – the ultimate objective being "to achieve a fair outcome," bearing in mind that the "first consideration" is the welfare of the children of the marriage.[16] But of course the position is a great deal more complex than that. For instance, in a landmark decision in 2000, *White v. White*,[17] the House of Lords rejected the previous doctrine that the content and limit of the courts' duty was to ensure satisfaction of the "reasonable requirements" of the spouses. There is now a double objective. First, to ensure that needs are met; second, once needs are met, there must be a good reason not to distribute assets equally, irrespective of need, "if, in their different spheres, each contributed equally to the family."[18] Distribution matches contribution as a matter of earned entitlement, at least with respect to those assets that remain after needs, including those of the children, have been met. But Lord

[12] PRINCIPLES § 4.12.

[13] PRINCIPLES § 4.05.

[14] PRINCIPLES § 4.05 cmts. d, e, at 672–73 (discussing application of the rule to owning and nonowning spouses).

[15] Matrimonial Causes Act 1973, s. 25.

[16] *White v. White* [2001] 1 All ER 1 at 8.

[17] [2001] 1 All ER 1.

[18] *White v. White* [2001] 1 All ER, speech of Lord Nicholls.

Nicholls denied that the decision creates a presumption, or even "starting point" of equal distribution of assets. Nevertheless, the decision has propelled English law strongly in the direction of the "balance-sheet" approach, though the lack of formal structure means that it is finding its way forward with uncertainty.

One problem is deciding what value to attribute to homemaking. True, there is to be no discrimination between homemaking and income earning: they are to be afforded equal worth. But Lord Nicholls's words, "if, in their different spheres, each contributed equally to the family," indicate that the extent of the contributions must be valued. In *Cowan v. Cowan*[19] the Court of Appeal allowed a husband who possessed "stellar" qualities as a businessman to take away a larger share than his wife of the assets built up in a thirty-seven year marriage. Shortly afterwards it was realized that, since the genius of a homemaker could not generally be measured by wealth acquisition, that way of measuring the respective contributions of the spouses against one another was biased against women, and should be used only in exceptional circumstances.[20] How, then, does one value homemaking as against wealth creation? Some suggest that it should always be given equal value, leading to presumptive equal allocation of assets in all cases.[21] This method could overvalue the homemaker's contribution in short marriages;[22] duration therefore is an intrinsic element in the value to be accorded to homemaking. On this view, a short period of homemaking would not necessarily constitute an equivalent entry on one side of the balance sheet as the value of assets rapidly acquired on the other side.

The point may be of little significance were it not for the fact that English law makes no systematic distinction between marital and separate (for example, premarital) property. All property (including inheritances) owned by either spouse at time of dissolution is in principle available for allocation. This approach can be defended where resort to such property is necessary to meet the needs of the spouses and their children.[23] But under the balance sheet approach it is hard to find a rationale why the relative economic circumstances of the partners after they separate should match a position prior to separation that incorporated the premarital and inheritance property of one of them. Such property should be kept off the sheet, and the PRINCIPLES (and many European systems) follow this practice. In fact, so flexible are the English courts' powers that, in one case involving a short-term marriage, the court returned to each party the value of properties they brought into it, taking them off the balance sheet, and distributed the rest of the assets, including inflationary gains, equally.[24] In another case, where a farm which had been in the husband's family for generations constituted the sole asset, the judge abandoned any pretense at asset sharing and based the award entirely on needs.[25] But the flexibility means that the courts have in some cases been able to spell out from the context that premarital or even inherited property should be treated as being contributions to the marriage, and therefore be appropriately placed on the balance sheet and available for distribution.[26] The PRINCIPLES would allow

[19] [2001] 2 FLR 192.

[20] *Lambert v. Lambert* [2003] 1 FLR 139.

[21] See Rebecca Bailey-Harris, Comment on *GW v. RW* [2003] EWHC 611 (Fam) (2003) 33 FAM. L. 386, supported by *Foster v. Foster* [2003] EWCA Civ 565.

[22] John Eekelaar, *Asset Distribution on Divorce – Time and Property*, (2003) 33 FAM. L. 828, supported by *GW v. RW* [2003] EWHC 611 (Fam).

[23] "The nature and value of the property, the time when and circumstances in which it was acquired, should be considered. In the ordinary course, it will carry little weight, if any, in a case where the other party's needs cannot be met without recourse to it": *Foster v. Foster* [2003] EWCA Civ 565, per Hale LJ at para 21. page 30.

[24] *Foster v. Foster* [2003] EWCA Civ 565.

[25] *P v. P (Inherited Property)* [2004] EWHC 1364 (Fam); [2005] 1 FLR 576.

[26] *Norris v. Norris* [2002] EWHC Civ 2996 (Fam); [2003] 1 FLR 1142.

this as well, of course, through recharacterization as marital property over time, but only following the duration formula.

Apart from allocating assets, English law directs courts to consider the needs of the parties. These may be met by capital transfers or income orders. Professor Ira Ellman, the principal drafter of the PRINCIPLES, has usefully contrasted the obscurity of the process by which the English courts in *McFarlane v. McFarlane* and *Parlour v. Parlour*[27] determined the quantum of the sums necessary to meet future "needs" and the compensation concept of the PRINCIPLES.[28] However, payments for needs are the functional equivalent in English law to the PRINCIPLES' compensation payments. The concept of "needs" is relative, allowing for consideration of the respective postseparation financial situations of the parties.[29] But the starting off point is different. It does not lie in an overt attempt to close the disparities between the partners' financial circumstances at separation, but in an effort to look forward and assess how the obligee will experience her new standard of living in the light of what she had been used to during the marriage. If the result will be too great an imbalance, need will be made out and the gap narrowed. Hence both the calculation of needs in English law and of compensatory payments under the PRINCIPLES can take into account the prospective financial position of the obligee at the time of separation, and recipients of both needs-based and compensatory payments will be under a duty to mitigate their losses. Neither consideration is relevant in the allocation of property. And, like compensatory payments, the duration of needs payments is also likely to be related to the length of the cohabitation and the exercise of child care because it has been held that the appropriateness of limiting the duration of needs payments[30] will be defeated where there are young children, or in the case of lengthy marriages.[31] It would not, therefore, be a large move for English law to reduce the subjectivity of the assessment of need by following an approach closer to that of the PRINCIPLES' compensatory model.

The unstructured nature of English law also threatens to blur the important distinction between earned entitlements and needs or compensatory awards. In *McFarlane v. McFarlane*; *Parlour v. Parlour*[32] the courts posed the question whether a partner's earning capacity after separation might be treated as capital and subject to allocation on the balance-sheet approach. The answer seemed to be negative, as it is under the PRINCIPLES, but the reasoning of the lower courts was unclear. The confusion arose as a result of the fact that the husbands were asked to accumulate part of their future earnings into a capital sum that would meet their former partners' future needs through a "clean break." But remarks were made in the judgments that the wives had earned a "fair share" in such capital by their efforts during the marriage. This suggests that a partner might be able to "earn" a share in the other's income after separation, and in this way avoid the duty to mitigate. In short, the judgments risked blurring a necessary bright line between balance sheet asset allocation and compensatory payments.[33]

27 [2004] EWCA Civ 872.

28 Ira Ellman, *Do Americans Play Football?*, (2005) 19 INT/J. L. POLY & FAM. 257. *See also* Joanna Miles, *Principle or pragmatism in ancillary relief? The Virtues of flirting with academic theories and other jurisdictions*, (2005) 19 INT/J. L. POLY & FAM. 242.

29 "The proposed standards of living of both spouses must be a relevant consideration and, where finances permit, they should not be wholly out of proportion to each other": *Gojkovic v. Gojkovic* [1990] 2 All ER 84, at 88.

30 The court must expressly consider the appropriateness of putting a limit of the duration of needs payments. Matrimonial Causes Act 1973, s. 25A(1).

31 *Suter v. Suter and Jones* [1987] 2 FLR 232; *SRJ v. DWJ (Financial Provision)* [1999] 2 FLR 176.

32 [2004] EWCA Civ 872.

33 *See* John Eekelaar, *Shared Income after Divorce: A Step too Far*, (2005) 121 LAW Q. REV. 1.

For the balance sheet approach to work fully, elements other than the contributions that are relevant to earning a reward need to be kept off the sheet, or at least reduced to a minimum. Hence, for the PRINCIPLES, marital misconduct is irrelevant, except in narrowly defined circumstances termed "financial misconduct."[34] This stance has created misgivings among American commentators.[35] But virtual exclusion of marital misconduct has been accepted in England ever since Lord Denning robustly declared in 1973 that it was to be taken into account only if "obvious and gross."[36] It is true that this expression has fallen out of favor, and by statute courts now may take conduct into account where it is "equitable" to do so,[37] but in practice courts strongly discourage the introduction of arguments about misconduct unless it relates to financial matters. Consistently with the broadly equitable nature of the jurisdiction, however, and unlike the PRINCIPLES, the English courts have avoided defining these issues too precisely.[38]

More significant, to English eyes, is the PRINCIPLES' limited reference to the welfare of the children. The English statute makes this the "first consideration." It is not "paramount," as it is in cases concerning with whom the child will reside and the degree of contact (visitation) the child will have with the nonresidential parent, and the broad objective remains doing justice between the parties,[39] but the requirement allows courts readily to depart from the equality outcomes indicated by the balance sheet approach where the children's welfare demands. It is not uncommon for the matrimonial home to be transferred entirely to the children's care giver if this is deemed to be in their interests.[40] In contrast, the PRINCIPLES merely allow the sale of a home to be deferred temporarily "in order to avoid significant detriment to the child."[41] Under the PRINCIPLES, it seems that the balance sheet must prevail, even to the (nonsignificant) detriment of a child, whereas the long-held approach of the English law will allow the balance sheet approach (as possibly imperfectly applied) to determine the matter only in residual cases where the children's interests have been fully met. It is therefore possible that, in England, the balance sheet approach will only be relevant in relatively rare "big money" cases: for the most part, the consequences of achieving the optimal outcome for the children will leave little on the balance sheet.

C. The Balance Sheet Approach and the Question of Legitimacy

It has been notoriously difficult for courts to justify the exercise of coercive powers over former spouses after divorce, for the simple reason that the marital status, in which a spouse's duties might be grounded, has now disappeared. So the courts have referred to such things as deterrence against divorce, returning property which would otherwise constitute an unfair windfall, protecting former wives from resorting to prostitution, and

34 PRINCIPLES § 4.10; PRINCIPLES § 4.10; PRINCIPLES § 1, Topic 2, at 42–85.

35 See, for example, Silbaugh, this volume; Westfall, this volume; Wardle, this volume.

36 *Wachtel v. Wachtel* [1973] Fam.

37 Matrimonial Causes Act 1973, s. 25 (2) (g), inserted by Matrimonial Proceedings and Property Act 1984.

38 *Beach v. Beach* [1995] 2 FLR 160 (financial recklessness); *Clark v. Clark* [1999] 2 FLR 498 (a "gold-digging" spouse).

39 *Suter v. Suter and Jones* [1987] Fam 111.

40 *Clutton v. Clutton* [1991] 1 FLR 242; *B v. B (Financial Provision: Welfare of Child and Conduct)* [2002] 1 FLR 555 (total proceeds of sale of house transferred to wife).

41 PRINCIPLES § 3.11.

relief of need (with a possible concern for depleting state welfare funds).[42] The balance sheet approach seeks legitimacy in the general principle of justice that contributions to a common enterprise should be fairly rewarded. This can be seen as at once treating the claimant as empowered by virtue of (her) efforts; and the obligee as under a responsibility to respond to those claims. This is broadly consistent with the direction in which family law appears to be moving. As the drafters' Overview to the PRINCIPLES nicely puts it: "... reconceptualizing the [alimony's] award's purpose as the equitable allocation of a joint loss changes it from a plea for help to a claim of entitlement."[43] Perhaps this is not quite true, because one could understand the satisfaction of need as an entitlement, too. However, that is not an earned entitlement: it rests on paternalistic judgments of desert, both moral and material. It is astonishing that at about the same time, but almost certainly without knowledge of the drafters' deliberations, English law, in *White v. White*,[44] moved sharply in the same direction. However, the PRINCIPLES are not completely consistent on the basis for the entitlement claim. The predominant basis seems to be that it is earned through the claimant's efforts. An alternative explanation, that it flows from duties inherent in the marital obligation, seems ruled out by the application to domestic partnerships. An explanation premised on earning also fails to explain why recharacterization of separate property does not also apply in domestic partnerships. There is an alternative basis of legitimacy for the exercise of these powers: the intentions of the parties. However, the PRINCIPLES are consistent in refusing to ground the justifications for property allocation or compensation on prior intentions of the parties,[45] except insofar as they are free to enter into contracts about them, which the PRINCIPLES allow subject to procedural safeguards.[46] English law is more suspicious of the operation of contract, either premaritally or with regard to nonmarital cohabitation. The closest England and Wales have come to giving effect to premarital contracts was in a government paper in 1998 stating that it was "considering whether there would be advantage in allowing couples, either before or after their marriage, to make written agreements dealing with their financial affairs which would be legally binding on divorce."[47] This did not find favor, even as applied to the unmarried,[48] although attitudes may have recently shifted in some parts of the legal profession.[49] The courts' attitude is that agreements do not restrict judicial discretion, but judges may implement an agreement, or certain aspects of the agreement, if they consider this to be fair.[50] Analytically, there seems no reason why entitlements based on earned shares should not be controlled by prior agreement. One may set the terms of the rewards for one's labor. But where awards are for compensation for loss, or, especially, to meet need, particularly in relation to children, one would expect greater reluctance to allow the matter to be controlled by prior agreement. Since need still plays an important part in the English scheme, this may explain the reluctance to recognize agreements as binding.

[42] *See* John Eekelaar and Mavis Maclean, *Maintenance after Divorce* (Oxford University Press, 1986), ch. 1; PRINCIPLES, ch. 1, overview of chs. 4 and 5.

[43] PRINCIPLES ch. 1 (discussing overview of Chapters 4 and 5, section II (b)).

[44] [2001] 1 All ER 1.

[45] PRINCIPLES §§ 4.12; 5.04.

[46] PRINCIPLES § 7.04.

[47] *Supporting Families: A Consultation Document* (1998), para. 4.21.

[48] *See* the Law Society, *Cohabitation: the Case for clear law: Proposals for Reform* (Law Society, 2002), at 42.

[49] Solicitors' Family Law Association, *Recognition of Pre-Marital Agreements in England and Wales* (SFLA, 2004).

[50] *M v. M* [2002] 1 FLR 654; *K v. K* [2003] 1 FLR 120.

D. Unmarried Domestic Partners

It has already been remarked that the PRINCIPLES allow the same provisions for property allocation and compensation payments to be applied to unmarried domestic partnerships, except for the recharacterization of separate property.[51] The reason given for the exception is simply that no state presently recharacterizes separate property.[52] It is not clear why the PRINCIPLES held back from the logic of the whole structure for this reason. Nevertheless, the proposals as they stand reveal a much more systematic approach to such partnerships than is found in English law. The English legal provisions applicable to opposite sex and same-sex domestic partnerships range from general principles of property and trust law which govern their property relationships, through a wide range of scattered statutory enactments applying various legal provisions to persons living together "as husband and wife," such as compensation for injury to one partner by the estate of the deceased partner. But three important developments have come close to transforming the picture.

The gay marriage issue falls well outside the drafters' charge, although same-sex partners will comprise a significant proportion of domestic partners covered by the PRINCIPLES. The Civil Partnership Act 2004 has cleverly created an institution for England and Wales for same-sex partners that is equivalent to marriage with hardly a murmur of protest. This may have been achieved, first, by assiduously avoiding the word "marriage" in the legislation, and simply copying into it almost every word of law which applies to marriage; and, second, by explicitly enacting that (unlike in the case of marriage) the formation of the partnership cannot take place in religious premises[53] and that "no religious service is to be used while the civil partnership registrar is officiating at the signing of a civil partnership document."[54] There is nothing, of course, to stop the civil partners from participating in a religious ceremony after the partnership is concluded. For same-sex partners who do not enter civil partnerships, the House of Lords, applying its duty under the Human Rights Act 1998 to interpret legislation as far as possible consistently with the European Convention on Human Rights and Fundamental Freedoms, has held that the expression "living together as husband and wife" should be read as, "living together as if husband and wife," thus extending the same protections to same-sex cohabitants as to opposite sex ones where that wording is used.[55]

The third development concerns a much larger group of domestic partners: those who are parents to a common child. Since they are unmarried, the courts have no power to order outright transfers of assets from one to another, so they cannot transfer ownership of the home from husband to wife where this is in the children's interests, as they can for divorcing spouses, as described earlier. However, they can order a temporary transfer[56] (as the PRINCIPLES provide between married parents). Despite these provisions, there are calls for injecting more coherence into the law relating to unmarried domestic partners, including the extension to unmarried parents of the judicial powers currently exercisable with respect to married parents.[57]

[51] PRINCIPLES § 6.05.

[52] PRINCIPLES § 6.04 cmt. b.

[53] Civil Partnership Act 2004, s. 6(1)(b).

[54] *Id.* s. 2(5).

[55] *Ghaidan v. Godin Mendoza* [2004] UKHL 30; [2004] 3 All ER 411.

[56] Children Act 1989, s. 15 and Schedule 1.

[57] The Law Society, *Cohabitation: the case for clear law: Proposals for Reform* (The Law Society, 2002) para. 96.

II. Parenthood and the Allocation of Custody Allocation

The themes underlying the PRINCIPLES' approach to financial and property issues reappear in their treatment of parents and children. Just as the source of obligation to a large extent breaks loose from an institution source, marriage, so also the parent-child provisions extend beyond "legal" parental relationships to embrace parents by estoppel (broadly, when someone has lived with a child in the belief they are the parent, or held out as they are) and de facto parents (broadly, where someone lives with child for more than two years exercising the same or more caretaking functions as the other parent).[58] English family lawyers would be comfortable with these provisions, though predictably English law is both simpler and more discretionary. Married stepparents who have treated the child as a "child of the family"[59] have a right to apply for any of the main orders[60] dealing with the upbringing of children: a "residence" order would confer on them "parental responsibility" (and married stepparents can now acquire this simply by agreement with the other parent).[61] Any other person can apply for such an order with the leave of the court. In deciding whether to give such leave, the court must take into account the nature of the application made (for example, is it for a residential arrangement or only for contact (visitation)?), the applicant's "connection with the child" and "any risk there might be of that proposed application disrupting the child's life to such an extent that he would be harmed by it."[62] If leave is given, the substantive issue is decided according to the "best interests" test.[63]

This flexibility[64] does not seem to have caused the kind of anxiety which the PRINCIPLES have generated.[65] This may be because of the way the PRINCIPLES treat the best interests test. They draw on an idea originally put forward by Professor Elizabeth Scott in 1992[66] which looks surprisingly similar to the balance sheet approach. This is that, where agreement cannot be reached, the court should allocate "custodial responsibility" so that "the proportion of custodial time the child spends with each parent approximates the proportion of time each parent spent performing caretaking functions for the child prior to the parents' separation or, if the parents never lived together, before the filing of the action."[67] Professor Scott's arguments, as enshrined in the PRINCIPLES, are beguiling. The maternal preference presumption exhibits gender stereotyping; the primary caretaker presumption downplays the role of secondary caretakers; the joint custody presumption is an unrealistic aspiration. In contrast, the approximation presumption minimizes disruption to children and is more likely to reflect parental preferences. The PRINCIPLES in particular stress the

[58] PRINCIPLES § 2.03.

[59] This test should be easy to satisfy in most cases of step-parenthood. *See* ANDREW BAINHAM, CHILDREN: THE MODERN LAW 234 (3d ed., 2005).

[60] These are "residence", "contact," "prohibited steps," or "specific issue" orders under section 8 of the Children Act 1989.

[61] Adoption and Children Act 2002, inserting new section 4A into the Children Act 1989. "Parental responsibility" means "all the rights, duties, powers, responsibilities and authority which by law a parent of a child has in relation to the child and his property." Children Act 1989, s. 3(1).

[62] Children Act 1989.

[63] *Id.*

[64] This flexibility appears to exist in France, through a flexible use of the concept of *possession d'état.* M.-T. MEULDERS-KLEIN, LA PERSONNE, LA FAMILLE, LA DROIT (Brussels, Bruylant 1999), p. 205.

[65] Robin Fretwell Wilson, this volume.

[66] Elizabeth S. Scott, *Pluralism, Parental Preferences and Child Custody,* 80 CAL. L. REV. 615 (1992).

[67] PRINCIPLES § 2.08.

greater certainty it is claimed such a presumption would promote. It is therefore rather ironic that there should be particular concerns about its application in the case of de facto parents.[68]

The issue of presumptions in the case of contact disputes has recently been under debate in England.[69] The statutory prescription is that "the child's welfare shall be the court's paramount consideration."[70] The only statutory presumptions are that delay in reaching decision is likely to prejudice the child's welfare and that if the court wishes to make an order, it must be satisfied that it is better to do so than to make no order at all.[71] Otherwise, the statute merely sets out "considerations" to be taken into account. But, as in the case of financial and property matters, reality is more complex. Three legal points are particularly important. First, in 1970 the House of Lords interpreted "paramount" as if it meant "sole," so that any other considerations were relevant only insofar as they had a bearing on the child's welfare.[72] Second, the courts have operated on certain "factual" presumptions, or "assumptions," of which the clearest are that children are generally better off with their biological parents than with strangers and that contact with a nonresidential parent is generally "a good thing." Third, the right to respect for family life enshrined in the European Convention on Human Rights and Fundamental Freedoms[73] has been interpreted by the European Court of Human Rights as requiring states to take all reasonable measures to ensure the continuation of contact between nonresidential parents and their children.[74] Since human rights jurisprudence is now part of English law, it is unlikely that the interpretation given to "paramount" by House of Lords in 1970 still represents English law.

This new emphasis on the "rights" of nonresidential parents is in line with the generally more pronounced rights discourse of contemporary family law, although the European Court of Human Rights has been criticized for relative neglect of children's rights.[75] That court has, however, said that the parents' rights are subject to the children's interests which "depending on their nature and seriousness" may override those of the parents,[76] and even that the children's interests are "paramount."[77] Of greater political impact has been a campaign by a father's rights pressure group, Fathers4Justice, one of whose members hurled a condom with purple dye at the Prime Minister, Tony Blair, in the House of Commons. That group and its supporters demanded a presumption of equal sharing. The government, however, resisted the introduction of any additional statutory presumptions, taking the view that problems lay not in the formulation of the law but in improving "advice, information, mediation, conciliation and enforcement processes."[78]

[68] *See* Wilson, *supra* note 65.

[69] *See* Fourth Report of the Constitutional Affairs Committee, *Family Justice: the Operation of the Family Courts,* Department for Constitutional Affairs, 2 March 2005.

[70] Children Act 1989, s. 1(1).

[71] Children Act 1989, s. 1(2) and (5).

[72] *J v. C* [1970] AC 668.

[73] 1950 European Convention on Human Rights and Fundamental Freedoms, Nov. 4, 1950, art. 8.

[74] There are many cases: see, for example, *Hansen v. Turkey* [2004] 1 FLR 142.

[75] Jonathan Herring, *The Human Rights Act and the welfare principle in family law: conflicting or complementary?*, (1999) 11 Child & Fam. L. Q. 223; Jane Fortin, *The HRA's impact on litigation involving children and their families* (1999) 11 Child & Fam. L. Q. 237; John Eekelaar, *Beyond the Welfare Principle* (2002) 14 Child & Fam. L. Q. 237.

[76] *Elsholz v. Germany* [2000] 2 FLR 486.

[77] *Yousef v. The Netherlands* [2003] 1 FLR 210.

[78] HM Government, *Parental Separation: Children's Needs and Parents' Responsibilities: Next Steps* Cm 6452 (2005), para. 14.

The government was influenced by arguments that if one new statutory presumption was created, there would be pressure for qualifications and counterpresumptions, such as exclusions in cases of violence (how defined?)[79] or of severe conflict, which would lead to a drafting nightmare and inhibit progress on more practical measures. This conclusion is in line with the position taken in Canada, where the "one size fits all" approach was rejected.[80]

It is unlikely that the "approximation" approach was considered by the UK Government. However, it is hard to think that it would have been found attractive. The PRINCIPLES do of course, see the approach as furthering children's interests. But if it is to be presumed that an arrangement will be in a child's best interests, it must be clear that this will be so in an overwhelming majority of cases. In the absence of clear evidence that time matching will satisfy this, or even that this is what parents usually do by agreement, it fails as a presumption. There are simply too many exceptions and qualifications. The PRINCIPLES recognize them, and attempt to restrict them to cases where the arrangements would be "extremely impractical" or would "substantially" interfere with the child's need for stability.[81] These seem potentially heavy penalties for a child to pay. Of course, it is likely that many arrangements, at least in their early stages, will in fact turn out as envisaged by the approach: but the mechanics of the arrangements should be driven by the substantial goal of sustaining beneficial and workable relationships rather than as ends in themselves.

III. Overview and Conclusion

The PRINCIPLES reveal some striking insights. Perhaps the most important is the recognition that family law has to respond to personal relationships which are not determined by social or legal institutions. Parallel to that is the recognition of the dynamics of those relationships. In important empirical studies on the nature of family responsibilities in England, Janet Finch has stressed the way a sense of obligation accumulates over time.[82] The PRINCIPLES respond to this, though more in terms of building up reward for investment of personal capital than of recognizing a growing sense of obligation. This may be wise, because the enforcement of an obligation after separation, especially if it is to meet needs, runs into major problems of assessment of desert. Here, another powerful insight of the PRINCIPLES comes into play: recognizing the limits of law. Although made explicit only in relation to child custody determinations,[83] this surely underlies the unwillingness to become involved in assessments of postseparation need and preseparation marital behavior. If someone's former spouse suffers misfortune unconnected with the marriage or separation, it is probably right to leave it to the parties' own sense of morality about whether the "ex" should help out rather than to embroil the law. On these points the

[79] The English courts have declined to endorse a *presumption* against contact even with a violent parent: *re L; re V (Contact: Domestic Violence)* [2000] 2 FLR 334.

[80] *See* Helen Rhoades and Susan B. Boyd, *Reforming Custody Laws: A Comparative Study*, (2004) 18 INT'L J. L. POLY & FAM. 119.

[81] *See e.g.*, PRINCIPLES § 2.08 (f).

[82] Janet Finch, *Family Obligations and Social Change* (London, Polity Press, 1989); J. Finch and J. Mason, *Negotiating Family Responsibilities* (London, Routledge, 1993).

[83] *See* PRINCIPLES ch. 1, intro. III.

PRINCIPLES have much to teach English law, which once ordered a former husband to increase financial support to his former wife when she had a child after the separation by a different man (who had left the scene).[84] English law needs also to learn from the separation between the conceptual bases of property allocation and postseparation compensatory payments, and might with profit reduce the subjectivity of the needs criterion by adopting something like the PRINCIPLES' compensation model. However, the English prioritization of the child's welfare, and the flexibility allowed by taking into account severe misconduct (with strong judicial discouragement from interpreting this too widely) may be advantages.

There are two features of the PRINCIPLES where it is possible that the nobility of the vision might need a practical corrective. Professor Elizabeth Scott saw the "approximate time" approach as a "continuation of the intact family." In 1993, the French sociologist, Irène Théry, remarked that the mediation movement was premised on the idea that, although a marriage might be over, the family, once constituted by cohabitation, nevertheless continued.[85] The balance sheet approach is a strong manifestation of that belief. But in many cases this may be a delusion. There is a strong countervision that sees separation as changing everything and the divorce process as about managing that change. This may require departures from the financial and property balance sheet where the children's interests require it, and acceptance that parental roles are bound to be different.

The other noble vision is the pursuit of greater certainty, to be achieved by detailed provisions for many eventualities. Professor Ira Ellman, the principal drafter, has frankly stated that, in view of the inherently uncertain nature of the outcomes of legal interventions in family law, it matters less what rules are chosen than that whatever is done is clear and applied with consistency, for that, at least, will be fair.[86] He is surely right about the limits of legal interventions in family matters. But has the quest for certainty been subverted by complexity of application? It is hard to imagine many divorcing couples getting together with the PRINCIPLES and sorting matters out by themselves. They may not be intended to be used that way. The ALI certainly was attempting to provide guidance across a vast country with many jurisdictions. Still, when state legislatures fill in details, will the results be less complex? Will not lawyers, or other negotiators, be encouraged to argue about the many formulations of law, and the many matters of fact that need to be placed on the balance sheet: from time expended on separate property to hours devoted to playing with children? Courts, and couples, do need principles to follow. English courts have been too slow to articulate these. But the principles need not be very elaborate. Property arrangements must aim to secure stability for the children. Subject to this, the balance sheet approach works well for the allocation of property, where it could be broadly stated that all contributions to family wealth are to be treated as being of equal worth, with nontangible contributions (generally) gaining value with the passage of time (including the actual and potential time spent caring for children). Postseparation support should be seen as compensatory. Arrangements for children should aim to sustain a stable environment, reduce conflict

[84] *Fisher v. Fisher* [1989] 1 FLR 423. The wife was looking after her former husband's child, so the award could be justified as a form of child support: but the court simply referred to its discretionary assessment of the circumstances. *Id.*

[85] IRÈNE THÉRY, LE DÉMARIAGE (Paris, Editions Odile Jacob, 1993).

[86] Ira Ellman, *Why Making Family Law is Hard*, 35 ARIZ. ST. L. J. 699 (2003).

and maintain, as far as possible, the child's beneficial relationships with parents or parent-figures, whose independent interests should be recognized as far as possible, but as being subordinate to those of the children. Such principles will play themselves out in different ways for different sets of people. They should provide sound guides for separating parties, their advisers, mediators, and lawyers. Sometimes decisions will need to be made which require the exercise of judgment on the application of the principles: the courts are there to make them.

24 The Past Caretaking Standard in Comparative Perspective

Patrick Parkinson

The PRINCIPLES advocate a radical new approach to determining parenting arrangements after separation.[1] The central concept is found in Section 2.08: "(T)he court should allocate custodial responsibility so that the proportion of custodial time the child spends with each parent approximates the proportion of time each parent spent performing caretaking functions for the child prior to the parents' separation."[2] This is the "past caretaking" standard. It should be seen as a 'standard,' rather than a rule, since the 'rule' can be modified on many different grounds. The past caretaking standard is based on the concept of continuity between the intact and separated family.

The presumptive allocation of custodial responsibility that results from this assessment can be modified, but only to the extent necessary to achieve other objectives contained in Section 2.08(1).[3] There are eight objectives in Section 2.08 and a number of exceptions provided in Section 2.11. This latter sets out a number of justifications for limiting the parental responsibility of a parent in order to protect the child, the other parent, or other

[1] For an explanation and defense of the past caretaking standard, see Katherine T. Bartlett, *Preference, Presumption, Predisposition, and Common Sense: From Traditional Custody Doctrines to the American Law Institute's Family Dissolution Project*, 36 FAM. L.Q. 11 (2002).

[2] PRINCIPLES § 2.08.

[3] PRINCIPLES § 2.08(1). The objectives are as follows:

(a) to permit the child to have a relationship with each parent which, in the case of a legal parent or a parent by estoppel who has performed a reasonable share of parenting functions, should be not less than a presumptive amount of custodial time set by a uniform rule of statewide application;

(b) to accommodate the firm and reasonable preferences of a child who has reached a specific age, set by a uniform rule of statewide application;

(c) to keep siblings together when the court finds that doing so is necessary to their welfare;

(d) to protect the child's welfare when the presumptive allocation under this section would harm the child because of a gross disparity in the quality of the emotional attachment between each parent and the child or in each parent's demonstrated ability or availability to meet the child's needs;

(e) to take into account any prior agreement, other than one under § 2.06, that would be appropriate to consider in light of the circumstances as a whole, including the reasonable expectations of the parties, the extent to which they could have reasonably anticipated the events that occurred and their significance, and the interests of the child;

(f) to avoid an allocation of custodial responsibility that would be extremely impractical or that would interfere substantially with the child's need for stability in light of economic, physical, or other circumstances, including the distance between the parents' residences, the cost and difficulty of transporting the child, each parent's and the child's daily schedules, and the ability of the parents to cooperate in the arrangement;

(g) to apply the Principles set forth in § 2.17(4) if one parent relocates or proposes to relocate at a distance that will impair the ability of a parent to exercise the presumptive amount of custodial responsibility under this section;

(h) to avoid substantial and almost certain harm to the child.

member of the child's household from harm, including abuse, neglect, or abandonment of a child, domestic violence, and abuse of drugs or alcohol. Given the overlap between Sections 2.08 and 2.11, some factual circumstances may be argued on more than one ground.

The past caretaking approach is also relevant to the allocation of responsibility for making significant parental decisions. Section 2.09 provides that in the absence of parental agreement, the court should allocate responsibility for making significant life decisions on behalf of the child, including decisions regarding the child's education and health care, to one parent or to two parents jointly, in accordance with the child's best interests. Factors in making this allocation include the allocation of custodial responsibility under Section 2.08 and the level of each parent's participation in past decision-making for the child.

The past caretaking standard clearly represents a bold new direction in the law of parenting after separation. Of course, not everything in Chapter 2 is new. The chapter reflects many ideas that are expressed in postseparation parenting laws across America and beyond, for example, parenting plans,[4] restricting parental involvement because of domestic violence or child abuse,[5] and proposals for dealing with relocation.[6] Like many jurisdictions in which major family law reform has occurred in recent years, the PRINCIPLES also avoid the outdated language of custody and visitation. Custodial responsibility, in the PRINCIPLES, differs from the traditional notion of custody because it does not imply the necessity for a binary choice between the mother and father as care giver. Rather, both parents are likely to have "custodial responsibility"[7] and the parenting plan should include "a custodial schedule that designates in which parent's home each minor child will reside on given days of the year" or a method for determining such a schedule.[8] In this way, the either/or choice between parents that marks traditional custody adjudication is abandoned in favor of an approach which recognizes that in the absence of reasons to restrict one parent's contact with the child, both will have caring responsibility for the child, and the parent who is not the primary care giver is nonetheless more than a visitor in the child's life.

This chapter first examines the origins of the past caretaking standard and then reviews some significant difficulties in the interpretation of how the standard will be applied in practice. It is argued that while the standard may be appropriate in determining who should be the primary care giver, it is out of step with both international trends and social science research when it comes to the allocation of time to the secondary parent. In particular, the standard is inappropriate in its application to role-divided marriages where both parents want to remain actively involved in their children's lives following separation. The focus now is on shared parenting around the western world. The chapter explores why this is so, and why for these reasons, the ALI approach is unlikely to achieve widespread support overseas.

[4] PRINCIPLES § 2.05.

[5] PRINCIPLES § 2.11. A presumption against joint custody or generous visitation where there is proven domestic violence is a common feature of American statutes. *See, e.g.*, Illinois, "Unless the court finds the occurrence of ongoing abuse as defined in Section 103 of the Illinois Domestic Violence Act of 1986, the court shall presume that the maximum involvement and cooperation of both parents regarding the physical, mental, moral, and emotional well-being of their child is in the best interest of the child." 750 ILL. COMP. STAT. ANN. 5/602(c) (West 1999 & Supp. 2005).

[6] PRINCIPLES § 2.17.

[7] PRINCIPLES § 2.05(5).

[8] PRINCIPLES § 2.05(5)(a). *Compare* WASH. REV. CODE ANN. § 26.09.184(5) (West 2005).

I. Origins: The Primary Caretaker Presumption and the Approximation Standard

The notion that past caretaking ought to be relevant to which parent will have physical custody of a child is not new. Whether articulated expressly in legislation or not, courts around the Western world tend to give great weight to the claims of the primary caretaker. This is reflected in the predominance of mothers as primary caretakers of children following separation both as a result of court orders and by agreement.

The past caretaking standard is a variant on the approach adopted first by the West Virginia Supreme Court in *Garska v. McCoy*.[9] In this case, the Court held that there should be a presumption in favor of the primary caretaker, if he or she met the minimum, objective standard for being a fit parent.[10] Chief Justice Neely's opinion enumerated a list of practical tasks to be examined in determining who was the primary caretaker.[11] The presumption was an absolute one for children of tender years, replacing the maternal preference rule. The trial judge was required to give such weight to an older child's opinion as he or she considered justified. It is an approach that has been strongly advocated by some feminist scholars.[12]

The *Garska* ruling was adopted by the Minnesota Supreme Court in *Pikula v. Pikula* in 1985.[13] However, it survived for only four years before it was overturned by legislation. Legislative amendments in 1990 designed to overcome continuing judicial support for the presumption, were emphatic in abolishing it. The legislation stated: "The primary caretaker factor may not be used as a presumption in determining the best interests of

[9] *Garska v. McCoy*, 278 S.E. 2d 357 (W. Va. 1981). Chief Justice Neely, who wrote the court's opinion, has written extrajudicially in support of the presumption. Richard Neely, *The Primary Caretaker Parent Rule: Child Custody and the Dynamics of Greed*, 3 YALE L. & POL. REV. 168 (1984).

[10] One difficulty with the primary caretaker presumption is identified by Professor Laura Sack in a study of reported decisions in Minnesota and West Virginia. *See* Laura Sack, *Women and Children First: A Feminist Analysis of the Primary Caretaker Standard in Child Custody Cases*, 4 YALE J. L. & FEM. 291 (1992). Professor Sack found numerous examples of trial judges using the unfit parent exception to disqualify women from custody on the basis of their sexual conduct. *Id.* at 292–93. While generally these decisions were overturned on appeal, Sack noted that the need for appellate intervention undermines one of the proposed benefits of the presumption, and the cost of an appeal might well deter many women from seeking to do so. *Id.* at 297–98.

[11] *Garska*, 278 S.E.2d at 363 (directing the trial court to "determine which parent has taken primary responsibility for, *inter alia*, the performance of the following caring and nurturing duties of a parent: (1) preparing and planning of meals; (2) bathing, grooming and dressing; (3) purchasing, cleaning, and care of clothes; (4) medical care, including nursing and trips to physicians; (5) arranging for social interaction among peers after school, i.e. transporting to friends' houses or, for example, to girl or boy scout meetings; (6) arranging alternative care, i.e. babysitting, day-care, etc.; (7) putting child to bed at night, attending to child in the middle of the night, waking child in the morning; (8) disciplining, i.e. teaching general manners and toilet training; (9) educating, i.e. religious, cultural, social, etc.; and, (10) teaching elementary skills, i.e., reading, writing and arithmetic.").

For strong critiques of the primary caretaker presumption, *see* Bruce Ziff, *The Primary Caretaker Presumption: Canadian Perspectives on an American Development*, 4(2) INT'L J.L. & FAM. 186 (1990); *see also* Carl E. Schneider, *Discretion, Rules and Law: Child Custody and the UMDA's Best-Interest Standard*, 89 MICH. L. REV. 2215, 2283–88 (1991).

[12] Martha Fineman, *Dominant Discourse, Professional Language, and Legal Change in Child Custody Decision-making*, 101 HARV. L. REV. 727 (1988); Katherine Munro, in *The Inapplicability of Rights Analysis in Post-Divorce Child Custody Decision-Making* 30 ALBERTA L. REV. 852 at pp. 893–895 (1992) (summarizing the advantages of the primary caretaker presumption). For a recent discussion from an Australian perspective, *see* Juliet Behrens, *The Form and Substance of Australian Legislation on Parenting Orders: A Case for the Principles of Care and Diversity and Presumptions Based on Them*, 24(4) J. SOC. WELFARE & FAM. L. 401 (2002). The primary caretaker presumption has not gained universal approval from feminist writers. *See* Susan Boyd, Helen Rhoades & Kate Burns, *The Politics of the Primary Care Giver Presumption*, 13 AUSTL. J. FAM. L. 233 (1999).

[13] *Pikula v. Pikula*, 374 N.W.2d 705 (Minn. 1985).

the child."[14] Eventually the primary caretaker presumption was abolished by statute in West Virginia as well, and was replaced by the past caretaking standard advocated in the PRINCIPLES.[15]

The past caretaking standard itself has its origins in a seminal article by Professor Elizabeth Scott published in 1992.[16] Professor Scott examined the primary caretaker preference, as well as the joint custody approach that was popular in the late 1970s and 1980s.[17] She found both to be lacking and proposed instead an "approximation" standard that is very similar to the past caretaking standard adopted in the PRINCIPLES.

The approximation or past caretaking standard differs from the primary caretaker presumption in that in the former, the history of past caretaking is not only relevant to the decision about who should have primary care giving responsibility, but also to the amount of time that the other parent will spend with the child. To the extent that the past caretaking standard is used to select who should be the primary care giver, it is indistinguishable from the primary caretaker presumption. Professor Scott acknowledged the relevance of the *Garska v. McCoy* factors in determining who has been the primary care giver.[18]

In preparing the successive drafts of the PRINCIPLES during the 1990s, the drafters preferred Professor Scott's approach to other approaches that were available to them in American jurisdictions or elsewhere.

II. The Past Caretaker Standard and the Claim to Predictability

One major claim made for the PRINCIPLES' past caretaking standard is that it will promote more predictable and easily adjudicated results, thereby advancing the best interests of children.[19] The commentary to Section 2.08 indicates:

> While each parent's share of past caretaking will in some cases be disputed, these functions encompass specific tasks and responsibilities about which concrete evidence is available and thus offer greater determinacy than more qualitative standards, such as parental competence, the strength of the parent-child emotional bond or – as the general standard simply puts it – the child's best interests.[20]

Unless one of the exceptions applies, then, the patterns of past caretaking will be determinative of the issue of custodial responsibility. The PRINCIPLES seek to limit the discretion of judges to determining a series of relatively closed questions. What was the proportion of time that each parent spent performing caretaking functions while they were together? Do any of the exceptions listed in Section 2.08(1) apply, and if so, to what extent should the presumptive allocation be modified? How should the custodial schedule best be organized to reflect the amount of custodial time allocated to each parent, given their postseparation

[14] 2004 Minn. Laws 518.17(1)(A)(13).

[15] W. VA. CODE ANN. § 48–9–206 (LexisNexis 2004).

[16] Elizabeth S. Scott, *Pluralism, Parental Preference, and Child Custody*, 80 CALIF. L. REV. 615 (1992) [hereinafter Scott, *Pluralism*].

[17] H. Jay Folberg & Marva Graham, *Joint Custody of Children Following Divorce*, 12(2) U.C. DAVIS L. REV. 523 (1979); Holly L. Robinson, *Joint Custody: An Idea Whose Time Has Come*, 21(4) J. FAM. L. 641 (1983); Sheila F. G. Schwartz, *Toward a Presumption of Joint Custody*, 18 FAM. L.Q. 225 (1984); JOINT CUSTODY AND SHARED PARENTING (Jay Folberg, ed.), (1984); Andrew Schepard, *Taking Children Seriously: Promoting Cooperative Custody after Divorce*, 64 TEX. L. REV. 687 (1985); Katharine T. Bartlett & Carol B. Stack, *Joint Custody, Feminism and the Dependency Dilemma*, 2 BERKELEY WOMEN'S L.J.9 (1986).

[18] Scott, *Pluralism*, *supra* note 16, at 638 n.71.

[19] PRINCIPLES § 2.08, cmt. b, at 181–83.

[20] PRINCIPLES § 2.08 cmt. b, at 182.

circumstances? Whether the past caretaking standard is likely to reduce litigation depends on the circumstances of the case, and the issues that are before the Court.

A. The Past Caretaking Standard and the Choice of Primary Care Giver

The past caretaker standard ought to be a reasonably straightforward principle in cases in which both parents seek an order for what has traditionally been called sole physical custody. If the issue is which parent will be the primary care giver following separation, then the answer provided by this standard is that it generally will be the parent who was the primary care giver during the marriage or cohabiting relationship. Application of the test to custody disputes is, of course, not entirely free from difficulty. The commentary to Section 2.08 addresses a number of issues that could arise, including how the test should be applied when the division of caretaking functions has changed over time,[21] in which arguments may arise over who was the primary caretaker. However, other tests for determining custodial responsibility are also fraught with difficulty, not least the best interests standard. It is not a convincing argument against the past caretaking standard that it may at times be difficult to apply.

Nonetheless, the history of the primary caretaker presumption in Minnesota indicates that the test may not create the certainty proponents suggest. Minnesota's experience with the presumption was analyzed by Judge Gary Crippen of the Minnesota Court of Appeals.[22] He found a dramatic increase in the numbers of custody appeals to the intermediate appellate court in the period during which Minnesota adopted the standard, from nine in the year before *Pikula* to an average of thirty per year after. Judge Crippen also found that practitioners and judges with extensive experience perceived that, while the preference was effective in some cases in discouraging litigation, in others it had the effect of inducing litigation. Trial judges sought to get around the test in favor of outcomes that they considered more justifiable. One lesson from Minnesota, perhaps, is that a custody rule that does not have general acceptance among those entrusted with its application is unlikely to succeed as intended.

B. Are the Exceptions Actually the Rule in Cases That Will Go to Trial?

Even if the past caretaking standard does promote greater predictability, this is only likely to occur when it is the rule itself, rather than one of the exceptions, that is the major issue at trial. Arguably, the exceptions to the standard are so many that they threaten to swallow up the rule.

There are many common situations where the exception, rather than the rule, is likely to be the focus of litigation. A father may concede that the mother was the primary care giver during the marriage, but argue that the determining factor ought to be the child's wishes.[23] The mother may counter that those wishes are the consequence of manipulation by the

[21] *See* PRINCIPLES § 2.08 cmt. c, at 183–85.

[22] Gary Crippen, *Stumbling Beyond Best Interests of the Child: Reexamining Child Custody Standard–Setting in the Wake of Minnesota's Four Year Experiment With the Primary Caretaker Preference*, 75 MINN. L. REV. 427 (1990).

[23] PRINCIPLES § 2.08 cmt. f, at 190–91. The drafters indicate that the rule-maker may reasonably choose the age of 11, 12, 13, or even 14 as the appropriate age.

father and should not displace the past caretaking standard.[24] Alternatively, the father may argue that while the mother has been the primary caretaker, she is not able to fulfil this role adequately because she is incapacitated by drug and alcohol abuse or mental illness. He may therefore argue that there is a gross disparity in each parent's "demonstrated ability or availability to meet the child's needs."[25]

Another dispute may turn on the quality of the relationship between the child and each parent. Although one parent has been the primary care giver, the other argues that there is a gross disparity in the "quality of the emotional attachment between each parent and the child."[26] Another dispute may be about whether one parent should have contact with the child at all, or should only have supervised contact. The issue here is not the relative involvement of the parents in past caretaking, but the risk of harm to the child if unrestricted contact takes place. This falls within exception (h), the need to avoid substantial and almost certain harm to the child, and Section 2.11.

Together, the exceptions in Section 2.08 and Section 2.11 account for the issues that are central to a very substantial proportion of cases that go to trial in Australia.[27] Because the primary caretaker is usually the obvious parent to continue in that role after separation, it takes some other significant factor like those given in the PRINCIPLES to displace the natural tendency of courts to preserve the status quo.[28] Consequently, if the PRINCIPLES were to be introduced into Australia, it would probably make very little difference to the kinds of disputes that trial courts hear day in and day out. The exceptions given in the PRINCIPLES are the rule when it comes to litigated cases.

C. When the Past Caretaking Has Been Shared Equally

This issue of equal caretaking clearly caused the drafters a great deal of difficulty. The logic of the ALI's approach is that if the parents have shared in the care of the child more or less equally, then the presumptive allocation of custodial responsibility between them should also be more or less equal, at least if the parents' circumstances permit.[29] Surprisingly, however, the commentary and illustrations that accompany Section 2.08 indicate a great

[24] For further discussion of the problems in interpreting children's wishes in the midst of parenting disputes, *see* Richard A. Warshak, *Payoffs and Pitfalls of Listening to Children*, 52(4) FAM. RELATIONS 373 (2003); Joan B. Kelly, *Psychological and Legal Interventions for Parents and Children in Custody and Access Disputes: Current Research and Practice*, 10 VA. J. SOC. POL'Y & L. 129 (2002); Robert E Emery, *Easing the Pain of Divorce for Children: Children's Voices, Causes of Conflict and Mediation. Comments on Kelly's "Resolving Child Custody Disputes,"* 10 VA. J. SOC. POL'Y & L. 164 (2002).

[25] PRINCIPLES § 2.08 cmt. h, at 193–99 (indicating that this exception is only intended to cover "exceptional cases").

[26] PRINCIPLES § 2.08(1)(d).

[27] In Australia, issues of domestic violence and child protection feature prominently in the matters that go to trial. THEA BROWN ET AL., VIOLENCE IN FAMILIES: REPORT NO 1 – THE MANAGEMENT OF CHILD ABUSE ALLEGATIONS IN CUSTODY AND ACCESS DISPUTES BEFORE THE FAMILY COURT OF AUSTRALIA (1998). *See also* Helen Rhoades, *The "No Contact Mother": Reconstructions of Motherhood in the Era of the "New Father,"* 16 INT'L J.L. POL'Y & FAM. 71 (2002). Regarding problems in the courts' handling of cases involving domestic violence in Australia, *see* Miranda Kaye, Julie Stubbs & Julia Tolmie, *Domestic Violence and Child Contact Arrangements*, 17 AUSTL. J. FAM. L. 93 (2003).

[28] An empirical study of closely contested custody disputes in Australia found that unfitness of the child's primary care giver is the major reason why fathers win custody disputes. Lawrie Moloney, *Do Fathers "Win" or Do Mothers "Lose?" A Preliminary Analysis of Closely Contested Parenting Judgments in the Family Court of Australia*, 15 INT'L J.L. & POL'Y & FAM. 363 (2001).

[29] PRINCIPLES § 2.08(1)(f) (indicating that the presumptive allocation may have to be modified in light of the parents' economic, physical, or other circumstances, including the distance between the parents' residences and each parent's schedule).

deal of confusion about what the outcome should be in this situation. There are three different views in the commentary.

The first view is that the past caretaking standard is not applicable at all. Illustrations 13 and 20 both involve a situation where the two parents shared approximately equally in the caretaking responsibilities while they were living together. The commentary indicates that because the parents shared caretaking equally in the past, the allocation of primary caretaking responsibility cannot be resolved by means of the presumptive standard and the court must apply the best interests of the child test.[30] This, the drafters say, is an application of the principle contained in Section 2.08(3), that the best interests test should apply because the history does not establish a sufficiently clear pattern of caretaking.

The second view is that the outcome depends on whether there was a prior agreement between the parents. It appears from Illustration 27[31] that if the parents had an agreement to share the care of the child on an equal basis during the marriage and carried this into effect, then this would support an equal division of custodial responsibility between the parents.

The third view is that the past caretaking standard ought to dictate an allocation of equal custodial time unless one of the exceptions applies. In Illustrations 34 and 35, it is accepted that if the parents have shared equally in the caretaking of the children, then an allocation of equal custodial time would ordinarily be warranted.[32]

These illustrations are followed, almost immediately, by Illustrations 38 and 42, in which the drafters return to an interpretation given in Illustrations 13 and 20 that if the parents have shared custodial responsibility equally, then the best interests test should apply.[33]

Any jurisdiction considering legislation along the lines of the PRINCIPLES would need to make a clear choice between these conflicting interpretations of the past caretaking standard.

D. The Past Caretaking Standard and Visitation or Contact Arrangements

It is also less than clear from the illustrations and commentary to Section 2.08 how exactly the custodial responsibility of the nonresident parent is to be allocated in accordance with the past caretaking standard. For the most part, the illustrations establish who should be the primary caretaker following separation, not how much time the other parent will get to spend with the children. In Illustration 2, the drafters provide their main illustration of how the primary caretaker standard might be applied to allocate the custodial responsibility of the nonresident parent.[34] In this illustration, Shira was a stay-at-home parent, while Duncan worked ten-to-twelve hour days in full-time employment and spent three to four hours per week playing with his children while the parents were living together. The

[30] PRINCIPLES § 2.08 cmt. f, at 190–91; PRINCIPLES § 2.08 cmt. h, at 193–95.

[31] PRINCIPLES § 2.08 illus. 27, at 200; PRINCIPLES § 2.08 cmt. i, at 199–200.

[32] PRINCIPLES § 2.08 illus. 34–35, at 203; PRINCIPLES § 2.08 cmt. j, at 202–03. This approach is supported by one of the drafters, Professor Katherine Bartlett. She writes: "If parents equally shared caretaking responsibilities, that fact will be reflected in the custodial allocations." Katherine T. Bartlett, *U.S. Custody Law and Trends in the Context of the ALI* Principles of the Law of Family Dissolution, 10 VA. J. SOC. POL'Y & L. 5, 18 (2002).

[33] PRINCIPLES § 2.08 illus. 38, at 205–06; PRINCIPLES § 2.08 cmt. m, at 205; PRINCIPLES § 2.08 illus. 42, at 208; PRINCIPLES § 2.08 cmt. n, at 207; PRINCIPLES § 2.08 illus. 13, at 192; PRINCIPLES § 2.08 cmt. f, at 190–91; PRINCIPLES § 2.08 illus. 20, at 196; PRINCIPLES § 2.08 cmt. h, at 193–95.

commentary in Illustration 2 suggests that if the nonresident parent only spent three to four hours per week playing with his children while the parents were living together, then that is all the time he is entitled to have with them after separation under the past caretaking standard. However, the drafters go on to say that the ordinary operation of the past caretaking standard is displaced because this would be lower than the presumptive amount of custodial time set under the state rule which aims to ensure that the child is permitted to have a relationship with each parent.

In other parts of the commentary, however, it is clear that the issue is not how much time the parent spent in caretaking responsibilities, but rather the proportion this bears to the caretaking responsibilities of the other parent. Section 2.03(5) defines caretaking responsibilities as "tasks that involve interaction with the child or that direct, arrange, and supervise the interaction and care provided by others."[35] Families engage in many other activities that do not involve caretaking as so defined except incidentally, such as going shopping, doing the washing and ironing, doing other chores around the house and garden, and engaging in recreational activities. One parent may spend four hours per week in caretaking responsibilities while his partner, who was the primary care giver, spends twelve hours in caretaking responsibilities as defined by the PRINCIPLES. If the proportionality test is applied, then the first parent ought to have the children staying with him for approximately 25 percent of the time and the primary care giver for 75 percent of the time.

In Illustration 2, what matters for Duncan is the presumptive amount of custodial time required by a rule of statewide application in an enacting jurisdiction, since this modifies the application of the past caretaking standard. The drafters do not specify what that should be. However, the commentary indicates that in the drafters' opinion, "a presumptive period of four to six hours a week for children under the age of six months is a reasonable guideline, whereas for a child over the age of six, six to eight days per month is a more reasonable minimum."[36]

Other illustrations, to the extent that they address the issue at all, posit a situation where the parents have shared equally in the caretaking tasks. Taking the illustrations as a whole, it is less than clear how precise the past caretaking standard is meant to be in allocating parenting time between two involved parents where one does more of the caretaking than the other, but where both are actively engaged in caretaking tasks in the course of the marriage. This lack of clarity is unfortunate.

The question of how to allocate parenting time was dealt with more fully by Professor Scott in her 1992 article.[37] She wrote that for the standard to have practical application, the courts would need to "characterize pre-divorce family arrangements by using simplifying categories or rules of thumb to ease the judicial task of applying the rule."[38] She thought that three categories could be constructed that would roughly reflect various patterns of parental involvement, spanning "a continuum from a family in which both parents equally share [caretaking] responsibility to one in which one parent is uninvolved while the other shoulders most of the burden."[39] In the first category, an arrangement for joint physical and legal custody would be appropriate. Where one parent is uninvolved in caretaking, the

[34] PRINCIPLES § 2.08 illus, 2. at 185.
[35] PRINCIPLES § 2.03(5).
[36] PRINCIPLES § 2.08 cmt. e, at 189.
[37] Scott, *Pluralism*, *supra* note 16, at 640–41.
[38] *Id.* at 640.
[39] *Id.*

appropriate order would be for sole custody and visitation. Professor Scott also described a third category as follows:

> [It would] include families with two involved parents, one of whom bears the greater burden of child care responsibility. A family in this third category might have a custody arrangement that is similar to joint legal custody, with the child's principal residence being with the primary caretaker and secondary residence with the other parent. The actual time allocation between residences would be based on each parent's participation in the child's life before divorce. Thus, a court ordering custody for a family in this group might use a variety of formulas to allocate the child's time between households, designating time with each parent as a proportion of the month or week. For example, the order might direct that the child live with an actively participating secondary caretaker twelve days a month (or three days a week), while a less involved secondary parent might be awarded physical custody eight days a month (or two days a week).[40]

In this formulation, the past caretaking or "approximation" standard is very approximate indeed. Contact arrangements are only loosely based on an examination of the amounts of time each parent spent in caretaking functions. The main purpose of that analysis is to choose who should be the primary care giver following separation. In relation to the amount of time the other parent should spend with the children, the approximation standard can be otherwise expressed by saying that the more involved the parent was in caregiving during the marriage, the more time he or she should be allocated after separation. If this is all the approximation standard means, then it is little different from the primary caretaker standard with an additional principle to give guidance about contact arrangements.

III. The Past Caretaking Standard and the Role-Divided Marriage

Role-divided marriages remain a very common form of marital partnership. While fathers are playing a more active role in their children's lives, mothers continue to carry most of the family's domestic responsibilities. The common pattern remains for women and men as parents to make differential life-course investments, with fathers' primary investment being in the marketplace of career or self-employed business, while women's life investments are more diversified and include a major orientation toward the care of children.[41]

Professor Scott's approach to the application of the approximation standard, if adopted by courts applying the ALI approach, would at least ensure that those nonresident parents who were most active and committed to caretaking during the marriage should also have a significant level of care following separation.

However, what is so controversial about the PRINCIPLES is how nonresident parents in role-divided relationships fare in the drafters' illustrations. Duncan, the father in Illustration 2, worked ten- or twelve-hour days in full-time employment and receives the presumptive amount of custodial time with his children after separation that the state rule deems appropriate.[42] However, the same is true for Randy, a father of two children, ages

[40] *Id.*

[41] The difference in roles does not necessarily indicate a difference in total hours spent in paid and unpaid work. For United States research *see* BETH SHELTON, MEN, WOMEN, AND TIME: GENDER DIFFERENCES IN PAID WORK, HOUSEWORK AND LEISURE CH 5 (1992) (suggesting in the U.S. that men and women have approximately the same amount of leisure time although patterns of availability and use are different). *See also* MICHAEL BITTMAN, JUGGLING TIME: HOW AUSTRALIAN FAMILIES USE THEIR TIME (1991).

[42] PRINCIPLES § 2.08 illus, 2. at 185.

two and four, who is introduced in Illustration 10.[43] Randy and Dawn had a role-divided marriage. Dawn was a stay-at-home parent while Randy worked outside the home, "interacting with the children in the evenings when he was at home and on weekends." The description of Randy is one of a loving and involved father who engages with the child rearing as much as his full-time work routine allows. Randy, however, will only be awarded the presumptive amount of custodial time that the statutory rule stipulates for those who have performed a reasonable share of parenting functions.

In comment e, the drafters acknowledge that the presumptive amount of time stipulated should be set at a level that includes time for family routines and not merely recreational activity. What is clear, however, is that the nonresident parent who has been in a role-divided marriage is only entitled to the presumptive amount of custodial time necessary to sustain a relationship with the children. This is expressed in terms of a minimum level of contact sufficient to remain involved still as a parent, rather than a level of contact that maximizes his involvement. The past caretaker standard is thus prejudicial to the primary earning parent in role-divided marriages. That prejudice can be alleviated to some extent if the rule of statewide application sets a generous amount of time for the nonresident parent to see the children.

The past caretaking standard has had an enthusiastic reception from many U.S. academics. Professor Herma Hill Kay welcomes it as offering "both mothers and fathers a way to retreat from this particular battlefield [of custody law] with their honor intact."[44] The standard has also been praised for being gender-neutral.[45] However, neither claim withstands careful scrutiny. There can be no question that the division of roles in the intact marriage is, and ought to be, a very significant factor in deciding who should be the primary care giver after separation. Children are likely to have developed a closer attachment to the parent who has been their primary care giver, and that parent is more likely to be attuned to the needs of the children. Primary care givers also play an anchor role emotionally in the lives of children.[46] The primary care giver's better qualifications to continue in that role justify allocating to them primary caring responsibility after separation in the majority of cases.

However, a fundamental issue about this standard is whether past caretaking patterns should dictate the amount of contact that nonresident parents should have when they have been in a role-divided marriage.

A. Should Levels of Contact Follow Pre-Separation Patterns?

What then, are the arguments against the use of past caretaking patterns to determine the amount of contact that a nonresident parent will have? First, this strict continuity approach equates practical caretaking with emotional closeness. A child may spend much more time with one caretaker than another and yet feel close to both and want to spend time with them both. This desire needs to be reflected in the contact arrangements.

[43] Principles § 2.08 illus. 10, at 189–90.

[44] Herma Hill Kay, *No-Fault Divorce and Child Custody: Chilling Out the Gender Wars*, 36 Fam. L.Q. 27, 40 (2002).

[45] Kathy T. Graham, *How the ALI Child Custody Principles Help Eliminate Gender and Sexual Orientation Bias from Child Custody Determinations*, 8 Duke J. Gender L. & Pol'y 323 (2001).

[46] In the aftermath of separation, the great majority of children and young people in families report that they feel close to their mothers. Christy M. Buchanan et al., Adolescents After Divorce 85 tbl. 5.1, 188 (1996). The picture with regard to fathers is more mixed. For example, recent British research with children of divorce found that half of the children interviewed reported that their fathers knew nothing, or very little, of their feelings about the divorce, while this was true of only 20 percent of mothers. Ian Butler et al., Divorcing Children: Children's Experience of Their Parents' Divorce 39 (2003).

Second, the argument that fathers should not have a greater role in parenting after separation than they had before separation ignores the significance of the change that separation can make to fathers' attitudes to the parenting role. Professors Smart and Neale found in Britain that some fathers adjust to divorce by making a new commitment to parenting.[47] Some leave the workforce or adjust their workforce participation in order to invest in a relationship which they feel could not be sustained without a substantial new investment of time and energy. Divorce, then, causes them to reorder their priorities in ways that were not required before their separation.

This is far from a belated conversion on the road to Damascus. Role division within marriage makes sense for many couples as long as the relationship remains intact. A law that determines postseparation parenting arrangements on the basis of parenting patterns before separation may be appropriate to the extent that the primary care giver is better attuned to the needs of the children. However, it may act unfairly if the strength of a presumption in favor of the primary care giver operates to the prejudice of men who fulfilled their role as primary breadwinners within a role-divided partnership, but who want to restructure their working arrangements significantly after separation to ensure that they can remain actively involved with their children's lives.[48]

Another flaw in the past caretaking standard is that it assumes the coparenting arrangement after separation can mirror the patterns of care giving within an intact relationship. This takes too little account of the emotional, geographical, and financial earthquake that separation can involve for parents. Coparenting after divorce, whatever form it takes, requires new patterns of parenting to be developed in the very different circumstances that exist for the separated family.

In particular, when parents live apart, it may not be practicable to replicate the arrangements in place that were there when the marriage was intact. There is a big difference between parenting together in the same household, and parenting apart where each parent must be the sole care giver during the times that the child is living with him or her. As Professors Smart and Neale observe: "[p]re-divorce parenting may be a poor preparation for post-divorce parenting, and the skills, qualities and infrastructural supports required for the former may be rather different to those required for the latter."[49]

When each parent is the primary care giver during the periods that a child lives with him or her, it may be much more difficult to organize roles in the same way as during the intact relationship. Taking children to and from school, arranging meetings with friends, and taking children to extracurricular activities may be much more difficult for a parent working full-time rather than part-time. Postseparation parenting means reorganizing parenting roles rather than a continuation of parenting roles.

B. The Past Caretaking Standard and the Rise of Shared Parenting Laws

In its application to parents who have had role-divided marriages, the reform proposed by the PRINCIPLES goes in the opposite direction to the trend, not only in the United States but all over the Western world, toward the encouragement of shared parenting after divorce.[50]

[47] CAROL SMART & BREN NEALE, FAMILY FRAGMENTS? (1999) Ch. 3 [hereinafter SMART ET AL., FAMILY FRAGMENTS].
[48] *See* John Guidubaldi, minority report, U.S. COMMISSION ON CHILD AND FAMILY WELFARE, PARENTING OUR CHILDREN: IN THE BEST INTEREST OF THE NATION, A REPORT TO THE PRESIDENT AND CONGRESS, 87 (1996).
[49] SMART EL AL., FAMILY FRAGMENTS, *supra* note 47, at 46.
[50] Helen Rhoades, *The Rise and Rise of Shared Parenting Laws*, 19 CAN. J. FAM. L. 75, 75 (2002).

Awarding a presumptive amount of custodial time to the nonresident parent sufficient for maintaining a relationship with the child stands in marked contrast to the law in a number of United States jurisdictions, where the emphasis is on facilitating the nonresident parent's role to the fullest extent that is consistent with the best interests of the child. These provisions are self-consciously aspirational.[51] Although aspirational or normative statements are not an established part of the tradition of legislative drafting in common law countries, laws concerning parenting after separation provide an exception. In the United States, it is common to have statements of legislative policy about the involvement of both parents. Missouri declares it is the public policy of the state that there should be "frequent, continuing and meaningful contact with both parents" following separation, unless the best interests of the child dictate otherwise.[52] In Iowa, postseparation parenting arrangements must be such as to "assure the child the opportunity for the maximum continuing physical and emotional contact with both parents."[53]

This kind of positive language about the importance of the secondary parent's role is not entirely absent from the PRINCIPLES. In Section 2.02, one of the objectives is that there should be "meaningful" contact between the child and each parent. However, this falls short of the emphasis present for years in many United States jurisdictions regarding frequent and continuing contact. The significance of the secondary parent for the child's well-being is understated, to say the least, in the PRINCIPLES.

C. Alternating Residence: The New Frontier

Legislative encouragement in many jurisdictions to share parenting after separation has been accompanied by a significant increase in the numbers of families in which the children alternate between the parents' homes. In rare cases, the parents even alternate in living with the children in the matrimonial home, a practice known as "bird-nesting."

In Wisconsin, the incidence of joint physical custody among divorced couples increased from 2.2 percent to 14.2 percent between 1980 and 1992.[54] Their most recent research indicates that the proportion of shared parenting arrangements is now 32 percent.[55] They define a shared parenting arrangement as involving at least 30 percent of the time with each parent. Equal time arrangements are not as common. A retrospective study of the living arrangements of college students who had experienced parental divorce found that 8 percent of respondents reported that they lived equal amounts of time with each parent.[56]

[51] In systems influenced by the civil law tradition, contact between the nonresident parent and the child may even be expressed in terms of a parental duty, in contrast to the common law focus upon rights. The Children Act 1995 in Scotland offers an example. Section 1 provides that where a child is not living with a parent, the parent has the responsibility "to maintain personal relations and direct contact with the child on a regular basis."

[52] MO. ANN. STAT. § 452.375(4) (West 2003 & Supp. 2005). *See also*, CAL. FAM. CODE § 3020 (West 2004 & Supp. 2005); FLA. STAT. ANN. § 61.13(3)(a) (West 1997 & Supp. 2005); ME. REV. STATE. ANN. tit. 19-A, § 1653(1)(C) (West 1998 & Supp. 2004); OKLA. STAT. § 43–110.1 (West, 2004).

[53] IOWA CODE ANN. § 598.41(1)(a) (West 2001 & Supp. 2005).

[54] Marygold S. Melli et al., *Child Custody in a Changing World: A Study of Postdivorce Arrangements in Wisconsin*, 1997 U. ILL. L. REV. 773.

[55] Marygold S. Melli, Steven T. Cook & Patricia Brown, *Recent Trends in Children's Placement Arrangements in Divorce and Paternity Cases in Wisconsin*, (March 2006), *available at* http.//www.irp.wisc.edu/. In 59% of cases, the mother had sole custody and in 7% the father had sole custody. These figures from the Institute for Research on Poverty, University of Wisconsin-Madison are taken from cases with final judgments dated 2000–2002.

[56] William V. Fabricius & Jeff A. Hall, *Young Adults' Perspectives on Divorce: Living Arrangements*, 38 FAM. & CONCILIATION CTS. REV. 446, 451 (2000). In contrast, a study in Oregon of 274 cases resolved by mediation in one county in 1995–96 found that joint physical and legal custody was awarded without allocating a primary care giver

At the political level, there has been pressure for change in a number of jurisdictions based upon the idea that for parents to be treated equally, there ought to be a presumption of joint physical custody, and that children should have an equal amount of time with each parent after separation.[57] In Louisiana, there is now a presumption in favor of joint custody,[58] and the courts are instructed that "to the extent it is feasible and in the best interest of the child, physical custody of the children should be shared equally."[59] This may be little more than a rhetorical flourish, however, as the Court is also required to identify a "domiciliary parent" with whom the child "shall primarily reside."[60]

The domiciliary parent also has the authority to make all decisions affecting the child unless an implementation order provides otherwise, and there is a statutory presumption that all major decisions made by the domiciliary parent are in the best interest of the child.[61] Thus Louisiana, while including a presumption in favor of equal time arrangements, also assumes there will always be a primary care giver with the major decision-making powers. Such legislative schizophrenia illustrates the tensions lawmakers must grapple with in determining custody policy, and the impact of inconsistent amendments over time.

Other U.S. jurisdictions also encourage consideration of equal custody. Oklahoma courts are required to order "substantially equal access"[62] when making temporary orders, if requested by one parent. A statutory amendment in Iowa in 2004 stipulates that if joint legal custody is awarded to both parents, and one parent seeks an award of joint physical care, the court that declines to make such an award must make specific findings of fact and conclusions of law that the awarding of joint physical care is not in the best interests of the child.[63] A similar provision, requiring reasons for rejecting shared primary residential care, exists in Maine.[64] These provisions, however, fall short of a presumption in favor of joint physical custody. In Australia at least, it would be seen as fundamental to the judicial duty to give reasons for or against any proposal that was put forward by one of the parties.

in only 9 cases (3.3%). Kathy T. Graham, *Child Custody in the New Millennium: ALI's Proposed Model Contrasted with Oregon's Law*, 35 Willamette L. Rev. 523, 543 (1999). However, these figures exclude consensual equal time arrangements reached without the need for mediation.

[57] The United States Commission on Child and Family Welfare, *supra* note 48, considered this option but did not adopt it, to the disappointment of the minority. *See* John Guidubaldi, minority report, 87, 93–97.

[58] La. Civ. Code Ann. art. 132 (1999 & Supp. 2005) ("If the parents agree who is to have custody, the court shall award custody in accordance with their agreement unless the best interest of the child requires a different award. In the absence of agreement, or if the agreement is not in the best interest of the child, the court shall award custody to the parents jointly; however, if custody in one parent is shown by clear and convincing evidence to serve the best interest of the child, the court shall award custody to that parent.").

[59] Civil Code Ancillaries 9–335 A(2)(b). Arizona and Georgia also define joint physical custody as substantially equal time, but, unlike in Louisiana, there is no presumption in those states in favor of joint physical custody. *See* Ariz. Rev. Stat. § 25–402(3) (Matthew Bender 2004); Ga. Code Ann. § 19–9–6(3) (West 2004).

[60] Civil Code Ancillaries 9–335 B(2). Professor Katherine Spaht writes that "the principal provision is para. B which establishes the default 'implementation plan'. That default plan designates a 'domiciliary parent', defined as the parent with whom the child primarily resides. That definition would make co-domiciliary parents and equal physical custody an oxymoron." She explains further that the "legislative history of the language [about the physical custody of children being shared equally] suggests the language is purely hortatory." Professor. Katherine Spaht, personal communication to author, (Jul. 7, 2003) (on file with author). Professor Spaht is the Reporter, Persons Committee of the Louisiana State Law Institute. The custody provisions in the Civil Code are based upon recommendations made by this Committee.

[61] Civil Code Ancillaries 9–335 B.

[62] 43 Okl. St. § 110.1 (2004).

[63] Iowa Code Ann. § 598.41 (West 2004).

[64] 19A Me. Rev. Stat. Ann. § 1653.

Agitation for an equal time presumption is also occurring elsewhere. In Britain, pressure for such a change[65] has been given particular impetus by the advocacy of singer Sir Bob Geldof, whose personal struggles to gain custody of his two children attracted considerable media attention.[66] In Australia, the issue was examined through a Parliamentary Inquiry.[67] The terms of reference required the Family and Community Affairs Committee of the House of Representatives to examine whether there should be a presumption that children will spend equal time with each parent and, if so, in what circumstances such a presumption could be rebutted.[68]

Although members of the committee began the inquiry with some sympathy for an equal time presumption, in the end they recommended against it, concluding that "the goal for the majority of families should be one of equality of care and responsibility along with substantially shared parenting time."[69] Nonetheless, they recommended that the legislation should require mediators, counselors, and legal advisers to assist parents to first consider a starting point of equal time where practicable. The committee also recommended that courts should also first consider substantially shared parenting time when making orders in cases where each parent wishes to be the primary care giver.[70] Legislation to give effect to these recommendations has been enacted in 2006.[71]

France has adopted an intermediate position. While 1993 amendments established joint parental authority after separation, the legislature rejected the idea of alternating residence.[72] However, some judges were persuaded to fix a primary residence, while giving contact with the nonresident parent that was so extensive that the arrangements were equivalent, in practice, to an alternating residence system.[73]

[65] *See, e.g.*, Ann Buchanan & Joan Hunt, *Disputed Contact Cases in the Courts, in* CHILDREN AND THEIR FAMILIES: CONTACT, RIGHTS AND WELFARE (Andrew Bainham, Bridget Lindley, Martin Richards & Liz Trinder eds., 2003) at 371, 380 [hereinafter CHILDREN AND THEIR FAMILIES]. For an examination of the earlier case law on shared residence in England, compared with New Zealand, *see* Caroline Bridge, *Shared Residence in England and New Zealand – a Comparative Analysis*, 8 CHILD & FAM. L. Q. 12 (1996).

[66] Bob Geldof, *The Real Love that Dare Not Speak its Name, in* CHILDREN AND THEIR FAMILIES, *supra* n. 65, 171.

[67] The announcement of the inquiry followed an indication from the Prime Minister, The Hon. John Howard MP, in June 2003 that he wanted to explore the option of a rebuttable presumption of "joint custody." He expressed concern that many boys growing up in single parent families lack male role models both at home and in school until their teenage years: THE AUSTRALIAN, Jun. 18, 2003, at 3. The Government utilized the traditional language of "custody" despite its removal by the Family Law Reform Act, 1995 (Austl.). This Act adopted reforms on similar lines to the Children Act, 1989 (Austl.), with the terms "custody" and "access" being replaced by "residence" and "contact," and the rhetoric of "parental responsibility" driving out notions of parental rights. *See* John Dewar, *The Family Law Reform Act 1995 (Cth) and the Children Act 1989 (UK) Compared – Twins or Distant Cousins?*, 10 AUSTL. J. FAM. L. 18 (1996).

[68] The Committee was also asked to consider whether changes should be made to the formula for calculating child support liabilities and issues concerning grandparents' rights to contact.

[69] HOUSE OF REP. STANDING COMMITTEE ON FAMILY & COMMUNITY AFFAIRS, EVERY PICTURE TELLS A STORY: REPORT OF THE INQUIRY INTO CHILD CUSTODY ARRANGEMENTS IN THE EVENT OF FAMILY SEPARATION (2003) at 30.

[70] Id at 43 (Recommendation 5).

[71] Family Law Amendment (Shared Parental Responsibility) Act 2006.

[72] This was implicit in the text, since the principle of a primary or usual residence was maintained, but explicit in the legislative debates: Hugues Fulchiron in *L' autorité parentale renovée*, RÉPERTOIRE DU NOTARIAT DEFRÉNOIS 959 (2002).

[73] Hugues Fulchiron & Adeline Gouttenoire-Cornut, *Réformes législatives et permanence des pratiques: à propos de la généralisation de l'exercice en commun de l'autorité parentale par la loi du 8 janvier 1993*, 1997 RECUEIL DALLOZ CHRONIQUES 363 and the cases cited therein.

Two commissions were established to advise the Government concerning possible reforms to the law of parental authority in the 1990s. One took a sociological view, under the presidency of Irène Théry.[74] The other focused more on legal issues under the presidency of Françoise Dekeuwer-Défossez.[75] President Dekeuwer-Défossez recommended that the notion of principal residence be removed from the French Code because it led judges to refuse shared residence arrangements when such arrangements would not have been contrary to the child's best interests.[76]

The consequence of these proposals for reform, and subsequent governmental consideration, was legislation on parental authority passed in 2002. This legislation was intended to promote alternating residence arrangements. The Minister for Family Affairs, Mme Ségolène Royal, indicated in the legislative debates that the reform's purpose was to encourage parents to reach agreement on the principle of alternating residence, arguing that it had the advantage of maintaining parity between them.[77] However, in the Senate, concerns were expressed about the imposition of an alternating residence arrangement on parents without their agreement.[78]

This led to the 2002 compromise in Article 373-2-9 of the Civil Code. The residence of a child may now be fixed alternately at the domicile of each of the parents or at the domicile of one of them. The listing of alternating residence first, before sole residence, was intended to indicate encouragement of this option. At the insistence of the Senate, the same Article also provides that alternating residence should not be imposed on the parties without their joint agreement unless there has first been a temporary alternating residence arrangement to determine its workability.[79]

The strong legislative encouragement toward shared parenting in many jurisdictions, and the increasing acceptance of the option of equal time provisions, stands in stark contrast to the ALI's approach. The past caretaking standard can yield a result similar to the shared parenting statutes of other jurisdictions, but not for parents in role-divided marriages. Jurisdictions around the world with statutes encouraging shared parenting are moving away from traditional patterns of custody and visitation. In contrast, the provisions on custodial responsibility in the PRINCIPLES reinforce those old patterns, giving many devoted fathers nothing more than a presumptive amount of custodial time set by the State legislature. The world is going one way. The ALI, it seems, is going another.

[74] IRÈNE THÉRY, COUPLE, FILIATION ET PARENTÉ AUJOURD'HUI: LE DROIT FACE AUX MUTATIONS DE LA FAMILLE ET DE LA VIE PRIVÉE (1998).

[75] FRANÇOISE DEKEUWER-DÉFOSSEZ, RÉNOVER LE DROIT DE LA FAMILLE: PROPOSITIONS POUR UN DROIT ADAPTÉ AUX RÉALITÉS ET AUX ASPIRATIONS DE NOTRE TEMPS (1999).

[76] *Id.* at 82.

[77] Assemblée Nationale, session of Jun. 14, 2001, J.O. 15 Juin 2001, Bebat Ass. Nat. at 4251. *See also* for an examination of the parental agreements since the March 4, 2002 reform, Olivier Laouenan, *Les Conventions sur L'autorité Parentale Depuis la Loi du 4 Mars 2002*, 28 J.C.P. (2003). *See also* Fulchiron, above, note 72.

[78] This position was expressed particularly by the Senate's reporter on the Bill, Mr. Béteille. He emphasized that it was important to be careful about the adoption of an alternating residence schedule without the agreement of the parents because of the practical constraints in terms of housing, the constant collaboration needed, and the uncertainties of the experts about the consequences of alternating residence for the child's development. Rapport Sénat, 71, Session Ordinaire 2001–2002, 18.

[79] Despite the emphasis on alternating residence in the debates leading up to the 2002 legislation, such arrangements remain uncommon in France. Only 10% of the cases concerning minor children in 2003 involved such a request, whether it originated from both parents or only one of them. In the context of consensual divorces, these requests were much more frequent (15.8%) than in the contested divorces, where they represented only 6.1% of the cases. DEPARTMENT OF JUSTICE, ETUDES ET STATISTIQUES JUSTICE, 23, LA RESIDENCE EN ALTERNANCE DES ENFANTS DE PARENTS SEPARÉS (2003).

IV. The Inevitability of Shared Parenting

How are we to understand this new legislative emphasis on shared parenting and the equally profound changes in patterns of parenting after separation? The legislative changes are all the more remarkable because they have not gone unchallenged. In some jurisdictions in particular, custody laws have been the subject of great public controversy.[80] Politicians' interest in custody law reform has been galvanized by the pressure of groups representing fathers, while women's groups and feminist advocates have been prominent in opposing reforms such as presumptions in favor of joint custody and shared parenting laws.[81]

However, seeing issues of postseparation parenting primarily in terms of gender politics diverts attention from the cultural factors and attitudinal changes which have led to the pressure for shared parenting laws. Away from the dust of battle in legislatures and the rhetoric of law reviews and internet sites, it is evident that there has been a quiet sea-change occurring in the hearts and minds of the general population concerning parenting after separation, including those who are separated or divorced, at least in Australia. This change is buttressed by research findings and evidence of what children and young people themselves say that they want, which is consistent across countries.

A. Changes in Community Attitudes toward Parental Responsibility

The extent of change in community attitudes about parenting after separation is illustrated by Australian studies indicating that shared parenting has very widespread support in the Australian population, including in the divorced population. Significant legislative change occurred in Australia with the enactment of the Family Law Reform Act 1995, which was intended to bring about a much greater emphasis on shared parenting.[82] The Reform Act, particularly in its statement of objects and principles, emphasized the equal responsibility of both parents after divorce, and the child's right of contact with both parents unless it was contrary to the child's best interests.[83]

Around this time, the Australian Institute of Family Studies was commissioned to research Australian attitudes to parental responsibility.[84] The study found that the 1995 legislation, far from being just a response to pressure groups representing a minority of

[80] *See, e.g.*, in Canada, Nicholas Bala, *A Report from Canada's 'Gender War Zone': Reforming the Child Related Provisions of the Divorce Act*, 16 CAN. J. FAM. L.163 (1999). For an analysis of the views and influence of different pressure groups in Canada from the late 1960s to the mid-1980s, *see* Susan B. Boyd & Claire F. L. Young, *Who Influences Law Reform? Discourses on Motherhood and Fatherhood in Legislative Reform Debates in Canada*, 26 STUDIES IN LAW, POLITICS & SOCIETY 43 (2002).

[81] For an analysis of the competing arguments and rhetorical devices used by fathers' groups and mothers' groups respectively in the United States, *see* Scott Coltrane & Neal Hickman, *The Rhetoric of Rights and Needs: Moral Discourse in the Reform of Child Custody and Child Support Laws*, 39 SOC. PROB. 400 (1992). For an international discussion of the issues from a feminist perspective *see* CHILD CUSTODY AND THE POLITICS OF GENDER (Carole Smart & Selma Sevenhuijsen eds., 1989). *See also* Joyce A. Arditti & Katherine R. Allen, *Understanding Distressed Fathers' Perceptions of Legal and Relational Inequities Post-Divorce*, 31 FAM. & CONCIL. CTS. REV. 461 (1993).

[82] *See generally*, PATRICK PARKINSON & JULIET BEHRENS, AUSTRALIAN FAMILY LAW IN CONTEXT (3d ed., 2004); TOM ALTOBELLI, FAMILY LAW IN AUSTRALIA – PRINCIPLES & PRACTICE (2003); ANTHONY DICKEY, FAMILY LAW (4th ed. 2002).

[83] Family Law Act, 1975 § 60B (Austl.).

[84] KATHLEEN FUNDER & BRUCE SMYTH, EVALUATION OF THE IMPACT OF PART VII (1996). The research was conducted mostly in November 1995 with some further interviewing done in January 1996. *Id.* at 14. The legislation commenced

divorced fathers,[85] reflected views already held by the great majority of the population. When parents are married, 78 percent of Australians think children should always be cared for by both parents, sharing the duties and responsibilities for their care, welfare and development and another 20 percent think this should mostly be the case.[86] When parents are separated or divorced, assent is still strong for this proposition, although somewhat more conditional; 50 percent of Australians think this should always be the case and another 33 percent think this should mostly be the way parents care for their children under these conditions.[87] These were the views of respondents in the survey taken as a whole. But even among the subset of those who had experienced separation and divorce, the results were very similar.[88]

B. The Benefits of Closeness to Nonresident Parents

The desirability of shared parenting is also supported by research on the outcomes for children of divorce. While there is a large body of research on outcomes of divorce for children based on psychological testing that has failed to show that more frequent contact with the nonresident parent in itself leads to improved well-being for the children of divorce,[89] children do benefit from a close relationship with the nonresident parent. In a 1999 metaanalysis of sixty-three prior studies on parent-child visitation, Amato and Gilbreth confirmed that frequency of contact in itself does not appear to be associated with better outcomes for children.[90] However, emotional closeness, and in particular, "authoritative parenting," is highly beneficial to children.[91] Authoritative parenting includes helping with homework, talking about problems, providing emotional support to children, praising children's accomplishments, and disciplining children for misbehavior. The researchers concluded that "how often fathers see children is less important than what fathers do when they are with their children."[92]

Parental separation and divorce is a significant risk factor for children both in terms of long-term emotional well-being and educational performance.[93] Greater involvement of fathers in postseparation parenting has at least the potential to ameliorate these risks, particularly the risk of depression and other indications of emotional distress. Adolescents who have no contact with their nonresident parent, and those who have infrequent contact,

in July 1996. *See also* Kathleen Funder, *The Australian Family Law Reform Act 1995 and Public Attitudes to Parental Responsibility*, 12 INT'L J. L. POL'Y & FAM. 47 (1998).

85 For this view of the etiology of the Act *see, e.g.*, HELEN RHOADES, REGINA GRAYCAR & MARGARET HARRISON, THE FAMILY LAW REFORM ACT 1995: THE FIRST THREE YEARS 23 (2000).

86 FUNDER & SMYTH, *supra* n. 84, at Table 3.1.7.

87 *Id.* at Table 3.1.10.

88 *Id.* at Tables 3.7.8, 3.7.9, 3.7.12, 3.7.15, 3.7.17, 3.7.18.

89 *See, e.g.*, SUSAN B. BOYD, CHILD CUSTODY, LAW, AND WOMEN'S WORK (2003).

90 Paul Amato & Joan Gilbreth, *Nonresident Fathers and Children's Well-being: a Meta-analysis*, 61 J. MARRIAGE & FAM. 557 (1999).

91 Authoritative parenting refers to a style of parenting which is neither authoritarian nor permissive. *See* Diana Baumrind, *Authoritarian v. Authoritative Control*, 3 ADOLESCENCE 255 (1968). *See also* E. MAVIS HETHERINGTON & JOHN KELLY, FOR BETTER OR FOR WORSE: DIVORCE RECONSIDERED 127–130 (2002); ELIZABETH SEDDON, CREATIVE PARENTING AFTER SEPARATION 26–28 (2003). Further research is needed to determine what aspects of authoritative parenting by a nonresident parent after separation are particularly beneficial to children and young people. Susan Stewart, *Nonresident Parenting and Adolescent Adjustment: The Quality of Nonresident Father–child Interaction*, 24 J. FAM. ISSUES 217 (2003).

92 Amato & Gilbreth, *supra* n. 90, at 569.

93 PAUL AMATO & ALAN BOOTH, A GENERATION AT RISK (1997); Paul Amato, *The Consequences of Divorce for Adults and Children*, 62 J. MARRIAGE & FAM. 1269 (2000); Jane Elliott & Martin Richards, *Children and Divorce: Educational Performance and Behaviour Before and After Parental Separation*, 5 INT'L J.L. & FAM. 258 (1991).

have been shown to be more depressed than those in frequent-visit and married families.[94] Although the research evidence is not unequivocal, closeness to nonresident fathers has also been found to be related to less depression in adolescents, better school performance, and a perception that their worst problem was less severe, independently of the effect of closeness to the mother.[95] Measures to encourage a continuing relationship between nonresident parents and their children should therefore be seen as highly desirable in the absence of high levels of ongoing conflict between the parents, irrespective of the division of roles between the parents when the marriage was intact.[96]

These generalizations about what is likely to benefit children and young people after parental separation and divorce must, however, be qualified by the extensive evidence that serious ongoing conflict between the parents after separation is likely to be harmful for children.[97] There is evidence, for example, that contact with nonresident fathers decreases boys' behavior problems when parental conflict is low but increases their behavior problems when levels of conflict are high.[98] In particular, when children are caught up as messengers or spies in these conflicts, contact may impact negatively on children's well-being.[99] The risk of ongoing emotional harm to children is particularly great where the relationship between the parents after separation is characterized by ongoing violence.[100] These research findings provide strong support for the PRINCIPLES' provisions

[94] Bonnie L. Barber, *Support and Advice from Married and Divorced Fathers: Linkages to Adolescent Adjustment*, 43 FAM. REL. 433 (1994).

[95] BUCHANAN ET AL., *supra* n. 46, 193, 204 (Fig.10.6) (1996). Buchanan et al. could not say whether a better relationship with the nonresidential parent leads to better adjustment in the adolescent, or whether adolescents who are better adjusted maintain better relationships with their nonresident parent. They theorized that both processes are at work (*Id.* at 198). They also found that the better adjustment of adolescents in dual residence families compared to single residence families was a reflection of the level of closeness they felt to both parents (*Id.* at 204–5). *See also* Susan Stewart, *Nonresident Parenting and Adolescent Adjustment: The Quality of Nonresident Father-child Interaction*, 24 J. FAM. ISSUES 217 (2003) (closeness to nonresident fathers after separation associated with significantly less emotional distress in young people independently of the effect of closeness to the resident mother). *But see* Frank F. Furstenberg, S. Philip Morgan & Paul D. Allison, *Paternal Participation and Children's Well-being After Marital Dissolution*, 52 AM. SOC. REV. 695 (1987) (closeness to fathers was not associated with lower levels of delinquency or distress, although the association between emotional closeness and children's reports of dissatisfaction approached significance); ELAINE WELSH, ANN BUCHANAN, EIRINI FLOURI AND JANE LEWIS, 'INVOLVED' FATHERING AND CHILD WELL-BEING: FATHERS' INVOLVEMENT WITH SECONDARY SCHOOL AGE CHILDREN (2004) (no relationship found between nonresident parent involvement and young people's well-being).

[96] For reviews of the literature *see* JAN PRYOR & BRYAN ROGERS, CHILDREN IN CHANGING FAMILIES: LIFE AFTER PARENTAL SEPARATION (2001); Joan B. Kelly, *Legal and Educational Interventions for Families in Residence and Contact Disputes*, 15 AUSTL. J. FAM. L. 92 (2001); Robert Emery, *Post-divorce Family Life for Children: An Overview of Research and Some Implications for Policy*, *in* THE POST-DIVORCE FAMILY: CHILDREN, PARENTING AND SOCIETY (Ross A. Thompson & Paul R. Amato eds., 1999); Michael Lamb, *Noncustodial Fathers and Their Impact on the Children of Divorce*, *in* THE POST-DIVORCE FAMILY: CHILDREN, PARENTING AND SOCIETY (Ross A. Thompson & Paul R. Amato eds., 1999).

[97] Michael E. Lamb, Kathleen J. Stemberg & Ross A. Thompson, *The Effects of Divorce and Custody Arrangements on Children's Behavior, Development, and Adjustment*, 35 FAM. & CONCIL. CTS. REV. 393 (1997); Jennifer McIntosh, *Enduring Conflict in Parental Separation:Pathways of Impact on Child Development*, 9 J. FAM. STUD. 63 (2003).

[98] Paul Amato & Sandra J. Rezac, *Contact with Nonresident Parents, Interparental Conflict, and Children's Behavior*, 15 J. FAM. ISSUES 191 (1994). The findings in relation to girls were in the same direction, but did not reach significance. *Id.* at 200.

[99] Christy M. Buchanan, Eleanor E. Maccoby & Sanford M. Dornbusch, *Caught Between Parents: Adolescents' Experiences in Divorced Homes*, 62 CHILD DEV. 1008 (1991).

[100] Catherine Ayoub, Robin Deutch & Andronicki Maraganore, *Emotional Distress in Children of High-Conflict Divorce. The Impact of Marital Conflict and Violence*, 37 FAM. & CONCIL. CTS. REV. 297 (1999); Claire Sturge & Danya Glasser, *Contact and Domestic Violence – The Experts' Court Report*, 30 FAM. L. 615 (2000); PETER JAFFE, NANCY LEMON & SAMANTHA POISSON, CHILD CUSTODY AND DOMESTIC VIOLENCE: A CALL FOR SAFETY AND ACCOUNTABILITY (2003). Recent research, however, has demonstrated the importance of distinguishing between different types or

that limit the parental responsibility of a parent where there has been a history of violence or abuse.[101]

While frequency of contact is not in itself beneficial to children, some degree of frequency of contact is a precondition for the kind of parenting that is beneficial to children.[102] When fathers have only brief or relatively infrequent contact with their children, they are less likely to feel comfortable about disciplining their children and engaging in other aspects of involved, authoritative parenting. Instead, they tend to make the visits "fun" and entertaining so that the children want to continue the visits.[103] A minimum amount of time is necessary to foster and maintain a "real parenting" relationship instead of merely a visiting relationship, whether it is through frequent and regular contact arrangements[104] or sustained periods of visiting during school holidays.[105] Regular overnight stays play an important role in fostering emotional closeness between children and nonresident parents.[106] Indeed, new thinking is emerging about the value of overnight stays with the nonresident parent even for infants, with proponents arguing that this will promote stronger attachments.[107]

The PRINCIPLES may provide a basis on which parents who have been involved in their children's lives prior to separation have enough time after separation to engage in authoritative parenting. However, this is in spite of, rather than because of, the past caretaking standard. Under the PRINCIPLES, many nonresident parents would maintain a parental role in their children's lives only because a rule of statewide application is allowed to override the past caretaking standard.

C. Children's Voices

Research on what children and young people say from their own experience fortifies the case for rethinking conventional notions of custody and visitation.[108] Recent studies in

contexts of violent behavior: Michael P. Johnson & Kathleen J. Ferraro, *Research on Domestic Violence in the 1990s: Making Distinctions*, 62 J. MARRIAGE & FAM. 948 (2000).

101 PRINCIPLES § 2.11.

102 Judy Dunn, *Contact and Children's Perspectives on Parental Relationships, in* CHILDREN AND THEIR FAMILIES, *supra* n. 65, at 15 (more contact associated with closer relationships with nonresident fathers).

103 As Thompson and Wyatt argue: "Divorced from the routines, settings and everyday activities of the child's usual life, a visiting relationship with the nonresidential parent quickly becomes constrained and artificial, making it easier for fathers and their children to drift apart as their lives become increasingly independent." Ross A. Thompson & J. M. Wyatt, *Values, Policy, and Research on Divorce: Seeking Fairness for Children, in* THE POST-DIVORCE FAMILY, *supra* n. 96, at 222. The artificiality of the contact relationship may help to explain why some fathers disengage from their children after separation and divorce: Bob Simpson, Julie Jessop & Peter McCarthy, *Fathers After Divorce, in* CHILDREN AND THEIR FAMILIES *supra* n. 65, at 201.

104 William V. Fabricius, *Listening to Children of Divorce: New Findings that Diverge from Wallerstein, Lewis and Blakeslee*, 52 FAM. REL. 385, 389 (Fig. 3) (2003).

105 Eleanor E. Maccoby et al., *Postdivorce Roles of Mothers and Fathers in the Lives of Their Children*, 7 J. FAM. PSYCH. 33 (1993). *See also* BUCHANAN ET AL., *supra* n. 46.

106 Bruce Smyth & Anna Ferro, *When the Difference is Night and Day: Parent-child Contact After Separation*, 63 FAM. MATTERS 54 (2002).

107 Joan B. Kelly & Michael E. Lamb, *Using Child Development Research to Make Appropriate Custody and Access Decisions for Young Children*, 38 FAM. & CONCIL. CTS. REV. 297 (2000); Richard A. Warshak, *Blanket Restrictions: Overnight Contact Between Parents and Young Children*, 38 FAM. & CONCIL. CTS. REV. 422 (2000). For the debates on this issue see the articles and rejoinders in response to these articles published in the Family Court Review in 2001–02. *See also* Judith T. Younger, *Post-Divorce Visitation for Infants and Young Children – the Myths and the Psychological Unknowns*, 36 FAM. L. Q. 195 (2002).

108 There is now a substantial literature on the importance of hearing children's voices in working out postseparation parenting arrangements. *See, e.g.*, Carol Smart, Amanda Wade, & Bren Neale, *Objects of Concern? – Children and*

Australia and New Zealand have shown that substantial numbers of children and young people would like to see their nonresident parents more than they do. In Australia, a study of sixty young people aged twelve to nineteen who had experienced their parents' separation a few years earlier found that 50 percent said that they did not have enough time alone with the nonresident parent.[109] In contrast, most young people (72 percent) said they had enough time alone with their resident parent.[110] A New Zealand study, which interviewed 107 children and young people from 73 families who had experienced divorce, found that 52 percent of the children felt that the levels of contact were about right, 34.7 percent wanted to see the other parent more often, and 11 percent wanted to see the other parent much more often. Only 2 percent wanted less time with the other parent.[111]

This is consistent with earlier research in Australia,[112] Britain,[113] Canada,[114] and the United States.[115] It is also consistent with the available evidence of young adults' views in the United States. Professors Laumann-Billings and Emery found that young adults who lived in sole custody arrangements expressed more feelings of loss, and more often viewed their lives through the lens of divorce, compared to those young adults who grew up in more shared physical custody arrangements.[116] In another study, Fabricius and Hall interviewed students in psychology classes at Arizona State University over a four-year period about their experiences of parental divorce and their views on what would have been the best custody and visitation arrangements.[117] Participating in the study were 344 men and 485 women. The researchers found that both men and women wanted significantly more time with their fathers than they actually had, although men reported wanting more time with their fathers than women.[118] When asked what they thought would be the best living arrangement for children after divorce, 70 percent said an equal time arrangement was optimal. There were no significant differences between men and women in this response.[119]

This is not to say that an equal time arrangement is the optimal arrangement for post-separation parenting. In Fabricius and Hall's study, only just over 20 percent of respondents wanted equal time given their particular family circumstances.[120] In that study, 93 percent of the eighty young adults who had actually lived in an equal time arrangement believed

Divorce, 11 Child & Fam. L. Q. 365 (1999); Megan Gollop, Anne B. Smith & Nicola J. Taylor, *Children's Involvement in Custody and Access Arrangements After Parental Separation*, 12 Child & Fam. L. Q. 383 (2000); Ian Butler et al., *Children's Involvement in Their Parents' Divorce: Implications for Practice*, 16 Children & Society 89 (2002); Carol Smart, *From Children's Shoes to Children's Voices*, 40 Fam. Ct. Rev. 307 (2002).

[109] P. Parkinson, J. Cashmore & J. Single, *Adolescents' Views on the Fairness of Parenting and Financial Arrangements After Separation*, 43 Fam. Ct. Rev. 429 (2005).

[110] Id. This did not differ according to whether they lived mostly with their mother or father, or by their age or gender.

[111] Anne Smith & Megan Gollop, *Children's Perspectives on Access Visits*, 2001 Butterworths Fam. L. J. 259; *see also* Gollop, Smith & Taylor, *supra* n. 108.

[112] M. McDonald, Children's Perceptions of Access and Their Adjustment in the Post-Separation Period, (Family Court Research Report No. 9, 1990).

[113] Y. Walczak & S. Burns, Divorce: The Child's Point of View (1984). *See also* A. Mitchell, Children in the Middle: Living Through Divorce (1985).

[114] R. Neugebauer, *Divorce, Custody and Visitation: The Child's Point of View*, 12 J. Divorce 153 (1989).

[115] Judith S. Wallerstein & Joan B. Kelly, Surviving The Breakup (1980); Buchanan et al., *supra* n. 46.

[116] Lisa Laumann-Billings & Robert Emery, *Distress Among Young Adults From Divorced Families*, 14 J. Fam. Psychol. 671 (2000).

[117] Fabricius & Hall, *supra*, n. 56.

[118] *Id.* at 451.

[119] *Id.* at 453–4.

[120] *Id.* at 457. It was more common for respondents to indicate that they would have liked to have lived with their mother while seeing their father a lot of the time. *Id.* at 452.

it was best.[121] However, British research has found that children in equal time parenting arrangements had a more diverse range of reactions, with some finding the arrangement oppressive and constricting, particularly if the parents were rigid in maintaining schedules and not focused on the needs of the children.[122] There is also the risk that children's support for an equal time arrangement has more to do with their concern to be fair to each parent than to be fair to themselves.[123]

As noted previously, the PRINCIPLES are less than clear on what the operative rule should be when the past caretaking of the parents has been approximately equal. One view is that the parents should have equal custodial responsibility. That may be fair as between the parents, but what if it is not fair to the child? The PRINCIPLES so constrain judicial discretion that it may be difficult for a judge, applying the law faithfully, to avoid ordering equal custodial responsibility even in the face of evidence that it is not an optimal arrangement for the child.

Children may also speak against extensive contact in certain situations. Some children do not want more time with their nonresident parent. Children may blame one parent for the marriage breakdown, or find that the nonresident parent does not do enough interesting things with them. Some fathers do not make enough time for their children because of the demands of work or new relationships. Others cannot be more involved because of the tyranny of distance. Listening to children involves listening to their individual needs and views, without romanticizing the parent-child relationship in such a way that it is assumed that children want to have a close relationship with the nonresident parent. Listening to children also involves being sensitive to their needs as circumstances change. An alternating residence arrangement may work well at a certain stage of a child's life but not as he or she grows older.[124] The ALI's past caretaking standard may be overridden to the extent necessary to accommodate the firm and reasonable preferences of a child who has reached a specific age, set by a uniform rule of statewide application.[125] However, this exception to the rule may be insufficiently flexible to ensure that children's voices influence the outcome of cases.

While children's voices do not speak in favor of any one custody rule or standard, they do indicate that traditional patterns of visitation are utterly inconsistent with the needs of most children as a general rule. While the most practical and sensible arrangement usually will be to have a primary care giver with whom the children live the majority of the time, children's interests are best served if we can find ways of encouraging active parenting by both parents following separation,[126] at least where the nonresident parent wants this and there are no concerns about the mother's or children's safety. Although the PRINCIPLES may allow for this through the statutory provision setting a presumptive amount of custodial time for an involved parent, they certainly do not encourage it.

[121] *Id.* at 454. The number of students who had lived in equal time arrangements is reported in a later review of the research. William V. Fabricius, *Listening to Children of Divorce: New Findings that Diverge from Wallerstein, Lewis and Blakeslee*, 52 FAM. REL. 385, 387 (2003).

[122] CAROL SMART, BREN NEALE & AMANDA WADE, THE CHANGING EXPERIENCE OF CHILDHOOD: FAMILIES AND DIVORCE (2001); Bren Neale, Jennifer Flowerdew & Carol Smart, *Drifting Towards Shared Residence?*, 33 FAM. L. 904 (2003).

[123] Parkinson, Cashmore & Single, *supra* n. 109.

[124] Neale, Flowerdew & Smart, *supra* n. 122.

[125] PRINCIPLES § 2.08(1)(b).

[126] Marsha B. Freeman, *Reconnecting the Family: A Need for Sensible Visitation Schedules for Children of Divorce*, 22 WHITTIER L. REV. 779 (2001).

D. Changes in the Attitudes of Fathers

It is clear that the major reason for the shift in favor of shared parenting arrangements is pressure from fathers for more time with their children. Despite the rhetoric of equality, more fathers want to assist in the parenting role after separation than to take over as primary care giver.[127] Over time, there have been significant changes in the ideal of fatherhood, with a greater emphasis on emotional closeness and active involvement with the children.[128] This has led to greater involvement in parenting in intact relationships, with a consequential impact upon fathers' attitudes toward postseparation parenting.[129]

This can be seen in research in a number of countries. For example, Fabricius and Hall found in interviews with college students who had experienced parental divorce that both men and women reported that their fathers had wanted more time with them than they had or their mothers wanted them to have. Forty percent reported that their fathers had wanted them to spend equal time or more with them.[130] There is similar evidence from Australia. In one study, 41 percent of fathers contacted in a random telephone survey of divorced parents in 1997 indicated that they were dissatisfied with the residence arrangements for the children.[131] Two-thirds of this group said they wanted to be the primary residence parent, and the remaining third wanted to have equal time with their children. On average the interview occurred about five years after the divorce. The study also indicated a very high level of dissatisfaction with levels of contact. In a study of a nationally representative sample of separated parents in Australia, interviewed in 2001, three-fourths of the nonresident fathers indicated dissatisfaction with the amount of contact they had.[132] In the study, 57 percent of fathers indicated that they had nowhere near enough time with their children and a further 18 percent said they did not have quite enough time with their children.

This does not mean that there has been a complete change in fathers' attitudes toward postseparation parenting. There remain a large number of fathers living apart from their children who do not see them often. In the United States, the picture is relatively consistent over time. For example, a national survey in the United States conducted in 1987–88 by Seltzer found that almost 60 percent of nonresident fathers saw their children less than once per month, according to mothers' reports.[133] Her findings were consistent with other

[127] Carl Bertoia & Janice Drakich, *The Fathers' Rights Movement: Contradictions in Rhetoric and Practice*, 14 J. Fam. Issues 592 (1993) (presenting interviews with members of fathers' groups in Canada).

[128] Graham Allan & Graham Crow, Families, Households And Society (2001).

[129] Carol Smart, *Towards an Understanding of Family Change: Gender Conflict and Children's Citizenship*, 17 Austl. J. Fam. L. 20 (2003).

[130] Fabricius & Hall, *supra* n. 56.

[131] Bruce Smyth, Grania Sheehan, & Belinda Fehlberg, *Patterns of Parenting After Divorce: A Pre-Reform Act Benchmark Study*, 15 Austl. J. Fam. L. 114 (2001).

[132] Patrick Parkinson & Bruce Smyth, *Satisfaction and Dissatisfaction with Father-Child Contact Arrangements in Australia*, 16 Child & Fam. L. Q. 289 (2004). The greatest levels of satisfaction for both mothers and fathers were with shared parenting arrangements. The data came from the Household Income and Labour Dynamics in Australia survey (HILDA). Interviews were conducted with 13,969 members of 7,682 households. It is not only fathers who want more time with their children. Mothers also want to see more contact between the children and their fathers. In this study, although the majority of resident mothers expressed satisfaction with the contact arrangements, 25% reported that they thought there was nowhere near enough father-child contact taking place, and a further 15% said there was not quite enough contact. Only 5% thought that there was too much contact.

[133] Judith A. Seltzer, *Relationships between Fathers and Children Who Live Apart: The Father's Role after Separation*, 53 J. Marriage & Fam. 79 (1991). She concluded that "for most children who are born outside of marriage or whose parents divorce, the father role is defined as much by omission as commission." *Id.* at 97.

general population studies in the United States conducted in the 1980s and early 1990s that revealed a pattern of disengagement by a majority of nonresident fathers over a period of years.[134] Another study reporting on data collected from young people between 1994 and 1996 in the National Longitudinal Study of Adolescent Health found a similar level of disengagement. Sixty-one percent of these young people saw their fathers less than once a month.[135]

However, as the Australian research shows, disengagement does not necessarily mean disinterest.[136] There have been similar findings in Britain. In one study, 76 percent of fathers who never saw their children were dissatisfied with this.[137]

One explanation for the growth in fathers' desire to be actively involved in their children's lives after separation is that it represents a reaction to the disappointment about failed adult relationships. German sociologists Beck and Beck-Gernsheim observe that following marriage breakdown:

> The child becomes the last remaining, irrevocable, unique primary love object. Partners come and go, but the child stays. Everything one vainly hoped to find in the relationship with one's partner is sought in or directed at the child. If men and women have increasing difficulty in getting on with one another, the child acquires a monopoly on companionship, sharing feelings, enjoying spontaneous physical contact in a way which has otherwise become uncommon and seems risky. Here an atavistic social experience can be celebrated and cultivated which in a society of individuals is increasingly rare, although everyone craves it. Doting on children, pushing them on to the centre of the stage . . . and fighting for custody during and after divorce are all symptoms of this. The child becomes the final alternative to loneliness, a bastion against the vanishing chances of loving and being loved. It is a private way of 'putting the magic back' into life to make up for general disenchantment. The birth-rate may be declining but children have never been more important.[138]

To some extent then, the new focus on parenting after separation reflects nonresident parents' desire for meaning and connection. The cultural battle over postseparation parenting reflects deep-seated emotions and values. Of course, as feminist scholars have pointed out, there is a difference between caring about and caring for children, and the majority of the "caring for" in parenting after divorce remains a female responsibility.[139] Yet "caring about" matters to children. On the whole, the greater willingness of nonresident fathers to be involved in their children's lives is a very positive development in terms of children's well-being.

[134] Frank Furstenberg et al., *The Life Course of Children of Divorce: Marital Disruption and Parental Contact*, 48 Am. Soc. Rev. 656 (1983); Judith A. Seltzer & Suzanne M. Bianchi, *Children's Contact with Absent Parents*, 50 J. Marriage & Fam. 663 (1988); J. Munsch, J. Woodward & N. Darling, *Children's Perceptions of Their Relationships with Coresiding and Non-Coresiding Fathers*, 23 J. Div. & Remarriage 39 (1995). Research with divorced parents, however, presented a different picture, with most fathers remaining involved in their children's lives in the first few years after divorce. Maccoby et al., *supra* n. 105.

[135] Stewart, *supra* n. 95.

[136] Parkinson & Smyth, *supra* n.132. In this study, only 20% of those fathers with no contact, and only 8% of the group that saw the child for 1–17 nights or days per year considered that the level of contact was about right.

[137] B. Simpson, P. McCarthy & J. Walker, Being There: Fathers After Divorce 32 (1995).

[138] U. Beck & E. Beck-Gernsheim, The Normal Chaos of Love 37 (Mark Ritter & Jane Wiebel translation, 1995).

[139] *See, e.g.*, Carol Smart, *Losing the Struggle for Another Voice: The Case of Family Law*, 18 Dalhousie L. J. 173 (1995).

E. Governments and Shared Parenting

There is a final reason why shared parenting legislation seems inevitable. Just as governments were once persuaded under the tutelage of the Church[140] to keep marriages together through laws prohibiting or restricting divorce, now they are inclined to keep families together after separation.

Why is it that numerous governments in the western world have embraced the ideology of shared parenting? The influences on government are no doubt many and various. Pressure groups, mainly those of fathers, have certainly played their role in making family law reform an issue.[141] Shared parenting offers an answer to the difficult politics of divorce. It speaks in the language of compromise in contrast to the "winner takes all" concept of custody. It draws upon the cultural persuasiveness of the idea of equality between men and women. Shared parenting, if it can be made to work, also reflects widely held beliefs about what is desirable after separation.

While all these factors have no doubt assisted the passage of laws promoting shared parenting, one rationale has made shared parenting virtually inevitable. This is the financial desirability, from the taxpayers' point of view, of privatizing maintenance obligations, especially the support of children, given the growth in the number of one-parent families.[142] This has occurred not only as a consequence of the rise in divorce rates following the no-fault divorce revolution, but also because of the massive increase in the numbers of children born outside marriage in Western countries.[143] Many of these children are born to cohabiting couples, but since the rate of breakdown of cohabitating relationships is so much greater than that for marriages,[144] a substantial proportion of these children will experience parental separation.[145]

The support of children provides a compelling, and arguably the only justification, for ongoing income transfers between nonmarried couples following separation. As Professor Dewar notes: "Parenthood is a way of tying men into the non-marital family."[146] Concern about the feminization of poverty has led to greater efforts at child support enforcement in particular. If nonresident parents are not contributing to their children's support, the State

[140] For a history, *see* MARY ANN GLENDON, STATE, LAW & FAMILY (1977).

[141] William C. Smith, *Dads Want Their Day: Fathers Charge Legal Bias Towards Moms Hamstrings Them as Full-Time Parents*, 89 A.B.A.J. 38 (2003). In Australia, *see* Miranda Kaye & Julia Tolmie, *Fathers' Rights Groups in Australia*, 12 AUSTL. J. FAM. L. 19 (1998). In Britain, *see* Richard Collier, *'Coming Together?': Post-heterosexuality, Masculine Crisis and the New Men's Movement*, 4 FEM. LEG. STUD. 3 (1996).

[142] Stephen Parker & Margaret Harrison, *Child Support in Australia: Children's Rights or Public Interest?*, 5 INT'L J. L. & FAM. 24 (1991).

[143] In 1998, two-thirds of births in Iceland and half or more of births in Norway and Sweden were out of wedlock. In the United States, the proportion was one-third: Stephanie J. Ventura & Christine A. Bachrach, *Nonmarital Child bearing in the United States, 1940–99*, 48 NAT. VITAL STATS. REP. 16 (2000), *available at* http://www.cdc.gov/nchs/data/nvsr/nvsr48/nvs48_16.pdf (last visited March 5, 2006). This is a relatively new phenomenon. There has been a dramatic rise, in many countries, in the numbers of children born exnuptially. In the United States, the percentage of births to unmarried women increased from 14.8 percent in 1976 to 33.0 percent in 1999. *Id.* at Table 1. In Britain, the rate of increase has been much greater. The proportion of births outside of marriage rose from 9.2% in 1976 to 40.6 percent in 2002: *available at* http://www.statistics.gov.uk/STATBASE/Expodata/Spreadsheets/D8264.xls (last visited March 5, 2006).

[144] *See* Garrison, this volume (summarizing research on rates of dissolution).

[145] Larry L. Bumpass & Hsien-Hen Lu, *Trends in Cohabitation and Implications for Children's Family Contexts in the United States*, 54 POPULATION STUDIES 29 (2000); *Robin Fretwell Wilson, Evaluating Marriage: Does Marriage Matter to the Nurturing of Children?*, 42 SAN DIEGO L. REV. 847 (2005).

[146] John Dewar, *Family Law and its Discontents*, 14 INT'L J. L. POL'Y & FAM. 59, 63 (2000).

is left as the default provider for low-income, female-headed households with children, placing a considerable strain on welfare budgets.[147]

Whereas courts were once willing to allow nonresident parents to prioritize the needs of second families over first families,[148] the massive rise in the numbers of first families dependent on welfare benefits made it impossible to sustain a policy of allowing nonresident fathers to be divorced from financial commitments to children of former relationships.

This need to ensure child support is paid does not have to be connected with shared parenting laws, but the evidence from many studies is that there is an association between regularity of contact and child support compliance, giving governments a motivation for encouraging continued father-child involvement.[149] Furthermore, it is difficult for governments to regularize the payment of child support while turning a deaf ear to nonresident parents' complaints about the little time they are able to spend with their children. This has become a driver for law reform.

V. Conclusion

One of the surprising elements of the PRINCIPLES' custody and visitation provisions is the lack of attention to the detail of applying the past caretaker standard in practice. The commentary and illustrations confuse matters more than they illuminate. Any criticisms of the past caretaker standard must be qualified therefore by the observation that the ALI has left much to the discretion of legislatures and trial judges about how the PRINCIPLES should be applied in practice.

What ought to be clear from this analysis is that the past caretaker standard is a much better approach to determining who should be the primary care giver, especially for young children, than it is as a means of determining how much contact the other parent should have. The past caretaker standard has an appearance of fairness between the parents. However, in its application to role-divided marriages, the standard may be insensitive to the commitment that the primary earning parent has shown or would show to the children, and the bond of love between them.

Even if the rule were fair as between the parents, that would not be enough to commend it. What matters most is that the standard is fair to children and that the law is aligned with social science knowledge about what is likely to benefit children in the aftermath of separation. It is not obvious that the past caretaking standard is well aligned with that knowledge base or that it is sufficiently sensitive to the needs of children following parental separation.

As a general principle, the idea is sound that the more involved a parent has been with his or her children in the intact relationship, the more that parenting should be shared after

[147] In Australia, according to the 2001 census, 18% of children under 15 years (over 660,000 children) lived in a household with no employed parent, with over one-half (61%) of these living in one-parent families. In 83.5% of one-parent families where the parent was not in the workforce, that parent was not looking for work. Australian Bureau of Statistics, *Families with no Employed Parent, in* AUSTRALIAN SOCIAL TRENDS (2004) *available at* http://www.abs.gov.au (last visited March 5, 2006).

[148] Mavis Maclean, *The Making of the Child Support Act of 1991: Policy Making at the Intersection of Law and Social Policy*, 21 J. L. & SOC. 505 (1994). *See also* Carol Smart, *Wishful Thinking and Harmful Tinkering? Sociological Reflections on Family Policy*, 26 J. SOC. POL'Y. 301, 311–15 (1997).

[149] Judith A. Seltzer et al., *Family Ties After Divorce: the Relationship Between Visiting and Paying Child Support*, 51 J. MARRIAGE & FAM. 1013 (1989); Bruce Smyth & Belinda Fehlberg, *Child Support and Parent-child Contact*, 57 FAM. MATTERS 20 (2000).

separation if the parents' circumstances permit it. Whether or not the parenting should be substantially shared ought to depend on a range of factors beyond past caretaking, including the relationship between the parents and the perceived needs of the child. If the past caretaking standard is thus reduced to a general principle, to be weighed against countervailing factors, it is entirely reasonable. However, expressed as a rule which aims to focus on past caretaking as the normal basis for postseparation parenting, the past caretaking standard does not seem adequately attuned to the degree of change in parents' circumstances that occurs following separation, to the needs of children, or to the direction that the law of parenting after separation is taking both in the United States and in other countries.

The author would like to thank Edwina Dunn, Severine Kupfer, Tharini Mudaliar, Annett Schmiedel and Kari Theobald for their excellent research assistance and translation work.

25 Compensating Gain and Loss in Marriage: A Scandinavian Comment on the ALI Principles

Tone Sverdrup

Introduction

Traditionally, both marital property rules and maintenance rules had their justifications in broader notions of "community," "solidarity," "equal treatment," and "marital partnership." As long as divorce occurred rarely and most families consisted of only one breadwinner, society could live with such broad justifications. Both spouses were presumed to have made a balanced effort in this community of living. In the case of divorce for such families, the stay-at-home wife was obviously in need of support, and since the norm was life-long marriage – the husband was expected to take responsibility for that support. However, because these justifications are so broad and vague, it is not always clear what constitutes the essence of the justification: Is the core justification one of need – "from each according to his abilities, to each according to his needs," or one of desert, according to the spouses' work efforts or their contributions to the surplus acquired during marriage? In society at large, these two factors are often contradictory: Persons who contribute the most in the form of taxes have, as a rule relatively, few unsatisfied needs and consequently receive little in return from, for example, social security. In marriage, the two factors overlap more often. Normally, the reason one of the spouses, usually the wife, has a greater need for money is that she cares for the children and does the housework[1], and not because her actual contributions are small. She has made a non-financial work effort, and this is the very reason for her need for marital property or financial support from her husband. Because both justifications often support a duty in the same case, the basic conflict between the two criteria in marriage often escape notice. Nevertheless, a conflict exists, and comes more to the surface in modern marriages. Both divisions, according to need and according to desert, are examples of so-called distributive justice, where a benefit (marital property or future earning capacity) is allocated according to the relative merits of the spouses. One could, however, look at justification from a different angle and ask whether one of the spouses has contributed to the other spouse's accumulation of wealth or earning capacity during marriage, and *therefore* is entitled to a share of his or her assets or income in return – so-called corrective justice.[2] Due to the fact that the benefits in marriage come from, and

[1] In this chapter, housework without child care is named "housework" or "household chores." A generic term for child care and/or housework is "domestic work" or "domestic labor." A person who performs domestic work is named "homemaker," "housewife." or "domestic worker."

[2] For a distinction between these Aristotelian conceptions of justice, *see e.g.*, E. J. Weinrib, The Idea of Private Law, Cambridge, Mass.: Harvard University Press, 56–114, T (1995); Eckhoff, Justice. Its Determinants in Social Interaction, 3–10, 206 Rotterdam University Press, (1974).

are distributed among, the same two parties, the distinction between distributive and corrective justice can be diffused in practice. The idea of corrective justice, however, is marked by the fact that one transfer is the reason (or part of the reason) for the other transfer. This construction of equality highlights the interaction between the spouses.

As the number of divorces increased dramatically in the 1970s, it was no longer self-evident that one spouse should bear any economic responsibility for the other after divorce. During this time, women started to take up paid work on a larger scale. In many countries, they were expected to be self-sufficient and to support themselves after divorce, even though they had not done so during marriage. In this situation, there was a need for more explicit and precise justifications for why marriage should impose economic duties on the parties after divorce.

Today, the trend in legal policy is to replace the broader terms of solidarity, community, and so forth, by more explicit justifications, such as compensation for contributions made during marriage and for losses suffered. The fundamental justification for the division of property is now more closely linked to the contributions of the spouses than it is to the broader concepts of solidarity or community. In the majority of European countries, property is divided equally according to fixed rules, and many of these countries exclude the value of inheritance, gifts, and premarital assets from the property subject to division. The most striking common feature of the three items exempt from equal division is that the other spouse is not presumed to have contributed to the property's acquisition. In other words, contribution appears to be the essence of the justification. When the property subject to division is limited to assets acquired during marriage, the option is open to conceive transfers between spouses on divorce in the perspective of corrective justice. In many countries in Southern and Eastern Europe exclusion of the value of inheritance, gifts, and premarital assets from equal division has long been the case. Germany introduced a property regime that excluded such items after the Second World War ("Zugewinngemeinschaft") and Norway introduced a similar system in 1991. In the Netherlands, Denmark, Sweden, and Finland, all property is subject to equal division, but such limitations have been discussed in these countries as well.[3] In England, Wales, and Ireland, the court has discretionary power to divide all property however defined upon the termination of marriage. However, one can even trace the tendencies to exclude inheritance, gifts, and premarital assets from division in English law in recent cases,[4] as well as in the United States.[5]

The PRINCIPLES also evidence this move from distributive justice, where "need" and "desert" are important criteria, to corrective justice, where "contribution" "gain" and "loss" are the key words. An equal division rule is proposed in the PRINCIPLES Section 4.09(1). Under Section 4.03, premarital assets, as well as gifts and inheritance, are not subject to division – such assets are characterized as separate property. Chapter 5 of the PRINCIPLES governing compensatory spousal payments also follows this development. The remedy it provides is recharacterized as compensation for loss rather than relief of need.[6] However, the ALI is reluctant to justify these property and compensatory rules by the parties' contributions.

[3] As regards the Scandinavian countries, *see* A. AGELL, *Nordisk äktenskapsrätt* (Nordic Marriage Law) Nord 2003:2, Copenhagen, 404–12 (2003).

[4] Notably White v. White [2001] 1 AC 596.

[5] PRINCIPLES § 1 Topic 1, Overview of Chapter 4, at 22–23.

[6] PRINCIPLES § 5.02 cmt. a, at 789.

This chapter discusses some of the effects of the ALI's proposed marital property and spousal maintenance rules in the light of the rationales behind these rules and the vision of marriage embedded in them. The first issue examined is how the PRINCIPLES understand the concepts of "contribution." Subsequently, gain and loss of the spouses are discussed in relation to the proposed compensatory payments. Although the PRINCIPLES are well in line with recent developments in social conditions, a recurrent theme of these examinations is the failure of the ALI to pay attention to the economic interactions of the spouses. In this "relational" light, certain consequences of the proposed equal division rule are finally discussed.

I. Valuation of the Spouses' Contributions

As mentioned, the common feature of the assets not subject to division is that the other spouse is presumed not to have contributed to the acquisition, and in some countries, the rationale for equal division is explicitly linked to the spouses' contributions – financial or nonfinancial.[7] The ALI, however, rejects such a justification. The ALI is of the opinion that spouses often do not make equal financial contributions, and maintains that the factual premise of an equal-contribution rationale does not become more plausible by redefining contribution to include contributions of domestic as well as market labor. The drafters reason as follows:

> Much of the spousal earnings during marriage are consumed, and only the surplus remaining is available for division at divorce. For domestic labors to contribute to that surplus, they must not only enhance the financial capacity of the other spouse or the value of marital property but do so by an amount that exceeds the consumption attributable to the spouse performing those labors. For domestic labors to contribute *equally* to that surplus would require, further, that this excess enhancement equal the excess of the higher-earning spouse's income over that spouse's consumption. Neither data nor intuition support such inferences.[8]

The PRINCIPLES do not explain in what way the domestic workers "enhance the financial capacity of the other spouse or the value of marital property." The ALI simply states that the contribution of the stay-at-home spouse is lower, when consumption attributable to the spouses is deducted.[9]

A common way of looking at the spouses' contribution is to take the value of each spouse's labor as starting points, both labor inside and outside the home, and deduct consumption costs attributable to each spouse. The net results are then compared – they are regarded as each spouse's contribution to the surplus available for division at divorce. In such an account, the value of domestic work is often deemed lower than that of work outside the home – whether domestic work is valued in terms of services purchased in the market or according to payment by the hour. In my view, this "comparison model" is not a realistic indicator of the domestic worker's contributions to the wage earner's

[7] For Norway, *see* NOU (Official Norwegian Report) 1987: 30,79 (1987); Innst. O. Nr. 71, 14 (1990–91).

[8] PRINCIPLES § 4.09 cmt. c, at 735.

[9] Accordingly, the ALI maintains that it "makes far more sense to ground an equal-division presumption on the spouses' contribution to the entire marital relationship, not just to the accumulation of financial assets." One spouse may, for example, "have contributed more than the other in emotional stability, optimism or social skills, and thereby enriched the marital life." PRINCIPLES § 4.09 cmt. c, at 735.

acquisition of marital property; the model rather indicates an account of the two spouses' net input to this surplus. Thus, the model implies an idea of distributive justice, where the surplus is divided according to deserts. It is hard to tell whether such a comparison (intuitively) lies behind the drafters' reasoning; however the two ways of reasoning have one common feature. They do not explain how the domestic worker has contributed to the wage earner's acquisitions. In order to give such an explanation, an economic connection has to be established between the wage earner's direct contribution to the surplus acquired during marriage and the housewife's domestic labor. The only economic connection that is apparent is the factual assumption that the wife has enabled part of his work effort, and thus his income, by taking more than her share of domestic work. When a spouse covers more than his or her share of domestic work, and thus enables the other spouse to earn more or spend more money, and this enabled income is invested, an economic connection is established between domestic work and the other spouse's acquisitions.[10] When such an indirect contribution is acknowledged, it is taken for granted that a given quantity of work effort has to be done in the family. If one of the spouses performs less, the other must perform more. The valuation method proposed under this "contribution model" considers these efforts as dependent upon each other. This is a departure from the "comparison model" which regards the spouses' efforts as autonomous entities.

The question of recognizing indirect contribution in the form of domestic work or payment of current expenses has been raised in several European legal systems. The question comes to a head in countries where co-ownership during marriage is established on the basis of the parties' contributions to the acquisition of the property. In England in the 1960s and 1970s, the question was raised whether a wife's indirect contribution in the form of payments for consumption expenses or child care should give her a beneficial interest like co-ownership, in the family home formally owned by the husband. A broad doctrine acknowledging indirect contribution within the framework of a remedial constructive trust has not been adopted in English law, contrary to other common law jurisdictions, such as Canada and Australia.[11] Instead, in England, once a spouse or cohabitant has established some beneficial interest by making a direct contribution by paying off the loan, by making a deposit, or assuming mortgage liability, the quantification of that interest is determined by the whole range of conduct during the relationship – including indirect contributions in the form of consumption expenses and such.[12] Conceptually, the quantification of the beneficial interest is founded on inferred intention. Thus, in theory, the contribution is not decisive in itself, only its significance for the parties' common understanding concerning the ownership of the property. In reality, however, as long as the threshold condition is satisfied, indirect contributions seem to be of great importance in determining rights of ownership in English law. Because division of property upon divorce is governed by other rules, this legal development is first and foremost of significance in relation to the spouses' creditors and between unmarried cohabitants.

In 1975, the Norwegian Supreme Court went a step further. It acknowledged indirect contribution in the form of child care and housework, and made no distinction between entitlement and quantification. The Court ruled a wife who stays at home and minds small

[10] In this chapter the word "contribution" is employed in an economic sense. Two forms of contributions are described: Direct contribution (by paying the purchase price of property, paying off the loan on a house, investing in stocks and so forth) and indirect contribution (domestic work and covering of consumption expenses).

[11] S. M. Cretney, J. M. Masson and R. Bailey-Harris, Principles of Family Law, 112–23 (7th ed.) (2002).

[12] *Id.* at 122–31.

children as coowner of the house purchased during the marriage by her husband with only his income earned during marriage.[13] This method of acquisition departs sharply from the traditional methods of acquiring co-ownership, as the justification is not linked to a "common intention" requirement.[14] The rule has since been codified in the Marriage Act of 1991.[15] Co-ownership is based on what the parties contributed to the acquisition of the property, and a homemaker's indirect contributions in the form of care for small children are sufficient in the majority of cases to make her an equal coowner of the family home or other items of common personal use bought by the husband with his income earned during marriage.[16] The fundamental thinking appears to be that if they had performed equal shares of work inside the home, the husband would have had to reduce his working hours – and earned less. On the other hand, the homemaker would have had free time for a paid job and thus would have made a direct contribution to the acquisition or made an indirect contribution in the form of covering more than her share of consumption expenses. It is worth noting that, under this "contribution model", the spouses' work efforts may be equal at any given moment, yet inequality is generated over time because one performance is consumed and the other is invested. Consequently, the homemaker need not perform extraordinarily to contribute equally to the surplus – an effort at a normal level will suffice.[17]

Both the ALI's proposed valuation method and this method of acknowledging indirect contributions justify the valuation of nonmarket contributions with economic reasoning.[18] One might think that consumption is not taken into account in the latter case, but that

[13] *Norwegian Supreme Court Reports* 1975, p. 220. The house in question was acquired during the marriage and the husband held the title. *Id.*

[14] Even if the spouses have agreed to a separate property regime, this rule relating to the acquisition of property applies, as long as the spouses have not agreed upon who is to be deemed the owner of the particular items of property. *Norwegian Supreme Court Reports* 1403 (1980); *Norwegian Supreme Court Reports,* 1269 (1982).

[15] Marriage Act 1991, Section 31, third paragraph. This rule applies not only to the family house, but also to other items of property for common personal use, e.g., a cabin, a car, or a boat, and holds good unless the spouses have expressly agreed upon who is to be considered the owner. Ownership is obtained regardless of title.

[16] The same principle is also applied judicially to *unmarried cohabitation. See Norwegian Supreme Court Reports* 1978, p. 1352 and 1984, p. 497. The Norwegian Supreme Court has also determined that *creditors* must respect co-ownership rights of this nature; cf. *Norwegian Supreme Court Reports* 1978, p. 871. In Scandinavia, spouses have separate property during marriage, but an equal division takes place on divorce (deferred community property). A similar course of legal development was in progress in the lower courts of Denmark and Sweden until the higher courts of these countries halted its development. It is understandable that this legal development took place in separate property regimes, where rights of ownership have some significance – mainly in relation to the spouses' creditors. In community-property countries like Italy, Spain, and countries in Eastern Europe, co-ownership in property acquired during marriage is embedded in the marital property regimes.

[17] Experience from lower courts in Norway shows that legal practitioners do not always come to terms with the fact that an effort at normal level will suffice. The difficulties may stem from the fact that they are influenced by the use of causal reasoning in tort law, penal law, and contract law, cf. Hart and Honoré who point out that "when causal language is used of the provision or failure to provide another with an opportunity, it is implied that this is a deviation from a standard practice or expected procedure", H. L.A. HART AND T. HONORÉ, CAUSATION IN THE LAW 60, (Oxford 1985). When measuring contribution, the purpose is quite different, namely to accredit a given amount or surplus to two cooperating parties.

[18] In the "Housewife Case," discussed above, the husband, in addition to performing the work from which he derived his income, had built a part of the house himself in his spare time. The judge who was the first to vote stated that it was the wife's housework and her caring for three small children "that has enabled the husband to devote so much work to building," *Norwegian Supreme Court Reports* 1975, p. 220, at p. 226. The legislative history of the new Marriage Act of 1991 state's likewise that the homemaker's co-ownership is based on "economic realities" and emphasize's that no transfer of property occurs by declaring that the wife is a co-owner. The same text also states that "co-ownership is based on the contribution from each of the spouses that lies behind the acquisition." cf. NOU (Official Norwegian Report) 1987: 30 p. 70–71.

is not so. Suppose the wife takes care of small children below compulsory school age and performs household chores. The husband is employed earning $40,000 per year after taxes. From his income, he pays the family's total expenses including principal payments on a mortgage, which constitute the "surplus" subject to division on divorce. The husband would have to reduce his working hours by one half, and consequently halve his income, if he were to take responsibility for his half of domestic work and child care, as the children are below school age and thus need round-the-clock care. We must presuppose that the children should have just as much contact with their parents in the comparative situation as follows. Given this premise, a wife has made half of his earnings possible. However, the total of this sum cannot be regarded as her yearly investments in the house. Part of this enabled income must also be deemed to have been spent on covering consumption expenses. In our case, it is reasonable to assume that the wife has contributed to one-half of the total consumption expenses and one-half of the total investment in the house. In other words, she has contributed on an equal footing to the surplus subject to division on divorce, as well as to the consumption expenses. The consumption attributable to the spouse performing domestic labor is thus taken into account.[19]

If the children are of compulsory school age and the wife still works full-time at home she will normally enable less than one-half his earnings. However, in modern marriages, women assume paid work after a shorter period at home, and they normally contribute directly to property acquisitions, or indirectly by covering consumption expenses.[20] Thus, in the great majority of marriages spouses could be regarded as equal contributors to the surplus created during marriage according to this "contribution model."

One could argue that the husband would often have earned just as much even if she had not performed "his" share of the child care duties, instead he would have paid for a nanny or placed the children at the child care center, and therefore she does not facilitate half of his earnings. The question is whether or not one should presuppose that the children should have just as much total contact with their parents in the hypothetical posed. The question could be rephrased as to whether the homemaker has freed time or capital for the wage earner. In the first instance, she has enabled him to work more, and thus enhanced his

[19] However, the share of consumption expenses attributable to each spouse is open for debate; even if the spouses' factual amount of consumption is more or less the same (this is taken as a premise in the following). Attributing one-half to each is unproblematic when the spouses' real work efforts are equally large. But if the one's work effort is greater than the other's, two principles could guide the debiting of consumption expenses: either one can deduct half of the consumption expenses or one can deduct expenses proportionately, in proportion to the size of each of the spouses' respective work efforts, that is according to ability. One also has to choose between the two methods when calculating *indirect contribution in the form of covering consumption expenses.* The question that arises is when has the spouse paid *more than her share* of the family's total consumption expenses? In these cases, the latter method of calculation (according to ability) better tracks the economic relationship between the spouses during marriage. The spouses must eat the same food, go on the same holidays, be responsible for their children's expenses, and so forth. In other words, they form a consumption unit *and the one with the higher income will pull the total consumption expenses upward.* Therefore, it may seem unreasonable if one-half the family's total consumption expenses are to be debited against the spouse who has the lower income. On the other hand, they have in fact consumed one-half the material goods each. In every circumstance, if their income just cover the bare necessities, the one with the higher income will not pull the total consumption expenses upwards and the above argument fails, cf. T. Sverdrup, *Stiftelse av sameie i ekteskap og ugift samliv* (Co-ownership in Marriage and in Unmarried Cohabitation), Oslo, 1997, p. 394–98, and 422–24.

[20] It is interesting to note that Professor Katharine Silbaugh found that courts took inadequate account of "women's most common labor pattern, a combination of paid and unpaid labor," when interpreting the homemaker provision in the Uniform Marriage and Divorce Act. *See*, Katharine Silbaugh, *Turning Labor into Love: Housework and the Law*, 91 Nw. U. L. Rev. 1, 62, 63 (1996).

gross income; in the latter case, she has enhanced his net income disposable for investments by saving him the cost of (half) the child care, nanny, housekeeper, and so forth. Normally, the enabled income is lower when conceived of as freed capital rather than as freed time. Whether this question is addressed one or the other way, the same deliberation takes place. Consider first child care, the care of parents and others are not fully replaceable. The reason is not that one kind of child care is necessarily better than the other. A variety of opinions exists on this matter in the society, and the legal system should therefore take the *parents' choice of child care* as a given starting point. Thus, the amount of contact between children and their parents should be kept constant in the comparative situation.[21] A different result occurs with household chores; as such work can be substituted more easily by market services without significantly changing the character of the service. The housewife's labor could therefore be regarded as freeing capital for the husband. However, if most of the household chores were to be substituted over a longer period of time, the distinctive character of that particular marriage would change substantially, and freeing of capital is no longer an obvious alternative.[22]

In the same way, it could be presupposed that the person working outside the home should have just as much spare time as in the hypothetical situation where work outside and inside the home is divided equally. Whether the contributions should be measured under such a premise, is a matter of opinion. As I see it, there may be good grounds to suggest such a premise – otherwise, a built-in welfare loss is present in the comparative situation. The purpose is not to find out what would most probably have happened in the alternative instance, but to trace the economic significance of domestic labor for the acquisition. If leisure is kept constant, one sees that a husband would have had to reduce his working hours if his wife had not performed some of "his" share of child care. From this point of view, she has made possible part of his earnings, and if these additional earnings result in investments or greater pension benefits, she has indirectly contributed thereto.

According to this "contribution model," co-ownership during marriage as well as an equal division rule upon divorce could be justified with reference to the spouses' indirect contributions, as they contribute on an equal footing in the great majority of marriages. The rationale for property division upon divorce is significant in determining whether a certain allocation of property should be viewed as an entitlement or a charitable transfer. The ALI maintains that if "the presumption of equal contribution were based on the factual assumption that the parties contributed equally to the property's acquisition, then it would seem appropriate to allow its rebuttal with evidence of unequal contribution."[23] In my opinion, it is unproblematic to justify an equal division rule with reference to the parties' contribution, and at the same time bar a rebuttal based on evidence of unequal contribution, as group data can establish equal contributions on the general level, but it is costly to prove this fact in the particular case. One exception could be made: Some argue that the housewife contributes less in cases where the husband has a very high salary and invests in property far above average, as explained more fully as follows with regard to

[21] This is also the position of the Norwegian Supreme Court. The Court speaks of the freeing of time and not of the freeing of capital where children are concerned, *Norwegian Supreme Court Reports* 1975 p. 220, 1976 p. 694, 1980 p. 1403 and 1983 p. 1146.

[22] The Supreme Court has regarded household chores in both ways in these cases, cf. *Norwegian Supreme Court Reports* 1978 p. 1352 (both time and capital) and 1979 p. 1463 (time).

[23] PRINCIPLES § 4.09 cmt. c, at 735.

future earning capacity. In those few cases, another justification for equal division than the parties' contributions might be appropriate.

II. Spousal Support – Compensating Loss or Gain?

It is no surprise that the question of indirect contribution to the acquisition of property was raised in the 1960s and 1970s. Before occupational work became a realistic alternative for many married women, gender or "the natural order of things" appeared to explain why the housewife could not invest directly in capital accumulation. The idea that a random or unjust benefit arises where the right of ownership is determined by who happens to go out to work and who happens to be at home, appears more likely when work outside the home is a viable alternative for women. The thinking is that the chosen division of labor shall not in itself entail that the homemaker acquires ownership of less than she would otherwise have had: where equal distribution of effort between the spouses both inside and outside the home would have given her a right of co-ownership, a skewed distribution should not lead to a different result. It is now more plausible to consider both the full-time and part-time homemaker as having made possible parts of the husband's income, and thus contributed indirectly to his acquisitions.

But, when one window is opened, another is closed. The same realistic expectancy of paid employment for women may eliminate the possibility of long-term maintenance after divorce. In Europe, the frequency of granting maintenance varies considerably – from countries in Eastern Europe and Scandinavia where maintenance is the exception, to Germany, Austria, Switzerland, and others where it is quite common. The overall trend seems to be a decline in the granting of maintenance, and a shift from permanent to short-term awards.[24] As fault-divorce is no longer the rule, maintenance as a sanction is less relevant; and as life-long marriage is declining, solidarity wanes as a justification.[25] Today, compensation for losses relating to marriage seems to be the most plausible justification both for long-term maintenance and for short-term maintenance.

The ALI proposal for compensatory spousal payments follows this development. The remedy it provides is re-characterized as compensation for loss rather than relief of need. The drafters refer to the historical failure to provide any satisfactory explanation for placing the obligation to support a needy person on his or her former spouse, and claim that the law, as a result, is unable to provide any consistent principle for determining when and to

[24] See K. European Family Law in Action. Volume II: Maintenance between Former Spouses, EFL Series, No. 3, Intersentia, Antwerp (K. Boele-Woelki, B. Bratt, I. Summer eds., 2003). Especially in Scandinavia, the self-sufficiency principle prevails, and both in Sweden and Norway it is normally required that the marriage as such has resulted in the need for maintenance. In Norway, as a general rule, the ability and opportunity of the spouse to ensure support must have been reduced *as a result of caring for children of the marriage or of the distribution of joint tasks* during marriage (Norwegian Marriage Act § 79 second paragraph). In other cases maintenance may only be ordered if special reasons so indicate, for example, if the former spouse is sick or disabled. The amount of maintenance shall be assessed on the basis of the need for maintenance of the person entitled thereto, and the ability of the person liable to pay maintenance, cf. § 80. In practice, maintenance after divorce is granted in a limited number of cases.

[25] Dieter Martiny identifies four different justifications for spousal maintenance after divorce. In addition to support during the transitional period, he identifies sanction, solidarity, and compensation for losses suffered during marriage. D. Martiny, Divorce and Maintenance between Former Spouses – Initial Results of the Commission on European Family Law, in K. Boele-Woelki (ed.), *Perspectives for the Unification and Harmonisation of Family Law in Europe*, EFL Series, No. 4, Intersentia, Antwerp (2003) p. 545–46.

what extent a former spouse is in need.[26] For entitlements based on the parties' disparate financial capacity, the PRINCIPLES recognize two different kinds of compensable loss: loss of living standard[27] and loss of earning capacity.[28]

Whether spousal earning capacity should be regarded as property subject to division on divorce is controversial. Future earning capacity is not treated as property in the European jurisdictions – instead, spousal claims on future earnings are made under the rubric of maintenance, as is normally the case in the United States, as well.[29] The crux of the argument for division seems to be that because both parents are not fully able to pursue a career out of consideration for the children, the choice of one of the spouses partly to give up a career should not be at the peril of that spouse alone. Future income is, however, regarded by many as too closely linked to individual autonomy and the personal characteristics of the earner, and therefore not suitable for division. Moreover, as the PRINCIPLES point out, division of property is final and raises great valuation difficulties. Maintenance, on the other hand, is more flexible because of the possibility of termination of the award, but does not accord with the self-sufficiency principle.[30] In terms of future income, "property" and "maintenance" are two different expressions of the same phenomenon: the spouses' adjustment of work efforts to each other during marriage that have effects after marriage. One can therefore imagine a new form of benefit on the dissolution of marriage under a new name, which cannot be characterized as either "property division" or "maintenance." Such a rehabilitative measure need not carry with it the traditional legal and political understanding that lies embedded in these two concepts. This new benefit may be tailor-made to address the particular problems that arise when compensating future gain or loss. The proposed provisions in chapter 5 of the PRINCIPLES attempt to create such a new remedy.

[26] PRINCIPLES § 1, Topic 1, Overview of Chapter 4, at 25; PRINCIPLES § 5.02 cmt. a, at 789.

[27] PRINCIPLES § 5.04.

[28] PRINCIPLES §§ 5.05 and 5.11. The ALI also recognizes entitlements *not* based on the parties' disparate financial capacity, such as contributions to the other spouse's education or training, PRINCIPLES § 5.12, as well as certain sacrifices during a short marriage, PRINCIPLES § 5.13. A few possible components of spousal support are dealt with elsewhere, e.g., the allocation of the costs of postdissolution childcare is provided as part of the child-support award in the PRINCIPLES' Chapter 3. Vested pension rights earned during the marriage are subject to division upon divorce under Section 4.08. This is appropriate since such assets could be compared to other forms of savings, such as bank deposits. Generally, there seems to be an increasing tendency to split pensions in European countries. Today, pension rights are subject to division in several European countries, like Germany, Switzerland, and the Netherlands and to some extent in England. Pension splitting is a much-debated question in the Scandinavian countries. Pensions are not subject to division in Norway. In Sweden and Denmark, pensions are divided to a limited degree. See M. BRATTSTRØM, *Makars pensionsrättigheter* (Spouses' Pension Rights), Iustus Forlag, Uppsala (2004) English Summary p. 317–330.

[29] PRINCIPLES § 4.07 cmt. a, at 694–95.

[30] A number of legal scholars have claimed that the principle of self-sufficiency does not take adequate account of the fact that the earning capacity of the majority of wives has been permanently reduced due to childcare and the work patterns during marriage. They have argued that society should rethink the "premature abandonment" of maintenance, and that maintenance should be granted as compensation for these losses. See, e.g., L. J. WEITZMAN, *Alimony: Its Premature Demise and Recent Resurgence in the United States,* in ECONOMIC CONSEQUENCES OF DIVORCE (L. J. Weitzman & M. Maclen Clarendon Press Oxford (1992); M. A. GLENDON, THE TRANSFORMATION OF FAMILY LAW, 233–38 (The University of Chicago Press 1989). A similar debate took place in Norway relating to the duration of maintenance. According to The Marriage Act § 81, maintenance shall be ordered for a limited period not exceeding three years. If special reasons so indicate, maintenance may, however, be ordered for a longer period or without any time limit. These rules were criticized because they did not pay enough attention to wives who had been working at home for a long period and had little opportunity to support themselves. As a result, Section 81 was amended in 1998, and the section now explicitly states that maintenance, as a main rule, shall be ordered for a longer period of time or without any time limit if the marriage has lasted for a long time, (which, however, was the rule in practice even before 1998).

The term "compensatory payment" is used instead of "alimony" and "maintenance" which helps to avoid the historic association with relief of need.[31] Additionally, the conditions for the granting of an award are standardized, and the difference between the spouses' post-divorce earnings is divided according to a durational factor.[32] In this respect, the benefit resembles an allocation of property upon divorce. In other respects, the benefit resembles maintenance, for example, the provisions regarding duration and automatic termination of the awards.[33]

The compensatory awards allocate certain financial losses equitably between the spouses, primarily the loss of marital living standard according to Section 5.04, and the loss of earning capacity by the primary caretaker, according to Section 5.05. Even though these two sections seek to compensate different losses, the basic measure employed by both sections is the same: the amount is calculated by applying a percentage (called durational factor or child care durational factor) to the difference between the incomes the spouses are expected to have at dissolution. The measure in Section 5.05 is an approximate proxy measure of the loss in earning capacity. In this way, the two sections "gradually merge the financial fates of the spouses as the marriage or child-care period lengthens through a durational factor that proportionately reduces any gap in their individual post-divorce earnings."[34]

The rationales for the claims recognized by the two sections are not the same. The rationale for claims recognized by Section 5.05 is primarily linked to the loss of future earning capacity due to child care, but two other rationales are mentioned as well: loss of a supportive spouse and the caretaker's contribution to the earning capacity of the other spouse. The latter rationale applies the same line of thought that lies behind the recognition of indirect contribution to the surplus acquired during marriage described above: "By fulfilling their joint responsibility for their children's care, the claimant under this section has allowed the other parent to have a family while also developing his or her earning capacity."[35]

In Section 5.04, the rationale is linked to "relationships as a source of obligation for the differential risk of marriage."[36] This rationale is based neither on economic nor on contractual thinking, but on a moral obligation: the obligation "develop[s] over time as the parties' lives become entwined."[37] The drafters point out that in "sharing a life together they mold one another."[38] This seems like a sensible and intuitively correct way of describing a long-term marriage; the argument, however, conceals the economic nature of this molding. The PRINCIPLES do not link this entwining to the division of labor and the fact that the primary homemaker normally is freeing up time for the person working outside the home. Even though division of labor is not mentioned in Section 5.04, it is the long-term homemaker in particular who is covered by this section.[39] As the PRINCIPLES point out, the long-term homemaker usually serves as the primary caretaker of the children of the marriage as well,[40] and the two awards are therefore coordinated. In practice, child care and household work are inseparably connected, and one could therefore ask why these two components of domestic work are not dealt with in the same award. The answer could be related to the fact the drafters are of the opinion that it is difficult to show that the

[31] PRINCIPLES § 5.02 cmt. a, at 790.

[32] PRINCIPLES §§ 5.04(3), 5.05 (4).

[33] PRINCIPLES §§ 5.06, 5.07.

[34] PRINCIPLES § 5.13 cmt. a, at 897.

[35] PRINCIPLES § 5.05 cmt. d, at 841.

[36] PRINCIPLES § 5.04 cmt. b, at 808.

[37] PRINCIPLES § 5.04 cmt. c, at 809.

[38] PRINCIPLES § 5.04 cmt. c, at 809.

[39] PRINCIPLES § 5.04 cmt. a, at 806.

[40] PRINCIPLES § 5.04 cmt. a, at 806.

homemaker covered in Section 5.04 has contributed to the other spouse's earning capacity although this difficulty does "not cast doubt on the observation that, in assuming that role, the homemaker incurs a significant economic loss."[41] The drafters state that because "there are many cases in which the facts would not suggest that the claimant contributed to the potential obligor's earning capacity," the contribution rationale would leave many awards unexplained.[42] In this reasoning, the drafters posit a hypothetical situation where the husband is single: "Such cases do not usually suggest that the trial court examine each particular case to determine whether the obligor might avoid or reduce the award by showing that he would have done as well without his spouse."[43] In my view, the question is not whether the husband would have done as well without his spouse, but whether he would have done as well if he had borne his share of homemaking in the family, as discussed earlier under the "contribution model."

The next question asks which factors should be kept constant in this comparative situation. If the spouses have agreed upon the division of labor – and a strong presumption that they have agreed should exist if they have practiced this division of labor for some years – their existing quality of life, in terms of spare time and standard of homemaking should be taken as a given when valuing the homemaker's contribution to the other spouse's earning capacity. In this way, the moral obligation to post-divorce support that arises in a long-term relationship, which serves as ALI's rationale for Section 5.04,[44] is taken into account as a premise in the economic reasoning. By taking spare time and the standard of homemaking as givens in cases where the division of labor is agreed upon, the moral relationships and commitments of the spouses are taken seriously. Given these premises, a husband would have had to reduce his working hours if his wife had not performed some of "his" share of the homemaking. From this point of view, she has contributed to his earning capacity. However, in those marriages where there are no children, the homemaking is less time-consuming, and the homemaker's contribution as well as her loss is limited. In the great majority of long-term marriages, children are present, and the homemaker has contributed to the other spouse's earning capacity in a substantial way.

The PRINCIPLES substitute "loss" for "need" as a rationale for compensatory payments after divorce, and argue that such payments should be viewed as an entitlement rather than a charitable transfer.[45] However, entitlements originate as much from the contribution side as from the loss side. According to the "contribution model" described above losses sustained and contributions made during marriage are two sides of the same coin. The wife's child care and homemaking has enabled the husband to pursue his own career and consequently obtain higher future earning capacity outside the family. The "coin" is the child care and household work, which from one side constitutes an indirect contribution to the breadwinner's acquisitions and future earning capacity and from the other side an obstacle for the homemaker to taking up paid work, which results in a loss of income and,

[41] PRINCIPLES § 5.04 cmt. b, at 808. With childcare, the contribution side is recognized. See PRINCIPLES § Section 5.05, cmt. e, at 841.

[42] PRINCIPLES § 5.04 cmt. b, at 808.

[43] PRINCIPLES § 5.04 cmt. b, at 823 ("Such a contribution is, however, difficult to show. It is clear that married men earn more than single men. The problem for the researchers is to determine whether their earning advantage results from a) marriage itself [or other factors]").

[44] PRINCIPLES § 5.04 at 808–12. See also Carl E. Schneider, *Rethinking Alimony: Marital Decisions and Moral Discourse,* 1991 BYU L. REV. 197, 248–49, 257.

[45] PRINCIPLES § 5.02 cmt. b, at 790.

subsequently, of earning capacity. Gain and loss are two sides of the same coin, although one sometimes gets the impression that one has to choose between them. There is no reason to conceal one side at the expense of the other. Simultaneous gain and loss constitute a powerful justification for transfers between the spouses in modern marriages. Thus, it seems clear that indirect contribution to the other spouse's earning capacity in the form of child care and household work is an important rationale for the granting of compensatory payments upon divorce. Another matter is whether this contribution could justify a division of future earning capacity after divorce. An important counterargument is the fact that future earning capacity is closely linked to individual autonomy and personal makeup of the higher-earning spouse, and therefore not so suitable for division. This discussion is not elaborated in this chapter.

Even though loss and gain are two sides of the same coin, they do not always go equally far. There may be differences in the quantification, according to whether one sees things from the gain side or from the loss side: Should the spouses split the increase in earning capacity that is a result of the wife's enabling him to devote himself more fully to his occupational work, or should the husband compensate the wife for her loss of earning capacity due to the fact that she has spent more time on child care and household chores? Apart from a small percentage of high-income families, however, these two methods of calculation lead to more or less the same result. In the hypothetical assessment, we must take it as established that she could have had a more lucrative career development if the roles were reversed from the beginning.[46] It is only in those cases in which the wife's alternative future income, given these conditions, would have been markedly lower than the husband's future income, that there is a difference of any significance. In those cases the husband can argue that his wife has not lost as much as he has gained, and her compensation should in any case be limited to her loss, or, put in other words, his future earning capacity is primarily related to his personal abilities, and not to his wife's child care and the chosen division of labor.[47] On the other hand, it may be claimed that the homemaker has freed time for the person who goes out to work to earn high as well as low pay, and consequently any increment in earning capacity should be credited both spouses accordingly. There is no "correct" answer to this question of causation. In cases where the husband has a much higher income than his wife would have had, the spouses have chosen a more efficient division of labor during marriage. The question of who shall be ascribed this efficiency gain cannot be solved on the basis of simple causal considerations – it is a matter of legal-political choice. Small and moderate differences in income should in any case be left out of account, due to the multifaceted character of marital relationships. There may be good grounds to suggest an exception in cases in which one of the spouses has an extraordinarily high income, as it is most probable that a greater part of the higher-earning spouse's future earning capacity is related to his or her personal abilities.

III. The Equal Division Rule and the Spouses' Adjustment of Behavior

The previous sections concluded that in the great majority of marriages the nonmarket contribution equals the financial contribution as long as the work efforts of the spouses

[46] PRINCIPLES § 5.05 cmt. e, at 840.

[47] See among others ALLEN M. PARKMAN, *No-Fault Divorce: What Went Wrong?* Boulder-San Francisco-Oxford 1992, pp. 39–42 and p. 143–44.

are viewed as dependent on each other. The key to this understanding is the adjustment of behavior that takes place in marriage. A certain quantity of domestic work has to be done in the family, and if one of the spouses performs less, the other must perform more. Given the premise that outsourcing of childcare and a substantial amount of housework is not an appropriate alternative, if one spouse performs more than her share of the services that are consumed, she has contributed indirectly to the other spouse's investments of his income during marriage. The PRINCIPLES recognize the loss side of domestic work, but they more seldom recognize the contribution side. The PRINCIPLES do not discuss the *interdependence between the spouses' work efforts* in any depth – they focus on the moral relationships rather than the economic relationship.

People do not view marriage primarily in terms of economic advantage, and rightly so. Nevertheless, economic contributions should not be concealed. Professor Katharine Silbaugh maintains regarding property division that while one might decide that the amount of contribution should not be the decisive factor, one nonetheless benefits from a clearer examination of those contributions in deciding proper outcomes.[48]

Spouses form a work unit, but also a consumption unit and an investment unit. The fact that spouses adjust consumption and investments to each other is an important recognition when analyzing the effects of the property division rule. As mentioned earlier, the ALI proposes an equal division rule, where premarital assets, as well as gifts and inheritance, are excluded from division.[49] The failure to acknowledge the spouses' economic adaptation has some unfavorable effects regarding property division, when only the assets acquired during marriage are divided equally. A fundamental adaptation lies solely in the fact that most spouses must be content with one dwelling; it is in the nature of family life that both parties live in one family home. If both have previously owned a house, one of them will in most cases sell his or her house when they start living together. If only one of them owned a house before the marriage, the other is in most cases prevented from future investments (savings) in a house. Whether the parties are independent of each other or not, the majority can afford only one house. If the dwelling has been paid off at the start of the marriage, this adjustment of behavior can lead to unfortunate results in cases where only assets acquired during marriage are divided. Owing to the increase both of wealth and in the frequency of remarriage, it is not uncommon for one spouse to bring a house, a car, or other property into the marriage, while the other spouse brings little property. If such basic investments are already available to the family, it is natural for the spouses to apply most of their disposable income to current expenses during marriage. The party without property will benefit from the other party's investments during the marriage, but will be hard hit when nothing is saved for equal distribution when the spouses part company. In order that one party shall not come out of the marriage empty-handed, the less wealthy party (or the other party) must put aside part of his or her income during the marriage in case of a possible breach. But how many people would do such a thing in practice? Spouses live in a community of life, one of the consequences of which is that they form a consumption unit, the parties eat the same food, they go on the same holidays and so forth. And the parties adjust this level of consumption to the fact that basic investments, like a family home, are already available. The prerequisite

[48] Katharine Silbaugh, *Commodification and Women's Household Labor*, 9 YALE J.L. & FEMINISM 81, 119 (1997).

[49] PRINCIPLES §§ 4.09(1), 4.03.

for equal division rules where only the assets acquired during marriage are divided seems to be that the spouses should make dispositions with a view to their long-term financial gain.[50]

If the house is acquired before the relationship starts, but the mortgage is paid off during marriage with the spouses' earnings, which are marital property, the nonowning spouse is better off, for such assets are divided equally irrespective of the ownership of the dwelling.[51] However, to the extent that the principal balance of the loan is not reduced during marriage, a home acquired on credit before marriage is presumed to be separate property, which means that the appreciation on that portion of the house is characterized as separate property.[52] As long as most couples must be content with one dwelling, the nonowning spouse should share in the price rise (and fall) in the real estate market. The family home holds a unique position and the appreciation on this portion of the house should be divided equally, whether or not the appreciation is related to any effort of the spouses. If the nonowning party cannot share in the rise in the market, he or she will be "trapped by" the housing market and be poorly equipped disproportionately to acquire a new dwelling on the dissolution of marriage (and vice versa regarding price fall). For a similar reason, the question may also be raised whether, as Section 4.06 (2)(a) provides, it ought to be the case that the paying spouse alone should benefit from the appreciation on a corresponding share of the dwelling when a mortgage on a house bought during marriage is paid off with separate property. Normally, the appreciation of that portion of the house is caused by the original acquisition of the house (and the borrowing), and not by the kind of property (separate or marital) that is used to pay off the loan.

Sometimes it is fortuitous whether a spouse consumes or invests an inheritance or a gift, which is separate property, during marriage – and the fortuity of this depends on factors that seem irrelevant when viewed *ex post.* Say, for example, that the husband uses his inheritance to pay off his consumer loan because this loan has a higher rate of interest than the mortgage. The husband acts on the basis of what appears profitable and rational at the time of the disposition, and not with a view to what he himself would have earned most from, that is, keeping his inheritance invested in the house. Or consider a second example: often both spouses will inherit in the course of the marriage, and in such cases, it is not unusual to see that the first inheritance is saved, while the second is consumed. For when the second inheritance comes into being, the spouses considered as a unit already have a capital reserve, and seen in this light it is rational behavior to consume inheritance number two. A third example: the family spends the husband's inheritance because it is composed of liquid assets, but keeps the wife's inheritance, which is real property. The factors that in relation to the PRINCIPLES appear as extraneous circumstances or matters of chance have their basis in rational behavior seen from the spouses' point of view. When it depends on matters of chance or irrelevant factors as to whether separate property is consumed

[50] T. SVERDRUP, "Marriage and Cohabitation: Community of Life or Community of Work? *Working Papers in Women's Law* No. 51, Department of Public and International Law University of Oslo (1999) and T. SVERDRUP, Maintenance as a Separate Issue – The Relationship between Maintenance and Matrimonial Property, in K. BOELE-WOELKI (ed.) *Common Core and Better Law in European Family Law*, EFL Series, No. 10, Intersentia, Antwerp (2005) pp. 119–34.

[51] PRINCIPLES § 4.06 (3).

[52] PRINCIPLES § 4.04. The same holds good even for cases where the house is acquired during the marriage, see PRINCIPLES § 4.06 illus. 4, reporter's note, at 687–91.

or invested during marriage, fact-finding about whether an inheritance was consumed becomes important. The spouses will easily feel estranged in such a legal system.[53]

These examples have a common feature; they arise from the fact that spouses adjust their behavior during the marriage, with regard to savings, investments, and consumption. This behavior leads to inadequate results in economic settlements based on the thinking that there should be a balance between contributions and returns, namely, that only those assets acquired during marriage by means other than gifts and inheritance is subject to equal division. Spouses adjust their economy according to the total amount of income, investments, and expenditure. When only assets acquired during marriage are subject to division, this mirrors a concept of reciprocation between contributions and returns that overlooks this adjusting behavior. As we have seen, one spouse's behavior is also a reflection of the starting position of the other spouse, as both form an investment and consumption unit. A spouse adjusts the level of consumption to the fact that basic investments are already available to the family.

Sections 4.12 and 4.03(6) should alleviate some of these unfortunate effects of the PRINCIPLES. Section 4.12 gives spouses in long-term marriages a share in one another's separate property.[54] According to Section 4.03(6), property acquired during a relationship between the spouses that immediately preceded their marriage is treated as if it were acquired during marriage.[55] These are important provisions that to a greater degree take into consideration the fact that spouses interact within the framework of an economic unit.

Section 4.12 is justified by the fact that spouses after many years of marriage do not think of their separate-property assets as separate.[56] Their expectations of sharing in one another's greater assets increase correspondingly. The longer the marriage, the more likely it is that the spouses will have made economic decisions premised on such expectations.[57] The PRINCIPLES maintain that the rationale for Section 4.12 is consistent with the approach taken in Section 5.04 to compensatory payments.[58] The spousal sense that property is communally, rather than individually, owned has its source in the relationship of the parties; the duration of marriage provides an administrable measure of that relationship.[59]

The problems described above are not so much related to the duration of the marriage as to the unique position of the family home as a dwelling and capital reserve, and to the fact that one spouse's separate property could be a hindrance for the spouses' investments during marriage. Because of the rationale for Section 4.12, this section aims both too low and too high to address these problems. The section fails to financially secure those spouses in medium-length marriages of seven to fifteen years, where divorce is frequently occurring. If the wife owned a house at the time of their marriage, and they as a result consumed most of their income during the marriage, the husband will receive 8 percent of the value of the house after nine years of marriage, and the wife will retain 92 percent.[60]

[53] Fact-finding has become a dominant part of property division cases in Norway since 1991 when the country introduced a rule that excluded the value of inheritance, gifts, and premarital assets from the property subject to equal division.

[54] PRINCIPLES § 4.12, at 769.

[55] PRINCIPLES § 4.03 (6), at 650.

[56] PRINCIPLES § 4.12.

[57] PRINCIPLES § 4.12 cmt. a, at 771.

[58] PRINCIPLES § 4.12 cmt. a, at 771–72.

[59] PRINCIPLES § 4.12 cmt. b, at 773.

[60] In this case 16% of the house is marital property according to the proposed section (a) in Illustration 1 of the PRINCIPLES at page 774. After fifteen years of marriage, he will receive 20% and she will retain 80% of the house (40% is marital property).

On the other hand, the full value of separate property is normally subject to recharacterization, and recharacterization takes place whether the separate property in question was an impediment to capital accumulation during the marriage or not. A recharacterization rule that is connected both to the family home and to the duration of marriage seems more appropriate.

IV. Conclusion

Overall, the equal division of property rule in the PRINCIPLES may seem appropriate. Fixed rules for the division of assets harmonize best, for procedural economic reasons, with today's high divorce figures, and because many marriages dissolve after a relatively short time, it seems natural to limit the divisible assets to those created during the relationship. The PRINCIPLES' justification for equal division is, however, marked by the fact that the spouses' contributions are considered independently of each other. The interplay and the reciprocal dependence between work outside and inside the home are not taken as a basis for the valuation of the parties' contributions, with the consequence that the value of domestic work is deemed lower than that of work outside the home. Spouses form an investment and consumption unit, as well, and adjust their level of consumption to the fact that basic investments, like a family home, are already available. If only one owned a house before marriage, there is often nothing to divide at dissolution of marriage. Spouses arrange their common economy according to the total amount of investments, expenditures, and their joint earning capacity. There is reason to believe the ALI's failure to regard the spouses' dispositions as interdependent of each other also could mark the content of some of the particular rules, for example, the extent to which separate property is recharacterized according to Section 4.12. In a corresponding manner, the ALI justifies the rules concerning compensatory payments primarily by the moral obligation that arises from the relationship itself and the loss of career opportunities due to child care, and only to a limited extent by the contributions of the parties. Viewed in the perspective of the "contribution model," loss and gain are two sides of the same coin, and in the great majority of marriages, they go equally far. The ALI does not view gain and loss due to domestic work as two sides of the same coin, and the PRINCIPLES therefore miss a powerful justification for the granting of spousal compensatory payments.

As mentioned earlier, when the property subject to division is limited to assets acquired during marriage, the option is open to conceive transfers between spouses on divorce in the perspective of corrective justice. One spouse has enabled part of the other's income by taking more than her share of domestic work and/or consumption expenses. In the great majority of marriages, her indirect contribution to the assets acquired during marriage equals the real contribution of the direct contributor, and she is therefore entitled to an equal share of the surplus created during marriage.

Even though the drafters are reluctant to justify the rules on equal division and compensatory payments with the parties' contributions, they are more willing to accept the loss side. In this respect, they are in line with the general development, where family law seems to increasingly resemble the rest of private law. Reciprocity is the fundamental way of thinking in private law, contract law; torts and the theory of unjust enrichment are all based on reciprocation. Spouses, however, have often not thought along these legal lines during marriage, and it is often unnatural for them to do so. In commercial transactions, a contract is a prerequisite for the effective exchange of goods and services. A transaction occurs in which one gets nothing unless one provides something. In a family, the transfers of goods and services are normally not mutually conditioned in this way. Rather than being conditioned in a contractual sense, in a number of cases, a service would lose its value if it were conditional upon a counterservice. Nevertheless, an idea of reciprocation seems to exist in many marriages – spouses appear to expect an overall balance between service and counterservice during the marriage. Likewise, it is reason to believe that many spouses would expect an overall balance between contributions during marriage and returns after marriage. The concept of corrective justice seems to be in accordance with at least one of the ideas of normative behavior that prevails in marriage; therefore one could ask why the legal system has to correct so many inequalities upon divorce.

One reason is the time factor: Spouses typically view the balance between service and counterservice on a short-term or day-to-day basis. Consumption and investments are viewed as equal services in this ad-hoc perspective, but in the end, they are not. As we have seen regarding indirect contributions, a balance might exist between any service and counterservice at any given moment, yet inequality is generated over time because one service (domestic work) is consumed and another (income) is invested. Moreover, a spouse can spend all his or her earnings on consumer goods for the family if, in that particular marriage, there is no need for investments, even though the investments are separately owned by the other spouse, and therefore not subject to division on divorce. The spouses often act regardless of the long-term return on individual dispositions. On the economic level, this adaptation is the essence of living together in a unity, and I assume it is deeply rooted in many marriages – it is the "logic of marriage."

Spouses view consumption and investments as equal contributions in their ad-hoc perspective. In this respect, one could argue that the equal division rule in the PRINCIPLES are built on a presupposition that spouses normally make dispositions with a view to their long-term financial gain and not based on what is rational during the marriage. This builds into the rules a kind of "system error." An invariable rule of equal division of property acquired during marriage is based on the rationality of individuals, and not on the logic of marriage.

I would like to thank Tom Andrews, Professor of Law at the University of Washington School of Law, and Peter Lødrup, Professor of Law at the University of Oslo, for valuable comments to my chapter.

Afterword: Elite Principles: The ALI Proposals and the Politics of Law Reform

Carl E. Schneider

> God forbid I should insinuate anything derogatory to that profession which is another priesthood, administrating the rights of sacred justice. But whilst I revere men in the functions which belong to them, and would do as much as one man can do to prevent their exclusion from any, I cannot, to flatter them, give the lie to nature. They are good and useful in the composition; they must be mischievous if they preponderate so as virtually to become the whole. Their very excellence in their peculiar functions may be far from a qualification for others. It cannot escape observation that when men are too much confined to professional and faculty habits and, as it were, inveterate in the recurrent employment of that narrow circle, they are rather disabled than qualified for whatever depends on the knowledge of mankind, on experience in mixed affairs, on a comprehensive, connected view of the various, complicated, external and internal interests which go to the formation of that multifarious thing called a state.
>
> Edmund Burke
> *Reflections on the Revolution in France*

I. Of This Time, of That Place

> It was the expert who benefited most directly from the new framework of politics. The more intricate such fields as the law and the sciences became, the greater the need for men with highly developed skills. The more complex the competition for power, the more organizational leaders relied on experts to decipher and to prescribe. Above all, the more elaborate men's aspirations grew, the greater their dependence upon specialists who could transcribe principles into policy.... Only the professional administrator, the doctor, the social worker, the architect, the economist, could show the way.
>
> Robert H. Wiebe
> *The Search for Order*

The Reporters of the PRINCIPLES were distinguished legal scholars who produced a serious and ambitious document. The contributors to the present volume subject the PRINCIPLES to probing, thoughtful, and illuminating analysis. At the volume's beginning, Professor Glendon puts the problems of family law in a broader perspective by examining the challenges families today face in living good lives. Now, at the volume's close, I want to put both the PRINCIPLES and the essays in a broader perspective. I need not vivisect the PRINCIPLES; that is admirably done by the essayists. Rather, I proffer a tool for understanding the PRINCIPLES more richly by situating them in their time and place.

"Now and then," Lionel Trilling wrote, "it is possible to observe the moral life in process of revising itself."[1] So it is today. American ways of thinking about the moral lives of families have been in turmoil for decades, and our ways of thinking about the legal regulation of families are correspondingly being disturbed and reconceived. The PRINCIPLES reflect these processes and are part of them, for law truly is the witness and external deposit of our moral life. But the PRINCIPLES can also rewardingly be understood as a new instance of an old tradition-elite law reform. In this Afterword, that is how I will try to understand them.

With some diffidence, I will draw on a quarter century's observation of the discipline of family law from the vantage of a professor at – I confess it – an elite law school. I began my career as a specialist in family law and found in it not what I had feared – the laborious study of a dry and technical system – but what I had sought – the opportunity for a large survey of causes.[2] However, as the field's center of gravity shifted from scholarship to advocacy, the narrowed range of opinion and tolerance in it became parching. I found in the neighboring discipline of law and bioethics a nourishing assortment of professional backgrounds and outlooks. Nevertheless, I have never ceased writing in family law and watching it from a safe distance. More largely, my calling has made me a witness to the process by which the moral life – the ideological, political, cultural life – of elite law schools is being revised. That too will be part of our story.

II. Introduction

> It may be objected that the progressivism espoused by corporation lawyers on a moral holiday would be a rather conservative sort of thing.... [T]his was not out of harmony with the general tone of the Progressive movement, especially in the Eastern states.... There Progressivism was a mild and judicious movement, whose goal was.... the formation of a responsible elite, which was to take charge of the popular impulse toward change and direct it into moderate and, as they would have said, "constructive" channels – a leadership occupying, as Brandeis so aptly put it, "a position of independence between the wealthy and the people, prepared to curb the excesses of either."
>
> Richard Hofstadter
> *The Age of Reform*

Elite law reform has a long and honorable tradition abroad and at home. In England, Whig aristocrats brought a measure of democracy to politics in the nineteenth century. In America, upper-middle-class Progressive reformers brought a measure of social welfare to life in the twentieth century. A late but typical fruit of the latter effort was the American Law Institute, which was founded "to promote the clarification and simplification of the law and its better adaptation to social needs, to secure the better administration of justice, and to encourage and carry on scholarly and scientific legal work."

The ALI's incorporators were flamboyantly elite; they included William Howard Taft, Charles Evans Hughes, and Elihu Root. The ALI remains emphatically elite. It comprises an elected membership of eminent lawyers, judges, and law professors and an *ex officio* membership of the Chief Justice of the United States, the Associate Justices of the Supreme Court, the Chief Judges of the United States Courts of Appeals, the Attorney General and Solicitor General of the United States, the chief justices of the state supreme courts, law

[1] LIONEL TRILLING, SINCERITY AND AUTHENTICITY 1 (Harvard U Press, 1982).

[2] *See* Carl E. Schneider, *Definition, Generalization, and Theory in American Family Law,* 18 J. L. REFORM 1039 (1985).

school deans, and the presidents of various legal organizations, including the national and state bar associations. Elite indeed.

The ALI has wielded influence beyond the fantasies of its founders. The Model Penal Code and the Restatements are as close to binding precedent as nongovernmental authority can be, and they are only part of the Institute's agenda. The ambition of ALI programs has expanded impressively over the years. The founders rather modestly thought that the law's uncertainty and complexity had produced a "general dissatisfaction with the administration of justice." They rather modestly assumed that those problems could be ameliorated if experts collaborated to solve essentially technical problems in interpreting the law. Behold the Restatements. At their heart was an attempt to understand a body of law in light of the complexities time had produced in it and to rationalize its doctrines cogently and acutely. This is the kind of work lawyers are trained to do, it is work skillful lawyers do better than mediocre lawyers, and it raises relatively few concerns about how elites exercise their powers.

But elites can hardly be so cabined. The ALI has long since ceased to regard itself as just a source of technical proficiency in the law and has come to value itself as a source of social policy. How could it not? Even technical analysis of precedents in private law asks the analyst to make choices that affect social policy. And once you begin to improve the law by rationalizing it, you notice other sorts of defects in the law, defects you are conveniently located to repair. When you have disposed of subjects that present "technical" issues, your search for more labors to perform leads you to subjects that implicate broad issues of public welfare. So having restated the law of contracts, you find yourself proposing a model penal code, and you then realize you must decide what the law of abortion should be. And from thence, where can you not go?

And so the ALI's expertise – whatever that is now thought to be – has been brought to bear on family law, and the ALI now offers its PRINCIPLES for the edification of the institutions that govern us. The PRINCIPLES are of their time and place. The time is the time when the generation whose elite excoriated elitism has become the nation's elite and enjoys its elite powers even while denying its elite status. The place is the American law school: The membership of the ALI approves the Institute's products and often modifies them before approving them, but the bulk of the work is done by the Reporters and, to a much lesser extent, the committees that advise them. The committee that assisted the drafters comprised family law scholars, practicing lawyers, and judges.

III. Elites and Masses: *Quis Custodiet Ipsos Custodes?*

> The culture wars that have convulsed America since the sixties are best understood as a form of class warfare, in which an enlightened elite (as it thinks of itself) seeks not so much to impose its values on the majority (a majority perceived as incorrigibly racist, sexist, provincial, and xenophobic), much less to persuade the majority by means of rational public debate, as to create parallel or "alternative" institutions in which it will no longer be necessary to confront the unenlightened at all.
>
> Christopher Lasch
> *The Revolt of the Elites*

The overriding challenge for elite law-making is normative and plain. Democracy is "government of the people, by the people, for the people." Elites have interests of their own, and their advantages – their education, their wealth, their experience, their economic, social, and political power – permit them to drown out their social inferiors when law is debated. As the examples of the Whig aristocracy and the Progressive reformers suggest, elite government can mean government for the people. Exactly because elites are elites, they benefit from the flourishing (at least as they understand the term) of the society they wish to lead. (That's why Engine Charlie Wilson thought that what's good for the country is good for General Motors.) Furthermore, when elites let slip the laboring oar, the ship of state often falters. Nevertheless, there is (as lawyers like to say) a tension between the democratic ideal of government by the governed and the exercise of elite authority. Even if elites are benevolent oligarchs, even if their contributions to law-making are essential, the democratic ideal dreams of a world in which nonelites join in their own government.

Assuring that people of all kinds can participate in making family law is particularly troublesome because several factors stimulate elite law professors to maximize their own influence and to minimize the influence of their opponents. On these issues, solicitude for their social inferiors appeals little to the academic elite. On the contrary, on these issues, that elite sees itself not as triumphing but as assailed. It must smite the infidels to the uttermost, since, as Harry Truman put it so clearly, "they are wrong and we are right."

To explain all this, I need to sketch the culture of the elite legal academy. Briefly, its ideology is the ideology of the contemporary American left, so much so that "radical academics, firmly entrenched in university life, dismiss conservative critics of themselves as 'marginal intellectuals.'"[3] Allegiance to that ideology is not just the norm; it is deep-seated and intensely felt, sometimes to the point of intolerance. Some of the reasons for this need to be understood. They grow out of the ideological evolution of the academic left. That left is not what it was. Historically, the predominant characteristic of the left here and in Europe was a concern for class and for the people at the nether reaches of the class structure. In the 1950s and early 1960s, when the first tier of the baby boom generation (from which come most of the actors in our story) was growing up, this meant allegiance to the working class, unions, and the poor, an allegiance which culminated in President Johnson's war on poverty. At the same time, of course, the civil rights movement was aborning. It increasingly became the template for thinking about social problems. At first, this fit easily into traditional leftist class thinking. Eventually, however, the left came to think less about class and more about disadvantaged and stigmatized groups. As is well known, this has in recent years led the left increasingly toward what are loosely called identity politics.

The shift from class to identity has transformed elite academic thinking about its politics and its role in making policy. When class was the issue, leftist academics tended to align themselves with the poor and the workers. Distance from, dislike for, and disdain toward those classes certainly existed; but it affronted the principal principles of the left and had to be suppressed. Likewise, distance from, dislike for, and disdain toward the right certainly existed and was certainly expressed, but while rightists might be mean-hearted, misguided, and selfish, their opinions were not outside the sphere of decent morality.

Now that identity is the template, the attitude of the left toward their social inferiors and toward their opponents has changed crucially. The left is no longer united with other classes and is, if anything, alienated from them. True, the left is committed to the welfare of "minorities," but from the vantage of the elite law professor, the left's agenda deals most directly with the welfare of relatively prosperous members of those minorities, especially

[3] Alan Wolfe, Marginalized in the Middle 7 (U of Chicago Press, 1996).

through the program that affects academics most – affirmative action for faculty and students. Similarly, another prominent part of the academic left's agenda deals with cultural matters (like multicultural education) which are not specific to the poor members of minorities.

Not only has the trend from class to identity frayed the ties that bound the leftist elite with other classes; the trend has also given that left multiplying reasons to condemn the behavior and beliefs of those classes. A century ago, moderate forms of ethnic prejudice were regarded even in genteel society as, at worst, a lapse in character not conspicuously more dreadful than others. Today, however, the twentieth-century travail of religious and racial bigotry has made invidious ethnic distinctions the outward sign of the basest inward depravity. Bigotry is not just wrong; it is evil. And in recent decades "bigotry" has expanded in two ways. First, it embraces invidious treatment of a lengthening list of groups. Second, it encompasses increasingly refined kinds of prejudice: "subtle" racism, "institutional" racism, and even racial "insensitivity" have been assimilated with more virulent and vicious forms of racism.

Elite law professors believe the programs they favor are not just wise; they are essential if bigotry and its consequences are to be purged from American life. If this is so, are not the left's opponents at least dupes of bigots, if not actually bigots themselves? Many parts of the academic left's agenda, then, are not just issues of policy; they are moral issues on which only one opinion can be tolerated. Decent people can only favor affirmative action, bans on military recruiting, and *Roe v. Wade*. Once to every man and nation...

There is a class element in all this. Since elite academics associate the working class and the lower-middle class with opposition to identity politics, the class gulf between the elite and the rest is wide and widening. Christopher Lasch, for example, concluded that "'Middle America'... has come to symbolize everything that stands in the way of progress: 'family values,' mindless patriotism, religious fundamentalism, racism, homophobia, retrograde views of women."[4] Academics also associate those classes with religious faith, and, as Lasch writes, "the elites' attitude to religion ranges from indifference to active hostility. It rests on a caricature of religious fundamentalism as a reactionary movement bent on reversing all the progressive measures achieved over the last three decades."

Let me give some life to this otherwise abstract description with an example of the first minutes of a first meeting with an academic from another institution. The Terri Schiavo case had been preoccupying the news, and I mentioned that illness had doomed me to grueling hours of Schiavo television. Certain I shared his political opinions, my interlocutor made some scoffing remarks about Republicans in Congress. I said he seemed quite contemptuous of his fellow citizens. He seemed startled that I could think of Republicans as fellow citizens: "Sometimes contempt is the only response.... " Republicans were not only stupidly wrong; they were self-serving and hypocritical. Their ideas were best explained in terms of social pathology, since the ideas were intellectually absurd. Modernity had passed these Middle Western and middle-class yokels by, and their status anxiety led them to cling to pathetic religious beliefs and social delusions.[5]

[4] Christopher Lasch, The Revolt of the Elites: And the Betrayal of Democracy 29 (W.W. Norton, 1995).

[5] *Plus ça change*: "[T]he effect of [Mr. Mencken's] polemic is to destroy, by rendering it ridiculous and unfashionable, the democratic tradition of the American pioneers. This attack on the divine right of demos is an almost exact equivalent of the earlier attack on the kings, the nobles, and the priests. He strikes at the sovereign power, which in America today consists of the evangelical churches in the small communities, the proletarian masses in the cities, and the organized smaller business men everywhere. The Baptist and Methodist sects, the city mobs, and the

In sum, the problem of elite authority and democratic participation presents itself with particular force when family law is formulated. No small part of the elite concludes that in this area their social inferiors espouse positions that they "loathe and believe to be fraught with death." And "[i]f you have no doubt of your premises or your power and want a certain result with all your heart you naturally express your wishes in law and sweep away all opposition."[6]

Elite law-making is perhaps least dangerous when elites have "technical" skills and expertise to contribute to "technical" analysis of "technical" issues of law. Not only do elites have special advantages in making policy in these areas, the public is disadvantaged. The public ordinarily has little idea that those issues exist, much less any idea of what is at stake in them and how they ought to be handled. Nor is it practical to bring people up to speed on every item of governmental policy.

Elite law-making is also relatively benign where the elite must work within established authority, as was the original intention of the Restatements. Even then law reformers will have room to make policy, but in those areas we may say of elites what Justice Holmes said of judges: "I recognize without hesitation that judges must and do legislate, but they do so only interstitially; they are confined from molar to molecular motions."[7] In these areas, that is, we need worry less about elites imposing their own perspectives and preferences on the rest of society and rejoice in their labors for us.

Family law, on the other hand, falls within neither category. The laws that currently govern the family are not especially technical or complex. They do not regulate arcane corners of life. Nor were the drafters of the PRINCIPLES confined within constricting authority; the PRINCIPLES do not even pretend to be a restatement of the earlier law, and professional incentives and inclinations drew the drafters away from the established and toward the fresh, the iconoclastic, and the radical. The point can be made even more emphatically: the PRINCIPLES do not raise questions about legal doctrine as much as they ask us what kinds of lives in families we want to promote and how social resources should be used to achieve our goals. As legal issues go, these are topics citizens are well-equipped to understand because they involve the lives citizens live. And for just that reason these are issues citizens should be able to decide. If ever democracy is to work, if ever people should be able to participate widely and truly in shaping policies under which they live, it should be here.

Perhaps these considerations should have given the ALI pause when it considered writing an elite prescription for family law. These considerations, after all, become yet more troubling when seen in light of a principal element in the modern law of the family – the removal of critical aspects of that law from legislative resolution and their transfer to courts acting under the authority of the Constitution. Government by the Supreme Court is elite government *in excelsis*. It is government by nine unelected shamans with unreviewable authority. Only lawyers may address the Court, and only litigants may hire lawyers to address the Court. It is elite government with many of its worst respects, not least its narrowness of experience and perspective, a narrowness that directly interferes with the

Chamber of Commerce are in power. They are the villains of the piece." Walter Lippman, The Saturday Review of Literature (December 11, 1926).

[6] Abrams v. United States, 250 U.S. 616, 630 (1919) (Holmes, J., dissenting). I analyze these issues at strenuous length in Carl E. Schneider, *State-Interest Analysis in Fourteenth Amendment "Privacy" Law: An Essay on the Constitutionalization of Social Issues*, 51 LAW & CONTEMP. PROBS. 79 (1988).

[7] Quoted in BENJAMIN N. CARDOZO, THE NATURE OF THE JUDICIAL PROCESS 69 (Yale U Press, 1975).

Court's ability even to anticipate the reactions to their rulings. (I strongly suspect, for example, that the Court was astonished when *Roe v. Wade* provoked a passionate response, astonished because most of the Justices lived in circles in which they rarely had to confront right-to-life opinions.)[8]

The distance between judicial government and democratic government is currently exacerbated by the recent interest in having the Supreme Court join courts from other countries in building an international body of human-rights law, no small part of which would affect our family law. My colleague Christopher McCrudden writes, "It is now commonplace for courts in one jurisdiction to refer extensively to the decision of other courts in interpreting human-rights guarantees."[9] America is much reviled for its parochial failure to follow suit. But how is it democratically decent to hand over law-making power to unelected judges guided not by policy electorally established, not by American law and tradition, but by what they and their upper-middle-class confreres from abroad think true at the opening of the twenty-first century?

IV. The View from the Tower, The Wisdom of Crowds

> The human understanding is not a dry light, but is infused by desire and emotion, which give rise to 'wishful science'. For man prefers to believe what he wants to be true. He therefore rejects difficulties, being impatient of inquiry; sober things, because they restrict his hope; deeper parts of Nature, because of his superstition; the light of experience, because of his arrogance and pride, lest his mind should seem to concern itself with things mean and transitory; things that are strange and contrary to all expectation, because of common opinion.
>
> Francis Bacon
> *Novum Organum*

Elites will always dominate law-making; this is one corollary of the iron law of oligarchy. But can we say anything more about the proper sphere of elite activity? This leads us to the second basic problem with elite law-making – some things it does well, some things it does badly. I have already mentioned some of the former. What of the latter?

Democracy is not only just because it lets the governed govern; it is wise because it consults the experience and insights of all parts of society. This elite policymaking can hardly do even in good circumstances. And these are not good circumstances. Family law affects almost everyone, but elite law professors generally come from and inhabit an isolated sliver of society. Too little in their lives dips them in the great streams of American society; too much in those dips confirms their prejudices about their fellow citizens.

The culture of law schools is astoundingly homogeneous. This is true even demographically. Because I was a member of our hiring committee, I recently browsed through the website biographies of colleagues who joined our faculty in the last couple of decades. Half of those who had a law degree received it from Yale, a third from Harvard, three from Columbia, one from Virginia, and one from Cardozo. (The last of these also had a

[8] I expatiate generously on the problem of judicial government in *State-Interest Analysis in Fourteenth-Amendment "Privacy" Law: An Essay on the Constitutionalization of Social Issues*, 51 Law & Contemp. Probs. 79 (1988).

[9] J. Christopher McCrudden, *A Part of the Main? The Physician-Assisted Suicide Cases and Comparative Law Methodology in the United States Supreme Court*, in Law at the End of Life: The Supreme Court and Assisted Suicide (Carl E. Schneider ed., U of Michigan Press, 2000).

Harvard Ph.D.) Roughly half are Jewish; apparently one is Catholic; few are religious (in the most religious country in the industrialized world). They seem largely to come (like our students) from the class of which they are now members – the professional upper-middle class. These fine colleagues and first-rate scholars boast a marvelously wide range of expertise in disciplines outside law, but otherwise it is hard to imagine a much more homogeneous group in such a heterogeneous society.[10]

The field of family law is astonishingly homogeneous as well, although in a different way. When I joined the field in 1981, both men and women were prominent figures in it. In the years since then, many – although certainly not all – of the men who had been doing exciting work in the field gradually left it. I can think of only three men who have achieved prominence who entered the field since then, and not all of them have stayed.

Similar in origin, elite law professors are similar in thought. The range of political views among them is so straitened that the greater part of American political opinion is virtually excluded. On many social issues opinion is so standard that, in my long and consistent experience, professors automatically assume you agree with them and will enjoy sharing their contempt for the knaves who disagree with us.

How might it matter that the most crucial work of producing the PRINCIPLES was performed by such cultural isolates? No single fact about the PRINCIPLES should have been more salient, more arresting, more daunting, more chastening to the Institute and its agents than this: The history of family law reform is the history of savaged hopes. Those reforms have regularly failed to achieve the ends for which they were proposed. They have regularly produced results that were unanticipated and unwanted. What made the ALI think their reforms would fare better? What did they do to understand the reasons for the record of failure? What did they do to avoid the traps into which their predecessors had fallen? What could they have done?

The ALI should have been alerted to this problem by, if nothing else, the fact that the law in general chronically fails, conspicuously and crucially fails. Its record of thwarted plans encompasses many areas of law and many techniques of regulation. For example, most of the central legal features of the law of bioethics have fallen strikingly short of the expectations that justified their adoption.[11] A favorite legal technique – requiring the stronger party in a transaction to provide the weaker party with information (as in the law of informed consent) rarely seems to affect behavior significantly, much less give the weaker party the authority the advocates of this technique fondly imagine.[12] Family law reforms, however, have particularly severe enforcement problems. They are of two general

[10] On the day this Afterword was due, my attention was drawn to a symposium in the first number of Volume 23 of the *Yale Law and Policy Review* which discusses the homogeneity of elite law school faculties. The pieces in the symposium appear to confirm quite impressively the experience I describe above.

[11] On the failure of the law of bioethics to achieve its purposes, see, e.g., Carl E. Schneider, *The Best-Laid Plans*, 30 HASTINGS CENTER REPORT 24 (July/August 2000); Carl E. Schneider, *Gang Aft Agley*, 31 HASTINGS CENTER REPORT 27 (January/February 2001). On the miserable failure of one of that law's showpieces, see Angela Fagerlin & Carl E. Schneider, *Enough: The Failure of the Living Will*, 34 HASTINGS CENTER REPORT 30 (March/April 2004).

[12] Take *Miranda* warnings: They "'have little or no effect on a suspect's propensity to talk'. Next to the warning label on cigarette packs, *Miranda* is the most widely ignored piece of official advice in our society.... Not only has *Miranda* largely failed to achieve its stated and implicit goals, but police have transformed *Miranda* into a tool of law enforcement...." Richard A. Leo, *Questioning the Relevance of* Miranda *in the Twenty-First Century*, 99 MICH. L. REV. 1000 (2001). Similar gloom surrounds studies of informed consent, product-liability warnings, health-insurance report cards, financial-privacy disclosures, and many other areas in which disclosures are legally mandated.

kinds – first, a failure of legal institutions to respond as reformers anticipate; second, a failure of legal rules and institutions to affect people's behavior in the ways intended.

Can things really be this bad? Let me lend verisimilitude to an otherwise bald and unconvincing narrative with several examples. Changing lives by changing judicial behavior should be the easy kind of reform. Judges are trained and obliged to take instruction. Law reformers imagine themselves like the centurion: "I say to this man, Go, and he goeth; and to another, Come, and he cometh; and to my servant, Do this, and he doeth it." In fact, they are more like Harry Truman's prophecy of Dwight Eisenhower, "He'll sit here, and he'll say, 'Do this! Do that!' *And nothing will happen.* Poor Ike – it won't be a bit like the Army. He'll find it very frustrating." Consider two examples of legal reform through judicial instruction.

Exhibit A: One of the worthiest goals of family law is to improve the lives of the children of divorce, not least by rescuing them from the penury in which they often languish. One of the most active subjects for family law reform has been that enterprise. One of the areas of widest agreement has been that the core reform should be substituting guidelines for judicial discretion. Yet "[w]hile Congress adopted the numerical guidelines requirement with the aim of significantly increasing award levels and decreasing award variability, available evidence suggests that these goals have not been met. Awards calculated under existing guidelines do not appear to differ dramatically from those produced under earlier discretionary standards."[13]

Exhibit B: Few areas of family law have been of more interest in the current era than the rules governing the division of marital wealth. In few areas has there been as much change in legal doctrine. To what end?

> California replaced its equitable property distribution regime with a rule requiring equal division of marital property on the assumption that equitable distribution typically produced relatively equal awards for husband and wife. The change was expected to curb case variation without altering overall outcomes. But researchers later determined that wives had typically received more than half of the marital property under the old law, and they also discovered that deferred distribution of the marital home in cases involving minor children declined dramatically under the new one.[14]

The enforcement problems of family law extend beyond the recalcitrance of judges. Many reforms have gone awry because the people regulated have not reacted to the law's incentives as intended. For example, Michael Wald's study of legal responses to parents who abuse or neglect their children raises the possibility that those responses matter less than anyone had supposed. He concluded that, considering only "what happened to the children from the time we first saw them until the end of the study, two years later, there was not a great deal of difference between home and foster care."[15] For another example, the contributors to *In the Interest of Children* reported that people avail themselves of the due-process mechanisms so beloved of the law far less than courts and scholars fondly contemplate.[16]

[13] Marsha Garrison, *Autonomy or Community?: An Evaluation of Two Models of Parental Obligation*, 86 Cal. L. Rev. 41, 44 (1998).

[14] Marsha Garrison, *The Economic Consequences of Divorce: Would Adoption of the ALI Principles Improve Current Outcomes?*, 8 Duke J. Gender L. & Pol. 119, 122 (2001).

[15] Michael S. Wald, J. M. Carlsmith, & P. H. Leiderman, Protecting Abused and Neglected Children 183 (Stanford U Press, 1988).

[16] Robert H. Mnookin et al, In the Interest of Children: Advocacy, Law Reform, and Public Policy (W. H. Freeman, 1985).

Nothing will assure that the law works properly. Making law is as supremely challenging as any human enterprise. James Scott correctly says that even a

> prudent, small step, based on prior experience, yields new and not completely predictable effects that become the point of departure for the next step. Virtually any complex task involving many variables whose values and interactions cannot be accurately forecast belongs to this genre: building a house, repairing a car, perfecting a new jet engine, surgically repairing a knee, or farming a plot of land. Where the interactions involve not just the material environment but social interaction as well – building and peopling new villages or cities, organizing a revolutionary seizure of power, or collectivizing agriculture – the mind boggles at the multitude of interactions and uncertainties (as distinct from calculable risks).[17]

How are law-makers to survey that "multitude of interactions and uncertainties"? Empirical study of the way people encounter the law, surely. Unhappily, few law professors relish that work. Theory and doctrine, not empirical research, are their metier.[18] This is tantalizing, because, as the research I just reviewed shows, laws repeatedly perform in counterintuitive ways.

In the absence of adequate empirical research, what is a law-maker to do? If law depends on the ways many kinds of people respond to many kinds of incentives and sanctions, sensible law-makers draw on the insights of many kinds of people about many kinds of experience. Here elite law-making falls short almost by definition, for it tends to consult just the insights of a few kinds of people with a few kinds of experience. Which is only to say that the straightened experience and perspective of elite law professors is a sadly deficient basis for making policy that affects everyone.

There is another respect in which family law needs the participation of all manner of people: If the PRINCIPLES are actually to shape people's behavior, people must understand, respect, and accept them. This need for public collaboration is more generally true of the law than law propounders think. As one eminent elitist knew:

> The amount of law is relatively small which a modern legislature can successfully impose. The reason for this is that unless the enforcement of the law is taken in hand by the citizenry, the officials as such are quite helpless.... [I]nsofar as a law depends upon the initiative of officials in detecting violations and in prosecuting, that law will almost certainly be difficult to enforce.... For what gives law reality is not that it is commanded by the sovereign but that it brings the organized force of the state to the aid of those citizens who believe in the law.[19]

So what chance would the PRINCIPLES have of attaining the collaboration of the people regulated by it? The first, and simplest, condition for the PRINCIPLES' success is that people will know what the PRINCIPLES say. However, few people know anything reliable about the law of the family when they marry. Nor do they care to learn, since they lovably assume that the law will never apply to them.

[17] JAMES C. SCOTT, SEEING LIKE A STATE: HOW CERTAIN SCHEMES TO IMPROVE THE HUMAN CONDITION HAVE FAILED 327 (Yale U Press, 1998).

[18] See Carl E. Schneider & Lee E. Teitelbaum, *Life's Golden Tree: Empirical Scholarship and American Law*, forthcoming in 2006 Utah Law Review, which explicitly and relentlessly explores the extent of and need for empirical research in family law.

[19] WALTER LIPPMANN, A PREFACE TO MORALS 276–77 (Macmillan, 1929).

This is actually a pervasive problem in the law. A sobering literature "reveals that, to the lawyer's chagrin, businesses resist using contracts, ranchers do not know what rules of liability govern damage done by wandering cattle, suburbanites do not summon the law to resolve neighborhood disputes, engaged couples do not know the law governing how they will own property when they marry, citizens repeatedly reject the due process protections proffered them, and, what is worse, all these people simply don't care what the law says."[20]

Popular knowledge about, comprehension of, and acquiescence in family law is especially problematic. People have their own moral and social norms of family behavior, norms that are often deeply considered and warmly embraced. Since people have adequate precepts of their own, why study the law's? Furthermore, people assume that they know what the law is. They have heard stories. Besides, people commonly suppose that their values are widely shared and thus expect that the law enacts what they believe. All this means that people will not inquire into what the law is and instead will rely on mistaken assumptions about it, if they think about it at all.

On divorce, things are hardly better. At this point, people must come to grips with legal institutions. This does not, however, mean that people will then learn the law or that the law will be applied as its drafters intended. Studies suggest that when divorcing couples meet their lawyers, they are eager to persuade their lawyers to see the case as they see it – in terms of the couple's moral relations (as the client sees them). Lawyers struggle to persuade their clients to abandon that preoccupation and to accept the law's terms, terms the clients often find misconceived and perverse. Few lawyers find it rewarding to teach the client the law, and they often settle for inducing the client to be practical.[21]

The understanding and acquiescence of clients in the PRINCIPLES might not be so necessary if clients litigated and judges decided divorce cases. In fact, most divorce cases are settled after negotiations, so that what judges do is much more marginal than reform proposals ordinarily assume. It was once thought that these negotiations were conducted "in the shadow of the law," but this supposition has lost ground. For example, Robert Mnookin, one of the early proponents of this theory, discovered in his empirical work that his speculations about it were not confirmed.[22] One reason for this is that most families cannot afford to pay lawyers and consequently must do the negotiating themselves in relative ignorance of (and indifference to) what the law says.

I have been discussing a number of reasons people will not understand, accept, apply, and live with the ALI proposals. Suppose, absurdly, that a citizen truly wanted to do all those things. How accessible would the PRINCIPLES be to even the most earnest person? Suppose someone actually tried to study the PRINCIPLES. What then? First, levels of literacy being what they are, few Americans could read them. (Eighty percent of the country cannot understand a written definition for jurors of "peremptory challenge.")

Second, even were literacy no problem, our earnest citizen would be wholly befuddled by the PRINCIPLES' complexity and obscurity. I know, because I assigned my (elite) first-year students the marital property section of the PRINCIPLES and then included in the final exam a copy of that section and a simple hypothetical in which the PRINCIPLES were

[20] CARL E. SCHNEIDER, BIOETHICS IN THE LANGUAGE OF THE LAW, 24 Hastings Center Report 16 (Jul/Aug 1994).

[21] See AUSTIN SARAT & WILLIAM L. F. FELSTINER, DIVORCE LAWYERS AND THEIR CLIENTS: POWER AND MEANING IN THE LEGAL PROCESS (Oxford U Press, 1995).

[22] ELEANOR E. MACCOBY & ROBERT H. MNOOKIN, DIVIDING THE CHILD: SOCIAL AND LEGAL DIMENSIONS OF CUSTODY (Harvard U Press, 1992).

the sole authority. Disaster. There were few decent answers. Some students were deceived by language that looked dispositive but was not; some stopped reading too early; many were just confused by the proliferating mass of rules. I need hardly say the obvious: if law students are baffled, how will the hapless untrained citizen fare?

But suppose our earnest citizen is so virtuous as to consult a lawyer about the meaning of the PRINCIPLES. "Am I living in a domestic partnership, with all the ominous consequences that seems to have?," our friend reasonably asks. No lawyer could say. Take just one *simplified* example. Domestic partners are "two persons of the same or opposite sex, not married to one another, who for a significant period of time share a primary residence and a life together as a couple." There is a presumption that unrelated people who have "maintained a common household" long enough are a domestic partnership. That presumption is rebuttable "by evidence that the parties did not share life together as a couple." We are then told, "Whether persons share a life together as a couple is determined by reference to all the circumstances, including. . . . " Here follows a list of *thirteen* factors to be considered. Not one of those factors is defined with enough specificity to give it reliable meaning. Nor is there any way of telling how to weigh the factors against each other. This analysis is only part of one provision of a wickedly complex document shot through with indeterminate phrases like "just" and "equitable" and "improper."

A third reason citizens will not easily comprehend the PRINCIPLES is that they are too distant from the population's ideas about how people should behave in families and how the law should regulate them. In order to understand a body of law, you need to understand the ideas that animate it. Even if the PRINCIPLES are animated by an orderly set of ideas (which I have searched for in vain), they will generally seem so counterintuitive that making sense of them will be insuperably difficult.

V. To Bind and Loose[23]

> [A]lthough it may be that no convention is any longer coercive, conventions remain, are adopted, revised, and debated. They embody the considered results of experience. . . . [T]hey are as necessary to a society which recognizes no authority as to one which does. For the inexperienced must be offered some kind of hypothesis when they are confronted with the necessity of making choices: they cannot be so utterly open-minded that they stand inert until something collides with them. In the modern world, therefore, the function of conventions is to declare the meaning of experience. A good convention is one which will most probably show the inexperienced the way to happy experience.
>
> Walter Lippman
> *A Preface to Morals*

Historically, elites have striven to impose order and discipline on their society generally and their social inferiors particularly. Even when elites have imagined they were motivated by altruism, historians have insisted that they really wanted social control.[24] Today, however,

[23] "[A] culture survives principally . . . by the power of its institutions to bind and loose men in the conduct of their affairs with reasons which sink so deep into the self that they become common and implicitly understood. . . . " PHILIP RIEFF, THE TRIUMPH OF THE THERAPEUTIC: USES OF FAITH AFTER FREUD 2 (Harper & Row, 1966).

[24] E.g.: "To many of those who could not accept the changing America, evangelical Protestantism seemed an excellent means of keeping the nation under control." Clifford S. Griffin, *Religious Benevolence as Social Control*, in ANTE-BELLUM REFORM 83 (David Brion Davis ed., Harper & Row, 1967).

a potent element of elite dogma advocates just the opposite – freedom, release from social constraint, autonomy – in private life and in public policy.[25] That dogma crucially shapes the PRINCIPLES.

Marriage is a repressive institution. It is, to be sure, much more. Goethe thought it "the beginning and the pinnacle of all culture."[26] But it is crucially a repressive institution. What do I mean by this statement, so unfashionable, so provoking? To answer this question, we return to first principles as they have historically been understood. Those principles talk about the depravity of human nature. Human nature is irredeemably self-interested, self-indulgent, and sadic. It therefore must be cabined, cribbed, and confined.

Nowhere are we more vulnerable to human depravity nor more disposed to it than in family life. In family life, we are beset by emotions and drives we do not understand and can not acknowledge. In family life, we live with those who mean the most to us and can do the most for us. In family life, harsh words, blows, betrayal, and desertion hurt most keenly. In family life, we can injure each other in ways we cannot elsewhere, as through sexual infidelity. In family life the most vulnerable people – children – live at the mercy of parents who are themselves made vulnerable by their affection for their children. And in family life, success demands (and fabulously rewards) a lifetime of labor and love, compassion and concession.

One goal of human society is to moderate human depravity; to deprive it of occasions of sin; to channel it from cruelty toward benignity. Society tries to do this directly, through the criminal law. But "[t]o try to regulate the internal affairs of a family, the relations of love or friendship, or many other things of the same sort, by law or by the coercion of public opinion, is like trying to pull an eyelash out of a man's eye with a pair of tongs. They may put out the eye, but they will never get hold of the eyelash."[27] Because the state cannot effectively prevent people from harming each other in the privacy of families through direct prohibitions, indirect means are critical.

Preeminent among these indirect means is the social institution. A social institution is "a pattern of expected action of individuals or groups enforced by social sanctions...."[28] Social institutions shape human behavior by rewarding virtue and penalizing vice, by making virtue natural and vice unthinkable. People need not enter social institutions, although there may be incentives to do so. Primarily, rather, it is their very presence, the social currency they have, and the governmental support they receive which combine to make it seem reasonable and even natural for people to use them. Thus people can be said to be channeled into them. As Berger and Luckmann write, "Institutions..., by the very fact of their existence, control human conduct by setting up predefined patterns of conduct, which channel it in one direction as against the many other directions that would theoretically be possible."[29] Or as James Fitzjames Stephen wonderfully wrote, "The life of the great mass of men, to a great extent the life of all men, is like a watercourse guided this

[25] For an account of this development in law and life, see CARL E. SCHNEIDER, THE PRACTICE OF AUTONOMY: PATIENTS, DOCTORS, AND MEDICAL DECISIONS (Oxford U Press, 1998).

[26] JOHANN VON GOETHE, ELECTIVE AFFINITIES (1809).

[27] JAMES FITZJAMES STEPHEN, LIBERTY, EQUALITY, FRATERNITY 162 (U Chicago Press, 1991).

[28] ROBERT N. BELLAH, ET AL., THE GOOD SOCIETY 10 (Alfred A. Knopf, 1991).

[29] PETER L. BERGER & THOMAS LUCKMANN, THE SOCIAL CONSTRUCTION OF REALITY: A TREATISE IN THE SOCIOLOGY OF KNOWLEDGE 52 (Anchor, 1966).

way or that by a system of dams, sluices, weirs, and embankments. . . . [I]t is by these works, that is to say, by their various customs and institutions – that men's lives are regulated."[30]

Social institutions, then, are a kind of soft regulation. They are not compulsory. They work more by inducement than by punishment. They spare people the burden of reinventing the forms of social life by offering them patterns of behavior, and they help people organize and coordinate their relations with family, friends, neighbors, colleagues, and strangers.[31] In the absence of social institutions, "a successful marriage depends wholly upon the capacity of the man and the woman to make it successful. They have to accomplish wholly by understanding and sympathy and disinterestedness of purpose what was once in a very large measure achieved by habit, necessity, and the absence of any practicable alternative."[32] Crucially, the patterns of behavior propounded in social institutions embody a set of norms, of moral understandings about how people should treat each other. People are channeled into accepting these norms because their institutions are so ordinary a part of social customs. Thus are people socialized.

The preeminent institutions of family life are marriage and parenthood. They inhibit us from abandoning each other, from betraying each other, from destroying our children's home. In marriage and parenthood, people give hostages to destiny. In marriage and parenthood, people cede freedom. Marriage and parenthood proffer a fount of blessings, their yoke can be easy and their burden light; but in marriage begins responsibility, and responsibility chains liberty. Andrew Sullivan writes, "Marriage provides an anchor, if an arbitrary and often weak one, in the maelstrom of sex and relationships to which we are all prone. It provides a mechanism for emotional stability and economic security. We rig the law in its favor not because we disparage all forms of relationship other than the nuclear family, but because we recognize that not to promote marriage would be to ask too much of human virtue."[33]

Today, however, marriage and parenthood are losing their power to bind. Law cannot by itself create or define social institutions; they arise out of and are sustained by social attitudes and practices. Law can only operate at the margin (for example, through divorce laws) to affirm, to assist, to adjust institutions. For some years, marriage and parenthood as social institutions have been weakened by a prolonged historical movement toward a new conception of moral duties and social institutions, a movement which has been particularly favored in the elite upper-middle class.

At the heart of this historical movement have been long-advancing trends in the moral life of America and indeed of the industrialized west. They begin in proud and venerable elements of the American ethos. That ethos is famously individualistic, and that individualism is remarkable for the special homage it has paid to self-reliance. Tocqueville believed American democracy reared men "intoxicated with their new power. They entertain a

[30] *Liberty, Equality, Fraternity* 63-4 (1967).

[31] "[I]n the absence of models that define what is expected of them, Americans will increasingly have to define for themselves the rules by which they will structure their lives. What this means concretely is that things once taken for granted will increasingly be subject to complex and difficult negotiations." Alan Wolfe, America at Century's End 468 (U California Press, 1991). Even more broadly, communities are built not just by "a spirit of benevolence, or the prevalence of communitarian values, or even certain 'shared final ends' alone, but a common vocabulary of discourse and a background of implicit practices and understanding within which the opacity of the participants is reduced if never finally dissolved." Michael J. Sandel, Liberalism and the Limits of Justice 172–3 (Cambridge U Press, 1982).

[32] Walter Lippmann, A Preface to Morals 311 (Macmillan, 1929).

[33] Andrew Sullivan, Virtually Normal: An Argument About Homosexuality 182 (Alfred A. Knopf, 1995).

presumptuous confidence in their own strength, and as they do not suppose that they can henceforward ever have occasion to claim the assistance of their fellow creatures, they do not scruple to show that they care for nobody but themselves."[34] And as the nineteenth century gave way to the twentieth, this strong version of individualism took on fresh vigor from the gathering power of a vision of the liberated and fulfilled self. That vision has assumed many forms, but at its core is a therapeutic ethos that has flourished in a prosperous, consumer society.

The upshot of these developments is an ideal of individual autonomy in which free choice is central. In this ideal, choice

> must be "free" in a strong sense. Choices must be the agents' own, and they must be based on the agents' critical reflection on their own choices, actions, and conceptions of a good life. This excludes the substitution of the judgment of some political, religious, moral, charismatic, or whatever authority for the agents' own. And it excludes as well the agents' judgments being based on indoctrination, compulsion, unexamined prejudice, uncontrolled passion, and the like. Autonomy requires that the agents should judge how they should exercise their freedom and that their judgments should involve the application of some standards that they have come to accept as a result of critical reflection on them and on how they should live.[35]

In this tradition of what might be called therapeutic individualism, people are admonished to pursue an independent "search for personal well-being, adjustment, and contentment – in short, for 'health'"[36] – a search that requires people to peel off the false social constraints that keep them from discovering their own true natures and living their own lives.[37]

Associated with therapeutic individualism is a transformation in attitudes toward moral thought and language. Americans have become, Himmelfarb rightly says, "suspicious of the very idea of morality. Moral principles, still more moral judgments, are thought to be at best an intellectual embarrassment, at worst evidence of an illiberal and repressive disposition".[38] As I wrote recently,

> The Americans who today most influence our cultural tone – and particularly the well-educated young Americans in whom these attitudes are most readily perceived – find they do not even know what is meant by a moral duty (unless perhaps it be a duty to oneself)

[34] Alexis de Tocqueville, 2 Democracy in America 107 (Vintage, 1957).

[35] John Kekes, Against Liberalism 20 (Cornell U Press, 1997).

[36] Carl E. Schneider, *Moral Discourse and the Transformation of American Family Law*, 83 Mich. L. Rev. 1803, 1847 (1985).

[37] The roots of these attitudes run much deeper than my abbreviated summary can suggest. (*Brevis esse laboro, obscurus fio.*) For example, James Fitzjames Stephen said in responding to John Stuart Mill's *On Liberty*: "It is one of the commonest beliefs of the day that the human race collectively has before it splendid destinies of various kinds, and that the road to them is to be found in the removal of all restraints on human conduct, in the recognition of a substantial equality between all human creatures, and in fraternity or general love." James Fitzjames Stephen, Liberty, Equality, Fraternity 52 (U Chicago Press, 1991).

[38] Gertrude Himmelfarb, The De-Moralization of Society: From Victorian Virtues to Modern Values 240 (Alfred A. Knopf, 1995). Himmelfarb's illustration of this point is telling:

> When members of the president's cabinet were asked whether it is immoral for people to have children out of wedlock, they drew back from that distasteful word. The Secretary of Health and Human Services replied, "I don't like to put this in moral terms, but I do believe that having children out of wedlock is just wrong." The Surgeon General was more forthright: "No. Everyone has different moral standards.... You can't impose your standards on someone else."

Id. at 240–241. These passages are quite typical of what I encounter in my conversations with my students on this subject. In particular, there is the assumption that if you speak in moral terms you must necessarily intend to "impose" your "morality" on other people.

> and are loath to speak in the outmoded, confining, small-minded, and even dangerous language of morality. They are moral relativists of a pronounced stripe who consider their own moral views just as happenstantial and even factitious as other people's. They see in moral obligation a cloak for the "judgmental." They believe that to visit the breach of a moral duty with sanctions is to be "punitive." And they detest the punitive.[39]

The therapeutic sources of contemporary individualism account for no small part of the changing attitudes toward moral thinking: "[T]he habit of forbearance, once having established itself as the first principle of psychiatric therapy, soon became a kind of automatic reflex regulating all forms of interpersonal exchange. A 'nonjudgmental' habit of mind, easily confused with the liberal virtue of tolerance, came to be regarded as the *sine qua non* of sociability."[40] The traditions of liberal tolerance and egalitarianism contribute as well: The upper-middle class men Lamont interviewed "often expressed their belief in the cultural sovereignty of the individual. They argued that 'the way you choose to dress and spend your money is your business,' that 'if you feel comfortable with it, that's fine,' and that it is wrong to be judgmental regarding other people's lifestyles and tastes...." They espoused a relativism which led them to "consider all opinions to be equally valuable and to be grounded in personal preferences..."[41]

Therapeutic individualism and the attitudes toward social constraint and moral duty which are associated with it erode social institutions. They reflect a sanguine view of human nature and make the discovery and expression of one's individual authentic nature the linchpin of life. This understanding attributes evil not to human nature but to the failure of societies "to foster the autonomy of individuals who live in them. The view of human nature at the core of the liberal faith is thus that human beings are by their nature free, equal, rational, and morally good."[42] On these principles, public policy should free people from any social force that promotes inauthenticity. As Sullivan writes of what he calls the liberationist view of marriage, "the full end of human fruition is to be free of all social constructs."[43] This movement sees law as empowering, not socializing; as liberating, not repressing.

Changes in social practices work in concert with changes in social theory to corrode marriage as a socializing institution. Divorce proliferates; out-of-wedlock births burgeon; family forms multiply. "Deinstitutionalization is even celebrated, on the grounds that all forms of family life should be encouraged and treated equally... Justice Brennan recently cited a string of cases he believed indicated that 'we have declined to respect a State's notion, as manifested in its allocation of privileges and burdens, of what the family should be.'"[44] This hardly begins to state the contempt some writers have had for family institutions. Sullivan writes, "Marriage of all institutions is to liberationists a form of imprisonment; it

[39] *Fixing the Family: Legal Acts and Cultural Admonitions*, in Alan J. Hawkins, Lynn D. Wardle, & David Orgon Coolidge, eds., *Revitalizing the Institution of Marriage for the Twenty-First Century* (Praeger, 2002). Lest this seem harsh, see my attempt to understand morality *à la mode* in Carl E. Schneider, *Marriage, Morals, and the Law: No-Fault Divorce and Moral Discourse*, 1994 Utah L. Rev. 503.

[40] Christopher Lasch, The Revolt of the Elites: And the Betrayal of Democracy 218 (W.W. Norton, 1995).

[41] Michèle Lamont, Money, Morals, & Manners: The Culture of the French and the American Upper-Middle Class 116 (U Chicago Press, 1992).

[42] John Kekes, Against Liberalism 39 (Cornell U Press, 1997).

[43] Sullivan, *supra* note 33, at 57.

[44] Carl E. Schneider, *The Law and the Stability of Marriage: The Family as a Social Institution*, in David Popenoe, Jean Bethke Elshtain, & David Blankenhorn (eds) *Promises to Keep: Decline and Renewal of Marriage in America* 192 (Rowman & Littlefield, 1996) (quoting *Michael H. v. Gerald D.*, 491 U.S. 110 (1989)(dissent)).

reeks of a discourse that has bought and sold property, that has denigrated and subjected women, that has constructed human relationships into a crude and suffocating form."[45] Thus Paula Ettelbrick invokes the wisdom of a t-shirt: "Marriage is a great institution . . . if you like living in institutions."[46]

Recent decades have also seen the weakening of elements of family law that help make marriage work as an institution. That institution centrally concerns moral duties people take on to each other. But family law has increasingly been stripped of occasions for moral discourse and has increasingly tried to transfer moral decisions from the state to individuals.[47] For example, in our no-fault age, the court from which you seek divorce need no longer address the justifiability of the divorce; it lets you decide whether you are morally entitled to a divorce or, for that matter, to ignore the moral aspects of the divorce altogether. This is not to say that there is no moral basis for no-fault divorce. There plainly is. But it is to say that the law's ability to reinforce the moral duties of familial institutions is inhibited when those duties cannot be discussed.

The PRINCIPLES reflect the elite distrust of social institutions. No small part of the force of those institutions comes from their distinctiveness. Social institutions offer special benefits and impose special burdens. People who enter those institutions choose to do so, they know that they have done so and treat themselves differently because of it, and other people recognize that they have done so and respond accordingly. One of the most arresting features of the PRINCIPLES is that they do just the opposite. They blur the distinction between marriage and cohabitation and between de jure and de facto parenthood.

This blurring is problematic not just because social institutions are sustained by their distinctiveness; it is also troubling because social institutions are formed by the way people in them think and act. How would people behave when they became "married" involuntarily, by the operation of law? People who choose not to marry may do so because they reject its social meaning, including the centrality of sexual fidelity. How would their behavior alter social expectations of marriage?

Furthermore, the broader the scope of marriage, the weaker its principles. And the scope of marriage could expand in the ordinary way of the slippery slope: Each extension of a rule makes the next step smaller and easier. This particular slope is waxed by several factors that have already helped ease our slide down: Much of the argument for broadening the scope of marriage draws on our contemporary discomfort with distinctions and judgments. Much of that argument partakes of the wish to accommodate within the term "family" what Kath Weston calls the "families we choose." Furthermore, as Chambers speculates, "By ceasing to conceive of marriage as a partnership composed of one person of each sex, the state may become more receptive to units of three or more . . . and to units composed of two people of the same sex but who are bound by friendship alone. All desirable changes in family law need not be made at once."[48]

The more broadly you define marriage, the less stringent the demands you can make of people in it. Weston writes that "most chosen families are characterized by fluid

[45] Sullivan, *supra* note 33, at 87.

[46] Paula Ettelbrick, *Since When Is Marriage a Path to Liberation?*, in Andrew Sullivan, ed, *Same-Sex Marriage: Pro and Con* 118 (Vintage Books, 1997).

[47] I identify and analyze this development in *Moral Discourse and the Transformation of American Family Law*, 83 MICH. L. REV. 1803 (1985).

[48] David Chambers, *What If? The Legal Consequences of Marriage and the Legal Needs of Lesbian and Gay Male Couples*, 95 MICH. L. REV. 447, 491 (1996).

boundaries, eclectic composition, and relatively little symbolic differentiation between erotic and nonerotic ties."[49] But where boundaries are fluid, where one family barely resembles another, where erotic and platonic ties are hardly distinguishable, marriage is no longer special. Yet making marriage special is part of making it work as a social institution.

I have been suggesting that the PRINCIPLES are animated by the antinomian and anti-institutional ethos of elite legal academia. But the PRINCIPLES reflect one more change in elite attitudes about family law that cuts in just the opposite direction. Several decades ago, much family law scholarship exalted the principle of family autonomy. That principle called for a law that intruded on people's lives in families as little as possible. Hope was cherished that allowing spouses to arrange the terms of their marriage contractually would create a world in which legal norms matched private wants. Fear was nurtured that the state would always abuse its authority in enforcing the law of child abuse and neglect. The state was the enemy, freedom the victim.

Today, the elite view of family law looks quite different. The family autonomy principle has been battered by the argument that the enemy is not the state but a culture that gives family members power over each other. In particular, the central problem became the power that husbands had over wives. Family autonomy became not a bulwark against the state but a grant of authority to husbands to abuse their wives physically, socially, and economically. It became conventional academic wisdom that domestic violence should be policed more actively, prosecuted more adamantly, and defined more broadly.

The PRINCIPLES strikingly reflect this dirigiste ethos. Contract is no longer the touchstone. The PRINCIPLES' provisions for the distribution of marital wealth seem to reflect a confidence that the drafters have analyzed the moral relations of the parties more decently than the parties themselves (even while many of those principles are somewhat eccentric[50]). The PRINCIPLES righteously impose the duties of spouses on cohabitants who had rejected the opportunity to assume those duties. Perhaps worst of all, the PRINCIPLES harshly fail in one of the first duties of law: to give citizens notice of the law's rules so that they can plan their lives. Can it be that a document clothed in the language of liberty represents the kind of expansion of governmental authority all too familiar in the history of elite law reform?

[49] KATH WESTON, FAMILIES WE CHOOSE: LESBIANS, GAYS, KINSHIP 206 (Columbia U Press, 1991).

[50] I criticize an earlier version of them in *Rethinking Alimony: Marital Decisions and Moral Discourse*, 1991 BYU L. REV. 197.

Index